# A COMPANION TO THE
# CLASSICAL GREEK WORLD

# BLACKWELL COMPANIONS TO THE ANCIENT WORLD

This series provides sophisticated and authoritative overviews of periods of ancient history, genres of classical literature, and the most important themes in ancient culture. Each volume comprises between twenty-five and forty concise essays written by individual scholars within their area of specialization. The essays are written in a clear, provocative, and lively manner, designed for an international audience of scholars, students, and general readers.

ANCIENT HISTORY

**Published**

A Companion to the Roman Army
*Edited by Paul Erdkamp*

A Companion to the Roman Republic
*Edited by Nathan Rosenstein and Robert Morstein-Marx*

A Companion to the Roman Empire
*Edited by David S. Potter*

A Companion to the Classical Greek World
*Edited by Konrad H. Kinzl*

A Companion to the Ancient Near East
*Edited by Daniel C. Snell*

A Companion to the Hellenistic World
*Edited by Andrew Erskine*

A Companion to Late Antiquity
*Edited by Philip Rousseau*

A Companion to Ancient History
*Edited by Andrew Erskine*

A Companion to Archaic Greece
*Edited by Kurt A. Raaflaub and Hans van Wees*

A Companion to Julius Caesar
*Edited by Miriam Griffin*

A Companion to Byzantium
*Edited by Liz James*

A Companion to Ancient Egypt
*Edited by Alan B. Lloyd*

**In preparation**

A Companion to Ancient Macedonia
*Edited by Ian Worthington and Joseph Roisman*

A Companion to the Punic Wars
*Edited by Dexter Hoyos*

A Companion to Sparta
*Edited by Anton Powell*

LITERATURE AND CULTURE

**Published**

A Companion to Classical Receptions
*Edited by Lorna Hardwick and Christopher Stray*

A Companion to Greek and Roman Historiography
*Edited by John Marincola*

A Companion to Catullus
*Edited by Marilyn B. Skinner*

A Companion to Roman Religion
*Edited by Jörg Rüpke*

A Companion to Greek Religion
*Edited by Daniel Ogden*

A Companion to the Classical Tradition
*Edited by Craig W. Kallendorf*

A Companion to Roman Rhetoric
*Edited by William Dominik and Jon Hall*

A Companion to Greek Rhetoric
*Edited by Ian Worthington*

A Companion to Ancient Epic
*Edited by John Miles Foley*

A Companion to Greek Tragedy
*Edited by Justina Gregory*

A Companion to Latin Literature
*Edited by Stephen Harrison*

A Companion to Greek and Roman Political Thought
*Edited by Ryan K. Balot*

A Companion to Ovid
*Edited by Peter E. Knox*

A Companion to the Ancient Greek Language
*Edited by Egbert Bakker*

A Companion to Hellenistic Literature
*Edited by Martine Cuypers and James J. Clauss*

A Companion to Vergil's *Aeneid* and its Tradition
*Edited by Joseph Farrell and Michael C. J. Putnam*

A Companion to Horace
*Edited by Gregson Davis*

**In preparation**

A Companion to Food in the Ancient World
*Edited by John Wilkins*

A Companion to the Latin Language
*Edited by James Clackson*

A Companion to Classical Mythology
*Edited by Ken Dowden and Niall Livingstone*

A Companion to Sophocles
*Edited by Kirk Ormand*

A Companion to Aeschylus
*Edited by Peter Burian*

A Companion to Greek Art
*Edited by Tyler Jo Smith and Dimitris Plantzos*

A Companion to Families in the Greek and Roman World
*Edited by Beryl Rawson*

A Companion to Tacitus
*Edited by Victoria Pagán*

A Companion to the Archaeology of the Ancient Near East
*Edited by Daniel Potts*

# A COMPANION TO THE CLASSICAL GREEK WORLD

*Edited by*

Konrad H. Kinzl

A John Wiley & Sons, Ltd., Publication

This paperback edition first published 2010
© 2010 Blackwell Publishing Ltd

Edition history: Blackwell Publishing Ltd (hardback, 2006)

Blackwell Publishing was acquired by John Wiley & Sons in February 2007. Blackwell's publishing program has been merged with Wiley's global Scientific, Technical, and Medical business to form Wiley-Blackwell.

*Registered Office*
John Wiley & Sons Ltd, The Atrium, Southern Gate, Chichester, West Sussex, PO19 8SQ, United Kingdom

*Editorial Offices*
350 Main Street, Malden, MA 02148-5020, USA
9600 Garsington Road, Oxford, OX4 2DQ, UK
The Atrium, Southern Gate, Chichester, West Sussex, PO19 8SQ, UK

For details of our global editorial offices, for customer services, and for information about how to apply for permission to reuse the copyright material in this book please see our website at www.wiley.com/wiley-blackwell.

The right of Konrad H. Kinzl to be identified as the Author of the editorial material in this work has been asserted in accordance with the UK Copyright, Designs, and Patents Act 1988.

Wiley also publishes its books in a variety of electronic formats. Some content that appears in print may not be available in electronic books.

Designations used by companies to distinguish their products are often claimed as trademarks. All brand names and product names used in this book are trade names, service marks, trademarks or registered trademarks of their respective owners. The publisher is not associated with any product or vendor mentioned in this book. This publication is designed to provide accurate and authoritative information in regard to the subject matter covered. It is sold on the understanding that the publisher is not engaged in rendering professional services. If professional advice or other expert assistance is required, the services of a competent professional should be sought.

*Library of Congress Cataloging-in-Publication Data*

A companion to the classical Greek world / [edited by] Konrad H. Kinzl.
    p. cm.
Includes bibliographical references and index.
ISBN: 978-0-631-23014-4 (hard cover : alk. paper)
ISBN: 978-1-444-33412-8 (pbk. :          )
1. Greece—History—To 146 B.C. I. Kinzl, Konrad H.

DF214.C58 2006
938—dc22
                                        2005013103

A catalogue record for this book is available from the British Library.

Set in 10/12pt Galliard by SPi Publisher Services, Pondicherry, India.

1   2010

# Contents

# Illustrations

# Notes on Contributors

**Zofia Halina Archibald** is Lecturer in Classical Archaeology at the School of Archaeology, Classics and Egyptology, University of Liverpool. Her research has focused on the history and material culture of late Iron Age south-eastern Europe and the Black Sea. Her most recent book, with J. K. Davies and V. Gabrielsen (co-editors), is *Making, moving, and managing: the new world of ancient economies, 323–31 BCE* (Oxford 2005).

**Roger Brock** is Senior Lecturer in Classics at the University of Leeds. He is particularly interested in political aspects of Greek history, especially political imagery, and has most recently published, with Stephen Hodkinson (co-editor), *Alternatives to Athens: varieties of political organization and community in ancient Greece* (Oxford 2000).

**Kai Brodersen** is Professor of Ancient History at the University of Mannheim, and was a Visiting Fellow at the Universities of Newcastle-upon-Tyne and St Andrews. He has worked on Hellenistic history, Greek and Roman historiography and geography, epigraphy, texts on marvels and wonders, and making Classical Antiquity more accessible to a wider audience. His most recent books deal with Phlegon of Tralleis (Darmstadt 2002), Palaiphatos (Stuttgart 2003), Antiphon's *Against a Stepmother* and Pseudo-Demosthenes' *Against Neaira* (Darmstadt 2004), and the mythographer Apollodoros (Darmstadt 2004).

**Stanley M. Burstein** is Professor Emeritus of History at California State University, Los Angeles. His research focuses on the history and historiography of Greek contact with peoples living on the periphery of the Mediterranean world, particularly the Black Sea and ancient north-east Africa. He is the author of *Outpost of Hellenism: the emergence of Heraclea on the Black Sea* (Berkeley 1976), *Agatharchides of Cnidus*, On the Erythraean Sea (London 1989), and *Ancient African civilizations: Kush and Axum* (Princeton 1998).

**Nick Fisher** is Professor of Ancient History in the Cardiff School of History and Archaeology, Cardiff University.

His research interests focus on the political, social and cultural history of Archaic and Classical Greece. His books include *Hybris: a study in the values of honour and shame in ancient Greece* (Warminster 1992), *Slavery in classical Greece* (London 1993) and *Aeschines, Against Timarchos, Translated, with introduction and commentary* (Oxford 2001).

**Björn Forsén** is Director of the Finnish Institute at Athens. His research deals mainly with the dedication of votive offerings in Greek sanctuaries, settlement patterns, population fluctuations and the formation of poleis. Recent publications include the monographs *Griechische Gliederweihungen* (Helsinki 1996); with J. Forsén, *The Asea valley survey: an Arcadian mountain valley* (Stockholm 2003); and, with G. Stanton (coeditor), *The Pnyx in the history of Athens* (Helsinki 1996).

**Lin Foxhall** is Professor of Greek Archaeology and History at the University of Leicester. She has published extensively on gender in classical antiquity, as well as on agriculture and the ancient economy. She has written *Olive cultivation in Ancient Greece: seeking the ancient economy* (in press) and co-edited *Greek law in its political setting: justifications not justice* (Oxford 1996), *Thinking men: masculinity and its self-representation in the Classical tradition* (London 1998) and *When men were men: masculinity, power and identity in Classical Antiquity* (London 1998).

**Peter Funke** is Professor of Ancient History at the Westfälische Wilhelms-Universität, Münster. The focus of his research is the political history of the Greek states from the archaic to the hellenistic period, ancient constitutions and interstate relations, and the study of the Greek world in its geographical and topographical setting. His most recent book is *Athen in klassischer Zeit* (Munich ²2003).

**Thomas Harrison** is Rathbone Professor of Ancient History and Classical Archaeology at the University of Liverpool. He is the author of *Divinity and history: the religion of Herodotus* (Oxford 2000) and *The emptiness of Asia: Aeschylus' Persians and the history of the fifth century* (London 2000), and the editor of *Greeks and barbarians* (Edinburgh 2002).

**Waldemar Heckel** is Professor of Ancient History at the University of Calgary. His most important publications include *The last days and testament of Alexander the Great* (Stuttgart 1988) and *The marshals of Alexander's empire* (London 1992). His most recent work is *Who's who in the age of Alexander the Great* (Oxford 2005). He is a Fellow of the Centre for Military and Strategic Studies at the University of Calgary.

**J. Donald Hughes** is John Evans Professor of Ancient History at the University of Denver. He is the author of *Pan's travail: environmental problems of the ancient Greeks and Romans* (Baltimore 1994) and *The Mediterranean: an environmental history* (Santa Barbara 2005). A founding member of both the American Society for Environmental History and the European Society for Environmental History, he is also author of *An environmental history of the world: humankind's changing role in the community of life* (London 2001).

**Emily Kearns** is currently a Senior Research Fellow at St Hilda's College, Oxford. Her publications include *The heroes of Attica* (London 1989) and, with Simon Price (co-editor), *The Oxford dictionary of classical myth and religion* (Oxford 2003).

**Bruce LaForse** is an Assistant Professor of Classics at Wright State University, Dayton, Ohio. He is interested in fourth-century Greek history and has published articles on Xenophon's writings.

**Steven Lattimore** is Professor Emeritus of Classics and Classical Archaeology at the University of California, Los Angeles. He has worked mainly on Greek sculpture of the fourth century BCE, with some attention also to Greek literature and history. Recent publications include 'Skopas and the Pothos' in: *American Journal of Archeology* 91 (1987) 411–20; *Isthmia*, vol. 6: *Marble sculpture 1967–1980* (Princeton 1996); and *Thucydides*: The Peloponnesian War (trans. with intro. notes, and glossary) (Indianapolis 1998).

**John W. I. Lee** is Assistant Professor of History at the University of California, Santa Barbara. His research focuses on the social and cultural aspects of classical Greek warfare. He has published articles on ancient urban battle and on women in Greek armies, and is currently finishing a book on community life in Xenophon's *Anabasis*.

**Kathryn Lomas** is Research Fellow at the Institute of Archaeology, University College London. Her research focuses on the urbanization of Italy, and on issues of cultural and ethnic identity in the ancient world. She is the author of *Rome and the Western Greeks* (London 1993) and *Roman Italy, 338 BC–AD 200* (London 1996), and has published numerous articles on pre-Roman and Roman Italy, urbanism and colonization in the Greek and Roman world, and ethnic and cultural identity. Her current research is a study of the development of literacy in pre-Roman Italy.

**Lynette G. Mitchell** is Senior Lecturer in Classics and Ancient History at the University of Exeter. Her work is concerned with the impact on each other of social norms and political life in Greece in the archaic and classical periods. She is the author of *Greeks bearing gifts* (Cambridge 1997).

**G. J. Oliver** is Lecturer in Ancient Greek Culture in the School of Archaeology, Classics and Egyptology, University of Liverpool. His main research interests are Classical and Hellenistic history, the Greek economy and epigraphy. He is the author of *War, food and politics in early Hellenistic Athens* (Oxford 2006). Currently he is completing for publication, after a period of research funded by the UK Arts and Humanities Research Board, a fascicle of state decrees and laws of Athens from 321 to 301 BCE for the third edition of *IG 2/3²*.

**Sarah B. Pomeroy**, Distinguished Professor of Classics Emerita, Hunter College and the Graduate School, CUNY, is the author of many books on women and ancient history, including *Goddesses, whores, wives, and slaves: women in classical antiquity* (New York 1975/1995), *Women in Hellenistic Egypt from Alexander to Cleopatra* (New York 1984), *Xenophon*, Oeconomicus: *a social and historical commentary; with a new English translation* (Oxford 1994), *Families in classical and Hellenistic Greece: representations and realities* (Oxford 1997), and *Spartan women* (New York 2002). She is also co-author of *Women's realities, women's choices: an introduction to women's studies* (New York ³2005), *Women's history and ancient history* (Chapel Hill 1991), *Women in the classical world: image and text* (Oxford 1995), *A brief history of ancient Greece* (New York 2004), and *Plutarch's* Advice to the bride and groom, *and* A consolation to his wife (Oxford 1999).

**Susan Prince** is Assistant Professor of Classics at the University of Colorado, Boulder. Her research is in the history of Greek philosophy, rhetoric, myth and prose literature. She is completing a book on the literary fragments and persona of Antisthenes, which demonstrates his intellectual relationships with his teacher Socrates, contemporary thinkers of the Sophistic movement, and his heirs Diogenes of Sinope and the Cynics.

**Kurt A. Raaflaub** is David Herlihy University Professor and Professor of Classics and History at Brown University, where he is also director of the Program in Ancient Studies. His main fields of interest are the social, political and intellectual history of archaic and classical Greece and the Roman republic. He most recently published *The discovery of freedom in ancient Greece* (Chicago 2004) and, with J. Ober and R. Wallace (co-authors), *Origins of democracy in ancient Greece* (Berkeley 2006).

**P. J. Rhodes** retired in 2005 as Professor of Ancient History at Durham. He has worked on Greek history, especially politics and political institutions, and has edited and commented on literary (Thucydides, the Aristotelian *Athenian Constitution*) and epigraphic texts; his *History of the Classical Greek world* was published by Blackwell in 2005.

**Robert Rollinger** is Professor of Ancient History at the University of Innsbruck. His primary research focus is Archaic Greek and Ancient Near Eastern History, including Greek historiography (especially Herodotos), intellectual history and intercultural contacts between the Greek and Near Eastern worlds. His most recent publications are, with C. Ulf (co-editor), *Das Archaische Griechenland* (Berlin 2004) and *Commerce and monetary systems in the Ancient world* (Stuttgart 2004); further monographs and other publications are in press.

**Robert W. Wallace** is Professor of Classics at Northwestern University. Recent publications include, with L. Edmunds (co-editor), *Poet, public and performance in ancient Greece* (Baltimore 1997); with E. Harris (co-editor), *Transitions to empire: studies in Greco-Roman history 360–146 B.C. in honor of Ernst Badian* (Norman OK 1996); with J. Ober and K. A. Raaflaub (co-authors), *Origins of democracy in ancient Greece* (Berkeley 2005); and, with M. Gagarin (co-editor), *Symposion 2001: Akten der Gesellschaft für griechische und hellenistische Rechtsgeschichte* (Cologne (forthcoming)).

**Uwe Walter** is Professor of Ancient History at the University of Bielefeld. He has worked on the early Greek polis, Roman historiography, the culture of historical memory in the Roman Republic, and the history of classical scholarship. His most recent book is *Memoria und res publica: Zur Geschichtskultur der römischen Republik* (Frankfurt 2004).

**Karl-Wilhelm Welwei** is Professor Emeritus of Ancient History at the Ruhr-Universität Bochum. His books range from *Unfreie im antiken Kriegsdienst*, 3 vols (Wiesbaden 1974–88), and *Die griechische Polis* (Stuttgart ²1998), to the most recent titles: *Die griechische Frühzeit: 2000 bis 500 v. Chr.* (Munich 2002), *Res publica und Imperium: Kleine Schriften zur römischen Geschichte* (Stuttgart 2004), and *Sparta: Aufstieg und Niedergang einer antiken Groamacht* (Stuttgart 2004).

# Preface

It is the editor's hope that this volume will offer, by its structure, organization and concept, an inspiring perspective, and will serve that audience well which Blackwell had in mind when they embarked on this enterprise: as 'a personal reference source for specialist historians, particularly those operating in adjacent fields of history, and as a "vade mecum" for undergraduate and graduate students'.

It is hoped that readers will in particular find much assembled here between the covers of one volume which they could otherwise locate only in a widely scattered variety of scholarly publications; and which they will not find in other volumes on this difficult period of ancient Greek History: chapters on government, the environment, art, philosophy, rhetoric, religion, society; on far distant regions to which ancient Greek civilization had spread or by which it was influenced, from the 'Pillars of Hercules' to Persia and India, and from the Crimea to North Africa. The historical narrative, while in many ways the backbone of any historical investigation, has been placed at the end of the volume in order to allow attention to be drawn to the many other aspects – not to negate its essential function.

A special and personal debt of gratitude is owed by me to Al Bertrand, without whose untiring support I would not have been able to complete the volume; to all others who worked at or for Blackwell Publishing on this volume; and last but not least to both Dr Thomas Elliott for generously creating the original blank maps and Dr Jörn Kobes for thoroughly reworking them for use in this book. The most deeply felt expression of gratitude, however, must go to the contributors of the chapters, *who collectively are the authors of this book.*

Konrad H. Kinzl

# Abbreviations and
# a Note on Spelling

This list resolves or explains abbreviations of frequently cited ancient authors or their works, editions and translations of inscriptions, books, and journals.

## Ancient Authors

| | |
|---|---|
| *Ath. Pol.* | (1) Aristotle (some contributors who wish to indicate that they question his immediate authorship write Aristotelian or Pseudo-Aristotle or [Aristotle]) *Constitution of Athens* (*Athenaion Politeia*); normally, *Ath. Pol.* without author's name refers to this treatise<br>(2) [Xenophon] or Pseudo-Xenophon (i.e., the work was transmitted amongst the genuine ones by Xenophon but wrongly ascribed to him in antiquity) *Constitution of Athens* (*Athenaion Politeia*); often referred to as 'The Old Oligarch' |
| Athenaios | Athenaios (or Athenaeus) *The Learned Banquet* (*Deiphnosophistai*) |
| Diodoros | Diodoros (or Diodorus Siculus) *Historical Library* (*Bibliotheke Historike*) |
| Hdt. | Herodotos (or Herodotus) *Histories* |
| *Lak. Pol.* | Xenophon *Constitution of Sparta* (*Lakedaimonion Politeia*) |
| Polyainos | Polyainos (or Polyaenus) *On Stratagems* (*Strategemata*) |
| *Suda* | Byzantine period lexicon (sometimes, erroneously, referred to as the author Suidas) |
| Thuc. | Thucydides *History of the Peloponnesian War* |

## Collections of Authors (Largely only Fragmentary)

| | |
|---|---|
| Diels-Kranz | Diels, H. (⁶1951–2) *Die Fragmente der Vorsokratiker* ed. W. Kranz, 3 vols (numerous repr.) (Berlin: Weidmann; now Hildesheim: Olms) |
| *FGrHist* | Jacoby, F., et al. (1923–) *Die Fragmente der griechischen Historiker* [in progress], parts A and B (Berlin: Weidmann; parts A–C now: Leiden: Brill; CD-Rom ed. Leiden: Brill 2004; new part '4' Leiden: Brill 1998–) |

(Worthington, I. (ed.-in-chief), et al.) (2006–) *Brill's New Jacoby*, parts A–C (updated text, with trans. and new comm.) (Leiden: Brill))

Kassel & Austin    Kassel, R., & C. Austin (1983–) *Poetae Comici Graeci*, 8 vols [in progress] (Berlin: de Gruyter)

# Inscriptions

## Greek texts

IG    *Inscriptiones Graecae* (Berlin: de Gruyter (formerly Reimer) 1873–)

IG 1³    Lewis, D. M. (ed.) *Inscriptiones Atticae Euclidis anno anteriores*, fasc.1: *Decreta et tabulae magistratuum*; fasc. 2: *Dedicationes, catalogi, termini, tituli sepulcrales, varia, tituli Attici extra Atticam reperti, addenda*; fasc. 3: *Indices* (Berlin: de Gruyter ³1981–98)

IG 2²    Kirchner, J. (ed.) *Inscriptiones Graecae*, editio minor, vol. 2/3: *Inscriptiones Atticae Euclidis anno posteriores* (Berlin: de Gruyter (formerly Reimer) 1924–40)

SEG    *Supplementum Epigraphicum Graecum*

Staatsverträge    Bengtson, H. (1975) *Die Staatsverträge des Altertums*, vol. 2 (Munich: Beck ²1975)

## Greek texts with commentaries

M&L    Meiggs, R., & D. M. Lewis (1988) *A selection of Greek historical inscriptions to the end of the fifth century B.C.* (revised ed.) (Oxford: Clarendon 1988)

R&O    Rhodes, P. J., & R. Osborne (2003) (eds) *Greek historical inscriptions, 400–323 BC* (ed. with intro., trans., and comm.) (Oxford: Oxford University Press)

Tod    Tod, M. N. (1933–48) *A selection of Greek historical inscriptions*, 2 vols (Oxford: Clarendon)

## Translations (including otherwise inaccessible literary texts)

Fornara    Fornara, C. W. (1983) *Archaic times to the end of the Peloponnesian War* (Cambridge: Cambridge University Press ²1983) (Translated Documents of Greece and Rome 1)

Harding    Harding, P. (1985) *From the end of the Peloponnesian war to the battle of Ipsus* (Cambridge: Cambridge University Press) (Translated Documents of Greece and Rome 2)

# Standard Works of Reference

CAH²4    Boardman, J., N. G. L. Hammond, D. M. Lewis, M. Ostwald (eds) *The Cambridge ancient history*, vol. 4: *Persia, Greece and the western Mediterranean* (Cambridge: Cambridge University Press ²1988)

CAH²5    Lewis, D. M., J. Boardman, J. K. Davies, M. Ostwald (eds) *The Cambridge ancient history*, vol. 5: *The fifth century B.C.* (Cambridge: Cambridge University Press ²1992)

CAH²6    Lewis, D. M., J. Boardman, S. Hornblower, M. Ostwald (eds) *The Cambridge ancient history*, vol. 6: *The fourth century B.C.* (Cambridge: Cambridge University Press ²1994)

OCD³    Hornblower, S., & A. Spawforth (eds) *The Oxford classical dictionary* (Oxford: Oxford University Press ³1996)

# Journals

| | |
|---|---|
| *AJAH* | *American Journal of Ancient History* |
| *AJAH* ns | *American Journal of Ancient History* new series (vols 1– (2002–)) |
| *AJPh* | *American Journal of Philology* |
| *BCH* | *Bulletin de correspondence hellénique* |
| *CJ* | *Classical Journal* |
| *CPh* | *Classical Philology* |
| *CQ* | *Classical Quarterly* |
| *CR* | *Classical Review* |
| *CSCA* | *California Studies in Classical Antiquity* |
| *G&R* | *Greece and Rome* |
| *GRBS* | *Greek, Roman and Byzantine Studies* |
| *HSPh* | *Harvard Studies in Classical Philology* |
| *JFA* | *Journal of Field Archaeology* |
| *JHS* | *Journal of Hellenic Studies* |
| *JMA* | *Journal of Mediterranean Archaeology* |
| *LCM* | *Liverpool Classical Monthly* |
| *NC* | *Numismatic Chronicle* |
| *PCPhS* | *Proceedings of the Cambridge Philological Society* |
| *TAPhA* | *Transactions* [formerly: *Transactions and Proceedings*] *of the American Philological Association* |
| *ZPE* | *Zeitschrift für Papyrologie und Epigraphik* |

# A Note on Spelling

Ancient Greek names are as far as possible rendered in what might be labelled moderate transliteration. As a model I cite J. K. Davies' *Athenian propertied families, 600–300 B.C.* (Oxford: Clarendon 1972). I also transliterate familiar names which in English *pronunciation* are identical to the Latinized/Anglicized forms, e.g., Sokrates, Herodotos, Attika. The common English is retained only for names which are to all intents and purposes part of the English language, such as Macedonia, Athens, Plutarch, Thucydides. Cases of doubt must inevitably remain.

The various chapters were written using UK or US spelling; it would have been presumptuous for the editor to impose 'foreign' spelling rules on the authors' work. The same difference occurs in the chapter bibliographies, in which a UK author will cite the UK publisher and the US author the US publisher of one and the same title: any library or bookseller's catalogue will provide instant clarification.

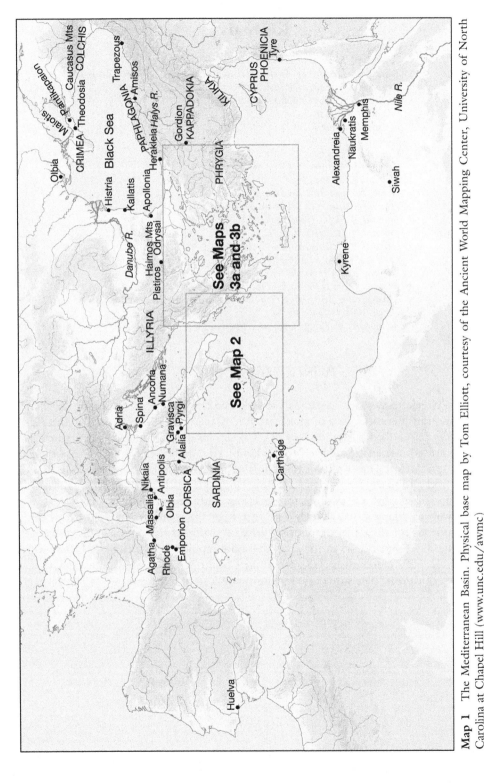

**Map 1** The Mediterranean Basin. Physical base map by Tom Elliott, courtesy of the Ancient World Mapping Center, University of North Carolina at Chapel Hill (www.unc.edu/awmc)

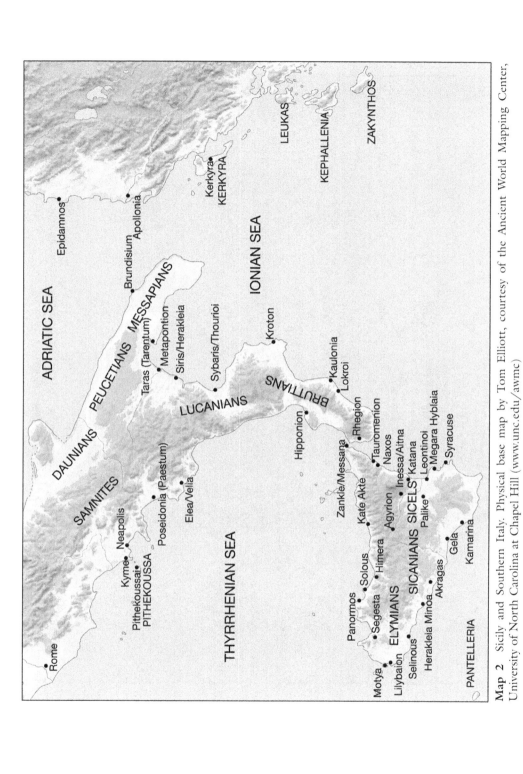

**Map 2** Sicily and Southern Italy. Physical base map by Tom Elliott, courtesy of the Ancient World Mapping Center, University of North Carolina at Chapel Hill (www.unc.edu/awmc)

ADRIATIC SEA

IONIAN SEA

THYRRHENIAN SEA

Rome

Kyme
Neapolis
Pithekoussai
PITHEKOUSSA

Poseidonia (Paestum)

Elea/Velia

SAMNITES

DAUNIANS

PEUCETIANS

MESSAPIANS

LUCANIANS

BRUTTIANS

Epidamnos

Brundisium
Apollonia

Kerkyra
KERKYRA

LEUKAS

KEPHALLENIA

ZAKYNTHOS

Taras (Tarentum)
Metapontion
Siris/Herakleia

Sybaris/Thourioi

Kroton

Kaulonia
Lokroi

Hipponion

Rhegion

Zankle/Messana

Kate Akte

Panormos
Solous
Segesta
Himera

Motya
Lilybaion
Selinous

Herakleia Minoa

Akragas

ELYMIANS

SICANIANS

SICELS

Agyrion

Palike

Gela

Kamarina

Inessa/Aitna
Katana
Leontinoi
Megara Hyblaia
Syracuse

Tauromenion
Naxos

PANTELLERIA

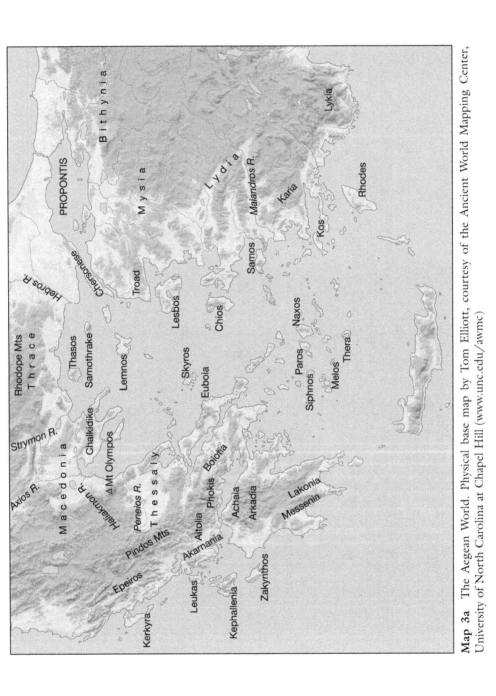

**Map 3a** The Aegean World. Physical base map by Tom Elliott, courtesy of the Ancient World Mapping Center, University of North Carolina at Chapel Hill (www.unc.edu/awmc)

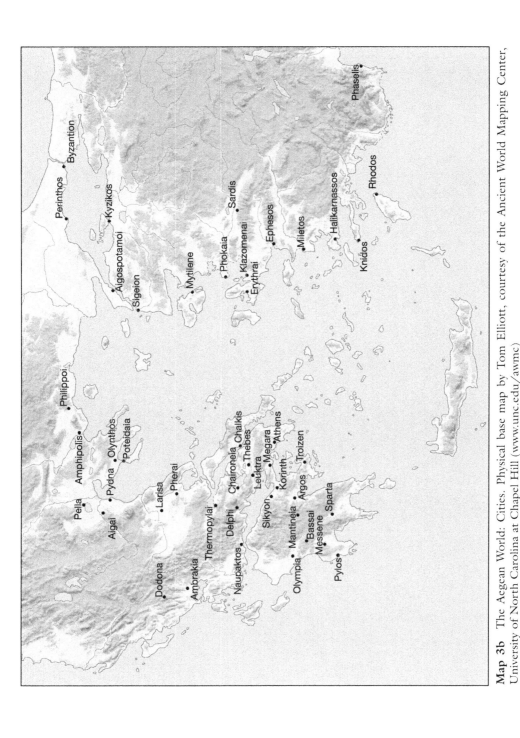

**Map 3b** The Aegean World: Cities. Physical base map by Tom Elliott, courtesy of the Ancient World Mapping Center, University of North Carolina at Chapel Hill (www.unc.edu/awmc)

CHAPTER ONE

# The Classical Age as a Historical Epoch

*Uwe Walter*

## 1  Introduction

To call the epoch in Greek history between the end of the great Persian War in 479/8 and the death of Alexander the Great in 323 the 'Classical Age' poses a problem. This is, admittedly, not a problem waiting to be solved and then set aside – rather, this problem is provocative, insolubly imprecise and perhaps still a challenge. The use of the term 'Classical' for a particular epoch in Greek history and 'Classics' for a branch of higher learning, and the term 'Classical Studies' for an entire discipline, makes one thing unmistakably clear: modern study of ancient history was at the very outset, for a long time continued to be, and indeed has ever since been inextricably associated with aesthetic, qualitative and normative ideas. When in the middle of the eighteenth century, i.e., long before the major archaeological excavations in Greece, Johann Joachim Winckelmann (1717–68) began his study of ancient art, far fewer remains of this art existed or were accessible than is the case today. The relatively few pieces of sculpture which had not become buried – all Roman copies of original Greek masterpieces – were for Winckelmann, however, not only the remains of a bygone era, but above all examples of a consummate artistic view of man. His description of the Apollo Belvedere begins with the sentence: 'The statue of Apollo represents the highest artistic ideal of all the surviving works of antiquity.' In his *Reflections on Painting and Sculpture of the Greeks* (1755, English trans. 1765), Winckelmann formulated the credo of a new Humanism: 'The only way for us to become great, or even inimitable if possible, is to imitate the Greeks' (on all this in general, Marchand 1996).

The rediscovery of Greece, fostered primarily by the drawings and descriptions of buildings in Athens by James Spratt and Nicholas Revett (*The Antiquities of Athens*, 4 vols, 1762–1808), and the championing of freedom by the Philhellenes increased the feeling of affinity with the ancient Greeks. This was expressed most succinctly in the famous words of the Romantic poet Percy Bysshe Shelley (1792–1822): 'We are all

Greeks. Our laws, our literature, our religion, our arts, have their roots in Greece' (on Shelley, Wallace 1997). When in the wake of the French Revolution in Europe political parties began to take shape, they all sought and found their political and cultural guarantors in the Greeks (Morris 1994: 29–30). From the perspective of conservatives, Greece stood for order, tradition and self-discipline, while for liberals like George Grote, the ancient Athenians in particular were the ideal of the active citizen, whereas for radicals like Shelley, the Hellenes represented the combination of republicanism, liberty and living life to the full. Even kings could attain self-glorification by formal recourse to the Greeks: in 1802, Antonio Canova created a colossal nude marble portrait statue of Napoleon, in a Greek pose, holding Victory on a sphere in his outstretched hand, striking the same pose as Pheidias' Athena in the Parthenon (Boardman 1993: pl. IV).

This power of the Greek ideal exerted a very significant influence on the study of the Hellenes, at least at the outset. For instance, Ernst Curtius (1814–96), the excavator of Olympia and author of a widely read *History of Greece* (English ed. in 5 vols, 1868–73), in a public lecture in 1844 still emphasized completely in this spirit the importance of the Akropolis in Athens: 'The breath of new life has crossed from there into our art *and scholarship* [my emphasis].' To this very day every serious definition of the term 'classical' (for a general discussion, Porter 2006, intro., with further bibliography) must place this idea of impulse and dynamics in the foreground. 'Classical' means something old, which has stood the test of time and speaks to every generation as if it had been designed for precisely that generation. It is obvious, however, that not all previous eras could be regarded as equally creative in this sense. The Apollo Belvedere, Winckelmann's model, was produced about 330–320 (Figure 1.1; Boardman 1993: no. 133), and the buildings on the Akropolis in the second half of the fifth century – accordingly, both in the 'Classical Period' of Greek art and Greek history. In connection with the structures from the time of Perikles – not only those on the Akropolis – Plutarch offered the following comment in the second century CE:

> For every particular piece of his work was immediately, even at that time, for its beauty and elegance, antique; and yet in its vigour and freshness looks to this day as if it were just executed. There is a sort of bloom of newness upon those works of his, preserving them from the touch of time, as if they had some perennial spirit and undying vitality mingled in the composition of them. (Plutarch *Perikles* 13.2; trans. J. Dryden)

By contrast, in modern study of classical antiquity, especially in Greek and Roman history, this value-laden affinity between classical Greece and our own time is cited as a mere convention or vigorously denied. A statement by the German ancient historian Christian Meier may suffice for the first position:

> In describing the characteristic features of Greek civilization, it is customary to invoke the concept of the 'classical' – a model for many, the attraction of which lay in all that had been achieved, experienced and represented, within the narrow confines of the world of the polis, in terms of accomplishments, of intellectual questions and matching up to the questioning, of human greatness and commensurability with events. (Meier 1990: 25)

In opposition to this convention, it is currently fashionable to emphasize precisely the strangeness of the Greeks. According to Cartledge, the object is 'to defamiliarize

**Figure 1.1**    The Apollo Belvedere, c. 330–320 BCE. Ht. 2.24 m. Roman marble copy of the original bronze. Vatican Museums, Rome. Photo: Hirmer Verlag München.

Classical Greek civilization, to fracture that beguilingly easy identification with the
ancient Greeks which reached a climax in post-Enlightenment Germany, Second
Empire France, and Victorian Britain, and which still has its residual adherents today,
partly no doubt for political rather than purely academic reasons' (Cartledge 1993:
175). This historicizing often takes on the character of vigorous iconoclasm, in which
exclusion and suppression of slaves, women, foreigners and the underprivileged in
everyday life and in the mentality of the Greeks are emphasized (e.g., Cohen 2000; von
den Hoff & Schmidt 2001). Moreover, the concerted efforts since the mid-1980s to
conduct a 'more realistic discourse which treats Greek and Eastern Mediterranean
history as a continuum and thereby begins to dissolve the intrinsically racist distinction
between "Greek" and "oriental" ' (Davies 2002: 235–6) point in this direction. The
relevant specialized studies admittedly concentrate rather on the Archaic Period. More
recent general introductions to Greek history, in which the word 'classical' appears in
the title (e.g., Davies 1993; cf. Osborne 2000), are not, however, essentially different
in their conceptual orientation from those studies which avoid the term and indicate
their subject by means of simply a neutral date (e.g., Hornblower 2002; *CAH*$^2$ 5 and
6). In the political and 'realistically' written grand narrative histories of the nineteenth
and early twentieth centuries by George Grote, Karl Julius Beloch and Eduard Meyer,
and even in Jacob Burckhardt's four-volume *Griechische Kulturgeschichte* (1898–1902;
Burckhardt 1998), the term 'classical' is not found in either the title or the chapter
heading of a single one. For these authors, however, the principal importance of
ancient history and culture was still completely self-evident. Then, however, within
the context of the new intellectual approach after the First World War, scholars adopted
the concept of 'classical' (see Jaeger 1931; Reinhardt 1941; Borbein 1995).

## 2   Classical – Primarily as a Feature in Literature and Art

The word 'classic', which means 'regarded as representing an exemplary standard'
and 'outstanding of its kind', is derived from the Latin adjective *classicus*, 'member of
a tax class (*classis*)'; *classicus* belongs to the vocabulary of Roman social hierarchy. The
learned Roman writer Cornelius Fronto (second century CE) used it in an evaluative
and superlative sense to designate outstanding writers (*classicus, assiduusque scriptor,
non proletarius*: 'a high-ranking and authoritative writer, not one of the common
herd', Aulus Gellius *Noctes Atticae* 19.8.15). In the sense of 'first class', and therefore
by inference also 'exemplary', the word appears for the first time in French. In 1548,
Thomas Sébillet (1512–89), in his *Art poétique françois*, spoke of *les bons et classiques
poètes françois* ('the excellent and classic French poets'); he had in mind a number of
the 'exemplary' poets of the Middle Ages. Since only ancient writers, however, were
regarded as exemplary within the context of humanist education, the adjective
'classical' was soon reserved only for them – and referred almost exclusively to non-
Christian writers. Accordingly, the term 'Classical antiquity' refers to the pagan
Greeks and Romans from Homer to late antiquity. The concept 'classical' retained
its qualitative meaning, but could be identified with a very specific period or several
periods, whose cultural achievements were regarded as outstanding and exemplary.
Voltaire (1694–1778), accordingly, called the era of Perikles, the Age of Augustus

**Table 1.1** The Classical Age

| | Art: Epoch | Art: Style | Art: Significant sculptures and buildings | Political History: Epoch | Political History: Significant events | | |
|---|---|---|---|---|---|---|---|
| 490 | | | | Persian Wars (499–479) | Battle of Marathon (490) | 490 | |
| 480 | Early Classical | 'Severe style' | Critian Boy (c. 485–480) | | Battle of Salamis (480) | 480 | |
| 470 | | | Tyrannicides (476) | | Rise of the Athenian Empire (since 478) | 470 | Bipolar Greece (478–404) |
| 460 | | | Temple of Zeus in Olympia (c. 465–460) | | | 460 | |
| 450 | | | | Pentekontaetia (478–432) | | 450 | |
| 440 | High Classical | | Parthenon (448–432) | | 'Age of Perikles' (450–429) | 440 | |
| 430 | | | Doryphoros (c. 440) | | | 430 | |
| 420 | | | Kresilas' portraiture of Perikles (c. 430) | Peloponnesian War (431–404) | | 420 | |
| 410 | | | | | | 410 | |
| 400 | | 'Rich style' | | | Thirty Tyrants (404/3) | 400 | |
| 390 | Late Classical | | | Sparta | 'King's Peace' (387/6) | 390 | Multipolar Greece (394–361) |
| 380 | | | | | | 380 | |
| 370 | | | Eirene of Ke-phi-so-do-tos (c.375) | Struggle for hegemony (404–338) | Battle of Leuktra (371) | 370 | |
| 360 | | | | Thebes | Battle of Mantineia (362) | 360 | |
| 350 | | | | | | 350 | |
| 340 | | | | | | 340 | |
| 330 | | | | Macedonian hegemony | Battle of Chaironeia (338) | 330 | Greece dominated (since 338) |
| 320 | | | Apollo Belvedere | | Alexander in Asia (since 334) | 320 | |

HELLENISM

and that of Louis XIV each a 'Golden Age' – and associated with them 'classical' authors who were a characteristic feature of each of these cultural high-points. In the nineteenth century this emphasis in terminology, which was at the same time accompanied by a narrowing in meaning, entered the field of Classical Studies. Now works written in the fifth and fourth centuries, chiefly in Athens and in the Attic dialect, were designated as 'classical Greek literature'. While the nature of our sources, mostly written in the Attic dialect, determined the Athenocentricity of the Classical model, it was only too easy to corroborate it by quoting from the ancient authors. The historian Thucydides (c. 460–400) called Athens the 'School of Hellas' (*paideia tes Hellados*) (Thuc. 2.41.1), and Plato (428–347) praised his home town as the 'very sanctuary of the wisdom of Greece' (Plato *Protagoras* 337D).

As could already be learned from Winckelmann, Stuart and Curtius, Greek antiquity of the fifth and fourth centuries did not exert a lasting influence in art in only the eighteenth and nineteenth centuries. This is not the place to discuss the periods and the problem of Classicism (for a succinct overview, see *Encyclopedia Britannica* (Deluxe Edition CD-ROM 2001): entries 'Classicism' and 'Neoclassicism'). In all the branches of Classical Studies, however, it is probably Classical archaeology that is most profoundly characterized by the 'Classical' ideal of form and expression. At the same time, it was influenced by literature on the history of art, and again by Winckelmann, who was exclusively engaged in clarifying the development of styles in the various art genres. Since the 1920s the normative, and therefore, strictly speaking, the timeless notion of 'classical' simultaneously denotes a specific phase in a historical development (the fifth and fourth centuries) – a phase which is regarded as the qualitative pinnacle. Scholars attempted to explain the outstanding virtues of Classical art – harmony, balance and

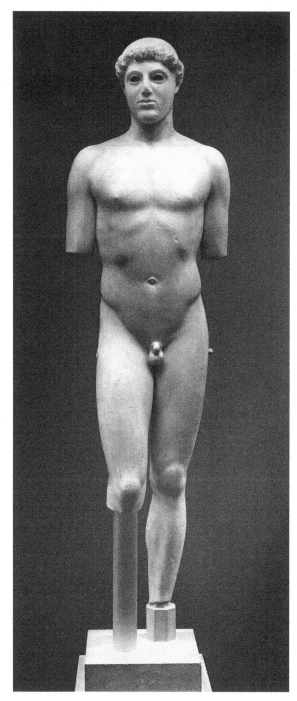

**Figure 1.2**   The Critian Boy, c. 485–480 BCE. Athens Akropolis Museum. Ht. 1.17 m. DAI, Athens. Neg. No. 1972/2938. Photographer: Hellner.

general validity – by claiming that the Classical Period lay between an Archaic era mired in tradition and a Hellenistic Period characterized by individualism. In the Classical Period the tensions between tradition and self-determination, between adherence to the polis and individualism, self-control and striving for power, it was argued, developed into a dialectic process. Sculpture no less than tragedy, historiography and philosophy strove to express these tensions, to reflect them, and to overcome them (see Pollitt 1972; Borbein 1993). Such explanations may be of interest as documents of a meta-historical character. No one nowadays, however, would consider the Archaic Period merely as an epoch of departure rather than fulfilment (a stage that could by definition be reached only during the Classical Period), or see Hellenism as the dissolution and decay of the zenith reached by the classical forms.

Archaeologists, however, believe themselves to be on firmer ground when it comes to working out an internal division of the Classical Period on the basis of prominent works of sculpture. The diagnostic starting point was contraposition, which gave a more natural appearance than the stiff poses of the older figures. By shifting the weight to the supporting leg, the figure created the impression of actually moving. Contraposition affected the entire figure, so that it now emerged as a unified organism. In this sense the Critian Boy (Figure 1.2; Boardman 1993: 88) represents a decisive step from the Archaic to the Classical Period.

Classical art strives for perfection, but at the same time provides scope for change and creative competition. On the one hand, this quality corroborates Winckelmann's idea and that of the Neo-Humanists, but, on the other, it warns against the danger of inertia which threatens everything Classical. The Classical archaeologist John Boardman describes this feature as follows:

> The 'classical orders' of architecture carry connotations of fixed rules and forms which, however, as study shows, were not blindly followed as a pattern-book, but which served as models within which subtleties of design and proportion could be exercised. In 'classical art' there are rules too, including a certain agreement to observe realistic rendering of the human figure, but generally in terms of ideal forms which might be rendered with as great precision as the architectural forms, and yet leave the artist the fullest scope for individual expression. What the neo-classicists did not realize was that idealization and a degree of truth to nature were not incompatible, and had been successfully reconciled in the Classical Period . . . This was the message of the Parthenon marbles. In some ways there were more rules in classical art than in arts of other cultures, but they were not restrictive. Indeed, they provided a basis for the development of the widest range of expression, both formal and humane. They guaranteed continuity without stifling change, and herein must lie their strength and durability, the reason why time and again artists have returned to them for inspiration and guidance (Boardman 1993: 8–9).

## 3 Could the Greeks of the Classical Period have Known the Concept We Describe as 'Classical'?

Although, as noted above, 'classical' is essentially a modern concept, the actual phenomenon already existed much earlier – i.e., in the 'Classical Period' itself. It is therefore legitimate to continue to use the term, and this not simply for reasons of convention. Already in the second half of the fifth century at least one artist and one historian each boasted of having created a work that could claim to be a model and would be a standard for future activity far beyond their own day. First, the sculptor Polykleitos of Sikyon produced exclusively statues of a single type – the nude standing youth. He perpetually produced works characterized by pose, rhythm and vivid articulation. Polykleitos was also the first artist ever to discuss this type in a (lost) work entitled *Kanon*. This treatise probably gave guidelines on the proportion of the ideal male body on the basis of a mathematical ratio designed to guarantee a supernatural beauty. Second, the historian Thucydides of Athens claimed that with his *History of the Peloponnesian War* he was writing a practical manual for statesmen, 'compiled not for a contest of the moment, but as a possession for all time' (*ktema es aiei*: Thuc. 1.22.4). It is no accident that Polykleitos and Thucydides were sooner or later to become the centre of the discussion on Classicism.

In retrospect, especially after the turning point of the Peloponnesian War (431–404), the extraordinary achievements of the three preceding generations were readily acknowledged, although in general there was no let-up in creativity, and in some areas, e.g., in rhetoric and philosophical prose, the greatest achievements still lay in the future. In respect of tragedy, the view soon became widespread that after Aischylos, Sophokles and Euripides, only second-rate poets were still active, who were no longer able to hold a candle to the three great tragedians (cf. Aristophanes *Frogs* 71–2; 96–7, written in 405).

From 386 the staging of earlier plays was also permitted in the tragic competitions, and in 338 Lykourgos, one of the leading politicians in Athens, took it upon himself to ensure that official texts of these 'classical' plays were established and stored in the state archives. These texts were to be mandatory for future re-runs. Otherwise, statues of the three tragic poets were erected in the newly renovated Theatre of Dionysos. This measure, along with others, was designed both to preserve Athens' great past and also to rekindle it (Hintzen-Bohlen 1996). Then, in the Hellenistic Period, it was the great schools and libraries, especially the Mouseion in Alexandreia (from 280 BCE), where inventories and texts were drawn up of those Greek authors who were regarded as most representative of each category: the nine lyric poets, the three tragedians, the ten Attic orators, etc. These authors, 'who had stood the test of time' (*qui vetustatem pertulerunt*, Quintilian *Institutio* 10.1.40), became 'canonical', and much of the scholarship of the time was devoted to their preservation, classification, and exegesis (Easterling 2002). In combination with the concept of *paideia*, the Alexandrians presented themselves, as a certain Andron puts it, as 'educators of all the world, of both Greeks and barbarians' (*FGrHist* 246 F 1; on *paideia*, still fundamental, Jaeger 1954–61).

In Attic sculpture, too, there were already in the fourth century stylistic references back to the fifth century, which conveyed a political statement. Thus the Eirene (the goddess of peace), produced by Kephisodotos about 370, was designed to celebrate Athens' rise once again after the defeat of 404 (Figure 1.3; Stewart 1990: 173–4, 275–6, plates 485–7). The arrangement of the drapery recalls the style of Pheidias, who in the heyday of Athens, between 460 and 430, produced, among other works, the bronze statue of Athena Promachos, at least seven metres high, and the chryselephantine Athena Parthenos, more than twelve metres high (for a reconstruction of the latter, see Boardman 1993: no. 106A). Otherwise, it is precisely in the most

**Figure 1.3**  The Peace Goddess Eirene and the Boy Pluto. Ht. 2.01 m. Roman marble copy after a statue by Kephisodotos the Elder, active c. 375 BCE. Staatliche Antikensammlungen und Glyptothek, Munich. Photo: akg- images.

advanced works by the artists of the late Classical Period, like Praxiteles and Lysippos, that there is an unmistakable flashback to works of the fifth century. These were viewed as models – in other words, 'classical'. Lysippos is said to have regarded the famous Doryphoros ('spearbearer') of Polykleitos (Figure 1.4; Boardman 1993: no. 93) as his model (Cicero *Brutus* 296).

From the last third of the fifth century the Athenians regarded their own exploits in the legendary past and in the period of the Persian wars as exemplary. Within a short time the orators who extolled the ancestors in the funeral speeches (*epitaphioi logoi*) at the annual public burial of those who had fallen in battle developed a canon of exploits which were repeated over and over (Loraux 1986). Lavish praise was heaped in particular on the generation of those who fought at Marathon. Despite the great pride which these orations evoked, it is possible to detect a certain regret that the great former days were probably no longer attainable, at least morally.

In political philosophy it was possible to go a step further, and not seek the 'classical' model in a superlative past, but construct it rationally, and this in an ideal form. It is noteworthy that in this context ideas which were also definitive in art played an important role, i.e., the striving for proportion, the mean and proper balance. A polis, too, or a specific constitution, could gain a 'classical', i.e., an appropriate form in this discussion, which can be illustrated by analogies in art. As the following passage from Aristotle's *Politics* aptly illustrates, 'suitable' or 'appropriate' does not mean 'perfect':

> Neither should we forget the mean (*to meson*), which at the present day is lost sight of in perverted forms of government; for many practices which appear to be democratical are the ruin of democracies, and many which appear to be oligarchical are the ruin of oligarchies. Those who think that all virtue is to be found in their own party principles push matters to extremes; they do not consider that disproportion destroys a state. A nose which varies from the ideal of straightness to a hook or snub may still be of good shape and agreeable to the eye; but if the excess be very great, all symmetry is lost, and the nose at last ceases to be a nose at all on account of some excess in one direction or defect in the other; and this is true of every other part of the human body. The same law of proportion equally holds in states. (Aristotle *Politics* 5,1309b19–31; trans. B. Jowett)

There were similar connections between art and politics in other areas. For instance, Damon of Athens, who was a member of the Periklean circle, reflected on the effect which the different styles in music had on ethical and political behaviour. The ideas of Hippodamos of Miletos were concerned with the connection between the form of a city and socio-political organization.

# 4   The Significance of the Classical Period

As in art, literature and philosophy, so also in the sphere of politics Athens unquestionably made the greatest contribution in the Classical Period. This polis was not only larger in population than all the others, and territorially the second largest (after Sparta), but the citizens of Athens were ever intent on undertaking something novel,

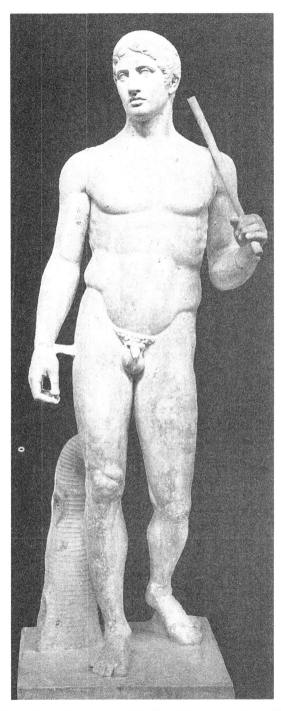

**Figure 1.4**   The Doryphoros ('spearbearer') by Polykleitos, c. 440 BCE. Ht. 2.12 m. Roman marble copy of the original bronze. Museo Archeologico Nazionale, Naples. © Scala/Art Resource, NY.

and exploiting all possibilities in order to attain power, fame and prosperity for themselves. At least that is how Thucydides saw it – as he permits a Korinthian envoy in 432 to portray Athenian mentality, granted critically, but by no means wide of the mark:

> The Athenians are addicted to innovation, and their designs are characterized by swiftness alike in conception and execution; you have a genius for keeping what you have got, accompanied by a total want of invention, and when forced to act you never go far enough. Again, they are adventurous beyond their power, and daring beyond their judgment, and in danger they are sanguine; your wont is to attempt less than is justified by your power, to mistrust even what is sanctioned by your judgment, and to fancy that from danger there is no release. Further, there is promptitude on their side against procrastination on yours; they are never at home, you are never from it: for they hope by their absence to extend their acquisitions, you fear by your advance to endanger what you have left behind. They are swift to follow up a success, and slow to recoil from a reverse. Their bodies they spend ungrudgingly in their country's cause; their intellect they jealously husband to be employed in her service. A scheme unexecuted is with them a positive loss, a successful enterprise a comparative failure. The deficiency created by the miscarriage of an undertaking is soon filled up by fresh hopes; for they alone are enabled to call a thing hoped for a thing got, by the speed with which they act upon their resolutions. Thus they toil on in trouble and danger all the days of their life, with little opportunity for enjoying, being ever engaged in getting: their only idea of a holiday is to do what the occasion demands, and to them laborious occupation is less of a misfortune than the peace of a quiet life. To describe their character in a word, one might truly say that they were born into the world to take no rest themselves and to give none to others. (Thuc. 1.70.2–9; trans. R. Crawley)

There was unquestionably a close link between political developments in Athens and the manner in which new ways of thinking and new expressions were created in this city, which were then regarded as 'classical'. For instance, one can cite in particular the monumental buildings on the Akropolis. These could scarcely have been possible without the revenues which the Athenians obtained from their naval empire (Kallet 1998).

The identification of 'classical' with Athens must not, however, mislead one into missing the fact that in the 'Athenian Century' Hellas was also much more than this one city. There was a world 'beyond Athens and Sparta' (Gehrke 1986; Brock & Hodkinson 2000); Greek history in the fifth and fourth centuries was the history of more than 1,000 states, mostly small, which placed great importance on their political independence (*autonomia*), but at the same time had close ties with each other (for a comprehensive inventory, see Hansen & Nielsen 2004). Thus the Peloponnesian War was due chiefly to the conflict between Sparta and Korinth, on the one hand, and Athens, on the other – but the grounds of complaint (*aitias kai diaphoras*: Thuc. 1.23.5), which led to the outbreak of the war, were spread over a large geographical area. These 'grounds of complaint' included Epidamnos on the Illyrian coast (Roman Dyrrhachium, today the Albanian port city of Durrës), Poteidaia on the Chalkidike peninsula in northern Greece, and Megara, wedged between Korinth and Athens. The decisive events of this war, however, took place outside the Peloponnese – and in its very last phase, in 404, even before the gates of Athens. The principal theatres of conflict were Central Greece and Thrace, Sicily and the region of the Hellespont, as well as the Aegean Sea between Asia Minor and mainland Greece. Poleis like Argos and Korinth, Chios and Samos, and also regions like Boiotia and Messenia played more than a secondary role in political and military events in the fifth and fourth centuries.

The world of Greek states was also polycentric in the Archaic Period. But it was in the fifth and fourth centuries that the Greeks in their citizen-states (*poleis* and *koina*: see below) 'were prominent players' (Heuß 1963: 23–4). In this period the Greeks were on an equal footing with the great powers of the day, i.e., in the first instance with the Persian empire, the only world power up to that time. Before 500 Greece was confined to the margins of larger events. At that time, only a few individuals exerted an influence beyond the confines of their own polis. After 338, when Philip II of Macedon had conquered most of the Greek states and used the Korinthian League to secure their dependence on him (Harding 99), the Greeks as individual states no longer initiated any major action – rather, henceforth they had to relinquish this to the monarchs. On occasion, within the framework of a new political configuration, that of the federal state, which had admittedly already come about in the Classical Period (see below), some of them could still play along with the great figures – until, in the second century, the whole of Greece was conquered (and pacified) by the Romans.

## 5   Chronology and Subdivisions within the Period

On the basis of these considerations we can also determine the chronological boundaries of the Classical Period, for which I would like to set different dates from the ones separating the 'Blackwell Companion' volumes on the Archaic and Classical Ages. The military conflict between the Greeks and the Persian empire began with the Ionian revolt, 499–494 (Murray 1988). The first direct attack on the Greek mainland occurred in 490: the Persians were defeated in the battle of Marathon by the Athenians and the Plataians. The Persian wars reached their climax in the invasion of the Great King, Xerxes, but he was decisively defeated in the naval battle of Salamis in 480 (Strauss 2004). In 479 the Persian army was defeated in the land battle at Plataiai, and driven out of Greece (Lazenby 1993; Green 1996). At the same time, the Persian wars formed the catalyst for Athens' rise to become a great power. As rowers, it was broad sectors of the poorer population that made possible the victory of the Greek ships. As a consequence, they gained self-confidence and an interest in politics. Thanks to Athens' position as a great power, there were now substantially more things to discuss and decide in the Athenian assembly: politics became much more important and much more interesting than hitherto. These were the reasons why the citizen-state of Athens, whose intellectual founder was Solon and institutional creator was Kleisthenes, could now, within a short time, become an egalitarian democracy – thanks to intensive participation on the part of virtually every citizen. Consequently, there are many grounds for regarding the sixth and fifth centuries as a unit, at least in the case of Athens (Stahl 2003a: 228–66; 2003b: 13–63; for a summary of Archaic Athens, Stahl & Walter (forthcoming)). Apart from this, there was much afoot in Greece at the latest by the time of the Persian wars, but in fact already in the previous decade, as is also attested by a decisive break in sculpture: the Critian Boy (Figure 1.2) dates from before the great Persian War of 480/79.

The battle of Chaironeia in 338, in which a coalition led by Athens and Thebes was crushed by the Macedonian king, Philip II, is a reasonable date for the lower limit of the Classical Period. The Hellenistic Period began with the conquest of Asia by Philip's son, Alexander III (beginning in 334). George Grote's arguments for placing the break at this point in his monumental *History of Greece* (1846–56) have therefore not been superseded:

> Even in 334 B.C., when Alexander first entered upon his Asiatic campaigns, the Grecian cities, great as well as small, had been robbed of all their free agency, and existed only as appendages of the kingdom of Macedonia. Several of them were occupied by Macedonian garrisons, or governed by local despots who leaned upon such armed force for support. There existed among them no common idea or public sentiment, formally proclaimed and acted on, except such as it suited Alexander's purpose to encourage. The miso-Persian sentiment – once a genuine expression of Hellenic patriotism . . . – had been converted by Alexander to his own purposes, as a pretext for headship, and a help for ensuring submission during his absence in Asia. (Grote 1907, vol. 12: 199)

By comparison, the subdivisions within the Classical Period are less controversial. The Persian wars (499 or 490–479) were followed by the Pentekontaetia (the period of 'fifty years' between the two great wars, i.e., 478–431) (Badian 1993). The Pentekontaetia was followed by the Peloponnesian War (431–404). The fourth century was characterized by attempts on the part of various Greek states to establish or re-establish separate hegemonies, by renewed Persian influence on Greek affairs, and by the rise of Macedonia as the dominating power (cf. Tritle 1997; Buckler 2003). The major turning points in the political culture of democratic Athens are disputed. Did the so-called fall of Kimon and the reforms of Ephialtes in 462/1 constitute a revolution that resulted in radical democracy (Stahl 2003b: 64–86; bibliography Boedeker & Raaflaub 1998: 349 n. 36)? Was Athenian fourth-century democracy qualitatively different from that of the fifth century, as a consequence of both the changes in its laws and constitution, and because it could no longer call on the imperial resources of its first (the 'Delian') naval alliance (bibliography Boedeker & Raaflaub 1998: 345 n. 4)?

## 6   The Significance of the Peloponnesian War

The Peloponnesian War took place precisely in the middle of the Classical Period. Thanks to the nature of the conflict, the phase which preceded and the one which followed the war appear at the same time to be connected with and yet separated by it. The war meant a serious blow for many Greek states. For instance, it could come about that a small polis could lose its entire citizen levy in a single battle (Thuc. 3.113.6: Ambrakia in Epeiros). Thucydides gives vivid examples of the process of moral decay precipitated by the war, which became particularly evident in the civil wars (Thuc. 3.69–85, especially 82–3: Kerkyra). Immediately after the end of the war the Thirty Tyrants established their despotic rule in Athens: 'For the sake of their private gain [they] have killed in eight months more Athenians, almost, than all the Peloponnesians in ten years of war' (Xenophon *Hellenika* 2.4.21; trans. C. L. Brownson (Loeb)) – i.e., about 1,500 citizens (Aristotle *Ath. Pol.* 35.4). Nor was any mercy shown in conducting war. For instance, in the summer of 414 a force of 1,300 Thracian mercenaries under an Athenian general struck down the undefended Boiotian city of Mykalessos:

> The Thracians bursting into Mycalessus sacked the houses and temples, and butchered the inhabitants, sparing neither youth nor age but killing all they fell in with, one after the other, children and women, and even beasts of burden, and whatever other living creatures they saw…Everywhere confusion reigned and death in all its shapes; and in particular they attacked a boys' school, the largest that there was in the place, into which the children had just gone, and massacred them all. In short, the disaster falling upon the whole town was unsurpassed in magnitude, and unapproached by any in suddenness and in horror. (Thuc. 7.29.4–5; trans. R. Crawley)

Fighting with light armed troops, and no longer exclusively with hoplites; mercenaries alongside traditional citizen levies; virtually continuous warfare, which all but totally feeds on itself, in place of short-term warfare, in which it was possible for even the vanquished to survive – these developments, alongside increasing professionalism, were the most noteworthy ones in the wake of this great conflict, triggering what was perhaps the most significant transformation in the conduct of war. Mercenaries were roving about everywhere. The first manuals on strategy and tactics appeared. Even commanders of a citizen levy often acted like warlords, i.e., largely independent of instruction and control by political panels of their poleis (Hornblower 2002: 189–97). Their model was the Spartan Lysander. The individual who destroyed the Athenian fleet in the final battle of Aigospotamoi (405) had a sculptural group erected at Delphi as a victory monument. In contradistinction to the other naval commanders, on this monument he alone appeared amongst the gods, in the act of being crowned by Poseidon (Pausanias 10.9.7). The inscription on the base illustrates a mentality of victory and power which forms an essential prerequisite for such a thirty-year war: 'He dedicated his statue [upon] this monument, when, victorious with his swift ships, he had destroyed the power of the sons of Ke[k]rops (i.e., Athens), Lysandros (is his name), having crowned unsacked Lacedaemon, his fatherland with its beautiful dancing-grounds, the acropolis of Greece' (Harding 4).

## 7   The Persistent Problems of Power and Freedom

As decisive as the effects of the Peloponnesian War were (excellent on this topic, Hornblower 2002: 184–209), there were, on the other hand, many features that demonstrate continuity. Accordingly, even after the defeat of Athens, the 'tyrannical city-state' (*polis tyrannos*, Thuc. 1.124.3; 2.63.2), war and reckless ambition did not diminish. Indeed, many Greeks expected that the world of two opposite camps would come to an end and usher in a great longing for freedom (Xenophon *Hellenika* 2.2.23). In fact, however, Sparta's victory did not even produce a lasting peace. The new hegemon had to concede that it was more difficult to establish a stable postwar state of affairs than it was to defeat the enemy. And the attempt, as the new champion of the freedom of the Greeks in Asia Minor, to resume the war against Persia was too much for a state which had a total of only slightly more than 2,000 full citizens fit for military service (Cartledge 1987, convincingly). The Spartans, however, lacked not only adequate resources, but also the 'know-how' and imagination necessary for successfully playing the role of a great power. They had too little knowledge of the world they wanted to govern. Moreover, their own institutions were scarcely exportable abroad. Nor did they possess a trained bureaucracy by which an empire could be administered. The leaders in Sparta were well aware that they were overstretched for running an empire, but were incapable of coming up with a satisfactory solution. But most importantly, it was impossible to stop. This characteristic feature linked the period before with the one after 404. The Spartans, no less than the Athenians (e.g., Walter 2003), fell under the spell of the thirst for power.

We shall advance some abstract considerations in an attempt to explain the structural 'inability of the Greeks to carry out foreign policy' (Stahl 2003b: 253–60), as this became particularly evident in the Classical Period. Three fixed objectives characterized the policies of all protagonists – hegemony, autonomy and peace with other states. The combination of all three factors was impossible under the prevailing circumstances. From time to time two of the objectives could be harmonized, but at no given time could the third be combined with the other two. By considering the three possibilities that arose from this configuration, the multifarious nature of events can be construed and explained in the form of patterns:

1   All states strove for freedom (*eleutheria* and *autonomia*) vis à vis other poleis, with the larger states at the same time also striving for power (*hegemonia* or *arche*) over as many other states as possible. Since these two principles were diametrically opposed to each other, they could only be pursued at the price of continual discord.

2   Peace and hegemony would have been reconcilable if a sufficiently strong power could have established itself on a permanent basis. But even Athens, whose naval empire encompassed only part of the Greeks, was never free from attack; in any event, her empire collapsed in 404, and, despite all her efforts, she could not restore her power to its former state. The idea of autonomy continued unabated, and became even stronger through the rise of new powers, such as Thebes. The following attempts to establish and maintain hegemonic power were therefore of even shorter duration. Despite at least thirty years as hegemon, Sparta went down in a single battle (Leuktra 371), and Thebes after no more than nine years, through the death of Epameinondas, the 'architect' of the Theban hegemony (Mantineia 362). After this the last major battle between two contenders for hegemony had been fought, the historian Xenophon stated with resignation that, despite the military victory of Thebes, no clear decision had been reached; confusion and disorder, he maintained, were even greater than hitherto (Xenophon *Hellenika* 7.5.27).

3   The fundamental idea behind the so-called Common Peace (*koine eirene*) was the attempt to blend autonomy and peace (Jehne 1994), but the existence and efforts of hegemonic powers were still a factor. Furthermore, it was the demand that the principle of autonomy should be unconditionally observed which repeatedly gave the powers acting as 'guarantors' of the peace accords, above all Sparta, a pretext to intervene in the affairs of other states. Compared with this, the instruments devised to regulate inter-state relations with a view to peace remained underdeveloped and ineffective in real conflicts.

# 8  The Obstacles to Integration

In the case of domestic affairs in the Classical Period it is possible to note a development which was probably closely connected with the cul-de-sac delineated above. Compared with the Archaic Period, citizens in the Classical Period identified considerably more with the citizen-states to which they belonged. The feeling of being part of their state and of integration with it was very strong. This was naturally most conspicuously the case in democratic Athens. There, the daily involvement of the *demos* in politics ensured that the awareness of being a citizen superseded all other identities. Jochen Bleicken has elucidated this relationship in his fundamental study on Athenian democracy, and at the same time emphasized the Classical position of this ancient political culture compared with ours today:

> There is no doubt that the greatest achievement of Athenian democracy lies in the realization of a society of citizens enjoying equal rights. The idea of equality may have already existed amongst the Greeks and other nations, but the organization of the whole body of the free-born inhabitants of a polis as a community of equals and their practical fulfilment is an original Athenian achievement. Nor was it only the idea, nor merely a lofty declaration of equality, but also the fact that it was formally implemented by hundreds of officially sanctioned regulations. Every governing body in Athens, and every norm of community life, demonstrate nothing less than a fanatic determination to anchor the notion of equality in the organizational structure of the citizenry. Since the notion of political equality was inextricably interwoven into the very implementation of this equality, it included at the same time responsibility on the part of the individual for the common good. Participation in politics and public spirit were part and parcel of this democracy, and this was so intertwined with it, and implemented to such a degree that it can still operate as a model today – and not least in light of the political apathy in our popular democracies. The public expression of politics can also be viewed as a result of the notion of equality. What many critics of antiquity as well as their modern counterparts found so repugnant, strange and even ridiculous, the drive of the Athenians, the hustle and bustle in the Agora and on the Pnyx, the dynamic energy of the masses – these are much more the unique characteristics of Athens' democracy and amongst her greatest achievements: accountable and public involvement in the rough-and-tumble of politics . . . Such a degree of civic involvement has never occurred again down to the present day, and is probably no longer possible. (Bleicken 1994: 411–12; trans. from the German original)

Athenian citizens had untold opportunities to experience their community life – in conversations and in collective actions in the Agora and in the Theatre, and in celebrations and festivals. This applied to the polis as a whole as well as to the smaller units of this 'grass-roots democracy', i.e., in the *phylai*, the *phratriai* and the *demoi* (bodies like these were part of the official organization in all Greek states: Jones 1987). In this context, the buildings of the Classical Period, especially of the fifth century, also had political significance: 'to say that the Athenians built the Parthenon to worship themselves would be an exaggeration, but not a great one' (Lewis *CAH*[2] 5 139). On Perikles' initiative a new Citizenship Law was passed in 451/0, spelling out that only those children whose parents were both full citizens could legally claim to be also Athenian citizens (Aristotle *Ath. Pol.* 26.4). Although the motives behind this bill are controversial (bibliography Boedeker & Raaflaub 1998: 355 n. 146), the acute political identity which distinguished Athenian citizens as citizens from foreigners and metics may have played a role.

As a result of the steady decrease in the number of full citizens, Sparta was from the end of the fifth century compelled to draw increasingly on very different groups within her population for military service and civic duty – such as the *perioikoi*, *neodamoi* and mercenaries. The Spartans did not, however, abandon the idea of involving the 'Spartiates', who actually formed the very core of the Spartan state. The national legends and the 'Return of the Herakleidai', the lawgiver Lykourgos and Leonidas, the hero of Thermopylai, further bolstered solidarity.

Elsewhere, the development of statehood had not been completed before the Classical Age. For example, Elis in the Peloponnese was constituted as a polis as late as 471 BCE (Roy 2002).

In a number of regions of Greece in which the autonomous city-state (polis) did not come about, the small village communities and cities formed larger unions, whose purpose was to enable them to conduct foreign policy and undertake military defence. The federal states (*koina*: Beck 2000: 612–13; also Beck 2003) were actually very modern creations, since in them civic duties were shared: each member state had control of its own domestic affairs, whereas foreign policy was in the hands of a federal board, in which all members enjoyed proportional representation. Accordingly, there was also such a thing as double citizenship. Integration of the populace, however, took place not only at the political level, but acceptance of a common ancestry and common festivals also played a major role, as did religious games and mythical topographies. The oldest (from 519) and most important federal state emerged in Boiotia under the leadership of Thebes. But it is at the same time also precisely in the case of Boiotia that the limits of this 'alternative to a polis' become evident, for the actual hegemon, Thebes, repeatedly sought to exploit the league for its own ends – i.e., to transform it into a hegemonic league. The reason why the federal states failed in the Classical Period was primarily because the bond of the individual citizen with his native polis remained as strong as ever. It was not until the Hellenistic Period that two federal states emerged which succeeded for a considerable period of time and were able to wield a certain measure of power in the shadow of the great powers: the Aitolian League in Central Greece, and the Achaian League in the Peloponnese.

The great extent to which citizens identified with their state in the Classical Period brought to the fore yet another threat to peace and stability: the fact that the citizenry was split up into a number of interest groups, each of which claimed political power for itself. In this respect the polis resembled a joint-stock company. In the world of large and small shareholders the consciousness of belonging to a common enterprise was accompanied by repeated efforts to gain control and sideline the other shareholders or squeeze them out of the enterprise altogether (cf. Ampolo 1996: 322). The concomitant of a deeply rooted determination to win a victory at any price or to seek revenge for wrongs (McHardy 1999) repeatedly resulted in fierce *stasis*, civil war (Gehrke 1985), which led to banishments, expropriations and massacres. Since the warring factions regularly appealed to other states for help, internal conflicts also destabilized inter-state relations.

# 9   A Common Past and a Better Future

The Greeks themselves were well aware of the actual military and political developments in the fifth and fourth centuries as sketched above (for a further excellent discussion, Schulz 2003). Historical memories of the Archaic Period as collected and recounted by Herodotos in the first part of his *Histories* featured individual poleis such as Sparta, Athens, Korinth, Kyrene or Samos, and certain prominent nobles and tyrants. It was not until the great military conflicts of the Classical Period, the Persian wars and the Peloponnesian War, that all, or virtually all, Greeks became involved in a single event. Moreover, poleis no longer joined in these wars singly, but for the most part as members of an alliance (*symmachia*). Of these, only the Peloponnesian League under Spartan leadership had already come about in the Archaic Period. In contrast, the Hellenic Alliance of 481 and especially the Delian League of 478 were new creations (succinct overview: Beck 2000: 1055–7). The conflict with Persia, the Hellenic Alliance and the subsequent division of a large part of the Greek world into allies of Sparta and allies of Athens created the awareness that there was a history of all Greeks, and that such a history had also to be written. Accordingly, Herodotos recounted 'the great and marvellous deeds, some displayed by the Hellenes, some by the Barbarians' (Hdt. 1.1). The Western Greeks, who for the most part marched to a different beat from those of the motherland, were at a notable juncture drawn into the united struggle. While the Hellenic Alliance triumphed over the Persians at Salamis in the summer of 480, the Western Greeks under the command of Gelon ostensibly at the same time defeated Carthage (Hdt. 7.166).

Thucydides regarded the Peloponnesian War as the greatest armed conflict ever – for:

> He could see the rest of the Hellenic world taking sides in the quarrel; those who delayed doing so at once having it in contemplation. Indeed this was the greatest movement (*kinesis*) yet known in history, not only of the Hellenes, but of a large part of the barbarian world – I had almost said of mankind. (Thuc. 1.1.1–2; trans. R. Crawley)

Authors like Xenophon and Theopompos, who began their accounts where Thucydides' narrative breaks off in the middle of 411, and followed events down into the fourth century, simply called their accounts *Hellenika* ('*Greek Affairs*'). At the end of the Classical Period this focus disappeared again – initially from titles, and then also from subject matter. The later *Histories* concentrated on either the new rulers (thus the *Philippika* of Theopompos and the works of the various Alexander historians), or broadened their perspective into that of 'universal histories' ('Universalgeschichte' in scholarly parlance). Thus even in terms of historiographical productions (for a brief overview, Hornblower *OCD*³ 714–15, entry 'Historiography, Greek') we witness the end of that period during which the Greek poleis themselves were the movers and shakers in grand political schemes, in alliance with or – more often than not – in opposition to each other.

*Ta Hellenika*, 'Greek Affairs', were also the object of a political utopia in the minds of some intellectuals in the fourth century. This utopia was called panhellenism.

The idea of panhellenism in this period rested on a specific perspective. Great importance was to be placed on that which united the Greeks as Greeks rather than on what divided them and brought them into conflict. Panhellenism therefore began from the premise of a fundamental antithesis between Greeks and Barbarians. At the same time, it contained a Classical idea at the historical-political level: one ought to begin with the (alleged) unity of the Greeks in the great Persian wars. Isokrates in particular in his political pamphlets cast in the form of speeches (Rhodes, below, Chapter 2, Section 3) vigorously championed this notion, which also promised to alleviate the economic and social ills of the severely battered Hellenes. Thus in his *Panegyrikos*, published in 380, he claims:

> One may best comprehend how great is the reversal in our circumstances if he will read side by side the treaties which were made during our [viz. Athens'] leadership and those which have been published recently [viz. especially the so-called King's Peace of 387/6], for he will find that in those days we were constantly setting limits to the empire of the King, levying tribute on some of his subjects, and barring him from the sea; now, however, it is he who controls the destinies of the Hellenes, who dictates what they must each do, and who all but sets up his viceroys in their cities. For with this one exception, what else is lacking? Was it not he who decided the issue of the war, was it not he who directed the terms of peace, and is it not he who now presides over our affairs? Do we not sail off to him as to a master, when we have complaints against each other? Do we not address him as 'The Great King' as though we were the captives of his spear? Do we not in our wars against each other rest our hopes of salvation on him, who would gladly destroy both Athens and Lacedaemon? Reflecting on these things, we may well be indignant at the present state of affairs, and yearn for our lost supremacy... So whenever we transport thither a force stronger than his, which we can easily do if we so will, we shall enjoy in security the resources of all Asia. Moreover, it is much more glorious to fight against the King for his empire than to contend against each other for the hegemony. It were well to make the expedition in the present generation, in order that those who have shared in our misfortunes may also benefit by our advantages and not continue all their days in wretchedness. (Isokrates 4.120–2; 166–7; trans. G. Norlin)

For the Athenian patriot Isokrates, it was self-evident that, thanks to her earlier services on behalf of the Greeks, Athens should play a leading role in the panhellenic expedition against the Persian king. Here the propaganda and ideological character of the slogan became very clear (Vatai 1984: 99–111). Consequently, panhellenism could not but remain a mere formula and a utopia, because it would have meant a radical change on the part of the Greek poleis – i.e., in their habits and objectives (Baynes 1955: 144–67; Perlman 1976).

Another slogan was also employed to recall the past – which was seen as a model, and therefore worthy of resurrecting. The 'ancestral constitution' (*patrios politeia*) played a central role in the polemics of the oligarchs against the abuses and alleged failure of the 'radical' democracy in Athens since the beginning of the Peloponnesian War (e.g., Aristotle *Ath. Pol.* 29.3; 34.3; Xenophon *Hellenika* 2.4.20–21; Finley 1971). The revolutionary attempt to overthrow the democracy gave promise of a better state of affairs. It was only in the time of Drakon (c. 620) or Solon (tradition-ally, 594/3, but more likely c. 580/70) or Kleisthenes (c. 510), at any rate before Perikles, that Athens allegedly had had a good constitution, because then the 'have-not' masses did not make all the decisions. The bloody excesses of the Thirty Tyrants

(404/3), however, put paid to the propaganda – but it was revived during oligarchic rule after 322, and played a certain role in the Early Hellenistic Period. Demetrios of Phaleron, the 'strong man' in Athens under Macedonian supremacy between 317 and 307, even characterized himself as the third great lawgiver of the polis – after Theseus and Solon (Lehmann 1997: 72)!

## 10   What Went Before and What Came After the Classical Period

In the case of the Ancestral Constitution, its champions looked back from the time of 400 and 300 to the early period of the Athenian polis, i.e., back to the late seventh and early sixth centuries, and even to a remote mythical age. This demonstrates that certain features of Greek history and culture in the Classical Period did not begin and end with it. One of these features was the citizen-state as the cardinal form of Greek community life in all of its various aspects. The beginnings of the polis are already perceptible in the Homeric epics, while the federal states enjoyed their best days in the third century (see above). *Stasis* (civil strife) and striving for hegemony over other states, as Sparta began to organize along these lines in the Peloponnesian League from the middle of the sixth century, were also features of this continuity.

In an impressive example, albeit in a completely different sphere, Hornblower underscores the importance of such phenomena, i.e., overlapping epochs, which represent a structure in the sense of Braudel's *longue durée*, but are at the same time subject to changes:

> No treatment of the main period of Greek civilization should end without emphasizing the continuity both with what went before and with what came after. Continuity is clearest in the sphere of religion, which may be said to have been 'embedded' in Greek life. Some of the gods alleged to have been relatively late imports into Greece can in fact be shown to have Mycenaean origins. For instance, one Athenian myth held that Dionysus was a latecomer, having been introduced into Attica from Eleutherae in the 6th century. There is reference to Dionysus (or di-wo-no-so-jo), however, on Linear B tablets from the 2nd millennium BC. Looking forward, Dionysus' statue was to be depicted in a grand procession staged in Alexandreia in the 3rd century BC by King Ptolemy II Philadelphus. (The iconographic significance of the king's espousal of Dionysus becomes clear in light of the good evidence that in some sense Alexander the Great had identified himself with Dionysus in Carmania.) Nor was classical Dionysus confined to royal exploitation: it has been shown that the festivals of the City Dionysia at Athens and the deme festival of the Rural Dionysia were closely woven into the life of the Athenian empire and the Athenian state. Another Athenian, Euripides, represented Dionysus in a less tame and 'official' aspect in the *Bacchae*; this Euripidean Dionysus has more in common with the liberating Dionysus of Carmania or with the socially disruptive Dionysus whose worship the Romans in 186 BC were to regulate in a famous edict. The longevity and multifaceted character of Dionysus symbolizes the tenacity of the Greek civilization, which Alexander had taken to the banks of the Oxus but which in many respects still carried the marks of its Archaic and even prehistoric origins. (*Encyclopedia Britannica* (Deluxe Edition CD-ROM 2001): entry 'Ancient Greek Civilisation')

As an epoch, the Classical Period – not surprisingly – bears the image of a Janus figure, for it is an integral component in the continuum of Greek history. What began in the Archaic Period, e.g., the citizen-state or the panhellenic games at Olympia and elsewhere, continued in the Classical Period, when it also acquired its definitive form. What was later to become the hallmark of Hellenism, i.e., the spread of Greek culture into many non-Greek regions, would not have become possible without the sense of identity and the general awareness which had developed hitherto. There still remains the question of what was by definition Classical. In conclusion, I should like to formulate a clear position. Deconstruction and inversion, whether motivated by political correctness or by the desire to be intellectually avant-garde, do not bring a clearer focus – rather they breed indifference and a callous attitude to the question of what it is in the Greek heritage that is worth being studied and internalized by us in today's world.

# Further reading

Only the more general books are mentioned here. Davies (1993) is a good introduction, although its main focus is Athens. Different in design is Hornblower (2002), where equal weight is given to the most important regions and to the Persian empire; it is rich in detail, with many ideas, and so more suited for the advanced student. Indispensable are $CAH^2$ 5 and 6; the latter volume, covering the fourth century, is much more comprehensive and also more modern. Although the 'classical' works of Grote (1846–56/1907) and Burckhardt (1898–1902/1998) are distinctly dated, they are still worth reading.

When approaching the history of Classical Greece, readers with some knowledge of German will find Heuß (1963: 214–400) particularly stimulating, thanks to its profound intellectual level. Schulz (2003) deserves to be translated into English, especially because of its clear presentation and style; this little volume also compellingly dispenses with a number of current theories. The same holds true for Stahl (2003b), which concentrates solely on Athens. The thoughtful book by Meier (1998) has been translated into English; it covers Athens from Solon to 404, and is particularly strong on the correlation between politics and culture. On Sparta, Cartledge (1987) is much broader in scope than the title implies. Buckler (2003) meticulously depicts the multipolar world of the fourth century – an 'Iron Age', as it were, compared to the 'Golden Age' of the fifth century.

The recent debate on the quality of Classical Greece is reflected in Heilmeyer (2002): it contains a wealth of material and many perspectives, but is heavily influenced by the destructive approach criticized above. Therefore, older works such as those by Jaeger (1954–61), Langlotz (1956) and Schefold (1967) are still indispensable as a corrective to the new orthodoxy; for the American context see Knox (1993).

# Bibliography

Ampolo, C. (1996) 'Il sistema della "polis": elementi costitutivi e origini della città greca' in: Settis, S. (ed.) (1996) *I Greci: storia, cultura, arte, società*, vol. 2.1: *Una storia greca: definizione (VI–IV secolo a.C.)* (Turin: Einaudi) 297–342

Badian, E. (1993) *From Plataea to Potidaea: studies in the history and historiography of the Pentecontaetia* (Baltimore: Johns Hopkins University Press)

Baynes, N. H. (1955) *Byzantine studies and other essays* (London: Athlone)

Beck, H. (2000) in: Speake 2000: 612–13 (entry 'Federal States'); 1055–7 (entry 'Military League')

Beck, H. (2003) 'New approaches to federalism in ancient Greece: perceptions and perspectives' in: Buraselis, K., & K. Zoumboulakis (eds) *The idea of European community in History*, vol. 2: *Aspects of connecting* poleis *and* ethne *in ancient Greece* (Athens: University of Athens & Greek Ministry of Education and Religious Affairs 2003) 177–90

Bleicken, J. (1994) *Die athenische Demokratie* (Paderborn: Schöningh [2]1994)

Boardman, J. (ed.) (1993) *The Oxford History of classical art* (Oxford: Oxford University Press)

Boedeker, D., & K. A. Raaflaub (eds) (1998) *Democracy, empire, and the arts in fifth-century Athens* (Cambridge MA: Harvard University Press) (Center for Hellenic Studies Colloquia 2)

Borbein, A. H. (1993) 'Die klassische Kunst der Antike' in: Vosskamp, W. (ed.) (1993) *Klassik im Vergleich: Normativität und Historizität europäischer Klassiken* (Stuttgart: Steiner 1993) 281–316

Borbein, A. H. (1995) 'Die Klassik-Diskussion in der klassischen Archäologie' in: Flashar, H. (ed.) (1995) *Altertumswissenschaft in den 20er Jahren: Neue Fragen und Impulse* (Stuttgart: Steiner 1995) 205–245 (cf. review article by H. Lloyd-Jones in: *International Journal of the Classical Tradition* 4 (1998) 580–613)

Brock, R., & S. Hodkinson (eds) (2000) *Alternatives to Athens: varieties of political organization and community in ancient Greece* (Oxford: Oxford University Press)

Buckler, J. (2003) *Aegean Greece in the fourth century BC* (Leiden: Brill)

Burckhardt, J. (1998) *The Greeks and Greek civilization* (abridged ed. and intro. O. Murray; trans. S. Stern) (New York: St Martin's)

Butler, E. M. (1935) *The tyranny of Greece over Germany: a study of the influence exercised by Greek art and poetry over the great German writers of the eighteenth, nineteenth and twentieth centuries* (Cambridge: Cambridge University Press)

Cartledge, P. (1987) *Agesilaos and the crisis of Sparta* (London: Duckworth)

Cartledge, P. (1993) *The Greeks: a portrait of self and others* (Oxford: Oxford University Press)

Cohen, B. (ed.) (2000) *Not the classical ideal: Athens and the construction of the other in Greek art* (Leiden: Brill)

Davies, J. K. (1993) *Democracy and classical Greece* (Cambridge MA: Harvard University Press [2]1993)

Davies, J. K. (2002) 'Greek history: a discipline in transformation' in: Wiseman 2002: 225–46

Easterling, P. (2002) 'A taste for the classics' in: Wiseman 2002: 21–37

Finley, M. I. (1971) 'The ancestral constitution' in: idem *The use and abuse of history* (London: Pimlico 2000) 34–59

Gehrke, H.-J. (1985) *Stasis: Untersuchungen zu den inneren Kriegen in den griechischen Staaten des 5. und 4. Jhs. v.Chr.* (Munich: Beck) (Vestigia: Beiträge zur Alten Geschichte 35)

Gehrke, H.-J. (1986) *Jenseits von Athen und Sparta: Das dritte Griechenland und seine Staatenwelt* (Munich: Beck)

Green, P. (1996) *The Greco-Persian wars* (Berkeley: University of California Press)

Grote, G. (1907) *A history of Greece*, 12 vols (London: Dent & Dutton) (Everyman's Library)

Hansen, M. H., & T. H. Nielsen (eds) (2004) *An inventory of archaic and classical poleis: an investigation conducted by the Copenhagen Polis Centre for the Danish National Research Foundation* (Oxford: Oxford University Press) 885–99

Heilmeyer, W.-D. (ed.) (2002) *Die Griechische Klassik: Idee oder Wirklichkeit: Katalog zur Ausstellung Berlin und Bonn 2002* (Mainz: von Zabern)

Heuß, A. (1963) 'Einleitung'; 'Hellas' in: Mann, G., & A. Heuß (eds) (1963) *Propyläen Weltgeschichte: Eine Universalgeschichte*, vol. 3: *Griechenland: Die hellenistische Welt* (Frankfurt: Propyläen 1963) 9–24; 69–400

Hintzen-Bohlen, B. (1996) 'Retrospektive Tendenzen im Athen der Lykurg-Ära' in: Gehrke, H.-J., & M. Flashar (eds) (1996) *Retrospektive: Konzepte von Vergangenheit in der griechisch-römischen Antike* (Munich: Biering & Brinkmann 1996) 87–112

Hornblower, S. (2002) *The Greek world 479–323* BC (London: Routledge ³2002)

Jaeger, W. (ed.) (1931) *Das Problem des Klassischen und die Antike* (1931; repr. Darmstadt: Wissenschaftliche Buchgesellschaft 1961)

Jaeger, W. (1954–61) *Paideia: the ideals of Greek culture* (trans. G. Highet from the 2nd German ed.), 3 vols (Oxford: Blackwell)

Jehne, M. (1994) *Koine Eirene: Untersuchungen zu den Befriedungs-und Stabilisierungsbemühungen in der griechischen Poliswelt des 4. Jahrhunderts v. Chr.* (Stuttgart: Steiner)

Jones, N. F. (1987) *Public organization in ancient Greece: a documentary study* (Philadelphia: American Philosophical Society)

Kallet, L. (1998) 'Accounting for culture in fifth-century Athens' in: Boedeker & Raaflaub 1998: 43–58

Knox, B. M. W. (1993) *The oldest dead white European males and other reflections on the classics* (New York: Norton)

Langlotz, E. (1956) 'Antike Klassik' in: Oppermann, H. (ed.) (1956) *Humanismus* (Darmstadt: Wissenschaftliche Buchgesellschaft ²1977) 353–411 (Wege der Forschung 17)

Lazenby, J. F. (1993) *The defence of Greece, 490–479 B.C.* (Warminster: Aris & Phillips)

Lehmann, G. A. (1997) *Oligarchische Herrschaft im klassischen Athen: Zu den Krisen und Katastrophen der attischen Demokratie im 5. und 4. Jahrhundert v. Chr.* (Opladen: Westdeutscher Verlag)

Lewis, D. M. (1992) 'The thirty years' peace' in: *CAH*² 5 121–46

Loraux, N. (1986) *The invention of Athens: the funeral oration in the classical city* (trans. A. Sheridan) (Cambridge MA: Harvard University Press)

Marchand, S. L. (1996) *Down from Olympus: archaeology and Philhellenism in Germany, 1750–1970* (Princeton: Princeton University Press)

McHardy, F. M. (1999) 'The ideology of revenge in ancient Greek culture: a study of ancient Athenian revenge ethics' (unpublished PhD thesis University of Exeter)

Meier, C. (1990) *The Greek discovery of politics* (trans. D. McLintock) (Cambridge MA: Harvard University Press)

Meier, C. (1998) *Athens: a portrait of the city in its golden age* (trans. Kimber, Robert, & Rita Kimber) (New York: Holt)

Morris, I. (1994) 'Archaeologies of Greece' in: Morris, I. (ed.) (1994) *Classical Greece: ancient histories and modern archaeologies* (Cambridge: Cambridge University Press 1994) 8–47

Murray, O. (1988) 'The Ionian revolt' in: *CAH*² 4 461–90

Osborne, R. (ed.) (2000) *Classical Greece 500–323* BC (Oxford: Oxford University Press)

Papenfuss, D., & V. M. Strocka (eds) (2001) *Gab es das Griechische Wunder? Griechenland zwischen dem Ende des 6. und der Mitte des 5. Jahrhunderts v.Chr.* (Mainz: von Zabern)

Perlman S. (1976) 'Panhellenism, the polis and imperialism' in: *Historia* 25: 1–30

Pollitt, J. J. (1972) *Art and experience in classical Greece* (Cambridge: Cambridge University Press)

Porter, J. I. (ed.) (2006) *Classical pasts: the classical traditions of Greece and Rome* (Princeton: Princeton University Press)

Reinhardt, K. (1941) 'Die klassische Philologie und das Klassische' in: Reinhardt, K. (1962) *Die Krise des Helden* (Munich: Deutscher Taschenbuch Verlag) 115–43

Roy, J. (2002) 'The synoikism of Elis' in: Nielsen, T. H. (ed.) (2002) *Even more studies in the ancient Greek 'polis'* (Stuttgart: Steiner 2002) 249–264 (*Historia* Einzelschriften 162 = Papers from the Copenhagen Polis Centre 6)

Schefold, K. (1967) *Classical Greece* (trans. J. R. Foster) (London: Methuen) (Art of the World)

Schulz, R. (2003) *Athen und Sparta* (Darmstadt: Wissenschaftliche Buchgesellschaft)

Speake, G. (ed.) (2000) *Encyclopedia of Greece and the Hellenic tradition*, 2 vols (London: Fitzroy Dearborn)

Stahl, M. (2003a) *Gesellschaft und Staat bei den Griechen: Archaische Zeit* (Paderborn: Schöningh)

Stahl, M. (2003b) *Gesellschaft und Staat bei den Griechen: Klassische Zeit* (Paderborn: Schöningh)

Stahl, M., & U. Walter (forthcoming) 'Athens' in: Raaflaub, K. A., & H. van Wees (eds) (forthcoming) *A companion to the archaic Greek world* (Oxford: Blackwell) (Blackwell Companions to the Ancient World)

Stewart, A. (1990) *Greek sculpture: an exploration* (New Haven: Yale University Press)

Strauss, B. (2004) *The battle of Salamis: the naval encounter that saved Greece – and western civilization* (New York: Simon & Schuster)

Tritle, L. A. (ed.) (1997) *The Greek world in the fourth century* (London: Routledge)

Vatai, F. (1984) *Intellectuals in politics in the Greek world: from early times to the Hellenistic age* (London: Croom Helm)

von den Hoff, R., & S. Schmidt (eds) (2001) *Konstruktionen von Wirklichkeit: Bilder im Griechenland des 5. und 4. Jahrhunderts v. Chr.* (Stuttgart: Steiner)

Wallace, J. (1997) *Shelley and Greece* (London: Macmillan)

Walter, U. (2003) '*Isokrates metanóôn*? Traditionen griechischer Kriegs-und Außenpolitik bei Isokrates' in: Orth, W. (ed.) (2003) *Isokrates: Neue Ansätze zur Bewertung eines politischen Schriftstellers* (Trier: Wissenschaftlicher Verlag 2003) 78–94

Wiseman, T. P. (ed.) (2002) *Classics in progress: essays on ancient Greece and Rome* (Oxford: Oxford University Press)

# CHAPTER TWO

# The Literary Sources

## P. J. Rhodes

## 1  Introduction

For students of, say, the causes of the Second World War the amount of relevant material is such that no one person could master the whole of it; but one person can master the whole of the material on the causes of the Peloponnesian War. For recent times, in Europe and North America, there has not been either the lapse of time or an upheaval so great as to destroy most of the documents that were placed in archives or retained by families, and since the invention of printing there has been a fair chance that a copy will survive somewhere of any text that has been printed. But classical Greece is separated from us by many centuries and major upheavals. Only a fraction survives of texts which we know were written – the works of many fourth-century historians including Ephoros and Theopompos are known only from quotations and from later works making use of theirs; of the works of the second-century historian Polybios and the first-century historian Diodoros parts survive but not the whole; the account by Diodoros, written nearly three hundred years later, is the earliest account of Alexander the Great to survive – and many other texts must have been written of which we know nothing at all. The literary works which have survived are those which were thought worth copying, in generation after generation, and are not always what we should most like to survive. It is important for historians of antiquity to make as much use as we can of all the evidence which does survive – literary, to be discussed in this chapter, other kinds of written text, to be discussed in Chapter 3, non-written sources, to be discussed in Chapter 4 – and if we are to approach a correct understanding of classical Greece it is important to realize how the evidence should and how it should not be interpreted.

# 2   Historians

History – establishing and explaining what has happened in the past – as a form of intellectual activity and a genre of writing was invented in the fifth century, and three major works which do survive complete, by men of successive generations, take us down to the year 362.

Herodotos was a member of an aristocratic family in Halikarnassos, in Asia Minor; the traditional date of 484 for his birth must at any rate be near the truth. After involvement in political feuding in his own city he set out on his travels, visiting the near east and the Greek world including the Greek colonies in the west. The book he has given us sets out the result of his *historie* (enquiry: the word from which 'history' is derived), to preserve the memory of famous deeds, and in particular the wars between the Greeks and Persians at the beginning of the fifth century and how they came about (Hdt. 1 prooem.): this allowed him a general context of conflict between east and west, and ample scope for digressions. His account is fairly full from the rise of the Persians in the mid sixth century to the failure of their invasion of Greece in 480–479; there is some mention of things earlier and things later, but nothing later than 430, and most scholars think that his history was finished soon after then.

He had a wide range of interests, in the history and religion and customs and habitats of different peoples. He had his doubts about anthropomorphic gods of the Homeric kind, but he believed in a divine power which rewards great goodness and punishes great wickedness, is jealous of great human success, and has an overarching plan into which the actions of human beings are fated to fit. When the Persian King Xerxes invaded Greece in 480, he did so to avenge the defeat at Marathon in 490, because he was incited by some of his courtiers and by some disaffected Greeks, and because the gods sent a dream (7.5–19) – because it was fated that he should overreach himself by invading Greece, and be defeated (cf. 7.17.2). Again and again in Herodotos' history things happen both for intelligible human reasons and in accordance with a divine plan.

Where they were available he made use of earlier writers, in particular Hekataios of Miletos, who had a range of historical and geographical interests similar to his own; but most of his material was oral, acquired by talking to people, and he seems to have distinguished between a historical period, from the middle of the sixth century (as far back as the oldest people he met would remember), and a prehistoric period: thus his whole work begins in the legendary past but quickly makes a fresh start with Kroisos, king of Lydia in the mid sixth century (1.1–5 contr. books 1.1–9). Herodotos distinguishes between what he has verified and what he has merely been told (2.99.1), and between accounts of witnesses and mere hearsay (4.16.1). He sometimes stresses that he does not necessarily believe all that he records (e.g., 2.123.1), and often gives more than one account of a matter, indicating his preference (e.g., 3.9). On one occasion his reason for rejecting a story seems now to be a good reason for accepting it: men who claimed to have circumnavigated Africa stated that in part of their journey the midday sun was to the north of them (4.42–3). He can be sceptical about the remote past: Helen cannot really have been in Troy, because the Trojans would not have endured a ten-year war to keep her – but the Greeks did not believe their denials, because it was fated that they would destroy the city and make an example of the Trojans (2.112–20).

Fifth-century Greek attitudes and beliefs are very different from the attitudes and beliefs of our own society, so Herodotos has not written the kind of book which a modern investigator would write. Sifting oral traditions to arrive at the truth is difficult, and it is not surprising that we do not think he always did arrive at the truth. But he set about the task energetically and intelligently – critics who think that he cannot have seen the places and things of which he gives exaggerated reports, or that his attributions of biased accounts to the obvious sources are simply a device to make his fictions more plausible, misunderstand the circumstances in which he was working – and he was certainly engaged in what we should consider historical enquiry. But he was doing other things too. He was a story-teller, telling of actual events as Homer told of legendary events: his account of Solon's visit to Kroisos (which almost certainly is an invention, though of his informants rather than himself), in 1.29–33, has many echoes of Odysseus' visit to Phaeacia in *Odyssey* 7–8. He was a teacher of moral lessons – human success is ephemeral, the gods are jealous, the gods' plans are fulfilled in the end if not immediately – and may in particular have been trying to teach that lesson to the Athens of his own day, more prosperous and more powerful than any Greek state had been before. When we read him as historians, we inevitably ask, 'Is it true?' In asking that question we also need to ask, from various angles, 'What is he doing with his material, and why?'

Thucydides belonged to an Athenian family which included Miltiades, general at the battle of Marathon, and Kimon and another Thucydides, leading opponents of Perikles in the middle of the fifth century. He was born not later than 454, was a general in 424/3 but was exiled for failing to keep Amphipolis out of the hands of the Spartans, returned under the amnesty at the end of the Peloponnesian War (Thuc. 4.102–7, 5.26.5), and died not long afterwards.

Despite his background, Thucydides became a great admirer of Perikles and of Athens' democracy and empire under Perikles' leadership (esp. 2.65.5–13), but except where Perikles was involved he was not a lover of democracy (2.65.4; 8.97.2) or of demagogic leaders (3.36.6; 4.21.3; 28.5). Nearly always he gives the impression of having no religious belief – the plague did not spare the pious, and religion did not prevent people from misbehaving when they thought they would escape punishment (2.47.4, 53.4), oracles are significant only for their influence on people's behaviour (e.g., 1.25.1), natural phenomena have no further significance (e.g., 2.28; 3.89) – and sometimes he suppresses a religious explanation (the men escaping from Plataiai with one foot bare and one shod, 3.22.2); but there are occasional gaps in the curtain (1.23.3 on natural phenomena, 5.26.3–4 on an oracle). His history has no room for fate or divine plans: beyond human explanations for human actions he recognizes only *tyche*, 'chance' (e.g., 1.140.1; 2.61.3). For the conduct of individuals he believed in moral standards, though not in a divine backing for them (e.g., 2.53; 3.82–3); for the conduct of states I suspect he was torn between thinking Athens' empire a great achievement and thinking it the result of lawlessness on the largest scale, which is why he returns to the subject so often.

His history is an account of the Peloponnesian War fought between Sparta and its allies and Athens and its allies from 431 to 404. From the beginning of book 2 to the breaking-off of the text in book 8 (autumn 411: the division into books is not his own) he proceeds strictly half a year at a time, with very few digressions; but book 1 is more complex. Thucydides begins with the claim that he started work at the beginning of the war, expecting it to be greater than any previous war (1.1), and then in what is called his 'archaeology' he provides an outline of Greek history from the earliest times to the Persian Wars, to justify that claim (1.2–23.3). Within that are two digressions: on the difficulty of getting history right, with the claim that he unlike others has made the effort to do so (1.20); and on how he has written his history, ending with the claim that it lacks the attraction of the fabulous but he will be satisfied if readers find it useful (1.22). He then distinguishes between particular grievances and the 'truest explanation' for the war (1.23.4–6), and, 'so that no one need ever have to enquire', he launches into an account of the events leading up to the war from 435 onwards (1.24 to end of book 1), interrupted by an account of the growth of Athens' power after the Persian Wars, to justify his 'truest explanation' (1.89–118.2), and a digression on Kylon, Pausanias and Themistokles (1.126.2–138), whose ostensible purpose is to explain the exchange of propaganda in 432/1 but which takes on a life of its own.

In the digressions in the 'archaeology' and elsewhere Thucydides proudly insists that, unlike others, he has taken the trouble to get the facts right. Most of the time we cannot check him – almost always he states only what he believes, without indicating the source or the degree of certainty or alternative versions (exceptions 2.5.5–6, 8.87) – but in the few cases where we can check we find he is not infallible (an inscription, M&L 61 = *IG* 1³364 ~ Fornara 126, supports 1.45.2 on the commanders of Athens' first expedition to Kerkyra in 433 but not 1.51.4 on the commanders of the second). On the other hand, in the 'archaeology' he frequently gives arguments to support his beliefs, and they are the right kinds of argument even if they do not always lead him to what we should consider the right conclusions.

Ancient historians regularly include speeches in their works. Herodotos' speeches are part of his story-telling manner, like the speeches of Homer or of drama, and nobody supposes them to be authentic reports. Thucydides begins his chapter on method with a frustrating account of his speeches:

> The words uttered by individual speakers, both before the outbreak of the war and once the war was under way, I could not easily report with accuracy either in cases where I heard the speeches myself or in cases where I depended on reports made to me from the various places. The speeches here represent what I judged it most appropriate for the individual speakers to say with regard to the current circumstances [contrast §2: 'The actions performed in the war I did not think it right to narrate . . . in accordance with my own judgment'], while keeping as closely as possible to the general sense of what was actually said. (1.22.1)

There has been unending argument as to what mixture of reporting what was said and inventing what he thinks appropriate has resulted: he has at least selected and edited; he sometimes makes a speaker in one place respond to an earlier speaker in a different place as cannot have happened in fact. The best indication of what he may have done comes from the Roman empire: we possess an inscription giving the speech delivered (or, strictly, the version published afterwards) by the emperor Claudius recommending the admission of Gallic notables to the senate (*ILS* 212 = Smallwood, *Gaius, Claudius and Nero* 369 ~ LACTOR 8. 34), and a version of that speech in Tacitus' *Annals* (11.24): Tacitus has thoroughly rewritten the original, but his version is recognizably a version of the original, using the kind of argumentation which Claudius used, not simply an invention of his own. I believe that the arguments in Thucydides' speeches are arguments which the original speeches actually did use or genuinely could have been expected to use – but that we can never rely on the silences, since Thucydides could easily have omitted what he considered unimportant.

Like Herodotos, Thucydides made some use of earlier writings but relied mostly on first-hand knowledge and oral material. He used documents where he could, and in parts of his history quoted documents, but documents would not have supplied much of the material which he wanted: for instance, they would tell him who commanded on a campaign but not what happened in that campaign. To modern readers his criteria of relevance to a history of the Peloponnesian War are disappointingly narrow, and we often find ourselves wishing for more background information of various kinds.

Thucydides can seem deceptively like a modern historian; but, despite his frequently authoritative and sometimes deadpan manner, he cannot have been a totally accurate chronicler of facts. First, he was only one generation later than Herodotos; like Herodotos, he was writing about 'the greatest war ever'; not all his history is low-key but he was very fond of superlatives. He wrote up some episodes and played down others; like other early Greek writers he led readers to see things as he wanted through his presentation of the material more than through explicit comments. Second, he cannot have been unprejudiced: he was an Athenian, from one of the city's leading families, who had broken from his family background to support Perikles, who had served as a general but had been exiled for his failure. There is no reason to think he was deliberately dishonest, but we may well think that, despite his honest intentions, his history is slanted as a result of his prejudices. In reading Thucydides, we should believe him on concrete facts where there is no reason for doubt, but not with the blind faith that he could not be wrong; beyond that we must be alert for his literary devices, for biased presentation, for omissions. His history is a work of the highest quality, but it should not be read uncritically.

Thucydides' history breaks off in the autumn of 411. What we have is all that was ever made public: several writers deliberately started their histories at that point, and one such history survives, Xenophon's *Hellenika* ('*Greek Affairs*').

Xenophon was another Athenian, born c. 430. He had oligarchic sympathies, and was in exile from the early 390s, living in the Peloponnese, for much of the time as a pensioner of the Spartans, and afterwards in Korinth (his exile was eventually revoked, and he then had some contact with Athens). The first part of the *Hellenika*, to 2.3.10 (Lysander's return to Sparta in 404), was written early in the fourth century; the remainder, covering 404–362, in the 350s. Though he could criticize the Spartans on occasion, notably for their occupation of Thebes in 382 (Xenophon *Hellenika* 5.4.1), his account tends to be favourable to Sparta in general and to king Agesilaos in particular; he is not much interested in Greek history where Sparta is not involved. He deals with some uncongenial matters by omitting them: he says nothing of the foundation of the Second Athenian League or of the Arkadian city of Megalopolis; he says as little as possible about the Theban leaders Pelopidas and Epameinondas.

He was a moralistic writer, interested in depicting virtue (e.g., 2.3.56), and this led him to differ from other historians on what was most worth recording (e.g., 7.2.1). For him, unlike Thucydides, the gods intervene in human affairs (e.g., 7.5.13), and men's neglect of religious duties is punished (e.g., 4.8.36; cf. the comment on

Sparta's occupation of Thebes, cited above); everybody had hoped that the battle of Mantineia in 362 would resolve the power struggle in Greece, but 'the god produced such a result...' (7.5.26). He was not particularly intelligent, or energetic in the search for truth; he was probably willing to invent details for the sake of a more vivid narrative, but there is no reason to think that he did not care about the truth, and that he wrote what he knew was false or invented except at a trivial level. Some scholars have tried to save his reputation by suggesting that he was writing not history but something else, perhaps his memoirs or a didactic work, but this is a misguided approach. In our world the kind of history that is published by a university press and weighed down by footnotes is not the only kind of history; similarly Xenophon's *Hellenika* is not Thucydides' kind of history (even though in the earlier part of it Xenophon was consciously continuing Thucydides), and is less appealing to an academic historian than Thucydides' kind of history, but it is still a kind of history, an attempt to establish and explain what happened in the past.

Xenophon wrote much else, as well as the *Hellenika*. The Persian Kyros recruited a Greek mercenary army to help him challenge his brother for the throne; after Kyros was defeated and killed the mercenaries had an exciting journey back to the Greek world, in which Xenophon played a leading part, and in the *Anabasis* ('journey up-country' from the Aegean to Mesopotamia) he gives us his memoirs of that campaign. He wrote a pamphlet on the *Spartan Constitution*, or rather the Spartan way of life. And he wrote much more: amateur philosophy to match his amateur history (he was a disciple of Sokrates); handbooks on horsemanship and the like; a historical novel based on the sixth-century Persian king Kyros; under the influence of Euboulos, policy recommendations for Athens in the 350s, in his *Poroi* ('Revenues').

No comparable history by a contemporary survives for the period of Philip and Alexander; nothing, indeed, until we reach the partially preserved history of 264–146 by Polybios. One later work which survives in part and is important for what it preserves from earlier works which do not survive is the universal history of Diodoros (Diodorus Siculus, 'the Sicilian'), written about 60–30: the surviving part includes books 11–20, covering 480/79–302/1. Diodoros was a writer who in most stretches of his narrative followed one main source, with limited use of others and moralizing additions of his own, forcing the material into an annalistic framework even when his source was not annalistically organized. His importance as a source for today's historians depends on the sources he used and on what else is available for the different stretches.

For the fifth century and the first half of the fourth his main source for Greek history was the fourth-century historian Ephoros of Kyme. On the Persian War of 480–479 disagreements with Herodotos seem likely to be due to invention rather than to a good alternative source. Between the Persian Wars and the Peloponnesian Wars, treated briefly by Thucydides (1.89–118.2), Diodoros has a good deal which is not in Thucydides, mostly about episodes which Thucydides mentions rather than episodes which Thucydides does not, and it is hard to be sure what we can believe; some dates which we can check (particularly in the 430s) are demonstrably wrong, so it is unwise to put much faith in dates which we cannot check. For the period treated in detail by Thucydides, 435–411, what he gives is largely a rewriting of Thucydides, with some variation for variation's sake. But after the end of Thucydides Diodoros becomes much more important. From 411 to (perhaps) 386 Ephoros was following the *Hellenika Oxyrhynchia*, to be discussed below; after 386 Ephoros was writing from his own direct knowledge. Here we have an alternative, independent account to set against that of Xenophon: Diodoros can make silly mistakes, killing a man who still has a long career ahead of him, or attributing a man to the wrong city, but even in his hands the alternative account is more balanced than that of Xenophon, and in many episodes where there is a serious disagreement between the two this alternative is more likely to be right.

For the reign of Philip of Macedon Diodoros' account (book 16) is the only narrative apart from the summary by Justin (variously dated between the second and the fourth century A.D.) of the *Philippic History* of Diodoros' younger contemporary Pompeius Trogus (in Latin: books 7–9). For the reign of Alexander the accounts by contemporaries and near-contemporaries have been lost; Diodoros (book 17), Q. Curtius Rufus (first century A.D.: Latin) and Pompeius Trogus/Justin (books 11–12) had a common source in Kleitarchos; Arrian's *Anabasis* (named in imitation of Xenophon: second century A.D.) is based on the accounts of Ptolemy and Aristoboulos, who took part in Alexander's campaign and were in a position to know the truth (if not as certain to tell the truth as Arrian believed: *Anabasis* 1, pref. 2); and we have a life and short essays by Plutarch (below, p. 33).

Ephoros for the late fifth and early fourth centuries used the *Hellenika Oxyrhynchia*, the Greek history of which papyrus fragments were found at Oxyrhynchos in Egypt. A section on the mid 390s was found first; more recently two shorter sections on the last years of the Peloponnesian War have been added. This is one of the histories written in continuation of Thucydides, and the surviving fragments show it to be detailed and serious. We do not know who the author was: the candidate most favoured is the Athenian Kratippos, but we know so little about Kratippos that we are not much enlightened if the work is attributed to him.

Many Greeks wrote not general histories but local histories. Athens as a major city elicited several: they are known as *Atthides* (singular *Atthis*), and their authors as Atthidographers. Some of them were antiquarians, concentrating on the legends of early Athens; others were serious historians, starting with early Athens but becoming more detailed as they reached their own time. The first of them was not an Athenian: Hellanikos of Mytilene, criticized by Thucydides (1.97.2) for his lack of chronological precision on the mid fifth century. The two who are most important for the fifth and fourth centuries are Androtion (mid fourth century) and Philochoros (early third century), both of them involved in the history of their own time. The fragments preserved in quotations by later writers suggest that their accounts were dry and factual.

I mention at this point because the *Atthides* were among its sources the Aristotelian *Athenian Constitution*. Aristotle (cf. below, pp. 40–1) in the fourth century collected instances as a basis for generalization in many fields – among them *Politics*, for which his school compiled 158 *Constitutions*. None of these has survived through the western manuscript tradition, but a papyrus text of the *Athenian Constitution* was first published in 1891: the first two thirds give a history of the constitution to the end of the fifth century, the final third gives an account of the working of the constitution at the time of composition (330s, with revisions in the 320s). The first part was based on written sources: Herodotos and Thucydides, where they provided relevant information (not very often); the *Atthides*, especially that of Androtion (the most recent at the time); whatever else was available. The second part, for which there was no precedent, was based on the laws of Athens and direct observation. The work was written in Aristotle's school in Athens; I believe the author was a pupil, not Aristotle himself, but that matters more for our view of Aristotle than for our view of the *Athenian Constitution* as a historical source.

I conclude this section with one much later writer, Plutarch, a widely read gentleman living in Greece under the Roman empire (late first – early second century A.D.). We have two sets of works by him. The *Moralia* is a collection of essays on a variety of topics, some of them relevant to Greek history: for instance, *The Malice of Herodotos*, *Spartan Sayings*, *Sayings of Kings and Generals*, works of guidance for politicians. The *Parallel Lives* is a series of biographies of famous Greeks and famous Romans: for example, *Perikles* paired with *Fabius Maximus*, *Demosthenes* with *Cicero*, *Alexander the Great* with *Julius Caesar*. The *Lives* are based on a wide range of sources, sometimes remembered rather than open on Plutarch's desk as he wrote; and their purpose is to illustrate the subjects' characters, so they devote as much space to personal matters as to public actions and sayings. They often tell us things which we do not find in earlier surviving texts, and then we have to ask what Plutarch's source is (he tells us sometimes, but not systematically), whether it is serious and likely to be well informed or rhetorical and likely to be inventing.

# 3   Orators and Pamphleteers

In the Greek world in the second half of the fifth century the travelling teachers known as sophists ('wise men') claimed to teach the skills necessary for success in public life, especially the art of making speeches in political meetings and law courts. Perikles is said to have been the first Athenian to have written out a speech (article on Perikles in the Byzantine lexicon called *Suda* Π 1180 Adler); after his death, in the late fifth and fourth centuries, a gap opened between politicians active in Athens and generals carrying out Athenian policy abroad, and *rhetor* ('speaker') came to be a word used to mean 'politician'. Between about 420 and 320 a number of leading orators revised and published speeches which they had written for their own or for others' use (litigants in the courts were expected to plead their own cases: there were no professional advocates, but there were professional speechwriters).

Speeches provide important material for historians, but for a number of reasons they have to be used with caution. First, the texts we have are not the exact speeches delivered but were revised afterwards, we cannot tell how much. An extreme case comes from the Roman Republic, with Cicero's defence of Milo in tense circumstances in 52: Cicero broke down in court, Milo was condemned, and our *Pro Milone* is the version written up afterwards of the speech which Cicero wished he had delivered (cf. Cassius Dio 40.54). Second, most published speeches were delivered in an adversarial context, in the assembly or a law court; usually we have no speech on the other side; often we do not know the outcome (exceptionally, we not only know the outcome but do have speeches on both sides for the trial of Andokides in 400 and the clashes between Demosthenes and Aischines in 343 and 330: see below, pp. 34–5). Third, Athenian juries voted immediately after listening to the speeches, with no cross-examination, no expert guidance and no discussion: orators could try to get away with lies even on recent, public facts where we might think it impossible, and also with slinging mud at opponents; what an orator says is not necessarily true.

Andokides was an upper-class Athenian with oligarchic leanings, from whom we have three speeches written for his own use. He was involved in Athens' religious scandals in 415 and went into exile; he failed to be allowed back in the last years of the Peloponnesian War (2 (*On His Return*)); he did return under the amnesty at the end of the war, but made enemies, who tried unsuccessfully to argue in 400 that the amnesty did not apply to him (1 (*On the Mysteries*)); in 392/1 he was a member of a delegation sent to a peace conference in Sparta, and recommended acceptance of a treaty which the assembly nevertheless rejected (3 (*On the Peace*)). What is preserved as his speech 4 (*Against Alkibiades*) is not by him but is probably a fourth-century rhetorical exercise.

Antiphon was the *éminence grise* behind Athens' oligarchic revolution in 411; he was put on trial afterwards, and delivered a speech which was greatly admired by Thucydides (8.68.2), but which unfortunately does not survive. He was a professional speechwriter, and the speeches which do survive are all concerned with homicide: three speeches written for individual clients; and three *Tetralogies*, short sets of sample speeches on each side in tricky cases (the attribution to him of these is disputed). These speeches are not much help for the main line of Athenian public history, but they allow us to see late-fifth-century Athens from another angle. It is disputed whether 'Antiphon the Sophist' was the same man (I think he was not): he was an extreme exponent of the view, to be discussed below, that laws and such distinctions as between Greeks and barbarians or between free men and slaves are not part of the natural order but mere human conventions which could have been decided otherwise.

Lysias spent much of his life in Athens but was from a Syracusan family; he was active in the late fifth and early fourth centuries. We have one speech written for his own use, against a member of the oligarchy of the Thirty in 404–403 who was responsible for his brother's death (12 (*Against Eratosthenes*)). We have a *Funeral Oration* (2), and Dionysios of Halikarnassos quotes the beginning of an *Olympic Oration* (33), but most of his speeches are speeches for clients, sometimes in purely private matters, sometimes connected in various ways with public affairs. One is 6 (*Against Andokides*), written for his trial in 400.

The best-known orators of the fourth century are Demosthenes and Aischines. Demosthenes learned the art of oratory in order to prosecute the guardians who had misappropriated his property; he wrote speeches for clients in private and in some major public lawsuits. From the end of the 350s he became obsessed with Philip of Macedon as a major threat to Athens: we have a series of assembly speeches, the *Philippics* and others (Demosthenes is the only orator from whom assembly speeches survive), and the speeches written for his two great clashes with Aischines. Aischines had at first favoured resistance to Philip when Philip directly threatened Athens but not otherwise; when circumstances forced Athens to make peace with Philip, in 346, he wanted to trust Philip and keep the peace, while Demosthenes backed the peace in a cynical spirit and looked for further conflict. Aischines 1 (*Against Timarchos*) was an attack on a man who was going to prosecute him on Demosthenes' behalf. Demosthenes' unsuccessful prosecution of Aischines in 343 produced Demosthenes 19 (*On the Embassy*) and Aischines 2 (*On the Embassy*); Aischines' unsuccessful prosecution in

330 of a man who had proposed honours for Demosthenes produced Aischines 3 (*Against Ktesiphon*) and Demosthenes 18 (*On the Crown*); these range over the public careers of Aischines and Demosthenes, and Athens' dealings with Philip, and eliciting the truth behind them is difficult.

Other fourth-century orators are Isaios, who specialized in inheritance cases; Hypereides and Lykourgos, supporters of Demosthenes' hard line against Macedon; Deinarchos, a Korinthian who wrote speeches for the prosecution of men charged with misappropriating money brought to Athens by Harpalos, the fugitive treasurer of Alexander the Great.

Somewhat different is Isokrates, who was born in the 430s and lived to be nearly a hundred. He wrote some speeches for clients at the beginning of the fourth century, but is best known for his political pamphlets cast in the form of speeches, and as a teacher of rhetoric (but it is hard to be sure how many of the men said to be his pupils actually were so). Some have regarded him as a major thinker, but more probably he was not an original thinker himself but a reflector of ideas current in certain circles. One theme in many of his works is that the great days of the Greeks were at the beginning of the fifth century, when they united (not totally, in fact) to fight the Persians, and that to recover their greatness they need to stop fighting amongst themselves and unite to fight the Persians again. From one decade to the next he looked to a different state or man to accomplish this, finally settling on Philip of Macedon. In the 350s in his *Areopagitikos* (speech 7) he wrote of rather vague Good Old Days in Athens when the council of the Areopagos was powerful – and in the 340s and 330s the Areopagos rose to new prominence.

One other pamphlet which survives is the *Athenian Constitution* preserved with the works of Xenophon but not written by him, the pamphlet of the 'Old Oligarch'. This is a short essay on the theme that Athenian Democracy is a Bad Thing, because it promotes the interests of the nasty people rather than of the nice people, but it is appropriate to Athens, because Athens' power depends on the lower-class men who row the navy's ships, it is successful and stable, and it could not easily be overthrown. Proposed dates have ranged from the 440s to the late fifth century or even to the fourth (as an academic exercise pretending to be written in the fifth century), but I am one of those who think chapter 2 points clearly to the early years of the Peloponnesian War, 431–424. It is a perverse piece of work, which should not be taken seriously as a factual report; its value lies in what it tells us about the author, that in the 420s (if that is the right date) there were men in Athens who could discuss the rival merits of democracy and oligarchy in an academic way, without any serious expectation of bringing about a change in the constitution. In 415, however, some Athenians saw behind the religious scandals a plot against the democracy (Thuc. 6.27.3), and in 411 the democracy actually was overthrown.

We have the work without a context, and can only guess how it came to be written and circulated. We know that there was discussion of the different forms of constitution in the fifth century, and that men like Antiphon the Sophist (see above) made great play with the contrast between nature and convention; this led to the argument that there is no universally right constitution but different men prefer the constitution which suits their different interests (e.g., Lysias 25 (*Subverting Democracy*) 7–14). The Old Oligarch's essay belongs here: it is an exercise by a pupil of the sophists.

# 4   Poets

To the end of the fifth century historians of Greece have to pay attention to poetry. Poetry was written down from the eighth century onwards, while there was no prose literature before the fifth century and none which now survives before the second half of the century; and a good deal of early poetry touches on themes of interest to historians.

Homer, at the climax of a tradition of oral poetry, probably in the eighth century, told stories connected with a Trojan war which (when they started calculating) the Greeks dated to the twelfth century. Troy was discovered in the nineteenth century by Heinrich Schliemann, but we can still entertain doubts at various levels. Was there a war in which the Greeks united against Troy at all? If so, were the people and events of the *Iliad* and the *Odyssey* – or at any rate some of them (much of the *Odyssey* is fairy-tale) – part of it? Is the background – the organization of households and cities, the style of fighting, and so on – correct for the time of the Trojan war, or the poet's time, or some time in between? Is there enough consistency, enough connection with reality at some time, to make it feasible to discuss 'Homeric society'? For classical Greeks Homer was writing about their past; they realized there were problems, but were not prepared to doubt as fundamentally as we do. Herodotos believed that there was a Trojan war, but not that the Trojans would have endured that war to keep Helen, so Helen was not in Troy (Hdt. 2.112–20: cf. above). Thucydides believed that there was a Trojan war, and that poets exaggerate but with a rational approach one can still extract history from them; and he thought that we can calculate from the 'catalogue of ships' in *Iliad* 2.484–760 how many Greeks went to Troy (Thuc. 1.10.3–4).

We have some material from a number of poets active between 800 and 500. Those of interest to historians include Hesiod (probably seventh century), whose *Works and Days* is set in agricultural society in Boiotia; Tyrtaios of Sparta (mid seventh century) and Solon of Athens (early sixth century), who were involved in and wrote about public affairs in their cities; Theognis of Megara (perhaps later seventh century), who was – or posed as – an aristocrat who saw his world destroyed by the rise of the *nouveaux riches*.

Early in the fifth century Simonides wrote epigrams and longer poems, some connected with the Persian Wars. A recent discovery gives us part of a poem comparing the Greeks who fought in the battle of Plataiai in 479 with the Greeks who fought at Troy (Simonides F 1–22 West[2]). Pindar of Thebes wrote (among other things) odes for victors in the great games: rich aristocrats in cities like Thebes, Korinth and Aigina; in Athens too; at the other extreme, the kings of the Greek settlement in Kyrene, and tyrants in Greek cities in Sicily. He had to manoeuvre tactfully, to flatter his current patron but not say things which might offend potential future patrons elsewhere. There is a good collection of *scholia*, ancient commentaries, on Pindar, explaining the background to and the allusions in the various poems: for Sicily in the early fifth century Diodoros (above, pp. 31–2) is our only continuous narrative source, and it is useful to have these *scholia* to set beside his account.

But the largest body of fifth-century verse literature is Athenian drama – tragedies spanning most of the century and 'old' comedies from the late fifth century and the beginning of the fourth. How, if at all, this is to be used by historians has become contentious. Traditional 'literary' interpretations, willing to recognize allusions to or comments on contemporary events of a straightforward kind, have been rivalled by newer approaches: some scholars have concentrated on the works as plays performed rather than texts to be read; others have focused on the festivals in connection with which the plays were performed, some studying them as festivals of the god Dionysos, while others emphasize the civic nature of the festivals and see the plays – the tragedies as well as the more obviously topical comedies – as engaging with civic concerns.

That one approach is valid and enlightening does not mean that others are invalid or unprofitable: drama may legitimately be interpreted in various ways. However, many of the 'civic' interpreters of drama have seen a strong connection between the plays and the circumstances of their performance on one side and the Athenian democracy on the other – but it can be argued that, while there is of course something Athenian in the plays and in the particular setting in which they were performed, to a considerable extent the circumstances are an Athenian version of circumstances which could be found in other Greek poleis too, and many of the issues addressed in tragedy are issues which would concern Greek polis-dwellers in general and not only the citizens of democratic Athens (see, for instance, below on the themes of Sophokles' *Antigone*).

There were three great tragedians of whom plays survive. The oldest, Aischylos, was active from the 470s to the 450s. Most tragedies known to us are on themes from the legendary past, though there may be contemporary relevance in the choice and the handling of the theme; but Aischylos' earliest surviving play, *Persians* of 472, is on a subject from the recent past (and his older contemporary, Phrynichos, wrote more than one play on a recent subject). *Persians* treats the Greeks' defeat of the Persian invaders in 480, specifically the reception at the Persian court of the news of Persia's defeat in the battle of Salamis. It can be interpreted on more than one level, not mutually exclusive: as a patriotic Greek play (though some interpreters have judged it sympathetic to the defeated Persians); as a patriotic Athenian play, since the victory at Salamis was particularly an Athenian achievement; as a partisan Athenian play, choosing to focus on Salamis, the victory of Themistokles and the navy, rather than Marathon (490), the victory of Miltiades, father of Themistokles' rival Kimon, and the army. The play includes an account of the battle of Salamis, which is somewhat different from and perhaps preferable to that of Herodotos; and it makes some of the contrasts between Greeks and Persians which were to become standard.

In *Suppliant Women* (commonly dated 463) the fifty daughters of Danaos flee to avoid being forced into incestuous marriages with their cousins, the sons of Aigyptos, and seek refuge in Argos. The characterization of Argos is striking: the king to whom they appeal is a very unkingly king, and insists emphatically that the right to grant sanctuary belongs not to him but to the assembly of the people. It can hardly be accidental that this emphasis on the democratic principle occurs shortly before 462/1, when the reforms of Ephialtes took powers from the council of the Areopagos (comprising all living ex-archons) and transferred them to more representative bodies, leaving homicide trials as the most important function of the Areopagos and making Athens self-consciously democratic.

In 458 Aischylos produced the trilogy (set of three plays) known as the *Oresteia*, the last play of which was *Eumenides*. Orestes, who had killed his mother Klytaimnestra because she had killed his father Agamemnon, was pursued by the furies and came to Athens; the goddess Athena instituted the Areopagos as a homicide court to try him, and he was acquitted by her casting vote. There is good evidence for what we may call a Themistokles–Ephialtes–Perikles set, with which Aischylos was linked: *Persians* supported Themistokles, and Perikles was its *choregos*, the rich citizen paying for the production; *Suppliant Women* stresses the democratic idea; *Eumenides* cannot have been written in innocent unawareness of the recent reform of the Areopagos. We should expect *Eumenides* to favour the reform: some eminent interpreters have thought that it does; but other eminent interpreters have thought that it deplores the reform, or at any rate fears that the reformers may continue too far; and one scholar has argued recently that Aischylos was intentionally ambiguous.

Sophokles was active from 468 to his death in 406. His first success was in a political context: in 468 Kimon and his fellow generals were called on to act in place of the normal judges, and awarded the prize to Sophokles although Aischylos was competing (Plutarch *Kimon* 8.7–9). It is, of course, possible that Sophokles' were uncontroversially the better plays; but in view of the link between Aischylos and Kimon's opponents this outcome is at least interesting.

Sophokles played some part in public life: he was one of the *hellenotamiai* (treasurers of Athens' Delian League) in 443/2 (*IG* 1³ 269); he was a general in 441/0 and again later (Androtion *FGrHist* 324 F 38; Plutarch *Nikias* 15.2); he was one of the ten *probouloi*, Athens' emergency cabinet of older citizens, in 413–411 (Aristotle *Rhetoric* 1419a26–30). In the sense of alluding to particular events, he is the least political of the three tragedians (the one likely allusion is *Oedipus Coloneus* 616–23, foreseeing a time when Athens and Thebes will be enemies); but he does more generally reflect issues which were of interest in the current intellectual climate, for instance, in *Antigone*, the clash between human law and divine law, and between obligations to the family and obligations to the state.

Euripides was active from the 450s, and died in 406, the same year as Sophokles. He was not involved in public life (except that he may once have served on an embassy to Syracuse: Aristotle *Rhetoric* 1384b15–16 with *scholion*), but there is more contemporary relevance in his plays. At a general level, though his plots are traditional stories involving interventions by the traditional gods, the handling of the story is apt to make readers question the rightness of the gods' justice; his versions of the stories give greater prominence to ordinary people (in his *Electra*, for instance, Orestes' sister Elektra has been forced to marry an ordinary peasant); there are various traces of ideas fashionable among the sophists.

A change in attitude can be detected in the course of the Peloponnesian War between Sparta and Athens. Euripides' plays towards the beginning of the war – *Heraclidae, Andromache, Suppliant Women, Hecuba* – show both a patriotic dislike of Sparta and a consciousness of the horrors of war; later in the war, either the horrors are still on display but the patriotism is not, as in *Trojan Women* and *Phoenician Women*, or else he turns away from the harsh realities to produce melodramatic plays with happy endings, such as *Iphigenia Among the Tauri, Helen, Ion*. The suppliants of his *Suppliant Women* are the mothers of the Seven Against Thebes, who appeal to Athens when the Thebans will not allow their sons to be buried (this may be a reflection of the Thebans' refusal to let the Athenians recover their dead after the battle of Delion in 424: Thuc. 4.97.2–4), and in this play there is a remarkable political intrusion: there is a scene (Euripides *Suppliant Women* 399–466) in which the Athenian king Theseus defends the principle of democracy against a Theban herald who has come to demand the handing-over of the women.

There is a great deal of obvious concern with contemporary issues in Athens' 'old' comedy, from which we have a number of surviving plays by Aristophanes and fragments quoted from plays by others, but how the plays are to be interpreted has been much disputed. At the beginning of the twentieth century scholars simple-mindedly saw the characters as speaking for the poet. In the middle of the twentieth century it became fashionable to stress that the poet was writing to amuse a mass audience, not to spread propaganda or to enlighten us, and the most extreme champion of this approach claimed that the poet's political views are irrecoverable and would not help us to appreciate the plays if we could recover them. More recently there has been a variety of approaches, and no consensus.

There is no doubt about Aristophanes' interest in current issues. His *Babylonians* (426) does not survive, and reconstruction of its contents is hazardous, but we know that it landed him in trouble with the democratic leader Kleon (Aristophanes *Acharnians* 377–82 with *scholion* 378, 502–8, 630–1). In *Acharnians* (425, six years into the Peloponnesian War) the hero makes a private peace treaty with Sparta. In *Knights* (424) Kleon, the principal slave of Demos, the Athenian people personified (other slaves are Nikias and Demosthenes), is a vulgar leather-seller, to be supplanted by an even more vulgar sausage-seller. *Clouds* (423) represents or misrepresents Sokrates as a typical sophist, who can teach how to make a bad argument defeat a good. *Wasps* (422) focuses on the Athenians' love of litigation. *Peace* was produced in 421, at the point when the war seemed to be at an end. In *Birds* (414) men who are tired of Athens found a city in the sky, Cloudcuckooland, which reproduces the familiar faults of Athens. In *Lysistrata* (411, when Athens was in difficulties) the women break off sexual relations with their husbands to force the men to make peace with Sparta. *Thesmophoriazusae* (411) deals with Euripides' treatment of women. *Frogs* (405) was written when Sophokles and Euripides had died: the god Dionysos goes to Hades to bring back a good tragedian, and the play turns into a contest between Aischylos and Euripides as to which was the better or more useful poet. *Ecclesiazusae* (late 390s) explores the ideas of government by women and community of property and family relations. In *Plutus* (388) the god of wealth, who is bestowing his favours on the undeserving because Zeus has blinded him, has his sight restored.

Aristophanes is interested in the war, politicians, jurors, sophists, women, literature and much more. Is he just making jokes? Is he attacking any one prominent enough to make a good target? Or is his aim more specific? I am one of those who believe that it is. His Kleon is obviously a caricature, but that means that he displays features possessed by the real Kleon (there is reasonable consistency between Aristophanes' Kleon and Thucydides' Kleon). Aristophanes does seem consistent in preferring aristocratic leaders to vulgar upstarts (but men who laughed at Aristophanes' Kleon were happy to back Kleon in the assembly), in disliking some features of trendy cleverness (but he had a love–hate relationship with Euripides, and of course Aristophanes himself was clever), in disliking extreme bellicosity (without being a pacifist or a traitor).

In *Acharnians* (514–38) and *Peace* (605–18) Aristophanes alludes to the causes of the Peloponnesian War, each time focusing on Athens' sanctions against Megara, and (in different stories) suggesting that Perikles was obstinate over Megara for disreputable reasons of his own. The stories are no doubt Aristophanes' own inventions, though they were taken seriously by later Greek writers (that in *Acharnians* involves a parody of the beginning of Herodotos' history; to that in *Peace* the chorus responds, 'I never heard that before'), but they may well reflect a view prevalent in Athens at the time that Athens had to endure the miseries of the war because of Perikles' obstinacy over Megara. Thucydides considered Athens' power and Sparta's fear of it to be the 'truest explanation' for the war (Thuc. 1.23.4–6: cf. above, p. 29), and among the particular grievances Megara is one about which he says little: he was perhaps in part reacting against the kind of view reflected by Aristophanes – and he was an admirer of Perikles who would not take seriously suggestions that Perikles had acted improperly.

Comedy can be useful to historians for more than its main themes and the targets of its jokes. The plays are not only concerned with but are set in the contemporary world, and contain a great deal of interesting background material. We learn, for instance, about the red-dyed rope used to herd reluctant citizens into meetings of the assembly in the fifth century (Aristophanes *Acharnians* 19–22), about the prayer-cum-curse which began every meeting of the assembly (a parody in Aristophanes *Thesmophoriazusae* 295–311 and 331–51), about the gate at the entrance to the council-house and the railings which separated the members from spectators (Aristophanes *Knights* 641, 674–5), about the payment made for attending the assembly in the fourth century, which one would fail to obtain if one arrived after a specified time or after the number qualifying for payment had been reached (Aristophanes *Ecclesiazusae* 300–10). We learn from the hero's festival after he has made his private peace treaty with Sparta (Aristophanes *Acharnians* 1000–end) and from the celebrations after the rescue of Peace and her attendants Harvest and Festival (Aristophanes *Peace* 871–end) about proceedings at Greek festivals.

# 5  Philosophers

From the fourth century we have a large body of material in the works of Plato and Aristotle. Their significance as philosophers is discussed in Chapter 21, but a little should be said here about their significance as historical sources.

In Plato's dialogues there are a few allusions to historical events, presumably based not on research but on what Plato thought he knew. One point has attracted some attention. In *Laws* 692D, 698D–E, it is claimed that the Spartans delayed going to Marathon in 490 because they were fighting the Messenians, whereas according to Hdt. 6.106.3 they delayed for religious reasons. Some scholars have been inclined to believe Plato; but more probably the explanation which had been acceptable in the early fifth century seemed less credible in the less religious fourth, and so an alternative was invented. Plato was an Athenian, but his one attempt to involve himself in public life was not in Athens but in Syracuse, in the time of Dionysios I and Dionysios II. *Letters* 3, 7 and 8, if not by Plato himself (which some but not all believe), are certainly by a well-informed writer, and they are an important source for the history of Syracuse in the early fourth century.

Aristotle was from Stagira, in Chalkidike, but spent much of his life and established a school in Athens, covering a wide range of subjects. *Politics* contains a great many allusions to particular historical events, to illustrate Aristotle's general points, and so too does *Rhetoric*; not all the allusions can be linked securely with episodes which we know from other sources. As with Plato, it is likely that many of these allusions were based simply on what Aristotle thought he knew, or remembered from one of the detailed works compiled in the school. For that reason, in the notorious disagreement between *Politics* 1273b35–1274a17, 1281b25–34, and *Athenian Constitution* 8.1 on Solon's provisions for the appointment of the Athenian archons, I believe we should follow the *Athenian Constitution*, which had a detailed source on Solon, rather than the *Politics*.

## Further reading and bibliography

### In general

There are Loeb translations (Cambridge MA: Harvard University Press) of nearly all continuous texts, and Penguin Classics (Harmondsworth: Penguin); and other translations of many.

Pelling, C. (1999) *Literary texts and the Greek historian* (London: Routledge 1999)

### Historians

Rhodes, P. J. (1994) 'In defence of the Greek historians' in: *G&R* ns 41: 156–71 – moderate defence against extreme doubts as to reliability
Gould, J. (1989) *Herodotus* (London: Weidenfeld & Nicolson)
Hornblower, S. (1994) *Thucydides* (corrected repr.; originally publ. 1987) (London: Duckworth)
Gray, V. (1989) *The character of Xenophon's* Hellenica (London: Duckworth)
Dillery, J. (1995) *Xenophon and the history of his times* (London: Routledge)
Harding, P. (1994) *Androtion and the* Atthis: *the fragments trans. with intro. and commentary* (Oxford: Clarendon)
Russell, D. A. (1973) *Plutarch* (London: Duckworth)

### Drama

Pelling, C. (ed.) (1997) *Greek tragedy and the historian* (Oxford: Oxford University Press)
Podlecki, A. J. (1999) *The political background of Aeschylean tragedy* (London: Bristol Classical Press [2]1999)
MacDowell, D. M. (1995) *Aristophanes and Athens* (Oxford: Oxford University Press)

### Inscriptions

Fornara – English translations
*IG*; *IG* 1[3]; *IG* 2[2] – Greek texts
*ILS* – Dessau, H. (ed.) (1892–1916) *Inscriptiones Latinae selectae*, 3 vols (Berlin: Weidmann) – Latin texts
*LACTOR 8* – Miller, S. J. (1971) *Inscriptions of the Roman empire*, A.D. *14–117* (London: London Association of Classical Teachers) (Lactor 8) – English translations

M&L – Greek texts, with commentary
R&O – Greek texts, with trans. and commentary
Smallwood, *Gaius, Claudius and Nero* – Smallwood, E. M. (1967) *Documents illustrating the
  principates of Gaius, Claudius and Nero* (Cambridge: Cambridge University Press) – Greek
  and Latin texts

## Herodotos

Fornara, C. W. (1971) 'Evidence for the date of Herodotus' publication' in: *JHS* 91: 25–34 – later
  date
Evans, J. A. S. (1979) 'Herodotus' publication date' in: *Athenaeum* ns 57: 145–9 – orthodox date
Shimron, B. (1973) 'πρῶτος τῶν ἡμεῖς ἴδμεν' in: *Eranos* 71: 45–51 – prehistoric and
  historical periods
Armayor, O. K. (1978) 'Did Herodotus ever go the Black Sea?' in: *HSPh* 82: 45–62 – doubts
  about travels
Fehling, D. (1989) *Herodotus and his 'sources'* (trans. J. G. Howie) (Leeds: F. Cairns) (origin-
  ally published in German as *Die Quellenangaben bei Herodot: Studien zur Erzählkunst
  Herodots* (Berlin: de Gruyter 1971)) – doubts about source attributions
Moles, J. L. (1996) 'Herodotus warns the Athenians' in: Cairns, F., & M. Heath (eds) (1996)
  *Papers of the Leeds International Latin Seminar 9: Roman poetry and prose, Greek poetry,
  etymology, historiography* (Leeds: Cairns) 259–84 (ARCA Classical and Medieval Texts,
  Papers and Monographs 34)

## Thucydides

Woodman, A. J. (1988) *Rhetoric in classical historiography* (London: Croom Helm) 1–69 (ch.
  1) – Thucydides a writer of historical literature rather than recorder of truth
Badian, E. (1993) *From Plataea to Potidaea: studies in the history and historiography of the
  pentecontaetia* (Baltimore: Johns Hopkins University Press) 125–62 with 223–36 (ch. 4) –
  Thucydides a dishonest journalist

## Xenophon

Cawkwell, G. L. (1979) in: *Xenophon:* A history of my times (trans. R. Warner) (Harmonds-
  worth: Penguin, revised 1979) 22–8 – *Hellenika* memoirs
Tuplin, C. (1993) *The failings of empire: a reading of Xenophon* Hellenica *2.3.11–7.5.27*
  (Stuttgart: Steiner) (*Historia* Einzelschriften 76) – *Hellenika* didactic

## Aristotelian *Athenian Constitution* (*Athenaion politeia*)

Rhodes, P. J. (1981) *A commentary on the Aristotelian* Athenaion Politeia (rev. ed.; originally
  publ. 1981) (Oxford: Oxford University Press) 58–63 – Aristotelian authorship rejected

## [Andokides] 4 (*Against Alkibiades*)

Rhodes, P. J. (1994) 'The ostracism of Hyperbolus' in: Osborne, R., & S. Hornblower (eds)
  (1994) *Ritual, finance, politics: Athenian democratic accounts presented to David Lewis*
  (Oxford: Clarendon) 85–98 (ch. 5) at 88–91 – rhetorical exercise

## Antiphon the orator and Antiphon the sophist

Gagarin, M. (2002) *Antiphon the Athenian: oratory, law, and justice in the age of the sophists* (Austin: University of Texas Press) – same man

Pendrick, G. J. (2002) *Antiphon the sophist: the fragments* (Cambridge: Cambridge University Press) (Cambridge Classical Texts and Commentaries 39) – different men

## Isokrates

Mathieu, G. (1925) *Les idées politiques d'Isocrate* (Paris: Belles Lettres) – Isokrates a thinker

Baynes, N. H. (1955) 'Isocrates' in: Baynes, N. H. (ed.) (1955) *Byzantine studies and other essays* (London: Athlone) 144–67 (ch. 8) – Isokrates not a thinker

## 'Old Oligarch'

Bowersock, G. W. (1966) 'Pseudo-Xenophon' in: *HSPh*. 71 33–46 – 440s

Forrest, W. G. (1970) 'The date of the pseudo-Xenophontic *Athenaion Politeia*' in: *Klio* 52: 107–16 – 431–424, and probably 424

Hornblower, S. (2000) 'The *Old Oligarch* (Pseudo-Xenophon's *Athenaion Politeia*) and Thucydides' in: Flensted-Jensen, P., T. H. Nielsen, L. Rubinstein (eds) *Polis and politics: studies in ancient Greek history, presented to Mogens Herman Hansen on his sixtieth birthday, August 20, 2000* (Copenhagen: Museum Tusculanum) 362–84 – fourth century

## Civic interpretation of Athenian drama

Griffin, J. (1998) 'The social function of Attic tragedy' in: *CQ* ns 48: 39–61, esp. 47–50 – opposed to civic interpretation

Goldhill, S. (2000) 'Civic ideology and the problem of difference: the politics of Aeschylean tragedy, once again' in: *JHS* 120: 34–56, esp. 34–41 – democratic interpretation

Rhodes, P. J. (2003) 'Nothing to do with democracy: Athenian drama and the *polis*' in: *JHS* 123: 104–19 – polis in general rather than Athenian democracy in particular

## Aischylos

Scullion, S. (2002) 'Tragic dates' in: *CQ* ns 52: 81–101 at 87–101 – *Suppliant Women* earlier than 463

Dover, K. J. (1957) 'The political aspect of Aeschylus' *Eumenides*' in: *JHS* 77: 230–7 = idem *Greek and the Greeks* (Oxford: Blackwell 1988) 161–75 – *Eumenides* favours reform

Dodds, E. R. (1960) 'Morals and politics in the "*Oresteia*"' in: *PCPhS* ns 6: 19–31 – *Eumenides* at any rate hostile to further reform

Sommerstein, A. H. (1996) *Aeschylean tragedy* (Bari: Levante) 391–421 (ch. 12) (Le rane, Studi 15) – *Eumenides* deliberately ambiguous

## Euripides

Bowie, A. M. (1997 ) 'Tragic filters for history: Euripides' *Supplices* and Sophocles' *Philoctetes*' in: Pelling, C. (ed.) *Greek tragedy and the historian* (Oxford: Oxford University Press) 39–62 (ch. 3) at 45–56 – *Suppliant Women* and battle of Delion

## Aristophanes

Murray, G. (1933) *Aristophanes: a study* (Oxford: Oxford University Press) – characters speaking for poet

Gomme, A. W. (1938) 'Aristophanes and politics' in: *CR* 52: 97–109 = Gomme, *More essays in Greek history and literature* (Oxford: Blackwell 1962) 70–91 – political interpretation illegitimate

Sommerstein, A. H. (1996) 'How to avoid being a *komodoumenos*' in: *CQ* ns 46: 327–56 – Aristophanes kinder to upper-class politicians

## Plato on the Spartans and Marathon

Wallace, W. P. (1954) 'Kleomenes, Marathon, the helots and Arkadia' in: *JHS* 74: 32–5 – believing

den Boer, W. (1956) 'Political propaganda in Greek chronology' in: *Historia* 5: 162–77 – disbelieving

## Aristotle's *Politics* and the *Athenian Constitution* on Solon

Rhodes, P. J. (1981) *A commentary on the Aristotelian* Athenaion Politeia (rev. ed.; originally publ. 1981) (Oxford: Oxford University Press) 146–8 – *Athenian Constitution* to be preferred

# CHAPTER THREE

# The Non-Literary Written Sources

*P. J. Rhodes*

## 1 Inscriptions

The non-literary written sources which first come to the mind of the student of classical Greece are those commonly meant when we talk of inscriptions – often on slabs of stone, about the size of a modern tombstone, occasionally on bronze plates or other media (it is conventional to use the word *stele* of stone slabs, but the Greek word was wider in its application and could indeed be used of a bronze plate). At all times and places the largest number of inscriptions are set up by private individuals – mostly dedications and funerary monuments – and these private inscriptions can be exploited in various ways as historical evidence; but the inscriptions cited most often in general histories are public documents – such as laws and decrees, alliances and peace treaties, inventories of temple treasuries, accounts of public expenditure, com-memorations of battles and lists of those who died in them, lists of officials or of victors in competitions.

Just as Athens is the city with which most of the literature surviving from the fifth and fourth centuries is connected, though it was not similarly predominant earlier or later, Athens is the city which produced the largest numbers of public inscriptions and of all inscriptions in the fifth and fourth centuries, though it was not the earliest state to produce public inscriptions and some other states became large-scale producers of inscriptions later. Athens was, of course, one of the largest Greek cities, and that helps to explain its large number of private inscriptions; but its large number of public inscriptions in the classical period seems at least in part to be due to public policy. Within a few years of the reforms of Ephialtes in 462/1 the Athenians were suffi-ciently self-consciously democratic to impose democratic constitutions on some of the member states of their alliance, the Delian League, and within a few years of those reforms they started inscribing public documents on a large scale: it looks as if the democrats had decided that it was important for the democracy that the *demos* should be kept informed about public business. Running the alliances which Athens led in the fifth and fourth centuries, the Delian League and the Second Athenian League, gave rise to many of the documents that have been inscribed; but the Peloponnesian League under Spartan leadership did not similarly generate inscribed documents.

As Chapter 2 has made clear, what we learn of the past from the literary sources is indirect. Historians had to obtain information, about their own time or about what was already the past, and they had to interpret it, which they did on principles which were not the same as those of a modern academic historian. Orators, philosophers, dramatists and writers of other kinds of literature were writing for their immediate audiences, and not with the intention of serving as historical sources either for them or for us: they may allude to historical events (on which they may or may not have taken trouble to get the facts right); they can provide information of various kinds about the society in and for which they were writing; but we can be led badly astray if we believe uncritically what they seem to be telling us.

Inscriptions, by contrast, are direct. The inscribed text of a decree or a treaty is (nearly always: cf. below, p. 50) a text which was made public by the authorities shortly after the decree had been enacted or the treaty had been agreed and sworn to. Inventories of a temple treasury or of ships in the dockyards, accounts of expenditure on a public building project or sales of confiscated property, are the texts which were made public by the relevant authorities for a particular year, to demonstrate the latest state of affairs in their field of responsibility and the fact that they themselves had done their duty in that field. When battles were commemorated, poets might be commissioned to compose suitable verses, in which they would enjoy the usual poetic licence, but the casualty lists would have to withstand the scrutiny of families which expected to find their deceased relative included. Lists of officials and victors are direct and should be accurate for the names added year by year (though a decision, for instance, to regard one office-holder as irregular and to leave one year blank might well be controversial: see *Athenian Constitution* 13.2 for years in the early sixth century when there is said to have been no Athenian archon); but such lists might start with more or less adventurous reconstructions of who had held offices or won victories long before the inscription was begun.

Caution is still needed, however, for a number of reasons. First of all, inscriptions do not give us access to the complete minutes of the Athenian assembly or any other body. Only a fraction of the literature written in antiquity has survived, and some works have survived in part but not entire (we have parts only of the major Roman histories of Livy and Tacitus; of histories used in the study of classical Greece, the relevant part of the world history of Diodoros ('Diodorus Siculus') has survived but not the whole, and Diodoros' source Ephoros has not survived at all). Because of the errors made in transmission by generations of copyists, editors have to do their best to reconstruct the exact wording of the texts as originally written. Similarly, not every document which could have been inscribed to be displayed in public was inscribed, and only a fraction of those which were inscribed have been found by archaeologists; in many cases a part or parts of an inscribed *stele* have been found but not the whole. And, where literary scholars have to cope with the errors of copyists (and stone-cutters can make mistakes too: for an example see below, p. 48), epigraphists have to cope with stones which may not only be incomplete but whose surface may be so badly damaged that the letters engraved on it may be hard to read. Familiarity with the body of material can help: the Greeks did not have computers with a cut-and-paste facility, but they did develop standard ways of saying standard things (while allowing variations within the basic pattern). If part of a standard expression can be identified on the part of a *stele* which survives and is legible, it becomes possible to reconstruct what is likely to have been in the gaps. The practice found in many public documents of using a *stoichedon* pattern, with letters regularly spaced on a grid and the same number of letters in each line, means that, if the use of a standard expression enables us to reconstruct the whole of one line, we know how many letters there should have been in every line. Over time the repertoire and the use of standard expressions increased: in particular, there are fewer such expressions and reconstruction is therefore more hazardous before c. 400 than after.

When a public document was inscribed, we must remember that the inscribed document is not the original but a copy made from an original on papyrus or some other medium – which may then have been kept in an archive, more or less efficiently, for a longer or shorter time. When more than one inscribed copy was made, they tend not to be identical word for word and letter for letter. For instance, M&L 45 ~ Fornara 97, an Athenian decree on weights, measures and coinage, is a text published in all the cities of the Delian League, and what we have is a composite text assembled from fragments found in different cities, but the discrepancies are such that some have doubted whether all the fragments are in fact from the same enactment. There are discrepancies between Thucydides' text, 5.47, and an inscribed text, Tod 72, of an alliance made by Athens with Argos and other Peloponnesian states in 420, but, for all we know, Thucydides may have reproduced perfectly the text which he saw.

We must assume that there could be similar discrepancies between the original text and an inscribed text, and indeed we must allow for the possibility that the inscribed text omits (e.g., in the dating and other details in the preamble) or modifies material in the original.

Nevertheless, when a text was published, the published version was in some sense the official version: the Thirty in Athens in 404/3 'took down from the Areopagos hill the laws of Ephialtes and Archestratos about the council of the Areopagos' (*Athenian Constitution* 35.2), and there are references to the demolition of other inscriptions to annul their content (e.g., R&O 22 ~ Harding 35.31–5; R&O 44 ~ Harding 59.39–40). When inventories had to be reviewed, in Athens and in Delos, what was taken to the council and assembly was not a set of original documents but a copy made from the inscribed text which had been based on those documents (*IG2²* 120.17–32, cf. *IG 9* 287. *A*. 197, *I. Delos* 399. *A*. 97). Some public documents, such as decrees honouring states or individuals, were published on private initiative (e.g., *IG1³* 17 provides for the publication of a decree honouring the city of Sigeion, at the request and the expense of Sigeion), and we may suspect that, in terms of inclusion and omission, if not actual modification, greater liberties could be taken in these cases than in cases of documents for which the state paid. (It is unsafe, however, to assume that a decree cannot have been inscribed at public expense except when the inscribed text includes a clause ordering that to be done.)

As we are well aware in an era in which journalists expose the activities of government 'spin doctors', an official document does not necessarily tell the whole story or an uncontroversial story. Very rarely we are told in a decree how many votes were cast (to demonstrate that a quorum requirement had been satisfied), and even more rarely how the votes were divided between the supporters and opponents of a measure (most of the instances that we do have are later than the classical period): usually we have the mere fact that it was passed.

Decrees do not normally indicate the circumstances which led to their enactment, or the purpose which their enactment was to serve; and, when a state or a man is honoured, the reason for the award is often expressed in bland and uninformative language: 'Praise the people of Clazomenae because they have been enthusiastic towards the city of Athens both now and in time past' (R&O 18 ~ Harding 26.4–6); 'Since Coroebus the Spartan has been a good man towards the people of Athens both now and in time past' (Tod 135 11–13). Some texts, however, are more informative: the decree ordering the reassessment of the Delian League's tribute in 425 explains, not at the beginning but after several lines, that the current level is not sufficient (M&L 69 ~ Fornara 136.16–17); in the 320s Athens honoured Eudemos of Plataiai because 'Eudemos previously offered to the people to make a voluntary gift towards the war of 4,000 (?) drachmas if there were any need, and now has made a voluntary gift towards the making of the stadium and the Panathenaic theatre of a thousand yoke of oxen, and has sent all these before the Panathenaia as he promised' (R&O 94 ~ Harding 118.12–20), and it honoured Herakleides of Salamis in Cyprus for selling grain in Athens at a reasonable price and donating money to a fund for buying grain (R&O 95). Most remarkable is an Athenian decree for Phanokritos of Parion in the 380s: the original motion, which has been lost, was presumably bland and uninformative; but an amendment specifies that Phanokritos 'passed over to the generals a message about the passage of the ships, and if the generals had believed him the enemy triremes would have been captured: it is in return for this that he is to receive the status of *proxenos* and benefactor' (R&O 19.11–16).

Inventories and accounts, even when published in a permanent medium, were intended for immediate purposes, not to serve as a quarry for historians. Demonstrating that the officials who had published the document had done their duty was as important as giving a clear picture of the current situation. The 'Athenian tribute lists' record not the total sums collected each year from the Delian League in tribute but the one sixtieth of the tribute which was given as an offering to the treasury of Athena – conveniently for historians, calculated not on the total but separately on each state's payment (*IG*1$^3$ 259–90: short extracts from first list M&L 39, Fornara 85). A detailed account of loans from Athens' sacred treasuries to the state from 426/5 to 423/2, with interest due on the loans and a summary going back to 433/2, does not tell us how much money there was in those treasuries, at the beginning or the end or any other time; it also ends with an arithmetical error, resulting from one wrong character, in the totals (M&L 72: beginning and end only Fornara 134). Inventories of temple treasuries vary between treasuries and over time for the same treasury in what they include and how their contents are organized. The order in Athens' first decree of Kallias that the gold and the silver kept in the *opisthodomos* are to be listed separately (M&L 58 ~ Fornara 119.A.21–4) is not obeyed in the inventories for the three chambers of the Parthenon in the late fifth century (*IG*1$^3$ 292–362: an example M&L 76 ~ Fornara 143). It appears that owing to clerical carelessness there is a 5–10 per cent chance that an item listed formerly will be missing from one list but reappear subsequently. When items are reweighed, the results often change; and, when they are not, there is often an error in copying the weight from a previous list.

There are some episodes for which literary and epigraphical evidence can be put together to give us a fuller picture: most strikingly, there are strong correspondences between Diodoros 15.28–9 and a series of inscriptions concerned with the foundation of the Second Athenian League in 378/7 (R&O 22, cf. R&O 20, Tod 121, R&O 23, Tod 124 ~ Harding 35, cf. 31, 34, 37, 38). On other occasions the possibility of combining literary and epigraphic evidence might have arisen but in fact has not: the earliest tribute lists and Athenian decrees concerning individual member states of the Delian League, or the whole League, in the middle of the fifth century reveal developments in the League on which we have nothing from Thucydides' account of the period, and only passing allusions from later writers. Often, however, inscribed documents add to our knowledge of Greek history by giving information on subjects about which our literary sources not only do not say anything but, in view of their interests, could not be expected to say anything.

Temple inventories fall into this category, and these records of objects dedicated in and retained by temples will interest both religious and economic historians. Religious and economic interests are served also by such texts as leases of sacred property (e.g., M&L 62 ~ Fornara 121.15 to end of text, Delos and Rheneia, fifth century; $IG1^3$ 84, Athens, fifth century). For the economic historian there are also, from the fourth century, leases for working the silver mines of Attika (Lalonde et al. 1991: pp. 5–16, 18–30, 32–41, 43–4, 50–1). Athens' religious scandals of 415 and the trials to which they led are of both political and religious interest, and we have literary evidence for them; the trials resulted in the sales of confiscated property which are recorded in the 'Attic *stelai*' ($IG1^3$ 421–30; extracts M&L 79 ~ Fornara 147.D), and these provide invaluable information on the kinds and quantities of property owned by rich Athenians in the late fifth century, and the prices which they fetched when sold in these somewhat unusual circumstances. There are inscriptions of various kinds connected with public buildings, such as contracts specifying the work to be done and the arrangements made with those who undertook to do it, and records of the collection and expenditure of money on a project. From the building programme on the Athenian akropolis in the 440s–430s, on which we also have literary evidence, there are annual accounts of expenditure – dated, as a result of which these are among the few classical Greek buildings which can be dated precisely (e.g., M&L 54, 59, 60 ~ Fornara 114, 120, 118.B). From the rebuilding of the temple of Apollo at Delphi in the fourth century, to which there are also a few literary references, there are documents of various kinds (collection of funds Bousquet 1989: 2.1–30: example R&O 45; itemized expenditure Bousquet 1989: 2.34–5, 46–66: example R&O 66). Other texts to interest religious historians are sacred laws (e.g., R&O 97, Kyrene, fourth century), calendars of festivals (e.g., R&O 62, Kos, fourth century), and records of those whose illnesses were cured when they visited a sanctuary (e.g., R&O 102, Epidauros, fourth century). On the production of Aischylos' earliest surviving tragedy, the *Persians*, an ancient introduction gives the date (473/2), the fact that Aischylos won first prize and the titles of the four plays which he entered on that occasion; an inscription listing the victors in the various contests at the Great Dionysia (the surviving fragments span 473/2–329/8) confirms the date and adds the information that the *choregos*, the rich citizen who took responsibility for the production, was Perikles ($IG2^2$ 2318.9–11). Another aspect of Greek society is illuminated by documents emanating from bodies within a state, such as a set of decrees of an Athenian phratry in the early fourth century on the procedures for checking the eligibility of those claiming membership (R&O 5).

I remarked above that the inscribed text of a decree or treaty is nearly always a text which was made public by the authorities shortly afterwards; but there are some notorious exceptions, texts inscribed at one date which purport to be authentic documents of a much earlier date, whose integration with our other evidence is therefore particularly problematic. One of the best known is the text found in 1959 in a local collection at Troizen in the north-eastern Peloponnese, which was inscribed in the early third century but appears to be an Athenian decree proposed by Themistokles in 480, embodying several of the major decisions taken in the face of the Persian invasion, and which if totally authentic would seriously undermine the chronology which we derive from Herodotos (M&L 23 ~ Fornara 55). It is in fact one of a number of fifth-century documents for which we have no fifth-century evidence but allusions in the literary texts from the fourth century onwards, as they were used to provide ammunition for the debates of the time. Another is the alleged Peace of Kallias between Athens and Persia in the middle of the century: the fourth-century historian Theopompos saw and was suspicious of an inscribed text, but that has not been found (evidence *Staatsverträge* 152, Fornara 95: Theopompos *FGrHist* 115 F 154 = *Staatsverträge* p. 65, Fornara 95.E). Are these authentic texts which survived underground for a century before being rediscovered? Were they invented to make more vivid what people thought they knew about the past? At least in the case of Themistokles' decree, the truth probably lies somewhere between the extremes: various features of the inscribed Greek text show that it cannot be word for word and letter for letter a text written in Athens in 480 but has at least undergone some editing – and we have seen (above, p. 47) that even when documents were inscribed immediately the inscribed text was not always a totally faithful copy of the original; on the other hand, the major decisions contained in it are decisions which actually were taken in 481–480, and even if it is largely reconstruction the construction may embody some authentic material rather than being pure invention – but, if we accept that an editor could easily have combined in a single text separate decisions which were taken on separate occasions, then even if the separate items are largely authentic the inscription cannot be used to undermine Herodotos' chronology.

Even more remarkable is an inscription set up in western Asia Minor, upstream from Magnesia on the Maiandros, in the second century AD, which gives in Greek what purports to be a letter from the Persian King Dareios I (522–486) to a satrap, praising him for cultivating fruit trees but threatening him with punishment for his treatment of the sacred gardeners of Apollo (M&L 12 ~ Fornara 35). The original will presumably have been written in Aramaic; there is nothing obviously inauthentic in the Greek text, which was presumably published by the officials of the sanctuary (for which cf. Pausanias 10.32.6) to serve their purposes at the time.

The inscriptions which survive for us to study were engraved on durable materials, but they were not set up in an antiquarian spirit. Recently some scholars have stressed their symbolic function, seeing the tribute lists, for instance, as a display of the greatness and piety of the Athenian empire (analogous to the pictures of tribute-bearers carved on a staircase of the Persian king Dareios' palace at Persepolis) rather than as documents which people were likely to read attentively. (The *stele* containing the lists of the first fifteen years was more than 3.5 m high, with letters about 1 cm high: its upper part could not easily have been read without the aid of a step-ladder.) Symbolic monuments, however, could have been produced in less laborious ways, and these detailed monuments could only have been produced because there were detailed records on which they could be based. One indication that texts were, at least in principle, published in order to be read, and that people were conscious of what was said in the texts, is that inscribed documents were demolished in order to annul them (cf. above, p. 47). About ten years after the prospectus of the Second Athenian League had been published, containing a favourable reference to the Persian king and the King's Peace, when the Persians adopted a policy unfavourable to Athens, the Athenians went back to the prospectus and erased the favourable reference (R&O 22 ~ Harding 35.12–15). Similarly, at the end of the third century, the Athenians set about deleting as many references as they could find to the Macedonian kings Antigonos and Demetrios, of a century earlier (reported by Livy 31.44.2–9; surviving inscriptions show many deletions, and a few references which the deleters failed to find).

We know from references both in literary texts and in inscriptions that documents for temporary use and notices for temporary display were written on non-permanent materials, sheets of papyrus, wax tablets or whitewashed boards. When they had served their purpose these were destroyed or cleaned and reused: thus we read that contracts for the collection of Athenian taxes were written on whitewashed boards and filed according to the date when payment was due, and when the payment was made the record was deleted (*Athenian Constitution* 47.2–48.1). Those objects have not survived for us to see. However, from near the building in the south-west corner of the Athenian Agora for which various identifications have been proposed (most often, *heliaia*; most recently and most persuasively, the Aiakeion) fragments of wall plaster have been found with letters in thin red paint, and it has been suggested that they are from the wall of the Aiakeion facing the Agora, and that this was used for temporary notices of court cases, which could be erased and replaced with new notices.

Private inscriptions are far more numerous than public: in particular, dedications to one or more gods in thanksgiving for and celebration of success achieved in any of a number of fields (e.g., an office held or victory gained in a competition; but often the reason for a dedication will not be stated), and funerary inscriptions. Sometimes one of these texts can be combined with evidence of other kinds. A family group of monuments in the Kerameikos at Athens includes that of Dexileos, who died as one of five cavalrymen at Korinth in 394/3 (R&O 7.*B* ~ Harding 19.C); a public inscription includes him in a list of eleven cavalrymen who died at Korinth (R&O 7.A ~ Harding 19.B); we also have a fragment of a full Athenian casualty list for the campaigns of that year (*IG* $2^2$ 5221 ~ Harding 19.A), and there are accounts of the campaign at Korinth in Xenophon (*Hellenika* 4.2.9–23) and Diodoros (14.83.1–2). It is possible though not certain that the eleven were the only Athenian cavalrymen killed in that campaign, but we do not know how to account for the smaller body of five mentioned in Dexileos' monument. More often those who set up or are commemorated in private inscriptions are people for whom we have no other evidence; but there are still things which historians can learn from these inscriptions, e.g., if inscribed funerary monuments at a particular site are more frequent at one time than another, or are of different kinds at different times.

## *Excursus: the three-bar* sigma

To be interpreted correctly, inscriptions must be dated correctly, so that they may be seen in the right context. In a system in which years are not numbered, dates are most easily specified by the use of an 'eponymous' annual official, in Athens the archon, but (although there are some earlier instances) it was not until c. 420 that the Athenians formed the regular habit of naming the archon in the preambles of their decrees. Therefore, even when the preamble survives complete and legible (which is not always the case), there are many fifth-century Athenian decrees whose dating remains problematic.

Various approaches to a solution are possible. If the chairman or secretary bears a reasonably uncommon name, and there are other decrees enacted under the same chairman or secretary, they should have been enacted on the same day (chairman) or (for the fifth century and the early fourth) in the same prytany, i.e. tenth of a year (secretary), and a date for one will be the date of all. If the proposer is an identifiable individual, the decree must have been enacted during that man's period of political activity. There may be something in the subject-matter of the decree which allows us to link it to a particular occasion.

Another possible approach is through the style of the lettering with which the texts are inscribed. There have been various attempts, most thoroughly by S. V. Tracy, to identify the individual styles of particular letter-cutters; and, as with the proposers of decrees, the known period of a cutter's activity will limit the possibilities of dating. More generally, it is clear that the form given by Athenian cutters to certain letters of the alphabet changed in the course of the fifth century: in particular, *beta* and *rho* began as angular letters, ßℝ, and became rounded letters, BP; *phi* began as a letter with either a vertical or a horizontal line which did not project beyond the circle, ⊕ ⊖, and became a letter with a vertical line which did project beyond the circle, Φ; *sigma* was originally carved with three strokes, ⊰, but came to be carved with four strokes, Σ. The exercise is in principle valid, if (as here) there is a reasonable body of dated material and that material indicates reasonably clearly when we can expect to find only the older forms, when either and when only the newer forms.

German editors of Athenian inscriptions more than a century ago worked out that the changes in *sigma*, *beta*, *phi* and *rho* took place about the middle of the fifth century, and it came to be standard doctrine that texts using the older forms of *sigma*, *beta* and *phi* should have been inscribed not later than c. 445, and those using the older form of *rho* not later than c. 435. The tribute lists are numbered and dated; but a number of other inscriptions important for the history of the Delian League are not dated and have been assigned to the middle of the fifth century on the basis of their letter-forms; and if the assignments are right the Athenians were already at that time using strongly imperialistic language (e.g., τὸν πόλεον ὅσον Ἀθεναῖοι κρατôσιν, 'the cities which the Athenians control', *IG* 1³ 19.8–9, 27.14–15) and behaving in strongly imperialistic ways (e.g., imposing democratic constitutions, M&L 40 ∼ Fornara 71; treating all the allies as colonists and requiring them to send offerings to the Panathenaia, M&L 46 ∼ Fornara 98.41–3).

An attack on that standard doctrine was first made by H. B. Mattingly at a conference in 1957 and in an article published in 1961, beginning to argue that many inscriptions which have been dated to the middle of the century make better sense if dated after

430. Although he has changed his mind on some points, he has persisted in this general line of argument ever since; and, particularly after M. H. Chambers' work on Athens' alliance with Egesta (cf. below), he has gained a number of adherents. If he is right, we have fewer Athenian public inscriptions from the middle of the century than would otherwise be the case, and no evidence for strongly imperialistic language and behaviour in Athens until about 430. Imperialism can therefore be blamed not on Perikles, of whom (following Thucydides) scholars tend to approve, but on Kleon, of whom (again following Thucydides) scholars feel able to disapprove.

The debate has involved language as well as letter-forms, with attempts to use as dating criteria such changes as *-a(i)si* to *-ais* in the first declension dative plural, *chsyn-* to *syn-* in compounds, and the use or non-use of movable *nu* at the end of such verbal forms as *egrammateue(n)*. There is perhaps a little support here for Mattingly's position on some texts, but not enough to tip the balance of the argument.

Two texts deserve special mention. I have referred in section 1 to M&L 45 ~ Fornara 97, a decree which (on the normal and almost certainly correct interpretation, though this has been challenged) requires the member states of the League to use Athenian weights, measures and silver coins and to cease issuing silver coins of their own. This was published in all the states of the League, and our text is an amalgam put together from fragments found in different places. There is a parody of a decree like this in Aristophanes *Birds* 1038–45, of 414, and because of that editors used to date it c. 430–415. In 1938, however, a fragment from Kos was published, on what was thought to be Attic marble, with Athenian lettering including the older form of *sigma*. Consequently some scholars dated the decree c. 450–445, and some numismatists (both before and after the discovery of that fragment) thought that date appropriate for what was known of the history of fifth-century coinages. Since then it has become accepted that the stone in question may well not be Attic; and that (while certainty is impossible since fifth-century coins cannot be precisely dated) the number of states issuing their own coinage was in any case declining during the fifth century; there does not seem to be any one date at which the issuing of coins by the states of the League ceased, but some states seem to have continued issuing coins to the 440s or later. In 1988 a fragment from the Troad was published, in Athenian lettering including the newer form of *sigma*, which Mattingly has identified as a fragment of this decree (but in *IG* 1$^3$, where the decree is no. 1453, this fragment is printed separately as 1454 *ter*). A date in the 420s for this decree now seems the more likely, but it might be possible to accept a late date for this without abandoning the orthodox doctrine otherwise.

There is an alliance between Athens and Egesta, in the west of Sicily, with a transitional *rho* and the old *sigma*, whose preamble included an archon's name (M&L 37 ~ Fornara 81), but the only letters of the name which have been read uncontroversially are the last two, *-on*, and there were many fifth-century archons whose names ended with those letters. Earlier editors restored [Arist]on, the archon of 454/3, under which year Diodoros 11.86.3 mentions a war involving Egesta – but that was a time when Athens was retrenching rather than expanding. In 1944 A. E. Raubitschek claimed to see traces of BP, from [Ha]bron, the archon of 458/7, a time when it is easier to suppose that the Athenians would have made an adventurous new alliance; but in 1963 Mattingly read the traces as IΦ, from [Ant]iphon, the archon of 418/7 – in which case Thucydides' failure to mention the recent alliance as part of the background to Athens' Sicilian expedition of 415 would be shocking, but Thucydides is capable of shocking his readers in such ways.

In response to Mattingly a number of scholars re-examined the fifth-century Athenian public documents which can be securely dated on other grounds. There was a transitional period, and older and newer forms of letters can coexist in the same inscription. The new forms of all four letters are found not later than the tribute list of 451 (*IG* 1³ 261); the old *beta* and *phi* are not found after c. 445; later than that there is one inscription with the old *sigma* (*IG* 1³ 440, of 443/2), and there are two with transitional *rho* (*IG* 1³ 445 and 460, both of 438/7). This seemed to confirm the old doctrine, since if the doctrine works for texts which can be dated on other grounds, it ought to work for texts which cannot: there is no particular significance in the latest dates at which the old forms are currently attested, and it would not be disturbing to find them in a text that could be dated slightly later, but on that evidence it seemed unwise to suppose that they were used in a number of texts to be dated after c. 430. Next M. H. Chambers and colleagues brought modern technology to bear on the question, using digital enhancement of photographs and shining a laser beam through the stone. They claimed to have confirmed Mattingly's reading in the Egesta alliance, and they convinced many scholars but not all. Most recently, however, two Greek scholars, A. P. Matthaiou and M. Korres, have been able to make out on the stone not only the IΦ of Antiphon but also the T before that, and so it appears that after nearly half a century of argument the dating of this alliance to 418/17 must be accepted.

This does not mean that the later date must necessarily be accepted for all texts for which a later date has been proposed; but the argument from letter-forms can no longer be used to rule out a later date, and the other arguments must be considered individually on their merits for the individual texts. Apart from the decree about weights, measures and coinage, two others for which a later date probably should be accepted are the decree for Miletos (*IG* 1³ 21 ~ Fornara 92) and Kleinias' decree about the collection of tribute (M&L 46 ~ Fornara 98).

M. I. Finley once complained that 'the problems and issues of the empire have been reduced to a question of the date when the Athenian stone-cutters began to carve the letter *sigma* with four bars instead of three' (*Times Literary Supplement* (7 April 1966) 289). That was unfair, and R. Meiggs justifiably responded, 'Finley has made a molehill out of a mountain' (*JHS* 86 (1966) 98). It is important to know not only what Athenian imperialism was like but what it was like at different dates; to do that we must be able to date the inscriptions correctly; and the alternative datings which have been canvassed result in markedly different pictures of the development of Athenian imperialism. Agreement has not yet been reached as to which texts should retain an early date and which should not, but the outcome may well be that some of the controversial texts settle after 430 but there remains evidence of strong imperialism twenty years earlier.

## 2   Lead Letters

So far I have dealt with the texts on stone or bronze of which we are normally thinking when we refer to inscriptions; but there are various other texts which come within the scope of this chapter.

A number of private letters have been found, particularly from traders, scratched on sheets of lead (one example translated, Austin & Vidal-Naquet 1977: 41, in which a trader writes to his son, to say that he is being enslaved and his goods confiscated and to ask his son to inform the man on whose behalf he was carrying the goods; the most recently published, Jordan (2000), in which a boy working for bronze smiths complains of being maltreated).

# 3  Coinage

The designs stamped on coins include lettering, referred to by numismatists as legends, as well as pictorial and other devices (for other aspects of coinage see Chapter 14). From this point of view Greece has less to offer in the classical period than later, and much less than Rome. It is now believed that the earliest of all coins, in electrum (a natural alloy of gold and silver) from Asia Minor, date from c. 600, and that the Greeks started coining silver shortly before 550. The first and most frequent use of lettering on Greek coins was to identify the issuing state (which commonly used a distinctive pictorial device also). Thus Athens' well-known owl coins, introduced in the second half of the sixth century, have to the right of the owl AΘE, the first three letters (in the Athenian version of the Greek alphabet) of ʼΑθεναίον, 'of the Athenians' (Kraay 1976: 177 etc.). Coins of Korinth, from the very earliest issues, before 550, have ϙ for ϙορινθίων (*koppa*) for *Qorinthion* (Kraay 1976: 220 etc.); and by the fifth century we find some colonies of Korinth using similar designs but their own legends: A for Ambrakia (Kraay 1976: 229), ΛΕΥ for Leukas (Kraay 1976: 247), E for Epidamnos (Kraay 1976: 248) and so on. From Euboia in the sixth century we have E for Eretria (Kraay 1976: 270) and KAP for Karystos (Kraay 1976: 271), while in the late fifth century there are 'federal' Euboian coins with EYB (Kraay 1976: 273–5).

For much of the fifth century there was an Arkadian coinage, bearing ΑΡΚΑΔΙΚΟΝ (in full or abbreviated) and apparently emanating from three different mints (e.g., Kraay 1976: 288–91), and there has been considerable discussion of the dating and significance of these coins: the latest study concludes that they are probably 'festival' coins issued in connection with the Arkadian festivals of Zeus Lykaios, and cannot be used as evidence for a political federation at any date. Another series of coins bearing a legend whose historical interpretation has been disputed is the so-called ΣΥΝ coinage, a series of coins issued by a number of east Greek states from Byzantion to Rhodes, which have on one face the design and legend of the issuing state and on the other Herakles strangling two snakes and the letters ΣΥΝ. It is agreed that the coins should be dated c. 400, but different interpretations have been offered: an alliance of liberated states formed after Sparta's supremacy in the Aegean was ended by the battle of Knidos in 394; or else a pro-Spartan alliance, either to be dated to a period of Spartan recovery c. 391/0 or (the best view) formed by Lysander about the end of the Peloponnesian War.

Athens' owl coinage became so popular that imitations of it were produced elsewhere, within the Greek world and even beyond it. Some imitations kept the legend AΘE (e.g., Kraay 1976: 204–5), but others used their own lettering: for instance, there is a version bearing ΒΑΣ for βασιλέως, 'of the king', speculatively attributed to Tissaphernes, the Persian satrap of Lydia who subsidized Sparta's war effort against Athens in the late fifth century (Kraay 1976: 206). From the late sixth century there is one surviving specimen of an owl coin with the letters ΗΙΠ – perhaps issued by the former tyrant Hippias when in exile.

The other main use of lettering on classical Greek coins is to give an individual's name. A principal local official would perhaps be named for dating purposes rather than because he had a particular responsibility for the coinage (e.g., Abdera, in Thrace: Kraay 1976: 530–42). Other men named may be officials who were responsible for the coinage (assumed, e.g., for Zakynthos, off the west coast of the Peloponnese: Kraay 1976: 313, 316). Particularly in Sicily and southern Italy, there are coins on which a name in small characters seems to be the signature of the die-engraver, sometimes made clear with the verb ΕΠΟΙΕ, 'made it' (an example of that from Klazomenai, in Asia Minor: Kraay 1976: 929).

Rarely before the hellenistic period, letters are used to number coins in a sequence of years, or simply to number the dies from which the coins were struck (years, e.g., Zankle in Sicily, while occupied by Samians in the early fifth century, Kraay 1976: 770, and Samos itself during the fifth century, Kraay 1976: 881–2; dies: Poseidonia in Italy, Kraay 1976: 654–6). Occasionally denominations are specified, particularly the smaller denominations over which confusion could most easily arise (e.g., Korinth, Kraay 1976: 36; Poseidonia, Kraay 1976: 35). Finally, just as Greek vases often have legends identifying the characters depicted on them (see below), this is occasionally done on coins (e.g., the river god Hypsas at Selinous in Sicily, Kraay 1976: 788).

# 4   Pottery

Texts to be found on pottery fall into two categories: legends included before firing, as part of the original decoration, and texts added subsequently.

The most frequent use of writing before firing was (especially in the sixth century) to supply captions to the pictures. In one of the best-known scenes on a Greek vase, painted by Exekias, Achilles and Ajax are playing dice – and we know that that is what is represented by this picture of two warriors with hands stretched out to a box between them because the men are identified, and the word 'four' comes from Achilles' mouth and 'three' from Ajax' (Boardman 1974: pl. 100). In an extreme instance of labelling, the scene of Troilos on the François Vase has captions for the well-house, Polyxena's water-pot and Priam's seat (κρένε, hυδρία, θᾶκος: Arias et al. 1962: pl. 44 top, middle, bottom respectively).

Second, we have the signatures of potters and/or painters, often with ἐποίησε, 'made', to identify the potter and ἔγραψε, 'drew', to identify the painter. On one Athenian red-figure vase of the late sixth century the painter, Euthymides, proudly proclaims hος οὐδέποτε Εὐφρόνιος, 'as never Euphronios' (Boardman 1975: pl. 33.2). Dedications and owners' names are usually added after firing, but there are a few bespoke pieces on which these texts were painted before firing.

Occasionally mottoes such as χαῖρε καὶ πιεῖ σ[ύ], 'hail and drink, you' (Boardman 1974: pl. 121.1), are used, particularly as in that example on drinking-cups. A particular kind of motto, of more interest to historians, is found on Athenian vases, especially between the third quarter of the sixth century and the third quarter of the fifth: a name (nearly always a man's name, but occasionally a woman or a god or hero is celebrated) with the adjective καλός, 'X is beautiful'. The assumption is that those celebrated are upper-class young men at the stage in life when they are subject to homosexual admiration; but it appears that the vases in question were not bespoke items commissioned by the admirers, since some names appear frequently, and many of the vases were sold, for instance, in Etruria, where the man praised must have been unknown. Some of the men can be identified as men who became public figures later in life: Leagros, praised on more than sixty vases at the end of the sixth century, is probably the Leagros who died as a general commanding the Athenians at Drabeskos in 465 (Hdt. 9.75 with Thuc. 1.100.3).

Special vases were made to hold the olive oil awarded in prizes at the Athenian festival of the Panathenaia. These continued to be decorated in the black-figure style when otherwise it had been superseded by red-figure; they all bore the legend τῶν ᾿Αθήνηθεν ἄθλων, 'of the prizes from Athens'; each vase depicts one of the competitions, and some also specify in words the competition for which the prize was awarded; and in the fourth century the archon's name might be given, so that we have some vases which can be precisely dated (Boardman 1974: pl. 301.2 shows the Panathenaic label clearly; pl. 307 has part of the name of Pythodelos, archon 336/5).

Texts added after firing are occasionally painted but usually incised. Commonly they identify the person who dedicated the vase and the god to whom it was dedicated, or else the owner (particularly on vases buried in the owner's grave). There are also some vases with merchants' or dealers' marks. Herodotos 4.152.3 mentions as an exceptionally successful trader Sostratos of Aigina. Not only has a votive anchor dedicated to Aiginetan Apollo by a man called Sostratos been found at Graviscae in Etruria, but a large number of Athenian vases of the late sixth century have been found in Etruria with the letters ΣΟ incised on the base. It is an interesting possibility, though not a certainty, that Herodotos' Sostratos dedicated the anchor and was the trader who took the ΣΟ vases to Etruria. Two vases have been found at Naukratis, in Egypt, with the name Herodotos on them; but Herodotos is a common name, and one is too early and the other too late for them to serve as confirmation of the historian's travels.

# 5   Ostraka

There is one particular use of pottery which is of considerable importance for fifth-century Athenian history. In the institution of ostracism, by which they had the opportunity each year to send one man into exile for ten years, without finding him guilty of any offence, the Athenians voted by writing the name of the man they wished to exile on an *ostrakon*, a fragment of pottery – and more than 11,000 of these *ostraka* have now been found, mostly from the 480s and (probably) 470s. The one essential was the name of the intended victim; often the patronymic and/or the demotic would be added; occasionally there is also some kind of comment, sometimes of an ambiguity which puzzles interpreters (some of the more interesting texts M&L 21, Fornara 41.D), and/or a drawing. We have *ostraka* bearing the names of all the men who are known from literary texts to have been ostracized, and of very many more (about 140 in all); for some names we have very large numbers (4,462 for

Megakles, 2,279 for Themistokles); for others, including some who are known to have been serious candidates, only one or two (until recently there were none for Nikias, known to have been one of the serious candidates in ?415). For a man to be ostracized, there had to be at least 6,000 votes cast, and the man with the largest number of votes had to go. It is clear from the range of surviving *ostraka* that there was no list of candidates but each voter submitted the name of the man he most wanted to be rid of. Those who attracted large numbers of votes will have been public figures, voted against (largely) because of their public *persona*; but it is likely enough that some men voted against private enemies – e.g., the man who had diverted a watercourse to flood his land or damaged his vines – with no chance of success.

The institution of ostracism presupposes reasonably widespread literacy, but does not positively require it. An illiterate man could always ask for help. Plutarch *Aristeides* 7.7–8 has a story of an illiterate voter who did not recognize Aristeides and asked him to write Aristeides' own name (if the story is true, was Aristeides honest enough to do what he was asked?); a hoard of 191 *ostraka* with Themistokles' name written by about fourteen hands (Lang 1990: 1146–1336) must have been prepared in advance to be issued to voters; on the other hand, joining fragments with different names on them (e.g., one pot from the Kerameikos yields one vote against Hippokrates, one against Themistokles and two against Megakles) must have been issued blank and marked by or for the individual voters.

A recent book by S. Brenne has used the evidence of *ostraka* to study the names of Athenians, and the extent to which candidates for ostracism were men attested in various other connections. Further work on the *ostraka* should add to our understanding of various aspects of Athenian society.

# 6   Other Documents

By the fourth century, writing was being painted or engraved on various objects used in the working of the Athenian democracy. For the allotment of jurors to serve on particular days, and also for appointment to some offices, in the early fourth century a mechanism was devised which involved the issue to candidates of a bronze ticket (*pinakion*), bearing his name and deme, one of the ten letters A–K, denoting which of ten subsections of his tribe he had been assigned to, and various official stamps (*Athenian Constitution* 68.2–69.1: Boegehold et al. 1995: plates 7–8). At the time of the allotment, these were placed in *kleroteria*, 'allotment machines', which in the case of jurors had ten columns headed A–K (Boegehold et al. 1995: 6, 33 ill. 3), and black and white balls were used to decide which candidates were to serve (white) and which were not. By the second half of the fourth century *pinakia* of boxwood had replaced *pinakia* of bronze for the allotment of jurors (cf. *Athenian Constitution* 63.3: none of these has survived).

Various other inscribed objects were used in the law courts in the fourth century. Courtrooms were denoted both by letter (beginning with Λ) and by colour, and each juror was given an acorn (*balanos*), or a token resembling an acorn, bearing the letter and a staff bearing the colour of the court in which he was to sit (*Athenian Constitution* 63.2, 64.4–65.3); perhaps also a token bearing one of 25 letters (the 24 of the Ionian alphabet and one additional) to assign him to a seating area within his court

(*Athenian Constitution* 65.2: Boegehold et al. 1995: plates 9–12). Each juror was given two bronze ballots, consisting of a disc with an axle (one hollow, to vote for the plaintiff, one solid, to vote for the defendant; if he held them with his fingers and thumbs over the ends of the axles, he could feel but nobody could see which was which), and the words *psephos demosia*, 'public ballot', were inscribed on the discs (*Athenian Constitution* 68.2–69.1: Boegehold et al. 1995: plates 15–22). When he had voted, he was given another token, this time with the design of a 3-obol coin, which he afterwards exchanged for his day's stipend of 3 obols (*Athenian Constitution* 68.2, 69.2).

Speeches in the courts were timed by water-clocks; and one has been found (which cannot itself have been used in a court, since every jury contained men from all the tribes) which bears the name of a tribe, *Antiochidos*, and the letters HH, denoting a capacity of 2 *choes* (the *chous* being about 3.4 l) (Boegehold et al. 1995: pl. 13). For some kinds of lawsuit, perhaps for many, the documents to be cited were placed in a sealed jar (*echinos*) and could not be added to at a later stage: the jars were labelled so that the relevant jars for a particular case could be identified (*Athenian Constitution* 53.2), and what appears to be the lid of such a jar has been found, with a text painted on it (Boegehold et al. 1995: pl. 14).

Another kind of inscribed object is the curse tablet, a tablet usually of lead, bearing a text which invokes a curse on one or more personal enemies: about twenty-five from Athens in the classical period seem intended to influence the outcome of lawsuits (an example, Boegehold et al. 1995: 55–7 with ill. 4).

## Further reading and bibliography

### Inscriptions

Collections from which texts are cited

Bousquet, J. (1989) *Corpus des inscriptions de Delphes*, vol. 2: *Les Comptes du quatrième et du troisième siècle* (Paris: de Boccard) – Greek texts
Fornara – English translations
Harding – English translations
*IG*; *IG* 1³; *IG* 2² – Greek texts
Lalonde, G. V., M. K. Langdon, M. B. Walbank (1991) *Inscriptions: horoi, poletai records, leases of public lands* (Princeton: American School of Classical Studies at Athens) (*The Athenian Agora* 19) – Greek texts
M&L – Greek texts
R&O – Greek texts and English translations
*Staatsverträge* – Greek texts
Tod – Tod, M. N. *A selection of Greek historical inscriptions*, vol. 2 (Oxford: Clarendon ²1948) – Greek texts

In general

Bodel, J. (ed.) (2001) *Epigraphic evidence: ancient history from inscriptions* (London: Routledge)
Cook, B. F. (1987) *Greek inscriptions* (London: British Museum Publications)

Woodhead, A. G. (1992) *The study of Greek inscriptions* (Cambridge: Cambridge University Press ²1981; reissued Bristol: Bristol Classical Press 1992)

## On various aspects of archival and published texts

Davies, J. K. (1994) 'Accounts and accountability in classical Athens' in: Osborne, R., & S. Hornblower (eds) (1994) *Ritual, finance, politics: Athenian democratic accounts presented to David Lewis* (Oxford: Clarendon) 201–12

Hamilton, R. (2000) *Treasure map: a guide to the Delian inventories* (Ann Arbor: University of Michigan Press) – Also, for comparison, discusses Athenian akropolis inventories

Harris, D. (1994) 'Freedom of information and accountability: the inventory lists of the Parthenon' in: Osborne, R., & S. Hornblower (eds) (1994) *Ritual, finance, politics: Athenian democratic accounts presented to David Lewis* (Oxford: Clarendon) 213–25

Osborne, R. (1999) 'Inscribing performance' in: Goldhill, S., & R. Osborne (eds) (1999) *Performance culture and Athenian democracy* (Cambridge: Cambridge University Press) 341–58

Rhodes, P. J. (2001) 'Public documents in the Greek states: archives and inscriptions' in: *G&R* ser 2, 48: 33–44 and 136–53

## On the Aiakeion and the lettering on its north wall

Stroud, R. S. (1998) *The Athenian grain-tax law of 374/3 B.C.* (Princeton: American School of Classical Studies at Athens) 84–104, esp. 99–101 with fig. 6 (*Hesperia* Suppl. 29)

## On the decree of Themistokles

Burn, A. R. (1984) *Persia and the Greeks: the defence of the west, c. 546–478 B.C. With a postscript by D. M. Lewis* (London: Duckworth ²1984) 364–77

## The three-bar *sigma* (§2)

### *Fifth-century letter-cutters*
Tracy, S. V. (1984) 'Hands in fifth-century B.C. Attic inscriptions' in: (1984) *Studies presented to Sterling Dow on his eightieth birthday* (Durham NC: Duke University Press) 277–82 (Greek, Roman, and Byzantine Monograph 10)

### *Orthodox doctrine on letter-forms first found, to my knowledge, in:*
Köhler, U. (1867) 'Attische Inschriften' in: *Hermes* 2: 16–36 at 17 – First publication of Athens' alliance with Egesta: four-bar *sigma* was used from the tribute list of 443/2 onwards

### *Many of Mattingly's articles reprinted*
Mattingly, H. B. (1999) *The Athenian empire restored* (Ann Arbor: University of Michigan Press) – The first: Mattingly, H. B. (1961) 'The Athenian coinage decree' in: *Historia* 10: 148–88

### *Linguistic criteria*
Henry, A. S. (1978) 'The dating of fifth-century Attic inscriptions' in: *CSCA* 11: 75–108

### *Athens' decree on weights, measures and silver coinage (M&L 45 ~ Fornara 97)*
Georgiades, A. N., & W. K. Pritchett (1965) 'The Koan fragment of the monetary decree' in: *BCH* 89: 400–40 at 400–25 – The stone of the fragment not Attic and probably Parian

Figueira, T. J. (1998) *The power of money: coinage and politics in the Athenian empire* (Philadelphia: University of Pennsylvania Press) – A detailed study, with controversial new interpretations

Mattingly, H. B. (1993) 'New light on the Athenian standards decree' in: *Klio* 75: 99–102 – *IG* 1³ 1454 *ter* restored as a fragment of this decree

## Athens' alliance with Egesta (M&L 37 ~ Fornara 81)

Raubitschek, A. E. (1944) 'Athens and Halikyai' in: *TAPhA* 75: 10–14 at 10 n. 3 – Habron

Mattingly, H. B. (1963) 'The growth of Athenian imperialism' in: *Historia* 12: 257–73 at 268–9 (= Mattingly, H. B. (1999) *The Athenian empire restored* (Ann Arbor: University of Michigan Press 1996) 87–106 at 99–101) – Antiphon

Chambers, M. H., R. Gallucci, P. Spanos (1990) 'Athens' alliance with Egesta in the year of Antiphon' in: *ZPE* 83: 38–57 – Modern technology used to support Antiphon

Henry, A. S. (1992) 'Through a laser beam darkly: space age technology and the Egesta decree (*IG* i³ 11)' in: *ZPE* 91: 137–46 – Antiphon still not certain

Chambers, M. H. (1992–3) 'Photographic enhancement and a Greek inscription' in: *CJ* 88: 25–31 – Antiphon

Matthaiou, A. P. (2004) 'Περί τῆς *IG* I³ 11' in: Matthaiou, A. P. (ed.) (2004) *Attikai Epigraphai: Symposion eis mnemen Adolf Wilhelm (1864–1950)* (Athens: Greek Epigraphic Society / Hellenike Epigraphike Hetaireia) 99–121 – Antiphon

## Orthodox doctrine on letter-forms upheld

Meritt, B. D., & H. T. Wade-Gery (1962) 'The dating of documents to the mid-fifth century' in: *JHS* 82: 67–74

Meritt, B. D., & H. T. Wade-Gery (1963) 'The dating of documents to the mid-fifth century' in: *JHS* 83: 100–17

Meiggs, R. (1966) 'The dating of fifth-century Attic inscriptions' in: *JHS* 86: 86–97

Walbank, M. B. (1978) 'Criteria for the dating of fifth-century Attic inscriptions' in: Bradeen, D. W., & M. F. McGregor (eds) (1974): φόρος: *tribute to Benjamin Dean Meritt* (Locust Valley NY: Augustin) 161–9 (revised as 'Criteria for dating' in: Walbank, M. B. (1978) *Athenian proxenies of the fifth century B.C.* (Toronto & Sarasota: Stevens) 31–51 ch. 2)

## Lead letters

The nine previously published catalogued, one from Athens published, and the existence noted of three still unpublished:

Jordan, D. R. (2000) 'A personal letter found in the Athenian agora' in: *Hesperia* 69: 91–103

One example translated:

Austin, M. M., P. Vidal-Naquet (1977) *Economic and social history of ancient Greece: an introduction* (trans. and rev. M. M. Austin) (London: Batsford) (originally published in French, *Économies et sociétés en Grèce ancienne* (Paris: Armand Colin 1972)) 41

# Coinage

Kraay, C. M. (1976) *Archaic and classical Greek coins* (London: Methuen), discussion of legends 5–8

## On Arkadia

Nielsen, T. H. (1996) 'Was there an Arkadian confederacy in the fifth century B.C.?' in: Hansen, M. H., & K. A. Raaflaub (eds) *More studies in the ancient Greek polis* (Stuttgart: Steiner) 39–61 (*Historia* Einzelschriften 108 = Papers from the Copenhagen Polis Centre 3)

## On Tissaphernes

Robinson, E. S. G. (1948) 'Greek coins acquired by the British Museum, 1938–1948' in: *NC* ser. 6, 8: 43–59 at 48–56 – Tissaphernes
Harrison, C. (2002) 'Numismatic problems in the Achaemenid west: the undue influence of "Tissaphernes" ' in: Gorman, V. B., & E. W. Robinson (eds) *Oikistes: studies in constitutions, colonies, and military power in the ancient world, offered in honor of A. J. Graham* (Leiden: Brill) 301–19 (*Mnemosyne* Suppl. 234) – fourth century, and head is not a portrait

## On Hippias

Boardman, J. (1999) *The Greeks overseas* (London: Thames & Hudson [4]1999) 266 with fig. 312

## On the ΣΥΝ coinage

Cawkwell, G. L. (1956) 'A note on the Heracles coinage alliance of 394 B.C.' in: *NC* ser. 6 16: 69–75 – Anti-Spartan, after Knidos
Cook, J. M. (1961) 'Cnidian Peraea and Spartan coins' in: *JHS* 81: 56–72, at 66–72 – Pro-Spartan, c. 391/0
Cawkwell, G. L. (1963) 'The ΣΥΝ coins again' in: *JHS* 83: 152–4
Karwiese, S. (1980) 'Lysander as Herakliskos Drakonopnigon' in: *NC* ser. 7 20: 1–27 – Pro-Spartan, end of Peloponnesian War

# Pottery

Boardman, J. (1974) *Athenian black figure vases* (London: Thames & Hudson)
Boardman, J. (1975) *Athenian red figure vases: the archaic period* (London: Thames & Hudson)
Arias, P. E., M. Hirmer, B. B. Shefton (1962) *A history of Greek vase painting* (London: Thames & Hudson)
Cook, R. M. (1997) *Greek painted pottery* (London: Routledge [3]1997) – Discussion of inscriptions 241–8 (ch. 10), with bibliography 353–4

## On Sostratos

Torelli, M. (1971) 'Il santuario di Hera a Gravisca' in: *La Parola del Passato* 26: 55–60 – Anchor at Gravisca
Johnston, A. W. (1972) 'The rehabilitation of Sostratos' in: *La Parola del Passato* 27: 416–23 – SO on vases
Boardman, J. (1999) *The Greeks overseas* (London: Thames & Hudson [4]1999) 206 with fig. 245 (both)

## On Herodotos

Hogarth, D. G. (1905) in: Hogarth, D. G., H. L. Lorimer, C. C. Edgar (1905) 'Naukratis, 1903' in: *JHS* 25: 105–36 at 116 nos. 5–6
Boardman, J. (1999) *The Greeks overseas* (London: Thames & Hudson [4]1999) 132 – Wanting to believe
Gill, D. W. J. (1986) 'Two Herodotean dedications from Naucratis' in: *JHS* 106: 184–7 – One vase late sixth century, the other early fourth

## Ostraka

Fornara 41 – English translations

M&L 21 – Greek texts, with commentary

Thomsen, R. (1972) *The origin of ostracism* (Copenhagen: Gyldendal) – The most comprehensive general account in English of the surviving *ostraka*; now out of date as a result of new finds and further work on the Kerameikos *ostraka*

Lang, M. L. (1990) *The Ostraka* (Princeton: American School of Classical Studies at Athens) (*The Athenian Agora* 25) – Full publication of the Agora *ostraka*, with the total numbers for each man for whom there are Agora *ostraka*

Brenne, S. (2002) in: Siewert, P. (ed.) (2002) *Ostrakismos-Testimonien*, vol 1 (Stuttgart: Steiner) 36–166 (*Historia* Einzelschriften 155) – List of all surviving *ostraka* (43–71) and associated studies

Brenne, S. (2001) *Ostrakismos und Prominenz in Athen* (Vienna: Holzhausen) (*Tyche* Suppl. 3) – Various investigations on the basis of the Kerameikos *ostraka*

Lewis, D. M. (1974) 'The Kerameikos ostraka' in: *ZPE* 14: 1–4, at 4 (= idem *Selected papers in Greek and near eastern history* (Cambridge: Cambridge University Press 1997) 110–13 at 113) – Votes on fragments of same pot

Brenne, S. (1994) 'Ostraka and the process of ostrakophoria' in: Coulson, W. D. E, O. Palagia, T. L. Shear, Jr., H. A. Shapiro, F. J. Frost (eds) (1994) *The archaeology of Athens and Attica under the democracy: proceedings of an international conference celebrating 2500 years since the birth of democracy in Greece, held at the American School of Classical Studies at Athens, December 4–6, 1992* (Oxford: Oxbow) 13–24 (Oxbow Monographs 37) – Votes on fragments of same pot

## Objects used in the law courts

Boegehold, A. L., et al. (1995) *The lawcourts at Athens: sites, buildings, equipment, procedure, and testimonia* (Princeton: American School of Classical Studies at Athens) (*The Athenian Agora* 28)

CHAPTER FOUR

# The Contribution of the Non-Written Sources

*Björn Forsén*

## 1 Introduction

The scarcity of written sources is one of the characteristic features of ancient history. This is also true for the Greek classical period, although it is much richer in written sources than the preceding archaic period. Although the scarcity of written sources makes the use of non-written sources especially important, many scholars of ancient history are not trained in the use of non-written sources and rather prefer to leave this part of the field to other disciplines such as art history, archaeology, numismatics, etc. This is in many ways regrettable, not least because non-written sources may need to be put into their correct historical context in order to become intelligible. Or, in other words, it may be difficult to make the non-written sources speak to us meaningfully unless we have a certain command of written sources.

On the other hand there has definitely been a change in attitude among historians towards the use of non-written sources. During the twentieth century, history in general expanded its original primary focus on the political and military aspects of the past to encompass all aspects of the past. Concurrently with the growing interest in economic and social history, scholars of ancient history have also accepted the material culture as an integral and natural part of their field. One can see this change in attitude very well by comparing the treatment of the fifth and fourth centuries in the first edition of the *Cambridge Ancient History* with that of the second edition (*CAH²* vols 5 and 6). In the first edition, published in 1927, no attention at all was paid to material culture, whereas the second edition, from 1992 to 1994, has reserved generous space to several areas (e.g., art, architecture, civic life in Athens, agriculture, communications, economy and trade, etc.), where our knowledge depends to a large degree on non-written sources.

The written sources give us a somewhat skewed picture of reality, being heavily centred on urban life and sanctuaries with special emphasis on the conditions in Athens and Sparta. Especially those who want to learn more about classical Greece 'beyond Athens or Sparta' (Gehrke 1986) or about rural reality within the Greek poleis, i.e., the history 'beyond the akropolis', have much to learn from the increasing amount of available non-written data. As a result, it is clear that future research in some genres of ancient history, such as economic and social history, will increasingly depend on non-written sources.

Non-written sources have been used to some degree by scholars of ancient history for a long time. For instance, there is a long tradition of attempting to identify sculptures found in excavations with works of art described by ancient authors. Soon it was noted that sculpture and vase paintings could give information additional to that of the literary sources about the beliefs of the ancient Greeks. Iconographical studies are still very popular and they have added considerably to our knowledge of many aspects of ancient life, such as of the Athenian attitudes towards death and the afterlife (e.g., Sourvinou-Inwood 1995: 321–61), or of the performance of sacrificial rituals (e.g., van Straten 1995). The extent to which public art relates to civic ideology has also been discussed. How should we understand the Parthenon sculptures, for instance, and what do they tell us about how the Athenians viewed themselves, their patron goddess and their place in the world (Hurwit 1999: 222–8 with further references)?

Most of the ancient art objects have been found in excavations – indeed one of the main objectives of early excavations was to bring more ancient art and architecture to the light of day. Since those early days however, archaeological excavations have become far more comprehensive and nowadays aim at recording the entire material culture. An ever-growing palette of scientific methods is giving us more and more information about how people lived, what they ate, how healthy they were, etc. As recording all this information in an accurate way is very time-consuming, large-scale excavations will probably become less common in the future. On the other hand, a growing number of sites that were previously considered less interesting, such as farmsteads or urban residences, are now receiving closer attention (Hoepfner 1999). New types of sites are also being explored by underwater archaeology, opening up a completely new world. After decades of painstaking work, the results of several important large-scale excavations begin to be thoroughly published (Athens (Agora and Kerameikos), Korinth, Delphi, Olympia, Olynthos, etc.), providing us with valuable databases that can be analysed in several comparative ways.

Each excavation gives us information about just one site, and although the results from several excavations can be compared and thus give us a broader and more general picture, it remains difficult to discern regional patterns and to understand the interplay between settlements and topography. This was already realized by the first Western travellers in Greece, who set out to identify settlements and battlefields mentioned by ancient authors in the contemporary landscape. Topographical studies soon led to the development of a discipline in its own right, i.e., landscape archaeology. Since the late 1970s, extensive surveys of complete regions, concentrating on looking for settlements in logical places in the landscape, such as on hills or close to well-known springs, have commonly been replaced by detailed surface surveys of small areas that are intensively searched for all signs of human activity.

Intensive surveys have many advantages over extensive surveys. Above all they give us a more complete picture of the use of the landscape, as they are normally carried out by teams of experts, including geologists, botanists, geophysicists, etc. Small sites, such as farmsteads or other kinds of 'special purpose sites', are seldom found in extensive surveys. Intensive surveys also accumulate information about how the landscape was used outside the settlements proper, for instance by collecting sherds that have been dispersed as a result of manuring the fields (Alcock et al. 1994). Finally they help us to understand how the environment and climate have changed, and whether natural causes (Rackham 1996) or human agents have contributed to the occurrence of ecological catastrophes such as large-scale erosion. On the other hand one should not altogether disregard the importance of extensive surveys, because only through them can we obtain information about larger regions, thereby enabling us to understand the ekistic networks better. Extensive surveys are still carried out and published (e.g., Fossey 1988), and this approach has recently proved to be very productive in studying ancient road networks (e.g., Pikoulas 1999).

The enormous amount of archaeological material collected by intensive surveys has unfortunately resulted in very slow progress in publications. Until now only a few of the so-called 'new wave' survey projects have been fully published (the only ones being the surveys of Keos, Methana, Lakonia, Atene in southern Attika, Berbati-Limnes in Argolis and the Asea Valley in Arkadia). Others remain unfinished despite having contributed extensively to our knowledge through a large number of preliminary publications or occasionally even through several volumes in the final publication series. The Argolid Exploration Project (Jameson et al. 1994) has, for instance, still not produced the final publication of the pottery and small finds of classical date, and the Cambridge/Bradford Boiotia expedition has brought only one sector of its survey area to final publication (Bintliff et al. forthcoming). Another problem is that some of the completed intensive projects have not presented any data on aspects related to site and off-site densities, find visibility and the like. This makes it difficult for non-specialists, such as historians, to use the data, and above all to compare the final results of the different projects.

It is not possible within the scope of this chapter to give a full picture of all the manifold ways in which non-written sources can be and/or have been used to throw light on the history of classical Greece. Instead I will concentrate on some areas in which the contribution of non-written sources has lately been especially important, viz. sanctuaries, funerary practices, trade, settlement patterns and demography. The common denominator of this research is the comparative and structural approach, through which we may gain new historical knowledge of seemingly mute, non-written sources. I shall focus on some of the methodological problems historians may face when using non-written sources.

## 2   Sanctuaries

Recent studies of religious practices have had an immense impact on our understanding of the relationship between the development of sanctuaries and territorial consolidation and the rise of the polis during the late geometric and archaic period. Historians working with the classical period have so far paid less attention to the location of sanctuaries or to patterns of votive offerings. However, a change is here clearly taking place concerning the interest of votive offerings. Snodgrass has drawn attention to the fact that the prolificacy of dedications that occurred in connection with the development of sanctuaries during the late geometric period and continued throughout most of the archaic period came to a noticeable end in the sixth and fifth centuries, when there was a sharp drop in the number of dedications. He links this change with the seemingly synchronous shift in the composition of votive offerings from everyday objects (raw dedications) to more expensive objects that were produced only in order to be dedicated to the gods (converted dedications), and thus also less frequently given (Snodgrass 1989–90).

How then, should this clear change in dedication practice be interpreted? According to Snodgrass, social and economic factors must have played a central role, although other factors, such as a more sophisticated attitude towards religion, should not be ruled out. Above all he emphasizes the increased social differentiation and polarization of society during the classical period (Snodgrass 1989–90). However, this change has also been interpreted in terms of restrictions of the use of wealth. Thus, Morris explains the decline as a sign of the collapse of the elitist style of life characteristic of the Orientalizing Period (Morris 1997). It has also been pointed out that there are considerable variations in the timing of the decline, including its generally later occurrence in sanctuaries of international character (e.g., Olympia, Isthmia, etc.) than in local polis sanctuaries, which could indicate that for some time, wealthy individuals circumvented restrictions at home by making dedications abroad (Hodkinson 2000).

It is of course very tempting to try to draw conclusions regarding economic or social history on the basis of a seemingly clear change in the distribution of objects, such as the decline in votive offerings. However, one has to remember that using non-written sources of this kind involves several methodological problems. First, we have to ask ourselves whether the evidence really is representative or if it possibly could have been skewed by post-depositional factors. Snodgrass (1989–90: 289–90) already pondered whether the decline in preserved votive offerings could be due to a widespread change of practice in the disposal of existing, unwanted dedications. Although he ultimately rejected this idea as a possible explanation, metal offerings that according to him would have ceased to be offered in the sixth to fifth centuries nevertheless still occur in inventory lists of dedications stored on the akropolis of Athens during the fourth century. This paradox may perhaps partly be explained by the fact that converted dedications of classical date were more expensive than the raw dedications and thereby also more prone to looting and expropriation. On the other hand the inventories from the late fifth and fourth centuries also include everyday objects, such as arms and weapons, jewellery, musical instruments, furniture and different tools, none of which has survived to our days although similar objects from the sixth century have been preserved (Harris 1995).

The scholarly discussion of the decline in offerings has mainly focused on the decline in the number of metal dedications recorded in sanctuaries that had experienced a proliferacy of similar dedications in the late geometric and archaic periods. Such an approach is dangerous, as it does not take into account the possibility that a general shift took place from metal to terracotta offerings and/or that the personal cult was no longer practised in panhellenic or state sanctuaries, but shifted towards smaller, new sanctuaries. Snodgrass refers to 'a certain diversion of cult' from the sanctuaries of Olympic deities towards 'assisting deities' such as Asklepios, Pan and the Nymphs, the Kabeiroi or the Great Gods of Samothrake. But he disregards this diversion, on the basis that a similar decline in the number of metal offerings can be seen in the sanctuaries of the 'assisting deities' at the end of the archaic period, after which terracottas and vases took over (Snodgrass 1989–90: 291).

Snodgrass may, however, underestimate the importance of a diversion of cult. The monumentalization of panhellenic sanctuaries and sanctuaries belonging to the principal deities of the poleis in the sixth and fifth centuries was accompanied by a virtual explosion in the number of offerings dedicated to deities and heroes who can be connected with fertility, birth and healing. New sanctuaries were also founded to these deities. As an example one can mention the immense popularity of sanctuaries dedicated to Demeter between the sixth and fourth centuries. Extensively excavated sanctuaries in Korinth, Eretria, Knossos, Kyrene and elsewhere have revealed copious amounts of modest dedications from individual women consisting of thousands of terracotta figurines and tens of thousands of miniature vessels (Cole 1994). In Tegea it has even been suggested that when the Athena Alea sanctuary was monumentalized and the number of small offerings decreased sharply, the aspects of a simple fertility and nature goddess were transferred to the sanctuary of Demeter at Agios Sostis (Voyatzis 1990: 271), where thousands of female terracotta figurines dating from the sixth to fourth centuries have been found (Jost 1985: 154–6).

Another example that should be mentioned in this connection is the increased popularity of healing gods and heroes during the classical period. In the late fifth or fourth century a new type of votive offering appears, viz. anatomical ex votos, i.e., depictions of body parts made of terracotta, metal or stone (Forsén 1996). But healing gods do not only receive anatomical ex votos. Rich inventory inscriptions from the Athenian Asklepieion dating to the fourth and third centuries record not only small metal plaques in repoussé with depictions of the dedicants or the healed body parts, but also coins, jewellery, strigils, medical equipment, different types of vases, etc. The number of metal plaques, which were apparently prefabricated and sold according to standard weights, increased sharply from the mid-fourth to the mid-third century at the same time that the popularity of dedications consisting of jewellery and different types of tools declined (Aleshire 1989). We have thus a sanctuary where the transfer from 'raw' to 'converted' dedications did not occur until the early Hellenistic period, and where small metal offerings show no signs of decreasing. Ironically, none of the almost one thousand plaques recorded has survived!

On the basis of these few examples one could possibly suggest another explanation for the seemingly abrupt decline of votive offerings in panhellenic and state sanctuaries. The reason may be found in the formalization of the cult practices, whereby increasingly expensive, specially manufactured votive offerings were financed by the state and influential persons while individual worshippers turned to other gods and heroes. However, we need much more quantified data on the distribution of votive offerings in different types of sanctuaries in order to support our explanatory models.

## 3   Funerary Practices

Athens during the late archaic period is characterized by graves marked by elaborate marble *stelai* (often with relief decoration and crowned by sphinxes) and sculptures of youths and maidens (*kouroi* and *korai*). However, around 500 major changes occurred in the Athenian funerary procedure. The elaborate grave markers, which have been interpreted as signs of aristocratic *kalokagathia*, disappeared and were not replaced by new grave monuments. At the same time the number of uncovered graves increased considerably (Figure 4.1) while the number and quality of the grave goods became modest, with insignificant differences between individual graves. After 430 the Athenians once again began to erect sculptured grave monuments and there was a virtual explosion in the number of funerary sculptures and epitaphs during the fourth century (Figure 4.2). Parallel to this development there was a revival in the use of *peribolos* tombs (family grave enclosures). There was no end to the sequence of monuments until 317 with the legislation of Demetrios of Phaleron, outlawing lavish sculptural display in funerary monuments.

How then are the major changes in funerary practices that occurred around 500 and 430/25 to be explained? Traditionally a sharp increase in the number of graves has been linked to an increase in population. On the other hand, the marked lack of distinctions based on wealth between the graves in combination with the absence of lavish funerary monuments indicates that burial rituals were not, as in the archaic period, reserved for the aristocracy, but extended to others as well. As a result, it has been suggested that the change in burial practices reflects an Athenian anti-luxury decree which has not been preserved (e.g., Clairmont 1993: 13), or the general advance of an ideology of equality brought about by the introduction of democracy in 509 (Whitley 2001: 364–6). But such explanations have the disadvantage of being too limited to Athens itself. As a matter of fact most of Greece witnessed a similar collapse of monumental burial practices around 500 (Morris 1992: 145), although there are some exceptions (e.g., Morris 1998). For instance in Sparta the decline had already occurred around 550 (Hodkinson 2000: 242, 255–6).

The end of the burial restraint in Athens around 430/425 has also been explained in local terms. Some have proposed that the revival in sculptured grave monuments was a spin-off effect of the completion of the Parthenon, which had left large numbers of

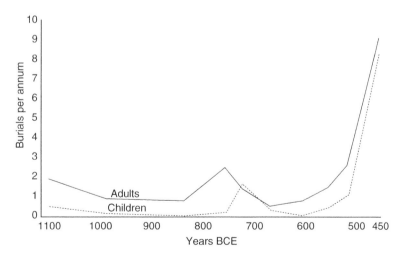

**Figure 4.1**   Number of adult and child burials at Athens, 1100–450 BCE.

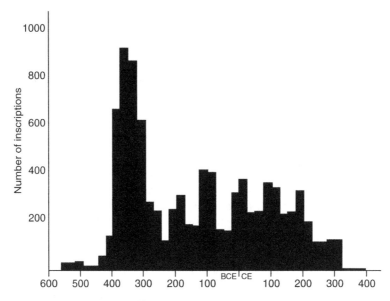

**Figure 4.2** Athenian epitaphs, 575 BCE–400 CE.

sculptors without occupation in Athens. Others have stressed the effect of the plague that hit Athens in 430, or of the new mid-fifth-century Athenian reforms emphasizing the importance of the family, such as the edict that in order to acquire Athenian citizenship one needed not only an Athenian father but also an Athenian mother (Morris 1992: 129; Whitley 2001: 369–70 with additional references). But these explanations are again heavily focused on Athenian circumstances, paying little attention to the fact that the rapidly increasing popularity of funerary display at the turn of the fifth to the fourth century is a genuinely panhellenic phenomenon (Morris 1992: 145–6), with Sparta (where no graves dating between 550 and 200 have been found) as the most notable exception (Hodkinson 2000: 243, 255–6).

The widespread changes in funeral practice occurring at the turn of the sixth to the fifth and then again at the turn of the fifth to the fourth centuries are without doubt of great importance for our understanding of the social and economic structures in the Greek poleis at that time. Ian Morris was the first one to look for these general patterns (Morris 1992; 1998). According to him the Greek world in the fifth century reached a peak in 'group-orientation', characterized by a strong communal ideal that discouraged personal display and encouraged chauvinism and expenditure on public architecture and monuments. The austerity in funeral practices may be connected with the possibly contemporaneous change in votive practices (see above) and the monumentalization of panhellenic and state sanctuaries. Taken together, these factors in a way characterize the beginning of what could be described as the apogee of the Greek polis.

It is even more difficult to explain why the burial restraint came to an end, starting in Athens around 430/25. We cannot see any connections to changes in the construction of temples or in the dedication patterns of votive offerings According to

Morris (1992: 130–55) the revival of monumental display is to be interpreted as a reflection of the expanding Greek world, in which the group-oriented polis turned out to be too small to manage on its own. The elite began to create social structures in which contacts outside their own poleis played an increasingly important role. The communal ideal eroded at the same time that the individual and the family became more important. The absence of a revival in Sparta could again be taken as an indication that the social structures and customs of classical Sparta remained valid, possibly as long as until 200.

Morris's interpretation shows very clearly how much information we may gain from a closer study of funerary practices. Much more detailed information about the distribution of wealth, age and gender of the deceased could be obtained from the graves if we just had better publications of excavated cemeteries, including more osteological analyses of skeletal remains. Likewise, more detailed regional comparative studies of burial practices outside Attika are definitely needed.

# 4   Trade

Our picture of ancient economic history, and thereby also of trade, has for a long time been heavily influenced by Finley's 'primitivist' view, according to which the ancient economy was underdeveloped, showing little tendency for, e.g., technological development, profit-oriented growth and long-distance trade in non-luxury items (Finley 1985). Although it is still largely accepted that trade probably never played a very important role in the ancient economy, the latest trend in the economic history of the classical period has been to stress that a more extensive integration and economic interdependence between different regions and poleis, and thereby also a greater volume of trade, must have existed than previously thought (e.g., the various papers in Parkins & Smith 1998). The development of research on ancient trade has to a large degree depended on the use of non-written, archaeological sources, the interpretation of which exemplifies the methodological problems involved in drawing conclusions on the basis of such source material.

Trade over land has usually been assumed to be limited as compared to sea-borne trade, because of the problems involved in transporting heavy freight overland. There is no need to doubt this in general, but the recent path-breaking contribution of Pikoulas on ancient Greek roads has shown that land links between individual communities must have been far more extensive than earlier assumed. Pikoulas has discovered the existence of a whole network of cart roads consisting of rock-cut wheel-ruts with a standard gauge of 1.40 m (e.g., Pikoulas 1999 for a summary of the road network in Arkadia). Roads of this type have so far been detected in the Peloponnese, in Attika, in central Greece and on several Aegean islands, seemingly connecting every single polis or larger settlement with its neighbours. Pikoulas believes that the roads were built mainly to facilitate the rapid movement of Spartan troops starting back in the archaic period. No matter who built the roads, it is clear that they must have greatly facilitated economic exchange between the communities they connected. An interesting parallel is the recent suggestion that the well-known Korinthian *diolkos* was built and used mainly for transporting cargo across the Isthmus and not for transporting warships, as earlier believed (Raepset 1993).

Scholars studying ancient economic trade patterns have to face several methodological problems. One is the 'positivist fallacy', which according to Snodgrass (1980: 126) is characterized by the assumption 'that the importance of a class of evidence...stands in some relation to the quantity in which it survives to be studied today'. According to him, painted pottery is an example of such a class of evidence. It has been assumed that painted pottery was traded as objets d'art, or even that it played an important role in the Athenian economy during the classical period, partly paying for the importing of grain. However, an evaluation of the underfoot marks on Attic pots, frequently giving the price of the pots, has shown that painted pottery was not considered intrinsically valuable during antiquity (e.g., Gill 1994). The growing number of excavated shipwrecks in the Mediterranean has furthermore showed that fine pottery was exported alongside other commodities, perhaps as 'space-fillers', in a way resembling the role of Chinese porcelain in the ships of the East India Companies of the seventeenth and eighteenth centuries (Gill 1991). But this does not invalidate the importance of painted pottery for understanding ancient trade patterns. Instead, its widespread distribution should be seen as an indicator of the vitality of trade in other commodities that are no longer extant.

Distribution patterns of transport amphorae provide a more valuable record of commerce than fine ware. The fact that such amphorae are found in large quantities in shipwrecks indicates that they played an important role in trade. Additionally, the fact that they, as opposed to painted pottery, which in the classical period was heavily dominated by Athens, were made in a large number of places (the Chian, Corinthian, Mendean and Thasian amphorae belonging to the most important at this time) expands the possibility of tracing different trade routes. Nevertheless, the contribution of the study of amphorae to our overall picture of classical trade is surprisingly small compared to the following Hellenistic and Roman periods. Finley, who made relatively little use of archaeological evidence in *The ancient economy* (Finley 1985), already called for more quantification of excavated finds of pottery in order to assess the scale of ancient trade. This again requires that the origin of pottery can be established. The origin of transport amphorae has traditionally been identified on the basis of stamps on the handles. There exist today several large stamp collections at large centres of importation, the ones from Alexandreia and Athens containing as many as some 85,000 and 20,000 stamps, respectively. However, several methodological problems are connected with the use of these collections as sources for economic history (e.g., Garlan 1983; Whitbread 1995).

A fundamental issue in connection with the study of trade in transport amphorae is to what extent stamped remains are representative of the total number of imported jars. Some types of amphorae were regularly stamped, the Rhodian ones even on both handles. Others were less regularly stamped. The figure for Thasian amphorae varies between c. 40 per cent and c. 80 per cent depending on the workshop, the earlier ones being stamped on both handles, the later ones only on one handle. Finally some types of amphorae were only rarely stamped, and it has been suggested that possibly as few as one out of 88 Koan amphorae were stamped, whereas Corinthian A and B amphorae were never stamped. This clearly shows that stamp collections cannot give a complete and unbiased picture of the commercial activity involving amphorae. This problem can be solved only by documenting all fragments of transport amphorae, establishing their origin with the help of fabric, shape and possibly petrographic analyses. However, as this is no easy task, studies involving unstamped amphorae often document only the presence or absence of a type without giving more detailed quantitative information, and it is not until lately that there have started to appear studies assessing the quantitative aspects also (e.g., Lawall 1998).

Another question is whether the presence of a large number of transport amphorae from place A in place B conclusively documents the importing of, for instance, oil or wine from A to B. Unfortunately there exist certain factors that may distort the picture. First, amphorae were commonly reused. This was, for instance, documented by Herodotos (3.6–7), who tells us that although wine was imported regularly to Egypt from Greece and Phoenicia, no empty amphorae could be found in Egypt because they were collected and reused to transport water to Syria! The contents of the amphorae could also be repacked into skins or smaller jars in order to be transported overland from the harbours. The large number of Greek amphorae found in Elizavetovskoe close to the mouth of Don have been explained in this way, suggesting that their contents were repacked there for further transport overland to the Middle Don or the Lower Volga (Garlan 1983; Whitbread 1995).

Trade is usually quantified in terms of the value of the goods, and when working with transport amphorae one has to remember that the value of the cargo depended on the contents of the jars and not on the jars themselves. Unfortunately we are mostly left without any hint of what the amphorae contained. It is often assumed that it was wine and oil, but finds in shipwrecks suggest the possibility of a wide range of other goods, such as vinegar, preserved fish, olives or even almonds and other kinds of nuts. The growing number of excavated shipwrecks has also helped to challenge earlier assumptions that the nationality of the traders could be identified by the origin of the pottery found on board, as it has been shown that the ships often contained a mixture of amphorae. Thus, on board the 'Porticello' wreck Mendean, Punic and a class of amphorae from the Bosporos were found, whereas the 'Kyrenia' ship contained amphorae of eleven different classes, the majority of which originated from Rhodes, Samos and Paros.

# 5   Settlement Patterns

On the basis of large databases created by intensive surveys we can draw conclusions about settlement patterns. There are many reasons why this is so important. Knowledge of settlement hierarchies gives indications of the political structures in regions for which we have few or no historical sources. The distribution of settlements in the landscape also enables us to understand in what ways and how intensively the countryside was exploited, and to what degree regional and temporal differences exist. This again constitutes an important basis for our knowledge of demographic trends in antiquity (below).

Most intensive surveys have divided the sites found into a three-tier hierarchy (towns, hamlets and/or villages, farmsteads). One of the main criteria for this hierarchical division is the area covered by the settlements, according to which towns are usually expected to be larger than 5 ha, hamlets and/or villages between 0.5–1 and 5 ha, and farmsteads smaller than 0.5 or 0.3 ha. The main exception to this three-tier hierarchy has been put forward by the Lakonia Survey, which introduces a five-tier hierarchy (towns, villages/forts, hamlets/large villas, villas/clusters of farmsteads, single farmsteads). However, in reality, their villages/forts and hamlets/large villas can be merged together into the second level of the three-tier hierarchy (hamlets and/or villages) and villas/clusters of farmsteads and single farmsteads perhaps into the third level (farmsteads).

Most controversy around the results of the intensive surveys has been concentrated on the occurrence of isolated farmsteads in the countryside, as this so clearly deviates from the traditional picture of ancient Greece, according to which the population lived in nucleated settlements such as towns, villages and/or hamlets. However, the realization that the population to a considerable degree lived in second-order, politically subordinated villages/hamlets not only in large poleis such as Athens (the *demoi* of Attika, not all of them necessarily nucleated, though), but also in several smaller poleis – for instance in Boiotia (e.g., Bintliff 1999a; 1999b), Arkadia (Forsén & Forsén 2003), the Argolid (e.g., Mee & Forbes 1997) or the Cyclades (Hoepfner 1999: 132–3) – offers valuable information for our understanding of the origin and nature of the Greek city-state. A pattern is revealed with villages/hamlets located at a distance of c. 4–6 km from each other, of which some develop into poleis, sometimes incorporating other villages/hamlets into their territory.

The second general feature of the classical period detected by intensive surveys is the existence of isolated farmsteads. Some have also been reported by extensive surveys. As a result we know of isolated farmsteads in most regions, including, e.g., Boiotia, southern Attika, Argolido-Korinthia (southern Argolid, Methana, Berbati-Limnes, Nemea), Arkadia, Lakonia, Messenia, Euboia, Keos, Melos, Delos and Chios (Catling 2002; Forsén & Forsén 2003). Additionally farmsteads occur commonly in the colonies, for instance in Metapontion in Magna Graecia or in Chersonesos on Crimea (Carter 1990; Pečírka 1973). Some have even been excavated, the most frequently cited examples being the Vari house and the Dema house in Attika.

The results of the intensive surveys have been variously interpreted. Some scholars believe that the small settlements found scattered around the landscape, especially towards the end of the classical period, are isolated farmsteads, each supporting one family or perhaps two. Others, however, argue that what we know from other sources about Greek inheritance systems (partible inheritance being the normal case), in conjunction with Greek farmers' tendency to exploit fragmented holdings in a wide range of micro-environments, makes such an interpretation unlikely. According to them, such sites were more likely to have been used on a temporary or seasonal basis as storage sheds, field buildings or animal folds by residents in nearby towns and/or villages/hamlets. According to them it is symptomatic that ancient Greek lacks a single word that means 'farm' in the sense of a farmhouse located on its own in the middle of some fields. Even the excavated Dema and Vari houses have been interpreted as agricultural installations inhabited only seasonally in connection with summer grazing or bee-keeping (Osborne 1987; Foxhall 2002).

Although it may very well be that some of the farmsteads were used only on a temporary or seasonal basis, there are still several factors that may be used as arguments for extended human occupation. Many of these small sites produce a wide range of finds, such as fine table ware, cooking ware, storage jars, as well as olive presses, grinding stones, mortars, loom-weights, etc. Soil chemistry in some cases has revealed abnormal concentrations of phosphate and trace metals indicating prolonged human occupation in connection with the localities (Bintliff 1999a; For-sén & Forsén 2003). In Metapontion small necropoleis, seemingly used by single families for two or three generations, have been discovered in close proximity to several of the farmsteads (Carter 1990). Furthermore, the full analysis of the excavated Pantanello necropolis shows that the numbers of burials in general follow the numbers of datable farmsteads, though often with a time lag of 50 years (Sbonias 1999b). A special case could also be made with respect to areas with large numbers of small, dispersed farmsteads that cannot be connected to any nucleated settlement in the vicinity (e.g., as revealed by the Lakonia, Nemea or Berbati-Limnes surveys). In these cases the long distances to nucleated settlements speak in favour of the farmsteads being permanently settled.

Unfortunately several questions that historians have about the ancient countryside cannot be answered on the basis of what we know of different settlement patterns. The difficulties involved in dating archaeological finds more exactly than within a range of some 20–30 years at best makes it impossible to prove that the farmsteads in a certain area really were contemporaneous. And even if we assume permanent occupation of the farmsteads, this tells us nothing of the social status of the residents, i.e., whether they owned the property or were just tenants. Neither can archaeology give any clues to whether the residents of the farmsteads in Lakonia were Spartiates, perioikoi or helots. On the other hand archaeology can sometimes confirm or refute assumptions made on the basis of written sources. For example, the fact that small, dispersed farmsteads do not seem to appear in Messenia until after 370 clearly challenges previous hypotheses according to which the helots lived isolated from each other in order to increase the security of their Spartan masters (Alcock 2002).

Even though the character of the data gathered with the help of landscape archaeology will never suffice to answer some of our specific historical questions, this does not imply that we cannot draw any historical conclusions from this material. More work will probably be done in the future to compare the settlement patterns of different Greek regions. Furthermore, regional studies can also contribute to the understanding of the non-agricultural usage of the countryside. Thanks to extensive exploration and analyses of written sources, we have a very good idea of how marble was quarried in Pentelikon and then transported from there to Athens (Korres 1995), or of how silver was produced at Laureion (Rihll 2001). But we know little about other quarries or mines, like the ones on Thasos or the marble quarry at Doliana in Arkadia, to mention just a couple of examples. Above all, we know far too little about how the settlement patterns were affected by large-scale quarrying or such industrial activities as silver production at Laureion, which may have employed as many as 10,000 slaves. Intensive surveys of quarrying or mining areas are definitely a desideratum for the future.

Isolated towers can be mentioned as examples of structures that seem to have some connection with the activity in quarries and mines. Such towers are notoriously difficult to date, although most appear to be classical. They have been detected in large numbers, not only on the islands of Amorgos, Lesbos, Siphnos, Thasos, Keos, but also in Attika and along the borders between the Argolid, Korinthia and Arkadia. The frequency of these towers in Thasos, Siphnos and southern Attika, all areas renowned for their mineral wealth, may indicate that they played a role in protecting the mines and ore-processing facilities or in providing security for the supervisors of the slaves. The fact that the towers also are common in borderlands and along the coasts points towards a more general defensive function. At the same time, many of the towers have some association with agriculture and may be parts of isolated farmsteads (Cherry et al. 1991). According to Morris & Papadopoulos (2005) the towers may even have served as places where the slaves were confined. The ongoing discussion about these towers once again illustrates how difficult it is to explain how archaeological structures were used, i.e., all structures of the same kind do not need to have had the same function, and some of the structures may have had multiple functions.

# 6  Demography

So far I have avoided the question of how to date the isolated farmsteads. Although they in general can be considered a characteristic feature of the classical Greek landscape, clear differences have been noticed between different regions as to when they start to occur and when their numbers peak. The peak is usually accompanied by an increase of off-site scatter in the landscape, possibly the result of intensive manuring of the fields. Even those who believe that the isolated farmsteads were not settled permanently agree that the parallel occurrence of dispersed small sites alongside nucleated settlements indicates an intensification of land use and thus also a population climax. The fact that many of the small, dispersed settlements are located in marginal lands provides further support for such an interpretation.

By studying the occurrences of farmsteads at different times across ancient Greece we can thus establish divergent regional demographical trajectories (Bintliff 1997). Thus, small isolated farmsteads occur already during the archaic period in Attika, Lakonia, Boiotia, parts of Argolido-Korinthia, as well as on Melos and Keos. However, the number of these settlements peaks during the classical to early Hellenistic period in a wide arc of south-eastern Greece, not only throughout all of the regions mentioned above, but also in Arkadia, Euboia and on other Aegean islands (with the exception of Melos, which shows a decrease) and possibly also on the islands of Leukas and Kephallenia. In Messenia the first farmsteads do not appear until after 369. In a similar way the peak appears in the early Hellenistic period in Aitolia and Epeiros, and possibly even later in the Hellenistic or early Roman period in Achaia and on Crete. In most of the rest of Greece there is a marked decrease in the number of rural sites during the late Hellenistic and early Roman period.

Landscape archaeology's main contribution to ancient demography is the fact that it is the only way in which we can detect changes in population size across time. Landscape archaeology can also be of some help when estimating the size of population at a given point in time, but it cannot give us any information about nativity and mortality rates, the distribution of population among sex and age groups, life tables or the average life expectancy, all basic concepts in historical demography. A close study of the epigraphical and skeletal data from cemeteries can help us to approximate some of these rates, but not all, thus invalidating any attempt at a full demographic analysis (Sbonias 1999a).

Lately it has also become fashionable to use the data collected by intensive surveys to estimate the size of population in a region at a given point in time. First, the total settled area (including all types of settlements) at a certain point in time has to be established. Then, the probable population density per hectare is estimated with the help of information from the residential quarters of urban settlements that have been excavated. On the basis of these two factors the number of people living in the region can finally be calculated. However, it must be pointed out that this method is full of pitfalls and should be used with care. When it has been applied (in Southern Argolid, Lakonia, Boiotia and on Keos), it has always been possible to compare the results with some sort of written demographic evidence. This may give some confirmation of the estimated settlement density, but cannot tell us whether the density was the same 100 years later, or, for that matter, in a totally different region.

Analogous with the method described above, it is often argued that it is possible to calculate the population of a city on the basis of the area inside its walls. Consequently it would also be possible to estimate the difference in population size between poleis for which we know the size of the walled area. The Copenhagen Polis Centre has collected all available data of this kind and presented it in a most useful article (Hansen 2004). For a total of 233 poleis of archaic or classical date there are sufficient remains of the circuit wall to allow an assessment of the area enclosed by the walls. Twenty-three of these poleis have a walled area exceeding 150 ha. In Table 4.1 they are arranged according to size.

Hansen assumes that all 23 of these poleis had a population larger than 10,000. This may very well be the case, but does Table 4.1 necessarily give the correct internal order of the poleis in terms of population? Was the population of Athens, for instance, really of the same size as that of Sybaris and Taras, and only slightly larger than that of Maroneia? It is also clear that some regions are over-represented in the table. It includes a total of eight poleis from Magna Graecia and three from Arkadia, but none, or, very few, e.g., from the Black Sea region, the Aegean islands and the Ionian colonies in Asia Minor. Important poleis surprisingly excluded from the table include Kos (112 ha), Mytilene (140 ha), Miletos (130 ha), Samos (103 ha), Eretria (81.5 ha) and Thasos (70 ha), just to mention a few. These examples clearly show the deficiencies of the method and the danger of using a standard figure for the relationship between population and space. The fact that certain regions are over-represented whereas others are totally absent in Table 4.1 could indicate that the population densities varied between the different regions for some economic or social reason. Thus, the method may perhaps be considered reliable only when comparing poleis of similar general character within one and the same region.

Despite these methodological caveats, the method brought forward by landscape archaeology to estimate the size of the population at a given point of time should not be fully rejected. Such data may confirm or refute figures quoted in written sources, and in those cases where no written information exists they constitute the only available 'guesstimate'. Furthermore, they can also give us some idea of how the population of a certain region was distributed over the landscape. In this case most of the intensive surveys seem to end up with similar results, i.e., that the majority of the population lived in the urban centres and that the rural population generally only constituted a small part of the total population (Hansen 2004 suggests a figure between 10 per cent and 33 per cent). The proportion of the rural population may perhaps be larger in the colonies – one thinks of the 400 or more farmsteads recorded outside the walls of Chersonesos on Crimea (Pečírka 1973) or the 870 farmsteads

**Table 4.1** The 23 Greek poleis of archaic and classical date with an area enclosed by walls larger than 150 ha (according to Hansen 2004).

| Name of polis | Region | Size (ha) |
| --- | --- | --- |
| Kyrene | Libya | 750 |
| Korinth | Korinthia | 600–700 |
| Akragas | Sicily | 625 |
| Kroton | Southern Italy | 620 |
| Taras | Southern Italy | 530 |
| Athens with Piraeus | Attika | 211 + 300 = 511 |
| Sybaris | Southern Italy | c. 500 |
| Maroneia | Thrace | c. 425 |
| Thebes | Boiotia | 350 |
| Megalopolis | Arkadia | 350 |
| Rhodos | Dodecanese | 300 |
| Messene | Messenia | 290 |
| Amphipolis | Macedonia | 250 |
| Lokroi | Southern Italy | 240 |
| Halikarnassos | Asia Minor | 220 |
| Argos | Argolid | 200+ |
| Gela | Southern Italy | 200 |
| Phigaleia | Arkadia | 195 |
| Tegea | Arkadia | 190 |
| Kaunos | Asia Minor | 190 |
| Sikyon | Korinthia | 175 |
| Syracuse (akropolis) | Sicily | 150 |
| Kamarina | Sicily | 150 |

outside the walls of Metapontion (Carter 1990). Then again, much depends on whether the farmsteads were occupied permanently and on the number of residents assumed to live on each farm.

# 7  Concluding Remarks

The five fields examined in greater detail in this chapter exemplify not only the way non-written sources can contribute to our understanding of the social, economic and religious history of classical Greece, but also which methodological problems historians face when using sources of this kind. Especially problematic are cases in which archaeology is used to corroborate written testimonia. Historians easily overlook the fact that the archaeologists in their turn may have reached their interpretation of the archaeological remains due to what they considered reliable written testimonia. Therefore it is important that historians do not altogether leave the interpretation of non-written sources to other disciplines. In order to be able to draw historical conclusions on the basis of non-written sources we also need to understand the methodological problems involved.

# Further reading

## Environment and ecological changes

Grove, A. T., & O. Rackham (2001) *The nature of Mediterranean Europe: an ecological history* (New Haven: Yale University Press)

## Shipwrecks

Parker, A. J. (1992) *Ancient shipwrecks of the Mediterranean and the Roman provinces* (Oxford: Tempus Reparatum) (British Archaeological Reports, International Series 580)

## The state of archaeology in Greece

Shanks, M. (1996) *Classical archaeology of Greece: experiences of the discipline* (London: Routledge)
Whitley, J. (2001) *The archaeology of ancient Greece* (Cambridge: Cambridge University Press)

## Archaeology and ancient history

Morris, I. (ed.) (1994) *Classical Greece: ancient histories and modern archaeologies* (Cambridge: Cambridge University Press)

## Methodologies and techniques of archaeological surveys

Francovich, R., H. Patterson, G. Barker (eds) (2000) *Extracting meaning from ploughsoil assemblages* (Oxford: Oxbow) (The Archaeology of Mediterranean Landscapes 5)
Alcock, S. E., & J. F. Cherry (eds) (2003) *Side by side survey: comparative regional studies in the Mediterranean world* (Oxford: Oxbow)

## Votive offerings

Boardman, J. (2004) 'Greek dedications' in: *Thesaurus cultus et rituum antiquorum*, vol. 1: *Processions, sacrifices, libations, fumigations, dedications* (Los Angeles: J. Paul Getty Museum) 269–318
Hägg, R. (ed.) (1998) *Ancient Greek cult practice from the archaeological evidence: proceedings of the fourth international seminar on ancient Greek cult, organised by the Swedish Institute at Athens, 22–24 October 1993* (Stockholm: Svenska Institutet i Athen) (Acta Instituti Atheniensis Regni Sueciae ser. in 8° 15)

## Amphora stamps

Garlan, Y. (2000) *Amphores et timbres amphoriques grecs entre erudition et idéologie* (Paris: de Boccard)

## Trade

Garnsey, P., K. Hopkins, C. R. Whittaker (eds) (1983) *Trade in the ancient economy* (Berkeley: University of California Press)
Parkins, H., & C. Smith (eds) (1998) *Trade, traders and the ancient city* (London: Routledge)

## Economies of ancient Greece

Cartledge, P., E. E. Cohen, L. Foxhall (eds) (2002) *Money, labour and land: approaches to the economies of ancient Greece* (London: Routledge)
Mattingly, D. J., & J. Salmon (eds) (2001) *Economies beyond agriculture in the classical world* (London: Routledge)

## Landscape and agriculture

Shipley, G., & J. Salmon (eds) (1996) *Human landscapes in classical antiquity: environment and culture* (London: Routledge)
Isager, S., & J. E. Skydsgaard (1992) *Ancient Greek agriculture: an introduction* (London: Routledge)
Wells, B. (ed.) (1992) *Agriculture in ancient Greece: proceedings of the seventh international symposium at the Swedish Institute at Athens, 16–17 May, 1990* (Stockholm: Åström) (Acta Instituti Atheniensis Regni Sueciae ser. in 4° 42)

## The classical farmstead

Pettigrew, D. K. (2001) 'Chasing the classical farmstead: assessing the formation and signature of rural settlement in Greek landscape archaeology' in: *JMA* 14: 189–209, with following responses and discussion by R. Osborne & L. Foxhall (2001) in: *JMA* 14: 212–22, and by J. Bintliff et al. and D. K. Pettigrew (2002) in: *JMA*: 15, 259–73

## Demography

Hansen, M. H. (1985) *Demography and democracy: the number of Athenian citizens in the fourth century BC* (Gjellerup: Systime)
Bintliff, J. (1997) 'Further considerations on the population of ancient Boeotia' in: Bintliff, J. (ed.) *Recent developments in the history and archaeology of central Greece: proceedings of the 6th International Boeotian Conference* (Oxford: Archeopress) 231–52
Bintliff, J., & K. Sbonias (eds) (1999) *Reconstructing past population trends in Mediterranean Europe* (Oxford: Oxbow) (The Archaeology of Mediterranean Landscapes 1)

# Bibliography

Alcock, S. E. (2002) 'A simple case of exploitation? The helots of Messenia' in: Cartledge, P., E. E. Cohen, L. Foxhall (eds) (2002) *Money, labour and land: approaches to the economies of ancient Greece* (London: Routledge) 185–99

Alcock, S. E., J. F. Cherry, J. L. Davis (1994) 'Intensive survey, agricultural practice and the classical landscape of Greece' in: Morris, I. (ed.) (1994) *Classical Greece: ancient histories and modern archaeologies* (Cambridge: Cambridge University Press) 137–70

Aleshire, S. B. (1989) *The Athenian Asklepieion: the people, their dedications, and the inventories* (Amsterdam: Gieben)

Bintliff, J. (1997) 'Regional survey, demography, and the rise of complex societies in the ancient Aegean: core–periphery, neo-Malthusian, and other interpretive models' in: *JFA* 24: 1–38

Bintliff, J. (1999a) 'Pattern and process in the city landscapes of Boeotia from Geometric to late Roman times' in: *Territoires des cités grecques: Actes de la table ronde internationale, organisée par l'École française d'Athènes 31 octobre–3 novembre 1991* (Paris: de Boccard) 15–33 (*BCH* Suppl. 34)

Bintliff, J. (1999b) 'The origins and nature of the Greek city-state and its significance for world settlement history' in: *Les princes de la Protohistoire et l'émergence de l'État: Actes de la table ronde internationale de Naples, organisée par le Centre Jean Bérard et l'École française de Rome, Naples 27–29 octobre 1994* (Paris: de Boccard) 43–56 (Collection de l'École française de Rome 252)

Bintliff, J., & K. Sbonias (eds) (1999) *Reconstructing past population trends in Mediterranean Europe* (Oxford: Oxbow) (The Archaeology of Mediterranean Landscapes 1)

Bintliff, J., P. Howard and A. Snodgrass (eds.) (forthcoming) *The Boeotia project*, vol. 1: *The Thespiae south and Leondari south-east sector* (Cambridge: Cambridge University Press) (Monograph Series of the MacDonald Institute, Archaeology Department of Cambridge University)

Carter, J. C. (1990) 'Metapontum – land, wealth and population' in: Descoeudres, J-P. (ed.) *Greek colonists and native population: proceedings of the First Australian Congress of Classical Archaeology held in honour of emeritus Professor A. D. Trendall, Sydney, 9–14 July 1985* (Canberra: Humanities Research Centre & New York: Oxford University Press) 405–41

Catling, R. W. V. (2002) 'The survey area from the early Iron Age to the classical period' in: Cavanagh, W., J. Crouwel, R. W. V. Catling, G. Shipley (eds) (2002) *Continuity and change in a Greek rural landscape: the Laconia survey*, vol. 1: *Methodology and interpretation* (London: British School at Athens) 151–256 (*Annual of the British School at Athens* Suppl. 26)

Cherry, J. F., J. L. Davis, E. Mantzourani (eds) (1991) *Landscape archaeology as long-term history: northern Keos in the Cycladic islands* (Los Angeles: UCLA Institute of Archaeology) (Monumenta Archaeologica 16)

Clairmont, C. W. (1993) *Classical Attic tombstones* (Kilchberg: Akanthus)

Cole, S. G. (1994) 'Demeter in the ancient Greek city and its countryside' in: Alcock, S. E., & R. Osborne (eds) (1994) *Placing the gods: sanctuaries and sacred space in ancient Greece* (Oxford: Clarendon) 199–216

Finley, M. I. (1985) *The ancient economy* (Berkeley: University of California Press [2]1985)

Forsén, B. (1996) *Griechische Gliederweihungen: Eine Untersuchung zu ihrer Typologie und ihrer religions-und sozialgeschichtlichen Bedeutung* (Helsinki: Finnish Institute at Athens) (Papers and Monographs of the Finnish Institute at Athens 4)

Forsén, J., & B. Forsén (2003) *The Asea valley survey: an Arcadian mountain valley from the palaeolithic period until modern times* (Stockholm: Svenska Institutet i Athen) (Acta Instituti Atheniensis Regni Sueciae ser. in 4° 51)

Fossey, J. M. (1988) *Topography and population of ancient Boeotia* (Chicago: Ares)

Foxhall, L. (2002) 'Access to resources in classical Greece: the egalitarianism of the polis in practice' in: Cartledge, P., E. E. Cohen, L. Foxhall (eds) (2002) *Money, labour and land: approaches to the economies of ancient Greece* (London: Routledge) 209–20

Garlan, Y. (1983) 'Greek amphorae and trade' in: Garnsey, P., K. Hopkins, C. R. Whittaker (eds) (1983) *Trade in the ancient economy* (Berkeley: University of California Press) 27–35

Gehrke, H.-J. (1986) *Jenseits von Athen und Sparta: Das dritte Griechenland und seine Staatenwelt* (Munich: Beck)

Gill, D. W. (1991) 'Pots and trade: spacefillers or objets d'art?' in: *JHS* 111: 29–45

Gill, D. W. J. (1994) 'Positivism, pots and long-distance trade' in: Morris, I. (ed.) (1994) *Classical Greece: ancient histories and modern archaeologies* (Cambridge: Cambridge University Press) 99–107

Hansen, M. H. (2004) 'The concept of the consumption city applied to the Greek *polis*' in: Nielsen, T. H. (ed.) *Once again: studies in the ancient Greek polis* (Stuttgart: Steiner) 9–47 (*Historia* Einzelschriften 180 = Papers from the Copenhagen Polis Centre 7)

Harris, D. (1995) *The treasures of the Parthenon and Erechtheion* (Oxford: Clarendon Press)

Hodkinson, S. (2000) *Property and wealth in classical Sparta* (London: Duckworth & The Classical Press of Wales)

Hoepfner, W. (ed.) (1999) *Geschichte des Wohnens*, vol. 1: *5000 v. Chr.–500 n. Chr. Vorgeschichte, Frühgeschichte, Antike* (Stuttgart: Deutsche Verlags-Anstalt)

Hurwit, J. M. (1999) *The Athenian acropolis: history, mythology and archaeology from the neolithic era to the present* (Cambridge: Cambridge University Press)

Jameson, M. H., C. N. Runnels, T. H. van Andel (1994) *A Greek countryside: the southern Argolid from prehistory to the present day* (Stanford: Stanford University Press)

Jost, M. (1985) *Sanctuaires et cultes d'Arcadie* (Paris: Vrin) (Études Péloponnésiennes 9)

Korres, M. (1995) *From Pentelicon to the Parthenon: the ancient quarries and the story of a half-worked column capital of the first marble Parthenon* (Athens: Melissa)

Lawall, M. (1998) 'Ceramics and positivism revisited: Greek transport amphoras and history' in: Parkins, H., & C. Smith (eds) (1998) *Trade, traders and the ancient City* (London: Routledge) 75–101

Mee, C., & H. Forbes (1997) *A rough and rocky place: the landscape and settlement history of the Methana peninsula, Greece* (Liverpool: Liverpool University Press)

Morris, I. (1992) *Death-ritual and social structure in classical antiquity* (Cambridge: Cambridge University Press)

Morris, I. (1997) 'The art of citizenship' in: Langdon, S. H. (ed.) (1997) *New light on a dark age: explaining the culture of geometric Greece* (Columbia MO: University of Missouri Press) 9–43

Morris, I. (1998) 'Archaeology and archaic Greek history' in: Fisher, N., & H. van Wees (eds) (1998) *Archaic Greece: new approaches and new evidence* (London: Duckworth & The Classical Press of Wales) 1–91

Morris, S. P. & J. K. Papadopoulos (2005) 'Greek towers and slaves: an archaeology of exploitation' in: *American Journal of Archaeology* 109: 155–225.

Osborne, R. (1987) *Classical landscape with figures: the ancient Greek city and its countryside* (London: George Philip)

Parkins, H., & C. Smith (eds) (1998) *Trade, traders and the ancient city* (London: Routledge)

Pečírka, J. (1973) 'Homestead farms in classical and Hellenistic Hellas' in: Finley, M. I. (ed.) *Problèmes de la terre en Grèce ancienne* (Paris: Mouton) 113–47 (Civilisations et sociétés 33)

Pikoulas, Y. (1999) 'The road net-work in Arkadia' in: Nielsen, T. H., & J. Roy (eds) (1999) *Defining ancient Arkadia: symposium, April, 1–4 1998* (Copenhagen: Munsksgaard) 248–319 (Historisk-filosofiske Meddelelse 78 = Acts of the Copenhagen Polis Centre 6)

Rackham, O. (1996) 'Ecology and pseudo-ecology: the example of ancient Greece' in: Shipley, G., & J. Salmon (eds) (1996) *Human landscapes in classical antiquity: environment and culture* (London: Routledge) 16–43

Raepset, G. (1993) 'Le diolkos de l'Isthme à Corinth' in: *BCH* 117: 233–56

Rihll, T. E. (2001) 'Making money in Classical Athens' in: Mattingly, D. J., & J. Salmon (eds) (2001) *Economies beyond agriculture in the classical world* (London: Routledge) 115–42

Sbonias, K. (1999a) 'Introduction to issues in demography and survey' in: Bintliff & Sbonias 1999: 1–20

Sbonias, K. (1999b) 'Investing the interface between regional survey, historical demography and paleodemography' in: Bintliff & Sbonias 1999: 219–34

Snodgrass, A. M. (1980) *Archaic Greece: the age of experiment* (London: Dent)

Snodgrass, A. M. (1989–90) 'The economics of dedication at Greek sanctuaries' in: *Anathema: Regime delle offerte e vita dei santuari nel Mediterraneo antico* (Roma: Università degli Studi 'La Sapienza') 287–94 (Special issue of *Scienze dell'Antichità* 3–4)

Sourvinou-Inwood, C. (1995) *'Reading' Greek death to the end of the classical period* (Oxford: Clarendon)

van Straten, F. (1995) *Hierà kalá: images of animal sacrifice in archaic and classical Greece* (Leiden: Brill) (Religions in the Graeco-Roman World 127)

Voyatzis, M. E. (1990) *The early sanctuaries of Athena Alea at Tegea and other archaic sanctuaries in Arcadia* (Göteborg: Åström) (Studies in Mediterranean Archaeology and Literature, Pocket-Book 97)

Whitbread, I. K. (1995) *Greek transport amphorae: a petrological and archaeological study* (London: British School at Athens) (British School at Athens Fitch Laboratory Occasional Paper 4)

Whitley, J. (2001) *The archaeology of ancient Greece* (Cambridge: Cambridge University Press)

CHAPTER FIVE

# Athens, Sparta and the Wider World

*Roger Brock*

## 1 Introduction

By the standards of mainland Greece, Sparta and Athens were enormous states. While the great majority of poleis had a territory of no more than 200 km$^2$, Attika covered some 2,500 km$^2$ and Lakonia twice that, and after the conquest of Messenia Sparta commanded some 8,500 km$^2$. In both cases the historical polis was a product of a process of aggregation in very early times: the Athenians attributed the political unification of Attika to their mythical king Theseus and celebrated it annually in the festival of the Synoikia, while the amalgamation of villages to form the Spartan polis was symbolized by her unique dual kingship. The abundance of resources in land and manpower which both enjoyed meant that neither followed the typical pattern of expansion through overseas settlement in the archaic period. In the late eighth century, Sparta annexed neighbouring Messenia by virtue of her superior manpower (according to later tradition (Plutarch *Lykourgos* 8), her lawgiver Lykourgos established a citizen body of 9,000), and her one major colony at Taras (modern Taranto) in 706 was principally a safety valve for social tensions.

At Athens, signs of overseas activity appear later: by the end of the seventh century, she was involved in a protracted struggle with her neighbour Megara for control of the island of Salamis, which implies a degree of pressure on land, and the establishment of footholds on the Hellespont at Sigeion and Elaious before 600 perhaps indicates that frustration locally turned her energies outward. The choice of a site that could control the Black Sea approaches also hints at an interest in trade: it is unlikely that Athens had already developed her later dependence on imported corn, but Solon's regulation of trade in cereals implies that there may well have been problems of supply. It is also possible that an ideology of territorial expansion developed at an early date, since the Ephebic Oath sworn by all Athenians on entering manhood

(R&O 88), which though only attested in the fourth century may well go back to an early date and is echoed in Athenian funeral orations (Siewert 1977), includes an undertaking to maintain and if possible increase the ancestral territory. We may note that territorial friction continued over the northern border between Attika and Boiotia, particularly at Oropos, throughout the classical period.

How far we can describe such overseas expansion at this date as 'foreign policy' is a moot point; the orthodox picture of colonial settlements as initiatives of a given polis has recently been called into question (Osborne 1998), and the literary sources are scanty and, in the case of the struggle between Sparta and Messenia, contaminated by romanticized myth-making under the influence of later events. However, inasmuch as both Spartan and Athenian troops fought to acquire and defend their new possessions, there is a clear sense of a community engagement with external relations and of a consensus over community interest. Elsewhere we can detect the beginnings of diplomacy in the religious associations called Amphiktyonies (*amphiktyon* = 'dweller around'), groupings of communities around a common sanctuary. Athens belonged to two such affiliations: one, the Kalaurian Amphiktyony, made up of states around the Saronic Gulf (plus Boiotian Orchomenos) and centred on a sanctuary of Poseidon on the island of Poros, and the other the influential Delphic Amphiktyony, though this had originally had its centre at the sanctuary of Demeter at Anthela, near Thermopylai. These associations formed regional networks with a potential for religious and, by extension, political influence, though this did not preclude squabbles between members, as events in the reign of Philip II proved. At Delphi, Athens held one of the two seats for Ionians, a reflection of her status as the metropolis (mother-city) of the Ionian Greeks, particularly in Asia Minor. This bond of kinship, marked by shared features such as tribe-names and the festival of the Apatouria which Thucydides mentions (2.15.4) as well as dialect, runs as a thread through Athenian foreign policy, for example in a persistent interest in Delos, the centre of a Cycladic network where the Ionians gathered at the festival of Delian Apollo. The Athenians twice demonstrated their concern with the island by 'purifying' it, first in the time of Peisistratos and again during the Peloponnesian War (Thuc. 3.104), and they remained perennially concerned with Delos in the fourth century (R&O 28). On a grander scale, the sentimental bond of kinship was evidently a factor in Athenian decisions to intervene in the Ionian Revolt and to take on the protection of the Asian Greeks in 478. Strictly speaking, these were divided into Ionians, Dorians and Aeolians, each with their own regional grouping and ethnic – particularly linguistic – identity, but Athenian foreign policy here and elsewhere was never ethnically exclusive, just as it was pragmatic over constitutional arrangements. This was helped by a tendency to extend the reference of the title 'Ionians' to refer to the Greeks of Asia Minor at large as well as the specific ethnic group, which allowed a degree of equivocation as to the nature of the Athenian alliance.

By contrast, neither of the Dorian seats at Delphi was occupied by Sparta: one belonged to the Dorian metropolis (i.e., the region in central Greece called Doris), while the other rotated among the 'Dorians of the [north-west] Peloponnese', notably Argos. Sparta could probably exercise influence indirectly, through the former; in the mid-fifth century, she unsuccessfully tried to change arrangements at Delphi by military force (the so-called 'Second Sacred War'), but when the Peloponnesian War broke out, Apollo's oracle at Delphi favoured Sparta – another reason for Athens to cultivate

Delian Apollo. Competition for primacy among Dorian cities and the presence of non-Dorians such as the Arkadians and Achaians in the Peloponnese may explain why in the mid-sixth century Sparta purportedly acquired the bones of Orestes from Tegea as the basis of a broader claim to rule the whole Peloponnese as Achaians (Hdt. 1.67–8, 5.72). However, in the fifth century the growing polarity between Athens and Sparta sharpened the ethnic opposition between Dorians under Spartan leadership and Ionians headed by Athens: the Spartan dedication after the battle of Tanagra in 457 celebrated victory over 'Argives, Athenians and Ionians' (Fornara 80), and Thucydides treats ethnicity as a natural basis for alliances in the Sicilian expedition while noting how other factors might cut across it (7.57–8, cf. 3.86). The relationship between the various Greek ethnic subdivisions had been exploited in support of claims to pre-eminence through the construction and manipulation of competing genealogies of their eponymous ancestors and of the other heroes. The process is most clearly visible in the Hesiodic *Catalogue of Heroines* of the early sixth century (Fowler 1998), but the ending of Euripides' *Ion* (first produced c. 413) shows that such propaganda was still viable in the classical period. The relationships between heroes could also be manipulated and exploited in the service of 'kinship diplomacy' (Jones 1999: esp. 1–49; Mitchell 1997: 23–8), the appeal to purported familial ties which might create a bond of sympathy. Here the wide-ranging travels of Herakles, especially in the western Mediterranean, were an asset to Dorians (Malkin 1994).

## 2   Spartan Primacy

In the late archaic period, Athens' foreign policy consisted more of what we might term diplomacy, in other words the cultivation of influence, than of gains in territory or power. According to Herodotos, this was only to be expected of a polis which was subject to a tyrant (5.78), for whom a citizen army was at best a risky asset. Indeed, it is arguable that we should speak in terms of the policies of Peisistratos and his sons in this period rather than of Athens. In one area they resumed earlier initiatives: Peisistratos recaptured Sigeion from the Mytileneans – it was to serve as a refuge for his exiled sons – and the elder Miltiades established an Athenian settlement in the Thracian Chersonese, doubtless with at least the assent of the tyrant. The other major development, the voluntary surrender to Athens of Boiotian Plataiai, is dated by Thucydides (3.68) to 519, though this has been disputed by some modern scholars; according to Herodotos, who relates it in the context of Plataian support for Athens at Marathon (6.108), it was the work of the Spartan king Kleomenes, who foresaw the friction it would provoke between Athens and Thebes. Certainly Sparta in this period was no friend of tyrants, and the growth of the network of alliances that became what we call the Peloponnesian League owed much to the fall of tyrannies and their replacement by sympathetic client oligarchies. How far Sparta actively promoted the process is disputed – her fifth-century reputation for overthrowing tyranny is entangled with her pose in the Peloponnesian War as liberator of the Greeks from the 'tyrant city' Athens– but she indubitably assisted in the suppression of the Peisistratids at Athens in 510. Presumably Athens briefly became an ally of Sparta (though perhaps not a member of the Peloponnesian League), and it is clear that in favouring the leadership of Isagoras Sparta was following the same model, and that his deposition by the Athenian masses in support of Kleisthenes was regarded by the Spartans as base ingratitude and disloyalty on the part of an inferior state, hence her violent if abortive response. The mistrust sown then will have persisted, and not just at Sparta: one reason why the Spartans held command against the Persians at sea as well as on land was the widespread suspicion of Athens in the Greek alliance (Hdt. 8.2–3). In any case, the build-up of Athens' navy was a very recent phenomenon: less than twenty years before Salamis, she had had to beg ships from Korinth by a form of lease-lend to be able to match her neighbour Aigina at sea (Hdt. 6.89). By contrast, Sparta was unquestionably the leading military power on land, and her nascent league offered the only viable basis on which to organize resistance to Persia. It was Spartan ambivalence about undertaking a long-term commitment to the Asian Greeks, caused in part by individual shortcomings in her commanders, which offered Athens the opportunity to take the first steps to becoming an imperial power and so to usurp her previously dominant position.

All this, however, came later. In 480 Athens and Sparta were allies, and the alliance clearly remained in force, since Sparta appealed to Athens as an ally for aid against the helots; it was only after the ensuing debacle that Athens repudiated it, in 462/1. It was not only her military prowess which made Sparta the natural head of the Hellenic League against Persia; despite her later tendency to introspection, Sparta in the late archaic period had a wide range of contacts in the Mediterranean world, including supposed colonial links such as those with Thera, Crete and Italian Lokroi, diplomatic contacts like those with Kyrene, whose king Arkesilas is depicted on a Spartan cup supervising the weighing of her valuable export silphium, and an interest through Taras in affairs in southern Italy and Sicily; the abortive colonial career of the Spartan prince Dorieus (Hdt. 5.42–8) notably touches on many of these areas. Sparta had also been at the forefront of contacts with the emergent powers of the Near East: she had formed an alliance with King Kroisos of Lydia against the Persians, and probably also had direct links with Kroisos' ally, the Pharaoh Amasis (Hdt. 3.47), who himself had connections with Kyrene (though also with Polykrates of Samos, against whom the Spartans mounted an expedition, an illustration of the potential for complications in such matters). Sparta had not actually intervened in eastern affairs: she was too late to help Kroisos, and confined herself to issuing a warning to the victorious Kyros not to harm any of the Greek cities in Asia, though he was not greatly impressed by it (Hdt. 1.152–3). Herodotos gives accounts of leading Athenian families which had *xenia* relations with Kroisos, notably the Alkmeonidai and Philaidai, but Athens does not appear to taken action against Persia at this stage either, and despite the self-serving account of his actions preserved by Herodotos, Miltiades seems to have ruled the Chersonese as a Persian nominee from the time of Dareios' Scythian expedition, and his seizure of Lemnos would make sense as a piece of opportunism while the Persians were distracted by the Ionian Revolt. It was at this point that the intervention of Athens and Eretria entangled the Greek mainland with Persian affairs and precipitated the retaliatory invasions of Dareios and Xerxes.

# 3   Athenian Ascendancy

The latter marked an ideological watershed. Not only did the Persian onslaught inspire a collective response in defence of Greece, however incomplete, fragile and short-lived Greek unity may have been, but the Greek victory encouraged a self-definition in cultural terms as Greeks in antithesis to a hostile barbarian 'other', a development which is particularly marked in Athenian tragedy (E. Hall 1989). Consequently for a generation any kind of compromise with Persia was unthinkable, as the Delian League pursued its retaliatory mission. Whether that was concluded by a formal peace (the 'Peace of Kallias') is one of the great controversies in ancient history, but there is an attractive alternative which styles it a 'détente' (Holladay 1986): while overt hostilities ceased, the Athenians continued to maintain a naval deterrent and to patrol the Aegean (Plutarch *Perikles* 11.4), and indeed show the flag further afield, as when Perikles led an expedition into the Black Sea (Plutarch *Perikles* 20). In many ways this was a 'Cold War', with defectors in both directions (Themistokles to Persia, Zopyros son of Megabyzos to Athens, for example), low-level hostilities pursued or fomented by satraps and attempts to stir up trouble by funding dissidents (the revolt of Samos in 440 is a good example of both, and the rumours and uncertainties about the possible involvement of the Phoenician fleet point to continuing fear of an outright attack from the east). Nevertheless, in Greece itself attitudes were changing, as growing tension between Athens and Sparta and the increasing prospect of major hostilities encouraged some in both states to think the unthinkable; by 431, when war broke out, Thucydides tells us (2.7.1) that both sides were seeking support from the Great King.

Thucydides also tells us that the principal reason for the increase in tension was the steady expansion of Athenian power. One aspect was territorial, which in part was driven by economic interest, and is exemplified by the establishment of cleruchies, overseas settlements of citizens (Figueira 1991). These were not a new phenomenon – cleruchs (*klerouchoi*) had been settled on the territory of Chalkis in Euboia after her defeat in 506 – but the fifth century saw their use on a much larger scale, particularly a clutch around 450, and not only as a reprisal, but on the territory of compliant allies who were compensated by a reduction in tribute. Cleruchs will have been largely poor citizens, but rich Athenians too evidently took advantage of Athenian power, since the inscriptions known as the *Attic Stelai* (e.g., Fornara 147) which list the confiscated property of those guilty of mutilating the herms in 415 mention estates overseas in Thasos, Euboia and Abydos; this contravened the normal link between citizenship and landholding, and the fact that the decree which established the Second Athenian Confederacy in 378/7 (R&O 22) explicitly abjures both private and public landholding in allied territory makes it clear how unpopular they had been.

Other settlements served strategic ends, notably the protracted attempt to establish a colony which would command the crossing of the river Strymon in Thrace and so secure land communications to the Hellespont. A Persian garrison was dislodged from Eion at the river mouth by the Delian League, probably in 476, and the Athenian settlers who replaced it established a foothold. One attempt at colonization about 465 by ten thousand Athenian and allied settlers was annihilated by the Thracians at Drabeskos, but an all-Athenian colony probably gained a foothold at Brea (Fornara 100), perhaps in 446, though date and location alike are uncertain, before the foundation of Amphipolis in 437/6. The majority of settlers here seem to have been non-Athenians (Thuc. 4.106.1), hence the initiative after the town fell to the Spartans in 424/3 to honour as founder the recently deceased Brasidas in place of the original Athenian founder Hagnon (Thuc. 5.11) and the failure of the Athenians ever to recover the place, which seems to have obsessed them for the rest of the classical period. The inclusion of so many non-Athenians was evidently an attempt to present the foundation of Amphipolis as an act on the part of and of benefit to all Greeks, though on Athenian initiative, a line of propaganda which had been deployed at the slightly earlier settlement at Thourioi. However, it clearly served Athenian strategic interests, since Athens was becoming increasingly reliant on imported corn, particularly from the northern Black Sea; the re-establishment of settlements on the Thracian Chersonese, Lemnos and Imbros (see Figueira 1991: 253–6 for the complexities of their status) fits the same pattern of securing communications, as do attempts to suppress piracy, particularly on Skyros, which lay on the natural route to the Piraeus, and the place of the grain supply in Perikles' strategic calculations is likely to have been a factor in his diplomatic initiative in the Black Sea, especially if it is to be dated to the 430s.

To the west, the foundation of Thourioi in the toe of Italy in 444/3 was another Athenian project which was opened to all Greece, and the most conspicuous evidence of a move to expand Athenian influence in this direction of which there are hints as early as the year of Salamis, when Herodotos (8.62) makes Themistokles, who had named two of his daughters Sybaris and Italia (Plutarch *Themistokles* 32), threaten a complete withdrawal of the Athenians to Siris, which according to certain oracles was destined to be colonized by them. Athens had also begun to make alliances in the region: the inscriptions which supply the evidence are unfortunately all problematic to interpret, particularly that recording an alliance with Egesta (which was to play an important role in precipitating the Athenian expedition to Sicily in 415). This (Fornara 81) has normally been dated to 458/7, which would make it the earliest of these alliances, though this continues to be disputed (above, pp. 53–4); the alliances with Rhegion and Leontinoi (Fornara 124; 125) are dated to 433/2, just before the outbreak of war, but are probably renewals of agreements originally made in the 440s. Overall, it seems likely that Athenian diplomatic activity was on the increase in the west after 450. So too was commerce, to judge from the wealth of Athenian pottery excavated at Spina, in the southern Po delta; this includes white-ground lekythoi, a type of funerary vase which is almost exclusively confined to Athenian graves, and therefore implies that in the fifth century Athenians were living and being buried in this entrepôt on the edge of the Etruscan zone of influence. Both developments encroached on Korinth, which as a colonial metropolis and a commercial power had hitherto been dominant in the west, and this was not the only respect in which the traditionally friendly relations between Athens and Korinth (encouraged in part by a common rivalry with Aigina) had been turning sour: the defection of Megara to Athenian protection in 459 and the settlement of Messenian rebels at Naupaktos on the northern shore of the Gulf of Korinth paved the way for open hostilities in the so-called 'First Peloponnesian War', in which Korinth bore the brunt of the fighting, and the Spartan response was late and limited, and culminated in a peace (the 'Thirty Years' Peace') which suited Sparta rather better than her allies. It appears that in these years Athens was trying to add a land empire to her maritime hegemony, seeking to control the Isthmus of Korinth and supporting anti-Theban regimes to gain control of Boiotia. All this rapidly unravelled: there were uprisings in Boiotia and Megara, and Athens was compelled to cede her remaining strongholds on the Isthmus of Korinth. Since Athenian imperial consolidation hardly missed a beat, the loss was clearly minimal in strategic terms, though the fact that a claim to the lost strongholds was floated in 425 (Thuc. 4.21.3) shows that aspirations in that direction had not been entirely abandoned; likewise the designs on Boiotia which led to the Athenian misadventure at Delion. Korinth, however, gained nothing from the peace, and matters came to a head when Athens took the side of her recalcitrant daughter-city Kerkyra; faced with veiled threats from her leading ally that her hegemony might fall apart, Sparta was forced to act. The Kerkyra episode, which on Thucydides' account precipitated a war that was to involve the whole Greek world, is also a conspicuous instance of the fact that the network of alliances which had begun life as the Delian League was only one element in Athenian foreign policy, and often not the dominant one, since the Athenians tended to give priority to their own interests (and continued to do so even in the fourth century).

Quite apart from the commitment to Kerkyra, Athenian interest in the west continued, and the opportunity was taken to intervene militarily when Leontinoi appealed to her ally for assistance against Syracuse. Syracuse was disproportionately large (probably at this time the largest polis after Athens herself) and under her late archaic tyrants had caused great disruption through the destruction and displacement of smaller cities and the forcible movement of populations on a large scale (behaviour otherwise associated with oriental absolutism). Ethnic divisions between Greeks were also a factor (above, p. 86), but divisions between Greeks and non-Greeks mattered much less: Egesta was not Greek but Elymian, while her neighbour Selinous reveals considerable Punic influence. Since the Dorian colonies had tended to be more aggressive towards the indigenous populations (Syracuse had a class of serfs, the *killyrioi*, the enslaved indigenous inhabitants), there was considerable scope for Athens to pose as a defender of the oppressed, both Greek and native. In the event, the first Athenian intervention (427–424) was unproductive, and the Syracusans were able to patch together a peace by persuading their fellow-Sicilians that Athens was the greater threat. Less than a decade later, a much larger expedition was launched, officially in response to an appeal from Egesta for aid against Selinous and to re-establish Leontinoi; in both cases, however, Syracuse was ranged on the other side, and the underlying objectives were clearly broader. This time many of the Greek cities responded guardedly; Thucydides' account of the debate at Kamarina (6.75–88) brings out the complex cross-currents between appeals to ethnicity and interest and suspicion of both great powers which led to Kamarina's decision to remain neutral. In contrast to many similar situations on the Greek mainland, however, political ideology played little or no part, since Athens, Syracuse and probably Kamarina all had some form of democratic constitution at this point; Athens' position as champion of democracy had much less purchase in the west. Just how ambitious Athenian aims in Sicily were is not clear; Thucydides credits them with ambitions to control the whole island as early as the first expedition, and puts in the mouth of Alkibiades (whom he associates with designs on Carthage: Thuc. 6.15) the assertion that this was only a stepping-stone on the way to subjugating the western Mediterranean and then the whole Hellenic world (Thuc. 6.90), though since this was in a speech at Sparta advocating aid to the embattled Syracusans, it would be wise to be sceptical. Although Thucydides likewise makes the Syracusan Hermokrates claim that the Carthaginians feared Athenian attack (Thuc. 6.34), in reality the Athenians sent envoys to Carthage (Thuc. 6.88), and a frustratingly fragmentary inscription (Fornara 165) reveals the presence of Carthaginian envoys at Athens as late as 406. Athens also attracted support from the Etruscans, old opponents of the Syracusans (Thuc. 6.88, 103, 7.53–4, 57), and from Campania (Diodoros 13.44.2). Another tantalising inscription (*IG* 1³ 291), the fragments of which record monetary contributions from Athens' allies, probably in 415, makes one wonder whether what was envisaged at some stage was a kind of western league, with Syracuse and her Dorian henchmen as the enemy rather than the barbarian. Athens' willingness to deal with all sorts of non-Greeks demonstrates how much less tidy the Greek–barbarian antithesis was in the west; although the propaganda of the Deinomenid tyrants sought to present their victories over Carthaginians and Etruscans as contributing to the cause of Greek freedom (Harrell 2002: 450–4), and the fourth-century historian Ephoros saw a full-blown conspiracy between eastern and western barbarians, Herodotos is already aware that the Carthaginian invasion of 480 was sparked by a quarrel between Greeks (Hdt. 7.165), and in the fourth century Lysias in his Olympic oration (33) denounced Dionysios I and Artaxerxes II in the same breath as enemies of Greek freedom.

# 4   Sparta Resurgent

In the end, the Athenians despite their weaknesses and errors came close to conquering Syracuse outright, but the huge costs of ultimate failure led to a radical shift in outlook at Sparta: at last it looked as though Athens could be defeated at sea, and that made a deal with Persia, the only realistic source of the necessary funds, a viable proposition. Hitherto, negotiations had made no progress: one embassy was intercepted early in the war en route to Persia (Thuc. 2.67), as five years later was a Persian envoy to Sparta, who bore dispatches in which the Persian king complained of Spartan vagueness and inconsistency and invited them to make some concrete proposals (Thuc. 4.50). The Athenians took advantage of the latter coup to send their own mission to Persia, and although this was frustrated by the death of Artaxerxes I, they subsequently renewed friendly relations with his successor (Lewis 1977: 69–77; M&L 70 and Addenda). By 413, relations between Athens and Persia had been soured by Athens' support for Amorges, bastard son of the rebel satrap Pissouthnes. How this came about is not clear from Thucydides; in the fourth century it could be treated as an instance of folly in Athenian foreign policy, but it is possible that the advent of the new satrap Tissaphernes, who was under pressure to produce arrears of tribute (Thuc. 8.5), was a significant factor. At all events, there was a flurry of diplomatic activity which saw the satraps Tissaphernes and Pharnabazos and their associates among the Greek cities competing to lobby for Spartan intervention, and a series of attempts to agree on satisfactory terms between Persia and Sparta (Thuc. 8.18; 36–7; 58). At the same time, Alkibiades was intriguing with Tissaphernes and Athenian oligarchs for Persian aid for Athens, holding out the inducement of a non-democratic government there, but the complex machinations into which Alkibiades' self-interest led him helped in the end to thwart that initiative, though the coup went ahead (and rapidly failed too). Even so, in practice the Persian response was rather equivocal, particularly on the part of Tissaphernes, whom Thucydides represents as seeking to play off either side against the other, and Athenian hopes remained alive until the arrival in Ionia of the young prince Kyros (Xenophon *Hellenika* 1.4); the genuine bond of friendship which he established with the Spartan commander Lysander led in turn to the effective support of the Spartan navy which paved the way for the defeat of Athens.

Spartan success in turn immediately exposed the ideological tensions implicit in the deal with Persia, whereby the leader of Greece against Xerxes and now self-professed liberator of the Greeks had abandoned the Greeks of Asia to the control of the Great King in exchange for Persian gold. The problem had clearly been evident from the start, hence Spartan indecision in her early negotiations with Persia, and even after pragmatism had prevailed, there were always those like the admiral Kallikratidas (Xenophon *Hellenika* 1.6.7) who objected on principle to 'flattering barbarians for the sake of money'. Once Sparta had got what she wanted, this element prevailed: Sparta reneged on her agreement by annexing the Asian Greeks, and compounded this by assisting (albeit unofficially) the revolt of Kyros against his brother Artaxerxes II and then sending troops when the Asian Greeks appealed for help against Tissaphernes. Although Kyros was defeated and killed at Kounaxa, the sequel, the famous march to the Black Sea of the Ten Thousand Greek mercenaries, contributed greatly to the anti-Persian movement we call Panhellenism, since their escape suggested that Persia was militarily weak and hence open to attack. The other major stimulus for this movement was paradoxically the tangible effectiveness of the Great King in intervening in Greek affairs, the clearest evidence of which was the series of Common Peaces brokered by Persia, and in particular the first of these, the so-called King's Peace of 386. While the principal motive for this was to stabilise Persian control of Asia Minor in the face of interference from both Sparta and a resurgent Athens, later Common Peaces were also influenced by a desire to free up Greek mercenaries to quell revolts in the satrapies, particularly the prolonged insurrection in Egypt (a weak point for Persia in the fifth century too), where at times a proxy war was being conducted by Greek troops commanded by Greek generals on both sides. The clear superiority of Greek hoplites in turn reinforced the suggestion of Persian vulnerability, as did the revolts of satraps and satrapies.

Nevertheless, the outright contempt for barbarians which typified fifth-century attitudes becomes much more muted in fourth-century sources, and Plato, for example, treats the Great King as the type of the powerful autocrat (e.g., *Republic* 553C), though naturally he does not regard him as a model for imitation. In the *Kyroupaideia* ('*Education of Kyros*') of Xenophon, on the other hand, the elder Kyros is used as the basis for an account of an ideal ruler. Xenophon had encountered enough Persians, above all the younger Kyros, to make his attitude to barbarians and Panhellenism complex and ambivalent, but his writings, like those of Plato and Isokrates, also reflect the renaissance of monarchy as an effective form of government on the edges of the Greek world (Sicily, Thessaly, Macedon, Cyprus) and beyond. Persia's effectiveness was partly economic, since she was the only available source of funds on a scale sufficient for decisive naval action, particularly given the generally diminished level of resources brought about by the Peloponnesian War – even Athens had Konon's association with Pharnabazos (and a Persian fleet) to thank for victory at Knidos in 394 and the reconstruction of her walls – and the difficulty which Greek cities had in paying for military action is nicely illustrated by the frequency with which fourth-century generals appear in the catalogue of devices for raising money in the Aristotelian *Oikonomika* 2. The result was that Persia was constantly courted by the three great powers, Athens, Sparta and Thebes. In this the Spartans were most generally successful, probably because they were culturally best placed to form friendships with Persians, while for the same reason the Athenians were generally least successful both because of their suspicion of monarchy and as a result of the mistrust among the demos of those who did establish good relations (Mitchell 1997: 111–33). The continuing deference of the leading Greek states to Persia and their lack of real power made it less and less likely that one or more of them would ever take effective action against the barbarian: Isokrates, who in his *Panegyrikos* of 380 had looked to a coalition of Athens and Sparta for leadership, turned his eyes north towards the new military autocrats, first Alexandros of Pherai (allegedly: Speusippos *Letter to Philip* 13) and then Philip II of Macedon, to whom he commended the unification of Greece for the crusade in the *Philip* of 346. It should be pointed out, however, that the objective which Isokrates regards as realistic is not outright conquest of Persia, but rather the annexation of Asia Minor for Greek settlement. It is ironic that Philip's need for a naval force to put such ideas into practice obliged him (and Alexander after him) to be tolerant of Athenian interference and opposition, though after Chaironeia Athens was constrained within the structures of the League of Korinth (which formally precluded an independent foreign policy) and compelled to acknowledge the hegemony of Philip and then Alexander.

## 5 Regional Interests: The North and the West

Indeed, all the leading states meddled in the affairs of northern Greece in the fourth century. Sparta had already signalled her ambitions in this direction in 426 with the foundation of Heraklea in Trachis (Thuc. 3.92–3; in this case the association with Herakles was authentic), and took the opportunity to intervene in the conflict between Thessalian dynasts as soon as her victory allowed. Spartan foreign policy in these years is remarkably dynamic and expansive, which may be due to the continuing influence of Lysander; however, in 395–394 they were dislodged from Thessaly (another established interest: Hdt. 6.72 and Plutarch *Moralia* 859d: *On the Malice of Herodotos* 21, for Leotychidas' expedition of 478) having achieved nothing of substance other than to incur the hostility of Thebes, on whose traditional sphere of influence they had encroached, and Lysander died in battle at Haliartos in Boiotia in the same year. They also lost Heraklea, from which they had already been expelled once and supplanted by Thebes (Thuc. 5.51–2). In the following decade their response to an appeal from Amyntas, king of Macedon, had more substantial consequences, since not only did they lose a king, but the dismantling of the Chalkidian League centred on Olynthos removed a potential check on the growth of Macedonian power. In the fifth century, Macedon's chronic weakness had left her vulnerable to the intrigues of the great powers, chiefly the Athenians, for whom the high-quality ship timber of Macedon made the region of strategic interest (the same was true of southern Italy). During the Peloponnesian War Perdikkas II had attempted to protect his kingdom by equivocation; Athenian public opinion regarded him as duplicitous (Hermippos F 63 Kassel & Austin (below, p. 95)), but in truth they had provoked him by allying with his enemies (Thuc. 1.57). Early in the war they also put pressure on him by cultivating the rulers of the Odrysian Thracians in a piece of kinship diplomacy noted by Thucydides (2.29); the Thracian prince Sadokos was even made an Athenian citizen, to the amusement of Aristophanes (*Acharnians* 141–50), though the policy bore little fruit.

Athenian manoeuvring in the north was clearly shaped from the restoration of the democracy in 403 by the ambition to reinstate her empire as quickly and fully as possible. Here, however, they found themselves in competition not only with Sparta but with Thebes, especially in her decade of hegemony, and then with Philip of Macedon. Athens started off on the wrong foot by backing a pretender to the Macedonian throne; having made peace with them at the outset to buy time, Philip then with a deft blend of force and diplomacy (the latter exploiting their fixation with Amphipolis) dislodged them from their footholds on the coast of Macedon. These included the cleruchy at Poteidaia, one of a number established in the 360s and 350s. Technically, these did not breach the undertakings Athens had made to its allies (above, p. 88), since none was placed on the territory of an ally, but like the need for Athenian commanders to fund their own expeditions, which according to Demosthenes (4.45) put their allies in mortal fear of them, these footholds were symptomatic of the way in which lack of resources inclined Athens to exploit where she could. In so doing she forfeited the fragile trust of her allies and undermined her own attempts to become an imperial power again, which were finally undone by the 'Social War'. It is significant, too, that her confederacy included the Molossians Alketas and Neoptolemos and perhaps Iason of Pherai, who appeared (with Alketas) as a character witness for the Athenian general Timotheus in 373. Especially in the north, Athens was having to come to terms with the emergence of powerful individuals who could have a major political impact but who originated in a culture rather different from that of the polis-centred Greek world. The hostility of Demosthenes, mingled with a grudging respect for Philip's dynamism and power, reveals an ambiguous attitude not confined to Athens: Theopompos of Chios (*FGrHist* 115), who began his history by stating that Europe had never borne a man like Philip, went on to include scathing exposés of the moral corruption of his court.

By contrast, Sicily, the other theatre in which autocracy flourished in the fourth century, saw a gradual decline in its engagement with politics in the Greek mainland. In the immediate aftermath of the Athenian defeat at Syracuse, the Syracusans in particular were energetic allies of Sparta in the naval war even after Hermokrates was exiled from the city (Selinous sent a small contingent too). Sparta maintained the connection by helping the tyrant Dionysios I consolidate his position and pursue the war with Carthage, and he reciprocated by supporting Sparta in the Korinthian War. Athens tried to woo him away from Sparta by bestowing honours on him (R&O 10), but only won him over in 368/7 (R&O 34, cf. 33), shortly before he died, and after a rapprochement between Sparta and Athens. This was also the year in which Dionysios won a victory in the tragic contest at the Lenaia, and it is worth noting the degree to which tragic drama was a cultural and diplomatic asset for Athens (Taplin 1999). On the one hand, Athenian playwrights attracted foreign patronage: Aischylos ended his life in Sicily after being commissioned by Hieron, and Euripides migrated to Macedon, where he wrote an *Archelaos* about the mythical origins of the royal house. He was followed by his younger contemporary Agathon (it is interesting that both were innovative rather than conservative figures), and the fragments of unidentified tragedies indicate that there must have been a number of Macedon-related plays by these or other authors. The high status of drama also led to the use of actors as envoys between Athens and Macedon (Csapo & Slater 1995: 223, 232–6). After Dionysios I, Syracuse became increasingly embroiled in internal struggles for power, while Greek Sicily as a whole was bogged down in hostilities with Carthage which dragged on without resolution, and the attention and ambitions of the major Greek poleis were directed elsewhere; it was left to Korinth to respond to the appeal of her daughter-city with the mission of Timoleon. Curiously, Sparta found herself in similar circumstances about the same time, though in a form which reflected her reduced circumstances, when Archidamos III died fighting for the Tarentines against their indigenous neighbours: he was fulfilling the Delphic prophecy that the Spartan colony would be 'a plague on the Iapygians', but he was serving for pay. So too in Egypt, which at the beginning of the century had supported Sparta's war against Persia (Diodoros 14.79.4), Agesilaos ended his days fighting Persia as a mercenary general.

# 6   Beyond Politics

Both these royal deaths far from home tellingly illustrate how Sparta's involvement in the world of power-politics inevitably entailed a need for money, especially once the loss of Messenia and disintegration of her alliance after Leuktra left her isolated in the Peloponnese. Internally, however, Sparta remained much less monetarized than many poleis; even if recent scholarship (Hodkinson 2000) has demonstrated a disparity between the ideological construction of Spartan austerity and the realities of Spartan life, the retention of an iron currency and the institution of *xenelasiai*, periodic expulsions of foreigners, reflect a society only partially open to the wider world, at least below the level of the élite. By contrast, domestically Athens displays an extraordinarily wide range of overseas contacts apparently little constrained by the ideological divide between Greek and barbarian. The boom in Athenian overseas trade and the growth of the Piraeus as a commercial centre which resulted from the rise of Athens as an imperial power in the fifth century connected the Athenians to most of the Mediterranean world, a development beautifully exemplified by a fragment of the comic poet Hermippos (F 63 Kassel & Austin) from the early years of the Peloponnesian War, which is worth quoting in full:

> Tell me now, Muses who have your home on Olympos, since Dionysos has been sailing over the wine-dark sea, how many good things he has brought here for men in his black ship. From Kyrene silphium and ox-hide, from the Hellespont mackerel and all kinds of dried fish, and from Thessaly coarse salt and sides of beef; from Sitalkes a plague for the Spartans, and from Perdikkas many shiploads of lies. Syracuse supplies pork and cheese . . . [1 or more lines missing] and may Poseidon obliterate the Kerkyreans in their hollow ships, because their heart is divided [i.e. they are duplicitous]. These goods [come] from there, and from Egypt rigging and papyrus, and from Syria incense. Beautiful Crete sends cypress-wood for the gods, Libya offers abundant ivory for sale, Rhodes raisins and dried figs which bring sweet dreams. Then from Euboia come pears and fat sheep, slaves from Phrygia, mercenaries from Arkadia. Pagasai provides slaves and branded runaways. Paphlagonia supplies Zeus's acorns [filberts] and shining almonds, ornaments of the feast, Phoenicia dates and fine wheat flour, Carthage carpets and embroidered cushions.

The capacity of trade, especially in the exotic and luxurious, to cut across ideology extended even to Persian goods such as dress and the accoutrements of parasol, fan and fly-whisk, which clearly appealed to the Athenian élite, perhaps with the allure of forbidden fruit (one might perhaps compare the appeal of the Havana cigar to Americans, or Leonid Brezhnev's collection of American cars). To a great extent this was a matter of individual indulgence among the wealthy, though pottery imitations of Persian metal drinking vessels certainly extended the social range of those following Persian fashions, and the Periklean Odeon may have been an attempt to appropriate Persian royal architecture for imperial Athens at large (see Miller 1997 for the whole phenomenon). Certainly in the fifth century Thucydides could make Perikles present the central place of the Piraeus in Mediterranean trade as a benefit of empire for Athens (Thuc. 2.38); it is a sign of the changed circumstances of the fourth century when Isokrates lauds it as a benefit for all Greece (4.42). Some realities persisted, however: Athens' continued dependence on imported corn encouraged the continued cultivation of the Spartokid rulers of the Crimean Bosporos (R&O 64), a good instance of the way in which her commercial and political interests could require her to deal with kings, the ideological antithesis of democracy. The problem was exacerbated when the essential link relied, as it often did, on a personal relationship, as when Andokides exploited his hereditary connection with the kings of Macedon to obtain oar-timber in the crisis of 411 (Andokides 2.11; in general: Mitchell 1997; Braund 2000). Such connections might also provide a refuge for Athenians in trouble, as Euagoras did for Konon and Andokides in Cyprus or the Bosporan kingdom for Lysias' client Mantitheos (Lysias 16.4), and perhaps for Gylon, father of Demosthenes. Iphikrates even married into a Thracian royal family in a way that harks back to a time before the citizenship law of Perikles sought to make the citizen body a closed circle of privilege. Yet insofar as the law was effective, it did not cause Athens to become exclusive as a community: the fact that trade was very largely in the hands of metics must have meant that Athens was always highly cosmopolitan, and the gravestones of non-Athenians found in Attika in this period offer a sample of the origins of those who visited Athens or chose to settle there. Almost 350 monuments (some for more than one person), dating very largely from the fourth century, cite more than 130 ethnics from a host of Greek cities and as far afield as Bithynia, Bosporos, Pontos, Cyprus (and more specifically Kition, Kourion, Salamis and Soloi), Sidon, Lykia, Phaselis, Mysia, Kilikia, Paphlagonia, Macedon, Paionia, Epeiros, Thesprotia, Sicily, Syracuse, Gela, Italy, Rhegion, Thourioi, Egypt, Naukratis, Kyrene, and even one apiece from Media and Persia. In most cases, only a few individuals are concerned, but where there are a dozen or more (e.g., Ephesos, Herakleia, Thebes, Miletos, Olynthos), one is tempted to think of an expatriate community like the Cypriot merchants from Kition (six tombstones) to whom the Athenians granted land in 333 on which to build a temple of Aphrodite (R&O 91 – the inscription also makes passing reference to a similar grant to Egyptians for a temple of Isis). Such windows on the experience of individuals remind us that relations between individual citizens were always more varied and complex than those between the states which they composed, and that to speak simply in terms of the latter is to obscure much of the subtlety and ambiguity of the topic.

# Further reading

Adcock, F., & D. J. Mosley (1975) *Diplomacy in ancient Greece* (London: Thames & Hudson)

Andrewes, A. (1978) 'Spartan imperialism?' in: Garnsey, P. D. A., & C. R. Whittaker (eds) (1978) *Imperialism in the ancient world* (Cambridge: Cambridge University Press) 91–102

Badian, E. (1995) 'The ghost of empire: reflections on Athenian foreign policy in the fourth century BC' in: Eder, W. (ed.) (1995) *Die Athenische Demokratie im 4 Jhdt. v. Chr.* (Stuttgart: Steiner) 79–106

Cartledge, P. (1987) *Agesilaos and the crisis of Sparta* (London: Duckworth)

Finley, M. I. (1978) 'The fifth-century Athenian empire: a balance-sheet' in: Garnsey, P. D. A., & C. R. Whittaker (eds) (1978) *Imperialism in the ancient world* (Cambridge: Cambridge University Press) 103–26

Griffith, G. T. (1978) 'Athens in the fourth century' in: Garnsey, P. D. A., & C. R. Whittaker (eds) (1978) *Imperialism in the ancient world* (Cambridge: Cambridge University Press) 127–44

Herman, G. (1987) *Ritualised friendship and the Greek City* (Cambridge: Cambridge University Press)

Hornblower, S. (2002) *The Greek world 479–323 BC* (London: Routledge [3]2002)

Lewis, D. M. (1997) 'The origins of the first Peloponnesian war' in: Shrimpton, G. S., & D. J. McCargar (eds) (1981) *Classical contributions: studies in honour of Malcolm Francis McGregor* (Locust Valley NY: Augustin) 71–8 = Lewis, D. M. (1997) *Selected papers in Greek and near eastern history* (ed. P. J. Rhodes) (Cambridge: Cambridge University Press) 9–21

Tritle, L. A. (ed.) (1997) *The Greek world in the fourth century* (London: Routledge)

Two general volumes which give proper weight to the regional perspective are Hornblower (2002) and Tritle (1997). For the broad narrative, the relevant chapters below will provide pointers for further reading, though discussion of foreign policy, especially for Athens, tends to centre on the hegemonic leagues. A broader survey of Spartan foreign policy is provided by Lewis (1977) and Cartledge (1987, especially chapters 6, 11, 13); Athens is less well served, but Lewis (1981 = 1997) illuminates the mid fifth century, highlighting the role of Korinth, while Badian (1995) argues that her ambitions and actions in the fourth century were haunted by the lost empire of the fifth. Whether either should be considered truly imperialistic is discussed by Andrewes (1978), Finley (1978) and Griffith (1978). On diplomacy, Adcock & Mosley (1975) is still useful, but to be supplemented by the more recent studies by Herman (1987) and Mitchell (1997), which highlight the importance and implications of personal connections. J. Hall (1997) is the best starting-point for concepts and uses made of ethnicity.

# Bibliography

Alty, J. H. M. (1982) 'Dorians and Ionians' in: *JHS* 102: 1–14

Braund, D. (2000) 'Friends and foes: monarchs and monarchy in fifth-century Athenian democracy' in: Brock, R., & S. Hodkinson (eds) (2000) *Alternatives to Athens* (Oxford: Oxford University Press) 103–18

Csapo, E., & W. J. Slater (1995) *The context of ancient drama* (Ann Arbor: University of Michigan Press)

Figueira, T. J. (1991) *Athens and Aegina in the age of imperial colonization* (Baltimore: Johns Hopkins University Press)

Fowler, R. L. (1998) 'Genealogical thinking, Hesiod's *Catalogue* and the creation of the Hellenes' in: *PCPhS* 44: 1–19

Hall, E. (1989) *Inventing the barbarian: Greek self-definition through tragedy* (Oxford: Clarendon) (Oxford Classical Monographs)

Hall, J. M. (1997) *Ethnic identity in Greek antiquity* (Cambridge: Cambridge University Press)

Harrell, S. (2002) 'King or private citizen: fifth-century Sicilian tyrants at Olympia and Delphi' in: *Mnemosyne* 55: 439–64

Hodkinson, S. (2000) *Property and wealth in classical Sparta* (London: Duckworth & The Classical Press of Wales)

Holladay, A. J. (1986) 'The détente of Kallias?' in: *Historia* 35: 503–7

Jones, C. P. (1999) *Kinship diplomacy in the ancient world* (Cambridge MA: Harvard University Press)

Lewis, D. M. (1977) *Sparta and Persia* (Leiden: Brill) (Cincinnati Classical Studies 2.1)

Malkin, I. (1994) *Myth and territory in the Spartan Mediterranean* (Cambridge: Cambridge University Press)

Miller, M. C. (1997) *Athens and Persia in the fifth century* B.C.: *a study in cultural receptivity* (Cambridge: Cambridge University Press)

Mitchell, L. G. (1997) *Greeks bearing gifts: the public use of private relationships in the Greek world, 435–323* BC (Cambridge: Cambridge University Press)

Osborne, R. (1998) 'Early Greek colonisation?: the nature of Greek settlement in the west' in: Fisher, N., & H. van Wees (eds) (1998) *Archaic Greece: new approaches and new evidence* (London: Duckworth & The Classical Press of Wales) 251–69

Siewert, P. (1977) 'The ephebic oath in fifth-century Athens' in: *JHS* 97: 102–11

Taplin, O. (1999) 'Spreading the word through performance' in: Goldhill, S., & R. Osborne (eds) (1999) *Performance culture and Athenian democracy* (Cambridge: Cambridge University Press) 33–57

CHAPTER SIX

# Aegean Greece

*Kai Brodersen*

## Introduction: The Sea and the Land – An Attempt at a Classification of the 'Third Greece'

The Classical Age as a historical epoch, it may be argued, is the most important period of Greek history. It certainly has traditionally been a focus of scholarly debate, and popular imagination, mainly because of the two most important political powers of the time: Athens and Sparta. The present chapter, however, sets out to explore the other regions of mainland Greece as well as the Aegean islands and western Asia Minor: the 'Third Greece beyond Athens and Sparta' around the Aegean Sea, as Gehrke (1986) has called it in an influential work. Given the bias of the extant literary and non-literary sources towards Athens and, at least indirectly, Sparta, our survey can only be based on scarce and very unbalanced evidence (for which see, e.g., Fornara, Harding, M&L, R&O). Generalizations are therefore especially risky, but an attempt may still be of some use if we try to organize the uneven material and thus to contribute to an understanding of this 'Third Greece'.

What is it then that makes the 'Third Greece' a more or less coherent entity? The usual 'historical' answer is that, during the Classical Age, large parts of it belonged to one of the two main leagues, either the Peloponnesian League comprising Sparta and her allies, formed in the sixth century and active until 365 (cf. Wickert 1961; Baltrusch 1994), or the first (or Delian) Athenian League comprising Athens and her allies (480/79 – 404; cf. Meiggs 1979); to which one must add, during the fourth century, the Second Athenian League (378/7 – 338; see R&O 23; Cargill 1981), and the Korinthian League formed by Philip II of Macedon after his victory over the combined Greek forces at Chaironeia in 338 (R&O 76).

However, a far more fundamental coherence is based on the geographical facts: the first and foremost factor connecting Aegean Greece is of course the Aegean Sea, which has always encouraged fishing and sailing (both in voyages along the coast, and in 'island hopping'), and has enabled lively communications between the Greek mainland, the islands and western Asia Minor throughout history. Hardly of less importance, however, were the common natural conditions for the communities' subsistence, which in the 'Third Greece' is often quite similar, as stated by Herodotos (3.1), who notes a uniformity of natural conditions in Greece: 'The most outlying nations of the world have somehow drawn the finest things as their lot, exactly as Greece has drawn the possession of far the best seasons.'

In fact, most of its regions lack mineral resources such as iron (let alone precious metals), but have three factors in common: (1) the sea, allowing for fishing and communications; (2) alluvial plains in 'far the best seasons', that is in a Mediterranean climate, often not well watered, but fertile enough to enable the cultivation of grain, olives, vines, fruit and vegetables, and less commonly animal husbandry of cattle and the prestigious horses; (3) mountain ranges for firewood and timber (cf. already Homer *Iliad* 23.114 – 22), for transhumance (especially goats and sheep) or – in the rougher areas – only for hunting.

Although the physical world and the economic realities will be dealt with in later chapters, it seems necessary to state at the outset the two single most important environmental – and therefore, as in any pre-industrial society, economic – factors which tied the Aegean world together and the varying qualities of which may help towards a classification of the regions under discussion: ease of access to the sea, and the availability and fertility of agricultural land.

Variations in these two factors allow us to organize our survey along the lines of a simplified systematic classification – a necessarily simplistic approach which cannot be more than a first attempt to identify comparable communities in the classical Greek World around the Aegean.

> Section 1: rich in agricultural land – easy access to sea
> Section 2: medium size agricultural land – easy access to sea
> Section 3: little agricultural land – easy access to sea
> Section 4: rich in agricultural land – less than easy access to sea
> Section 5: medium size agricultural land – less than easy access to sea
> Section 6: little agricultural land – less than easy access to sea
> Section 7: rich in agricultural land – difficult access to sea
> Section 8: medium size agricultural land – difficult access to sea
> Section 9: little agricultural land – difficult access to sea

# 1   Rich in Agricultural Land – Easy Access to Sea

The only community which easily falls into this category in Aegean Greece is Athens, with 'the finest and safest accommodation for shipping, since vessels can anchor here and ride safe at their moorings in spite of bad weather' (Xenophon *Poroi* 3.1), especially the Piraeus, and its large and generally fertile hinterland, Attika. Xenophon also states:

> One might reasonably suppose that the city lies at the centre of Greece, nay of the whole inhabited world. For the further we go from her, the more intense is the heat or cold we

meet with; and every traveller who would cross from one to the other end of Greece passes Athens as the centre of a circle, whether he goes by water or by road. Then, too, though she is not wholly sea-girt, all the winds of heaven bring to her the goods she needs and bear away her exports, as if she were an island; for she lies between two seas: and she has a vast land trade as well; for she is of the mainland. Further, on the borders of most states dwell barbarians who trouble them: but the neighbouring states of Athens are themselves remote from the barbarians. (Xenophon *Poroi* 1.6 – 8)

Athens, however, as well as the Greek colonies in the Black Sea region, in Sicily and Southern Italy and elsewhere, which typically approached the optimum in these two qualities – Panormos (modern Palermo), for example, which has an excellent harbour, and a large and very fertile hinterland – are not the subject of our chapter.

# 2 Medium Size Agricultural Land – Easy Access to Sea

This type of community is the most frequent in the 'Third Greece'. Given the geographical facts – many mainland regions and, obviously, all islands border on the sea, and large continuous fertile plains are rare, but mediocre ones reasonably common – it is not surprising that most agricultural communities near a good port and most larger islands fall into this category. Typically the disadvantage of the limitations of arable land led to a concentration on specific agricultural goods to be produced, in amounts exceeding what was needed for subsistence, for export thanks to easy access to the sea.

One might consider the example of Korinth on the coast of the Korinthian Gulf in a fertile coastal strip east of Sikyon, and west of (but including) the Isthmus of Korinth, with several terraces north of Akrokorinth and some more land on the Isthmus. Korinthia (c. $900 \, \text{km}^2$), not abundant in agricultural land if compared to Athens, 'not very fertile, but rifted and rough' (Strabon 8.6.23), was able not only to support its own sizeable community but also to export some of its agricultural production. However, it was the land-bridge of the Isthmus with its road, the harbours on both the Korinthian Gulf (Lechaion) and the Saronic Gulf (Kenchreai) and the *diolkos* (a well-paved 'road' for pulling boats across the Isthmus on a kind of sledge) which supported 'wealthy Korinth' (Pindar F 122 Snell; cf. *Olympian Odes* 13.4). Strabon (8.6.20) states:

> Korinth is called 'wealthy' because of its commerce, since it is situated on the Isthmus and is master of two harbours, of which the one leads straight to Asia, and the other to Italy; and it makes easy the exchange of merchandise from both countries that are so far distant from each other. … It was a welcome alternative, for the merchants both from Italy and from Asia, to avoid the voyage to Malea (around the Peloponnese) and to land their cargoes here. And also the duties on what by land was exported from the Peloponnese and what was imported to it fell to those who held the keys.

Trade and tolls brought in extra money, and surplus agricultural as well as specifically manufactured goods (from small pots to large boats) could be sold, or even delivered to the customers, in both East and West. It is obvious, then, why the rise of Athens in the fifth century brought Korinth into conflict with this city in the Peloponnesian War. Korinth's successes were shared by Sparta, which, however, soon became more oppressive towards the city, and the so-called Korinthian War (395 – 386) led to the destruction of the city, and for some time to a complete loss of independence. Korinth regained it, but henceforth mainly kept a 'low profile' in international politics throughout the Classical Age, while expanding its agricultural and trading activities again. After 338, Philip II made it the centre of his Korinthian League (see above); later events (notably the Roman destruction in 146, and the wealth of the city refounded by the Romans in 44) seem to repeat the lessons of the Classical Age (cf. Salmon 1984).

Similarly, the mountainous Aegean island of Chios, which had limited agricultural lands, clearly could grow enough to feed its population. But the fact that the Chians were even referred to as 'the richest of the Greeks' (Thuc. 8.45) was the result of specialization in agricultural goods exported via the island's fine harbours: a prized wine (cf. Athenaios 1.32 – 3) for which the vines even grew on the slopes of the mountains, and the so-called mastix, which was widely used throughout the Greek world as a drug, as a kind of 'chewing gum' and as a perfume (cf. Dioskurides 1.70.3). As at Korinth, some specialized manufacturers (e.g., producing ceramics for storage and transport), and some wood workers and furniture makers, also supported themselves, and consequently the islands' community, well beyond subsistence. But despite its affluence through trade Chios never became an important power. A member of the Delian League, the island had its own fleet, but when it tried to break away from Athens after the Sicilian disaster in 413, internal strife ensued. Chios also joined the Second Athenian League, and eventually developed a growing dependence on the Karian dynast Maussolos.

Even the three poleis on the largest of the Aegean islands, Rhodes (Ialysos in the north, Kamiros in the north-east, Lindos in the south-east), remained mainly self-sufficient farming communities surviving on the lands, and on fishing and hunting; individually, they were members of the Athenian-led Delian League. Near the end of the Peloponnesian War, in 408/7, they united forces in an anti-Athenian move, which led to a *synoikismos*, forming a new city, called Rhodos like the island, at its northernmost corner, and a new artificial harbour (Strabon 14.2.5). At the time, this was mainly used for trading some of the surplus agricultural goods; it was only after the Classical Age that Rhodes became one the most important trading harbours, dealing with exports from and imports to Hellenistic Egypt.

Like Rhodes, the Aegean islands of Samos, Lesbos, Kos and Naxos (the least famous for its wine among these islands) fall into the category discussed here, but having looked at communities on the Greek mainland and in the Aegean Sea, it remains in this section to single out one community in western Asia Minor which equally enjoyed easy access to the sea and medium size agricultural lands: Miletos. It had fertile, but – when compared to Athens – not abundant agricultural land; olive oil and wool (raw and manufactured into textiles) were produced in surplus. Most important, however, was the fact that the city boasted excellent access to the sea; Strabon (14.1.6) exclaims: 'The city has four harbours, each one of which is large enough for a fleet!' Like Korinth, Miletos engaged in trading both its own products and goods produced elsewhere, in its case in the Persian Empire. Increasingly under pressure from the Persians, it rose against them in the so-called Ionian

Revolt (499 – 494), but was conquered and destroyed, and its population deported to Persia or sold into slavery. The quality of the site's agricultural land, however, and especially the very easy access to the sea, led to a resettlement of Miletos soon afterwards, though during the Classical Age it never returned to its former affluence; rather than enjoying its former independence, it remained a prize in the conflicts between Athens, Sparta and Persia, and concentrated on farming and trading activities throughout the Classical Age. The silting up of the harbour led to a decline of the city in later times (cf. Kleiner 1968). A similar basic structure characterized other communities in Asia Minor as well, e.g., Erythrai, Klazomenai, Teos and Knidos, to name but the most obvious examples for this category.

It has become clear, then, that communities with easy access to the sea, but only mediocre agricultural lands, tended to concentrate on the benefits of their harbours, by selling some specialized agricultural products of which they generated a surplus, and otherwise concentrating on trading other people's goods. None of the communities in this type became strong enough to pursue a truly independent foreign policy; economic success was, however, continuously possible, especially when keeping a 'low profile' in what we might want to call the 'world conflicts' of the Classical Age. Significantly, most of these communities began to flourish when these conflicts had ceased, in Hellenistic and especially Roman times, and when easy access to the sea became the most important asset for a community which could safely import foodstuffs beyond what the mediocre lands in its possession could supply.

## 3   Little Agricultural Land – Easy Access to Sea

It is obvious that a community cannot grow on an insufficient agricultural base, unless food is imported; in order to guarantee such imports, something must be exported. While successful cases are infrequent in Aegean Greece, we can single out a few communities which supported themselves well beyond what subsistence farming on the small agricultural lands could provide – through specialization.

First, there are two identifiable cases where some natural wealth in metal and fine stone (so rare elsewhere in the 'Third Greece') encouraged such specialization. Siphnos, an island in the Cyclades archipelago, was among the richer communities in the Aegean world at the beginning of the Classical Age (cf. *Praktika* (etc.) 1998): not only was the centre of the polis adorned with prestigious architecture, but the community could also afford to build the famous 'Treasury of the Siphnians' at Delphi (cf. Daux and Hansen 1987). Herodotos (3.57.2) admired their prosperity:

> The Siphnians were very prosperous and the richest of the islanders, because of the gold and silver mines on the island. They were so wealthy that the treasure dedicated by them at Delphi, which is as rich as any there, was made from a tenth of their income; and they divided among themselves each year's income.

The wealth which was thus displayed could not be based on what the sea and the land provided in foodstuffs alone, but was owed to the exceptionally rich mines on the island where metal (iron, lead, gold and silver) was found, and marketed, via the good harbour, across the Greek world: 'Their island contained gold mines, and the god ordered them to pay a tithe of the revenues to Delphi' (Pausanias 10.11.2). An early member of the Delian League, Siphnos eventually suffered from the increasingly systematic exploitation of Athens' own silver-mines at Laureion, against which the island's exhausted mines could not compete. Pausanias goes on to say: 'so they built the treasury, and continued to pay the tithe until greed made them omit the tribute, when the sea flooded their mines and hid them from sight.' This decline of the island's economic base entailed a collapse of the community's stability: by the fourth century, Siphnos features in the extant sources mainly because of social unrest, expulsions and civil war, and all that Strabon (10.5.1), writing at the end of the first century BCE, says about Siphnos is that 'because of its worthlessness' it had inspired the proverbial 'Siphnian knuckle-bone' (parts of a slaughtered animal which were usually discarded).

Paros (cf. Carson & Clark 1980) on the other hand had just enough agricultural land to support its small community. The conspicuous wealth of this island, like that of Siphnos, however, was owed not to agriculture and fishing (and some ship-building) but to exporting a natural commodity: the famous Parian marble: 'On the island of Paros is the so-called "Parian stone", the best one for sculpting statues' (Strabon 10.5.7). The island's good harbours, its central location in the Aegean, and most of all the perfectly white and smooth quality of the stone made Parian marble a commodity which was sought after for art and architecture throughout the Greek world. If the extant sources illuminate what is typical, the islanders' interests focused on exports, and apart from some quarrels with neighbouring islands (notably Naxos), they made no serious attempt at an independent foreign policy: a member of the Delian League from its inception in 478/7, Paros remained untouched by the events of the Peloponnesian War; after Athens' defeat it fell under Spartan supremacy in 404, but joined the Second Delian League and later the Korinthian League.

While Siphnos and Paros exported their own natural commodities (metal or marble), other communities which had nothing comparable to export, and were equally disadvantaged by the small size and/or bad quality of their agricultural lands, supported themselves well beyond subsistence by trading *other* communities' goods. Unlike in the poleis we have surveyed in Section 2, the small agricultural base in these did not allow for a sizeable community to stay within the city and run a port of trade; rather, substantial numbers of the communities' members were highly mobile, or even altogether based abroad.

Many a Cretan community is probably most typical for this kind of trading, but an early example is Phokaia in western Asia Minor, the terminus of a road from Sardis through the Hermos valley to the Aegean coast. Its agricultural land is small, but its harbour is an ideal base for both trading and the more versatile pirate vessels (the difference remained blurred until well into the post-classical period). Before the Classical Age Phokaian boats sailed as far as Egypt and Spain, trading in silver and tin (the latter necessary for producing bronze) from even further beyond; Phokaia also became the mother city of several colonies in the western Mediterranean, the most famous of which was Massalia (Marseille; cf. Blistène et al. 1995). After Phokaia's conquest by the Persians around 500, however, most inhabitants left Asia Minor for Corsica, and later for Elea (Hyele) in southern Italy (like Phokaia a settlement with little hinterland but a good harbour). What remained of Phokaia joined the Delian League, but it never regained importance.

Similarly, Aigina relied on its fleet. The island itself lacks substantial agricultural lands and thus could not support more than a couple of thousand subsistence farmers: 'The country of Aigina is fertile at a depth below the level part, but rocky on the surface, and particularly barren' (Strabon 8.6.16). Aigina, however, supported probably ten times this figure of inhabitants in the Classical Age, and was rich enough to build a magnificent city and the famous temple of Aphaia (Walter 1993). As in the example of the Cretans or the Phokaians, the Aiginetans' excellent seamanship supported trade as far as Spain – and piracy. The historian Ephoros (*FGrHist* 70 F 176) is cited by Strabon (8.6.16) on the consequences:

> Ephoros says that silver was first coined in Aigina, by Pheidon; for the island, he adds, became a merchant centre, since, on account of the poverty of the soil, the people employed themselves at sea as merchants, and hence, he adds, petty wares were called 'Aiginetan merchandise'.

The decline of Phokaia, Samos and Miletos (see above) enabled further growth in Aigina's trade, gradually allowing the richer Aiginetans to live off the income from tolls and businesses without themselves having to brave the seas. The rise of Athens, however, led inevitably to conflict with Aigina, which was forced to become a member of the Delian League in 456. In 431 its population was expelled by the Athenians and Athenian cleruchs replaced the Aiginetan population, 'wiped off like butter from the eyes' (Plutarch *Perikles* 8.7). Only few of them survived and returned after the Peloponnesian War, but the island's economy never quite recovered, not least because of the competition of nearby Piraeus.

Rather than exporting or trading goods, the third kind of community with easy access to the sea but only small agricultural lands was one which, as it were, imported people, as a centre of pilgrimage. The prime example is of course Delphi (cf. Bommelaer 1991), which had no agricultural hinterland of its own to speak of, but was accessible from the Korinthian Gulf via the harbour of Kirrha/Krisa. After its conquest in the so-called First Sacred War in the early sixth century and throughout the Classical Age, Kirrha/Krisa belonged to the sanctuary, and its plain was to remain uncultivated (Aischines 3.108), leaving Delphi altogether without a sizeable agricultural base. The income which supported Delphi instead came from the pilgrims, and the participants and visitors at the Pythian Games which were celebrated every fourth year. After all (and despite the similar claim made for Athens in the quotation from Xenophon in Section 1), according to Strabon (9.3.6):

> Delphi is almost in the centre of Greece taken as a whole, between the country inside the Isthmus [viz. of Korinth] and that outside it; and it was also believed to be in the centre of the inhabited world, and people called it the navel of the earth. . . . Such being the advantages of the site of Delphi, the people easily came together there.

Repeatedly, Delphi had to fight for its independence from Phokis and Lokris; this eventually allowed Philip II to intervene and exert direct influence on the oracle.

Similarly, the oracle of Apollo on the tiny island of Delos, with no natural sources of fresh water, clearly could not survive on what the soil provided. In the Homeric *Hymn to Delian Apollo* (51 – 60), the god's mother, Demeter, says:

Delos, if you would be willing to be the abode of my son Phoibos Apollon and make him a rich temple; for no other will touch you, as you will find: and I think you will never be rich in oxen and sheep, nor bear vintage nor yet produce plants abundantly. But if you have the temple of far-shooting Apollon, all men will bring you hecatombs and gather here, and incessant savour of rich sacrifice will always arise, and you will feed those who dwell in you from the hand of strangers; for truly your own soil is not rich.

The island nevertheless very successfully supported its community through incoming pilgrims, however, and the yearly festival of the Ionians (ibid. 146 – 55):

In Delos do you [viz. Apollon] most delight your heart; for there the long robed Ionians gather in your honour with their children and shy wives: with boxing and dancing and song, mindful, they delight you so often as they hold their gathering. A man would say that they were deathless and unageing if he should then come upon the Ionians so met together. For he would see the graces of them all, and would be pleased in heart gazing at the men and well-girded women with their swift ships and great wealth.

As the focus of the Athenian League (originally referred to as the 'Delian League'), Delos housed the league's treasury from 478/7 until its transfer to Athens in 454. Delos continued to be a cult centre, living mainly off the income generated by the steady flow of visitors; later, this became the nucleus of the commercial centre and slave market into which the Romans converted the island in the second century (cf. Strabon 10.5.4; cf., in general, Bruneau & Ducat 1983).

Exporting natural riches like metal or marble, running long-distance trade for others or importing, as it were, pilgrims and visitors helped these communities to grow well beyond the meagre size of their agricultural land, by using the easy access to the sea they enjoyed. However, when their specialization failed (as at Siphnos, above) or foreign powers interfered (as at Phokaia or Aigina), these communities' existence was soon endangered.

## 4   Rich in Agricultural Land – Less than Easy Access to Sea

While the three types of communities in Aegean Greece discussed so far all enjoyed good harbours and made the best use of them to grow beyond a subsistence economy, the three types which we shall look at next are characterized by only limited access to the sea. This is rarely combined with plentiful agricultural lands, as such rich communities would usually strive to improve their access to the sea to win the chances described in Section 2. Sparta, however, for a long time spurned such options, but it falls outside the compass of this chapter.

## 5   Medium Size Agricultural Land – Less than Easy Access to Sea

A combination of only mediocre qualities in both access to the sea (usually employed for fishing or regional trade) and the size of cultivable soil is quite frequent in the

'Third Greece'. When speaking about such communities, some authors may tend to exaggerate: Isokrates, for example, contrasts the Thessalians with 'the Megarians, who had small and insignificant resources to begin with and who possess neither land nor harbours nor mines but are compelled to farm mere rocks' (8.116); and Strabon (9.1.8) says about Megara: 'The country of the Megarians . . . has rather poor soil, and the greater part of it is occupied by the Oneian Mountains.' During the Classical Age, Megara (cf. Legon 1981) indeed only possessed lands of limited usefulness (in the seventh century it had unsuccessfully fought Korinth for possession of the relatively fertile land between the two communities) and the harbour of Nisaia, which was too small (and too close to its more powerful neighbours Athens and Korinth) to attract sizeable trade. One way out of the dilemma was large-scale emigration, in Megara's case to colonies in the North-east (Chalkedon, Selymbria, Byzantion) and the West (Sicilian Megara Hyblaia). The Megarians who stayed specialized in non-agricultural activities like fishery and sea-salt production, animal husbandry (goats and sheep) and exporting salted or dried fish, raw wool or textiles, while importing grain from the Black Sea region or Egypt, mainly via the Piraeus at Athens, which smaller vessels could reach from Nisaia. In the Classical Age, Megara, while traditionally mainly on Sparta's side (though equally traditionally an enemy of Sparta's ally Korinth), had to rely on Athens economically, and was faced with increasing pressure from there (the 'Megarian decree', banning trade, was one of the major causes that led to the outbreak of the Peloponnesian War), eventually settling for a 'low profile' in foreign politics, while trying to make good in the shadow of mightier neighbours, 'continually in a state of peace' (Isokrates 8.117).

Similarly, Sikyon, the western neighbour of Korinth on the northern shore of the Peloponnese in the Korinthian Gulf, had fertile land only along the coast; this, however, is at most 5 km wide (plains further inland belonged to different communities), and, as at Megara, there is no harbour suitable for larger seagoing vessels (again, the success of Korinth could have prevented development). In what went beyond subsistence farming (and fishing) Sikyon generated income with metal work (including bronze sculpture), items for everyday use, and shoes which were sold elsewhere, as were certain types of fish. Sikyon's aristocratic oligarchy stayed on Sparta's side even after the latter's defeat at Leuktra in 371, but soon afterwards a tyrant, Euphron, took power and changed allegiances to Thebes; internal strife followed. After the Classical Age the city was relocated from the plain to a securer position further inland; it noticeably gained importance only after the Roman destruction of Korinth in 146 (cf. Griffin 1982).

Sikyon's western neighbours, the communities of Achaia (Aigeira, Aigion, Patrai, Dyme, etc.) on the south shore of the Korinthian Gulf, faced similar problems in transcending the level of mere subsistence. Some income was generated by ferry services along the shore and across to Delphi. Like the Megarians, the Achaians attempted to solve further problems by sending away colonists (to, e.g., Kroton and Sybaris); later, they were known to be selling their manpower as mercenaries. To counteract their individual lack of influence outside the region, the communities formed a federation, which first Athens, then after 417 Sparta, and after 367 Thebes tried to win over to their side; the federation was dissolved after 324 (it was later refounded and was to become an important regional power only in the third century; cf. Larsen 1968).

Communities with less than easy access to the sea and mediocre agricultural lands are known not only along the coastlines but also on islands. Karystos (cf. Wallace 1972) on Euboia, for example, which is separated from the remainder of the island by a difficult mountainous region and thus forms a kind of island of its own, had only limited agricultural land and a small harbour which mainly supported fishery: tuna and pickled fish from Karystos were sold as far away as Athens. It was the strategic position of Karystos, however, as a jumping-off point, as it were, for boats serving the western Aegean, which brought Karystos under Persian sway in 490. After the Persian Wars it fell under the direct control of Athens, first in the Delian League and then in the Second Athenian League, interrupted only by an interval of supporting Thebes. It was only later that the city was relocated closer to the shore and that its green marble began being exploited after construction of an artificial harbour, suitably called Marmarion (cf. *Corpus Inscriptionum Latinarum* (*CIL*) 14 14301) and in use well into imperial times (*CIL* 6 8486). Karystos thus survived on the model described in Section 3 above.

In sum, less than easy access to the sea and agricultural lands of mediocre quantity and quality made life rather difficult for the communities, especially when larger powers threatened to take advantage of their weakness (which in turn was frequently exacerbated by internal strife). Large-scale emigration as colonists or men's serving as mercenaries was one way out; forming larger units in federations was another option; but otherwise a 'low profile' in international conflicts allowed agricultural activities to secure subsistence and some specialized exports.

# 6   Little Agricultural Land – Less than Easy Access to Sea

Even smaller agricultural lands than at Karystos characterize the last type of communities with less than easy access to the sea. Halieis/Halike, for example, a community in the southern Argolid (in the bay of modern Portoheli), separated from the main plain of Argos by mountainous territory, was founded by exiled men from Tiryns in 479, when all better lands had already been occupied: it had only small plains and terraces, which could be used for producing grain and olives; the sea shore and the harbour, however, supported the production of sea-salt and fisheries, including the highly valued (because of its dye) purple snail; Halieis rose above mere subsistence mainly because of this luxury item, but only while the supply lasted; the place was apparently given up altogether soon after the Classical Age (cf. Pausanias 2.36.1).

With Karystos and Halieis, we have discussed coastal communities separated from the hinterland by mountains; rather than repeating similar observations for other marginal places of the Argolid like Hermione, Troizen and Methana, or similar ones in Aitolia or western Lokris, it must be stated that most of the smaller islands in the Aegean, and the smaller poleis on the Aegean islands (Keos had four of them, Lesbos four small ones in addition to Mytilene), fall into this category, usually surviving hardly beyond a subsistence level, unless fishing or transport (as for instance at Tenedos) generated some extra income. How fragile their subsistence remained is clearly shown by the fact that some of these settlements were simply abandoned during or soon after the Classical Age.

# 7    Rich in Agricultural Land – Difficult Access to Sea

In contrast, communities with plentiful agricultural lands but only difficult access to the sea were able to support relatively large populations and were typically ruled by a landowning aristocracy.

A prime example is Thessaly (cf. Stählin 1924; Philippson vol. 1 1950), where the 'plains are the middle parts, a country most blest, except so much of it as is subject to inundations by rivers' (Strabon 9.5.2). The plain was indeed watered throughout the year by the Peneios and its tributary, the river Epineus, and surrounded by high mountain ranges, the Olympos in the north, the Pindos in the west, and the Othrys, Ossa and Pelion in the south; the coastline towards the Aegean in the east provided some small and unimportant harbours only in the Pagasitic Gulf. While other parts of Greece were threatened by drought, parts of Thessaly were so well watered that they were swampy for at least part of the year. Most of the land, however, was used for producing grain (the climate with its searing-hot summers is unsuitable for the olive tree); animal husbandry included not only the usual goats and sheep, but cattle and especially horses, the pride of the landowning Thessalian aristocracy. Unlike other parts of Greece, Thessaly remained a rather loosely connected federation of communities, which through internal strife slowly disintegrated: in the fifth century, some aristocratic groups favoured a pro-Athenian policy, while others supported Sparta. The federation continued to be weak, and foreign powers attempted to put themselves at its centre. The most successful of them was Philip II of Macedon in 352, who eight years later reorganized the federation, and in 338 incorporated Thessaly as a distinct unit in the Korinthian League and thus his realm.

Further to the south, Boiotia (cf. Buck 1979) consisted mainly of fertile plains surrounded by mountainous territory, while the sea was difficult to reach from the interior. Like Thessaly, it had a good water supply – so abundant, in fact, that Lake Kopaïs rendered large areas marshy for most of the year and separated western Boiotia (around Chaironeia, Orchomenos and Lebadeia) from the larger eastern part (around Thebes), whose plains and rolling hills allowed not only for production of grain, olives and wine, fruit and vegetables, but also, like Thessaly, for raising cattle and horses (which, again, were sought after by the ruling aristocracy); beyond this part of Boiotia, there were the smaller but exceptionally fertile plains of Thespiai and Plataiai. Given the desirability of the land and its position as the only land-bridge between Attika and central Greece – Epameinondas is said to have called it 'a stage (*orchestra*) of war' (Plutarch *Moralia* 193e) – Boiotia formed a rather loose federation under Theban leadership, which had sided with the Persians in the Persian wars, but it lost its influence (or was even dissolved) for a generation after the battle of Plataiai in 479. Athens' conflict with Sparta lead to the latter's support of Thebes (in 421 Boiotia, though geographically well outside the Peloponnese, was a member of what we call the Peloponnesian League: Thuc. 5.17.2). In the course of the fourth century it rose to become an independent new power, joining the Second Athenian League, defeating Sparta at Leuktra in 371 and thus becoming a leading power for nearly a decade; eventually it was conquered by the Macedonians in 338, and Alexander the Great destroyed the city of Thebes three years later.

A similar combination of large and fertile lands and difficult access to the sea can be found in Elis in the north-western Peloponnese. Enclosed by high mountain ranges towards the north-east and east and elsewhere looking towards the sea, with hardly a useful natural harbour, Elis grew grain, vines and olives, flax and hemp, and raised cattle and horses, but the lack of easy lines of communication to the outside world forced Elis to be self-sufficient. Unlike the equally self-sufficient regions of Thessaly and Boiotia, however, it had little strategic importance and thus remained untouched by the Persian Wars and later events. Formally belonging to the Peloponnesian League, it sided first with Sparta, later with Athens; after the latter's defeat it was forced back into Sparta's league, becoming independent after Sparta's defeat at Leuktra in 371 – but, in sum, it remained a self-contained and self-sufficient marginal region throughout the Classical Age (cf. Rizakis 1991).

For further examples one could also look to Messenia, 'good for ploughing' (Tyrtaios F 5 West), in the south-western Peloponnese, whose fertile lands – cf. Euripides F 1083 Nauck$^2$ on a country full of 'beautiful fruit and good irrigation' – had been completely conquered by Sparta by the late seventh century to serve as an agricultural resource for the Spartans; central Euboia with Chalkis, and Eretria with the Lelantine plain; and Kolophon in western Asia Minor. It is not surprising that communities with difficult access to the sea and plentiful agricultural lands remained self-sufficient, and, unless they were of strategic relevance, remained very much marginal in the world as far as it is illuminated by our sources for the Classical Age.

# 8   Medium Size Agricultural Land – Difficult Access to Sea

Difficult access to the sea made communities which could not compensate for this problem with agricultural lands face more problems than others. Argos may serve as an example:

> The city of the Argives is for the most part situated in a plain, but it has for a citadel the place called Larisa...and near the city flows the Inachos, a torrential river that has its sources in Lyrkeios, the mountain that is near Kynouria in Arkadia.... 'Waterless Argos' [Homer *Iliad* 4.171] is also a fabrication, ...since the country lies in a hollow, and is traversed by rivers, and contains marshes and lakes. (Strabon 8.6.7)

As swamps separated the agriculturally useful land from the coastline (which has extended further southwards since antiquity) and Nauplia did not belong to the polis, access to the sea was difficult from Argos, but the land itself was fertile, and allowed to grow a balanced mix of grain, fruit, vegetables, olives and vines (obviously, today's main agricultural products of the plain, oranges and tangerines, were un-known in antiquity) providing subsistence for a sizeable community, but not being put to use for export. Argos in fact was so isolated that it missed the trend towards aristocracies or even democracies so prevalent in the century or so before the Classical Age and still had a monarchy in the early fifth century (cf. Wörrle 1964; Carlier 1984). Later in the Classical Age, Argos tended to side with Athens against Sparta, or follow a policy of neutrality.

While the sea was close, if difficult to reach, for Argos, most communities which fall into this category are situated inland, such as Mantineia and Tegea in Arkadia. The territories of these poleis, which had only been formed in the fifth century by combining several villages (*synoikismos*), are at a relatively high elevation (c. 800 m plus) and suffer cold winters. The land, however, is exceptionally fertile; the winter rains and spring runoff from the surrounding mountains provide good irrigation. This enabled the cultivation of grain, fruit and vegetables, and even some vines, for subsistence. The individual poleis remained independent. Mantineia took an anti-Spartan stance from 420 onwards. Tegea by contrast was compelled to be a member of Sparta's Peloponnesian League. Sparta forced Mantineia to be dissolved into villages in 385, but after Sparta's demise after the battle of Leuktra in 371 the city was refounded. A new pan-Arkadian federation and a new 'great city', Megale Polis (known today by its Latin name Megalopolis), were also created; the latter's territory was as large as that controlled by Argos (cf. Callmer 1943). It can be argued that this foundation was an innovative solution to the problems of the individual poleis' undersized lands in a part of the Greek world with very difficult access to the sea. To conclude with a quotation from Strabon (8.8.1):

> On account of the complete devastation of the country it would be inappropriate to speak at length about these tribes; for the cities, which in earlier times had become famous, were wiped out by the continuous wars, and the tillers of the soil have been disappearing even since the times when most of the cities were united into what was called the Great City. But now the Great City itself has suffered the fate described by the comic poet [Comica Adespota F 913 Kassel & Austin]: 'The Great City is a great desert'.

It has become clear, then, that difficult access to the sea, when combined with only mediocre agricultural land, enabled the support of self-sufficient communities, but did not allow for any kind of expansion; an innovative way to compensate for the problems was the formation of larger units, such as the Great City, although it did not enjoy permanent success.

# 9   Little Agricultural Land – Difficult Access to Sea

'There has never been a time when poverty was not a factor in the rearing (*syntrophos*) of the Greeks', said an advisor to the Persian king, according to Herodotos (7.102), to characterize the Persians' opponents, and with communities which were disadvantaged both in their access to the sea and in the size of the agriculturally useful land we finally look at poleis which fit Herodotos' description especially well.

Akarnania, for example, does indeed have a long coastline along the Ionian Sea, but could not make use of this, as the coast is too steep, or too flat, to allow for the building of useful harbours (apart from the small, and anyway more often than not independent, one at Oiniadai). Using the pockets of arable land behind that coast enabled subsistence farming, and the more mountainous hinterland could be used for transhumance, but the reputation of the Akarnanians as brigands (Thuc. 1.5.3) and mercenaries (Thuc. 7.31.5) demonstrates that living off the land was difficult enough. Given the roughness of the hinterland, many conflicts with neighbouring Aitolia and other communities (including even Athens) concerned access to the sea and especially possession of Oiniadai (see above). Apart from this harbour and Stratos as the central place, Akarnanian settlements are small, and widely dispersed. Probably influenced by the Arkadian example, and for similar reasons, the communities began to form a federation (*koinon*) in the fourth century (cf. Larsen 1968: 89 – 95), but Akarnania never became an affluent part of the 'Third Greece'.

Central Aitolia, to the east of Akarnania, represents an equally mountainous region in central Greece: while it is rich in forests, there are only small pockets of arable land. Apart from hunting (and brigandage), transhumance was one of the few ways of avoiding dire poverty. Settlements were few and small; the Aitolians were regarded as uncivilized until well into the Classical Age. The only coherent fertile patch, near Thermos by Lake Trichonis, served as winter quarters for the flocks. In the late fifth century Aitolia (as did other regions) reorganized itself as a federation (*koinon*) with Thermos as its cultic and political centre. The federation changed sides, first from Sparta to Thebes, and eventually it sided with Philip II; only then did it succeed in improving its access to the sea by conquering Oiniadai in 330 (Diodoros 18.8.6).

Further to the east, Phokis – having lost its only (small) harbour at Kirrha/Krisa to Delphi in the sixth century (above, Section 3) – has to contend with a very mountainous terrain and a harsh climate. Pockets of arable land and some olive cultivation, using the forests for hunting and cutting wood, and transhumance characterize the region. Not only the areas suitable for transhumance existence in summer but also their strategic importance (Phokis controls the passages from Boiotia to Eastern Lokris and on towards Thermopylai) joined the nearly two dozen small poleis of Phokis in a federation to ensure mutual military support; the league was repeatedly under pressure from Thessaly and Boiotia, but also from the Delphic Amphiktyony. A successful attack on the wealthy sanctuary in 356 allowed the Phokians to become, as it were, their own mercenaries, who for a decade fought against neighbouring Thessaly, and Macedonia. The defeat in the so-called Third Sacred War in 346, however, led to the destruction of the settlements, and opened up a route for the Macedonian control of Greece, leading to the victory achieved by Philip II of Macedon at Chaironeia in 338.

Difficult access to the sea and only undersized agricultural lands allowed merely for the bare subsistence of small self-sufficient communities, which supplemented their income by brigandage or as mercenaries. Unless access to the sea was improved (as with the conquest of Oiniadai), or federations were formed, there was little chance of improving, let alone expanding, the communities, some of which simply had to be abandoned altogether.

# Conclusion

Our attempt at a classification of the 'Third Greece beyond Athens and Sparta' around the Aegean Sea, which necessarily had to be based on very unbalanced evidence, has highlighted the ease of access to the sea, and the quantity and quality of agriculturally useful land, as relevant features of that (in many ways quite uniform) Greek world. These were the two most important factors for the challenges faced by individual communities and their chances of survival. A plenty of agricultural lands – so characteristic of Athens and (especially after the conquest of Messenia) Sparta – was also enjoyed by Thessaly, Boiotia and Elis, central Euboia,

Kolophon and other communities, notably also beyond Aegean Greece in the so-called colonies (*apoikiai*). Unless combined with quite easy access to the sea (as especially at Athens), or in a strategically important position, these communities remained merely self-sufficient. Greater difficulties were faced by poleis with only mediocre agricultural lands, which tried to solve some of their problems of sustaining their members by sending some of them away, as colonists, mercenaries or traders – which, however, required good or at least less than difficult access to the sea. Another solution, and indeed the only one when access to the sea was difficult, was the forming of federations, or even newly founded cities (*synoikismos*) combining the lands of several communities to gain a 'critical mass', as it were; the only and inevitable alternative was isolation. Finally, lack of agricultural lands could only be compensated for if easy access to the sea permitted the exploitation and export of valuable natural resources, long-distance trade, or the 'import', as it were, of pilgrims. Failing this, subsistence was fragile, and even attempts at forming federations usually could not prevent such communities with little land and at best difficult access to the sea from justifying – especially for the 'Third Greece' – Herodotos' astute observation (7.102): 'There has never been a time when poverty was not a factor in the rearing (*syntrophos*) of the Greeks.'

## Further reading and bibliography

For relevant inscriptions see the selections by M&L, R&O, Fornara, and Harding.

### Sites

Brodersen, K. (ed.) (1999) *Antike Stätten am Mittelmeer: Metzler-Lexikon* (Stuttgart: Metzler) – Survey of archaeological sites of the Mediterranean, with bibliographies

Lauffer, S. (ed.) (1989) *Griechenland: Lexikon der historischen Stätten; von den Anfängen bis zur Gegenwart* (Munich: Beck) – Excellent individual entries for ancient sites within the borders of today's Greek state

Stillwell, R., W. L. MacDonald, M. Holland McAllister (eds) (1976) *The Princeton encyclopedia of classical sites* (Princeton: Princeton University Press) – Also available on-line; access: www.perseus.tufts.edu/cgi-bin/ptext?doc=Perseus% 3Atext%3A1999.04.0006

Talbert, R. J. A. (ed.) (2000) *Barrington atlas of the Greek and Roman world* (accompanied by map-by-map directory) (Princeton: Princeton University Press) – Up-to-date atlas, with invaluable gazetteer providing full bibliography on the classical sites

### General studies

Gehrke, H.-J. (1986) *Jenseits von Athen und Sparta: Das Dritte Griechenland und seine Staatenwelt* (Munich: Beck) – Systematic work exploring the 'Third Greece', i.e., the Aegean world 'beyond Athens and Sparta'

Philippson, A. (1950 – 59) *Die griechischen Landschaften: Eine Landeskunde* (ed. E. Kirsten) (Frankfurt: Klostermann)

## Studies on individual regions discussed in this chapter (beyond the reference works quoted)

Baltrusch, E. (1994) *Symmachie und Spondai: Untersuchungen zum griechischen Völkerrecht der archaischen und klassischen Zeit (8. – 5. Jahrhundert v. Chr.)* (Berlin: de Gruyter) (Untersuchungen zur antiken Literatur und Geschichte 43)

Blistène, B., et al. (1995) *Phocée et la fondation de Marseille* (Marseille: Musées de Marseille)

Bommelaer, J.-F. (1991) *Guide de Delphes: le site* (Paris: de Boccard) (Sites et monuments 7)

Bruneau, P., & J. Ducat (1983) *Guide de Délos* (Paris: de Boccard ³1983) (Sites et monuments 1)

Buck, R.J. (1979) *A history of Boeotia* (Edmonton: University of Alberta Press)

Buckler, J. (2003) *Aegean Greece in the fourth century* BC (Leiden: Brill)

Callmer, J. A. C. (1943) *Studien zur Geschichte Arkadiens bis zur Gründung des arkadischen Bundes* (Lund: Gleerup)

Cargill, J. (1981) *The second Athenian league: empire or free alliance?* (Berkeley: University of California Press)

Carson, J., & J. Clark (1980) *Paros* (German trans. Jacobs, J., & J. Maus) (Athens: Lycabettus ³1980)

Carlier, P. (1984) *La royauté en Grèce avant Alexandre* (Strasbourg: A.E.C.R. [Association pour l'étude de la civilisation romane]) (Etudes et travaux: publiés par le Groupe de recherche d'histoire romaine de l'Université des sciences humaines de Strasbourg 6)

Daux, G., & E. Hansen (1987) *Fouilles de Delphes*, tome 2: *Le trésor de Siphnos*, 2 vols (Paris: de Boccard)

Figueira, T. J. (1981) *Aegina: society and politics* (New York: Arno) (Monographs in Classical Studies)

Griffin, A. (1982) *Sikyon* (Oxford: Clarendon) (Oxford Classical and Philosophical Monographs)

Kleiner, G. (1968) *Die Ruinen von Milet* (Berlin: de Gruyter)

Larsen, J. O. A. (1968) *Greek federal states: their institutions and history* (Oxford: Clarendon)

Legon, R. P. (1981) *Megara: the political history of a Greek city-state to 336* B.C. (Ithaca NY: Cornell University Press)

Meiggs, R. (1979) *The Athenian empire* (repr. with corrections) (Oxford: Clarendon)

Praktika A. *Diethnous Siphnaikou Symposiou: Siphnos, 25 – 28 Iouniou 1998/Proceedings of the First International Siphnean Symposium* (Athens: Hetaireia Siphnaïkon Meleton 1998)

Rizakis, A. D. (ed.) (1991) *Archaia Achaïa kai Eleia: anakoinoseis kata to proto diethnes symposio, Athena, 19 – 21 maïou 1989* (Athens: Kentron Hellenikes kai Romaïkes Archaiotetos, Ethnikon Hidryma Ereunon) (Kentron Hellenikes kai Romaïkes Archaiotetos, Meletemata 13)

Salmon, J. B. (1984) *Wealthy Corinth: a history of the city to 338* BC (Oxford: Clarendon)

Stählin, F. (1924) *Das hellenische Thessalien: Landeskundliche und geschichtliche Beschreibung Thessaliens in der hellenischen und römischen Zeit* (Stuttgart: Engelhorn)

Tomlinson, R. A. (1972) *Argos and the Argolid: from the end of the Bronze Age to the Roman occupation* (London: Routledge & Kegan Paul) (States and Cities of Ancient Greece)

Wallace, M. B. (1972) 'The history of Karystos from the sixth to the fourth centuries B.C.' (unpublished PhD thesis University of Toronto)

Walter, H. (1993) *Ägina: Die archäologische Geschichte einer griechischen Insel* (Munich: Deutscher Kunstverlag)

Wickert, K. (1961) 'Der Peloponnesische Bund von seiner Entstehung bis zum Ende des archidamischen Krieges' (PhD thesis University of Erlangen-Nürnberg)

Wörrle, M. (1964) 'Untersuchungen zur Verfassungsgeschichte von Argos im 5. Jahrhundert vor Christus' (PhD thesis University of Erlangen-Nürnberg)

CHAPTER SEVEN

# The Central and Northern Balkan Peninsula

*Zofia Halina Archibald*

## 1  Travelling to the North

If we, readers of the early twenty-first century, could be transported backwards in time to southern Europe in the 470s, how might the vast block of land between the Adriatic and Black Seas have looked to a visitor who had just left Delphi, for instance? What might he (it would inevitably have been a he) have thought as he travelled northwards, in the direction of the Dalmatian coast, or eastwards, to the Thermaic Gulf and beyond, as far as the Black Sea? We divide the region up using maps, but our notional traveller would have had no map in his head. There were no maps of the Balkans, no systematic knowledge; only better-known and more obscure areas. So he would have configured distances in terms of journey days from his point of reference.

This is what the historian Thucydides does in his summary of the Odrysian kingdom of Thrace, when he estimates the distance from Abdera (at the mouth of the River Nestos, on the north Aegean coast), skirting the shoreline to the mouth of the Danube, as being four days and nights with a following wind, while an overland journey from Abdera to the Danube would have taken eleven days by the shortest route (2.97.1–2). Presumably he means a journey at speed on foot, but on horseback would have been preferable. Alexander the Great took ten days to reach the Haimos range in spring 335 (Arrian *Anabasis* 1.1.5), using seasoned troops, but in considerable numbers. The fourth-century historian Theopompos apparently calculated that it would take thirty days to walk the length of Illyrian country; that is, from the Keraunian Mountains that shield the Gulf of Orikos, north of the island of Kerkyra, as far as the head of the Adriatic (Strabon 7.5.9 = *FGrHist* 115 F 129). The implication is that while most people might travel along the sea route, others who had business in the interior would want to know about inland traffic. The strategic importance of roads was appreciated not just for military purposes (Thuc. 2.98.1: the Odrysian king Sitalkes; 2.100.1–2: Archelaos of Macedon as road builders), but for commercial ones as well (see the waiver of road tolls on the Pistiros inscription: Velkov & Domaradzka 1994; Chankowski & Domaradzka 1999).

The geographical space under consideration here has no boundaries as such. So the scope of this chapter is quite arbitrary. Its limits are the confines created by contemporary written sources, the extended narrative histories of Herodotos and Thucydides, fragments of other fifth- and fourth-century writers (most but not all of whom lived and worked in Athens), passages in some later Greek and Latin authors, and a small, but significant, and growing, body of inscriptions in Greek. The framework created by these sources does not fully reflect the activities of travellers – sailors, merchants, adventurers, but also ambassadors, even suitors, whose paths, whilst being silent to us, are nevertheless charted by various material and abstract symptoms: presents exchanged (Andronicos 1984: 180–6; Rolle 1985: 485–7; Bouzek & Ondrejová 1987: 91–2; Vasić 1993: 1683, 1687–8; Archibald 1998: 85, and chapters 7, 11); votives deposited in local sanctuaries (Figure 7.1) (Hammond 1967: 428–43; Dakaris 1971; Tsetskhladze 1998b: 53; Domaradzka 2002); the names of distant but important friends commemorated in those of the next generation (Herman 1987: 31–4).

The material culture of the regions under consideration is suffused with elements, ideas and actual imported objects familiar from southern Greece and the Aegean, as well as items that are related to the latter, but differ in varying respects from them. It is clear that we are dealing with a number of different phenomena, across time and space, only some of which are as yet apparent to the modern observer. The archaeology of Greece has been investigated far more intensively and systematically than the material remains of neighbouring areas to the north. So comparison with Greece is an

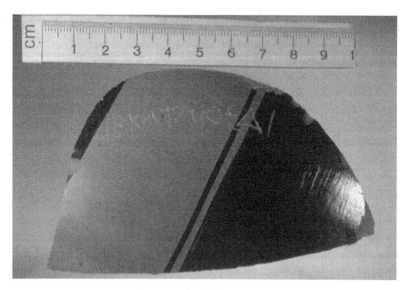

**Figure 7.1**  Vetren-Pistiros, Thrace (central Bulgaria): sherd of a Panathenaic amphora wall inscribed 'Hekataios Di' (Hekataios, to Zeus), found in a pit in the northern part of the site. Archaeological Museum, Septemvri, API 215; copyright: Z. H. Archibald.

understandable starting point for investigating these cultures. All the regions encom-passed here are at an early stage of archaeological investigation compared with the Aegean as a whole. The land area occupied by the Illyrians, Macedonians, Thracians and Scythians, taking into account only those areas that writers knew something about, is, on a conservative estimate, approximately three times the size of the Greek-speaking Aegean world. Yet research is on a far smaller scale, and far fewer sites are currently being investigated per annum. Analytical techniques, scientific procedures, newer methods of spatial survey have been introduced much more recently than in central and southern Greece. Current assessments of these northern regions are accordingly necessarily provisional. New data, even from a single source, can have considerable impact on the way we interpret the record.

In some cases what we can detect are symptoms of physical exchange, especially the movement of organic produce, detectable from the inorganic containers that are left behind, particularly large storage jars for wine and oil (amphorae), fine ceramic perfume flasks and toilet boxes, as well as other types of inorganic containers (table and kitchenware), glass, marble, ceramic roof tiles, and finished objects in both precious metals (mainly tableware and jewellery) and base metals (bronze and iron tools and weaponry). The physical exchange of commodities did not consist simply of moving consignments from a production centre in place *a* to a recipient in place *b*. Nor was the traffic moving in one direction only, or in a simple reciprocal manner. Different rules applied to different commodities. We have as yet only rudimentary notions of how demand and supply were managed, and a great deal would have depended on the organization of transport. Shipwrecks suggest that many different commodities would have travelled together by sea and by river (Stanimirov 2003). This makes it likely that much of the material that did travel was, in effect, 'down the line' traffic, commodities manufactured or containers filled elsewhere, travelling with local shippers or carriers, rather than with producers or merchants from source (cf. Horden & Purcell 2000: 137–43, 149–52; cf. below, Chapter 14). Athenian Red Figure and black gloss tableware is ubiquitous in larger settlements throughout the whole northern region, from the second half of the fifth century to the end of the fourth century. But it is equally ubiquitous in similarly sized sites on much of the Greek mainland, throughout the Aegean, and is very widely disseminated in both the eastern and western Mediterranean. These exceptional fabrics generally appear as a variable component of the ceramic repertoire in any northern town or large village location, alongside locally made or regional household pots (Figure 7.2). Chian and Thasian amphorae are found in substantial quantities in lower Macedonia, Thrace and Scythia during the fifth and fourth centuries, dominating the bulk traffic in liquids until they were superseded by Rhodian, Koan and also Pontic, such as Herakleian, production centres, beginning in the final third of the fourth century but especially during the third century (Garlan 1999). Chian and Thasian wine jars were equally well known along the Ionian coast of Epeiros and Illyria. Theopompos apparently thought that a subterranean passage must link the Adriatic and Aegean seas (Strabon 7.5.9 = *FGrHist* 115 F 129 found this hard to believe). The traffic in people – mercenary soldiers, craftsmen, especially masons and metalsmiths, painters, dyers, entertainers (musicians and poets), is harder to detect, though echoes in Greek literature abound (*Suda* E 3695 Adler; Ailianos *Varia Historia* 2.21, 13.4: Euripides, Agathon; Ailianos *Varia Historia* 14.17: Zeuxis at the court of Archelaos of

**Figure 7.2** Selection of locally made, regional, and imported Aegean ceramics excavated from a single late fourth- to early third-century BCE context at Vetren-Pistiros, Thrace (central Bulgaria). Adjiyska Vodenitsa, D19 [1031]; copyright: Z. H. Archibald.

Macedon; Athenaios 8.345D: epic writer Choirilos of Samos; Plutarch *Moralia* 177b: Timotheos of Miletos, writer of choral poetry; Athenaios 4.131B–C: entertainers at the wedding of Iphikrates to king Kotys I's daughter).

## Different norms

Most of the ancient writers who give voice to this evidence of interaction, mainly between Aegean Greeks and various natives of the north, approached this topic at a high level of abstraction. Relations are couched in a language and a mythology of difference – different cultural norms, different approaches and expectations, different values. Different norms constituted significant intellectual challenges, and it should come as no surprise to find that writers and poets were preoccupied with questions of norm and variety (Hartog 1988). But such abstract preoccupations are no guide to how individuals and groups succeeded in negotiating the social and commercial links that are manifested in the material and cultural evidence. The taste, even demand, for certain kinds of products of Mediterranean origin in these northern regions shows a considerable openness to these products at a local level. It would be inaccurate to suggest that such taste was widespread. Incoming commodities and luxury goods (originating either in the Aegean or in Continental locations) may well have been socially manipulated by politically astute or powerful individuals. But access to such commodities was not controlled or monopolized, at least not in those areas closer to the coast where systematic fieldwork has taken place over many years. In the rural hinterland of the great waterways that connected the Continental landmasses to the Black Sea, there are traces of communities whose material remains make it hard to decide whether they were immigrant Greeks or indigenous natives (Maslennikov 2001 on the eastern Crimean peninsula; Bylkova 2000 on the lower Dnieper estuary; Okhotnikov 2001 on the lower Dniester).

## *Uncharted territory*

Beyond this peripheral zone, accessible with comparative ease to Mediterranean travellers, lay the Continent of Europe proper. Connections between these much more distant regions and the Mediterranean are still very poorly understood, and tend to be seen through the eyes of a Strabon (7.2.4), that is, agnostically. But although Classical writers virtually ignore the Continent of Europe beyond the Danube, archaeological evidence reflects significant social and technological inter-changes between the Mediterranean coastal zone and the Continental interior (Kristiansen 1998, chapters 6 and 7; Bouzek 1997: 108, 110–23, 200–14, 232–51). These contacts were not restricted to occasional high-level embassies, accompanied by ostentatious presents, although such formal meetings are very likely to have taken place. The variety and scope of attested connections indicates numerous less formal contacts, in many separate regions. Perhaps the most visible symptom of such informal connections is the spread of a hard, often grey ceramic fabric made on the fast potter's wheel. Only a few decades ago it was assumed that this technological development became established, at a range of key centres, in the sixth century or thereabouts (Alexandrescu 1977). But new evidence is consistently pushing this fundamental transformation back into the first half of the first millennium BCE (Nikov 1999; Dordević-Bogdanović 1999).

Long-distance traffic was, for the most part, sea-borne. The logical way for anyone to travel was by sea. Much of the evidence at our disposal, whether written or archaeological, confirms the vitality of sea-borne relations, and explains the pattern of intensive coastal settlement. The majority of known ancient sites in the north are located on coastal plains or near the estuaries of rivers. There is an ecological explanation for this pattern. The alluvial soils that cover large parts of the coastline around the Balkan peninsula provide good conditions for arable farming. It would be surprising not to find concentrations of population within such areas. But what we

**Figure 7.3** Dodona, Epeiros: the sanctuary of Zeus (copyright: C.B. Mee).

know of prehistoric settlement patterns in the Balkans shows that the ancestors of the Illyrians, Macedonians, Thracians and their neighbours exploited a wide variety of ecological niches deep into the interior of this landmass (Hammond 1967: 476–83, 487–524; Wilkes 1992, 91–104, 126–36; Andrea 1993 with earlier bibliography; Tasić 1999 and other contributions to the same volume). So our notional visitor may have had good reasons for travelling overland, as well as along the coast.

Most of the evidence for inland exchanges is material. Traces of overland human traffic are much rarer in the written sources than reports of maritime transport. Strabon found an account, in the fourth century BCE *Histories* of Ephoros, of how the people of Boiotia were obliged by an oracle to steal a bronze tripod annually, from a local sanctuary, and convey it to the shrine of Zeus at Dodona in Epeiros (Figure 7.3) (*FGrHist* 70 F 119; Strabon 9.2.4, p. 401). This bizarre tale was intended to explain a well-established custom linking the Boiotians with Dodona (Roesch 1987). Other anecdotes of this kind, when viewed alongside the demonstrable evidence from inscriptions (mainly third- and second-century), show that we should not underestimate the capacity and determination of those who chose, for whatever reason, to travel by road, and to engage with communities at some distance from the coastline. This applies as much to traffic across the Pindos Mountains (cf. Homer *Iliad* 2.748–50; 16.233), or from Macedonia and Thrace as far as the Danube, as it does to traffic between the Epeirotes and Central Greece.

## Witnesses and guides

The principal historians, travel writers and geographers of Classical antiquity knew far less about inland areas than they did about the coasts. The tendency of Hellenistic and Roman geographers was to concentrate on the theatres of grand political affairs, which increasingly became congruent with Roman imperial expansion. Regions, such as the Balkans, that were seen by such writers as playing a lesser part in the imperial project attracted less scholarly attention and less active research. As a result, general knowledge about these areas diminished. Our own perception of the Balkans as a geographical region of antiquity is hampered by the absence of a sustained narrative work concentrating on this area. No surviving prose work takes the Balkan interior as its focus. Some sections are missing from Book 7 of Strabon's *Geography*, which approximates most closely to a general account of the peninsula. Strabon's work is partly structured along the lines of practical travel guides, *periploi* or 'sailings around', and thus provides far more information about harbours, headlands and coasts than about inland areas. But his interest in economic resources (as well as material that would contribute to a good read) makes the absence of sections that might have dealt with such matters a serious loss. The historical excerpts from various writers that have survived constitute a mosaic whose pieces can be aligned in different ways. It is hard to give structure to the history of this region, or even to find suitable cues for investigation. Interpretations of the Balkan landmass and its peoples have been even more prone to changing styles and fashions in the hands of individual historians than have other parts of the Aegean and adjacent areas. As the quantity and range of archaeological evidence have increased over the last half century, more coherent arguments have emerged, not just about what gave the region its distinctive characteristics, but about what these areas had in common with their more southerly neighbours.

Historians are more cautious now than they once were about the scientific or objective knowledge to be derived from early narrative texts. Whereas the texts of the founding fathers of Greek history used to be examined according to various criteria of veracity, what contemporary readers are most anxious to discover are the assumptions and preoccupations of the authors, assumptions that shaped the thrust as well as the content of their narratives. Our own concepts of factual knowledge rely on a broad appreciation of what is known and what can be known about other people and places. Fifth-century writers were surrounded by personal and collective stories that incorporated various experiences, as well as what we might call externally referenced facts. But there was no epistemological framework by reference to which systematic information could be evaluated. These stories to some extent floated freely, except insofar as they could be confronted by other stories (esp. Luraghi 2001). Nor should we assume that authors were necessarily anxious to convey the sort of information that we would like to have. Thucydides disciplined his account of the Peloponnesian War with a variety of devices. It would be naïve to imagine that he gives anything close to a comprehensive picture. This was not his intention. The absence of key topics from his account, and the structure of certain episodes, suggest that in some respects he was being economical with the range of facts at his disposal (Badian 1993). Herodotos' digressions on Scythia and Thrace are highly selective, and focus on what he thought to be particular differences between them and communities with which he was more familiar. The effect of his narrative is to render the customs and practices of these peoples even more bizarre and exotic than they might otherwise have appeared to passing travellers. Details were chosen for their specific narrative possibilities. Above all, Herodotos did not try to summarize cumulative data.

What he has to say about the Danube reveals both the strengths and weaknesses of his approach in terms of conveying objective information (cf. Murray 2001: 321):

> The Istros (Danube) river arises among the Celts and the polis of Pyrene, cutting Europe across the middle. The Celts are to be found beyond the Pillars of Herakles (as the Greeks called the Straits of Gibraltar) and are neighbours of the Kynetes, who live furthest to the west of any Europeans. The Istros flows through the whole of Europe as far as the Black Sea, near Histria, which was settled by Milesians. For the Istros flows through inhabited country, familiar to many people. (Hdt. 2.33.3)

The information about Histria is unexceptionable, as is the idea that the Danube flows west–east across Europe. But 'Pyrene' is surely a transformation of the Pyrenees, just as 'Carpis' (Carpathians?) and 'Alpis' (Alps?) are taken to be tributaries of the Danube flowing northwards, although 'beyond the Umbrians' (4.49.2) is not how we would express the sources of the Danube. (Two rivers, the Brigach and the Breg, unite to form the upper Danube not far from the Swiss and French borders, in Donaueschingen in south-western Germany.) Nor do we get to hear more than this tantalizing but vague snippet about undifferentiated 'Celts'. Geographical and ethnic imprecision is understandable. The spatial relationships of peoples and places in continental areas were then, and continued to be in later times, rather sketchy. Nevertheless, Herodotos' bold, if broad-brush, speculations do not invalidate other kinds of information. On the contrary, Herodotos' descriptions of customary practices, particularly burials, in Thrace as well as Scythia have been abundantly confirmed, though in more varied forms than he indicates. The historian was not being fanciful and did not invent imaginary elements in these particular descriptions of distant regions. But there is a great deal of evidence, known from archaeological sources, that he omits, or side-steps (see Rolle et al. 1998; Reeder 1999; Archibald 1998: 151–76). Provided that we do not expect a one-to-one relationship between Herodotos' story and the material evidence to which it relates, we are less likely to confuse his narrative vision with historical communities.

Since narrative texts are frequently used as the structural cores around which the history is shaped, it is by no means easy to detect whether texts can be downright misleading. Yet the very paucity of such material with regard to our northern regions demands caution. A key example of misleading rhetoric is the passage in a speech attributed to Alexander the Great at Opis, near the River Tigris, during the summer of 324, in which the king claims that his father Philip exchanged the Macedonians' skin garments for cloaks, made them city dwellers, and established order on the basis of good laws and customs (Arrian *Anabasis* 7.9.2; Hatzopoulos 1996: vol. 1 49–50, 431–4, 479–82). Notwithstanding the rhetorical context as well as the late authorship of the passage (whatever its relationship to earlier biographical literature), it has exerted a disproportionate influence on historians, generating the impression that law-making and urban development in general were products of recent administrative changes, rather than of long-term socio-political evolution, as discussed below. Historians exploring these subjects should not merely be encouraged to look at other sources of information. Without the assistance of epigraphy and material remains, the structure and characteristics of northern societies would remain largely opaque.

# 2 Regional Identities

Our written sources refer to the various peoples inhabiting the Balkans with collective nouns – Chaonians, Dardanians, Macedonians, Paionians and the like – that sound much like the categories these same sources use for more familiar communities (Athenians, Korinthians). But whereas we have a fair idea of what it meant to be an Athenian, or a Spartan, or a Boiotian, in the fifth and fourth centuries, it is still difficult to picture what it felt like to be a Lynkestian, or an Odrysian, or a Royal Scythian. Not only are these groups difficult to locate on a map with any precision, but it is not always clear when, or whether, we are dealing with local communities, or with larger entities. Our principal sources talk about Macedonians, Thracians or Illyrians as though these were clear, well-defined categories. In fact, these large collectives are rather elusive groupings. Detailed study of place- and personal names has revealed interesting patterns of concentration or preference, but has not furnished the evidence of well-defined cultural distinctions that our authors have led us to anticipate (see, e.g., the contributions to Cabanes 1993b; Wilkes 1992: 67–87; *SEG* 45 696). Thus, for example, there is no scholarly agreement about the specific relationship between the language spoken by Macedonians and Aeolic or West Greek, or Illyrian, although they were indubitably closely related (Hall 2001 for a summary of the evidence; Hatzopoulos 2000). Similarly, there is uncertainty about the relative admixture of Greek and Illyrian elements in Epeiros and the north-west Balkans, although there were more Greek-speakers in Epeiros and southern Illyria, and more Illyrian-speakers further north. These uncertainties are not just a reflection of lacunose evidence, although it would undoubtedly be easier to make sense of such linguistic inter-relationships if a reasonable range of vocabulary and grammatical examples were available to us. They demonstrate, on the one hand, the relative imprecision of 'ethnic' groupings as such, and, on the other, the comparative fluidity and dynamism between members of different 'ethnic' categories.

I use the term 'ethnic' advisedly, because the Greek word *ethnos* lacked many of the connotations that our word 'ethnicity' holds (Morgan 2003: 10–18). Collective identities depend on a set of collective ideas that can be communicated and renewed at regular intervals and are maintained and invigorated by various mutual institutions. The *ethne* reported in our sources were sometimes small, nucleated groups, such as those in the Chalkidike peninsula (e.g., Bottiaioi), but elsewhere the term is applied to much larger and more diffuse entities, apparently disseminated over several hundred kilometres or more – the Illyrians, Thracians, Macedonians or Scythians. The Scythians were less like the others, insofar as many Scythian communities continued to be nomadic or semi-nomadic throughout the fifth and fourth centuries, even though durable settlements had existed for many centuries in the grass and forest steppe regions, as well as closer to the coastlines. The settled character of Scythian culture (Kovpanenko et al. 1989) and the importance of extractive and production activities (Rolle 1989 and fig. 7 in Rolle) have been seriously under-appreciated, because of the preoccupation with nomadic rather than sedentary themes, as well as the merging of distinctive communities under an all-embracing pan-Scythian label (Yablonsky 2000; Bashilov & Yablonsky 2000).

The larger, more diffuse kinds of *ethne* referred to by ancient writers were unlike modern nations (leave alone nation states). States – complex socio-political entities composed of many different nucleated or extended communities – were beginning to emerge in the fifth century. The larger ones were often organized as kingdoms, notably those of the Argead dynasty in Macedonia, the Molossian house in Epeiros, and the Odrysian dynasty in Thrace. The 'Royal' Scythians held a similar kind of power over settled and nomadic communities in the grass steppe regions of Ukraine and south Russia. The power holders of the steppe regions, together with the native princes of Thrace, provided a model for the dynastic rulers of the Bosporan kingdom based in the Crimean peninsula, who were styled *archontes* (chief magistrates) in a civic Greek milieu, and *basileis* (kings) among the purely native communities of the Taman peninsula and around the Sea of Azov (Hind 1994: 496–7).

## Emergent powers

The 470s to 450s were a period of significant political transformation in areas that had been occupied by Persian troops, or that had been restricted in one way or another by the Persian occupation. Changes in political organization and territorial administration are particularly apparent in Macedonia and Thrace south of the Balkans. The withdrawal of imperial troops created new opportunities for political leaders who could offer protection against Persian, or indeed other, opportunistic reprisals. The uncertainties of the wider political situation in the northern Aegean were undoubtedly one of the factors that enabled Alexander I of Macedon to expand beyond the modest realm in Lower Macedonia that he had inherited from his forebears, and that had constituted the Argead kingdom for a century or more. This included the slopes of Mount Bermion and the Pierian range, either side of the River Haliakmon, the low-lying regions of Bottiaia and Pieria, as far as the River Axios in the east, and the hill country of Almopia in the north. Alexander acquired a large slab of territory east of the River Loudias after the Persian withdrawal, extending into the western half of the Chalkidic peninsula (Hatzopoulos 1996: vol. 1 171–9). Similarly, the Odrysian Teres made the traditional lands of his family in the middle reaches of the River Hebros (modern Maritsa) the nucleus of a much larger territory, which was consolidated by his son, Sitalkes, probably from the 440s onwards. Under Sitalkes the Odrysian kingdom extended from the hinterland of the Aegean coast around Abdera in the south to the Balkan mountains and the Danube estuary in the north (Thuc. 2.97.1; Archibald 1998: 93–125). The power of the Molossian dynasty of Epeiros is more difficult to specify in the fifth than in the early fourth century, when we find Molossian rulers negotiating with neighbouring regional communities (Illyrians), cities and sanctuaries of the mainland (notably Athens, Epidauros, Delphi) and beyond (Syracuse) (Cabanes 1988; 1996; 1999a; Davies 2000). The degree of organizational momentum implied by such negotiations must have evolved during the second half of the fifth century at least. By c. 400 the Molossoi had extended their control over the most important sanctuary in the north-western part of the Greek peninsula, that of Zeus at Dodona, which had previously been controlled by the Thesprotoi. There were three large tribal groupings north of the Ambrakian Gulf in the Classical Period – the Thesprotoi, who lived inland from the coast opposite Kerkyra and its archipelago; the Chaones, north of the Thesprotoi, behind the

'Keraunian' mountains and either side of the River Aöos; and the Molossoi, east of these two major groupings, but west of the Pindos mountain range. Meanwhile, on the northern shores of the Black Sea, a man called Spartokos replaced an autocratic dynasty, perhaps of Milesian origin, called 'Archaianaktidai' ('ancient rulers'), which had monopolized decision-making in the city of Pantikapaion, then the most important city of the Crimean peninsula (Diodoros 12.31.1, dated under 438/7). Spartokos is a Thracian name, and it is likely that this was a member of the Odrysian house ruling in Thrace. (Sitalkes had a brother called Sparadokos: Thuc. 2.101.5; Hind 1994: 491; Archibald 2002a: 60; Graham 2002: 90–1, 98–9.) Spartokos' successors, who came from the same family, also had Thracian names that betray a similar connection. The circumstances of the changeover are unknown, but as this event coincided with attempts by the Athenians, during the early 430s, to exert more political power on the communities of the Black Sea coasts (Plutarch *Perikles* 20), it suggests a realignment between some of the northern coastal cities and at least one emerging inland power. (The Odrysians also had family connections with the Royal Scythians, who dominated the steppe regions north of Crimea.)

The nascent Bosporan kingdom did not impinge on the consciousness of contemporary metropolitan historians before the fourth century. Thucydides does not refer to the Molossian kingdom directly, and what he has to say about leadership relates to military campaigns (operations in 430–429), which may well reflect different organizational principles from those that pertained to ordinary community matters. On campaign, the Thesprotoi were subordinate to the Chaones, the Atintanes to the Molossoi, and the Orestai (a 'tribe' located east of the Pindos range) were subordinate to the Parauaioi (Thuc. 2.80 5–6). Most of what we know about developments in Macedon and Thrace was written down during the final third of the fifth century, and related retrospectively by Herodotos and Thucydides. These accounts telescope gradual developments and make them look, in either case, like an inevitable and progressive expansion.

In reality, political expansion functioned as a consequence of negotiations between communities and political leaders. The ruling élites of Macedon and Thrace were still in an embryonic state in the post-war years. They did not have the power to enforce their command over these territories. Before the time of Philip II of Macedon, when the creation of a full-time professional army, inflated by mercenary forces paid from newly captured crown property and revenues from the Pangaion gold mines, gave one man irresistible resources (Hammond & Griffith 1979: 405–49; Garlan 1994: 686–8; Hatzopoulos 1996: vol. 1 434–5), public authorities in these regions could afford systematic military campaigns only in limited circumstances. In the fifth century, the Macedonian army consisted of a small permanent corps of professional cavalrymen, drawn from the wealthier families of the kingdom, who could supply their own beasts and breastplates (Thuc. 2.100.5), together with levies of Macedonian irregulars, who served as infantrymen, equipped probably from their own resources. External attack of any kind would have required co-operation with neighbouring communities, notably the Lynkestians and Elimiotai (Thuc. 2.99.2).

In each of the areas under consideration, decisions concerning international or inter-regional policy seem to have been the primary responsibility of the regional authority, not of individual communities (Hatzopoulos 1996: vol. 1 365–9; idem 1999; Davies 2000: 251–7; Archibald 2000: 230–1). Documents often give the impression that rulers, or chief representatives, spoke on behalf of community groups with respect to external relations (Hatzopoulos 1996: vol. 1 365–9, 371; Velkov & Domaradzka 1994; Chankowski & Domaradzka 1999 on the mid fourth-century Pistiros inscription). But this need not mean that local communities lacked the power to take initiatives with other states. Rather, individual communities that belonged to a larger, confederate grouping (Brock & Hodkinson 2000: 25–30, esp. 27 n. 62 on appropriate terminology) necessarily had to defer, in some cases, to other bodies. Hatzopoulos has compared the collective organisation of Macedonian communities to the confederate mechanisms of Thessaly and Epeiros, distinguishing between the 'monarchical' polities of Macedonia, Thessaly, Epeiros (we may add Odrysian Thrace: Archibald 2000) and the 'republican' *ethne* of Aitolia, Achaia, Arkadia and elsewhere in the central and southern Greek mainland (Hatzopoulos 1996: vol. 1 491–6; 1999; cf. Cabanes 1996; 1999a).

Some features of collective decision-making in the Molossian kingdom are reflected in a remarkable dossier of inscriptions from the sanctuary of Zeus at Dodona (Davies 2000: 245–51). The earliest documents date from the second quarter of the fourth century. They contain a form of preamble, including the name of the reigning king, of a leading magistrate (*prostatas*), and a secretary (*grammateus*), together with their 'ethnics', which reflects a systematization of administrative duties, at once resembling north-west Greek preferences, as well as wider Greek practice. Over the course of the following century and a half, the names of the officials in whose name decisions were taken became more nuanced. These officials (*hieromnameuontes, synarchontes*: respectively 'sacred remembrancers', 'co-rulers') stand in for wider communities, implied by the 'ethnic' identifiers that each individual is given. Whom these 'ethnic' names refer to is difficult to pin down, historically and spatially. The lists of sacred envoys from all over the Aegean world, chosen to announce religious festivals (notably those of Asklepios at Epidauros c. 360, and of Hera at Argos c. 330), combine local and regional designations from the north in a list that suggests rapidly evolving political mechanisms and entities. By the final quarter of the fourth century, 'Apeirotai' had replaced 'Molossoi' as a collective term for the kingdom and its dependencies, and decisions are articulated as those of an assembly of the Molossians. What might be termed refined regional, or sub-regional, designations (Thesprotoi, Chaones, Prasai-boi) were nevertheless used to denote decision-making of a more explicitly local kind.

Systematic publication of pre-Hellenistic epigraphic documents is beginning to reveal the complexity and sophistication of inter-community relations in these north-ern regions. The period between the end of the Persian wars and the demise of Alexander the Great witnessed the rapid development of political institutions at regional and inter-community level. This is best exemplified in the monuments and inscriptions displayed at panhellenic sanctuaries (notably at Delphi, but from the middle decades of the fourth century at Olympia, Isthmia, Nemea), as well as Argos and later Delos, together with what were to become the respective communal archives at Dodona for Epeiros (Figure 7.4) and Dion for Macedonia (Mari 2002: 50–60; Le Bohec-Bouhet 2002: 45–7). At Dodona, a *prytaneion*, as well as a Council House, was built towards the end of the fourth century (Dakaris et al. 1999). Decrees issued by Argead kings before the second century are not numerous, but many of the decision-making procedures documented in Hellenistic times evolved in the fourth if not the fifth century. It is not yet clear whether all state officials, such as the *epistates*,

**Figure 7.4**   Dodona, Epeiros: the theatre constructed originally under king Pyrrhos of Epeiros (297–272 BCE) and rebuilt by Philip V of Macedon soon after 219 BCE. A building programme begun early in the fourth century, with the construction of the first temple of Zeus, culminated in the theatre. Copyright: C. B. Mee.

were principally royal servants, or whether they also exercised a more independent intermediary role between the crown and individual cities, particularly those in the territories acquired after the mid fourth century that enjoyed more independence than those of the kingdom of Macedonia proper (cf. Hatzopoulos 1996: vol. 1 372–96; Errington 2002). The dramatic increase in the number of epigraphic documents recovered from excavations and issued by civic communities in Macedonia is beginning to illuminate different levels of decision-making, those of purely local significance and those requiring the intervention of a higher body. As yet we know very little about the machinery of state power in Thrace and Scythia, but increasing evidence of local decision-making in these regions, as in Macedonia, has implications for how we envisage the relationship between cities or towns on the one hand, and the central administration on the other (esp. Hatzopoulos 1997; Archibald 2000).

## 3   Local Identities

One of the most intriguing questions regarding the north during the Classical Period is the nature of local organization. The greatest single discovery of recent decades has been the proliferation of towns and cities. In Macedonia epigraphy and narrative sources name as many as fifty cities with independent status, in territories acquired between the reigns of Alexander I and Alexander III. The tally within the much larger territory of the kingdom itself must have been much higher. Thucydides refers to a mere handful, without specifying anything about their status (1.61.2–4: Therme, Pydna, Beroia, Strepsa; 2.100.3: Doberos, Eidomene, Gortynia, Atalante, Europos, Pella, Kyrrhos; Hatzopoulos 1996: vol. 1 108–23; Hatzopoulos & Paschidis 2004). An intensive programme of archaeological investigation has not only extended the number of known civic centres, but revealed the longevity of many, stretching well back into the early first millennium (Archibald 2000: 220–8). Although the character of many fifth- and early fourth-century civic centres is still largely unknown, this has more to do with the extensive redevelopment of major Macedonian cities from the beginning of the third century than with the absence of earlier civic activity (Figure 7.5) (Pella, Dion, Amphipolis: Ginouvès 1994: 91–104; Aigai: Kottaridi 2002 with bibliography; Pella: M. Lilimpaki-Akamati 2002; Dion: Stephanidou-Tiveriou 1998; Pandermalis 1999).

The existence of such centres, and the provision of public buildings, is illustrated at Aiane, near Kozani, from the sixth century at least (Karamitrou-Mentessidi 1993; Ginouvès 1994: 29–32). In the prefecture of Voïon, which corresponds broadly to the ancient districts of south Orestis and part of Elimeia, thirty-five towns and villages have been identified by systematic survey work, nineteen of which are in the vicinity of Voïon itself (Karamitrou-Mentessidi 1999). These discoveries confirm on the ground what Hatzopoulos has argued on the basis of epigraphic documents, namely that rural sites in Macedonia participated in civic status (Hatzopoulos 1996: vol. 1 51–123; Karamitrou-Mentessidi 1999: 260–62; cf. Mari 1999: 629–31). The *politeia* enjoyed by these communities would have entitled them to make decisions about property, inheritances, local justice or collective norms. As yet we have sparse evidence of specific decision-making machinery, but the comparative complexity of many inland sites, even in upland areas around Grevena, and further north, at Florina, close to the Prespa lakes and the northern border of modern Greece (an area covering the ancient districts of Derriopos, Lynkos, Eordaia and Orestis), shows that community organization was well advanced before Alexander's reign (Drougou & Kallini 1999; 2000 (Kastri, Polyneri); Lilimpaki-Akamati & Akamatis 1999 (Florina)).

In Epeiros there has been an analogous increase in the number and range of sites investigated belonging to the Classical Period. At the village end we can detect series

**Figure 7.5**  Vergina (Palatitsa): the royal palace, late fourth to second centuries BCE. Copyright: C. B. Mee.

of hut foundations, enclosed by an irregular circuit wall, which constituted the focus of a community group, on the banks above the River Girmos, close to the main communication routes along the Aoös and Drinos river valleys (Andréou & Andréou 1999). Although some Epeirotes, like the inhabitants of Vitsa, were long-distance transhumant farmers (Vokotopoulou 1986), others were, increasingly from the late fifth and markedly from the first half of the fourth century, settling on larger defensible proto-urban sites. Many of these became the central places for *koina*, confederate communities, which acquired regular street plans and public buildings and were progressively fortified (Dakaris 1987; Andréou 1999). Ambrakia, which became the seat of king Pyrrhos (319–272 BCE), was several times larger than most at over 100 ha, but almost a dozen were 20–60 ha in size, including Amantia, Byllis, Kassope and Torone (cf. also Preka-Alexandri 1999 on Gitani).

Investigations of urban sites in Thrace have been less developed. Data are currently limited to less than a dozen centres, although the quality of information even in this limited number suggests that the overall pattern of community development was similar to what we see in Macedonia (Archibald 1998: 126–50, 213–39; 2000: 228–33; 2004). The river port at Adjiyska Vodenitsa, near Vetren, on the River Hebros in central Thrace, has been the most informative single site (Figure 7.6) (Bouzek et al. 1996; 2002; Domaradzki 1996; Domaradzka & Domaradzki 1999; Domaradzka 2002; Archibald 2002b). It is an atypical urban location, being liable to periodic flooding. Chance finds here date from the late sixth century, but the circuit wall was built in the final quarter of the fifth century, and remodelled early in the second quarter of the fourth (Domaradzki 1996). Quantities of transport amphorae, imported Attic tableware, evidence of metallurgy (smithing and smelting) using base and precious metals, weights and measures, and above all, almost a thousand coins illustrate the main features of an *emporion* (Bresson & Rouillard 1993). The

**Figure 7.6** Vetren-Pistiros, Thrace (central Bulgaria): the principal east–west road through the *emporion*. The cobbled street represents the latest of three street levels, the earliest of which belongs to the late fifth century BCE. Copyright: Z. H. Archibald.

inscription found 2 km to the north-east, at a Roman roadside *mansio*, was probably taken from Vetren and reused there (Velkov & Domaradzka 1994; Chankowski & Domaradzka 1999; Archibald 1999 for other epigraphic documents; Archibald 2001). Much of what we know about other urban centres in Thrace is confined to a tiny number of excavated sites, including Seuthopolis in the Valley of the Roses and Sboryanovo in north-east Bulgaria (Archibald 2004, with further references).

Urbanized sites in the Scythian hinterland have been investigated in the lower Dnieper, where a series of detailed surveys and excavations has been conducted since the mid 1980s. In the Kiev-Cherkassk region at least three proto-urban sites already existed in the seventh century, along with twenty-five other settlements. Over the next two centuries, the number of urban sites increased to fifteen, with fourteen sites of other kinds (Kovpanenko et al. 1989). Botanical evidence confirms the fact that Scythian farmers had adopted similar methods and cereal varieties to those known in Greek settlements on the coast (Pashkevich 1997).

The societies of the north are better known for the spectacular burials of their élite members, which form one of the most distinctive differences between the northern and southern Balkans. Where examples have survived in a relatively intact condition, the quality and imagination bestowed on individuals with no apparent connection to the crown can be astonishing (Agios Athanasios: Tsibidou-Avloniti 2002; high-status burials at Aineia: Vokotopoulou 1990). The prominence of high-status burials throughout the north has focused much research on mortuary data, and the social importance of this material has not yet been adequately interpreted in relation to what has been learned more recently about social organization. But systematic investigation of cemeteries, and the application of scientific methods, are beginning to yield important new information about discrete social groups (Lungu 2000; Simion & Lungu 2000; Archontiko, Giannitsa: Chrysostomou & Chrysostomou 2001; 2002). The societies of the north are no longer quite as strange as they appeared a few decades ago in relation to their more southerly neighbours.

The most impressive, though equally the most enigmatic, tomb from the whole northern region dating to the Classical period is Tomb 2 in the Great Tumulus at Vergina. It is remarkable not only for the exceptional preservation of its grave goods, but also for the distinguished identity of its occupants (Andronicos 1984). Who the royal male personage was whose cremated remains were deposited inside the gold casket of the main chamber, and which female came to be associated with him in the analogous casket found within the antechamber, are questions that have aroused lively debate. The excavator's view, that the man was Philip II, has been corroborated by close study of the skeletal material (Prag & Neave 1997). The identification has been controversial partly because our impressions of the north have until recently been rather sketchy. Excavations at Vergina have shown that Macedonia had moved into centre stage during Philip's reign, not just in military terms, but in cultural and social terms too.

# Further reading

Since the area covered by this chapter coincides with territory belonging to eight different modern states, information is necessarily fragmented, and only a limited amount of primary data is available in western European languages. Some monographs and general accounts provide syntheses of less accessible material (Rolle 1989; Wilkes 1992; Hammond 1994; Hind 1994; Archibald 1998; Reeder 1999; Tsetskhladze 1998a; 2001). Introductory primers for the history, geography and/or archaeological background of Epeiros in the Classical Period are Hammond (1967; 1994) and Cabanes (1988; 1996), together with the papers from four international symposia (Cabanes 1987; 1993a; 1993b; 1999a) and Davies (2000). Hatzopoulos's *Macedonian institutions under the kings* (1996), notwithstanding the controversial character of some of his propositions, is now the standard work on the history of Macedonia and its institutions in pre-Imperial times, complementing the political accounts in Hammond & Griffith (1979) and Errington (1990). New discoveries in Macedonia and the Greek coastal parts of Thrace are published in the annual *To Archaiologiko ergo ste Makedonia kai Thrake*, usually in Greek with English summaries.

# Bibliography

Alexandrescu, P. (1977) 'Modèles grecques de la céramique thrace tournée' in: *Dacia* 21: 113–37

Andrea, Z. (1993) 'Aspects des relations entre l'Albanie et la Macédoine durant l'Âge du Fer' in: *Ancient Macedonia: V, Papers read at the fifth international symposium held in Thessaloniki, October 10–15, 1989* (Thessaloniki: Institute of Balkan Studies 1993) 1: 109–23 (Institute for Balkan Studies 240)

Andréou, E., & I. Andréou (1999) 'Les villages préhistoriques fortifiés de la vallée de Girmos à Pogoni d'Épire' in: Cabanes 1999a: 51–5

Andréou, I. (1999) 'D'Ambracie à Nicopolis: les villes – jalons de l'urbanisme en Épire' in: Cabanes 1999a: 343–9

Andronicos, M. (1984) *Vergina: the royal tombs and the ancient city* (trans. L. Turner) (Athens: Ekdotike Athenon; repr. 1987 etc.)

Archibald, Z. H. (1998) *The Odrysian kingdom of Thrace: Orpheus unmasked* (Oxford: Clarendon) (Oxford Monographs on Classical Archaeology)

Archibald, Z. H. (1999) 'Thracian cult: from practice to belief' in: Tsetskhladze, G. R. (ed.) (1999) *Ancient Greeks west and east* (Leiden: Brill) 427–68 (*Mnemosyne* Suppl. 196)

Archibald, Z. H. (2000) 'Space, hierarchy and community in archaic and classical Macedonia, Thessaly and Thrace' in: Brock & Hodkinson 2000: 212–33

Archibald, Z. H. (2001) 'The Odrysian river port near Vetren, Bulgaria, and the Pistiros inscription' in: *Talanta* 32–3 (2001–2) (*The Black Sea region in the Greek, Roman and Byzantine periods*) 253–75

Archibald, Z. H. (2002a) 'The shape of the new commonwealth: aspects of the Pontic and eastern Mediterranean regions in the Hellenistic age' in: Tsetskhladze, G. R., & A. M. Snodgrass (eds) *Greek settlements in the eastern Mediterranean and the Black Sea* (Oxford: Archaeopress) 49–72 (British Archaeological Reports, International Series 1062)

Archibald, Z. H. (2002b) 'A river port and emporion in central Bulgaria: an interim report on the British Project at Vetren' in: *Annual of the British School at Athens* 97: 309–51

Archibald, Z. H. (2004) 'Inland Thrace' in: Hansen & Nielsen 2004: 885–99

Badian, E. (1993) 'Thucydides and the *arche* of Philip' in: Badian, E. (1993) *From Plataea to Potidaea: studies in the history and historiography of the Pentekontaetia* (Baltimore: Johns Hopkins University Press) 171–85 and 239–44 (notes)

Bashilov, V. A., & L. T. Yablonsky (2000) 'Some current problems concerning the history of early iron age Eurasian steppe nomadic societies' in: Davis-Kimball et al. 2000: 9–12

Boardman, J. (1999) *The Greeks overseas: their early colonies and trade* (London: Thames & Hudson ⁴1999)

Borza, E. (1990) *In the shadow of Olympus: the emergence of Macedon* (Princeton: Princeton University Press)

Bouzek, J. (1997) *Greece, Anatolia, and Europe: cultural interrelations during the early Iron Age* (Jonsered: Åström)

Bouzek, J., and I. Ondrejová (1987) 'Some notes on the relations of the Thracian, Macedonian, Iranian and Scythian arts in the fourth century B.C.' in: *Eirene* 24: 67–93

Bouzek, J., M. Domaradzki, Z. H. Archibald (eds) (1996) *Pistiros I: excavations and studies; the result of the excavations conducted in Vetren-Pistiros in the collaboration of Bulgarian, Czech and British teams* (Prague: Karolinum)

Bouzek, J., L. Domaradzka, Z. H. Archibald (eds) (2002) *Pistiros II: excavations and studies; the result of the Joint Project of Excavations and Studies by the Bulgarian Academy of Sciences, Charles University in Prague, University of Liverpool, École française d'Athènes and Archaeological Museum Septemvri* (Prague: Karolinum)

Bresson, A. (1993) 'Les cités grecques et leurs *emporia*' in: Bresson & Rouillard 1993: 163–226

Bresson, A., & P. Rouillard (eds) (1993) *L'emporion* (Paris: de Boccard) (Publications du Centre Pierre Paris: (URA 991) 26)

Brock, R., & S. Hodkinson (eds) (2000) *Alternatives to Athens: varieties of political organization and community in ancient Greece* (Oxford: Oxford University Press)

Bylkova, V. P. (2000) 'On the cultural traditions in the lower Dnieper region during the Scythian period', *Rossiyskaya Arkheologiya* 2: 26–39 (in Russian; English summary)

Cabanes, P. (ed.) (1987) *L'Illyrie méridionale et l'Épire dans l'Antiquité: actes du colloque international de Clermont-Ferrand (22–25 octobre 1984)* (Clermont-Ferrand: ADOSA)

Cabanes, P. (1988) *Les Illyriens de Bardylis à Genthios (IV–II s. av. J.C.)* (Paris: Sedes) (Regards sur l'Histoire) (Histoire Ancienne 65)

Cabanes, P. (ed.) (1993a) *L'Illyrie méridionale et l'Épire dans l'Antiquité: II, Actes du IIe colloque international de Clermont-Ferrand (25–27 octobre 1990)* (Paris: de Boccard)

Cabanes, P. (ed.) (1993b) *Grecs et Illyriens dans les inscriptions en langue grecque d'Épidamne-Dyrrhachion et d'Apollonia d'Illyrie: actes de la table ronde internationale (Clermont-Ferrand, 19–21 octobre 1989)* (Paris: Éd. recherche sur les civilisations)

Cabanes, P. (1996) 'La Grèce du Nord (Épire, Macédoine) en plein développement au IVe siècle avant J.-C.' in: P. Carlier (ed.) *Le IVe siècle av. J.-C.: approches historiographiques* (Paris: de Boccard) 195–204 (Études Anciennes 15)

Cabanes, P. (ed.) (1999a) *L'Illyrie méridionale et l'Épire dans l'Antiquité: 3, Actes du 3e colloque international de Chantilly (16-19 octobre 1996)* (Paris: de Boccard)

Cabanes, P. (1999b) 'États fédéraux et *koina* en Grèce du nord et en Illyrie méridionale' in: Cabanes 1999a: 373–82

Chankowski, V., & L. Domaradzka (1999) 'Réedition de l'inscription de Pistiros et problèmes d'interprétation' in: *BCH* 123: 247–581

Chrystostomou, A., & P. Chrysostomou (2001) 'Anaskaphe ste dytike nekropole tou Pellas kata to 2001' in: *To archaiologiko ergo ste Makedonia kai Thrake* 15: 477–88

Chrystostomou, A., & P. Chrysostomou (2002) 'Excavations in the west cemetery of Arhondiko near Pella in 2002' in: *To archaiologiko ergo ste Makedonia kai Thrake* 16: 465–78

Dakaris, S. I. (1971) *Archaeological guide to Dodona* (Ioannina: Cultural Society 'The Ancient Dodona')

Dakaris, S. I. (1987) 'Organisation politique et urbanistique de la ville dans l'Épire antique' in: Cabanes 1987: 71–80

Dakaris, S., C. Tzouvara-Souli, A. Vlachiopoulou-Oikonomidou, K. Gravani-Latsiki (1999) 'The prytaneion of Dodona' in: Cabanes 1999a: 149–59

Davies, J. K. (2000) 'A wholly non-Aristotelian universe: the Molossians as ethnos, state, and monarchy' in: Brock & Hodkinson 2000: 234–58

Davis-Kimball, J. (2002) 'Statuses of eastern early Iron Age nomads' in: *Ancient West and East* 1: 332–56

Davis-Kimball, J., E. Murphy, L. Koryakova, L. T. Yablonsky (eds) (2000) *Kurgans, ritual sites, and settlements: Eurasian Bronze and Iron Age* (Oxford: Archaeopress) (British Archaeological Reports, International Series 890)

Domaradzka, L. (2002) 'Catalogue of graffiti discovered during the excavations at Pistiros-Vetren 1988–1998. Part one: graffiti on imported fine pottery' in: Bouzek et al. 2002: 209–28

Domaradzka, L., & M. Domaradzki (1999) 'Population structure of Pistiros' in: *Archaia Makedonia, VI: anakoinoseis kata to hekto Diethnes Symposio, Thessalonike, 15–19 Oktovriou 1996: Archaia Makedonia VI (Symposium) (1996: Thessalonike, Greece)* (Thessalonike: Hidryma Meleton Chersonesou tou Haimou 1999) vol. 1: 383–92

Domaradzki, M. (1996) 'Interim report on archaeological investigations at Vetren-Pistiros, 1988–94' in: Bouzek et al. 1996: 13–34

Dordević-Bogdanović, B. (1999) 'Some features of pottery production of the sixth and fifth centuries BC in the central Balkans' in: Vasić 1999: 24–7

Drougou, S., & C. Kallini (1999) 'Kastri Polyneriou Grenevon, protes anaskaphikes erevnes', *To archaiologiko ergo ste Makedonia kai Thrake* 13: 579–86

Drougou, S., & C. Kallini (2000) 'Excavation of Kastri near Polyneri, Grevena prefecture' in: *To archaiologiko ergo ste Makedonia kai Thrake* 14: 575–9

Errington, M. (1990) *A history of Macedonia* (Berkeley: University of California Press) (Hellenistic Culture and Society 5)

Errington, M. (2002) 'König und Stadt im hellenistischen Makedonien: Die Rolle des Epistates' in: *Chiron* 32: 51–63

Garlan, Y. (1994) 'Warfare' in: *CAH*² 6 678–92

Garlan, Y. (ed.) (1999) *Production et commerce des amphores anciennes en mer Noire: colloque international organisé à Istambul, 25–28 mai 1994* (Aix-en-Provence: Publications de l'Université de Provence)

Ginouvès, R. (ed.) (1994) *Macedonia: from Philip II to the Roman conquest* (English edition ed. M. B. Hatzopoulos, trans. D. Hardy) (Princeton: Princeton University Press)

Graham, A. J. (2002) 'Thasos and the Bosporan kingdom' in: *Ancient West and East* 1: 87–99

Hall, J. M. (2001) 'Contested ethnicities: perceptions of Macedonia within evolving definitions of Greek identity' in: Malkin, I. (ed.) (2001) *Ancient perceptions of Greek ethnicity* (Cambridge MA: Harvard University Press) 159–86 (Center for Hellenic Studies Colloquia 5)

Hammond, N. G. L. (1967) *Epirus: the geography, the ancient remains, the history and the topography of Epirus and adjacent areas* (Oxford: Oxford University Press)

Hammond, N. G. L. (1994) 'Illyrians and north-west Greeks' in: *CAH*² 6 422–43

Hammond, N. G. L., & G. T. Griffith (1979) *A history of Macedonia*, vol. 2: *550–336 B.C.* (Oxford: Clarendon)

Hansen, M. H. (1997) '*Emporion*: a study of the use and meaning of the term in the archaic and classical periods' in: Nielsen 1997: 83–105

Hansen, M. H., & T. H. Nielsen (eds) (2004) *An inventory of archaic and classical poleis: an investigation conducted by the Copenhagen Polis Centre for the Danish National Research Foundation* (Oxford: Oxford University Press)

Hartog, F. (1988) *The mirror of Herodotus: the representation of the other in the writing of history* (trans. L. Janet) (Berkeley: University of California Press) (The New Historicism 5)

Hatzopoulos, M. B. (1996) *Macedonian institutions under the kings*, 2 vols (Athens: Research Centre for Greek and Roman Antiquity, National Hellenic Research Foundation) (Meletemata 22)

Hatzopoulos, M. B. (1997) 'L'état macédonien antique: un nouveau visage' in: *Comptes Rendus de l'Académie des Inscriptions et Belles Lettres* 1: 7–25

Hatzopoulos, M. (1999) 'Formes d'état et régimes politiques du Nord et en Illyrie Méridionale' in: Cabanes 1999a: 383–7

Hatzopoulos, M. (2000) ' "L'histoire par les noms" in Macedonia' in: Hornblower, S., & E. Matthews (eds) (2000) *Greek personal names, their value as evidence* (Oxford: Oxford University Press) 99–117 (Proceedings of the British Academy 104)

Hatzopoulos, M., & P. Paschidis (2004) 'Makedonia' in: Hansen & Nielsen 2004: 794–809

Herman, G. (1987) *Ritualised friendship and the Greek city* (Cambridge: Cambridge University Press)

Hind, J. (1994) 'The Bosporan Kingdom' in: $CAH^2$ 6 476–511

Horden, P., & N. Purcell (2000) *The corrupting sea: a study of Mediterranean history* (Oxford: Blackwell)

Karamitrou-Mentessidi, G. (1993) *Kozani, city of Elimiotis: archaeological guide* (Thessaloniki: Thanases Altintzes)

Karamitrou-Mentessidi, G. (1999) *Voïon – Notia Orestis: archaiologike ereuna kai historike topographia* (Thessaloniki: De Novo)

Kottaridi, A. (2002) 'Discovering Aegae, the old Macedonian capital' in: Stamatopoulou & Yeroulanou 2002: 75–81

Kovpanenko, H. T., S. S. Bessonova, S. A. Skoryj (1989) *Pamjatniki skifskoi epokhi Dneprovskogo Lesostepnogo Pravoberež'ja (Kievo-Cerkasskij region)* (Kiev: Naukova Dumka)

Kristiansen, K. (1998) *Europe before history* (Cambridge: Cambridge University Press) (New Studies in Archaeology)

Le Bohec-Bouhet, S. (2002) 'The kings of Macedon and the cult of Zeus in the Hellenistic period' in: D. Ogden (ed.) *The Hellenistic world: new perspectives* (London: Duckworth & Classical Press of Wales 2002) 41–57

Lilimpaki-Akamati, M. (2002) 'Recent discoveries in Pella' in: Stamatopoulou & Yerolanou 2002: 83–90

Lilimpaki-Akamati, M., & Y. Akamatis (1999) 'The Hellenistic city of Florina' in: *To archaiologiko ergo ste Makedonia kai* Thrake 13: 587–96

Lungu, V. (ed.) (2000) *Pratiques funéraires dans l'Europe des XIIIe–IVe s. av. J.-C.: actes du IIIe Colloque international d'archéologie funéraire org. à Tulcea, 15–20 septembre 1997, par l'Association d'études d'archéologie funéraire, avec le concours de l'Institut de recherches éco-muséologiques de Tulcea* (Tulcea: Publications de l'Institut de recherches éco-muséologiques de Tulcea)

Luraghi, N. (ed.) (2001) *The historian's craft in the age of Herodotus: papers presented at the workshop 'The Dawn of Historiography', held in Turin at the beginning of September 1997* (Oxford: Oxford University Press)

Mari, M. (1999) 'Potere centrale e poteri locali nella Macedonia dei re: realtà istituzionali e imagine letteraria' in: *Mediterraneo Antico* 2: 627–49

Mari, M. (2002) *Al di là di Olimpo: Macedoni e grandi santuari della Grecia dall'età arcaica al primo ellenismo* (Athens: National Hellenic Research Foundation) (Meletemata 34)

Maslennikov, A. A. (2001) 'Some questions concerning the early history of the Bosporan state in the light of recent archaeological investigations in the Eastern Crimea' in: Tsetskhladze 2001: 247–60

Misailidou-Despotidou, V. (1997) 'Taphoi klasikon chronon apo to nekrotapheio tes Sindou' in: *Mneme Manole Andronikou* (Thessalonike: Hetaireia Makedonikon Spoudon) 153–86 (Parartema Makedonikon 6)

Morgan, C. (2003) *Early Greek states beyond the polis* (London: Routledge)

Murray, O. (2001) 'Herodotus and oral history reconsidered' in: Luraghi 2001: 314–25

Nielsen, T. H. (ed.) (1997) *Yet more studies in the ancient Greek polis* (Stuttgart: Steiner) (*Historia* Einzelschriften 117 = Papers from the Copenhagen Polis Centre 4)

Nikov, K. (1999) ' "Aeolian" Bucchero in Thrace?' in: *Archaeologia Bulgarica* 3: 31–42

Okhotnikov, S. B. (2001) 'Settlements in the lower reaches of the Dniester (6th–3rd centuries BC)' in: Tsetskhladze 2001: 91–115

Pandermalis, D. (1999) *Dion: he anakalypse* (Athens: Ekdoseis Adam)

Papazoglou, F. (1978) *The central Balkan tribes in pre-Roman times: Triballi, Autariatae, Dardanians, Scordisci and Moesians* (trans. M. Stansfield-Popovic) (Amsterdam: Hakkert)

Pashkevich, G. A. (1997) 'Early farming in the Ukraine' in: Chapman, J., & P. Dolukhanov (eds) (1997) *Landscapes in flux: central and eastern Europe in antiquity* (Oxford: Oxbow) 263–73 (Colloquia Pontica 3)

Prag, J. N., & R. Neave (1997) *Making faces using forensic and archaeological evidence* (London: British Museum)

Preka-Alexandri, K. (1999) 'Recent excavations in ancient Gitani' in: Cabanes 1999a: 167–9

Reeder, E. D. (ed.) (1999) *Scythian gold: treasures from ancient Ukraine* (New York: Abrams)

Roesch, P. (1987) 'Y eut-il des rapports entre les Béotiens, les Épirotes et les Illyriens?' in: Cabanes 1987: 179–83

Rolle, R. (1985) 'Der griechische Handel der Antike zu den osteuropäischen Reiternomaden aufgrund archäologischer Zeugnisse' in: Düwel, K., H. Jankuhn, H. Siems, D. Timpe (eds) (1985) *Untersuchungen zu Handel und Verkehr der vor-und frühgeschichtlichen Zeit in Mittel-und Nordeuropa*, Teil 1: *Methodische Grundlagen und Darstellungen zum Handel in vorgeschichtlicher Zeit und in der Antike: Bericht über die Kolloquien der Kommission für die Altertumskunde Mittel-und Nordeuropas in den Jahren 1980 bis 1983* (Göttingen: Vandenhoeck & Ruprecht) 460–89 (Abhandlungen der Akademie der Wissenschaften in Göttingen, Philologisch-historische Klasse 3,143)

Rolle, R. (1989) *The world of the Scythians* (trans. F. G. Walls) (London: Batsford)

Rolle, R., V. J. Murzin, A. J. Alekseev (1998) *Königskurgan Certomlyk: Ein skythischer Grabhügel des 4. vorchristlichen Jahrhunderts* (Mainz: von Zabern) (Hamburger Forschungen zur Archäologie 1)

Simion, G., & V. Lungu (eds) (2000) *Tombes tumulaires de l'Age du fer dans le Sud-Est de l'Europe: actes du IIe Colloque International d'Archéologie Funéraire organisé à Tulcea, Braila, Calaraşi et Slobozia, 18–24 septembre 1995, par l'Association d'Études d'Archéologie Funéraire avec le concours de l'Institut de recherches éco-muséologiques de Tulcea, le Musée de Braila, le Musée du Bas-Danube de Calarasi, le Musée de Slobozia* (Tulcea: Institut de recherches éco-muséologiques de Tulcea) (Publications de l'Institut de recherches éco-muséologiques de Tulcea 1)

Stamatopoulou, M., & M. Yeroulanou (eds) (2002) *Excavating classical culture: recent archaeological discoveries in Greece* (Oxford: Archaeopress) (British Archaeological Reports, International Series 1031) (Studies in Classical Archaeology 1)

Stanimirov, S. (2003) 'Underwater archaeological sites from the ancient and Middle Ages along the Bulgarian Black Sea coast' in: *Archaeologia Bulgarica* 1: 1–34

Stephanidou-Tiveriou, T. (1998) *Anaskaphe Diou*, vol. 1: *He ochyrose* (Thessaloniki: Archaiologika Ergasteria Diou)

Tasić, N. (1999) 'Die jugoslawische Donauniederung vom Zerfall des Basarabi-Komplexes bis zum Erscheinen der Kelten, 6–4. Jahrhundert' in: Vasić 1999: 18–23

Tsetskhladze, G. R. (ed.) (1998a) *The Greek colonisation of the Black Sea area: historical interpretation of archaeology* (Stuttgart: Steiner) (*Historia* Einzelschriften 121)

Tsetskhladze, G. R. (1998b) 'Greek colonisation of the Black Sea area: stages, models, and native population' in: Tsetskhladze 1998a: 9–68

Tsetskhladze, G. R. (ed.) (2001) *North Pontic archaeology: recent discoveries and studies* (Oxford: Oxbow) (Colloquia Pontica 6)

Tsibidou-Avloniti, M. (2002) 'Excavating a painted Macedonian tomb near Thessaloniki: an astonishing discovery' in: Stamatopoulou & Yeroulanou 2002: 91–7

Vasić, M. (ed.) (1999) *Le Djerdap/les Portes de Fer à la deuxième moitié du premier millenaire av. J. Ch. jusqu'aux guerres daciques: Kolloquium in Kladovo-Drobeta-Turnu Severin, September–October 1998* (Belgrade: Arheoloski Institut & Bucarest: Rumänisches Institut für Thrakologie) (Jugoslawisch-rumänische Kommission für die Erforschung der Region des Eisernes Tores 3)

Vasić, R. (1993) 'Macedonia and the central Balkans: contacts in the archaic and classical period' in: *Ancient Macedonia: V, Papers read at the fifth international symposium held in Thessaloniki, October 10–15, 1989* (Thessaloniki: Institute of Balkan Studies 1993) 1683–91 (Institute for Balkan studies 240)

Velkov, V., & L. Domaradzka (1994) 'Kotys I (383/2–359 av. J.-C.) et l'emporion Pistiros de Thrace' in: *BCH* 118: 1–15

Vokotopoulou, I. P. (1986) *Vitsa: ta nekrotapheia mias Molossikes komes* (Athens: Tameio Archaiologikon Poron kai Apallotrioseon) (Dimosieumata tou Archaiologikou Deltiou 33)

Vokotopoulou, I. P. (1990) *Oi taphikai tymboi tis Aineias* (Athens: Ekdose tou Tameiou Archaiologikon Poron kai Apallotrioseon) (Dimosieumata tou Archaiologikou Deltiou 41)

Wilkes, J. (1992) *The Illyrians* (Oxford: Blackwell)

Yablonsky, L. T. (2000) '"Scythian Triad" and "Scythian World"' in: Davis-Kimball et al. 2000: 3–8

CHAPTER EIGHT

# The Greek Cities of the Black Sea

*Stanley M. Burstein*

## 1  Introduction

The emergence of the polis system in Greece coincided with the beginning of an extraordinary emigration of Greeks from the Aegean homeland. This emigration began about the middle of the eighth century and continued for over two centuries. When it ended around 500, the Greek world extended from eastern Spain in the west to Colchis in the east. The primary causes of this remarkable expansion were twofold: the search for sources of metal to satisfy the Greeks' growing need and the hope of acquiring the land required to live the life of a citizen in the new poleis, as opportunities for land at home dwindled.

The Black Sea was the last major area colonized by the Greeks. Attracted first by the rich fishing and agricultural potential of the Hellespont and the Pontos and then by its remoteness, which offered refuge from Lydian and Persian pressure, various Ionian and Aeolian states founded colonies in the area. The most active of these was Miletos, credited by the ancient sources with seventy colonies, though the actual number was probably much smaller. Among Miletos' numerous colonies were such important cities as Kyzikos (675) near the entrance of the Hellespont, Sinope (c. 631) on the north coast of Anatolia, Olbia (c. 550) at the mouth of the Bug River in southwestern Ukraine, and Pantikapaion (c. 600) in the Crimea. Megara also colonized in this area, occupying the important sites of Byzantion and Chalkedon on both sides of the Bosporos as well as founding the city of Herakleia Pontike (560) in northwest Anatolia near one of the reputed entrances to Hades.

Because they had no rivals in this area, the Greeks were able to establish new colonies throughout the Archaic and Classical periods until the Black Sea was almost entirely ringed by prosperous Greek cities equipped with fine public buildings and temples and linked by steadily growing ties of trade. The Black Sea seemed to be on the verge of becoming a Greek lake like the Aegean. Instead, the fifth century opened with unprecedented threats to the survival of the Greek cities of the region that resulted in fundamental changes in their organization and relations to each other and the world around them. Reconstruction of the history of these developments is difficult, not least because of the lack of sources that plagues the historian of Greek colonies everywhere.

## 2   Sources for the History of the Greek Cities

The literary sources for the history of the Black Sea in the fifth and fourth centuries are limited in quantity and uneven in coverage. Although evidence exists for local historical traditions dealing with the Bosporan kingdom in the eastern Crimea and the Taman peninsula and the city of Herakleia Pontike and its colony Chersonesos, only fragments remain. References to the Black Sea cities occur also in numerous classical authors such as the historians Herodotos, Xenophon, and Diodoros, the geographer Strabon, and the Athenian orators, especially Isokrates and Demosthenes. Their value for the history of the Black Sea cities is limited, however, by their strongly Atheno-centric biases. As a result, while relatively full evidence survives concerning the dates, founding cities (*metropoleis*), and founders of the Black Sea cities as well as the legends that were invented to connect them to the Heroic Age and to establish divine sanction for their foundation, the evidence for the fifth and fourth centuries primarily concerns issues related to Athenian history, such as the return of the Ten Thousand and the grain trade, rather than the internal history of the cities themselves.

Fortunately, archaeology has compensated for much of the deficiencies of the literary sources. Although excavation of the cities of northern Turkey has barely begun, there is a long and rich archaeological tradition dealing with those of the west and north coasts of the Black Sea. Almost a century of excavation of cities such as Istria, Olbia, Chersonesos, and Pantikapaion has produced a wealth of epigraphical and material evidence illuminating their society and economy, culture, institutions, and urban development. Moreover, since studying the Greek cities in their geo-graphic and ethnographic contexts is a hallmark of the Black Sea archaeological tradition, archaeology has also involved the exploration of the cities' hinterlands, producing a wealth of information about the structure and history of their *choras* (rural hinterlands) and their relations with their non-Greek neighbors, and illumin-ating basic trends in the history of the region as a whole.

## 3   Greeks and Non-Greeks in the Black Sea

The history of the Greek cities of the Black Sea is usually written in terms of the spread of Greek life and culture in the region, and there is some truth in such reconstructions. Cities such as Herakleia Pontike, Sinope, and Olbia proudly affirmed their "Greek-ness" by working their foundations into Panhellenic saga, maintaining close ties with their *metropoleis*, patronizing the Delphic oracle, celebrating their military triumphs at Olympia, and keeping abreast of cultural developments in the Aegean. Such Helle-nocentric accounts, however, ignore an equally important truth: these cities formed a thin fringe on the edges of a vast "barbarian" world. Although a few cities such as Herakleia Pontike succeeded in dominating their non-Greek neighbors, most were not so fortunate and had to find accommodations with their "barbarian" neighbors, trading and intermarrying with them and sometimes even seeking their protection in order to survive. The negotiation and renegotiation of these accommodations is central to the history of the Greek cities of the Black Sea, especially during the fifth and fourth centuries, when they assumed the form that they would maintain for the rest of antiquity.

During the sixth century the cities had grown and prospered, building their first stone temples and expanding and settling their *choras*. Olbia, for example, founded over a hundred subsidiary agricultural settlements in its *chora* in the lower reaches of the Dnieper and Bug Rivers. The good times ended, however, in the first third of the fifth century. Although literary evidence is lacking, evidence of the change is clear in the archaeology of the cities. The situation is clearest at Olbia, where the city acquired new defensive walls at the same time that virtually all the settlements in its *chora* were abandoned. New walls and evidence of widespread destruction have also been found at Istria in levels dated about 500 by the excavators. Finally, there are remains of an extensive system of fortifications intended to defend the cities of the Kerch peninsula dating to this period. Russian and Ukrainian scholars explain these development by the efforts of powerful non-Greek states located in the hinterlands of the Black Sea – those of the Odrysian Thracians in the Balkans and the "Royal Scythians" in the Ukraine – to extend their control over the Greek cities on their coasts, and their view is supported by the character and extent of the changes (Vinogradov 1997c: 20–1).

For much of the late sixth century the Persian Empire had protected the Greek cities of the south and west coasts of the Black Sea, albeit at the price of their paying tribute and providing troops for Persian military campaigns. Unsuccessful efforts by Kyros the Great (c. 530) and Dareios I (c. 513) to extend Persian power north of the Black Sea were followed by withdrawal of Persia from the region in the wake of the defeat of Xerxes' invasion of Greece in 480/79 and its aftermath. In northern Anatolia the result was political fragmentation as various local populations vied for control of the coast and its hinterlands, while elsewhere the Odrysians and Scythians hastened to fill the vacuum created by the collapse of Persian power. Herodotos (4.80) refers to hostilities – probably in the 470s – between the Thracians and Scythians near Olbia that ended with the mutual surrender of rival claimants to the thrones of the two peoples and recognition of the Danube as the boundaries between their kingdoms, thereby freeing them to turn their attention to the Greek cities of the coasts of Thrace and Scythia.

The cities' responses to the changed political environment of the Black Sea varied according to the peculiarities of their local situation. The lack of a dominant non-Greek power in northern Anatolia to replace the Persians encouraged the cities there to try to expand their influence over their neighbors. First to take advantage of these possibilities was Herakleia Pontike. Founded about 560 by colonists from Megara and Boiotia near the mouth of the Lykos River about 150 km east of the Bosporos, Herakleia had co-existed uneasily with the natives of the region – a people of probably Thracian origin called the Mariandynoi – for most of the first century of its existence, recognizing Persian suzerainty and possibly even participating in Xerxes' ill-fated Greek campaign.

The weakening of Persian power in the area, however, freed the city to turn on the Mariandynoi, and by the second half of the fifth century at the latest, Herakleia had conquered its neighbors, a victory it celebrated with a monument in Olympia. Following their victory, the Herakleotes reduced their new subjects to a form of agricultural servitude that reminded other Greeks of the condition of Sparta's helots and the Thessalian *penestai*. Henceforth the Mariandynoi were bound to the soil as hereditary tenants protected only by the guarantee that they would not be sold out of their homeland.

The conquest of the Mariandynoi enriched Herakleia and provided the city with a strong foundation for future economic growth. References by Aristotle and other sources to demands for redistribution of land, conflicts between "oligarchs" and "democrats," and a short-lived tyranny by an otherwise unknown Euopios suggest, however, that it was Herakleia's aristocracy that had profited most from the city's victory. The result was *stasis* and political instability that probably contributed to the city's decision to colonize outside its *chora*, first in the late 420s when it founded Chersonesos near modern Sevastopol in the southwestern Crimea, and again in the early fourth century when it founded Kallatis on the site of modern Mangalia in the Dobruja (Graham 1994: 6). Equally important, domination of Mariandynia provided Herakleia with an extensive labor force to work the citizens' estates and numerous rowers to man its fleet, making it the most powerful of the cities of northern Anatolia.

The situation was more complex east of Herakleia. Sinope was the principal city on the Paphlagonian coast. Founded by Miletos in the second half of the seventh century, Sinope had flourished, founding a series of colonies of her own further east on land seized from the Paphlagonians, including Kotyora, Kerasous, and, most importantly, Trapezous. Not surprisingly, relations between Sinope and her colonies and the Paphlagonians were tense throughout the city's history. Xenophon (*Anabasis* 5.5.7–12) reveals that by the end of the fifth century Sinope had been able to exploit that tension and bind her colonies tightly to her, forcing them to accept Sinopean harmosts and pay tribute to Sinope. Epigraphic and archaeological evidence indicates Sinope's influence was not limited to northern Anatolia but that the city established economic and political ties with the cities of the north and west coasts of the Black Sea, most notably with Olbia, where Sinopean pottery and decrees honoring Sinopeans and granting special trading privileges have been found. At the same time, the presence of a tyranny at Sinope in the 430s suggests that the city had experienced internal tensions similar to those documented at Herakleia Pontike and elsewhere in the Black Sea.

Significantly different from the experience of Herakleia Pontike and Sinope was that of the cities of Colchis – modern Georgia – at the eastern end of the Black Sea. Unlike their kinsmen to the west, whose neighbors were small-scale polities capable of being conquered as Herakleia had done or held at bay as was the case at Sinope, the Colchian Greek cities had been founded on the coast of rich states with a long tradition of urbanism and close ties with the various empires of their hinterlands, such as Urartu, Assyria, and, of course, Persia.

Three cities are mentioned in the sources as founded in this remote area – Dioskourias, Gyenos, and Phasis – while archaeology has added two more, whose ancient names are still unknown, one at the important site of Pitchvnari and another nearby at Tsikhisdziri. The sources suggest, therefore, that the Colchian Greek cities were virtual dependencies of the various kingdoms of the interior, whose precarious survival depended on their usefulness as commercial gateways to the outside world; Phasis is even described as an *emporion* – a market – for the Colchians. Although the earliest written sources for the Colchian cities date to the fourth century, archaeo-logical evidence indicates Greek activity in the region began as early as the sixth century. Excavations at Pitchvnari and interior sites such as Vani indicate that by the late fifth century there was an unusually high degree of intermingling of Colchian and Greek traditions in the region, so "that the culture of the gymnasium coexisted at Pitchvnari with a local culture exemplified by its tools, wares, and dwellings"; while "deep in the hinterland, at least some of the elite sported an identity that was both Colchian and Greek" (Braund 1994: 116, 118).

The central theme of the history of the west coast of the Black Sea in the fifth century was the emergence of the Odrysian Thracians as the dominant power in the region. Freed from Persian suzerainty, the Odrysian kings rapidly expanded their power in the Balkans. The details of the process are unknown, but Thucydides (2.96–7) describes their empire in the 420s as extending over the whole of the eastern Balkans from the Propontis to the Danube and including both the tribes of the interior and the Greek cities of the Black Sea coast, all of whom paid tribute to the Odrysian high king. The amount of their tribute is unknown, but it is likely to have been substantial since Thucydides says that Sitalkes realized an income of four hundred talents a year in gold and silver, a sum almost comparable to that of the Athenian empire at the beginning of the Peloponnesian War. Although evidence concerning relations between the Greek cities and their Odrysian suzerains is lacking, it is likely that, just as would be the case in the Hellenistic Period, the burden of their tribute was offset by the protection afforded them against raids on their *choras* by neighboring tribes and increased trading opportunities with the peoples of the interior.

For the cities of the coasts of the Ukraine and the Crimean and Taman peninsulas, the central fact of the early fifth century was the pressure put on them by the kingdom of the Royal Scythians, which dominated the steppes north of the Black Sea. As elsewhere in the Black Sea, the responses of the south Russian cities to the new situation were not uniform. The evidence is fullest for Olbia (Vinogradov and Kryžikij 1995: 130–4). In a famous passage of his fourth book Herodotos (4.78–9) tells the pathetic story of the Scythian king Skyles, who resided in Olbia for half of the year in a Greek-style palace with his Olbian wife, until his nobles learned of his participation in the rites of Dionysos and assassinated him. Herodotos' purpose in telling the story of Skyles is to illustrate the Scythians' hostility to foreign customs. The fact that Skyles had a Greek wife and regularly spent part of the year in Olbia, however, suggests that the Olbian aristocracy had recognized Scythian authority in return for a privileged position for the city in the kingdom, perhaps as one of the royal residences where the kings would stay during their annual migrations throughout their vast territories.

Olbia's function as a royal residence probably ended with the death of Skyles but not the city's subjection to the Scythians. Initially the Scythians ruled through the agency of Greek tyrants who governed the city in the interests of their Scythian masters, such as the Tymnes who Herodotos says was *epitropos* of Olbia for Skyles' predecessor Ariapeithes, or a certain Pausanias who held the eponymous office of *aisymnetes* of the Molpoi, suggesting that as elsewhere Olbia's tyrants governed by manipulating rather than suppressing the city's polis institutions. Thereafter, however, Olbian coins with non-Greek names such as Arichos and Eminakos suggest that the Scythians replaced their Greek puppet tyrants and imposed their own administrators on the city. But whatever the modalities of Scythian rule, the evidence for substantial public building, including a new temple for Apollo Delphinios, suggests that Olbia prospered during much of the fifth century thanks to Scythian protection and her function as the primary center for the export of the products of the Scythians' steppe subjects and the provision of Greek manufactured goods to the peoples of the interior.

The most original response to the rise of Scythian power, however, was that of the cities bordering the Straits of Kerch at the entrance to the Sea of Azov, which united in a military alliance led by the Milesian colony of Pantikapaion about 480/79 (Vinogradov 1997c: 21). Unfortunately, the sole evidence for this important development is provided by a brief note that the historian Diodoros (12.31) entered under the year 438/7: "In Asia the dynasty of the Kimmerian Bosporos, whose kings were known as the Archaianaktidai, ruled for forty-two years: and the successor to the kingship was Spartokos, who reigned seven years (438/7–432/1)." It has long been recognized that this note taken from Diodoros' chronological source anachronistically treats the founders of the Bosporan state as kings, a status they first acquired in the Hellenistic Period. Although scholarship is divided as to whether the origin of the Archaianaktidai should be sought in Mytilene or Miletos, it is agreed that their rule took the archaic form of the collective rule of an aristocratic lineage like the Korinthian Bakchiads that monopolized key political and military offices, and not a simple tyranny. Information about the internal organization of the Archaianaktid state is lacking, but the existence of coins minted by Phanagoreia suggests that it was organized as a loose alliance rather than an integrated territorial state. Its extent is also unknown, but the fact that the cities of Nymphaion (south) and Theodosia (west) of Pantikapaion remained independent throughout the fifth century points to its initially being limited to a few cities on either side of the Straits of Kerch, most probably including Pantikapaion, Hermonassa, Kepoi, and, possibly, Phanagoreia. Finally, while the manner in which the rule of the Archaianaktidai came to an end is unknown, the fact that their successors bear Thracian names such as Spartokos and Pairisades, well attested among members of the Odrysian dynasty, suggests that the new dynasty was Thracian in origin, possibly being descendants of the leaders of Thracian military units, who originally came to Pantikapaion as allies against the Scythians.

# 4   Athenian Intervention in the Black Sea

For most of the fifth century relations between the Black Sea cities and the Aegean were limited. Trade increased, particularly with Athens, but political involvements were avoided. The Aegean and Black Sea basins formed two relatively self-contained political universes, a situation that Athens recognized when it conceded the Black Sea to Persia in the Peace of Kallias (most commonly dated to 449). The situation changed, however, in the 430s when Perikles led a powerful Athenian fleet into the Black Sea. The evidence for this event is limited to a single passage in Plutarch's *Life of Perikles*:

> He once made a naval expedition into the Euxine Sea with a large and exceptionally well-equipped fleet, where he saw to it that the Greek cities got what they wanted and treated them kindly, made the surrounding non-Greek tribes and their kings and chieftains aware of the extent of Athenian power, proved their fearlessness and courage, in that they sailed wherever they wished and made themselves masters of the whole sea, and left thirteen

ships along with Lamachus and troops to help the people of Sinope against their tyrant Timesilaus. Once Timesilaus and his supporters had been overthrown, he got a decree passed to the effect that 600 volunteers would leave for Sinope and settle there alongside the Sinopians, taking over the houses and estates which had previously belonged to the tyrant and his men. (Plutarch *Perikles* 20; trans. R. Waterfield (Oxford: Oxford University Press 1998) 163)

Plutarch's source for his account of Perikles' Pontic Expedition is unknown, but attacks on its historicity have not been convincing. More contentious has been the question of the expedition's date and purpose. For over a century scholars have argued that it should be dated to 437/6 and connected to Spartokos' assumption of power at Pantikapaion, maintaining that Perikles' goal was to establish cordial relations between Athens and the new ruler of Pantikapaion and secure for Athens a privileged position in the Black Sea grain trade, similar to that enjoyed by the city in the fourth century. Despite its wide acceptance, this interpretation is seriously flawed. The problems are twofold: first, epigraphic evidence suggests a date later than 437/6 for the expedition (Clairmont 1979: 123–6); and, second, it rests on an anachronistic overestimation of Athenian dependence on Black Sea grain, retrojecting late fifth- and fourth-century conditions into the 430s, when Athens was able to import grain freely from a wide variety of Mediterranean sources (Noonan 1973: 231–42; Burstein 1999: 93–104). More probable is the explanation provided by Plutarch's source, namely, that Perikles opportunistically responded to appeals for help from factions in the Black Sea cities. Certainly, the most tangible result of the expedition was an expansion of Athenian influence in the region with its center on the south coast at Sinope and Amisos, both of which received substantial bodies of Athenian colonists and the latter even renamed itself Peiraieus after Athens' port.

Athenian influence in the Black Sea basin increased with the outbreak of the Peloponnesian War in 431. As the region did not become a significant theatre of military operations, references in the sources are few, but the trend is clear. The Assessment Decree (*IG* $1^3$ 71) reveals the existence in 425 of a Euxine district containing at least forty cities on the south, west, and north coasts of the Black Sea; and the fact that Nymphaion was still paying tribute and had an Athenian garrison throughout most of the Peloponnesian War indicates that doubts concerning the reality of the Euxine district are unjustified. It is likely, however, that as in the Aegean the reaction of Pontic cities to the growth of Athenian power was pragmatic.

Cities threatened by the ambitions of more powerful neighbors such as Theodosia and Nymphaion probably welcomed Athenian protection, while by the same token cities with expansionist aspirations of their own, such as Pantikapaion, Olbia, and Herakleia, were less enthusiastic, if not openly hostile. So the new Thracian rulers of Pantikapaion are described as "enemies" in Athenian sources. Likewise, Herakleia refused to pay her assessment, maintaining her long-standing policy of loyalty to Persia. The situation at Olbia is less clear, but the fact that the city had already given sanctuary to the exiled tyrants of Sinope in the 430s points to the existence of a desire to maintain Olbian independence (Vinogradov 1997d: 172–89). At the same time, however, numismatic and epigraphic evidence suggests that Olbia's aristocrats took advantage of Athenian protection to escape from Scythian rule and replace the city's Scythian governor with a native tyrant.

Athenian power in the Black Sea – as elsewhere – quickly declined after the Syracusan disaster. Although the details are unknown, the decision in 410 to raise revenue by levying a 10 percent toll at Chalkedon on shipping in and out of the Black Sea suggests that tribute collection in the region had effectively ceased. Athens' final defeat and surrender in 404 left the remaining Athenians in the Black Sea to fend for themselves. Despite the peace treaty's requirement that Athenian colonists and cleruchs return to Athens, some Athenians clearly decided to remain in the region. So Demosthenes' maternal grandfather Gylon surrendered Nymphaion to Satyros, the tyrant of Pantikapaion, in exchange for the city of Kepoi on the Taman peninsula, while the fact that Amisos was still known as Peiraieus in the fourth century suggests that some of the Athenian colonists decided to stay there as well.

More important in the long run than the continued residence of a few Athenians in the region were the effects of Athenian intervention in the Black Sea on the life of the Black Sea cities. Some changes were cultural, such as the strong influence of Athenian sculptural and epigraphic styles on local workshops and the growing interest of local elites in intellectual developments in the Aegean, as indicated by Xenophon's (*Anabasis* 7.5.14) reference to books in the cargoes of ships wrecked on the west coast of the Black Sea about 400, and the appearance of evidence about the same time for students coming from the region to study at Athens. More fundamental, however, was the growth in trade between Athens and the Black Sea and its influence on the economic life of the Pontic cities.

Trade between Athens and the Black Sea Greek cities grew steadily during the fifth century, but for most of the century it was primarily a trade in luxuries, as is indicated by the prominence of Athenian painted pottery of all types and other manufactured goods in the archaeological record. As the Peloponnesian War turned against Athens, however, the city lost access to her traditional Mediterranean grain sources, becoming as a result increasingly dependent on Black Sea grain to survive. The result was a fundamental change in the nature of trade between Athens and the Black Sea cities. From a luxury trade it changed to a trade in staples with grain as its primary focus. Although the Spartan blockade of the Hellespont in 405/4 interrupted the growth of the grain trade, it quickly resumed its growth with the conclusion of peace, reflecting Athens' continuing dependence on Black Sea grain. The Black Sea cities responded by increasing grain production to meet the new demand. Clear evidence of the changed character of Black Sea trade with the Aegean is provided by the sharp increase in the number of agricultural settlements in the cities' hinterlands beginning in the late fifth and fourth centuries, as documented by archaeological surveys at Olbia, Chersonesos, and in the Kerch and Taman Peninsulas (Noonan 1973: 233–5; Saprykin 1994; Vinogradov & Kryžickij 1995: 67–74). Not surprisingly, it was the major cities such as Pantikapaion and Herakleia Pontike that most benefited from the new situation.

# 5   The Fourth Century

From 432 to 389 Pantikapaion was ruled by Spartokos' eldest son, Satyros I. Although evidence for Satyros' reign is limited to brief notes dealing with events just before his death, it is clear that he had already established the foreign policy framework that his successors would follow for the rest of the century: expanding

Pantikapaian power over the Greek cities and native populations on both sides of the Straits of Kerch while cultivating good relations with Athens by providing grain on favorable terms in times of shortage. Satyros' success in implementing this policy was, however, limited. Thus, while the Athenians responded to his generous gifts of grain by granting him privileges, which are, unfortunately, unspecified (Burstein 1993: 81–3), his attempts to extend his influence east and west of the Straits of Kerch ended in failure. Polyainos (8.55) recounts how Satyros' bid to gain control of the Sindians by forcing their king Hekataios to replace his Maiotian queen Tirgatao with his daughter resulted in a war with the Maiotians that only ended after Satyros' death, when his son Gorgippos accepted Tirgatao's terms for peace. Equally unsuccessful was his attack on the city of Theodosia in 389, which ended with his death.

Although Satyros seems to have been succeeded jointly by his sons Leukon I and Gorgippos, Leukon (389/8–349/8) was clearly the dominant figure and his forty year reign was remembered as being of decisive importance for the history of the dynasty, so much so, indeed, that historians named it after him: the Leukonidai (Strabon 7.3.8; Ailianos *Varia Historia* 6.13). The emphasis on the epochal significance of Leukon's reign, however, should not obscure the continuities between his policies and those of Satyros, particularly in the area of foreign policy. So his first major foreign policy achievement was the conquest of Theodosia. After an initial failure, most likely in the 370s, caused by the intervention of Herakleia Pontike, which probably feared for the safety of its colony Chersonesos (Burstein 1974: 416), Leukon succeed in conquering the city. The date of Theodosia's conquest is unknown, but it occurred sometime before 354, when Demosthenes (20.33) refers to it as being under Leukon's control.

Leukon also resumed his father's expansionist policy in the Taman Peninsula. A recently published inscription reveals that Leukon, like Satyros, first sought to bring the Sindians under his influence by supporting Hekataios against Tirgatao and her children (Graham 2002: 95–9). Diplomacy soon was replaced by force, and by the end of his reign Leukon had conquered and made himself king of the Sindians and their neighbors, the Toretai, the Dandarioi, and the Psessoi. Unfortunately, epigraphic evidence indicates only that these important events, which extended Leukon's power over the peoples of the Taman Peninsula and their neighbors immediately to the north and south, occurred sometime after the conquest of Theodosia.

Leukon's reign was also marked by a dramatic political reorganization that is reflected in his adoption for the first time of a formal titulary for the tyranny: Archon of Bosporos and Theodosia. Although scholars have argued that the title "Archon" as opposed to "Basileus" reflects Leukon's desire to disguise his real position by claiming to be holding a normal polis office, this is unlikely since none of the cities under his rule used the term "Archon" for their chief political office. Rather, as has long been recognized, Leukon's new title reflects a political conception similar to that embodied in his contemporary Dionysios I of Syracuse's title Archon of Sicily, namely, autocratic rule of a territorial state centered at Pantikapaion in which the subject Greek cities had lost their independent identity. Confirmation of this interpretation is provided by three facts. First, in contemporary epigraphic and literary sources all the political decisions of the Bosporan state are treated as the result of personal decisions by Leukon and his successors, and only they represent Bosporos in diplomatic relations with other states. Second, signs of polis sovereignty such as the minting of coins by cities ruled by Leukon cease. Third, and finally, individuals from the region are consistently described as Bosporans and not citizens of a particular polis in non-Bosporan documents. The distinction between the titles used by Leukon to describe his rule of his Greek and non-Greek subjects in the final form of his titulary – Archon of Bosporos and Theodosia and King of the Sindians, Toretai, Dandarioi, and Psessoi – are to be explained, therefore, not so much by a difference in the nature of his rule of the two groups of subjects as by the previous use of the title "Basileus" or its equivalent by the native rulers he supplanted.

As has long been recognized, the effect of Leukon's reforms was to create a multi-ethnic quasi-monarchy centered on the Straits of Kerch that foreshadowed the Hellenistic kingdoms in many ways, including treating important aspects of the economy as governmental monopolies – most notably, the export of grain from Bosporan territory. Thus, Demosthenes notes that Leukon and successors personally granted tax exemptions and priority loading of grain for ships bound for Athens, while inscriptions attest grants of similar privileges to other cities (*Sylloge Inscriptionum Graecarum*[3] 212: Mytilene). Moreover, although Demosthenes' claim (20.32–3) that Leukon provided Athens with 400,000 *medimnoi* of grain per year, or half its annual imports, or Strabon's (7.4.6) that he made the city a one-time gift of 2,100,000 *medimnoi* of grain, are controversial, it is clear that Leukon and his successors grew rich on the revenues generated by the grain trade. Archaeological evidence of the growth of the trade and the extent of the wealth it generated is provided by the expansion of agricultural settlements, particularly in the Taman peninsula and by the monumental tombs of the dynasty and extensive building projects undertaken by the tyrants at Pantikapaion and elsewhere in their realm.

Nor was their role in the trade passive. As already mentioned, Demosthenes (20.33) also remarked that Leukon transformed Theodosia into a major grain exporting center, and he probably also encouraged expansion of agricultural settlement in the hinterlands of the Greek cities of his realm, particularly in the Taman peninsula. It is unfortunate, therefore, that neither the date nor the circumstances in which Leukon's reforms took place are known. The fact that Leukon is still called a Pantikapaian and not Bosporan in a decree of the Arkadian League (*CIRB* (Struve 1965) 37) may, however, provide a *terminus post quem* of 369 for their completion, while Polyainos' (6.9.2–3) references to conspiracies against Leukon by his "friends" and "trierarchs" and his reliance on non-Greek troops during the war with Herakleia Pontike suggests that his plans met strong resistance among his Greek subjects.

Leukon was succeeded in 349/8 jointly by his sons Spartokos II (349/8–344/3) and Pairesades I (349/8–311/10), who followed their father's policies, exploiting their control of the export of Bosporan grain to maintain good relations with Athens, while continuing to extend Bosporan power eastward until by the end of Pairesades' rule it included all the Maiotians and the Thateis and reached, according to a Bosporan poet, the Caucasus Mountains (*CIRB* 113). Pantikapaion was not the only Greek city to build an empire by conquering other Greek cities. Another was Chersonesos, which carved out a place for itself in the grain trade by annexing Kerkinitis and Kalos Limen in the western Crimea, and reorganizing their *choras* by dividing them into regular plots protected from Scythian and Taurian raids by rural fortresses. Even more successful was Chersonesos' mother city, Herakleia Pontike.

Herakleia's emergence as the pre-eminent Greek city on the south coast of the Black Sea was delayed until the late fourth century. Although the city did intervene on the side of Theodosia in its struggle with Leukon and founded a colony at Kallatis in the Dobruja, severe *stasis* dominated Herakleia's political life for much of the first half of the century. The problem was rooted in the unequal division of the land conquered from the Mariandynoi and led to increasingly serious agitation for cancellation of debts and redistribution of land. By 364 the situation had become so threatening that in desperation the leaders of Herakleia's ruling oligarchy invited a political exile named Klearchos, who was serving as a mercenary commander for a nearby Persian military official, to return and bring order to the city. Once in the city, however, Klearchos turned on his putative employers and used his mercenaries to become tyrant. The estates of the oligarchs were confiscated and their slaves freed, while those members of Herakleia's aristocracy who managed to escape Klearchos' purge, and their descendants, were to remain in exile until 281.

The dynasty founded by Klearchos lasted for eighty years, until it was overthrown and Herakleia was annexed by Lysimachos in 284. After a period of consolidation under the rule of the first two tyrants, Klearchos (364–352) and Satyros (352–346), Herakleote foreign policy became openly expansionist during the reigns of Timotheos (346–337) and Dionysios (337–305), resulting in the creation of an empire that extended eastward along the north Anatolian coast from the Rhebas River in Bithynia to central Paphlagonia and included the cities of Tieion, Sesamos, Kromna, and Kytoros, giving Herakleia control of the principal ports along the route followed by grain ships sailing from the Crimea to the Hellespont. Numismatic evidence indicates that the expansion of Herakleote territory in northern Anatolia was accompanied by an extension of the city's diplomatic influence beyond the limits of its empire to include Amisos in northern Anatolia and the cities of the western Crimea, while the abundance of Herakleote amphora stamps found on sites throughout the Black Sea attests to the city's emergence as one of the principal wine-exporting centers in the region.

The Greek cities were not the only powers to take advantage of the withdrawal of Athens from the Black Sea. Pressure on the Greek cities of the region by the non-Greek states of their hinterlands also revived in the fourth century. As was true a century earlier, the greatest of these states was that of the Royal Scythians, which threatened Bosporos and Chersonesos and its neighbors from its center north of the Crimea. Unfortunately, the sources preserve only scattered references to hostilities between the Scythians and Bosporos and Chersonesos, with little indication of their scale or seriousness. A clearer indication of the magnitude of the threat posed by the Scythians is provided, however, by the elite residences, monumental tombs, and spectacular gold and bronze art works that were created by Greek craftsmen for Scythian kings and aristocrats (Tsetskhladze 1998: 55–92).

These wonderful objects have primarily been viewed as works of art and ethnographic documents since they were first discovered in the eighteenth century. They have been and continue to be admired for their superb craftsmanship and their illuminating depiction of Scythian life, and treated as evidence for the closeness of cultural interaction between Greeks and Scythians, with little concern for their political implications. All of this is undeniably true, but such interpretations ignore an important fact: the most likely mechanism by which these objects reached the

Scythians is diplomatic gift exchange. Their abundance and richness is, therefore, also clear evidence of the high price Bosporos and the other Greek cities that provided them had to pay for protection against raiding by their Scythian neighbors.

Although the price the north Pontic Greek cities paid for protection from Scythian raiding was high and the security they gained was precarious, it was still worth the expense. Safety for the new settlements in the cities' hinterlands was essential to the expansion of agricultural production that fed the growing grain trade with the Aegean and the trade in wine between the cities that is well documented both archaeologically and epigraphically. Even more important, however: it opened the interior of Scythia to trade with the Pontic cities. How far into the interior that trade actually reached is suggested by the remarkable discovery of a boat that had sunk with its cargo of fifteen fine bronze vessels and the body of its owner about 350 km north of the coast of the Black Sea on one of the tributaries of the Dnieper River (Graham 1984: 8). Unfortunately, the ethnicity of the boat's owner cannot be determined, but the existence at major Scythian settlements scattered between the Dnieper and the Don of what can only be called Greek quarters, complete with Greek-style fortifications and houses and large amounts of Greek pottery, is clear evidence that Greek traders settled for long periods in the Scythian interior (Tsetskhladze 2000: 236–8). Unfortunately, what they traded for is nowhere made clear, but the recognition that the prime source of grain for the grain trade was the Pontic cities' own hinterlands suggests that it probably consisted of typical steppe products such as animal hides and tallow, fine textiles, and especially slaves for which the Black Sea is known to have been a major source (Finley 1962: 51–9).

Similar conditions faced the Greek cities elsewhere in the Black Sea cities. Most difficult was the situation of south-coast cities such as Herakleia Pontike and Sinope, which attempted to maintain a delicate balance between local independence and loyalty to Persia in an environment dominated by ambitious satraps freed from central control by the chronic instability that characterized the long reign of Artaxerxes II. Equally complicated but far more dangerous was the situation of the cities of the west coast, which found themselves after the withdrawal of Athens increasingly serving as both pawns and prizes in an ongoing struggle for domination between the Odrysians in the south and recently emerged Getic and Scythian states in the north. Because of the lack of sources it is impossible to reconstruct in detail the history of this struggle, but the fact that by the middle of the century major cities throughout the area were ruled by non-Greeks – Apollonia Pontike by the Odrysians, Istria by the Getai, and Kallatis by the Scythians – strongly suggests that most had lost their independence by that time. What the ultimate result of these developments would have been is, however, unknown, because the political environment of the Black Sea was changed fundamentally by the sudden and forceful intervention of a new power into the region in the 340s: Macedon.

Two factors induced Philip II of Macedon (360–336) to intervene in the Black Sea: his hope of finally ending Odrysian meddling in Macedonian affairs and his desire to secure the rich land and mineral resources of Thrace for Macedon. By the late 340s Philip had decisively defeated the Odrysians and annexed Thrace, thereby extending Macedonian power north to the Danube, where it threatened both the Getai and the Scythians. Divide and conquer had been the key to Philip's success in northern and central Greece, and the same policy served him well in the Black Sea. Finding the

Scythians and Getai at loggerheads over control of the city of Istria, Philip initially responded favorably to the Scythian king Atheas' offer to make him his heir in return for his support against the Getai, only to betray his would-be ally's hopes by agreeing to an alliance, brokered by the city of Apollonia Pontike, that was sealed by marriage to the Getic king's daughter. Philip then followed up his diplomatic success with an equally decisive military campaign against now isolated Atheas in 339 that left the Scythian king dead on the field and Macedon the dominant power in the northern Balkans and ruler of the west coast Pontic cities from the Bosporos to the Danube.

Philip's triumph was short-lived, however. Less than a decade later his achievements were undone as a result of his son Alexander's dramatic conquest of the Persian Empire. The south-coast cities suddenly found themselves in a new and particularly threatening environment, since the collapse of Persian power in Anatolia freed their non-Greek neighbors from the last vestiges of Persian authority and facilitated the emergence of new and potentially dangerous states such as the kingdoms of Bithynia and Pontos. A similarly unstable situation was created on the west and north coasts, where the death of Zopyrion, Alexander's governor of Thrace, and the destruction of his army under the walls of Olbia in 326 by the Scythians (Vinogradov 1997a: 322–35), was followed by a major Thracian revolt and the reestablishment of an Odrysian kingdom by Seuthes III (c. 326–300) that was to last well into the Hellenistic Period, and once again to threaten the independence of the west Pontic cities (Burstein 1986: 21–4). Although some of his ancient biographers suggested that Alexander may have intended to campaign in the Black Sea after returning from India, his sudden death in 323 aborted any such plans, leaving it to his successors to try to restore Macedonian power in the region; but that is another story.

# 6   Conclusion

The fifth and fourth centuries were formative in the life of the Black Sea Greek cities. During these two centuries they emerged as full-fledged poleis with rich and dynamic cultures. They were not, however, simply replicas of the cities of their Aegean homelands. Archaic features remained part of their culture, such as funerary blood sacrifice and feasts at Bosporos, and the epigraphical use of the Doric dialect at Chersonesos long after ceasing to be current practice in the Aegean. But as the events treated in this chapter make clear, the hallmark of their political and cultural environment was intense and ongoing interaction between the Greek cities and the native peoples of their hinterlands. Although that interaction was often turbulent and dangerous, it decisively shaped the culture and politics of the Pontic cities.

The result is most obvious in art, where, for example, the empathy for Scythian life evident in the objects created for the Scythians by Black Sea Greek artisans has no parallel in Aegean Greek art, with its stereotyped portrayals of barbarian "others." It is evident also in the Pontic cities' ready acceptance of intermarriage between Greek and non-Greek and their willingness to include local deities in pantheons of polis deities. Obvious examples are the "Parthenos," a Taurian goddess once claimed to have demanded the sacrifice of all Greek sailors wrecked on the coasts of Taurian territory, which became the principal deity at Chersonesos, and a Scythian goddess syncretized with Aphrodite Ourania at Pantikapaion. Not surprisingly, the Pontic cities strongly resisted involvement in the affairs of the Aegean and readily invoked the aid of the city's non-Greek neighbors against extra-Pontic powers, as Olbia did when threatened by Alexander's general, Zopyrion. The Black Sea, in other words, was not merely an extension of Aegean Greece but home to an original and distinctive form of Hellenism. It is not surprising, therefore, that the accounts of visitors to the region, from Herodotos in the fifth century BCE to Dion Chrysostomos in the first century CE, reveal a certain puzzlement and ambivalence about the Greekness of the society and culture of the Black Sea cities.

# Further reading

Archibald, Z. H. (1998) *The Odrysian kingdom of Thrace: Orpheus unmasked* (Oxford: Clarendon) (Oxford Monographs on Classical Archaeology) – Comprehensive archaeologically based history of Thrace from the early fifth century to the early Hellenistic Period

Boardman, J. (1999) *The Greeks overseas: their early colonies and trade* (London: Thames and Hudson ⁴1999) – Standard archaeological history of Greek colonization

Braund, D. (1994) *Georgia in antiquity: a history of Colchis and Transcaucasian Iberia 550 BC–AD 562* (Oxford: Clarendon) – History of ancient Georgia based on Soviet- and post-Soviet-period archaeological discoveries

Burstein, S. M. (1976) *Outpost of Hellenism: the emergence of Heraclea on the Black Sea* (Berkeley: University of California Press) (University of California Publications: Classical Studies 14) – Text-based history of Herakleia Pontike from its foundation to the early Hellenistic Period

Christian, D. (1998) *A history of Russia, central Asia and Mongolia*, vol. 1: *Inner Eurasia from prehistory to the Mongol empire* (Oxford: Blackwell) (The Blackwell History of the World) – Standard textbook of the ancient and medieval history of the Eurasian steppe countries and their peoples

Davis-Kimball, J., V. A. Bashilov, L. T. Yablonsky (eds) (1995) *Nomads of the Eurasian steppes in the early Iron Age* (Berkeley: Zinat) – Volume of translations of articles by leading Russian archaeologists and historians of steppe nomads and their cultures

Gajdukevič, V. F. (1971) *Das Bosporanische Reich* (Berlin: Akademie-Verlag ²1971) – Comprehensive history of the Bosporan kingdom with emphasis on its society and economy by the leading Soviet historian of Bosporos

Graham, A. J. (2001) *Collected papers on Greek colonization* (Leiden: Brill) (*Mnemosyne* Suppl. 214) – The collected papers of the principal English historian of Greek colonization

Hind, J. (1994) "The Bosporan kingdom" in: *CAH*² 6 476–511 – Lucid and up-to-date survey of the history of Bosporos

Krapivina, V. V., et al. (2001) *Ancient Greek sites of the northwest coast of the Black Sea* [*Anticnye pamjatniki Severo-Zapadnogo Pricernomor'ja*] (Kiev: Mystetstvo) – Well-illustrated and up-to-date survey of the archaeology and history of the cities of the northwest coast of the Black Sea from Odessos to Olbia (contributions in Russian and English)

Minns, E. H. (1913) *Scythians and Greeks: a survey of ancient history and archaeology on the north coast of the Euxine from the Danube to the Caucasus* (Cambridge: Cambridge University Press) – Large scale and still valuable survey of Czarist-period Russian scholarship on the archaeology and history of the cities of the north coast of the Black Sea and their hinterlands

Pippidi, D. M. (1971) *I Greci nel Basso Danubio: dall' età arcaica alla conquista romana* (trans. G. Bordenache) (Milan: Il Saggiatore) – Standard history of the Greek cities of the Dobruja by a leading Romanian historian

Reeder, E. D. (ed.) (1999) *Scythian gold: treasures from ancient Ukraine* (New York: Abrams) – Lavishly illustrated catalogue of an exhibition of Scythian art at the Walters Gallery in Baltimore with essays on various aspects of Scythian culture by leading scholars

Rolle, R. (1989) *The world of the Scythians* (trans. F. G. Walls) (Berkeley: University of California Press) – Lucid general survey of Scythian history and culture

Rostovtzeff [Rostovcev], M. (1930) "The Bosporan kingdom" in: *CAH*[1] 8 561–89 – Still valuable synthesis by a major pre-Soviet historian

Saprykin, S. J. (1994) *Ancient farms and land-plots on the khora of Khersonesos Taurike (research in the Herakleian peninsula, 1974–1990)* (Amsterdam: Gieben) (Antiquitates Proponticae, Circumponticae et Caucasicae 1; McGill University Monographs in Classical Archaeology and History 16) – Valuable synthesis of the results of archaeological surveys of the *chora* of Chersonesos by Soviet archaeologists

Saprykin, S. J. (1997) *Heracleia Pontica and Tauric Chersonesus before Roman domination (VI–I centuries B.C.)* (Amsterdam: Hakkert) – General history of Herakleia Pontike and Chersonesos with particular emphasis on social and economic history

Struve, V. V. (ed., for Akademiia nauk SSSR; Institut istorii, Leningradskoe otdelenie; Institut arkheologii, Leningradskoe otdelenie) (1965) *Corpus Inscriptionum Regni Bosporani* (*CIRB*) (*Korpus bosporskikh nadpisei: polnoe sobranie vsekh do sikh por izvestnykh epigrafi-cheskikh tekstov, naidennykh za poslednie poltorasta let*) (Leningrad: Nauka [Leningradskoe otdnie])

Tsetskhladze, G. R. (ed.) (1998) *The Greek colonisation of the Black Sea area: historical interpretation of archaeology* (Stuttgart: Steiner) (*Historia* Einzelschriften 121) – valuable collection of articles on all aspects of the history and archaeology of Greek colonization of the Black Sea by leading contemporary Russian and Western scholars

Vinogradov, J. G. (1997) *Pontische Studien: Kleine Schriften zur Geschichte und Epigraphik des Schwarzmeerraumes* (ed. and trans. H. Heinen) (Mainz: von Zabern) – Volume of German translations of the major articles of a leading contemporary Russian historian and epigraphist

# Bibliography

Bilde, P. G., J. M. Højte, V. F. Stolba (eds) (2003) *The cauldron of Ariantas: studies presented to A. N. Ščeglov on the occasion of his 70th birthday* (Århus: Aarhus University Press) (Black Sea Studies 1)

Braund, D. (1994) *Georgia in antiquity: a history of Colchis and Transcaucasian Iberia 550 BC–AD 562* (Oxford: Clarendon)

Burstein, S. M. (1974) 'The war between Heraclea Pontica and Leucon I of Bosporus' in: *Historia* 23: 401–16

Burstein, S. M. (1986) 'Lysimachus and the cities: the early years' in: *The Ancient World* 14: 19–24

Burstein, S. M. (1993) 'The origin of the Athenian privileges at Bosporus: a reconsideration' in: *Ancient History Bulletin* 7: 81–3

Burstein, S. M. (1999) '*IG* 1[3].61 and the Black Sea grain trade' in: Mellor, R., & L. Tritle (eds) (1999) *Text and tradition: studies in Greek history and historiography in honor of Mortimer Chambers* (Claremont CA: Regina) 93–104

Clairmont, C. (1979) 'New light on some public Athenian documents of the 5th and 4th century' in: *ZPE* 36: 123–6

Doonan, O. P. (2004) *Sinop landscapes: exploring connection in a Black Sea hinterland* (Philadelphia: University of Pennsylvania Museum of Archaeology and Anthropology)

Finley, M. I. (1962) 'The slave trade in antiquity: the Black Sea and Danubian regions' in: *Klio* 40: 51–9

Graham, A. J. (1984) 'Commercial interchanges between Greeks and natives' in: *The Ancient World* 10: 3–10

Graham, A. J. (1994) 'Greek and Roman settlements on the Black Sea coasts: historical background' in: Tsetskhladze, G. R. (ed.) *Greek and Roman settlements on the Black Sea coast: a workshop held at the 95th Annual Meeting of the Archaeological Institute of America, Washington, D.C., USA, December 1993* (*Colloquenda Pontica*) (Bradford: Loid 1994) 4–10

Graham, A. J. (2002) 'Thasos and the Bosporan kingdom' in: *Ancient West and East* 1: 87–101

Grammenos, D. B., & E. K. Petropoulos (eds) (2003) *Ancient Greek colonies in the Black Sea*, 2 vols (Thessaloniki: Archaeological Institute of Northern Greece, Archaeological Receipts Fund) (Publications of the Archaeological Institute of Northern Greece/Demosieumata tou Archaiologikou Institoutou Boreias Elladas 4)

Noonan, T. S. (1973) 'The grain trade of the northern Black Sea in antiquity' in: *AJPh* 94: 231–42

Saprykin, S. J. (1994) *Ancient farms and land-plots on the khora of Khersonesos Taurike (research on the Herakleian peninsula, 1974–1990)* (Amsterdam: Gieben) (Antiquitates Proponticae-Circumponticae et Caucasicae 1 = McGill University Monographs in Classical Archaeology and History 16)

Saprykin, S. J. (1997) *Heracleia Pontica and Tauric Chersonesus before Roman domination (VI–I centuries B.C.)* (Amsterdam: Hakkert)

Struve, V. V. (ed., for Akademiia nauk SSSR; Institut istorii, Leningradskoe otdelenie; Institut arkheologii, Leningradskoe otdelenie) (1965) *Corpus Inscriptionum Regni Bosporani* (*CIRB*) (*Korpus bosporskikh nadpisei: polnoe sobranie vsekh do sikh por izvestnykh epigraficheskikh tekstov, naidennykh za poslednie poltorasta let*) (Leningrad: Nauka [Leningradskoe otdnie])

Tsetskhladze, G. R. (1998) 'Who built the Scythian and royal élite tombs?' in: *Oxford Journal of Archaeology* 17: 55–92

Tsetskhladze, G. R. (2000) 'Pistiros in the system of Pontic emporia (Greek trading and craft settlements in the hinterland of the northern and eastern Black Sea and elsewhere)' in: Domaradzki, M. (ed.) (2000) *Pistiros et Thasos: structures économiques dans la péninsule balkanique aux VIIe–IIe siècles avant J.C.* (Opole: Université d'Opole) 233–46

Vinogradov, J. G. (1997a) 'Eine neue Quelle zum Zopyrion-Zug' in: Vinogradov 1997b: 323–35

Vinogradov, J. G. (1997b) *Pontische Studien: Kleine Schriften zur Geschichte und Epigraphik des Schwarzmeerraumes* (ed. and trans. H. Heinen) (Mainz: von Zabern)

Vinogradov, J. G. (1997c) 'Pontos Euxeinos als politische, ökonomische und kulturelle Einheit und die Epigraphik' in: Vinogradov 1997b: 1–73

Vinogradov, J. G. (1997d) 'Zur politischen Verfassung von Sinope und Olbia im fünften Jahrhundert v. u. Z.' in: Vinogradov 1997b: 165–229

Vinogradov, J. G., and S. D. Kryžikij (1995) *Olbia: Eine altgriechische Stadt im nordwestlichen Schwarzmeerraum* (Leiden: Brill) (*Mnemosyne* Suppl. 149)

# CHAPTER NINE

# Western Greece (Magna Graecia)

## *Peter Funke*

## 1 A 'Greater Greece' (*Megale Hellas*): Southern Italy and Sicily

### *The region*

> While at the same time the Greeks were holding possession of both seaboards as far as the Strait of Messana, the Greeks and the barbarians carried on war with one another for a long time . . . Later on . . . the Greeks had taken away from the earlier inhabitants much of the interior country also, and indeed had increased in power to such an extent that they called this part of Italy, together with Sicily, *Megale Hellas* ['Greater Greece'].
> (Strabon 6.1.2)

In these few words the ancient geographer and historian Strabon (c. 64 BCE–25 CE) describes the close connections that existed between the Greek states in southern Italy and Sicily from their foundation in the colonization period to the Roman conquest. There was evidently, at least for Strabon, no doubt that Sicily too had to be subsumed under the term *Megale Hellas* or 'Greater Greece', commonly referred to in English as 'Magna Graecia', even though most other ancient authors seem to have restricted it to the southern part of the Italian peninsula (Polybios 2.39.1; Athenaios 523E). Accordingly, the term 'Greater Greece' signified the unity of a region which was not merely geographical in character, but was also a sphere of activity, and has retained this character down to our own day. The area south of a line stretching from the Gulf of Gaeta and the Gulf of Naples in the west to Monte Gargano and the Gulf of Manfredonia in the east forms, together with Sicily, a regional unit that in the course of history always preserved its own distinct – also political – character, and thus clearly differentiated itself from the central and northern regions of the Italian peninsula. What was called *Megale Hellas* in antiquity continued to be a region which European powers incessantly fought to control, down into modern times. Nor was it by chance that the spatial extent of Strabon's *Megale Hellas* corresponded – at least approximately – to that of the Royal Kingdom of 'Naples-Sicily' established by the Bourbons in 1735, and then at the Congress of Vienna in 1815 was revived under the name of the 'Kingdom of the Two Sicilies'. To this very day the so-called 'Mezzogiorno' forms a world of its own and is separated from the rest of Italy by an imaginary boundary that was, however, concealed during the centuries of the Roman Empire and then again after the national unification of Italy in the nineteenth century, but was not actually obliterated, as Carlo Levi has impressively delineated in his novel *Cristo si è fermato a Eboli*.

The division of Italy into a northern region and into a southern one was at all times also determined by factors resulting from the way in which power politics played itself out: just as the Papal State of the Holy Roman Empire marked the boundary between the two from the Middle Ages until 1871, in like manner the Etruscans in the Archaic period prevented the Greeks from advancing further into the mineral-rich districts of the north of the peninsula. It was, however, in fact also geographical features that gave southern Italy and Sicily a distinct character, and thereby also created a specific sphere of action and a distinct environment (Kirsten 1975: 1–33). In the west, the southern foothills of the Apennines extend closer and closer to the coast of the Tyrrhenian Sea, and therefore act as an impediment to northbound traffic, since at the coast they fall precipitously to the sea, and in the interior they form an east–west barrier. At the same time, however, in this region, especially at river estuaries, many small coastal plains have formed, but which are accessible only from the sea, as they are cut off from the hinterland by mountain ranges. In other words, it is a landscape which is very similar to that along the coasts of the eastern Mediterranean, but found everywhere also in Sicily. By contrast, the east coast of southern Italy facing the Adriatic Sea is completely different. Here, southwards from Monte Gargano to the extreme south-east, there is a flat, narrow coastal plain which adjoins the arid Apulian plateau in the interior. Consequently, for the Greek colonists from the motherland who surged towards the west in the first half of the first millennium BCE, this coastal strip was much less inviting than the much more fertile coastline stretching around the boot of Italy from Tarentum in the east to Naples in the west, and around the whole of Sicily.

Moreover, it was only here that there were convenient harbours and favourably protected bays, but most of all fertile land for agriculture. In the fifth century the Greek poet Pindar refers to 'fertile Sicily' (Pindar *Nemean Odes* 1.15), and Strabon extols the fertility of the soil in Sicily: 'it is on the lips of all men, who declare that it is not a whit inferior to that of Italy. And in the matter of grain, honey, saffron and certain other products, one might call it even superior to Italy' (Strabon 6.2.7).

A glance at today's economic conditions in this area, often referred to as the 'poverty-stricken' region of Italy, makes it difficult to visualize the immense wealth which in the Archaic period drew wave after wave of Greeks to this 'New World'. It was not until the latter part of the Middle Ages and then above all in the early modern period with the wholesale exploitation of the natural resources, especially the clearing of large tracts of forests in the interior, that the agricultural foundations of the soil were continually undermined. In the Classical period, however, it was not least the growth in economic strength that prompted talk about 'Greater Hellas' (Athenaios 523E). Like pearls on a chain, the Greek colonial cities were strung along the coasts of southern Italy and Sicily. They formed a region whose economic prosperity could scarcely be rivalled, and which, because of its geographical location in the middle of the Mediterranean and at the point where Greek, Etruscan and Carthaginian-Phoenician spheres of influence intersected, was actually predestined to far-reaching trade connections. The early, very rapid spread of commerce based on coinage precisely in this region is a reflection of its economic potential. Innumerable, therefore, were the tales that circulated about the proverbial wealth of these cities. The philosopher Empedokles of Akragas described the life-style of his fellow-citizens as follows: 'The Akragantinians revel as if they must die tomorrow, and build as if they would live for ever' (Diogenes Laertios 8.63), and Diodoros, who was born in Agyrion on Sicily, called the city of Akragas: 'well-nigh the wealthiest of the Greek cities of that day' (Diodoros 13.90.4), and devoted a detailed discussion to its wealth (Diodoros 13.81–84.7; cf. also Athenaios 37B–D).

The geographical, economic and political realities turned southern Italy and Sicily into a world whose cohesion became well known throughout the whole of 'Greater Greece'. This name shows beyond doubt, however, that, despite the degree of independence that it asserted, this region had, at least in the eyes of the Greeks from the time of the colonization, become an integral part of the world of Greek states – i.e., of what Herodotos called *to hellenikon* (Hdt. 1.4.4). It is for this reason too that the envoys who came from the Greek motherland in 481 to the tyrant Gelon to enlist him as an ally against the Persian advance on Greece could appeal to this cohesion:

> Your power is great; as lord of Sicily you possess no inconsiderable portion of the Greek world; we ask you, therefore, to help us, and to add your strength to ours in our struggle to maintain our country's liberty. Greece united will be strong and a match for the invader; but if in the body of our country there is but one limb . . . then there is reason to fear that all Greece may fall. (Hdt. 7.157.2)

Treasuries and votive offerings in Olympia, Delphi and many other large Panhellenic centres, as well as the victor lists of the Panhellenic games, offer abundant evidence of the integration of the 'Golden West' within the Greek world. How close these ties were is illustrated by a recently published bronze tablet bearing a sacred law from the Sicilian city of Selinous (*SEG* 48 630; Jameson et al. 1993). According to this inscription, the *ekecheiria*, an armistice proclaimed every four years for the duration of the Olympian games and binding on all Greek states, was in force even in the distant West already in the early fifth century, and, as in this instance in Selinous, quite unmistakably constituted a paramount fixture 'on the calendar' in the life of a city. Many other examples could be cited to show that there were close ties between the Greek motherland and the daughter-cities on the other side of the Ionian Sea. But these ties certainly did not produce any feelings of forced dependence. The poleis 'in the West' claimed for themselves the same political independence and freedom as the poleis on the Greek mainland; and although they as daughter-cities always remained fully conscious of the special bonds that existed between them and the mother-cities, and that their foundation legends were based on *syngeneia*, i.e., their common ancestry, political relations between them were just as much characterized by friendship and hostility as in all other Greek states. Indeed, it may have been precisely because of the special bonds – as in the case of neighbouring states – that in a love-hate relationship the pendulum between co-operation and confrontation often swung even further than was normal.

## *The melting pot*

Neither for the Greeks who cast their gaze across the sea from the motherland to the West nor for those who had found a new homeland in southern Italy and Sicily was there the slightest doubt that this region of the Mediterranean was an integral part of the Greek *oikoumene*. And if today we speak of the 'Western Greeks', we too take this Greek perspective no less into consideration. Southern Italy and Sicily, however, had not merely become a new home for many Greeks. At the crossroads between East and West, already at an early date Sicily in particular became a jumping-off point also for the Phoenicians – initially from the Levant and then above all from Carthage. Later they actually established a permanent settlement on the island. As immediate neighbours of the Greek poleis they secured the north-west coast of Sicily as a sphere of influence and at the same time also as a link with their possessions on Sardinia and Corsica, and as a bridgehead for their commercial activities. The core of Carthaginian power, her *epikrateia*, rested on three bases on Sicily (Thuc. 6.2.6): in the extreme west there was the small offshore island of Motye, 'the Phoenician beachhead from which to attack Sicily' (Diodoros 14.47.4) which, after its destruction by Dionysios I in 397, was replaced by strongly fortified Lilybaion; with possession of Panormos (modern Palermo) on the north coast the Carthaginians had control of 'the finest harbour in all Sicily' (Diodoros 22.10.4), whose coastal plain – it is still called 'conca d'oro' ('golden shell') – was known as a 'garden', thanks to its fertility and wealth in forests (Athenaios 542A); east of Panormos, Solous served as a Carthaginian military outpost.

While referring to the Greeks and the Carthaginians here, it is very easy to lose sight of the actual political and to some extent also of the ethnic diversity which existed in this region. By reason of their close ties with Carthage, however, the Punic colonies formed a relative homogeneity. By contrast, the situation in the Greek cities was different. Their inclusion in the Panhellenic community was only one side of the coin, as it were. To begin with, membership amongst the Greeks secured no more than a cultural identity, from which it was possible to gain political significance only seldom and only in very specific circumstances. It was at this Panhellenic level that in the West – apparently much more persistently than in most other parts of the Greek world – the awareness survived in the Classical period of belonging to one of the old Hellenic tribes, the Ionians or the Dorians. Alliances between individual cities were a distinct outgrowth of such tribal mentality. The rousing cry with which Hermokrates of Syracuse in the winter of 415/14 appealed to the opposition between Ionians and Dorians in his attempt to mobilize the inhabitants of Kamarina against the Athenians (Thuc. 6.77; cf. Thuc. 4.61.2–3) shows that this tribal mentality, which was rooted in the traditions of the colonial period, was still alive and still found political resonance. Beyond that, however, there was a supra-polis identity amongst the western Greeks – in any event in cases where convenient political alliances came about, as, e.g., amongst the Greek cities of southern Italy, who in the fifth and fourth centuries united against their indigenous neighbours. In this respect, however, there were narrow limits, for the same Hermokrates cited above employed the slogan 'Sicily for the Siceliots [*Sikeliotai*, viz. the Greek inhabitants in Sicily]' at the Peace Congress at Gela in 424 in his attempt to persuade the Sicilian Greeks to put aside their internal conflicts (Thuc. 4.58–64). But he failed to achieve a lasting success, as it was not long until the old rivalries amongst the poleis broke out afresh.

The polis of the day continued to be the actual centre-piece. In this respect too Magna Graecia exactly replicated the motherland, and to that extent the large number of its poleis structurally meshed precisely with the world of Greek states – with the result that here the same areas of conflict prevailed as characterized interstate relations in other parts of the Mediterranean where Greeks were a factor. The divergent interests of many smaller and medium-sized states which at any given time sought to attain the highest possible degree of freedom and political independence opposed the efforts of larger poleis (they were competing no less amongst each other) to expand their own sphere of influence and establish a hegemony. The prosperity of the country fostered greed. Intense conflicts over territory, to which powerful cities like Siris and Sybaris fell victim already in the Archaic period, continued to be an enduring source of tension in the Classical period in inter-state relations. These conflicts were aggravated by reason of the fact that the tyrants at Syracuse in particular were determined to expand their sphere of influence beyond the confines of their polis and bring the largest territory possible under their control. In addition, there were the ongoing tensions from the struggle for involvement in the decision-making process within the individual poleis, which all too often culminated in violent civil wars. Although we can gain only a very fragmentary picture of events in the West from the ancient sources, it is impossible to avoid the impression that the conflicts amongst the poleis as well as within individual poleis in many instances exceeded what was otherwise regarded as normal, and went to great extremes – not least because of the imperialistic ambitions of the individual tyrants, who resorted to acts of brutality that can scarcely be exaggerated. The total destruction and obliteration of cities, the forcible resettlement of tens of thousands of inhabitants, but also the founding of new cities by newly constituted citizen groups, into which large numbers of non-Greeks, especially mercenaries, were integrated – these created an atmosphere of permanent instability and political insecurity.

Instability was further accentuated by the fact that the major 'sister states' in the motherland, like Athens, Sparta and Korinth, were all too ready to allow themselves to be drawn into the conflicts of their kindred poleis in the West in an effort to extend their own influence also over this region. The readiness of these 'foreign' powers, to which Carthage also belonged, to become involved only heightened political tension in the West. The picture which the Greek historian Thucydides (c. 460–400) paints, using the civil war on Kerkyra as an example of the cruel machinations in the political struggles in the Greek poleis (Thuc. 3.82–3), is often corroborated in the history of Magna Graecia in the Classical period. The outlines are often even clearer here since the potential for conflict was even greater in one fundamental point: the local population exerted a much greater influence here than in other parts of the Greek world. Alkibiades also drew attention to this factor in his speech in 415 while attempting to persuade the Athenians to embark on the Sicilian expedition: 'The Sicilian cities have swollen populations made out of all sorts of mixtures, and there are constant changes and rearrangements in the citizen bodies . . . Such a crowd as this is scarcely likely either to pay attention to one consistent policy or join together in concerted action' (Thuc. 6.17.2–4).

What Alkibiades in an indisputably negative undertone characterizes as 'motley rabbles' were the result of much more varied and much more complex interrelations which existed over many centuries from the beginning of colonization in southern Italy and Sicily, and which involved Greeks, Phoenicians and the native population.

It is very difficult to give an accurate description of the local population. The sources admittedly provide a plethora of names, but even ancient authors had already great difficulty in explaining descent, specific identity and the precise localities of individual peoples. This is not, however, surprising, since the emergence of ethnic groups does not necessarily follow any prescribed pattern and hard-and-fast rule, but is the result of a highly dynamic process and subject to constant change. This is particularly true of Magna Graecia in the fifth and fourth centuries. Despite the fact that our sources are extremely fragmentary, a synopsis of the historiographical, epigraphical and archaeological evidence (see below) makes it possible to conclude that during this period fundamental changes came about in the ethnic character of southern Italy and Sicily. These changes resulted in tension in relations between the local inhabitants – the *Sikanoi*/Sicanians and *Sikeloi*/Sicels – and those who came as settlers and conquerors – such as Greeks (*Sikeliotai*/Siceliots), Phoenicians but also Etruscans, and later the Romans. But this tension was by no means always of a hostile nature.

The conflicts arising from this new dynamic led to a process of confrontation and accommodation, which in part led to political reforms and changes in ethnic identity. Accordingly, in the course of the fifth century successive waves of Oscians left the arid mountain region of the Apennines and pushed their way into the fertile coastal region of Campania, and gradually took control of the cities there. In a counter-effect, this 'urbanization' led to the dissolution of the old tribal structures and also a merging into Mediterranean urban culture. Other tribes in the region of the Apennines joined together to form larger federations in order to reinforce their military strength, and in this way exert greater pressure on the Greek coastal cities in the south and west as well as on the 'Oscianized' cities of Campania – i.e., on their former kinsmen. In the higher ranges of the Apennines, Samnite tribes such as the Hippinians, Pentrians, Caudinians and Frentanians joined together to form a league in the fourth century. And in the south of the Italian peninsula the Oenotrians had merged with the earlier immigrants, the Lucanians, as early as the fifth century. Then, about 357, the Bruttians, who themselves were part of the Lucanians, separated from these (Diodoros 16.15; Strabon 6.1.5; Justin 23.1.3–12) in order to found a separate alliance with a number of indigenous tribes – namely at the extreme south-west toe of Italy. On the east coast, in what is today Apulia and Calabria, the archaeological finds attest an increasing differentiation amongst the resident population, composed of immigrant tribes from across the Adriatic in Illyria – i.e., the Daunians, the Peucetians and the Messapians, who in the ancient sources are in part grouped together under the umbrella term of Iapyges (Hdt. 4.99.5; Strabon 6.3.2; differently, only Polybios 2.24.10). It is possible that here close contact with the Greek cities, particularly in the Gulf of Tarentum, led to politicization and a greater move towards independence on the part of these tribes. In Sicily it is possible to distinguish three chief indigenous groups: the Elymians in the extreme north-west, and the Sicanians and the Sicels in the west and central interior. The origin of the individual tribes was disputed even in antiquity (Thuc. 6.2), and still cannot be precisely clarified today, especially since the few, apparently Indo-European linguistic remains still elude a more precise identification, and – in part in contrast to earlier archaeological evidence – do not evince any particular connection with Italic dialects. As a result of the extremely close contacts with the Greeks and Phoenicians, all three tribes underwent an acculturation process, especially from the fifth century, whose impact on the political, social and cultural institutions of these indigenous tribes was probably more far-reaching than in comparable instances on the Italic mainland. While the Sicanians and the Sicels succeeded in apparently preserving their identity, the Elymians are no longer mentioned as an ethnic entity from the fifth century onwards. It seems that increasing urbanization in the wake of distinct Hellenization to a large degree undermined tribal cohesion, with the result that membership in a given city (among others, Segesta, Entella, Eryx) became the decisive factor for political identity, so that awareness of being Elymian faded into the background.

In other words, two quasi counter trends characterize the political restructuring of the indigenous peoples of southern Italy and Sicily. On the one hand, under external pressure individual tribes joined together in larger unions and formed strong tribal alliances. On the other, however, old tribal structures completely disappeared in favour of the formation of polis societies on the Greek model. The two developments do not differ that much, as the points of transition were fluid and in their manifold character the result of constant shifts between antagonism and accommodation. Nor does this in any way apply only to the process of political change described here, but on a much greater scale to the whole cultural realm. Those involved used the Greek script and in many instances also the Greek language. Along with the adoption of the idea of the Greek polis, its external manifestations were also taken over – such as architecture and art. As unmistakable as much that is Greek may appear, it is possible to observe a tendency to persist in old ways and to implement independent reforms. There was no firm line of demarcation between the Greek poleis and the Phoenician cities on the one hand, and, on the other, between the Greek poleis and the barbarian hinterland. Asheri has rightly talked about a 'dynamic model of cultural osmosis from the primary apoikiai on the coast to the indigenous interior, creating various intermediate forms of cultural life along the way' (Asheri 1988: 742–3).

The above sketch, although brief and punctuated by examples, should nonetheless suffice to demonstrate the tremendous dynamic energy which was released between foreigners and the indigenous population, and which led to lasting changes on all sides. For it was not only the indigenous peoples who were exposed to a strong transforming pressure. And it would be completely inappropriate to describe these interrelations exclusively as a product of Hellenization. The dominance of Greek influence is indeed beyond question. It was not, however, a one-sided give-and-take, but a manifold acculturation process, whose dimensions only gradually emerge – not least by reason of the fact that archaeological research has intensified. It was in the religious realm in particular that the melting pot of Magna Graecia produced a great wealth of syncretic results, in which Greek, Phoenician, Etruscan and indigenous elements blended in a complex manner with each other, and in doing so became a dynamic witness to accommodation with the other foreigners at any given time.

## *The distorted view: the sources*

The prime witnesses for the history of the fifth century, the historians Herodotos (c. 480–420) and Thucydides (c. 460–400), provide astonishingly little information on the history of the Greek West. In Herodotos this region actually assumes greater importance only within the context of the Greek preparations for the defence of Hellas against the Persians in 481, when the Greeks of the motherland sought to draw Syracuse, the new powerhouse in the West, into the anti-Persian coalition (Hdt. 7.153–67). And in his historical survey of the period between the Persian wars and the Peloponnesian War, Thucydides (Thuc. 1.89–118) completely omits any reference to southern Italy and Sicily. Not until the introduction to his account of Athens' Sicilian expedition in 415 does he give an extremely brief overview of the early history of the island, but without in any way taking developments in southern Italy into consideration. Thucydides offers an ethnographic excursus which is essentially restricted to a plain list of names and places connected with the history of the early settlement of the island by 'Hellenes and Barbarians'. Despite the great political importance of the Greek West in the Classical period, it received remarkably little mention in contemporary historiography in the motherland.

There was, however, no lack of efforts on the part of the 'Western Greeks' to correct this deficit in the history of the Greek states and to guarantee that their own history was given its proper place. A historiographical tradition actually began to develop in the West at a very early date, which was neither confined to the history of individual cities nor dwelt exclusively on ethnographic descriptions, but from the very outset took the history of the whole of Sicily within its scope, including also southern Italy (*FGrHist* 3b pp. 479–82). This too is proof that this geographical region was at the same time also considered to be a separate political realm. Accordingly, already in the last third of the fifth century Antiochos of Syracuse (*FGrHist* 555) stepped forward as the immediate successor to Herodotos, and quite deliberately sought to fill the gaps left by him – namely by giving an account of the entire history of the Greek West from its mythical beginnings down to the Peace Congress at Gela in 424. Philistos of Syracuse (*FGrHist* 556) (c. 430–356/5), an *imitator Thucydidi* (Quintilian *Institutio* 10.1.74), denies his support to this 'Herodotos of the West' (*FGrHist* 3b p. 480). His *Sikelika* also started with the earliest beginnings, but the emphasis was, entirely in the tradition of Thucydides, on the history of his own time. As an intimate confidant of and advisor to Dionysios I and Dionysios II, he was seen as a '*philotyrannotatos*', i.e., as an 'ultra pro-tyrant' (Plutarch *Dion* 36.3). Thanks to his great mastery of factual information, later writers used his *History* as an important source, but because of his otherwise extreme pro-tyrannical bias it was rejected. This was not the least reason why Philistos' *History* was soon forced into the background by Timaios of Tauromenion (*FGrHist* 566) (c. 350–260). He was the last and at the same time also probably the most influential author in the line of Greek historians whose works encompassed the history of the entire West.

Western Greece could therefore boast of a rich historiographical tradition, all the more since, in addition to the three authors cited above, there was a great number of other writers whose *Histories* are no longer extant *in toto*, and of whom in most instances we consequently know little other than their names and occasionally also the titles of their works. But the accounts of Antiochos, Philistos and Timaios became irretrievably lost in the period after the end of antiquity, and are today accessible only second-hand, in the works of later writers of the Roman period who used them as models for their own works. First and foremost in this respect are Diodoros, Dionysios of Halikarnassos and Strabon, but also the biographers Cornelius Nepos and Plutarch, and the learned man of letters Athenaios of Naukratis; moreover, the many quotations and references to be found in the geographical lexicon of Stephanos of Byzantion – these demonstrate that the works of historians of the Greek West were extant at least well into the sixth century. What have survived are rather paltry fragments and the accounts of later writers, and these afford only a dim reflection of the original works. This loss of historiographical knowledge cannot be made up for by relevant reports and references in contemporary poetry – these above all in the works of Pindar, Simonides, Bacchylides and also Aischylos – or by the philosophical writings of Plato, Xenophon or Aristotle. Granted that, e.g., the historical importance of Plato's *Letters* (3, 7, 8 and 13) – quite apart from the question of their authenticity – is undisputed, they represent only a single instance, one portion of a much larger whole, which in its diversity is inaccessible. This applies to some extent also to the major problem of determining just what was the Pythagorean influence on the politics of the south Italian poleis in the first half of the fifth century – namely on the basis of the only extant late sources, i.e., of the Roman imperial period (Diogenes Laertios, Porphyrios and Iamblichos).

The extremely fragmentary state of the historiographical tradition causes our view of the history of the Greek West in the Classical period to be distorted. Consequently, every attempt to reconstruct it as a historical continuum must remain as patchy as the sources themselves, in which the Syracusan perspective all too often prevails, with the result that the history of the rest of Western Greece – especially southern Italy – fades into the background and is scarcely perceptible. Much of this is, however, offset by the increasing number of epigraphical finds and especially the extraordinary wealth of highly informative numismatic material. Moreover, in just the most recent decades excavations which have been carried out with great vigour have produced an unexpected harvest of historical information. Despite this, it is still impossible to close the gaps in the historiographical tradition, which in view of our knowledge of the lost wealth makes that loss all the more painful. Consequently, the discussion to follow here will perforce be selective and to a certain degree also random.

# 2 From Tyranny to Democracy: The Fifth Century

## *Supremacy in the West*

It is customary to equate the end of the Persian wars in 480/79 with the beginning of a new era in Greek history and to regard the defeat of Xerxes as the boundary between the Archaic and the Classical period. Even if such an approach perhaps overemphasizes the break which the Persian wars constitute, it will be impossible to deny that there were changes and transformations involved in these historical events which were already in antiquity regarded as fundamental turning-points. What appears to be entirely clear in respect of the motherland and the Greek East, however, is by no means as evident when it comes to the Western Greeks. Ancient historians nonetheless sought to integrate the events in the Greek West into this picture in as seamless a manner as possible – by, e.g., dating the Carthaginian attack on Sicily in 480 in the same year as Xerxes' offensive against Greece. Both military expeditions were allegedly the result of a co-ordinated strategy, with the object of conquering the whole Greek world by means of a gigantic pincer-movement (Diodoros 11.1.4–5; 20.1). With a view to linking both military events as closely as possible with each other, historians actually placed the Carthaginian defeat at Himera and the Persian defeat at Salamis on the same day (Hdt. 7.166; Thermopylai instead of Salamis, Diodoros 11.24.1); and Pindar compared the victory over the Carthaginians with the battles of Salamis and Plataiai (Pindar *Pythian Odes* 1.75–79; cf. also Diodoros 11.23.1).

Independent of the question of the authenticity of a Persian–Carthaginian joint strategy, still disputed today, it is necessary to interpret the events of 480 differently in respect of the Greek West as compared with the East. It is true that the outcome of the battle at Himera represented a decisive break in that for the next 70 years Carthage refrained from any military intervention, but it would be difficult to argue for a fundamental historical break. With his victory over the Carthaginians, Gelon was able to 'round off' his political ambitions, which had begun with his capture of Gela in 491. At the time, Gelon, a leading member of the noble family of the Deinomenids, had seized the inheritance of his predecessor Hippokrates after his death, and in the following years built up what Hippokrates had established on a firm foundation between 498 and 491. Aided by a superbly organized bodyguard, an efficient mercenary force and a cavalry unit commanded by Gelon, Hippokrates had succeeded in expanding his rule far beyond Gela, indeed virtually over the entire south-east of Sicily. After conquering Katana, Naxos and for a time even Zankle (Messana), as well as many Sicel cities, he could only be prevented from seizing Syracuse because of the mediation of Korinth on behalf of her daughter-city.

Gelon then followed in the footsteps of Hippokrates with unflinching determination. And so in 485, when in Syracuse the protracted conflict between the leading oligarchic faction of the *gamoroi* and the democratic faction, allied with the *killyrioi* (the enslaved indigenous inhabitants), escalated into open hostilities, Gelon took advantage of the situation to invade, and conquered the city and reinstated the banished *gamoroi*, but without relinquishing power in Syracuse once he had seized it. Indeed, he now systematically turned Syracuse into his capital. At virtually the same time as Themistokles in Athens, Gelon in Syracuse too laid the foundations for the new supremacy in the West by building a harbour and fortifications, and by a comprehensive naval programme. The area encompassed by the city was greatly expanded and the size of the population significantly increased. From Gela alone, where Gelon installed his brother Hieron as tyrant, half the inhabitants were forced to resettle in Syracuse. Further mass deportations followed from previously conquered cities, from whose inhabitants the wealthy were granted Syracusan citizenship, while the members of the poorer classes were sold into slavery – since Gelon was persuaded that 'the masses are very disagreeable to live with' (Hdt. 7.156). In addition, Diodoros speaks of Gelon giving citizenship to 10,000 mercenaries (Diodoros 11.72.3).

The power which Gelon acquired by seizing Syracuse he expanded even further by means of adroit marriages. His marriage to Damarete, the daughter of Theron the tyrant of Akragas (he, in his turn, in a second marriage wed one of Gelon's nieces), sealed a political alliance whose strength could not be trumped, since Theron's power encompassed virtually the whole of northern Sicily. This constellation drove the other tyrants – most particularly Anaxilaos of Rhegion, who with Zankle/Messana had brought the straits between Sicily and southern Italy under his control, and Terillos, who had been driven out of Himera – into the arms of the Carthaginians, who were no longer willing to tolerate a further unification of Sicily under Syracusan initiative without taking action, and so proceeded to attack in 480. The large-scale military advance, however, ended in a devastating defeat for the Carthaginians at Himera (Hdt. 7.165–7; Diodoros 11.20–6). Gelon emerged from the war in a strengthened position. The polygamous relations of his brother Hieron are an indication of how firmly his power was established. In a second marriage he took the daughter of Anaxilaos of Rhegion as his bride, and in a third marriage a niece of Theron of Akragas.

The marriage connection with the tyrant family in Rhegion is an indication that Hieron was already casting his eyes across the straits, to the mainland of Italy, in accordance with his expansionist foreign policy – i.e., after he took the place of his brother in 478, who had just died. In 477/6 he actively supported the inhabitants of Lokroi in a conflict with his father-in-law Anaxilaos of Rhegion (*scholion* to Pindar *Pythian Odes* 2.36), and at approximately the same time came to the aid of Sybaris in her fight against Kroton (Diodoros 11.48.4). Then in 474 Hieron responded to a call for help from Kyme against the Etruscans, and came away the triumphant victor in a naval battle in the Gulf of Naples. Pindar compared this victory with that of Gelon over the Carthaginians at Himera, and painted it as 'Hellas' deliverance from grievous slavery' (Pindar *Pythian Odes* 1.75). That Hieron's victory over the Etruscans paved the way for the rise of Rome is something which at the time probably could still not be foreseen. Hieron's successes in foreign policy expanded the sphere of influence of the Deinomenids deep within Italy. Through the friendly connection with Kyme and the temporary establishment of a military colony on the island of Pithekoussai (today Ischia) (Strabon 5.4.9) the southern sector of the Tyrrhenian Sea had gradually become a 'Syracusan lake' (Asheri 1992: 149).

Developments in the political realm were matched by flourishing activity in the cultural sphere, which continued to thrive even after the collapse of the tyrant regimes. The tyrants on Sicily summoned poets, artists and philosophers to their Courts, pursued a vigorous building programme and sought to raise their international profile by numerous victories at the Panhellenic games. Although their conduct may correspond at least in part to that of the tyrants in the motherland and in the Aegean in the Archaic period, their rule was characterized by fundamental differences and therefore took on a completely different style – one that in many respects approximated what was later to characterize the Hellenistic monarchies. This may explain the unquestionably anachronistic statement in Diodoros (it probably goes back to Timaios) that following his victory at Himera, Gelon, in a genuinely Hellenistic manner, was greeted as 'Benefactor, Saviour and King' (*euergetes, soter, basileus*) (Diodoros 11.26.6). Consequently, *tyrannis* in the West cannot be made to conform to the approach that prevailed in the nineteenth century, i.e., as divided into different phases along chronological lines: an 'older *tyrannis*' in the Archaic period, and a 'younger *tyrannis*' towards the end of the fifth century. In view of the great diversity in the instruments of government, a division into 'old' or 'young', 'atavistic' or 'modern' simply will not go down. The recruiting of bodyguards and mercenaries, the organization of spy networks, as well as political marriages and the promotion of art and culture were all part and parcel of the conduct of tyrants, although the polygamy of the Sicilian tyrants went far beyond the bounds of what was customary at the time, and already anticipated the practices of Hellenistic rulers.

The Sicilian tyrants, however, struck out into completely new paths by creating inclusive territorial states. Accordingly, the Deinomenids of Syracuse and the Emmenids of Akragas had succeeded in bringing large parts of Sicily under their direct rule in the first third of the fifth century. Even they, however, could not of course deprive the individual cities completely of their autonomy, but by pursuing a rigorous 'city policy', in which they did not shy away from radical intervention in the makeup of the citizenry or from the total destruction of cities, they did make sure that the cities they conquered remained docile. We have already mentioned Gelon's settlement policy in Syracuse. In 476 Hieron adopted a similar strategy in connection with the city of Katana, which may be cited as an example of the fate which overtook it: After initially transplanting her inhabitants as well as those of Naxos to Leontinoi, Hieron settled 10,000 new inhabitants – half from the Peloponnese and from Syracuse – and changed the name of the city from Katana to Aitna, and installed his son Deinomenes there as ruler. Hieron's new foundation, which Pindar celebrated in his first Pythian Ode and Aischylos in his play *The Women of Aitna*, however, lasted only a few years. After the fall of the Deinomenids, the original inhabitants returned to the city, which was once again called Katana, while Hieron's colonists settled in Inessa, which they renamed Aitna (Diodoros 11.49.1–2; 76.3; Strabon 6.2.3). In 403 the inhabitants of Katana once more became the victims of Syracusan policy, when Dionysios I conquered the city, had the inhabitants sold into slavery and settled Campanian mercenaries in their place. But after only a few years they too were transplanted to Aitna/Inessa.

The poleis and their inhabitants thus became a disposable mass, subject to the whims of the tyrant, whose goal continued to be that of securing his rule over the widest territory possible. Nonetheless, the tyrants were ever intent on not flaunting their personal power in public, but sought to integrate themselves into the discipline of the polis community and present themselves as part of the citizen body. Titles which the rulers assumed and by which they were addressed by the people, such as Diodoros ascribes to the Syracusans (see above), are not attested either in contemporary inscriptions or on coins. Instead, 'Gelon, son of Deinomenes, the Syracusan' dedicates to Apollo in Delphi a tripod as a thank offering for the victory at Himera (M&L 28), and the bronze helmets which Hieron dedicated to Zeus at Olympia from the booty from the naval battle at Kyme were engraved as follows: 'Hieron, son of Deinomenes, and the Syracusans for Zeus from the Etruscan booty from Kyme' (M&L 29; *SEG* 23 253; 33 328). It is not until we reach Dionysios I that we have evidence for a title, in official decrees. In Athenian honours from 393 and 368 he is referred to as '*archon Sikelias*' (R&O 10; 33; 34). But this title too, which no doubt had to have the endorsement of Dionysios I himself, reflects the attempt to paraphrase his political power in as neutral a language as possible. Employing the term *archon*, which could serve as a completely general designation for military or high civil office also in a polis, showed the intent of attempting to avoid any association with terms such as *basileus* (king), *tyrannos* or *dynastes* (Lewis 1994: 136–9). Thus *tyrannis* in Sicily, after its revival in the fourth century, took the same route for which the first tyrants had shown the way at the turn from the sixth to the fifth century. It therefore retained its entirely distinct character, which could not conceal its archaic roots, but at the same time already foreshadowed what was to become its essential expression in the Hellenistic period.

## *The road to democracy – an interlude?*

The successors did not succeed in maintaining the inheritance of their predecessors. Within a single decade (471–461) the three major tyrant regimes in Syracuse, Akragas and Rhegion were eliminated, and the realms over which they had ruled collapsed like a house of cards. Upon succeeding his father, Thrasydaios of Akragas was able to maintain his rule for only one year (472/1). After a vain attempt to challenge the supremacy of Hieron of Syracuse, the people of Akragas forced him to flee to Megara in Greece, where he was condemned to death and executed. In the following years the successors of Hieron and of Anaxilaos of Rhegion were both overthrown, after only a brief rule – i.e., after having themselves seized power from Hieron and Anaxilaos, respectively. As in a domino effect the tyrants were simply swept away. Their abrupt end clearly demonstrated that *tyrannis* was inextricably bound up with the personality of the individual holding power in the first instance, but also that *tyrannis* had simply become out of date and was shunted aside: the wealth and prosperity which increased significantly under the tyrants, and from which the rest of the population no doubt profited, strengthened the desire within the citizenry for greater participation in political decisions.

    In addition, there was the pent-up opposition to the arbitrary manner in which the tyrants treated the cities. Mass deportations and the forced integration of tens of thousands, as well as the creation of new citizens including non-Greeks, led to serious tensions with the 'old citizens'. After the fall of the tyrants, these tensions culminated in prolonged conflicts bordering on civil war, until an agreement was reached which guaranteed the return to their original cities of those who had been deported and banished, and the settlement of all foreigners who had been granted citizen rights by the tyrants – mostly mercenaries – in Messana (Diodoros 11.72.2–73.3; 76.4–6). The coins of the period demonstrate the impressive revival of autonomy amongst the cities of Sicily, some of which – like Naxos and Kamarina – had to be completely rebuilt after having been destroyed by the tyrants (on the redistribution of the citizenry in Kamarina, see now the approximately 150 bronze tablets from the period, *SEG* 41 846; also *SEG* 47 1431). But the restoration of the poleis apparently proceeded all the more smoothly because the political unrest evidently did not have any serious negative effect on prosperity (Diodoros 11.72.1). Moses Finley offers the following pertinent summary:

> The end of tyranny saw no cessation in the outward signs of prosperity: in agriculture, in continuation of the tradition established by the tyrants of minting the finest coins, in the scale and quality of temple-building and of other public works. On the material side, it seemed as if Syracuse and Akragas had the necessary conditions to follow the path of Athens, where the tyranny had been overthrown in 508. (Finley 1979: 57)

The same path was in fact followed. From everything we can deduce from the highly fragmentary information in the ancient sources, as a rule democratic factions came to power in the newly constituted poleis, and insisted on greater participation by the citizens in political decision-making. Many details – such as the introduction of *petalismos* in Syracuse (Diodoros 11.87.4), similar to ostracism in Athens – corresponded to those in democratic institutions known in other parts of the contemporary Greek world. To that extent the West was following the trends of the time.

Nonetheless, conditions in the West were fundamentally different. Indeed, the tyrants in the Greek West did not attempt to secure the support of the lower classes, as was the case elsewhere (Hdt. 7.156.2–3), but always remained closely aligned with the nobles. Although social changes came about from the tyrants having intervened in the very structure of the poleis, no consolidation of the lower classes took place. Consequently, after restoration of the poleis the aristocratic factions were able to re-establish themselves, under a democratic guise. Just how strong the influence was which they exerted is shown by the fact that in Syracuse the *petalismos* was, under pressure from the aristocrats, abolished not long after having been introduced (Diodoros 11.87.4). With this, certain social structures became consolidated, which thwarted any lasting political change and left little prospect for democratic development within the lower classes. Here we may also look for the reason why, after a promising beginning in overthrowing the tyranny, 'the end-product proved to be weak and short-lived' (Finley 1979: 5), and why democracy remained an 'interlude' – if not indeed in the entire West, then at least in Sicily (Finley 1979: 58–73).

No less of an interlude, albeit much shorter, was the attempt of the Sicel Douketios to exploit the confusion to establish a dominion of his own in the wake of the collapse of the tyrant regimes. Stemming from an eminent Sicel family (Diodoros 11.78.5), he sought to unite his fellow-Sicels into a kindred alliance – Diodoros refers to a *synteleia* or a *koinon* (Diodoros 11.88.6) – and thereby create a powerful counter-weight to the Greek poleis. Initially supported by Syracuse, Douketios was able to score substantial successes in the years after 461, and in 453/2, with the founding of the city of Palike in the immediate vicinity of a leading Sicel sanctuary, he established an urban centre for his newly created Sicel league (Diodoros 11.88.6–90.1). Even though Douketios may have played the Sicel card, it is scarcely possible to speak of a national Sicel revolt. Douketios' action doubtless bears the stamp of Greek tyrants, whom he used as his model. Indeed, 'Ducetius' models were Gelon and Hieron, not Kokalos or Hyblon of old' (Asheri 1992: 165). The founding of a Sicel league was therefore much more the result of an already highly advanced Hellenization of the Sicels than a conscious return to indigenous origins.

The constitutional changes in the Sicilian cities altered but little in respect of the struggles for supremacy. Thus, after the situation in domestic politics had become stabilized, Syracuse – along with Akragas – moved decisively against the growing power of Douketios. He was finally defeated in 450. After Douketios had been sent into exile in Korinth for several years, he returned to Sicily in 448/7 in order to found the Greek-Sicel city of Kale Akte. It is uncertain to what degree Douketios was acting with the connivance of the Syracusans or was being used by them to further their own political ambitions. At all events, this affair led to conflict between Syracuse and

Akragas, in which the other poleis also became involved. Douketios, who once more – admittedly in vain – announced his claim to the leadership of the Sicels, became a player in the power politics of the rival cities until his death in 440. In this drama Syracuse was able to re-establish her former hegemonic position until the end of the 430s. At the same time, there was a sharp increase in the conflicts amongst the various poleis: the call for outside help became increasingly more pronounced, and brought the major powers of mainland Greece upon the scene – above all Korinth and Athens, but eventually Sparta as well.

Although the Athenians had not participated in the colonization of the West, as had the Korinthians and the Spartans, they nonetheless had cast their gaze on southern Italy and Sicily ever since the time of the Persian wars. Themistokles is said to have named two of his daughters Sybaris and Italia (Plutarch *Themistokles* 32.2), and before the battle of Salamis Themistokles threatened to resettle all Athenians in Siris, which had been destroyed by her neighbours in the sixth century, and, as an Ionian city, 'has long been ours, and the oracles have foretold that Athenians must live there some day' (Hdt. 8.62.2).

In the middle of the fifth century Athens headed up a Panhellenic colonization venture, and carried out the founding of Thourioi at the site of Sybaris, which had been destroyed in 510. And the treaties which Athens made with Rhegion, with Leontinoi (M&L 63, 74) and eventually also with Segesta (M&L 37 – possibly not until 418/17) and the Messapian leader Artas (Thuc. 7.33.4) go back to approximately the same period.

Within this configuration of events southern Italy was without fail also pulled into the undertow of the political conflicts which in the end engulfed the entire Greek world, i.e., the Peloponnesian War. Despite this, our sources provide extremely little information on the history of this region, which seems to have taken a very similar course to that of Sicily. In any event, it is possible to observe very similar developments in the constitutional history of the poleis in southern Italy, where, against the background of social tensions, the aristocratic-oligarchic regimes were also plunged into a crisis after the end of the sixth century. Here too demands for the extension of political participation by the citizenry had fostered the rise of tyrant regimes. According to later tradition, Pythagoras is said to have played a central role in the internal conflicts. He had emigrated from Samos c. 530 and settled in Kroton, where he founded a religious community, whose adherents attained great political influence in many poleis in the Greek West. 'Did not many of them act as guardians of the laws and govern Italic cities by proclaiming what in their view was best, and gave advice . . . It was evidently at this time that the best forms of government existed in Italy and Sicily' (Iamblichos *Life of Pythagoras* 129).

The rigorous and sectarian conduct of these aristocratically inclined men led to bitter internal conflicts, which culminated in a pogrom against the Pythagoreans about the middle of the fifth century:

> When, in the district of Italy, then known as Greater Hellas, the club-houses of the Pythagoreans were burnt down, there ensued, as was natural, a general revolutionary movement, the leading citizens of each city having thus unexpectedly perished, and in all the Greek towns of the district murder, sedition and every kind of disturbance were rife. (Polybios 2.39.1–3; cf. also Iamblichos *Life of Pythagoras* 249)

To all appearances, these political upheavals fostered the breakthrough of democratic forces, but without it becoming possible for us to discern more precisely the forms which these democracies assumed. Aristotle's reference to the democratic constitution of Taras (Tarentum) (Aristotle *Politics* 1320b9–16) at least suggests that it was a case of more or less moderate forms of democracy, which still afforded many opportunities for the aristocrats to exert their influence. But one had adjusted to the demands of the times and to political necessity. Beyond that, in the case of Tarentum events in foreign policy left the aristocrats no alternative after they had suffered a devastating defeat against the Messapians in a 'great bloodbath that was so common amongst Greeks' (Hdt. 7.170.3). Aristotle offers the terse comment: 'In Tarentum, following the defeat in which many eminent citizens were killed by the Iapyges (= Messapians) not long after the Persian wars, a democracy replaced the government' (Aristotle *Politics* 1303a3–5).

Enduring internal disputes within the poleis and constant rivalries amongst the poleis are characteristic features of conditions in both Sicily and southern Italy. On the other hand, in southern Italy conflicts with the indigenous population became accentuated in the course of the fifth century, while in Sicily Syracuse succeeded in thwarting Sicel ambitions. The cities of southern Italy came increasingly under the pressure of native tribes who – as already noted – united together in strong alliances and thereby presented great potential for aggression. In order to confront this threat, the Greek cities came closer together. In the last third of the fifth century at the latest, the cities of Kroton, Kaulonia and Sybaris (re-founded after civil strife had erupted in Thourioi by citizens who consequently chose to leave their city) formed the nucleus of an alliance that was modelled on the institutional structures of the federal principles of the Achaian League in the Peloponnese (Polybios 2.39.4–6). This league not only became effective in terms of foreign policy, but may at the same time also have contributed decisively to stabilizing democratic constitutions in the member states of the league.

# 3   The Return of the Past? The Fourth Century

## *A kingdom of two Sicilies*

The experiences of the military conflicts of the last three decades of the fifth century must have come as a shock to the Syracusans. Thanks to military skill and also to luck and chance, they had succeeded within a short time in extricating themselves from the imperial advances of two major states. For neither Athens nor Carthage was it any longer merely a question of lending support to their Sicilian allies. The pleas for help from Leontinoi (427) and Segesta (416/15) were for Athens little more than a pretext for their attempt to extend their supremacy also to the West (Thuc. 6.6.1). And when in 409 the Carthaginians – so to speak in the aftermath of the Athenian defeat – took up Segesta's cause, and after 70 years of peaceful restraint carried on war in Sicily, there could no longer be any doubt, in the face of the escalation of the conflict, that in the final analysis what was at issue was hegemony and no longer the protection of an Elymian city. The mighty military hardware which in 415 – after the prelude of 427 – Athens threw into action and the devastating consequences of

Carthage's military campaigns since 409, which culminated in the massacre of 3,000 Greeks in Himera – as revenge for 480 – and in the destruction of Akragas, made the Syracusans all too aware of the threat to their very existence. The resultant prevailing mood may have been a decisive factor in preparing the way, in the confusion of the most intense internal disputes, for Dionysios to be acclaimed *strategos autokrator* (i.e., chief commander with plenipotentiary powers) in 405.

This office, which in the Syracusan constitution was designed to come into effect in political crises, Dionysios used to establish his personal power base and organized it into the 'greatest and longest tyranny in history' (Diodoros 13.96.4). It is undeniable that here Gelon and Hieron were his models, for he employed the same tools for governing, except that he wielded them with far greater rigour and severity, and on a much greater scale – in accordance with his unquestionably greater ambitions. A mercenary army, drawn from virtually all parts of the Mediterranean, but especially from the Peloponnese and central and northern Italy, constituted the foundation of his power. These mercenaries served Dionysios not only in the capacity of fighting troops, but also as a bodyguard, as occupation troops in conquered cities and, after disarmament of the Syracusan citizenry, as a substitute for militiamen. Syracuse, celebrated already by Pindar as a *Megale Polis* (Pindar *Pythian Odes* 2.1), was provided with gigantic fortifications and turned into the largest city in the Greek world. Thanks to a defence industry of the most modern type, it resembled a massive munitions factory (Diodoros 14.18.2–8; 41.3–43.4).

After Dionysios had relinquished almost half of Sicily to the Carthaginians in the peace treaty of 405, and, in addition, granted autonomy to other parts of the island, and at least secured Carthaginian recognition to implement his rule over Syracuse (Diodoros 13.114.1), he took decisive action against the cities of Sicily in the following years. By means of large-scale forced settlements and by giving citizen rights to soldiers and former slaves, Dionysios succeeded step by step in breaking down the resistance of the cities and in bringing them under his control. He did not, however, confine himself to Sicily, but, in an alliance with Lokroi – even more decisively than Hieron had in his day – also crossed over to Italy. As a result, the Greek cities in southern Italy found themselves caught between two fronts: they had to defend themselves, on the one hand, against the increasingly aggressive attacks of the local tribes of the Lucanians and Samnites, and, on the other, against the attacks of Dionysios. In this situation, at the beginning of the fourth century, Thourioi, Hipponion, Rhegion, Elea and perhaps Naples, along with other cities, joined the existing League composed of Kroton, Sybaris and Kaulonia, and formed the Italiote league. With his victory at the Eleporos river in 388, however, Dionysios put a quick end to this league. The Syracusan territory stretched as far as the Isthmus of Catanzaro, and with the seizure of Rhegion (386) Syracuse ultimately gained control of the straits between Sicily and Italy, especially also after the destruction of Hipponion and Kaulonia and the deportation of their inhabitants to Syracuse, put an end to her most determined adversaries. The toe of Italy, however, served Dionysios merely as a bridgehead for much more ambitious plans. An alliance with the Lucanians as well as a reorganization of the Italiote League, the leadership of which passed to Tarentum, expanded the Syracusan sphere of influence over many parts of southern Italy. And with the founding of Ankon (Ancona), Hatria, Issa and possibly Lissos, Dionysios extended his net of colonies across the Adriatic. Attempts by the

Carthaginians to set foot in southern Italy, however, in the end came to nothing, whereas in Sicily they had a number of successes, and finally secured their *epikrateia* in a line running from Himera to Herakleia Minoa (Diodoros 15.17.5).

What could still be construed as liberation of the Greeks from the yoke of barbarism in the war against the Carthaginians between 398 and 392 (Diodoros 14.46.5) soon came up against a fundamental contradiction in the Greek world: e.g., in a passionate speech by the Athenian Lysias (Lysias 33) in 388, during the Olympian games, containing his call to arms against both suppressers of Greek freedom, the Great King and the 'tyrants of Sicily'; and Isokrates' complaint in 380: 'Italy has been devastated, Sicily enslaved' (Isokrates 4.169). Dionysios, however, trumped all his critics in the power game, and succeeded in working his way even into the politics of the motherland – at first on the side of Sparta, and then also as a friend (and citizen) of Athens (R&O 33; 34). And until his death he held an empire together 'in iron chains' (Diodoros 16.5.4; Plutarch *Dionysios* 7.6) which, at least in terms of its geographical dimensions, but perhaps also in respect of its political aims, came close to what in 1815 was singled out from the remains of the Napoleonic empire as the 'Kingdom of the Two Sicilies'.

## Futile new beginnings

Things seemed to repeat themselves in Syracuse. As scarcely a hundred years earlier, so once again the successors were incapable of maintaining the inheritance of their predecessors. Dionysios I had scarcely died in 367 when the 'iron chains' snapped with which he had held the kingdom he had created together. The tyranny of his son and successor Dionysios II was doomed to failure, since his father had kept him well clear of state affairs. He was unfortunate in his foreign policy, and became the helpless victim in the growing Court intrigues and power conflicts, in which Dion, both brother-in-law and son-in-law of Dionysios I, played a leading role. Dion, a friend of the philosopher Plato, saw in the change of throne from father to son an opportune occasion, under the influence of Platonic ideas, to put into practice his own political theories in Syracuse. In the face of the political realities, however, the experiment ended in a lamentable failure, despite several attempts. Nor did the fact that Plato was present in person, twice summoned to the Court of the tyrant (366 and 361), make any difference. On the instigation of his opponents, who included the historian Philistos, Dion was forced to flee into exile to Greece in 366. In 357, however, he returned to Syracuse with a small mercenary force, and after fluctuating battles succeeded in overthrowing Dionysios II, and forced him to flee into exile in Lokroi. But Dion's renewed attempt to carry out a radical change in the constitution of Syracuse met with growing opposition, and led to his assassination in 354, by his most intimate confidants.

With Dion's death Syracuse was plunged into anarchy. In quick succession a number of individuals took over as tyrants: first Dion's assassin Kallippos, then two half-brothers of Dionysios II, namely Hipparinos (in 353) and Nysaios (in 351), and finally Dionysios II once more himself (in 347). This disintegration of political power was not without its effect on foreign policy. The 'Kingdom of the Two Sicilies' collapsed and revealed the same lack of unity as in the Greek motherland, where in the words of Xenophon, 'chaos and discord were greater than ever before'

(Xenophon *Hellenika* 7.5.27). In southern Italy the Bruttians broke away from the Lucanians, and expanded their power over former Syracusan territory at the tip of south-west Italy. Thanks to the fact that Syracuse had become powerless, the Italiotes had lost rear cover, and so had to defend themselves all the more against attacks from their local neighbours. On Sicily, virtually all cities had broken away from Syracuse and were under the rule of local tyrants, who with the support of mercenary alliances carried on war against each other. In addition, 'the Carthaginians turned up on the shores of Sicily with a huge fleet and, hovering over the Greeks of the island, posed a permanent threat' (Plutarch *Timoleon* 2.1).

In this situation the Syracusans followed a time-worn pattern: they sought help from without. As so often in the past, they turned to their mother-city, Korinth, which in 345 sent Timoleon as a mediator. His mission was to lead Sicily once more to a new period of power. The 'revival of Sicily' (Talbert 1974) associated with Timoleon's name no doubt belongs to one of the most astonishing moments in Greek history in the Classical period. In less than a decade he not only restored the old frontiers of Syracuse's *epikrateia*, but also liberated Syracuse and all the other cities of Sicily from tyranny. Syracuse became the centre of a league of free cities, whose political and economic base Timoleon completely overhauled. He pursued a very deliberate policy of reviving the urban diversity of Sicily, and thereby counter-checked the policies of the Syracusan tyrants. For the resettlement of Syracuse alone he is said to have drawn 60,000 new colonists from Greece, Italy and Sicily (Plutarch *Timoleon* 23.6), but all the other cities also experienced a new period of flowering. The accounts of ancient authors, however, reflect only the beginnings of the extent of this restoration policy, and it is not until we turn to the numismatic and above all the archaeological evidence that we get a clearer picture of the enormous dimensions it assumed. This also explains why Timoleon upon his death was buried as an *oikistes*, the founder of a colony, in the market place in Syracuse and why annual games were decreed in his honour, 'because he overthrew the tyranny, conquered the barbarians, rebuilt the largest of the cities which had been destroyed and restored to the Siceliots their freedom' (Plutarch *Timoleon* 39.4).

This freedom did not, however, last very long. Soon after Timoleon's death Sicily – as earlier also the rest of the West – was plunged into fresh political chaos, which was once more finally to lead back to *tyrannis*. Plato's warning, which he published already in his eighth *Letter* (8.353D–E), was to be valid for a long time:

> but what seems to be the end of the old is always being linked on to the beginning of a new brood; and because of this endless chain of evil the whole tribe of tyrants and democrats alike will be in danger of destruction. But should any of these consequences ... come to pass, hardly a trace of the Greek tongue will remain in all Sicily, since it will have been transformed into a province or dependency of Phoenicians or Oscans.

## Further reading

An excellent survey of the state of research can be found in the regularly published Acts of the Convegni di studi sulla Magna Grecia (organized annually since 1961), as well as in the Acts of the Congressi internazionali di studi sulla Sicilia antica, which are published in the journal *Kokalos*. The results of archaeological research are published regularly in *Archaeological Reports* – the latest by de Angelis (2001) and Ridgway (2002). The Bibliography to follow here is confined almost exclusively to studies in English, but it must be emphasized that for any detailed investigation in the history of the Greek West research published in Italian is mandatory. Additional literature can readily be found in the bibliographies in the studies cited below.

# Bibliography

Asheri, D. (1988) 'Carthaginians and Greeks' in: *CAH²* 4 739–80
Asheri, D. (1992) 'Sicily, 478–431 B.C.' in: *CAH²* 5 147–70
Berger, S. (1992) *Revolution and society in Greek Sicily and southern Italy* (Stuttgart: Steiner) (*Historia* Einzelschriften 71)
Caven, B. (1990) *Dionysius I: war-lord of Sicily* (New Haven: Yale University Press)
Cerchiai, L., L. Jannelli, F. Longo (2004) *The Greek cities of Magna Graecia and Sicily* (Los Angeles: J. Paul Getty Museum)
De Angelis, F. (2001) 'Archaeology in Sicily 1996–2000' in: *Archaeological Reports* 47: 145–201
De Angelis, F. (2003) *Megara Hyblaia and Selinous: the development of two Greek city-states in archaic Sicily* (Oxford: Oxford University School of Archaeology) (Oxford University School of Archaeology Monograph 57)
Dunbabin, T. J. (1948) *The western Greeks: the history of Sicily and south Italy from the foundations of the Greek colonies to 480 B.C.* (Oxford: Clarendon)
Finley, M. I. (1979) *Ancient Sicily* (revised edition) (London: Chatto & Windus 1979)
Gabba, E., & G. Vallet (eds) (1980) *La Sicilia antica*, vol. 2, part 1: *La Sicilia greca dal sesto secolo alle guerre puniche* (Palermo: Lombardi)
Hall, J. (2004) 'How "Greek" were the early western Greeks?' in: Lomas, K. (ed.) (2004) *Greek identity in the western Mediterranean: papers in honour of Brian Shefton* (Leiden: Brill) 35–54 (*Mnemosyne* Suppl. 246)
Jameson, M. H., D. R. Jordan, R. D. Kotansky (1993) *A 'lex sacra' from Selinous* (Durham NC: Duke University Press)
Kirsten, E. (1975) *Süditalienkunde: Ein Führer zu klassischen Stätten*, vol. 1: *Campanien und seine Nachbarlandschaften* (Heidelberg: Winter)
Lewis, D. M. (1994) 'Sicily, 413–368 B.C.' in: *CAH²* 6 120–55
Lomas, K. (2000) 'The polis in Italy: ethnicity and citizenship in the western Mediterranean' in: Brock, R., & S. Hodkinson (eds) (2000) *Alternatives to Athens: varieties of political organization and community in ancient Greece* (Oxford: Oxford University Press) 167–85
Pugliese Carratelli, G. (ed.) (1996) *The western Greeks: classical civilization in the western Mediterranean* (London: Thames & Hudson)
Purcell, N. (1994) 'South Italy in the fourth century' in: *CAH²* 6 381–403
Ridgway, D. (2002) 'Archaeology in Sardinia and south Italy 1995–2001' in: *Archaeological Reports* 48: 117–38
Rutter, N. K. (1997) *The Greek coinages of southern Italy and Sicily* (London: Spink)
Sjöqvist, E. (1978) *Sicily and the Greeks: studies in the interrelationship between the indigenous populations and the Greek colonists* (Ann Arbor: University of Michigan Press) (Jerome Lectures 9)

Smarczyk, B. (2003) *Timoleon und die Neugründung von Syrakus* (Göttingen: Vandenhoeck & Ruprecht) (Abhandlungen der Akademie der Wissenschaften zu Göttingen, Philologisch-historische Klasse 3, 251)

Smith, C. J., & J. Serrati (eds) (2000) *Sicily from Aeneas to Augustus: new approaches in archaeology and history* (Edinburgh: Edinburgh University Press) (New Perspectives on the Ancient World 1)

Talbert, R. J. A. (1974) *Timoleon and the revival of Greek Sicily, 344–317* B.C. (London: Cambridge University Press) (Cambridge Classical Studies)

Talbert, R. J. A. (1997) 'The Greeks in Sicily and south Italy' in: Tritle, L. A. (ed.) (1997) *The Greek world in the fourth century: from the fall of the Athenian empire to the successors of Alexander* (London: Routledge) 137–65

Walbank, F. W. (1968–9) 'The historians of Greek Sicily' in: *Kokalos* 14–15: 476–98

Westlake, H. D. (1994) 'Dion and Timoleon' in: *CAH*² 6 693–722

CHAPTER TEN

# Beyond Magna Graecia: Greeks and Non-Greeks in France, Spain and Italy

*Kathryn Lomas*

## 1   Introduction

The study of the Greek western Mediterranean has sometimes been regarded as marginal to mainstream Greek history but at the same time not entirely accepted within the study of the native populations – a problem especially acute in Italy, where Magna Graecia tended to fall into a gap between the study of Greek history and that of Roman Italy. This is due in part to artificial boundaries created by the structures of Classical education, and in part to a rather Athenocentric approach to Greek history which took the mainland classical democracies as the norm and dismissed the western poleis, which had a different line of development, as an aberration. In doing so, scholarship was following the lead of Thucydides (Thuc. 6.17), who dismissed the Sicilians as being weakened by their demographic flexibility and lack of a strong bond between land and citizenship; but at the same time, this focus on fifth- and fourth-century Athens as the norm has drawn attention away from areas which provide fascinating evidence for culture-contact with the non-Greek world and for the development of alternative state identities and forms of political behaviour within the Greek communities. The Greeks of the western Mediterranean lived in a multi-cultural region, interacting with a wide variety of non-Greek populations. Their settlement history spanned a wide range of experiences from migration by individuals and small groups such as that which gave rise to Pithekoussai, through piecemeal settlement leading to the formation of a polis, to planned colonizations such as the foundation of Thourioi. As a result, study of these areas gives us a rich insight into the development of Greek communities and into the processes of cultural contact and exchange with their indigenous neighbours and with other immigrants such as the Phoenicians, and later the Carthaginians, in Sicily, Spain and North Africa.

The areas on which this chapter will focus are even more peripheral to mainstream Greek history than the settlements of Sicily and Magna Graecia. Both Spain and France had some Greek settlement which developed into poleis, much of it taking place later than that in southern Italy and Sicily, but both areas also had a long history of Greek contact which was not polis-based – settlement by individuals and small groups, formation of emporia, and regular economic and cultural contacts via trade networks. North Africa and the islands of the western Mediterranean are part of a complex network of economic and cultural contacts, including settlement by a number of different ethnic groups – notably Greek and Phoenician in the Classical period – which formed an intricate pattern of cultural contacts, exchanges and hybridization (van Dommelen 1997). Finally, central and northern Italy – and in particular the Adriatic coast – were regions of considerable economic, social and cultural contact with the Greek world.

The concept of colonization has become deeply problematic and there has been a vigorous debate about the nature of settlement in the West, particularly that of the early archaic period, but which is also relevant to our understanding of the region in the Classical period. Recent studies (e.g. Osborne 1998; van Dommelen 1997; De Angelis 2004) have emphasized the extent to which scholarship on ancient colonization has been refracted through the colonial experiences of western Europe in the nineteenth and twentieth centuries. This lent itself to a 'top-down' approach to the settlement process which viewed indigenous societies as less advanced but transformed by exposure to the economic and cultural benefits of a superior society, disseminated from a planned and structured city-state. The ancient sources could all too easily be used to support this model, presenting the act of settlement as a structured, state-driven event which results in the founding of a polis. Necessary components of the foundation process were identified as consultation of an oracle, appointment of an oikist or founder, the demarcation of boundaries and division of land, and the location of key ritual sites (Hdt. 5.42–8; Cicero *De Divinatione* 1.1.3; Diodoros 8.21.3, 8.23; Strabon 4.1.4). More recently, it has been argued that Greek communities in the Mediterranean evolved as part of a long-term process of migration and settlement rather than being founded as the result of a specific event or at a specific point in time (Osborne 1998). There are still many uncertainties about whether the concept of the polis had even crystallized in Greece itself at the time of the early colonizations (for contrasting views see Snodgrass 1994 and Malkin 1994) and new evidence from Italy and Sicily has opened up the likelihood that early settlement in the western Mediterranean was a fluid and piecemeal process. The earliest phases of Megara Hyblaia, Policoro, Metapontion (Metaponto) and other sites are much less structured than previously thought, and examination of early burials seems to point to a mixed population of Greeks and indigenous peoples which did not develop into something resembling a Greek polis until at least the end of the seventh century. Most recently, a vigorous series of counter-arguments have been put forward, defending the idea that Greek cities outside Greece were for the most part founded communities, and seeking to re-evaluate both the literary and archaeological evidence for the establishment of such communities (Malkin 2002).

This debate has fundamentally changed the way in which Greek settlement outside Greece and the Aegean is studied, and has to some extent outlawed the term 'colonization' in favour of more neutral terms such as 'colonialism' (van Dommelen

1997) or 'settlement' (Osborne 1998). It is, however, something which we need to consider in the context of Greek settlement in the areas and time-frames covered by this chapter. Greek contact with the western Mediterranean in the Classical period took place in a very different context from that of the eighth and seventh centuries and was driven by a complex mixture of economic and political motivations. The Phokaians, for instance, brought a well-defined sense of their own cultural identity as a polis with them to the West in the middle of the sixth century. Nevertheless, much Phokaian settlement was in small emporia of mixed ethnicity, only a few of which went on to form a fully developed polis identity, and despite the arguments for a common Phokaian identity, they fissured into several different groups with different settlement histories in various parts of the western Mediterranean. They were also notable for their ability to absorb and assimilate non-Greek populations into their community. There are areas of the western Mediterranean, however, in which Greek contact never crystallized into full-scale polis settlements even during the Classical period, or in which those which did evolve had a problematic trajectory of development. A significant amount of Greek settlement in Spain, for instance, was the result of individuals or small groups settling in indigenous communities rather than forming their own poleis (De Hoz 2004), while the Greeks at Spina and Hatria (Adria) at the head of the Adriatic remained part of ethnically mixed communities. Ankon (Ancona), despite being founded as a colony by Syracusans in 387, failed to flourish as a Greek polis, and the settlers seem to have remained as a fairly self-contained and isolated group in an otherwise Picene cultural environment (Mercando 1976: 164–70; Sebastiani 2004: 22–3; Colivicchi 2000: 135–40). The question of whether we are examining a self-conscious colonization or a process of individual or group settlement is by no means clear even in the Classical era, and the Greeks of the western Mediterranean represent a wide range of different experiences of settlement and contact.

## Greeks beyond Magna Graecia: Adriatic Italy and the Greek world

Greek contacts with Italy are mostly addressed in terms of the Greek cities of the south coast and Campania, but in fact this is only a part – albeit a major one – of the subject. From the Mycenaean period onwards, there had been close contacts between many other areas of Italy and the Greek world, attested by imported artefacts and cultural influences (Vagnetti 1983; Kilian 1990). During the Classical period, there was significant Greek contact with the Italic populations well beyond Magna Graecia, which took the forms of both settlement and less structured commercial and cultural contacts. These commercial contacts are particularly prominent in the Adriatic. There is evidence of Greek contact along this coast of Italy dating back to the Bronze Age, in the form of Mycenaean pottery found at many locations along the Adriatic coast, possibly as far north as Venice (Braccesi 1988), although whether it was transmitted via Greeks or local exchange networks remains open to question. In the Classical period, however, this region becomes an interesting case-study of contact and exchange. These contacts between Greeks and Italians are driven by socio-economic factors rather than large-scale colonization. During the last quarter of the sixth century, an upsurge in quantities of Greek material goods and evidence of Greek settlement on the Adriatic coast points to the development of a major trade route disseminating Greek goods – a phenomenon which continued throughout the fifth century and did not begin to tail off until c. 350. However, this took place via a number of multi-ethnic emporia and local trade networks, not via exclusively Greek settlements.

One important point which needs stressing is that the populations of Adriatic Italy are significant players in this relationship, which was driven to a large extent by demand for Greek luxury goods by the status-conscious Italic elites. Greek and Roman historians identify several different ethnic groups in this region, ranging from the Messapians, Peucetians and Daunians in what is now Puglia, through the Picenes in central Adriatic Italy, to the Veneti north of the Po delta (on the problems of self-identity among the indigenous populations, see Dench 1995; Bradley 2000; Herring 2000; Lomas 2000). Although there are significant cultural differences between these populations, there are some common features. At the beginning of the fifth century, these regions are all in the process of developing complex state societies, characterized by increasingly large and dominant central settlements which served as economic, ritual and administrative centres for their territories. Socially, these were highly stratified societies dominated by very wealthy and powerful elites, to the point where leading men are often described by Greek authors as kings (*basileis*) or autocrats (*dynastai*) (Pausanias 10.13.10; Thuc. 7.33; Strabon 6.3.4; Justin 12.2.5). Some of the sites in these areas (notably in south-east Italy, and possibly also in the Veneto) were in the process of developing urban settlement in the course of the fifth and fourth centuries, and were indisputably wealthy and complex societies dominated by elites with wide-ranging international connections, both within Italy and beyond.

Greek contact with the Adriatic is represented in two fields of activity – a modest level of permanent Greek settlement (although no exclusively Greek poleis), and copious evidence for the import of Greek goods, especially luxury goods, by the elites of these areas. Permanent settlement was restricted, and consisted principally of the growth of Greek communities at Adria, on the Po delta, in the late sixth century (Pseudo-Skylax 17.3; Pliny the Elder *Naturalis Historia* 3.16; Strabon 5.1.7; Dionysios of Halikarnassos 1.18.2–5), and the foundation of a colony at Ancona by refugees from Dionysios I in 387 (Strabon 5.4.2). These communities reflect a variety of different modes of Greek settlement and interaction with the non-Greek populations. According to our sources, Ancona was founded by Syracusans, but in fact there was a flourishing Picene community there dating back to the Bronze Age, and the Greek portion of the population seems to have remained relatively small. It also seems to have remained fairly self-contained and to have had little impact on the culture of the city. There is evidence for Greek goods found at Ancona and a series of Greek grave stelai of the late fourth to first centuries, but the culture of Ancona in the Classical period remained basically Picene, with only a few traces of Greek structures (Mercando 1976; Sebastiani 2004: 22–3; Colivicchi 2000: 135–8).

More important, from a commercial point of view, was the nearby Picene settlement of Numana. From c. 510 onwards, this site seems to have acted as an *entrepôt* for Greek goods and an emporion for trade between the Greeks and the Picenes. The Picene aristocrats were large-scale consumers of Greek luxury goods, and between the late sixth and mid fourth century, there is evidence of flourishing commercial and cultural contacts with Greece (Shefton 2003). Corinthian pottery was imported in significant quantities in the late sixth century, and is found in elite burials both in Numana itself and in the settlements in its hinterland (Luni 2001: 147–50). By the early fifth century, Attic wares are the most numerous pottery imports, along with Peloponnesian and Etruscan bronzes, south Italian pottery and Greek and Graeco-Italic transport amphorae, which provide evidence for importation of wine (Luni 2001: 145; on the distribution of Greek pottery in Picenum, see Naso 2000: 202–7). Much of the pottery is sympotic in function. Princely burials of the sixth and fifth centuries, such as those at Numana, Filottrano and Sirolo, contained spectacular Attic red figure kraters, oinochoai and various types of drinking cup, providing a strong indication of the adoption of Greek vessels for ritual feasting by the wealthy Picene elite. The presence of Greek transport amphorae also indicates a trade in wine and olive oil (Landolfi 2001: 148–50). During the fourth century, the number of Greek imports decreases somewhat from its fifth-century peak, but Attic red figure and black glaze wares continued to be imported in significant quantities (Landolfi 2001: 147). As at Ancona, there is also the question of whether Numana had a resident Greek community. The presence of assemblages of early fifth-century grave goods similar to those found in the Kerameikos cemetery at Athens, and of Greek inscriptions on some ceramics, raises the question of whether there was a settled Greek presence in Numana, but the evidence for this is inconclusive (Landolfi 2001: 147).

Further north, there is strong evidence for Greek settlement at Adria and Spina, both major emporia in the fifth century, but these were ethnically mixed communities rather than exclusively Greek foundations. Both began to develop in the sixth century and by the later sixth century Spina was sufficiently established, and sufficiently embedded in Greek cultural networks, to build a treasury at Delphi (Strabon 5.1.7) to advertise its aspirations to membership of the wider Greek cultural community. In the fifth and fourth centuries, both expanded significantly, and in the Classical period, they played a major role as points on a major trade route up the Adriatic, and points of contact for Greeks and the populations of north-east Italy. Adria appears to have been a Greek (possibly Aiginetan) emporion, but it also had a substantial Etruscan population, and possibly also Venetic and Celtic elements (Fogolari and Scarfi 1970). Greek inscriptions on pottery, mostly of the fifth–fourth century, attest to the presence of a substantial Greek population, as does the existence of a cult of Apollo, and the large quantity of imported Attic pottery confirms Adria's role as an important centre for trade with Greece. In the fourth century, however, Adria's contacts with Etruria become more prominent and the commercial and cultural influence of Volterra becomes especially marked. Spina, despite references to Greek foundation myths (Pliny the Elder *Naturalis Historia* 3.16), its treasury at Delphi, and the copious quantities of Greek pottery found there, was principally an Etruscan settlement. The excavated areas of the city – principally the cemeteries and one area of the settlement – indicate that it was laid out in orthogonal fashion, in a similar manner to Marzabotto (Rebecchi 1998). Both burials and settlement areas produced large quantities of both Greek and Etruscan pottery and other goods, attesting to the mixture of ethnic and cultural influences.

Both Adria and Spina seem to have been essentially emporia of mixed Greek and Etruscan population and culture, and both acted as a means of diffusing Greek and Etruscan goods up the Po valley and into the Veneto. The effects can be traced in the quantities of Greek imports found at the important Venetic settlements of Este and Padova, where there is evidence of imported fifth- and fourth-century Greek pottery (Calzavara Capuis 1993), and also traces of wider Greek cultural influence. Greek inscriptions have been found at Padua, and Greek influence can arguably be detected in the styles of local pottery and sculpture (Zampieri 1994). The routes taken by them up the Adriatic can also be charted by the finds of Greek inscriptions, mostly short graffiti on pottery, in Adriatic Italy and also on the Adriatic islands and Dalmatian coast. As in other areas of central and northern Italy, as well as in France and Spain, the dynamics of Greek settlement and contact in the Classical period seem centred on emporia with mixed populations and wide networks of economic and cultural contacts, rather than on the foundation of colonies.

## 2   Tyrrhenian Italy and the Islands

Tyrrhenian Italy and the islands of the western Mediterranean had played an important part in Greek contacts with the region throughout the archaic period, but from the end of the sixth century, these decline markedly and the classical period is one of contraction and change. In Etruria, the presence of imported Greek pottery both changes in emphasis and declines in quantity. The east Greek and Corinthian wares which were characteristic of the seventh and early sixth centuries disappear and are replaced by Attic pottery. In the early fifth century, Attic imports remain significant but are increasingly restricted in distribution to the major coastal centres such as Gravisca and Pyrgi, and to their immediate hinterland. From c. 480, these imports decline markedly in quantity, even at these centres. Graviscae and Pyrgi were both sanctuaries which acted as emporia for a large quantity of Greek, Phoenician and eastern imports throughout the sixth century and votive deposits indicate that they were major points of contact, used by Greeks and Phoenicians as well as Etruscans. Large numbers of Greek votives, mainly pottery and lamps of Greek manufacture, are found in the sixth-century levels at Gravisca, and the number of votives inscribed in Greek (mainly Attic dialect) with Greek personal names may suggest a Greek population there until c. 480, although it is also possible that these are the results of a transient population of Greek visitors (Dubois 1995). After this date, however, Greek inscriptions disappear from the archaeological record, and the incidence of Attic pottery declines sharply, although it revives briefly at the end of the fifth century. This coincides with changes to the structure of the sanctuary and also an overall decline in the richness and quantity of the Etruscan votives, suggesting a period of general economic decline as well as diminution of contact with the Greek world (Torelli 1971, 1977 and 1999). A similar pattern can be found at Pyrgi, with a decline in imported Greek votives during the course of the fifth century (Baglione 1989–90).

Greek contact with Corsica and Sardinia also undergoes a decline during the course of the fifth century. The important centre of Alalia on Corsica flourished during the sixth century as a substantial settlement with a mixed population of Greeks, Etruscans, Phoenicians and indigenous inhabitants (Jehasse & Jehasse 1994). In 540, however, it was sacked following a major sea battle in which the Phokaians who had settled there after the Persian invasion of Ionia were defeated by a combined Etruscan and Carthaginian fleet (Hdt. 1.166), and the Greek population abandoned the site. The Carthaginian expansion of the late sixth century also had a major impact on Greek relations with the other islands of the western Mediterranean and with southern Spain. By the beginning of the fifth century, most of Sardinia was also under Carthaginian control (Diodoros 11.20.4–5, 14.63.4 and 14.77.6; D'Oriano 1990: 148–9). Greek contact is still discernible in the fifth and fourth centuries, but mainly with the Greek settlements of Italy and Sicily. Contact with the Aegean world appears to be indirect, at best. Attic pottery found in burials at Sulcis may have been imported via Ischia rather than direct from Athens (D'Oriano 1990: 148–9). In the fourth and early third centuries, this pattern intensifies, and the Greek goods found are mainly imported from other western Greek settlements. Iberian pottery, including grey ware from Emporion, is found in a fourth-century cemetery at Nora, and Tarentine jewellery and Apulian red figure pottery were buried in Punic graves at Monte Luna (D'Oriano 1990: 151–6). These, along with Graeco-Italic amphorae, seem to suggest that although Greek goods were still arriving in Sardinia in the fourth century, they were doing so via a Carthaginian network of exchange, not through the direct presence of Greeks. Recent studies of western Sardinia have revealed a very complex pattern of culture contact and exchange in the fifth–third centuries BC. Evidence from settlements and burials indicates a strong Carthaginian culture, with some Greek influence, but examination of votives from sanctuaries in this area shows the development of a very distinctively local ritual culture, absorbing influences from Greek and Carthaginian artefacts but transforming them into hybridized local forms (van Dommelen 1997: 313–20).

## 3   Phokaian Settlement in the West: Southern France

Much of the Greek contact with the far western Mediterranean was controlled by a single group of Greeks – the Phokaians. Their role, from the seventh century onwards, both in trade and exchange networks and in establishment of colonies in the region is considerable, but difficult to quantify, and the concept of a Phokaian 'thallasocracy' in the seventh and sixth centuries is being increasingly challenged (on the nature of Phokaian contact Morel 1966; 1975; Kerschner 2004). By the Classical period, they were also a disparate group without a mother-city, as Phokaia itself was destroyed c. 540 by the Persian invasion of Ionia, leaving the Phokaian diaspora to settle at Alalia, then at Elea, Massalia and Emporion. Nevertheless, it has been strongly argued (Domínguez Monedero 2004) that they retained a strong sense of Phokaian identity as a major component of their own individual civic identities.

Phokaians have a long history of contact with Spain, Tyrrhenian Italy and the islands of the western Mediterranean, dating back to the seventh century and attested both by East Greek imports such as pottery and by the testimony of Herodotos (1.163–5), who describes the mercantile activities of the Phokaians in southern Spain and a close relationship with Tartessos. Similar traditions of close social and economic connections with indigenous populations are also attached to the foundation of Massalia (Hdt. 1.163–5; Thuc. 1.13.6; Plutarch *Solon* 2.7; Athenaios 13.36.2–17; Justin 43.3.4–5.10; Aulus Gellius *Noctes Atticae* 10.16.4.2; Hyginus

7.11; Livy 5.34.8; Pomponius Mela 2.77.3–4; Pliny the Elder *Naturalis Historia* 3.34.6–35.1; Strabon 3.4.6–8, 4.1.4, 14.2.10). During the archaic period, however, their presence took the form of relatively small-scale settlement, much of it in indigenous communities, with only a small number – the most important of which were Elea, Massalia and Emporion – developing into full-scale poleis.

The close links between Phokaian settlement and patterns of trade and interaction with non-Greeks is illustrated by both Massalia and Emporion. Massalia, founded c. 600 on the Rhone delta, dominated contacts with the interior of Gaul via the Rhone valley as well as routes to Spain and an extensive network of maritime trade routes, while Emporion (discussed below, at pp. 184–8) acted as an *entrepôt* for Greek goods into north-east Spain, possibly under the control of Massalia for at least part of its history. The mechanisms by which these networks operated, and the extent to which the Greeks adopted a dominant role, are open to question. Traditional models stress the proactive role of the Greeks as both providers and traders of luxury goods, but examination of patterns of distribution of these goods has increasingly called this into question. Dietler (1989), for instance, notes that the greatest density of both Massaliote goods and Massaliote settlement is along the coast and around the Rhone delta, suggesting that the city's strongest social, political and economic links were with the immediate hinterland. During the sixth and early fifth centuries, Massaliote grey-ware pottery spreads rapidly throughout the area, as do Greek sympotic pottery and Greek wine amphorae. Further up the Rhone valley, however, patterns of Greek luxury goods such as the bronzes and Attic pottery found at Vix, Seurre, Chatillon-sur-Glane etc. suggest that they may have been transmitted via local indigenous exchange mechanisms, and Dietler argues strongly that patterns of exchange in the region in the sixth–fifth centuries should take into account a proactive indigenous population as well as the activities of the Phokaians (Dietler 1989; Bats 1998: 624–30; cf. also Shefton 1989; Morel 1990: 277–92).

It should also be borne in mind that the Phokaians were not the only sources of Greek goods and products such as wine, or the only groups operating in the western Mediterranean. There were extensive Etruscan contacts with southern France, and wrecks of Etruscan ships, many of them filled with wine amphorae, have been found off the coast of southern France. An Etruscan ship which was wrecked off Cap d'Antibes in the late sixth century (c. 540–530), to cite only one example, was carrying a cargo of bucchero and Etrusco-Corinthian pottery and Etruscan wine amphorae (Bouloumié 1990). In Spain, and in particular in southern Spain, the Phoenicians (and later the Carthaginians) had a strong presence which may have cut the Greeks out of direct trade with the area from the early fifth century onwards, and it is possible that many Greek imports dating to the fifth century may have been shipped by Phoenicians (see below, pp. 187–90). Despite these caveats, however, Massalia in the fifth century maintained a central role in economic and cultural contacts between the Greek world and the non-Greek hinterland in southern France and northern Spain, as demonstrated by the shipwrecks off Porquerolles, which contained large cargoes of Attic pottery and wine amphorae of a wide variety of Aegean and Massaliote types (Long, Miro and Volpe 1992; on the general importance of Massalia as a trading centre, see Shefton 1994: 68–74). Further evidence of extensive trade networks in the fifth and fourth centuries is provided by the Giglio shipwreck (Bound 1991) and a fourth-century wreck off Majorca.

The city of Massalia itself developed into the largest and most important of the Greek settlements of the far west. The topography of Greek Massalia is not fully determined, but it occupied the promontory on what is now the north side of the Vieux Port, defended by a wall across the landward side (Figure 10.1). The earliest settlement seems to have been concentrated on the area around the Fort St-Jean, on the tip of the promontory, and on the Butte St-Laurent (Gantès 1992: 72–7). By the end of the archaic period, the city seems to have expanded further inland, and during the fifth–fourth centuries, it was extended again to the north and east. By the Hellenistic period, the enclosed area was of c. 50 ha (Tréziny 1997: 189–91, 194–6). There were major concentrations of habitation and public buildings on the Butte St-Laurent and the Butte des Moulins, which may have been the akropolis of the Greek city, by the beginning of the fifth century (Gantès 1992: 72–5). The agora was probably located on a saddle of lower ground between the two hills on the side of the modern Place de Lenche. A stadium is known only from a Greek inscription, and may have been located close to the Cathédrale de la Major, but many of the key monuments of Greek Massalia – in particular its temples – are known only from literary sources (Strabon 4.1.4–5). The area to the north of the archaic city seems to have developed as an artisan quarter in the fifth century, marked by finds of kilns, but evolved into a residential area in the later fourth and third centuries (Tréziny 1997:

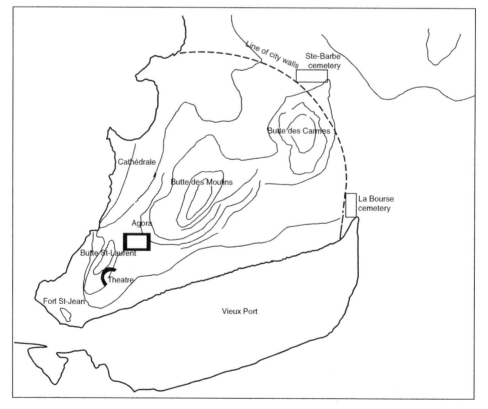

**Figure 10.1**   Greek Massalia: key archaeological sites.

197). One major problem is the continuous occupation of the site. For instance, the theatre and the so-called 'wall of Crinas', which were found during the excavations at the Bourse, both date to the first century CE, but are almost certainly built over earlier fourth-century walls and an earlier Greek theatre (Benoît 1972; Tréziny 1997: 188–91; Hodge 1998: 79–88).

Since the 1990s, substantial areas of burials have been discovered outside the gates of the city. An area of elite burials near the Bourse was contained within a terraced area, the retaining wall of which was decorated with triglyphs, and organized into what appear to be family groups. The graves, dating from the fourth to the second century, all contain cremations, housed within lead, bronze or ceramic urns and accompanied by grave-goods, although these are not lavish (Tréziny 1997: 197–9). The Ste-Barbe cemetery is considerably bigger and contains over 500 graves, also mostly cremation, dating from the fifth century to the mid-second century CE. There is a mixture of cremations and inhumations in simple *fossa* graves. Most burials contained only modest grave-goods, usually pottery, glass, lamps and sometimes coins, and were marked – if at all – by a simple stone stele, mostly undecorated and carrying only a simple inscription (Moliner 1999: 107–24; Hermary et al. 1999: 81–5; Bertucchi 1992: 124–37). This plain style of burial seems to bear out ancient sources for the emphasis on simplicity of lifestyle at Massalia, and in particular for Valerius Maximus' assertion (2.6.7) that mourning and funerary ritual was strictly limited.

The literary tradition about Massalia is also more copious than that for other settlements in France and Spain, although the fact that ancient authors focus on several very specific features, and that our sources are mostly of Hellenistic or Roman date, raises the problem of how far they represent the realities of the fifth and fourth centuries, and how far they enshrine later traditions and *topoi* about Massalia (Rougemont & Guyot-Rougemont 1992; Lomas 2004a: 478–82). In particular, both Greek and Roman authors stress the foundation myths which describe the intermarriage between the ruling family of the Gallic Segobriges and the leaders of the Phokaian settlers (Hdt. 1.163–5; Thuc. 1.13.6; Plutarch *Solon* 2.7; Athenaios 13.36.2–17; Justin 43.3.4–5.10; Strabon 4.1.4; Aulus Gellius *Noctes Atticae* 10.16.4.2; Hyginus 7.11; Livy 5.34.8; Pomponius Mela 2.77.3–4; Pliny the Elder *Naturalis Historia* 3.34.6–35.1). They also stress the supposedly austere moral climate of Massalia, which was reputed to have had strict sumptuary laws controlling display of personal wealth in areas such as dowries, marriage ceremonies and funerals (Valerius Maximus 2.6.7b–8; Athenaios 10.33.26; Tacitus *Agricola* 4.3.4; Strabon 4.1.5), although other references ascribe a very different moral character, making reference to the occurrence of luxury and decadence of the city (Athenaios 12.25.3–7; Pseudo-Plutarch *Proverb. Alex.* 60).

The constitution of Massalia was also an object of fascination amongst ancient authors. It is said to have consisted of an assembly of 600 men (*timouchoi*) who hold office for life, an executive of fifteen *timouchoi*, and three supreme office-holders, chosen from people of at least three generations of citizenship (Strabon 4.1.5), and was widely admired, although not uncritically. Aristotle, who wrote a monograph about it (now lost), acknowledges that the power base was too narrow and had to be modified, under pressure from excluded citizens, creating what he describes as a *politeia* rather than oligarchy (Aristotle *Politics* 1305b4, 1321a30), and Cicero thought that it had the potential to become oppressive (Cicero *Pro L. Valerio Flacco* 63.8, *De Re Publica* 1.43–4). It is also unclear how long it lasted in the form described by Strabon, and Aristotle's comments indicate that it was by no means static and unchanging.

The history of Massalia in the Classical period is, therefore, one of economic and territorial development, with the continued domination of the immediate area around the mouth of the Rhone and of smaller neighbouring Greek settlements such as Agatha, Antipolis (Antibes) and Nikaia (Nice/Nizza). The urban development of the city itself continued, with extension of the settlement to new habitation areas, the construction of new walls, and the continued development of the cemetery areas. At the same time, its early control over Emporion seems to have weakened during the fifth century, and it has been suggested (Mierse 1994) that the urban development of Emporion in the fifth century is a reflection of its new independence. Nevertheless, Massalia continued to play an important role in trade with both the Gallic hinterland and Spain throughout the Classical period, and to be a major trading power in the north-west Mediterranean (Jully 1980; Shefton 1994).

# 4  The Greeks in Spain

The nature of Greek settlement in Spain in the Classical period and earlier has been a matter of considerable academic debate. In the archaic period, there is evidence of extensive Greek contact with southern Spain, especially in the area around Tartessos. East Greek and Etruscan prestige objects, notably fine pottery and bronzes, are found in large quantities throughout the region in the seventh and early sixth century (Shefton 1982: 337–53; Kerschner 2004). From c. 570 onwards, these are replaced by extensive imports of Corinthian and Attic pottery, a pattern which persists throughout the sixth century (Shefton 1982: 337–55; Tsirkin 1996). The processes by which these imports arrived there are, however, hotly debated. Literary sources make reference to the foundation of Greek settlements in the region at Mainake, Hemeroskopeion, Alonis and Akra Leuke (Strabon 3.4.2; Pseudo-Skymnos 203–4; Braun 2004: 303–13), but there is little or no archaeological evidence to support the presence of significant Greek settlement this far south (Garcia y Bellido 1948; Clavel-Lévêque 1977: 25–30; Morel 1983: 127; Niemeyer 1990: 33–8). It is likely that the process which underpinned this diffusion of Greek goods was one of trade and exchange, not settlement, but the details of the mechanisms by which they arrived in Spain are uncertain. It has been suggested, in the light of the important Phokaian connections with the region, that the distribution of Greek prestige goods was the result of a Phokaian-dominated trade network. Although there is reason to believe that the Phokaians were very active in trade in the region, this ignores the complexities of interactions in the region, and it is extremely likely that at least some of the Greek material in Spain arrived with Phoenician traders (Shefton 1982: 359; Niemeyer 1990: 40–46; Domínguez Monedero & Sanchez 2001). At Huelva, for instance, the pottery recovered from excavations in the harbour area is 70 per cent Phoenician and 20 per cent indigenous wares, with only 10 per cent of pottery finds being of Greek manufacture (Fernandez Jurado and Cabrera Bonet 1987), suggesting a relatively small Greek presence in a predominantly Phoenician and indigenous settlement.

From the beginning of the fifth century, however, there is a major change in the nature and focus of the Greek contacts with Spain. In the south, the number of Greek imports drops sharply in the early fifth century. It recovers somewhat by c. 450, but in a form which suggests very different patterns of contact. The dominant form of imported pottery is Attic, and castulo cups, a type of black glaze cup made specially for export, are found in large numbers in Spain in the early fifth century. The distribution of Greek material, however, is now less widespread and more concentrated in the Guadalquivir valley. Both the changes in distribution and the evidence of growing Carthaginian dominance in the area may suggest that Greek imports were now being disseminated by indigenous Iberian networks of trade and exchange rather than by Greeks themselves (Shefton 1982: 365–7; Rouillard 1991: 317–30). The few references to southern Spain in fifth-century Greek literature also indicate that the Greeks of the Classical period regarded southern Spain as a very remote and distant region, suggesting that contact with it was not frequent (Pindar *Olympian Odes* 3.43, *Nemean Odes* 3.20, *Isthmian Odes* 4.12; Euripides *Hippolytos* 1–10, 745–5; Shefton 1982: 367–70; Prontera 1990).

The main focus of Greek activity in Spain in the Classical period undergoes a marked shift to the north-east, where it is centred on the demonstrably Greek settlements of Emporion and Rhode. Emporion was founded by the Phokaians at some point in the sixth century, although the exact date is not entirely clear. The traditional foundation date given in ancient literature is 575 (Strabon 3.4.8; Pseudo-Skylax 2–3; Pseudo-Skymnos 203–4; Polybios 1.3.76; Pomponius Mela 2.87–90; Pliny the Elder *Naturalis Historia* 3.21–23; Rouillard 1991: 244–51) but so far, there have been few finds earlier than the middle of the sixth century, and it is possible that it was established around the time of the destruction of Phokaia itself by the Persians in 540. In its first phase, in the sixth and early fifth centuries, it was a small settlement situated on an island off the coast of Spain, named as Palaipolis by Strabon (3.4.8) and close to the indigenous Iberian site of Ullastret. There have been conjectures that the motivation for placing the settlement in this area was to give access to the mineral resources of south-west Spain, and also to trade routes between Spain and southern France. It seems to have acted as an *entrepôt* for Greek goods, as large quantities of Attic pottery have been found both at Ampurias itself and in burials at Ullastret and other indigenous sites in the hinterland (Mierse 1994: 792–3; Rouillard 1991: 244–81).

Little is known of the early settlement, but in the Classical period there is evidence of significant urban expansion, and the number and distribution of Greek finds (notably Attic pottery) at Emporion itself and on neighbouring indigenous sites suggests that it continued and enhanced its role as an *entrepôt* and redistribution centre for imported Greek goods (Mierse 1994: 792–3). A new settlement, known as Neapolis, was established on the mainland and together with the original island settlement (which continued to be inhabited until the second century) formed the city of Emporion. The date at which this took place is unclear. There is evidence of settlement at Neapolis from the sixth century, but there is an important new phase of development from the beginning of the fourth century. It was heavily fortified c. 375 with walls of cyclopean masonry with double gateways, enclosing a relatively small area of c. 2.75 ha. The presence of the walls, together with the appearance of fortifications at neighbouring indigenous sites, may point to a period of tension and stress within the region in the early fourth century. The construction techniques also point to a complex history. The use of cyclopean masonry is also found at a number of indigenous sites, notably Gerona, although the plan of the gateways follows a very standard fourth-century Greek pattern (Mierse 1994: 794–6; Sanmartí 1988). The rest of the Classical city is poorly documented, but Greek sources note that it was a mixed community of Greeks and non-Greeks, who are described as living in adjacent settlements separated by a wall (Strabon 3.4.8; Silius Italicus 3; Livy 34.9). Although there is no certain evidence for this demarcation of urban space on ethnic grounds, analysis of the cemeteries of Emporion confirms that there was a significant non-Greek presence within the city (but cf. Jones 1997 for the difficulties of mapping ethnic divisions onto material culture). The Bonjoan cemetery (c. 525–475) consists mainly of inhumations accompanied by lekythoi, mostly of Attic origin, and small items of jewellery (Almagro Basch 1953; Domínguez Monedero 2004: 438–40), and has been identified as the cemetery of the Greek settlers. The contemporary and slightly earlier burials by the north-east wall of the city contain rather different grave goods – local and imported pottery, along with armour and weapons – and may be burials of the indigenous population (Almagro Basch 1955; Sanmartí-Grego 1992). There appears to have been an erosion of this distinction over time, however, as the fourth-century Marti cemetery contains burials with both Greek and non-Greek types of grave-goods (Domínguez Monedero 2004: 438–41).

The small size of the settlement has also given rise to speculation about its status and organization. Greek sources refer to it as a polis (Pseudo-Skylax 2–3; Strabon 4.1.4; *SEG* 37 838.3), but estimates of its population based on the size of the enclosure indicate that it may have been a very small community. Domínguez (1986: 3–5) calculates that the area enclosed by the walls at Emporion could have accommodated only c. 2,000 people in the fifth century, and raises the question of whether it should be regarded as a polis or classified as an emporion, possibly under the control of Massalia. Size in itself would not disqualify Emporion as a polis and references in both ancient literature and the occurrence of the ethnic *Emporitanon* in inscriptions suggest that it was viewed as such, by the Emporitans and outsiders (Pseudo-Skylax 2–3; *SEG* 37 838.3; Hansen 2000). It also minted its own coinage, using a Massaliote weight standard but its own iconography (Head 1911). However, the small size of the community and the doubts about its status and organization are a stark reminder of the low levels of permanent Greek colonial settlement in Spain in this period.

Despite this relatively low level of actual Greek settlement, Greek contacts with Spain remained significant in the fifth and early fourth centuries, and there is a lively ongoing debate about the nature of Greek contacts with indigenous society and the impact of Greek culture on that of the Iberian population. Inscriptions, written in Greek and containing Greek names, from indigenous contexts seem to indicate that there was a significant level of settlement by individuals and small groups of Greeks in otherwise indigenous settlements. The famous lead tablet from Pech Maho, dating to the middle of the fifth century, records a complex mercantile transaction which seems to have involved both Iberians and Greeks with a long-term presence in the area (Lejeune, Pouilloux and Solier 1988; Rodríguez Somolinos 1996). In addition, inscriptions in both Greek and Iberian continue to be found at Emporion in contexts as late as the fourth century, suggesting that it continued to be a city with a mixed population rather than developing into a culturally 'Greek' polis in the manner of the Greek cities of Italy and Sicily (Almagro Basch 1952). The occurrence of inscriptions written in Greek in an Iberian context could potentially point to the adoption of Greek as a form of 'link language' used as a *lingua franca* by Greeks, Iberians and other groups such as Phoenicians, but in practice, this role seems to have been taken by Iberian rather than Greek (De Hoz 2004: 419–20).

The influence of Greek culture can be traced in numerous other fields of activity, but by no means as an indication of straightforward Hellenization. Iberian sculpture adopts Greek decorative motifs such as palmettes, volutes and orientalizing animals, and also Greek techniques, but the uses to which these are put are distinctively Iberian (Niemeyer 1990: 41–3; Domínguez Monedero 1999: 302–5). Stone sculptures of the early fifth century onwards from Obulco, Pozo Moro, Cabezo Lucero and Elche all show the influence of Greek sculptural techniques and styles, and comparison with contemporary sculptures from Emporion suggest that this was the point from which Greek influence was disseminated (Sanmartí-Grego 1992: 27–41; Boardman 1994: 69–70; Croissant & Rouillard 1996: 55–66; Domínguez 1999: 304–5). However, these Greek elements were combined with Phoenician influences and with distinctively Iberian styles and iconography to create a specifically Iberian form of representation (Almagro Gorbea 1983: 177–93; Domínguez 1999: 305). Greek pottery shapes were also adopted by Iberian craftsmen, particularly those such as kraters and cups which were associated with feasting, but it is significant that Greek decorative forms were not necessarily adopted along with them (Niemeyer 1990: 41–3; Domínguez Monedero 1999: 313–16). Where the influence of Greek decorative motifs can be seen, as on the white-painted pottery produced at Indiceta in north-east Spain in the late fifth century, they are developed into a very distinctive local style which is in no sense an attempt to copy the Ionian and Attic pottery from which they were derived (Domínguez Monedero 1999: 312–13). The emphasis was on selectively adopting aspects of Greek culture and adapting them to Iberian needs and cultural practices, not on simply copying Greek objects, styles or manufacturing techniques. The distribution of Greek pottery types also suggests that Greeks and non-Greeks were using these objects in very different ways. Assemblages of Greek or Greek-style pottery in Iberian contexts, notably burials, are mostly collections of kraters and drinking cups, all vessels connected primarily with wine-consumption and ritual feasting. In Greek burials, in context, these dining or sympotic assemblages are rare and the most commonly found type of pottery is the lekythos (Domínguez Monedero 1999: 319–20). A similar pattern of the adoption and adaptation of Greek technologies can be seen in the development of writing in Iberia. In the early fifth century, inscriptions in Iberian begin to appear in the so-called 'Graeco-Iberian' script, adapted from the Greek alphabet, but by c. 450, this is beginning to disappear in favour of a more specifically Iberian script developed from the Phoenician alphabet (De Hoz 1985–6: 285–98; Domínguez Monedero 1999: 306–7).

The implication of all of these developments is that Greek technologies and artefacts were well represented in Iberian contexts in the fifth and fourth centuries, but they do not necessarily bear the traditional interpretation of 'Hellenization'. It has been argued that the extensive adoption of some aspects of Greek culture, such as pottery shapes, sculptural motifs or alphabet, is indicative of a fairly strong and extensive phase of Hellenization in the development of Iberian society. However, the extensive differences highlighted above in the ways Greeks and Iberians used these strongly suggests that it was a more interactive process than one-way adoption of Greek cultural norms. In all these cases, the Iberian elite seems to be using aspects of Greek culture to express their own concerns and adapting it extensively to meet their own needs (Domínguez 1999: 323–4). Greek contacts with Iberia, therefore, appear to be a process of interaction with indigenous elites who are selectively taking on and transforming Greek culture into something which can be used to represent their own Iberian identity.

# 5   Conclusions: Greek Settlement and Acculturation in the West

The patterns of Greek contact and settlement in the western Mediterranean seem, therefore, to have significant differences from those with Sicily and southern Italy. To some extent, this is to be expected, as Greek settlement in France, Spain and Adriatic Italy takes place later than that in these regions and in a different context. By the time Emporion, Adria and Massalia were established, the concept of the polis and of polis identity was well established in Greece and the Aegean, in a way it was not when the earliest settlements in Sicily and Magna Graecia were formed, and there was already a long history of Greek contact with the areas settled. Nevertheless, these differences raise interesting questions about the nature of Greek settlement overseas, and the extent to which it constituted 'colonization'.

The most striking feature of Greek settlement north and west of Magna Graecia, and in the Adriatic, is that much of it does not involve the foundation of Greek poleis and the establishment of a permanently settled Greek population. It is impossible to know for certain how many of the Greeks who left archaeological traces in the West, such as Greek pottery or inscriptions, were permanent residents – Greeks who had left Greece to settle permanently in the West and their descendants – and how many were temporary migrants, visiting Spain, France and the various ports of Italy and then returning to Greece. Ports would inevitably have attracted a large transient population, and the Greek artefacts from settlements such as Pyrgi and Graviscae – and particularly those which come from votive contexts rather than burials or habitation areas – may well indicate a large but migratory population of Greek traders and sailors rather than a sizeable permanent settlement. Elsewhere, in places where we do have secure evidence of permanent Greek settlement, there is a much greater tendency for Greeks to settle in mixed communities, living alongside the indigenous population, rather than to form culturally homogeneous units with strong cultural demarcations. This level of cultural plurality is well demonstrated by Greek settlement in Adriatic Italy. Adria and Ancona both have a substantial Greek population, and in the case of Adria, it may have been originally a Greek foundation, but neither develops into a straightforward Greek polis. At Ancona, the Greek population seems to have maintained a cohesive Greek identity while living in what remained basically a Picene community, while at Adria, the Greeks lived in a mixed, and apparently unsegregated, community of Greeks, Etruscans, Veneti and Celts. In Spain, recent research has highlighted the extent to which there was a substantial Greek population which did not live in Greek settlements (De Hoz 2004), and the one settlement which did develop a self-consciously Greek polis identity – Emporion – did so while apparently incorporating a substantial Iberian population which remained culturally distinct from the Greeks until at least the fourth century. This contrasts markedly with the pattern of development in Italy and Sicily, where indigenous populations seem to have co-existed with the Greeks in the earliest phases of sites such as Metapontion and Policoro, but disappear from the archaeological record (either by departure or by adoption of Greek culture) at the point at which they begin to establish a fully urban identity (Carter et al. 1998; Osborne 1998).

The explanation for this phenomenon is still not clear, but it raises a number of interesting questions. A recent article by Domínguez Monedero (2004: 446–50) has put forward the suggestion that since many of the Greeks settled in France and Spain (and especially at Massalia and Emporion) were of Phokaian origin, we can trace the development of a specifically Phokaian identity in the far western Mediterranean, which co-existed with the development of specific polis identities and was analogous to the communal Achaian identity suggested for Achaian colonies in Italy (Hall & Morgan 1996; Hall 2002: 58–62). One of the features which he defines as an important element in this identity is that of co-existence and co-operation with the non-Greek populations. It is clear that this element of Massalia and Emporion was regarded as unusual and interesting by Greek writers. Strabon (3.4.8) and Livy (34.9) both comment on the close interactions between Greeks and Iberians at Emporion, and the foundation myths of Massalia place considerable emphasis on the intermarriage of Greek settlers with the local population (Justin 43.3.4–5.10, quoting the Gallo-Roman historian Pompeius Trogus). This interpretation, however, places a strong emphasis on the culture and group identity of the Greeks, but gives too little space to that of the indigenous populations. The Greeks along the Adriatic and in Spain were settled in areas, and at a time, in which there were already strong and developing indigenous states with distinctive cultural identities of their own. Etruscan Spina was already represented at major Greek sanctuaries as an equal of the Greek city-states, as demonstrated by the establishment of a treasury at Delphi, by the end of the sixth century, and the Iberians in the hinterland of Emporion were very clearly adopting and manipulating Greek goods and cultural features for their own purposes rather than assimilating to Greek cultural norms. What this suggests is that Greek settlement in the sixth–fourth centuries was taking place in the context of more complex and developed indigenous societies, with well-defined cultural identities of their own, than had been the case for settlement in the eighth and seventh centuries, and also in the context of interaction and competition with other external groups such as Phoenicians and Etruscans. The corollary was that the Greeks were not able to impose their own political, social and cultural structures to anything like the same extent as was the case in Sicily and Magna Graecia, but instead their communities developed into multi-ethnic communities, whether emporia or poleis.

The separate issue of whether Greek settlers in Spain and France maintained a distinct sense of Phokaian identity alongside the developing polis-identities of their own communities remains open to question. The close connections between Massalia and other Phokaian colonies such as Emporion and Lampsakos in Asia Minor may also suggest a strong sense of connection to other settlements of Phokaian origin (Domínguez Monedero 2004: 448). In addition, they maintained a common cult, that of Ephesian Artemis, and shared architectural styles, while inscriptions reveal a conservatism in personal names which seems to hark back to the Phokaian origins of these cities (Manganaro 1992; Robert 1968). All of these features seem to point to at least some element of shared Phokaian identity embedded within the different development trajectories and identities of the individual cities.

One of the important themes of any study of Greek settlement in the non-Greek Mediterranean is that of the interaction of Greeks and non-Greeks and the nature of culture-contact. It is clear, particularly when examining areas such as Iberia, where the patterns of Graeco-Iberian contact are very complex, that this can no longer be approached as a case of 'Hellenization' in which the indigenous population takes on a package of Greek artefacts and the social and cultural behaviours (such as Greek-style symposia) which go with them as a one-way transaction. In particular, it is clear that much more consideration needs to be given to the indigenous populations as proactive participants in any form of contact and exchange (De Angelis 2004: 19–21). The pattern in most of the areas covered by this chapter appears to be one of intense cultural and economic interaction between Greeks and non-Greeks over a long time-span, but one in which the indigenous populations, together with other external groups such as the Etruscans in northern Italy and the Phoenicians in Corsica, Sardinia and Sicily, play a full and proactive role. Complex patterns of interaction and adaptation of Greek culture to indigenous uses can be seen in fields as widely varied as language, writing and its uses, burial practices, sculpture and pottery. In addition, the role of Phoenicians, Etruscans, Iberians, Gauls and others must be fully recognized in the patterns of trade and economic exchange throughout the western Mediterranean. The history of the Greeks in the western Mediterranean demonstrates, perhaps more fully than any other part of the Greek world, the diversity of Greek culture and forms of statehood in the Classical period, and the need to examine these in their wider regional context.

# Further reading

The bibliography on the Greeks in the far western Mediterranean is vast, but there are relatively few books available which offer an overview of this region in the fifth and fourth centuries. Two works which provide overviews of particular regions within the western Mediterranean are Hodge (1998) and Harrison (1988). Rouillard (1991) gives a comprehensive and detailed review of the evidence for Greek settlement in Spain up to the end of the fourth century. For those wishing to explore the Phoenician settlements in the West and their relations with the Greeks, the best starting point is Aubet (2001), while Niemeyer (1982) includes a series of more specialist studies.

The starting point for the recent debate about the nature of settlement in the western Mediterranean is Osborne (1998), while an alternative viewpoint to this can be found in Malkin (2002). Both of these papers focus on Italy and Sicily and on a rather earlier period than this chapter, but they provide a good introduction to recent thinking about the nature of settlement and foundation in the West.

In addition to the more general works cited above, there are a very large number of conference publications, exhibition catalogues and collections of papers on aspects of the Greeks in France, Spain and the western Mediterranean. It would be impossible to review them all here, but the following are some of the most useful. Pugliese Carratelli (1996) focuses mainly on Italy and Sicily but also includes chapters on the Greeks in France, Etruria, the Mediterranean islands and the Po Valley. Bats et al. (1992) include papers on many aspects of Greek settlement in southern France and contact with the indigenous populations, while Cabrera Bonet & Sánchez Fernández (1998) presents an important collection of the evidence for the Greeks in Spain, and Krinzinger (2000) contains an important collection of papers on contact between the Aegean and the West. Finally, two conferences dedicated to aspects of Greek colonization in the West, Tsetskhladze (1999) and Lomas (2004b), include a number of papers exploring aspects of Greek settlement in France and Spain.

# Bibliography

Alfieri, N. (1994) *Scritti minori*, vol. 1: *Spina e la ceramica attica* (ed. S. Patitucci) (Rome: Kappa)

Almagro Basch, M. (1952) *Las inscripciones ampuritanas: griegas, ibéricas y latinas* (Barcelona: Departamento de Barcelona del Instituto Rodrigo Caro de Arquelogía) (Monografías ampuritanas 2)

Almagro Basch, M. (1953) *Las necrópolis de Ampurias*, vol. 1: *Introducción y necrópolis griegas* (Barcelona: Seix y Barral) (Monografías ampuritanas 3)

Almagro Basch, M. (1955) *Las necrópolis de Ampurias*, vol. 2: *Necrópolis romanas y necrópolis indígenas* (Barcelona: Seix y Barral) (Monografías ampuritanas 3)

Almagro Gorbea, M. (1983) 'Pozo Moro: El monumento orientalizante, su contexto socio-cultural y sus paralelos en la arquitectura funeraria ibérica' in: *Mitteilungen des Deutschen Archäologischen Institutes (Abteilung Madrid)* 24: 177–293

Aubet, M. E. (2001) *The Phoenicians and the West: politics, colonies and trade* (trans. M. Turton, from Spanish ed. *Tiro y las colonias fenicias de Occidente* (Barcelona ²1994)) (Cambridge: Cambridge University Press)

Baglione, M. P. (1989–90) 'Considerazioni sui santuari di Pyrgi e di Veio-Portonaccio' in: *Scienze di Antichità* 3–4: 651–67

Bats, M. (1998) 'Marseille archaïque: Étrusques et Phocéens en Méditerranée nord-occidentale' in: *Mélanges de l'École Française de Rome, Antiquité* 110: 609–33

Bats, M., et al. (eds) (1992) *Marseille Grecque et la Gaule: actes du Colloque international d'histoire et d'archéologie et du Ve Congrès archéologique de Gaule méridionale (Marseille, 18–23 novembre 1990)* (Aix-en-Provence: Université de Provence) (Travaux du Centre Camille Jullian 11 = Études massaliétes 3)

Benoît, F. (1972) 'Topographie antique de Marseille: le théâtre et le mur de Crinas' in: *Gallia* 24: 1–22

Berti, F, & P. G. Guzzo (1993) *Spina: storia di una citta tra Greci ed Etruschi (Catalogo della mostra tenuta a Ferrara nel 1993–1994)* (Ferrara: Comitato Ferrara arte)

Bertucchi, G. (1992) 'Nécropoles et terrasses funéraires à l'époque grecque: bilan sommaire des recherches' in: Bats et al. 1992: 124–37

Boardman, J. (1994) *The diffusion of classical art in antiquity* (London: Thames & Hudson) (A. W. Mellon Lectures in the Fine Arts 1993)

Boitani, F., & M. Torelli (1999) 'Un nuovo santuario dell'emporion di Gravisca' in: *La colonisation grecque en Méditerranée Occidentale: Actes de la rancontre scientifique en hommage* à Georges Vallet organisée par le Centre Jean-Bérard, l'École française de Rome, l'Istituto Universitario Orientale et l'Università degli Studi di Napoli "Federico II": (Rome-Naples, 15–18 novembre 1995) (Paris: de Boccard) 93–101 (Collection de l'École française de Rome 251)

Bouloumié, B. (1990) 'L'épave étrusque d'Antibes' in: [Centre de la Vieille Charité] (1990) *Voyage en Massalie: 100 ans d'archéologie en Gaule du Sud* [Catalogue de l'exposition organisée dans le cadre de l'année de l'archéologie au Centre de la Vieille Charité du 19 novembre 1990 au 24 février 1991] (Marseille: Musées de Marseille)

Bound, M. (1991) *The Giglio wreck: a wreck of the archaic period (c. 600 BC) off the Tuscan island of Giglio, an account of its discovery and excavation: a review of the main finds* (Athens: Hellenic Institute of Marine Archaeology) (*Enalia* Suppl. 1)

Braccesi, L. (1988) 'Indizi per una frequentazione micenea dell'Adriatico' in: Acquaro, E. (ed.) (1988) *Momenti precoloniali nel Mediterraneo antico: questioni di metodo, aree d'indagine, evidenze a confronto: atti del convegno internazionale (Roma, 14–16 marzo 1985)* (Rome: Consiglio Nazionale delle Ricerche) 133–45 (Collezione di studi fenici 28)

Bradley, G. J. (2000) *Ancient Umbria: state, culture and identity in central Italy from the Iron Age to the Augustan era* (Oxford: Oxford University Press)

Braun, T. (2004) 'Hecataeus' knowledge of the western Mediterranean' in: Lomas 2004b: 287–348

Cabrera Bonet, P., & C. Sánchez Fernández (eds) (1998) *The Greeks in Spain: in the footsteps of Herakles* in: Cabrera Bonet & Sánchez Fernández (1998): *Oi archaioi Ellenes sten Ispania: sta ichne tou Erakle = Los Griegos en España: tras las huellas de Heracles* (Madrid: Ministerio de Educación y Cultura; Athens: Hellenic Republic, Ministry of Culture) 429–605 (= Cabrera Bonet, P., & C. Sánchez Fernández (eds) (2000) *Los Griegos en España: tras las huellas de Heracles: Museo Arqueológico Nacional, 2000* (Madrid: Secretaría de Estado de Cultura))

Calzavara Capuis, L. (1993) *I Veneti: società e cultura di un popolo dell'Italia preromana* (Milan: Longanesi) (Biblioteca di archeologia 19)

Carter, J. C., J. Morter, A. Parmly Toxey (eds) (1998) *The chora of Metaponto: the necropoleis* (Austin: University of Texas Press)

Clavel-Lévêque, M. (1977) *Marseille grecque: la dynamique d'un impérialisme marchand* (Marseille: Laffitte)

Colivicchi, F. (2000) 'Dal "pallium" alla "toga": Ancona fra ellenismo e romanizzazione' in: *Ostraka* 9: 135–42

[Comitato Promotore Ferrarese] (1959) *Spina e l'Etruria padana : atti del 1. Convegno di studi etruschi : (Ferrara, 8–11 settembre 1957)* (Florence: Olschki) (*Studi Etruschi* vol. 25: Suppl.)

Croissant, F., & P. Rouillard (1996) 'Le problême de l'art "gréco-ibère": état de la question' in: Olmos, R., & P. Rouillard (eds) (1996) *Formes archaïques et arts ibériques = Formas arcaicas y arte ibéric* (Madrid: Casa de Velázquez) 55–66 (Collection de la Casa de Velázquez 59)

De Angelis, F. (2004) 'Equations of culture: the meeting of natives and Greeks in Sicily (*ca.* 750–450 BCE)' in: *Ancient Greeks East and West* 3: 19–32

De Angelis, F., & G. R. Tsetskhladze (eds) (1994) *The archaeology of Greek colonisation: essays dedicated to Sir John Boardman* (Oxford: Oxford University Committee for Archaeology) (Oxford University Committee for Archaeology Monographs 40)

De Hoz, J. (1985–6) 'La escritura greco-ibérica' in: *Veleia* 2–3: 285–98

De Hoz, J. (1987) 'La escritura greco-ibérica' in: Gorrachategui, J., J. L. Melena, J. Santos (eds) (1987) *Studia paleohispanica: actas del IV Coloquio sobre Lenguas y Culturas Paleohis-pánicas: (Vitoria-Gasteiz, 6–10 Mayo 1985)* (Vitoria: Instituto de Ciencias de la Antigüedad, Universidad del País Vasco) 285–98 (*Veleia: revista de Prehistoria, Historia Antigua, Arqueo-logía y Filología clásicas* 2–3)

De Hoz, J. (2004) 'The Greek man in the Iberian street' in: Lomas 2004b: 411–28

Dench, E. (1995) *From barbarians to new men: Greek, Roman, and modern perceptions of peoples from the central Apennines* (Oxford: Clarendon) (Oxford Classical Monographs)

Dietler, M. (1989) 'Greeks, Etruscans and thirsty barbarians: early Iron Age interaction in the Rhone basin of France' in: Champion, T. C. (ed.) (1989) *Centre and periphery: comparative studies in archaeology* (London: Unwin Hyman) 127–41 (One World Archaeology 11)

Domínguez Monedero, A. J. (1986) 'La ciudad griega de Emporion y su organización política' in: *Archivo Español de Arqueologia* 59: 3–12

Domínguez Monedero, A. J. (1999) 'Hellenisation in Iberia?: the reception of Greek products and influences by the Iberians' in: Tsetskhladze 1999: 301–29

Domínguez Monedero, A. J. (2004) 'Greek identity in the Phocaean colonies' in: Lomas 2004b: 429–56

Domínguez Monedero, A. J., & C. Sanchez (2001) *Greek pottery from the Iberian peninsula: archaic and classical periods* (Leiden: Brill)

D'Oriano, R. (1990) 'La Sardegna sulle rotte dell'Occidente: L'eta storica' in: Stazio 1990: 134–60

Dubois, L. (1995) *Inscriptions grecques dialectales de Grande Grèce*, vol. 1: *Colonies eubéennes, colonies ioniennes, emporia* (Geneva: Droz) (Hautes études du monde gréco-romain 21)

Fernandez Jurado, J., & P. Cabrera Bonet (1987) 'Comercio griego en Huelva a fines del siglo V a. C.' in: *Revue des Études Anciennes* 89: 149–59

Fogolari, G., & B. M. Scarfì (1970) *Adria antica* (Venice: Alfieri)

Franchi Dell'Orto, L., & C. Gobbi (eds) (2001) *Eroi e regine: Piceni popolo d'Europa (Catalogo della mostra tenuta a Roma, Galleria Nazionale d'arte antica, Palazzo Barberini dal 12 aprile al 1 luglio 2001)* (Rome: De Luca)

Gantès, L.-F. (1992) 'La topographie de Marseille grecque: bilan des recherches (1829–1991)' in: Bats 1992: 72–88

García y Bellido, A. (1948) *Hispania Graeca*, 3 vols (Barcelona: Instituto Español de Estudios Mediterráneos) (Publicaciones sobre arte y arqueologia)

Hall, J. M. (2002) *Hellenicity: between ethnicity and culture* (Chicago: University of Chicago Press)

Hall, J. M., & C. Morgan (1996) 'Achaian *poleis* and Achaian colonisation' in: Hansen, M. H. (ed.) (1996) *Introduction to an inventory of poleis: Symposium August 23–26, 1995* (Copenhagen: Munksgaard) 164–232 (Kongelige Danske Videnskabernes Selskab: Historisk-filosofiske meddelelser 74 = Acts of the Copenhagen Polis Centre 3)

Hansen, M. H. (2000) 'A survey of the use of the word *Polis* in archaic and classical sources' in: Flensted-Jensen, P. (ed.) (2000) *Further studies in the ancient Greek* polis (Stuttgart: Steiner) 173–215 (*Historia* Einzelschriften 138 = Papers from the Copenhagen Polis Centre 5)

Harrison, R. J. (1988) *Spain at the dawn of history: Iberians, Phoenicians and Greeks* (London: Thames & Hudson)

Head, B. V. (1911) *Historia numorum: a manual of Greek numismatics* (Oxford: Clarendon)

Hermary, A., A. Hesnard, H. Tréziny (1999) *Marseille grecque: 600–49 av. J.C: la cité phocéenne* (Paris: Errance) (Hauts lieux de l'histoire)

Herring, E. (2000) ' "To see ourselves as others see us!": the construction of native identities in southern Italy' in: Herring, E., & K. Lomas (eds) (2000) *Literacy and state societies in the ancient Mediterranean in the 1st millennium BC* (London: Accordia Research Institute) 45–78

Hodge, A. T. (1998) *Ancient Greek France* (London: Duckworth)

Huber, K. (1999) *Le ceramiche attiche a figure rosse* (Bari: Edipuglia) (Gravisca: scavi nel santuario greco 6)

Jehasse, J. & L. Jehasse (1994) 'La société Corse face a l'expansion phocéenne' in: Cabrera, P., R. Olmos, E. Sanmartí-Grego (eds) (1994) 'Iberos y Gregos – Lecturas desde la Diversidad: Simposio International celebrado en Ampurias, 3, al 5 de Abril de 1991' in: *Huelva arqueologica* 13 (1994) fasc. 2: 305–22

Jones, S. (1997) *The archaeology of ethnicity: constructing identities in the past and present* (London: Routledge)

Jully, J.-J. (1980) *Les importations de céramique attique (Vie–IVe s.) en Languedoc méditerranéen, Roussillon et Catalogne* (Paris: Belles Lettres) (Centre de recherches d'histoire ancienne 30 = Annales littéraires de l'Université de Besançon 231)

Kerschner, M. (2004) 'Phokäische Thalassokratie oder Phantom-Phokäer? Die frühgriechischen Keramikfunde im Süden der iberischen Halbinsel aus der ägäischen Perspektive' in: Lomas 2004b: 115–48

Kilian, K. (1990) 'Mycenaean colonization: norm and variety' in: Descoedres, J.-P. (ed.) *Greek colonists and native populations: proceedings of the first Australian Congress of Classical Archaeology held in honour of Emeritus Professor A. D. Trendall, Sydney 9–14 July 1985* (Oxford: Clarendon) 445–67 (Oxford University Press/Humanities Research Centre series)

Krinzinger, F. (ed.) (2000) *Akten des Symposions Die Ägäis und das westliche Mittelmeer: Beziehungen und Wechselwirkungen: 8. bis 5. Jh. v. Chr.: Wien, 24. bis 27. März 1999* (Vienna: Verlag der Österreichischen Akademie der Wissenschaften) (Archäologische Forschungen 4 = Denkschriften der Österreichischen Akademie der Wissenschaften, Philosophisch-historische Klasse 288)

Landolfi, M. (2001) 'I commerci greci nel Piceno' in: Franchi Dell'Orto & Gobbi 2001: 145–7

Lejeune, M., J. Pouilloux, Y. Solier (1988) 'Étrusque et ionien archaïques sur un plomb de Pech Maho (Aude)' in: *Revue Archéologique de Narbonnaise* 21: 19–59

Lomas, K. (2000) 'Cities, states and ethnic identity in south-east Italy' in: Herring, E., & K. Lomas (eds) (2000) *Literacy and state societies in the ancient Mediterranean in the 1st millennium* BC (London: Accordia Research Institute) 79–90

Lomas, K. (2004a) 'Hellenism, Romanization and cultural identity in Massilia' in: Lomas 2004b: 475–98

Lomas, K. (ed.) (2004b) *Greek identity in the western Mediterranean: papers in honour of Brian Shefton* (Leiden: Brill) (*Mnemosyne* Suppl. 246)

Long, L., J. Miro, G. Volpe (1992) 'Les épaves archaïques de la pointe Lequin (Porquerolles, Hyères, Var): des données nouvelles sur le commerce de Marseille à la fin due VIe s. et dans la première moitié du Ve s. av. J-C.' in: Bats 1992: 199–234

Luni, M. (2001) 'Le importazioni di ceramica greca' in: Franchi Dell'Orto & Gobbi 2001: 147–50

Malkin, I. (1994) 'Inside and outside: colonization and the formation of the mother city' in: D'Agostino, B., & D. Ridgway (eds) (1994) *Apoikia: i più antichi insediamenti greci in occidente: funzioni e modi dell'organizzazione politica e sociale: scritti in onore di Giorgio Buchner* (Naples: Istituto Universitario Orientale) 1–10 (Annali di archeologia e storia antica ns 1)

Malkin, I. (2002) 'Exploring the validity of the concept of "foundation": a visit to Megara Hyblaia' in: Gorman, V. B., & E. W. Robinson (eds) (2002) *Oikistes: studies in constitutions, colonies, and military power in the ancient world, offered in honor of A. J. Graham* (Leiden: Brill) 195–225 (*Mnemosyne* Suppl. 234)

Manganaro, G. (1992) 'Massalioti per il Mediterraneo: tra Spagna, Sardegna e Sicilia' in: Atzeni, E. (ed.) *Sardinia antiqua: studi in onore di Piero Meloni in occasione del suo settantesimo compleann* (Cagliari: della Torre) 195–206

Mercando, L. (1976) 'L'Ellenismo nel Piceno' in: Zanker, P. (ed.) (1976) *Hellenismus in Mittelitalien: Kolloquium in Göttingen vom 5.–9. Juni 1974* (Göttingen: Vandenhoeck & Ruprecht) 160–218 (Abhandlungen der Akademie der Wissenschaften in Göttingen, Philosophisch-historische Klasse 3, 97)

Mierse, W. E. (1994) 'Ampurias: the urban development of a Graeco-Roman city on the Iberian coast' in: *Latomus* 53: 790–805

Moliner, M. (1999) 'Les Faubourgs: les nécropoles' in: Hesnard, A., M. Moliner, F. Conche, M. Bouiron (eds) (1999) *Parcours de villes: Marseille: 10 ans d'archéologie, 2600 ans d'histoire: exposition, Vieille Charité, 3 novembre 1999–31 janvier 2000* (Marseille: Musées de Marseille) 107–24

Morel, J. P. (1966) 'Les Phocéens en Occident, certitudes et hypothèses' in: *La Parola del Passato* 21: 378–420

Morel, J. P. (1975) 'L'expansion phocéenne en Occident: dix années de recherches (1966–1975)' in: *BCH* 99: 853–96

Morel, J. P. (1983) 'Greek colonisation in Italy and the West' in: Hackens, T., N. D. Holloway, R. R. Holloway (eds) (1983) *The crossroads of the Mediterranean: papers delivered at the International Conference on the Archaeology of Early Italy, Haffenreffer Museum Brown University, 8–10 May 1981* (Providence RI: Brown University) 123–62 (Archaeologia Transatlantica 2 = Publications d'histoire de l'art et d'archeologie de l'Université catholique de Louvain 38)

Morel, J. P. (1990) 'Les échanges entre la Grand-Grèce et la Gaule di VIIe au Ier siècle avant J.-C.' in: Stazio 1990: 247–93

Naso, A. (2000) *I Piceni: storia e archeologia delle Marche in epoca preromani* (Milan: Longanesi) (Biblioteca di archeologia 29)

Niemeyer, H. G. (ed.) (1982) *Phönizier im Westen: Die Beiträge des Internationalen Symposiums über 'Die Phönizische Expansion im Westlichen Mittelmeerraum' in Köln vom 24. bis 27. April 1979* (Mainz: Zabern) (Madrider Beiträge 8)

Niemeyer, H. G. (1990) 'The Greeks and the far west: towards a revaluation of the archaeological evidence for Spain' in: Stazio 1990: 29–54

Osborne, R. (1998) 'Early Greek colonisation?: the nature of Greek settlement in the West' in: Fisher, N., & H. van Wees (eds) (1998) *Archaic Greece: new approaches and new evidence* (London: Duckworth & The Classical Press of Wales) 251–69

Prontera, F. (1990) 'L'estremo occidente nella concezione geografia dei Greci' in: Stazio 1990: 55–82

Pugliese Carratelli, G. (ed.) (1996) *The western Greeks: classical civilization in the western Mediterranean* (London: Thames & Hudson)

Rebecchi, F. (ed.) (1998) *Spina e il delta padano: riflessioni sul catalogo e sulla mostra ferrarese: atti del Convegno internazionale di studi Spina: due civilta a confronto, Ferrara, Aula magna dell'Universita, 21 gennaio 1994* (Rome: 'L'Erma' di Bretschneider) (Studia archaeologica)

Robert, L. (1968) 'Noms de personnes et civilisation grecque: I: Noms de personnes dans Marseille grecque' in: *Journal des Savants* 1968: 197–213

Rodríguez Somolinos, H. (1996) 'The commercial transaction of the Pech Maho lead' in: *ZPE* 111: 74–8

Rougemont, C., & R. Guyot-Rougemont (1992) 'Marseille grecque: les textes antiques' in: Bats 1992: 45–50

Rouillard, P. (1991) *Les Grecs et la péninsule ibérique du VIIIe siècle au IVe siècle avant Jésus-Christ* (Paris: de Boccard) (Publications du Centre Pierre Paris 21)

Sanmartí-Grego, E. (1988) 'Datación de la muralla griega meridional de Ampurias y caracterización de la facies cerámica de la ciudad en la primera mitad del siglo IV a. de J. C.' in: *Revue des Études Anciennes* 90: 99–137

Sanmartí-Grego, E. (1992) 'Massalia et Emporion: une origine commune, deux destins différents' in: Bats 1992: 27–41

Sebastiani, S. (2004) *Ancona: forma e urbanistica* (repr. with revisions) (Rome: 'L'Erma' di Bretschneider)

Shefton, B. B. (1982) 'Greeks and Greek imports in the south of the Iberian Peninsula' in: Niemeyer 1982: 337–70

Shefton, B. B. (1989) 'Zum Import und Einfluss mediterraner Güter in Alteuropa' in: *Kölner Jahrbuch für Vor- und Frühgeschichte* 22: 207–20

Shefton, B. B. (1994) 'Massalia and colonisation' in: De Angelis & Tsetskhladze 1994: 61–86

Shefton, B. B. (2003) 'Contacts between Picenum and the Greek world to the end of the fifth century B.C.: imports, influences and perceptions' in: Istituto nazionale di studi etruschi ed italici (ed.) (2003) *I Piceni e l'Italia medio-adriatica: atti del 22. Convegno di studi etruschi ed italici, Ascoli Piceno, Teramo, Ancona, 9–13 Aprile 2000* (Pisa: Istituti editoriali e poligrafici internazionali) 315–37 (Atti di convegni, Istituto nazionale di studi etruschi e italici 22)

Snodgrass, A. (1994) 'The nature and standing of the early Western colonies' in: De Angelis, F., & G. R. Tsetskhladze (eds) (1994) *The archaeology of Greek colonisation: essays dedicated to Sir John Boardman* (Oxford: Oxford University Committee for Archaeology) 1–10 (Oxford University Committee for Archaeology Monographs 40)

Stazio, A. (ed.) (1990) *La Magna Grecia e il lontano Occidente: atti del ventinovesimo Convegno di studi sulla Magna Greci: Taranto, 6–11 ottobre 1989* (Taranto: Istituto per la Storia e l'Archeologia della Magna Grecia)

Torelli, M. (1971) 'Il santuario di Hera a Gravisca' in: *La Parola del Passato* 26: 44–67

Torelli, M. (1977) 'Il santuario greco di Gravisca' in: *La Parola del Passato* 32: 398–458

Torelli, M. (1999) 'Un nuovo santuario dell'emporion di Gravisca' in *La colonisation grecque en Méditerranée occidentale: actes de la rancontre scientifique en hommage à Georges Vallet (Rome, Naples, 15–18 novembre 1995) organisé par le Centre Jean-Bérard [et al.]* (Rome: École française de Rome) 93–101 (Collection de l'École française de Rome 251)

Tréziny, H. (1997) 'Marseille grecque: topographie et urbanisme à la lumière des fouilles récentes' *Révue Archéologique* ns 1: 185–200

Tsetskhladze, G. R. (ed.) (1999) *Ancient Greeks west and east* (Leiden: Brill) (*Mnemosyne* Suppl. 196)

Tsirkin, J. B. (1996) 'The downfall of Tartessos and the Carthaginian establishment on the Iberian peninsula' in: *Rivista Studi Fenici* 24: 141–52

Vagnetti, L. (1983) 'Quindici anni di studi e ricerche sulle relazioni tra il mondo egeo e l'Italia protostorica' in: Vagnetti, L. (ed.) (1983) *Magna Grecia e mondo miceneo: nuovi documenti: Atti del 22° Convegno di studi sulla Magna Grecia: Taranto 7–11 ottobre 1982* (Taranto: Istituto per la Storia e l'Archeologia della Magna Grecia) 9–40

Valentini, V. (1993) *Le ceramiche a vernice nera* (Bari: Edipuglia) (Gravisca 6)

van Dommelen, P. (1997) 'Colonial constructs: colonialism and archaeology in the Mediterranean' in: *World Archaeology* 28: 305–23

Zampieri, G. (1994) *Il Museo archeologico di Padova: dal Palazzo della ragione al Museo agli Eremitani: storia della formazione del Museo civico archeologico di Padova e guida alle collezione* (Milan: Electa)

# CHAPTER ELEVEN

# The Eastern Mediterranean and Beyond: The Relations between the Worlds of the 'Greek' and 'Non-Greek' Civilizations

*Robert Rollinger*

## 1 Introduction: The Hellenocentric View of the East

To comprehend the points of contact between the so-called Greek world and that of the eastern Mediterranean and to describe it over a two-hundred-year period is no light undertaking. There are many reasons for this. First, the juxtaposition of 'Greeks' and 'non-Greeks' suggests these were two separate 'worlds', and the opposites of 'Greeks' and 'non-Greeks' implied therein clearly betrays a Hellenocentric point of view and one which is likely to detract from how this period must be more objectively approached. Yet this is a question which must be considered first and foremost: is this point of view grounded in historical fact or does it merely reflect an 'orthodoxy'? There is also the problem of historical methods, which must not be simply ignored.

Hellenocentrism has characterized the study of all aspects of classical antiquity for centuries. That there was one Greek World and on Greek Identity was regarded as being as much a fact as a unique Greek Way in world history. It was supposed to have generated itself essentially from within itself; in a special relationship with the so-called Western World. These premises have begun increasingly frequently to be questioned in recent years, even though mainstream scholarship remains wedded to them (Rollinger 2004a). As a result, the idea of the unity of the Greek world yielded to a conception which emphasizes regional differences and its special *identities*, and subjected any definition of 'Greekness' based on Sparta and Athens to critical re-examination. This observation is valid not only for the pre-archaic and archaic periods

(Gehrke 1986; Morris 1997; 1998; 2000), but also for the classical (P. Funke 1994; 1997; 1998; S. Funke 2000). Moreover the legend of the 'Greek wonder' as a self-generated process, which owed its suggestive power to an alleged uniqueness of the 'Greek spirit' and of the 'Greek character', yielded to a growing awareness that the drive towards advancement, observed in certain regions of Greece, is simply unthinkable without the external impulses of an extensively integrated Mediterranean world (Burkert 1992; Rollinger & Ulf 2004a). Any description of the contact between *the* 'Greeks' and *the* 'non-Greeks' in a set geographical area therefore meets with already nearly insurmountable difficulties. This subject and its problems become even more precarious because modern scholarship has largely exposed both the notion of the *ethnos* (Ulf 1996a; J. M. Hall 1997; McInerney 2001; Morgan 2001) and that of *culture* (J. M. Hall 2004) as constructs, which were themselves subject to strong diachronic fluctuations and falsely an only apparent measure of stability.

Although this chapter directs our attention to intercultural contact with the eastern Mediterranean in the fifth and fourth centuries BCE, the premise is not one of a collision of two distinct worlds, which are to be understood as 'Greek' and 'non-Greek', but rather under the auspices of contemporary patterns of awareness, their exploitation from within and without, and the historical implications bound to them (for panhellenic notions and their exploitation, cf. Flower 2000; for the actual lines of confrontation transcending 'national' frontiers, e.g., Ritter 2001). In the following our focus of attention will be the manifold interrelations with the Persian empire, which informed the Greek view of their eastern neighbour just as profoundly as the Greeks were bound to this vast empire in multiple patterns of exchange and contact (for this generally, Starr 1975; 1977; Vickers 1990; Jacobs 1994a; Briant 2002; de Jong 1997; Tuplin 1993; 1996; Duchesne-Guillemin 2002; Shaki 2002; Scheer 2003; Wiesehöfer 2002; 2003a).

## 2   Planes of Contact

As was noted above, patterns of awareness, according to which the Levantine neighbours were sorted and categorized, have been extensively analysed and adapted by modern scholarship (Lund 1990; E. Hall 1989; 1994; Georges 1994; Schmal 1995; Tuplin 1999a; Konstan 2001; Thomas 2001; Bichler & Rollinger 2002). The perceptual images of the barbarian, its genesis, and its position in life particularly for the fifth century have been thoroughly treated (Hutzfeldt 1999). This holds true in general terms also for the fourth century, for which a grand synthesis, aiming at exploiting all available written sources – as Hutzfeldt was able to accomplish – still constitutes a desideratum (cf., e.g., Rosselini & Saïd 1978; Saïd 1985; 2001).

Even the archaeological sources have been discussed intensively in that they contrast with the surviving written sources and that, as an independent source, they have appreciable value (Hölscher 2000a; Boardman 2000). Finally conceptions and images, which derive both from written and archaeological sources, of the eastern barbarians as foils to everyday life and experience are severely blinkered, and the broad influence of Persian-eastern custom and usage on even these conditions of life are stressed. Indeed, a distinct Persia-oriented trend (*Perserie*) in fashion, eating habits, luxury goods of every kind, and even in architecture, was evident in the distinguished circles of high society in the Greek polis (M. C. Miller 1997: 135–258; 2002; Wiesehöfer 2003b; 2004a).

The political and military contacts have already been picked out as major themes of historical consideration by older scholarship and therefore diplomatic interrelations were always broadly stressed (M. C. Miller 1997: 3–28, 109–33; for a general introduction, Hofstetter 1978). In addition to exchange as a medium of intercultural contact (Rollinger & Ulf 2004b) the role of theft and booty goods has now entered firmly into the view of scholarship (M. C. Miller 1997: 63–88). Because ceramics in particular have gained strong scholarly interest as archaeological evidence and as markers for transcultural connections of exchange (Haider 1996; Waldbaum 1997; Raptou 1999), a broad network of contacts that quite tightly meshed the Aegean world and that of the Levant together became visible behind the surface of warfare, hostility, and military confrontation. In this context particular attention has been directed to Cyprus, where modern scholarship – in contrast to earlier opinions – again reached a substantially different conclusion. There the conception of a national conflict between Greeks and Persians, which dominated older scholarship, could be exposed as a construct. Attention could then be directed behind the stereotypes and the propagandistically loaded conceptions of the world – both that of ancient sources and that of modern observers – to a broadly integrated and intermeshed everyday world, in which 'national ideals' play no role at all (Seibert 1976; Wiesehöfer 1990; Maier 1985; 1994).

If we consider how the actual sphere of contact is presented to us especially through the Greek sources, there results a broad range of connections, which far exceed the politico-diplomatic plane. In fact, we encounter both Greeks in the Persian empire and Persians in Aegean and Greek areas to such degree that a broad spectrum of mutual points of contact becomes clear. Certainly we are less adequately informed about the presence of Persians in the Greek poleis. Rather individual examples emerge from the sources, which already in antiquity were regarded as particularly terse. The most famous case is that of Zopyros, who entered into Athenian service shortly after the middle of the fifth century and died on campaign in Karia shortly after the beginning of the Peloponnesian War. Artaphernes, who was sent by Artaxerxes I in 425 as an envoy to Athens, can also be named in this context (Thuc. 4.50). Aristophanes among other things set a Persian legation on the stage in *Acharnians* 91–122 (Chiasson 1984). Moreover it is possible to isolate a set of offerings in the surviving inventory lists of the great Greek sanctuaries, which can be regarded as 'oriental'. The personal and national identity of the dedicants, how-ever, remains largely obscure (Kosmetatou 2004).

Leaving aside these brief glimpses into the presence of Persians in Greece, we come to the role of Greeks in the Achaimenid empire, about which we are substantially better informed. Our sources concentrate on two regions above all: Asia Minor west of the Halys river and the residences of the Persian king. Yet even here the sources provide only a conditionally representative insight into the manifold network of connections, to which Greeks of very different origin and social class were likely to have been bound. In the first place there are prominent individuals to whom the surviving tradition turned its attention. The fate of Miltiades, the victor of Marathon, for example, shows the manifold levels of interaction. He, as the owner of large estates in the Thracian Chersonese, was obliged to pay tribute to the Great King and later fled to Athens after his participation in the Ionian Revolt. These levels of interaction become still clearer in the case of Themistokles, who in the late 470s fled from Athens and placed himself under the protection of the Great King, where in the vicinity of Magnesia on the Maiandros River he was offered a sinecure as a tribute-paying lord over several cities and there was allowed even to strike his own coinage. Recent scholarship has shown that his eventual suicide and the alleged return of his family to Athens were, in fact, historical constructs. Rather Themistokles' son followed in his father's footsteps and exercised his rule as a Persian vassal (Nollé & Wenninger 1998–9).

That Greek–Persian mixed marriages occurred in such contexts need not be surprising, even if the sources for it provide little concrete evidence (Whitby 1998). Besides Alkibiades several other exiled Greeks can be named who found a convenient reception in the empire of the Great King, and can, therefore, expose the national contrast between Greeks and Persians as a surface for projecting specific political and ideological interests (Seibert 1979). This notion becomes quite evident when the contingents which the Greek poleis of Asia Minor contributed to the grand army of Xerxes are taken into account. As a result, the Persian Wars in no way offer themselves as purely 'national' confrontations (cf. Ritter 2001). In fact, we are woefully ill-informed about the actual motives of the Persian kings that motivated their massive offensives of 490 and 480/79 (Young 1980; Wiesehöfer 2004b).

In addition the Greek soldiers who constituted a fixed component of the armies led either by the satraps or by the Great King himself played a major role in the conflicts of the fifth and fourth centuries (Parke 1933; Seibt 1977; H. F. Miller 1984; Krasilnikoff 1992; 1993; McKechnie 1994; Ducrey 2000; Kaplan 2002). The comparatively well-documented difficulties Xenophon experienced in western Asia Minor likewise belong in this context. It involves the great civil war between Artaxerxes II and his brother Kyros the Younger, who led a force of Greek troops as far as the vicinity of Babylon. After the battle of Kounaxa, where Kyros died, the Greeks, led by Xenophon, were forced to make it on their own to the coast of the Black Sea. Xenophon has left for us an impressive testament to these events in his *Anabasis* (Lendle 1995; Tuplin 1999b; 2004a).

We are similarly well informed about the presence of Greek specialists at the court of the Great King (Walser 1967). To begin with, it is possible to identify a set of doctors, from among whom two examples are particularly conspicuous. Herodotos (3.129–37) relates in detail the fate of Demokedes of Kroton, who stayed at the court of Dareios for an extended period of time and supposedly embarked on a reconnaissance expedition commissioned by the Great King to Kroton in southern Italy (Griffiths 1987). Here, a remarkable affinity with the ladies of the Persian royal court becomes apparent in these Greek physicians – in this case Demokedes reportedly cured Atossa of a breast ailment. This affinity emerges still more clearly in the works of Ktesias of Knidos. Ktesias relates to us something of the medical skill of Apollonides of Kos, who allegedly devised a cure for a 'gynaecological disorder' of Amytis, the daughter of Amestris and Xerxes (*FGrHist* 688 F 14 = Lenfant 2004, 133–4). This distinguished Persian lady only too happily took up the remedy of penetration, in which even the doctor himself participated, until Amytis finally succumbed to her illness and Apollonides met a gruesome fate because of Amestris' vengefulness (Tuplin 2004b: 319, 332–5). Even Ktesias, however, preferred to practise as a doctor at the Persian royal court. His work unfortunately survives only in various fragments (Lenfant 2004), which treats the happenings of Asia from the rule of the Assyrians to his own time and in which his own presence at the royal court plays a special role. Ktesias paints a bewildering picture of the customs at the court: intrigues, harems, decadent and sumptuous lifestyles, excesses of cruelty and under-handedness – all the stereotypical elements that characterized and defined the mental edifice of oriental despotism, well into the present (Briant 1989). The reports of Ktesias confront modern scholars with notorious difficulties, so that not only the historicity of his accounts (Dorati 1995), but also the very characterization of Ktesias' work as historiography (Bichler 2004c), must remain of dubious value. No matter how these questions are evaluated, Ktesias has in each case profoundly helped in shaping a conception of oriental despotism that is recognizable even in our own day (Bichler 2005), a notion corroborated by the allegedly elaborate methods of torture and execution (Jacobs 2005; also Rollinger 2004b).

In addition to the physicians and diplomats another class of specialists appears in the sources, who are likely to have remained at the court of the Great King. It is again Herodotos who reports that the architect Mandrokles of Samos was in the service of Dareios (Hdt. 4.87). He was denounced as the one responsible for the rescue of the bridge that made it possible for Dareios' troops to cross the Bosporos. Pliny the Elder (*Naturalis Historia* 34.68) makes mention of the sculptor Telephanes, who was in the service of Dareios and Xerxes. Whether we enter into realm of the fabulous with the person of Poulydamas, the Thessalian pancratist and the Olympic victor of 408, is debatable. According to Pausanias, he went to Susa at the invitation of the Persian king, Dareios II, where he not only defeated two of the legendary 'immortals', but is also supposed to have killed them (Pausanias 6.5.1–8). At any rate, two large frag-ments of the base of a statue of the athlete with the wrestling scene before the Persian king are preserved (M. C. Miller 1997: 89).

The 'Ionian explorers', among whom Herodotos of Halikarnassos is by far the most famous, pose an even larger problem (Bichler 2000; Bichler & Rollinger 2000; Rollinger 2003b). During the course of the last third of the nineteenth century scholarship had clearly come to a general consensus, which found powerful expres-sion in Felix Jacoby's monumental 1913 article in Pauly-Wissowa's *Realencyclopädie der classischen Altertumswissenschaft* (Bichler & Rollinger 2000, 145–7). References in Herodotos to specific sources were now thought to be largely authentic and on that basis an itinerary was constructed which tied together his alleged sources with their respective localization. In this way a travel route originated, which allowed Herodotos to visit Asia Minor, Syria, Palestine, Babylon, and Egypt. Only in regard to the Persian homelands and their *metropoleis* – Media and Ekbatana, Susiana and Susa, Persia and Persepolis – did scepticism prevail against the possible presence of Herodotos. Arguments in favour of Herodotos' travels were first driven back by the provocative theses of Detlev Fehling, who preferred to understand all of Herodotos' sources as literary constructs (Fehling 1989). Even though this thesis was certainly overdone, it nevertheless suggested the need for a critical reconsider-ation of the question, by which the literary dimension of Herodotos' work could be thoroughly evaluated (Erbse 1992; Bichler 2000). With regard to the sources, attention was strongly focused on a literary technique directed at a Greek public. It is unlikely that this technique employed source quotations as guarantees of historical authenticity, but it was rather aimed at prevailing opinion and the cognitive association of information (Rollinger 2004c: 936–43). As a result, the historical anchoring of Herodotos' travels obviously disappears. Yet it is important in consideration of the present inquiry to recall the rightly emphasized argument of Margaret Miller: 'If we deny the travels of one Herodotos, we must posit the travels of other Herodotoi' (M. C. Miller 1997: 107). Therefore the likelihood of touring the Persian empire, collecting information, and assembling corresponding inquiries is in theory beyond question. Indeed, the ancient eastern evidence attests to this quite amply.

In addition to these particularly prominent individuals in the Greek sources it follows that the presence of Greeks in the Persian empire was relatively extensive. Besides the above-mentioned soldiers and craftsmen it is of course necessary to take into account those persons falling into captivity, a group to which the victims of mass deportation also belong. Such cases are attested at least twice. Herodotos mentions the deportation of the Greeks from Eretria and Miletos (Hdt. 6.20; 6.119) to Susa. Yet no further trace of them appears in the sources (cf. Diodoros 1.64.4).

Previous scholarship had depended particularly on the Greek sources in its description of the points of contact between the Greek world and that of the Persians as well as the manifold connections bound up with them. Because of this, a picture was offered that was inextricably tied to Greek perspectives. In the next section an attempt at a change in perspective will be undertaken and the reciprocal contact will be treated from the 'eastern' point of view. This is attractive not only because it breaks from the usual and trusted patterns of examination, but also because the sources, which are here treated extensively, remain otherwise largely ignored or are, at best, consulted only by specialists.

## 3   The View from the East: The 'Greek World' in the Reflection of Eastern Sources

From the eighth century the Greeks are known to us from eastern sources (Rollinger 2001b). There appears in Assyrian and Babylonian sources, in addition to the place name Yaman (pronounced 'Yawan'), an ethnic name Yamanaya (pronounced 'Yawanaya'), or Yamnaya (pronounced 'Yawnaya') (Rollinger 1997), which did not, of course, refer to the 'Greeks' in the modern sense, but rather to a people from the far-removed Aegean region, where Greek-speaking elements are likely to have constituted an essential component (Rollinger 2001b; 2003b; Rollinger & Korenjak 2001). Although the evidence clearly diminishes after the Assyrian empire's decline, similar evidence emerges during the time of the Achaimenid empire, from Dareios I to the fourth century (Del Monte 2001; Kuhrt 2002), predominantly mostly trilingual royal inscriptions. Therefore the Old-Persian forms Yauna and Yaunā as well as the Elamite Yauna and Yauna-ip correspond to the Babylonian Yaman and Yamanaya (Kuhrt 2002; Brinkman 1989: 63; evidence for this from Achaimenid inscriptions is incomplete).

The evidence begins with the inscriptions of Dareios I, which in many ways ought to be considered the template for later Achaimenid inscriptions (the abbreviations are explained in the first paragraph of the bibliography). On his tomb in Naqsh-i Rustam the Great King presents himself on a throne platform, which is supported by thirty representatives of subject peoples from various locations. These bearers have been identified by means of trilingual inscriptions, which are heavily damaged (DNe). Yet by comparing it with the comparably shaped layout of tomb V (probably that of Artaxerxes III but also attributed to Artaxerxes II) in Persepolis where the bearers are also given trilingual captions ($A^3Pb$) they have been largely identified (Hachmann 1995). Even the other three graves in Naqsh-i Rustam, which were assigned to Xerxes, Artaxerxes I, and Dareios II, demonstrate similar iconography. They are, however, missing the inscription just as is the second grave in Persepolis (Artaxerxes II (?); a third remains incomplete). According to the trilingual captions bearers number twenty-three and twenty-six are referred to as – in the Old-Persian forms – Yauna (23) and Yaunā takabarā (26) (DNe: Kent 1953: 140–1; Lecoq 1997: 22–6; Schmitt 1999a: 4, 11–12; 2000: 47–9. A3Pb: Kent 1953: 114, 155–6; Lecoq 1997: 271–2; Schmitt 2000: 119–22).

Sancisi-Weerdenburg described the outer appearance of both Yauna and Yaunā takabarā as follows: 'They are identically dressed in knee-length chitons, chlamides around their shoulders, bare lower legs, and (probably) low leather boots. Both have beards and probably short curly hair. The takabara Ionian wears a small hat usually identified as a petasos' (Sancisi-Weerdenburg 2001a: 325) (illustrations Schmidt 1970: figs. 39–50 and plate 67; see also Hachmann 1995). Only the 'Lydian' (Spardiya: no. 21) and the 'Karian' (Krka: no. 29) are likewise dressed in a chiton and chlamys. Moreover the tomb of Dareios is uniquely provided with a longer trilingual (Old-Persian, Babylonian, and Elamite) inscription, which among other things explicitly refers to the peoples there depicted:

> By the favour of Ahuramazda these (are) the countries which I have seized outside Persia; I ruled them; to me they brought tribute. What has been said to them by me, that they did. The law was mine, that held them (stable). (DNa 15–22 following the translation of the Old-Persian version by Schmitt 2000: 30)

There follows a listing of the peoples that corresponds to the pictorial representation and here again mention is made of both Yauna and Yaunā takabarā (DNa 28; 29). Finally the inscription makes a direct reference to the relief:

> Ahuramazda, when he saw this earth in turmoil, after that he bestowed it upon me; me he made king; I am king. By the favour of Ahuramazda I put it in its proper place. What I have said to them, that they did, as was my desire. But if you shall think: 'How many (are) those countries which Dareios the king held?', look at the sculptured figures which bear the throne platform. Then you shall perceive, then it shall become known to you: 'The spears of the Persian man has gone forth far away', then it shall become known to you: 'The Persian man has repulsed the enemy far away from Persia.' (DNa 31–47, following the translation of the Old-Persian version by Schmitt 2000: 30)

Besides the list of peoples, which Dareios presents in Naqsh-i Rustam, similar enumerations in other inscriptions of this king and his successors are also known (it is highly controversial to what extent in these lists it is a matter of peoples or of administrative units; Jacobs 2003). Not only are Yauna as well as Yaunā takabarā mentioned again – it is also possible to assume broader distinctions by geographical criteria (discussion further below).

In addition to these lists of lands, to which the admittedly fragmentary DSv inscription must be added, it is necessary to mention two inscriptions that include no lists in the formal sense, but rather integrate an enumeration of peoples in a building report, which has as its subject the supplies drawn from the entire empire for the palace of Dareios in Susa. If inscription DSaa merely offers a plain listing, then DSf and DSz record along with the participating peoples the part played by each in the construction of the palace. From this we learn:

> The cedar which was used here (for building) men principally, from Ebir-nāri (Syria) brought from a mountain called [Labnānu] to [Babylon]. From Babylon the Karians and 'Greeks' [brought (it)] to Susa. (DSf 21–4 (§ 9) following the translation of the Babylonian version by Brinkman 1989: 61; the supplements are corroborated by the Old-Persian and Elamite versions: Old-Persian text: Steve 1974b: 145–7; Babylonian text: Steve 1974b: 155–7)

Indeed, these 'Greeks' were also as well-known specialists employed in the building of the palace:

> The [stonecutters who] worked [the stone] were ['Greeks'] and [Lydia]ns. (DSf 32f (§ 12) (Babylonian version; the supplements are corroborated by the Old-Persian (DSf 47–9) and Elamite versions: see Steve 1974b: 146; Lecoq 1997: 236)

Moreover:

> The material for the [palace] reliefs [was brought from 'Greece']. (DSf 29 (§ 11) following the translation of the Babylonian version by Brinkman 1989: 61; the supplements are corroborated by the Old-Persian (DSf 42–3) and Elamite versions: Steve 1974b: 146; Lecoq 1997: 236. DSz is merely a variant of this and offers nothing new: Lecoq 1997: 243–5)

From all these sources it is possible to extract a set of weighty inferences. According to external criteria two groups of 'Greeks' are distinguished, both of which find expression in a representation differently depicted each time on royal tombs at Naqsh-i Rustam and Persepolis. The distinction between Yauna and Yaunā takabarā becomes clear in the first place through the headdresses. This seems to be confirmed by the terminology, although the difficult-to-interpret Old-Persian takabara and the corresponding Babylonian terminology – the other 'Greeks' (Yamanāja šanūtu) who wear maginnāta (plural) on their heads (Schmitt 1999a: 22) – still pose problems (*Chicago Assyrian Dictionary* M/1, 1977: 44b; *Akkadisches Handwörterbuch* 576b). Klinkott (2001: 121–32) on the one hand suggests that the term refers to a headdress, specifically, the *petasos*, a felt hat with a wide brim. Schmitt (1999a, 11, 23–24.) on the other hand raises the possibility that it refers to a shield, the *pelte*, because the wide brim does not seem to be a characteristic iconographical element. It is in any event significant that both 'types' can be applied to both Karians and Lydians, who were also characterized by a suitably uniform costume and because of this were clearly distinguishable from other peoples (Sancisi-Weerdenburg 2001a: 325).

The Yaunā, who are distinguished according to geographical criteria, are by far more difficult to identify. Therefore the ' "Greeks" of the mainland' appear alongside the ' "Greeks" who dwell by the sea' as well as the ' "Greeks" who dwell beyond the sea'. Greek territories have been presumed to be behind even such terms as the 'countries which (are) beyond the sea', '(the people) who (dwell) by the sea', and the 'countries which (are) by the sea', the last of which appears only in a Babylonian version (for this see the evidence in the Appendix at the end of this chapter).

Here recent scholarship has produced divergent attempt at identifications, none of which has been able to clarify the issue satisfactorily. Even though it is not possible to go further into detail at this point, it might be instructive to distinguish two models of interpretation, which have been presented recently. In one case the meaning of Yaunā is understood as a homogenous ethnic term and is the equivalent of the Greek world. Therefore Yaunā, with its various attributes, would refer to the regions that lie in the west and northwest of Asia Minor (Sancisi-Weerdenburg 2001b). The second interpretation construes the original meaning of Yaunā in a broader sense and interprets it as multiethnic. It refers to far-distant peoples in the west, who are to be found both in Asia Minor and in the northern Aegean. In addition to the Greeks this included the Phrygians, Mysians, Aeolians, Thracians, and Paionians (Klinkott 2001). Even in the definition of ethnic groups that are not clearly defined, such as the dahyāva tayā para draya (countries which [are] beyond the sea) and tayai drayahyā ([the people] who [dwell] by the sea) there is no agreement. The latter, for example, was referred to by Sancisi-Weerdenburg 2001b: 3–4, 11 with reference to Cyprus (different point of view: Sancisi-Weerdenburg 2001a).

However much one wishes to judge this incongruity, it is possible nevertheless to regard a few observations as certain. Yaunā refers to an *ethnos* or a conglomeration of peoples, who lived at the western fringes of the empire and possibly beyond. It is therefore likely that the various terms may go back to differing situations of conquest (Sancisi-Weerdenburg 2001a; 2001b: 9). The terminology may betray a constructed artificiality striving for order, such as one finds otherwise only for another border people, the Scythians (Klinkott 2001: 138; Sancisi-Weerdenburg 2001b: 2; different Jacobs 1994a: 129–30). The location becomes quite clear from the Yaunā's special proximity to the Karians and Lydians (Sancisi-Weerdenburg 2001a: 325; 2001b: 6). The spatial distance becomes recognizable in that inscription, in which the 'Greeks' do not appear, in which the endpoints of the empire in the west are marked with the Lydians (Kuhrt 2002, 20–2; also Jacobs 1994a: 127–30; 1997: 286). Its optional non-consideration did not, therefore, trace back to a specific historical situation, as for instance Calmeyer (1982; 1983a; 1983b; 1987) holds, but rather to the particular focus of any given inscription and its context (Sancisi-Weerdenburg 2001a: 328–9).

This special focus deserves closer examination. 'Greeks' first appear in Persian inscriptions in the texts of Dareios I, where they are quite notably attested. Beyond that they are mentioned only twice, once in an inscription of Xerxes and again in an inscription of Artaxerxes III. This certainly does not mean that the 'Greeks' in the reign of Dareios reached particular acclaim, which later appreciably diminished. Moreover such a conclusion is not supported by the way royal Achaimenid inscriptions evolved. This process began under Dareios. It was, with the Behistun inscription, linked to older, eastern narrative models in a unique way, and assumed a canonical form after the reign of Dareios had been established. Xerxes modified it only lightly (Sancisi-Weerdenburg 1999).

These forms should not therefore be misunderstood as an unimaginative repeating of ancient formulas, but rather as reflecting the fact that the Achaimenid kings resorted to firmly established forms of expression for a world rule which was considered to be secure. This holds true for the representation of the 'Greeks' as well as for that of other peoples. To this extent, evidence that appears in the reigns of Dareios and his successors ought to be considered representative for the image of the West, which was cultivated in inscriptions until the rise of Alexander the Great. Moreover, the fact that the Persian Wars are not mentioned in these inscriptions should not to be mistaken for an attempt to conceal the defeat in high official documents, but rather results from the character of the inscriptions themselves. If it is remembered that not one of the great conquests of the Persian kings was immortalized in an inscription – with the exception of the singular example of the Cyrus-Cylinder, which is attributable to Babylonian-Assyrian models – it becomes clear that the Achaimenids did not exalt the political or the military as a subject of their inscriptions. This assessment holds true for all of the royal inscriptions of the time except for the Behistun inscription. They reveal a world order that was thought of as static, which was established by higher powers for eternity, and in which the king operated as a divine agent. In this order Persia lies in the centre of a giant empire. From this perspective the Aegean is a remote region at the edge of the world (Kuhrt 2002).

It is in this context that a passage in Aristophanes' *Acharnians* assumes a crucial role. At lines 100–6 one Pseudartabas makes an appearance at the head of a Persian delegation. Speaking first a line (100) in Persian (Brandenstein 1964). Pseudartabas then addresses the Athenians in garbled Greek as Ionau: 'thou shalt not have gold, thou gaping-arsed Ionau' (*Acharnians* 104, cf. 106) is his devastating response to an Athenian request for Persian financial support. Ionau indubitably represents a rendition of Old-Persian Yaunā, no matter how we interpret the Yaunā named in the royal inscriptions and the fine geographical differentiations connected with that ethnonym, and no matter whether we take Ionau to refer to: the Athenians; to the Athenian and Ionians; to the Greeks in general; or even more broadly to any 'Westerner'.

As we have already seen, 'Greeks' appear not only in royal inscriptions, but also in pictorial representations of Achaimenid monumental art (on this, generally: Jacobs 2002). These representations do not simply affect the royal grave monuments in Naqsh-i Rustam and Persepolis where on the basis of the labels the identification of individual peoples hardly presents a problem. We find them moreover on the walls on both sides of the grand staircases leading up to the Apadāna, the Receiving Hall of the Great King, which display the lands and peoples of the empire as they bring gifts or tribute to the king (Walser 1966; 1981) The sequence of relief decoration on both flights of stairs is identical, even though the east side was worked with more detail than the north. Altogether twenty-three delegations are portrayed, whose identification in individual cases presents difficulties because the reliefs display no explanations (Hachmann 1995). Delegation XII, which has often been regarded as a Lydian delegation, however, clearly depicts 'Greeks' (a Greek delegation is also depicted on the reconstructed staircases of the palace of Artaxerxes I: Calmeyer 1983b: 154; Jacobs 2002: 358). The 'Lydians' are in fact present in delegation VI (Sancisi-Weerdenburg 2001a: 326: also, already, Barnett 1957: 69–70; Hinz 1969: 97).

A high Persian official presents seven delegation members, who can be described in the following way:

> Delegation XII wears short-sleeved dresses reaching the mid-calf. The lower part of the dress and the sleeves are pleated or wrinkled, and an overgarment with large folds has a slip thrown over the shoulder. All the individuals wear half boots and have beards and shoulder-length hair that is curly at the ends. Three delegates carry gold and silver vessels, two folded cloths (possibly the garments that they themselves are wearing), and the last two bundles that have been identified as wool. (Sancisi-Weerdenburg 2001a: 326)

Here too there is a great similarity to the Lydians, who – apart from their gifts – are dressed in like fashion and most notably differ from the 'Greeks' in wearing a conical hat. Even though the textile gifts, which are depicted as being given by the Greeks to the Great King, are at first glance likely to surprise, there nevertheless exists a continuity going back at least to Neo-Babylonian times. Even at that time 'Greek' purple wool, which was destined for Babylonian weavers, is mentioned in addition to the supply of bronze and iron located there (Kuhrt 2002: 12). 'Greek' craftsmen appear to have been found at the residence of Nebuchadnezzar, a fact that derives from corresponding ration lists and calls to mind those specialists who were employed in the building of the palace of Dareios at Susa.

In addition to the Apadāna reliefs there are finally two pairs of throne-carrier reliefs to mention, which evidently continue the depiction on the flights of stairs at Apadāna and embed it in a new iconographical context: the East Gate of so-called Tripylon (Central Building) and the South Gates to the Hall of the Hundred Columns, both of which show the Great King on his throne carried by representatives from the various peoples of the empire (Jacobs 2002: 357–61).

**Figure 11.1** Persepolis: Apadāna, eastern staircase, delegation XII: the Greeks. © photo archives Birgit Gufler.

**Figure 11.2**   Persepolis: southern entrance of the Hall of the Hundred Columns. Part of the minor thrones with representatives from the various peoples of the empire; from right to left: Saka haumavarga, Libyans, Arabians, Saka tigraxauda, Saka paradeaya, nos. 28, 26, 24, 22, 20. Copyright: R. Rollinger.

When we combine the sources presented above, it becomes clear that the 'Greeks' were primarily represented as a section of the population that belonged to the edge of the empire and appeared opposite the Great King as a tributary people. In this capacity, at least, they are present in the royal residence at the centre of the empire. A further aspect is shown by inscriptions from Susa that make mention of Greek specialists employed in the building of the palace of the Great King. This concerns not only their employment in transporting expensive building materials down the Euphrates – a fitting parallel to similar employment in the Neo-Assyrian period (Rollinger 2001b; 2003a) – but also their position as top specialists in construction.

This picture can, of course, be somewhat sharpened through a series of other sources. First of all an admittedly fragmentary document from Sippar, dated to 487, attests the presence of a Greek by the name of [LÚ]Ya-ma-na-a-a in Achaimenid Babylonia (Barton 1899–1900: 74 no. 17, line 11; cf. Brinkman 1989: 63). Equal weight should be given to an administrative tablet from Persepolis, which was composed in Greek. This tablet booked the shipment of two *maris* of wine for the Babylonian month Tebet (December/January) at some point between the years 509 and 494: *oino/s dyo/ ii/ marig/ tebêt* (Hallock 1969: 2; Lewis 1977: 12–15; 1985: 197; Balcer 1979: 280 with incorrect transcription; Boardman 2000: 133 with incorrect tablet identifier). *Marig* reproduces perhaps a unit of measure that may go back to Elamite *mari(k)s/mariš* (Balcer 1979: 280; Hinz & Koch 1987: 886), which corresponds to c. 9.7 litres, and which even Aristotle later attests (*Historia*

*Animalium* 8.9.1). The writer of the tablet, at any rate, not only had a command of Greek, but also was active in a central administrative unit of the Achaimenid empire and made use of terminology that was common within that context. Therefore he not only falls back on a Persian-Elamite system of measures, but more astonishingly he also makes use of the name of a Babylonian month. In connection with this, Balcer speaks of a Greek who is 'bilingual; a dragoman in the Persian court', whom he sought to identify as a Samian on the basis of the 'four-bar sigma and eta' as well as the 'lunate gamma' (Balcer 1979: 279a, 280b). Irrespective of the exact origin of the writer, there can be little doubt both that the milieu of the chancellery at Persepolis was polyglot and that Greeks were in contact with that bureaucracy as well, or rather that they were integrated into it. The administrative tablets from Persepolis sketch out a generally extremely heterogeneous milieu in terms of language (Uchitel 1991; Tavernier 2002; Schmitt 2003). The tablets fall into two large groups of archives, which belonged to the reigns of Dareios and his successor, Xerxes. Whereas the the 'Persepolis Fortification Tablets' date to between 509 and 494 (published by Hallock 1969 = PFT with the tablet identifiers PF, and Hallock 1978 with PFa; the identifier 'Fort' stands for the unpublished tablets; cf. Hinz & Koch 1987: 1369–92), the 'Persepolis Treasury Tablets' include the period of time from 492 to 458 BCE (published by Cameron 1948 = PTT with the tablet identifiers PT; cf. Cameron 1958; 1965). Both groups of archives show a multiethnic colouring that reflects not only the huge expanse of the Persian empire, but also an accompanying migration or relocation of people. This variety first becomes clear in the linguistic consistency of the surviving archival materials. Most texts are in Elamite; however, here are also some seven hundred texts in Aramaic, two tablets in Babylonian, one in Phrygian, and the one example (above) in Greek (Tavernier 2002; Roaf 2004: 408–10). If we direct our attention to ethnic names, a multiethnic character becomes substantially clearer. Besides the Persians, Medes, and Elamites the represented peoples came from almost the entire empire. One encounters Arabians, Assyrians, Babylonians, Egyptians, Kushites, Hattians, Indians, and ethnic groups coming from Asia Minor and beyond. In addition to the Karians, Lykians (under the name 'Turmirians'), Lydians ('Ispardians'), and Thracians ('Skudrians'), the latter category also includes Greeks classified as Yauna-ip (Tavernier 2002; Hallock 1969: 772, entries Yauna, Yaunā, Yaunap; Dandamaev & Lukonin 1989: 152–77; Hinz & Koch 1987: 1264–5). These 'Greeks' can be noted expressly as subsisting on rations or plainly as consumers (PT 15:6; for this, see Hinz & Koch 1987: 422 entry 'gal.ma-ki-ip'; 862 entry 'ma-ki-ip'). They can also be identified simply as 'workers' (PT 15: 5; PF 2072: 84), whose exact function is often left vague (Hinz & Koch 1987: 534, entry 'hh.kur-taš' and the forms derived from it; Aperghis 2000). It is interesting to note that in this context women outnumber men (Aperghis 2000: 133; cf. PF 2072: 86; Hinz & Koch 1987: 836 entry 'LÚ.lg' or 1044 entry 'ru-hu'). Women often appear collectively. They are in one case referred to as 'nu-ma-kaš-be' (PF 1224: 8–9):

32 BÁN [1 BÁN equals c. 9.7 litres] (of) grain, supplied by Ašbašuptiš, Šedda, the *hatarmabatti*š [a high priest according to Hinz & Koch 1987: 650] (at) Persepolis, for whom Abbateya sets the apportionments, received, and gave (it as) *kamaka*š ['desired food', 'bonus' according to Hinz & Koch 1987: 424] to post partum Ionian women (at)

Persepolis, irrigation (?) (workers) (nu-ma-kaš-be), whose apportionments are set by Abbateya and Miššabadda. Nine women (who) bore male children received (each) two BÁN, and fourteen women (who) bore girls received 1 BÁN. (PF 1224 as translated by Hallock 1969: 349)

What exactly is meant by 'nu-ma-kaš-be' remains unclear. Hallock's suggested translation as 'irrigation (?) (workers)' has been called into question (Hinz 1973: 95). The interpretation of 'kamakaš' as a special ration due only to those women who had borne a child was also important in this context (Koch 1992: 56). There appears to have been a difference whether a boy or a girl was born (Aperghis 2000: 133). For the latter there was only half the special ration (this fact suffices to expose the remark of Koch's 1992: 234 that supposes a far-reaching equality of the sexes in the Achaimenid empire as a romanticizing illusion: cf. generally Brosius 1996; Aperghis 2000: 140–1). It seems that Lewis wishes to see in the bearing of children one of the central occupations of these women, and he proposes the translation 'spinster' for this 'professional group': 'Since they are getting bonus rations for producing children, it should be clear that I use the word in its primary sense' (Lewis 1985: 107 with a reference to Hinz 1973: 95; following him, M. C. Miller 1997: 102). Hinz had proposed the translation 'spinning women', which he later repeated (Hinz & Koch 1987: 1009, entry 'nu-ma-kaš-be'). It is in any event obvious that we are here dealing with a dependent work force, whose freedom of action was quite restricted (Aperghis 2000). In these milieus it is quite possible that eastern Greeks played a dominant role (M. C. Miller 1997: 102–3).

Special attention is owed to those Greeks who appear in lofty positions and whose function could be described as 'secretarial' (see Lewis 1977: 12–15). These people

**Figure 11.3**   Persepolis: northern sector of the site. © photo archives Birgit Gufler.

appear simply as 'Yauna', where in this case Yauna is rightly interpreted as a person's name (PF 1798: 19–20; PF 1799: 18–19; PF 1800: 21–2; PF 1806: 20–1; PF 1807: 19–20; PF 1808: 15–16; PF 1810: 18–19; PF 1942: 27–8: PF 1965: 29; PT 21: 20–1). Administrative duty, which is connected to the writing down of documents and is classified as a drawing up of 'dumme', appears in this context as an area of responsibility for one or more of these individuals labelled Yauna (PF 1798: 19–20; PF 1799: 18–19; PF 1800: 21–2; PF 1806: 20–1; PF 1807: 19–20; PF 1808: 15–16; PF 1810: 18–19; PT 21: 20–1). This function may not only have been defined by writing rough drafts and dictating documents (Hinz & Koch 1987: 384, entry 'du-um-me'), but may also have included the responsibility for passing on and writing translations of instructions issued from higher up. This also implies contact with the heads of the administrative hierarchy (Lewis 1985: 108). This is, therefore, of importance because through it Greeks in high administrative positions, who cooperated closely with the writers of the documents (likewise individually named), come to light. Moreover their occupation also presupposes a thorough knowledge of Elamite, to which Old-Persian and Babylonian may also be added. There is probably disagreement as to whether they could be characterized as well versed in cuneiform. Yet an elementary knowledge, at least, appears to be a likely presupposition. Finally a Yauna appears in two documents as a 'grain handler' (Hinz & Koch 1987: 359, entry hh.tu-ma-ra: 'Kornkommissar', 'Ceralien-Beauftragter'), who performed his job at an outside station and there publicly signed for the distribution of grain (PF 1942: 27; PF 1965: 29):

> Three hundred (BÁN of) grain carried forward (as) balance (in) the twentieth year, at Battirakkan, entrusted to Yauna the grain handler and to Narezza his delivery man, (for) Iršena to apportion, in the twentieth year. (PF 1965: 28–31 according to Hallock 1969: 575; for the location of Battirakan, see Vallat 1993: 39)

Even personal names have been interpreted as Greek by more recent scholarship. Mayrhofer (1973, 245: 8.1717; 215: 8.1294; 215: 8.1296) saw a Eumenes behind Umanna (PF 1: 9; PF 54: 13–14; PF 1831: 1; Fort. 5206: 3), a Polyandros or Polyanor behind Parruna (PF 83: 1–2; PF 84: 2; PF 2035: 2–3; Fort. 8626: 3), and a Polys behind Parruš (PF 27: 3–4). Tavernier did not include these examples but draws attention to a 'hh.pi-ul-pi-su', who is identified as an accountant (PF 1276: 2–3) (Hinz & Koch 1987, entry mu-ši-in.zik-ki-ra: 'Abrechnungsaufsteller = Buchhalter, Rechnungsführer'). If it is actually possible to see in the name of this accountant the Greek name Philippos (Delauney 1976: 24; Tavernier 2002: 148; also Hinz & Koch 1987: 226–7 with a further possible example for the name: Fort. 1348: 2–3), then another Greek at a somewhat lower level of the administrative hierarchy would be identified, for whom an appropriate knowledge of writing and speaking is similarly to be assumed.

In this context it is remarkable that the Greek craftsmen, who have been identified in the inscriptions of Dareios and whom he would have called in for the building of his residence, do not appear in the administrative tablets. This is likely to be due to the vicissitudes of preservation. At any rate, Karian goldsmiths are present during the reign of Xerxes (PT 37), and in other cases peoples from the Anatolian provinces are well attested (Uchitel 1991). The archaeological record at any rate offers strong evidence for the presence of a specialized work force of Greeks in the construction of Achaimenid monumental buildings.

The archaeological evidence also suggests that Greek craftsmen were already involved in the buildings of Kyros the Great in Pasargadai (Nylander 1970). Columns with fluting and torus, for instance, and also other techniques of stone-masonry, are used in Pasargadai, but also later in Persepolis and elsewhere (Root 1991; Boardman 2000). The porticoes with columns appear indeed to be inspired by the Greek stoa, although an influence in the opposite direction cannot be ruled out (Boardman 2000: 61). The bas-reliefs of Persepolis also show the mark of Greek artists (Boucharlat 2002: 330). Several fragments of a scratch drawing preserved in the Greek style from Persepolis portray Apollo, Herakles, and Artemis. They represent a familiar motif from Greek vase painting, which seems to represent the struggle between Apollo and Artemis for possession of the tripod (Roaf & Boardman 1980). There is similar evidence from Susa for miniature sculpture such as ivory carvings (Boucharlat 2002: 330). Moreover, the presence of Greek artists at the Persian residence is likely to be reflected in the above-noted evidence from the classical tradition, in which Pliny the Elder tells the story of a certain Telephanes of Phokaia, who was in the service of Dareios and Xerxes (*Naturalis Historia* 24.68). It is of course likely that among these 'Greeks' people of other ethnic backgrounds from western Asia Minor were included, and especially Lydians (Sancisi-Weerdenburg 2001a: 330). This picture can be completed by means of five short Greek inscriptions, which were found in the quarry at Kuh-i Rahmat, near Persepolis (Pugliese Carratelli 1966: 31). This find corroborates the evidence of Greek stone masons at Persepolis and Susa (Nylander 1979).

Greek coins in Persepolis (Root 1988) as well as the infiltration of Greek motifs in the Babylonian glyptography of the Achaimenid period (Jakob-Rost & Freydank 1972; Collon 1996; Kuhrt 1999) are further indications, if not of the presence of Greeks, then of a far too little appreciated dimension of the East–West exchange. This becomes particularly clear in the sarcophagi of the royal necropolis of Sidon, whose showpiece, the so-called Alexander Sarcophagus, marks the completion of a development of sepulchral art imbued with Greek artistic creativity (Graeve 1970; Frel 1971).

Even though the evidence is, when considered together, still quite sparse, a coherent picture of a broad cultural fusion of the Greek world with those areas dominated by Persia nevertheless emerges. Contacts ranged from Egypt (Wirth 2000; Sternberg-el Hotabi 2002; Vittmann 2003) to the Levant and Anatolia and beyond, to include the heartlands of Babylonia, Media, Elam, and Persia. The Greek sources, by painting a picture characterized by stereotypes, provide only a one-sided picture. The eastern sources – especially the evidence gleaned from the royal inscriptions – are admittedly also stereotyped. Their archives with their numerous documents, however, as well as the archaeological record with its direct and indirect pointers demonstrate the existence of intense and multifaceted cultural interaction which was able to prevail, largely unaffected by geo-political friction.

**Table 11.1** Appendix: 'Greeks' in the Inscriptions of the Achaimenid Kings[1]

| | DB[2] | DNa[3] | DNe[4] | DPe[5] | DSaa[6] | DSe[7] | DSm | DSf[8] | DSz[9] | XPh[10] | A³Pb[11] |
|---|---|---|---|---|---|---|---|---|---|---|---|
| Y | I 15 (§ 6)[12] | 28 (§ 3) | 23 | | 24[13] (b) | | § 2 | 33f[14] 42f[15] 48[16] | 27 30f | | 23 |
| Yt | | 29 (§ 3) | [26] | | | | § 2 | | | | 26 |
| Ytu | | | | 12f (§ 2) | | | | | | | |
| Ytd | | | | 13f (§ 2) | | 27f[17] | | | | 23f (§3) | |
| Ytpd | | | | | | 29f[18] | | | | 24f (§ 3) | |
| dtpd | | | | 14f (§ 2) | | | | | | | |
| td | I 15 (§ 6)[19] | | | | | | | | | | |
| cs | | | | | 23 (b) | | | | | | |

Notes:

Y = Yauna ('Greece')/Yauna ('Greek'), Yaunā ('Greeks') (op)

Yt = Yaunā takabarā ('Greeks' *takabarā*) (op)

Ytu = Yaunā tayai uškahyā ('Greeks' of the mainland) (op)

Ytd = (Yaunā) tayai drayahyā (dārayanti) ( ('Greeks') who (dwell) by the sea) (op)

Ytpd = Yaunā tayā para draya (dārayanti) ('Greeks' who (dwell) beyond the sea) (op)

dtpd = dahyāva tayā para draya (countries which (are) beyond the sea) (op)

td = tayai drayahyā ((the people) who (dwell) by the sea) (op)

cs = matāta ša ina $^{ID2}$marratu: countries which (are) by the sea (b)

[1] The superscript numerals (with the exception of 'A³Pb') in this table refer to either lines or sections (§) of the following inscriptions: DB (b, op, e); DNa (op, b, e); DNe (op, b, e); DPe (op); DSe (op, b e); DSf (op, b, e); DSm (op, b, e); DSz ([op], e); DSv (b) DSaa (b); XPh (op, b, e). Old-Persian forms are the starting point (op); Babylonian forms, where extant, are recorded in the notes (b); Elamite forms are easily accessible in Hinz & Koch (1987: 1264–5, entry 'ya-u-na' (e)).

[2] Schmitt (1991). The Babylonian version von Voigtlander (1978); Elamite version Grillot-Susini, Herrenschmidt, Malbran-Labat (1993).

[3] Schmitt (2000: 25–32).

[4] Schmitt (2000: 47–9).

[5] Schmitt (2000: 60–2).

[6] Vallat (1986).

[7] Steve (1974a: 7–28). Elamite version Kent (1938: 119–20); Herzfeld (1938).

[8] Steve (1974b: 135–69). Elamite version Vallat (1972b: 8–10).

[9] Steve (1974b: 161–8). Elamite version cf. Vallat (1970: 149–60).

[10] Schmitt (2000: 8895). Elamite version cf. Herzfeld (1938).

[11] Schmitt (2000: 119–22).

[12] Babylonian: $^{KUR}$Ya-a-ma-nu (line 5).

[13] Babylonian: $^{KUR}$Ya-a-ma-ni.

[14] Babylonian $^{KUR}$Ya-ma-na-a-a (line 24).

[15] Babylonian: [ ] (line 29).

[16] Babylonian: LÚ[ ] (line 33).

[17] Babylonian: $^{KUR}$Ya-ma-na šá i-na A.A.BA (line 20).

[18] Babylonian exclusively: $^{KUR}$Ya-ma-na (line 21).

[19] Akkadian: ina marrati.

# Further reading

## Comprehensive studies and reference resources

For all matters concerning the Achaimenid empire: Briant (2002), a comprehensive study of the Achaimenid empire; also Wiesehöfer (2001). Briant (1997; 2001) are invaluable bibliographical tools; also Weber & Wiesehöfer (1996), for earlier literature. 'Achemenet.com' – access: http://www.achemenet.com – provides updates, new links to resources, and recent articles or previews. An excellent analysis of the 'mental map' of the Achaimenid empire: Kuhrt (2002). Indispensable for gender relevant questions: Brosius (1996). On Greek prosopography, unrivalled: Hofstetter (1978).

## Maps

Excellent overview of the Achaimenid empire and its provinces: Jacobs (1994b). For Persis/Fars in detail: Talbert (2000: 94).

## Archaeological evidence

Boardman (2000), most recent and comprehensive study of Persian-Greek relations (taking into account also older literature); also Boucharlat (2002). Achaimenid art in general: Jacobs (2002) and authoritative treatment of the topic.
Persepolis: Roaf (2004); also Jacobs (1997). Pasargadai: Boucharlat – access: http://www.achemenet.com/recherche/sites/pasargades/pasargades.htm – newest results of the French-Iranian excavations.
Schmidt (1970) is the authoritative publication for the royal tombs of the Achaimenids. Walser (1966) is still essential on the delegations of the various peoples on the Persepolis relief decorations; also Hachmann (1995).

## Achaimenid inscriptions and archives

For most Achaimenid inscriptions (Old-Persian as well as Babylonian and Elamite versions) Lecoq (1997); also Kent (1953) (most Old-Persian inscriptions). Detailed studies of every single text in *CII* (in progress: Schmitt 1991; 2000; von Voigtlander 1978).
The archives of Persepolis: Brosius (2003b) on their general organisation and structure. Foreign workers: Aperghis (2000) is basic; very useful are also Tavernier (2002); Uchitel (1991). Patterns of movements of migrants: Zaccagnini (1983).

## Greek relations with Persia and the Greek sources

The best treatment of Graeco-Persian matters is M.C. Miller (1997; also 2002); Walser (1984). The Greeks' views on their eastern neighbours: Hall (1989); Hutzfeldt (1999). A more general treatment on the basis of recent publications is Bichler

& Rollinger (2002); also Georges (1994). Bichler (2000) is an up to date in-depth study of Herodotos and the non-Greek world. Herodotos and the Persians: Rollinger (2003b); also Thomas (2001). Xenophon: the contributions in Tuplin (2004a), for the results of current research.

# Bibliography

Inscriptions are normally cited according to Kent (1953). Several corrections are found chiefly in Schmitt (2000; 2002). Unless stated otherwise (b = Babylonian; e = Elamite) only the Old-Persian versions are referenced (op = Old-Persian). For a tabulation of all evidence refer to the Appendix.

*EIR* – Yarshater, E. [Yāršātir, I.], & A. Ashraf (eds) (1985–) *Encyclopaedia Iranica*, vols 1–12 (in progress) (changing publishers; distr. Winona Lake IN: Eisenbrauns)

*CII* – *Corpus Inscriptionum Iranicarum*

Andraschenko, F. M., & K. Schmidt (1998) 'Orientalen und Griechen in Ägypten: Ausgrabungen auf Elephantine' in: Rolle, R., K. Schmidt, R. F. Docter (eds) (1998) *Archäologische Studien in Kontaktzonen der antiken Welt* (Göttingen: Vandenhoeck & Ruprecht): 49–67 (Veröffentlichungen der Joachim-Jungius-Gesellschaft der Wissenschaften Hamburg 87)

Antonaccio, C. M. (2001) 'Ethnicity and colonization' in: Malkin 2001: 113–57

Aperghis (2000), G. G. 'War captives and economic exploitation from the Persepolis Fortification Tablets' in: Andreau, J., P. Briant, R. Descat (eds) (2000) *Économie antique: la guerre dans les économies antiques* (Saint-Bertrand-de-Comminges: Musée archéologique départemental) 127–44 (Entretiens d'archéologie et d'histoire, Saint-Bertrand-de-Comminges 5)

Balcer, J. M. (1979) [Review of Hofstetter 1978] in: *Bibliotheca Orientalis* 36: 276–80

Balcer, J. M. (1991) 'The east Greeks under Persian rule' in: Sancisi-Weerdenburg & Kuhrts 1991: 57–65

Barnett, R. D. (1957) 'Persepolis' in: *Iraq* 19: 55–77

Barton, G. A. (1899–1900) in: *American Journal of Semitic Languages* 16: 74

Baslez, M.-F. (1985) 'Présence et traditions iraniennes dans les cités de l'Égée' in: *Revue des Études Anciennes* 87: 137–55

Baurain, C. & S. Destrooper-Gorgiades (1995) 'Chypre' in: Krings 1995: 597–631

Bettalli, M. (1995) *I mercenari nel mondo Greco*, vol. 1: *Dalle origini alla fine del V sec. a. C.* (Pisa: Edizioni ETS) (Studia e testi di storia antica 5)

Bichler, R. (1996) 'Wahrnehmung und Vorstellung fremder Kultur: Griechen und Orient in archaischer und frühklassischer Zeit' in: Schuster, M. (ed.) (1996) *Die Begegnung mit dem Fremden: Wertungen und Wirkungen in Hochkulturen vom Altertum bis zur Gegenwart* (Stuttgart: Teubner) 51–74 (Colloquium Rauricum 4)

Bichler, R. (2000) *Herodots Welt: Der Aufbau der Historie am Bild der fremden Länder und Völker, ihrer Zivilisation und ihrer Geschichte* (Berlin: Akademie Verlag) (Antike in der Moderne)

Bichler, R. (2004a) 'Das chronologische Bild der "Archaik" in der Historiographie der griechischen Klassik' in: Rollinger & Ulf 2004a: 207–48

Bichler, R. (2004b) 'Some comments on the image of the Assyrian and Babylonian kingdoms within the Greek tradition' in: Rollinger & Ulf 2004b: 499–518

Bichler, R. (2004c) 'Ktesias "korrigiert" Herodot: Zur literarischen Einschätzung der *Persika*' in: Heftner & Tomaschitz 2004: 105–16 (also online, access: http://www.achemenet.com/ressources/souspresse/annonces/RB.Herodotus&Ktesias.pdf)

Bichler, R. (2005) 'Phantastische Bauten in der Residenz "asiatischer" Despoten: Ein Essay zu Herodot, Ktesias und Platon' in: Gassner, V. (ed.) *Festschrift Fritz Krinzinger* (Vienna)

Bichler, R., & R. Rollinger (2000) *Herodot: Eine Einführung* (Hildesheim: Olms) (Studien-bücher Antike 3)

Bichler, R., & R. Rollinger (2002) 'Greece, relations with Persian empire VI: the image of Persia and Persian in Greek literature' in: *EIR* 11: 326–9

Bloedow, E. (2003) 'Why did Philip and Alexander launch a war against the Persian empire?' in: *L'Antiquité Classique* 72: 261–74

Boardman, J. (2000) *Persia and the west: an archaeological investigation of the genesis of Achaemenid art* (London: Thames & Hudson)

Boardman, J. (2001) *Cyprus between east and west* (Nicosia: Bank of Cyprus Cultural Foundation) (Annual Lecture on the History and Archaeology of Cyprus 16)

Boucharlat, R. (2002) 'Greece, relations with Persian empire VII: Greek art and architecture in Iran' in: *EIR* 11: 329–33

Bourriot, F. (1981) 'L'Empire achéménide et les rapports entre Grecs et Perses dans la littérature grecque du V siècle' in: *L'Information Historique* 43: 21–30

Brandenstein, W. (1964) 'Der persische Satz bei Aristophanes: *Acharnes*, Vers 100' in: *Wiener Zeitschrift für die Kunde Süd- und Ostasiens und Archiv für indische Philosophie* 8: 43–58

Briant, P. (1989) 'Histoire et idéologie: les grecs et la "décadence perse"' in: Mactoux, M.-M.., & E. Gery (eds) (1989) *Mélanges Pierre Lévêque*, vol. 2: *Anthropologie et société* (Paris: Les Belles Lettres) 33–47 (Centre de recherche d'histoire ancienne 82 = Annales littéraires de l'Université de Besançon 377)

Briant, P. (1997) *Bulletin d'histoire achéménide I* in: *Bulletin d'histoire achéménide* 1 (*Topoi* Suppl. 1)

Briant, P. (2001) *Bulletin d'histoire achéménide II, 1997–2000* in: *Bulletin d'histoire achéménide* 2 (Persika 1)

Briant, P. (2002) *From Cyrus to Alexander: a history of the Persian empire* (trans. P. T. Daniels) (Winona Lake IN: Eisenbrauns)

Brinkman, J. A. (1989) 'The Akkadian words for "Ionia" and "Ionian"' in: Sutton, R. F. (ed.) (1989) *Daidalikon: studies in memory of Raymond V. Schoder, S. J.* (Wauconda IL: Bolchazy-Carducci) 53–71

Brosius, M. (1996) *Women in ancient Persia, 559–331 BC* (Oxford: Clarendon) (Oxford Classical Monographs)

Brosius, M. (2003b) 'Reconstructing an archive. Account and journal texts from Persepolis' in: Brosius, M. (ed.) (2003a) *Ancient archives and archival traditions: concepts of record-keeping in the ancient world* (Oxford: Oxford University Press 2003) 264–83

Burkert, W. (1992) *The orientalizing revolution: near eastern influence on Greek culture in the early archaic age* (trans. Pinder, M. E., & W. Burkert) (Cambridge MA: Harvard University Press) (Revealing Antiquity 5)

Calmeyer, P. (1982) 'Zur Genese Altiranischer Motive: Die "Statistische Landcharte des Perserreiches" 1' in: *Archäologische Mitteilungen aus Iran* 15: 105–87

Calmeyer, P. (1983a) 'Zur Genese Altiranischer Motive: Die "Statistische Landcharte des Perserreiches" 2' in: *Archäologische Mitteilungen aus Iran* 16: 109–263

Calmeyer, P. (1983b) 'Zur Rechtfertigung einiger großköniglicher Inschriften und Darstellungen: Die Yauna' in: Koch, H., & D. N. Mackenzie (eds) (1983) *Kunst und Kultur der Achämenidenzeit und ihr Fortleben* (Berlin: Reimer) 153–69 (*Archäologische Mitteilungen aus Iran* Ergänzungsband 10)

Calmeyer, P. (1987) 'Zur Genese Altiranischer Motive: Die "Statistische Landcharte des Perserreiches" Nachträge und Korrekturen' in: *Archäologische Mitteilungen aus Iran* 20: 129–46

Cameron, G. G. (1942) 'Darius' daughter and the Persepolis inscriptions' in: *Journal of Near Eastern Studies* 1: 214–19

Cameron, G. G. (1948) *Persepolis treasury tablets* (Chicago: University of Chicago Press) 1948 (University of Chicago Oriental Institute Publications 65)

Cameron, G. G. (1958) 'Persepolis treasury tablets old and new' in: *Journal of Near Eastern Studies* 17: 172–6

Cameron, G. G. (1965) 'New tablets from the Persepolis treasury' in: *Journal of Near Eastern Studies* 24: 167–92

Chiasson, C. C. (1984) 'Pseudartabas and his eunuchs: *Acharnians* 91–122' in: *CPh* 79: 131–6

Collon, D. (1996) 'A hoard of sealings from Ur' in: Boussac, M.-F., & A. Invernizzi (eds) (1996) *Archives et sceaux du monde hellénistique/Archivi e sigilli nel mondo ellenistico: Torino, Villa Gualino, 13–16 gennaio 1993* (Paris: de Boccard) 65–84 (*BCH* Suppl. 29)

Dandamaev, M. A., & V. G. Lukonin (1989) *The culture and social institutions of ancient Iran* (English ed. by P. L. Kohl with the assistance of D. J. Dadson) (Cambridge: Cambridge University Press)

Delauney, J. (1976) 'Remarques sur quelques noms de personne des archives élamites de Persépolis' in: *Studia Iranica* 5: 9–31

Dorati, M. (1995) 'Ctesia falsario?' in: *Quaderni di storia* 21: 33–52

Duchesne-Guillemin, J. (2002) 'Greece, relations with Persian empire III: Persian influence on Greek thought' in: *EIR* 11: 319–21

Ducrey, P. (2000) 'Les aspects économiques de l'usage de mercenaires dans la guerre en Grèce ancienne: avantages et inconvénients du recours à une main-d'œuvre militaire rémunérée' in: Andreau, J., P. Briant, R. Descat (eds) (2000) *Économie antique: la guerre dans les économies antiques* (Saint-Bertrand-de-Comminges: Musée archéologique départemental) 197–209 (Entretiens d'archéologie et d'histoire, Saint-Bertrand-de-Comminges 5)

Elayi, J. (1988) *Pénétration grecque en Phénicie sous l'empire perse* (Nancy: Presses Universitaires de France) (Travaux et mémoires: études anciennes 2)

Elayi, J. (2000) 'Les sites phéniciens de Syrie au Fer III/Perse: bilan et perspective de recherche' in: Bunnens, G. (ed.) (2000) *Essays on Syria in the iron age* (Louvain: Peeters) 327–48 (*Ancient Near Eastern Studies* Suppl. 7)

Erbse, H. (1992) *Studien zum Verständnis Herodots* (Berlin: de Gruyter) (Untersuchungen zur antiken Literatur und Geschichte 38)

Fehling, D. (1989) *Herodotus and his 'sources'* (trans. J. G. Howie) (Leeds: F. Cairns) (originally published in German as *Die Quellenangaben bei Herodot: Studien zur Erzählkunst Herodots* (Berlin: de Gruyter 1971))

Flower, M. A. (2000) 'From Simonides to Isocrates: the fifth-century origins of fourth-century Panhellenism' in: *Classical Antiquity* 19: 65–101

Frel, J. (1971) 'The Rhodian workmanship of the Alexander sarcophagus' *Mitteilungen des Deutschen Archäologischen Institutes (Abteilung Istanbul)* 21: 121–4

Funke, P. (1994) 'Staatenbünde und Bundesstaaten: Polis-übergreifende Herrschaftsorganisationen in Griechenland und Rom' in: Buraselis, K. (ed.) (1994) *Henoteta kai Henotetes tes Archaiotetas: Anakoinoseis apo hena Symposio stous Delphous, 5–8.4.1992/Unity and units of antiquity* (Athens: Nea Synora) 125–35

Funke, P. (1997) '*Polis*genese und Urbanisierung in Aitolien im 5. und 4. Jh. v. Chr.' in: Hansen, M. H. (ed) (1997) *The polis as an urban centre and as a political community: symposium August 29–31 1996* (Copenhagen: Det Kongelige Danske Videnskabernes Selskab) 145–88 (Historisk-filosofiske meddelelser 75 = Acts of the Copenhagen Polis Centre 4)

Funke, P. (1998) 'Die Bedeutung der griechischen Bundesstaaten in der politischen Theorie und Praxis des 5. und 4. Jh. v. Chr.' in: Schuller, W. (ed.) (1998) *Politische Theorie und Praxis im Altertum* (Darmstadt: Wissenschaftliche Buchgesellschaft) 59–71

Funke, S. (2000) *Aiakidenmythos und epeirotisches Königtum: Der Weg einer hellenischen Monarchie* (Stuttgart: Steiner 2000)

Gehrke, H.-J. (1986) *Jenseits von Athen und Sparta: das Dritte Griechenland und seine Staatenwelt* (Munich: Beck)

de la Genière, J. (1999) 'De la céramique pour les mercenaries' in: *La colonisation grecque en méditerranée occidentale: actes de la rencontre scientifique en hommage à Georges Vallet, Rome–Naples, 15–18 novembre 1995* (Paris: de Boccard 1999) 121–30 (Collection de l'École française de Rome 251)

Georges, P. (1994) *Barbarian Asia and the Greek experience: from the archaic period to the age of Xenophon* (Baltimore: Johns Hopkins University Press) (Ancient Society and History)

Griffiths, A. (1987) 'Democedes of Croton: a Greek doctor at the court of Darius' in: Sancisi-Weerdenburg & Kuhrt 1990: 37–51

Grillot-Susini, F., C. Herrenschmidt, F. Malbran-Labat (1993) 'La version élamite de la trilingue de Behistun: une nouvelle lecture' in: *Journal Asiatique* 282: 19–59

Hachmann, R. (1995) 'Völkerschaften auf den Bildwerken von Persepolis' in: Finkbeiner, U., R. Dittmann, H. Hauptmann (eds) (1995) *Beiträge zur Kulturgeschichte Vorderasiens: Festschrift für Rainer Michael Boehmer* (Mainz: von Zabern) 195–223

Haider, P. W. (1996) 'Griechen im Vorderen Orient und in Ägypten bis ca. 590 v. Chr.' in: Ulf 1996a: 59–115

Hall, E. (1989) *Inventing the barbarian: Greek self-definition through tragedy* (Oxford: Clarendon) (Oxford Classical Monographs)

Hall, E. (1994) 'Drowning by nomes: the Greeks, swimming and Timotheus' Persians' in: Khan, H. A. (ed.) (1994) *The birth of the European identity: the Europe–Asia contrast in Greek thought, 490–322 BC* (Nottingham: Nottingham University Press) 44–80 (Nottingham Classical Literature studies 2)

Hall, J. M. (1997) *Ethnic identity in Greek antiquity* (Cambridge: Cambridge University Press)

Hall, J. M. (2004) 'Culture, cultures and acculturation' in: Rollinger & Ulf 2004a: 35–50

Hallock, R. T. (1969) *Persepolis fortification tablets* (Chicago: University of Chicago Press) (University of Chicago Oriental Institute Publications 92)

Hallock, R. T. (1978) 'Selected fortification texts' in: *Cahiers de la Délégation Archéologique française en Iran* 8: 109–36

Hayajneh, H. (2001) 'First evidence of Nabonidus in the ancient north Arabian inscriptions from the region of Tayma' in: *Proceedings of the Seminar for Arabian Studies* 31: 81–95

Heftner, H., & K. Tomaschitz (eds) (2004) *Ad Fontes! Festschrift für Gerhard Dobesch zum fünfundsechzigsten Geburtstag* (Vienna: Eigenverlag)

Herzfeld, E. (1938) *Altpersische Inschriften* (Berlin: Reimer) (Archäologische Mitteilungen aus Iran Ergänzungsband 1)

Hinz, W. (1950) 'The Elamite version of the record of Darius's palace at Susa' in: *Journal of Near Eastern Studies* 9: 11–17

Hinz, W. (1969) *Altiranische Funde und Forschungen; Mit Beiträgen von Rykle Borger und Gerd Gropp* (Berlin: de Gruyter)

Hinz, W. (1973) *Neue Wege im Altpersischen* (Wiesbaden: Harrassowitz 1973) (Göttinger Orientforschungen, Reihe 3, Iranica 1)

Hinz, W., & H. Koch (1987) *Elamisches Wörterbuch* (in 2 Teilen) (Berlin: Reimer) (Archäologische Mitteilungen aus Iran Ergänzungsband 17)

Hofstetter, J. (1972) 'Zu den griechischen Gesandtschaften nach Persien' in: Walser, G. (ed.) (1972) *Beiträge zur Achämenidengeschichte* (Stuttgart: Steiner) 94–107 (*Historia* Einzelschriften 18)

Hofstetter, J. (1978) *Die Griechen in Persien: Prosopographie der Griechen im persischen Reich vor Alexander* (Berlin: Reimer) (Archäologische Mitteilungen aus Iran Ergänzungsband 5)

Hölscher, T. (ed.) (2000a) *Gegenwelten zu den Kulturen Griechenlands und Roms in der Antike* (Munich: Saur)

Hölscher, T. (2000b) 'Feindwelten – Glückswelten: Perser, Kentauren und Amazonen' in: Hölscher 2000a: 287–320

Hutzfeldt, B. (1999) *Das Bild der Perser in der griechischen Dichtung des 5. vorchristlichen Jahrhunderts* (Wiesbaden: Reichert 1999) (Serta Graeca: Beiträge zur Erforschung griechischer Texte 8)

Jacobs, B. (1994a) *Die Satrapienverwaltung im Perserreich zur Zeit Darius' III.* (Wiesbaden: Reichert) (Beihefte zum Tübinger Atlas des Vorderen Orients, Reihe B, Geisteswissenschaften 87)

Jacobs, B. (1994b) *Die Satrapienverwaltung im Perserreich zur Zeit Darius' III* (Wiesbaden: Reichert) (Tübinger Atlas des Vorderen Orients, Karte B, 87)

Jacobs, B. (1997) 'Eine Planänderung an den Apadāna-Treppen und ihre Konsequenzen für die Datierung der Planungs- und Bebauungsphasen von Persepolis' in: *Archäologische Mitteilungen aus Iran* 29: 281–302

Jacobs, B. (2002) 'Achämenidische Kunst – Kunst im Achämenidenreich' in: *Archäologische Mitteilungen aus Iran* 34: 245–95

Jacobs, B. (2003) 'Die altpersischen Länder-Listen und Herodots sogenannte Satrapienliste (Historien III 89–94): Eine Gegenüberstellung und ein Überblick über die jüngere Forschung' in: Dittmann, R., C. Eder, B. Jacobs (eds) (2003) *Altertumswissenschaften im Dialog: Festschrift für Wolfram Nagel zur Vollendung seines 80. Lebensjahres* (Münster: Ugarit-Verlag) 2003 (Alter Orient und Altes Testament 306)

Jacobs, B. (2005) 'Grausame Hinrichtungen und friedliche Bilder bei den Achämeniden' in: Zimmermann, M. (ed.) (2005) *Kolloquium Munich 2003* (Stuttgart: Steiner)

Jakob-Rost, L., & H. Freydank (1972) 'Spätbabylonische Rechtsurkunden aus Babylon mit aramäischen Beischriften' in: *Forschungen und Berichte der Staatlichen Museen zu Berlin* 14: 7–35

Jong, A. de (1997) *Traditions of the Magi: Zoroastrianism in Greek and Latin literature* (Leiden: Brill) 1997 (Religions in the Graeco-Roman World 133)

Kaplan, P. (2002) 'The social status of the mercenary in archaic Greece' in: Gorman, V. B. & E. W. Robinson (eds) (2002) *Oikistes: studies in constitutions, colonies, and military power in the ancient world: offered in honor of A. J. Graham* (Leiden: Brill) 229–43 (*Mnemosyne* Suppl. 234)

Kapten, D. (2000) 'Perseus, Ketos, Andromeda and the Persians' in: Isik, C. (ed.) *Studien zur Religion und Kultur Kleinasiens und des ägäischen Bereiches: Festschrift für Baki Öğün zum 75. Geburtstag* (Bonn: Habelt) 135–44 (Asia-Minor-Studien 39)

Karageorghis, V., & I. Taifacos (eds) (2004) *The World of Herodotus: proceedings of an international conference held at the Foundation Anastasios G. Leventis* (Nicosia: Foundation Anastasios G. Leventis)

Kent, R. G. (1938) 'The restoration of order by Darius' in: *Journal of the American Oriental Society* 58: 112–21

Kent, R. G. (1953) *Old Persian: grammar, texts, lexicon* (New Haven: American Oriental Society) (American Oriental Series 33)

Klinkott, H. (2001) 'Yauna – Die Griechen aus persischer Sicht?' in: Klinkott, H. (ed.) (2001) *Anatolien im Lichte kultureller Wechselwirkungen: Akkulturationsphänomene in Kleinasien und seinen Nachbarregionen während des 2. und 1. Jahrtausends v. Chr.* (Tübingen: Attempto) 107–48

Koch, H. (1992) *Es kündet Dareios der König...: Vom Leben im persischen Groareich* (Mainz: von Zabern) (Kulturgeschichte der Antiken Welt 55)

Konstan, D. (2001) '*To Hellenikon ethnos*: ethnicity and the construction of ancient identity' in: Malkin 2001: 29–50

Kosmetatou, E. (2004) '"Persian" objects in classical and early Hellenistic inventory lists' in: *Museum Helveticum* 61: 139–70

Krasilnikoff, J. A. (1992) 'Aegean mercenaries in the fourth to second centuries BC: a study in payment, plunder and logistics of ancient Greek armies' in: *Classica et Mediaevalia* 43: 23–6

Krasilnikoff, J. A. (1993) 'The regular payment of Aegean mercenaries in the classical period' in: *Classica et Mediaevalia* 44: 77–95

Krings, V. (ed.) (1995) *La civilisation phénicienne et punique: manuel de recherche* (Leiden: Brill) (Handbuch der Orientalistik 1: Der Nahe und der Mittlere Osten 20)

Kuhrt, A. (1999) [Review of Wallenfels 1994] in: *Bibliotheca Orientalis* 56: 449–554

Kuhrt, A. (2002) *'Greeks' and 'Greece' in Mesopotamian and Persian perspectives: a lecture delivered at New College, Oxford, on 7th May, 2001* (Oxford: Leopard's Head Press) (J. L. Myres Memorial Lectures 21)

Lane Fox, R. (ed.) (2004) *The long march: Xenophon and the ten thousand* (New Haven: Yale University Press)

Lecoq, P. (1997) *Les inscriptions de la Perse achéménide: trad. du vieux perse, de l'élamite, du babylonien et de l'araméen, présenté et annoté par...* (Paris: Gallimard) (L'aube des peuples)

Lendle, O. (1995) *Kommentar zu Xenophons Anabasis (Bücher 1–7)* (Darmstadt: Wissenschaftliche Buchgesellschaft)

Lenfant, D. (ed.) (2004) *Ctésias de Cnide: [La Perse; L'Inde; Autres fragments] édition, traduction et commentaire historique des témoignages et fragments; sous la direction de J. Jouanna* (Paris: Belles Lettres) (Collection des universités de France, série grecque 435)

Lewis, D. M. (1977) *Sparta and Persia* (Leiden: Brill) (Cincinnati Classical Studies 2.1)

Lewis, D. M. (1985) 'Persians in Herodotus' in: Jameson, M. H. (ed.) *The Greek historians: literature and history: papers presented to A. E. Raubitschek* (Department of Classics, Stanford University: ANMA Libri) 101–17

Lewis, D. M. (1990) 'The Persepolis fortification texts' in: Sancisi-Weerdenburg & Kuhrt 1990: 1–6

Lewis, D. M. (1994) 'The Persepolis tablets: speech, seal and script' in: Bowman, A. K., & G. Woolf (eds) (1994) *Literacy and power in the ancient world* (Cambridge: Cambridge University Press) 7–32

Lund, A. A. (1990) *Zum Germanenbild der Römer: eine Einführung in die antike Ethnographie* (Heidelberg: Winter)

Maier, F. G. (1985) 'Factoids in ancient history: the case of fifth-century Cyprus' in: *JHS* 105: 32–9

Maier, F. G. (1994) 'Cyprus and Phoenicia' in: *CAH*² 6 297–336

McInerney, J. (2001) 'Ethnos and ethnicity in early Greece' in: Malkin 2001: 51–73

McKechnie, P. (1994) 'Greek mercenary troops and their equipment' in: *Historia* 43: 297–305

Malkin, I. (ed.) (2001) *Ancient perceptions of Greek ethnicity* (Cambridge MA: Harvard University Press) (Center for Hellenic Studies Colloquia 5)

Mayrhofer, M. (1973) *Onomastica Persepolitana: Das altiranische Namengut der Persepolis-Täfelchen* (unter Mitarbeit von J. Harmatta, W. Hinz, R. Schmitt, J. Seifert) (Vienna: Verlag der Österreichischen Akademie der Wissenschaften) (Österreichische Akademie der Wissenschaften, Philosophisch-historische Klasse, Sitzungsberichte 286 = Veroffentlichungen der Iranischen Kommission 1)

Mehl, A. (2004) 'Cypriot city kingdoms: no problem in the Neo-Assyrian, late Egyptian and Persian empires, but why to be abolished under Macedonian Rule?' (prepublication of Mehl (forthcoming) in: *Epeteris* (Leukosia: Kentron Epistemonikon Ereunon) 20: 9–21

Mehl, A. (forthcoming) 'Cypriot city kingdoms: no problem in the Neo-Assyrian, late Egyptian and Persian empires, but why to be abolished under Macedonian Rule?' in: *From Euagoras I to the Ptolemies: the transition from the classical to the hellenistic period in Cyprus: International Conference Nicosia, 29–30 November 2002* (forthcoming)

Mehl, A. (forthcoming *bis*) 'The relations between Egypt and Cyprus from Neo-Assyrian to Achaemenid rule (7/6th centuries B.C.)' in: *International Conference on 'Egypt and Cyprus in Antiquity' organised by the Cyprus American Archaeological Research Institute and the Archaeological Research Unit of the University of Cyprus, 3–6 April 2003* (forthcoming)

Miller, H. F. (1984) 'The practical and economic background to the Greek mercenary explosion' in: *G&R* 31: 153–60

Miller, M. C. (1997) *Athens and Persia in the fifth century BC: a study in cultural receptivity* (Cambridge: Cambridge University Press)

Miller, M. C. (2002) 'Greece, relations with Persian empire II: Greco-Persian cultural relations' in: *EIR* 11: 301–19

Del Monte, G. F. (2001) 'Da "*barbari*" a "*re di Babilonia*": i Greci in Mesopotamia' in: Settis, S. (ed.) (2001) *I Greci: storia, cultura, arte, società,* vol. 3: *I Greci oltre la Grecia* (Turin: Einaudi) 137–66

Moorey, P. R. S. (2002) 'Novelty and tradition in Achaemenid Syria: the case of the clay "Astarte Plaques"' in: *Iranica Antiqua* 37: 203–18

Morgan, C. (2001) 'Ethne, ethnicity, and early Greek states, ca. 1200-480 B.C.: an archaeological perspective' in: Malkin 2001: 75–112

Morris, I. (1997) 'Homer and the Iron Age' in: Morris, I., & B. B. Powell (eds) (1997) *A new companion to Homer* (updated ed.) (Leiden: Brill) 535–59 (*Mnemosyne* Suppl. 163)

Morris, I. (1998) 'Archaeology and archaic Greek history' in: Fisher, N., & H. van Wees (eds) *Archaic Greece: new approaches and new evidence* (London: Duckworth & The Classical Press of Wales) 1–91

Morris, I. (2000) *Archaeology as cultural history: words and things in Iron Age Greece* (Oxford: Blackwell)

Nollé, J., & A. Wenninger (1998–9) 'Themistokles und Archepolis: eine griechische Dynastie im Perserreich und ihre Münzprägung' in: *Jahrbuch für Numismatik und Geldgeschichte* 1998–9: 48–9, 29–70

Nylander, C. (1970) *Ionians in Pasargadae: studies on Old Persian architecture* (Uppsala: Almquist & Wiksell) (Acta Universitatis Upsaliensis, Boreas 1)

Nylander, C. (1979) 'Mason's marks in Persepolis' in: *Akten des VII. Internationalen Kongresses für Iranische Kunst und Archäologie: München, 7.–10. September 1976* (Berlin: Reimer) 236–9 (*Archäologische Mitteilungen aus Iran* Ergänzungsband 6)

Oppenheim, A. L. (1967) 'An essay on overland trade in the first millennium B.C.' in: *Journal of Cuneiform Studies* 21: 236–54

Parke, H. W. (1933) *Greek mercenary soldiers: from the earliest times to the battle of Ipsus* (Oxford: Clarendon)

Pugliese Carratelli, C. (1966) 'Greek inscriptions of the Middle East' in: *East and West* 16: 31–4

Raaflaub, K. A. (2004) 'Archaic Greek aristocrats as carriers of cultural interaction' in: Rollinger & Ulf 2004a: 197–217

Raptou, E. (1999) *Athènes et Chypre à l'époque perse (VIe–IVe s. av. J.-C.): histoire et données archéologiques* (Lyon: Maison de l'Orient) (Collection de la Maison de l'Orient, Série archéologique 14)

Ritter, S. (2001) 'Heracles, the symmachy and the Persians' in: Kuhn, D., & H. Stahl (eds) *Die Gegenwart des Altertums: Formen und Funktionen des Altertumsbezugs in den Hochkulturen der Alten Welt* (Heidelberg: edition forum) 183–201

Roaf, M. (1980) 'Texts about sculptures and sculptors at Persepolis' in: *Iran* 18: 65–74

Roaf, M. (2004) entry 'Persepolis' in: *Reallexikon der Assyriologie und Vorderasiatischen Archäologie,* vol. 10 (Berlin: de Gruyter) 293–412

Roaf, M., & J. Boardman (1980) 'A Greek painting at Persepolis' in: *JHS* 100: 204–6

Rollinger, R. (1997) 'Zur Bezeichnung von "Griechen" in Keilschrifttexten' in: *Revue d'Assyriologie* 91: 167–72

Rollinger, R. (2001a) 'Altpersische Herrscher – die Achämeniden: König der Könige' in: *Damals* 8/2001 (33. Jahrgang) 14–23

Rollinger, R. (2001b) 'The ancient Greeks and the impact of the ancient Near East: textual evidence and historical perspective' in: Whiting, R. M. (ed.) (2001) *Mythology and mythologies: methodological approaches to intercultural influences: proceedings of second annual symposium of the Assyrian and Babylonian intellectual heritage project held in Paris, October 4–7, 1999* (Helsinki: The Neo-Assyrian Text Corpus Project) 233–64 (Melammu Symposia 2)

Rollinger, R. (2003a) 'Homer, Anatolien und die Levante: Die Frage der Beziehungen zu den östlichen Nachbarkulturen im Spiegel der schriftlichen Quellen' in: Ulf, C. (ed.) *Der neue Streit um Troia: eine Bilanz* (Munich: Beck 2003) 330–48

Rollinger, R. (2003b) 'Herodotus' in: *EIR* 12: 254–88 (access: http://www.iranica.com/articles/v12f3/v12f3016.htm)

Rollinger, R. (2004a) 'Das fünfte internationale "Melammu-Meeting" in Innsbruck: Überlegungen zu Kulturkontakten und Kulturaustausch in der Alten Welt' in: Rollinger & Ulf 2004b: 20–30

Rollinger, R. (2004b) 'Herodotus, human violence and the ancient Near East' in: Karageorghis & Taifacos 2004: 121–50

Rollinger, R. (2004c) 'Herodot (II 75f, III 107–109), Asarhaddon, Jesaja und die fliegenden Schlangen Arabiens' in: Heftner & Tomaschitz 2004: 927–46 (also on-line, access: http://www.achemenet.com/ressources/souspresse/annonces/wolski.pdf)

Rollinger, R. (2004d) 'Von Griechenland nach Mesopotamien und zurück: Alte und neue Probleme in der Beschäftigung mit Fragen des Kulturtransfers, von Kulturkontakten und interkultureller Kommunikation (Zu den Beziehungen zwischen Mesopotamien und Griechenland im ersten Jahrtausend v. Chr.)' in: Schipper, F. (ed.) (2004) *Der Irak zwischen den Zeiten: Österreichische Forschungen zwischen Euphrat und Tigris* (Vienna: Institut für Orientalistik der Universität Wien) (Wiener Offene Orientalistik 3) 87–99

Rollinger, R., & M. Korenjak (2001) 'Addikritušu: Ein namentlich genannter Grieche aus der Zeit Asarhaddons (680-669 v. Chr.): Überlegungen zu ABL 140' in: *Altorientalische Forschungen* 28: 372–84

Rollinger, R., & C. Ulf (eds) (2004a) *Griechische Archaik: Interne Entwicklungen – Externe Impulse* (Berlin: Akademie Verlag 2004)

Rollinger, R., & C. Ulf (eds) (2004b) *Commerce and monetary systems in the ancient world: means of transmission and cultural interaction (proceedings of the 5th International Melammu Conference, 3rd–8th October 2002 in Innsbruck)* (Stuttgart: Steiner 2004) (Oriens et Occidens 6: Studien zu antiken Kulturkontakten und ihrem Nachleben ed. J. Wiesehöfer = Melammu Symposia 5)

Root, M. C. (1988) 'Evidence from Persepolis for the dating of Persian and archaic Greek coinage' in: *Numismatic Chronicle* 148: 1–12

Root, M. C. (1991) 'From the heart: powerful Persianisms in the art of the western empire' in: Sancisi-Weerdenburg & Kuhrt 1991: 1–29

Rosselini, M., & S. Saïd (1978) 'Usages des femmes et autres nomoi chez les "sauvages" d'Hérodote: essai de lecture structurale' in: *Annali della Sscuola Normale Superiore di Pisa, Classe di Lettere e Filosofia* 8: 949–1005

Saïd, S. (1985) 'Usages de femmes et sauvagerie dans l'ethnographie grecque d'Hérodote à Diodore et Strabon' in: *La femme dans le monde méditerranéen*, vol. 1: *Antiquité* (Paris: de Boccard) 137–50 (Travaux de la Maison de l'Orient 10)

Saïd, S. (2001) 'The discourse of identity in Greek rhetoric from Isocrates to Aristides' in: Malkin 2001: 275–99

Sancisi-Weerdenburg, H. (1980) 'Yauna en Persai: Grieken en Perzen in een ander perspectief' (unpublished PhD thesis University of Leiden)

Sancisi-Weerdenburg, H. (1999) 'The Persian kings and history' in: Kraus, C. S. (ed.) (1999) *The limits of historiography: genre and narrative in ancient historical texts* (Leiden: Brill) 91–112 (*Mnemosyne* Suppl. 191)

Sancisi-Weerdenburg, H. (2001a) '*Yaunā* by the sea and across the sea' in: Malkin 2001: 323–46

Sancisi-Weerdenburg, H. (2001b) 'The problem of the Yauna' in: Bakir, T. (ed.), H. Sancisi-Weerdenburg, G. Gürtekin, P. Briant, W. Henkelmann (associate eds) (2001) *Achaemenid Anatolia: proceedings of the first international symposium on Anatolia in the Achaemenid period, Bandirma 15–18 August 1997* (Leiden: Neederlands Instituut voor het Nabije Oosten) 1–11 (Uitgaven van het Neederlands Historisch-Archaeologisch Instituut te Istanbul 92)

Sancisi-Weerdenburg, H., & A. Kuhrt (eds) (1990) *Centre and periphery: proceedings of the Groningen 1986 Achaemenid History Workshop* (Leiden: Neederlands Instituut voor het Nabije Oosten) (Achaemenid History 4)

Sancisi-Weerdenburg, H., & A. Kuhrt (eds) (1991) *Asia Minor and Egypt: old cultures in a new Empire: proceedings of the Groningen 1988 Achaemenid history workshop* (Leiden: Neederlands Instituut voor het Nabije Oosten) (Achaemenid History 6)

Scheer, T. S. (2003) 'Die geraubte Artemis: Griechen, Perser und die Kultbilder der Götter' in: Witte & Alkier 2003: 59–85

Schmal, S. (1995) *Feindbilder bei den frühen Griechen: Untersuchungen zur Entwicklung von Feindbildern und Identitäten in der griechischen Literatur von Homer bis Aristophanes* (Frankfurt: Lang) (Europäische Hochschulschriften, Reihe 3, 677)

Schmeja, H. (1974) 'Griechen und Iranier' in: Mayrhofer, M., W. Meid, B. Schlerath, R. Schmitt (eds) (1974) *Antiquitates Indogermanicae: Studien zur Indogermanischen Altertumskunde und zur Sprach- und Kulturgeschichte der indogermanischen Völker: Gedenkschrift Hermann Güntert zur 25. Wiederkehr seines Todestages am 23. April 1973* (Innsbruck: Institut für Sprachwissenschaft der Universtät Innsbruck) 377–89 (Innsbrucker Beiträge zur Sprachwissenschaft 12)

Schmeja, H. (1975) 'Dareios, Xerxes, Artoxerxes: Drei persische Königsnamen in griechischer Deutung (Zu Herodot 6,98,3)' in: *Die Sprache* 21: 184–8

Schmidt, E. F. (1953) *Persepolis 1* (Chicago: University of Chicago Press) (University of Chicago Oriental Institute Publications 68)

Schmidt, E. F. (1957) *Persepolis 2: contents of the treasury and other discoveries* (Chicago: University of Chicago Press) (University of Chicago Oriental Institute Publications 69)

Schmidt, E. F. (1970) *Persepolis 3: the royal tombs and other monuments* (Chicago: University of Chicago Press) (University of Chicago Oriental Institute Publications 70)

Schmitt, R. (1977) 'Der Numerusgebrauch bei Länder- und Völkernamen im Altpersischen' in: *Acta Antiqua Academiae Scientiarum Hungaricae* 25: 91–9

Schmitt, R. (1984) 'Perser und Persisches in der alten attischen Komödie' in: *Orientalia J. Duchesne-Guillemin emerito oblata* (Leiden: Brill) 459–72 (Acta Iranica 23)

Schmitt, R. (1988) 'Achaimenideninschriften in griechischer literarischer Überlieferung' in: *Papers in honour of Jens P. Asmussen* (Leiden: Brill 1988) 17–38 (Acta Iranica 28)

Schmitt, R. (1991) *The Bisitun inscriptions of Darius the Great* (London: Published on behalf of *Corpus Inscriptionum Iranicarum* by the School of Oriental and African Studies) (*CII*, part 1: *Inscriptions of ancient Iran: Old Persian text*, vol. 1: *The Old Persian inscriptions: texts* 1)

Schmitt, R. (1992) 'Assyria grammata und ähnliche: Was wuaten die Griechen von Keilschrift und Keilschriften' in: Müller, C. W., K. Sier, J. Werner (eds) (1992) *Zum Umgang mit fremden Sprachen in der griechisch-römischen Antike: Kolloquium der Fachrichtungen klassische Philologie der Universitäten Leipzig und Saarbrücken am 21. und 22. November 1989 in Saarbrücken* (Stuttgart: Steiner) 21–35 (Palingenesia 36)

Schmitt, R. (1993) 'Die Sprachverhältnisse im Achaimenidenreich' in: Finazzi, R. B., & P. Tornaghi (eds) (1993) *Lingue e culture in contatto nel mondo antico e altomedievale: atti dell'8. Convegno internazionale di linguisti tenuto a Milano nei giorni 10–12 settembre 1992* (Brescia: Paideia) 77–102

Schmitt, R. (1999a) *Beiträge zu altpersischen Inschriften* (Wiesbaden: Reichert 1999)

Schmitt, R. (1999b) 'Zur Bedeutung von altpers. */dahyu-/*' in: Anreiter, P., & E. Jerem (eds) (1999) *Studia Celtica et Indogermanica: Festschrift für Wolfgang Meid zum 70. Geburtstag* (Budapest: Archaeolingua Alapítvány) 443–52 (Archaeolingua 10)

Schmitt, R. (2000) *The Old Persian inscriptions of Naqsh-i Rustam and Persepolis* (London: Published on behalf of *Corpus Inscriptionum Iranicarum* by the School of Oriental and African Studies 2000) (*CII*, part 1: *Inscriptions of ancient Iran*, vol. 1: *The old Persian inscriptions: texts* 2)

Schmitt, R. (2002) 'Greece, relations with Persian empire I. Greco-Persian political relations' in: *EIR* 11: 292–301

Schmitt, R. (2003) 'Lyder und Lyker in den achaimenidischen Quellen' in: Giorgieri, M., M. Salvini, M.-C. Trémouille, P. Vannicelli (eds) (2003) *Licia e Lidia prima dell'ellenizzazion Licia e Lidia prima dell'ellenizzazione: atti del Convegno internazionale, Roma, 11–12 ottobre 1999* (Roma: Consiglio nazionale delle ricerche) 291–300 (Monografie scientifiche, Serie Scienze umane e sociali)

Seibert, J. (1976) 'Zur Bevölkerungsstruktur Zyperns' in: *Ancient Society* 7: 1–28

Seibert, J. (1979) *Die Politischen Flüchtlinge und Verbannten in der griechischen Geschichte: Von den Anfängen bis zur Unterwerfung durch die Römer* (Darmstadt: Wissenschaftliche Buchgesellschaft) (Impulse der Forschung 30)

Seibt, G. F. (1977) *Griechische Söldner im Achaimenidenreich* (Bonn: Habelt) (Habelts Diss.-Drucke Reihe Alte Geschichte 11)

Shaki, M. (2002) 'Greece, relations with Persian Empire IV: Greek influence on Persian thought' in: *EIR* 11: 321–6

Starr, C. G. (1975) 'Greeks and Persians in the fourth century B.C.: a study in cultural contacts before Alexander: I' in: *Iranica Antiqua* 11: 39–99

Starr, C. G. (1977) 'Greeks and Persians in the fourth century B.C.: a study in cultural contacts before Alexander: II: The meeting of two cultures' in: *Iranica Antiqua* 12: 49–115

Stern, E. (2001) *Archaeology of the land of the Bible*, vol. 2: *The Assyrian, Babylonian and Persian periods (732–332 B.C.E.)* (New York: Doubleday)

Sternberg-el Hotabi, H. (2002) 'Die persische Herrschaft in Ägypten' in: Kratz, R. G. (ed.) (2002) *Religion und Religionskontakte im Zeitalter der Achämeniden* (Gütersloh: Kaiser, Gütersloher Verlagshaus) 111–49 (Veröffentlichungen der Wissenschaftlichen Gesellschaft für Theologie 22)

Steve, M.-J. (1974a) 'Inscriptions des Achéménides à Suse (Fouilles 1952 à 1965)' in: *Studia Iranica* 3: 7–28

Steve, M.-J. (1974b) 'Inscriptions des Achéménides à Suse (suite)' in: *Studia Iranica* 3: 135–69

Steve, M.-J. (1975) 'Inscriptions des Achéménides à Suse (fin)' in: *Studia Iranica* 4: 7–26

Talbert, R. J. A. (ed.) (2000) *Barrington atlas of the Greek and Roman world* (accompanied by map-by-map directory) (Princeton: Princeton University Press)

Tavernier, J. (2002) 'Non-Elamite individuals in Achaemenid Persepolis' in: *Akkadica* 123: 145–52

Thomas, R. (2001) 'Ethnicity, genealogy, and Hellenism in Herodotus' in: Malkin 2001: 213–33

Tuplin, C. (1993) *The failings of empire: a reading of Xenophon* Hellenica 2.3.11–7.5.27 (Stuttgart: Steiner) (*Historia* Einzelschriften 76)

Tuplin, C. (1996) *Achaemenid studies* (Stuttgart: Steiner) (*Historia* Einzelschriften 99)

Tuplin, C. (1997) 'Xenophon's *Cyropaedia*: education and fiction' in: Sommerstein, A. H., & C. Atherton (eds) (1997) *Education in Greek fiction* (Bari: Levante) 65–162 (Nottingham Classical Literature Studies 4)

Tuplin, C. (1999a) 'Greek racism? Observations on the character and limits of Greek ethnic prejudice' in: Tsetskhladze, G. R. (ed.) (1999) *Ancient Greeks: west and east* (Leiden: Brill) (*Mnemosyne* Suppl. 196) 47–75

Tuplin, C. (1999b) 'On the track of the ten thousand' in: *Revue des Études Anciennes* 101: 331–66

Tuplin, C. (2003) 'Heroes in Xenophon's *Anabasis*' in: Barzanò, A. (ed.) (2003) *Modelli eroici dall'Antichità alla cultura europea* (Rome: 'L'Erma' di Bretschneider) 115–56

Tuplin, C. (ed.) (2004a) *The world of Xenophon: papers from a conference held in Liverpool in July 1999* (Stuttgart: Steiner) (*Historia* Einzelschriften 172)

Tuplin, C. (2004b) 'Doctoring the Persians: Ctesias of Cnidus, physician and historian' in: *Klio* 86: 305–47

Uchitel, A. (1991) 'Foreign workers in the Fortification Archive' in: de Meyer, L., & H. Gasche (eds) (1991) *Mesopotamie et Elam: actes de la XVIème Rencontre assyriologique internationale, Gand, 10–14 juillet 1989* (Ghent: Rijksuniversiteit) 127–35 (Comptes rendus de la rencontre assyriologique internationale 36 = Mesopotamian History and Environment, Occasional Publications 1)

Ulf, C. (ed.) (1996a) *Wege zur Genese griechischer Identität: Die Bedeutung der früharchaischen Zeit* (Berlin: Akademie Verlag 1996)

Ulf, C. (1996b) 'Griechische Ethnogenese versus Wanderungen von Stämmen und Stammstaaten' in: Ulf 1996a: 240–80

Vallat, F. (1970) 'Table élamite de Darius' in: *Revue d'Assyriologie* 64: 149–60

Vallat, F. (1972a) 'L'Inscription cunéiforme trilingue' in: *Journal Asiatique* 260: 247–51

Vallat, F. (1972b) 'Deux inscriptions élamites de Darius Ier' in: *Studia Iranica* 1: 3–13

Vallat, F. (1986) 'Table accadienne de Darius Ier (Dsaa)' in: de Meyer, L., H. Gasche, F. Vallat (eds) (1986) *Fragmenta Historiae Elamicae: mélanges offerts à M.-J. Steve* (Paris: Éd. Recherche sur les Civilisations) 277–87

Vallat, F. (1993) *Les noms géographiques des sources suso-élamites* (Wiesbaden: Reichert) (Tübinger Atlas des Vorderen Orients Beihefte B 7) (Repertoire géographique des textes cunéiformes 11)

Vickers, M. (1990) 'Interactions between Greeks and Persians' in: Sancisi-Weerdenburg & Kuhrt 1990: 253–62

Vittmann, G. (2003) *Ägypten und die Fremden im ersten vorchristlichen Jahrtausend* (Mainz: von Zabern) (Kulturgeschichte der Antiken Welt 97)

von Graeve, V. (1970) *Der Alexandersarkophag und seine Werkstatt* (Berlin: Mann) (Istanbuler Forschungen 28)

von Voigtlander, E. N. (1978) *The Bisitun inscription of Darius the Great: Babylonian version* (London: published on behalf of *Corpus Inscriptionum Iranicarum* by Lund Humphries 1978) (*CII*, part 1: *Inscriptions of ancient Iran*, vol. 2: *The Babylonian versions of the Achaemenian inscriptions*, texts 1)

Waldbaum, J. C. (1997) 'Greeks *in* the east or Greeks *and* the east?: problems in the definition and recognition of presence' in: *Bulletin of the American Schools of Oriental Research in Jerusalem and Baghdad* 305: 1–17

Wallenfels, R. (1994) *Uruk: Hellenistic seal impressions in the Yale Babylonian collection*, vol. 1: *Cuneiform tablets* (pref. by W. W. Hallo) (Mainz: von Zabern) (Ausgrabungen in Uruk-Warka Endberichte 19)

Walser, G. (1966) *Die Völkerschaften auf den Reliefs von Persepolis: historische Studien über den sogenannten Tributzug an der Apadanatreppe* (Berlin: Mann) (Teheraner Forschungen 2)

Walser, G. (1967) 'Griechen am Hof des Grosskönigs' in: Walder, E., P. Gilg, U. im Hof, B. Mesmer (eds) (1967) *Festgabe Hans von Greyerz zum sechzigsten Geburtstag, 5. April, 1967* (Bern: Lang) 189–202

Walser, G. (1981) *Persépolis: la cité royale de Darius* (trans. J. Scheidegger) (Fribourg: Office du Livre)

Walser, G. (1984) *Hellas und Iran* (Darmstadt: Wissenschaftliche Buchgesellschaft) (Erträge der Forschung 209)

Watkin, H. J. (1987) 'The Cypriot surrender to Persia' in: *JHS* 107: 154–63

Weber, U., & J. Wiesehöfer (1996) *Das Reich der Achaimeniden: eine Bibliographie* (Berlin: Reimer) (*Archäologische Mitteilungen aus Iran* Ergänzungsband 15)

Wenning, R. (2001) 'Griechische Söldner in Palästina' in: Höckmann, U., & D. Kreikenbom (eds) (2001) *Naukratis: Die Beziehungen zu Ostgriechenland, Ägypten und Zypern in archaischer Zeit: Akten der Table Ronde in Mainz, 25.–27. November 1999* (Möhnesee: Bibliopolis) 257–68

Whitby, M. (1998) 'An international symposium? Ion of Chios fr. 27 and the margins of the Delian League' in: Dąbrowa, E. (ed.) *Ancient Iran and the Mediterranean world: proceedings of an international conference in honour of Professor Józef Wolski held at the Jagiellonian University, Cracow, in September 1996* (Kraków: Jagiellonian University) 207–24 (Electrum 2)

Wiesehöfer, J. (1990) 'Zypern unter persischer Herrschaft' in: Sancisi-Weerdenburg & Kuhrt 1990: 239–52

Wiesehöfer, J. (2001) *Ancient Persia: from 550 BC to 650 AD* (trans. A. Azodi) (London: Tauris)

Wiesehöfer, J. (2002) '"Griechenland wäre unter persische Herrschaft geraten..." Die Perserkriege als Zeitenwende' in: Sellmer, S., & H. Brinkhaus (eds) (2002) *Zeitenwenden: Historische Brüche in asiatischen und afrikanischen Gesellschaften* (Hamburg: EB-Verlag) 209–32 (Asien und Afrika 4)

Wiesehöfer, J. (2003a) '"Sie haben sich durch ihre Schlechtigkeit selbst überlebt" Barthold Georg Niehbuhr und die Perser der Antike' in: Stamm-Kuhlmann, T., J. Elvert, B. Aschmann, J. Höhensee (eds) (2003) *Geschichtsbilder: Festschrift für Michael Salewski zum 65. Geburtstag* (Stuttgart: Steiner) 201–11 (Historische Mitteilungen Beiheft 47)

Wiesehöfer, J. (2003b) 'Iraner und Hellenen: Bemerkungen zu einem umstrittenen kulturellen Verhältnis' in: Conermann, C., & J. Kusber (eds) (2003) *Studia Eurasiatica: Kieler Festschrift für Hermann Kulke zum 65. Geburtstag* (Schenefeld: EB-Verlag) 497–524 (Asien und Afrika 10)

Wiesehöfer, J. (2004a) 'Persien, der faszinierende Feind der Griechen: Güteraustausch und Kulturtransfer in achaimenidischer Zeit' in: Rollinger & Ulf 2004b: 295–310

Wiesehöfer, J. (2004b) '"*O master, remember the Athenians*": Herodotus and Persian foreign policy' in: Karageorghis & Taifacos 2004: 209–21

Wirth, G. (2000) 'Hellas und Ägypten: Rezeption und Auseinandersetzung im 5. bzw. 4. Jht. v. Chr.' in: Görg, M., & G. Hölbl (eds) (2000) *Ägypten und der östliche Mittelmeerraum im 1. Jahrtausend v. Chr.: Akten des Interdisziplinären Symposions am Institut für Ägyptologie der Universität München 25.–27.10.1996* (Wiesbaden: Harrassowitz) 281–319 (Ägypten und Altes Testament 44)

Witte, M., & S. Alkier (eds) (2003) *Die Griechen und der Vordere Orient: Beiträge zum Kultur- und Religionskontakt zwischen Griechenland und dem Vorderen Orient im 1. Jahrtausend v. Chr.* (Fribourg: Universitätsverlag) (Orbis Biblicus et Orientalis 191)

Young, T. C. (1980) '480/479 BC – a Persian perspective' in: *Iranica Antiqua* 15: 213–39

Zaccagnini, C. (1983) 'Patterns of mobility among ancient Near Eastern craftsmen' in: *Journal of Near Eastern Studies* 42: 245–64

CHAPTER TWELVE

# The Natural Environment

## J. Donald Hughes

## 1 Introduction

The natural environment of Greece presents a remarkable theater for human en-
deavors. In large part it formed Greek ways of life and thinking. The Greeks inhabited
Mediterranean landscapes and seascapes, experienced a Mediterranean climate, and
depended for their livelihoods on the Mediterranean ecosystems from which they
derived food and materials for clothing, shelter, and transport, and with which
they lived in close and constant interaction.

The geography of Greece is characterized by an intimate interplay between land
and sea. The Mediterranean Sea, especially the Aegean Sea, one of its basins, is the
central element of the Greek world. The Aegean Sea is spangled with scores of islands,
and its shores are complicated by bays, inlets, and straits. The land rises in mountain
chains that extend into the sea as peninsulas and emerge again as islands that are the
peaks of the same ranges, drowned by the Mediterranean in times long past. There is
no place on the Greek peninsular mainland that is more than 115 km from some
point on the seacoast. With a land mostly filled by formidable mountains – only one-
fifth of the area being arable plains – it is understandable that it was to the sea that
Greeks predominantly turned for trade, transport, and warfare.

Except for the narrow connection to the Atlantic Ocean at the Straits of Gibraltar,
which the Greeks called the Pillars of Herakles, the Mediterranean is almost completely landlocked, and that fact has a formative influence on the environment of
Greece. The oceanic tides do not enter the inland sea, so tides in Greece are local and
limited; along most coasts, less than a meter between low and high. This makes ports
accessible without major harbor works such as floating docks, and makes construction possible relatively close to the shoreline – although floods are not unknown.
Waters around Greece are relatively warm and saline, since they are heated by the sun
and subject to evaporation.

## 2   Climate

At the end of the Ice Age, about 12,000 years ago, the climate of Greece – itself never directly touched by the Ice Age glaciation – approached present conditions. In Classical times, it was like the mid-twentieth century with some minor variations. The Mediterranean climate is fairly dependable, characterized by a hot, dry summer (from April to October) and a mild winter punctuated by rainstorms and occasional snowstorms in the mountains and toward the north that bring almost all the annual precipitation. The storms move from west to east, bringing the heaviest precipitation to north-western Greece – over 1,400 mm near Ioannina – as the air masses strike the massive Pindos range, and cause a rain shadow in eastern Greece, including Athens, where the annual average is under 600 mm. Rainfall is quite variable and rarely lasts very long, although it can be quite heavy when it occurs. Its lack is often a severe problem in many Aegean islands.

The nearness of the sea moderates temperatures, and nights with frost are uncommon, but not unknown near sea level. The same could not be said of the mountains, where in winter shepherds wrapped themselves in heavy goatskin. Snow descended rarely to the lowlands in winter. Summers were another story, with temperatures rising to the high 20s or mid-30s C, which may explain why typical marketplace architecture was a colonnade simultaneously offering shade and breezes. Daytime heat in summer can be oppressive, although in Athens, for example, nights generally are cooler than days by around 10 degrees C. Sunshine is present during a high percentage of the possible time. The Greek sky is almost always blue, although Greeks would undoubtedly emphasize the "almost" in this sentence.

Winter storms made sailing dangerous, so the proper season for navigation was summer, with a prevailing north-east wind called "etesian" ("annual"). All statements about Greek weather have their exceptions, however. Violent summer thunderstorms, occasionally bringing tornados, can sweep out from the mountains, sending flash floods down streambeds and causing squalls at sea.

## 3   Geology

Geologically, the Mediterranean is a shrunken remnant of the Tethys Ocean, an immense tropical sea that existed in the Mesozoic Era more than 63 million years before our time. Over millions of years, plate tectonics moved Africa northward toward Eurasia, the continental plates collided and in the Aegean sector, the African continental plate began to slip under the European plate. As one result, the mountain ranges of Greece folded upward in a complex pattern. The chain of Pindos, the backbone of northern Greece, and Olympos, the highest mountain in Greece at 2,917 m, are among the results of this folding. The process continues today and is a reason why Greece has been an active earthquake zone throughout human history. Along with the folding, volcanic activity occurred and still occurs intermittently in the Aegean island arc at places such as Thera (Santorini), Nisyros, and Methana. There are many other sites of past volcanic activity, such as the islands of Melos, Lesbos, and Lemnos. In the late Tertiary Period, the Strait of Gibraltar closed and the

Mediterranean slowly evaporated, leaving saline lakes and deep salt beds behind. This probably happened several times. Remains of the products of evaporation can be seen in many locations because geologic uplift has raised former shorelines high above the present sea level in Cyprus, for example, and the Ionian islands. Then about 5.5 million years ago, the Atlantic found its way through the strait and filled the Mediterranean. Greece was not covered by the Ice Age glaciation, but the climate cooled, precipitation increased, and evaporation slowed. Evidence of valleys carved by large mountain glaciers is found on Olympos and other massifs such as the Pindos and Rhodope mountains.

The oldest rocks in Greece are fragments of the ancient continental plates dating back to the Precambrian era which are found in the mountains of Thrace and eastern Macedonia. The more prevalent and extensive strata are of limestone originally laid down as sediment under the Tethys Ocean. This limestone, under geologic pressure, has been formed into fine marble in places such as the islands of, e.g., Paros and Thasos. Other sedimentary formations such as sandstone, shale, and conglomerate exist. In the zones of volcanic activity, igneous rocks are evident. From surface rocks the process of soil formation began with the aid of vegetation; while there are limited areas of highly fertile soil in Greece, over much of the country soils are thin and poor.

## 4 Mineral Resources

In such a geologically active area, it is not surprising that ores containing metals including gold, silver, copper, lead, and iron were often found. There were coal seams, too, but they were little used in ancient times. The Greeks looked down on mining as degrading labor, and they were undoubtedly right; the life expectancy of the slaves who labored in the mines was regrettably short. The Athenians struck their famous coins, the drachmas bearing the image of an owl, from silver mined at Laureion. Silver mines on the island of Thasos had been worked by the Phoenicians before the Greeks. The Iron Age began about 1000 BCE, sparking a search for exploitable ores of that metal. The Spartans had an iron mine in southern Lakonia on Mount Taygetos, the source of steel that they manufactured into weapons, and from which they made the cumbersome Spartan iron money called obols ("spits"). Philip of Macedon conquered Mount Pangaion in order to exploit the placer gold there, thus gaining the riches he needed to hire spies and to bribe corrupt officials. Greek miners accomplished work on an amazing scale considering the level of their technology. Many mines were of considerable size even by modern standards. At Laureion, more than 2,000 vertical shafts gave access to over 140 km of tunnels. The methods used for extraction of the ores were washing them from the surrounding material by placer and hydraulic mining, open-pit mining, and tunneling into veins deep below the earth. A never-ending problem in mines was drainage, which along with the need for air supply limited the depth to which shafts and tunnels could be sunk. Where topography permitted, miners could dig tunnels as drains. Elsewhere, water was raised by bailing, or by means such as the Archimedean screw pump. Drainage from mines polluted water with many substances, some poisonous.

Quarrying presented many problems similar to those encountered in mining. Since large, potentially useful blocks of various kinds of stone had to be cut and removed, most quarries were of the open-pit type, but sometimes tunnels and galleries were excavated underground. A great weight and volume of substance removed from the earth was required for the production of concrete and mortar. Mortar was known as early as the Bronze Age in Greece.

Mining and quarrying had pervasive impacts on the ancient landscape. Herodotos (6.46–7) said that a whole mountain on the island of Thasos had been turned upside down by gold miners. Counting it together with other mines on the mainland at Skapte Hyle on the western flank of Mount Pangaion, where a forest was removed by the excavation and by felling for fuel and timber, the Thasians realized an annual profit of 200–300 talents. Wertime (1983: 448) says the mines at Laureion inflicted "a great scar upon the Attic landscape," and "by the time of Strabon the wooded surface of the region had been completely bared to provide timber for the mines and charcoal for the smelting of the ore." The ancient quarries of Mount Pentelikon are still visible. Mining also diverted enormous quantities of water, much of it near the headwaters in the mountains, which deprived farmers lower down of much of the supply and polluted what was left. Air quality was another concern in mines. Contamination came from gases trapped underground, and from the fumes of fires used for lighting the tunnels and for breaking rocks. Conditions in the workplace environment were appalling.

Metallurgical industries processed ores to recover the useful metals. They used furnaces that were often provided with chimneys. Other smelters were excavated as pits in the ground. Smelting required large amounts of fuel to reach the desired high temperatures. Metalsmithing required more fuel and produced additional pollution. Minting of coins generated demand for precious metals. Each ton of silver required removing about 100,000 t of rock from the mines.

Pottery was one of the most prolific industries of ancient times. Ceramic factories required prodigious quantities of fuel to heat the kilns. Brush and vine cuttings burned hot but fast, and fuel-wood from logs was used as well (Cato *De Agricultura* 38.4). Kilning of limestone for plaster and mortar got its material from quarries, but in times of war and social upheaval might also use fragments of buildings and statues. To supply one limekiln for one burn in the Greek mountains required a thousand donkey-loads of juniper wood, and fifty kilns required annually 6,000 t of wood (Wertime 1983: 452).

Along with household use in cooking and heating, industry produced a demand for fuel-wood and charcoal that contributed to deforestation. To smelt one ton of silver, however, required 10,000 t of wood. The centers of mining and smelting became the areas most depleted of forests; copper mining in Cyprus was especially destructive. In the latter area, now devoid of trees, archaeologists have found huge deposits of wood ashes (Thirgood 1981: 57). Air pollution came not just from wood and charcoal smoke, but also from the fumes of hazardous substances such as lead and mercury produced during metallurgical processes.

# 5   Plants

Biodiversity is high in Greece. The number of species of flowering plants alone is more than 6,000; this may be compared with 2,113 in the entire British Isles, which have an area well over twice as large as Greece.

Mediterranean ecosystems occur in zones with limits determined by a combination of such factors as latitude, elevation, exposure, and precipitation. The lowest zone extends from sea level to about 1,000 m elevation, and contains the typical vegetation of the Mediterranean climatic zone proper. Before human interference, this was in large part a belt of forests consisting mainly of pines and evergreen oaks, with thick shady galleries of broadleaved trees along watercourses.

Here also in dryer sections occurs the most distinctive plant association of the Mediterranean basin, the maquis, a brushy cover of hardy shrubs that varies from sparse to impenetrable. It is widespread in Greece and might be said to be the most typical cover of hillsides there. The bushes or small trees of which it is composed rarely exceed 8 m in height. Some students of plant succession regard maquis as a degenerate association, and it often becomes established after forest has been removed, but it is not always a sign of disturbance. In many districts it is the climax, that is, a biotic community that perpetuates itself under locally prevailing conditions of soil and climate. The most prominent species are broad sclerophylls, which are evergreen trees with leaves adapted to drought by thick hairy, leathery, oily, or waxy coverings. Some maquis plants survive in dry conditions by having extensive root systems, high osmotic pressure, and the evergreen ability to utilize winter moisture. Most importantly, maquis is a community of plants that is perfectly adapted to periodic fires, which are widespread in Greece. Each species possesses one or more adaptations that enable it to reestablish itself after fire: by recuperating rapidly, sprouting from buried root crowns, or germinating from seeds that respond to heat or spread into a burned area on the winds or by other means and find bare or scorched soil a congenial place to germinate. Typical maquis plants are holm-oak and kermes oak, junipers, arbutus, laurel, myrtle, tree heather, rockrose, broom, rosemary, and the shrubby mastic tree (*Pistacia lentiscus*), a widespread plant of the maquis that is cultivated on Chios.

After repeated destruction by clearing, browsing, or fire, or in harsh locations, maquis may be replaced by garigue or "rock heath," a tough, low association of shrubs that are often spiny. It is rarely more than 50 cm high, often lower than the rocks among which it grows. Among more than two hundred common species that occur in it are many spice-bearing herbs such as basil, garlic, hyssop, lavender, oregano, rosemary, rue, sage, savory, and thyme. Their pleasant odors waft far out to sea, especially in spring, the flowering season.

Garigue may be tough, but where conditions are even more extreme or overexploited, not even it can survive, and there a winter grassland or "steppe" may occur. It includes annuals adapted to the moister half of the year, and perennials that grow from rootstocks, tubers, or bulbs. Like garigue, grassland blooms in spring before the desiccating winds of summer. Species that survive grazing do best here; typical are asphodel, mullein, sea squill, thistle, and members of the buttercup, composite, grass, legume, lily, mint, mustard, parsley, pink, and rockrose families.

The deciduous forest zone occurs, where rainfall permits, above the zone just described, and up to around 1,400 m, and is sometimes called the upper Mediterranean zone. Dominant trees are deciduous oaks, elm, beech, chestnut, ash, and hornbeam. In Greece these forests are seen in the northern mountains; elsewhere they may have been eliminated by human use over the centuries.

At even greater altitudes the mountain zone, or coniferous forest zone, extends upward to the tree line, which is found at about 2,400 m on Mount Olympos. In rare pristine conditions, a high forest of pines, silver fir, cedars, and junipers survives, interspersed with open meadows. One such forest in Greece, which has apparently remained untouched since time immemorial, has been discovered in the Rhodope Mountains north of Drama near the Bulgarian frontier. Greece created a national park of 585 ha in 1975 to protect a portion of this unique forest of beech, fir, Norway spruce, and other trees, with its rich population of birds and mammals. Among the birds found there are the capercaillie, golden eagle, and black and griffon vultures, while the mammals include bear, wolf, lynx, red and roe deer, and chamois. The scenery is exquisite, with mountains, gorges, streams, and waterfalls. Precipitation is higher in this subalpine zone, taking the form of snow in the winter and thunderstorms in the summer. The growing season, limited by winter cold rather than dryness, takes place in the summer.

Above the tree line is an alpine tundra of dwarfed plants and lichens. Tiny flowering plants are adapted to a short summer growing season, during which they must bloom and set seed quickly before frosts return. On the bare rocks of the summits, snow may persist until the hottest part of the summer. Species in this zone are often narrowly endemic, occurring only on one mountain or range, a fact noted by the ancient botanist, Theophrastos (*Historia Plantarum* 3.18.1). Mount Olympos, for example, has a dozen or so species that grow only there among the 150 species that occur there above the tree line. Among the "locals" are a cerastium named after Theophrastos, an alyssum, a violet, and an Achillea.

# 6  Animals

The diversity of animals in Greece matched that of the plants described above. The forests and maquis formed advantageous habitats for wild animals. Plants are the main food producers of the ecosystems, and all animals, including humans, depend on them. Animals can be classified according to their trophic habits. Herbivores consume plants directly, while carnivores prey on other animals. All animals and plants, before and after they die, may provide nutriment for decomposers such as bacteria, molds, and microscopic animals. Under natural conditions, species do not destroy the other species they eat; they maintain a fluctuating balance of numbers. Plotinos (*Enneades* 3.2.15) recognized that predators and prey are different kinds of life, both essential to the world. Just as humans have changed plant communities in Greece, most notably by removing the forests, so they also have changed the distribution of animals by altering their habitats, reducing their numbers, causing extinction, and deliberately or inadvertently introducing exotic species, whether domestic or wild. "Species richness and distribution have been influenced by local human history, especially persecution and hunting, since the early or mid-palaeolithic" (Blondel & Aronson 1999: 79).

Some wild mammals of Greece were herbivores that are relatives of domestic animals such as goats, sheep, cattle, swine, donkeys, and horses. Other large herbivores including bison and deer ranged the forests and grasslands. Smaller plant eaters were ubiquitous, including rabbits, hares, mice, voles, porcupines, and squirrels. In prehistoric times, some of the islands including Crete and the larger Aegean islands had unusual mammalian faunas that had evolved there in isolation, including dwarf elephants and hippopotami, deer whose limbs indicate that they were not fleet of hoof, and large rodents. Most of these endemic species became extinct in a relatively brief period after human arrival, although a few persisted or even survive until the present, such as the spiny mouse of Crete.

The next trophic level consists of animals that eat other animals: carnivores and insectivores. The larger predators included lions, leopards, lynxes, hyenas, jackals, foxes, and wolves. Some present-day readers may be surprised to learn that there were lions in Greece, but lion bones were unearthed in the Bronze Age site of Tiryns, and lions are often represented in Mycenaean art (Sallares 1991: 401). Living lions are mentioned by Classical writers such as Herodotos (7.125–6), who says that they came down from the mountains to attack camels in the Persian baggage train during Xerxes' invasion, and Aristotle (*Historia Animalium* 579a31–b14). Both of the latter writers say that lions were found in their day from the Acheloos River to the Nessos, an area that covers most of northern Greece including Aristotle's birthplace at Stagira and Macedonia, where he lived for several years. In the second century CE, Dion Chrysostomos (21.1) wrote that lions had disappeared in Macedonia. Omnivores such as the bear ate both animal and vegetable foods. There are smaller carnivores such as wildcats and weasels, and insectivores like hedgehogs, shrews, and bats.

There was a variety of amphibians and reptiles greater than today's, including the many species of frogs that formed choruses in the ponds as well as in the famous comedy of Aristophanes. These, along with other amphibians such as toads, newts, fire salamanders, and others, as a rule are found near water and are insectivores. There were several kinds of tortoise, both herbivorous and insectivorous. Snakes of many species, poisonous and nonpoisonous, preyed mostly on small animals, thus helping to keep their numbers under control. Small lizards such as the insectivorous gecko and chameleon, including one poisonous species, could be found.

The Greeks were familiar with many species of birds, and observed them carefully, since they used them for divination. Some birds are herbivorous; finches, pigeons, and sparrows are seedeaters. Others are carnivorous, including eagles, owls, hawks, and other raptors. Some specialize in carrion: vultures, ravens, and magpies, for instance. Many are insectivores, and this makes them important to agriculture: swallows, thrushes, warblers, nightingales, starlings, and the crested hoopoe, to list a few. There are summer visitors (oriole, warblers), winter visitors (some owls, gulls), and year-round residents (buntings, wall creeper). One Mediterranean bird, the rock dove, adapted to human buildings and has spread around the world as the common pigeon.

Perhaps the majority of the animals in the ecosystem is made up of insects, whether one thinks of number of species, number of individuals, or total biomass. They perform many functions in ecological processes. Many of them, from bees, beetles, butterflies, and moths to the musical cicada, cricket, and locusts, eat plants. Insects that consume animal material include praying mantises, wasps, hornets, and some beetles. Literature pays attention with good reason to lice, fleas, flies, and mosquitoes, which include human blood in their diets. Various species of ants specialize in food sources; some are herbivorous, some carnivorous, and some practice mold agriculture or aphid pastoralism. Numerous insects, such as the dung beetle, assist in the process of decomposition. Among other herbivorous arthropods are the wood louse and millipede. Centipedes, spiders, and scorpions, which are poisonous to human beings to various degrees depending on the species, are predominantly insectivorous. Snails and slugs, which are land mollusks, are destructive to plants but serve as food for predators. Annelids like earthworms also perform the helpful function of soil aeration and fertilization, although the ancients did not discover this.

Another great ecosystem is found in the waters surrounding Greece: of the Aegean, Ionian, and Cretan Seas. The various climates, water depths, degrees of salinity, and benthic forms of these reaches of the Mediterranean Sea provide a variety of habitats for aquatic life. Here life depends on food producers such as algae and phytoplanktons, and also on nutrients washed down from the land. More than five hundred species of fish are found in the sea, along with algae, corals, shellfish, and sponges. Most sea life is found in the upper layers where light penetrates. The total quantity of marine organisms, however, is not particularly large compared to that of the oceans, either in number of species or in the total weight of living organisms per unit of volume of seawater. Still, it should not be supposed that Greek fisher-folk found their work unprofitable. Fishing was an important economic activity, and there were many species of economic importance, from sharks and rays to eels, sardines, and anchovies. Flounder and sole were caught on the sea bottom. The murex or rock whelk, source of the purple dye (*phoenix*) manufactured in Tyre in Phoenicia, was also found in Greek waters. Large quantities of sponges, brought up by divers, were exported from Greece.

Mammals of the Mediterranean waters included whales, seals, and dolphins, all of which were predators of other animal life of various sizes. Birds are well adapted to depend on the sea, whether frequenting the shore (snipe, sandpiper) or the surface (gulls, terns), or diving under the surface (cormorants). There are numerous other seabirds including grebes, pelicans, and puffins. There were several species of sea turtles.

Salt-water invertebrates are numerous and interesting, and some were considered delicacies. There are crustaceans (barnacles, shrimp, prawns, lobsters, crabs); mollusks, including univalves (limpets, tritons), bivalves (oysters, mussels, clams), and cephalopods (squid, octopus, nautilus); echinoderms (starfish, urchins, sea-cucumbers); and coelenterates (jellyfish, sea anemones, sponges, coral). Rivers and lakes provided habitats for freshwater ecosystems. The eels of Lake Kopaïs were famous. Other fish in lakes and streams included carp, perch, and catfish. Anadromous fish such as the salmon-trout and sturgeon spent most of their lives in salt water, but ascended rivers to spawn.

# 7   Deforestation

The most damaging environmental process that occurred during ancient Greek times was the widespread removal of forests and ensuing erosion. In a passage that has merited frequent quotation, Plato (*Critias* 111B–D) observed that the mountains of his homeland, Attika, were heavily forested not long before his own time, but had been laid bare by the cutting of timber and by grazing. The result was serious erosion that had washed away the rich, deep soil and consequently dried up the springs and streams that formerly existed there. Theophrastos (*Historia Plantarum* 3.2, 4, 6; 3.3.2; 4.5.5) recorded that wood of good quality, especially large trees useful for ships' masts and temple roof beams, had disappeared from some areas and had to be sought in less accessible mountains.

Wood was the basic material for buildings, tools, machines, means of transportation, and fuel. So important was wood that its name (*hyle* in Greek) was a synonym for "substance" or "material." Wood and its carbonized product, charcoal, were the most important fuels in households, public facilities, and industries, producing both heat and light. Consumption for fuel constituted the most extensive use of wood, accounting for perhaps 90 percent of its use. Metal refineries and pottery kilns used enormous amounts, placing great pressures on the forests. While some forestland was managed as coppice, where stems and branches are taken out selectively and the forest is allowed to regenerate, providing a sustained yield, it is hardly a coincidence that the areas around ancient mining centers became among the most deforested. Towns and cities demanded the services of woodcutters, charcoal burners, and haulers who brought fuels to market on the backs of mules or donkeys. Phainippos made twelve drachmas a day, then a large sum, by keeping six donkeys busy carrying firewood into Athens (Demosthenes 42.7).

Lumber for use as building material was a fundamental article of import to major Greek cities such as Athens. This commerce was carried on by water, and allowed the exploitation of forests along coastlands and rivers. Logs were floated down watercourses to ports, and there loaded on merchant ships. A typical lumber port would be located near the mouth of a river with a mountainous, forested watershed, like Thessalonike. Other ports important in wood export had the mountains right at their backs, like Antandros. Governments encouraged the timber trade through privileges, tax incentives, and advantageous leases.

The use of wood most often mentioned in Greek literature is shipbuilding. From keel to mast, almost everything in a ship came from trees, as did pitch to caulk the vessel. This applies to merchant vessels and warships alike, although authors give more attention to warships. Attempts to secure supplies of timber for the latter play a major role in ancient diplomacy and warfare. When Histiaios of Miletos founded a colony in Thrace, the Persian general Megabazos warned his king Dareios that the area was valuable because it had "abundance of timber for building ships and making oars" (Hdt. 5.23). In the Peloponnesian War, to give a second example, one of Athens' purposes in launching the Sicilian Campaign was to conquer a source of shipbuilding timber (Thuc. 6.90). Later in the war, the Persian governor of Asia Minor helped the Spartans win by giving them access to the forests of Phrygian Mount Ida and advising them "not to be discouraged over a lack of ship's timber, for there is plenty of that in the King's land" (Xenophon *Hellenika* 1.1.24–5). Timber was also used for siege engines and other military purposes. Detachments of soldiers were sent to cut wood for fortifications and fuel. Deliberate destruction of forests, usually by fire, was sometimes used as a tactic in warfare. For example, Kleomenes of Sparta set fire to the sacred grove of Argos and burned 5,000 Argives alive (Hdt. 6.75–80). Even accidental setting of fire must have happened in warfare, granted the extremely combustible character of Greek forests in summer, the season of warfare. This is exactly what Thucydides says happened to the Spartans on the island of Sphakteria during the Athenian attack, when the forest caught fire and burned off, revealing the size of the Spartan force to their enemies (Thuc. 4.30). The fire was so convenient to the Athenians, however, that it is difficult not to suspect them of starting it. It is quite clear that warfare in all of its various aspects was a major force in the process of deforestation.

Strategies of warfare and diplomacy were often aimed at obtaining supplies of timber and other forest products such as pitch, and guarding the sea-lanes and roads over which they were transported. Historians saw timber supply as a major factor determining naval strategy. One way to get forests was to conquer them; Alkibiades told the Spartans that this was one of the Athenians' major purposes in launching the Sicilian Campaign. Colonies were established as timber ports; thus Athens founded Amphipolis on the River Strymon below heavily forested mountains in Thrace, so it is understandable that there was consternation when the Spartans took that city.

Literature and inscriptions give considerable information, if limited in quantitative data, on the process of forest exploitation among the Greeks. Loggers took great pride in their work; a grave inscription on Mount Parnes announces, "I never saw a better woodcutter (*hylotomon*) than myself" (Zimmern 1961: 278). Such men knew the forests well; Theophrastos often takes advantage of the expertise of lumbermen from areas that supplied the Greek timber trade, including Macedonia, Mount Ida, and Arkadia. Trees were cut with double- or single-bitted axes, long metal saws with set teeth, and wedges. Smaller trees were uprooted by digging. The branches were then lopped off, and the logs pulled out by oxen or other draft animals. Large logs might have pairs of wheels attached to them to make hauling easier. After they arrived at a place where they could be prepared, logs were cut into sections of transportable length and split into thick beams and planks. Theophrastos (*Historia Plantarum* 5.1.5–12), guided by the experience of woodcutters he knew, gave directions for splitting pine and fir logs in the best way so as to take advantage of the grain. Those to be used as masts were kept whole. Finally, boards of the desired length and thickness could be sawn, with one man standing below, either in a pit or under a supported log.

Clearing of forests to make room for farming was a prominent feature of ancient history. New farms were established in forested regions. During the settlement of Cyprus, as noted below, in a kind of homestead guarantee, free land was offered for forest clearance and planting (Strabon 14.6.5). Lucretius said that woodcutters "made the woods climb higher up the mountains, leaving the foothills to be tilled and tended" (Lucretius *De Rerum Natura* 5.1247–9, 1370–1). A palynological study in the mountains of Macedonia indicates that pine forest was periodically cleared for planting wheat (Athanasiadis 1975). Trees were uprooted or cut down, the useful parts removed, and the rest burned and the ashes plowed under as fertilizer. Agriculture included some forestry; Greek farmers often did not clear all their land, but reserved sections as woodlots, so that the axe and saw were part of regular farm equipment. They planted trees for timber, and also to line roads, shelter fields, and mark boundaries. In spite of this, the archaeologist K. Greene (1986: 84) states, "The long-term environmental impact of both Roman and Greek farming appears to have been negative. Recent research has suggested that it was agricultural activity rather than climatic change which was responsible for the widespread soil erosion . . . of late Classical times."

Ancient writers were aware that cities stood where forests had once flourished. Forests of various types had covered most of the land surface at one time, however far in the past. Speaking of the disappearance of thyon trees from Kyrene, Theophrastos remarked (*Historia Plantarum* 5.3.7), "There was an abundance of those trees where now the city stands, and people can still recall that some of the roofs in ancient times were made of it." Place names often preserved the memory of forests that had been encompassed by the growth of cities and towns. An Athenian fortress was designated Peuke ("Pine"). Of course the effects of urbanization were more far-reaching than the clearing of sites for cities; through the ever-extending tentacles of the timber trade, the needs of the city for wood grasped and denuded forests many miles away.

Southern Greece, closest to the cities with the greatest demand for timber, was deforested first. Classical writers give the impression that the devastation was extensive, since they describe places as wooded which were not so in later times, or mention forests that had disappeared in their own day. Traces of vanished forests persist in names of places that once played a part in the lumber trade, such as Elatea ("Firtown"), Pityoussa ("Pineville"), Kastanea ("Chestnutburg"), and Xylopolis ("Timber City").

Exploitation of forests began near centers of demand such as cities and mining districts, and proceeded into more isolated places as time went on. The environs of Athens were mostly bare by the fifth century BCE, and the nearby island of Euboia, where the relict forests suggest abundant original growth, produced only inferior timber once the requirements of the silver mines at Laureion had stripped it of accessible wood. Forestlands that were more easily reached were cleared first. Lowlands lost their trees before the mountains, and forests near rivers were exploited rather than those further away. The areas most praised as sources of good timber in classical times tend to be mountainous regions with heavier than average rainfall: Macedonia is the chief example. But it would be misleading to suggest that the progress of forest removal was steady and cumulative. Some forests were leveled, grew again, and were cut again a number of times. Although forests were seriously depleted in ancient times, not all of them were destroyed. Many tracts of forest, often in association with temples, were regarded as sacred groves and thus preserved.

Literary sources are not the only evidence for forest history. Much information comes from palynology, the study of pollen grains contained in stratified deposits, often in waterlogged places such as lakebeds, but also in soils and accumulations of dust in caves. Pollen is well preserved under certain conditions, and the grains from various plant species usually can be distinguished from one another, so that scientists can recover from a column of accumulated material such as lake sediments or cave-floor deposits a record of the relative abundance of pine trees, say, or grain, over a long period of time. The deposits can be dated by the radiocarbon method, and they sometimes provide unbroken records going back hundreds of thousands of years, as the lake-bottom sediments of Lake Pamvotis (or Lake Ioannina) do. However, there is a margin of error sufficient to make it often difficult to relate changes in vegetation to specific historical events. General observations can be made, nonetheless. Wild forests were much more extensive before human occupation. Pollen diagrams make it clear, however, that forest history is far from simple. In northern Greece, for example, palaeobotanists have discovered a pattern indicating that forests survived best in settled times, but when invasions occurred, peasants moved into refuge areas in the mountains, cleared the forests, and planted fields of wheat and barley (Athanasiadis 1975: 106–24). When conditions became more stable, they abandoned these retreats and moved down to the richer plains, allowing forests at higher elevations to recover. Because movements of peoples occurred often over the centuries in Macedonia, this cycle was repeated several times there. Palynology also shows that forests persisted in parts of the north down to medieval times, whereas they were gone in some populated areas of southern Greece as early as the Bronze Age. For example, pollen cores from Messenia show that pinewoods had disappeared from coastal areas near Pylos by the Late Bronze Age (Wright 1972: 199). Textual evidence in treaties between Athens and the Macedonian kings shows that in Classical and Hellenistic times the city had to depend on the forested north for timber. Not all Mediterranean forests were exploited in ancient times; remote mountains, particularly those located on strategic borderlands, escaped.

Ancient writers knew that the destruction attendant upon pastoralism included fire to clear brush and forests. These fires, as well as wildfires started by lightning or volcanic eruptions, usually burned until they reached a natural barrier or were put out by rains; they would not be fought unless they threatened a settlement. Fires during a long, dry summer are often catastrophic and bare the slopes to erosion, though many typical Mediterranean plants are adapted to fire and show remarkable powers of recovery if not prevented by grazing.

Local climates, also called microclimates, change when forests are removed. Deforested tracts become more arid and windy. The aridification of many parts of the Mediterranean is in part due to human interference with regional environments. Theophrastos (*De Causis Plantarum* 5.14.5) recorded changes in local climates that he had observed: after the trees had been cut down around Philippoi, for example, the waters dried up and the weather became warmer.

Deforestation inflated the price of wood. As abundant sources near the centers of consumption disappeared, it became rarer and had to be imported over longer distances. Increased prices were particularly noticeable for fine woods, but affected timber and fuel as well. Detailed lists survive from a few periods and places, and these seem to show a pattern of rising prices. Pay in kind for Athenian jurors included fuelwood, the third necessity along with bread and *opson* (fish, fruit, etc.). The shortage and high cost of building timber due to deforestation contributed to a shift to stone construction; baked bricks were not used because they would have required wood fuels for firing; but stone construction in turn made buildings more dangerous in Greece's frequent earthquakes. Deforestation also increased costs of transportation, due not only to the greater distances merchants had to go to find wood, but also to scarcity of timber adjacent to shipbuilding centers, which drove up the price of the ships themselves. Warships had priority over merchant vessels in competition for materials.

The importance of timber supply and the effects of deforestation and erosion were evident to ancient observers, who often lamented them. Therefore it is not surprising that governments as well as private landowners exercised care in assuring a continued supply of wood from the forests under their control. A city generally asserted its ownership of all unoccupied forestland within its territory. Supervision of forests and watersheds included regulation of the forest products trade, the timber harvest, and the construction of works to provide or control water supply, drainage, and erosion. Responsibility for these matters was delegated to designated officials; in some cities the timber trade was under *agoranomoi* (overseers of commerce), while forestland in the countryside was supervised by *hyloroi* (custodians of forests) who, says Aristotle (*Politics* 6.5.4; 7.11.4), had "guard-posts and mess-rooms for patrol duty." It was a recurrent policy of governments to encourage private exploitation of forests by leasing the right to cut trees on public land, which was a source of revenue, or by sale or grant of public forestland to entrepreneurs. During the Greek settlement of Cyprus, rulers "permitted anyone who wished, or was able, to cut the timber and keep the land thus cleared as his own property, exempt from taxes" (Strabon 14.6.5). Aware of a diminishing wood supply, the state sometimes regulated private land to encourage conservation. Plato's recommendation that landowners be fined if fire spread from their property to a neighbor's timber doubtless represented actual law. Land leases might contain restrictions on timber cutting and stipulations for replanting.

A city had its own public forestlands. Although they were often granted to individuals or communities, large tracts remained in government hands, and measures were taken to prevent encroachment and assure their use for the good of the state. Wise administrators limited timber harvest; Theophrastos (*Historia Plantarum* 5.8.1) said that in Cyprus, "the kings used not to cut the trees...because they took great care of them and managed them." He added that later rulers of that island reaped the benefit of their predecessors' restraint; Demetrios Poliorketes cut timber of prodigious length there for his ships. Some magistrates were foresighted enough to protect public lands against greed-motivated exploitation, and found popular support for their efforts. Unfortunately such efforts were far from universal, were not always effective, and were vitiated by other policies that encouraged exploitation and destruction of forests.

# 8 Grazing

A major force of environmental degradation was the grazing of domestic animals. Every uncultivated tract, as well as fallow land, was used as pasture. The worst effects of grazing were making deforestation permanent and exacerbating erosion. Grazing animals by themselves will not destroy a mature high forest, although goats will climb into trees to eat foliage. But they can make a disturbed situation worse by eating the young trees before they can develop.

The four major grazing species were cattle, sheep, goats, and swine. Each has its own dietary preferences, and together they form a synergistic partnership that is destructive to virtually all vegetation within reach. Cattle prefer grass and leaves, so herders cut tree branches or whole trees to let them graze. Swine especially like acorns, chestnuts, and beechnuts, so swineherds drove them into the forest where they destroyed the means of reproduction of the trees. Sheep eat grass right down to the soil and also pull up the roots of all but the hardiest plants. Shepherds set fires to encourage the growth of grass. Goats are most destructive, and their ability to eat almost anything is proverbial, but given the choice they prefer woody plants such as bushes and young trees. Numerous herds of goats browsed almost everywhere in Greece, and they were adaptable, prolific, and easy to care for. Goats and sheep together can strip a hillside bare, opening it to erosion, driving away competing wildlife, and forcing the ecosystem to regress down the scale of succession and energy. Limitation of numbers could have prevented this, but was almost never practiced. If one herder left any vegetation untouched, others would no doubt have used it the same season.

The ancients observed that goats could damage plant cover. Plato (*Laws* 639A) knew how controversial the goat was, proposing an argument between a man who thought it a valuable animal and another who regarded it as a destructive nuisance. The comic poet Eupolis wrote a play with a chorus of goats, and had them bleat a list of their favorite foods:

> We feed on all manner of shrubs, browsing on the tender shoots
> Of pine, ilex, and arbutus, and on spurge, clover, and fragrant
> Sage, and many-leaved bindweed as well, wild olive, and lentisk,
> And ash, fir, sea oak, ivy, and heather, willow, thorn, mullein,
> And asphodel, cistus, oak, thyme, and savory.
> (Eupolis F 13 Kassel–Austin = Macrobius *Saturnalia.* 7.5–9)

This could serve as a botanical list of the most typical plants of the maquis, and it should be noted that a number of timber trees, consumed while young and small, are included on the goats' bill of fare. The effect of goats may be judged from the following statement (Greig & Turner 1974: 188): "In a place not far from Kopaïs we saw woody plants regenerating vigorously in a goat-proof enclosure, effectively demonstrating that the present sparse vegetation is due to grazing." The grazing of sheep, goats, and cattle often involved transhumance, the annual shift to moister pastures with a later growing season in the mountains during the dry summer. As a result, mountain vegetation was consumed at the time it was growing, and with the prevalent overgrazing, erosion was always a danger. In addition, manure was lost to the farms during the summer months.

# 9   Erosion

The most common results of deforestation in the Mediterranean basin are erosion of hillsides, flooding as the waters are no longer retarded and absorbed, interference with the water supply, and siltation of lowlands and coastlands. George Perkins Marsh (1801–82), who served in Constantinople, and in Rome for a period longer than any other American ambassador (1861–82), understood this form of environmental deterioration well: "Vast forests have disappeared from mountain spurs and ridges; the vegetable earth accumulated beneath the trees . . . the soil of alpine pastures . . . are washed away; . . . rivers famous in history and song have shrunk to humble brooklets: . . . harbors . . . are shoaled by the deposits of rivers at whose mouths they lie" (Marsh 1965 [1864]: 9).

Forests regulate the runoff of the precipitation they receive. Like a sponge, the plants and soil hold water, preventing floods and releasing a year-round supply to springs and streams. Ancient authors noted the connection between forests and water supply. Pausanias (7.26.4) visited a place "clothed with oak woods" and remarked of it, "No town in Greece is more abundantly supplied with flowing water than Phellai." Ancients also noted the effects of deforestation in light of this relationship. As Plato observed (*Critias* 111B), the water that rushed unimpeded down mountainsides was no longer available to feed the springs. Perhaps for this reason, he portrayed his ideal Atlantis as having springs surrounded by plantations of appropriate trees. Without forests, streams that formerly flowed clear all year long became intermittent and muddy, existing only as dry courses during the summer, while hundreds of springs dried up. Most of the erosion that occurs takes place in brief periods during torrential rains.

As Helen Rendell notes (1997: 52), "A vegetation cover is the most effective protection against erosion." Once the land was bare of trees, torrential rains washed away the unprotected earth. Erosion destroyed uplands that might have grown trees again, and the silt, sand, and gravel that reddened the rivers was deposited at their mouths along the shores of the virtually tideless Mediterranean Sea. This greatly altered coastlines, in some cases pushing them many kilometers farther out to sea, as is the case around the mouth of the Peneios River. The new wetlands were unhealthy to humans because they served as a breeding ground for malarial mosquitoes, but were useful as homes for water birds and other animals, and spawning places for some species of fish.

Erosion and siltation around the Mediterranean in ancient times were large in scale, although the amount of soil removed from the highlands is difficult to estimate. Deposits along the coasts and in valleys and lowlands can be measured, and dated from artifacts found in them or by radiocarbon analysis of organic materials. Such studies indicate that erosion was a complicated and highly localized process. Thermopylai, the famous pass between cliffs and sea near the mouth of the Spercheios River, was narrow enough in 480 to be defended by a small Greek army against a vastly superior Persian force. Subsequent accretion of river deposits has widened the land at least 8 km seaward from the battle site. Pausanias (8.24.5) compared the silt deposits laid down at the mouths of two rivers: the Acheloos, whose watershed was uninhabited and therefore forested, "does not wash down so much mud on the Echinadian islands as it would otherwise do," but the Maiandros, whose valley had been cleared, "had turned the sea between Priene and Miletos into dry land." Siltation clogged harbors at river mouths, as was true of Miletos in the case just mentioned, and Heraklean labors were needed in many places to retain them.

# 10   Conclusion

The histories of peoples have been shaped to a great extent by the natural environments within which those peoples lived. Just as significantly, peoples through history have altered their natural environments. The importance of these interactions is as true for Greece and the Greeks as it is of any landscape and society of ancient or modern times. To say this is not to invoke a rigid environmental determinism, but to recognize a process of interaction. From the viewpoint of the historian, anthropogenic and environmental factors must be seen in relationship, indeed in dynamic tension. Humans are not exempt from ecological causation, and in Greece, even in ancient times, there were few if any parts of the physical and biological world that were free from the effects of human activities.

These ideas received increasing attention among historians after the mid-twentieth century as a number of environmental issues emerged around the globe including land, air, and water degradation; depletion of resources; and threats to biodiversity. But to study ancient environmental relationships is not simply to read modern problems into the past. Instead, historians are finding that to study the past in its own terms also reveals the centrality of environmental issues. The Greek writers recognized some of these. Plato commented on the deforestation of the mountains of his native land and the effect of that process in the drying of springs of water, and as he sketched his ideal community in the *Laws* he described means of safeguarding its water supply. Thucydides (1.2.) began his account of war by speculating on the effect of the fertility or poverty of soil on the instability or stability of Greek states.

Examination of the evidence has increasingly convinced modern environmental historians of the major role of the ancients in the deterioration of their environments, and the effects of that deterioration on their societies. For example, J. R. McNeill judges (1992: 72–3), "Without a doubt a substantial measure of Mediterranean deforestation and consequent erosion happened in classical times, say between 500 BCE and 500 CE." He adds, "By the time the Roman Empire began to totter [third century CE] it is likely that no extensive forest remained in the plains or low hills surrounding the Mediterranean." Since forests provided essential resources for construction, transportation, and fuel, their loss in local districts and the necessity of importing forest products from distant sources undoubtedly affected the economy and military considerations. It was one factor among several, but a major one. When one considers all of the processes of interaction between the Greeks and their environments, it should be evident that they represent an aspect of history that cannot be minimized or ignored by anyone who seeks a balanced understanding of the past.

# Further reading

Attenborough 1987 – A good general introduction to the Mediterranean environment and history

Baumann 1993 – A fascinating study of the meaning of plants in ancient Greek culture and civilization

Blondel & Aronson 1999 – Covers ecosystems from the early holocene to the present, including human interactions with habitats and other species

Bradford, E. (1971) *Mediterranean: portrait of a sea* (London: Hodder & Stoughton) – A popular treatment, valuable as an introduction

Carrington, R. (1971) *The Mediterranean: cradle of Western culture* (New York: Viking) – Wide-ranging and comprehensive

Crouch 1993 – Relates the use of water to the geological setting of the Mediterranean limestone karst

Gallant 1991 – A fascinating look at the questions surrounding the grain trade and the adequacy of grain supply

Grant & Kitzinger (eds) 1988 – A monumental collection of articles on virtually every aspect of ancient civilization

Healy, J. F. (1978) *Mining and metallurgy in the Greek and Roman world* (London: Thames & Hudson) – An excellent guide to this specialized subject

Horden, P., & N. Purcell (2000) *The corrupting sea: a study of Mediterranean history* (Oxford: Blackwell) – An unconventional interpretation of the social construction of the meaning of the Mediterranean Sea through history

Hughes 1994 – Organized by subject on problems such as deforestation, wildlife depletion, industrial damage, agricultural decline, and urban troubles

Hughes 2001 – Includes chapters on ancient environmental history, including a case study on Athens

Isager, S., & J. E. Skydsgaard (1992) *Ancient Greek agriculture: an introduction* (London: Routledge) – A comprehensive introduction to agriculture practices, the role of the state, and the influence of religion

King et al. 1997 – Covers geology, geography, and history in relationship to the environment from ancient times to the present

Levi 1980 – A useful reference, as much a text as a book of maps

McDonald & Rapp 1972 – The use of archaeology to discover the ancient condition of a whole countryside

McNeill 1992 – Concentrates on five case studies of Mediterranean mountain ranges; the Greek example is the Pindos, the "backbone of Greece"

Meiggs 1982 – An interesting look at every variety of evidence about trees and the timber trade, with an excellent chapter on deforestation

Pollard, J. R. T. (1977) *Birds in Greek life and myth* (London: Thames & Hudson) – The appreciation, symbolism, and use of avian species

Polunin, O. (1966) *Flowers of the Mediterranean* (Boston: Houghton Mifflin) – A standard guide to the most prevalent Mediterranean plants, with notes on their distribution and use

Radcliffe, W. (1974) *Fishing from the earliest times* (Chicago: Ares) – A repr. of the 1921 classic on fishing in the ancient world, with emphasis on Greece and Rome

Strid 1980 – Illustrated with sumptuous photographs of plants and mountain scenery

Thirgood 1981 – A solid study by a forester, with an authoritative case study of Cyprus

van Andel, T. H., & C. N. Runnels (1987) *Beyond the Acropolis: a rural Greek past* (Stanford: Stanford University Press) – An informative archaeological survey

Westra & Robinson 1997 – Despite its general title, this is a series of articles on Greek philosophers and the environment, with emphasis on Plato and Aristotle

# Bibliography

Athanasiadis, N. (1975) *Zur postglazialen Vegetationsentwicklung von Litochoro Katerinis und Pertouli Trikalon* (Thessaloniki: World University Service)

Attenborough, D. (1987) *The First Eden: the Mediterranean world and man* (Boston: Little, Brown)

Baumann, H. (1993) *The Greek plant world in myth, art and literature* (Portland OR: Timber)

Blondel, J., & J. Aronson (1999) *Biology and wildlife of the Mediterranean region* (Oxford: Oxford University Press)

Crouch, D. P. (1993) *Water management in ancient Greek cities* (New York: Oxford University Press)

Fortenbaugh, W. W., & R. W. Sharples (eds) (1988) *Theophrastean studies: on natural science, physics and metaphysics, ethics, religion, and rhetoric* (New Brunswick NJ: Transaction Books) (Rutgers University Studies in Classical Humanities 3)

Gallant, T. W. (1991) *Risk and survival in ancient Greece: reconstructing the rural domestic economy* (Stanford: Stanford University Press)

Grant, M., & R. Kitzinger (eds) (1988) *Civilization of the ancient Mediterranean: Greece and Rome*, 3 vols (New York: Scribner's)

Greene, K. (1986) *The archaeology of the Roman economy* (London: Batsford)

Greig, J. R. A., & J. Turner (1974) "Some pollen diagrams from Greece and their archaeological significance" in: *Journal of Archaeological Science* 1: 188–206

Hughes, J. (1988) "Theophrastus as ecologist" in: Fortenbaugh & Sharples 1988: 67–75

Hughes, J. D. (1988) "Land and sea" in: Grant & Kitzinger 1988, vol. 1: 89–133

Hughes, J. D. (1994) *Pan's travail: environmental problems of the ancient Greeks and Romans* (Baltimore: Johns Hopkins University Press)

Hughes, J. D. (2001) *An environmental history of the world: humankind's changing role in the community of life* (London: Routledge)

Hsu, K. J. (1983) *The Mediterranean was a desert* (Princeton: Princeton University Press)

King, R., L. Proudfoot, B. Smith (eds) (1997) *The Mediterranean: environment and society* (London: Arnold)

Levi, P. (1980) *Atlas of the Greek world* (New York: Facts on File)

Marsh, G. P. (1864) *Man and nature: or, physical geography as modified by human action* (New York: Scribner; repr. Cambridge MA: Belknap Press of Harvard University Press 1965)

McDonald, W. A., & R. G. Rapp (eds) (1972) *The Minnesota Messenia expedition: reconstructing a Bronze Age regional environment* (Minneapolis: University of Minnesota Press)

McNeill, J. R. (1992) *The mountains of the Mediterranean world: an environmental history* (Cambridge: Cambridge University Press)

Meiggs, R. (1982) *Trees and timber in the ancient Mediterranean world* (Oxford: Clarendon)

Rendell, H. (1997) "Earth surface processes in the Mediterranean" in: King et al. 1997: 45–56

Sallares, R. (1991) *The ecology of the ancient Greek world* (Ithaca NY: Cornell University Press)

Strid, A. (1980) *Wild flowers of Mount Olympus* (Kifissia: Goulandris Natural History Museum)

Thirgood, J. V. (1981) *Man and the Mediterranean forest: a history of resource depletion* (London: Academics)

Tozer, H. F. (1882) *Lectures on the geography of ancient Greece* (London; repr. Chicago: Ares 1974)

Wertime, T. A. (1983) "The furnace versus the goat: the pyrotechnologic industries and Mediterranean deforestation in antiquity" in: *JFA* 10: 445–52

Westra, L., & T. M. Robinson (eds) (1997) *The Greeks and the environment* (London: Rowman & Littlefield)

Wright, H. E., Jr. (1972) "Vegetation history" in: McDonald & Rapp 1972: 199

Zimmern, A. (1961) *The Greek commonwealth* (New York: Oxford University Press)

CHAPTER THIRTEEN

# Environments and Landscapes of Greek Culture

## Lin Foxhall

## 1 The Mediterranean: The Geographical Parameters of the Greek World

By the beginning of the fifth century BCE the Greek heartland, the territory which now comprises mainland and island Greece and the west coast of modern Turkey, was only a small portion of the Greek world. From the eighth century onward Greeks had established communities spreading east–west across the Mediterranean from the Levant to southern France and Spain, and north–south from southern Russia to north Africa. Although most of these Greek communities were set in environments which were broadly 'Mediterranean' in terms of their climate, geography and vegetation, there is a huge range of local variation even over very short distances. The consequence is that though some practices were common over a wide area, Greeks exploited the environments they inhabited in many different ways, depending on both local traditions and local conditions.

## 2 Mediterranean Climates

In both the northern and southern hemispheres all areas with Mediterranean-type climates are on or close to the 35° latitude lines and bordering the sea (Grove & Rackham 2003: 11 and fig. 1.2). Ancient Greek settlement in fact ranged somewhat beyond the fringe of land surrounding the Mediterranean Sea. Mediterranean climates are characterized by relatively mild, wet winters and hot, dry summers. Except in the high mountains, few areas suffer from intense and regular frosts. Often the limits of the olive's cold tolerance are perceived as defining the extent of Mediterranean zone, though this is something of an over-simplification (Grove & Rackham 2003: 11). Certainly it is true that the olive and Greek culture have flourished in most of the same places.

Summers are largely sunny with temperatures often over 30 degrees C, and in many areas at altitudes under 200 m above sea level even dew is rare. This is wonderful for the modern tourist trade, which can usually guarantee its customers a vacation uninterrupted by rain, though humidity can be high in locations close to the sea, but it places severe constraints on other kinds of human activities. Summer temperatures are generally cooler at higher altitudes, and places only a few kilometres distant from each other but differing by several hundred metres in altitude can also differ perceptibly in temperature.

Precipitation in the Mediterranean is characterized by its unpredictability, and this has important implications for agriculture in the region. Generally the bulk of the year's rainfall occurs between mid-September and April and rainfall events may be very unevenly distributed over this time. Even over the summer, occasionally a sudden, violent thunderstorm may result in flash floods or damaging hailstorms. In addition, rainfall in any particular area may vary dramatically from year to year. And, often over short distances, especially over changes in altitude and aspect (the direction a place faces and to which it is exposed), rainfall can vary quite substantially from one place to another. Generally, precipitation increases (and the length of the dry season decreases) with altitude. West-facing locations such as the island of Kerkyra (modern Corfu) are usually wetter than east-facing ones such as the peninsula of Methana in the Saronic Gulf. Absolute amounts of annual precipitation rarely exceed 1,000 mm except in the more northerly parts of the region, and at high altitudes. In most parts of southern Greece, Italy and Spain average annual rainfall ranges from 400 to 650 mm, though in some significant places this figure is lower. Athens averages 385 mm per year, Thera (modern Santorini) 357 mm, close to the limits for un-irrigated cereal cultivation (Grove & Rackham 2003: 24–8).

# 3   Mediterranean Environments

Mediterranean environments and ecosystems are both fragile and resilient. For the most part they are creations of human culture. Many parts of the region have been cultivated for at least 8,000 years, and were inhabited and exploited by people for many thousands of years previously. It is therefore impossible to point to pristine 'natural' environments unaffected by human activities.

Although mountains in the region are often covered with forest, many of the slopes which are bare rock today were probably also bare in antiquity. The oak, chestnut and pine forests of the mountain zone are not the only kind of 'climax vegetation', insofar as the term is even appropriately applied to Mediterranean plant communities. In many areas maquis and garrigue (*phrygana*)—the scrubby, prickly plants adapted to arid conditions, regular fires and rocky soils—constitute the largest portion of the 'natural' vegetation. Wild or feral varieties of olive and pear, several species of oak (especially *Quercus coccifera*, prickly oak), juniper, cypress and wild pistachio (*Pistacia lentiscus*) are common. Along with these grow shrubby plants such as brooms (*Sparticum* and *Genista spp.*) and *Cistus spp.* (rock rose), and numerous smaller, short-lived perennials (mints, thyme, oregano, caper, bryony, smilax), annuals (*Inula viscosa*, vetches, wild carrot, wild fennel), tough grasses (esparto grass), bulbs (crocus, colchium, asphodel, squill, cyclamen) and the large and ubiquitous thistles.

This is vegetation with attitude. Equipped with vicious spines, toxins, hairy leaves, exploding seeds, heat-stimulated germination, extensive root systems, vigorous growth habits, aromatic resins and other features, these plants are well adapted to withstand earthquakes, drought, fire, grazing, cultivation and other natural disasters and human activities. Although Mediterranean vegetational communities are unstable and easily damaged, they also possess extraordinary powers of recovery. The 'Ruined Landscape' theories of Mediterranean environments promoted by many scholars from antiquity to the present to explain past and present 'environmental degradation', i.e. the notion that human impact on the landscape has been solely destructive to the pristine 'natural' environment, is far too simplistic. Historical and environmental evidence suggests that virtually all parts of the region have suffered repeated phases of 'destruction' (from both human and natural causes) and recovery over the long term (Grove & Rackham 2003: 60–5). In our present era, non-sustainable development and misuse of resources may have permanent environmental impact, but ancient Greek culture was not technologically equipped to inflict this level of damage.

Plato's depiction of the Attic landscape (*Critias* 110C–112E) is often cited by modern scholars to support the 'Ruined Landscape' paradigm. This imaginary account, however, set 9,000 years before his own time, is as much philosophical fantasy as is his description of the 'ancient' socio-political system in which the citizens were divided into classes by occupation and the elite military class held their property in common and were supported by the rest (an arrangement suspiciously similar to that of Plato's ideal state as portrayed in the *Republic* and the *Laws*).

[110C] Now at that time there dwelt in this country not only the other classes of the citizens who were occupied in the handicrafts and in the raising of food from the soil, but also the military class, which had been separated off at the commencement by divine heroes and dwelt apart. It was supplied with all that was required for its sustenance and training, and none of its members possessed any private property, but they regarded all they had [110D] as the common property of all; and from the rest of the citizens they claimed to receive nothing beyond a sufficiency of sustenance; and they practised all those pursuits which were mentioned yesterday, in the description of our proposed 'Guardians'. Moreover, what was related about our country was plausible and true…[110E] that all other lands were surpassed by ours in goodness of soil, so that it was actually able at that period to support a large host which was exempt from the labours of husbandry. And of its goodness a strong proof is this: what is now left of our soil rivals any other in being all-productive and abundant in crops and rich in pasturage for all kinds of cattle; [111A] and at that period, in addition to their fine quality it produced these things in vast quantity. How, then, is this statement plausible, and what residue of the land then existing serves to confirm its truth? The whole of the land lies like a promontory jutting out from the rest of the continent far into the sea and all the cup of the sea; round about it is, as it happens, of a great depth. Consequently, since many great convulsions took place during the 9000 years—for such was the number of years [111B] from that time to this—the soil which has kept breaking away from the high lands during these ages and these disasters forms no pile of sediment worth mentioning, as in other regions, but keeps sliding away ceaselessly and disappearing in the deep. And, just as happens in small islands, what now remains compared with what then existed is like the skeleton of a sick man, all the fat and soft earth having wasted away, and only the bare framework of the land being left. But at that epoch the country was unimpaired, and for its mountains it had [111C] high arable hills, and in place of the stony soil as it is now called, it contained plains full of rich soil; and it had much forest land in its mountains, of which there are visible signs even to this day; for there are some mountains which now have nothing but food for bees, but they had trees no very long time ago, and the rafters from those felled there to roof the largest buildings are still sound. And besides, there were many lofty trees of cultivated species; and it produced boundless pasturage for flocks. Moreover, it was enriched by the yearly rains from Zeus, [111D] which were not lost to it, as now, by flowing from the bare land into the sea; but the soil it had was deep, and therein it received the water, storing it up in the retentive loamy soil and by drawing off into the hollows from the heights the water that was there absorbed, it provided all the various districts with abundant supplies of spring waters and streams, whereof the shrines which still remain even now, at the spots where the fountains formerly existed, are signs which testify that our present description of the land is true. [111E] Such, then, was the natural condition of the rest of the country, and it was ornamented as you would expect from genuine husbandmen who made husbandry their sole task, and who were also men of taste and of native talent, and possessed of most excellent land and a great abundance of water, and also, above the land, a climate of most happily tempered seasons. And as to the city, this is the way in which it was laid out at that time. In the first place, the akropolis, as it existed then, was different from [112A] what it is now. For as it is now, the action of a single night of extraordinary rain has crumbled it away and made it bare of soil, when earthquakes occurred simultaneously with the third of the disastrous floods which preceded the destructive deluge in the time of Deukalion. But in its former extent, at an earlier period, it went down towards the Eridanos and the Ilissos, and embraced within it the Pnyx; and had the Lykabettos as its boundary over against the Pnyx; and it was all rich in soil and, save for a small space, level on the top. [112B] And its outer parts, under its slopes, were inhabited by the craftsmen and by such of the husbandmen as had their farms close by; but on the topmost part only the military class by itself had its dwellings round about the temple of Athena and Hephaistos, surrounding themselves with a single ring-fence, which formed, as it were, the enclosure of a single dwelling. (Plato *Critias* 110C–112B, trans. Lamb (Loeb) modified by Foxhall)

This is not a story that we should take at face value. What it does show is that classical Greeks recognized the general phenomena of deforestation and erosion. What it cannot prove is that Attika was *ever* a land of deep soils, abundant rain and forested hills: this is Plato's view of the 'golden age' of his homeland, as mythological as the tale of Atlantis which follows this passage in the dialogue (Plato *Critias* 113B–121C). Significantly, in both Plato's Attika of the remote past and Atlantis a decline in the moral calibre of the inhabitants and a breakdown of what Plato perceived as a desirable social system resulted in environmental degradation and disaster. It is therefore highly unlikely that this picture of ancient Attika is accurate.

As well as forests and maquis, marshes were a crucial resource for human communities in the region, their importance often underestimated by modern scholars (Horden & Purcell 2000: 186–90). Marshes offer different plant communities from much of the rest of Mediterranean vegetation, and are important resources for human communities, especially for grazing, hunting and gathering. Plants such as the giant reed (*Arundo donax*) were used for items from spears to roofing material. Marshes are important habitats for many birds, animals and fish. Near the sea, salt marshes were important for salt panning.

## 4   Polis and *Chora*: Greek Countrysides

In the world of classical Greece, the polis, both in the sense of city-state and in the sense of urban centre, was the main focus of political and social life. Most Greeks lived in towns. However, the inhabitants of the polis exploited the whole range of the land-scape by cultivating the land, keeping animals, hunting, fishing, gathering wild plants for many purposes, collecting wood and felling timber, mining, quarrying and extract-ing clay for pottery and building materials. Greek cities were largely dependent on their rural territories for the necessities of life (and many luxuries as well). Nonetheless, the impact of classical Greek cities on their environment was probably not great compared to the impact of Roman occupation or modern tourism. Most Greek poleis were small and few had territorial ambitions on any scale. Even in mining areas such as southern Attika, exploited for silver and lead, the individual mining operations were small, and the environmental impact was relatively short term and limited.

## 5   Land Ownership and Citizenship

Citizenship and the ownership of land were closely linked (see Oliver below, Chapter 14). In most cities, citizens and land owners were the same people: only citizens could own land and only land owners could be citizens. Democratic Athens was unusual in this respect: only citizens could own land, but citizenship was not limited to land owners. The effect, however, even in Athens, was to assign a high moral and social value to land ownership and farming, as an activity worthy of a politically empowered and active man. This positive view of farming appears in many Greek texts of the fifth and fourth centuries (for example Plato *Critias* 111E, quoted above, and Xenophon *Oikonomikos* 5.1–11).

> In that case, Sokrates, he [Ischomachos] said, you shall hear now about the beneficence of this craft [farming]. For it is most profitable and pleasant to work at, as well as the most lovely and dear to gods and men. Besides, it is very easy to learn—how could it not be noble? (Xenophon *Oikonomikos* 15.4)

Here, in Xenophon's Socratic dialogue about household management, the *Oikonomi-kos*, Sokrates has asked Ischomachos, the hard-working gentleman farmer with the ideal estate, to teach him farming and Ischomachos explains to Sokrates why he spends as much time as he can on his farm. In his answer, financial profit and moral gain are interlaced. Moreover, the characters in this dialogue assume that farming is central to the lives of most Greeks and that the basic techniques and principles are familiar to all:

> And I think, he said [Ischomachos to Sokrates], you know a great deal without realizing it. For other craftsmen conceal the most critical elements of their craft, but among farmers the one who is best at planting trees would be pleased if someone were watching him, so too the one who is best at sowing. Whatever you were to ask him about the things he does well, he would conceal nothing whatsoever. So, Sokrates, he said, farming appears to produce the most noble characters among those engaging in it. (Xenophon *Oikonomikos* 15.10)

The implication is that the good and noble citizen is a land owner and a farmer. In Xenophon's words (put into the mouth of Sokrates):

> Those who are able not only to manage their own households, but also to put something by so that they can adorn the city and back their friends, how could they not be deemed solid and sound? (Xenophon *Oikonomikos* 11.10)

# 6  Ordered Landscapes: Land Division and Land Holdings

From at least the eighth century BCE Greeks imprinted their culture on the landscapes they occupied by measuring out land into ordered plots. Although many of the best-known examples are 'colonial' cities, the phenomenon appears in old Greece as well. Sometimes these land divisions are visible on the ground, as in the countryside of Metapontion in southern Italy (Carter 1990). Sometimes they are revealed by archaeologists as the framework for urban landscapes, as at Megara Hyblaia and Selinous in Sicily, or Halieis in the southern Argolid (Figure 13.1 a–d). Even in an urban setting land divisions may have been inspired by rural principles and practical-

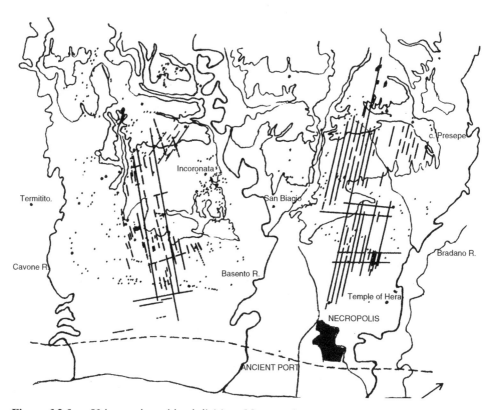

**Figure 13.1a**   Urban and rural land division: Metapontion.

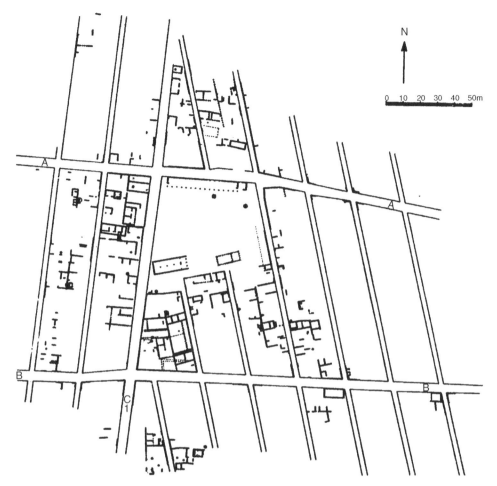

**Figure 13.1b** Urban and rural land division: Megara Hyblaia area around 'agora'.

ities: the earliest land divisions at both Megara Hyblaia (eighth century) and Halieis (sixth century) result in plots of about the right size for a day's ploughing. This suggests that these structured landscapes may originally have been intended as plots for farming rather than as part of an urban planning scheme (Foxhall 2003: 86–8).

Frequently, land divisions are understood by modern scholars to imply equality of land holdings (at least at some point in the city's past) as part of the egalitarian ethos of the polis community (Morris 1994: 362–5; Hanson 1999: 182, 186–96). This is most probably a mistake. Most Greek cities were not democratic and even in those that were, political egalitarianism certainly did not imply economic equality, as is well attested in classical Athens. Land was bought, sold, rented and leased in classical cities, but most people probably acquired most of their land through inheritance. Although there were many minor variations in inheritance customs, partible inheritance was practised throughout Greece. This means that sons inherited equal shares of their father's estate. How women fared was more variable, but generally they received

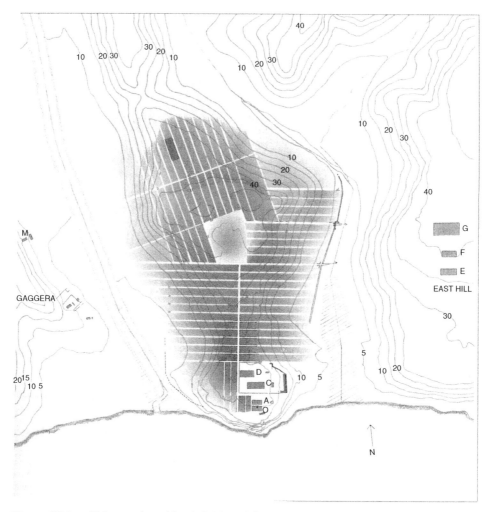

**Figure 13.1c** Urban and rural land division: Selinous.

smaller portions of the patrimony than the sons, often as dowry at marriage. If land were divided among siblings every generation, a man's holdings would almost inevitably consist of a collection of small plots scattered around the countryside, rather than a single, contiguous 'farm'. It is also likely that most people owned plots of land close to those of relatives, especially brothers or cousins. These plots did not necessarily become infinitely smaller over time: they might be 'rationalized' to some extent by selling land in less convenient locations or recombining plots by acquiring neighbouring ones. Similar traditions of partible inheritance fragmenting plots have persisted in many parts of Greece and elsewhere in the Mediterranean up to the present day (Figure 13.2). At Metapontion there may be archaeological evidence for the sub-division of plots (Carter 1990). Therefore what appear to be equal-sized plots in systems of land division do not automatically imply equal-sized holdings, since a single landholder might have possessed more than one plot or small fragments of plots.

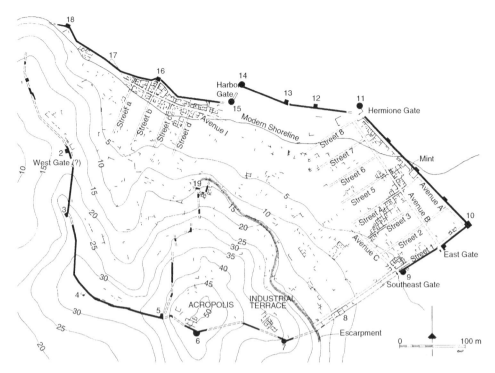

**Figure 13.1d**   Urban and rural land division: Halieis.

**Figure 13.2**   Methana, Greece: several families ploughing plots of vines in the 1970s. Here there are no visible field boundaries, but what appears to be a single large area of vines is actually divided into small plots owned by many different households.

Inevitably, the land holdings of wealthy farmers are far better attested than those of small-scale farmers. One of our most important documents for demonstrating the scattered land holdings of rich men is the so-called 'Attic Stelai' of fifth-century Athens. This is a series of Athenian inscriptions (*IG*1³ 420–430; Amyx 1958; Pritchett 1956) published by the *poletai*, the magistrates responsible for selling property confiscated by the state. The reason for full publication of their records on this occasion was the political and religious controversy surrounding those accused of mutilating the herms just before Athens' expedition to conquer Sicily embarked in 415, and subsequently accused of parodying the Eleusinian Mysteries (Thuc. 6.27–9, 60–1). Some of Athens' wealthiest and most eminent citizens and metics were implicated in these scandals, and their property was confiscated by the state and sold at auction. The 'Attic Stelai' contain inventories of the property sold and the price fetched at auction. However, the culprits had ample warning of their impending arrest and most appear to have disposed of or hidden as much of their property as possible before they fled Attika. It is likely therefore that the preserved lists represent only the relatively worthless items or property which they could not hide, not the full extent of their estates. Even so, it is possible to catch a glimpse of the wide range of agricultural and other property which a wealthy citizen might own, and its geographical spread.

Figures 13.3 and 13.4 show the property listed in the 'Attic Stelai' under the names of two different men, Adeimantos son of Leukolophides of Skambonidai and Axiochos son of Alkibiades of Skambonidai. Adeimantos owned land in at least two different parts of Attika, and it appears to have been divided into a minimum of six different plots. He also owned land abroad in Thasos, which itself may well have been divided into smaller plots. Axiochos owned land in at least seven different places in Attika (and some of these holdings must have consisted of several separate plots), as well as land overseas in Abydos, Klazomenai and elsewhere. However imperfect our knowledge of the full range of their property, it is clear that in both of these estates, agricultural land and enterprises were extremely important sources of wealth and income for these men, and that the range of their agricultural activities was diverse.

# 7   Rural Settlement and Land Use

From literary and epigraphical sources it has long been clear that classical Athenians valued and exploited the Attic countryside. Our understanding of rural settlement throughout Greece and the Greek world, however, has been transformed over the past twenty-five years by the prolific discoveries of intensive archaeological survey. Important field projects in Boiotia (Bintliff & Snodgrass 1985; 1988; Bintliff et al. 2004), Keos (Cherry et al. 1991), Lakonia (Cavanagh et al. 1996; 2002), Megalopolis (Lloyd et al. 1983), Aitolia (Bommeljé et al. 1987), Pylos in Messenia (Davis et al. 1997), Methana (Mee & Forbes 1996), the southern Argolid (Jameson et al. 1994), Berbati-Limnes near Mycenae (Wells & Runnels 1996), Attika (Lohmann 1992; 1993), Sphakia in Crete (Nixon et al. 2000) and elsewhere have revealed dynamic and complex countrysides. Outside Greece, archaeological projects in areas of Greek settlement such as the Crimea, Sardinia, Sicily and southern Italy have also clarified our picture of rural settlement.

*IG* 1$^3$ 422

    187–90   4 shadufs and a large trough on land in Xypetnaion

    182–6     land (specifications and location lost)

    178–81   land (specifications and location lost)

*IG* 1$^3$ 426 [skilled slaves and equipment – prices missing]

    10–39    Phrygian man

                  a man, Apollophanes

                  Charias, *obeliskopoios* [spit or nail maker]

                  Aristarchos, *skutotomos* [leather worker]

                        his equipment: small table, 2 couches, table, sleeping pallets, building timber, and 8 unpreserved and unidentified items

                  Satyros, *skytotomos* [leather worker]

                  [3 lines missing and 3 lines that seem to have been equipment]

    44–51    [Thasian farm specializing in vines]

    44         man, Aristomachos [bailiff?]

    45–6      land and *oikia* in Thasos in I–

                  large numbers of good and bad *pithoi* with lids

                  590(?) *amphorai* of wine (capacity: 3 *choai*) = 8.64 l each = 5,098 l wine total

    106–7   income from rents on land that had been owned by Adeimantos: 1,632 drachmai, 4 oboloi [if a rent of around 8 per cent of the capital value is assumed, this makes for a capital value of about 3 talanta, 2,408 drachmai]

    142       something unidentifiable worth 520+ drachmai

*IG* 1$^3$ 430 a

    1–4       'oakery' and 'pinery' and *oikia* in B–, 8 *pithoi* in the *oikia*, and Kydimakhos, slave of Adeimantos [who presumably managed the 'oakery' and 'pinery'].

    10–12   harvested crops [cereals or other arable?], worth 50 drachmai, from land in Ophryneion.

    27–8    sale of slave, Satyros, 170 drachmai

**Figure 13.3**   Adeimantos son of Leukolophides of Skambonidai: surviving possessions in the 'Attic Stelai'.

Archaeological survey is the process of closely scrutinizing a known area for remains of human occupation and use on the surface, generally in the form of broken bits of pottery (sherds) (Figure 13.5). Most of these are in poor condition, but some are sufficiently well preserved for it to be possible to assign a date, and to determine the shape and sometimes the function of the pot. In most areas many small sites (concentrations of sherds and sometimes architectural remains) with plain, coarse and fine pottery for cooking, storage, eating and drinking and roof tile have been found scattered across the landscape. Generally they have been identified by archaeologists as 'farmsteads', although their precise functions may have varied considerably and are not always clear from surface survey alone. In some areas smaller installations of agricultural equipment such as olive presses or treading floors for making wine are found out in the fields, isolated from residential housing (Figure 13.6a–c). These might have been similar to the kinds of rustic 'sheds' which appear in the 'Attic

*IG* 1³ 422

194–204 [slaves]

> Arete, Thracian woman (361 drachmai, for all 3?)
> Grylion, Thracian man
> Habrosyne, Thracian woman
> Dionysios, Scythian bronze smith (155 drachmai)
> income from rents on fields (*choria*) in Tho– which had been owned by Axiochos, 150 drachmai [if a rent of around 8 per cent of the capital value is assumed, this makes for a capital value of 1,875 drachmai]

*IG* 1³ 424

10–16 apartment house

> total of houses [*oikiai*] – large sum of money not preserved.
> foreign agricultural land – details not preserved

*IG* 1³ 426

101–2, income from rents on land owned by Axiochos
108–11 1,633 drachmai 2.5 oboloi [if a rent of around 8 per cent of the capital value is assumed, this makes for a capital value of about 3 talanta, 2,417 drachmai]

> item not preserved, more rents? 250 drachmai
> item not preserved, more rents? 162 drachmai, 4 oboloi.

*IG* 1³ 427

52–85 [equipment and fittings from a country house]

> 5 *phidaknai* [small *pithoi*]: 9 drachmai; 11 drachmai; 4 drachmai, 4 oboloi; 4 drachmai, 3 oboloi; 4 drachmai
> funnel [no price, goes with next item?]
> lead pipe 2 drachmai, 2 oboloi
> written board/picture 60 drachmai
> another small one 6 drachmai, 4 oboloi
> painted(?) picture 5+ drachmai
> land which had belonged to Axiochos ... [further details missing]
>> [poorly preserved entry] 2,040 drachmai (?)
>> [poorly preserved entry] 1,590 drachmai (?)
> area of land (in *plethra*) with *oikia*, another to the metics/merchants [no price]
> 3 *plethra* arable land with vines 1,900 drachmai [goes with last item?]
> *oikia* in the countryside [*agroi*]
> another piece of arable land, with olives(?), 3 *plethra* 6,100 drachmai
> [something unidentifiable] with vines; [something unidentifiable] in Abydos 310 drachmai
> [something unidentifiable] in Klazomenai 200 drachmai

*IG* 1³ 430

6–7 a man, Olas 195 drachmai
8–9 Messenian man 130 drachmai
24–5 Keph–, slave 195 drachmai
33–5 crops in the field(?) 20 drachmai.

**Figure 13.4** Axiochos son of Alkibiades of Skambonidai: surviving possessions in the 'Attic Stelai'.

**Figure 13.5**   Archaeologists on survey in Bova Marina, Calabria, Italy.

Stelai'—storage buildings for tools and agricultural produce (Figure 13.3 ~ $IG1^3$ 422.187–90, shadufs and trough; Figure 13.4 ~ $IG1^3$ 427.52–85, equipment and fittings from a country house). In addition, particularly in lowland areas, high levels of 'background' scatter (low levels of sherds found outside 'sites') suggest very intensive use of the fields, perhaps indicating regular manuring or other activities

**Figure 13.6a**   Lever press on black figure skyphos (Boston Museum).

**Figure 13.6b**   Rock-cut press located in Methana countryside.

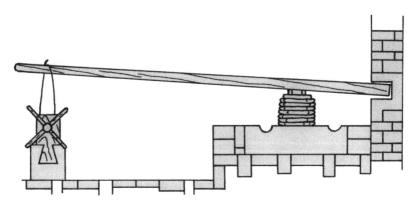

**Figure 13.6c**   Reconstruction of ancient olive press.

(Alcock et al. 1994; Pettegrew 2001, 2002 with discussion by Osborne 2001, Foxhall 2001, and Bintliff et al. 2002).

The most striking feature of classical countrysides of Greece is the pattern of dispersed settlement found in most parts of Greece and the Greek world in the fifth and especially the fourth centuries (Figure 13.7). Although most people plainly lived in towns and villages, these rural landscapes were intensively farmed. Some people probably lived out in the country all year round, but there is much debate on the extent to which some of these 'farmstead' sites many have been occupied for only part of the year. It is also possible that in some cases the owner lived in a town or village and commuted out to his fields in the countryside. In the case of wealthy farmers, slaves may have lived in the country house all year round, while the owner and his

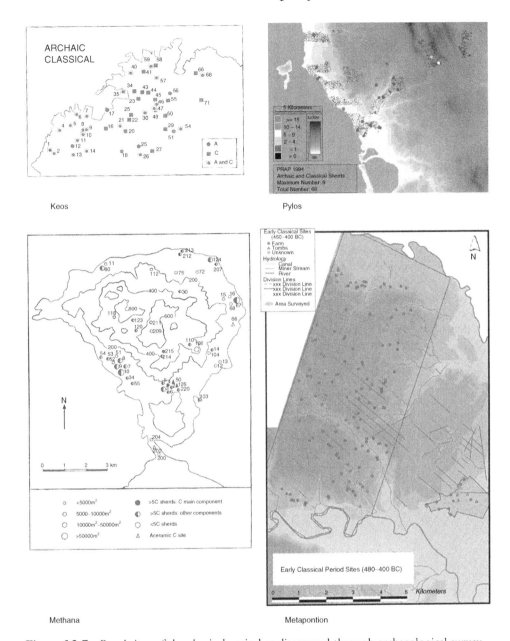

Keos

Pylos

Methana

Metapontion

**Figure 13.7**　Rural sites of the classical period as discovered through archaeological survey.

family spent only some of their time in the country, as suggested by the descriptions of country house management in Xenophon's *Oikonomikos* (11.14).

It is clear from archaeological survey that during the classical period the rural territories of cities in most parts of Greece were intensively exploited compared to other periods. Of course, not all of the sites dating to the 100 or so years of the time span were necessarily occupied simultaneously, nor on the other hand have archae-ologists discovered all of the sites in use at any one time. However, only in the late Roman period and the late nineteenth–early twentieth centuries CE does the extent of use of the countryside rival that of classical times. There are some interesting exceptions to this general pattern. The territory of Messenia, conquered by Sparta and worked by helots of slave status (perhaps as sharecroppers), is an empty landscape compared to those of other cities (Figure 13.7), and it is likely that the unusual political situation was the cause (Alcock 2002). In other areas, for example, on the peninsula of Methana (Figure 13.7), it is clear that the remote uplands (areas over 500 m above sea level) were less intensively exploited than the lowlands (altitudes of 200 m above sea level and below). However, it is clear that all types of land in the territories of Greek cities were exploited for their productive resources, even those areas which were uncultivable.

Although the information provided by survey has proven immensely valuable to our understanding of rural Greece in antiquity, many questions remain unanswered by surface remains alone. There are few excavated rural houses of the period, but the two best examples are in Attika: the Dema House and the Vari House.

The Dema House, dating to the last quarter of the fifth century BCE, was located north of Athens near the Dema Wall (Jones et al. 1962) (Figure 13.8). A large, residential courtyard house with a tiled roof, it may have been abandoned in the later stages of the Peloponnesian War, with some re-occupation in the fourth century. Part

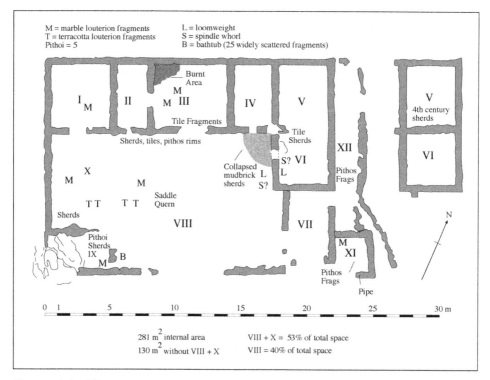

**Figure 13.8**   The Dema House: plan.

of the house may have had a second storey, but there is no tower, a feature regularly documented for other farmhouses (Figure 13.9). The courtyard was an important working area—note the saddle quern for grinding grain found in it. The stone bases were for (wooden?) columns, around which a vine might have grown, to provide shade in summer. The house faces south so that the courtyard and the northern rooms would catch the sun in winter, when the vine would have lost its leaves. The range of artefacts found is similar to that of contemporary urban houses, and there is no agricultural processing equipment or evidence of other kinds of activities to suggest that it was a working farm. It might have been the kind of country house portrayed in Xenophon's *Oikonomikos*, in which the character Ischomachos lived—part farm and part holiday home. If so, the farming activities must have been physically separated from the comfortable residential accommodation.

The Vari House was sited on the road up to a remote rural sanctuary (the Cave of Pan, a god special to shepherds and their flocks) on Mt Hymettos, above the ancient deme village of Anagyrous (Figure 13.10). Though the main period of the house dates to the early fourth century, there is some evidence of earlier fifth-century occupation on the site. This is also a courtyard house with a tiled roof, but smaller than the Dema House. The range of finds is closer to those of the rural sites discovered in survey than to those of the Dema House and urban houses, and there is more evidence for agrarian activities. The Vari House is set within a large enclosure wall, probably because livestock (most likely to have been sheep or goats) were kept in the yard. The area is highly suitable for summer grazing. The beehive sherds found near the door in the yard suggest that the occupants kept bees on the thyme-covered

**Figure 13.9**   Classical period farmhouse (?) tower, Methana.

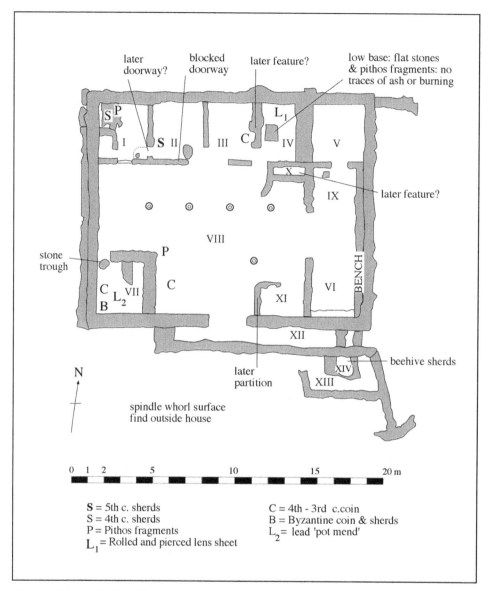

**Figure 13.10** The Vari House: plan.

slopes of Mt Hymettos, famous for its honey from antiquity to the present. Keeping bees by the back door seems highly unlikely and rather dangerous, and the broken beehives must have been thrown into the yard for the animals to lick once the honey had been removed. Grazing in the mountains and bee keeping are both summertime activities so it is probable that the occupants lived here only for only part of the year, at the time when the sanctuary would have been most regularly visited. As is the case for many farmers today, tourists might have provided a welcome stream of customers for honey, cheese and other farm products. In winter the occupants probably moved themselves and their animals down to the coast to where the ancient village of Anagyrous was located.

It is likely that, as in the written sources, the wealthier end of the socio-economic spectrum is over-represented in the archaeological record. Nonetheless, the archaeological evidence for the countryside of classical Greece offers a picture of a diverse and busy rural landscape, directly linked to urban centres and providing the livelihood for the citizens of the poleis. The following sections will explore in more depth the ways in which Greek farmers worked the land.

# 8   Farming the Land

In ancient Greek the word *chora* meant a piece of land of any size from the entire territory of a polis to a tiny field. Today and in the recent past, the agrarian landscapes of Greece and many other parts of the Mediterranean have been characterized by fields in small areas of plains land combined with a patchwork of terraces on the hill slopes (Figure 13.11). It is not clear, however, that the fields of classical Greece were farmed in the same way. Although several scholars claim to have discovered terraces dating to the classical period (Lohmann 1992), the chronological evidence for these is dubious. Indeed, it is not certain, except in very unusual circumstances, that an agricultural terrace from classical times would easily survive to the present day. Terraces are continuously built and re-built, even in more recent periods. These are landscapes which have been repeatedly re-sculpted by a combination of the people who worked the fields and natural forces such as tectonic activity, forest fires, floods, wind, erosion and alluviation. Among the few descriptions that we have in ancient literature and inscriptions of ancient fields, there are no unambiguous references to

**Figure 13.11**   Terraced landscape in modern Methana.

terraces or terrace walls (Foxhall 1996). In contrast, there are numerous references to other techniques for soil management on steep slopes.

The main purposes of terracing are not only to get rid of the rocks, but also to hold soil in place, to create a level area for cultivation and to slow run-off from the winter rains. Many of these aims can be achieved by other means. In the absence of terraces, many hill slopes were planted with all kinds of fruit trees and vines (Theophrastos *De Causis Plantarum* 3.6.7). The trees themselves helped to hold the soil in place. Wealthy farmers who had slave labour available were able to dig trenches around trees, shaped like basins sloping in towards the trunk, which caught precious rainwater and kept it where it would most benefit the tree. In areas where drainage was a problem in winter, these basins around trees could be connected by ditches dug across the slope (Theophrastos *De Causis Plantarum* 3.6.3–4). Repeated digging around trees also removed weeds which would compete for moisture and nutrients, and kept the top layer of soil dry and crumbly, thus reducing the loss of water from lower soil levels via capillary action and evaporation. Theophrastos, writing about plants in the fourth century, was clearly familiar with this practice and recommended a regime of regular digging around trees three times throughout the year (Theophrastos *De Causis Plantarum* 3.12.2; 3.16.2, 3). Indeed, repeated ploughing and digging were considered the best way to work land for arable crops as well as for trees, though this would have needed much labour, possibly more than a poorer household could manage on its own without the help of slave labour.

> Cultivation consists of ploughing in both seasons, both in summer and in winter, so that the soil may be exposed to winter and to the sun, a point we also made in treating the planting of trees. For by being turned up often the soil becomes open textured, light and free of woody plants, so that it can easily bring up the crop.... Snow is considered excellent for fields ploughed in winter, and hoar frost no less, for they say it eats through the ground and gives it an open texture. Again when farmers after the first ploughing plough again in spring they turn the earth to destroy the weeds that come up, and then plough in summer and plough lightly once more just before sowing, with the idea, as we said, that one must work the land before sowing and make this one's chief task. This is why the authorities prefer working the land with a mattock, and consider that working it with the plough misses much. (Theophrastos *De Causis Plantarum* 3.20.7–8)

It is therefore probable that such ideal regimes of cultivation reflect the practices of the rich and that less well-off farmers did not follow them closely, even though they may have aspired to them. Greek farmers were adept at managing to make the most of a wide range of soil types and conditions.

The tools of ancient farming were basic, as the passage of Theophrastos quoted above shows. Simple ard ploughs, appropriate for the shallow soils of the Mediterranean region, mattocks for digging (they did not have spades or shovels), sickles, axes and adzes, pruning knives, winnowing forks and baskets, and sometimes basic threshing sledges comprise virtually the entire repertoire (Figure 13.12). Very little metal was used in their manufacture, and even implements such as ploughs might be almost entirely made of wood. Though sickles were sometimes made of metal, the teeth could also be triangular flakes of obsidian (volcanic glass) set in a wooden haft—even stone tools still had their place (Figure 13.13). Transport and other motive power was supplied by cattle, donkeys and mules. Much of the agricultural machinery of

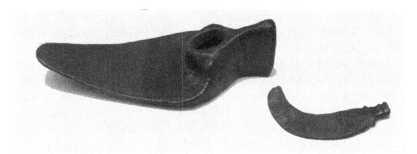

**Figure 13.12**  Farming tools and technology: (top) ploughing scene from a black figured Attic vase; (bottom) agricultural tools: mattock/hoe for digging and pruning knife. Kerameikos Museum, Athens.

**Figure 13.13**  Obsidian flake, probably from a sickle, found in a classical Greek farmhouse, Bova Marina, Calabria, Italy.

classical times, such as wine and oil presses, was simple and modular—assembled for the job in hand then taken apart so that the components could be used for other tasks (Figure 13.6c).

# 9    Crops and Choices: The Agricultural Year

The major crops of ancient Greece are often called the 'Mediterranean trinity': cereals, olives and vines, to which legumes and figs should be added. Cereals were the main staple crop, mostly processed as bread. Olives were probably eaten as table olives as much as they were pressed for oil—always a luxury product, and used for industrial purposes (in a petroleum-free world) as well as culinary ones. The vine was of course mostly used for wine, though table grapes were eaten too. Many other fruit trees, especially the fig, were important: figs produce far more calories per hectare than either cereals or olives. Almonds, quinces, apples, pears, walnuts, pomegranates and medlars were also commonly grown. Important leguminous crops were broad beans (fava beans), lentils, chickpeas, vetch and lathyrus pea (related to sweet peas and used for both fodder and human food). Garden vegetables included marrows, cucumbers, leeks, onions, garlic, and various leafy crops such as chicory and black nightshade (*Solanum nigrum*). However, many of the plants familiar in Mediterranean cooking today were unknown in classical times and were introduced from either the Near East (aubergine) or the Americas (tomato, sweet and chilli peppers, potato, and many types of beans).

The exploitation of a wide range of crops helped reduce risks for farmers since whatever the weather in any particular year, something was likely to do well and other things were likely to fare less well. Moreover, in a regime where farmers owned plots of land in different places, with different soils, aspects, altitudes, etc., farmers could choose crops and varieties (and there were many varieties of the major cultigens) which best suited specific situations.

Thucydides' (2.1) choice to organize his history of the Peloponnesian War by summers and winters was not a capricious one, but reflects the rhythm of the agricultural year (Figure 13.14). Summer was a relatively slack season, when men had time for war, sailing, craft work, building and all the other jobs that were difficult to fit into the busiest times in the agricultural year, but also a time for rest and enjoyment of seasonal pleasures:

> When the golden thistle is in flower and the noisy cicada sitting in the tree pours down its clear song thick and fast from under its wings in the fatiguing summer season, then goats are fattest and wine is best, women are most lustful, but men are weakest, because Sirios parches their head and knees, and their skin is dried out with the heat. Then you want rocky shade and wine from Byblos, barley bread made with milk and the goats' last milk, and meat of a scrub-grazed heifer and of firstling kids. (Hesiod *Works and Days* 582–92)

The Greek agricultural year begins in the autumn:

> When the keen sun's strength stops scorching and sweltering, after mighty Zeus begins the autumn rain, and human skin feels the change with relief—for then the star Sirios

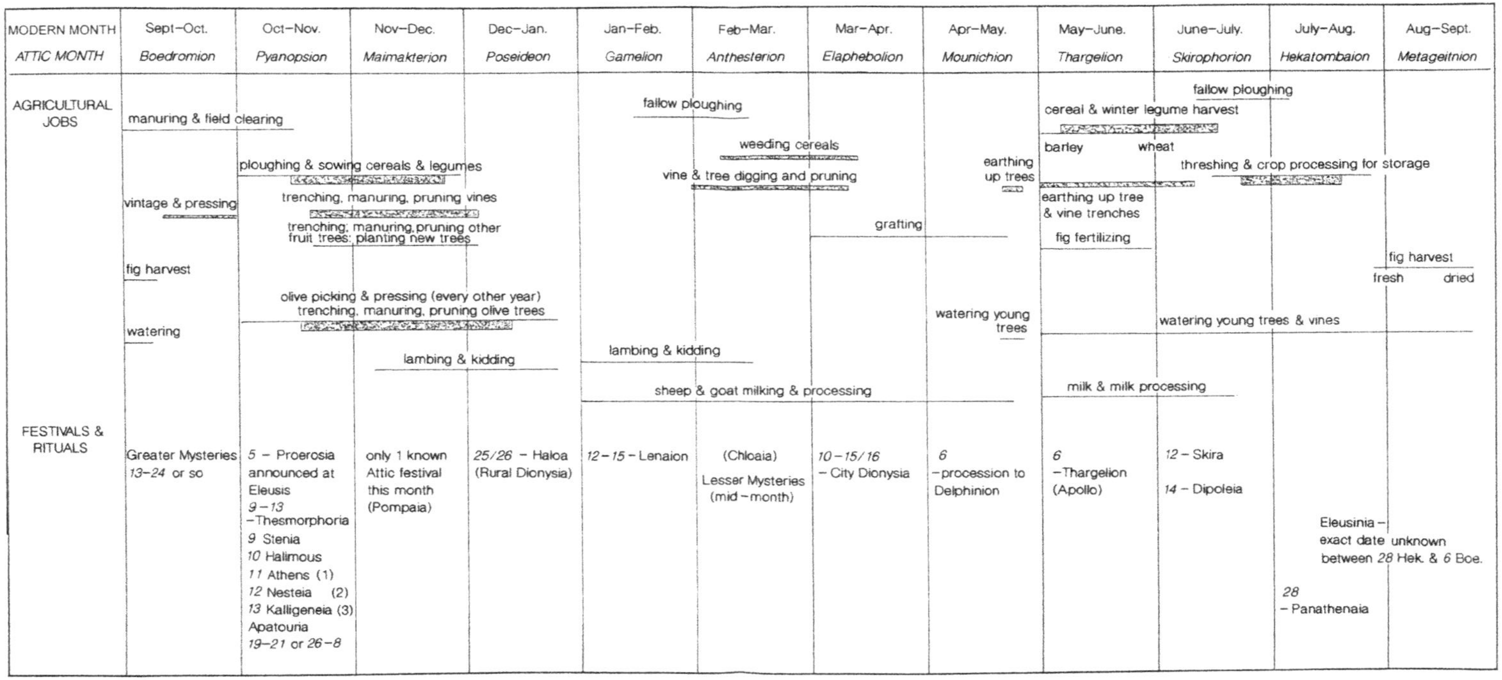

| MODERN MONTH | ATTIC MONTH | AGRICULTURAL JOBS | FESTIVALS & RITUALS |
|---|---|---|---|
| Sept–Oct. | Boedromion | manuring & field clearing; vintage & pressing; fig harvest; watering | Greater Mysteries 13–24 or so |
| Oct.–Nov. | Pyanopsion | manuring & field clearing; ploughing & sowing cereals & legumes | 5 – Proerosia announced at Eleusis; 9–13 – Thesmophoria: 9 Stenia, 10 Halimous, 11 Athens (1), 12 Nesteia (2), 13 Kalligeneia (3); Apatouria 19–21 or 26–8 |
| Nov.–Dec. | Maimakterion | ploughing & sowing cereals & legumes; trenching, manuring, pruning vines; trenching, manuring, pruning other fruit trees; planting new trees; olive picking & pressing (every other year); trenching, manuring, pruning olive trees; lambing & kidding | only 1 known Attic festival this month (Pompaia) |
| Dec.–Jan. | Poseideon | trenching, manuring, pruning vines; olive picking & pressing (every other year); lambing & kidding | 25/26 – Haloa (Rural Dionysia) |
| Jan.–Feb. | Gamelion | fallow ploughing; lambing & kidding; sheep & goat milking & processing | 12–15 – Lenaion |
| Feb.–Mar. | Anthesterion | fallow ploughing; weeding cereals; vine & tree digging and pruning; sheep & goat milking & processing | (Chloaia); Lesser Mysteries (mid-month) |
| Mar.–Apr. | Elaphebolion | weeding cereals; vine & tree digging and pruning; grafting | 10–15/16 – City Dionysia |
| Apr.–May | Mounichion | earthing up trees; watering young trees | 6 – procession to Delphinion |
| May–June | Thargelion | cereal & winter legume harvest (barley); earthing up tree & vine trenches; fig fertilizing; watering young trees & vines; milk & milk processing | 6 – Thargelion (Apollo) |
| June–July | Skirophorion | fallow ploughing; cereal & winter legume harvest (wheat); threshing & crop processing for storage; watering young trees & vines | 12 – Skira; 14 – Dipoleia |
| July–Aug. | Hekatombaion | fallow ploughing; threshing & crop processing for storage | Eleusinia – exact date unknown between 28 Hek. & 6 Boe.; 28 – Panathenaia |
| Aug.–Sept. | Metageitnion | fig harvest fresh; dried | |

Figure 13.14 The Greek agricultural year. (The Attic calendar year begins with Hekatombaion.)

goes but briefly by day above the heads of men who are born to die, having a larger share of the night. (Hesiod *Works and Days* 414–19)

This is the busiest time of the agricultural cycle, when the demands of ploughing the fields and sowing cereals, legumes and other arable crops; pruning, digging around and planting fruit trees and vines; and harvesting and pressing olives put enormous pressure on farmers' time and labour resources. At this period, access to labour beyond the family, notably slaves, could be crucial for Greek farmers. Given the limited window for ploughing, a family working with one yoke of oxen probably could not have worked more than five to six hectares of land per year (Foxhall 2003: 83). Even the business of religion and city politics sometimes had to be swept aside— during the height of the Attic sowing season in the month of Maimakterion (November/December) there were no major religious festivals in Athens and few recorded meetings of the Assembly and Council (Mikalson 1975: 86). In midwinter, when it was too cold and wet for farming tasks, there was a short lull when jobs such as woodcutting could be done. By February, however, the weather was usually suitable for planting spring-sown crops and for any pruning that had not been finished before the onset of winter. Hand weeding the autumn-sown cereals was a high priority. This is also the season for the second ploughing. Later in the spring vines needed to be dug again when the weather warms up, to encourage growth— this is one of the most arduous tasks of the year. Spring is also the season when sheep and goats begin giving milk, as lambs and kids are born, so animal husbandry and cheese-making are important tasks. The cereal harvest begins in May and, depending on the type of grain and the location of the field, may run as late as early July. Threshing and processing the crops for storage is less frenetic, as the onset of summer generally guarantees dry and sunny weather. At this time comes the third ploughing (called the 'dusting' by Theophrastos), to kill weeds and conserve soil moisture, and earth is heaped up around the trunks of trees and vines to protect them from the summer sun. Late in July and through August come the fig harvest, which is not particularly hard work, followed by the exuberance of the vintage and winemaking in September, finished before the winter rains start again in October.

# 10   Arable Crops

Cereals and other arable crops were generally grown in a two-year rotation system: one year the field was sown with a crop and the next year nothing was grown and the land was left fallow. In temperate regions fallowing is used primarily to conserve and restore soil fertility, and to prevent the build-up of pests and diseases. In the drier parts of the Mediterranean, the main purpose of fallowing is to conserve soil moisture. Sometimes fallow land was ploughed so that weed growth did not consume soil moisture and the dry top levels of soil acted as a blanket to stop the loss of water by capillary action and evaporation. However, fallow land with weeds growing on it could also be an important resource for grazing.

The most important cereal in much of the Greek world was barley. It is tolerant of drought, salt and alkaline conditions, and though it is sensitive to cold this is not generally a problem in the southern Mediterranean. The drawbacks are that (1) most types of barley grown in classical Greece had hulls which took considerable pounding to remove (although they protected the kernel from pests in storage) and (2) it makes truly terrible bread. Wheat was considered a much more desirable cereal by Greeks, because of its bread-making qualities, and several species were grown in classical antiquity. Because it does not produce as prolifically in less than optimal conditions, it was something of a 'luxury' cereal—perhaps not eaten as an everyday food by poorer people. One variety of wheat was spring sown, and was sometimes used as an emergency crop if the autumn rains had been inadequate. In damper areas millet (sown in the spring) was also grown, though it was not as important as wheat and barley. In addition to legumes (see above), other field crops regularly grown included sesame, fenugreek and, in damp areas with good soil, flax both for linseed and for rope and textiles.

For arable crops the field was ploughed and sown in the autumn, after the onset of the winter rains had sufficiently softened the ground. In Figure 13.12 (top), the sower is walking in front of the ploughman scattering the seed broadcast, while the plough breaks up the soil and covers it over. Cereals sown at higher altitudes and/or in warmer locations need up to two months more growing time than those planted at lower altitudes and/or in warmer locations. This is where the Greek habit of fragmenting plots could be advantageous: farmers could spread out the work of the busy sowing and harvest seasons by having plots in both cooler, wetter, higher places and warmer, drier, lower ones. This also incidentally spread the risks of crop failure: in dry years grain on damper plots grew better, while in wet years drier plots might produce more.

Important by-products of arable crops included chaff and straw which were used for animal fodder, and in the latter case also for stable bedding. Grain was normally harvested close to the ear, so the straw left in the field was generally quite long. This could be gathered separately, or it could have been used for grazing as stubble. The haulms (stalks) of leguminous crops also made nutritious fodder. Unsuccessful crops of cereals or legumes might be harvested early for fodder or hay, though sometimes crops such as vetch were grown specifically for hay. (Hay was never meadow grass, as was traditional in temperate Europe.)

## 11   Arboriculture

Although polycropping, growing trees with arable crops in between, has regularly been practised in the recent past in the Mediterranean, it may have been less common in classical antiquity, at least on the plots of wealthy farmers, because of the habit of trenching around trees, discussed above. Theophrastos certainly understood that repeated digging around trees throughout the year to direct water to the roots retained soil moisture and eliminated weed growth, improving the productivity of the tree. In consequence he did not generally recommend polycropping.

> Digging benefits all [trees], since it removes the things which block and intercept the food supply and makes the earth itself damper and lighter. Moreover, air gets mixed in with the soil, as it must when the earth is turned up, and gives some moisture and so provides food. This is why one must dig even dry and waterless ground and turn it up

frequently (as said earlier). However, digging is also good for land that is marshy and has surface water. (Theophrastos *De Causis Plantarum* 3.10.1)

Indeed, plants also that are planted or sown as neighbours are all of them injurious for this reason, some actually destroying a tree, except where they serve a curative purpose, for example when people sow barley or some other dry plant among vine cuttings to reduce the moisture, or sow bitter vetch (*orobos*) among radishes (*raphaneis*) so that they are not devoured [by caterpillars], and the like. (Theophrastos *De Causis Plantarum* 3.10.3)

Olives, vines and figs, like most fruit trees, do not grow true to type from seed. The Greeks propagated them vegetatively using cuttings, ovules (growths at the bases of old olive trees) and grafting. Theophrastos (*De Causis Plantarum* 1.6.1–10) has a long and detailed discussion of grafting techniques, which farmers clearly used with considerable sophistication (Figure 13.15, top).

It is rightly recommended to keep the bud and bark from getting torn and to trim the inserted scion so that no core wood is exposed at the join. This is why people also first bandage the join with layers of lime bark, then plaster mud over it mixed with hair, to keep it moist and to prevent damage from sun, rain and cold. So too after slitting the stock and making the scion wedge-shaped, they drive it in with a mallet to make the fit as tight as possible. (Theophrastos *De Causis Plantarum* 1.6.7–8)

Sometimes farmers used the wild forms of olives, figs or pears as rootstock because they were so vigorous, and grafted choice domestic varieties onto them.

It is also reasonable that trees so grafted should bear finer fruit, especially when the scion is from a cultivated tree and the rootstock from a wild tree of the same bark, since the scion is better fed because the stock is strong (this is why it is recommended to plant the wild olives first and later graft them with cultivated buds or twigs). (Theophrastos *De Causis Plantarum* 1.6.10)

Of course, tree crops were cultivated primarily for their fruit. However, there were many important by-products of arboriculture. Branches pruned from olives, vines, almonds and other fruit trees were an important source of fodder for animals. When all the leaves had been eaten, the branches could then be cut and stored for fuel. Vine prunings in particular made excellent fuel for kilns and ovens. Fallen fruit (e.g., maggot-infested olives and figs) and almond husks were also important supplements for animals in late summer when grazing was scarce. The residue from the pressing of grapes made nutritious fodder, and the residue from olive pressing could be used for either fodder or fuel.

## 12 Garden Crops and Gardens

Despite their focus on urban life, Greeks loved plants and flowers, and grew them ornamentally in gardens (Figure 13.15). Unlike Roman or modern gardens, Greek gardens were not attached to houses, but were simply small, accessible plots of land,

**Figure 13.15** Ancient Greek gardens: (top) detail of a krater by the Meidias Painter (British Museum, London E224), showing top-grafted tree; (bottom) women picking quinces, Attic red figured vase.

often situated along roads and surrounded by trees. They also differed from our gardens in that they contained mostly 'economic' plants, but grown in an ornamental way. Just as Greeks were partial to grid-planned towns and rural landscapes where this was possible, they also preferred grid-planned gardens: timber or fruit trees arranged in orderly rows, sometimes with vines or other climbing plants growing up them and flowers growing in between, protected by the shade from the burning summer sun. Flowers, such as roses, violets and lilies, also had economic uses, for perfume, garlands and flavouring.

Small garden plots were one of the few settings in which small-scale irrigation might have been possible, using a spring, well or cistern, perhaps in combination with

**Figure 13.16**  Dry garden (*xeriko bostani*) for summer vegetables in Methana in the 1980s.

some kind of water-lifting device, such as the shadufs mentioned in the 'Attic Stelai' above (Figure 13.3). This would have allowed the cultivation of cucumbers, flax, greens and other vegetable crops over the hot summer. However, judicious use of ploughed fallow on deep soils would allow the summer vegetables to exploit two years of rainfall, if planted far apart and constantly weeded (Figure 13.16). Theophrastos (*Historia Plantarum* 2.7.5; *De Causis Plantarum* 3.16.3, 4) describes the technique of 'dusting' dry-farmed summer vegetables, which seems to be similar to the dry gardens (*xerika bostania*) of modern Greek farmers.

## 13   Rivers, Springs and Water Management

Springs and wells, year-round sources of water, were always a precious resource in the Mediterranean, for humans and animals alike. In most parts of Greece and southern Italy rivers are seasonal, ranging from raging torrents in winter to dry beds used as roads in the summer. This is almost certainly the problem in Demosthenes 55, a speech from a fourth-century Athenian court case in which the speaker has been accused of obstructing a dry riverbed with a wall so that it flooded the field of his neighbour in winter:

> For the space between my property and theirs is a road, and as a hilly country encircles them, unluckily for the farms, the water that flows down runs, as it happens, partly into the road, and partly on to the fields. And in particular, that which pours into the road, whenever it has free course, flows down along the road, but when there is any stoppage,

then it of necessity overflows upon the fields. Now this particular piece of land, as it happened, was inundated after a heavy downpour had occurred. As a result of neglect, when my father was not yet in possession of the land, but a man held it who utterly disliked the neighbourhood, and preferred to live in the city, the water overflowed two or three times, wrought damage to the land, and was more and more making itself a path. For this reason my father, when he saw it (so I am informed by those acquainted with the circumstances), inasmuch as the neighbours also began to encroach upon the property and walk across it, built around it this enclosing wall. (Demosthenes 55.10–11)

Even the mighty Eurotas of Lakonia shrinks to a sluggish stream lurking in the reed beds around the sanctuary of Artemis Orthia in high summer. In some areas it is possible to slow down the flow of water in winter so that more sinks into the ground. Riverbeds may even then be used as plots for cultivation, though these are exposed to the risk of summertime flash floods. In areas where there were few permanent springs and wells, such as Methana, the inhabitants depended upon cisterns to collect rainfall in winter, often exploiting the runoff from tiled roofs. It is not surprising that springs may become sacred places, as in the case of the Pantenello spring at Metapontion. Equally understandable is the way in which rights of access to water may become a matter of contention.

# 14   Pastoralism

The role of livestock in Greek farming regimes has been much debated (Skydsgaard 1988; Hodkinson 1988; Forbes 1995). Certainly it is clear that the keeping of animals was closely integrated with other agricultural activities, and as noted above, animals exploited resources which humans could not otherwise use directly, such as plant growth on fallow and uncultivated land and agricultural by-products. The evidence is scanty for specialized transhumance, that is the movement of flocks seasonally from one environmental and/or climatic zone to another, and some scholars (Hodkinson 1988: 51–8) thus think that it was not widely practised. Certainly the kinds of long-distance transhumance routes found in later periods in some parts of the Mediterranean world seem inherently unlikely given the territoriality of classical Greek poleis, and the relatively constrained sizes of their territories (Hodkinson 1988: 53). In areas where borders were relatively clear-cut shepherds would have been unlikely to graze animals or walk them through land that was not deemed to be part of their own polis. On the other hand, there are indications that the movement of flocks over short distances from winter lowland grazing to upland summer grazing was regularly practised, as suggested in the discussion of the Vari House (see above). From the Temple of Athena Alea, located in the mountains of the central Peloponnese near Tegea, an early fourth-century inscription (*IG* 5 2) lays out the regulations for grazing livestock on both the land owned by the sanctuary and land within the sacred precinct. Certain officials of the temple are allowed grazing rights for restricted numbers of animals. However, there also seems to be provision for people who are not citizens of Tegea to stop overnight at the sanctuary with their flocks while moving animals from one area to another. This could imply that the sanctuary was located on a well-established trans-humance route in the broken upland landscapes of Arkadia.

In [the sanctuary of Athena] Alea there is to be no grazing [of animals] by either foreigners or citizens unless they are coming for a feast, but for foreigners leading down [flocks?] it is permitted to graze the animals for a day and a night, and if they should graze for longer they will owe a drachma per sheep for each day more, and their right of grazing will be revoked. (*IG* 5 2.11–15)

Similarly in Sophokles' tragedy *Oidipous the King*, the secret of Oidipous' (Oedipus) adoption is revealed by an old shepherd who explains how he met a fellow shepherd from the territory of an adjoining city when both were grazing their sheep (presumably in summer) up in the mountains in the no-man's-land between the two poleis (Sophokles *Oedipus Tyrannus* 1026–50; 1121–40).

> I am sure he knows well of the time we dwelled in the region of Kithairon for six month periods, from spring to Arktouros he with two flocks, and I, his comrade, with one. And then for the winter I used to drive my flock to my own fold, and he took his to the fold of Laios. Did any of this happen as I tell it, or did it not? (Sophokles *Oedipus Tyrannus* 1134–40)

The animals most commonly kept were sheep and goats, well adapted as they are to the rugged landscapes and the harsh, dry conditions. Flocks were probably relatively small—generally 50 animals or fewer—because of high mortality rates from disease and parasites in the absence of modern veterinary medicine. They were versatile and were exploited for wool, milk and meat, though it is clear that a number of specific breeds were recognized. Contrary to popular belief, goats are much fussier eaters than sheep, but both can survive on rough Mediterranean grazing when desperate in the dearth of midsummer, even consuming desiccated, prickly thistles. Nonetheless, they must have considerable amounts of water to survive.

Cattle were important as traction and transport animals, but are more difficult to maintain in the drier parts of the Mediterranean as they need good-quality grazing and/or browsing as well as very large amounts of water, far greater than the quantities needed by sheep and goats. Beef was a luxury as only small numbers of cattle were kept, except in localities where appropriate resources were available, such as marsh lands. Pigs were useful in areas of upland forests, as they could be left to forage for acorns, beech mast, arbutus and cornel fruits and a wide range of other foods. Sows and piglets could be kept in pens, but boars may have been too wild and dangerous to keep as domestic animals. Chickens arrived in Greece from the Near East in the eighth century and were ubiquitous by classical times.

# 15   Exploiting Uncultivated Landscapes

Greeks often represent the wild landscape as a scary place, far from civilized life in the city and, unlike cultivated fields, untamed by men. It is a place inhabited by wild powers, such as the god Dionysos and his followers, the maenads and satyrs, who, through the power of wine and the sacred mysteries of the god, overcome the normal rules of social behaviour:

> O Thebes nurse of Semele crown yourself with ivy, flourish, flourish with the verdant smilax bearing sweet fruit, and crown yourself in honour of Bacchos with branches of oak

or pine. Adorn your garments of spotted fawn-skin with fleeces of white sheep, and sport in holy games with outrageous thyrsoi. At once all the earth will dance—whoever leads the sacred band is Bromios—to the mountain, to the mountain, where the crowd of women waits, goaded away from their weaving by Dionysos. (Euripides *Bacchae* 105–19)

Ivy, smilax (*Smilax aspera*), oak and pine are all plants characteristic of wild mountain landscapes. The characters who inhabited it were as wild as the plants who grew there. Aristophanes portrayed the charcoal burners from the uplands of Acharnai as 'some old men from Acharnai, tough old folk, dense as prickly oak, unyielding Marathon fighters, men of maple' (Aristophanes *Acharnians* 179–81). Generally, shepherds, resin tappers, charcoal burners and others who worked in the wild were slaves or other low-status workers. Nonetheless, the resources of wild landscapes were important ones. As discussed above, forest, maquis and garrigue were important areas for grazing animals. Trees and shrubs provided timber and fuel (both wood and charcoal, Figure 13.17). In the well-known, and undoubtedly exaggerated, account of Phainippos' property in Attika (Demosthenes 42.7) the speaker suggests that 6 donkey-loads of brushwood per day were being transported away for sale. As donkey-load was about 50 kg, this make roughly 300 kg per day.

A wide range of other resources, too, came from the wild. Many plants useful for basketry, dying, medical and culinary uses were gathered. Birds and animals were hunted and trapped. However, the most important product was probably resin, tapped from pine trees (Figure 13.18) and a crucial product in ship building and other industries.

**Figure 13.17**   Charcoal burner, southern Argolid.

**Figure 13.18**  Resin tapping, Methana.

# 16   Conclusions: Landscapes of Greek Culture

Although the Greeks saw themselves as city folk, they were dependent on the rural hinterland of the polis for their livelihood. To those of us who are modern visitors from temperate zones, the Mediterranean may appear dry and poor, but in reality the cities of the Greeks were set in rich and variegated landscapes. For the most part the territories of Greek poleis were more than capable of supporting their people despite the vagaries of the weather and the hazards associated with semi-arid farming regimes.

For Greeks, taming the landscape was the first step towards civilization: the Athenians claimed cultural superiority over other Greeks because, according to the myth of Eleusis and the Eleusinian Mysteries, they had served as the intermediaries through whom Demeter had bestowed on humans the divine gifts of cultivating cereals and enacting her mysteries.

> And rich-crowned Demeter did not refuse but straightway made fruit to spring up from the rich lands, so that the whole wide earth was laden with leaves and flowers. Then she went, and to the kings who deal justice, Triptolemos and Diokles, the horse-driver, and to doughty Eumolpos and Keleus, leader of the people, she showed the conduct of her rites and taught them all her mysteries, to Triptolemos and Polyxeinos and Diokles also, awful mysteries which no one may in any way transgress or pry into or utter, for deep awe of the gods checks the voice. (*Homeric Hymn to Demeter* 2.470–9)

The Greeks saw themselves as human masters of the natural world around them, and exploited their landscapes, especially the lowlands, intensively. However, it is unlikely that that we can hold them to blame for any significant long-term damage to the Mediterranean lands they occupied. The city-states of the Greek world were small, and the technology by which they worked their lands had comparatively little impact, in contrast to the large-scale environmental changes wrought by later societies, most of all our own.

# Further reading

Grove, A. T., & O. Rackham (2003) *The nature of Mediterranean Europe: an ecological history* (New Haven: Yale University Press) (2nd printing, with corrections)—provides the best, as well as the most amusing, readable and reliable, introduction to the study of Mediterranean environments and ecology, ancient and modern

Horden, P., & N. Purcell (2000) *The corrupting sea: a study of Mediterranean history* (Oxford: Blackwell)—a comprehensive and quite breathtaking work covering many aspects of the inter-action of human and 'natural', environmental factors which shaped the Mediterranean world over the long term. Packed with brilliant ideas and useful information, but not always easy to read

## Ancient Greek agriculture and countrysides

Isager, S., & J. E. Skydsgaard (1992) *Ancient Greek agriculture: an introduction* (London: Routledge)—an excellent introduction, mostly based on written sources

Osborne, R. (1987) *Classical landscape with figures: the ancient Greek city and its countryside* (London: George Philip)—also remains excellent and useful, and incorporates more arch-aeological evidence

Useful collections of papers on Greek countrysides include:

Doukellis, P. N., & L. G. Mendoni (1994) Structures rurales et sociétés antiques: actes du colloque de Corfou, 14–16 mai 1992 (Paris: Belles Lettres) (Annales littéraires de l'Uni-versité de Besançon = 508 Centre de recherches d'histoire ancienne 126)—many papers are in English

Shipley, G., & J. Salmon (eds) (1996) *Human landscapes in classical antiquity: environment and culture* (London: Routledge)

Wells, B. (ed.) (1992) *Agriculture in ancient Greece: proceedings of the seventh international symposium at the Swedish Institute at Athens, 16–17 may, 1990* (Stockholm: Åström) (Acta Instituti Atheniensis Regni Sueciae ser. in 4° 42)

### 'Farm houses'

The only two fully published 'farm houses' remain:

Jones, J. E., L. H. Sackett, A. J. Graham (1962) 'The Dema house in Attica' in: *Annual of the British School at Athens* 57: 75–114

Jones, J. E., A. J. Graham, L. H. Sackett (1973) 'An Attic country house below the cave of Pan at Vari' in: *Annual of the British School at Athens* 68: 355–452

## Recent archaeological surveys

Useful reports of regional archaeological surveys, which provide primary data about Greek countrysides, include:

Bintliff, J., P. Howard, A. Snodgrass (eds) (2004) *The Boeotia project*, vol. 1: *The Thespiae south and Leondari south-east sector* (Cambridge) (Monograph Series of the MacDonald Institute, Archaeology Department of Cambridge University)

Cavanagh, W., J. Crouwel, R. W. V. Catling, G. Shipley (1996) *Continuity and change in a Greek rural landscape. the Laconia survey*, vol. 2: *Archaeological data* (London: British School at Athens) (*Annual of the British School at Athens* Suppl. 27)

Cavanagh, W., J. Crouwel, R. W. V. Catling, G. Shipley (2002) *Continuity and change in a Greek rural landscape: the Laconia survey*, vol. 1: *Methodology and interpretation* (London: British School at Athens) (*Annual of the British School at Athens* Suppl. 26)

Cherry, J. F., J. L. Davis, E. Mantzourani (eds) (1991) *Landscape archaeology as long-term history: northern Keos in the Cycladic islands* (Los Angeles: UCLA Institute of Archaeology) (Monumenta Archaeologica 16)

Jameson, M. H., C. N. Runnels, T. H. van Andel (1994) *A Greek countryside: the southern Argolid from prehistory to the present day* (Stanford: Stanford University Press)

Lohmann, H. (1993) *Atene: Forschungen zur Siedlungs- und Wirtschaftsstruktur des klassischen Attika*, 2 vols (Cologne: Böhlau)

Mee, C. B., & H. A. Forbes (eds) (1996) *A rough and rocky place: settlement and land use in the peninsula of Methana, Greece; results of the Methana Survey Project sponsored by the British School at Athens and the University of Liverpool* (Liverpool: Liverpool University Press) (Liverpool Monographs in Ancient and Oriental Studies)

'The Pylos Regional Archaeological Project: Internet Edition', access: http://classics.uc.edu/prap/

Runnells, C. N., D. J. Pullen, S.. Langdon (eds) (1995) *Artifact and assemblage: the finds from a regional survey of the southern Argolid, Greece*, vol. 1: *The prehistoric and early Iron Age pottery and lithic artefacts* (Stanford CA: Stanford University Press)

Wells, B., & C. Runnels (1996) *The Berbati-Limnes archaeological survey, 1988–1990* (Stockholm: Åström) (Acta Instituti Atheniensis Regni Sueciae ser. in 4° 44)

## Bibliography

Alcock, S. E. (2002) 'A simple case of exploitation? The helots of Messenia' in: Cartledge, P., E. E. Cohen, L. Foxhall (eds) (2002) *Money, labour and land: approaches to the economies of ancient Greece* (London: Routledge) 185–99

Alcock, S. E., J. F. Cherry, J. L. Davis (1994) 'Intensive survey, agricultural practice and the classical landscape of Greece' in: Morris, I. (ed.) (1994) *Classical Greece: ancient histories and modern archaeologies* (Cambridge: Cambridge University Press) 137–70

Amyx, D. A. (1958) 'The Attic stelai, III: vases and other containers' in: *Hesperia* 27: 163–310

Bintliff, J. S., & A. Snodgrass (1985) 'The Cambridge/Bradford Boeotian expedition: the first four years' in: *JFA* 12: 123–61

Bintliff, J. S., & A. Snodgrass (1988) 'Mediterranean survey and the city' in: *Antiquity* 62: 57–71

Bintliff, J. S., C. Farinetti, P. Howard, K. Sarri, K. Sbonias (2002) 'Classical farms, hidden prehistoric landscapes and Greek rural society: a response and an update' in: *JMA* 15.2: 259–65

Bintliff, J., P. Howard, A. Snodgrass (eds) (2004) *The Boeotia project*, vol. 1: *The Thespiae south and Leondari south-east sector* (Cambridge: Cambridge University Press) (Monograph Series of the MacDonald Institute, Archaeology Department of Cambridge University)

Bommeljé, S., P. Doorn, M. Deylius, J. Vroom, Y. Bommeljé, R. Fagel, H. van Wijngaarden (1987) *Aetolia and the Aetolians: towards the interdisciplinary study of a Greek region* (Utrecht: Parnassus) (Studia Aetolica 1)

Carter, J. C. (1990) 'Metapontum—land, wealth and population' in: Descoeudres, J.-P. (ed.) *Greek colonists and native population: proceedings of the First Australian Congress of Classical Archaeology held in honour of emeritus Professor A. D. Trendall, Sydney, 9–14 July 1985* (Canberra: Humanities Research Centre & New York: Oxford University Press) 405–41

Cavanagh, W., J. Crouwel, R. W. V. Catling, G. Shipley (1996) *Continuity and change in a Greek rural landscape. the Laconia survey*, vol. 2: *Archaeological data* (London: British School at Athens) (*Annual of the British School at Athens* Suppl. 27)

Cavanagh, W., J. Crouwel, R. W. V. Catling, G. Shipley (2002) *Continuity and change in a Greek rural landscape: the Laconia survey*, vol. 1: *Methodology and interpretation* (London: British School at Athens) (*Annual of the British School at Athens* Suppl. 26)

Cherry, J. F., J. L. Davis, E. Mantzourani (eds) (1991) *Landscape archaeology as long-term history: northern Keos in the Cycladic islands* (Los Angeles: UCLA Institute of Archaeology) (Monumenta Archaeologica 16)

Davis, J. L., S. E. Alcock, J. Bennet, Y. G. Lolos, C. W. Shelmerdine (1997) 'The Pylos Regional Archaeological Project 1' in: *Hesperia* 66: 391–494

Forbes, H. (1995) 'The identification of pastoralist sites within the context of estate-based agriculture in ancient Greece: beyond the "transhumance versus agro-pastoralism" debate' in: *Annual of the British School at Athens* 90: 325–38

Foxhall, L. (1996) 'Feeling the earth move: cultivation techniques on steep slopes in antiquity' in: Shipley, G., & J. Salmon (eds) (1996) *Human landscapes in classical antiquity: environment and culture* (London: Routledge) 44–67

Foxhall, L. (2001) 'Colouring in the countryside: response to David K. Pettegrew, "Chasing the classical farmstead"' in: *JMA* 14.2: 216–22

Foxhall, L. (2003) 'Cultures, landscapes and identities in the Mediterranean world' in: *Mediterranean Historical Review* 18.2: 75–92

Grove, A. T., & O. Rackham (2003) *The nature of Mediterranean Europe: an ecological history* (New Haven: Yale University Press) (2nd printing, with corrections)

Hanson, V. D. (1999) *The other Greeks: the family farm and the agrarian roots of western civilization* (Berkeley: University of California Press [2]1999)

Hodkinson, S. (1988) 'Animal husbandry in the Greek polis' in: Whittaker 1988: 35–74

Horden, P., & N. Purcell (2000) *The corrupting sea: a study of Mediterranean history* (Oxford: Blackwell)

Jameson, M. H., C. N. Runnels, T. H. van Andel (1994) *A Greek countryside: the southern Argolid from prehistory to the present day* (Stanford: Stanford University Press)

Jones, J. E., L. H. Sackett, A. J. Graham (1962) 'The Dema house in Attica' in: *Annual of the British School at Athens* 57: 75–114

Jones, J. E., A. J. Graham, L. H. Sackett (1973) 'An Attic country house below the cave of Pan at Vari' in: *Annual of the British School at Athens* 68: 355–452

Lloyd, J. A., E. J. Owens, J. Roy (1983) 'The Megalopolis survey in Arcadia' in: Keller, D. R., & D. W. Rupp (eds) *Archaeological survey in the Mediterranean area* (Oxford: British Archaeological Reports) 267–9 (British Archaeological Reports International Series 155)

Lohmann, H. (1992) 'Agriculture and country life in classical Attica' in: Wells 1992: 29–57

Lohmann, H. (1993) *Atene: Forschungen zur Siedlungs- und Wirtschaftsstruktur des klassischen Attika*, 2 vols (Cologne: Böhlau)

Mee, C. B., & H. A. Forbes (eds) (1996) *A rough and rocky place: settlement and land use in the peninsula of Methana, Greece; results of the Methana Survey Project sponsored by the British School at Athens and the University of Liverpool* (Liverpool: Liverpool University Press) (Liverpool Monographs in Ancient and Oriental Studies)

Mikalson, J. D. (1975) *The sacred and civil calendar of the Athenian year* (Princeton: Princeton University Press)

Morris, I. (1994) 'The Athenian economy twenty years after *The Ancient Economy*' in: *CPh* 89: 351–66

Nixon, L., J. Moody, S. Price, O. Rackham (2000) *Sphakia Survey: the internet edition*, access: http://sphakia.classics.ox.ac.uk/; a two-volume print edition (Oxford: Oxford University Press) is promised)

Osborne, R. (2001) 'Counting the cost: comments on David K. Pettegrew, "Chasing the classical farmstead"' in: *JMA* 14.2: 212–16

Pettegrew, D. K. (2001) 'Chasing the classical farmstead: assessing the formation and signature of rural settlement in Greek landscape archaeology' in: *JMA* 14: 189–209

Pettegrew, D. K. (2002) 'Counting and colouring classical farms: a response to Osborne, Foxhall and Bintliff et al.' in: *JMA* 15.2: 267–73

Pritchett, W. K. (1956) 'The Attic stelai, II' in: *Hesperia* 25: 178–317

'The Pylos Regional Archaeological Project: Internet Edition', access: http://classics.uc.edu/prap

Skydsgaard, J. E. (1988) 'Transhumance in ancient Greece' in: Whittaker 1988: 75–86

Wells, B. (ed.) (1992) *Agriculture in ancient Greece: proceeding of the seventh international symposium at the Swedish Institute at Athens, 16–17 May, 1990* (Stockholm: Åström) (Acta Instituti Atheniensis Regni Sueciae ser. in 4° 42)

Wells, B., & C. Runnels (1996) *The Berbati-Limnes archaeological survey, 1988–1990* (Stockholm: Åström) (Acta Instituti Atheniensis Regni Sueciae ser. in 4° 44)

Whittaker, C. R. (ed.) (1988) *Pastoral economies in classical antiquity* (Cambridge: Cambridge Philological Society) 35–74 (*PCPhS* Suppl. 14)

# Appendix to further reading

The following important works appeared too late for the author to incorporate their results into the text of this chapter:

Morris S.P., & J. K. Papadopoulos (2005) 'Greek towers and slaves: an archaeology of exploitation' in: *American Journal of Archaeology* 109: 155–225 – An extremely useful survey of work on 'farmhouse' sites, with excellent bibliography. It focuses on those with towers and their potential range of functions, especially their possible association with the use of slave labour.

Price, S., & L. Nixon (2005) 'Ancient Greek agricultural terraces: evidence from texts and archaeological survey' in: *American Journal of Archaeology* 109: 665–94 – An excellent survey, with a full and useful bibliography, of the evidence for pre-modern terracing in Greece. The article documents many good examples of post-classical but pre-modern terracing (only the excavated examples from Delos are securely dated to classical/Hellenistic times). The appendix of ancient literary references to possible field walls and terraces is exceptionally helpful.

CHAPTER FOURTEEN

# The Economic Realities

## *G. J. Oliver*

## 1  Introducing Economics to Classical Greece

Although the economy was not a subject that the ancient Greeks considered as a separate entity, it is wrong to assume that the ancient Greeks ignored economic realities or that economies did not matter in politics and Greek polities. In the fifth century financial strength and the management of finances became an essential occupation of Athens as it became an imperial power. Economic activities are either directly or indirectly linked with the main issues that should concern a politician: sources of revenue (*prosodoi*), war and peace, protection of the territory, importation and exportation, and legislation (Aristotle *Rhetoric* 1.4 1359b–60a; Bresson 2000: 119–29). Economic concerns were deeply rooted in many areas of life in a manner similar to the pervasiveness of religion.

However, there are differences. Greek poleis did not operate a fiscal policy that one sees typically in a modern state: national debt, balance of payments, trade deficits (at least in the modern sense) are anachronisms that do not apply directly to ancient Greece. There was a time when historians argued how 'modern' or 'primitive' the ancient economy was. That debate was modified when Moses Finley ([2]1999), embracing the cultural and economic anthropology of Hasebroek and Polanyi in the search for 'different concepts and different models, appropriate to the ancient economy, not (or not necessarily) to ours' (Finley [2]1999: 27), set the ancient economy within the cultural context and values of ancient society and argued therefore that the economy was not comprehensible unless it was seen within that context. This has been called a 'substantivist' approach (elsewhere 'neo-primitivist', Bresson 2000: 244). To some extent Finley's own position was a product of his view that there was insufficient evidence to attribute to the ancient economy precise descriptions and quantitative analyses of economic mechanism (Finley [2]1999: 22–34). This view was predicated on the idea that an economy should be defined as 'an enormous conglomeration of interdependent markets' (Finley [2]1999: 22), an idea that

remained fundamental in the second edition of *The ancient economy* (Finley
²1999: 177–8).

Finley concluded that the Greek economy was not very developed – the state was
not interested in the economy *per se*; for individuals, status was an important factor in
decision-making rather than economic profit.

The corollary of Finley's position has been the 'formalist' position. This emphasizes the independence of economic activity from other areas of life in ancient Greece.
Although it is dangerous to draw too many direct parallels between ancient and
modern economies, it is important to recognize economic behaviour. A degree of
rationality and logic defines *some* economic behaviour in ancient Greece (Christesen
2003) and even if the economy is not as developed or sophisticated as later economies, there are elements of the ancient economy that resemble those of more recent
historical cultures.

The polarity of the 'substantivist' and 'formalist' positions can be best illustrated in
the different approaches to and conclusions drawn from a common body of evidence.
In fourth-century Athens, oratorical evidence provides for the most part the information on which two scholars, Millett (1990; 1991) and Cohen (1992), published
studies of lending and borrowing. Millett argued that lending and borrowing in
Athens was not a widespread activity and that although there is evidence for it, such
activities were marginal and of little relevance to the economy at large. Cohen
considered that the same small amount of evidence for lending money by Athenians
and non-Athenians alike was significant: money-lending was a source of considerable
wealth for these early financiers or bankers as Cohen calls them, some of whom were
honoured by the Athenian state.

Millett emphasizes the social relations between the known examples of lenders and
borrowers, in which lending for profit was not well regarded. Cohen prefers to see the
lending of money as an essentially economic (rather than socio-culturally motivated)
activity and recognizes that money was lent to finance commercial operations that
were of real importance to the economies of polities. The evidence is confined largely
to the fourth century and to Athens where, according to Cohen, the first 'private
banks' appeared (Cohen 1992: 22). 'Public banks' are not found before the Hellenistic period (Cohen 1992: 42 n. 2), although in Athens there was an institution that
made payments from public funds (Stroud 1998: 18 with n. 10). The difference in
approach adopted by these two academics typifies the separation between what we
might call a 'cultural' view and a 'realities' view. Millett's emphasis on the socio-
cultural relations between lenders and borrowers is not a mirage, but at the same time
the economic importance of the lenders (albeit small in number) must not be
underestimated. It should be remembered that a small élite organized in private
partnerships had dominated banking in nineteenth-century Europe (Ferguson
2001: 121).

Although recent academic research into the economies of ancient Greece has
moved on from Finley's analysis, no monograph has replaced Finley's description of
what is in effect an anthropological approach to the economy of the ancient Greeks.
New presentations of the complexities of the ancient economy have displaced Finley
(cf. Davies 1998; Cartledge 1998). Commercial operations and economic behaviour
can be seen as economic activities in their own right rather than as actions embedded
only in social behaviour. The economy is now presented as more complex, diverse and

dynamic, so that we can speak of economies, not of a single economy (Cartledge 1998; Archibald et al. 2001).

The differing approaches to understanding these complexities – what I will call the 'cultural' and 'realist' approaches – respectively build on and diverge from the Finleyan traditions. The 'cultural' approach is post-Finleyan in that it draws heavily on anthropological methodologies and sees economics in terms of cultural activity (e.g., von Reden 1995; 2002). This view understands that 'realities' are, if not illusory, then difficult to discern in the 'text', the evidence from which one must try to draw conclusions about the economy. The other approach, more rooted in what one might call 'realities', emphasizes the dynamics of economic interactions or the range of activities that are implied by both simple and complex financial and commercial transactions (Davies 1998). The former cultural approach is postmodern in that it lays much more emphasis on ideology and the interpretation of 'text'. The latter, the realities approach, is positively heuristic and lays greater emphasis on the dynamics and economic realities that lie behind the processes that evidence either preserves or implies. The 'cultural economists' believe that evidence supports a 'construction' of economic analyses because evidence as text reflects mentalities before realities. This approach offers important insights into Greek society's cultural values but tends to suppress an overtly economy-for-economy's-sake approach. The 'realist' approach acknowledges but does not privilege the cultural context of economic behaviour and prefers to lay greater emphasis on the financial motivations and institutional structures rather than cultural modalities of economic activities. It is the second approach that provides the intellectual framework for this survey of 'economic realities'. This chapter therefore considers the economy of classical Greece in terms of its plural 'economies, with rules and regulations and even a measure of predictability' (Finley [2]1999: 23).

The progress since Finley has been made largely by returning to and embracing the literary, epigraphical and archaeological evidence in new ways. However, the diversity of evidence and different approaches to its treatment has tended to result in the avoidance of all-embracing models of how the economies of ancient Greece worked (on this problem, see Bresson 2000: 261). One attempt to outline the wider economic structures sees a complex matrix of operations (Davies 1998: 249). According to this view, Athens provides a possibly unique model (Descat 1989) of the complexity and dynamics of interaction that involved institutions and individuals within a polity and saw interactions extending beyond the confines of the polity to individuals, communities and polities. These interactions can be traced by different economic activities: making, moving and selling goods or products, the infrastructure that the labour and underlying activities of such operations require, and the values and cultural relationships within which these operations must be perceived. Such an approach appreciates cultural context but gives much greater emphasis to the raw economic drivers of price, profit and power.

Athens offers rich evidence, particularly epigraphical material, for the diverse economies found in a Greek polis. It must be remembered, however, that although this chapter focuses on Athens, not all polities in the Greek world displayed the same levels of complexity and sophistication in their behaviour. At the foundation of all Greek economies is agriculture, the key to understanding most aspects of economic behaviour. The range in size and difference in complexity of other Greek communities or poleis must not be overlooked. For example, at Athens the importation and sale of grain and grain-related produce will have involved numerous officials: the *agoranomoi* (market-place officers), *sitophylakes* (grain market supervisors), *metronomoi* (measures and weights officials) and *epimeletai tou emporiou* (inspectors of the commercial centre), and several other officials. In a smaller city such roles may have involved far fewer officials, typically the *agoranomos* (see below, section 6: Polis Economies and Institutions).

# 2   Perspectives on Evidence

This survey of methodologies and models for studying economic history in ancient Greece has been necessary because of the problems in dealing with the ancient evidence: there is no ancient Greek author offering a survey of economic history, just as there is no similar comprehensive ancient Greek study of religion.

The best ancient survey of economic history is the short treatise falsely attributed to Aristotle, the *Oikonomika*, which was written c. 320/10. From the mid-fourth century, Xenophon's *Poroi* and *Oikonomikos* offer insights respectively into a case-study for improving state revenues and guidelines to a rich Athenian for the ideal organization of one's estate-based household. Economics do, however, underpin much of what ancient authors understand in contemporary politics and history. So Thucydides recognized the importance of economic or financial power in his history of the Athenian Empire but not sufficiently to give full financial details (Kallet-Marx 1993; Kallet 2001).

The problem is always how to interpret the evidence that has survived. Athens in the second half of the fifth and fourth centuries, for example, provides rich epigraphical evidence much of which contains important information on economic activities – leases of land, sales of property, inscriptions detailing the financial status of property (the *horoi*), inventories listing contents in temple treasuries. But epigraphical evidence survives only through various filters. First, stones must survive and be discovered. Second, one has to ask why an inscription was written up. Third, one has to consider the authority behind the writing up of the inscription. However, inscriptions do provide information often absent from similar general surveys of the Greek economy.

In addition to epigraphy, archaeology offers important evidence. Archaeological excavation reveals not only buildings, their plan, construction and history, but also artefacts: fine ceramics and coarse ware, in particular amphoras, now offer new possibilities of uncovering economic histories not contained in written sources (Lawall 1998). Non-intrusive archaeology has also offered much for the economic historian. Archaeological survey has, since the 1970s, revealed much about the rural history of the Greek countryside in Sicily, mainland Greece, Greek islands, the northern Black Sea and some parts of Asia Minor (Alcock et al. 1994; Alcock & Cherry 2004). Survey allows the historian to observe over long periods of time the changing nature of rural activity, usually identifying 'sites of all sizes, types, and periods' (Jameson et al. 1994: 220). Often the lack of more targeted excavations in the course of surveys denies the historian tighter chronological evidence, but the accumulation of ceramic evidence does allow at least a broad picture of rural activity to be presented.

What follows draws heavily on that epigraphical and archaeological evidence because this material is often treated lightly by cultural economists, as Finley's own *Ancient economy* epitomizes. The rest of this chapter is divided into five interconnected sections. The first three, working up from the widest base on which ancient society was built, deal with in turn (section 3) the agricultural foundations of Greek economies (territory and land; labour; wealth and the farm); (section 4) the manufacturers and non-agricultural labour; and (section 5) traders and commerce. There follow two sections that suggest how these features fit into the institutional and political frameworks of Greek polities by considering (section 6) the economies and institutions of the polis and finally (section 7) the realities of economic power.

# 3   Land, Labour and Farmers

## *Territory and land*

Even in the most sophisticated and complex of the polis economies, such as Athens, a significant proportion of the population did not live in the urban centre (*asty*). The polis was almost always intrinsically linked with and dependent on its territory (the countryside or, to use the Greek word, the *chora*) and the agricultural produce of the countryside (Osborne 1987; Sallares 1991). Thucydides says that at the outbreak of the Peloponnesian war, 'from early times down to the present war most of the Athenians still lived in the country with their families and their households' (Thuc. 2.16). Attika was unusual in that its territory of around $2,400 \, km^2$ had only two urban centres (Athens and Piraeus). However, in other respects its *demes* were the same sort of size as the small or medium poleis that one finds in other regions of Greece. In this respect most other regions of Greece of a similar size would have been far more 'urbanized'. To illustrate this point one can consider Boiotia, a territory which occupied roughly the same area as Attika ($2,500 \, km^2$: Fossey 1988: 4) but was made up of many poleis. There were fourteen main poleis in Boiotia but many other smaller poleis which were often associated with or attached to the larger cities of the region. Hansen (1996: 74; Hansen & Nielsen 2004: 436–59) has found as many as twenty-five identifiable poleis of varying size in Boiotia. By definition the political structure of the region known as Boiotia is much more typical of Greece, in that a region was made up of several poleis or urban centres with a rural territory attached. In some regions 'nucleated' living may well have accounted for larger proportions of the population of the polis than at Athens before the Peloponnesian war. The authors of the southern Argolid survey suggest that less than half the population resided in the countryside, perhaps as few as 16 per cent (Jameson et al. 1994: 553). In the long course of its history (the *longue durée*), the Greek countryside was most heavily exploited during the Classical period and probably peaked in the fourth century. Archaeological surveys find consistently that the signs of the greatest activity fall in the Classical and early Hellenistic period (Alcock et al.1994: 142).

## *Land and property*

Ownership of land and property was usually restricted to citizens and a minority of people (non-citizens) given the right to own land (*enktesis*). An ideal *oikos* (household) owned sufficient land to feed itself and produce a surplus (Plato *Laws* 744B, in order to avoid *stasis*) but this ideal was probably far from the reality (see, e.g., Garnsey 1988:

43–6). Xenophon's *Oikonomikos* includes a fictionalized conversation between Sokrates and Ischomachos and a discussion of farming, in which Sokrates says: 'Not everyone does equally well, but some live in plenty and have a surplus, whereas others cannot provide themselves with the necessities, but even get into debt as well' (Xenophon *Oikonomikos* 20.3). Sokrates' intention here is to encourage Ischomachos to organize and run the household efficiently based on agriculture (Xenophon *Oikonomikos.* 6.4–8) – the essence of the treatise and a topos of conservative Greek thought ([Aristotle] *Oikononomika* 1343b). Sokrates refers to and Ischomachos reports differences in property holding and the running of estates (Xenophon *Oikonomikos* 20.4–5; 11.14–18) that probably reflect a reality (Foxhall 2002: 210–12).

Not all citizens ran estates of the same scale ([Aristotle] *Oikonomika* 1345a17). In some parts of the Greek world, communities had their roots in a more egalitarian control of *oikos*-sustaining property, such as at Metapontion (Metapontum), where the average property-plot covered 9 ha (Isager & Skydsgaard 1992: 76). It is widely believed that 5 ha of land was sufficient to sustain a typical household in ancient Greece. In the Hellenistic period a register of land in Larissa (Thessaly) allotted 5 ha to the settlers (Habicht 1976; *SEG* 26 672–6), and 5 ha is widely understood to have been the standard size of farm in classical Greece (Burford Cooper 1977–8; Gallant 1991: 86–7). In some regions, not only were individual properties large enough to produce a marketable surplus of agricultural products but wealthy individuals probably owned several properties. In the hinterland of Chersonesos Taurike (in south-west Crimea on the northern coast of the Black Sea) big estates of an average of 26 ha maximized the production of surplus in different crops (Saprykin 1994: 83–94). However, in Attika, a small minority of Athenians, perhaps as few as 9 per cent, may have held a large proportion of the agriculturally productive land (40 per cent) in the fourth century, according to one theory (Foxhall 1992: 156).

In Sparta, Hodkinson (2000: 123, 382–5) has shown that the estates of *ordinary* Spartiates were relatively large, around 18 ha. The Spartiate elite had considerably larger estates, on average 44 ha, and such property holding was considerably larger than that of most of the richer Athenians (Hodkinson 2000: 384–5 and [Plato] *Alcibiades I* 122D). As in other Greek societies, the Spartans enjoyed a fragmented and almost certainly geographically scattered property portfolio; in other words the average 44 ha was probably made up of several properties (Hodkinson 2000: 121–2).

The reality of the economics of property holding, the potential pressures of population increase (and decrease), the limit of property ownership to citizens, and the possible restrictions on the property available provide the background not only for farms, farming and farmers but also for our picture of the landed economy. In the Athenian economy it is highly likely that not all workers on the land were the property-owners. The Spartan economy was built on the fact that the Spartan citizens relied on other people to work the land, notably the helots (Hodkinson 2000: 113–43).

The question of labour, particularly in Athenian agriculture, is still highly contentious (Finley 1981: 99–100). There are grounds for believing that slave labour must be envisaged for larger farms, fundamentally farms larger than the subsistence farm of around 5 ha. Much of the activity in ancient agriculture was labour intensive and subject to peaks of activity coinciding with times of greatest activity, such as the harvest, when timing can be critical (Halstead & Jones 1989: 49). For the subsistence farm, one model suggests that the household maximized the labour of family members, even relatives and possibly neighbours, rather than buying slaves; if slaves were bought, then they might have been kept and sold on depending on the economic circumstances of the household (Gallant 1991). Whether the subsistence farmers did or did not ordinarily own slaves is important in terms of the extent of slave ownership. But one must also factor in social expectation and values: it is likely that most households desired to own a slave or slaves (Osborne 1995; Jameson 2002: 170–2). Both Xenophon (*Oikonomikos* 3.4) and Lysias (5.3–5) suggest that slave ownership was expected. It was a reality for the richer members of society, without doubt for those of hoplite status/wealth levels and upwards ('hoplites' owning slaves: Thuc. 3.17.3–4; 7.75.5) and only the poorest members of society could not afford slaves (Lysias 24.6; Aristotle *Politics* 1323a5). For the rich, slaves were no doubt owned and employed widely in agriculture (Lysias 7.34; Xenophon *Oikonomikos* 12.3; 14.1–2; 15.9–10; [Aristotle] *Oikonomika* 1.6.5), and given the likelihood that this group dominated much of the cultivable land there is some reason to believe that the largest number of slaves were employed in either agriculture or the silver mines (Hypereides F 29 Jensen). No doubt for the rest of the numerically significant members of slave-owning society, slaves would have been used in a variety of ways, including some agricultural work.

The agricultural foundation of Greek society ensured that slaves were a fundamental economic fact. Agriculture was the most widespread activity and the most intensive demand on free and non-free labour in the diverse economies of Greece. Chios had a highly developed economy. The evidence of Chian amphoras suggests a peak of exports to Athens in the middle of the fifth century, and supports a view that the Chian economy flourished for many decades up to the point of the oligarchic revolt against the Athenians in 412 (Thuc. 8.24; Lawall 1998: 88–90). Chios was probably one of the most extensive slave-based economies in the Greek world (Jameson 1992: 142). When the Athenians arrived to put down the oligarchic revolt in 412, the large numbers of slaves on Chios rebelled against their owners and considerable damage was done to the rural economy, the basis of the society's wealth (Thuc. 8.40). The island's economy was specialized and produced large quantities of an exportable commodity, wine, that could be sold abroad. The foundation for the surplus was an agricultural economy that was almost certainly dependent on slave labour.

In a different way the Spartan economies depended on agriculture and non-free labour. For Spartiates relied on helots to work their estates on Spartan territory that included Lakonia and, until 370/69, Messene. The helots were probably the property of one particular Spartiate and worked his land. For the most part they were relatively stable and identified with the property that they worked (Hodkinson 2000: 119–21), which in some cases may have consisted of separate portions of land that belonged to different owners. It is clear that many helots may have worked the land belonging to a Spartiate property-holder (Xenophon *Hellenika* 3.3.5).

## Farmers and wealth

Agriculture was one foundation for the wealth of the elite in any Greek community. The Athenians enjoyed many benefits from their Empire in the fifth century, in particular the ownership of land abroad. When several Athenians, including Alkibiades, were tried and found guilty in the mutilation of the herms in Athens, their property was confiscated and sold. Inscribed fragments of the sales from the Eleusinion have survived. Adeimantos, no doubt one of the richest Athenians of his generation, had at least eight slaves sold and lost considerable revenue from his rented property (M&L 79.53–61 = Fornara 147D; M&L p. 247). He also lost two very valuable vineyards on Thasos: one including a slave, farm and house, storage jars and stored local wine (possibly 230 hectolitres), and another with 93 storage jars, pressing table and wine vat (Salviat 1986: 150–2). The first property may have been 8 to 10 ha in size, and it and the highly valuable harvest of Thasian wine would have provided considerable wealth for Adeimantos.

In Lakedaimonia, land was owned by citizens, inferiors (former citizens, *hypo-meiones*) and *perioikoi* (free, non-citizen habitants of Lakedaimonian territory). The Spartan citizen land-owner owned sufficient land to fulfil his mess obligations (*syssi-tion*) and supported the helots who worked it. The inferior could still own land but by definition not to maintain his full citizen status (Hodkinson 2000: 146 n. 15). *Eisphora* in Lakedaimonian territory was collected not only from Spartiates but also from *perioikoi* (Hodkinson 2000: 190), which suggests that in some cases this category included individuals with significant property holding (on dedication of votives by *perioikoi* and production of bronzes in their territory, Hodkinson 2000: 296).

The distribution of property among Spartiates became increasingly unbalanced in the Classical period. The declining number of Spartan citizens is suggested by the number of Spartans serving in the army and indicates a fall in those Spartans able to perform the mess duties that were required of those who enjoyed Spartan citizenship (Aristotle *Politics* 1271a26–36; Hodkinson 2000: 399–400). The fall in citizen numbers meant that the rich became richer, and almost certainly their wealth increased because they owned more and more land (Hodkinson 2000: 416). The Spartans suffered from a shortage of citizens (*oliganthropia*) that was already evident in the fifth century, and by the fourth century they were *de facto* a plutocracy. The loss of Messenia in 370/69 deprived the Spartans of perhaps as much as 60 per cent of their territory, resulting in significant losses particularly for the less wealthy Spartan land-owners. From 370 to the middle third century the fall continued from 1,000 to 700 Spartans (Aristotle *Politics* 1270a29–31; Plutarch *Agis* 5.4; Hodkinson 2000: 436–7), and only served to intensify the already disproportionate concentration of property ownership among the ever smaller Spartan élite.

## Farming a profit

It should now be clear that by the fifth and fourth centuries, it is no longer helpful to consider the agricultural economies of Classical Greeks in terms only of subsistence farmsteads. Individual wealth and the wealth of whole communities existed in many instances because of agricultural productivity. At the same time, some of those communities as a whole presented economic vulnerabilities, most famously at Athens, where grain imported from outside of Attika helped to feed the population. Athens was probably not unusual in its importation of grain, as the example of Teos shows. There (c. 470) it was forbidden for anyone to prevent the importing of grain by land or sea into the city, and the subsequent re-exportation of grain was banned. In each case the penalty was death for the transgressor and his family (M&L 30.A = Fornara 63.A lines 6–12).

### Spreading the risk on the farm

A variety of agricultural and productive practices were pursued in many regions of the Greek world to spread the risk of crop failure (Gallant 1991: ch. 3). So a typical farm might grow at least one or a combination of the four main crops, the Mediterranean quartet: cereals (typically wheat and barley), olives, pulses and vines. Many farmers throughout the Greek world practised polyculture: legumes, figs, honey, other tree-fruits were all part of this picture. Most farmers or land-holders, even in urban contexts, might have had some animals (typically pigs). Animal husbandry was of considerable importance and exploited land that was not always best suited to agriculture: land that was, sometimes particularly, suited to animal husbandry (Hodkinson 1988; 2000: 133, 151–2). But the simple desire to have a varied diet could also have figured in the practice of polyculture (see Plato *Republic* 369D, 371C, 372C–D for a varied diet). The Spartiates had to provide for their mess (*syssition*) a simple diet of barley meal, wine, cheese and figs that already requires a reasonably diverse agricultural economy: cereals, vines, figs and animals (sheep/goats) for the cheese. Indeed the sophisticated rural economy practised by the Spartans produced sufficient agricultural surplus to supply the messes, the helot population and a tidy surplus that brought considerable financial benefit to the Spartan land-owners (Hodkinson 2000: 133–5). Polyculture was also a natural consequence of the agricultural calendar, in which different crops needed sowing or harvesting at different moments in the year (see Isager & Skydsgaard 1992: 160–3, fig. 11.1).

But sometimes necessity restricted the diversity. Not all regions were suited to one or a number of crops (for olives: Brun 2003: 126) and some regions positively favoured certain forms of cultivation that saw, indeed, an intensive cultivation of specific crops. For instance, on Amorgos, as on several other Cycladic islands such as Delos, the cold northern winds prevented productive olive cultivation. Olives are absent from the lease of the land belonging to the cult of Zeus Temenites at Arkesine (*IG* 12.7 62 = Pouilloux 2003 no. 35; Brunet et al. 1998: 222–31). But in Asia Minor, the people of Klazomenai, for example, enjoyed a highly productive olive harvest and stored (in amphoras) a considerable surplus that at one time was envisaged as a means of raising money to buy in cereals in the face of a shortage of rain ([Aristotle] *Oikonomika* 2.2.16; for the amphoras, Döger 1986).

Land-ownership remained the essential (and most conservative) source of wealth in the Greek world largely because of the importance of agriculture. However, the development of urban centres dependent on their neighbouring territory also produced complex non-agricultural economies. Not everyone in the Greek world was either a farmer or a land-owner, and we now turn to craftsmen and other forms of non-agricultural production.

# 4   Non-Agricultural Production: Manufacturers and Materials

In many communities the realities of the distribution of property among the citizen population meant that some citizens owned little or no land. A significant proportion of Athenians owned only small plots or none at all (Foxhall 1992).

What economic activities did those without sufficient land or without any land pursue? Indeed, did land-ownership preclude the pursuit of other economic activities? In a survey of 'professions' that provided goods or services that were exchanged in the market-place at Athens, Harris (2002) listed 170 different occupations. Only a small proportion involves agricultural activities or animal husbandry; while the majority identify other forms of non-agricultural production (Harris 2002: 69) on which this section focuses. In a sophisticated urban centre such as Athens, one of the largest in the Greek world and certainly the best documented, such a concentration of professions says a great deal about the diversity of economic activity and the specialization of individuals active in the economies of the polis in contrast with smaller poleis (Xenophon *Kyroupaideia* 8.2.5).

Harris' survey indicates a variety of professions that some (citizens and non-citizens alike) might have pursued. The market-place was in fact frequented by all levels of society and was not only a place where the elite bought luxury commodities (Harris 2002: 78).

## Craft specialization

What is striking about the nature of the professions identified by Harris in the literary and epigraphical sources is their specificity. He underlines that in the Athenian and therefore certainly in Greek economies as a whole, there is an absence of vertical specialization. Athenian and Greek society display a high degree, therefore, of horizontal specialization. A considerable variety of occupations were required to provide the wide demands of services and products that society required or demanded. Vertical specialization is required to create a product that demands several different levels of operation and skills. In ancient Greece only a limited number of 'products' required such 'vertical specialization'. Temple building probably demanded the highest levels of craftsmanship (Harris 2002: 81), but other complex operations included the construction and maintenance of a navy and mining processes.

Minting silver coinage is, on the surface, a simple operation. For example, at Olynthos two houses are known in which individuals may have been producing counterfeit coins (Cahill 2002: 259–61). But coin production required a supply of metal (bronze or silver or exceptionally gold) and craftsmen to design and produce the coins. Athens, unlike many communities in the Greek world, relied on its own local supply of silver from the Laureion hills to strike the 'owls', the name given to the city's coins because of the image of the owl depicted on the obverse of the coins. The different levels of labour that led ultimately to the striking of these coins are worth considering in a survey of non-agricultural labour and are an example of vertical specialization.

## From spade to anvil – silver coins

The processes whereby silver was extracted from the ground and turned into silver coins involved many different stages of labour-intensive activities (Rihll 2001; for the installations Jones 1982): 15–16 kg of ore had to be extracted to produce a silver coin weighing 4 g (Rihll 2001: 129, table 6.1)! In the earliest stages dangerous work required the extraction of rock which contained the rich silver-bearing ores from the hills of south-east Attika. A large slave-labour force was required to cut the vertical shafts and horizontal galleries to reach the metalliferous ores, dig them out and bring them to the surface. There the extracted ore was ground down into small pieces and washed on specially constructed 'washing tables' using vast quantities of water, which was collected in huge cisterns cut into the ground which captured rain water. Slaves performed the grinding, washing and water-carrying processes. Furnaces were built to separate the silver from the silver-bearing minerals by cupellation, and combustion was required to reach temperatures between c. 810° and 950° C. This last procedure required a plentiful supply of combustible material and it is likely that Laureion's local wood supply was quickly exhausted. Furnaces have been found on the coast, located not only to keep the noxious fumes from the cupellation process away but also to facilitate access to supplies of combustible material. These processes all required labour input, supervision and financing by speculators ready to invest in the mining operations. Finally the silver found its way to the state Mint in the Athenian Agora where public slaves produced the coins.

The production of silver coins in Attika from the local silver made heavy demands on the economies of the region. The slave-labour forces needed feeding and maintaining and may have consumed 4,000 kg of food per day (Rihll 2001: 115). The processing of ores required specially designed and dedicated installations (washing tables). The furnaces consumed natural resources (timber and charcoal). The industry depended on people to finance the operations. Such a complex operation provided Athens with vast amounts of silver in the fifth and fourth centuries and many other by-products from the smelting processes (Rihll 2001: 130–2, 136). The high-quality silver from Laureion rendered the Athenian owl a coin with an exceptionally high purity of silver content. The wide circulation of these silver owls in the Classical period saw the later adoption of the Athenian weight standard in the Hellenistic period.

### Workshops and the use of slaves

Large-scale operations like the mines of Attika were relatively unusual. A small number of people made a great deal of profit from hiring out slaves: Nikias, the Athenian politician and general in the fifth century, hired out 1,000 slaves, a number which the lessor was obliged to maintain should slaves die (Xenophon *Poroi* 4.14). Xenophon in the middle of the fourth century urged that the state should emulate such individuals by itself leasing out publicly owned slaves to provide revenues for the polis (Xenophon *Poroi* 4.1–18 = Austin & Vidal-Naquet 1977: 94). Slave owning was fundamental not only to the agrarian economy but also to the household and especially workshops (*ergasteria*). One of the largest *ergasteria* belonged to a metic, Kephalos, who had a shield-making establishment which had 120 slaves (Lysias 12.19 (*Against Eratosthenes*)).

While an Athenian might have owned a property, both the citizen and metic might have leased a property (on leases of land and property, Osborne 1988). Any workshop might have been dedicated to producing marketable commodities. Citizens and metics or even slaves might typically have used slaves for a workforce. Although the Athenians did not distinguish the financial activities and assets of their workshops from their household, slaves were identified usually with a specific task. So the estate of Demosthenes' father included two workshops. One, a workshop he had received as security for money he had lent, produced furniture and used 20 slaves. A second was a knife factory which had 32 or 33 slaves among whom there was clearly some distinction, probably in craftsmanship, as the value of the slaves ranged to up to 300–60 *drachmai* from at least 180 *drachmai* (Demosthenes 27.9). A typically priced slave probably cost in the region of 150 to 250 *drachmai* (cf. the price of the slaves of the metic Kephisodoros, confiscated in 414, Austin & Vidal-Naquet 1977: 74, 75).

### Producers and markets

Production of goods and the movement (and sale) of agricultural surplus require markets in both the notional and physical senses. Polities did not all necessarily produce everything they needed or everything that people wanted, but were able to satisfy these needs and desires by importing products and produce. It is in this context that we must understand the notion of *autarkeia* (literally: 'self-sufficiency'), a term that has been much discussed because of the importance attached to it by several ancient writers (Bresson 2000: 116). The most notable among them was Aristotle, who considered that *autarkeia* was 'the goal and the very best thing' (Aristotle *Politics* 1253a1–2); in other words an aim and an ideal. It was to be achieved by the export of surplus and import of what one does not find in the polity (Aristotle *Politics* 1328b5–3 with Bresson 2000: 111–19). According to Thucydides (1.37.3), Kerkyra fulfils these conditions. Korinthian ambassadors address the Assembly at Athens before the outbreak of the Peloponnesian war and describe Kerkyra as 'a polis . . . that enjoys by its location *autarkeia*'. They suggest that the Kerkyreans rarely leave but force others to come to them. Thucydides (3.70) reveals that the island in fact produced wine. Amphoras that carried this product are known from archaeological contexts (Bresson 2000: 122–4). The island is the sort of place that exports its surplus and imports what it needs, an ideal which is achieved by Byzantion (according to Polybios 4.38.8–9). The relationship between produce and products and commerce is an essential one and requires further thought about trade.

# 5   Traders and Markets

The varied production of commodities in workshops and the range of specialized crops produced on estates in different regions of the Classical world suggest that the sale of marketable commodities and the 'market' were complex. The production of crops for sale and the manufacturing of products in workshops for consumption require markets and movement of goods. Transportation and spaces in which to sell products are prerequisites of markets.

### Local commodities and the domestic market(-place)

Local markets provided a real range for the sale of commodities. The cost of overland transport was not a prohibitive factor. Phainippos, an Athenian land-owner, was able to make 12 *drachmai* a day by keeping six mules busy carrying wood to Athens, and proves that moving commodities by road or simple track was a fundamental feature of local economies ([Demosthenes] 42.7). It is therefore no surprise to find both a donkey driver and two muleteers on the manumission lists of fourth-century Athens (Harris 2002: 94).

## Market movers

The movement of goods by land was therefore an essential feature of most Greek cities, particularly those dependent on harbours. The movement of commodities by road from Piraeus to the city centre of Athens was a sine qua non of the city's survival. A law codifying the sale of the grain tax in 374 states explicitly that tax-farmers are to move grain (taxed in kind) from the harbour to the grain depot in the city of Athens at their own cost (Stroud 1998: 4, lines 12–15, 50–1). A recently published inscription from Bulgaria concerns the commercial relations in Thrace at Pistiros, an *emporion* where Thasians numbered among the favoured merchants. The decree of c. 359 grants exemption from taxes on the roads both from Pistiros to Maroneia and other *emporia* and also in the other direction (Velkov & Domaradzka 1994). The movement of commodities was fundamental to economies on both a local and a regional scale. Such movements also generated opportunities for communities both to extract revenues by taxing such movements into and out of commercial areas, as is clear at Pistiros, and ultimately to extract tax on the sale of commodities.

Extensive local road networks existed and facilitated the movement of commodities into, out of, and probably within regions throughout Greece. Arkadia, a mountainous region made up of several individual political communities (poleis), had an extensive network of roads (Pikkoulas 1999: 253–4; 305–9). Although there is not much evidence for trade between Arkadian communities, the evidence for the large movement of various commodities both into and out of the region as a whole suggests that there was considerable local and intra-regional movement of commodities facilitated by the road network (Roy 1999: 338–40).

## Intra- and inter-regional movement of commodities

Communication and movements within a region will have thrived, although they are not always apparent in the body of evidence. Phainippos' business moving wood by road to Athens is an example of this localized intra-regional trade. More typical is evidence for regional and especially long-distance commodity movements. In Aristophanes' *Acharnians* (719–22) Dikaiopolis wants to set up his own personal market so that all the Peloponnesians, Megarians and Boiotians have the right to trade with him. Such inter-regional trading movements were certainly disrupted in the Peloponnesian war. The shortage of Boiotian eels from Lake Kopaïs may have been a humorous reference but suggests that some desirable commodities were more difficult to procure in 425 (Aristophanes *Acharnians* 881–90).

Even if intra-regional trade was the most basic economic interaction within Greek communities, and the foundation of Greek economies, it is this inter-regional and especially maritime trade between regions over greater distances that has attracted most attention among scholars. Important commodities like grain were moved over considerable distances and could be important to a community's provision of food, as was probably the case for the fifty-one recipients of grain from Kyrene around 330 to

326 (R&O 96). Long-distance inter-regional trade allowed luxury or unusual commodities to find their way into many regions of the Mediterranean world and beyond.

## The infrastructure of maritime trade

Trade in the Mediterranean world demanded that commodities were moved by sea
and therefore required not only numerous levels of infrastructure but also different
agencies to sustain the infrastructure. Ships moving long distances required markets
for selling their cargo, harbours and adequate space for unloading it, and places to
store and then to sell the cargo.

However, traders in the Classical period could choose between several potential
markets, and so the creation of attractive and well-regulated 'market-places' was one
way to draw in such merchants. Communities developed all kinds of ways not only to
'encourage' traders to transport commodities to their market but to attract particular
goods. Among important factors for a trader was the ability to find a good market
where another cargo to fill the ship for the next leg of the voyage could be secured.
Athens in the Classical period provided these opportunities, as no doubt did several
other important emporia like Byzantion, Rhodes and Korinth. Emporia typically
enjoyed a good coastal location (Casevitz 1993: 20) but this was not always the
case (Pistiros, Thrace).

A Demosthenic speech records the loan of money by an Athenian and a Euboian to
two men from Phaselis for a maritime trading trip ([Demosthenes] 35.10–13). One
possible itinerary for the expedition was to take in the Thracian poleis of Mende or
Skione (on Pallene, the western finger of the Chalkidike peninsula) and then the
Bosporos on the northern coast of the Black Sea before returning to Athens. At
Mende or Skione the traders would probably buy up wine. In the Bosporos one can
assume that they were then required to return to Athens with grain, because Athenians and metics at Athens could only make loans that transported specific commodities including grain back to Athens ([Demosthenes] 35.51 = Austin & Vidal-Naquet
1977: 82).

## Financing maritime trade

Such trading expeditions were possible not only because of infrastructure but also
because individuals were ready to risk financing such operations for the profit that
could be gained (Cohen 1992). Maritime expeditions were risky but potentially
lucrative (Lysias 22 (*Against the Corndealers*) = Austin & Vidal-Naquet 1977: 84).
Athens was an attractive commercial centre where traders could find not only many
commodities for subsequent outward cargoes (Isokrates 4.42) but also a substantial
financial sector and legal system (Demosthenes 33.1–2) to protect such investments.
The same characteristics are found also in Thasos, where in the fourth century
monthly trials offered similar forms of commercial protection for traders (Salviat
1958). Personal contacts, trust and knowledge were a crucial factor in such operations (Isokrates 17.6), and traders could use such knowledge in financing operations
(Demosthenes 33.4–5). By the fourth century, the evidence for maritime trade shows
a level of sophistication in financing, with the raising of loans from individual bankers
and competition between potential markets.

## Risks at sea

Such sophistication marks a process that had been longstanding. Overseas trade had thrived throughout the Archaic period (Plutarch *Solon* 2.3–3.1) and by the Classical era was an everyday feature of most Greek economies (cf. Thuc. 1.5–19, who develops a maritime theme in his summary of Greek history). Moving by sea continued to be as dangerous as before, given the vulnerabilities of shipping to natural dangers. As potentially disruptive were pirates, but one should not necessarily think of such threats as marauding, eyepatch-wearing mavericks (De Souza 1999), for piracy was often a well-organized, even institutionalized mode of economic activity, as it has been in later periods of history (Ferguson 2003: 1–12: sixteenth- and seventeenth-century England). Some states practised regularly forced diversions of shipping and making passing ships unload their goods at their markets. The people of Byzantion, Chalkedon and Kyzikos redirected grain ships in the late 360s when their local food supplies were not adequate (Demosthenes 50.6, 17). In some instances communities formalized such arrangements; piracy (and plunder by land) had become institutionalized, as the fifth-century agreement between Knossos and Tylissos on Crete reveals (M&L 44.B 2–14) and Demosthenes explains in the fourth century (Demosthenes 8. 24–8; Garnsey 1988: 142–4).

## Markets and suppliers

Many of the trading contacts between Greece and, for example, the peripheries of the Greek world had already been established in the Archaic period: Aigina and the Peloponnese were receiving grain from the Black Sea in the early fifth century (Hdt. 7.147 = Austin & Vidal-Naquet 1977: 80). But clearly there were shifts in these patterns. Demosthenes, a major intermediary between the Athenian consumers and the Bosporan kings, claims in the mid-fourth century that Athens imports more grain from the Bosporos than from all its other sources of grain put together (Demosthenes 20.31–3 = Austin & Vidal-Naquet 1977: 81). In terms of such inter-regional trade, some cities and regions were renowned for their specialized commodities. Grain was one of the most important commodities coming from the Black Sea, in particular the Bosporos; timber was coming from Macedonia and Thrace (Xenophon *Hellenika* 6.1.11; Theophrastos *Historia Plantarum* 4.5.5); and wine was shipped in from numerous places in and around the Aegean – for example, Mende, Skione, Thasos, Kos, Chios.

## Supplying a demand

The movement of commodities can not only supply but also stimulate demands. One index of the diffusion of Greek culture is the symposium. At a typical Greek symposium, imported commodities might have included perfumes, cheeses, honey and eels as well as good wine such as that from Mende or Thasos (Menander F 224 Kassel & Austin). And in many communities the diffusion of the symposium not only meant the consumption of good wine but also required the use of ceramics, bowls and cups and other pieces of table ware to complete the ideal Greek banquet. Here perhaps we can see some of the cultural associations that can be attached to trade. The theme is worth pursuing and one can follow the trail left by the table ware. Ceramics became popular for a variety of reasons: quality, desirability, fashion, local tastes, ease of supply, low cost – in short, marketability. It is dangerous to privilege any one, but cultural choices will have been of considerable importance. It is useful to look at ceramics as an indicator of such choices amid the realities of commerce in the Greek world. The commercial importance of Athens as a magnet for maritime trade and the quality of its ceramics as a potential outward cargo-filler meant that Athenian pottery was widely traded throughout the Mediterranean world. The diffusion of Greek culture may also have helped this process. Archaeological evidence confirms the wide sale of Athenian pottery and suggests differences not only in 'markets' but also in producers and suppliers.

## The producers

Ceramic workshops at Athens have been recognized by the traces of kilns and other ceramic material, such as unfinished or misfired pieces or supports for firing the ceramics or moulds for terracottas. The evidence suggests that the workshops in rural Attika supplied pottery for domestic consumption while those workshops in and immediately around the urban centre of Athens produced ceramics, especially those of higher quality, for both local markets (e.g., Thorikos) and those beyond Attika (Jubier-Galinier et al. 2003: 39–40; Monaco 2000; cf. Blondé 2000: 273 n. 9).

Coarse ware and cooking ware may well have been bought on a more localized basis from nearby workshops, as evidence in Attika (Jubier-Galinier et al. 2003: 38) and Thasos suggests (Blondé & Picon 2000). Pottery production is a relatively simple technique and required little vertical specialization in terms of its labour. The diffusion of ceramics illustrates well both the intra- and inter-regional nature of trade and production. It is, however, less easy to establish if the value (price) of ceramics moved significantly depending on their ultimate destination.

The movement of commodities over long distances in ships required traders to fill their ships with a variety of marketable products. Pottery such as black-glazed ware from Athens was probably a useful product in this respect and was relatively cheap. When found in shipwrecks it is clearly being carried as part of a much larger cargo (Gill 1991). The presence of ceramics and amphoras also suggests something of the movements of traders. A ship carrying pottery and other commodities to one destination would certainly carry something back for the return or next lap of the voyage. The numerous movements of trading ships into Athens carrying grain in the fourth century meant that there was a subsequent exportation of commodities out of Attika. It is clear that here in the fourth century, for example, the pottery workshops flourished and they were providing potential return cargoes for commercial expeditions arriving in Piraeus. The environment was a good one, for grain was coming to Athens from a variety of distant markets and the Piraeus was a huge international commercial centre. The wide diffusion of Athenian ceramics almost certainly reflects the large-scale international movement of commerce into Athens and Piraeus.

## Distant markets and . . .

One particular phenomenon is the marked increase of Athenian pottery in the western Mediterranean. Phoenician traders sold Attic pottery on the Atlantic coast of Africa ([Skylax] 112, writing around the middle of the fourth century). Particular pottery shapes are found in greater quantities than others. For instance, in Spain and southern France, Athenian black-glazed tableware was successful (Spain: Principal-Ponce 2000: 220–3; fig. 4; France: Py & Sabattini 2000: 183 fig. 14). In both regions Attic fine black-glazed pottery seems to have increased in circulation from the fifth to the fourth centuries (Sanmartí Grego 2000: 238–9; Ugolini 2000: 202 fig. 2).

The appearance of Attic black-glazed ware from Carthage in North Africa in the form of circular *kernos* with seven circular depressions, known only here and in the El Sec shipwreck, suggests that Athenian workshops had produced pottery dedicated to the Punic market (Morel 2000: 263). Indeed Carthage may well have operated as a point from which Attic pottery was re-exported further west. It was understood to be a wealthy city (Thuc. 6.34.2) by the time of the Peloponnesian war and Athens certainly enjoyed at least sporadic contacts with Carthaginians on the political level in the fifth and fourth centuries (M&L 94 = Fornara 165). The El Sec shipwreck off the south-west coast of Majorca illustrates some aspects of trade in the western Mediterranean around the middle of the fourth century (date: Koehler in: Rouillard & Villanueva-Puig 1989: 132). The excavation of the wreck recovered a high concentration of Attic pottery: 358 black-glazed Attic vessels, 100 fragments of Attic red figure ware (*kraters, kylikes, skyphoi*), among a diverse cargo the bulk of which consisted of 474 amphoras. Around 30 per cent of these had come from Samos (Rouillard & Villanueva-Puig 1989: 21–116).

## ... How the West was one

The (re-)distribution of Athenian pottery in the fourth century in the western Mediterranean shows the complexity of the economies of the Classical Greece. Commodities were traded well beyond the confines of the 'Greek world' and almost certainly re-exported. The El Sec wreck carried a significant quantity of Punic coarse ware and bronze ware of Italo-Etruscan origin, as well as large quantities of Attic pottery and amphoras of Greek (especially Samian) origins (presumably carrying wine). The El Sec wreck was almost certainly a Punic vessel, a conclusion that can be drawn from the nature of the commodities and the mixture of Greek and Punic graffiti on some vases (Rouillard & Villanueva-Puig 1989: 117–30).

The risk-economies of maritime trade created an ascending spiral of commodity movements. The movement of commodities encouraged the movement of more commodities. A varied cargo made the commercial success of a cargo much more likely, but fundamentally allowed merchants to maximize the capacity of the ship (Gill 1991: 46 table C, on the ratio between volume and value of various commodities). Much pottery may not have been of great intrinsic cost at its point of manufacture, but it was a useful part of a merchant's cargo in a commercial voyage. It is likely that such pottery increased in value at the point of its final sale, but it is difficult to establish if this was in fact the case and if so to what extent its sale-price increased.

## Wine sales

Ceramic evidence also echoes the movement of other commodities, for amphoras, a coarse-ware container carrying mostly wines, survive in significant numbers (e.g., the

El Sec shipwreck). They could of course be re-used, typically as water-containers, and, on at least one occasion, were even employed for military purposes when the Phokians filled concealed pits with amphoras to trap enemy cavalry (Hdt. 8.28).

Pieces of amphoras from Chios are likely to indicate the circulation or sale of the island's wine. It not easy to explain changes in the circulation of the material, but economic (competition or stronger demand from other markets) and political factors are likely to have affected markets. Chian amphoras no longer circulate in the western Mediterranean after c. 525. In the east, for example at Gordion in Phrygia, they made up as much as 30 per cent of imported amphoras up to 475 and 50 per cent between 475 and c. 425, and fell to 5 per cent in 420–400. In the fifth century at Gordion imported ceramics declined steadily, reflecting changes in the market, but a relatively strong Chian element persisted among the imports. In the same period Chios benefited from the rise in the Athenian market (Lawall 1998: 88–9, fig. 5.2), where Chian wine seems to have been imported in increasingly greater quantities.

## Squeezing the markets: pots, grain and grapes on Thasos

The circulation of ceramics probably affected production patterns on a local level. The black-glaze ceramics of fourth-century Athens, for example, were extremely popular on Thasos. Excavations of a public well from the second and third quarters of the fourth century have revealed that the majority of the fine ware consisted of imported black-glaze Athenian vessels (Blondé 2000: 274–5). The Thasian workshops produced black-glazed ware, but archaeology reveals that the domestic market preferred imported Attic ware. Certainly the high quality and/or good value of Attic pottery were potential factors in its popularity on Thasos. But one should not exclude the possibility that incoming trading vessels had been exporting the highly desirable local wine to a major centre of consumption such as Athens and on their return leg back to the island carried a variety of products including plenty of Attic black-glaze pottery.

Thasos was a major trading centre. Its celebrated wine (Xenophon *Symposion* 4.40) enjoyed considerable success throughout the Greek world and notably in the Black Sea region from the second half of the fifth century (Bouzek 1989: 257; Salviat 1986: 189–90, fig. 2; Lazarov 1986: 404; [Demosthenes] 35.35). On an island rich in vines and mines, with specialized economies, it would not be surprising that some commodities such as grain were imported to supplement domestic or regional production, and the Black Sea was one likely source.

The local economies of many Greek cities were often supplemented by imported commodities such as grain from other regional sources. Agriculture was normally vulnerable to shortfalls in production such as, and in particular, that of wheat-grain. Some communities may have specialized in commodities, for example wine on Thasos and olives at Klazomenai, making them more dependent on imported grain but able to use the success of their specialized products to exploit the markets and so buy in the commodities that were required.

Short-term losses in harvest could result from climatic extremes. Too much cold or not enough rain or too much rain at the wrong times of the year could reduce the harvest just as they continue to do in the twenty-first century. In addition warfare could cause major disruption to the often time-critical operations such as harvesting and sowing (Hanson 1998). Delays in such fundamental tasks could also reduce production. The Classical period was no different from any other period of history. The food supply was a critical factor, and given the potential market it is no surprise to see the development of economies that supplied critical commodities such as grain. Some cities more than others relied on imported grain. Athens (Demosthenes 20.31; Whitby 1998: 118–19) imported (and re-exported) grain more than other cities, while cities such as Syracuse were able to supply their needs from the local harvests (Thuc. 6.20.4).

Given the variety of markets, it is no surprise that traders or buyers might have sought out markets or attempted schemes that could fetch a higher price for their shipment of grain (Demosthenes 56.8–10; Lysias 22). Even local grain prices must have varied (cf. Aristophanes *Acharnians* 758–9). Moreover, given the complexities of such market operations, cities resorted to policies and legislation which were designed to counteract the forces of what can only be described as profit maximization. Agricultural production, manufacturing and the markets all operated in contexts that involved institutions that were elements in the diverse economies of the polis.

# 6   Polis Economies and Institutions

Throughout this chapter the economic realities have involved not only the agents of the economies – individuals, the farmers, the manufacturers and the traders – but also the civic structures (poleis or kingdoms) in which for the most part these individuals operated. The politics of the Greek world and civic institutions provide another layer of understanding the complex dynamics of the Greek economies. Fundamental concerns of several institutions in most Greek polities were various aspects of direct or indirect economic significance. After considering examples of such institutions, a brief survey will be offered of money and coinage and weights and measures.

## *Institutions*

The ideal politician should be concerned with matters that have economic significance. The defence of the countryside essentially prevented the removal of produce (and people) from the territory of a polity. It was equally important to understand how long the grain harvest would support the people (Xenophon *Memorabilia* 3.5–6; cf. Aristotle *Rhetoric* 1359b–60a). By and large such fundamentally economic concerns were as relevant for Athenian politicians as they were for most leaders in the Greek world, and beyond. Defence of the territory was connected with the economies of the polis and especially its viability, its food supply: few cities were able to survive without their dependent territory.

A rural hinterland, the countryside, is virtually a distinguishing feature of the polis (Hansen 1998: 53–6) and its defence is almost a prerequisite of political concerns, one of the reasons why Perikles' apparent abandonment of Attika in the opening years of the Peloponnesian war might have received such lukewarm support (on this strategy Spence 1990). When the territory failed to provide an adequate food supply for the local population – citizens, foreigners and slaves – several interventions were possible.

Communities developed sophisticated and multi-faceted strategies to cope with this perennial vulnerability. At Athens the defence of the countryside and the food supply were permanent items on the agenda for the principal meeting of the Assembly held every month ([Aristotle] *Ath. Pol.* 43.4). Most of the other fixed items – confirmation that outgoing magistrates have served well when in office, the accounting of confiscated property, the confirmation of inheritance of properties and cases of inheritance involving childless daughters (*epikleros* in Athens, Karabélias 2002) – have some rapport with economic concerns, except for the presentation of cases of high treason. These agenda items confirm that the ideal politician outlined by both Xenophon and Aristotle was an ideal that was in touch with the real needs of the community.

Some other interventions in economic problems, not only the food supply, are worth reviewing. In the supply of grain to the city, both the external producers and those involved in moving and selling commodities were not necessarily under the control of a polis, unlike the community's markets, harbours, and to some extent the citizens and financial transactions that they conducted within the controlled space. Not only were there restrictions on the destination or sale of imported grain but loans for maritime commercial expeditions had to be used to import specific crops, and, probably in the fourth century, the Athenians started to appoint a 'grain buyer' (*sitones*) whose role seems to have been to secure grain purchases from foreign suppliers. Famously Demosthenes served as a *sitones* in 338 and no doubt was able to exploit his relationship with the Spartokid kings (Develin 1989: 344).

## *Magistracies*

In several ways, the institutions of the polis oversaw organization and matters of major economic importance. Institutions were created often to respond to economic concerns. Needless to say at Athens, as in many cities, numerous magistrates had responsibilities which involved the economies. Many were involved directly with the administration of markets. The market officials (*agoranomoi*) made sure that all commodities and goods sold were of high quality; the *sitophylakes* (grain market supervisors) made sure that unground corn was sold at a just price and that ground barley was sold at a weight determined by them and at a price that related to wheat, and presided over cases involving offences in the grain market; and the inspectors of the *emporion* (*epimeletai tou emporiou*) supervised the *emporia* in Piraeus and made sure that two-thirds of grain imported by sea was brought to the grain markets ([Aristotle] *Ath Pol.* 51.4 = Austin & Vidal-Naquet 1977: 89; Harding 45). Several other officials performed functions which had economic ramifications. *Astynomoi* at Athens made sure the dung collectors (*koprologoi*) kept the streets clean and free of human excrement by removing human and animal waste at least 1.8 km away from the city walls – where it was presumably used to fertilize the surrounding fields ([Aristotle] *Ath. Pol.* 50.2; Owens 1983). The *astynomoi* were also responsible in fourth-century Athens for submitting offences concerning illegal movements of ruddle, a valuable commodity with waterproofing properties used particularly in construction and ship-building, which was exported from the island of Keos (R&O 40 = Austin & Vidal-Naquet 1977: 86). In many other cities, especially later in the Hellenistic period, they had much wider duties often linked to commerce.

## Taxes and revenues

Greek polities were not only concerned with administrating markets and running the economies as much as they could to the benefit of the traders and buyers, they were also exploiting the economies to support the polity, usually in the form of taxes. The finances of Greek polities are sometimes difficult to detail but we can gain some understanding of how they operated. Indirect taxation (e.g., sales taxes), recurrent taxes (e.g., metic tax) and ad hoc raising of revenues (e.g., in some polities, *eisphora*) helped generate money which served as the financial income of a polity.

*Eisphora* was a tax on property and probably equates with one form of the first level of revenues indicated in the fourth-century treatise on east Mediterranean economies. For in his analysis of the four forms of ancient economies, the author of the *Oikonomika* ([Aristotle] 1346b5–8) distinguishes four majors forms of revenue in the polis economy. These are income derived from private property in the territory of the polis, revenues from centres of commerce (*emporia*), transit tolls, and finally recurrent taxes (farmed typically on an annual basis).

At Athens *eisphora* was first mentioned by Thucydides in 428 (Thuc. 3.19) to finance military activities and was paid by all those who owned or leased property assessed for payment and organized according to *deme* ([Demosthenes] 50.8). It existed in other communities such as the Boiotian Confederacy as a regular tax (*Hellenika Oxyrhynchia* 19.4). According to sources an assessment valued the property in Athens and Attika in the fourth century at 5,750 or 6,000 talents (Polybios 2.62.7; Demosthenes 14.19). There the *eisphora* was raised on an ad hoc basis and there were originally restrictions on its introduction (M&L 58.B lines 12–19 = Fornara 119). Both citizens and metics were therefore liable for *eisphora*, which became another service (*leitourgia* or 'liturgy') to the community that an individual could point to as worth mentioning among completed civic obligations (Lysias 12.20).

Liturgies were one way in which polities such as Athens 'taxed' its wealthiest members. The richest Athenians (and metics) were required not only to pay *eisphora* but also to perform other services. These included the financing and training of choruses for agonistic festivals such as the Dionysia (Wilson 2000). The winner of the choral events (the men's and boys' dithyramb) contested between all the Athenian tribes was entitled to set up a monument supporting the tripod that was awarded to the *choregos* for the victory (the Lysikrates monument set up in 335/4 in Athens is an example). Another service was the fitting out of a warship (trireme) – the trierarchy. The trierarch might have to pay for the crew, which could be very costly (Gabrielsen 1994). The liturgies were performed by members of the wealthiest families and they can be frequently identified with known politicians, magistrates and generals (Davies 1971; 1981). In most Greek communities, the wealthiest members performed many important services for the state; in an oligarchy, the principle of the political structure was that the wealthiest should also have the most power.

## Taxation

Let us return to other forms of revenue. Taxes on various sales in the markets, on purchases at auctions, on fees for public sales, all brought in money for the polity. Transit taxes brought in revenues on the movement of traders through ports. At

Chalkedon (opposite Byzantion) in 410/9 the Athenians established a station where they could charge 10 per cent transit duties on movements out of the Black Sea (Xenophon *Hellenika* 1.1.20).

Typically taxes were 'farmed' out to the highest bidders ([Aristotle] *Ath. Pol.* 47.2), meaning that individuals made bids to purchase the right to collect the tax, and if successful typically gave the state a down-payment of the sum bid, providing guarantors to pay the total sum. The successful bidder would collect the tax and make payments to the polis at dictated intervals: in the fourth century the 2 per cent tax (the *pentakoste*) that was collected was deposited every month ([Demosthenes] 50.27), but payments every prytany, three times a year and a one-off annual payment are also known ([Aristotle] *Ath. Pol.* 47.3). It was in the interests of the successful bidder(s) to collect more than he or they had paid. So Agyrrhios in c. 402/1 led a successful bid at Athens to collect the 2 per cent tax for 30 talents, and subsequently made a 3 talent profit (Andokides 1.133–4).

Taxes in kind are also known. At Athens a grain tax was raised in the form of an $8\frac{1}{3}$ tax on the islands of Lemnos, Imbros and Skyros and a separate 2 per cent tax in grain. The law establishing the tax was proposed in 374/3 by the wealthy and canny Agyrrhios (Stroud 1998: 27–39 on Athenian taxation). There is no doubt that this law was designed to secure the Athenians a reserve of affordable grain from three relatively rich sources of cereal crops (Garnsey 1988: 98, 101–2). It also provided security late in the agricultural year, outside of the sailing season in February/March, when grain prices may also have been rising (Stroud 1998: 73). The law probably offered the successful tax bidders opportunities to collect extra grain, assuming the harvest was a good one, which they could sell on.

## Income and controlled civic space

The institutions that organized and regulated economic activities in the polis operated within a spatial context too. The physical space where commerce took place, the Agora, and by extension the market in the abstract sense, was controlled by the community and these institutions. The existence and success of the Agora or *emporia* and therefore a community's 'markets' in the abstract sense was in essence a reflection of and extension of a polity's institutions. Another extension of a polity's control over commercial areas is their imposition of weights and measures and coinage.

## Coinage

The development of coinage in the Greek world in the Archaic period had already witnessed the adoption of small denominations for lower-cost transactions (Kim 2002). In 426 Aristophanes makes a joke in the *Wasps* (791) over the confusion of small silver obols and fish scales, suggesting the size and widespread use of coins. Clearly people were using coins for all levels of transaction throughout the Classical period. At Olynthos low-value bronze coins are found all over the excavated city (Cahill 2002: 266–9).

Coinage by the Classical period was a familiar feature of many Greek economies, but communities adopted different weight standards. For example, an Athenian silver tetradrachm (4 *drachmai*) weighed 17.2 g, whereas an Aiginetan *stater* (a didrachm, i.e., two *drachmai*) weighed 12.2 g. The Aiginetan *drachma* therefore weighed more in terms of silver content than the Athenian *drachma*. Differences in rates of exchange are suggested by the sources (Demosthenes 50.30). For example, it cost 28 *drachmai* to buy a *stater* in the Bosporos on the north coast of the Black Sea, compared to 21 *drachmai* at Athens (Cohen 1992: 150 n. 166). An individual may well have held coinage in different forms: Lysias held in a chest in his house 3 talents of (probably) Athenian silver, 400 Kyzikene staters and 100 Persian darics (*dareikoi*) (Lysias 12.11; Cohen 1992: 150). In addition to differences in standards, the purity of the precious metal content also varied. Some coinage became particularly widely accepted, probably because of the volumes in which it was produced and its intrinsic quality. These factors apply to the Athenian silver coinage of the Classical period and the fact that Philip II adopted this standard for his coinage.

Coinage was an essential feature of commerce and civic life. Coinage was required to pay mercenaries (the monies paid out in Athens during the Peloponnesian war, M&L 72 = Fornara 134) and finance most civic projects, such as paying for labour in construction (e.g., the Erechtheion at Athens, Austin & Vidal-Naquet 1977: 71; Salmon 2001). In some polities the domestic coinage enjoyed circulation only on a local level. For example, the Thasian coinage in the fourth century did not seem to enjoy a wide circulation (Picard 1994). The different standards and issuers of coinage clearly did not prevent commerce. In fact there was no real common Greek coinage until the silver tetradrachms of Alexander the Great began to dominate and become very widely accepted. Significantly, Alexander's coinage adopted the same weight for its tetradrachm as was being used by Athens for her issues.

The role that money played in Greek economies is illustrated in 364 when the Athenian general Timotheos was involved in the Olynthian campaign but ran out of finances. His troops needed to purchase food and supplies from merchants who were waiting to sell their goods. As a temporary measure, Timotheos minted an emergency coinage of small-denomination bronze coins, some examples of which have been found near Olynthos (Robinson & Price 1967). With this coinage, Timotheos' men could buy goods, the traders could purchase local goods and booty, and any bronze money they had left over could be exchanged with Timotheos for silver coins which he was expecting to be able to have later ([Aristotle] *Oikonomika* 2.2.23 = Austin & Vidal-Naquet 1977: 89.B; cf. Polyainos *Strategemata* 3.10.1). Coins had become an essential feature of the economy, but their value was essentially linked to the real metal content of the coinage.

The control of market-places and its regulation by institutions and laws was closely associated with coinage, as the decree concerning the importation of foreign coins at Olbia in the fourth century shows (Austin & Vidal-Naquet 1977: 99). The same interest in control and the provision of a good economic environment attractive to merchants is probably at the heart of the similar controls on weights and measures.

## Weights and measures

At Athens the *metronomoi* inspected weights and measures and made sure that all those selling goods used official ones ([Aristotle] *Ath. Pol.* 52 = Austin & Vidal-Naquet 1977: 89). The standardization of measures and the scrutiny of such procedures is well illustrated in the grain tax law of 374/3 at Athens. The grain brought by the tax collectors from Lemnos, Imbros and Skyros to the Agora is to be measured in accordance with the same methods that other traders have to follow (Stroud 1998: 56–61). It is quite likely that Thasos had standard measures to regulate its important wine 'industry', where an *amphoreus* was probably a vessel of around 20 l. The late fifth-century law regulating the wine sales seems to prevent the use of larger vessels in the selling of wine (Salviat 1986: 176–7 = *IG* 12 suppl. 347). Official measures, identifiable by the word *demosion* (or its abbreviation *de*), and weights have been found in the Agora (Lang & Crosby 1964). Official measures are also found in other commercial areas of Attika such as Vouliagmeni (bronze and lead weights: Stavro-poullou 1938).

One of the more controversial fifth-century documents is the so-called Athenian 'Standards' decree, an inscription made up of fragments of copies found in six different member-cities of the Empire (M&L 45 = Fornara 97). The decree realizes the well established association of weights, measures and coinage as three connected elements of some significance for commercial transactions ([Aristotle] *Ath. Pol.* 10). A new theory suggests that the Athenians sought to facilitate the collection of commercial revenues by harmonizing the weights, measures and coinage used in the Empire following the imposition in 413 of a 5 per cent tax on goods moved by sea, which replaced the collection of tribute (Thuc. 7.28.3–4; Kallet 2001: 205–26). The control of the Empire brought huge revenues to the Athenian polis and its economic power financed many of the buildings that remain today on the Akropolis, a demonstration of the connections between wealth and power and economics and politics.

# 7   The Realities of Economic Power in Classical Greece

In the history of Classical Greece two political entities present arguably the most fascinating and important economies respectively: Athens in the fifth and fourth centuries and Macedon in the fourth century. Although the evidence for the latter is sparse, discovery of inscriptions can add new information (Athens: Stroud 1998; Macedon: Missitzis 1985; *SEG* 34 664) and archaeology advances understanding of the rural economies of both regions (Attika: Steinhauer 2001; Macedonia: Adam-Veleni et al. 2003). But one of the greatest developments of the fourth century is the rise of Macedonia, a growth in power that was to shape the history not only of the Greek world but of the Persian Empire and beyond, heralding what since the nineteenth century has been known as the Hellenistic Age.

Economic might was of considerable importance to both Athens and Macedon as imperial powers. In the Classical period Athenian revenues collapsed with the loss of the Empire. From the heights of 1,000 talents in revenue in the fifth century (Xenophon *Anabasis* 7.1.27), of which probably 600 talents came from the tribute of the subject allies (Thuc. 2.13), Athens in the mid-fourth century had to exist with 130 talents a year, but increased annual revenues to 400 talents by c. 340 (Demosthenes 8.37–8 (*Fourth Philippic*)). The figures may not be exactly right but the degree of change seems appropriate to the city's financial capacity. Macedonia on the other hand enjoyed far greater resources (Billows 1995: 1–20; Le Rider 2003). In the mid-fourth century, Philip II used the revenues from the mines around Philippoi to finance his operations (Diodoros 16.8.6–7). The difference in the changing fortunes of Athens and Macedon in this period not only reflects the respective extent of their resources but offers a useful parallel to the central role of the economies in modern history and Empire building (Ferguson 2001; 2003).

Any understanding of the development of the history of the fifth and fourth century must take into account the economic strengths of the major polities. These strengths are determined by the resources that communities could exploit: the land, commodities such as timber, grain, vines, and natural resources such as silver. Political institutions developed to administer and care for many aspects of these economies. But underlying these high-level features were the people who drove the economic systems: farmers, workers, citizens, slaves and foreigners. Owners of land and workers of land; the craftsmen producing goods for sale; the merchants carrying those goods to local and distant markets by road and sea; all these activities fell in some way or other under the controls of polities that extracted revenues from the production of crops and goods and the movement and sale of commodities, and redirected the incomes in the political economies. These then were the economies of the Classical Greek world. Such economies were sophisticated and were considered as important factors that lay at the heart of the institutions of ancient Greek communities and their social and political history.

# Further reading

Students should start with the revised edition of *The ancient economy* (Finley [2]1999) and Morris's excellent introduction to the debates in response to Finley's work. Cartledge (1998) and Andreau (2002) show how thinking on the ancient economy has evolved since Finley and give important indications of future directions. Davies (1998) is a more concrete example of where one approach is leading and can be contrasted with more culturally focused studies of Greek economies (e.g., von Reden 1995; 2002; Kurke 1999; 2002).

Descat (2001; 2004) (in French) offer the best overviews of the Classical economies in the fifth and fourth centuries respectively. Other summaries worth consulting include Davies (1992) (fifth century) and Austin (1994) (fourth century). Austin & Vidal-Naquet (1977) is still the best collection of sources; Meijer & van Nijf (1992) is useful for trade but not limited to Classical Greece.

Several books cover various themes of the ancient economy although they do not focus exclusively on the Classical era. Osborne (1987; 1991) offer excellent studies of the economic interactions between city and countryside. For the role of wealth and the integrated economies of a complex society, see Hodkinson (2000) on Sparta. Collections of useful essays can be found in Cartledge, Cohen & Foxhall (2002); Mattingly & Salmon (2001); and Meadows & Shipton (2001). Scheidel & von Reden (2002) brings together a selection of useful articles published before in different books and academic journals. A new assessment of ancient economies is being prepared by an international team of academics under the direction of Ian Morris, *The Cambridge ancient economic history.*

# Bibliography

Adam-Veleni, P., E. Poulaki, K. Tsakalou-Tzanavari (eds) (2003) *Ancient country houses on modern roads: central Macedonia* (Athens: Archaeological Receipts Fund)

Alcock, S. E., & J. F. Cherry (eds) (2004) *Side-by-side survey: comparative regional studies in the Mediterranean world* (Oxford: Oxbow)

Alcock, S. E., J. F. Cherry, J. L. Davis (1994) 'Intensive survey, agricultural practice and the classical landscape of Greece' in: Morris, I. (ed.) (1994) *Classical Greece: ancient histories and modern archaeologies* (Cambridge: Cambridge University Press) 137–70 (New Directions in Archaeology)

Andreau, J. (2002) 'Twenty years after Moses I. Finley's *The ancient economy*' in: Scheidel & von Reden 2002: 33–49 (originally published in French, in *Annales: histoires, sciences sociales* 50 (1995) 947–60)

Archibald, Z., J. K. Davies, V. Gabrielsen, G. J. Oliver (eds) (2001) *Hellenistic economies* (London: Routledge)

Austin, M. M. (1994) 'Society and economy' in: *CAH²* 6 527–64

Austin, M. M., & P. Vidal-Naquet (1977) *Economic and social history of ancient Greece: an introduction* (trans. and rev. M. M. Austin) (London: Batsford) (originally published in French, *Économies et sociétés en Grèce ancienne* (Paris: Armand Colin 1972))

Billows, R. A. (1995) *Kings and colonists: aspects of Macedonian imperialism* (Leiden: Brill) (Columbia Studies in the Classical Tradition 22)

Blondé, F. (2000) 'La céramique attique du IVe siècle en Grèce du Nord: quelques commentaires' in: Sabattini 2000: 271–6

Blondé, F., & M. Picon (2000) 'Autour de la céramique du IVe siècle dans le Nord-Est de l'Égée: quelques approches différentes' in: *BCH* 124: 161–88

Bouzek, J. (1989) 'Athènes et la mer Noire' in: *BCH* 113: 249–59

Bresson, A. (2000) *La cité marchande* (Bordeaux: Ausonius) (Scripta Antiqua 2)

Brun, J.-P. (2003) *Le vin et l'huile dans la Méditerranée antique: viticulture, oléiculture et procédés de fabrication* (Paris: Errance) (Collection des Hespérides)

Brunet, M., G. Rougemont, D. Rousset (1998) 'Les contrats agraires dans la Grèce antique: bilan historiographique illustré par quatre exemples' in: *Histoire & Sociétés Rurales* 9: 211–45

Burford, A. (1993) *Land and labor in the Greek world* (Baltimore: Johns Hopkins University Press) (Ancient Society and History)

Burford Cooper, A. (1977–8) 'The family farm in Greece' in: *CJ* 73: 162–75

Burstein, S. M. (1999) '*IG* 1³.61 and the Black Sea grain trade' in: Mellor, R., & L. A. Tritle (eds) (1999) *Text and tradition: studies in Greek history and historiography in honor of Mortimer Chambers* (Claremont CA: Regina) 93–104

Cahill, N. (2002) *Household and city organisation at Olynthus* (New Haven: Yale University Press)

Cartledge, P. A. (1998) 'The economy (economies) of ancient Greece' in: *Dialogos* 5: 4–24 (repr. in Scheidel & von Reden 2002: 11–32)

Cartledge, P., E. E. Cohen, L. Foxhall (eds) (2002) *Money, labour and land: approaches to the economies of ancient Greece* (London: Routledge)

Casevitz, M. (1993) '*Emporion*: emplois classiques et histoire du mot' in: Bresson, A., & P. Rouillard (eds) (1993) *L'emporion* (Paris: de Boccard) 9–22 (Publications du Centre Pierre Paris 26)

Christesen, P. (2003) 'Economic rationalism in fourth-century BCE Athens' in: *G&R* 50: 31–56

Clinkenbeard, B. G. (1986) 'Lesbian and Thasian wine amphoras: questions concerning collaboration' in: Empereur & Garlan 1986: 353–62

Cohen, E. E. (1992) *Athenian economy and society: a banking perspective* (Princeton: Princeton University Press)

Davies, J. K. (1971) *Athenian propertied families 600–300 B.C.* (Oxford: Clarendon)

Davies, J. K. (1981) *Wealth and the power of wealth in classical Athens* (New York: Arno)

Davies, J. K. (1992) 'Society and economy' in: *CAH²* 5 287–305

Davies, J. K. (1998) 'Ancient economies: models and muddles' in: Parkins & Smith 1998: 225–56

Davies, J. K. (2001a) 'Temples, credit, and the circulation of money' in: Meadows & Shipton 2001: 117–28

Davies, J. K. (2001b) 'Rebuilding a temple: the economic effects of piety' in: Mattingly & Salmon 2001: 209–29

De Souza, P. (1999) *Piracy in the Graeco-Roman world* (Cambridge: Cambridge University Press)

Descat, R. (1989) 'L'économie d'une cité grecque au IVe siècle avant J.-C.: l'exemple athénien' in: Rouillard & Villanueva-Puig 1989: 239–52

Descat, R. (2001) 'L'économie' in: Briant, P., & P. Lévêque (eds) (2001) *Le monde grec aux temps classiques*, vol. 1: *Le Ve siècle* (Paris: Presses Universitaires de France ²2001) 295–352 (Nouvelle Clio: l'histoire et ses problèmes)

Descat, R. (2004) 'L'économie' in: Brulé, P., & R. Descat (eds) (2004) *Le monde grec aux temps classiques*, vol. 2: *Le IVe siècle* (Paris: Presses Universitaires de France) 353–411

Develin, R. (1989) *Athenian officials 684–321 B.C.* (Cambridge: Cambridge University Press)

Döğer, E. (1986) 'Premières remarques sur les amphores de Clazomènes' in: Empereur & Garlan (eds) 1986: 461–71

Empereur, J.-Y., & Y. Garlan (eds) (1986) *Recherches sur les amphores grecques: actes du colloque international organisé par le Centre national de la recherche scientifique, l'Université de Rennes II et l'École française d'Athènes (Athènes, 10–12 septembre 1984)* (Paris: de Boccard) (*BCH* Suppl. 13)

Ferguson, N. (2001) *The cash nexus: money and power in the modern world, 1700–2000* (London: Allen Lane)

Ferguson, N. (2003) *Empire: how Britain made the modern world* (London: Allen Lane)

Finley, M. I. (1981) *Economy and society in ancient Greece* (London: Chatto & Windus)

Finley, M. I. (1999) *The ancient economy* (Berkeley: University of California Press) (updated ed. with a foreword by I. Morris; originally published as Finley, M. I. (1973) *The ancient economy* (Berkeley: University of California Press) (Sather Classical Lectures 48))

Fossey, J. M. (1988) *Topography and population of ancient Boiotia* (Chicago: Ares)

Foxhall, L. (1992) 'The control of the Attic landscape' in: Wells 1992: 155–9

Foxhall, L. (1993) 'Farming and fighting in ancient Greece' in: Rich & Shipley 1993: 134–45

Foxhall, L. (2002) 'Access to resources in classical Greece: the egalitarianism of the polis in practice' in: Cartledge et al. 2002: 209–20

Gabrielsen, V. (1994) *Financing the Athenian fleet: public taxation and social relations* (Baltimore: Johns Hopkins University Press)

Gallant, T. W. (1991) *Risk and survival in ancient Greece: reconstructing the rural domestic economy* (Stanford: Stanford University Press)

Garnsey, P. D. A. (1988) *Famine and food supply in the Graeco-Roman world: responses to risk and crisis* (Cambridge: Cambridge University Press)

Garnsey, P. D. A., K. Hopkins, C. R. Whittaker (eds) (1983) *Trade in the ancient economy* (London: Chatto & Windus)

Gill, D. W. J. (1991) 'Pots and trade: spacefillers or objets d'art' in: *JHS* 111: 29–47

Habicht, C. (1976) 'Eine hellenistische Urkunde aus Larisa' in: Milojčić, V., & D. R. Theocharis (eds) (1976) *Demetrias*, vol. 1 (Bonn: Habelt) 157–73 (Beiträge zur ur- und frühgeschichtlichen Archäologie des Mittelmeer-Kulturraumes 12: Die deutschen archäologischen Forschungen in Thessalien)

Halstead, P., & G. Jones (1989) 'Agrarian ecology in the Greek islands: times stress, scale and risk' in: *JHS* 109: 41–55

Hansen, M. H. (1996) 'An inventory of Boiotian *poleis* in the archaic and classical period' in: Hansen, M. H. (ed.) (1996) *Introduction to an inventory of poleis: Symposium August 23–26, 1995* (Copenhagen: Munksgaard) 73–116 (Kongelige Danske Videnskabernes Selskab: Historisk-filosofiske meddelelser 74 = Acts of the Copenhagen Polis Centre 3)

Hansen, M. H. (1998) *Polis and city-state: an ancient concept and its modern equivalent* (Copenhagen: Munksgaard) (Kongelige Danske Videnskabernes Selskab: Historisk-filosofiske meddelelser 76 = Acts of the Copenhagen Polis Centre 5)

Hansen, M. H., & T. H. Nielsen (eds) (2004) *An inventory of archaic and classical poleis: an investigation conducted by the Copenhagen Polis Centre for the Danish National Research Foundation* (Oxford: Oxford University Press)

Hanson, V. D. (1998) *Warfare and agriculture in classical Greece* (Berkeley: University of California Press; revised ed., first published 1983 (Pisa: Giardini) (Biblioteca di Studi Antica 40))

Harris, E. M. (2002) 'Workshop, marketplace and household: the nature of technical specialization in classical Athens and its influence on economy and Society' in: Cartledge et al. 2002: 67–99

Hodkinson, S. (1988) 'Animal husbandry in the Greek polis' in: Whittaker, C. R. (ed.) 1988: *Pastoral economies in classical antiquity* (Cambridge: Cambridge Philological Society) 35–74 (*PCPhS* Suppl. 14)

Hodkinson, S. (2000) *Property and wealth in classical Sparta* (London: Duckworth & The Classical Press of Wales)

Isager, S., & J. E. Skydsgaard (1992) *Ancient Greek agriculture: an introduction* (London: Routledge)

Jameson, M. H. (1992) 'Agricultural labour in ancient Greece' in: Wells 1992: 134–46

Jameson, M. H. (2002) 'On Paul Cartledge, "The political economy of Greek slavery"' in: Cartledge et al. 2002: 167–74

Jameson, M. H., C. N. Runnels, T. H. van Andel (1994) *A Greek countryside: the southern Argolid from prehistory to the present day* (Stanford: Stanford University Press)

Jones, J. E. (1982) 'The Laurium silver mines: a review' in: *G&R* 29: 169–84

Jubier-Galinier, C., A.-F. Laurens, A. Tsingarida (2003) 'Les atelier de potiers en Attique: de l'idée à l'objet' in: Rouillard, P., & A. Verbanck-Piérard (eds) (2003) *Le vase grec et ses destins: ouvrage réalisé à l'occasion de l'exposition 'Le fabuleux destin du vase grec', présentée au Musée royal de Mariemont, 23 mai–28 septembre 2003, ... [et] au Musée Calvet d'Avignon, mars–juin 2004* (Munich: Biering & Brinkman) 27–43

Kallet, L. (2001) *Money and the corrosion of power in Thucydides: the Sicilian expedition and its aftermath* (Berkeley: University of California Press)

Kallet-Marx, L. (1993) *Money, expense, and naval power in Thucydides' History 1–5.24* (Berkeley: University of California Press)

Karabélias, E. (2002) *L'épiclérat attique* (Athens: Academy of Athens)

Kim, H. S. (2002) 'Small change and the moneyed economy' in: Cartledge et al. 2002: 44–51

Kurke, L. (1999) *Coins, bodies, games, and gold: the politics of meaning in archaic Greece* (Princeton: Princeton University Press)

Kurke, L (2002) 'Money and mythic history: the contestation of transactional orders in the fifth century BC' in: Scheidel & von Reden 2002: 87–113

Lang, M., & M. Crosby (1964) *Weights, measures, and tokens* (Princeton: American School of Classical Studies at Athens) (*The Athenian Agora* 10)

Lawall, M. (1998) 'Ceramics and positivism revisited: Greek transport amphoras and history' in: Parkins, H., & C. Smith (eds) (1998) *Trade, traders and the ancient city* (London: Routledge) 75–101

Lazarov, M. (1986) 'Les timbres amphoriques et les problèmes commerciaux' in: Empereur & Garlan 1986: 401–05

Le Rider, G. (2003) *Alexandre le Grand: monnaie, finances et politique*; préface de P. Chaunu (Paris: Presses Universitaires de France) (Histoires)

Mattingly, D. J., & J. Salmon (eds) (2001) *Economies beyond agriculture in the classical world* (London: Routledge)

Meadows, A., & K. Shipton (eds) (2001) *Money and its uses in the ancient Greek world* (Oxford: Oxford University Press)

Meijer, F., & O. van Nijf (eds) (1992) *Trade, transport and society in the ancient world: a sourcebook* (London: Routledge)

Millett, P. (1990) 'Sale, credit and exchange in Athenian law and society' in: Cartledge, P., P. Millett, S. Todd (eds) (1990) *Nomos: essays in Athenian law, politics, and society* (Cambridge: Cambridge University Press) 167–94

Millett, P. (1991) *Lending and borrowing in ancient Athens* (Cambridge: Cambridge University Press)

Missitzis, L. (1985) 'A royal decree of Alexander the Great on the lands of Philippi' in: *The Ancient World* 12: 3–14

Monaco, M. C. (2000) *Ergasteria: impianti artigianali ceramici ad Atene ed in Attica dal Protogeometrico alle soglie dell'Ellenismo* (Rome: 'L'Erma' di Bretschneider) (Studia archaeologica 110)

Morel, J. P. (2000) 'La céramique attique du IVe siècle en Afrique du Nord' in: Sabattini 2000: 259–64

Murray, O. (1993) *Early Greece* (London: Fontana [2]1993)

Nielsen, T. H., & J. Roy (eds) (1999) *Defining ancient Arkadia* (Copenhagen: Munksgaard) (Kongelige Danske Videnskabernes Selskab, Historisk-filosofiske Meddelelser 78 = Acts of the Copenhagen Polis Centre 6)

Osborne, R. G. (1987) *Classical landscape with figures: the ancient Greek city and its countryside* (London: Philip)

Osborne, R. G. (1988) 'Social and economic implications of the leasing of land and property in classical and Hellenistic Greece' in: *Chiron* 18: 279–323

Osborne, R. G. (1991) 'Pride and prejudice, sense and subsistence: exchange and society in the Greek city' in: Rich, J., & A. Wallace-Hadrill (eds) (1991) *City and country in the ancient world* (London: Routledge) 191–245 (repr. in Scheidel & von Reden 2002: 114–32)

Osborne, R. G. (1995) 'The economics and politics of slavery at Athens' in: Powell, A. (ed.) (1995) *The Greek world* (London: Routledge) 27–43

Osborne, R. G. (1996) *Greece in the making, 1200–479 BC* (London: Routledge)

Owens, E. J. (1983) 'The *koprologoi* at Athens in the fifth and fourth centuries B.C.' in: *CQ* 33: 44–50

Parkins, H., & C. Smith (eds) (1998) *Trade, traders and the ancient city* ('A collection of papers from a 1995 conference with the same working title') (London: Routledge)

Picard, O. (1994) 'Monnaies et commerce à Thasos' in: *Économie antique, les échanges dans l'antiquité: le rôle de l'État: Rencontres sur l'économie antique, Saint-Bertrand-de-Comminges, 1994* (intro. J. Andreau, P. Briant, R. Descat) (Saint-Bertrand-de-Comminges: Musée archéologique départemental) 31–45 (Entretiens d'archéologie et d'histoire 1)

Pikoulas, G. A. (1999) 'The road-networks of Arkadia' in: Nielsen & Roy 1999: 248–319

Pouilloux, J. (2003) *Choix d'inscriptions grecques* (Paris: Les Belles Lettres [2]2003)

Principal-Ponce, J. (2000) 'Panorama de la vajilla ática durante el siglo IV a.C. en la Cataluña Occidental' in: Sabattini 2000: 217–24

Py, M., & B. Sabattini (2000) 'La céramique attique du IVe s. à Lattes (Hérault)' in: Sabattini 2000: 167–200

Rich, J., & G. Shipley (eds) (1993) *War and society in the Greek world* (London: Routledge)

Rihll, T. (2001) 'Making money in classical Athens' in: Mattingly & Salmon 2001: 115–42

Robinson, E. S. G., & M. J. Price (1967) 'An emergency coinage of Timotheos' in: *Numismatic Chronicle* 1967: 1–6

Rouillard, P., & M.-C. Villanueva-Puig (eds) (1989) *Grecs et Ibères au IVe siècle avant Jésus-Christ: commerce et iconographie: actes de la table ronde tenue à Bordeaux, les 16–17–18 décembre 1986* (Paris: de Boccard) (Bordeaux: Publications du Centre Pierre Paris 19)

Roy, J. (1999) 'The economies of Arkadia' in: Nielsen & Roy 1999: 340–81

Sabattini, B. (ed.) (2000) *La céramique attique du IVe siècle en Méditerraneeé occidentale: actes du colloque international organisé par le Centre Camille Jullian, Arles, 7–9 décembre 1995* (Naples: Centre Jean Bérard) (Collection du Centre Jean Bérard 19; Travaux du Centre Camille Jullian 24)

Sallares, R. (1991) *The ecology of the ancient Greek world* (London: Duckworth)

Salmon, J. (2001) 'Temples the measures of men: public building in the Greek economy' in: Mattingly & Salmon 2001: 195–208

Salviat, F. (1958) 'Une nouvelle loi thasienne: institutions judiciaires et fêtes religieuses à la fin du IVe avant J.-C.' in: *BCH* 82: 193–267

Salviat, F. (1986) 'Le vin de Thasos, amphores, vin et source écrites' in: Empereur & Garlan 1986: 145–96

Sanmartí-Grego, J. (2000) 'Les importations de céramique attique du IVe s. av. J.-C. sur la côte centrale de Catalogne' in: Sabattini 2000: 233–41

Saprykin, S. J. (1994) *Ancient farms and land-plots on the khora of Khersonesos Taurike: research in the Herakleian Peninsula, 1974–1990* (Amsterdam: Gieben) (McGill University monographs in classical archaeology and history 16) (Antiquitates Proponticae, Circumponticae et Caucasicae 1)

Scheidel, W., & S. von Reden (eds) (2002) *The ancient economy* (Edinburgh: Edinburgh University Press) (Edinburgh Readings on the Ancient World)

Spence, I. G. (1990) 'Perikles and the defence of Attika during the Peloponnesian war' in: *JHS* 110: 91–1079

Stavropoullou, P. D. (1938) 'Hieratike oikia en Zosteri tei Attikei' in: *Archaiologike Ephemeris* 1938: 1–31

Steinhauer, G. (2001) 'The Classical Mesogaia (5th–4th century B.C.)' in: Aikaterinidis, G. (ed.) *Mesogaia: history and culture of Mesogeia* (Athens: Athens International Airport) 80–139

Stroud, R. S. (1998) *The Athenian grain-tax law of 374/3 BC.* (Princeton: American School of Classical Studies at Athens) (*Hesperia* Suppl. 29)

Ugolini, D. (2000) 'La céramique attique d'Agde dans le cadre du Languedoc central et occidental' in: Sabattini 2000: 201–7

Velkov, V., & L. Domaradzka (1994) 'Kotys I (383/2–359 av. J.-C.) et l'emporion Pistiros de Thrace' in: *BCH* 118: 1–15

von Reden, S. (1995) *Exchange in ancient Greece* (London: Duckworth; pb. 2003 with new intro. and additional bibliography)

von Reden, S. (2002) 'Money in the ancient economy: a survey of recent research' in: *Klio* 84: 141–74

Wells, B. (ed.) (1992) *Agriculture in ancient Greece: proceeding of the seventh international symposium at the Swedish Institute at Athens, 16–17 May, 1990* (Stockholm: Åström) (Acta Instituti Atheniensis Regni Sueciae ser. in 4° 42)

Whitby, M. (1998) 'The grain trade of Athens in the fourth century BC' in: Parkins & Smith 1998: 102–28

Wilson, P. (2000) *The Athenian institution of the* khoregia: *the chorus, the city, and the stage* (Cambridge: Cambridge University Press)

Zervoudaki, E. A. (1968) 'Attische polychrome Reliefkeramik des späten 5. und 4. Jahrhundert v. Chr.' in: *Mitteilungen des Deutschen Archäologischen Institutes (Athenische Abteilung)* 83: 188

CHAPTER FIFTEEN

# Religious Practice and Belief

*Emily Kearns*

## 1    Introduction

'Regarding the Gods, I have no means of knowing whether they exist or do not exist, or what they are like in form.' The statement of Protagoras of Abdera (c. 490–420; 80 B 4 Diels-Kranz) has often been taken as emblematic of fifth-century sophistic rationalism, but it may be less revolutionary than it sounds. Greeks of the classical period had a tendency to believe that no certainty was possible with regard to the divine. Thus Herodotos, whose work is full of 'god', 'gods' and 'the divine', remarks in connection with Egyptian religion that 'all people know an equal amount about the divine' (Hdt. 2.3.2) – by which he clearly means 'equally little'. But Protagoras' words certainly point up a paradox at the heart of Greek religion. For if the Greeks in reflective mood believed that they knew little about the Gods, in other contexts they acted as though they knew a lot. They knew the names of the Gods, or at least some of them; they knew that Poseidon had to do with the sea, with earthquakes and with horses, and Demeter to do with land cultivation and cereal crops; they knew that Hera was the protector of Argos, and Athena of Athens; they knew that pigs should not be offered to Aphrodite, but that she was, on the other hand, rather fond of pigeons. And these were not simply odd facts that could be neatly sorted into a category 'religion'; things to do with the Gods permeated pretty well every aspect of life. Whether it is Plato's Sokrates investigating the nature of some abstract quality, Pindar celebrating an athlete's victory, or the orators praising the city or vilifying their opponents, few are the texts which fail to indicate the closeness and importance of the Gods to human life and ways of thought. Even Thucydides, who famously removes the divine as a direct causal explanation from history, allows on occasion human beliefs about the Gods as a motivating factor (e.g., 7.18.2) and becomes quite discursive on the history of Delos as sacred island (3.104).

   In this respect at least, literature seems to have reflected life. It was impossible to pass through a Greek city without being aware of the presence of the Gods on every side, from the loftiest and most magnificent temples to wayside shrines, fountain-heads, and herms – ithyphallic markers of the way identical in name with the God Hermes, and sacred enough for their deliberate mutilation in Athens in 415 to be the cause of real outrage and panic. Similarly, a person's life was marked out with religious ritual – not just the obvious life-cycle events, but almost all their significant occupations. In Athens, for instance, men grouped themselves for political activity and mustered for military service under the watchful eye of their tribal eponymous hero, who was the object of cult; they prepared for battle with elaborate prayers and sacrifices; and well-born women left the house almost exclusively for funerals and religious rites.

Literary and epigraphic sources concur in showing that the Gods and their inter-action with humans (or the attempts of humans to interact with them) are to be found everywhere, and because in our period – or at least the earlier part of it – the majority of our sources are concerned primarily with public rather than private life, this makes Greek religion seem to be a very public, community-oriented affair. Indeed, while studies of mythology have often taken a different direction, over the last thirty years or so perhaps the main concern of writing on Greek religious *practice* has been 'polis religion'. And a model that works for the polis, in most areas of the Greek world the fundamental unit of society, works also for larger groups – Leagues, Amphiktyonies – and smaller (phylai, phratries, local groups such as demes). Reli-gious activity and sentiment, once tacitly dismissed (at least in much Anglo-Saxon scholarship) as a polite fiction, a mostly meaningless survival like the prayers in the Houses of Parliament, is now seen to be thoroughly 'embedded' in society.

Fashions in historical interpretation change, but it is hard not to suppose that this view is essentially more correct than that in which religion is no more than an ornamental periphery. At its most basic, religious organization can be seen to be operating throughout society in different but complementary ways, both as a defin-ing and limiting force and as a cohesive force. Greek society was full of interlocking and overlapping groups, and a group is maintained both by defining who is not a member and by strengthening the feeling of belonging which the members have. In almost all cases it was those who sacrificed with you who belonged to the same group, and those who didn't share sacrifices who were outside. 'Common sacrifices' were a potent emotional bond, from the level of 'Greekness' (Hdt. 8.144) down to the smallest local and family units.

We shall see that this role, fundamental as it is, is very far from exhausting the interactions of religion and society. Even so, the concept of 'polis religion' is not the key to understanding *everything* about Greek religion. To begin with a very simple point, it is clear even from fifth-century evidence that religious activity was carried out by the individual as well as the group, and the impression is strengthened in the fourth century by the greater willingness of the texts to engage with private affairs and everyday life. Indeed, it would be a very singular society where *no* religious practice or experience took place on an individual basis! More tellingly, we might remark that the individual's religious position was not entirely dictated by his or her place in society. Certainly, birth and (for women) marriage within a particular community determined many of the cults that one was able or obliged to take part in, but there were variations possible which had more to do with personal choice. The choice whether or not to receive initiation into various Mysteries (see below) might have something to do with whom you knew and whom you were related to, but equally it might not; in any case, it was emphatically not a consequence of your belonging or not belonging to a formally constituted group. The same might be said of the more radical decision to follow an Orphic or Pythagorean way of life. Seeing dreams and visions had more to do with the wish to satisfy personal needs and with the deity's relationship towards an individual than with that individual's formal position in city, tribe or phratry. And although serious atheism and total non-participation in cult was scarcely an option for Greeks of the classical period, the fundamental choice of less or more piety and observance was overwhelmingly a personal matter.

Another aspect of religion which can only partially be dealt with by the 'polis religion' idea is that of assumptions and speculations about the nature of the Gods. Here, we find in the classical period something of a dynamic between community and individual. However uncertain many Greeks may have been of what the Gods were *really* like, in practice some assumptions were accepted as necessary to the proper functioning of the community: that the Gods existed, that they took account of human affairs and (other things being equal) were likely to favour their worshippers, and that they were pleased with worship according to ancestral custom. Without such beliefs operating at least at some level, the public cult so conspicuous in Greek cities would have operated in a strange and implausible vacuum. But in more speculative contexts, there was room for a variety of individual approaches. In Protagoras' statement, we find an assertively personal note which is typical of fifth-century prose writers: 'Concerning the Gods, *I* have no means of knowing ...'. To be sure, the reasons given for this lack of resource are universal (the obscurity of the subject and the brevity of life), but Protagoras presents himself as the one who has understood this, in distinction from the mass of mankind – in this perhaps anticipating his adversary, the Platonic Sokrates. Not all such speculation was acceptable to the wider community, and the apparatus of state control could on occasion be brought in to curb its excesses. Hence, notoriously, the trials for impiety (*asebeia*) which occurred sporadically in Athens in the second half of the fifth century. Less adversarially, individual and community were both involved in the often disturbing presentations of the Gods in tragedy, which originated in the mind of an individual but were presented to the city as a whole, in the context of a public festival.

On the other hand, the religious thought of (say) Herodotos or Plato, although in certain contexts engaged with the community, in others went far beyond it. There has been something of a tendency since the mid-twentieth century to play down the thought and belief side of Greek religion in favour of religious practice, 'cult', which has been generally assumed to be primary and somehow more genuine. This has made it easier to see the religion of the Greeks as essentially public – and the public aspect is as we have seen important and characteristic – but it would probably have surprised the Greeks themselves.

## 2   Worship in the Community

As in any religious system, we can pick out certain tendencies and characteristics in the religion of fifth- and fourth-century Greeks, but these are far from defining that religion in its entirety. Perhaps we should try to define Greek religion in another way: geographically, with respect to its contemporary neighbours. Since the ancients lacked the concept of 'a' religion, a belief and practice system whose adherents could be counted and which excluded the adherents of rival systems, precision is not easy here either. In some ways it is tempting to adopt a minimalist approach. On the one hand, the cults practised within a Greek city were proper only to its citizens, and non-citizens, even though Greek, were very often barred from participation; on the other, some aspects of Greek practice do not seem to have been very different from those of their near neighbours in Asia, the Karians, Lykians and Mysians, while deities from other parts of Asia (Kybele, Adonis) and Thrace (Bendis) were taken over into the pantheons of the Greek cities.

But the Greeks themselves were – rightly or wrongly – conscious of the distinctness of their religious practices, at least by the classical period; it may well be, as many scholars surmise, that it was the Persian Wars which finally crystallized a sense of Greekness among Dorians, Ionians, Aeolians and others, and in the famous statement which Herodotos puts into the mouths of the Athenian envoys to Sparta common religious practice goes hand in hand with *to hellenikon* (Hdt. 8.144, alluded to above). 'Common sacrifices' were seen very obviously in the great panhellenic festivals at Olympia, Delphi, Nemea and so on, which brought participants together from all over the Greek world. Greeks of different cities also worshipped Gods with the same names, though the significance of this is somewhat diminished when we realize that in the usual conception foreigners did not worship different Gods, but rather the same Gods under different names: *Mylitta* (from Neo-Assyrian Mulissu) is the Assyrian word for Aphrodite (Hdt. 1.132.1) just as *bekos* is the Phrygian word for bread (Hdt. 2.2.4). Mythology was perhaps more helpful: thanks to Homer and Hesiod, most Greeks could agree about most of the relationships of the Gods to each other, and shared a common stock of stories about the Gods (with some local variations) which was not also common to Persians, Lydians or Egyptians. It is clear also that authors writing for a panhellenic audience seldom felt the need to explain cult practice in a particular Greek city – readers would fill in the blanks from experience in their own. For the modern historian of the ancient world, a review of some of the more prominent features is enough to indicate that there is indeed a more or less coherent whole which can be called 'Greek religion', even if its boundaries are markedly permeable.

Most of the Gods worshipped in a Greek city would be recognizable to Greeks from elsewhere, although the emphasis might be different: Persephone in the Italian city of Lokroi Epizephyrioi appears to have had more to do with marriage than with death, Demeter in Arkadia has apparently little connection with corn. Even in one city, the same God had often several manifestations. Pausanias, whose second-century CE view of the Greek cities reflects many of the conditions of a much earlier period, names at Argos for instance Apollo Lykios, Agyieus and Deiradiotes, and Zeus Hyetios, Meilichios, Nemeios, Phyxios and Larisaios, all with separate cult-places and all no doubt of different appearance: Zeus Larisaios, on the Argive akropolis, was depicted with three eyes. Or were these Zeuses and Apollos the same God? Often people spoke of the God in a particular sanctuary as different from a God of the same name in another: this Apollo, that Apollo. Just so the Virgin of Lourdes is often perceived as different from the Virgin of Fatima, whatever may be the case theologically, and however little anyone believes that Christ has more than one mother or that there are several Christ and Virgin sets.

It was location which defined the cult of a particular deity, in this narrow sense. The Gods might be called 'Olympian', and Homer might picture their houses on top of a massively high mountain or even in the sky, but as far as cult was concerned the God was located in his sanctuary: the word for temple, *naos*, means 'dwelling-place'. At the very least the God made his way there to receive sacrifice. Sanctuaries varied from the very large and elaborate, the object of civic ostentation, to tiny plots round makeshift altars. What they all had in common was a strict demarcation of their sacred space from the space outside. A *temenos* of this sort was a God's property, just as in earlier Greek a *temenos* was the land of a lord or chieftain (*anax, basileus*). The essential for cult was a place for sacrifice or, more rarely, to perform other offerings. The temple proper was a secondary development, its original function to house the cult statue. By the classical period, however, temples had become often magnificent structures, and certainly were more than just backdrops for action at the altar outside, as they have sometimes been described; the statue itself was probably the focus of much prayer and exchange between deity and worshipper (see below). Larger sanctuaries also contained shrines of subsidiary deities, altars, statues, and tombs of heroes, all places of cult.

Of cult activities, animal sacrifice was undoubtedly the most central and characteristic. The origins of the practice have been the subject of much discussion among historians of Greek religion, but for the Greeks themselves sacrifice was the obvious way of pleasing the deity to whom it was offered. It was the almost inevitable accompaniment, even climax, of whatever other rituals were performed at any regular observance, and it was also frequently performed in cases of individual or family need. The expense, and the time necessary from the preliminaries to the conclusion of the feast which usually followed the slaughter, meant that even for the most pious of ordinary individuals, sacrifice could not be a daily event; on the other hand, the smallest of usual sacrificial victims, a piglet, was well within the reach of even a poor family's occasional function.

Animal sacrifice, however common, had its disquieting elements. The 'drama of death' was certainly played up in the ritual, and some observers were led to ask unanswerable questions: why was it pious to shed sacrificial blood over the altars of the Gods, when other kinds of blood were impure and polluting? Why did the Gods so seldom receive the whole offering, and why were the pieces of meat they did receive such unappetizing ones? Very few, however, were led by such doubts to reject the practice altogether. To do so would be to reject the offering of the standard and most effective gift to the Gods, sanctioned by immemorial tradition, and the articulation of the community, large or small, that went with it. A complete withdrawal from normal religious practice, even more perhaps than the airing of disturbing views about the Gods, was generally regarded with suspicion.

We are best informed about those sacrifices which came round on a regularly recurring basis, as part of observances which are generally, if sometimes misleadingly, called festivals. This is due partly to chance mentions in literary sources, but also to the penchant of the Greeks for setting up regulatory inscriptions about cult, often in the form of calendars listing the victims to be offered at different dates in the year. A fair number of such calendars survive, either in whole or in part, mainly from

Attika, the islands, and the Greek cities of Asia Minor. These enable us to see clearly the range of possibilities in 'normal' sacrifice. The victim is one of the commonly domesticated animals, pig, sheep, goat or cow – without blemish, it goes without saying, as we know from the literary sources – and virtually without exception of the same sex as the deity to whom it is offered. A young animal may be specified (cheaper); sometimes, usually for deities concerned with fertility, a pregnant one (expensive). Indeed, one of the main purposes of these calendars was budgetary; they enabled those responsible in the group to whom the calendar belonged to see at a glance how much would have to be spent on each occasion – the price of the victim is normally given, and other expenses would not, presumably, vary a lot between occasions. Whether the event was paid for by common funds or by an individual benefactor, if the group concerned was the city or one of its local subdivisions, we can legitimately speak of *public* sacrifices, *public* festivals – these were the concern of the people as a whole.

Typically such occasions would involve a procession, several sacrifices – each with a specified and appropriate victim – often some ritual peculiar to that occasion, and a meal. Frequently some sort of contest was held, whether poetic or athletic. But exceptions to the usual pattern are not that uncommon. The victim's flesh might be burned completely (so no meal – at least not with sacrificial materials); the libations of liquid which accompanied sacrifice might omit wine, which was seen as changing the character of the rite; the meat might be distributed only to a certain group among the participants, for example women; the meat might have to be consumed entirely on the spot (it was clearly normal to take some away). Such variations played an important part in defining the distinctive nature of each observance.

In other respects, annual observances were very various in character. We are best informed about those of Attika, but there is no reason to suppose that the picture was substantially different elsewhere; a number of festivals, in fact, were common to many or most Ionian cities, though the exact details of their celebration no doubt sometimes diverged: such were, for example, the Thesmophoria (see below) and the Apatouria, the latter for Herodotos (1.148) a touchstone of Ionian identity. 'Public' festivals, public in the sense that their performance was a state responsibility, even necessity, ranged from huge celebrations involving much of the population to tiny but nonetheless vital rites in which only a handful of people took part. Athens had many of the former type: a well-known example is the City Dionysia, where the centrepiece and characteristic feature was the competitive production of tragedies, dithyrambs and comedies, where crowds were evidently huge and included bigwigs from many other cities. The classic 'tiny' rite is that of the Arrhephoria, celebrated in honour of Athena and Pandrosos, daughter of Kekrops, where the participants seem to have been limited to the priestess of Athena Polias and two or perhaps four little girls called *arrhephoroi*, who carried mysterious objects between certain sanctuaries – neither girls nor priestess knowing what these objects were, Pausanias tells us (1.27.3). Small though this ritual might be in terms of participation, it was an essential part of the cult complex of the akropolis, and a very great honour for the girls and their families.

Neither is there any contradiction between the idea of public cult and the insistence on secrecy. 'Things not to be spoken', *arrheta* (sometimes taken, in both ancient and modern times, as the origin of *arrhe-phoria*), are quite a conspicuous feature of Greek religious life and sensibility. A certain coyness in speaking about religious matters is observable in several authors, notably Herodotos, who is fond of signalling some myth or explanation for a rite as somewhat esoteric by stating that he himself knows it, but will not repeat it (e.g. 2.47.2, 48.3). Perhaps these *logoi* might sound foolish or risqué without proper exegesis; perhaps they were simply too holy to be passed on randomly. Whatever the reason, secrecy could be a feature both of things told and of things done. There were secret or unutterable names, often of underworld divinities whom you might not want to alert by naming them; secret tombs, like that of Dirke in Thebes (Plutarch *Moralia* 578a–b); and above all secret rites, known only to those who had taken part in them. In some of these, the participatory group might be quite large: 'women's festivals', discussed below, are an example, for in most of these there was at least an element of secrecy, something done which should not be divulged to men.

Another type of secret celebration was the rites known as 'mysteries', *mysteria*. Here the participants, other than the priestly officiants, underwent an 'initiation', *myesis*, consisting in seeing, doing and experiencing certain things, perhaps also being told things, which constituted the central part of the rite. The most famous Mysteries were of course those of Eleusis, which came to have unchallenged prestige in later times but which Athens was already pushing in the fifth century as a great Athenian benefaction – for although this too was very much a state cult, initiation was equally open to non-Athenians. Another famous celebration was that associated with the Kabeiroi, local Gods of Samothrake; but similarly structured cults existed all over the Greek world, some with more or less local reputations, others better-known.

The fundamental appeal of such initiations was presumably the seriousness and sense of importance hinted at by the secrecy. There were also well-publicized consequences of initiation; a better fate after death for Eleusinian initiates, or more modestly freedom from shipwreck for those of Samothrake. But what was actually experienced at initiation, or felt as a consequence afterwards, is impossible to recover. We know a certain amount about the preliminaries of some of these rites, which involved elaborate purifications, and Christian writers purport to reveal the sacred things done – but their testimony is obviously suspect, and no coherent overall picture can be formed. It does seem likely that at Eleusis the initiates in some way re-enacted or re-experienced the search of Demeter for her daughter, their reunion, perhaps the marriage of Kore/Persephone with the underworld God, all the elements of the central myth complex relating to the Two Goddesses; though the scraps of information and hints that we do have suggest a greater complexity than this simple summary might suggest. It was at any rate a powerful emotional experience. It may even be that a greater knowledge of these important rituals would considerably modify our impressions of how Greek religion worked. It is possible that after initiation a different sort of relationship with the God could have been felt, or a new understanding of 'things to do with the Gods'. This is speculation, of course, but we do have (once again) Herodotos' witness that initiation could affect the way one might look at other religious practices: speaking of ithyphallic statues of Hermes, Herodotos says 'Whoever has been initiated in the rites of the Kabeiroi which the Samothrakians celebrate … that man knows what I mean' (2.51).

Mysteries or otherwise, regular, major rites, and especially sanctuaries for their performance, demanded a religious personnel to carry out ritual and make sure things

were done properly. But the priest in the Greek world was a very different figure from
that of most ancient civilizations. There was no hereditary group of priests as such,
and a person was not simply 'a priest' but 'the priest of such-and-such a God' –
Artemis Limnatis, Apollo Pythios, or whatever, the deity of a particular sanctuary.
Typically a priesthood was held in one family, whether that was defined as a large or a
small kinship group, and might be strictly hereditary or else determined by drawing
lots among the eligible members – sortition being, among other things, a method of
discovering the God's own choice. But there were other methods. The Pythia at
Delphi needed only to be 'of good family', not to come from any particular family,
and the newer priesthoods established in Athens (and probably other democracies as
well) had also very wide eligibility – in practice, probably extending to those who
could afford the expenses. (At a later period, the sale of priesthoods was common in
many cities.) Priesthoods on the older model were usually held for life; the newer kind
were sometimes appointed annually, making them even more analogous to the
magistracies with which modern scholars sometimes compare priesthoods. Despite
this relative lack of priestly mystique, there remained something special about the
priest's office; he was after all the intermediary with the God, and in recognition of
this his person was supposed to be inviolable – it was an outrage to lay hands on a
priest wearing the characteristic holy headbands.

   The actual job of the priest would vary somewhat from sanctuary to sanctuary.
Larger places had numerous cult personnel, medium-sized ones at least a *neokoros*
(warden or caretaker); in the very smallest, perhaps most or all aspects of the day-to-day
worship and care of the shrine fell to the priest's own lot. The essential function of the
priest was to preside over sacrifices, directing operations and speaking the right prayers.
Most often he did not kill the sacrificial victim himself – that was the role of
the *mageiros* (butcher/cook), who then took charge of the processing of the meat.
It could also be assumed that the priest would somehow have acquired some knowledge about the traditions, practical and otherwise, of his shrine, but a priest was
not necessarily a religious expert; when facing a difficult question on general religious
practice, in Athens at least, you would probably be more likely to consult an *exegetes*,
a state official whose job it was to know and interpret a vast amount of religious lore.
(We have a few fragments of the works on religion and antiquities written by a fourth-
century Athenian exegete, Kleidemos or Kleitodemos.) This was as close as the
Greek world got to a group of cultic specialists, but in terms of historical development, the *exegetai* are clearly secondary to priests. On the other hand, we should not
form a picture of priests who simply performed the actions required of them with
no further thought. Some did, undoubtedly, but others we might expect to have been
more like Plutarch in later centuries, for whom his Delphian priesthood went hand
in hand with a deep interest in 'divine things' more generally. Nor was it perhaps
entirely whimsical that Plato chose to make Sokrates' instructor in the *Symposium* a
priestess, the no doubt fictional Diotima; in the *Meno* also (81A) Sokrates claims to
have heard his *logos* from 'wise men and women', whom he defines as 'those priests
and priestesses who have taken the trouble to be able to give an account (*logos*) of
the things they are occupied with'. We do not have to believe that this is actually
where Sokrates heard the doctrine of rebirth; the point is rather that some priests and
priestesses might reasonably be expected to have a degree of theological interest
and skill.

Priests *and priestesses*: the gender issue can no longer be postponed. Priestesses were as normal and everyday a phenomenon as priests, again in distinction from many, if not most, ancient societies, and apparently in stark contrast to women's lack of a public role in Greece in other spheres. The two were not interchangeable, of course; each cult required either a priest or a priestess. Most often the sex of the officiant was the same as that of the God, but there were numerous exceptions to this rule. In general terms the role of a priestess was identical to that of a priest, neither was there any sense that only minor priesthoods could be held by women. In Athens, the city's own special protector, Athena Polias, was served by a woman (we know the names of several of her priestesses, including Lysimache, who held office for 64 years in the fifth century). Within the category of females, however, further specifications could be made, since more than men women were defined by their stage in the life-cycle and potential sexual and reproductive role. Thus some cults were served by a virgin priestess, who given the norms of Greek marriage would be either a little girl or at most a young teenager. Other priesthoods were reserved for women who 'had finished with sex'. But very many had no such restrictions, as in the case of Lysi-mache. Since a priestess needed presumably to be on hand whenever the calendar demanded a special observance, this has the interesting consequence that menstru-ation could not have been regarded as a serious impurity – at least, not so serious that it could not be dealt with in some way.

The responsibilities assigned to women as priestesses seem to sit oddly with their severely circumscribed role in other spheres. But priestly roles for individuals did not exhaust women's public religious functions. Actual participation in a cult or festival was sometimes limited to one sex or the other. While certain sanctuaries (quite often those of Herakles, for example) did not allow women within their bounds, rather more widespread were those celebrations already alluded to which excluded men from all or part of what was done. These were often festivals in which the worship of Demeter was primary, and frequently had to do with fertility, whether human, animal or vegetable. Reproduction and the care of children was after all women's primary contribution to the life of the polis, and it was a process that could not be carried on without them; it was logical, therefore, that they should be the ones to take respon-sibility for sorting this out with the Gods. How far this was a conscious calculation is difficult to say, but everyone knew that these rituals must be performed, and could only be performed by women. This did not prevent men from feeling some anxiety about women getting together in this way, whether it was expressed comically in Aristophanes' treatment of the Thesmophoria (where the women's secret is wine-drinking), horrifically in the traditions of violence carried out by maenads, or pro-tectively in the myths of women at festivals carried off by raiders. Certainly in hellenistic times and probably earlier, many communities empowered a male *gynai-konomos* to supervise the proper carrying-out of women's rites, no doubt in part in a spirit of protection, to make sure that conditions were suitable and the women were undisturbed, and without compromising essential secrecy. Some male mediation was also necessary in order that such observances should fit smoothly into the pattern of public life, otherwise exclusively male. Thus in decrees of the fourth-century Attic demes, we find the *hieromnemones*, officials regulating many aspects of public cult life, also concerned in some way in the local Thesmophoria, and some male official, presumably the demarch, assisting the priestess of the Two Goddesses in maintaining proper order in and around the Thesmophorion – though his role seems to be curtailed when women gather to celebrate their festivals (*IG* 2² 1184; 1177).

Even at celebrations open to men and women, which were the majority, certain of the roles were differentiated between the sexes. At a sacrifice, it was a man who did the killing, but an unmarried girl who carried the basket containing the grains to sprinkle on the animal's head, and all the women present who cried out the *ololyge* or ululation. These roles can be seen as a continuation of roles assigned to the sexes in other areas of life. Men kill, women mark a death by lamentation. Men deal with meat, women with the grains and flour to make bread and cakes. If groups of girls sing and dance to please Artemis and other virgin Goddesses, that is because it is evidently a girlish occupation anyway; the chorus (*choros*) become the Goddess's own companions and playmates. Following on this line of thought, the priestess's work has been seen as analogous to that of a responsible housewife.

## 3   Individual Practice

So far we have been considering mainly the more public, group-oriented side of Greek religious practice, for which there is rather more evidence. But religion was not confined to the polis and its subdivisions, nor can 'private' cult all be subsumed under the neat-sounding but in practice vague label 'cults of the oikos'. Certainly, Gods such as Zeus Herkeios were worshipped to safeguard the family enclosure; certainly, each family hearth was sacred, and new family members had to be introduced to it, but much more would depend on individual circumstances and inclination. A house might stand next to a shrine; Apollo Agyieus ('of the streets') and Hermes were everywhere, or you might have a 'neighbour hero' like Lykos in *Wasps* or (in one interpretation) Alkmaion to Pindar (*Pythian Odes* 8.57–60). You might even discover a previously unknown shrine, perhaps a hero's tomb, on your own land. In such cases, it would be natural to take part in worship – without necessarily going so far as Theophrastos' 'Deisidaimon' (the man who exhibits 'cowardice with respect to the Gods'), who falls to his knees and anoints the stone at every crossroads. A person might also be a frequent visitor to a favourite sanctuary. Herodotos obviously does not think it particularly strange behaviour for the nurse of a Spartiate girl to take her charge every day to the sanctuary of Helen at Therapne (Hdt. 6.61), and Aristotle recommends for pregnant women a daily walk to a temple (*Politics* 1335b).

Sacrifice, we have seen, was not a daily occurrence, so what form did this worship take? First, there was the address to the deity. It was standard practice to speak a greeting to the God even when passing a sanctuary; the same, therefore, would have been done on entering. Prayer proper, the making of a request, may have followed. The Spartan nurse, according to Herodotos, prayed in front of the cult statue. But whereas elsewhere – in an emergency, say, or on the battlefield – prayer would have to be just prayer, accompanied perhaps by a hasty promise to give something later if spared, in a cult place some cult action would be the natural accompaniment. This could be the burning of a few grains of incense, the offering of a garland, the pouring of a libation or a gift of sweetmeats – all actions which accompanied animal sacrifice but were peripheral to it, now occupying centre stage. The simple piety evinced in such actions was sometimes thought to be particularly pleasing to the Gods. Of course, individuals might decide to offer a sacrifice too, if circumstances seemed to demand it. Thus in Menander's *Dyskolos*, the mother of Sostratos sees Pan in a dream, and following this a family party goes out to the appropriate country shrine with a sheep to sacrifice. Sometimes worshippers commemorated their sacrifices on stone, as countless votive reliefs testify from all over the Greek world; most sanctuaries must have been full of these. The dream, too, is amply confirmed by epigraphic testimony: 'So-and-so dedicated this having seen a dream' is a common formula from the fourth century onwards (see for instance *Hesperia* 29 (1960) 123–5). Comparative studies suggest, unsurprisingly, that where the divine is a part of 'everyday' life, dreams about God or Gods are indeed common. The waking vision was rarer, but more reliable. Both were important but unpredictable channels of individual communication with the divine.

Dreams and visions are God-initiated (in Menander, it is part of Pan's design to appear in Sostratos' mother's dream). Help, advice and instruction could also be solicited by humans, either as a simple request, or, particularly where the best course of action was not clear, through divination. Various signs could be used to discern the Gods' purpose, if only the interpreter had sufficient skill; omens from sacrifice and the flight of birds were common, but a sneeze or even an apparently chance word spoken could have mantic significance. For Aischylos, or whoever wrote *Prometheus Bound*, the art of *mantike* was the highest human achievement (lines 484ff.). Although a few sceptical voices are found, we might very roughly compare attitudes to weather forecasting today: in Britain at least, we see that the forecasts are very often inaccurate, yet hardly anyone will argue seriously that the predictions are not founded on a 'true' basis. That other kinds of prediction are possible follows fairly easily from the assumptions that the Gods have a connection with 'fate', what will happen, and that they are usually well-disposed towards their worshippers.

The oracular shrine was a much more elaborate development of the same idea. Beginning no doubt with the simple observation that a particular place was good for receiving signs, perhaps simultaneously with the idea that a God was specially present there, oracles developed into an important and characteristically Greek phenomenon; the Lydian Kroisos, in Herodotos' well-known account (1.46–52), made trial of all the well-known Greek oracles in order to find the most reliable source of knowledge about the future. Many more oracles must have existed than we can know about: Pausanias records some local ones in the second century CE, in which the God's answer was given by a mirror, or by the first words heard on leaving the agora (Pausanias 7.21.12, 22.2–3). The best-known oracle, of course, was that of Apollo at Delphi, closely followed by the more ancient oracle of Zeus at Dodona in northern Greece. Oracles of this level of repute did not confine themselves to the pressing concerns of individuals (though we have some individual queries from Dodona, on matters of theft, paternity, and so on), but were consulted as a matter of course on important state decisions. Hence Delphi in particular can be seen as playing a part in inter-state politics; a lot has been said about its apparent 'medizing' stance in the Persian Wars, much less about how the mechanics of such a position might have worked. Greeks recognized that responses might not always be accurate; human error or, not seldom, corruption might creep in, but the central process continued to carry conviction.

Consulting an oracle was indeed a very potent form of the encounter with divinity, hedged about with elaborate preliminaries and only possible in a restricted range of circumstances. What happened next might be far removed from everyday experience. It is a plausible assumption that the Delphic Pythia gave her prophecies in a state of altered consciousness. The mystical-sounding experiences which Plutarch relates of those who consulted the Boiotian oracle of Trophonios (Plutarch *Moralia* 590A–592E) may be anachronistic for his fifth-century setting, but already in the fifth century it was well known that 'going down to Trophonios' (it was an underground oracle) was a frightening experience (Aristophanes *Clouds* 506–8). Although oracular responses were often clear and simple (at Dodona, for instance, divination by lots was used in at least some cases), there is no reason to discard the pervasive and well-attested tradition of oracular ambiguity. As Herakleitos said (22 B 93 Diels-Kranz), perhaps comparing his own writings: 'The Lord whose oracle is at Delphi neither speaks nor conceals, but gives a sign (*semainei*).' It is up to the inquirer then to complete the process by working out the correct meaning.

An analogous process in some ways was the visit to a sanctuary to request healing. Indeed, some oracles, like that of Amphiaraos at Oropos on the Boiotian–Attic border, were primarily concerned with healing. The usual procedure, treated humorously in Aristophanes' *Wealth*, was for the worshipper after purification and sacrifice to sleep in the sanctuary, in the hope that the God would either effect a cure then and there or reveal in a dream the procedure to be followed. The Asklepieion at Epidauros, a major healing sanctuary, has yielded long inscriptions listing miraculous cures. Healing must be a matter of universal interest, but the fifth century seems to have seen a surge in the popularity of specialized healing-shrines. This was the time when Asklepios' cult spread rapidly from its centres at Epidauros in the Argolid and Trikka in Thessaly to establish places of worship all over the Greek world. In Athens also we have testimony of very many more local cults, mostly of heroes, which specialized in healing; the same may well have been true of other cities. Once again it is likely to have been the personal encounter with the deity which underlay the appeal of the cult and gave the experience conviction.

# 4   Patterns of Thought

It is indeed conviction which must lie at the heart of any religious system. This conviction need not take the shape of dogmatic certainties – how often have we been told that the Greeks had no creed, no sacred books even? It need not even suppose that human beings are capable of knowing very much about the Gods. What we see in the religion of the classical period (and this persists later, with certain modifications) is a twofold conviction: first, there is the sense of the rightness of religious practice; second, there is the feeling that the existence of the Gods and their relationship with human beings is a necessary, even central, part of the way the universe is. Neither of these points was without difficulties, but still they acted as foundations to which, consciously or unconsciously, thought would keep returning.

The first point is simple: any set of rituals carried on with more or less universal acceptance and potential participation will carry a strong authority. In Greece, this effect is complicated because of the high value placed on doing things *kata ta patria*, in accordance with ancestral custom, and because of the integration of so much of religious ritual with the city and its sub-groups. But essentially a process of circular confirmation is going on: the high value placed on the performance of rituals lends authority to the belief that the Gods will respond, and hence to the assumptions about the Gods which we reviewed at the outset; in turn, these assumptions will naturally entail the performance of ritual. Criticism and puzzlement over the procedure of animal sacrifice seldom involved non-performance. Even some of the Pythagoreans may have made an exception to their habitual vegetarianism to allow them to taste sacrificial meat – the tradition is unclear and divided on this point.

The second point is related to the first, for in the mutuality of the exchange between the Gods and their worshippers lies much of the perceived sense of the way things are. 'In return for this give wealth and long-lasting health' and 'make it possible for me to set up another offering' say fifth- and fourth-century dedications. Sokrates has little difficulty in leading Euthyphron to a position where he agrees that *to hosion*, piety, is a kind of *emporike techne*, exchange and bartering (Plato *Euthyphro* 14E). It is when this system of exchange appears to break down that its function as sense-provider is most clearly seen. Thus the chorus in Sophokles' *Oedipus Tyrannus* (863–910) observe crimes going unpunished and ask what point there is now in forming a chorus for the Gods. A whole system of explanation, based on the Gods and their unwritten laws, seems to be collapsing around them. Usually, the system reasserts itself. The chorus's disquiet at the apparent non-fulfilment of oracles is seen to have been misplaced, though with consequences that are no happier for them. Even Hekabe's cry at the destruction of Troy, 'In vain we sacrificed' (Euripides *Trojan Women* 1242), is eventually tempered – like all the disturbing elements of tragedy – by its appearance at a festival honouring the Gods. And Thucydides' observation (2.47.4) that during the plague at Athens people in despair ceased worshipping the Gods demonstrably cannot have held for long. 'What's the point?' is perhaps a natural reaction, but it is unlikely to be a permanent one.

Paradoxically, the Gods explained not only order, but the lack of it. Natural phenomena such as floods or earthquakes, and the sudden shattering of human expectations, were as a matter of course referred to divine action, which Herodotos famously calls 'envious and full of disturbance' (1.32.1). Most societies have comparable mechanisms for dealing with disasters and disappointments, but a pervasive Greek view created a further system out of the simple point. Too much of anything had to be levelled. Too much good luck or prosperity sooner or later would lead to disaster, either of its own accord or by leading its possessor into arrogant behaviour which demanded punishment. For natural disasters too, the explanation tended to be sought in some human wrongdoing which had angered the Gods. The apparent disorder and confusion was really a reaffirmation of order.

Another system which is often seen by moderns as explanatory caused the Greeks themselves a lot of difficulty. I refer of course to mythology. It is highly unlikely that there was ever a time when stories about the Gods were apprehended as 'true' in the same way that an account of what you did yesterday might be true. But by the classical period such stories were already an embarrassment. Xenophanes' caustic reference to Homer and Hesiod describing the Gods' indulgence in activities which were 'shame and disgrace among humans' (21 B 11 Diels-Kranz) sets the scene for a whole history of later criticism, from Pindar's self-conscious refusal to say unfitting things of the Gods (*Olympian Odes* 1.52) to Euripides' ironic, even metatheatrical (see especially *Hercules Furens* 1340–6) games with the absurdities of myth, to Plato's wholesale rejection of divine mythology and banishing of the poets (*Republic* 377E–92A). An alternative route, which flourished in the hellenistic period and later, but was already known to Plato, was to take the stories not as representing the actual doings of the Gods, but as allegories of some higher truth. Popular though this approach became, it was not enough to prevent a pervasive feeling that father-beating, theft, deception and adultery were not appropriately portrayed as pursuits of those who could be expected to punish bad behaviour in mortals. Whatever mythology might once have 'explained', by this stage it had been so heavily problematized that it raised more questions than it answered. In fact, for many thinkers, the Gods were better apprehended in quite other ways. Xenophanes posits 'one God … not like mortals in form or in thought (21 B 23 Diels-Kranz), and Herodotos reports with evident approval the Persians' supposed view that the making of statues, temples and altars is 'foolishness', 'because they do not habitually consider (*enomisan*) the Gods as having human form, as the Greeks do' (Hdt. 1.131.1).

We are thus brought back to the paradox with which we started: apparently radical ideas, and radical uncertainty, alongside equally apparent conservatism and certainty. But labels such as 'radical' and 'conservative' may be misleading, no more than an accident of our particular historical perspective, giving us in the fifth century and again in the fourth a sudden increase in the amount and change in type of evidence available. Just as in religious practice cults of Bendis, Adonis and Sabazios took root and flourished – with or without official approval – alongside those of Zeus, Artemis and Dionysos, so in thought, conceptions of the Gods flourished which were quite different from those of poetry, of assumptions about the city and its Gods, and to an extent those implied in cult, without, however, supplanting the latter in their appropriate contexts. It may equally be a mistake to see these alternative conceptions as a product of 'fifth-century enlightenment' or the sophistic movement, briefly anticipated by the Presocratics. It seems much more likely that Greek religion of its nature was, like most polytheisms, an open, pluralistic system able to 'contain multitudes', to accommodate many different, even seemingly incompatible, viewpoints and practices. In the fifth and fourth centuries we have simply a close-up view of the process at work, as it produces kaleidoscopic images which defy a simple summary.

# Further reading

Possibly the best really introductory work on classical Greek religion, with extensive quotation from ancient sources and good illustrations, is Mikalson (2005). This should be followed by Price (1999), an important and more debate-oriented account. The best comprehensive survey, full of useful insights, is still Burkert (1985). Invaluable also is the short, bibliographically based, overview in Bremmer (1999). (There is some more recent bibliography in Mikalson 2005.) Specifically on Athens, whence comes most of our evidence, see Mikalson (1983) and especially Parker (1996; 2005).

On the place of the city, Sourvinou-Inwood (1988; 1990) are classic and powerful statements; elements of the approach are to be found in Easterling & Muir (1985), and especially in Bruit Zaidman & Schmitt Pantel (1992), another 'introductory' treatment. Different ways of conceptualizing the Gods are discussed in Kearns (1995); see also ch. 2 of Mikalson (2005). Mythology would require a separate bibliographical note, but a good place to start is Graf (1993).

For sanctuaries, see Mikalson (2005: ch. 1), Alcock & Osborne (1994) and Corbett (1970). The writings of Burkert on sacrifice (1966; 1983) have generated much discussion; a different approach is Bowie (1995). For dedications, see van Straten (1976; 1981); for prayer, Pulleyn (1997). There is no satisfactory up-to-date treatment of Greek priesthoods, but Garland (1990) will serve for Athens. The last decades have seen a great deal of discussion on specific rituals performed by women, for which see Dillon (2002), and rather less on gender issues in religion generally: some aspects are explored in the essays in Blundell & Williamson (1998). Burkert (1987) deals with Mysteries, while Parker (1995) is a fairly recent survey and tentative interpretation of the evidence for 'Orphism'. Parker (1983) is fundamental on religious purity and its opposite.

# Bibliography

Alcock, S. E., & R. Osborne (eds) (1994) *Placing the gods: sanctuaries and sacred space in ancient Greece* (Oxford: Clarendon)

Blundell, S., & M. Williamson (eds) (1998) *The sacred and the feminine in ancient Greece* (London: Routledge)

Bowie, A. M. (1995) 'Greek sacrifice: forms and functions' in Powell 1995: 463–82

Bremmer, J. N. (1999) *Greek religion* (Oxford: Oxford University Press) (*G&R* New Surveys in the Classics 24)

Bruit Zaidman, L., & P. Schmitt Pantel (1992) *Religion in the ancient Greek city* (trans. P. Cartledge from the French original (¹1989)) (Cambridge: Cambridge University Press)

Burkert, W. (1966) 'Greek tragedy and sacrificial ritual' in: *GRBS* 7: 87–121

Burkert, W. (1983) Homo necans: *the anthropology of ancient Greek sacrificial ritual and myth* (trans. P. Bing from the German original (1972)) (Berkeley: University of California Press)

Burkert, W. (1985) *Greek religion: archaic and classical* (trans. J. Raffan from the German original (1977)) (Oxford: Blackwell)

Burkert, W. (1987) *Ancient mystery cults* (Cambridge MA: Harvard University Press)

Buxton, R. G. A. (ed.) (2000) *Oxford readings in Greek religion* (Oxford: Oxford University Press)

Corbett, P. E. (1970) 'Greek temples and Greek worshippers: the literary and archaeological evidence' in: *Bulletin of the Institute of Classical Studies* 17: 149–58

Dillon, M. (2002) *Girls and women in classical Greek religion* (London: Routledge)

Easterling, P., & J. Muir (eds) (1985) *Greek religion and society* (Cambridge: Cambridge University Press)

Garland, R. (1990) 'Priests and power in classical Athens' in: Beard, M., & J. North (eds) (1990) *Pagan priests: religion and power in the ancient world* (London: Duckworth) 73–91

Graf, F. (1993) *Greek mythology: an introduction* (trans. T. Marier from the German original (1987)) (Baltimore: Johns Hopkins University Press)

Kearns, E. (1995) 'Order, interaction, authority: ways of looking at Greek religion' in: Powell 1995: 511–29

Mikalson, J. D. (1983) *Athenian popular religion* (Chapel Hill: University of North Carolina Press)

Mikalson, J. D. (2005) *Ancient Greek religion* (Oxford: Blackwell)

Parker, R. (1983) *Miasma: pollution and purification in early Greek religion* (Oxford: Clarendon Press (reissued, with new preface, 1986))

Parker, R. (1995) 'Early Orphism' in: Powell 1995: 483–510

Parker, R. (1996) *Athenian religion: a history* (Oxford: Clarendon)

Parker, R. (2005) *Polytheism and society at Athens* (Oxford: Oxford University Press)

Powell, A. (ed.) (1995) *The Greek world* (London: Routledge)

Price, S. (1999) *Religions of the ancient Greeks* (Cambridge: Cambridge University Press)

Pulleyn, S. (1997) *Prayer in Greek religion* (Oxford: Oxford University Press)

Sourvinou-Inwood, C. (1988) 'Further aspects of polis religion' in: *Annali dell'Istituto Universitario Orientale di Napoli, Dipartimento di Studi di mondo classico e del Mediterraneo antico, Sezione di archeologia e storia antica* 10: 259–74 = Buxton 2000: 38–55

Sourvinou-Inwood, C. (1990) 'What is polis religion?' in: Murray, O., & S. Price (eds) (1990) *The Greek city* (Oxford: Clarendon) 295–322 = Buxton 2000: 13–37

van Straten, F. T. (1976) 'Daikrates' dream: a votive relief from Kos, and some other *kat'onar* dedications' in: *Bulletin Antieke Beschaving* 51: 1–38

van Straten, F. T. (1981) 'Gifts for the Gods' in: Versnel, H. S. (ed.) (1981) *Faith, hope, and worship: aspects of religious mentality in the ancient world* (Leiden: Brill) 65–151 (Studies in Greek and Roman Religion 2)

CHAPTER SIXTEEN

# Citizens, Foreigners and Slaves in Greek Society

## Nick Fisher

## 1  Introduction

Classical Greek states are often described as 'male clubs', societies where citizenship was tightly defined and regulated, and adult male citizens monopolized the right to vote, to hold public office and to own land. A variety of other people also lived in these cities: in addition to the citizens' children and wives, and the other women, of citizen, non-citizen and non-Greek backgrounds, discussed by Sarah Pomeroy in the next chapter, there would usually be officially registered foreign residents, immigrants from other Greek or non-Greek communities. All states depended on exploited, non-citizen, labour forces: in most cases these were chattel-slaves, the property of their masters, typically of non-Greek origin; in a few cases they were free but inferior labourers tied to particular estates, whose status is usually described as that of 'serfs' or 'community slaves', best known being the Spartan helots. All these non-citizens were excluded from participation in political life, and held at varying levels of legal disadvantage, but the free residents were not excluded from participating in a variety of forms of economic or social interaction on more equal levels, and there are clear signs of uncertainty and controversy on the issue of the proper application of these rules. This chapter considers some of the issues of interrelationships between these different groups and resulting tensions and contradictions; most of the discussion, like the evidence, is necessarily focused on Athens and Sparta.

## 2  Slave Societies?

Nature then intends to make the bodies of free persons and of slaves different from each other, those of slaves strong for their necessary duties, and those of the free upright and useless for such forms of work, but useful for the political life.

Aristotle *Politics* 1254b27–33

> It seems to be a law of nature, that slavery is equally destructive to the master and to the slave; for, while it stupefies the latter with fear, and reduces him below the condition of man, it brutalizes the former by the practice of continual tyranny; and makes him the prey to all the vices which render human nature loathsome.
>
>                                    The ex-slave Charles Ball, in Taylor (1999: vol. 1, 265)

While slavery was ubiquitous throughout the Greek world, it is less certain how many of the Greek states should be classified as 'slave societies', as that term is commonly used by contemporary historians of a society where slaves formed a significant proportion of the labouring population (say 20–5 per cent or more) or where at least the dominant class or the elite derived the majority of their surplus production and hence their wealth from enslaved labour (see, e.g., Finley 1998: 145–60; de Ste. Croix 1981: 52–7, 133–74; Cartledge 2001: 131–2). It is agreed that Athens (from at least the fifth century BCE onwards) was such a slave society, and so probably were a fair number of other poleis, amongst them those famous among the Greeks for the large numbers of their slaves, such as Chios (Thuc. 8.40) Korinth, and Aigina (Athenaios 272B–D, though the numbers quoted there from earlier authors for the slave populations of these states are impossibly exaggerated). One central feature of slave systems was accurately identified by Aristotle: 'a human being who by nature belongs not to himself, but to another person is a slave by nature, and a human belongs to another who is a piece of property as well as a human, and a piece of property is a tool which is used to assist some activity which has a separate existence from its owner' (Aristotle *Politics* 1254a14–18). As we shall see, this dual nature of the slave, conceived both as a tool owned by another, and as a human being, so clearly recognized by one of the greatest of Greek philosophers, is the fundamental contradiction which engenders many problems in any slave society – problems in terms of deciding how to treat slaves and how to justify the institution. This in itself made absurd Aristotle's sustained attempt in *Politics* book 1 to justify the institution as natural and legitimate (see the analyses of his treatment by Smith 1983; Cartledge 1993b; Garnsey 1996; Schofield 1999: 115–40). Many modern definitions of slavery follow Aristotle's lead, focusing on the issues of ownership and absolute power (e.g., de Ste. Croix 1981; Finley 1998); others, equally helpfully, develop analysis of the master–slave relationship in terms of a consequence of such absolute power exercised on alienated persons in the form of the regular imposition of shame and degradation exercised on them by force (see Patterson 1982). Here I explore how this insistence on the distinction between slave and free, and on reminding slaves or serfs of their inferiority, was a constant element in their management, but also how the need for the free to avoid seeming 'slavish' created systemic opportunities for some slaves and ex-slaves to attain positions of relative independence and even wealth.

## 3   Sparta and the Helots

Some Greek states depended primarily not on imported, mostly non-Greek, slaves, but on the labour of semi-free dependents tied to the land, mostly indigenous subordinate populations. Besides Sparta's helots, they include Thessaly, some or all of the states in Crete, and many 'colonial' poleis, for example Herakleia on the Black

Sea or Syracuse in Sicily. The origin of the term 'helots' is either from Helos on the south coast of Lakonia, from which some of them may originally have come, or as a word meaning 'captives' (or both). Two groups of subject peoples came to be distinguished, those descended from Lakonians, believed to have been suppressed by the Spartans in the eighth century, and those from Messenia, conquered during the seventh century (on the traditional interpretation of very uncertain ancient chronology). The Messenian helots were believed to be the larger population (Thuc.1.101), with the more tenacious religious and cultural traditions and memories of freedom, and hence the more likely to resist or revolt.

Unlike chattel-slaves, the helots were not solely the property of individual masters, bought and sold in slave markets; they lived with their families in their own local communities, while being assigned to work on the estates of their masters the Spartiates. As our earliest source suggests (the archaic Spartan poet Tyrtaios F 6 West, quoted by Pausanias 4.4), the helots were probably locked into a sharecropping scheme whereby they contributed 50 per cent of their produce to their masters and kept the other 50 per cent for themselves – such a scheme has many parallels. Quotas taken by the landlords under sharecropping schemes known across the world can vary between 10 per cent and 80 per cent of the main crop, but in many places 50 per cent has been standard. In the best-known, but still very obscure, case elsewhere in Greece, the *hektemoroi* ('sixth-parters') in Athens before the reforms of Solon, a probable view is that these 'serfs' paid one sixth of the crops of some or all of their lands to their richer neighbours in exchange for some help and protection. The Spartan system, though obviously exploitative, spread the risks and encouraged shared activity in developing the estates (Hodkinson 2000: 125–31). The Spartan state appears to have had the right to intervene regularly in the rights of the individual owners to sell, free or otherwise dispose of them:

> Ephoros says . . . : 'the Heleioi, those who held Helos, revolted and were conquered by force of arms and adjudged slaves (*douloi*) on fixed conditions. Their master was permitted neither to manumit them nor to sell them outside the boundaries.' The Spartans held the Helots as slaves (*douloi*) as it were belonging to the people (*demosioi*). (Strabon 8.5.4, quoting the fourth-century historian Ephoros *FGrHist* 70 F 117)

What exactly 'the boundaries' means here, and whether we should label these people 'serfs' or 'community slaves', are matters of debate (see recently, e.g., Hodkinson 2000: 113–31; Luraghi 2002), but these features distinguish them from chattel-slaves and had important consequences. The Spartans recognized a relationship of collective and official enmity, based on conquest: Aristotle reported (according to Plutarch *Lykourgos* 28) that the five new ephors would annually declare war on the helots, so that they might be killed without incurring a religious pollution. This statement authorized Spartiates to execute them without any moral and religious scruple, and suggests both that they felt a need to kill helots quickly and without trial, and that they wished to strike constant fear into the helots. We cannot be certain when this practice began; but two further reports strongly reinforce this state of perpetual war, though their interpretation is disputed. In the same chapter, Plutarch describes the activities of a 'secret service' (*krypteia*), though he doubts that it was part of ancient tradition, and prefers to believe it developed only after the 460s earthquake and Messenian helot revolt: on this account the overseers of the bands of youths completing their military and civic education sent the cleverest young men into the countryside, armed only with daggers and charged with killing any helots they met by night (thus in effect imposing a night curfew), and also killing those reported as being excessively strong or brave (and a third-century BCE historian, Myron of Priene, also stated that over-vigorous helots would be put to death, *FGrHist* 106 F 2). As has been argued by Vidal-Naquet (1986), this has the appearance of a transformation of a coming-of-age ritual, where young warriors were separated from their community and lived by hunting in the rough countryside, into a process for the exercise of helot-control by terror, employing both random and targeted killings. But it remains open when this transformation began (sixth century? fifth century?), how often this was done, how many were killed, and whether the practice became greatly intensified after the Messenian revolt of the 460s. Second, Thucydides reported an especially gruesome episode during a crisis period in the Archidamian War in 424, when 2,000 of the bravest helots were tricked into believing that they were to be honoured and set free, were taken garlanded around the sanctuaries, but then mysteriously 'disappeared' (Thuc. 4.80). Sceptical views that Thucydides adopted this horror story uncritically, either out of sympathy for Messenian helots or misled by Spartan propaganda (see Talbert 1989; Whitby 1994), seem unlikely, given his lack of sympathy shown elsewhere for the Messenians or for any other slaves, and the implausibility of the Spartans actively promulgating such a story. It seems preferable to suppose that Thucydides heard of this from helot sources (conceivably he might have talked to helot deserters who fled to Athenian protection at Naupaktos, Pylos or Kythera, or picked the story up from Athenians operating in those places, such as the general Demosthenes), and believed it because it fitted what he generally knew of Spartan methods of control (see Cartledge 2002: 128–30).

Spartan treatment of their helots was, however, systematically contradictory, mixing elements of integration and encouragement with terror and savagery. Helots were used as combatants in their armies at least from the time of the Persian Wars, and in large numbers; according to Herodotos there were 35,000 light-armed helots at the battle of Plataiai, perhaps fighting in the rear of the phalanx, and only 5,000 Spartiates (Hdt. 9.10.28–9). From the time of the Peloponnesian War, they increasingly armed and trained helots to serve as hoplites, with the promise of liberating them; intriguingly, at just the same time as the disappearance of the 2,000, a good number of helots agreed to serve in the Spartan land army in Brasidas' expedition in north east Greece, in Thrace, and a number of these were subsequently liberated and became the so-called 'new demos-members' (*neodamodeis*) (Thuc. 5.34). They did not in fact become Spartiates, but formed one of a large number of inferior status-groups between Spartiates and helots in Spartan society (see Hunt 1998: 170–5). Another 'liberated' group were the children of Spartiates and helot women; probably quite a large group, as one can only assume that such sexual abuse of power was frequent, as in all known systems of slavery and serfdom. These were probably called *mothones* and in many cases may have served as personal attendants of their Spartiate half-brothers; they may also have been called *mothakes*, though that term may rather refer to other 'inferior' Spartans whose family estates were no longer able to maintain the mess-dues necessary for citizenship (see Hodkinson 2000: 336–7, 355–6). Myron of Priene (*FGrHist* 106 F 2) gives further examples of Spartan humiliations, involving degrading dress and regular beatings, whether an offence had been committed or not; such reminders of the permanent state of inferiority, and satisfaction of masters' sadism, are standard in slave systems, which rest above all on the fear of the whip (for a telling mythical anecdote on that point, see Hdt. 4.1–4, with Finley 1998: 186–7). Plutarch adds that privileged helots were invited to attend meals in the messes, but then were encouraged to make drunken exhibitions of themselves, singing and dancing in vulgar fashion, for the young men to laugh at them; Plutarch (*Lykourgos* 28) claims the purpose was for the young men to learn 'what drunkenness was like', but it was doubtless also for the helots to be reminded, even when being given a privilege, of their permanent inferiority. On plantations in the southern states, masters commonly allowed encouraged slaves to make music and dance on Saturday nights (see Genovese 1974: 569–84); renewed humiliation could be involved, as in the case of the slave owner Edwin Epps of Louisiana, who, drunk himself, and whip in hand, would make his exhausted slaves dance and laugh all night (Solomon Northup, in Taylor 1999: vol. 2, 243–5).

From at least the mid-fifth century onwards, the Messenian helots claimed strong memories of their own cultural traditions; when they revolted in the 460s they established a stronghold on Mount Ithome (where there was a sanctuary sacred to Zeus which became their major shrine), and when liberated in 370 they successfully founded their new city on its slopes. The narratives of their earlier 'history' preserved in Pausanias book 4 seem to be mostly post-370 inventions, and some would even argue (perhaps with excessive scepticism) that the very idea of their ethnic identity was invented in the classical period to create a solidarity among the helots working and living in Messenia (Figueira 1999; Luraghi 2002). There had evidently been a large-scale revolt by helots in the archaic period (the 'Second Messenian War', traditionally located in the mid-seventh century, but the dates are seriously problematic). There may have been some troubles late in the sixth century and early fifth century (Hdt. 5.49; Plato *Laws* 692D, 698D–E), but this is debatable. The major revolt in the 460s followed an earthquake causing large loss of life at Sparta (Thuc. 1.101–3); and it seems that many helots were prepared to join the rebellion planned in 397 by Kinadon, a disaffected young 'Inferior', which was nipped in the bud by the cunning Spartan authorities (Xenophon *Hellenika* 3.3.4–11). Finally, all the Messenian helots, but not the Lakonians, were successfully liberated by the Thebans, after the battle of Leuktra (371), and helped by them to establish the new and lasting polis of Messene. Sparta was fundamentally weakened as a result.

This record seems to confirm, as ancient writers like Plato and Aristotle concluded after the events of 371–370, that the helots had been a constant danger to the Spartiates. When about to describe the 'disappearing' of the 2,000 helots, Thucydides generalized that 'most Spartan institutions have always been designed with a view to security against the Helots' (or that 'as far as the helots are concerned, most Spartan institutions have always been designed with a view to security', Thuc. 4.80: the Greek can be read either way, and both statements are defensible – see, e.g., Cartledge 2002: 88–9, 128–9). Among the institutions which should be seen as having at least as one aim security against the helots are the rigorous system of young Spartiates' upbringing (*agoge*), the adult men's messes with their concentration on uniformity and the suppression of economic and social individuality, and the cautious approach to the presence of foreigners in their state. Much of the time Spartiate cohesion, arrogant superiority, and the whip, on the one hand, and on the other economic security for all helots, and personal ties with their masters and inducements for some, maintained a relatively stable system of dominance; from the second half of the fifth century, however, a declining population of the Spartiate citizen-body, and internal social tensions produced by this demographic decline, exacerbated by an unwisely aggressive foreign policy, made Spartan control dangerously unstable. Even so, the force of the psychological ties of subservience can be glimpsed in two anecdotes of the Lakonian helot responses during the Theban invasion of Lakonia in 370. While the Messenian helots responded warmly to the Theban invitation to rebel, 6,000 Lakonian helots signed up to serve as hoplites, and fought loyally, though their very number initially worried the Spartans (Xenophon *Hellenika* 6.5.28; Diodoros 15.65.6 gives a figure of 1,000); and some of these Lakonian helots, when captured by the Thebans, did not dare sing traditional Spartan songs because their Spartan masters would not wish them to (Plutarch *Lykourgos* 28).

## 4   Slaves and Ex-Slaves in Athens

In the early fourth century, an Athenian defended a metic accused with others, primarily on the testimony of their own slaves, of some serious financial offence; only a few paragraphs have survived of the defence speech which the speechwriter Lysias (himself a metic) wrote to be delivered in court, but they include the following argument:

> The trial should not be considered, I believe, as a private affair of these participants, but a matter of common concern to everyone in the city. It is not just these men who have slaves, but everyone else does too; when slaves look at what has happened to these slaves, no longer will they calculate how they may do good services for their masters in order to become free men, but rather what lies they can use to denounce them. (Lysias 5.5)

This asserts as uncontroversial norms that every free man was likely to own one or more slaves, and that manumission as a reward for good behaviour was routinely operated as an incentive. In another Lysias speech a citizen defending his right to continue to receive a disability pension from the state claims that he has

> a craft which is little able to help me, which I can myself only work at with difficulty; and I cannot yet afford to buy someone to take it over from me. I have no other source of income apart from this grant; if you take that away from me, I will be in danger of suffering very great hardship. (Lysias 24.5)

He may well be lying about his disability and poverty, but the appeal is again to a general assumption that Athenians bought slaves if they possibly could, and it was an indication of serious poverty if one was unable to do so. How far removed this was from reality is hard to determine, and a matter of much modern debate. But the ideological points remain, that even if half or more of the Athenians owned no slaves, they would all hope to be able to afford one some day, and would like it to be thought they did or might; popular juries, many of whom were probably poor, liked to be appealed to as slave owners (see also Demosthenes 45.86), and above all did not want to be thought of as being like slaves themselves.

Evidence from the military sphere also suggests that a good many citizens possessed slaves, and that slaves often attended their masters and fought on campaigns. During the Peloponnesian War, those who were registered as infantry (hoplites; also probably classed as *zeugitai*), the majority of them farmers, were expected to take a slave with them as attendant and baggage-carrier (Thuc. 3.17 and 7.75). This is good evidence that not only the elite, who might serve in the cavalry or in the navy as trierarchs, but the rest of the registered hoplites as well were likely to own more than one slave (but estimates of the proportion of that group to the rest vary considerably: see, for an innovative, rather minimizing account, van Wees 2001). Similarly in the mercenary army of the Ten Thousand in Asia in 401–400 there were many slave baggage-carriers, some of whom appear to have been promoted to fighting roles in the long retreat (Xenophon *Anabasis* 2.5.32, 3.2.28, 3.4.32, and Hunt 1998: 165–70). In the navy, many of the rowers and normally the 'marines' (*epibatai*) who were armed came from the poorer Athenians classified as *thetes* (Thuc. 6.43, 8.24); many rowers came from the metic populations, from Athens' allies, or were slaves, some owned by these poorer Athenians. One inscription lists crews by name, perhaps because they were awarded honours after the battle of Aigospotamoi (405), and reveals over a hundred slaves; in nine cases their masters appear also on the lists, as *epibatai* or as ordinary rowers (*IG* 1$^3$ 1032 – with Laing 1965; Graham 1992; Osborne 1995: 29–30). The use of slaves in the military forces of many ancient states including Athens and Sparta has been systematically undervalued or obfuscated in both ancient and modern historiography (see Hunt 1998); some slaves may have resented the compulsion to risk their lives for their masters' city, but for others it may have helped to cement loyalty and given them hopes of being set free, either by their masters, or occasionally in large numbers by the state, as after the battle of Arginousai (406), when they were also, more unusually, given citizenship as well (see Xenophon *Hellenika* 1.6.24, Aristophanes *Frogs* 533, 693–4, with *scholia*; Graham 1992; Hunt 1998: 87–95).

Most Athenians owned some land, and all who could no doubt employed slaves to help them; on the argument above and others this would surely have included most registered hoplites (who may have numbered perhaps between 5,000 and 10,000 at various times) and the vast majority of rich Athenians, save only those like Demosthenes' father who chose not to own land. The disputed issue concerns how many of those poorer Athenians (*thetes*) who had smaller farms could afford a slave or two to help them. The leading male characters in Aristophanes' comedies, who seem to represent the ordinary, less politically active, citizen-farmers, and some of whom complain bitterly of their poverty, are shown owning a number of all-purpose slaves, who work on the farm among other duties. For example, Philokleon in the *Wasps*, who is presented as an old man neither rich nor sophisticated, and obsessive about jury-service (though his son seems comfortably off), often reminisces how he used to run his farm with his four or so slaves, and Chremylos in *Wealth*, who complains that he like many has been impoverished by the war, still has a faithful slave Karion, and others besides (*Wealth* 26–7). While this reinforces the idea that the typical citizens were small farmers who had slaves to help them, it does not give us any idea of the proportion, or how this proportion may have varied over time; the total number of slaves will no doubt have varied in relation to times of general prosperity or hardship, and fluctuations in the life-cycle of peasant families, in the number of active members of the family, will have affected the number of slaves needed at any one time. Further, the considerable demand for extra labour at peak times of ploughing and sowing, and harvesting, is likely to have created the demand for short-term hiring of labour (slave or free) by those with larger landholdings, and to have induced neighbourly collaboration among the poorer farmers (see on all this Gallant 1991; Sallares 1991; Jameson 1978; 1992; Fisher 1993; Osborne 1995).

There were few really large estates in Attika; the rich elite, the top 10 per cent, who may well have owned a third or more of the agricultural land (Osborne 1992; Foxhall 1992), seem on the evidence of listings of estates in the forensic speeches to have owned a number of middling estates across Attika rather than a single large one. A consequence may be that slaves who worked on a farm were not organized in large chain gangs, as on *latifundia* in classical Italy or large plantations in the Americas, but in small groups managed by the owner, or by his slave overseer, or by a farm-tenant (see, e.g., Xenophon *Oikonomikos* 12–14, with Pomeroy 1994; Osborne 1995: 32–4). Comic presentations of the relations between citizen farmers and their slaves give a plausible picture of the coexistence of contempt, frequent whippings, casual sexual abuse, yet also something approaching friendship, on the side of the slave owners, and an expectation in return of hard work and loyalty, but also of constant pilfering and sabotage, from the slaves. These two addresses to supposedly loyal slaves, from Aristophanes' poor farming heroes Philokleon and Chremylos, convey well the uneasy comedy to be made of these contradictions:

> Won't you let me go now, you worst of beasts,
> don't you remember the time when I found you stealing grapes
> and I tied you up to the olive tree and flayed you well and manfully,
> so that every one envied you? But I see you weren't grateful.
> (Aristophanes *Wasps* 438–51)

> Well, I will tell you; for of my slaves
> I hold you to be the most loyal . . . and the biggest thief.
> (Aristophanes *Wealth* 26–8)

There is as one would expect much advice on kind treatment and providing incentives for slaves in the surviving treatises of household management, including praise and extra privileges and honours, especially for the overseers, a share in religious sacrifices and festivals, and the hope of manumission (see Xenophon *Oikonomikos* 9.13–14; Aristotle *Politics* 1330a26–33; Pseudo-Aristotle *Oikonomika* 1344a20–1344b11). There are examples of kindness and good treatment of loyal ex-slaves in the orators: e.g., a family's nurse who had been manumitted, 'lived apart' with her husband, then returned when widowed to live again with the former owner's family, only to die from injuries inflicted when enemies of the household seized valuables in a raid on their farmhouse (Pseudo-Demosthenes 47.52–73). But the consciousness of the danger of slave resistance or revolt produces the repeated recommendation to employ non-Greek ('barbarian') slaves from different ethnic origins, and preferably from peoples not supposed to be too courageous; and the centrality of bodily punishments and the physical and symbolic power of the whip is never far from view, in these and in all our other texts:

> If you (the jury) wished to look into what makes the difference between a slave and a free man, you would find that the greatest distinction was that in the case of slaves it is the body which takes responsibility for all their offences, whereas it is possible for free men, however great their misfortunes, to protect their bodies. (Demosthenes 22.54)

This distinction runs throughout Greek culture; in comedy: slaves fear or boast about regular whippings, e.g., Aristophanes *Knights* 53–7, *Wasps* 428–9, 1292–8, where slaves envy tortoises their protective shells, and an apparently traditional pun plays on the appropriateness of slaves of all ages being called 'boy' (*pais*) because they are always being beaten (*paiein* = to beat) (see DuBois 1990; 2003; Golden 1992). Slaves may be casually addressed as 'whip-bait' (*mastigias*), and slapstick humour was frequently extracted from protracted flogging scenes: see both Aristophanes' ironic criticism of such comic exploitation of slave trickeries and savage punishments inflicted on them at *Peace* 741–7, and his resort to similar humour at *Frogs* 594–657. Similarly in Menander's plays characters regularly assume that all slaves are deceitful, may be primarily interested in thieving and sneaking in as much sex as they can, and deserve their whippings (e.g., *Dyskolos* 459–65). On the other hand Aristophanes' later plays began to develop the tradition of the loyal and cunning slave, which was greatly expanded in the plays of Menander and his contemporaries into that of the leading character scheming ceaselessly for the interests and concerns of the family – and especially the love-sick young hero – to which he is encouraged to feel he belongs. Any idea that these comic characters – the forerunners of Figaro or Jeeves – were based on a new reality of slave–master relations should be viewed very sceptically (Garlan 1988: 16–18). We should note also that the Greeks were fully aware that excessive bodily punishments inflicted on slaves, punishments inflicted in anger rather in reason, carried moral dangers to the soul of the masters and practical dangers to their security, as unjust savagery might provoke slaves to acts of sabotage, assault or flight (see Harris 2001: 318–38; DuBois 1990; 2003). Such humour and advice seem to rest on the perception, which we find echoed in ex-slave accounts from the Southern States of the USA, that the combination of the constant fear and reality of whippings, along with signs of paternalistic concern and the setting of moral standards by the master, often produced an acceptance of legitimate punishment and a deferential loyalty, as well as a bitter sense of injustice at arbitrary whippings (Genovese 1974: 63–149; Blassingame 1979: ch. 8; Patterson 1982: 11–13).

This bodily distinction is central to the legal system; slavery in Athens, as in Sparta and probably everywhere in Greece, was as institutionally violent and tolerant of the cruelty of masters as any other slave system, and operated with a similar, contradictory, view of the slave-personality (see MacDowell 1978: 79–83; Todd 1993: 184–200). If slaves committed offences outside their own household, the slave owners might be prosecuted and pay the damages, and might deliver the slaves for physical punishment or punish them themselves (e.g., Demosthenes 53.20); here slaves were not seen as legally significant persons. Similarly, they could not normally bring actions themselves, but masters or others would have to bring any action on their behalf, and they could not normally give evidence in the same way as could free adult males. In cases of public or religious concern, such as the investigation into the mutilation of the herms in 415, slaves might be invited to give evidence, with the prospect of freedom if their evidence proved to be true (Thuc. 6.27–8); or they might be compelled by commissioners to give evidence under judicial torture. But in general the principle was that slaves, and only slaves, should have their evidence taken only if they were first subjected to torture; and in legal disputes between individuals, each party had to agree to a challenge from the other for a slave's evidence to be presented in court after torture. There would naturally be a strong temptation for the challenged party to resist, because he feared what the slave might come up with (and where he was the owner, he might also not wish his property to be hurt or damaged). Hence in all the cases we know of, the challenge was not carried through, and the slave's evidence not heard; and the usual view is that in practice slave-torture was remarkably rare (e.g., Thür 1977; Gagarin 1996). There is an alternative argument that in cases where slave-torture took place, it was taken as decisive, and hence no further trial took place, hence no speeches survive in such cases (Mirhady 1991; 1996). But it is clear that in a great many cases the challenge to collect slave-evidence by torture was taken merely as a rhetorical opportunity for both sides to rehearse traditional arguments about the reliability or not of slave-torture, and that in general the Athenians subordinated the attempt to ensure that relevant evidence was heard by the court to the preservation of the twin principles that slaves, unlike the free, did not have the mental capacity or the stake in the country to be trusted to tell the truth in the public interest, and that their bodies, unlike those of the free, could be subjected to physical pain inflicted (see also Todd 1990; DuBois 1990; Hunter 1994; Mirhady 1996).

The laws recognized a need to offer some protection to slaves against ill treatment. Homicide by a slave owner might in theory be prosecuted by another citizen, but it is not easy to imagine this happening in view of the general solidarity among slave owners (see, e.g., Plato *Republic* 578D–9A; Xenophon *Hieron* 4.3), and the fact that an owner might ask the state to approve the execution of a disobedient slave, or merely perform a ceremony of purification if a slave died after punishment. Killing someone else's slave might perhaps incur a prosecution, either for homicide, or perhaps only for damages (see Pseudo-Demosthenes 47.70). The serious offence of grievous insult (*hybris*) envisaged the possibility of slaves (as of women and children) as victims of violent or sexual assaults (law cited in Demosthenes 21.47), and Athenian juries liked to be complimented on their humanity in allowing slaves' honour to be so protected. There seems an ideological contradiction here, in that permanent dishonour was seen as a defining feature of the existence of Greek slaves, like most slaves (see Patterson 1982); yet the essence of *hybris* is the infliction of dishonour. It seems that the Athenians did allow in principle that the slave had vestigial honour which deserved signalling by this law; but it should also be argued that one main purpose of this law was to indicate to all how grave an offence *hybris* was. Possible cases featuring slave victims were doubtless very rare, and where they occurred, they tended to involve either public or otherwise privileged slaves (e.g., Pittalakos in Aischines 1.56–64), or female musicians/entertainers, publicly assaulted in ways which also may have humiliated their citizen lovers (see Fisher 1995, and for a rather more optimistic assessment of how much genuine protection these laws offered to slaves, Cohen 2000: 160–7).

The literary evidence gives more abundant evidence for slaves as labour forces in silver mining, in craft workshops, in overseas and retail trade and in banking than in agriculture (e.g., Hopper 1979; Osborne 1985). In the lists of property-holdings from law court speeches we hear of 120 slaves, mostly shield-makers, owned by the very rich metic family of Lysias (Lysias 12.19), thirty-two or thirty-three knife-makers and twenty bed-makers owned by Demosthenes' father (Demosthenes 27.9–11), and the more typical smaller craft units owned by Timarchos' father (Aischines 1.97–9). In all, there was a fairly high degree of 'horizontal specialization'; over 200 different occupational terms, and at least 170 specialized occupations, have been identified, in farming and food production, retail, building, manufacture of clothes and household goods, metalwork, transport, services, banking, entertainment and the arts (see Harris 2002); slaves and ex-slaves might perform almost all of these roles. What is especially notable is that a good number of these slaves were trusted sufficiently to operate on their own in small workshops, as agents in retail or overseas trade, or in money changing and banking operations; they paid agreed amounts of their profit to their owners and might keep the rest. Some such slaves are occasionally described as *khoris oikountes*, those who are 'living separately' (and this phrase is also found of freedmen, or of those whose status is unclear, as at Pseudo-Demosthenes 47.72 and at Demosthenes 4.36); slaves hired out to other operators were labelled as 'fee-earning' (*andrapoda misthophorounta*) and paid their masters a fixed amount (*apophora*). Examples include the cobblers and weavers owned by Timarchos' father (Aischines 1.97), the perfumers who are sold to the speaker in Hypereides' speech *Against Athenagoras*, and most interestingly a character in Demosthenes 34 called Lampis, who is described as the 'domestic slave' (*oiketes*) of Dion, but who has his own ship, engages in trading, was probably registered as a metic in Athens, and can give evidence in this commercial case (see Cohen 1992: 240). There is, however, a faint possibility that by now he is a freedman, called in the speech 'slave', *oiketes*, to denigrate him, though the point is not developed (see Todd 1993: 192–4). It seems from this case and others that from the mid-fourth century special 'commercial courts' were established for the swift conduct of business, and it is likely that slaves engaged in trade and banking could give evidence there as free men did, without torture.

These slaves were also likely to have been among the most likely to be manumitted, often buying the privilege with accumulated savings. Much of our evidence for Greek manumission comes from Hellenistic inscriptions from Delphi and other places in central Greece (see Hopkins 1978: ch. 3; Darmezin 1999); different types of manumission are attested, but many are concerned to define continuing duties which will be owed to ex-owners (the status called *paramone*); sanctuaries may be involved in the regulation and in some cases slaves end up 'dedicated' to various deities. It is very difficult to assess relative rates of manumission, and judge whether in Greece it was on the high side, as for example in Roman Italy, or relatively low, as in the USA. For Athens, the most interesting evidence is provided by a set of inscriptions from Athens of the 320s. What seems to be going on in these obscure documents is the recording of a prosecution brought by a master against an ex-slave for not performing the agreed further obligations (a *dike apostasiou*), where in all cases the slave is acquitted and thus finally 'set free' from all obligations, and then dedicates to Athena a silver bowl (*phiale*) of a fixed weight of 100 drachmas (though we have no information on which party normally paid this 'tax'). It is not clear whether these were real cases of genuine disputes between ex-slaves and their former owners (if so there seem to be a surprising number of them handled at once), or, more probably, fictitious cases: this is plausibly seen as one of a number of revenue-increasing mechanisms designed by Lykourgos and his colleagues c. 330, here used to regularize one type of manumission and raise money (Lewis 1959; 1968; Todd 1993: 190–2). Lykourgos is reported also to have passed a law regulating what happened to ex-slaves convicted in this type of lawsuit, but the relation between the measures is unclear (see Klees 1998: 334–54). It is, however, interesting that manumissions, and issues of their continuing relations with owners, were becoming sufficiently numerous to engage the legislative and financial interest of politicians.

The inscriptions usually designate the occupation of the (ex)slave. The majority of women who appear are 'woolworkers' (either a general term for their domestic duties, or a sign that they worked in a more commercial operation), and there are a number of 'entertainers'. The males are mostly divided across a wide range of crafts, small businesses and overseas trade, with a smaller number engaged in farming. Where slaves have a deme of residence indicated it is most commonly in the city or Piraeus; their citizen owners in almost all cases come from a different deme, but it is impossible to estimate from this how many slaves 'lived apart' from their masters, since we cannot say of any citizen whether he still lived in the 'ancestral' deme in which he was registered for citizenship purposes. In some cases, however, metic slave owners appear as living in different demes from their slaves, and here it seems certain that the slaves had been operating independently before they were set free.

The relative freedom of such richer, independent and 'luxurious' slaves, who it was alleged showed no deference towards the free, and were indistinguishable in dress from them, seems to have caused resentment among some traditional Athenians, as is recorded by the 'Old Oligarch' (Pseudo-Xenophon *Ath. Pol.* 1.10–12); his explanation is that in Athens, a strong naval and trading city, it was advantageous for men to let their slaves make money by engaging in direct financial trading with free men; Plato (*Republic* 563B) linked this trend not very persuasively to 'democratic freedom'. A fuller explanation would focus on the ideological pressure on free men and especially on citizens to preserve their 'macho' honour from the slur of engagement in a 'slavish' occupation, by working directly for another individual (the ideal is expressed clearly in Aristotelian aphorisms, as at *Rhetoric* 1367a30–5, and also at Xenophon *Oikonomikos* 4.1–4, 6.4–8, *Memorabilia* 2.8; Demosthenes 57.30–4, 45). Hence bankers, traders or manufacturers could get harder and more loyal workers by training their slaves to operate as their underlings or agents, with the gradated incentives of a freer life-style and eventual freedom. Encouraging them to operate separate businesses with separate living arrangements might also prevent the slaves from having a potentially dangerous knowledge of all the owners' business activities (Cohen 2002). A further advantage was that manumission could always be conditional, and the ex-slaves legally bound to continue indefinitely to offer respect to and perform economic services (*paramone*) for their former master, now their legal champion and defender (*prostates*).

## 5   Metics and Foreigners in Athens

Geographical mobility both of large population groups and of individuals was extremely widespread from early times among Greek communities, as across the Mediterranean and the Near East generally. As Greek states developed regulations to deal with questions of citizenship and identity, they must have devised mechanisms to distinguish their citizens (*politai*), who typically had monopoly rights to ownership of land and to the polis' decision-making bodies, from slaves and serf-like groups like the helots, on the one hand, and from free outsiders (*xenoi* – which may designate 'guest-friends', or more generally 'foreigners') who (unlike slaves) chose to reside in the city, on the other. Two alternative strategies are neatly identified, a propos of two neighbouring cities on the Dalmatian coast, by the second to third-century CE writer Ailianos: 'They say that the Apollonians practice foreigner-expulsions (*xenelasiai*) in the Spartan fashion, whereas the Epidamnians leave it open to anyone who wishes to visit and to become metics' (Ailianos *Varia Historia* 13.16). At one extreme, Sparta, and perhaps a very few other cities, chose a cautious and restrictive policy, not normally welcoming settlers and occasionally indulging in 'foreigner-expulsions' see, e.g., Thuc. 2.39; Xenophon *Lak. Pol.* 14); again we cannot say whether this was a long tradition, or began only with the pressures of the Peloponnesian War, nor how frequent they were. At the other, Athens and probably a great many other cities gradually developed formal arrangements for the registration and organization of their resident foreigners. Each state which decided to create such a status-group – they were usually called metics (*metoikoi*) – had to determine how long a period of temporary residence was permitted before registration was required – something like a month or so may have been standard: a statement attributed to the Alexandrian scholar Aristophanes of Byzantion (F 303–5 Slater) speaks of it being a question of 'how many days' before a visitor had to register; a fifth-century decree from Lokris recording an agreement between the cities of Chaleion and Oiantheia stipulates a month before a citizen of each state staying in the other becomes subject to the laws of that state, Tod 34; for Athens, cf. the exemption from the need to register as metics and pay the tax offered to Sidonians, in *IG* $2^2$ 141 = R&O 21. Then they had to decide whether to create a separate status with differentiated rights and obligations for ex-slaves – Athens chose not to take that route but to merge the categories, but many other states probably decided differently (see Aristotle's general assumption of different categories at *Politics* 1277b33–1378a2, and an example from the island of Keos at *IG* 12 5.647). Third, they might choose to require metics to be registered with a citizen as their official representative – at Athens he was called a *prostates*, and in the case of ex-slaves these would normally be their last masters, for whom they might well be required to perform continuing services. Finally they might levy extra taxes and obligations on them, and/or offer them privileges. Athens imposed a poll tax at the relatively low rate of one drachma a month (half for females), which none the less had significant symbolic value in distinguishing metics from citizens; metics were expected to serve in the armed forces at the level appropriate to their wealth, and to contribute to the property taxes and some of the lesser festival 'liturgies' (*leitourgiai*), which were expected of the wealthier citizens and involved expenditure of money, time and effort in the running of many of the state festivals, such as the drama. General statements in late lexicographers, and some documents in relation to a few states, suggest that many of these elements were added fairly regularly (Aristophanes of Byzantion F 303–5 Slater; Xenophon *Hellenika* 1.2.10 (Ephesos); *IG* 12 5.647, Keos) but only Athens allows any detailed discussion of economic and social relations (for Athens, Whitehead 1977; Patterson 2000; for other states, Whitehead 1984).

The standard view is that Athenian institutions maintained in principle the strict political and legal distinctions between citizens (normally called *politai*, or sometimes *astoi* when distinguished from *xenoi*, foreigners) and metics; though there were constant fears that metics were gaining access illicitly to the deme lists by bribery and collusion with citizens, and occasionally revisions of the lists were ordered. Cohen (2000: ch. 2) has recently argued that deme lists routinely came to include both citizens by descent and some long-term well-established metics, and that the term *astoi*, as distinct from *politai*, came to include both these categories; but this view is not, I think, supported by the texts he cites in support (e.g., Pseudo-Xenophon *Ath. Pol.* 1.12; Lysias 12.35; Xenophon *Poroi* 2.2), and ignores the continuing concerns at the illicit infiltration by such established metics. Cohen is right, however, to argue that there were increasing business, social and associative connections between citizens and metics, some of which would be situated in a deme (on banking connections, see also Shipton 1997), and one may suggest that these often formed the basis for metics' attempts illegally to infiltrate themselves or their kin into deme membership.

Athenian attitudes towards metics and other foreigners were contradictory, and the balance struck between the poles of welcoming approval and suspicious hostility fluctuated, partly no doubt in response to political events and social perceptions (e.g., Whitehead 1977; Patterson 2000). Positively, Athenians were conscious of the contributions metics made to the economy and to community life, and of the importance of winning the support and loyalty of foreign rulers and other influential figures; they offered citizenship and other honours to those whose benefactions and displays of their proper ambition (*philotimia*) were thought to merit it, however unlikely they were to be used in practice in the case of foreign dignitaries: see, e.g., Demosthenes 20, 23, Pseudo-Demosthenes 59.88–107, and the many inscriptions at least from c. 350 onwards proclaiming the importance of the practice to encourage others (e.g., *IG* $2^2$ 222, stating that a grant of citizenship be awarded so that 'everyone should know that the Athenian people renders large-scale returns to its benefactors'). Metics might be rewarded for exceptional performances (usually in-volving large-scale financial contributions) by a range of honours, such as paying taxes and military service on a par with citizens, the right to own house and land (see Pečírka 1966), and culminating in citizenship itself. From the documentary and literary evidence for grants of citizenship (see Osborne 1981–3), it emerges that such grants were relatively rare in the fifth century, but increased somewhat in the difficult years of the Peloponnesian War (including the mass enfranchisement of the Samians in 405). At the restoration of democracy in 403, (probably) close to 100 foreigners and metics who had fought with Thrasyboulos to restore the democracy were rewarded with citizenship, while many more hundreds (including many slaves) were merely granted equality of taxation (see the difficult document, *IG* $2^2$ 10 + 2403; Krentz 1980; R&O 4); there then seems to have been an increase in grants from c. 370 on, especially to foreign kings or tyrants and their supporters (com-mented on by Demosthenes 23.199–203), and – especially perhaps in the Lykourgan period – a growth in grants to metic bankers and other business men. In general bankers, often ex-slaves, seem to have been the metics who found it easiest to accumulate resources and donate enough of them to the city, and perhaps to make helpful social contacts, to overcome opposition to their crossing the citizenship barrier (Davies 1981: 64–6; Shipton 1997).

In about 355 the elderly Xenophon included in his pamphlet on increasing Athenian revenues some recommendations to induce more metics – and especially rich ones – to settle in Athens and more foreigners to trade there (Xenophon *Poroi* 2 and 3);

the text too reveals an ambiguous attitude (Whitehead 1977: 125–9). Positively, he suggests removing some dishonouring restrictions on the metics (perhaps the obligation to have a *prostates*, or some other restrictions); allowing (rich) metics to serve in the Athenian cavalry; making it easier for metics to buy plots of land inside the urbanized area of Athens and the Piraeus on which to build houses (but not extended to the purchase of farming land); and instituting a board of magistrates charged with looking after the metics' interests (but he doesn't indicate their functions). On the other hand, he reveals a concern that now many metics are 'barbarians' from the 'softer' parts of the Persian Empire (Lydians, Syrians and Phrygians), and recommends that they be excluded from the hoplite infantry. It is not clear whether he supposes increased immigration into Athens from those regions in particular, or (more probably) an increase in manumitted ex-slaves; either way the remark reveals the persistence of the ideological belief in the inferiority of barbarians/non-Greeks which was the fundamental basis of Greek slavery.

The classic instance of upward mobility, though rare in its extent, was the banking family of Pasion. He began as a slave working his way up to be the trusted manager of the money changing and banking firm of Antisthenes and Archestratos; by the 390s he was manumitted and as a metic was left in control of the business; and by the 380s he had contributed enough in naval liturgies and lavish gifts of shields and naval equipment so that he (and his descendants) were given citizenship, with the sponsorship of a citizen, Pythodoros, who acted as his agent (Davies 1971: 427–31). He then built up his banking, shield-making and property businesses to become one of the richest Athenians, maintaining financial and social connections with figures like the general Timotheos and the politician Kallistratos (see Apollodoros' speech against Timotheos, Pseudo-Demosthenes 49). His son Apollodoros built on these foundations to become a politician himself, and he is well known to us from a series of law court speeches which (though ascribed to Demosthenes) he composed himself (see Trevett 1992). We find him engaged in bitter disputes with his younger brother Pasikles and his father's slave manager Phormion, to whom Pasion leased the businesses at his death and bequeathed his widow Archippe as wife. This act, apparently common among bankers, reveals a contradiction in the law, of which this bequest took advantage: there was no mechanism whereby Archippe, the slave wife of a slave granted citizenship, could herself be recognized as a woman of citizen status and she was left in an anomalous status. If she had been now reckoned of citizen family, she should not have been permitted to marry Phormion, now a metic, but if she were reckoned as a metic woman, she should not have received as she did the substantial property of a boarding house which Pasion left her (Whitehead 1986b; Cohen 1992: 102–6). Phormion followed Pasion along the path to citizenship, while Apollodoros ended up with a good share of Pasion's very rich estate. His speeches reveal well his consciousness of his ambiguous position in Athenian society, a continuing preoccupation with citizenship issues, and a vulnerable, yet vindictive, temperament. In his attacks on Phormion and on his own mother and brother, he claims to have been deeply insulted by this misalliance between a barbarian slave and his former owner, whom he allegedly seduced and then married; Apollodoros even insinuates that Phormion had fathered his younger brother Pasikles during Pasion's lifetime. In all this, he chose to overlook that Archippe too had been a slave (Demosthenes 45.71–84 – a speech probably written for Apollodoros by Demosthenes, but reflecting Apollodoros' anger at losing the first trial). He tried to be more Athenian than the Athenian elite he consorted with, enjoying a lavish life-style, building credit with the people through a generous performance of liturgies, pursuing quarrels and feuds in the law courts, and as he admits himself incurring some unpopularity among other members of the elite by his fast walk and loud mouth (Demosthenes 45.77). So ostentatious was his over-spending on his trierarchies that he made life problematic for other trierarchs: he reports how one of them mocked his pretensions with the phrase 'The mouse has tasted pitch – he did want to be an Athenian' (Pseudo-Demosthenes 50.26–7).

The latest of Apollodoros' speeches to survive constitutes an impassioned defence of Athens' citizenship laws, though his main purpose was to gain revenge on a political and personal enemy (Pseudo-Demosthenes 59 (*Against Neaira*)). He and his brother-in-law Theomnestos prosecuted Neaira, a notorious, now middle-aged, prostitute, whose career had begun as a very young slave in a high-class brothel in Korinth. She was then owned by and lived with two men from Korinth and Leukas, who set her free when they were getting married; after being briefly kept by Phrynion, a prominent Athenian, she lived for a long time with a minor politician called Stephanos. The alleged offence is that Stephanos, a citizen, and Neaira, a foreign prostitute, have been living as if they were legitimately married, for which the 'proof' is that 'their' three sons have been enrolled as citizens, and 'their daughter' Phano has been twice married to citizens as a woman of citizen family; if convicted (as usual we do not know the result), Stephanos would be fined 1,000 drachmas, and Neaira returned to slavery. The case hinged not on the status of Neaira as a foreign prostitute and long-term partner of Stephanos, both of which seem undeniable, but on whether she was in fact the mother of any of these children, or whether they were the legitimate offspring of Stephanos' now deceased wife. The Areopagos Council had apparently already investigated the possibility that Phano had committed impiety when she had performed sacred Dionysiac rituals on behalf of the city, as the wife of her second husband who was the King-Archon that year, and they seem to have found it difficult to decide whether Phano was indeed Neaira's daughter. Allegedly they felt there was sufficient doubt about her religious suitability – perhaps merely because she had been married before – to require the rituals to be performed again, and her marriage to Theagenes to be dissolved, but were not so certain that serious sacrilege had taken place that they imposed further penalties (see Kapparis 1999: 351–3; Hamel 2003: 102–13; but also the doubts about the whole episode in Carey 1992: 126–8). Apollodoros devotes the climax of his speech to the importance of protecting the principles of the citizenship laws, for the sake of the gods, the laws and the honour of citizens and their women. He adopts the pose of a new citizen who has fully immersed himself in the history of his city, including enfranchisements of the past (the Plataians in 427); and at the same time assumes the tone of a well-off man of the world who can proclaim that 'we' (i.e., he and the jury) have the leisure to pursue pleasure and physical comforts with other women, *hetairai* and *pallakai*, while reserving for the wives the honoured functions of producing legitimate children and safeguarding the households; this privileged position must not be endangered by the jury's toleration of the infiltration of illegitimate children such as Neaira's daughter (Pseudo-Demosthenes 59.107–26).

This speech was delivered sometime between 347 and 340. During 346/5 the Athenians carried through, in all the demes, a complete revision of their citizenship lists; apparently a fair number of alleged infiltrators were expelled, under a procedure where a condemnatory vote in a deme assembly might lead to an appeal heard in the courts (see Demosthenes 57 *passim*; Isaios 12; Aischines 1.77–8, 114–15). Evidently there was a widespread perception that many illegitimate or non-Athenian children had been admitted onto the deme lists, whether sons of male citizens and their mistresses, or the result of liaisons between poor Athenian males and daughters of richer metics. Apollodoros' speech was evidently trying to tap into the same fears and prejudice whether it preceded the scrutiny or followed it. We cannot easily determine whether most of those expelled were properly expelled, or whether the operations of Demophilos' law merely offered opportunities for score settling between enemies inside the demes (see Davies 1978; Whitehead 1986a: 99–109; Connor 1994). One may note that mid-fourth-century comedy could make jokes about the easy mobility from slavery to citizenship:

> There is no city anywhere, my dear chap, made up of slaves,
> But Fortune shifts their bodies around in all directions.
> Nowadays many people are not free men
> But tomorrow they'll be registered Sounians, and the next day
> They'll make full use of the agora. A daimon steers the helm
> For every man.
>             (Anaxandrides F 4 Kassel & Austin = Athenaios 262C)

In theoretical mode, Aristotle, writing not much later, held that in cities with large populations 'it is easy for foreigners and metics to acquire citizenship, as because of the size of the population it is not difficult to escape detection' (Aristotle *Politics* 1326b21–6). Given that citizens came into regular close contact with metics (including freedmen), it would not be surprising if a good few citizens were tempted to gain a financial or social advantage by helping non-Athenians to infiltrate the deme lists.

Citizens, metics and foreigners made complex financial deals with each other in the worlds of overseas and retail trade and in banking, and even ordinary peasant farmers would be likely to be involved to some extent in market operations with metics and foreigners (see Cohen 1992; 2000: 104–29). Metics and foreign visitors could train at the gymnasia and wrestling grounds which were the major daytime social settings, compete in the open events at the Panathenaic games, and participate in Panathenaic processions; and they could engage in less formal interactions at the many local and city festivals, though there were dangers of malicious scams for unsuspecting foreign visitors (e.g., Aischines 1. 43–8, with Fisher 2001 ad loc.; Cohen 2000: 171–7). The protocols of sexual relations are unsurprisingly complex. Slaves of both sexes were naturally subject to sexual abuse (though moral norms advised restraint at flaunting this before one's wife), but were themselves forbidden by law from actively pursuing free youths, as they were from training with free men in the *gymnasia* (Aischines 1.138–9; Plutarch *Solon* 1.34; Golden 1984). Athenians, as Apollodoros proclaimed in his man of the world mode, often engaged in sexual acts or relationships with foreign women or boys, as with slaves. Seducing respectable citizen girls or married women might be very dangerous, and affairs with citizen youths which could be represented as based on the exchange of money or lavish gifts and maintenance for sex could bring disrepute, and a possible serious charge for the youth if he later sought to enter active political life (Aischines 1 *passim*, with, e.g., Fisher 2001). Hence casual sex or affairs with prostitutes or *hetairai* might be officially encouraged, as Aischines at the end of his prosecution of Timarchos asks the jury to give this message to those citizens – probably many – who liked to engage in sex with young men or boys (without being classifiable as 'homosexuals' in our sense): 'tell those who are the hunters of such young men as are easily caught to turn themselves to the foreigners and the metics, so that they may not be deprived of their inclination, but you citizens are not harmed' (Aischines 1.195).

A final example of citizen–metic co-operation which turned sour, as well as of the continued popularity of appeals in the courts to xenophobia and racial prejudice against non-Greek metics, is provided by what remains of Hypereides' law court speech *Against Athenogenes* (c. 330–324); the prosecution story presented by the cunning speechwriter is that the speaker was an honest if foolish citizen farmer who was persuaded to enter into a contract to buy a small perfume business, with three slaves, an adult and two boys, from Athenogenes, a 'speechwriter, market operator and worst of all an Egyptian'. The allegation is presumably that Athenogenes, who has a perfectly Greek name, moved to Athens from Egypt, and has at least some non-Greek blood; Greeks had been settled in Egypt, e.g. at Naukratis, for centuries, and the truth of the slur cannot be assessed by us. The speaker's main interest was in acquiring a monopoly of the sexual services of one of the slave boys; but in his eagerness, he failed to discover in time that the perfume business came with un-declared debts; the deal was partially engineered through the deceptions of Antigona, 'the cleverest *hetaira* of her generation', now a brothel keeper and Athenogenes' lover and partner-in-crime. The speaker is now prosecuting (with what success as usual we do not know) Athenogenes for the damages incurred, on the grounds that he, a clever, devious and cowardly 'Egyptian', had tricked the speaker into an unfair deal (Patterson 2000: 105–9; Cohen 2002: 106–7). On the other hand, evidence of tolerance and encouragement of foreign groups – even an Egyptian group – can be found in this period. Not only are many foreign and metic traders and politicians given honours and privileges under the guidance of Lykourgos, the leading politician in Athens, but he had also had a law passed granting to the community of merchants from Kition in Cyprus the right to buy a plot of land for a sanctuary to Aphrodite, and cited as a precedent the previous grant given to the Egyptian community for their temple to Isis (*IG* $2^2$ 337 = R&O 91). Such communities evidently met together to honour their chosen deity and to reinforce solidarity through regular meetings and shared eating and drinking. Much epigraphic evidence demonstrates that there were in Athens and elsewhere a steadily increasing number and variety of voluntary groups or associations (typically called *thiasoi*, *eranoi* or groups of *orgeones*) which defined themselves usually in relation to some cult, managed themselves along the model of the democratic state and its official subgroups with their assemblies and elected officials, owned (and might lease out) their properties and buildings, met regularly, and might raise loans to assist their members in trouble (e.g., Parker 1996: 328–42; Jones 1999; Arnaoutoglou 2003). The membership of these associations was in most cases citizen and male, but there is evidence that occasionally women participated in the social activities, and that membership might include foreigners and metics; exclusively foreign clubs are also attested in small numbers from the later fifth century (especially honouring the Thracian goddess Bendis), but increased in the Hellenistic period. In general, then, these associations gave new and important social identities and sociability to large numbers of ordinary inhabitants of Athens, and contributed a good deal to social integration between citizens and non-citizens.


# Further reading

A useful sourcebook on ancient slavery is Thomas Wiedeman's (1981; repr. 1992) *Greek and Roman slavery.* For the general study of ancient slavery and its effects on Greek ideology in general, with a strong comparative perspective, fundamental are Finley (1980, new ed. 1998) and papers in Finley (1968); de Ste. Croix (1981); and Patterson (1982; 1991). General accounts of Greek slavery are provided by Garlan (1988) and (briefer) Fisher (1993). On Sparta and the helots, the many debates can be followed in Cartledge (2001), and his collected papers, Cartledge (2002); Ducat (1990); Hodkinson (2000); and various papers in Powell (1989), Powell & Hodkinson (1994), Hodkinson & Powell (1999; 2002), Luraghi & Alcock (2003). For slaves in Greek warfare, Hunt (1998) and van Wees (1995; 2001; 2004); for the roles of slaves in Athenian agriculture, Jameson (1978), Gallant (1991), Sallares (1991), and papers in Wells (1992); in manufacture, business, banking and trade: Hopper (1979), Osborne (1985), Millett (1991), Cohen (1992), papers in Cartledge et. al. (2002); on various legal and ideological issues, Todd (1993), Cartledge (1993a; 1993b), Osborne (1995), Fisher (1995), Garnsey (1996), Gagarin (1996), Cohen (2000; 2002). On the laws and attitudes relating to foreigners and metics in Athenian society, fundamental is Whitehead (1977), and for other Greek cities, Whitehead (1984); on material on grants of citizenship and other privileges to metics and foreigners, see above all Osborne (1981–3) and further discussions of the legal and social issues in Boegehold & Scafuro (1994), Cohen (2000), Hunter & Edmondson (2000).


# Bibliography

Arnaoutoglou, I. N. (2003) Thusias heneka kai sunousias: *private religious assocations in Hellenistic Athens* (Athens: Academy of Athens) (Epeteris tou Kentrou Ereunes tes Historias tou Hellenikou Dikaiou 37, 4)

Blassingame, J. W. (1979) *The slave community: plantation life in the antebellum South* (revised and enlarged ed.) (Oxford: Oxford University Press)

Boegehold, A. L., & A. C. Scafuro (eds) (1994) *Athenian identity and civic ideology* (Papers presented at a conference held at Brown University, in April 1990) (Baltimore: Johns Hopkins University Press)

Carey, C. (1992) Apollodoros against Neaira *[Demosthenes] 59: edited and translated by C. Carey* (Warminster: Aris & Phillips) (Greek orators 6)

Cartledge, P. (1993a) *The Greeks: a portrait of self and others* (Oxford: Oxford University Press)

Cartledge, P. (1993b) 'Like a worm i'the bud?: a heterology of classical Greek slavery' in: *G&R* 40: 163–80

Cartledge, P. (2001) *Spartan reflections* (London: Duckworth)

Cartledge, P. (2002) *Sparta and Lakonia: a regional history 1300–362 B.C.* (London: Routledge ²2002)

Cartledge, P., E. E. Cohen, L. Foxhall (eds) (2002) *Money, labour and land: approaches to the economies of ancient Greece* (London: Routledge)

Cohen, E. E. (1992) *Athenian economy and society: a banking perspective* (Princeton: Princeton University Press)

Cohen, E. E. (2000) *The Athenian nation* (Princeton: Princeton University Press)

Cohen, E. E. (2002) 'An unprofitable masculinity' in: Cartledge et al. 2002: 100–12

Connor, W. R. (1994) 'The problem of Athenian civic identity' in: Boegehold & Scafuro 1994: 34–44

Darmezin, L. (1999) *Les affranchisements par consécration: en Béotie et dans le monde hellénistique* (Paris: de Boccard) (Collection Études anciennes 22)

Davies, J. K. (1971) *Athenian propertied families, 600–300 B.C.* (Oxford: Clarendon)

Davies, J. K (1978) 'Athenian citizenship: the descent group and its alternatives' in: *CJ* 73: 105–21

Davies, J. K. (1981) *Wealth and the power of wealth in classical Athens* (New York: Arno) (Monographs in Classical Studies)

De Ste. Croix, G. E. M. (1981) *The class struggle in the ancient Greek world: from the archaic age to the Arab conquests* (London: Duckworth)

DuBois, P. (1990) *Torture and truth* (London: Routledge) (The New Ancient World)

DuBois, P. (2003) *Slaves and other objects* (Chicago: University of Chicago Press)

Ducat, J. (1990) *Les hilotes* (Paris: École française d'Athènes) (*BCH* Suppl. 20)

Figueira, T. J. (1999) 'The evolution of the Messenian identity' in: Hodkinson & Powell 1999: 211–44

Finley, M. I. (ed.) (1968) *Slavery in classical antiquity* (Cambridge: Heffer) (Views and Controversies about Classical Antiquity)

Finley, M. I. (1981) *Economy and society in ancient Greece* (London: Chatto & Windus)

Finley, M. I. (1998) *Ancient slavery and modern ideology* (expanded edition ed. B. D. Shaw) (Princeton: Marcus Wiener, [2]1998 (Penguin [1]1980))

Fisher, N. R. E. (1993) *Slavery in classical Greece* (Bristol: Bristol Classical Press) (Classical World Series)

Fisher, N. R. E. (1995) 'Hybris, status and slavery' in: Powell 1995: 44–84

Fisher, N. R. E. (2001) *Aeschines* Against Timarchos: *introduction, translation and commentary by Nick Fisher* (Oxford: Clarendon) (Clarendon Ancient History Series)

Foxhall, L. (1992) 'The control of the Attic landscape' in: Wells 1992: 155–9

Gagarin, M. (1996) 'Torture of slaves in Athenian law' in: *CPh* 91: 1–18

Gallant, T. W. (1991) *Risk and survival in ancient Greece: reconstructing the rural domestic economy* (Stanford: Stanford University Press)

Garlan, Y. (1988) *Slavery in ancient Greece* (revised and expanded ed.; trans. J. Lloyd) (Ithaca NY: Cornell University Press)

Garnsey, P. (1996) *Ideas of slavery from Aristotle to Augustine* (Cambridge: Cambridge University Press) (The W. B. Stanford Memorial Lectures)

Genovese, E. D. (1974) *Roll, Jordan, roll: the world the slaves made* (New York: Pantheon)

Genovese, E. D. (1979) *From rebellion to revolution: Afro-American slave revolts in the making of the modern world* (Baton Rouge: Louisiana State University Press; repr. New York: Vintage Books 1981) (The Walter Lynwood Fleming Lectures in Southern History, Louisiana State University)

Golden, M. (1984) 'Slavery and homosexuality at Athens' in: *Phoenix* 38: 308–24

Golden, M. (1992) 'Pais, "child" and "slave" ' in: *L'Antiquité Classique* 54: 91–104

Graham, J. W. (1992) 'Thucydides 7.13.2 and the crews of Athenian triremes' in: *TAPhA* 122: 257–70

Hamel, D. (2003) *Trying Neaira: the true story of a courtesan's scandalous life in ancient Greece* (New Haven: Yale University Press)

Harris, E. (2002) 'Workshop, marketplace and household: the nature of technical specialisation in classical Athens and its influence on economy and society' in: Cartledge et al. 2002: 67–99

Harris, W. V. (2001) *Restraining rage: the ideology of anger in classical antiquity* (Cambridge MA: Harvard University Press)

Hodkinson, S. (2000) *Property and wealth in classical Sparta* (London: Duckworth & The Classical Press of Wales)

Hodkinson, S., & A. Powell (eds) (1999) *Sparta: new perspectives* (London: Duckworth & The Classical Press of Wales)

Hodkinson, S., & A. Powell (eds) (2002) *Sparta: beyond the mirage* (London: Duckworth & The Classical Press of Wales)

Hopkins, K. (1978) *Conquerors and slaves* (Cambridge: Cambridge University Press) (Sociological Studies in Roman History 1)

Hopper, R. J. (1979) *Trade and industry in classical Greece* (London: Thames & Hudson) (Aspects of Greek and Roman life)

Hunt, P. (1998) *Slaves, warfare and ideology in the Greek historians* (Cambridge: Cambridge University Press)

Hunter, V. (1994) *Policing Athens: social control in the Attic lawsuits, 420–320 B.C.* (Princeton: Princeton University Press)

Hunter, V., & J. Edmondson (eds) (2000) *Law and social status in Athens* (revised papers from an international conference organized at York University, Ontario, in the spring of 1997) (Oxford: Oxford University Press)

Jameson, M. H. (1978) 'Agriculture and slavery in classical Athens' in: *CJ* 73: 122–45

Jameson, M. H. (1992) 'Agricultural labour in ancient Greece' in: Wells 1992: 13–46

Jones, N. F. (1999) *The associations of classical Athens: the response to democracy* (New York: Oxford University Press)

Kapparis, K. A. (1999) Apollodoros 'Against Neaira' *[D. 59]: ed. with intro., trans. and commentary* (Berlin: de Gruyter) (Untersuchungen zur antiken Kultur und Geschichte 53)

Klees, H. (1998) *Sklavenleben im klassichen Griechenland* (Stuttgart: Steiner) (Forschungen zur antiken Sklaverei 30)

Krentz, P. (1980) 'Foreigners against the Thirty: IG II$^2$ 10 again' in: *Phoenix* 34: 298–306

Laing, D. R. (1965) 'A new interpretation of the Athenian naval catalogue IG 2$^2$ 1951' (unpublished PhD thesis University of Cincinnati 1965)

Lewis, D. M. (1959) 'Attic manumissions' in: *Hesperia* 28: 208–38

Lewis, D. M. (1968) 'Dedications of *phialai* in Athens' in: *Hesperia* 37: 368–80

Luraghi, N. (2002) 'Helotic slavery reconsidered' in: Hodkinson & Powell 2002: 227–48

Luraghi, N., & S. E. Alcock (eds) (2003) *Helots and their masters in Laconia and Messenia: histories, ideologies, structures* (Cambridge MA: Harvard University) (Hellenic studies 4)

MacDowell, D. M. (1978) *Law in classical Athens* (London: Thames & Hudson) (Aspects of Greek and Roman life)

Millett, P. (1991) *Lending and borrowing in ancient Athens* (Cambridge: Cambridge University Press)

Mirhady, D. C. (1991) 'The oath-challenge in Athens' in: *CQ* 41: 78–83

Mirhady, D. C. (1996) 'Torture and rhetoric in Athens' in: *JHS* 116: 119–31

Osborne, M. J. (1981–3) *Naturalization in Athens: commentaries on the decrees granting citizenship*, 4 vols in 3 (Brussels: Paleis der Academiën) (Verhandelingen van de Koninklijke Academie voor Wetenschappen Letteren en Schone Kunsten van België, Klasse der letteren 98, 101, 109)

Osborne, R. (1985) *Demos: the discovery of classical Attika* (Cambridge: Cambridge University Press) (Cambridge Classical Studies)

Osborne, R. (1992) 'Is it a farm?: the definition of agricultural sites and settlements in ancient Greece' in: Wells 1992: 21–7

Osborne, R. (1995) 'The economics and politics of slavery at Athens' in: Powell 1995: 27–43

Parker, R. (1996) *Athenian religion: a history* (Oxford: Clarendon)

Patterson, C. (2000) 'The hospitality of Athenian justice: the metic in court' in: Hunter & Edmondson 2000: 93–112

Patterson, O. (1982) *Slavery and social death: a comparative study* (Cambridge MA: Harvard University Press)

Patterson, O. (1991) *Freedom*, vol. 1: *Freedom in the making of western culture* (London: Tauris)

Pečírka, J. (1966) *The formula for the grant of* enktesis *in Attic inscriptions* (Prague: Univerzita Karlova) (Acta Universitatis Carolinae, Philosophica et historica 15)

Pomeroy, S. B. (1994) *Xenophon*, Oeconomicus: *a social and historical commentary; with a new English trans.* (Oxford: Clarendon)

Powell, A. (ed.) (1989) *Classical Sparta: techniques behind her success* (with a foreword by P. Cartledge) (London: Routledge)

Powell, A. (ed.) (1995) *The Greek world* (London: Routledge)

Powell, A., & S. Hodkinson (eds) (1994) *The shadow of Sparta* (London: Routledge)

Sallares, R. (1991) *The ecology of the ancient Greek world* (London: Duckworth)

Schofield, M. (1999) 'Ideology and philosophy in Aristotle's theory of slavery' in: Schofield, M. (1999) *Saving the city: philosopher kings and other classical paradigms* (London: Routledge 1999) 115–40 (Issues in Ancient Philosophy)

Shipton, K. M. W. (1997) 'The private banks in fourth-century BC Athens: a reappraisal' in: *CQ* 47: 396–422

Smith, N. D. (1983) 'Aristotle's theory of natural slavery' in: *Phoenix* 37: 109–22

Talbert, R. J. A. (1989) 'The role of the helots in the class-struggle at Sparta' in: *Historia* 38: 22–40

Taylor, Y. (ed.) (1999) *I was born a slave: an anthology of classic slave narratives*, 2 vols (foreword by C. Johnson) (Edinburgh: Payback)

Thür, G. (1977) *Beweisführung vor den Schwurgerichtshöfen Athens: Die Proklesis zur Basanos* (Vienna: Verlag der Österreichischen Akademie der Wissenschaften) (Österreichische Akademie der Wissenschaften, Philosophisch-historische Klasse, Sitzungsberichte 317 = Veröffentlichungen der Kommission für antike Rechtsgeschichte 1)

Todd, S. C. (1990) 'The purpose of evidence in Athenian courts' in: Cartledge P., P. Millett, S. C. Todd (eds) (1990) *Nomos: essays in Athenian law, politics and society* (Cambridge: Cambridge University Press) 19–39

Todd, S. C. (1993) *The shape of Athenian law* (Oxford: Clarendon)

Trevett, J. C. (1992) *Apollodoros, son of Pasion* (Oxford: Clarendon)

van Wees, H. (1995) 'Politics and the battlefield: ideology in Greek warfare' in: Powell 1995: 153–78

van Wees, H. (2001) 'The myth of the middle-class army: military and social status in Ancient Athens' in: Bekker-Nielsen, T., & L. Hannestad (eds) (2001) *War as a cultural and social force: essays on warfare in antiquity* (Copenhagen: Kongelige Danske Videnskabernes Selskab) 45–71 (Historisk-filosofiske skrifter 22)

van Wees, H. (2004) *Greek warfare: myth and realities* (London: Duckworth)

Vidal-Naquet, P. (1986) *The black hunter: forms of thought and forms of society in the Greek world* (trans. A. Szegedy-Maszak with a foreword by Bernard Knox) (Baltimore: Johns Hopkins University Press)

Wells, B. (ed.) (1992) *Agriculture in ancient Greece: proceedings of the seventh international symposium at the Swedish Institute at Athens, 16–17 May, 1990* (Stockholm: Åström) (Acta Instituti Atheniensis Regni Sueciae ser. in 4° 42)

Whitby, M. (1994) 'Two shadows: images of Spartans and helots' in: Powell & Hodkinson 1994: 87–126

Whitehead, D. (1977) *The ideology of the Athenian metic* (Cambridge: Cambridge Philological Society) (*PCPhS* Suppl. 4)

Whitehead, D. (1984) 'Immigrant communities in the classical polis: some principles for a synoptic treatment' in: *L'Antiquité Classique* 53: 47–59

Whitehead, D. (1986a) *The demes of Attica 508/7–ca. 250* B.C.: *a political and social study* (Princeton: Princeton University Press)

Whitehead, D. (1986b) 'Women and naturalisation in fourth-century Athens: the case of Archippe' in: *CQ* 36: 109–14

Zelnick-Abramovitz, R. (2005) *Not wholly free: the concept of manumission and the status of manumitted slaves in the ancient Greek world* (Leiden: Brill)

# CHAPTER SEVENTEEN

# Women and Ethnicity in Classical Greece: Changing the Paradigms

*Sarah B. Pomeroy*

## 1 Introduction

How did the Greeks distinguish Greek women from foreigners, and how did they define ethnic groupings among Greek women? In this chapter I will survey Greek thinking about women and ethnicity in Greek society and among the non-Greeks they had encountered through colonization, or exploration, or had created through mythological speculation. For this investigation I will use post-colonial theory as currently applied by ancient historians, and feminist theory that has become traditional among historians of women (e.g., Pomeroy 1984).

## 2 Ethnic Identity of Women

Greek colonization used to be viewed primarily as a process of Hellenization, or the adoption of Greek culture by the natives, with Hellenism trickling down from the elite to lower social strata. Implicit in this paradigm was a colonialist assumption that indigenous culture would naturally be submerged in a superior Greek civilization (Shepherd 1999: 267, 271–4).

Nowadays some ancient historians are moving away from a vision of history centered on a glorified image of classical democracy, and looking at a broader picture that includes people on the fringes of the Greek world. In some areas contacts with Greeks produced a fusion of Greek and native elements, elsewhere they remained distinct. Although substantial ancient evidence exists for the agency of women in producing or resisting these changes, most of the recently published scholarly work on ethnic identity focuses on men (e.g., Hall 2002; Malkin 2001). Yet, as Aristotle (*Politics* 1269b14–19) recognized in his critique of Spartan society, women constitute half the community; therefore it should be obvious that views of women and their roles and status are undeniably a part of any ethnic identity.

By "ethnic identity" we mean inherited cultural traits that are often observable only by comparison with people who do not exhibit these traits. Ethnic identities can be carved out by members of the group being defined, or conferred by outsiders. The sources for historians exploring gender and ethnicity are archaeological and textual. Chief among Greek authors is Herodotos. Like many Greeks of his time, Herodotos tended to organize knowledge according to polar opposites, in sharply contrasted distinctions (Hartog 1988). From Herodotos' description of women in various barbarian societies, we may deduce the Greek norm for women, which was (simply put) the opposite (Dewald 1981).

# 3 Mixed Marriages

A few examples concerning intermarriage will make this identification clear. According to Herodotos (4.110–17) the Amazons and Scythians were the ancestors of the Sauromatians. The Amazons wore revealing dresses, rode astride, and lived mostly outdoors. According to the foundation myth of the Sarmatians, after the Amazons had killed some Greek men, they met the Scythians. The Amazons initiated proposals of dating and marriage. Their bridegrooms needed to get their parents' permission and to provide dowries for the marriages. This reversal of roles was not only bizarre, but threatening to Greek views of the appropriate behavior of women and men. Greeks told myths about heroes such as Herakles, Theseus, and Achilles who conquered Amazons, and the subject became common in Athenian visual arts. The Amazons were always vanquished, but not completely assimilated. Though the Amazons learned to speak their husbands' language, they spoke it imperfectly, and thus created a new dialect. Furthermore no Sauromatian woman could marry until she killed a male enemy (Hdt. 4.117). Thus the union of Amazons and Scythians produced a new mixed society to which both contributed: the Sarmatians.

Gender separatism was also part of the ethnic identity of Kyrene where Greek men had married indigenous women. The women of Kyrene did not eat meat, and maintained a different diet from their husbands' through subsequent generations (Hdt. 4.186, 3.99). When the Athenians founded Miletos, they killed the Karian men and married the women (Hdt. 1.146; also Pausanias 7.2.6). In revenge for the massacre, the women took an oath to preserve a tradition which they handed down through the female line. They swore that they would never dine with their husbands and never call them by name. Thus, the women's continual resistance produced a hybrid society, rather than a thoroughly integrated and Hellenized colony. Another tale of women's resistance involves men and women originally from the same region, but from two different ethnic groups. Pelasgian men exiled in Lemnos captured Attic women and brought them to Lemnos to serve as their concubines (Hdt. 6.138). The women bore children and were bringing them up in the Athenian way. In order to prevent the infusion of Attic customs into their society, the Lemnians killed both mothers and children. Despite the opinion found in some medical treatises and elsewhere in classical literature that the father is the true parent and the mother only the receptacle of his seed, the activities of the Greeks in these stories of

**Figure 17.1**  "Achilles kills Penthesileia." Black figure amphora (wine-jar) signed by Exekias as potter and attributed to him as painter. Greek. c. 540–530 BCE. © The Trustees of The British Museum, London.


Herodotos demonstrate that intermarriage and producing children was indeed a partnership to which male and female invariably contributed. Herodotos also reports that sometimes women alone were responsible for the establishment of their native cults in foreign lands. For example, women from Egypt founded oracles in Dodona and Libya, and the Danaides imported the Thesmophoria (Hdt. 2.54, 171).

Scholars debate whether intermarriage was the usual practice, or whether Greek women were regularly included from the start of any colonizing venture. Greek sources often ignore women, and certainly some priestesses had to participate in the original settlements, since the cults of goddesses required their ministration (Graham 1980–1). My view still is that the intermarriage of the archaic period as reported by Herodotos was the regular pattern in colonization, and that it continued in the Hellenistic period (Pomeroy 1975: 34–5). Few Greek women traveled to the frontiers in the original foundations, and not very many in subsequent generations. This conclusion is based on the following evidence: Herodotos reports that one adult man was selected by lot from every set of brothers in Thera and sent to colonize Kyrene (4.150–9). He does not mention Theran women, and later discusses the marriages of the settlers with native women. Archaic colonists included Archilochos who evidently was a young unmarried man, an illegitimate soldier of fortune. One of the motivations for Perikles' citizenship law in 451/0 was that Athenian cleruchs living in Delian League cities were marrying local women, causing the marriage market for Athenian girls to shrink (Pomeroy 1975: 78). Demosthenes' opponents alleged that his mother Kleoboule was the daughter of an exiled Athenian and a Scythian (Aischines 2.78; 3.172; Deinarchos 1.15, etc.). Hellenistic colonists included veterans of Alexander's campaigns who settled down with native women. The Delphinion inscriptions recording grants of citizenship to mercenaries in Hellenistic Miletos show that the immigrants had raised few daughters. The skewed sex ratio generally found among the Greeks as a result of female infanticide and neglect of girls created a surplus of Greek men available to settle in colonies and a dearth of young women to send out as brides (Golden 1981). Intermarriage was the obvious solution for many men.

## 4   Barbarian Women and Greeks

Herodotos also discusses foreign peoples, without referring to intermarriage with Greeks. Confrontation with Egypt through exploration and colonization produced a Greek view of a society in which gender and spatial division of labor was exactly the reverse of the Greek norm. Herodotos (2.35) reports that among the Egyptians men stay home and weave, while women go to market. He also includes briefer ethnographies of people on the fringes of the Greek world who did not prize the virginity of unmarried girls nor consider a wife the sexual partner exclusively of her husband (as did most Greeks), but who practice fraternal polyandry, or promiscuous intercourse, or among whom unmarried girls are free, but married women are guarded vigilantly (1.216; 4.104, 172, 180; 5.6). In Asia young girls work as prostitutes until they accumulate sufficient funds for a dowry (Hdt. 1.93–4). Then they are considered marriageable, and arrange their own marriages. The Eneti of Illyria buy their brides at auction (Hdt. 1.196). Once in a lifetime Babylonian wives must have intercourse with a stranger (Hdt. 1.199). The Libyan king deflowers a bride from each cohort of marriageable women (Hdt. 4.168). The Massagetai share wives (Hdt. 1.216). The Nasamones practice promiscuous intercourse starting on the wedding night (Hdt. 4.172). The Ausëes of Libya do not marry at all, but award a child to the potential father the child most resembles (Hdt. 4.180). Among the Gindanes women wear anklets to advertise the number of men with whom they have had intercourse (Hdt. 4.176). To further their political ambitions, or to ferret out other men's secrets, a series of Egyptians as well as some other barbarian fathers tell their daughters to sleep with any man who comes to them (Hdt. 2.121, 126, 3.69). Among the Lykians, children inherit their name and status as citizens through the mother (1.173). In contrast, among the Greeks it was essential for a bride to be a virgin, and the father supplied the dowry, arranged his daughter's marriage, and was the parent who conferred legitimacy on offspring. A major distinction between Greeks and barbarians is that the former are monogamous and the latter are polygynous.

# 5 Greek Women

In every case, both Greek and barbarian, and in all Greek societies, male and female function in separate spheres, and there is a sexual division of labor. Indications of respectability, such as nudity or concealing clothing, and ideas about promiscuity, virginity, and even the exercise of public power by women vary among ethnic groups. Descriptions of gender relations in other societies led some Greeks to realize that such relationships were not biologically determined or inevitable, and inspired them to articulate what was distinctive and original about their own.

Ethnic identities are contingent and change over time. Thucydides (1.5–6) described a progression of customs which were once practiced by both Greeks and barbarians alike, and were to be found in his day only among barbarians and a few unsophisticated Greek tribes. In the classical period some of the primitive practices of non-Greeks were still to be found in north-western and western Greece where the inhabitants did not live in settled political communities. There women could manage families and own slaves and other property without the assistance of a *kyrios* (Cabanes 1979: 193; 1980: 333–4). Although Thucydides does not mention Macedonia, these were probably the practices of the Macedonians who were migrant pastoralists before Philip II built cities for them. Thucydides does report that Greeks racing at Olympia discovered that clothing could trip them up, and that nude racing was more efficient. Thucydides goes on to contrast less civilized peoples who had not progressed to such knowledge. Thus in the visual arts Greek males are regularly nude, while barbarians are often heavily dressed, wearing concealing garments including pantaloons and caps. Similarly, at Sparta the helots – who were the lowliest members of society – were obliged to wear animal skins and leather hats as visual reminders that they were bestial and subhuman.

Xenophon, who was an eyewitness in Athens and Sparta, gives a picture of the women in both cities. Ischomachos, a wealthy Athenian, instructs his wife who is probably not more than fifteen years old:

(18) "The gods seem to have shown much discernment in yoking together female and male, as we call them, so that the couple might constitute a partnership that is most beneficial to each of them. (19) First of all, so that the various species of living creatures may not become extinct, this pair sleeps together for the purpose of procreation. Then this pairing provides offspring to support the partners in their old age, at least in the case of human beings. And finally, human beings do not live outdoors like cattle, but obviously have need of shelter. (20) Those who intend to obtain produce to bring into the shelter need someone to work at the outdoor jobs. For ploughing, sowing, planting, and herding is all work that is performed outdoors, and it is from these that our essential provisions are obtained. (21) As soon as these are brought into the shelter, then someone else is needed to look after them and to perform the work that requires shelters. The

nursing of newborn children requires shelters, and so does the preparation of bread from grain, and likewise, making clothing out of wool. (22) Because both the indoor and the outdoor tasks require work and concern," he said, "I think the god, from the very beginning, designed the nature of woman for the indoor work and concerns and the nature of man for the outdoor work. (23) For he prepared man's body and mind to be more capable of enduring cold and heat and travelling and military campaigns, and so he assigned the outdoor work to him. Because the woman was physically less capable of endurance," said Ischomachus, "I told her that I thought the god has evidently assigned the indoor work to her. (24) And because the god was aware that he had both created in the woman and assigned to her the duty of nourishing newborn children, he had measured out to her a greater share of affection for newborn babies than he gave to the man. (25) And because the god had also assigned to the woman the duty of guarding what had been brought into the house, because he realised that a tendency to be afraid is not at all disadvantageous for guarding things, he measured out a greater portion of fear to the woman than to the man. And knowing that the person responsible for the outdoor work would have to serve as defender against any wrong-doer, he measured out to him a greater share of courage. (26) Because it is necessary for both of them to give and to take, he gave both of them equal powers of memory and concern. So, you would not be able to distinguish whether the female or male sex has the larger share of these. (27) And he gave them both equally the ability to practise self-control also, when it is needed. And the god granted the privilege to whichever one is superior in this to gain a larger share of the benefit accruing from it – whether man or woman. (28) So, because each of them is not equally well-endowed with all the same natural aptitudes, then they are more in need of each other, and the bond is more beneficial to the couple, since one is capable where the other is deficient." (Xenophon *Oikonomikos* 7; trans. Pomeroy 1994: 141, 143, 145)

**Figure 17.2** In the women's quarters a mother reaches for her baby boy, the goal of marriage. Attic red figure lebes gamikos. Washing Painter. Courtesy Staatliche Antikensammlungen und Glyptothek, Munich.

Xenophon viewed the Athenian woman in terms of her relationship with her husband and his household, but he describes the Spartan in the context of her education in preparation for motherhood.

> (1.3) First, to begin at the beginning, I will take the begetting of children. In other states the girls who are destined to become mothers and are brought up in the approved fashion, live on the very plainest fare, with a most meagre allowance of delicacies. Wine is either withheld altogether, or, if allowed them, is diluted with water. The rest of the Greeks expect their girls to imitate the sedentary life that is typical of handicraftsmen – to keep quiet and do wool-work. How, then, is it to be expected that women so brought up will bear fine children? (4) But Lycurgus thought the labour of slave women sufficient to supply clothing. He believed motherhood to be the most important function of freeborn woman. Therefore, in the first place, he insisted on physical training for the female no less than for the male sex: moreover, he instituted races and trials of strength for women competitors as for men, believing that if both parents are strong they produce more vigorous offspring. (5) He noticed, too, that, during the time immediately succeeding marriage, it was usual elsewhere for the husband to have unlimited intercourse with his wife. The rule that he adopted was the opposite of this: for he laid it down that the husband should be ashamed to be seen entering his wife's room or leaving it. With this restriction on intercourse the desire of the one for the other must necessarily be increased, and their offspring was bound to be more vigorous than if they were surfeited with one another. (6) In addition to this, he withdrew from men the right to take a wife whenever they chose, and insisted on their marrying in the prime of their manhood, believing that this too promoted the production of fine children. (Xenophon *Lak. Pol.*: 137, 139, trans. Marchant (Loeb))

Athenian artists regularly showed women wearing several layers of clothing, tangible evidence of their hermetic seclusion from the world around them. Concealing clothing tainted barbarians with effeminacy, and Athenian women with barbarism, and both groups were categorized as primitive. Only in rendering a non-Greek mythical figure like an Amazon or a victim of violence did the Athenian artist show a semi-nude female. At Sparta, in contrast, physical training was obligatory for boys and girls, and athletic nudity was required of both.

## 6  Athenians and Spartans

Athens and Sparta are the chief representatives of Ionian and Dorian ethnicity respectively. The primary sources for the women of these two cities in the classical period are more abundant by far than those for the women of other Greek cities. Women's style of dress was used to characterize Dorians in general. Liddell & Scott define *doriazo* as "to dress like a Dorian girl, that is, in a single garment open at the side" and "to imitate the Dorians in life." In other words the dictionary views Dorian ethnicity in terms of the dress or semi-nudity of Spartan women.

Obviously clothing, as well as the lack of it, marked differences between Spartans and other Greek women. Because Spartans spent time out of doors, they needed warm garments in some types of weather. The Dorian *peplos* was a heavier dress than the Ionian *chiton*, and had to be fastened on the shoulders by fibulae. This

**Figure 17.3** Groom leads bride into the bridal chamber. He looks back at her but she casts her eyes down demurely. Athenian red figure loutrophoros. Sabouroff Painter. National Museum, Copenhagen, Department of Classical and Near Eastern Antiquities.

**Figure 17.4** Spartan girl runner from Prizren or Dodona. © The Trustees of The British Museum, London.

woolen dress is best called "Hellenic" for it had been worn by all Greek women in the archaic period (Hdt. 5.87, Harrison 1989: 42–4, 48). Like much else at Sparta, women's fashions were conservative and austere compared to what Greek women were wearing in other cities. The special identity of Spartan women was more stable than most, due to Spartan xenophobia, endogamy, and lack of colonization. The light linen *chitones* of the Ionian style were new fashions in Athens. These dresses were made of imported fabric, reminiscent of Eastern luxury, and appropriate for citizen women living mostly indoors in seclusion, or worn in public by less respectable women. In Athenian art women are shown wearing either the Ionian *chiton* or the *peplos*, or both. Herodotos (5.87) explains that the change came about when a sole survivor of a battle returned to Athens and told the women that all their men had died. They killed the bearer of this devastating news with their pins, which were subsequently associated with aggression on the part of women. Thereafter the women were forbidden to wear fibulae, and instead wore the *chiton* that was sewn on the shoulders.

**Figure 17.5** Hippodameia wearing woolen peplos pinned at the shoulders. East pediment, Olympia, second quarter of the fifth century. Olympia Archaeological Museum. Photo: Alison Frantz Collection, American School of Classical Studies at Athens.

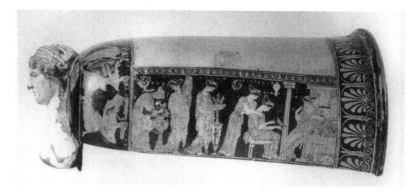

**Figure 17.6** Scene of the women's quarters showing a bride, her friends and family, and her guests. Athenian *epinetron* (vase placed over the knee when working wool). Circa 420. National Archaeological Museum, Athens. Photo TAP Service.

In fact the change in costume coincides with the loss of status and the increased seclusion of Athenian women that I have posited for the late archaic period (Pomeroy 1975: 78). Indeed some of the jewelry dedicated at the sanctuary of Artemis at Sparta resembles nails with very long spikes (Dawkins 1929). Wearing a Doric *peplos* meant always having a weapon to hand. Only when she was dressed in a man's costume as a bride was a clothed Spartan woman disarmed. Regulations attributed to Lykourgos banned the use of gold, silver, and cosmetics at Sparta. Interestingly enough, it was the men who wore the only luxurious item of clothing: soldiers wore a short cloak colored by expensive crimson dye (Xenophon *Lak. Pol.* 11.3).

In Aristophanes' *Lysistrata*, produced in 411, a female delegate from each of the major cities participating in the Peloponnesian War comes to an assembly at Athens. Every woman embodies her ethnic stereotype. Even before she speaks, the Spartan representative is recognizable by her strapping physique, and agility. A life spent outdoors and good nutrition give her a clear complexion, not needing any artificial enhancement. The Athenian women are characterized as unreliable, self-indulgent, and interested in cosmetics and luxurious clothing. Their youth is encapsulated in a cursus honorum of religious duties which are ritual versions of domestic chores including weaving, grinding grain, and carrying baskets of butchers' utensils (*Lysistrata* 870–4 Henderson). In contrast, the Spartan ambassador has a nostalgic vision of young girls racing like fillies beside the Eurotas (Aristophanes *Lysistrata* 641–5, 1307–10 Henderson). The Athenian Lysistrata is intelligent and a good speaker, but like Athenian men, domineering, self-confident, and convinced of her right to act as leader of the group. The humor about the women (like that about the men) is often ethnically specific. The Athenians are eager to drink the wine, doubtless because it is not available to them daily as it was to Spartan women. Jokes about adultery are also directed against them. Plutarch reports that there was no adultery at Sparta, although of course he knew of two notorious cases of the king's wife and the handsome stranger: Helen and Paris, and Timaia and Alkibiades. These, however, were exceptional.

# 7   The Legacy of Myth

Like the foundation myths of barbarian societies and Greek colonies, those of older Greek cities are a distinctive feature of ethnic identity, and also an indication of gender relations. The myth of Athens stresses continuity: theirs was a myth of autochthony. Athenian men had always inhabited the same land. They claimed that Erechtheus, one of their founding fathers, had not been born of woman, but rather had sprung up directly from the earth. The event used to rationalize women's exclusion from the political process also was said to have occurred in the remote past (Augustine *De Civitate Dei* 18.9). According to this aetiological myth when Athens was young, Athena and Poseidon competed to be the most important divinity. All the women voted for Athena, and all the men for Poseidon. Since one more woman than man was present, Athena won. Thenceforth women lost the right to vote. The structure of the state was a macrocosm of family structure and their ideologies were mutually consistent. Athenian women were citizens insofar as only they could be the mothers of citizens. Any woman would do, for according to Athenian ideas about parentage, the father was the true parent (Ogden 1996). The mother was merely the fertile field in which he sowed his seed. Women and metics were barred from owning land and permitted to own only movable property. Marriage was virilocal. When she moved to her bridegroom's house, a bride, like a newly purchased slave, would have to make sacrifices to his domestic gods, including Zeus and Hestia of the hearth, in order to gain acceptance in a household where she had not been carried around the hearth as a baby.

In contrast to Athens, the founding myths and history of the Dorians involved invasion and suppression of the existing native population, reducing them to the status of helots. Thus the distinctive authority and autonomy of Spartiate women may be attributed in part to the fact that the Spartans constituted an aristocracy. The Athenian style of democracy was oppressive to all women, for all were an underclass, like metics and slaves, whereas in Sparta it was all helots and perioikoi – men and women alike – who formed the populous underclass (Pomeroy 1975: 78). As I have mentioned above, the otherness of the helots was emphasized by their subhuman treatment.

In Sparta women could and did own land (Pomeroy 2002: 77–82). The ancient economy was based on agriculture, and land was the most valuable commodity. Though in Athens there were other sources of wealth including trade, banking, and manufacture, at Sparta wealth was based exclusively on land. Spartan women came to possess land through dowry and inheritance. Furthermore, unlike Athenians, who needed to have a male relative act as their legal guardian, as far as we can tell Spartans controlled their own property. As girls they had learned to drive horses for the festival of the Hyakinthia and it seems likely that they rode out in carriages to supervise their estates. Except for the costume, at Sparta the sight of a tall woman riding in broad daylight in a chariot would not have caused the consternation that the vision of Phye masquerading as Athena created at Athens (Hdt. 1.60). Eventually Spartan women owned two fifths of the land and, one assumes, the helots and slaves necessary to cultivate it. At Sparta royal women became not only the wealthiest women, but the wealthiest citizens in all Sparta.

Legends about Helen helped to shape the image of Spartan women and project it beyond Sparta. Helen was the most beautiful woman in the world. She was also wealthy and dominated men. Spartan art and Athenian literature indicate that she was able to subjugate her infuriated husband when they were reunited. Although Aristotle does not mention Helen, he repeats most of these attributes in his denunciation of Spartan women and their effect on the community (see above).

According to the myth of the judgment of Paris, Helen and her champion Aphrodite won a competition. From earliest times, Sparta was known as a land of beautiful women – in Homer's words: *Sparte kalligynaika* (*Odyssey* 13.412). In the seventh century the Delphic oracle declared: "Of all the earth, Pelasgic Argos is best, and Thessalian horses, and Lakedaimonian women" (Parke & Wormell 1956: 1.82–3; 2.1–2 no.1). Spending time out of doors in the nude meant that women were exposed to public scrutiny from the time when they were very young. They competed with their peers not only in formal athletic events, but also in the eyes of their beholders and in their own judgment. Although Lykourgos had outlawed cosmetics, Spartan women had mirrors. Some bronze mirror handles show young Spartan women wearing a sickle which identifies them as athletic victors. Young girls learned to evaluate the beauty of other girls, and to compare their own appearance with that of their peers. In Alkman (*Partheneion* 1), the chorus decide that Agido is first in beauty, and Hagesichora is second. Theokritos captured the same sentiment. The 240 girls who race in honor of Helen declare that when they compare themselves to Helen not one of them is faultless (Theokritos *Idyllia* 18.25). Men also prized beautiful women and sought them as brides, even breaking some of society's rules to win them. Unlike men in Athens where nubile girls were secluded and wore multiple layers of clothing when they went out, Spartans will have had many opportunities to look over potential brides who were completely nude. Herodotos (6.61) tells the story of a young girl who was afflicted with *dysmorphia* ("misshapenness"). More than ugly, she may have been deformed, for her parents had forbidden her nurse to show her to anyone. The nurse was so concerned that the daughter of fortunate parents was disfigured that she carried her every day up a mountain to the shrine of Helen and prayed to the goddess to free her from her ugliness. Helen appeared, and touched the child. Thereupon the ugliest girl grew up to be the most beautiful of Spartan women (Pausanias 3.7.7; Hdt. 6.61). The competitive phrase "most beautiful woman" occurs, often gratuitously, in many stories about historical Spartan women (e.g., Xenophon *Hellenika* 3.3.8; Plutarch *Kleomemens* 1.2, 22.1–2).

Greeks considered height an attribute of beautiful, noble women (Pomeroy 1994: 306). Homer (*Odyssey* 6.102–07) had described Nausikaa as towering over her handmaidens like a palm tree, and in the visual arts gods were depicted as taller than mortals. Thus, at Athens in a ruse staged by Peisistratos Phye's height helped to convince the crowds that she was Athena. The Spartan Timasimbrota, who is mentioned in a fragment of archaic poetry, was as tall as a man, for she is described as resembling a golden-haired youth in her noble stature (*Poetarum Melicorum Graecorum Fragmenta* 5 F 2, col. ii 17–18). Archidamos was fined for choosing a short woman, because it was expected that the children produced by the couple would take after their mother (Athenaios 566A–B; Theophrastos in Plutarch *Agesilaos* 2.3; *Moralia* 1d). Plutarch described a heroic woman who accompanied Kleomenes' family to Egypt as tall and robust (Plutarch *Kleomenes* 38.5). Diet reflected ethnic differences. Xenophon indicates that the Spartans were taller and stronger than other Greeks (Xenophon *Lak. Pol.* 1.10). The height of Spartan women probably resulted not only from heredity and eugenics, but also from their generous food rations. In ancient Greece a thin woman was not considered beautiful, but rather a pitiful creature who did not have enough food. Spartans were the only Greek women who were well-fed and drank wine. The Greeks viewed wine-drinking as a civilized activity, reserved for cultivated people high on the social scale (Lyons 1996: 110; Antonaccio & Neils 1995: 277). Since wine-drinking by women was not approved of elsewhere in Greece, the practice took on a negative connotation among critics of Spartan women. It was known that Spartan women drank wine as part of their regular diet, but there is no evidence that they were less temperate than the male revelers depicted on Lakonian cups (Kritias F 6 Diels-Kranz = Athenaios 10.432D; Plutarch *Lykourgos* 12.7).

# 8   Status of Women

People station themselves in a hierarchy of social status that provides an avenue to rights and disabilities. Thus Spartans were taught that they were superior to their helots, and the helots, in turn, were encouraged to feel themselves inferior by being treated as subhuman and forced to wear primitive clothing. Spartan women were also smugly secure in their feelings of superiority over other Greek women. Plutarch quotes many of them. Gorgo, daughter of one king and wife of another, is the first Spartan woman who is reputed to have participated in the construction of the special identity of Spartan women. When she was asked by an Athenian woman: "Why is it that you Spartans are the only women who can rule men?" she replied: "That is because we are the only ones who give birth to men" (Plutarch *Sayings of Spartan Women, Moralia* 240e5; cf. Plutarch *Lykourgos* 14, and *Sayings of Spartans* 7e13). In this story the interlocutor assumes the special identity before Gorgo replies. About a century later another royal Spartan, Kyniska, who was the first woman to own race horses that were victorious at pan-Hellenic festivals, emphasized her uniqueness by declaring: "I am the only woman in all of Greece to have won an [Olympic] crown" (Moretti 1953 no. 17; cf., e.g. Pausanias 6.1.6). Plutarch quotes an anonymous Spartan woman who was conscious of her ethnic distinctiveness and articulated it: When an Ionian woman was proud of something she had woven, a Spartan showed off her four well-behaved sons, and said: "these should be the work of a noble and honorable woman, and she should swell with pride and boast of them" (Plutarch *Moralia* 241). We observe, in passing, the competitive nature of the Spartan's retorts. Quotations from women were anthologized in the Hellenistic period when there was a revival and reassertion of Spartan self-definition. That Spartan women were taught to speak and were encouraged to do so distinguishes them from Spartan men, who did not debate in law courts or in their General Assembly, and also distinguishes them from Athenian women, who were expected to remain silent and by no means to speak to men who were not close relatives. Because Athenians were also not to be seen by men, there was no competitiveness about beauty at least in the eyes of men as there was at Sparta. In Athens, respectable women were brought up so that they might see and hear and speak as little as possible (Schaps 1977). Perikles declared that the best women were those who were least known among men whether for praise or blame

(Thuc. 2.56). Their names were not mentioned outside the family circle. Herodotos (5.72) does not give the name of the priestess of Athena who warns Kleomenes not to enter the akropolis, though he does name Phye, the Athenian whom Peisistratos costumes as Athena. She is selected because she is very tall; thus Phye from *phyo* "to grow" is doubtless a nickname. The daughter of Megakles who was married to Peisistratos may be considered the Athenian counterpart of Gorgo, daughter and wife of kings. Herodotos does not mention the former by name, but readily refers to the latter. The former is passive and talks to her mother; the latter assertive and articulate, even in the presence of foreign men. As a rule, with the exception of tyrants' mothers, wives, and daughters and some Spartan members of the royal family, Herodotos tends not to mention the names of Greek women, but readily gives the names of barbarian queens and royal consorts such as Semiramis, Tomyris, Atossa, Artemisia, and others. The names of such women needed to be known not only in order to validate the lineage of their children and their right to the succession, but also because in Herodotos more barbarian than Greek women were active in political and military affairs, often responsible for memorable deeds with important consequences for the Greeks.

Not only do people arrange themselves in hierarchies, but historians of women may rank groups of women. Herodotos does not express preferences when writing about women in various societies, but Xenophon and Plutarch, our two major textual sources on Spartan women, often compare Spartans explicitly or implicitly with other Greek women, and the Spartans are always superior. According to several criteria that may be applied to assess the status of women, including health, education, economic power, and freedom of verbal and sexual expression, Spartans earn high ranking.

Unlike other Greek women, Spartans are rarely depicted as passive. Their agency is manifest in both the public and private spheres. Spartan women understood and enforced societal norms. Even little Gorgo did so. They not only spoke, but jeered at cowards and bachelors. Of all Greek women they alone are depicted as wielding the power of life and death over their adult sons, ordering them to be brave in battle even at the cost of their lives. In the *Sayings of Spartan Women* Plutarch gives many examples of women's leadership and control over men throughout Spartan history. Aristotle (*Politics* 1269b) criticized Sparta for it, observing that a state is divided into two roughly equal bodies of people, one of men, one of women. Therefore it is obvious that to study women is not only to learn women's history, but also to have a more complete and accurate assessment of Greek ethnic identity.

# Further reading

Dean-Jones, L. A. (1994) *Women's bodies in classical Greek science* (Oxford: Clarendon)
Fantham, E., H. P. Foley, N. B. Kampen, S. B. Pomeroy, H. A. Shapiro (1994) *Women in the classical world: image and text* (New York: Oxford University Press)
Lacey, P. (1968) *The family in classical Greece* (Ithaca NY: Cornell University Press) (Aspects of Greek and Roman Life)
Lefkowitz, M. R., & M. Fant (1992) *Women's life in Greece and Rome: a source book in translation* (Baltimore: Johns Hopkins University Press [2]1992)

Pomeroy, S. B. (1997) *Families in classical and Hellenistic Greece: representations and realities* (Oxford: Clarendon)

# Bibliography

Antonaccio, C. M., & J. Neils (1995) "A new graffito from archaic Morgantina" in: *ZPE* 105: 261–77

Barnes, S. J., & W. S. Melion (eds) (1989) *Cultural differentiation and cultural identity in the visual arts* (Washington DC: National Gallery of Art) (Studies in the history of art 27 = Symposium papers/Center for Advanced Study in the Visual Arts 12)

Cabanes, P. (1979) "Frontière et rencontre de civilisations dans la Grèce du Nord-Ouest" in: *Ktèma* 4: 183–99

Cabanes, P. (1980) "Société et institutions dans les monarchies de Grèce septentrionale au IVe siècle" in: *Revue des Études Grecques* 93: 324–51

Dawkins, R. M. (ed.) (1929) *The sanctuary of Artemis Orthia at Sparta: excavated and described by members of the British School at Athens, 1906–1910* (London: Macmillan) (Society for the Promotion of Hellenic Studies Supplementary Paper 5)

Dewald, C. (1981) "Women and culture in Herodotos' *Histories*" in: Foley 1981: 91–125

Foley, H. P. (ed.) (1981) *Reflections of women in antiquity* (New York: Gordon & Breach) (Women's Studies 8)

Golden, M. (1981) "Demography and the exposure of girls at Athens" in: *Phoenix* 35: 316–31

Graham, A. J. (1980–1) "Religion, women and Greek colonisation" in: *Atti del Centro ricerche e documentazione sull'antichità classica* 11: 293–314

Hall, J. (2002) *Hellenicity: between ethnicity and culture* (Chicago: University of Chicago Press)

Harrison, E. B. (1989) "Hellenic identity and Athenian identity in the fifth century B.C." in: Barnes & Melion 1989: 41–61

Hartog, F. (1988) *The mirror of Herodotus: the representation of the other in the writing of history* (trans. L. Janet) (Berkeley: University of California Press) (The New Historicism 5)

Henderson, J. (ed. and trans.) (2000) *Aristophanes*, pt 3: *Birds; Lysistrata; Women at the Thesmophoria* (Cambridge MA: Harvard University Press) (Loeb classical library 179)

Lyons, C. L. (1996) *The archaic cemeteries* (Princeton: Princeton University Press) (Morgantina Studies 5)

Malkin, I. (ed.) (2001) *Ancient perceptions of Greek ethnicity* (Cambridge MA: Harvard University Press) (Center for Hellenic Studies Colloquia 5)

Marchant, E. C. (ed. and trans.) (1923) *Xenophon*: Memorabilia *and* Oeconomicus (Cambridge MA: Harvard University Press) (Loeb Classical Library)

Moretti, L. (1953) *Iscrizioni agonistiche greche* (Rome: Signorelli) (Studi pubblicati dall'Istituto italiano per la storia antica 12)

Ogden, D. (1996) *Greek bastardy in the classical and Hellenistic periods* (Oxford: Clarendon) (Oxford Classical Monographs)

Parke, H. W., & D. E. W. Wormell (1956) *The Delphic oracle*, 2 vols (Oxford: Blackwell)

Pomeroy, S. B. (1975) *Goddesses, whores, wives, and slaves: women in classical antiquity* (New York: Schocken; reissued with new foreword 1995)

Pomeroy, S. B. (1984) *Women in Hellenistic Egypt from Alexander to Cleopatra* (New York: Schocken, 1984; pb. with new foreword Detroit: Wayne State University Press 1990)

Pomeroy, S. B. (1994) *Xenophon*, Oeconomicus: *a social and historical commentary; with a new English translation* (Oxford: Clarendon)

Pomeroy, S. B. (2002) *Spartan women* (New York: Oxford University Press)

Schaps, D. M. (1977) "The woman least mentioned: etiquette and women's names" in: *CQ* 27: 323–30

Schaps, D. M. (1979) *Economic rights of women in ancient Greece* (Edinburgh: Edinburgh University Press)

Shepherd, G. (1999) "Fibulae and females" in: Tsetskhladze 1999: 267–300

Tsetskhladze, G. R. (ed.) (1999) *Ancient Greeks west and east* (Leiden: Brill) (*Mnemosyne* Suppl. 196)

CHAPTER EIGHTEEN

# Greek Government

*Lynette G. Mitchell*

To speak of 'government' in the context of classical Greece is an anachronism, since 'government' is not a Greek word (though it has some relationship in derivation to the Greek *kybernetes*, the helmsman). Nevertheless, in the fifth and fourth centuries the Greeks themselves did talk about 'constitution' (*politeia*), 'rule' (*arche*), 'to rule' (*kratein*) and 'sovereignty' (*to kyrion*), and were concerned with questions of who ruled and how they did it. One of the major movements in the archaic period which had radically affected ideas of statehood and which was probably the most significant phenomenon for the development of the polis is what Morris (1996) has called the 'strong principle of equality'. As a result, many states across the Greek world had moved towards systems of political administration in which 'rule' was conducted by magistrates (*archai*) from the citizen body, however that was defined. Although these magistrates 'ruled' in one sense, in Greek political thought they were answerable to a higher rule, and that was the 'rule of law' (*nomoi*), that body of custom which was enshrined as traditional and unwritten law (indeed Aristotle thought that unwritten law had more authority than written law: *Politics* 1287b4–8), which gave freedom and equality for all before the law (*isonomia*). To stand outside the law was to be a tyrant.

The present chapter will have three sections. In the first section we will look at ideas of sovereignty as they developed in fifth- and fourth-century political thought. This overview will provide the background for the second section, which will work through the chief magistracies of the constitutional forms which acted under the rule of law. In the final section, we will turn to those constitutions which were deemed not to exist under the rule of law, the models the Greeks (and particularly the Athenians) used to understand them, and how this understanding then affected perceptions of real-life politics in the city-states.

# 1  On Constitutions

The first instance we have in the extant literature of political theorizing is Herodotos' description of the alleged discussion between the three Persian conspirators on the virtues of the three types of constitution: the rule of the one (monarchy), the rule of the few (oligarchy), and the rule of the many (democracy) (Hdt. 3.80–2 with 6.43.3). Ironically, Herodotos puts this constitutional debate into the mouths of Persians, but the tripartite division of constitutions was a Greek construct, and provided the model for Greek constitutional thought down into the fourth century. Here, even monarchy is envisaged as rule according to ancient law, and Herodotos has Dareios say that it was monarchy that gave the Persians freedom (Hdt. 3.82.5), alluding to his story of Kyros the Great's 'liberation' of the Persians from the Medes (Hdt. 1.125–30). But it is important for Herodotos' narrative and for his thematic purposes that, although Persia was liberated by a monarch, it was later enslaved by a tyrant ('for soft lands breed soft men', as Kyros warns his advisers: Hdt. 9.122.3), and that cities that were once great have become small, and those that were small have become great, since for men prosperity (*eudaimonia*) never remains in the same place for long (Hdt. 1.5.4).

Although the tripartite model for describing constitutions remained influential into the fourth century and was greatly elaborated by Plato and Aristotle, a competing model emerged, probably under the influence of the Peloponnesian War and in an atmosphere in which monarchy generally meant tyranny, which defined democracy and oligarchy as the two principal and opposing styles of constitution (cf. Loraux 1986: 214–17). In fact Aristotle, who is trying to systematize the range of constitutional types by means of his extended version of the tripartite classification, says that some people try to reduce the model to only these two basic types of constitution (*Politics* 1290a13–29). While Herodotos was interested in the contrast between freedom before the law, whatever the constitutional form (cf. Hdt. 3.142–3, 5.78, 91, 7.104, 134–6), and the enslavement of arbitrary and non-constitutional tyranny, the antithesis between oligarchy and democracy is explored by Thucydides in his *History of the Peloponnesian War* (e.g., 5.31.6, 81.2; 6.39.1–2; 8.47.2, 48.4, etc.). Nevertheless, even Thucydides concedes that oligarchy can be isonomic (Thuc. 3.62.3), although in the same passage he also has the Thebans claim that rule by the few can be 'the form of government nearest to tyranny and farthest removed from law and the virtues of moderation', making for the first time the link between oligarchy and tyranny which was developed in the fourth century (cf. Thuc. 6.60.1).

In the fourth century, Xenophon, Isokrates and Plato provide encomia of kings and tyrants both of their own time and of the past, including Kyros the Great of Persia, and Euagoras and Nikokles of Salamis in Cyprus. On the other hand, Plato in the utopian world of the *Republic* imagines the state ruled by the philosopher king (an ideal he tried to translate into practice at the court of Dionysios II of Syracuse with disastrous results for himself: Diodoros 15.7.1), and in the *Laws* echoes Xenophon's (and Herodotos') treatment of Kyros as the good king, whose successors fall into decline because of their life of luxury (694C–696B).

Aristotle in the *Politics* in the late fourth century provides the most systematic treatment of constitutions and the political life. The basis of Aristotle's argument is that the city is an association, that it is the most sovereign of all associations, and that it is a political association (*Politics* 1252a11–7). However (he argues), while no city can exist without rulers (*Politics* 1291a35–8), political activity is unlike the activity of other associations in which there are ruler and ruled, because being a member of the polis involves both ruling and being ruled in turn (*Politics* 1252a7–16); the good citizen is one who learns how to rule and be ruled; and this kind of rule is called 'political rule' (*Politics* 1277a25–b16). In the best constitutions all citizens are also equal and think it right to take their turns in holding office (*Politics* 12791a8–13).

A constitution (*politeia*), on the other hand, he defines both as the organization of those who live in a city (*Politics* 1274b38) and at the same time as the organization of its magistrates, and particularly the magistracy which is sovereign in the state; it is this sovereign body which defines the constitution as rule by the one, the few or the many (*Politics* 1278b8–15). Yet Aristotle was aware of the plurality of constitutions that can be contained within this definition, and sought to classify them as the 'right kinds of constitution', kingship, aristocracy and 'politeia' (which was a mixed constitution), and the three perverted forms, tyranny, oligarchy and democracy (their perversion lying in the fact that they pursued the interests of the rulers and not the common good) (*Politics* 1289a26–1290a29, cf. 1279a22–1279b11). Yet for Aristotle, as for Herodotos and others before him, the best constitution is the one ruled by law (*Politics* 1282b1).

The rule of law was the theoretical principle of political life. In Herodotos the Spartan ex-king tells Xerxes that the Spartans are more afraid of the law than Xerxes' subjects of him (Hdt. 7.104.4), and Thucydides has Perikles declare that in democratic Athens all citizens were equal before the law (Thuc. 2.37.1). In the *Hellenika*, on the other hand, Xenophon explores the practical tension between the sovereignty of the assembly and the sovereignty of law in his description of the events at Athens after the disaster at Arginousai in 406 (Xenophon *Hellenika* 1.7.8–34). The assembly called for the prosecution of the eight generals, shouting out that 'it was a terrible thing if "the people" (*ho demos*) was not allowed to do what it wanted (1.7.12)', though Euryptolemos exhorted the Athenians to act legally, since '[t]he laws are yours, and it is the laws, above all, which have made you great. Guard them and never attempt to do anything without their sanction' (1.7.29).

While the law may have been the ultimate ruler, the citizens also shared in that rule. Aristotle says that it is the job of rulers (whether the one, the few or the many) to make pronouncements on matters that need a more precise judgement than the laws can naturally provide (*Politics* 1282b1–6). Indeed, for Aristotle, sovereignty at this level resides with citizens who participate in the administration of justice and the holding of office (*Politics* 1275a22–3). So it is to the holding of office and the administration of the constitution that we shall turn next.

## 2   The Administration of the Constitution

Aristotle formulates another definition of a constitution (*Politics* 1289a15–20): 'A constitution is the organization of the magistracies (*archai*) for the cities, in regard to how they should be divided up, and what part should be sovereign and what the purpose (*telos*) of each association is.' Indeed in many Greek states, citizens were involved directly in these magistracies, and there was little attempt to develop permanent bureaucracies (Rhodes 1996). Athens is the only city where we know much about the organization of administration, but here the liturgical class paid for such things as ships and festivals (Aristotle *Politics* 1291a33–4; [Xenophon] *Ath. Pol.* 1.13; cf. Isaios 11.40), and individuals were responsible for taking up prosecutions on behalf of the state. In the spirit of ruling and being ruled, administrative responsibilities, where they could not be devolved onto individuals, were held by boards of ten (one from each of the ten tribes), who were appointed for a year and were not eligible for re-election to the same board (cf. Rhodes 1996).

But Athens was not the only state to deem the holding of office to be a responsibility of citizens. Although different constitutions chose to distribute their principal magistracies in different ways, there were similar kinds of office (assemblies, probouleutic councils, councils of elders, etc.) across many Greek states, and in this section we will look at the various magistracies according to their function. Although these magistracies may have had family similarities, in different states different magistracies held more or less decision-making power according to the type of constitution.

## 2.1   Assembly

Aristotle says that membership of the assembly and participation in the law courts are two magistracies with permanent tenure (*Politics* 1275a26). In most states the assembly acted as the final decision-making body in the state, though it may not have had the right to form or change the resolutions put to it. However, while most Greek cities had assemblies, not all did (Rhodes with Lewis 1997: 502). While there is considerable evidence for the role of the assembly in Athens, the role that the assembly played in some other states is less clear. In Korinth, for example, it has sometimes been assumed that there was no assembly but only a council of *probouloi*. Diodoros (for what it is worth) does mention a *gerousia* and assembly (*syn(h)edrion*) in the fourth century (Diodoros 16.65.6–8), but Rhodes (Rhodes with Lewis 1997: 72–3) notes that the literary evidence is not conclusive either way, and we are not helped by the fact that there are so few inscribed decrees from Korinth and none relating to the classical period.

Federal states could also have assemblies. Although we have no decrees from the earlier phase of federation in Boiotia (447–386), decrees dating from the reformed Boiotian Federation of the mid fourth century indicate a federal assembly of citizens (in which there is no indication of the earlier four-council structure: Rhodes with Lewis 1997: 122–3; cf. Buck 1994: 106–7). Yet while the fourth-century Arkadian *koinon* issued decrees in the name of the assembly of the Arkadians (Tod 115 A), decrees could still be issued by individual cities within the federation: for example, during the period of federation there are decrees made by 'the city of the Lousiatai' (*IG* 5.2 388–90). On the island of Keos, decrees could also be issued either by individual cities or by the federal assembly of the Keans (e.g., *IG2²* 1128 = R&O 40; *IG* 12.5 542 with Suppl.; cf. *I. Delos* 98 = R&O 28), though this may reflect tension between Athens' desire for the Keans to be governed by cities, and the Keans' own wish to organize themselves in a federal state (R&O 200; 201).

In order for an active assembly to work efficiently and effectively, it needed to meet regularly, and the most common pattern for meetings across the Greek world seems to have been one a month (Rhodes with Lewis 1997: 503–4). Nevertheless, at Athens by the end of the fifth century there were probably four assembly meetings each prytany (the year was divided into 10 prytanies) (*Ath. Pol.* 43.3–4) (Hansen, e.g., 1983a, thinks there were three regular meetings, but see Harris (1986); cf. Rhodes 1993: 778–9, id. with Lewis 1997: 13–14). At Athens, the principal assembly meeting in each prytany, the *ekklesia kyria*, discussed whether magistracies were being conducted satisfactorily, the food supply and defence of the state (*Ath. Pol.* 43.4), and it was also possible to call additional extraordinary meetings (though Hansen does not think so).

Assemblies not only had to be regular but also needed to be attended in those states where they acted as the chief decision-making body. Attendance at meetings of the assembly could be encouraged by pay – Aristotle says that assemblies are most powerful in those states where there is a high rate of payment for attendance (*Politics* 1299b37–1300a4; cf. 1297a13–29) – but this was not universal. Even at Athens, while jurors had been paid since Perikles' reform of the 450s (*Ath. Pol.* 27.3–4), attendance at assemblies did not receive payment until about 400, and then apparently only for those who arrived early (Aristophanes *Ecclesiazusae* 372–93). When assembly pay was introduced, payment was made initially at a rate of one obol (Markle 1985 calculates that a family of four could be fed on two and a half obols a day), although this was raised to three obols between 393 and 390 (*Ath. Pol.* 41.3; Seager 1967: 107 with n. 110). Although the practice does not seem to have been common, Athens was not the only state to use assembly-pay (cf. Aristotle *Politics* 1297a35–8, 1299b38–1300a4): a decree from Iasos sets outs how payments are to be made for attendance at their monthly meetings (*SEG* 40 959; Rhodes with Lewis 1997: 509; de Ste. Croix 1975). But even at Athens where there was payment for attendance there are questions about who may or may not have been able to attend meetings of the assembly because of geographic or economic limitations (Osborne 1985: 64–72; cf. Davies 1993: 87–116), and there may have been many for whom the loss of labour caused by attendance may have imposed a severe restriction on participation.

The composition of the assembly varied across Greek states. In Athens the assembly comprised all citizens (cf. *Ath. Pol.* 7.3), who were defined as males of eighteen years and over (*Ath. Pol.* 42.1). All citizens had the right to speak in the assembly ([Xenophon] *Ath. Pol.* 1.6; Demosthenes 18.170), and voting was by show of hands (*Ath. Pol.* 44.3; Hansen 1983b). Some decrees, such as ostracism, required a quorum of 6,000 votes (Philochoros *FGrHist* 328 F 30; cf. Plutarch *Aristeides* 7.5). At democratic Argos in the fifth and fourth centuries, decrees were issued by the *aliaia* ('assembly') (e.g., *SEG* 13 239; M&L 43 B 44), but there may have been a property qualification for membership of the assembly (Tomlinson 1972: 193; cf. Piérart 2000: 308–9); similarly in democratic Erythrai (which had a democracy imposed on it by Athens in c. 453/2), there was a property qualification for membership of the jury-courts (*IK Erythrai und Klazomenai* 2).

In Sparta, on the other hand, all citizens could participate in the assembly, even if there was a property and educational qualification for membership of the citizen body (Cartledge 1987: 129–30). Votes were decided by acclamation, although in 432, when the assembly was deliberating about whether the Athenians had broken the thirty years' peace, Sthenelaïdas the ephor requested those who wanted war to stand on one side, and those who did not to stand on the other, since he claimed to be unable to decide which shout was the loudest, and wanted to force everyone to take a position on the question, showing clearly that the majority was on his side (Thuc. 1.87.1–2).

Under some oligarchic regimes only a part of the citizen body was made eligible for membership of the assembly. In the Boiotian federation of 447–386, there was a property qualification for membership of each of the city councils, and it is perhaps reasonable to presume that the same qualification applied to the federal councils (*Hellenika Oxyrhynchia* 19.2 with Thuc. 5.38.2). There may also have been a similar restriction in Arkadia (Rhodes with Lewis 1997: 502, 507). Some states also seem to have experimented with representative assemblies: the four Boiotian councils comprised 60 representatives from each of the 11 divisions of Boiotia (*Hellenika Oxyrhynchia* 19.3–4).

However, according to Aristotle, the difference between oligarchy and democracy was that in democracy the assembly was sovereign (*Politics* 1298a3–35). After 462/1 at Athens, when Ephialtes' reforms reduced the judicial powers of the Areopagos (the Council of ex-archons) and increased those of the assembly (*Ath. Pol.* 25), the assembly worked in conjunction with the courts (which after at least 415 provided a check through prosecutions for illegal decrees on decisions made in the assembly and monitored magistracies) as the sovereign body of the state (*Ath. Pol.* 41.2; cf. Thuc. 2.37.1; Aischylos *Suppliants*, esp. 365–9). Indeed, in the period of most radical democracy at the end of the fifth century, most matters were presented to the assembly for consideration (although reforms in the fourth century gave some of the assembly's powers in the making of laws to officials, the *nomothetai*: cf. Rhodes 1979–80).

Even in states where there were monarchs, it was possible for assemblies to issue decrees in their own name. In the later part of the fourth century the assembly of the Molossians enacted decrees (e.g., *SEG* 23 471 with 24 446), despite the hereditary monarchy, and in a decree awarding citizenship from earlier in the century the assembly is not mentioned but officials are, indicating that these grants are not simply in the gift of the king (cf. Davies 2000: 254). The assembly of the Macedonians, on the other hand, seems only to have been able to decide on the succession or to act as a court for capital offences (Arrian *Anabasis* 3.26.2; Q. Curtius Rufus 6.8.23–11.40; Justin 7.8–10; Diodoros 17.2.1–2; (Hammond & Griffith 1979: 383–92; Borza 1990: 241–8), the sovereign power being vested in the king.

But just because decrees were issued by the assembly did not mean that the assembly was the principal decision-making body in the state, and Sparta illustrates a particular problem in this regard. Thucydides provides the text of two decrees issued by 'the assembly (*ekklesia*) of the Spartans' concerning their relations with Argos in 418/17 (Thuc. 5.77, 79). On the other hand, Aristotle says that the assembly at Sparta was not a deliberative body, but simply ratified decisions made by the council of elders, the *gerousia* (Aristotle *Politics* 1272a4–12). Further, while the Great Rhetra suggests that the assembly had the ultimate decision-making power (Plutarch *Lykourgos* 6), this power seems also to have been modified so that the *gerousia* had the power of veto (cf. Cartledge 1987: 124–9). Also, although Thucydides in 432 gives the assembly the final word on whether or not the Athenians had broken the peace treaty (Thuc. 1.87), in 415 it is the ephors and 'those in office' who prepare to send ambassadors to Syracuse (Thuc. 6.88.10). Yet it is 'the Spartans' who deliberate on Alkibiades' advice and decide to send help to Sicily (Thuc. 6.93.1). Likewise

Xenophon recounts a number of instances when the Spartan assembly listened to foreign ambassadors, and formed a decision on the basis of what they heard (e.g., Xenophon *Hellenika* 5.2.11, 20, 24).

The apparently contradictory nature of this evidence has provoked considerable debate. On the one hand, Andrewes (1966: 1–8) argues that the *gerousia* seems not to play any part in any of the deliberations we have, and concludes that the assembly and not the *gerousia* was the sovereign body of state. De Ste. Croix (1972: principally 124–38 with 349–53), on the other hand, accepts Aristotle's statement, pointing out that there is no sign in any of these passages of any actual discussion in the assembly, and argues that the assembly could only ratify (or not) proposals put to it by the *gerousia* and had no power of amendment, and that individual Spartiates had no absolute right to speak in the assembly. Others since have tried to find a place somewhere between the two positions. Finley (1981: 33) and Lewis (1977: 36–9), for example, argue for a situation where the assembly made the decision when 'the leadership' (presumably the *gerousia* and 'those in office') was unable to decide (cf. Rhodes 1986: 76–80).

## 2.2  Probouleutic councils

But even in democratic Athens, the assembly did not deliberate unaided. At Athens, as elsewhere across the Greek world, material for discussion in the assembly was often prepared in advance by a council in a process called *probouleusis*, which, though not universal (Rhodes suggests that some states were too small to need such a body: Rhodes with Lewis 1997: 476), was widespread. While Aristotle notes that *probouleusis* is not democratic, he argues that in democratic constitutions the preparation of material for discussion by preliminary councils did not limit democracy because of the size of the council (at Athens it was a council (*boule*) of 500, at Elis a council of 600 (Thuc. 5.47.9), at Tegea (*IG* 5.2 6) and Thasos (M&L 83) a council of 300); further, councils of this kind were necessary in order that the assembly could deliberate on the things that were most important (Aristotle *Politics* 1299b30–1300a4, 1322b12–17). Small councils, on the other hand, he says, were oligarchic by nature (*Politics* 1299b34), and in some oligarchies the probouleutic council held sovereign power (he gives as examples Sparta and Crete: cf. *Politics* 1272a7–8).

The power of the probouleutic body to act executively varied from state to state, and in many states it was possible for the assembly to change or amend proposals put by the probouleutic council (Rhodes with Lewis 1997: 484–91). In Athens, the assembly deliberated on matters put to it in a *proboleuma* of the *boule*, which sometimes but not always incorporated a specific recommendation (Aischines 3.125–7; Rhodes with Lewis 1997: 13). In Chios in the classical period, on the other hand, the council (*bole*) seems to have held executive power (*IGA* 381; Michel 707; *SEG* 35 923), and there is no sign of an assembly (Rhodes with Lewis 1997: 230).

Yet even in constitutions where the assembly was powerful, some decisions could be taken solely by the probouleutic body, particularly in emergencies. For example, the Three Hundred in Tegea had some decision-making power during times of war (*IG* 5.2 6). One notorious example from Athens is the overtures of the *boule* to Philip in 358/7 concerning Amphipolis and Pydna, about which (according to Theopompos *FGrHist* 115 F 30 a–b) the assembly was told nothing so that the Amphipolitans and Pydnaians would not get to hear of it. As de Ste. Croix (1963: esp. 114) points out, however, a treaty could not have been made without the assembly's knowledge and approval.

In Sparta, on the other hand, the *gerousia* comprised the two kings and 28 men from those over 60 years old who served out their lives in office (Hdt. 6.57.5; Plutarch *Lykourgos* 26.1; Aristotle *Politics* 1270b35–1271a1). While there may have been no formal restriction on who could hold office, the sources are clear that it was thought to be the preserve of the 'best' families (e.g., Aristotle *Politics* 1270b24–5, 1306a16–19; de Ste. Croix 1972: 353–4). Members were elected by acclamation in a manner Aristotle regarded as 'childish', each candidate coming before the assembly and the one receiving the loudest shout winning (Plutarch *Lykourgos* 26.2–3; Aristotle *Politics* 1271b9–10).

Federal states could also have councils. This was certainly the case in the Arkadian federation (R&O 32; *SEG* 29 405), and the earlier Boiotian federation had four councils, each of which took it in turns to perform a probouleutic function for the other three (*Hellenika Oxyrhynchia* 19.2). In the restored federation, the college of Boiotarchs may have formed a probouleutic council which prepared material for consideration by the assembly (Buckler 1980: 30–1), though the fact that the Boiotarchs are named in decrees does not prove this. The Ionian *koinon*, which met at least in emergencies in the sixth century (Hdt. 1.141.4, 148, 170), seems to have had a council which could act executively: a fourth-century decree is issued in the name of the '*boule* of the Ionians' (*I. Priene* 139).

## 2.3   Council of Elders

A number of states, even democratic states, retained councils of elders into the classical period. At Sparta, this was the *gerousia*, and other states also had *gerousiai*, including Korinth and the Arkadian city of Stymphalos (*SEG* 11 1105). In a late sixth-century decree, the Council of Elders of one of the cities in Ozolian Lokris (the *preiga*) had voting powers (M&L 13). There was also a council of 80 in democratic Argos, which was possibly also a council of elders (Tomlinson 1972: 196), and which administered the oaths for the alliance between Argos, Athens, Mantineia and Elis in 418/17 (Thuc. 5.47.9). The Areopagos at Athens, on the other hand, originally comprised ex-archons who had been elected for this office on the basis of good birth and wealth (*Ath. Pol.* 3.6, cf. 8.2). By the beginning of the fifth century the selection process was by lot from an elected list (*Ath. Pol.* 22.5), though later election was replaced by lot for the first stage as well (Rhodes 1993: 472–4). Nevertheless, despite its reduction in power in the mid fifth century, members of the Areopagos continued to serve for life (*Ath. Pol.* 3.6).

Such councils also often had judicial functions. The *gerousia* at Sparta not only had a probouleutic function, but also was the highest court in the state (de Ste. Croix 1972: 132–7). It tried capital charges (Xenophon. *Lak. Pol.* 10.2), important cases (Aristotle *Politics* 1270b38–40) and homicide (Aristotle *Politics* 1275b9–11), and was not subject to public scrutiny (Aristotle *Politics* 1271a5–6). The Council of Elders at Athens, the Areopagos, on the other hand, was reduced to a homicide court after the reforms of 462/1 (*Ath. Pol.* 57.3; cf. Aischylos *Eumenides*), though it gained more power in the fourth century.

## 2.4 Public officials

Different states had different types of public officials, some of which had considerable power even in democratic states, such as Athens. The Athenians, indeed, had a large number of public officials serving both in the state and abroad (including the nine archons, The Eleven (viz. jailers), jury-men, magistrates in the Piraeus, auditors, arbitrators, road-builders, etc). Most of these were selected by lot and paid for out of the public purse (*Ath. Pol.* 24.3, 50–62). Only a few positions were elected, and these were principally military (*Ath. Pol.* 61; but note also ambassadors: Aischines 2.18–19).

Other states had officials, about whom we know less than those at Athens. Thucydides refers to the officials who administered and received the oaths of the alliance between Athens, Argos, Mantineia and Elis in 420 (Thuc. 5.47.9): at Athens the oaths were taken by the *boule* and the city magistrates; at Argos, by the *bola*, the 80, and the *artynai*; at Mantineia by the *damiourgoi*, the council, and the other magistrates; at Elis, by the *damiourgoi*, the magistrates, and the 600. We have already discussed the various probouleutic councils (the *boule* at Athens, the *bola* at Argos, and the 600 at Elis), as well as what is perhaps a council of elders at Argos, the 80. The *damiourgoi* (literally: 'public officials') of Mantineia and Elis (cf. *I. Olympia* 16; *SEG* 15 241) are also known elsewhere from inscriptions, and seem to be a western Greek phenomenon (Murakawa 1957; cf. Jeffery 1973–4). Tomlinson (1972: 198) also suggests that it may be an oligarchic office, since boards of *damiourgoi* are known from sixth-century inscriptions, which seem to have been replaced by the *artynoi* (Tomlinson suggests 'magistrates'), a magistracy known at Argos only from this passage of Thucydides, though an inscription dating to c. 480 from Halieis (see Jameson 1974 for attribution) also refers to *synartynoi* (*IG* 4 554). Nevertheless, he concedes that there are other possibilities.

In Sparta, the chief public officials were the five ephors, who Aristotle thought were the most democratic of the Spartan constitutional institutions, since they were drawn from the whole citizen body (Aristotle *Politics* 1265b38–40, 1272a6–7, 31–3, 1294b29–31; cf. 1270b8–10). They served for a year, and changes in the ephorate – though there was not always unanimity within a single board (e.g., Xenophon *Hellenika* 2.4.29–30; but note also 2.3.34) – could mean reversals in public policy, as evidenced in 421 just after the swearing of the Peace of Nikias between Athens and Sparta when two of the incoming ephors who were opposed to the peace sought to undermine it (Thuc. 5.36–9).

The ephors had far-reaching powers (Andrewes 1966: 8–14; Lewis 1977: 40–2), though this was limited by the annual tenure of the office, which probably could not be repeated (Westlake 1976). The selection process is unclear (all we know for certain is that Aristotle thought that, like the election of the Spartan *gerousia*, it was 'childish': *Politics* 1270b26–8), but ephors were likely to have been elected directly by the assembly from those over 30 years of age (Rhodes 1981 *contra* Rahe 1980).

According to Aristotle, the ephors held sovereign power in the most important matters (so that it was equal to a tyranny) and could act on their own discretion, and their duties included the scrutiny of all other officials (Aristotle *Politics* 1270b7–8, 13–16, 28–31, 1271a6–7; cf. Xenophon *Lak. Pol.* 8.4), and Xenophon says that they kept public order and were able to impose fines (Xenophon *Lak. Pol.* 8.4, cf. 13.5). They despatched armies on campaign (Thuc. 8.12.3, Xenophon *Hellenika* 5.1.33), and seem to have had the power of appointment of other officials, or at the very least played an important part in the appointing process: for example, the commander Eudamidas asked the ephors to allow his brother Phoibidas to bring troops to him at Olynthos (Xenophon *Hellenika* 5.2.24); and Xenophon says that Derkylidas was replaced as harmost of Abydos through no fault of his own, but because Anaxibios arranged to become harmost there through the ephors, who were his friends (*philoi*) (Xenophon *Hellenika* 4.8.32).

The principal magistrates in the cities of Thessaly were the *tagoi*. In an early decree from one of the cities of Thessaly the *tagoi* are responsible for making a dedication (*SEG* 27 183), in a fifth-century inscription from Thetonion a *tagos* is made responsible for driving out anyone who transgresses the immunity which is being awarded by the decree (*IG* 9.2 257), and a fourth-century decree from Lamia provides a list of magistrates: the archons (here probably equivalent to the *tagoi*), a *stratages* (a military commander), a hipparch and a secretary (*IG* 9.2 60).

The chief political position in the Thessalian *koinon*, on the other hand (which was first established in the seventh century: Aristotle F 497 Rose with Westlake 1935: 25 n. 1), was the *archon* (R&O comm. on 44). This was the title given to Philip II of Macedon (and inherited by Alexander) when he was appointed to the leadership of the *koinon* (Justin 11.3.2); the Thessalians opposed to Alexander also called themselves the *koinon* and continued to appoint an *archon* (R&O 44). *Tagos* in the context of the *koinon* was the name given to the military commander, and in the fourth century Iason (Jason) of Pherai claimed the title of the *tagos* of all Thessaly (Xenophon *Hellenika* 6.1.2–13, 18–19). In this he probably required the vote of all four Thessalian regions (Westlake 1935: 79), since Polydamas the tyrant of Pharsalos promised to persuade the Pharsalians to help Iason secure the vote (Xenophon *Hellenika* 6.1.18).

In other states military and naval commands could also be important politically in the formation and enacting of policy. Of the military positions at Athens, the board of ten generals, the *strategoi*, were the most important. The generals were elected on the principle of one from each of the ten tribes probably until the third quarter of the fourth century, although it was possible after the mid fifth century for one tribe to be represented by more than one general (Mitchell 2000). Generals were often from prominent families within the community, and, although there was no property qualification on holding office, there was a feeling that this was a job for men with appropriate experience (cf. Xenophon *Memorabilia* 3.4; Mitchell 1997: 96–108).

At least in the fifth century, the generals at Athens were often also important politicians. The *boule* had to include on the agenda for the assembly any matters raised by the *strategoi* (M&L 65.55–6; cf. Hignett 1952: 246), and Thucydides suggests that they also had the right (together with the *boule*) to summon the assembly (Thuc. 4.118.14), though Rhodes argues that this only applied during the Peloponnesian War (Rhodes 1985: 43–6). But generals principally held only the power of influence, were subject to the will of the assembly (Hamel 1998), and were subject to a vote of confidence by the assembly each prytany (*Ath. Pol.* 61.2). Although Perikles held the position of *strategos* for 15 years in succession (Plutarch *Perikles* 16.3), and Thucydides suggests that he had the power or the right to cancel meetings of the assembly as well as summon them (Thuc. 2.22.1), Perikles was nonetheless removed from office and fined in 430, though he was later reinstated (Thuc. 2.65.3–4). Further, by the fourth century a division of role occurred between military generals and politicians (Hansen 1989: 25–72), so that we find men becoming either professional generals on the one hand (e.g., Iphikrates, Chabrias, Timotheos and Chares), or career politicians on the other (e.g., Philokrates, Aischines and Demosthenes son of Demosthenes), though Phokion tried to be both.

At Athens a general or generals could also be elected to hold 'unrestricted power' (that is, to be *autokratores*), though this may not always have meant very much. The three generals who were sent to Sicily were given such powers (Thuc. 6.8.2, 26.1), though in fact they remained answerable to the assembly (cf. Thuc. 7.14.4). Alkibiades was also elected *autokrator* in 407 (Xenophon *Hellenika* 1.4.20), and this is the only example from Athens where one general was given more power than his colleagues. At Syracuse under their mixed constitution, during the Peloponnesian War the norm of fifteen generals was reduced to three, who were elected by the assembly with special powers (Thuc. 6.72.4–73.2), and in 405 Dionysios was appointed general *autokrator* (just before seizing the tyranny) because of the Carthaginian threat (Diodoros 13.95).

At Sparta, in the appointment of overseas commands and in the development of foreign policy, it was wealth and patronage, as in other areas of Spartan life, which spoke loudest and most powerfully. Hodkinson (1993: 157–9, 161) has noted that all non-royal commanders were drawn from the Spartan elite, and as we have seen the ephors seem to have played an important part in their selection. By the same token, some individuals holding these appointments could then have considerable influence on policy. This was particularly true at the end of the fifth century in the case of Lysander, probably of humble origins, who developed his position through the nauarchy, the principal naval command. The nauarchy seems to have been originally appointed in a fairly desultory fashion, but became increasingly important in the final throes of the Peloponnesian War, settling down into a regular annual (initially non-renewable) appointment by at least 409 (Sealey 1976: 335–58 and Piérart 1995; Bommelaer 1981: 66–79, however, thinks it became annual by 413/12). On the back of his success in bringing the Peloponnesian War to a Spartan victory, Lysander was able to pursue his own imperialist policies in Athens and the cities of Asia Minor by installing in power 'dekarchies' (Diodoros 14.10.1, 13.1; Plutarch *Lysander* 13.3–4), oligarchic governments of ten men (in Athens it was an administration of Thirty), though neither Lysander's influence nor his dekarchies lasted very long (Xenophon *Hellenika* 3.4.2 with Andrewes 1971: 106–16). Lysander tried to recoup his losses through the king Agesilaos (Xenophon *Hellenika* 3.4.2; Plutarch *Agesilaos* 6.1), but Agesilaos soon asserted his independence of Lysander and sent him away (Xenophon *Hellenika* 3.4.7–10). Lysander died at Haliartos in 395 in a battle against the Boiotians and Athenians (Xenophon *Hellenika* 3.5.7–25).

The Boiotarchs of the Boiotian federation were also essentially military officials, but became overtly political under the restored federation. In the earlier Boiotian federation, there had been 11 Boiotarchs, one for each of the divisions of Boiotia (*Hellenika Oxyrhynchia* 19.3), but under the restored federation there were seven (*IG 7* 2407 = R&O 43; *IG 7* 2408), who were elected by the assembly, and could be re-elected annually (see Buck 1994: 108–9). The Boiotarchs of the restored federation also seem to have been able to initiate policy. Thus we find Pelopidas and Epameinondas, two of the most prominent Boiotarchs of the middle years of the fourth century, fronting foreign policies which were aimed in (almost literally) opposite directions. While Epameinondas concentrated on invasions of the Peloponnese from 370 (Xenophon *Hellenika* 6.5, 7.1.13–22, 41–3; Diodoros 15.61.3–66.1, 68–9, 75.2), Pelopidas headed north in 369, interfering in Thessaly and Macedon in two successive campaigning seasons, though he was imprisoned by Alexandros of Pherai in 368 (Diodoros 15.67.3–4, 71.2–7), and Epameinondas won his release in 367 (Diodoros 15.75.2; Plutarch *Pelopidas* 29.2–6).

## 2.5  Kings (basileis)

Though not technically magistrates, the final group we need to consider in this section on the officials of government are the constitutional kings. As we saw in the opening section, monarchy (rule by the one) was one of the three traditional forms of constitution. There were traditions of kings in Greece (though the degree to which tradition reflects fact is another matter), and the Argive monarchy may have survived down to the sixth century, since a late tradition provides the story of Meltas, a descendant of Pheidon, who was driven into exile (Pausanias 2.19.2). Herodotos (7.6.2) calls the Aleuadai of Thessaly *basilees* (kings), but they were in fact just one of at least three baronial families in Thessaly (cf. Westlake 1935: 29–31).

The dyarchy at Sparta, however, still flourished in the classical period. The two Spartan royal houses had an ancient and distinguished heritage which (whatever their true origins) they traced back through genealogies as least as far as the tenth century (Hdt. 7.204, 8.131.2; Cartledge 1987: 100–3). Herodotos deemed the Agiads to be the more senior house (Hdt. 6.51), and Cartledge argues that he may well be right given that some of the names in the Eurypontid family tree (Prytanis – 'Chief', and Eunomos – 'Good law') seem to have been invented to extend the line, and in the fourth century a further name was added to square the tally of the two lists (Cartledge 2002: 91, 293–8).

The kings at Sparta did not hold sovereign power, but only had jurisdiction when they led the army out to war (Aristotle *Politics* 1284b35–1285b19, esp. 1285a3–6), although they were always accompanied in the field by two ephors (Xenophon *Hellenika* 2.4.36; Xenophon *Lak. Pol.* 13.5, 15.2). They were also responsible for religious observances on behalf of the state (Aristotle *Politics* 1285a6–7), and made the sacrifices and performed the omens before going into battle (Xenophon *Lak. Pol.* 15.2): Agesilaos notoriously tried to make sacrifices at Aulis in imitation of Agamemnon before setting out in his Asian campaign in 396, although the Boiotarchs sent him packing (Xenophon *Hellenika* 3.4.3–4). The kings were also members of the *gerousia* (and particularly influential members since they did not have to wait until they were of age 60 before they could serve), and there were also special observances on their death, the king's funeral being a large public affair (Hdt. 6.56–7; Xenophon *Lak. Pol.* 15.9). However, the kings themselves could face trial, and throughout the fifth and fourth century a number of kings were tried, six being exiled or going into voluntary exile (Lewis 1977: 43–4; cf. de Ste. Croix 1972: 140–7).

The kings potentially held a great deal of influence, particularly in foreign policy. Many, however, were too young to be effective when they came to the throne. Agesipolis, for example, had succeeded his father Pausanias (who was tried and given the death penalty though he escaped into exile: Xenophon *Hellenika* 3.5.25), while he was 'still a child' (Xenophon *Hellenika* 4.2.9). Agesilaos, who became one of the brightest lights of Greece in the first half of the fourth century, was in his mid forties when he came to the throne (he was born in c. 445: Cartledge 1987: 21), and is a good example of the way a king by building up networks of power and influence was able to pursue an independent policy, and become a focus for powerful and influential groups (cf. Hamilton 1979; David 1981; Cartledge 1987). At the very beginning of his reign, he was heavily influenced by his mentor and lover, Lysander, but soon broke away and became a central political figure in his own right, pursuing an independent and imperialistic policy in Asia.

The dyarchy at Sparta (though much lauded by Aristotle) was not the only model for kingship in Greece. Despite the fact that Aristotle claimed that hereditary kinship only existed among barbarian states (*Politics* 1285a16–29), there were states on the fringes of the Greek world (whose Greekness sometimes came under question), such as the Molossoi in Epeiros and the Macedonians, who maintained monarchy of this sort. Although the Molossoi retained their kings, they also had a working assembly and civic magistrates, including 10 *damiourgoi* (Cabanes *L'Épire* 1), and a college of 15 magistrates (*synarchontes*) (Cabanes *L'Épire* 2). Aristotle says that the reason the Molossian royal house survived was because it was less despotic, and the king was more of an equal with his subjects (*Politics* 1313a20–3).

The Macedonian monarchs were a different matter. Although the question of the relationship between king and assembly is muddied by the evidence, which relates mostly to Alexander, whose rule was by no means ordinary, the king seems to have been the absolute ruler, and the assembly acted only in limited circumstances (see Lock 1977; Errington 1978). Hammond (1987: 58–9, 166–77) thinks that the Macedonian monarchy was set within the framework of a formal constitution, although not everyone agrees.

Philip and Alexander (if not the kings before them) were surrounded by the *hetairoi*, their companions, who were drawn from the leading Macedonian families, and who ate and drank with the king, acted as his bodyguard, and advised him on matters of state and military tactics (e.g., Arrian *Anabasis* 1.24.4–4, 3.6.4–6, 4.10.5–12.5; Plutarch *Alexander* 10.2–3, 11). In fact, not only was the relationship between the king and his *hetairoi* personal (Hammond & Griffith 1979: 395–404), but also the relationship between the king and his subjects (cf. Borza 1990: 236–41), and the king ruled by persuasion rather than compulsion (Hammond 1981: 242–3). Or at least that was the theory. As Alexander's reign progressed and he tried to adapt to and meet the demands of a more oriental and autocratic style of monarchy, the relationship between the king and his companions and his army started to disintegrate, and Alexander's control of events, and his relationship between his men and himself, started to become less secure (cf. Badian 1962). In fact, although Aristotle was Alexander's tutor, he probably would not have approved the kind of king his pupil had become: the oriental king; to the Greek mind, a tyrant.

# 3   Unconstitutional Constitutions: Tyrants and Tyrannical Oligarchs

For Aristotle in the fourth century tyranny was a perverted form of monarchy (e.g., *Politics* 1279b4–6). It was a form of constitution that stood outside the law (cf. *Politics* 1285a16–29, 1287a1–1288a6), and was directed towards the interest of a single person (*Politics* 1279b6–7). Although in the early fifth century Pindar says that both tyranny and rule of the 'boisterous army' (*Pythian Odes* 2.86–9) are under law, tyranny was associated with slavery soon after the Persian Wars: Diodoros (11.33.2) says that the Greek victory dedications soon after the Persian Wars were framed in terms of deliverance from 'hateful slavery'. Certainly at Athens, freedom under the law became associated with liberation from tyranny at some point after the expulsion of the Peisistratids (though 'liberation' in popular thought was wrongly associated with the 'tyrant-slayers', Harmodios and Aristogeiton: F 893 Page *Poetae Melici Graecae*; cf. Thuc. 1.20.2, 6.54–9; *Ath. Pol.* 18).

In fact, after the Persian Wars, at least to the Athenian mind, tyranny became closely associated with the Persian king. In Athenian vase-painting from the middle of the fifth century all barbarian potentates became assimilated to the Persian king (Miller 1988; 2000), and Herodotos contrasted arbitrary rule by one man (as exemplified in Xerxes) with rule under the law, and equated this with the contrast between slavery and freedom (cf., e.g., Hdt. 1.62.1, 3.142–3, 7.104, 134–5). Thucydides also was interested in tyranny that brings enslavement, and compared Athens to Persia as the 'enslaver' of the Greek cities (e.g., Thuc. 3.10.2–4). Indeed, the Athenians themselves in their public art ostentatiously and shockingly represented themselves as the ultimate tyrants, being conquerors of both Persians and Greeks, as part of their self-propaganda (Hölscher 1998; cf. Miller 1997: 239–42).

Yet in the fifth and fourth centuries there were a number of tyrannies among the Greek states. There had been tyrants in Sicily in the sixth and early fifth centuries, though these had been expelled around 466/5 (Hdt. 7.153–6; Diodoros 11.38, 67–8). Again in 405, Dionysios had seized control of Syracuse and established himself as tyrant, and, though he ruled ruthlessly, attempted to deal with the Carthaginian threat. He was succeeded by his son, Dionysios II, in 367 (Diodoros 15.74.5), who was, Diodoros says, 'inferior by far to his father' (Diodoros 16.5.1), and was ousted by his uncle by marriage, Dion, within ten years (Diodoros 16.9–15).

However, the erratic and ruthless administrations of Dionysios and his son were not the only kind of tyranny. Having defeated Dionysios II, Dion was elected general with full powers (*strategos autokrator*, Diodoros 16.30.5). But Dion himself was soon assassinated (Diodoros 16.31.7), and thereafter there was a run of would-be tyrants in Syracuse. Then the Korinthian Timoleon was sent to Syracuse, since the Syracusans had asked the Korinthians (their mother-city) for help. But Timoleon's role in Syracuse is not clear. Timoleon had been involved in the assassination of his brother, who had tried to seize the tyranny in Korinth. But while it was good to kill a tyrant it was bad to kill a brother, and Timoleon was despatched to Syracuse in order to prove himself (Diodoros 16.65). He defeated the Carthaginians (the old enemy of the Greeks in Sicily), and liberated the other Greek cities on the island from their tyrants (Diodoros 16.65–90). And yet Plutarch's account suggests another side to the story, and if his stories are to be relied upon Timoleon may have had a great deal of power and influence in decisions made by the state (Plutarch *Timoleon* 22.4, 38).

Indeed it seems there was room for constitutional tyranny (although in Aristotle's terms that is not really possible). In fourth-century Thessaly, Lykophron was the first in a tyrannical dynasty at Pherai, and there was also a tyrant at Pharsalos, Polydamas, though he may have been imposed by Sparta (Westlake 1935: 48–50, 76–8). Nevertheless, Polydamas' position seems to have had some kind of constitutional basis: when Jason presented him with an ultimatum to hand over the city, he went first to Sparta for help (they regretfully declined), and then (significantly) told Iason that he would try to persuade the Pharsalian assembly (Xenophon *Hellenika* 6.1.2–18). He was a tyrant subject to the assembly, and therefore (at least on one level) the law.

Nevertheless, tyranny was a bad word in Athens in particular, although Athens itself could *be* tyrannical. Aristotle says that tyranny is a system dear to the wicked (*Politics* 1314.1–2), and for Herodotos, Aristotle and others, Greek tyrants lived lives of luxury and ruled cruelly, holding their people in subjection (e.g., Kypselos and Periander of Korinth, and Polykrates of Samos: Hdt. 3.39–56, 5.92; Aristotle *Politics* 1311a20–2). For Thucydides, anticipating Aristotle, the tyrant was one who thought first of himself and his own safety, and the greatness of his family, so that personal security was his main concern (Thuc. 1.17). Lysias, in a speech which – or at least as much as we have of it – made liberal use of the panhellenic rhetoric of war against the barbarian as exemplified by the Persian Wars, declared in his *Olympic Oration* (delivered at the Olympic Games of 384) that the Greeks should unite in order to expel the barbarian (by which he means the Persian King, who controlled parts of Asia Minor) and to crush despotism, and in particular the tyrant of Sicily (in this case Dionysios I) (Lysias 33, esp. 33.3, 5–6).

In fact tyranny came to be a way of thinking about any regime which was opposed to the perceived interests of Athenian democracy, or just Athens. In the fifth century, Thucydides had already associated tyranny with oligarchy, and in the fourth century Demosthenes picks up this association and develops it. For Demosthenes oligarchy is brutal (Demosthenes 22.52; 24.24), and brings wealth to its adherents (Demosthenes 20.15). Oligarchy is opposed to the rule of law, and those who choose to live under it are cowards and slaves (Demosthenes 24.75–6). In the speech on the Rhodians (in which Demosthenes is only vaguely aware of the Macedonian threat and is much more preoccupied with Persia and its satrapies in Asia Minor) he says that war with oligarchs was an ideological war or a war about freedom, and that oligarchy was equal to slavery (Demosthenes 15.17–18). In fact, oligarchs (like the Persian King) are the common and natural enemy. 'When men overthrow democracies (here *politeiai*) and change to oligarchies', he says, 'I recommend you consider them to be the common enemies of all who desire freedom (*eleutheria*)' (Demosthenes 15.20).

It was probably in this context that oligarchs at Athens became stigmatized as tyrants, particularly the oligarchs involved in the oligarch coups at the end of the fifth and beginning of the fourth centuries. For two periods, in 411/10 and 404/3, democracy was overthrown or (at least in 411) replaced (the assembly thought in 411 that democracy could be restored once the crisis was over: Thuc. 8.54.1; *Ath. Pol.* 29.1). Both periods of oligarchy were extreme, but the second more so than the first, and many were put to death for little reason or on trumped-up charges (Xenophon *Hellenika* 2.3–4; Lysias 12; *Ath. Pol.* 34.3–39.6; cf. Thuc. 8.70.2 (411)). Certainly Xenophon says of the Thirty that, after the death of Theramenes (one of their number who objected to the executions), they began to act like tyrants (Xenophon *Hellenika* 2.4.1).

So oligarchs could be tyrants. But enemies of Athens could also become tyrants. It was as a tyrant and enslaver that Demosthenes (who had recognized the Persian

King as 'the common enemy of all' in the speech *On the Symmories* in 354/3: 14.3) described Philip of Macedon, transforming the Macedonian monarch into the traditional enemy of Athenian democracy (cf. Demosthenes 1.5). 'Do you seek freedom?' Demosthenes (6.25) says to the Argives and Messenians in the *Second Philippic*, 'Do you not see that Philip has titles which are irreconcilable to this? King and tyrant are all enemies of freedom and are the opposite of law. Will you not be on your guard lest in seeking to change from war you find a despot?' Likewise, he claims that the Greek cities are 'enslaved' to Philip (Demosthenes 3.20), that the Athenians too have become 'enslaved' to him (Demosthenes 8.49, 59–60), that Athens must stand for the 'freedom' (*eleutheria*) of Hellas (18.80, 100; 23.124), and that Philip is the enemy of constitutional government (*politeia*) and democracy (Demosthenes 8.43). And once Philip becomes the enemy, those who support him are traitors who have pledged away their freedom to the Macedonian (Demosthenes 18.296).

Constitutional theory was based on rule by the one, the few, or the many. But in Athens rule by the one, or at least one type of one-man rule, had become a way of understanding rule by the many, both by opposing tyranny to democracy and making tyranny antithetical to everything that democracy stood for, and by assimilating to tyranny oligarchy, the other constitutional form. As a result, not only did oligarchy become a form of constitution which was unacceptable, taking to itself all the attributes of the despised tyranny, but also democracy (and particularly Athenian democracy) was raised to the status of the only constitution which stood for justice, freedom, and the Athenian way.

# Further reading

There are no up-to-date synthetic monographs on Greek constitutional practice, though Ehrenberg (1969) provides a starting point. Most recent treatments on constitutions have focused on the practice of democracy, on which, a recent and accessible collection of essays, has been edited by Rhodes (2004), but see also Raaflaub in this volume's next chapter. Oligarchy as a constitutional form has attracted little scholarly interest in recent years, and, except for Ostwald (2000), the standard text is still Whibley (1896). For oligarchs and oligarchy at Athens, see Rhodes (2000). The practice of monarchy and tyranny in Greece and its representation in the sources has started to be reappraised; McGlew (1993) provides a useful starting point, while the essays in Morgan (2003) start to unpick the sources and representations, although they concentrate on tyrants and tyranny in Athenian literature and drama. A volume of essays edited by Lewis (2006) on tyranny and autocracy in the ancient world is also useful.

For an overview of the procedures and practice of Greek government, 'Part III' in Rhodes with Lewis (1997) discusses assemblies and *probouleusis*. The volume also offers a way into the inscriptional evidence through the gazetteer and discussions of patterns of procedure as reflected in the decrees. Hansen & Nielsen (2004) now also gives a brief overview and analysis of the available evidence, including constitutional matters, for all the Greek poleis.

# Bibliography

Cabanes *L'Épire* – Cabanes, P. (1976) *L'Épire de la mort de Pyrrhos à la conquête Romaine (272–167 av. J.C.)* (Paris: Belles Lettres) (Centre de Recherches d'Histoire Ancienne 19 = Annales littéraires de l'Université de Besançon 186

*I. Délos.* – *Inscriptions de Délos* (1926–) (Paris: Champion)

*I. Olympia* – Dittenberger, W., & K. Purgold (eds) (1896) *Die Inschriften von Olympia* (Berlin: Asher)

*I. Priene* – Hiller von Gaertringen, F. (ed.) (1906) *Inschriften von Priene* (Berlin: Reimer)

*IGA* – Roehl, H. (1882) *Inscriptiones Graecae antiquissimae praeter Atticas in Attica repertas* (Berlin: Reimer)

*IK Erythrai und Klazomenai* – Engelmann, H., & R. Merkelbach (1972) *Inschriften griechischer Städte aus Kleinasien*, vol. 1: *Die Inschriften von Erythrai und Klazomenai* (Bonn: Habelt)

Michel – Michel, C. (1900–27) *Recueil d'inscriptions grecques* (with 2 supplements) (Paris: Leroux)

Andrewes, A. (1966) 'The government of classical Sparta' in: Badian (ed.) 1996: 1–20

Andrewes, A. (1971) 'Two notes on Lysander' in: *Phoenix* 25: 206–26

Badian, E. (1962) 'Alexander the Great and the loneliness of power' in: *Journal of the Australasian Universities Language and Literature Association* 17: 80–91 (repr. in: Badian, E. (1964) *Studies in Greek and Roman history* (Oxford: Blackwell) 192–205)

Badian, E. (ed.) (1966) *Ancient society and institutions: studies presented to Victor Ehrenberg on his 75th birthday* (Oxford: Blackwell)

Bérard, C. (2000) 'The image of the other and the foreign hero' (trans. J. Curtiss Gage) in: Cohen 2000: 390–412 (originally published as 'L'image de l'Autre et le héros étranger' in: *Sciences et Racisme* fasc. 67 (1985–6) 5–22)

Boedeker, D., & K. A. Raaflaub (eds) (1998) *Democracy, empire, and the arts in fifth-century Athens* (Cambridge MA: Harvard University Press) (Center for Hellenic Studies Colloquia 2)

Bommelaer, J-F. (1981) *Lysandre de Sparte: histoire et traditions* (Paris: de Boccard) (Bibliothèque des Écoles françaises d'Athènes et de Rome 240)

Borza, E. N. (1990) *In the shadow of Olympus* (Princeton: Princeton University Press)

Bradeen, D. M., & M. F. McGregor (eds) (1974) Phoros: *tribute to Benjamin Dean Meritt* (Locust Valley NJ: Augustin)

Brock, R., & S. Hodkinson (eds) (2000) *Alternatives to Athens: varieties of political organization and community in ancient Greece* (Oxford: Oxford University Press)

Buck, R. J. (1994) *Boiotia and the Boiotian league, 423–371 BC* (Edmonton: University of Alberta Press)

Buckler, J. (1980) *The Theban hegemony, 371–362 BC* (Cambridge MA: Harvard University Press)

Cartledge, P. (1987) *Agesilaos and the crisis of Sparta* (London: Duckworth)

Cartledge, P. (2002) *Sparta and Lakonia: a regional history 1300–362 B.C.* (London: Routledge ²2002)

Cartledge, P., & F. D. Harvey (eds) (1985) *Crux: essays presented to G. E. M. de Ste. Croix on his 75th birthday* (First issued as *History of Political Thought* 6.1–2 (1985) Exeter: Imprint Academic) (London: Duckworth) 265–97

Cohen, B. (ed.) (2000) *Not the classical ideal: Athens and the construction of the other in Greek art* (Leiden: Brill) 413–42

David, E. (1981) *Sparta between empire and revolution (404–323 BC): internal problems and their impact on contemporary Greek consciousness* (New York: Arno)

Davies, J. K. (1993) *Democracy and classical Greece* (London: Fontana ²1993) (Fontana History of the Ancient World)

Davies, J. K (2000) 'A wholly non-Aristotelian universe: the Molossians as ethnos, state and monarchy' in: Brock & Hodkinson 2000: 234–58

De Ste. Croix, G. E. M. (1963) 'The alleged secret pact between Athens and Philip II concerning Amphipolis and Pydna' in: *CQ* 13: 110–119 (repr. in Perlman 1973: 35–45)

De Ste. Croix, G. E. M. (1972) *The origins of the Peloponnesian War* (London: Duckworth)

De Ste. Croix, G. E. M. (1975) 'Political pay outside Athens' in: *CQ* 25: 48–52

Ehrenberg, V. (1969) *The Greek state* (London: Methuen ²1969)

Errington, R. M. (1978) 'The nature of the Macedonian state under the monarchy' in: *Chiron* 8: 77–133

Finley, M. I. (1981) 'Sparta and Spartan Society' in: Finley, M. I. (1981) *Economy and society in ancient Greece* (London: Chatto & Windus) 24–40

Flensted-Jensen, P., T. H. Nielsen, L. Rubinstein (eds) (2000) *Polis and politics: studies in ancient Greek history, presented to Mogens Herman Hansen on his sixtieth birthday, August 20, 2000* (Copenhagen: Museum Tusculanum)

Hamel, D. (1998) *Athenian generals: military authority in the classical period* (Leiden: Brill) (*Mnemosyne* Suppl. 182)

Hamilton, C. D. (1979) *Sparta's bitter victories: politics and diplomacy in the Corinthian war* (Ithaca: Cornell University Press)

Hammond, N. G. L. (1981) *Alexander the Great: king, commander and statesman* (London: Chatto & Windus)

Hammond, N. G. L. (1987) *The Macedonian state: the origins, institutions and history* (Oxford: Clarendon)

Hammond, N. G. L., & G. T. Griffith (1979) *A history of Macedonia*, vol. 2: *550–336 B.C.* (Oxford: Clarendon)

Hansen, M. H. (1983a) 'How often did the *ecclesia* meet?' in: Hansen, M. H. (1983) *The Athenian ecclesia: a collection of articles 1976–83* (Copenhagen: Museum Tusculanum 1983) 35–72 (= *GRBS* 18 (1977) 43–70)

Hansen, M. H. (1983b) 'How did the Athenian *ecclesia* vote?' in: Hansen, M. H. (1983) *The Athenian ecclesia: a collection of articles 1976–83* (Copenhagen: Museum Tusculanum 1983) 103–21 (= *GRBS* 18 (1977) 123–37)

Hansen, M. H. (1986) 'The origin of the term *demokratia*' in: *LCM* 11: 35–6

Hansen, M. H. (1989) '*Rhetores* and *strategoi* in fourth-century Athens' in: Hansen, M. H. (1989) *The Athenian ecclesia II: a collection of articles 1983–1989* (Copenhagen: Museum Tusculanum 1989) 25–72

Hansen, M. H., & T. H. Nielsen (2004) *An inventory of archaic and classical poleis: an investigation conducted by the Copenhagen Polis Centre for the Danish National Research Foundation* (Oxford: Oxford University Press)

Harris, E. H. (1986) 'How often did the Athenian assembly meet?' in: *CQ* 36: 363–77

Hignett, C. (1952) *A history of the Athenian constitution* (Oxford: Clarendon)

Hodkinson, S. (1993) 'Warfare, wealth, and the crisis of Spartiate society' in: Rich & Shipley 1993: 146–76

Hölscher, T. (1998) 'Images and political identity: the case of Athens' in: Boedeker & Raaflaub 1998: 153–83

Jameson, M. H. (1974) 'A treasury of Athena in the Argolid' in: Bradeen & McGregor 1974: 67–75

Jeffery, L. H. (1973–4) 'Demiourgoi in the archaic period' in: *Archaeologia Classica* 25–6: 319–30

Lewis, D. M. (1977) *Sparta and Persia* (Leiden: Brill) (Cincinnati Classical Studies 2.1)

Lewis, S. (2006) *Ancient tyranny* (Edinburgh: Edinburgh University Press)

Lock, R. (1977) 'The Macedonian army assembly in the time of Alexander the Great' in: *CPh* 72: 91–107

Loraux, N. (1986) *The invention of Athens: the funeral oration in the classical city* (trans. A. Sheridan) (Cambridge MA: Harvard University Press)

Markle, M. M. (1985) 'Jury pay and assembly pay at Athens' in: Cartledge & Harvey (eds) 1985: 265–97

McGlew, J. F. (1993) *Tyranny and political culture in ancient Greece* (Cambridge: Cambridge University Press)

Miller, M. C. (1988) 'Midas as the Great King in Attic fifth-century vase-painting' in: *Antike Kunst* 31: 79–89

Miller, M. C. (1995) 'Persians: the oriental other' in: *Source: notes in the history of art* 15.1 (*Special issue: Representations of the 'other' in Athenian art, c. 510–400 BC*) 39–44

Miller, M. C. (1997) *Athens and Persia in the fifth century BC: a study in cultural receptivity* (Cambridge: Cambridge University Press)

Miller, M. C. (2000) 'The myth of Bousiris: ethnicity and art' in: Cohen 2000: 413–42

Mitchell, L. G. (1997) *Greeks bearing gifts: the public use of private relationships in the Greek world (435–323 BC)* (Cambridge: Cambridge University Press)

Mitchell, L. G. (2000) 'A new look at the election of generals at Athens' in: *Klio* 82: 344–60

Morgan, K. A. (ed.) (2003) *Popular tyranny: sovereignty and its discontents in ancient Greece* (Austin TX: University of Texas Press)

Morris, I. (1996) 'The strong principle of equality and the archaic origins of Greek democracy' in: Ober & Hedrick 1996: 19–48

Murakawa, K. (1957) 'Demiurgos' in: *Historia* 6: 385–417

Ober, J., & C. Hedrick (eds) (1996) *Demokratia: a conversation on democracies ancient and modern* (Princeton: Princeton University Press)

Osborne, R. (1985) *Demos: the discovery of classical Attika* (Cambridge: Cambridge University Press)

Ostwald, M. (2000) *Oligarchia: the development of a constitutional form in ancient Greece* (Stuttgart: Steiner) (*Historia* Einzelschriften 144)

Perlman, S. (ed.) (1973) *Philip and Athens* (Cambridge: Cambridge University Press)

Piérart, M. (1995) 'Chios entre Athènes et Sparte: la contribution des exilés de Chios à l'effort de guerre lacédémonien pendant la guerre du Péloponnèse *IG* V, 1 + (*SEG* XXXIX 370*)' in: *BCH* 119: 253–82

Piérart, M. (2000) 'Argos: une autre démocratie' in: Flensted-Jensen et al. 2000: 297–314

Raaflaub, K. A. (1994) 'Democracy, power and imperialism in fifth-century Athens' in: Euben, J. P., J. R. Wallach, J. Ober (eds) *Athenian political thought and the reconstruction of Athenian democracy* (Ithaca: Cornell University Press 1994) 103–46

Rahe, P. A. (1980) 'The selection of ephors at Sparta' in: *Historia* 29: 385–401

Rhodes, P. J. (1979–80) 'Athenian democracy after 403 BC' in: *CJ* 75: 305–23

Rhodes, P. J. (1981) 'The selection of ephors at Sparta' in: *Historia* 30: 498–502

Rhodes, P. J. (1985) *The Athenian boule* (re-issued with additions and corrections) (Oxford: Clarendon)

Rhodes, P. J. (1986) *The Greek city-states: a source book* (London: Croom Helm)

Rhodes, P. J. (1993) *A commentary on the Aristotelian* Athenaion Politeia (rev. ed. 1993) (Oxford: Clarendon)

Rhodes, P. J. (1994) 'The polis and the alternatives' in: $CAH^2$ 4 365–91

Rhodes, P. J. (1996) in: $OCD^3$ 644, entry 'Government/Administration (Greek)'

Rhodes, P. J. (2000) 'Oligarchs in Athens' in: Brock & Hodkinson 2000: 119–36

Rhodes, P. J. (ed.) (2004) *Athenian democracy* (Edinburgh: Edinburgh University Press) (Edinburgh readings on the ancient world)

Rhodes, P. J., with D. M. Lewis (1997) *The decrees of the Greek states* (Oxford: Clarendon)

Rich, J., & G. Shipley (eds) (1993) *War and society in the Greek world* (London: Routledge)

Seager, R. J. (1967) 'Thrasybulus, Conon and Athenian imperialism, 396–386 BC' in: *JHS* 87: 95–115

Sealey, R. (1976) 'Die spartanische Nauarchie' in: *Klio* 58: 335–58

Tomlinson, R. A. (1972) *Argos and the Argolid: from the end of the Bronze Age to the Roman occupation* (London: Routledge)

Tuplin, C. (1996) *Achaemenid studies* (Stuttgart: Steiner) (*Historia* Einzelschriften 99)

Westlake, H. D. (1935) *Thessaly in the fourth century* BC (London: Methuen)

Westlake, H. D. (1976) 'Re-election to the ephorate' in: *GRBS* 17: 343–52

Whibley, L. (1896) *Greek oligarchies: their character and organisation* (London: Methuen; repr. Chicago: Ares 1975)

# CHAPTER NINETEEN

# Democracy

## Kurt A. Raaflaub

## 1 Introduction

We begin with three late-fifth-century comments on democracy. In 411, two years after an Athenian army perished in Sicily, a group of elite Athenians succeeded in persuading the assembled citizens to abolish democracy in favor of an oligarchy. The historian Thucydides emphasizes that this was possible only because the people were terrified by a conspiratorial terror campaign, convinced that crucial Persian assistance in the war against Sparta could be secured only by changing the constitution, and certain that this decision could be reversed at any time (Thuc. 8.53–4). Even so, and although some highly intelligent and astute politicians were involved, Thucydides writes, it "was no easy matter about 100 years after the expulsion of the tyrants to deprive the Athenian people of its liberty – a people not only unused to subjection itself, but, for more than half of this time, accustomed to exercise power over others" (Thuc. 8.68.4, trans. Warner (Penguin)). When the oligarchs initiated peace negotiations with the Spartan king Agis, he too did not believe that the Athenian "people would give up their ancient liberty so quickly" (Thuc. 8.71.1).

Probably in the 420s, an anonymous Athenian opponent of democracy wrote a pamphlet on the *Constitution of the Athenians* (*Athenaion politeia*), which is preserved among Xenophon's works and thus commonly attributed to "Pseudo-Xenophon" or the "Old Oligarch." His purpose is to explain why democracy, in his view the worst possible political system, is so successful, "how well they preserve their constitution and handle the other affairs for which the rest of the Greeks criticise them," and why under present circumstances the chances of overthrowing it are minimal (Pseudo-Xenophon *Ath. Pol.* 1.1; cf. 3.1; trans. Moore 1975). His main objection concerns the right of every citizen who wants (*ho boulomenos*) to serve in the council (*boule*) and to speak in the assembly (*ekklesia*) and, in doing so, to advance the interests of the likes of himself rather than those of the "better ones," the elite (1.2–7):

A city would not be the best on the basis of such a way of life, but the democracy would be best preserved that way. For the people do not want a good order (*eunomia*) under which they themselves are slaves; they want to be free and to rule. Bad order (*kakonomia*) is of little concern to them. What *you* consider not *eunomia* is the very source of the people's strength and freedom. If it is *eunomia* you seek, you will first observe the cleverest men establishing the laws in their own interest. Then the good men will punish the bad; they will make policy for the city and not allow madmen to participate or to speak their minds or to meet in assembly. As a result of these excellent measures the people would swiftly fall into slavery. (Pseudo-Xenophon *Ath. Pol.* 1.8–9; trans. Bower-sock (Loeb), modified by Raaflaub)

In the fall of 431, the Athenians buried those who had died in the first year of the war against the Peloponnesians in a solemn ceremony in the public cemetery (Thuc. 2.34). Perikles, the foremost leader of Athens at the time, was chosen to give the traditional Funeral Oration (*epitaphios*) honoring the fallen soldiers. Thucydides is likely to have heard this speech. In the condensed version he includes in his *History* (2.35–46), Perikles focuses not on wars, battles, and the exploits of ancestors and contemporaries, traditional subjects familiar to all, but on "the spirit in which we faced our trials and also our constitution and the way of life which has made us great" (2.36.4). He says:

Athens' constitution is called a democracy because it respects the interests not of a minority but of the whole people. When it is a question of settling private disputes, everyone is equal before the law; when it is a question of putting one person before another in positions of public responsibility, what counts is not membership of a particular class, but the actual ability which the man possesses. No one, so long as he has it in him to be of service to the state, is kept in political obscurity because of poverty. And, just as our political life is free and open, so is our day-to-day life in our relations with each other...We are free and tolerant in our private lives; but in public affairs we keep to the law...We obey those whom we put in positions of authority and the laws themselves, especially those which are for the protection of the oppressed, and those unwritten laws which it is an acknowledged shame to break. (Thuc. 2.37; trans. Warner (Penguin), modified by Raaflaub)

These passages illustrate how deeply democracy was entrenched among the Athenian people, how profoundly it was despised by its opponents, and how positively it could be viewed by its supporters. Democracy, as it existed in Athens from about the mid-fifth century, was, in the landscape of Greek polis constitutions, a unique and truly revolutionary system that realized its basic principle to an unprecedented and quite extreme extent: no polis had ever dared to give all its citizens equal political rights, regardless of their descent, wealth, social standing, education, personal qualities, and any other factors that usually determined status in a community. As a result, democracy was both tremendously exciting and offensive; it unleashed among its citizens enormous enthusiasm and energy, it elicited unheard-of levels of civic involvement, and it shaped the lives and mentalities of individuals and community alike. The Athenians developed a primary political identity and a collective character that distinguished them from other Greek polis citizens and especially from their perennial opponents, the Spartans (Thuc. 1.70–1). As contemporaries observed, in a democratic polis not only laws and politics but the entire way people lived and interacted with each other and with the outside world differed radically from those in an oligarchic community. Democratic Athens was, as its supporters liked to stress, a model for others (a "school for Hellas" – *paideia tes Hellados* – Thuc. 2.41.1) but with its aggressive, interventionist policies it also represented a constant threat to others. It did not allow anyone to remain passive, and intellectuals of all stripes and colors (tragedians, comedians, historians, political theorists, and philosophers) felt challenged to cope with it in their works.

All this raises a number of questions. How did this system work on a day-by-day basis? What were its origins and how did it develop? Even if the Athenians called it a democracy, to what extent does it correspond to modern conceptions of democracy, and does this matter? To what extent was it really unique, and in what ways did it differ from other democracies? What exactly did this system offer the Athenian people and why were they so supportive of it? Who exactly were "they" in this context, who were their opponents, and what were the latter's motives and goals? In other words, what were the differences, politically and ideologically, between democracy and oligarchy, and what role did this contrast play in Athenian politics? To what extent were constitutional and ideological differences recognized, formulated, and discussed, and what did political theory contribute to this? How is all this reflected in political terminology? What was democracy's impact on Athenian society, not least the nonpolitical classes (women, resident aliens called metics (*metoikoi* – "settlers from abroad"), and slaves), religion, law and the judicial system, culture, economic life, warfare, foreign relations, and other aspects of Athenian life and politics? And finally, what are the sources that inform us about this system and its working, and how reliable are they? These are the main questions to be examined in this chapter.

So far we have only mentioned Athens. For various reasons, Athens probably produced the most fully developed form of democracy. But this form emerged out of earlier types of polis constitutions that were broadly egalitarian ("isonomic" from *isonomia*, "equality before the law" or "equality of distribution, participation," hence "political equality") and fairly widespread by the late sixth century (Robinson 1997). Partly imposed and often influenced by Athens, partly independently, democracies emerged during the fifth century in various parts of the Greek world (e.g., in Argos and Syracuse), although they probably always remained a minority (O'Neil 1995; Robinson (forthcoming)). Indeed, as Aristotle's systematic analysis in *Politics*, based on broad empirical research, shows, both democracy and oligarchy existed in many versions, and the most moderate forms of each overlapped considerably (Dolezal 1974; Robinson 1997: 35–44; see also Ober 1998: ch. 6). Moreover, institutions, values, and customs were often closely related in communities with both types of constitutions (Kurke 1998; Morris 1998; Rhodes 2003). Unfortunately, for very few other democracies (or oligarchies) does sufficient evidence survive to permit a substantial reconstruction. However much we would prefer to break the Athenocentric pattern, for most questions that interest us in this chapter only Athenian evidence offers reasonably clear answers.

## 2   The Nature of the Evidence

We begin with the sources (see Rhodes, above, Chapter 2, with bibliography): how, and how reliably, do we know about the history and workings of Athenian democracy? Depending on the time period, this question prompts different answers.

The fourth century is illuminated mainly by three categories of evidence. One is the *Constitution of the Athenians*, produced late in the century in Aristotle's school (whether by the master himself or one of his pupils: Rhodes 1993: 58–63). It is the only survivor of a set of over 150 constitutions that formed the empirical base of Aristotle's *Politics* (*Nicomachean Ethics* 10.9 1181b18–24), even if the *Ath. Pol.* (and probably the entire collection of constitutions) was in fact published after *Politics* (Rhodes 1993: 58–61). It is not to be confused with its namesake, by Pseudo-Xenophon, mentioned above. Its first part sketches the evolution of democracy from the late seventh to the early fourth century (1–41), the second its working in the author's time (42–69). Both parts are invaluable, although the latter takes much for granted and the former needs to be used with caution: it is organized too schematically around a sequence of competing "progressive" and "conservative" leaders, reflects the strengths and weaknesses of the sources employed, and reveals all too clearly the scarcity of available information and the author's lack of awareness about the differences between his own and earlier times. Recent commentaries (Rhodes 1993; Chambers 1990), translations (Moore 1975; Rhodes 1984), and interpretations (Keaney 1992; Piérart 1993; Maddoli 1994) make the work accessible and help us navigate through the many difficulties it poses, although a great deal of work remains to be done here.

Beginning at the end of the fifth century and throughout the fourth many political speeches, whether given in the assembly or council, law courts, or at communal celebrations (such as the funeral ceremony), were recorded and published (Kennedy 1963). About 150 of these survive, by Antiphon, Andokides, and Lysias (a metic and speechwriter) from early in this period, by Demosthenes, Aischines, and a few others from later, and by Isokrates, who was not an active politician himself and wrote sample or literary speeches. About two thirds are forensic orations. That they were generally addressed to large groups (hundreds or thousands) of Athenian citizens makes this "corpus of Attic orators" immensely valuable. The orators knew the attitudes and concerns of their audiences and used the language and arguments they expected to be most effective. Especially prosecution speeches in public trials often contain "long passages about the structure and working of democratic institutions and well-formulated defenses of the ideals of popular government" (Hansen 1999: 13). The corpus offers unique insights (Ober 1989). (It is easily accessible in bilingual editions in the Loeb Classical Library and by Aris & Phillips, and in a new series of annotated translations published by the University of Texas Press.)

By the early fifth century, Athenians began to record important public decrees and documents in stone. The number of such inscriptions increased greatly with the multiplication of political decisions necessitated by the Athenian empire, and again in the fourth century. Their subject matter comprises political decrees, laws, financial and other public accounts of officials and committees, treaties, contracts, honors bestowed on citizens and non-citizens, lists of inventories, state debtors, victors at athletic and dramatic competitions, officials, councilmen, war casualties, and much more. As Hansen (1999: 12) observes, "over 20,000 inscriptions have been found just in Attika, most of them fragmentary, and several thousand of them are public documents from the golden age of democracy. For the fourth century alone we have some 500 decrees, ten laws, over 400 accounts and inventories, and fifty odd inscriptions with the names of *prytaneis*" (members of the council's executive committee) and other councilors. The restoration and interpretation of these texts requires special skills and experience; the discipline that specializes in these tasks is called epigraphy (Bodel 2001). The Attic inscriptions to 403 are available in *IG* 1³ (for those later than 403: *IG* 2²); for the more important ones, we have good translations (e.g., Fornara; Harding) and Greek texts with commentaries (M&L; R&O). We should add here that, unlike their Hellenistic and especially Roman counterparts, Greek coins of the archaic and classical period offer little political information (Howgego 1995: 63–4).

With the partial exception of inscriptions, the types of evidence discussed so far have no equivalent in most of the fifth century. Hence the most detailed analyses of democracy (e.g., Ober 1989; Hansen 1987, 1999) focus on the fourth century. Yet other categories of sources, themselves mostly absent in the fourth century, illuminate the democracy of the fifth from different perspectives: the political pamphlet by the "Old Oligarch," history, and drama.

Herodotos, a citizen of Halikarnassos in Asia Minor and later of Thourioi in southern Italy, spent time in Athens and was closely familiar with this city (Moles 2002; Fowler 2003). Writing in the 430s and 420s about the Persian Wars and their long prehistory (Lateiner 1991), he does not cover events after 479 but throws light on the early stages of democracy and offers pointed comments that reflect contemporary judgments of it; in fact, signs of his constant interaction with democracy's impact on Greek society and politics in his own time are quite pervasive (Fowler 2003; Bakker et al. 2002: 185 n. 111). Recent work illuminates his intellectual and political context (Thomas 2000; Munson 2001; Raaflaub 1987; 2002).

Thucydides, a politician and general who was forced to leave Athens in 424 and spent the rest of the war in exile (5.26.5), started to collect material and draft his report early in the long and bitter "Peloponnesian War" (1.1; 5.26), but wrote or revised much of it after the war (de Romilly 1963; Hornblower 1987). The work is unfinished, breaking off abruptly in 411. It focuses on power politics, foreign relations, and war; domestic issues and constitutional developments, like religion and social or economic aspects, enter the picture only when they are immediately relevant to the progress of the war. Naturally, political decisions concerning the war were highly relevant; so were the circumstances and methods in and by which they were reached. Thucydides therefore comments frequently on "democracy in action," mostly through a series of often antithetical speeches that explain crucial decisions (e.g., concerning the Sicilian expedition in 415, 6.8–26). Such episodes, together with Perikles' Funeral Oration or the eulogy on Perikles (2.65), contribute to an analysis of the nature, strengths, and weaknesses – or the ideal and deterioration – of democracy. Vignettes on the civil war in Kerkyra (3.82–4) and the plague in Athens (2.47–55) dissect the illness and disintegration of society and community under extreme pressures imposed by war and epidemic. Similarly, Thucydides uses a debate in Syracuse about how to react to Athens' aggression (6.32–41) and the oligarchic coup in Athens in 411 (8.45–98) to analyze the ideological differences between democracy and oligarchy and the nature of oligarchy (Raaflaub forthcoming). Although incorporating what could be learned about the arguments actually used, Thucydides' speeches are his own products, highlighting motives, goals, and specific problems, and serving as interpretive tools (1.22.1; Stadter 1973; Hornblower 1987: ch. 3; Rusten 1989: 7–17). Two sets of thorough historical commentaries (Gomme

et al. 1945–81; Hornblower 1991–6) help illuminate his often difficult text, and a
*Brill Companion on Thucydides* is forthcoming.

Xenophon's *Greek History* (*Hellenika*) picks up where Thucydides breaks off, and
ends in 462. The author shows less depth and analytical acumen than his predecessor
(Gray 1989; Dillery 1995), but contributes importantly to the history of democracy
as well as oligarchy by describing the final phase of the Peloponnesian War (1.1–2.2)
as well as the tyranny of the Thirty and its overthrow (2.3–4; Krentz 1995).
A fragment, preserved on two papyri, of another, anonymous, continuator of Thucydides (the *Hellenika Oxyrhynchia*) is valuable not least because it illuminates the early
fourth-century oligarchic constitution of the Boiotian Confederacy (16.2–4;
McKechnie & Kern 1988). Otherwise, the rich historical production of the fourth
century survives only in numerous fragments.

Old Comedy, represented by Aristophanes' eleven extant plays (MacDowell 1995;
Cartledge 1995), was highly and immediately political. Taking advantage of a culture
of almost unlimited freedom of speech (Henderson 1998), the poet assaulted and
parodied not only intellectuals (Euripides in *Thesmophoriazusae*, Sokrates and the
sophists in *Clouds*) and the city's predilection for war and failure to seek peace (in
*Acharnians, Peace,* and *Lysistrata*) but also the practices of democracy and its corrupt
demagogues or fanatically committed jurors (especially in *Knights* and *Wasps*), and
the demos' habits in assembly (in *Acharnians* and *Ecclesiazusae*). Comic humor feeds
on wild exaggeration, but the plays identify some of the major problems the (or
some) Athenians perceived in their democracy (Henderson 1990, 2003; Ober 1998:
ch. 3 with bibliography; McGlew 2002; Spielvogel 2003). By contrast, tragedy, older
in origin and more dignified, chose its plots almost exclusively from myth; it very
rarely took a stand on current political issues but, by dramatizing problems that
agitated the community at the time, it helped raise political awareness and, in turn,
informs us about some of these issues. The extent to which tragedy's political and
ethical dilemmas reflect specifically Athenian or even democratic concerns is much
debated (e.g., Goldhill 2000; Rhodes 2003; cf. Saïd 1998; Boedeker & Raaflaub
2005), but some of Aischylos' (*Suppliants, Eumenides*), Sophokles' (*Antigone*), and
Euripides' plays (*Suppliants, Phoenician Women*) unquestionably throw light on then
current discussions on political and constitutional issues (Meier 1990: ch. 5; 1993;
Gregory 1991; Croally 1994).

These, however, are just the main groups of sources. Because democracy had a
broad and deep impact on every aspect of Athenian life, politics, and culture, and its
policies affected most of the rest of Greece, reactions to democracy are visible in
virtually all extant authors (Raaflaub 1989).

# 3   How Athenian Democracy Worked

As explained above, we know Athenian democracy best in the form that emerged in
the early fourth century, after a comprehensive revision of laws (410–399, Hansen
1999: 162–5), and is described in the Aristotelian *Ath. Pol.* By then it could be
understood as a system approaching a "constitution" consisting of defined institutions that operated according to legally determined rules (Bleicken 1994; Hansen
1999). The assembly (Hansen 1987) met at least forty times a year, usually for less

than the entire day, often to deal with an agenda that was partly prescribed by law (*Ath. Pol.* 43.4–6). The presidents of assembly and council, selected by lot, served for only one day (44.1–3). The assembly place on the Pnyx hill, opposite the Akropolis, had space for about 6,000 citizens (Hansen 1999: 128–32); the number 6,000 apparently was considered representative, although the citizen body comprised at least 50,000–60,000 adult men in 431, some 30,000 in the fourth century after the terrible losses of the Peloponnesian War. Hence 6,000 jurors were selected annually to staff the *dikasteria* and the quorum for important decisions (such as ostracism or decrees on naturalization and remission of debt) was 6,000. Attendance thus probably quite often reached this level.

The 500 members of the *boule* were selected by lot (*Ath. Pol.* 43.2) and limited to two (non-successive) years of service. On the basis of a sophisticated formula devised in the late sixth century, they represented the population of 139 districts in Attika (*demoi*, demes, consisting of villages and sections of towns and of the city of Athens) that were divided into three regions (city and central plain, hills, and coast) and combined into thirty "Thirds" (*trittyes*) and ten tribes (*phylai*) (Traill 1975; 1986). Each tribe thus comprised citizens from various regions of Attika; their collaboration in the army (organized into tribal regiments, Siewert 1982), in festivals (where tribal contingents competed with each other), in cults, and in politics was decisive for integrating Athens' unusually large polis territory (Anderson 2003). In the *boule* a tribe's fifty members formed the council's executive committee for a tenth of the year, while those of one *trittys* (called a prytany) were continuously present during one third of that time in the round Tholos adjacent to the council building (*bouleuterion*) on the west side of the Agora (Camp 1986: 52–3, 90–7). The council broadly supervised the officials and administrative committees and heard their reports and accounts (*Ath. Pol.* 45–9), dealt with foreign policy issues, and prepared the agenda and motions for the assembly (Rhodes 1985). The *ekklesia* deliberated such motions and accepted them with or without amendments, referred them back to the council for further deliberation, or rejected and replaced them with different ones. On specific policy issues it adopted *psephismata* (decrees), while it passed *nomoi* (laws with general validity, Ostwald 1969) in a procedure that resembled a trial; the latter were drafted by a board of *nomothetai* (lawgivers) and could be challenged in the people's court (Hansen 1999: ch. 7). These distinctions and procedures were introduced in the early fourth century, which has prompted the suggestion that by then the Athenian political system had made the transition "from popular sovereignty to the sovereignty of the law" (thus the title of Ostwald 1986; cf. Sealey 1987 and the comments by Eder 1998).

Assisted by the *boule* and the law courts (*dikasteria*), the *ekklesia* made policy decisions, supervised their execution, and tightly controlled the officials in charge of realizing them. Whether in administration, religion, or the maintenance of public order, professional personnel was minimal; most conspicuous were a few hundred state-owned slaves who served in specific functions at the disposal of various officials or as a rudimentary police force (Hunter 1994: 3). Numerous committees of various sizes (serving for one year and totaling about 700 members) handled virtually all administrative business; they assisted the council and various officials and were in turn supervised by both. Several hundred other officials served in various functions throughout the empire (Aristotle *Ath. Pol.* 24.3; Hansen 1999: 239–40; Meiggs

1979: ch. 11). Of all these officials only a few, holding major financial and military responsibility (such as the generals and cavalry commanders), were elected (Aristotle *Ath. Pol.* 43.1; 44.4); all others were selected by lot (43.1; 47–8; 50–5.1). This applies as well to the chief magistrates (archons) who emerged from a double sortition procedure (8.1) and to the thousands of jurors who were needed on every court day to staff variously large juries (or rather, assemblies of jurors) in several cases tried simultaneously in various locations (Todd 1993; Boegehold 1995; Hansen 1999: ch. 8). These jurors were chosen in a sophisticated mechanical procedure (by an allotment machine, *kleroterion*) that eliminated tampering and made bribery virtually impossible (*Ath. Pol.* 63–66; Boegehold 1995: 58, 230–4; Demont 2003). Democracy was famous for the litigiousness of its citizens. The law courts were an important part of democratic life and procedures: much political business was conducted there, one might say, in a continuation of politics by different means. In fact, Aristotle thought that the people's power in democracy rested essentially in the courts (*Ath. Pol.* 9.1; Hansen 1990).

Clearly, then, several thousand citizens – a remarkably large proportion of a surprisingly limited population of adult male citizens – were politically active every year in ways that far exceeded occasional attendance at the assembly, and many of them probably did this quite regularly year after year (Hansen 1999: 90–4, 313, 350). Rotation of offices ("ruling and being ruled in turn," Euripides *Suppliants* 406–7; Aristotle *Politics* 1317b2–7) made sure that those not involved in one year would be in another (if they wished to) and that through their varied involvement the citizens achieved a high level of familiarity with the administration of their community and its policies. Most impressively, as Hansen states (1999: 249), "over a third of all citizens over eighteen, and about two thirds of all citizens over forty" served at least one year-long term in the *boule*, a time-consuming office. To facilitate participation by lower-class citizens who were not financially independent, pay for certain political and judicial functions was introduced between 462 and 450 and expanded later, to include, by the early fourth century, even the *ekklesia* (Markle 1985; Hansen 1999: 240–2). This democracy, we conclude, was not only "direct" but the "most direct" imaginable in the sense both of active participation and of exertion of power: the people not only made decisions but through assembly, council, offices, and law courts controlled the entire political process. Moreover, these same citizens also regularly served in their polis' infantry army or helped row its fleet, even if mercenaries played a more significant role in naval and fourth-century infantry warfare than they did earlier (Burckhardt 1996).

Because of the distribution of evidence described above we do not know how much of all this was realized already in the fifth century. Some offices or committees did not yet exist, others had different functions, while others (those connected with controlling the empire) disappeared with the empire; assembly meetings were perhaps less frequent and not yet fixed in number, and before the Peloponnesian War the number of adult male citizens was much larger. Despite much debate about the differences between fifth-century and fourth-century democracy (Rhodes 1980; Bleicken 1987; Eder 1995b; 1998), in the fifth century the citizens were hardly less involved in running their democracy than in the fourth. This probably was especially true during those periods in the Peloponnesian War when a large number of the rural population were evacuated to the confined space between the Long Walls, were unable to work on their fields, and thus lived close to the political center. In fact, if one of the goals of the reforms at the turn of the century was to make the political process more objective, transparent, and subject to the law, we might conclude, as elite complaints seem to confirm, that before then the citizens' control over this process was even more immediate and intense.

# 4 The Evolution of Democracy

Although opinions diverge over when exactly we should date and how we should explain the "origin" or "breakthrough" of democracy, the main phases of its evolution are reasonably clear (Bleicken 1994: part 1; Hansen 1999: ch. 3; detailed discussion in Raaflaub et al. 2006). Democracy "Athenian style" resulted from a long development that was punctuated by three "rupture points" of rapid change and incisive reform. It originated in a core of basic egalitarianism and "people's power" that, despite the predominance of evolving aristocracies, was essential for the fabric of the early Greek polis (city-state or, rather, citizen-state) and shared widely through-out Greece (Morris 1996; 2000; Raaflaub & Wallace 2006 in: Raaflaub et al. 2006). In a period of severe economic crisis and social conflict, Solon was elected archon and mediator in 594 (Aristotle *Ath. Pol.* 5–12; Plutarch *Solon*; Andrewes 1982a; Blok & Lardinois (forthcoming)). Besides mandating debt relief, abolishing debt bondage, and regulating by legislation areas that were likely to cause conflict, he increased the citizens' civic responsibility and involvement in politics by permitting third party prosecution and appeals to a popular court and by correlating in a "timocratic system" (from *time*, honor, status) the citizens' social, economic, military, and political capacity. Henceforth, office holding was tied to property rather than descent. Whether active citizenship (including speaking and voting in the assembly) was available to all citizens or limited, by tradition and prevailing values rather than law, to those who were qualified for the heavy infantry (hoplite) army (Rhodes 1993: 140–1) is debated. Although Aristotle recognized in Solon's system crucial elements typical of democracy (*Ath. Pol.* 9.1, 22.1; Wallace 2006 in: Raaflaub et al. 2006), certain statements preserved in Solon's own poetry seem to suggest that Solon's goal was to establish justice for all rather than government by the demos. In fact, he was quite emphatic about the demos' limitations: leadership was to remain the elite's prerogative, although all citizens needed to be protected from abuses of power (Morris & Raaflaub 1998: 38–9).

Renewed factional strife eventually prompted the usurpation of sole power (tyranny) by Peisistratos (Hdt. 1.59–64; Aristotle *Ath. Pol.* 13–17; Andrewes 1982b). His regime, later remembered as a "Golden Age," brought the Athenians domestic peace and increasing prosperity, while the aristocracy's political power was curtailed; through cults, festivals, and buildings Peisistratos emphasized the role of Athens as the polis' center, at the expense of local centers in Attika that were dominated by elite families. As a result, paradoxically, in weakening aristocratic control and fostering communal integration, tyranny contributed importantly to preparing the ground for democracy (Stahl 1987; McGlew 1993). After Peisistratos' death, the regime of his sons, disrupted by the assassination of Hipparchos in 514, turned oppressive. Hippias was overthrown by Spartan intervention in 510 (Hdt. 5.55, 5.63–5; Aristotle *Ath.*

*Pol.* 18–19; Lewis 1988). Tyranny henceforth had a bad press in Athens, especially since the community in subsequent years twice faced the threat of Hippias' reinstatement by Spartan or Persian intervention. Such threats enhanced communal solidarity. Anachronistically, the tyrannicides of 514, soon honored by a monument in the Agora, became symbols of liberation and, eventually, democracy.

After the fall of tyranny, aristocratic families resumed their traditional rivalries for predominance. In 508/7 Kleisthenes turned defeat into victory by appealing to the Athenian demos with an apparently popular reform proposal. His opponent, Isagoras, in traditional aristocratic fashion summoned help from a powerful "guest-friend" (*xenos*), king Kleomenes of Sparta, who promptly arrived with a company of soldiers, expelled Kleisthenes and his supporters, and proceeded to place Isagoras and his faction in power. The existing council resisted and the Athenian demos rose in revolt, forcing Kleomenes to leave and eliminating Isagoras' faction. Kleisthenes returned and implemented the promised reforms. These were remarkably comprehensive and sophisticated. At their core was a reorganization of the citizen body and territory of Attika (mentioned above) that served as basis for the hoplite army and the Council of 500, which came to represent the entire citizen population of Attika. Now for the first time even the fringes of Attika were fully integrated into the polis (Hdt. 5.66, 5.69–73; Aristotle *Ath. Pol.* 20–2; Ostwald 1988; Meier 1990: ch. 4; Ober 1996; Anderson 2003).

According to Herodotos, Kleisthenes "established for the Athenians the tribes and the democracy" (6.131.2). Whether the latter is correct in a specific sense and whether the Athenian citizens who did not qualify for the hoplite army (the lowest property class called thetes) enjoyed full political equality in this new political system – all this remains debated (chapters by Ober and Raaflaub in Morris & Raaflaub 1998 and in Raaflaub et al. 2006). Even so, unquestionably the late-sixth-century reforms, apparently supported by the entire community, had a broadly integrative effect and enhanced civic equality and political participation among a large part of the citizen body. All this was a necessary condition for Athens' ability to repel attacks by hostile neighbors and Sparta in 506 and by Persia at Marathon in 490, and to play a crucial role in Greek victories over Persian armies in 480/79. And it served as an indispensable platform for another breakthrough, fifty years later, that fully established democracy both in institutions and in public consciousness (Martin 1974).

In the generation after the Persian Wars Athens underwent profound changes in all spheres of life (Raaflaub 1998). As the head of a new alliance (the "Delian League") comprising a wide range of members, from Asia Minor, the Aegean islands, and the mainland, it continued the war against the Persians, eventually eliminating their control over the west coast of the Aegean and far beyond. Gradually it transformed this alliance into a tightly ruled and remarkably centralized empire (Meiggs 1979; Fornara & Samons 1991: ch. 3; Rhodes 1992a). All these developments depended on Athens' large fleet and on those who manned it: thousands of lower-class citizens (besides metics, mercenaries, and slaves). The Athenian thetes thus assumed a crucial and permanent importance for their community's security, power, and prosperity. By the late 460s the Athenians accepted the obvious consequences. Led by Ephialtes and soon by Perikles, they passed another set of reforms that weakened the political influence of the traditional aristocratic Areopagos Council and strengthened the power of those institutions that represented the entire citizen body (assembly, Council of 500, and law courts), introduced pay for certain offices and political or judicial functions, thereby making it possible for lower-class citizens to spend their time in service for the community, and redefined citizenship (Aristotle *Ath. Pol.* 25–26; Fornara & Samons 1991: ch. 2; Rhodes 1992b).

Henceforth, with very few exceptions, all political functions were accessible to and spread widely among all citizens. The whole demos, constituted as an exclusive political elite irrespective of wealth, descent, and education, now participated equally in making all decisions and controlling the entire political process. In Euripides' words, the demos now was lord and monarch, power had been popularized (*Suppliants* 352, 406; *Cyclops* 119). By the 440s, the citizens must have been accustomed to their political role, the impact of the reforms fully visible. Naval power continued to be crucial for Athens' imperial success, especially during the Peloponnesian War. As long as it was successful, democracy essentially remained unchallenged and open opposition was impossible. All this explains why democracy became deeply entrenched in the citizen body and was, as contemporaries observed (introduction above), so difficult to uproot.

Constitutional development continued, though much more slowly, until, because of the Athenian disaster in Sicily, other setbacks in the war, and increasing financial pressure on the elite, opponents of democracy found broader support and finally prevailed in imposing a narrow oligarchy in 411. Even so, they succeeded only in the context of an extraordinary set of political conditions and as the result of massive terror. Their "oligarchy of the 400" was overthrown after a few months and its successor, a more moderate oligarchy based on 5,000 full citizens, even sooner (Thuc. 8.63–98; Aristotle *Ath. Pol.* 29–33). The restored democracy, although fortified by strict controls, proved vengeful, unstable, and incapable of capitalizing on military successes to end the war honorably. Defeated and humiliated, Athens in 404 lost its empire and suffered through the terror regime of an even narrower oligarchy (the "thirty tyrants"), civil war, and a split of the polis, before in 403 reunification and reconciliation were achieved (Aristotle *Ath. Pol.* 34–41.2; Xenophon *Hellenika* 2.3–4; Ostwald 1986: chapters 7–9; Bleckmann 1998; Munn 2000: part 2; Krentz 1982).

Even earlier, in 410, the Athenians initiated an ambitious process of reviewing and revising their laws. The law code that was completed and passed in 399 and a new procedure for the creation of new laws (mentioned earlier) limited demotic arbitrariness and objectivized the process of legislation. To what extent this changed the nature of democracy and enhanced the "sovereignty of the law" is much debated. By contrast, the introduction of pay for attendance at the assembly (Aristotle *Ath. Pol.* 41.3) cemented the principle of universal citizen participation in and control of politics. Aristotle (*Politics* 1274a7–11; *Ath. Pol.* 41.2) thus considered the form democracy reached in the fourth century the completion of its long development. The centralization of financial administration under the elected directors of the Theoric Fund from the 350s (Aristotle *Ath. Pol.* 43.1), which bestowed great power on the holders of this office, did not change the working of democracy. As Ober concludes:

> There were various constitutional adjustments made in the period between the Peloponnesian and Lamian Wars, but there were no major changes in the sociology of Athenian politics. There were no compromises made with the basic principles of the

political equality and exclusivity of the citizen body, of the lottery, or of pay for state service ... Compared with the fifth century, the fourth century is remarkable less for its constitutional evolution than for its social and political stability. (Ober 1989: 95–103, quotation from 103)

# 5   Ideology, Debate, and Criticism

Democratic ideology rested on three pillars: equality, inclusiveness, and freedom. In the late sixth century, at least the hoplite farmers achieved political equality; half a century later this was true for all citizens. Terms denoting such equality (*isonomia*; *isegoria*, equality of speech), variously attested in the second half of the sixth century, may have been catchwords used to characterize the political system introduced by Kleisthenes (Raaflaub 1996: 143–5). By the last third of the fifth century much evidence documents that both terms, although in principle applicable to any non-tyrannical regime (Thuc. 3.62.3–4 speaks of an "isonomic oligarchy"), had become prime values of democracy. As Herodotos puts it, "rule by the masses has the most beautiful name of all, *isonomia*" (3.80.6). In particular, the Athenians singled out equality of speech, soon complemented by a specific term for "freedom of speech" (*parrhesia*, saying everything, unlimited speech), as the democratic citizen's most important privilege (Raaflaub 2004b: 221–5). These notions come close to our "rights" or "civil liberties" (Raaflaub 2004b: 231–3; Ostwald 1996). In Athens, such equality was understood in the most comprehensive and inclusive sense. Accordingly, the democrats emphatically interpreted demos inclusively as the entire citizen body (Thuc. 6.39.1).

Freedom (*eleutheria*) emerged in the Persian Wars as a highly valued political concept that denoted both the community's independence from outside domination and the citizens' freedom from oppression within the community (Raaflaub 2004b: ch. 3). In the latter sense, it was initially contrasted with tyranny and thus applicable to any non-tyrannical constitution. When exactly freedom was specifically claimed for democracy is uncertain; explicit evidence connects the two concepts in the 420s, and political conflicts in the 440s and late 430s provide the most likely contexts (Raaflaub 2004b: ch. 6). Aristotle observes that the "foundation of the democratic constitution is liberty." This implies "that only in this constitution is there any share in liberty at all; every democracy, they say, has liberty for its aim" (Aristotle *Politics* 1317a40ff.). He distinguishes two elements of liberty: ruling and being ruled in turn (rotation in office) and the "live as you like" principle. Both are attested much earlier: the latter in Thucydides (2.37.2), the former in Euripides (*Suppliants* 406–7), where freedom and equality, represented by the demos' sovereignty in the assembly, rotation in office, and equality before the law, of political opportunity, speech, and vote, appear intertwined as the bulwarks of democracy (Euripides *Suppliants* 352–3, 403–8, 429–41). They are embodied in the herald's opening call in the assembly: "This is freedom: 'Who has some good advice for the community and wants to bring it in the middle?' ... What greater equality than this could there be for the polis?" (Euripides *Suppliants* 438–41; cf. Finley 1983: ch. 5).

The Old Oligarch confirms that every citizen who wanted (*ho boulomenos*) was entitled to, and in fact did, speak in the assembly (Pseudo-Xenophon

*Ath. Pol.* 1.2–9, quoted at the beginning). Yet the communal ideology promoted by democracy was more comprehensive. In the Funeral Oration, Thucydides lets Perikles sketch an idealized portrait of democratic Athens. It is a community characterized by civic harmony, mutual tolerance, and respect for law and office holders (2.37, also quoted earlier). In other words, the qualities of *aidos* (respect for others) and *dike* (justice) that Plato's Protagoras (*Protagoras* 320D–22D) emphasizes as indispensable for communal well-being are realized perfectly here. The Athenian citizen is interested both in his own affairs and in those of the state; he is well informed on general politics; he is used to considering all aspects of an issue before making a decision and taking action (Thuc. 2.40.2); he is independent and self-sufficient (41.1) and in this respect mirrors the community (36.3). Most importantly, he is supposed to be a lover (*erastes*) of his polis, putting communal interests above his own (43.1). "We alone consider a citizen who does not partake in politics not only one who minds his own business (*apragmon*) but useless" (40.2). The democratic citizen, that is, is expected to be constantly active and involved (*polypragmon*), and thus to display individually the character trait that is typical of the entire polis (1.70; Raaflaub 1994). His political identity is to have priority over his social identity (Meier 1990: ch. 6; Monoson 2000: ch. 3).

This ideal picture, intentionally ambivalent and serving a programmatic function for the entire work (Grethlein 2005), did not remain uncontested. Thucydides himself dismantles it systematically in the course of his *History* (Farrar 1988: ch. 5; Ober 1998: ch. 2), beginning with the impact of the plague, which he intentionally juxtaposes to the Funeral Oration: under extreme pressure the Athenian citizen proves anything but self-sufficient and law-abiding, communal integration crumbles, and the veneer of socialization peels off (2.47–55). Under similar pressure, caused by brutal civil strife between factions claiming to be democratic or oligarchic, social and political order collapses disastrously in Kerkyra (3.69–85), as it will later in Athens (8.45–98, esp. 63–70). A comparison between Perikles (portrayed by Thucydides as an ideal democratic leader) and his inferior successors (2.65) reveals the tensions between democracy's need and intolerance of strong leadership, the qualities required of a politician that can foster communal well-being, and the negative impact of competition between unscrupulously self-serving demagogues. Ultimately, Thucydides concludes, Athens flourished under Perikles because it was only "in name a democracy but in reality rule by the first man" (2.65.9). Yet even he became a victim of the fickleness and emotionality of the masses (2.65.2–4). Illuminating the decision-making process at crucial junctures of the war (3.36–48 on the punishment of Mytilene in 427; 4.17–22, 27–8, 41 on the conduct of war at Pylos and peace negotiations in 425/4; 6.8–26 on the expedition to Sicily in 415), Thucydides exposes further weaknesses of democracy, especially in the manipulation of the assembly by demagogues and the demos' inability to recognize good advice and make rational decisions. The Athenian defeat in 404, the historian believes, was due not to a lack of communal resources or an erroneous calculation and wrong choice of strategy by Perikles, but to multiple bad decisions by the assembly under the influence of rivaling demagogues: "they did not give in until they stumbled over themselves in their internal disputes and in that way came to ruin" (2.65.12).

Other authors were equally critical of democracy. It suffices to mention the corrupt demagogues' manipulation of Old Man Demos in Aristophanes' *Knights* and his parody of obsessed jurors in *Wasps* (Konstan 1995; MacDowell 1995). *Lysistrata*, performed just before the oligarchic coup of 411, challenges the core of democratic ideology by emphasizing that the values of polis and *oikos* and the citizens' public and private functions, political and social identities need to be integrated if the community is to recover and prosper (Henderson 1980). Euripides, although criticized in the competition among the dead poets in *Frogs* as too "democratic" (948–79), abounds in critical comments about the assembly's decision making (*Orestes* 884–945) and vile demagogues (*Hecuba* 106–36, 217–327; *Iphigenia in Aulis* 511–33). In the Old Oligarch's view, democracy, serving the interests of the masses, is the very embodiment of a "bad order" (*kakonomia*) and run by "people lacking a sound mind" (*mainomenoi*, cf. Alkibiades in Thuc. 6.89.6: democracy as "generally acknowledged madness," *homologoumene anoia*). It is so profoundly rotten that it can only be improved by being abolished and replaced by a "good order" (*eunomia*), dominated by and serving the interests of the upper classes. Fearing this, the masses prefer to live in a bad order, to rule and be free, and they so skillfully preserve this system that under present conditions no radical change seems possible (Pseudo-Xenophon *Ath. Pol.* 1.1–9, 13–18; 2.9–10, 17–20, and *passim*; Ober 1998: 14–27). Plato, though more subtle and complex than is often assumed (Rowe 1998; Monoson 2000: part 2), shares the fifth-century authors' critical attitude toward democracy, and in Aristotle's systematic analysis of constitutions and constitutional change the same issues remain prominent (Roberts 1994: ch. 4; Ober 1998; Mulgan 1991).

Aristocrats vigorously challenged democracy's appropriation of equality, inclusiveness, and freedom. They countered its concept of numerical with one of proportional equality that was based on social status (Harvey 1965). They trumped the undifferentiated democratic notion of freedom (*eleutheria*) with an aristocratic concept of "full freedom" (*eleutheriotes*) that took social status and economic independence into account (Raaflaub 2004b: 243–7). And they set against the democrats' inclusive interpretation of *demos* (all citizens) their own exclusive understanding (only the lower classes): in their view, *demokratia* was rule by the masses, the rabble (*ochlos*, hence later *ochlokratia*, Polybios 6.4.6, 57.9). The only exception is "freedom of speech," which did not fit into the aristocratic canon of political values and thus remained a specifically democratic achievement (Raaflaub 2004a).

Democracy created new realities, within the polis and in its dealings with others. It shaped its citizens and transformed their attitudes and mentalities. Nobody could escape being affected by it. Hence we find components of an intense debate about democracy scattered in many works of fifth-century literature. They were apparently never combined into a coherent, comprehensive, and theoretically founded comparative analysis, but most of the arguments that Aristotle later incorporated in his analysis in *Politics* are attested already in the fifth century (Raaflaub 1989). Here it is possible only to mention a few examples.

Thucydides (6.38–40) lets a Syracusan demagogue refute oligarchic criticism of democracy's egalitarianism and the limitations it imposes on the elite by stressing inclusiveness and the demos' cumulative qualification (below). Herodotos (3.80–2) and Euripides (*Suppliants* 399–455) insert formal constitutional debates into unlikely historical and mythical contexts. In both democracy is starkly contrasted with tyranny; while the supporters of democracy emphasize values (equality and liberty) and the role of institutions, the opponents disparage the demos' ability to participate rationally and responsibly in government. One response, that the citizens' individual shortcomings are more than balanced by their collective or cumulative qualities (Hdt. 3.80.6: "in the many is all"; Thuc. 6.39.1), is of questionable validity, despite Aristotle's partial endorsement (*Politics* 1281a40–b20). Democracy's most compelling defenses appear in different contexts. On a theoretical level, Plato's Protagoras argues that in principle all citizens, even all human beings, carry the seed, the potential to develop the qualities required for social integration and political participation (justice, respect for others, and political skills, *politike arete*, Plato *Protagoras* 322B–23A). On a practical level, supporters emphasized two aspects. One is democracy's success: the freedom guaranteed by democracy empowers and energizes the citizens, enabling them to realize their full potential and, in their own *and* the community's interest, previously unthinkable achievements (Hdt. 5.78). The other is the entitlement derived from such achievements: the citizens' continual commitment to their polis' success entitles all of them (including the lower classes) to full political participation (Aischylos *Suppliants*; Raaflaub et al. 2006: ch. 5). Because they rule in their polis and, through their polis, over an empire, the Athenians proudly claim to be citizens of "the greatest and freest city" (Thuc. 6.89.6; cf. 7.69.2; Raaflaub 2004b: 187–90). As even the Old Oligarch admits (Pseudo-Xenophon *Ath. Pol.* 1.2), the community's success and power and the lower classes' full enfranchisement, power, and liberty in democracy are interconnected. Not accidentally, democracy's deep crisis is linked with the loss of such legitimation by success.

# 6    Opposition and Revolution: The Rise and Failure of Oligarchy

Although in the Greek world constitutions based on a restricted franchise probably were more frequent than democracies, we are poorly informed about oligarchies. The short-lived Athenian oligarchies of 411/10 and 404/3 are the only reasonably well-documented cases, and even there many questions remain open. That they maintained their power by oppressive terror and did not rule out, or even depended on, collaboration with Sparta tainted them forever. The oligarchies imposed by Macedonian intervention in the late fourth century differed in nature and collapsed as soon as outside support vanished (Lehmann 1997). Scattered references (most notably the description of the Boiotian constitution in the *Hellenika Oxyrhynchia*, mentioned earlier) and Aristotle's discussion in *Politics* offer additional information. Overall, though, little can be said about oligarchic theory or constitutional thought (Whibley 1896; Larsen 1955; Ostwald 2000). Again, the evidence forces us to focus on one case: oligarchy in Athens. But a warning is in place: Thucydides' portrait of the Athenian oligarchy of 411/10 shows us only the contorted face of a political system fighting for its survival in a hostile environment; so do his analysis of civil war on Kerkyra and Xenophon's description of the "tyranny of the Thirty" in 404/3. No historical source survives to tell us how a stable and "normal" oligarchic or aristocratic system was perceived or justified itself. Thucydides offers no oligarchic equivalent of Perikles' Funeral Oration, and – a remarkable but perhaps telling shortcoming of his *History* – he neglects to scrutinize thoroughly the social and political system, the decision-making processes, and the relations between leaders and citizen body in

Sparta (the report about how the Spartans and their allies decided for war in 432 remains unique, 1.66–88), although he is clearly impressed by Sparta's long-lasting domestic stability (1.18; Rawson 1969: 20–4; Hornblower 1987: 161–5).

The oligarchic coup in 411 occurred rather suddenly, after a short time of open agitation and preparation (Thuc. 8.45–70; Ostwald 1986: ch. 7; Munn 2000: ch. 5; on the sources, Gomme et al. 1945–81: vol. 5 184–256). Scholars often surmise, therefore, that before the acute crisis that prompted it opposition to democracy was minimal and ineffectual. The latter may be true but does not mean much (Wolff 1979; Bleicken 1994: 371–9). For good reasons, opposition to democracy did not operate in the open: democracy was protected by laws against subversion (Ostwald 1955), and politicians consistently opposing popular leaders and their policies (and thus not even the system itself) risked ostracism or denigration as would-be tyrants. Opposition therefore was forced underground; those unwilling to collaborate with democracy had no choice but to withdraw into an internal exile and become, in Perikles' words, useless to the community (Thuc. 2.40.2; cf. 8.68.1; Xenophon *Memorabilia* 3.7; Euripides *Hippolytus* 986–9, 1016–18; Heftner 2003: 7). If the breakthrough of democracy in the reforms of 462–450 was already violently contested (Thuc. 1.107.4–6; Ostwald 1986: 177–81), from then on a core of elite persons probably stood in constant opposition; their numbers fluctuated according to the level of democracy's success and political tensions caused by its policies. Such opposition must have been substantial in the 440s, during a protracted power struggle between the factions of Perikles and Thoukydides son of Melesias that ended in the latter's ostracism, and again in the late 430s, when Perikles (apparently against strong resistance) prevailed with his intransigent political strategy that accepted the inevitability of war with Sparta. In the mid to late 420s, when the war dragged on and peace opportunities were debated emotionally and squandered frivolously, Kleon, as Aristophanes attests (Henderson 2003), fostered a climate of fear of tyranny (a shorthand for any threat to democracy: Raaflaub 2003) – perhaps not entirely without reason. In 415, on the eve of the departure of the armada to Sicily, religious scandals raised the specter of a conspiracy aiming at tyranny or oligarchy (Thuc. 6.27–8, 53, 60.1; Furley 1996). In the crisis after the destruction of this armada, increasing financial pressure on the elite caused rapidly growing dissatisfaction; combined with Alkibiades' promise of Persian assistance that was tied to constitutional change, this swelled the ranks of oligarchic sympathizers.

Probably in the 420s, the Old Oligarch made no secret of his antipathy to democracy. Although he sees no real possibility yet of overthrowing it, he knows exactly what this would entail: the incompetent and "crazy" masses must be eliminated from politics, power and government restricted to the few, the elite. He was hardly alone in thinking like this. In the 420s as well, Herodotos' and Euripides' constitutional debates attest to the issue's importance in public discourse: the Athenians were familiar with criticisms leveled against democracy and arguments used to defend it. Moreover, some sophists (itinerant philosophers and teachers) were explicitly critical of democratic egalitarianism (Wallace 1998). In theoretical discussions of law, they contrasted laws founded in nature (*physis*) with man-made conventions (*nomoi*). They emphasized the right of the strong to rule over the weak and the natural entitlement of the most capable to ignore the fetters imposed on them by the cumulative will of the weak (Kerferd 1981: ch. 10; Hoffmann 1997: ch. 3).

Disgruntled young aristocrats took this to heart, apparently causing a veritable "conflict of generations" (Thuc. 6.12.2, 18.6, 38.5; Forrest 1975).

Hence intellectually, ideologically, and politically, the ground was well prepared for rising oligarchic opposition against democracy. Institutions capable of supporting a coup had long been in place: *hetaireiai* (groups of followers of elite leaders) were a traditional feature of aristocratic society; *xynomosiai* (conspiratorial "clubs") had spread as well. Such groups had long been used "for mutual support in lawsuits and in elections"; now they served to organize revolutionary cadres (Thuc. 8.54.4; Gomme et al. 1945–81: vol. 5 128–31). When the time came, they were ready to strike. Political murders of democratic leaders and other persons opposed to the oligarchic cause spread terror and paralyzed the supporters of democracy (8.65–6). Overall, then, led by a group of committed leaders (Thuc. 8.68.1 singles out Antiphon, but there surely were others), uncompromising opponents of democracy had long been waiting for their opportunity. When it arrived in the crisis of 413–411, they seized it with ruthless determination. The oligarchic coup of 411 was so well prepared and supported by "so many intelligent men" (Thuc. 8.68.4) that it succeeded despite great difficulties and serious resistance (Thuc. 8.53–54; Lehmann 1973; Heftner 2001).

Still, the oligarchs' ideas about the constitution they hoped to realize were surprisingly vague. Understandably, they advertised their plans cautiously and spoke more about "not having the same kind of democracy" (Thuc. 8.53.1), seeking out an "ancestral constitution" or the "ancestral laws" of Kleisthenes' time, that is, returning to an earlier, less corrupted type of democracy (Thrasymachos 85 B 1 Diels-Kranz, trans. Freeman 1948: 141–2; Aristotle *Ath. Pol.* 29.3), or, as is attested elsewhere, establishing a responsible and moderate "government by the best men" (Hdt. 3.81.3; Thuc. 3.82.8). They also made sure that the suspension of the democratic constitution was sanctioned by a legitimate decree passed – although under great pressure – in the assembly (Thuc. 8.53–4, 67). The exclusion of the crazy and irresponsible masses (advertised by the Old Oligarch) was realized by restricting full citizenship to those who contributed most with their bodies (*somasin*) and money (*chremasin*), that is, the wealthy bearing arms, the horsemen and hoplites (Thuc. 8.65.3, Aristotle *Ath. Pol.* 29.5), as opposed to the poor who manned the ships (Pseudo-Xenophon *Ath. Pol.* 1.2). Pay for military service remained intact, that for political functions was, with few exceptions, abolished (Thuc. 8.65.4; Aristotle *Ath. Pol.* 29.5).

The execution of this program left much to be desired. The franchise was restricted to the 5,000 wealthiest citizens. This number was much smaller than that of the hoplites (of whom a few months later more than 9,000 were registered; Lysias 20.13); the criterion thus probably was the ability to make major contributions to communal expenses known as liturgies (such as funding for warships or performances at festivals). The democratic council was replaced by a smaller Council of Four Hundred consisting of members co-opted by an initial core of oligarchs. This is essentially all we know. The oligarchic constitution adopted at the time in Boiotia was based on a rotation among four councils drawn from among the wealthiest citizens (*Hellenika Oxyrhynchia* 16.2–4) and probably influenced the conceptions discussed among the Athenian oligarchs, but it is unclear how the "constitution for the future" sketched in Aristotle *Ath. Pol.* 30, which shows such influences, is related to the moderate oligarchy of the Five Thousand established after the fall of the Four Hundred (Gomme et al. 1945–81: vol. 5 8–26). What is clear is that the "radical" core among the Four Hundred aimed at ruling autocratically and preserving their power by any means necessary, that their methods and aims were soon opposed by a more moderate group, and that they were deposed and, if they had not fled the country, convicted and executed. In this effort the moderates enjoyed the support of large numbers of hoplite-citizens, although others initially were prepared to defend the radical regime (Thuc. 8.89–98).

The oligarchy of the Five Thousand received Thucydides' qualified approval: he describes it as "a moderate mixture (*xynkrasis*)" that took the interests of the few and the many into account; "the initial period (of this regime) was one of the periods when the affairs of Athens were conducted best, at least in my time" (8.97.2; trans. Andrewes in: Gomme et al. 1945–81: vol. 5 339, with commentary at 331–9). The idea that a mixture between, or collaboration of, extremes (here oligarchy and democracy) was necessary to establish balance and lasting stability occurs in other authors of the time (Euripides F 21 Nauck) mentions a *xynkrasis* between rich and poor, and Alkibiades in Thuc. 6.18.6 urges the collaboration of young and old and all types of citizens). The concept of a mixed constitution was developed further by Plato and Aristotle and received its fullest elaboration in Polybios (von Fritz 1954; Nippel 1980). It is related to another proposal to strengthen stability and cohesion of a polis torn by civil strife: to enhance the role of the *mesoi* ("those in the middle"; e.g., Euripides *Suppliants* 238–45; de Romilly 1975: 138–40); unfortunately, as Thucydides observes (3.82.8), it was precisely the moderates in the middle that tended to be destroyed in the fights between the extremists. Other proposals (stressing the traditional constitution, concord, or commitment to the common good) were no less idealistic and unrealistic (Raaflaub 2001: 99–117). Real solutions became possible only after several more years of infighting, a defeat and capitulation following upon terrible losses, famine, and complete exhaustion, an even more radical and terroristic oligarchy, and civil war. As pointed out earlier, the fourth-century democracy, somewhat more regulated and less immediate, proved remarkably stable and enduring.

# 7  Democracy's Impact on Society and Community

We return to a statement made earlier. Athenian democracy was a unique system, unprecedented and never fully imitated in history. It transformed values and relationships, created a new type of citizen (whom Plato characterizes sarcastically in *Republic* book 8, alongside his oligarchic counterpart, the *oligarchikos*, whom Theophrastos portrayed in one of his character sketches, *Charakteres* 26), and shaped the polis' policies and relations to the outside world.

Thucydides, dissecting the phenomena that influence the course of history, formulates this pointedly twice, both times in comparison with Sparta, the idol of democracy's opponents (Xenophon *Lak. Pol.* offers a good illustration). The contrast with Sparta pervades Perikles' Funeral Oration, explicitly and proudly when the issue is military training and education (Thuc. 2.39), implicitly and more defensively when attention turns to respect for the law (2.37.3) – a sore point in critical discussions of democracy (Cohen 1995; Millender 2002). Trying to rouse Sparta to action, the Korinthians draw a collective character portrait of the hyperactive, aggressively interventionist Athenians, models of *polypragmosyne* and the total opposite of the slow and cautious Spartans:

> An Athenian is always an innovator, quick to form a resolution and quick at carrying it out ... Athenian daring will outrun its own resources; they will take risks against their better judgement, and still, in the midst of danger, remain confident ...; they never hesitate ..., they are always abroad, for they think that the farther they go the more they will get ... If they win a victory, they follow it up at once, and if they suffer a defeat, they scarcely fall back at all. As for their bodies, they regard them as expendable for their city's sake, as though they were not their own; but each man cultivates his own intelligence, again with a view to doing something notable for his city ... They prefer hardship and activity to peace and quiet. In a word, they are by nature incapable of either living a quiet life themselves or of allowing anyone else to do so. (Thuc. 1.70)

Much of this is echoed in the Funeral Oration, culminating in Perikles' demand that the citizen be a "lover of his city" (*erastes*, Thuc. 2.43.1), just as democratic leaders in the post-Periklean period present themselves as "friends of the city" or "friends of the demos" (*philopolis, philodemos,* Connor 1971: 99–108). A strong link between democracy, naval power, and Athens' propensity to pursue aggressive and expansionist policies seems undeniable (Raaflaub 1994), and thus democracy was a crucial condition for the radical transformation of warfare in the fifth century (Strauss 1996; Hanson 2001).

Democracy emerged in interaction with naval power and the empire. Together, these developments transformed Athenian society profoundly in the generation after the Persian Wars (Raaflaub 1998). To determine precisely what impact democracy itself had on Athenian society is more difficult. Because of imperial and other revenues, the polis disposed of exceptionally large resources and was used to paying its sailors and soldiers, which again was exceptional; both conditions are likely to have facilitated the introduction of state pay for political and judicial functions. Moreover, both empire and naval power caused exceptional amounts of business for council, assembly, and law courts, and necessitated the establishment of numerous committees and offices, both in Athens/Attika and abroad (Schuller 1984). As a result, the level of regular citizen involvement in politics, public administration, and military duties was staggeringly high. So was that of the citizens' familiarity with the ordinary aspects of state business and the empire (the demos' ignorance, noted acidly by critics, became a serious problem only when campaigns aimed at conquests far beyond the polis' traditional sphere of influence; Ober 1993). No other polis came even close to matching these conditions. Politically, Athenian democracy thus must have been markedly different from democracies operating in other poleis.

The transformation of Athens in the generation after the Persian Wars went far beyond politics. As its fleet dominated the seas, piracy was eliminated, trade was facilitated, and Athens became the hub of trade in the Aegean and far beyond. The fleet of triremes, each manned by up to 200 men, and the shipyards that built and maintained hundreds of triremes required enormous manpower resources; Garland (1987: 68) estimates 20,000 for the latter in the fourth century. Many men may have rowed in the summer and worked in the shipyards in the winter (Finley 1983: ch. 3). Weapons manufacturers flourished. Athens and its harbor, the Piraeus, became places of opportunity for foreign immigrants and migrants from the Attic hinterland.

The population of this large metropolitan and port area increased dramatically; it needed to be housed, fed, and entertained. The Piraeus became a city in its own right and was connected with Athens by the Long Walls in the 450s. Moreover, the ruling demos assumed the functions traditionally held by tyrants and aristocracies in sponsoring festivals and authorizing the construction of public buildings and temples (Kallet 1998; 2003). All this added to an economic boom and had important demographic and political consequences.

Although most citizens continued to live a rural life in the villages and towns of Attika (Thuc. 2.14–16), an extraordinary proportion now became urban dwellers and earned their living by working in state-funded enterprises. Their number increased even more when during the Peloponnesian War the population of Attika was evacuated into the fortress Athens–Piraeus, while the Spartans ravaged the Attic country. As a result, a much larger than usual part of the citizen body was able to attend meetings of the assembly and law courts and had a direct interest in decisions that were made there. According to Thucydides, the expectation of rich revenues and guaranteed pay for years to come was a major factor in fueling the masses' enthusiasm for the Sicilian expedition (6.24). At the same time, the proportion of "industrialists" and entrepreneurs among the wealthy elite and of politicians coming from this part of the elite increased dramatically (Rhodes 2000: 131): Kleon the tanner, mercilessly satirized in Aristophanes' *Knights* (Lind 1990), and Nikias, the owner of thousands of slaves hired out to work in the silver mines of Laureion, are good examples. The number of resident aliens increased dramatically, making it necessary to define their status (Whitehead 1977; Bakewell 1997) and eventually prompting the Athenians to adopt a more restrictive concept of citizenship (Patterson 1981; Boegehold 1994; Blok 2003). The number and importance of slaves must have grown exponentially as well, although these aspects are even more elusive and much debated (Osborne 1995; summary in Raaflaub 1998: 26–8). The Old Oligarch comments that the Athenians' involvement in public matters increased their dependence on metic and slave labor to such an extent that they were forced to give them a unique degree of independence (freedom of speech, Pseudo-Xenophon *Ath. Pol.* 1.10–12).

The impact of democracy on Athenian families is more difficult to gauge. A long-standing scholarly debate turns on the question of whether or not the political empowerment of all male citizens caused them to treat their womenfolk more oppressively and, if so, how exactly the interaction between democracy and the status of women should be defined (summarized in Raaflaub 1998: 32–6). Aristophanes' *Lysistrata* (mentioned above) seems to undercut a democratic ideology that placed the polis and public sphere over the family and private sphere, demanding a reintegration of both for the good of all. Otherwise it must have been the war rather than democracy that caused families to suffer. In the disguise of myth, Euripides presents their misery on stage (*Andromache, Hecuba, Suppliants, Trojan Women*) – without noticeable effect on Athenian policies. Finally, scholars have searched, mostly in vain, for indications of any direct impact of democracy on Athenian religion. With very few exceptions (such as the modes of selecting priests for new cults), the relationship seems to be rather general (visible in an increase of festivals and sacrifices and, therefore, of meat offered for consumption to the citizens) and indirect: it was rather the polis' imperial and war policies that necessitated, and provided the means for, generous and ostentatious propitiation of the state's divine supporters through the construction and sumptuous decoration of magnificent sanctuaries (summarized in Raaflaub 1998: 36–40; see Boedeker (forthcoming)).

# 8   Conclusion

Adjectives used in this chapter to characterize Athenian democracy (such as "remarkable" or "unique") are not intended to convey praise or admiration. We need not subscribe to Perikles' Funeral Oration to find the polity he led and the political system he helped realize worthy of close study. Undoubtedly, the latter had major flaws and prompted questionable or even bad decisions: it is not only the trial of the generals after the battle of Arginousai (Munn 2000: 181–8; Giovannini 2002) and the condemnation of Socrates (Hansen 1995; Munn 2000: ch. 11) that offer rich fodder for critical minds (Samons 2004).

Moreover, the Athenian political system was radically different from just about anything we moderns understand under democracy. Few examples of direct democracy have survived to be studied by modern scholars (one example, Hansen 1983: ch. 12); even these fit the Athenian model only in the most elementary respects. Obvious differences, among others, lie in the assembly's role as governing body, the level of citizen involvement in the political process and public administration, and the definition of the citizen body. To focus on the last of these, not only slaves and foreigners but also women were excluded from politics (although they had important communal responsibilities, for example, in religion). The adult male citizens entitled to be actively involved in politics represented a small minority (perhaps between 10 and 20 percent) of the total population. Scholars sometimes conclude, therefore, that the Athenian constitution was not really a democracy. This invites two responses. One is that, historically, the Athenians who invented the word *demokratia* own the "copyright" on it. Thucydides (2:37.1: "Our constitution . . . by name is called a democracy") and the Old Oligarch use the word frequently; their contemporaries allude to it (Sealey 1974; Farrar 1988). It is left to us to define and explain the differences and to use distinctive terminology for modern democracies (such as "representative," "parliamentary," or "popular"). The other point is that, sociologically, progress beyond Athenian exclusiveness is a recent phenomenon. In most European and North American democracies women were granted the right to vote only sometime in the twentieth century. Slaves were, in the USA, freed and legally enfranchised as late as the 1860s, although political discrimination against their descendants continued until the 1960s. Non-citizens have no voting rights in any of the modern democracies. Athenian parameters of thought and action were generally accepted throughout antiquity and far beyond (Strauss 1998: 147–54). Within these limitations, their definition of "citizenship" was extremely broad – and unacceptable to the vast majority of contemporaries and to posterity for over two millennia (Roberts 1994). Moreover, democracy's record, impressive though it was in many respect, had its dark sides: most conspicuously, the Arginousai trial (Ostwald 1986: 431–45) and the conviction and execution of Sokrates (Hansen 1995; Parker 1996: ch. 10) tainted it forever (Samons 2004).

For these and other reasons, like many others, the Founding Fathers of the American Constitution rejected the Athenian model (Richard 1994; Roberts 1994: ch. 9). It therefore served only to a very limited extent as a model for modern democracy. Ancient and modern democracy are not connected by a direct line of development, even if scholars try to trace the latter to Athens (Hansen 1994) or Sparta (Hornblower 1992: 1–2). Modern democracy has a varied and ambiguous or ideologically tainted ancestry (Wood 1994; Strauss 1998) that is much more recent. In terms of constitutional history, Athenian democracy, suppressed by Macedonian rule in the late fourth century, was an evolutionary dead-end – even if Greek political theory and philosophy, decisively provoked by the experience of democracy (Meier 1990; Farrar 1992), stimulated political thinkers, theorists, and philosophers through the centuries and does so even today.

## Further reading

The interested reader might begin with a survey of the classical period in Greek history that pays close attention to democracy (such as Davies 1993 or Jones 1984) or with Meier's "biography of Athens" (1998). More detailed discussions of democracy's history and crisis in the fifth century and of the critical period between 415 and 395 will be found in Ostwald (1986) and Munn (2000), respectively. Hansen's many works on the working of Athenian democracy (esp. 1987; 1999) and Bleicken's magisterial analysis of all aspects of democracy (1994) offer useful and detailed surveys and analyses. They include sketches of democracy's evolution, which is also discussed, controversially and from various aspects, in Raaflaub et al. (2006). Ober (1989) dissects the complex relationship between leaders and masses and thus illuminates the working of democracy, as do, from various angles, Jones (1957) and, for the fourth century, Eder (1995a). Sinclair (1988) and Carter (1986) deal with participation in and withdrawal from democracy.

For democratic ideology and terminology, one should consult Meier (1990) and Raaflaub (1996; 2004b), for political thought and theory connected with democracy, Farrar (1988) and Meier (1993). Roberts (1994) and Ober (1998) pay close attention to criticism leveled at democracy at the time and later, while Brock & Hodkinson (2000) investigate alternative forms of political organization and community, and Ostwald (2000) presents a systematic analysis of oligarchy.

Raaflaub (1998; 1999) offers richly annotated surveys of social, economic, and military aspects connected with democracy (on the last of these, see also Hanson 2001). Sakellariou (1996) and Boedeker & Raaflaub (1998) discuss manifold questions connected with the cultural impact of democracy.

## Bibliography

Anderson, G. (2003) *The Athenian experiment: building an imagined political community in ancient Attica, 508–490 B.C.* (Ann Arbor: University of Michigan Press)

Andrewes, A. (1982a) "The growth of the Athenian state" in: *CAH*² 3, pt. 3 360–91

Andrewes, A. (1982b) "The tyranny of Pisistratus" in: *CAH*² 3, pt. 3 392–416

Bakewell, G. W. (1997) "*Metoikia* in the *Supplices* of Aeschylus" in: *Classical Antiquity* 16: 209–28

Bakker, E. J., J. F. I. de Jong, H. van Wees (eds) (2002) *Brill's companion to Herodotus* (Leiden: Brill)

Bleckmann, B. (1998) *Athens Weg in die Niederlage: Die letzten Jahre des Peloponnesischen Kriegs* (Stuttgart: Teubner)

Bleicken, J. (1987) "Die Einheit der athenischen Demokratie in klassischer Zeit" in: *Hermes* 115: 257–83

Bleicken, J. (1994) *Die athenische Demokratie* (Paderborn: Schöningh ²1994)

Blok, J. (2003) "Oude en nieuwe burgers" in: *Lampas* 36: 5–26 (with English summary)

Blok, J., & A. Lardinois (eds) (forthcoming) *Solon: new historical and philological perspectives*

Bodel, J. (ed.) (2001) *Epigraphic evidence: ancient history from inscriptions* (London: Routledge)

Boedeker, D. (forthcoming) "Athenian religion in the age of Pericles" in: L. J. Samons (ed.) *The Cambridge companion to the age of Pericles* (Cambridge: Cambridge University Press (forthcoming))

Boedeker, D., & K. A. Raaflaub (eds) (1998) *Democracy, empire, and the arts in fifth-century Athens* (Cambridge MA: Harvard University Press) (Center for Hellenic Studies Colloquia 2)

Boedeker, D., & K. A. Raaflaub (2005) "Tragedy and the city" in: Bushnell, R. (ed.) (2005) *A companion to tragedy* (Oxford: Blackwell) 109–27

Boegehold, A. (1994) "Perikles' citizenship law of 451/0 B.C." in: Boegehold, A. L., & A. C. Scafuro (eds) (1994) *Athenian identity and civic ideology* (Baltimore: Johns Hopkins University Press) 57–66

Boegehold, A. L. (1995) *The lawcourts at Athens: sites, buildings, equipment, procedure, and testimonia* (Princeton: American School of Classical Studies at Athens) (*The Athenian Agora* 28)

Brock, R, & S. Hodkinson (eds) (2000) *Alternatives to Athens: varieties of political organization and community in ancient Greece* (Oxford: Oxford University Press)

Burckhardt, L. (1996) *Bürger und Soldaten: Aspekte der politischen und militärischen Rolle athenischer Bürger im Kriegswesen des 4. Jh. v.Chr.* (Stuttgart: Steiner)

Camp, J. McK. (1986) *The Athenian agora: excavations in the heart of classical Athens* (London: Thames & Hudson)

Carter, L. B. (1986) *The quiet Athenian* (Oxford: Clarendon)

Cartledge, P. (1995) *Aristophanes and his theatre of the absurd* (corr. ed.) (Bristol: Classical Press)

Chambers, M. (1990) *Aristoteles: Staat der Athener, übersetzt und erläutert* (Berlin: Akademie-Verlag)

Cohen, D. (1995) "The rule of law and democratic ideology in classical Athens" in: Eder 1995b: 227–44

Connor, W. R. (1971) *The new politicians of fifth-century Athens* (Princeton: Princeton University Press)

Croally, N. T. (1994) *Euripidean polemic*: The Trojan Women *and the function of tragedy* (Cambridge: Cambridge University Press)

Davies, J. K. (1993) *Democracy and classical Greece* (Cambridge MA: Harvard University Press ²1993)

Demont, P. (2003) "Le '*kleroterion*' ('machine à tirer au sort') et la démocratie athénienne" in: *Bulletin de l'Association Guillaume Budé* 2003.1: 26–52

De Romilly, J. (1963) *Thucydides and Athenian imperialism* (trans. P. Thody) (Oxford: Blackwell 1963; repr. Salem NH: Ayer 1988)

De Romilly, J. (1975) *Problèmes de la démocratie grecque* (Paris: Hermann) (Collection Savoir 14)

Derow, P., & R. Parker (eds) (2003) *Herodotus and his world* (Oxford: Oxford University Press)

Dillery, J. (1995) *Xenophon and the history of his times* (London: Routledge)

Dolezal, J. P. (1974) *Aristoteles und die Demokratie* (Frankfurt am Main: Akademische Verlagsgesellschaft)

Dunn, J. (ed.) (1992) *Democracy: the unfinished journey 508 BC to AD 1993* (New York: Oxford University Press)

Eder, W. (1995a) "Die athenische Demokratie im 4. Jahrhundert v. Chr.: Krise oder Vollendung?" in: Eder 1995b: 11–28

Eder, W. (ed.) (1995b) *Die athenische Demokratie im 4. Jahrhundert v. Chr.: Vollendung oder Verfall einer Verfassungsform?* (Stuttgart: Steiner)

Eder, W. (1998) "Aristocrats and the coming of Athenian democracy" in: Morris & Raaflaub 1998: 105–40

Euben, P., J. Wallach, J. Ober (eds) (1994) *Athenian political thought and the reconstruction of American democracy* (Ithaca NY: Cornell University Press)

Farrar, C. (1988) *The origins of democratic thinking: the invention of politics in classical Athens* (Cambridge: Cambridge University Press)

Farrar, C. (1992) "Ancient Greek political theory as a response to democracy" in: Dunn 1992: 17–39

Finley, M. I. (1983) *Economy and society in ancient Greece* (ed. with an intro. by B. D. Shaw & R. P. Saller) (New York: Penguin)

Fornara, C. W., & L. J. Samons (1991) *Athens from Cleisthenes to Pericles* (Berkeley: University of California Press)

Forrest, W. G. (1975) "An Athenian generation gap" in: *Yale Classical Studies* 24: 37–52

Fowler, R. (2003) "Herodotos and Athens" in: Derow & Parker 2003: 305–18

Freeman, K. (1948) *Ancilla to the pre-Socratic philosophers* (Cambridge MA: Harvard University Press)

Furley, W. (1996) *Andokides and the herms: a study of crisis in fifth-century Athenian religion* (London: Institute of Classical Studies)

Garland, R. (1987) *The Piraeus from the fifth to the first century B.C.* (Ithaca NY: Cornell University Press)

Giovannini, A. (2002) "Xenophon, der Arginusenprozess und die athenische Demokratie" in: *Chiron* 32: 15–50

Goldhill, S. (2000) "Greek drama and political theory" in: Rowe, C., & M. Schofield (eds) (2000) *The Cambridge history of Greek and Roman political thought* (Cambridge: Cambridge University Press) 60–88

Gomme, A. W., A. Andrewes, K. J. Dover (1945–81) *A historical commentary on Thucydides*, 5 vols. (Oxford: Clarendon)

Gray, V. (1989) *The character of Xenophon's Hellenica* (Baltimore: Johns Hopkins University Press)

Gregory, J. (1991) *Euripides and the instruction of the Athenians* (Ann Arbor: University of Michigan Press)

Grethlein, J. (2005) "Gefahren des *logos*: Thukydides' Historien und die Grabrede des Perikles" in: *Klio* 87: 41–71

Hansen, M. H. (1983) *The Athenian ecclesia: a collection of articles 1976–83* (Copenhagen: Museum Tusculanum)

Hansen, M. H. (1987) *The Athenian assembly in the age of Demosthenes* (Oxford: Blackwell)

Hansen, M. H. (1990) "The political powers of the people's court in fourth-century Athens" in: Murray, O., & S. Price (eds) (1990) *The Greek city from Homer to Alexander* (Oxford: Clarendon) 215–43

Hansen, M. H. (1994) "The 2500th anniversary of Cleisthenes' reforms and the tradition of Athenian democracy" in: Osborne, R., & S. Hornblower (eds) (1994) *Ritual, finance, politics: Athenian democratic accounts presented to David Lewis* (Oxford: Clarendon) 25–37

Hansen, M. H. (1995) *The trial of Sokrates: from the Athenian point of view* (Copenhagen: Det Kongelige Danske Videnskabernes Selskab) (Historisk-filosofiske meddelelser 71)

(= Hansen, M. H. (1996) "The trial of Sokrates from the Athenian point of view" in: M. Sakellariou (ed.) (1996) Colloque international "Démocratie athénienne et culture" organisé par l'Académie d'Athènes en coopération avec l'UNESCO (23, 24 et 25 novembre 1992) (Athènes: Académie d'Athènes 1996) 137–70)

Hansen, M. H. (1999) *The Athenian democracy in the Age of Demosthenes* (expanded ed.) (Norman: University of Oklahoma Press)

Hanson, V. D. (2001) "Democratic warfare, ancient and modern" in: McCann, D., & B. Strauss (eds) (2001) *War and democracy: a comparative study of the Korean war and the Peloponnesian war* (Armonk NY: Sage) 3–33

Harvey, F. D. (1965) "Two kinds of equality" in: *Classica et Mediaevalia* 26: 101–46

Heftner, H. (2001) *Der oligarchische Umsturz des Jahres 411 v. Chr. und die Herrschaft der Vierhundert in Athen* (Stuttgart: Teubner)

Heftner, H. (2003) "Oligarchen, Mesoi, Autokraten: Bemerkungen zur antidemokratischen Bewegung des späten 5. Jh. v.Chr. in Athen" in: *Chiron* 33: 1–41

Henderson, J. (1980) "*Lysistrate*: the play and its themes" in: *Yale Classical Studies* 26: 153–218

Henderson, J. (1990) "The *dêmos* in the comic competition" in: Winkler, J. J., & F. I. Zeitlin (eds) (1990) *Nothing to do with Dionysus? Athenian drama in its social context* (Princeton: Princeton University Press) 271–313

Henderson, J. (1998) "Attic old comedy, frank speech, and democracy" in: Boedeker & Raaflaub 1998: 255–73, 405–10

Henderson, J. (2003) "Demos, demagogue, tyrant in Attic old comedy" in: Morgan 2003: 155–79

Hoffmann, K. F. (1997) *Das Recht im Denken der Sophistik* (Stuttgart: Teubner)

Hornblower, S. (1987) *Thucydides* (Baltimore: Johns Hopkins University Press)

Hornblower, S. (1991–6) *A commentary on Thucydides*, 2 vols (Oxford: Clarendon)

Hornblower, S. (1992) "Creation and development of democratic institutions in ancient Greece" in: Dunn 1992: 1–16

Howgego, C. (1995) *Ancient history from coins* (London: Routledge)

Hunter, V. J. (1994) *Policing Athens: social control in the Attic lawsuits, 420–320 B.C.* (Princeton: Princeton University Press)

Jones, A. H. M. (1957) *Athenian democracy* (Oxford: Blackwell; repr. Baltimore: Johns Hopkins University Press 1986)

Jones, N. F. (1999) *The associations of classical Athens: the response to democracy* (New York: Oxford University Press)

Jones, P. V. (ed.) (1984) *The world of Athens: an introduction to classical Athenian culture* (Cambridge: Cambridge University Press) (Joint Association of Classical Teachers' [JACT] Greek Course Background Book)

Kallet, L. (1998) "Accounting for culture in fifth-century Athens" in: Boedeker & Raaflaub 1998: 43–58, 357–64

Kallet, L. (2003) "*Demos tyrannos*: wealth, power, and economic patronage" in: Morgan 2003: 117–53

Keaney, J. J. (1992) *The composition of Aristotle's* Athenaion Politeia: *observation and explanation* (New York: Oxford University Press)

Kennedy, G. A. (1963) *The art of persuasion in Greece* (Princeton: Princeton University Press)

Kerferd, G. B. (1981) *The Sophistic movement* (Cambridge: Cambridge University Press)

Konstan, D. (1995) *Greek comedy and ideology* (New York: Oxford University Press)

Krentz, P. (1982) *The Thirty at Athens* (Ithaca NY: Cornell University Press)

Krentz, P. (1995) *Xenophon:* Hellenika II.3.11–IV.2.8: *edited with an introduction, translation and commentary* (Warminster: Aris & Phillips)

Kurke, L. (1998) "The cultural impact of (on) democracy: decentering tragedy" in: Morris & Raaflaub 1998: 155–69

Larsen, J. A. O. (1955) "The Boeotian confederacy and fifth-century oligarchic theory" in: *TAPhA* 86: 40–50

Lateiner, D. (1991) *The historical method of Herodotus* (Toronto: University of Toronto Press) (*Phoenix* Suppl. 23)

Lehmann, G. A. (1973) "Überlegungen zur Krise der Demokratie im Peloponnesischen Krieg" in: *ZPE* 69: 33–73

Lehmann, G. A. (1997) *Oligarchische Herrschaft im klassischen Athen* (Opladen: Westdeutscher Verlag)

Lewis, D. M. (1988) "The tyranny of the Pisistratidae" in: *CAH*[2] 4 287–302

Lind, H. (1990) *Der Gerber Kleon in den "Rittern" des Aristophanes: Studien zur Demago-genkomödie* (Frankfurt am Main: Lang) (Studien zur klassischen Philologie 51)

MacDowell, D. (1995) *Aristophanes and Athens* (New York: Oxford University Press)

Maddoli, G. (ed.) (1994) *L'Athenaion politeia di Aristotele, 1891–1991: per un bilancio di cento anni di studi: incontri perugini di storia della storiografia antica e sul mondo antico 6* (Naples: Edizioni scientifiche italiane) (Studi di storia e di storiografia)

Markle, M. M. (1985) "Jury pay and assembly pay at Athens" in: Cartledge, P., & F. D. Harvey (eds) (1985) *Crux: essays presented to G. E. M. de Ste. Croix on his 75th birthday* (First issued as *History of Political Thought* 6.1–2 (1985) Exeter: Imprint Academic) (London: Duckworth) 265–97

Martin, J. (1974) "Von Kleisthenes zu Ephialtes: Zur Entstehung der athenischen Demokratie" in: *Chiron* 4: 5–42

McGlew, J. F. (1993) *Tyranny and political culture in ancient Greece* (Ithaca NY: Cornell University Press)

McGlew, J. F. (2002) *Citizens on stage: comedy and political culture in the Athenian democracy* (Ann Arbor: University of Michigan Press)

McKechnie, P. R., & S. J. Kern (1988) Hellenica Oxyrhynchia, *ed. with trans. and commentary* (Warminster: Aris & Phillips)

Meier, C. (1990) *The Greek discovery of politics* (trans. D. McLintock) (Cambridge MA: Harvard University Press)

Meier, C. (1993) *The political art of Greek tragedy* (trans. A. Webber) (Baltimore: Johns Hopkins University Press)

Meier, C. (1998) *Athens: a portrait of the city in its golden age* (trans. Kimber, Robert, & Rita Kimber) (New York: Metropolitan Books)

Meiggs, R. (1979) *The Athenian empire* (repr. with corrections) (Oxford: Clarendon)

Millender, E. G. (2002) "*Nomos despotes:* Spartan obedience and Athenian lawfulness in fifth-century thought" in: Gorman, V., & E. Robinson (eds) (2002) *Oikistes: studies in constitutions, colonies, and military power in the ancient world offered in honor of A. J. Graham* (Leiden: Brill) 33–59 (*Mnemosyne* Suppl. 234)

Moles, J. (2002) "Herodotus and Athens" in Bakker et al. 2002: 33–52

Monoson, S. (2000) *Plato's democratic entanglements: Athenian politics and the practice of philosophy* (Princeton: Princeton University Press)

Moore, J. M. (1975) *Aristotle and Xenophon on democracy and oligarchy: translations with introductions and commentary* (Berkeley: University of California Press)

Morgan, K. A. (ed.) (2003) *Popular tyranny: sovereignty and its discontents in ancient Greece* (Austin TX: University of Texas Press)

Morris, I. (1996) "The strong principle of equality and the archaic origins of Greek democracy" in: Ober & Hedrick 1996: 19–48

Morris, I. (1998) "Beyond democracy and empire: Athenian art in context" in: Boedeker & Raaflaub 1998: 59–86, 365–71

Morris, I. (2000) *Archaeology as cultural history: words and things in iron age Greece* (Oxford: Blackwell)

Morris, I., & K. A. Raaflaub (eds) (1998) *Democracy 2500? Questions and challenges* (Dubuque IA: Kendall/Hunt) (Colloquia and Conference Papers 2)

Mulgan, R. (1991) "Aristotle's analysis of oligarchy and democracy" in: Keyt, D., & F. D. Miller, Jr. (eds) (1991) *A companion to Aristotle's* Politics (Oxford: Blackwell) 307–22

Munn, M. (2000) *The school of history: Athens in the age of Socrates* (Berkeley: University of California Press)

Munson, R. V. (2001) *Telling wonders: ethnographic and political discourse in the work of Herodotus* (Ann Arbor: University of Michigan Press)

Nippel, W. (1980) *Mischverfassungstheorie und Verfassungsrealität in Antike und früher Neuzeit* (Stuttgart: Klett/Cotta)

Ober, J. (1989) *Mass and elite in democratic Athens* (Princeton: Princeton University Press)

Ober, J. (1993) "Thucydides' criticism of democratic knowledge" in: Rosen, R., & J. Farrell (eds) (1993) *Nomodeiktes: Greek studies in honor of Martin Ostwald* (Ann Arbor: University of Michigan Press) 81–98

Ober, J. (1996) "The Athenian revolution of 508/7 B.C.: violence, authority, and the origins of democracy" in: Ober, J. (ed.) (1996) *The Athenian revolution: essays on ancient Greek democracy and political theory* (Princeton: Princeton University Press) 32–52. (See also Ober, J. in: Morris & Raaflaub 1998: ch. 4; Ober, J. in: Raaflaub et al. 2006: ch. 4.)

Ober, J. (1998) *Political dissent in democratic Athens: intellectual critics of popular rule* (Princeton: Princeton University Press)

Ober, J., & C. W. Hedrick (eds) (1996) *Demokratia: a conversation on democracies, ancient and modern* (Princeton: Princeton University Press)

O'Neil, J. (1995) *The origins and development of ancient Greek democracy* (Lanham MD: University Press of America)

Osborne, R. (1995) "The economics and politics of slavery at Athens" in: Powell, A. (ed.) (1995) *The Greek world* (London: Routledge) 27–43

Ostwald, M. (1955) "The Athenian legislation against tyranny and subversion" in: *TAPhA* 86: 103–28

Ostwald, M. (1969) *Nomos and the beginnings of the Athenian democracy* (Oxford: Clarendon)

Ostwald, M. (1986) *From popular sovereignty to the rule of law* (Berkeley: University of California Press)

Ostwald, M. (1988) "The reform of the Athenian state by Cleisthenes" in: *CAH*[2] 4 303–46

Ostwald, M. (1996) "Shares and rights: 'citizenship' Greek style and American style" in: Ober & Hedrick 1996: 49–61

Ostwald, M. (2000) *Oligarchia: the development of a constitutional form in ancient Greece* (Stuttgart: Steiner) (*Historia* Einzelschriften 144)

Parker, R. (1996) *Athenian religion: a history* (Oxford: Clarendon)

Patterson, C. B. (1981) *Pericles' citizenship law of 451–450 B.C.* (New York: Arno) (Monographs in Classical Studies)

Piérart, M. (ed.) (1993) *Aristote et Athènes: [table ronde] Fribourg, Suisse, 23–25 mai 1991: [organisée par] l'Université de Fribourg* (Paris: de Boccard)

Raaflaub, K. A. (1987) "Herodotus, political thought, and the meaning of history" in: Boedeker, D., & J. Peradotto (eds) (1987) *Herodotus and the invention of history: papers and commentaries presented at the conference held at the College of the Holy Cross, Worcester, Mass., in April 1986* (Buffalo: Department of Classics, State University of New York at Buffalo) 221–48 (*Arethusa* 20.1–2)

Raaflaub, K. A. (1989) "Contemporary perceptions of democracy in fifth-century Athens," in: *Classica et Mediaevalia* 40: 33–70

Raaflaub, K. A. (1994) "Democracy, power, and imperialism in fifth-century Athens" in: Euben et al. 1994: 103–46

Raaflaub, K. A. (1996) "Equalities and inequalities in Athenian democracy" in: Ober & Hedrick 1996: 139–74

Raaflaub, K. A. (1998) "The transformation of Athens in the fifth century" in: Boedeker & Raaflaub 1998: 15–41, 348–57

Raaflaub, K. A. (1999) "Archaic and classical Greece" in Raaflaub, K. A., & N. Rosenstein (eds) (1999) *War and society in the ancient and medieval worlds: Asia, the Mediterranean, Europe, and Mesoamerica* (Cambridge MA: Harvard University Press) 129–61 (Center for Hellenic Studies Colloquia 3)

Raaflaub, K. A. (2001) "Political thought, civic responsibility, and the Greek polis" in: Árnason, J. P., & P. Murphy (eds) *Agon, logos, polis: the Greek achievement and its aftermath* (Stuttgart: Steiner) 72–117

Raaflaub, K. A. (2002) "Philosophy, science, politics: Herodotus and the intellectual trends of his time" in Bakker et al. 2002: 149–86

Raaflaub, K. A. (2003) "Stick and glue: the function of tyranny in fifth-century Athenian democracy" in: Morgan 2003: 59–115

Raaflaub, K. A. (2004a) "Aristocracy and freedom of speech in the Greco-Roman world" in: Sluiter, I., & R. Rosen (eds) (2004) *Free speech in classical antiquity* (Leiden, Brill) 41–61

Raaflaub, K. A. (2004b) *The discovery of freedom in ancient Greece* (Chicago: University of Chicago Press)

Raaflaub, K. A., J. Ober, R. W. Wallace (2006) *Origins of democracy in ancient Greece* (Berkeley: University of California Press)

Raaflaub, K. A. (forthcoming) "Thucydides on democracy and oligarchy" in: Rengakos, A., & A. Tsakmakis (eds) (forthcoming) *Brill's companion to Thucydides* (Leiden: Brill (forthcoming))

Rawson, E. (1969) *The Spartan tradition in European thought* (Oxford: Clarendon)

Rhodes, P. J. (1980) "Athenian democracy after 403 B.C" in: *CJ* 75: 305–23

Rhodes, P. J. (1984) *Aristotle*, The Athenian Constitution, *trans. with intro. and notes* (Harmondsworth: Penguin)

Rhodes, P. J. (1985) *The Athenian boule* (re-issued with additions and corrections) (Oxford: Clarendon)

Rhodes, P. J. (1992a) "The Delian league to 449 B.C." in: *CAH*² 5 34–61

Rhodes, P. J. (1992b) "The Athenian revolution" in: *CAH*² 5 62–95

Rhodes, P. J. (1993) *A commentary on the Aristotelian* Athenaion Politeia (rev. ed) (Oxford: Clarendon)

Rhodes, P. J. (2000) "Oligarchs in Athens" in: Brock & Hodkinson 2000: 119–36

Rhodes, P. J. (2003) "Nothing to do with democracy: Athenian drama and the *polis*" in: *JHS* 123: 104–19

Richard, C. J. (1994) *The founders and the classics: Greece, Rome, and the American enlightenment* (Cambridge MA: Harvard University Press)

Roberts, J. T. (1994) *Athens on trial: the antidemocratic tradition in western thought* (Princeton: Princeton University Press)

Robinson, E. (1997) *The first democracies: early popular government outside Athens* (Stuttgart: Steiner) (*Historia* Einzelschriften 107)

Robinson, E. (forthcoming) *Classical democracy beyond Athens* (forthcoming)

Rowe, C. (1998) "Democracy and Sokratic-Platonic philosophy" in Boedeker & Raaflaub 1998: 241–54, 400–5

Rusten, J. S. (1989) *Thucydides*, The Peloponnesian War, *Book II* (Cambridge: Cambridge University Press)

Saïd, S. (1998) "Tragedy and politics" in: Boedeker & Raaflaub 1998: 275–95, 410–15

Sakellariou, M. (ed.) (1996) *Colloque international "Démocratie athénienne et culture" organisé par l'Académie d'Athènes en coopération avec l'UNESCO (23, 24 et 25 novembre 1992)* (Athènes: Académie d'Athènes 1996)

Samons, L. J. (2004) *What's wrong with democracy? From Athenian practice to American worship* (Berkeley: University of California Press)

Schuller, W. (1984) "Wirkungen des Ersten Attischen Seebunds auf die Herausbildung der athenischen Demokratie" in: Schuller, W. (ed.) (1984) *Studien zum Attischen Seebund* (Konstanz: Universitätsverlag) 87–101 (Xenia: Konstanzer Althistorische Vorträge und Forschungen 8)

Sealey, R. (1974) "The origins of *demokratia*" in: *CSCA* 6: 253–94

Sealey, R. (1987) *The Athenian republic: democracy or the rule of law?* (University Park: Pennsylvania State University Press)

Siewert, P. (1982) *Die Trittyen Attikas und die Heeresreform des Kleisthenes* (Munich: Beck) (Vestigia 33)

Sinclair, R. K. (1988) *Democracy and participation in Athens* (Cambridge: Cambridge University Press)

Spielvogel, J. (2003) "Die politische Position des athenischen Komödiendichters Aristophanes" in: *Historia* 52: 3–22

Stadter, P. A. (ed.) (1973) *The speeches in Thucydides: a collection of original studies with a bibliography [of scholarship on the speeches in Thucydides, 1873-1970, by W. C. West III]* (Papers presented at a colloquium sponsored by the Dept. of Classics of the University of North Carolina at Chapel Hill, March 26–7, 1972) (Chapel Hill: University of North Carolina Press)

Stahl, M. (1987) *Aristokraten und Tyrannen im archaischen Athen* (Stuttgart: Steiner)

Strauss, B. S. (1996) "The Athenian trireme: school of democracy" in: Ober & Hedrick 1996: 313–25

Strauss, B. S. (1998) "Genealogy, ideology, and society in democratic Athens" in: Morris & Raaflaub 1998: 141–54

Thomas, R. (2000) *Herodotus in context: ethnography, science, and the art of persuasion* (Cambridge: Cambridge University Press)

Todd, S. C. (1993) *The shape of Athenian law* (Oxford: Clarendon)

Traill, J. S. (1975) *The political organization of Attica: a study of the demes, trittyes, and phylai, and their representation in the Athenian council* (Princeton: American School of Classical Studies at Athens) (*Hesperia* Supplement 14)

Traill, J. S. (1986) *Demos and trittys: epigraphical and topographical studies in the organization of Attica* (Toronto: Athenians)

von Fritz, K. (1954) *The theory of the mixed constitution in antiquity* (New York: Columbia University Press)

Wallace, R. W. (1989) *The Areopagus council, to 307 B.C.* (Baltimore: Johns Hopkins University Press)

Wallace, R. W. (1998) "The sophists in Athens" in: Boedeker & Raaflaub 1998: 203–22, 392–5

Whibley, L. (1896) *Greek oligarchies: their character and organisation* (New York: Putnam; repr. Chicago: Ares 1975)

Whitehead, D. (1977) *The ideology of the Athenian metic* (Cambridge: Cambridge Philological Society) (*PCPhS* Suppl. 4)

Wolff, H. (1979) "Die Opposition gegen die radikale Demokratie in Athen bis zum Jahre 411 v. Chr." in: *ZPE* 36: 279–302

Wood, E. M. (1994) "Democracy: an idea of ambiguous ancestry" in: Euben et al. 1994: 59–80

CHAPTER TWENTY

# Law and Rhetoric: Community Justice in Athenian Courts

*Robert W. Wallace*

## 1   Introduction: Litigation – Ancient and Modern

Written law, equal for everyone and enforced by people's courts, was one of archaic Greece's most enduring innovations. From the seventh century, many Greek communities appointed lawgivers to remedy the "crooked justice" of "gift-devouring princes" (Hesiod *Works and Days* 38–9). In 594, Athens' great lawgiver Solon proclaimed that his new statutes were equal for all Athenians, "lower and upper classes alike" (F 36.18 West). The Athenians carefully preserved the *axones*, the wooden "axles" on which he inscribed his laws; Plutarch was shown their "meager remains" some 750 years later (*Life of Solon* 25). In the Classical period, the Athenians wrote their laws on marble pillars and displayed them around the city.

Solon also established a people's court, which became in Classical times the *dikasteria* ("places for justice"), to administer justice and enforce the laws. Between 200 and 1,500 citizen judges (*dikastai*, dicasts) staffed each *dikasterion*. The dicasts judged after listening to the opposing speeches (*antilogoi*) by courtroom litigants and their supporters (*synegoroi*). The central role of antilogies in the process of adjudication helped spawn the development of forensic rhetoric in the fifth and fourth centuries.

In an oral culture where texts were performed and often fluid, laws were a unique genre: they were written, permanent, and often called authoritative (*kyrioi*). The ephebes, Athens' soldier recruits, each year swore "to obey the officials and the laws. If anyone seeks to destroy the laws I will oppose him as far as I am able myself, and with the help of all" (R&O 88 lines 11–16 = Tod 204). The dicasts' oath began, "I shall vote according to the laws and the decrees of the Athenian demos" (Demosthenes 24.150). Dicasts were often called "guardians of the laws" (e.g., [Demosthenes] 25. 6–7). Litigants and rhetors had the city clerk read out the texts of laws in court. They interpreted these laws but never read out the legal texts themselves, thus making patent the distinction between law and rhetoric. In the later fifth century, the Athenians instituted the *graphe paranomon*, a public suit for proposing a decree that conflicted with existing laws. When the Athenians collected and republished their laws in the decade after 410, they carefully preserved the archaic wording of older statutes. Officials were forbidden to use "unwritten laws" (Andokides 1.85–87). It was a capital offense for a courtroom speaker to cite a non-existent law ([Demosthenes] 26.24). Reflecting their belief in law, democratic Athenians loved to litigate, and in contrast to other Mediterranean societies, they frequently proclaimed their commitment to law and legal procedure rather than private vendetta (Herman 1996). In Thucydides' Funeral Oration Perikles proclaims that the Athenians "do not transgress the law, but obey the officials and the laws" (2.37). His words find parallels in many other public texts (see, e.g., Lysias 2.18–19, Andokides 4.19, Aischines 3.6, Euripides *Suppliants* 429–34). Because of the importance of the law in Athenian litigation, the presentation and interpretation of laws were a major component of many forensic speeches (Harris 1994).

The modern West shares with Athens the administration of justice by written laws, people's courts, and opposing speeches. Yet despite any historical connections and many similarities, Athenian justice was distinct from ours in important ways. In particular, many modern scholars and some Athenians contend that in reaching verdicts, Athens' courts did not always follow the law but sometimes their emotions or other considerations not strictly relevant to the case in hand. Extraneous elements were introduced especially in the rhetoric of courtroom speakers. Lysias says that his enemies "cannot even do what has become the custom in this city, whereby defendants make no defense against the charges, but sometimes deceive you with irrelevant statements about themselves, showing that they are fine soldiers, or have captured many enemy ships" (12.38, trans. Todd). In 30.1, Lysias says that even if a defendant seems guilty he could be acquitted if he mentions valiant deeds by ancestors and proves that he had served the city well. Isokrates, a wealthy man, says that in early Athens judges enforced the laws on money lending instead of making use of *epieikeia* ("decency"? "equity"?) (7.33–4). In [Demosthenes] 25.76 the speaker states, "before now I have seen some men on trial being convicted by the actual facts and unable to show that they had not done wrong, take refuge in the moderation and self-control of their lives, others in the achievements and public services of their ancestors, or in similar pleas, through which they induced their judges to pity and goodwill." The speaker in Demosthenes 44.8 says that "generosity and justice" sometimes triumph over the laws. Lykourgos complains that it is unjust for prosecutors to raise irrelevant charges but "you judges have granted this possibility to those who appear before you" (1.13). In Xenophon's *Apology* (or *Defense of Socrates*) (4), Hermokrates asks Sokrates, "Do you not see that the *dikasteria* of the Athenians have often been carried away by a speech and killed those who have done no wrong, or else have often freed the guilty because their speech aroused pity or because they spoke agreeably?" Such statements can be multiplied.

In Anglo-American courts also, impassioned speeches and personal circumstances sometimes sway jury verdicts. At the same time, verdicts are formally required to be consistent with the law. The judge instructs the jury that if they find that the defendant has broken the law, they must vote to convict. Most conspicuously today, mandatory sentencing reflects an effort to eliminate juridical inconsistencies based on extra-legal factors. On "jury nullification," Allen (2000: 5–9): "The 1992 Federal

U.S. criminal jury instructions read: 'you will . . . apply the law which I will give you. You must follow that law whether you agree with it or not.' And in forty-eight U.S. states judges and lawyers are not allowed to tell the jury that they have the power and legal right to set aside the law."

These differences between Athenian and modern adjudication have led to a long-standing scholarly debate whether Athenian justice represented "the rule of law," or whether, as many recent scholars have argued, the legal resolution of disputes was not so important as other factors. "Between the judicial, where a man invested with authority and responsibility decides and his decision is enforced, and the political, where a decision is reached and a settlement made as a result of the relative strengths of the two parties to the dispute as they are shown and tested in social action," Robin Osborne (1985: 53) concludes, "we would do well to look more closely at the possibility that [the Athenian situation] has strong 'political' characteristics, rather than assume that it is a modified judicial system without a judge." According to Herman (1996: 12–13), "it was not the [Athenian] jurors' concern to find out the truth. Theirs was the task of weighing the relative merits of the arguments they heard with an eye to the city's best interests . . . Any idea of ascertaining the 'facts', and then testing them against the letter of the law, was given short shrift." David Cohen (1995) contends that the immediate legal disputes were not necessarily central to court cases: the extraneous elements in litigants' speeches reveal that these were contests for social honor and the prosecution of longstanding feuds, here carried out through the courts.

The many discussions of law in Athenian courtroom speeches surely indicate that the legal aspects of forensic rhetoric should not be disregarded. What are the implications of the "extraneous" arguments?

In a 2004 article reversing recent trends, Peter Rhodes addresses this issue in detail, arguing that most of the "extraneous" material is in fact relevant to "the larger story" of the case in dispute. Even more recently, Lanni (2005) argues that the extraneous materials helped provide the dicasts with important information about the contexts of disputes, enabling them to "take into account the particular circumstances of the individual case." In many instances, the interpretations of these scholars certainly seem justified. For example, in "scrutinies" (*dokimasiai*) for public office, the laws may have mentioned certain specific kinds of forbidden behavior, but a wider discussion of character would obviously not have been out of place. Yet questions remain. Why should an ancestor's brave deeds in war have any relevance to a financial dispute a century later? Why should the dicasts ignore the law in favor of "decency," in lending or inheritance cases? Rhodes admits that many speeches have at least some irrelevant passages. As we have seen, again and again the Athenians state that they follow the law. It is equally clear that Athens' courts were sometimes influenced by factors that were not strictly relevant to the case at hand. Were the Athenians simply being inconsistent, or "amateurs" (Lanni 2005: n. 19)?

I shall argue that conceptual similarities between law and the kinds of extraneous considerations raised in court cases make Athenian practice both consistent and clear. Lysias, Isokrates, Xenophon, and the other writers I have quoted not only contrast the law with factors such as personal character or past history, but point to a more profound distinction between Athenian justice and our own. The evolution of modern law has steadily reinforced ever sharper distinctions regarding relevance in court. When it was to their advantage, Athenian litigants also made such distinctions, as we have seen. However, because of the historical factors that shaped their approach to adjudication, the Athenians were prepared to view laws and certain kinds of not immediately relevant materials from similar perspectives and as directed toward similar goals. Such materials were therefore judged to be appropriate in reaching verdicts. Even litigants who protest against irrelevant arguments include these kinds of materials, often within the same speech.

Athenian perspectives become clearer in the light of several fundamental contrasts between Athens' judicial system and the United States'. The US legal system is intended to function within the framework of the values of modern liberal society. Central tenets of liberalism include the primacy of the individual over the state and the paramount importance of protecting individual liberties against public interference. This orientation is in part the product of the continuous struggle against religious oppression since the Roman period. It is also the product of the ongoing struggle against so-called "heavy states," where regimes or faceless bureaucrats dominate an alienated populace by what Max Weber (1972: 822) called a monopoly of legitimate violence, including censorship, taxation, and the police. In the eighteenth century, liberalism itself emerged out of debates over the extent to which any state might restrict citizens' freedoms. For John Locke, the founding father of liberalism, freedom meant shielding a realm of personal life from interference by the government. Although the US Constitution permits states to set aside individuals' rights when "the public safety may require it" (Article I, section 9), the legal system of the United States is so far oriented toward protecting individuals that in some instances even known criminals (even if non-citizens) are freed if representatives of the state have inadvertently committed some minor procedural mistake. The American Civil Liberties Union opposes indiscriminate security screening of passengers at airports, and police sobriety checkpoints against drunk drivers (*Policy Guide of the ACLU* #270 (1986); *Washington Post* June 30, 1990, p. A29; G. Guerrero, speech before the American Society of Industrial Security, November 8 (1989) 11). Individuals are not required to testify against themselves, or spouses against their mates; individuals can refuse to speak to investigating authorities; individuals have the right to have a lawyer. These rights and laws help to guard individuals against abuse by the state or the majority population. For that reason, as a society and even sometimes in court, we are sometimes prepared to tolerate illegal actions when the law is deemed to represent the oppressive power of the state or of the majority against individuals, acting especially in accordance with personal conscience. In a longstanding tradition of civil disobedience, many Americans feel entitled to violate the law for reasons of conscience. A significant number refuse to pay taxes in support of the military. A significant number refused induction during the Vietnam War. As Mohammed Ali remarked, "I got no quarrel with them Viet Cong." For years no jury would convict one Dr. Kevorkian for assisting others to commit suicide. In other contexts, strict adherence to the law is considered egalitarian and fair. For example, in conspicuous contrast with Athens, in US courts when guilt or innocence is at issue, it is forbidden to mention any past misdeeds by a defendant, even if they might demonstrate that he is a serial offender.

Athens' laws, its judicial system, and in a wider frame its democracy developed in reaction to abuses not by the state or the majority population but by powerful individuals, including tyrants, "gift-devouring princes," and other members of the elite. When reform came, the essential point was that the community, the people together, be empowered. Law emerged within this context as a means to protect the community against powerful or dangerous individuals. The community, coming together in court, enforced the laws which they saw as their common protector. Andokides 4.19 proclaims, "Obeying the authorities and the laws is safety for all. Whoever ignores these has destroyed the greatest protection of the city." Aischines' third speech begins by excoriating contemporary rhetors whose actions fly in the face of the law. "If the laws are faithfully upheld for the polis, the democracy also is saved" (3.6). Euripides' *Suppliants* calls "fairly preserving the laws" "the bond of all men's cities" (429–34). Demosthenes (25.20) explains the need to obey the laws in terms of the benefits which they bring to the community:

> I shall say nothing novel or extravagant or peculiar, but only what you all know as well as I do. For if any of you wishes to inquire what is the cause and the motive-power that calls together the Council, draws the people into the Assembly, fills the *dikasteria*, makes the old officials yield readily to the new, and enables the whole life of the polis to be carried on and preserved, he will find that it is the laws and the obedience that all men yield to the laws.

Although the argument cannot be fully developed here, virtually no Attic text questions the prior importance of the community over any individual: this was a central tenet of Athenian political ideology. Thucydides' Perikles remarks "When the whole polis is on the right course it is a better thing for each separate individual than when private interests are satisfied but the polis as a whole is going downhill" (2.60.2; also 1.141.7). Thucydides' Nikias claims that a person who cares for his own safety and property is still a "good citizen," because in his own interests he "would be most anxious that the city's affairs prosper too" (6.9.2). Thucydides himself remarks that after Perikles' death the city suffered because politicians acted "in accordance with their personal ambition for honor and personal gain" (2.65.7). In the debate on saving Athens in Aristophanes' *Frogs* (1427–9), Euripides says "I hate the kind of citizen who'll prove to be | Slow to assist his country, swift to harm her greatly | For his own good astute, but useless for the City's." According to Xenophon (*Hellenika* 1.7.21), Euryptolemos called it "disgraceful" to put the interests of his relatives over the interests of the whole polis. The democrat Lysias, the oligarch Andokides, the fourth-century speech in [Andokides] 4 all proclaim the priority of the community over individual concerns. As Andokides states, "those who do not identify their interests as individuals with yours as a community can only be hostile to the city" (2.2–3; cf. Lysias 31.6, 31.17–18, 21.18, 22.14; [Andokides] 4.1, 19). In Aristotle's more abstract terms, "no one of the citizens must think that he belongs just to himself, but rather that everyone belongs to the city…and the care of each part naturally looks to the care of the whole" (*Politics* 1337a27–30). "The polis has priority over the household and over any individual among us. For the whole must be prior to the part" (*Politics* 1253a18–29).

Community sentiment also drove Athens' system of public values. *Philotimia*, "ambition," was good if directed toward the community, bad if it benefited only oneself (Whitehead 1983).

In the forensic speeches cited earlier in this chapter and in many other texts as we shall see, litigants are said to have received favorable albeit "extra-legal" treatment especially because of their service to the community and their upstanding characters. Lysias mentions brave combat, valiant deeds, and serving the city well; [Demosthenes] mentions "the achievements and public services of their ancestors." Litigating itself was considered responsible communal activity. As Herman (1996: 31) observes: "the victim of aggression was expected rationally to subordinate his behavior to considerations of communal utility: rather than reacting impulsively and violently, he was expected to forbear, to exercise self-restraint, to reconsider or re-negotiate the case, and to compromise."

As we have seen, many Attic sources attest that the purpose of law was to safeguard the community. In light of that purpose, actions either harmful or beneficial to the community, even including brave military service by a litigant's ancestors, were judged relevant to his case. Of course some litigants tried to weaken the force of such evidence by claiming that the law alone was important. However, the claim that everyone must strictly obey the law arose in the context of contesting aristocratic or other claims to special privilege. In the egalitarian, community world of Classical Athens, many litigants stress the importance and relevance of character and community service. They do not include this material because of ongoing feuds or contests for honor, but because both in law and for the dicasts the welfare of the community was a central concern. The frequency with which issues of community or wider personal character are addressed shows their importance in the administration of justice. For its different historical reasons, our society is sometimes willing to tolerate illegal actions by individuals against the public or its government, for reasons of personal conscience. The Athenians completely rejected any such conception.

## 2   In Athenian Courts

The community nature of the Athenian judiciary is apparent first in the composition of its courts. Each year, from an eligible group of perhaps 30,000 male citizens over 30 years of age, 6,000 were chosen to serve as dicasts in the ten *dikasteria*. These courts were in session between 175 and 225 days a year (Hansen 1979). As I have noted, hundreds of citizens heard each case. As cases never lasted more than one day and private cases were much shorter, dicasts will have heard numerous cases during their year of service. Many scholars condemn Athens' mass dicasts as amateurs. Yet unlike our jurors, most dicasts will have gained a good deal of legal experience from the many court cases they adjudicated.

More important, the Athenians were proud of being amateurs, and suspicious of legal experts. Our courts are supervised by an expert judge, who decides issues of law and thus helps to make law. Our juries then apply the law to the facts as they determine them, and thereby decide whether defendants are guilty of the charges brought against them. Athenian courts had no expert judge to state the law. Each dicast was both judge and juror. Each came to his own understanding of the law, and decided guilt or innocence. In consequence, Athens' laws were reinterpreted each day, according to the circumstances of each case in the eyes of ordinary citizens.

Although modern jurists will worry that non-experts sometimes fail to understand the law, the Athenian arrangement was again no oversight. The point of written law was to remove judicial authority from any powerful individual. As Demosthenes says, "the private citizen should not be confused and at a disadvantage compared with those who know all the laws, but all should have the same ordinances before them, simple and clear to read and understand" (20.93). In Euripides' *Suppliants* Theseus observes, "There is nothing more hostile to a polis than a tyrant. In the first place, there are no common laws in such a city, but one man rules, keeping the law in his own hands. This is not equality. When the laws have been written down, both the weak and the rich have equal justice" (429–34). Dicasts were even forbidden to discuss cases among themselves, presumably lest powerful or influential men exercise undue influence (Aristotle *Politics* 1268b7–11). The many presentations of laws in court speeches show that the dicasts sought to judge in accordance with them. In the democracy, each citizen was charged with understanding the laws for himself.

For similar reasons, the substantive – but I note, not the procedural – provisions of Athens' legal statutes were often left general. Laws outlawing "impiety" or "idleness" did not further define that offense. This quality has often been called "open texture": both litigants and dicasts could interpret laws according to the circumstances of each case. Thus, most famously, Sokrates was accused of "not believing in the gods of the city but in strange new spiritual beings, and corrupting the youth." The rubric under which he was charged was almost certainly impiety. However, his prosecutors gave that charge an individual, even idiosyncratic definition: in particular, the charge of "corrupting the youth" can have reflected no language in the law. Absent such detailed specifications by the prosecutors, dicasts came to their own sense of the meaning of each statute. Even more egregiously from modern legal perspectives, in their oath the dicasts also swore "where there are no laws, I shall decide as seems best to me." Verdicts in such cases can only have represented the majority of dicasts' general sense of right and wrong.

The Athenians understood open texture but did not change it and did not consider it problematic. *Ath. Pol.* 9.2 comments that because Solon's laws

> were not written simply and clearly, but were like the law on inheritance and heiresses, it was inevitable that many disputes should arise and that the *dikasterion* should decide all things both public and private. Some people think that he made his laws unclear deliberately, in order that the power of decision should rest with the people. However, it is not likely that he was unclear for that reason, but rather because it is impossible to define what is best in general terms. It is not right to estimate his intentions from present day practice. (trans. Rhodes (Penguin))

This passage indicates that in the "present day" (the later fourth century), at least some Athenians were aware that "unclear" statutes empowered the people. In this same judicial context, *Ath. Pol.* 9.1 observes that "when the demos is master (*kyrios*) of the vote, it is master of the polity." The Roman period saw the emergence of jurisprudence, the science of law, through which over centuries professional experts have worked to make laws clearer, more precise, and more consistent, and to define their uses and scope. In Athens the community, the mass of dicasts, themselves preferred to decide what was just.

Again for similar reasons, legal expertise was normally suspect except in the field of sacred law. Litigants sometimes apologize for seeming to possess too great a knowledge of the law. According to Hypereides *Against Athenogenes* 13,

> Athenogenes will presently tell you that in law whatever agreements one man makes with another are binding [e.g., Demosthenes 47.77]. Yes, my friend, just agreements. But if they are unjust, the opposite is true: the law forbids that they be binding. From the laws themselves I shall make this clearer to you. For you have reduced me to such a state of fear lest I be ruined by you and your cleverness [*deinotes*] that I have been searching the laws night and day, and studying them to the neglect of everything else. (trans. Burtt (Loeb))

In Demosthenes 57.5, Euxitheos remarks that "since this fellow [Euboulides], who knows the laws, and knows them more than is proper, has made his charges with injustice and greed, I must first tell you of the outrageous treatment which I received..." Even if such sentiments were influenced by the fear of seeming to be a sycophant (a professional blackmailing prosecutor), they also show how the law should ideally serve ordinary citizens. As we have seen, in 20.93 Demosthenes says, "the private citizen should not be confused and at a disadvantage compared with those who know all the laws, but all should have the same ordinances before them, simple and clear to read and understand."

A related sentiment involves the announcement that a litigant was forgoing (or at any rate was claiming to forgo) legal advantage if the other side makes a reasonable case. In [Demosthenes] 44.8, the speaker states that even if his opponents "do not have the support of the laws, but it seems to you that what they say is in accordance with justice and generosity, even so we withdraw our claim." According to [Demosthenes] 56.14, the speaker's party agreed to a concession in a dispute: "we were not unaware, dicast men, of what was just from the agreement, but we thought that we should suffer some loss and make a concession, so as not to appear litigious." Litigation was thus "embedded" within the frame of wider community values.

Finally, trials in Athens were not always initiated when crimes were committed, but when the community was affected. Sokrates was no less guilty of impiety in 399 than he had been for decades. He was charged chiefly because some of his students among the Thirty tyrants helped to overthrow the democracy in 404 and killed some 1,500 persons to steal their money. Afterwards, he will have continued to say that democracy was a bad form of government – dangerous words in difficult times (see Hansen 1995).

The courts themselves were loci for community sentiment. Even if the dicasts were forbidden to confer with each other, hubbub (*thorybos*) was common (Bers 1985). According to Aristophanes' *Wasps*, the dicasts shouted *kataba, kataba, kataba, kataba*: "get down!" which Bdelykleon says many litigants misunderstand, thinking they have won their case (lines 979–81). The dicasts' oath to listen to both sides (Demosthenes 24.151) has been interpreted as a measure against *thorybos* (Bers 1985: 7 with references). The litigant in Demosthenes 57.1 begs the judges to please listen quietly to his presentation. In [Demosthenes] 45.6, Apollodoros says that the judges were so impressed by his opponents' false evidence that they "refused to hear a single word from me." He was "denied the opportunity to speak and was outraged as no other man had been."

In our courts, the judge immediately silences any outburst by the public. Although speakers in Athens' courts or Assembly sometimes beg not to be interrupted (e.g., Demosthenes 5.15), no speaker voices objections to hubbub once the people have spoken. On the contrary, Aischines states that some politicians "shamelessly" refuse to yield to the people's shouting and step down (1.34). Demosthenes reports that when he tried to counter Aischines in an Assembly in 346, "Aischines and Philokrates posted themselves on either side of me and kept shouting and interrupting, and finally jeering at me. You were all laughing, you would not listen to me...and by the gods I think your feelings were quite natural" (19.23–4). In [Demosthenes] 45.6–7, Apollodoros says that at first he was bitter at his treatment by the dicasts, but on reflection he thought "there was abundant excuse for those who gave that verdict." In both ideology and practice, the obligation to sit quietly without speaking was a hated characteristic of monarchy, tyranny, and oligarchy. In Aischylos' *Persians*, the defeated Persian elders lament, "no longer for mortals is the tongue under guard. For the people have been set loose, to bark out free things now that the yoke of military might has been loosed" (lines 591–4). In *Prometheus Bound*, the chorus warns Prometheus that he is "too free in his speech" (*eleutherostomein*) for tyrant Zeus' liking (line 180). In Sophokles' *Antigone*, Kreon's son Haimon tells his increasingly tyrannical father, "your presence frightens any man of the people from saying things you would not care to hear. But in the dark corners I have heard them say...You expect to be listened to, but not to listen" (lines 690–2). Thucydides reports that in the oligarchic coup of 411, all the speakers in the Assembly and Council came from the oligarchs. "People were afraid when they saw their numbers, and no one now dared to speak in opposition to them...Instead the people kept quiet" (8.66.1). The Athenians had no experience of the heavy bureaucratic state. They did know about tyranny.

The communal quality of court disputes is further indicated by the often large numbers of spectators, "people standing around" (*hoi periestekotes*) the courts, listening to judicial proceedings (see Lanni 1997). These spectators ranged from ordinary citizens and visiting foreigners to Athens' principal politicians and rhetors. They are often mentioned and were sometimes addressed by court speakers (e.g., Demosthenes 18.196; 44.41). The speaker in Antiphon 6.14 states, "Many of the spectators know all these things quite precisely; they hear the oath; and they are paying attention to my defense. I would like them to think that I respect your oath and that by telling the truth I persuade you to acquit me."

To demonstrate their close ties to both family and community, defendants sometimes brought their children into court, to gain sympathy (Aristophanes *Wasps* 568–70; Demosthenes 21.99; 25.84; cf. 48.57; Aischines 2.159). Parodying this convention, Plato's Sokrates purports to apologize for not doing so (*Apology* 34C). After the main speeches, friends and relatives might, with the dicasts' permission, briefly address the court, usually to supply character evidence (see Rubinstein 2000). These elements were extra-legal and circumstantial, but influenced verdicts. Such material is normally forbidden in modern courts except to mitigate or augment sentences. It is not used to determine guilt.

Finally and above all, court speeches were oriented toward the community (for a general introduction, see also above, Chapter 2, section 3). In more than just their treatment of law, these speeches are anti-expert and reflect the perspectives of ordinary citizens. First, every litigant had to speak for himself. To be sure, more prosperous litigants could purchase speeches (which they memorized) from professional speech-writers, "logographers," who were knowledgeable in the ways of the court. Anti-phon, Lysias, Isaios, Isokrates, Demosthenes, and other famous orators had all been logographers. Although never one himself, Aischines had been a court clerk, gaining knowledge of the law and legal procedures. He also attended court as a spectator to learn his craft: "whenever I go to the court and hear the litigants, I notice that you always find the same argument persuasive" (1.77). However, litigants tried to conceal their relationship with logographers, and logographers tried to write in ways appro-priate to their clients (*ethopoieia*: "writing in character").

Popular suspicion of "making the worse *logos* seem the better" sprang from similar sentiments against elite courtroom expertise. Demosthenes states, "I never reproached my enemy for being a sophist and paying silver to Isokrates, but people should not look down on others and covet the property of others, trusting in *logos*. That is the part of a rascally sophist, who should be made to suffer for it." His opponent is "clever" (*deinos*) and "trusts in speaking and in the 1000 drachmas he has paid to his teacher" (35.40–3). Aischines called Demosthenes "the pirate of politics, who sails on his craft of words over the sea of state" (3.253). Demosthenes retorted that Aischines "bids you be on your guard against me, for fear that I should mislead and deceive you, calling me a clever speaker, a mountebank and a sophist and so forth." Demosthenes admits his *deinotes*, which he renames "experience" (*empeiria*) and says he uses only to benefit the demos (18.276–7; see also Demosthenes 51.20–2; Aischines 1.173–5; Isaios 10.1; Isokrates 15.4–5; Hypereides 4.25–6 and F 80 Jensen (*rhetores* are like snakes)).

On the Athenian model, citizens spoke to their peers in a simple, straightforward way. By contrast, our courts virtually require individuals to employ legal experts to represent them in court, and lawyers are obliged to use any strategy within the bounds of the law to win a verdict for their clients. In modern criminal cases inadequate counsel is grounds for a new trial. In modern courts defendants need not even testify. As one lawyer famously remarked, 95 percent of his clients "are guilty as hell." The Athenians would never have tolerated a system in which so many culpable offenders escape justice. In our liberal society, guarding the individual is paramount. My students invariably agree that it is far better to let 99 murderers walk free than to execute a single innocent man. The Athenians did not agree. The community's safety came before any individual's.

An Athenian litigant's task was to convince the dicasts of the merits of his case. To that end, speakers had the clerk recite laws which in their view were relevant and which they interpreted. They also discuss the circumstances of the case (their side of the story), and adduce in support various kinds of arguments, for example from likelihood (*eikos*). They discuss the past history of the litigation if any, and the long-term relations between the parties. They also play on the dicasts' human sympathies. In particular, inheritance cases frequently hinged on discrepancies between Athenian laws that fixed the order of precedence for heirs, and natural human emotions within families, such as friendship or enmity toward the deceased, with which dicasts might sympathize (esp. Hardcastle 1980). While much of this material is consistent with what Rhodes (2004) calls "the larger story" and Lanni (1997) "the context of the dispute," in fact the litigants' general aim is to embed their immediate disputes within a wider social frame which they proceed to construct.

As Lanni (2005) says, even if extraneous material was formally prohibited in the *dikasteria*, any such prohibition "appears to have had no effect." I hope to argue elsewhere that for many types of charges, there were no legal restrictions. Stricter rules seem to have applied in the Areopagos and other homicide courts, for reasons I shall consider elsewhere, and in the maritime courts as Lanni describes. Therefore, in the following pages I discuss only cases heard by the *dikasteria*.

In his 2004 essay, Rhodes quickly surveys all the orators with these issues in mind. Here I limit myself to Lysias, but in somewhat greater detail. First, in 12.38–9, which in part I have already quoted, Lysias mentions how frequently litigants go outside the immediate dispute to discuss extraneous matters such as distinguished military service on land or at sea. Rather than objecting to this, however, he tells the dicasts they should ask the defendant Eratosthenes about these matters. "You must insist that he show you where they have killed as many of the enemy as they have citizens, or where they have captured as many ships as they have betrayed" (trans. Todd). Hoping simultaneously to exploit the prejudice originally directed against elite citizens who ignore legal issues and to ignore those issues himself, Lysias 9 begins:

> What on earth did my opponents have in mind when they ignored the point at issue and sought to defame my character? Are they unaware that they are supposed to keep to the point? Or do they recognize this, but devote more attention to other matters than they should, thinking you will not notice? . . . I had expected, gentlemen of the jury, that I would face trial on the basis of the indictment and not of my character. However, since my opponents are defaming me, I am forced to make my defense on the basis of all these topics. (trans. Todd)

Just so, the speaker begins by discussing the *apographe* (list of property to be confiscated) and then remarks:

> You have learned how my name was handed over and I was fined, but you need to know not simply the reason for the indictment but also the pretext for their hostility. Before their hostility developed, I was a friend of Sostratos, because I knew that he had been prominent in public life. Even while I was becoming well known through his influence, I did not take vengeance on an enemy or confer benefits on a friend. During his lifetime, I necessarily took no part in public affairs because of my age, and after he died, I did not hurt any of my accusers in word or action. Indeed, I could recount events showing how I should much more justly receive benefits than suffer harm from my opponents. (trans. Todd)

The speaker expatiates on the wider issue of his personal character in Athenian society. Although he rightly says that these topics were not necessarily relevant to the charge, their inclusion shows their relevance to the community of dicasts.

Rhodes himself (2004: 138) calls attention to Lysias 14 (*Against Alkibiades I*) on a charge of desertion, the bulk of which deals with matters entirely extraneous to the charge, in particular the behavior of this Alkibiades' famous ancestor. "Since you allow defendants to recount their own virtues and their forebears' benefactions, it is reasonable that you should also listen to the accusers, if they reveal that the defendants have done many wrongs against you and their forebears have been responsible for many evils" (14.24, trans. Rhodes). Community service is the important point. In

Lysias' fragmentary speech *Against Hippotherses* (F 7 Carey), a speaker asks the dicasts "to give whatever verdict you choose as to which of the [litigants] behaves better toward your city."

What remains of Lysias 21 (*On a Charge of Taking Bribes*) consists almost entirely of a recitation of the speaker's services to Athens. Rhodes speculates and could well be right that this was part of an argument, that after "such an exceptional record of public service ... he is not likely to have used a public position to enrich himself." In fact, the speaker has asked the dicasts to view him from the extra-judicial perspectives of the community he claims he has served. The speaker in Lysias 25.12 says that he had been generous to the city so that he would fare better if he ever had to appear in court.

Lysias 21.12 was written against a charge of accepting bribes:

> It is not so much the prospect of losing my property that concerns me, but I would not be able to endure the insult. Nor could I put up with those who avoid their liturgies [public service], if the money spent on you wins me no gratitude, and their decision to spend none of their resources on you is thus regarded as sensible. If you accept my argument, you will be voting for what is just and choosing what is beneficial to yourselves. (trans. Todd)

Lysias' lengthy speech 12 (*Against Eratosthenes*), which Rhodes (2004: 140) rightly calls "all ... reasonably relevant," is directed against a member of the Thirty who wanted to remain in Athens after they had been suppressed. Lysias rehearses in detail Eratosthenes' involvement with Athenian oligarchic activities and crimes, in pages that have become prime sources for Athenian history between 411 and 404. Passage after passage details history sometimes only tangential to Eratosthenes, but implicating him in the wider political crises of the period and showing him to be a wicked citizen. These pages are entirely relevant to the issue of whether the community should allow this person to remain in the city.

On Lysias's second long speech 13 (*Against Agoratos*), Rhodes (2004: 140) writes:

> the passages claiming that Agoratus' victims were good men but Agoratus and his family were bad (62–9), and that it can neither be true nor have been accepted as true by the Thirty that in 411–410 Agoratus had killed Phrynichus and had been rewarded with citizenship on the restoration of the democracy (70–6), may be regarded as straying too far from the accusation that Agoratus was responsible for the death of one of the Thirty's victims; but the rest of the speech, though much of it is not concerned with that particular charge, is concerned with Agoratus' attempts to manoeuvre between the democrats and the oligarchs in 405–403, and is acceptably relevant if the formal charge is regarded as a sample charge against a man who is essentially accused of involvement in the misdeeds of the Thirty.

Beyond "contexts" and "larger stories," many forensic speeches range well outside the immediate issue in dispute, especially to address community concerns including litigants' personal qualities and their benefit or harm to Athens. Prosecutors commonly interpret private criminal actions as crimes against the polis, and the prosecution of private offenses as helping the community. Demosthenes calls "every deed of violence a public offense" (21.44–5). The dicasts were interested to hear whether a litigant was worth voting for. Was he a good democrat? Had he served the polis?

Did he have an innocent family that would suffer from a harsh sentence? Defendants were judged according to the law but also quite consciously in the commonsense light of the community in which all Athenians shared.

As we have seen, as a point of rhetorical strategy some litigants contrast such arguments with strict enforcement of the law. Some complain that when their opponents are losing on the merits of the case, they recite their personal contributions to Athens. A client of Antiphon remarks, "neither should a man's good deeds save him from conviction if guilty, nor his evil deeds, apart from the charge in the indictment, convict him if innocent" (5.11; cf. 6.11). The speaker of [Demosthenes] 25.76 states that those who "take refuge" in personal appeals do so when it is clear that in court they are losing on the merits of the case.

Other speakers put a more positive spin on citations of wider civic status. At the same time that he complains that prosecutors too often make irrelevant accusations, Hypereides has Lykophron remark in his defense that a judicial verdict should be based on a man's whole life, and then proceed to give an account of his entire career (Hypereides 1.8–11; 14–18). Just before begging the judges not to listen to irrelevancies (1.176), Aischines (1.152–3) paraphrases with approval a passage from Euripides' *Phoenix* (F 812 Nauck):

> Examine the sentiments, fellow citizens, which the poet expresses. He says that before now he has been made a judge of many cases, as you today are dicasts, and he says that he makes his decisions not from what the witnesses say, but from the habits and associations of the accused. He looks at this, how the man who is on trial conducts his daily life, and in what manner he administers his own house, believing that in like manner he will administer the affairs of the city also, and he looks to see with whom he likes to associate. And finally he does not hesitate to express the opinion that a man is like those whose company he loves to keep. (trans. Adams (Loeb))

Lykourgos (1.13) stresses the importance of speaking to the charge, and then proceeds to discuss many other points. Are these speakers simply being inconsistent, blind to their own protests against irrelevancies? On the contrary, violating the community's laws raises the question of the defendant's relations with the polis. That wider topic was relevant.

Several scholars have rightly understood the importance of the community in Athenian litigation, but downplay the importance of law. David Cohen states, "the rule of law was inextricably linked to the court's perception of the interests of the demos" (1991: 192). Stephen Todd writes, "our assumption that democracy requires the independence of the judiciary would have made no sense whatever to a citizen of Classical Athens, who would probably have responded that you cannot have a democratic constitution without the lawcourts being controlled by and in the interests of the democracy" (1993: 6). K. J. Dover (1989: 39) remarked,

> the Greeks did not take kindly to the idea that a man of bad character should be acquitted on a technicality or through a deficiency in explicit testimony; on the contrary, they were quite willing to try and to sentence people whose offense was to behave in ways which aroused resentment but could not easily be subsumed under precise legal prohibitions.

> The question to which our own courts address themselves is, "Has the defendant done what he is alleged to have done, or has he not?" and "If he has done it, is it forbidden by law?" An Athenian court seems rather to have asked itself "Given this situation, what treatment of the persons involved in it is most likely to have beneficial consequences for the community?"

Although these and other scholars (Herman 1996: 12–13) rightly stress the court's community concerns, administering the law was also important and for the same reason. Both laws and courts guarded the community: that was the essential point.

Notwithstanding the Athenians' commitment to legal process, their system of adjudication sometimes functioned outside the narrow confines of law. It never functioned outside the concerns of the community. In the Mysteries scandal of 415, following the doubtful testimony of a prisoner, the Athenians

> brought to trial those against whom he had given evidence and all who were secured were put to death. The death sentence was passed on all who managed to escape and a price was put on their heads. In all this it was impossible to say whether those who suffered deserved their punishment or not, but it was quite clear that the rest of the city benefited greatly. (Thuc. 6.60, trans. Warner)

Aischines claimed, "autocracies and oligarchies are administered according to the tempers of their lords, but democracies according to the established laws ... In a democracy the laws guard the person of the citizen and the government of the polis" (1.4–6). This claim, we now see, is less than compelling. Demosthenes (21.224) more rightly remarks:

> Where is the strength of the laws? If one of you is wronged and cries aloud will the laws run up and stand at his side to assist him? No. They are only writings and could not do this. Wherein then lies their power? In yourselves, if only you support them and make them all-powerful to help whoever needs them. So the laws are strong through you and you through the laws. (trans. Vince (Loeb), adapted)

In administering the law, Athens' people's courts could sometimes be as emotional as Aischines' oligarchs; but harshness was dictated by the greater needs of the community. Legal verdicts were shaped by an ever-shifting blend of legalism, a broader sense of community justice, and the interests of Athens.

Even Sokrates endorsed the greater claim of the polis and at the cost of his own life, refusing to escape the death sentence of a dikastic court. In *Crito* 51A–C, Plato's "Laws" say to him,

> Are you too wise to realize that your fatherland is more to be honored ... than your mother, father, and other ancestors? ... You must persuade your fatherland or do what it commands, and endure in silence what it orders you to endure, whether you are beaten or bound, whether you are led into war to be wounded or killed ... for there justice lies.

Once a democratic majority had made its decision, the community most often united behind it. Thucydides often records disputes in the Assembly. Once decisions are reached, we rarely hear of further dissention. In a court of perhaps 500 dicasts, Sokrates was condemned by 30 votes. At the second, penalty stage of his trial, a somewhat greater majority voted to execute him. This discrepancy has often been considered a sign of the demos' irresponsibility: some dicasts who voted to acquit Sokrates then voted to execute him. Yet once the community had decided that Sokrates was guilty, it was reasonable for some of those who had thought him innocent to accept the majority judgment and vote to have him killed. In the speech that Plato writes for him, Sokrates' principal point is the benefits he believes he has conferred upon his city. Straying far from the charge of impiety, he details many of these benefits. He was charged with not believing in the city's gods and in corrupting the young: offenses against the community. As I have noted, behind these charges lay the murderous terror that some of his students had visited upon Athens. The dicasts decided that he had harmed the city. In Athens' courtrooms as elsewhere, the welfare of the community was paramount.

# Acknowledgment

I am grateful to Jon Everett, Michael Gagarin, and Peter Rhodes for comments on this chapter.

# Further reading

## On the law in classical Athens

Christ, M. R. (1998) *The litigious Athenian* (Baltimore: Johns Hopkins University Press)
Gagarin, M., & D. Cohen (eds) (2005) *Cambridge companion to Greek law* (Cambridge: Cambridge University Press)
MacDowell, D. M. (1978) *The law in classical Athens* (London: Thames & Hudson) (Aspects of Greek and Roman life) – Briefer than Todd (1993), but still useful

## On rhetoric

Yunis, H. (1996) *Taming democracy: models of political rhetoric in classical Athens* (Ithaca NY: Cornell University Press)
Worthington, I. (ed.) (1994) *Persuasion: Greek rhetoric in action* (London: Routledge) – An excellent introduction; includes a useful selection of essays

## Translations

A series of new translations of the Attic orators is being published by the University of Texas Press, under the general editorship of Michael Gagarin

# Bibliography

Allen, D. S. (2000) *The world of Prometheus: the politics of punishing in democratic Athens* (Princeton: Princeton University Press)

Bers, V. (1985) "Dikastic thorubos" in: Cartledge, P., & F. D. Harvey (eds) (1985) *Crux: essays presented to G. E. M. de Ste. Croix on his 75th birthday* (First issued as *History of political thought* 6.1–2 (1985) Exeter: Imprint Academic) (London: Duckworth) 1–15

Cohen, D. J. (1991) *Law, sexuality, and society: the enforcement of morals in classical Athens* (Cambridge: Cambridge University Press)

Cohen, D. J. (1995) *Law, violence and community in classical Athens* (Cambridge: Cambridge University Press) (Key Themes in Ancient History)

Dover, K. J. (1989) *Greek homosexuality* (updated and with a new postscript) (Cambridge MA: Harvard University Press)

Hansen, M. H. (1979) "How often did the Athenian dicasteria meet?" in: *GRBS* 20: 243–6

Hansen, M. H. (1995) *The trial of Sokrates: from the Athenian point of view* (Copenhagen: Det Kongelige Danske Videnskabernes Selskab) (Historisk-filosofiske meddelelser 71) (= Hansen, M. H. (1996) "The trial of Sokrates from the Athenian point of view" in: M. Sakellariou (ed.) (1996) *Colloque international "Démocratie athénienne et culture" organisé par l'Académie d'Athènes en coopération avec l'UNESCO (23, 24 et 25 novembre 1992)* (Athènes: Académie d'Athènes) 137–70)

Hardcastle, M. (1980) "Some non-legal arguments in Athenian inheritance cases" in: *Prudentia* 12: 11–22

Harris, E. M. (1994) "Law and oratory" in: Worthington, I. (ed.) *Persuasion: Greek rhetoric in action* (London: Routlege) 130–50

Herman, G. (1996) "Ancient Athens and the values of Mediterranean society" in: *Mediterranean Historical Review* 11: 5–36

Lanni, A. M. (1997) "Spectator sport or serious politics? *hoi periestēkotes* and the Athenian lawcourts" in: *JHS* 117: 183–9

Lanni, A. M. (2005) "Relevance in Athenian courts" in: Gagarin, M., & D. Cohen (eds) (2005) *Cambridge companion to Greek law* (Cambridge: Cambridge University Press)

Osborne, R. (1985) "Law in action in classical Athens" in: *JHS* 105: 40–58

Rhodes, P. J. (2004) "Keeping to the point" in: Harris, E. M., & L. Rubinstein (eds) (2004) *The law and the courts in ancient Greece* (London: Duckworth) 137–58

Rubinstein, L. (2000) *Litigation and cooperation: supporting speakers in the courts of classical Athens* (Stuttgart: Steiner) (*Historia* Einzelschriften 147)

Todd, S. C. (1993) *The shape of Athenian law* (Oxford: Clarendon)

Weber, M. (1972) *Wirtschaft und Gesellschaft: Grundriß der verstehenden Soziologie* ("5., revidierte Auflage, von Johannes Winckelmann") (Tübingen: Mohr)

Whitehead, D. (1983) "Competitive outlay and community profit: *philotimia* in classical Athens" in: *Classica et Mediaevalia* 34: 55–74

CHAPTER TWENTY-ONE

# The Organization of Knowledge

*Susan Prince*

## 1   Introduction

By the end of the Persian Wars in 478, Greeks from the east (Asia Minor, especially Miletos, Ephesos, and Kolophon) and the west (southern Italy, especially Kroton and Elea) had laid important foundations for the intellectual achievements in philosophy and science that were to become one of the Greeks' lasting contributions to human culture. But Athens, the eventual home of the most important thinkers of the classical period – Sokrates, Plato, and Aristotle – and the spawning ground for all the major philosophical schools and movements that continued beyond the classical period, was not yet an important intellectual center, nor had "knowledge" been articulated into fields anything like the array Aristotle and his school, the Lyceum (*Lykeion*), would have discerned by the time of Aristotle's death in 322. Although the development of knowledge continued throughout the Greek world in the classical period, and the famous individuals who are remembered as Pre-Socratics, Sophists, ethnographers, doctors, and mathematicians tended still to hail from cities other than Athens and to travel widely, it was in classical Athens, as far as we can tell from the evidence that we have, that intellectual activity developed toward a conception of knowledge in general. From various stimuli in the democracy arose the Sophistic movement, the Socratic movement, the Platonic Academy, and the Lyceum of Aristotle, whose writings communicate the comprehensive and structured overview of "knowledge" that rates as one of the most impressive achievements of the Greeks.

Athens' importance in this development was surely the result of its political and economic power in the so-called Periklean period: indeed, Perikles himself is portrayed as a personal devotee of new learning and an eager associate of the leading contemporary intellectuals. The thinkers who tended to gather in Athens from about the middle of the fifth century represent, from all appearances, both those interested in exchanging theories and views for their own sake and those attracted to the financial benefits of promulgating their knowledge in the democracy, among relatively wealthy individuals who themselves stood to gain socially and politically from the skills and clout arising from intellectual education. Yet, for all the historical credibility that an Athenocentric picture of the development of classical knowledge bears, we must remain mindful of the Athenocentrism of our sources, which, for the pre-Platonic period (to about 390), are largely Plato's dialogues, Aristotle's brilliant but self-centered histories of previous thought, and scholarly exegeses within the traditions of the Peripatetics, as Aristotle's followers were called. Thinkers who could not be usefully imagined by Plato in discussion with Sokrates (with or without historical accuracy), or who did not fit conveniently into Aristotle's histories of his predecessors, are unlikely to have left much trace in the historical record, and those who did meet these criteria were submitted to the filtering that these criteria brought along. The more directly historical reports of Aristotle's colleagues in the Peripatos, such as Eudemos on astronomy and mathematics, have by and large not survived, although we have, by chance, a history of medicine by Menon (late fourth century) partially preserved on papyrus. Outside the philosophical literature, we have good evidence for a general intellectual upheaval in Athens in the tragedies of Euripides, the comedies of Aristophanes, and the *History* of Thucydides, and the Athenian provenance of this material leaves us with a circular problem: was this literature produced in Athens because Athens was special, or does Athens appear to be special because this literature happens to survive? Although a final answer remains elusive, the traditional assumption has been that Athens was indeed the center of intellectual progress in the classical period, and remained the center until Alexandria took its place in the course of the Hellenistic period (but see Thomas 2000: 10–12, with further bibliography, for arguments against excessive Athenocentrism).

In this chapter I will describe, in four categories, the "Pre-Socratic" intellectual landscape at the beginning of the classical period, then proceed to a brief chronological account of the "Sophistic" developments of Periklean Athens, the intellectual response to Sokrates' execution in 399 (as well as, perhaps, the crises of the Peloponnesian Wars and the oligarchic revolutions of 411 and 404), and the basic approaches of the major schools that emerged from the Sophistic and Socratic movements through the first three-quarters of the fourth century. I will emphasize fields of inquiry and the methods and assumptions that direct the inquiries as well as the individuals whose names have been attached to these inquiries. Further detail on both the knowledge and the knowers is readily available in a number of recently published general reference works on ancient Greek philosophy and thought as well as more specialized studies.

## 2 Greek Knowledge in 478

Greek knowledge, originally called *sophia* or "wisdom," was the domain of poets – traditionally named as Homer, Hesiod, and the legendary figures of Orpheus and Musaios – and sages – who traditionally number seven, though the exact names vary from list to list – until a group of thinkers in sixth-century Miletos developed universalizing, naturalizing models of the world, or *kosmos*, its constitution, origins, and operation: these thinkers, connected with Thales, are identified by Aristotle (*Metaphysics* 1.3–10) and his heirs as the first Greek philosophers, also called *physikoi* or "physicists" since their field of inquiry was the physical world. The old knowledge embedded in the pre-philosophical, pre-scientific expertise of the poet and the sage was surely broader than cosmology, covering, at least in a practical aspect, most of the fields of knowledge that would become differentiated over the philosophical and scientific period: the nature of the divine and its interactions with humans (Hesiod's *Theogony*, and presupposed by the myths that function in our earliest literature as the media for saying anything at all), justice on a corporate level (Homer's *Iliad*) and on the scale of human morality (*Iliad*, Homer's *Odyssey*, Hesiod's *Works and Days*), geography and ethnography (in the Homeric catalogue of ships, *Iliad* 2.484–877), implicit arts of language and tactics of persuasion (*passim* in the four great epic poems), the physiology of humans, animals, and plants (to be inferred from Homeric narrative and similes), as well as the origin and nature of the physical kosmos, including astronomy, meteorology and weather signs (*Theogony* and *Works and Days*, with references in the *Iliad* and *Odyssey*).

In distinction from what should be called philosophical or scientific knowledge, though, this early wisdom rested on the authority of tradition, divine inspiration, and respected individual men. Insofar as it depended on a narrative of divine acts to explain phenomena or social practices, it was arbitrary, unfit for generalization, unverifiable, and justifiable only circularly, through its own modes of myth or divine will. Its relationship to repeatable human experience and observation was, however, probably closer to empiricism, valued highly in later science, than were the highly speculative practices in early philosophy and science, which were based on reason, analogy, and symmetry sooner than perception. Indeed, the practical orientation of information preserved in Homer and anecdotes about the seven sages suggests that pre-philosophical knowledge had a tighter connection to experience than most of Greek knowledge in its abstracted, generalized, justified guises. Nor, of course, did this "pre-philosophical" knowledge perish in the philosophical period, but survived, probably with a high level of continuity right through antiquity, as the main mode of popular, sub-literate, non-elite belief and thought.

At the end of the Persian Wars the philosophical turn, so to speak, was about a century underway. (Laks 2005 responds to recent proposals that Greek "philosophy" began with Plato.) Although the precise chronology of the late archaic thinkers is obscure, as are their communications and interrelations, at least four self-conscious traditions of "knowledge" were in play in 478, differentiated partly by subject matter but also, importantly, by epistemological attitude. These traditions included, in addition to Milesian cosmology and natural philosophy, the mathematical and proto-logical approach of the Pythagoreans, the skeptical and argumentative approach that culminated in the Eleatics, and a tradition based in the rationalization of traditional myth that would give rise to history.

## Science of the Milesians

The three major cosmologists from Miletos, Thales, Anaximandros, and Anaximenes, by 478 all dead for fifty years or more (Anaximenes, the youngest, is traditionally said to have been active 546–525), had set the stage for further physical and cosmological inquiries. Their views may have been confronted by Herakleitos of Ephesos (traditional period of activity c. 500) and Parmenides of Elea (traditional period of activity

c. the 69th Olympiad, 504–501), who will feature more prominently below, but were not significantly developed by any thinker known by name until the mid-fifth century, at the hands of Anaxagoras of Klazomenai (c. 500–428) and Empedokles of Akragas (c. 492–432).

Thales, the oldest of the Milesians (mature around 585, when he is said to have predicted an eclipse) and probably the teacher of the other two, had posited that the world came to be out of water and was still supported by water: since by Aristotle's time there was no trace or record of a written work agreed to have been authored by Thales, we depend ultimately on oral tradition for information about his radical departure from the mythical tradition regarding the origin of the world. It is possible, indeed, to understand his theory as a direct rationalization of myth, since the origin of the world from a mixture and separation of water gods is claimed in Babylonian and Egyptian myth, reflected in the Hebrew Genesis, and implied at *Iliad* 14.201: but Thales understood water as a physical substance (albeit possibly divine) rather than a set of anthropomorphic gods.

Anaximandros next, writing in prose, had proposed that the world is bounded by, and composed of, the *apeiron* or "indefinite," by which he may have meant an undifferentiated substance composed of a pair of opposed qualities – such as the hot and the cold, or the wet and the dry – in an unspecified proportion or mixture: the birth of the world then amounted to the separation of these qualities, perhaps into what would later be recognized as the four basic elements, fire, water, air, and earth. This is one way Aristotle understands Anaximandros' cosmology, operating under the assumption of a law of conservation of matter that took hold in the wake of Parmenides. Alternatively, the evidence supports the interpretation that the indefinite has produced the world of opposites, in a generative act that does not imply a conservation of matter. In several respects Anaximandros appears to have responded to the views of his master Thales: although our sources are especially problematic, this explanation of the material composition of the world seems to extend the views of his predecessor, solving a problem left open by the thesis that the world was created from water. In opposition to Thales, however, Anaximandros claimed that the earth is not supported by water, but floats freely in the *apeiron* by a cosmic symmetry, being caused by nothing to move one way or another. This reasoned refutation of a predecessor was a second key development in the formation of Greek philosophy and science.

Anaximenes, finally, revising Milesian cosmology into the form that was influential in the fifth century, posited air as both the origin, and possibly basic composite, of the world and the body that supported the earth. Anaximenes went further than the other Milesians in naming a process, condensation and rarefaction, by which the differentiated matter of the world came to be from the original air. As with the other Milesians, the persistence of the original stuff in the present constitution of the world is unclear: it could be that differentiated matter, such as fire, water, and earth, really *is* air, under various appearances, or it could be that fire, water, and earth have been generated from air, which is something different. (Stokes 1971: 43–8 shows that the concepts of condensation and rarefaction need not have implied the persistence of the air.) Air was the element most frequently posited as the material of the world by later monists, thinkers who believed there was just one basic stuff that, under various appearances, really constituted the world.

## *Mathematics and mysticism of the Pythagoreans*

The second tradition of knowledge in play in 478 was the more mystical knowledge of the Pythagoreans, followers of the sage Pythagoras of Kroton, who had migrated to southern Italy around 530 from his birthplace in Samos. Pythagoras was leader of a sect based on religious and dietary principles probably connected to the transmigration of souls, and the Pythagoreans seem to have enjoyed leadership in the political life of Kroton. Although many aspects of Pythagorean knowledge differ little from the embedded knowledge of the poets and other sages, the Pythagoreans bequeathed two important ideas to general developments of the classical period. First, they asserted the importance of number, obscure as it is, to the constitution of all that exists: physical bodies, their physical properties (such as straight and bent), the animate world (male and female), and the moral realm (good and bad). Hence they were credited in the classical period with laying foundations for the fields of knowledge that are readily understood as mathematical, especially music, geometry, and astronomy. Second, they understood polar oppositions as the basic modes of phenomenal existence, the way the world appears to humans who perceive it through their sensory faculties rather than their minds. Although all things are number in basic reality, their phenomena consist in members of pairs of opposed states, such as male or female: according to Aristotle (*Metaphysics* 1.5), the ten canonical oppositions were, in addition to the three mentioned above, the limited and unlimited, odd and even, unity and multiplicity, right and left, still and moving, light and dark, square and oblong. Although Aristotle seems to attribute this so-called "Table of Opposites" to Pythagoreans of the classical period, polar thought was characteristic of much early speculation and argument, and the early Pythagoreans, whose insistence on the centrality of number would have given them a ready basis for perceiving fundamental, mutually exclusive oppositions, like that between odd and even, seem good candidates for promoting this mode of thought (Lloyd 1966).

## *Skepticism, argument, and proof: the Eleatics*

The third tradition, overlapping in subject matter with the others, is distinctive for its epistemological attitude: it featured a strong skeptical aspect and an insistence that true knowledge differs from any rival claims, whether the beliefs of the many or the *polymathia* ("much learning") of the traditional poets and sages. Most of the Pre-Socratics, to judge from the fragments (normally referred to by the numbers assigned in Diels-Kranz), were dogmatic and confident in their knowledge. Herakleitos of Ephesos and Parmenides of Elea, mentioned above, were the immediate representatives of this tradition to the early classical period; both may have been still alive in 478, and Plato even represents Parmenides in Athens conversing with a young Sokrates at a date that cannot much precede 450 (*Parmenides*). In their skeptical and polemical bent these figures were both preceded by, and possibly influenced by, the Ionian Xenophanes of Kolophon (mature c. 545), whose writings in a variety of poetic verse forms addressed topics in cosmology and natural philosophy reminiscent of the Milesians, but stand out for their hostility to the anthropomorphic gods of Homer and Hesiod (Diels-Kranz 21 B 11), to anthropomorphism in general (B 14–16), and to humans' ability to know in general (B 18, 34). He said that there is one god supreme in the world, and this figure turns out to resemble the impersonal, natural deity later posited by Plato and especially Aristotle (B 23–6). Xenophanes allegedly left his home at the age of twenty-five and wandered the world for sixty-seven years, and thus he could have made contact with both Herakleitos in the west and Parmenides in the east.

Regardless of the historical connections, these younger figures shared Xenophanes' interest in second-order questions, that is, the problems surrounding how we know what we claim to know. Herakleitos, like Xenophanes, attacked famous wise men of the Greek tradition (e.g., Diels-Kranz 22 B 40, 42, 56, 57) as well as his contemporary conventional thinkers, whom he compared to deaf people (B 34). Writing in short prose aphorisms, Herakleitos most famously claimed the counter-intuitive (and possibly counter-Pythagorean) unity of opposites: that is, he pointed to an underlying identity behind apparent oppositions in the world, such as the way up and the way down. Though the examples of identical opposites mentioned in the fragments vary significantly in the ways they are opposed (for example, alternating phases such as day and night are also said to be the same), it seems that the critical unity of opposites should be thought of as a tension, just as two opposing stress forces are in tension in the constitution of the lyre, or the bow. The world as a whole, according to Herakleitos, is in a constant state of change or flux, and thus its unity might amount to a constant tensional force among elements which itself creates a system, the world. In a more Milesian mode, Herakleitos also claimed that fire was the single basic principle of process in the world. From yet another point of view, it was *Logos* ("Reason") that unified the world: this may have been another way to think of the tension between opposites, which can be understood from an intellectual perspective, but not from the appearances of the senses. It was the *Logos* to which the truly wise man was attuned and to which the multitudes of the people were deaf.

Parmenides, finally, offered a perspective of the world even more counter-intuitive than that of Herakleitos, and his claims about ultimate reality posed the most lasting challenge to thinkers of the classical period, especially the atomists, some of the Sophists, and Plato. Writing, like Xenophanes, in verse which many scholars believe has poetic qualities, and under the instruction of an unnamed goddess, Parmenides used the logic of polar oppositions, especially the jointly exhaustive and mutually exclusive alternatives of "what is" and "what is not," to prove through an extended argument (Diels-Kranz 28 B 8) that the underlying reality of the world is single, unchanging, and indivisible. Even more radically than the Milesians, the Pythagoreans, or Herakleitos, Parmenides posited a fundamental disconnection between the reality that truly exists, which can be discerned and known only by the intellect, and the world of appearances, which can be perceived, albeit falsely, through the senses and believed in through mechanisms of human convention and human language. Thus he described an apparently dualist world, which he represented in his poem as two textually separated parts or "Ways," labeled by modern scholars as the Way of Truth (B 1–8) and the Way of Seeming (B 9–19). (One can also understand the Way of Seeming as the appearance, to humans, of the one world that is accurately described in the Way of Truth.) Consistent with his claim (B 2, 6) that what is must be the same as what can be thought, which must in turn be the same as what can be said (presumably in a purely logical discourse, since ordinary human language is part of the Way of Seeming), the Way of Truth uses logic and argument to trace out the nature of what really is. For the first time in recorded Greek thought, a developed argument usurped all other forms of access to the truth, especially sense experience and ordinary language, to reveal a reality that flew in the face of the conclusions likely from any other method. The role of divine revelation in Parmenides' "knowledge" of the truth remains unclear, but it is clear that the authority Parmenides claims for his conclusions lies in his argument, not with the goddess who helped steer him to the beginning of the correct path. With Parmenides' argument, epistemological questions were privileged as they had never been before. Even if Xenophanes and Herakleitos had been aiming in the same direction, in a certain way Parmenides' poem first enabled a clear distinction between natural science and philosophy.

## *The rationalization of myth*

The fourth tradition of knowledge inherited by the Greeks of the classical period was a rationalizing approach to the traditional "knowledge" of human history, ethnography, and geography that had been the subject matter, we assume, for an originally vast amount of oral epic poetry, including local epics (Fowler 1996). Although this tradition is not part of Greek philosophy, it is a critical tradition of Greek knowledge. On the one hand, it shares with Greek philosophy and natural science an effort of the human mind to submit inherited "truth" to external, generalized standards such as consistency, non-contradiction, and correspondence with the relevant phenomena. On the other hand, it was a practice called in many accounts *historia*, or "investigation," the same word used of investigations in natural science that followed strict empirical standards (Thomas 2000).

As city-states developed through the archaic period, local historians endeavored to record continuous genealogies of leading families that would be chronologically plausible, positing the correct number of human generations from the divine paternities to the Trojan War and from the returns of the heroes from Troy down to the present day, and geo-politically authoritative, representing geographical proximity, ethnic identity, and political alliance through mythical relationships. Thus we see in Athenian myth, for example, doublings of names (Erechtheus and Erichthonios, two Pandions, among others) that must be the inventions of anonymous rationalizing mythographers trying to fill the missing generations; we see the Trojan War hero Aias of Salamis, who in Homeric poetry bore no relationship to Athens, naturalized as an Athenian hero with a local cult and indeed as forefather of one of the ten tribes of Kleisthenes.

In a different sort of rationalizing turn, we see the mythographer Pherekydes of Syros (active around 544) writing cosmogonic myth in prose rather than transmitting it in verse, as Hesiod and the oral tradition had: this choice indicates self-conscious differentiation from the epic poets, and the fragments, though sparse and difficult, bear comparison with the cosmological fragments of Anaximandros (Schibli 1990), even while Aristotle treated Pherekydes among mythologists rather than Milesians. Other archaic mythographers such as Akousilaos of Argos (who, we are told by Josephus *Contra Apionem* 1–13, "lived before the Persian Wars") made a career of correcting other poets, such as Hesiod's poetic catalogues of human genealogy. Crowning this tradition, finally, and laying the groundwork for further progress in history, ethnography, and geography during the classical period, was Hekataios of

Miletos (active 500–494), who wrote in prose a *Circumnavigation of the World* (a catalogue of information about peoples encountered on a coastal journey around the Mediterranean and Black Seas) and the *Genealogies*, which rationalized traditional myths such as stories in the life of Herakles by claiming that they had been exaggerated or had reinterpreted original metaphors as literal truths. His revision of a map of the world allegedly handed down by his fellow Milesian Anaximandros shows his connection to the Milesian traditions of investigation and improvement on the work of predecessors, and the polemical mention of his name by Herakleitos (22 B 40) shows that he was recognized by his contemporaries as a practitioner of knowledge, even if his version of knowledge is among those Herakleitos scorned.

# 3 Physics, Natural Philosophy, and Logic in the Classical Period

Most pursuits of knowledge in the fifth century were directly continuous with the beginnings laid down in the archaic period, and much of early classical knowledge is classified with late archaic thought under the not always chronologically accurate label "Pre-Socratic." The natural philosophers of the Milesian tradition became more sophisticated, in the wake of Parmenides' argument for absolute monism as well as the growing awareness of past achievement enabled by literacy and communication, and most took issue with some aspect of Parmenides' *Truth*. Pythagorean wisdom was applied in studies of music, astronomy, mathematics, and also the newly emerging field of medicine. Investigation into the human past and into the causes of great events became more self-conscious of method and more critical of "mythical" approaches. The interest in argument, authority, and proof apparent in Parmenides' work was reflected in the new arguments about natural philosophy but also continued by the so-called "Sophists," a group of thinkers with more connections to Greek traditions than many scholarly treatments account for. Although Protagoras, Gorgias, Hippias, and their contemporaries, including Sokrates, may have taken an original impetus from social conditions outside the traditions of formal knowledge, and may have reappropriated the traditional term *sophistes* to designate a new kind of teacher, both their fields of interest – ethics and justice – and their modes of thought are continuous with those of their Greek predecessors. Developments in knowledge also continued outside of Athens, but from about the mid-450s we see major thinkers drawn to Athens from other Greek cities, whether to visit or to settle.

## *Cosmology in the fifth century*

Perhaps the most influential group of fifth-century natural philosophers were the so-called Neo-Eleatics, those who continued Parmenides' project sympathetically, especially two famous pupils, Zenon of Elea and Melissos of Samos. Zenon, portrayed by Plato in *Parmenides* as Parmenides' close associate twenty-five years his junior, was famous for four paradoxes of motion, apparently intended to refute both the possibility of motion or change in itself and also certain physical theories, such as the infinite divisibility of continua of time and space, that were in dispute along with

Parmenidean monism. More generally, Zenon was credited by Plato and Aristotle with an innovative method in argument, to reveal the deficiencies in an interlocutor's case by deriving contradictory consequences from it. Melissos, on the other hand, who served as a general for Samos in 441 and so was probably younger than Zenon, seems to have favored physical theory over logic, but, like Zenon, he was chiefly concerned to defend the Eleatic theory from its many challengers. In addition to Zenon and Melissos, it seems that many minor figures (e.g., the brothers Euthydemos and Dionysodoros in Plato's *Euthydemos* and many figures named or implied in Aristotle's *Topics* and *Sophistical Refutations*) exploited Eleatic arguments without regarding themselves as part of the Eleatic tradition. These men, in some ways the quintessential "sophists," were not physicists at all but experts in logic and argument or "eristic," who framed paradoxes by assimilating language to material entities. Since they seem to delight in the paradoxes for their own sake, and seem to lack good faith for the pursuit of the truth, they are given pejorative portrayals by both Plato and Aristotle.

Most strands of fifth-century physics attempted to challenge Parmenides' argument, as developed by Zenon and Melissos, not always directly, but rather by accounting for its central justified claim against generation and destruction in more plausible ways. Anaxagoras of Klazomenai, the first major thinker known to have settled in Athens (probably about 456/5), where he stayed for about twenty years, and Empedokles of Akragas, who has no known connection to Athens but is said to have traveled widely and to have visited the south Italian city Thourioi, founded in 444/3 as a panhellenic project under Athenian leadership, continued the cosmological speculations of the Milesians in light of the Eleatic argument. Anaxagoras is distinctive for his identification of *nous*, "mind," as the cause of the differentiation of the cosmos. Like his predecessors Anaximenes and Parmenides, he thought the world began from a unified original state. Like Anaximandros, he thought this original state was a kind of undifferentiated stuff, which Anaxagoras clearly thought of as a mixture. Anaxagoras departed from his predecessors in the way he explained the separation: Mind, its mechanism, was not an element in the mixture but a discrete entity. Like Parmenides, he ruled out the possibility of any ultimate origin or destruction of what exists. Rather, he innovated previous theories of composition by claiming that all elements of everything are present within everything: it is only the prominence of the black, for example, that makes a thing appear black: the white is also present. Thus he has affinity also with Herakleitos. In fundamental disagreement with Parmenides, and much of tradition, he held that the phenomena accessible to sense perception are roughly similar to real nature. Anaxagoras is said by Plato (*Phaedo* 97B) to have attracted the interest of the young Sokrates to natural philosophy precisely for his acknowledgement of Mind, presumably because of its anthropomorphic, non-mechanistic, teleological suggestiveness. However, Anaxagoras' concept of Mind seems not to have been anthropomorphic enough for Sokrates, who demanded that natural philosophy should explain why the composition of the world was for the best, that is, that it should be more fully teleological and non-mechanistic (Hankinson 2003). Anaxagoras is reported to have instructed also Euripides the tragic playwright and Perikles, and the latter allegedly supported him through his trial for impiety c. 437/6, after he shocked the Athenians by claiming that the sun was not a divinity but a stone, and helped him to settle in Lampsakos.

Empedokles, too, accepted the Parmenidean thesis that whatever exists must exist without ultimate origin or destruction, but, like Anaxagoras, he recognized a multiplicity of physical elements, in this case just four – earth, air, fire, and water – and two further elements fundamentally different from these which were responsible for their combination and separation – love and strife, again anthropomorphic, though in an emotional rather than intellectual way. Again like Anaxagoras, he defended the reliability of sense perception, even if his theory required more difference between phenomena and reality than the theory of Anaxagoras. Empedokles was positively influenced by Pythagoreanism and advocated some of its mystical claims, especially the transmigration of souls. His interest in the mechanisms of sense perception, which remained influential for the atomists, may have been connected with the physiological interests of Pythagoreans also reflected in early western (Sicilian and south Italian) medicine. His theory of four elements may have contributed to the further development of medical thought in the newer tradition of eastern doctors, the Hippocratics from Kos who emerged in the mid-fifth century. At the same time, Empedokles is picked out by some Hippocratics as an example of the sort of natural philosopher whose *a priori* and non-empirical theories are useless and indeed distorting when accepted into the study of medicine.

Anaxagoras and Empedokles had important followers in the second half of the fifth century, who seem to have continued to include humanizing elements in their views of physics, though as far as we know these successors did little to innovate the boundaries of Greek fields of knowledge. Anaxagoras' pupil Archelaos, apparently Athenian born and, if so, the first known native Athenian philosopher, seems to have followed Anaxagoras in his physics but taken interest also in ethics. Diogenes Laertios claims (2.16) that Archelaos became the teacher of Sokrates after Anaxagoras was forced into exile and that Sokrates' moral interests were inspired by Archelaos' discussion of "laws, the fine and the just." Diogenes of Apollonia (well known by 423, when Aristophanes parodied his views) was probably the most famous late-fifth-century advocate of air as the fundamental principle of everything: it seems to be his views that are reflected in Hippocratic literature (especially *Breaths*), as well as Aristophanes' *Clouds*, and Xenophon's *Memorabilia* 1.4 and 4.7. Diogenes, like Anaxagoras, emphasized a principle of intelligence in the composition of things: the Xenophon passages, whatever their source, imply that the intelligence is divine and provident. In both Aristophanes' *Clouds* and Xenophon's *Memorabilia* we see these views attributed to Sokrates, but Plato's insistence on a very restricted and short-lived Socratic interest in natural philosophy (*Phaedo* 96A–99D) has normally been accepted. The theological argument from design in the *Memorabilia*, if Socratic, need not imply a detailed engagement with natural science.

The clearest and most lasting dissenting response to Parmenidean monism, though, was the atomism of Leukippos (birthplace disputed, dates unknown) and Demokritos of Abdera (c. 460–380 or later), who again accepted Parmenidean requirements of changelessness and indivisibility for what exists, but in place of the one existing thing of Parmenides posited indefinitely many tiny, identical *atoma*, or "uncuttables," which existed in an infinite universe of empty space and formed the phenomenal world through various combinations. Though the atoms were identical to each other in material composition, they varied in shape and size, and their position and orientation also determined variety in the phenomenal world. This physical theory was a basis for astronomy and meteorology, but also for atomist theories of the soul, psychology, and epistemology. The ancient catalogue of Demokritos' writings (preserved by Diogenes Laertios 9.46–9) includes lengthy sections on ethics, mathematics, literature and music, and the practical arts, including divination, medicine, agriculture, painting, and military tactics. These titles are supported by very few fragments, however: only in ethics were some of Demokritos' ideas preserved, and then only in late, aphoristic paraphrases, which resonate suspiciously with Epikurean doctrine of the Hellenistic period in privileging a peace of mind achieved through self-control and self-understanding. Since it is likely that the Epikureans, who saw Demokritos as a predecessor, shaped the epitomizers' choices of texts and the terminology of their paraphrases, we can know little about the connections, if any, Demokritos posited between the atomic theory and these other fields of knowledge. If the connection with ethics is like that we find in Epikureanism, then it is knowledge of the true nature of things that is supposed to free the wise man from false and distracting superstitions. Nor can we attribute to Demokritos certain innovations in developing these other fields: since his lifespan overlaps with the Sophistic and Socratic periods, it is plausible that he was a polymath, engaging in discussion of all the topics of his day. But the conjunction between natural philosophy and ethics apparent not only in Demokritos but in many figures of the fifth century shows the potential shortcomings of our standard view about the history of Greek thought, which assigns natural philosophy to the Pre-Socratics and ethics to the Sophists.

## 4   More Forms of *Historia* in the Fifth Century

Extension of the various Milesian projects in investigation or *historia*, which favored the collection of information over theoretical speculation, and of the Pythagorean project in discovering the numerical bases for things, continued also in the fifth century. Hekataios' ethnography and rationalized genealogy gave direction to the historian of the Persian Wars, Herodotos of Halikarnassos, mature in the mid-440s, when he is said to have performed readings from his work in Athens and, like Empedokles and others, to have participated in the foundation of Thourioi. Herodotos mentions Hekataios polemically and in dissent, but he probably owed to him the starting points in skepticism toward tradition and source, rationalization of myth, correction of Homer, and reliance on autopsy that characterize his historical method. But Herodotos' work also reflects intellectual currents of the time: the discussion of the reasons for the flooding of the Nile (2.20–4), the constitutional debate set among the Persian usurpers (3.80–3), ethnographical theory similar to what appears in the medical writers (book 4 and *passim*; Thomas 2000), and, most relevantly for the outstanding new debate of the mid-fifth century, the dominance of *nomos* or custom over *physis* or nature (3.38; Thomas 2000). This polarity, together with the insight that the human mind can in at least some sense create its own "reality" and/or "truth," is the major marker of the so-called "Sophistic" movement, to which Herodotos is a witness if not also a participant.

Thucydides of Athens (c. 460–c. 400), historian of the Peloponnesian Wars who was inspired in turn by Herodotos, extends in some ways Herodotos' skepticism about evidence and reports (famously scorning the *mythodes* or "myth-like" at 1.22

and omitting all appeals to divine causation), but also, in reducing historical explanation from the multiple options often offered by Herodotos to a single, clear view of human nature organized by his dominating intellect, makes the study of history less an investigation and more a lesson. Thucydides' text reflects sophistic culture in Athens more specifically than Herodotos' does: the debate between Kleon and Diodotos over the fate of the Mytileneans at 3.37–48, with its charge by Kleon that the Athenians are spectators of words, and the dialogue between the empowered Athenians and the powerless Melians at 5.84–114, with its claim by the Athenians that "it is a general and necessary law of nature to rule whatever one can" (5.84), are clear references to sophistic controversy of the late fifth century.

## Hippocratic medicine

The field of medicine, the most obvious case of knowledge that developed outside of Athens, came of age in the middle-to-late fifth century by differentiating itself on the one hand from traditional, often supernatural, modes of cure and on the other hand from natural philosophy. Hippokrates of Kos (probably contemporary with Sokrates) was recognized by the ancients as the founder of rationalist medicine: correspondingly, a collection of over sixty medical treatises in Ionian prose was attributed by the ancients to Hippokrates. We know now that this picture is simplistic in many respects. First, there is good evidence that figures predating Hippokrates, especially Alkmaion of Kroton, probably working in a Pythagorean tradition, also made starts in rationalist medicine (Longrigg 1993). Second, the so-called Hippocratic corpus is too heterogeneous in both outlook and date to have been composed by one thinker: every text in the corpus is subject to well-founded doubts about Hippocratic authorship, though most scholars agree that some part of our corpus was probably written by Hippokrates. Third, a formerly prevailing view that medicine on Kos was practiced under the guidance of the god of healing, Asklepios, until Hippokrates forged the path away from deference to the divine has been undermined by archaeological evidence that the major temple of Asklepios on Kos was not constructed until the fourth century: thus it seems that rationalist medicine may have contributed to divine modes of healing, at least on Kos, rather than effacing them.

Although the connection of the Greek medical tradition to the ancient legend of Hippokrates is problematic, the Hippocratic corpus itself shows that this tradition was working between the last third of the fifth century and the first third of the fourth to become a distinct field of knowledge. Fifth-century treatises are highly polemical in their insistence that medicine is not natural philosophy (*On Ancient Medicine*, esp. 1.15.20) and is not a divine method of "purifications and incantations" (*On the Sacred Disease* 1). Although the writer of *On Ancient Medicine* states that those who try to use philosophical "hypotheses" are following a *new* method (13), and implies that the empirical approach he endorses is the older way, it is clear that the main trend is separation from philosophy. Biological thought was prominent in early, Milesian natural philosophy but was being eliminated from natural philosophy as a consequence of the fifth century's preference for cosmology and logic. Empedokles, the main counter-example to this trend, is indeed named by the Hippocratic writer as the natural philosopher whose main concern, the origin of humans, is really another subject (20). Thus the writer may be defending empirical medicine against new-fangled theories, but the separation from natural philosophy is still in progress: despite the claims of this and other texts, the approach of the Hippocratic doctors was not exactly empirical by modern standards (Lloyd 1979: 126–225). The writer of *On the Sacred Disease* is concerned throughout to show that epilepsy has natural causes (heredity and blockages of air in the veins, 5–10) and must be treated with natural remedies (21).

The body of knowledge controlled by the Hippocratic doctors seems to have been primarily a prognostic knowledge of the progress of diseases, assembled through observation. Although the sixty-odd Hippocratic treatises taken together are some-times thought to constitute a doctor's library, and in their variety to contain the many things a doctor needs to "know" (including how to defend the profession), most scholars understand the clinical histories collected in the seven books of *Epidemics* (not held to be a unified composition) to be typical of the knowledge that defined the Hippocratic doctor. These histories merely record what happened in the course of various ailments, even when the outcome is death. Although the goal of medicine in some treatises is cure and treatment (often entailing "regimen," i.e., diet and exer-cise), and other texts discuss anatomy with the implication that this knowledge is useful for treatment (*On Fractures* and *On Joints*, where bandaging and anatomical manipulation are recommended), it seems that the authority of the doctor derived principally from his ability to predict accurately the course of disease.

# 5   The Sophistic Movement and Sokrates

The varied intellectual activity of the fifth century included a newly vigorous interest in questions of language and rhetoric, especially its connections with human percep-tion and thought and with the ultimate reality that is the object of human perception and thought. The questions were inspired in part by the Eleatic argument, including its confidence in the power of argument to discern and posit fundamental truth, but also gained a new urgency from the increasingly democratic politics in Athens, where justice in the law courts and policies of state in the assembly were determined through verbal debate and ultimately one argument's victory over another. In an environment where success in arguing carried such high stakes, there arose a group of intellectuals offering themselves as professional teachers of virtue, justice, and success. These men, labeled since Plato the "Sophists," were understood in the popular imagination as advocates of positions threatening to traditional wisdom: the view that *nomos* or convention was opposed to *physis* or nature, together with a belief that, when it comes to human practice, "*nomos* is king"; a claim that for every matter there existed two opposing valid arguments, and that through instruction "the weaker" argument could be made "the stronger"; and a belief that popular justice was a virtue of convention rather than nature, whereas real justice was "the interest of the stronger." Fifth-century writers such as Herodotos (e.g., 3.38), Aristophanes (*Clouds*), Thucydides (especially the Mytilenean debate and the Melian dialogue), the Hippocratics (*On Ancient Medicine, On the Art, On the Nature of Man*), and more broadly Euripides (e.g., *Medea, Hippolytus, Helen*, and *passim*) attest to the novelty and popularity of these ideas, often casting them as destructive of civic morality.

Whereas these articulations of current thought tend not to attribute the new ideas to named historical individuals, Plato, writing a generation later (late 390s to the early 340s), devoted his full literary and intellectual genius to showing that his own teacher Sokrates, executed by the Athenians in 399 for "corrupting the youth," had no share in the dangerous nominalism of the Sophists: indeed, whereas they engaged in intellectual activity for purposes of winning – winning money and reputation as well as arguments – Sokrates did so in pure pursuit of the truth. Plato thus provides in his dialogues of Sokrates unique detail about the identities and arguments of the particular men whom Sokrates allegedly made it his mission to oppose and confront (*Apology*, taking issue with *Clouds*, where Sokrates himself was represented as the main "Sophist"). In *Protagoras* he names Prodikos of Keos and Hippias of Elis as the most important Sophists in Athens next to the title character Protagoras of Abdera (c. 490–20); in *Republic* book 1 he attributes a noxiously conventionalist, or possibly nominalist, view of justice to the famous rhetorician Thrasymachos of Chalkedon (at his prime c. 430–400), and in *Gorgias* he portrays Kallikles of Athens, a (possibly fictional) admirer of the well-known title character Gorgias of Leontinoi (c. 485–post 399), defending the claim that the rule of the stronger is natural justice (like the Athenian speakers in Thucydides' Melian dialogue): hence conventional justice would be a fiction set up by agreement among the weak to curb the power of the strong. Xenophon, like Plato an apologist for Sokrates, adds the Athenian Antiphon of Rhamnous to Sokrates' "sophistic" interlocutors – assuming that Antiphon of Rhamnous is identical to Xenophon's Antiphon "the sophist" (Nails 2002: 32–4) – and Antiphon, too, is associated with the power of argument on the one hand and the superiority of "natural" to "conventional" justice on the other.

Not all the famous older "Sophists" were proponents of the dangerous "sophistic" positions, however: Plato and others present Prodikos and Hippias not as skeptics or relativists, but as advocates of positive doctrines. Prodikos was famous for views about linguistic correctness, especially the distinction of apparent synonyms, and he re-interpreted the labors of Herakles allegorically to demonstrate the superiority of virtue to pleasure (Xenophon *Memorabilia* 2.1). Hippias was famous for his confident claims to know and speak about almost every contemporary field of knowledge, from mathematics to genealogy to Homeric literature, and his "self-sufficiency" (*Hippias Maior*) was supposed to extend even to his elaborate wardrobe, which he crafted with his own hands. Hippias was credited with creating lists of Olympic victors that became the basis for historical chronology. In two senses, then, Hippias might be recognized as an important predecessor to Aristotle and the Peripatetics in the "organization of knowledge": first, he collected information and organized it for presentation and application, and, second, he organized a wide range of fields of knowledge into a repertoire of speeches or, perhaps, a curriculum he could offer to others. Prodikos and Hippias are portrayed disdainfully by Plato because they are somehow charlatans, claiming to know what they really do not know or what is not worth knowing. The implication that the "sophist" has a pseudo-knowledge, especially when it is achieved through short cuts and fallacious argument, becomes the leading idea in Aristotle's frequent use of the term (Classen 1981).

Protagoras and Gorgias are the most likely individual candidates for views that laid open the ways to the challenge to objective ethical values that so inflamed

Plato's hostility to the sophists. Protagoras allegedly advocated relativism, and Gorgias apparently disregarded moral issues altogether: by a possible reading of his text *On Not Being*, Gorgias denied that there is any reality at all, let alone an ethical reality. At the same time, it is difficult to attribute the right sort of dangerously relativist or nihilist positions to either without trusting Plato's already biased presentation (Bett 1989). Like Anaxagoras, Protagoras is closely associated by our sources with Perikles (Plutarch *Perikles* 36.3); like Empedokles and Herodotos, he was associated also with the colony at Thourioi: Perikles allegedly invited Protagoras to design its constitution. The leading interest of Protagoras seems indeed to have been politics, namely, the ways individuals who differ in intellectual and affective disposition can cooperate as a unified community. Protagoras' interest in language and argument should, then, probably be subordinated to his interest in political justice and constitution. In Plato's respectful but ultimately hostile portrayals, Protagoras is shown in conversation with Sokrates about the coherence of the position of the professional teacher of excellence, as Protagoras claims to be (*Protagoras*), and the nature of knowledge (*Theaetetus*). In *Protagoras*, the title character defends his profession explicitly against the view that virtue cannot be taught, or indeed formalized in any way that could render it teachable, and implicitly against the view that all citizens who have the capacity for human virtue are equally excellent, and hence have no need for a paid expert in excellence. In the more technical *Theaetetus*, the Protagoras character is made to defend the view that knowledge is perception, that is, that "man is the measure of all things," a subjectivist view of truth that Plato adamantly refutes throughout his corpus. Although this claim by Protagoras may have been made in connection with political "truth," such as deliberations about the best constitution or course of action for the city (Farrar 1988), Plato and his followers tend to assess it in reference to physical truth and sense perception of the physical truth, such as whether the wind is cold or warm.

The analogy between physical truth and political "truth" is, however, not complete, and the type of "relativism" that can be plausibly reconstructed in each case is fundamentally different. Modern discussion of Protagorean and Sophistic relativism, which seeks to understand both the appeal of the Sophistic views and the fervency of the Platonic renunciation, distinguishes three types of relativism that could have been at stake (Kerferd 1997). First, the privileging of "private" truths could imply that no public, or objective, truth exists: this is objective nihilism. Second, the private truth might be not an independent thing, but a phenomenal interface between a perceiver and an object, perhaps really caused by a public object, but caused differently for different recipients: this is a relativism – or, better, subjectivism – of some qualities, or predicates, but not objective nihilism. Third, the real object might really have conflicting qualities within itself, whether because it is always changing (as in the "secret doctrine," associated with Herakleitos, which Plato ascribes to his Protagoras character in *Theaetetus*) or because its complexity, regardless of change, exceeds the capacity of a human thinker to posit completely true propositions about it: this is, then, less a problem about what exists (existence becomes richer than it was on a naïve view) than another type of subjectivism, together with pessimism about human knowledge. In charting out these different "relativisms" it is important, we see, to distinguish between absolute versus relative *existence* or *ontology* on the one hand and objectively versus subjectively true *judgments* on the other. The point Protagoras makes at *Protagoras* 334A–B, that olive oil is bad for plants but good for people, demonstrates, more so than the discussion in *Theaetetus*, a true relativism. This example is not an epistemological matter, but an ontological one: the good quality in the olive oil really is relative to the consumer of the olive oil, regardless who perceives it, or how it tastes. If Protagoras was interested primarily in questions such as the temperature of the wind, his relativism was most probably of the second type, actually a subjectivism. If he was interested primarily in moral and political issues, however, the first and third types of relativism become more plausible, and the fact that he exerted himself over constitutions and teaching renders it unlikely that he was an objective nihilist. The question then arises how physical "facts" and political or ethical "facts" are to be compared. If Plato's strict, homogeneous objectivism is an extreme position, this would explain his vehemence against plausible views of Protagoras and the other Sophists.

Gorgias, said to have come to Athens in 427 on an embassy from Leontinoi, is never called a "sophist" but is associated most commonly with the most damning positions of sophistry. In Plato's *Gorgias* he represents, sometimes indirectly through his associates Polos and Kallikles, the position that the skills of rhetoric supersede all others, and rhetoric is somehow the supreme knowledge: at the same time, rhetoric is amoral, and the teacher of rhetoric is not responsible for whatever immoral applications his pupils might give to his teachings. Three works of Gorgias himself survive in more or less original form, and these can be read as articulations of views that fit well into the picture of the relativist, nihilist sophist. The *Defense of Helen*, written, amid contemporary consensus that Helen of Sparta was responsible for the Trojan War, as an apparent exercise in making the weaker argument the stronger, affirms that language or *logos* is a "great lord" which through its essentially deceptive powers overrules like a drug all competing modes of mental input and thus controls thought and choice. The fictional defense speech of the mythical Palamedes against Odysseus' charge of treason demonstrates the powerful potential of argument from probability in a situation where eyewitness knowledge of the historical facts of the matter is unavailable. The fragmentary work *On Nature*, sometimes called *On Not Being*, which survives in two paraphrases by other thinkers, argues in Eleatic style for the three paradoxical theses that (1) nothing exists; (2) if it (anything) does exist, it cannot be known; (3) if it can be known, it cannot be communicated from one mind to another through speech. On the face of it, this argument seems equivalent to the nihilism that makes the sophist so threatening to traditional wisdom and social order. But the overall structure of the three-pronged argument, which proceeds onward only in the case that each thesis is false, and presents itself overall as a compelling argument for the audience of the words only if the final thesis is false, makes it likely that Gorgias is interested in demonstrating second-order points about how arguments work, not the first-order points that he uses as his content, which might instead count as a ridiculous joke at the expense of Parmenides and his very different assumptions about the power of argument (e.g., Long 1984). Gorgias does in general depend on the existence, knowability, and communicability of truth; at the same time, if one is willing to read excerpts out of context, the stereotypical "sophistic" views associated with rhetoric can be found throughout his work.

# 6   The Socratic Movement and Plato

Radical thinking about conventions and the relationships among language, reality, perception, belief, and convention were associated by Thucydides with the mistakes of the Athenian citizenry in the Peloponnesian Wars and by later thinkers of the fourth century with the similarly great mistakes of the two oligarchic revolutions of 411 and 404–403. After the first restoration of the democracy in 411, Antiphon of Rhamnous was put on trial as a traitor and executed. After the second restoration in 403, a general amnesty prevented similar treatment of the surviving oligarchs, but the trial and execution of Sokrates in 399 on charges of impiety and corruption of the youth were surely motivated by popular anger at the intellectual presumptions of Sokrates, and especially of his associates Kritias of the Thirty Tyrants and Alkibiades, the wily and treacherous Athenian aristocrat (Xenophon *Memorabilia* book 1). Unlike Antiphon or any other figure in the intellectual enlightenment of the late fifth century, however, Sokrates had inspired a wide array of disciples to rise to his defense against the Athenians for their unfair treatment and to continue his intellectual goal of provoking individuals to think for themselves and to understand the bases of their own moral character (Vander Waerdt 1994; Kahn 1996). This goal was continuous with, and probably shared by, the sophistic culture and its response to the moral crises of the late Peloponnesian War (Raaflaub 1989), but, in its pursuit of true knowledge, fundamentally opposed to the stereotypes of "sophistry."

Sokrates wrote nothing himself. He practiced the activity Plato would dub "philosophy" without any institutional basis, but by wandering the streets of Athens and engaging the people he met in conversation. In several passages of the Platonic corpus he even claims that his wisdom consists in not believing that he knows what he does not know (*Apology* 21D); his purpose is above all negative, to test the professed ideas of others to see whether they are real ideas (*Theaetetus* 150B–D). At the same time, the dialogues imply consistently that there does exist a truth to be discovered by those who are able (Vlastos 1991; 1994). The historical Sokrates thus remains no less a conundrum than any other of the pre-Socratic or Sophistic thinkers, and it appears from anecdotes (e.g., Diogenes Laertios 3.35) that the very definition of Socratic philosophy was disputed among his followers after his death. The views and writings of the many Socratic disciples survived into Hellenistic times to become perceived as the heritage of all philosophy in its many varieties, including the hedonism of the Epikureans, supposed to derive from Sokrates through Aristippos; the anti-hedonist moralism of the Cynics and Stoics, supposed to derive from Sokrates through Antisthenes; and the skepticism of the Academics, probably first attributed to Sokrates in Arkesilaos' reading (mid-third century) of certain passages in Plato (Long 1988). But Plato had emerged by the 380s as the dominant spokesman.

Like Sokrates, Plato aimed primarily to convert others to the pursuit of truth for its own sake and for the sake of a just moral and political order: like the conversations of the Sokrates he portrays, his literary dialogues, especially the early ones, were meant not primarily to lay out dogma but to inspire readers to undertake their own reasoned inquiry into the truths of ethics, politics, epistemology, ontology, the soul, and the kosmos. In many ways, however, Plato was far more dogmatic and formal than Sokrates. Certainly by the time he wrote his most lengthy, so-called "middle" dialogues (classified as such primarily on the basis of style), Plato was teaching in the formal setting of the Academy, the educational institution he founded in the 380s, possibly in rivalry with Isokrates, one of many known fourth-century disciples of Gorgias, who remained skeptical about human access to ultimate truth and continued a more sophistic education in argument and rhetoric in a large institution of his own (Eucken 1983). In the Academy, if not in his "exoteric" dialogues intended for publication, Plato seems to have taught substantial doctrine: Aristotle of Stagira, a member of the Academy from his arrival in Athens in about 367 at the age of 17 to Plato's death in 348/7, reports many doctrines of his master with which he variously agrees or takes issue. The major modern debate about Plato concerns the degree to which his surviving dialogues communicate positive doctrine or recommended courses of argument, at one extreme, or remain largely aporetic or even arbitrary stimuli to the reader's personal engagement in philosophy, at the other.

In the early, Socratic dialogues, where he may have been still trying to establish his voice as a Socratic authority, Plato presents Sokrates in conversation with self-proclaimed experts about the meaning of moral concepts such as courage, piety, friendship, or justice. Sokrates offers no positive views of his own, but uses the so-called "elenctic" method – the reduction of any view articulated to a logical contradiction or other absurdity, compared by Aristotle to the tactics of Zenon and the Eleatics – to demonstrate to others the incoherence of their views. In the middle dialogues, Plato attributes to Sokrates not only interrogating dialogue, but also longer expositions of positive doctrine regarding the range of topics that interest him, and especially the ontological theory of forms and a theory of the soul which explains how the forms can be known. In *Phaedo* and *Republic*, especially, Plato has Sokrates lay out the view that the fundamental reality which underlies the changeable, conflicting appearances of the world apparent to our senses is constituted by a set of so-called "forms," or objective entities corresponding to concepts such as beauty, courage, and, ultimately, the good, which are eternal, unchanging, and causative of the various instances of goodness etc. in the physical world. In *Meno* and *Phaedrus*, Plato has Sokrates outline a theory of recollection, whereby a soul can know the forms, which are not accessible through ordinary empirical means, through recollection of an acquaintance with the forms that it enjoyed before it was joined with the body in its present incarnation. The doctrine of recollection has a clear Pythagorean, Orphic, or other mystical background. The theory of forms, in its commitment to the ontological priority of an imperceptible world over a perceptible one, clearly follows the Eleatics, and indeed much of Pre-Socratic natural philosophy.

It remains controversial, within a naïve reading of the Platonic corpus as well as in modern debate, both which forms exist and how exactly they are related to perceptible particulars or individuals. At some places in the corpus it seems that moral concepts are the primary type of form: these are the forms most obviously related to the Socratic project of the early dialogues, as well as the sophistic challenges. Elsewhere it seems that craftsman's artifacts such as beds are the primary model, or mathematical entities such as numbers, or, in the debates of the early Academy as reflected in the late dialogues, the Pseudo-Platonic *Definitions* and Aristotle's *Metaphysics*, biological kinds such as men or horses, or even individuals such as Sokrates. The problematic relationship between the forms and the particulars is examined by Plato himself in *Parmenides*, where the view that a form is the perfect paradigm of the perceptible individuals, but itself also an individual, is apparently refuted in the so-called "Third-Man Argument," whereby we are forced to generate yet another level of entity to explain how the form is the same as the perceptible individuals. Alternatively, if the form is not an individual, then it must be somehow identical to all the perceptible individuals, and in that case one appeals to an unclear relationship of "participation" between forms and perceptible objects.

Plato's late dialogues are often characterized by critique, rejection, or negligence of the theory of forms, as in *Parmenides* and also in *Theaetetus*, where questions about knowledge lead anew to *aporia*. However, since the theory of forms is so variously expressed in various dialogues, and since its clearest expression comes in *Phaedo*, which in its presentation of the famous intellectual biography of Sokrates as well as his death raises acute questions about what Socraticism is and what persists as its true afterlife, this theory may be taken wrongly, even by Aristotle, as the linchpin of Plato's views and should be seen more as a hypothetical answer to the Socratic and sophistic problems to which Plato is not committed in any particular way. The "late" dialogues are, then, less likely to be a true philosophical – or even chronological – grouping than the early dialogues: one finds only various radical conflicts with the relatively unified doctrine of the middle dialogues. Thus *Timaeus* admits a close union between the physical, perceptible world and the forms, which constitute the world on a micro-level. *Statesman* allows fiction and myth as explanation in a more serious way than early dialogues. Arguments are in general more technical and detailed than in the middle dialogues, perhaps reflecting progress in the Academy, and the Sokrates character is simplified further, sometimes becoming a univocal expounder of doctrine, sometimes, as in *Laws*, dropped altogether. The later works, too, tend to separate topics or perhaps fields of knowledge more discretely than before – thus, e.g., *Laws* by contrast with *Republic* is a program for politics rather than a program of politics, moral psychology, education, and ontology all wrapped together. This trend could show a progressing differentiation of disciplines of "political" knowledge from an original unity, at least in Plato's view, of the sophistic problem.

Unlike Aristotle, who would pursue and organize virtually all fields of knowledge opened by the Greeks until his time, the interests of Plato and the Academy remained limited to political and ethical issues and their ontological basis, which turned out to involve mathematics. Natural science remained largely excluded, although Plato shows knowledge of contemporary medical theory in *Timaeus*, and also largely outside the scheme is contemporary research into historical cultural topics such as poetry. Plato certainly knew his Homer, and put forward or criticized theories of interpretation and poetics in many texts (e.g., *Ion*, *Hippias Minor*, *Protagoras*, *Republic*, *Phaedrus*), but, as in the case of names in *Cratylus* or rhetoric in *Phaedrus*, the point seems to be more a demonstration that most claims to knowledge are insufficient without the right philosophical basis than a serious investigation of these fields in their own right. Incidentally, they allow us intimations of an increasingly diversified intellectual approach in the late fifth and early fourth centuries to the humanist fields that most interested the sophists, Sokrates, and Plato.

After Plato's death in 348/7, leadership of the Academy was turned over to the Athenian Speusippos, who unlike the metic Aristotle was qualified to own property. A series of successors largely continued and refined the researches into definition, mathematics, and ethics begun by Plato, until 269, when the Academy under Arke-silaos turned to skepticism in a phase known to historians as the Middle Academy.

# 7  Aristotle and the Lyceum

Aristotle left Athens upon the death of Plato and spent about twelve years in eastern and northern Greece under the patronage of former associates, including the Mace-donian court, where his father had been a physician. When he returned to Athens in 335, he founded his own school, the Lyceum, later nicknamed the "Peripatos" from its teachers' habit of "walking around" (according to ancient explanations), or possibly from the fact that the building had walkways. There he apparently delivered lectures on a wide array of empirical, theoretical, and practical topics, which by some avenue became the basis for his extant works, largely in the form of treatises. Although Aristotle also wrote dialogues, which like Plato's dialogues were meant to attract members of the public to the study of philosophy, these have survived in only a few fragments.

At *Metaphysics* 6.1 (1025b25) Aristotle asserts that science is either practical, productive, or theoretical. This scheme was probably also Academic (suggested in Plato's *Politicus*), and may have underlain the ancient organization of Plato's dia-logues by Thrasyllos (Diogenes Laertios 3.41) (Hadot 1979), but remains at best implicit in Platonic "knowledge." Aristotle's own work, on the other hand, is by and large conscious of its place within this scheme and exemplary of the differences. Practical science includes the directly ethical and political studies, the *Ethics* (in two editions, the *Nicomachean Ethics* and the *Eudemean Ethics*) and the *Politics*, which examine how best to live and how best to run a city. The productive fields study how to create a product rather than engage in a practice, and in this class the *Poetics* and *Rhetoric* survive as reasoned instruction in how to write tragedy (a second book on comedy is lost) and how to write speeches for the law court, the assembly, or display. These works include theories of poetry, psychology, argument, and diction, which held authority into modern times, even if they are not admitted by Aristotle into the properly theoretical studies, identified in *Metaphysics* 6.1 as natural science, math-ematics, and "first philosophy" or theology. Both texts, like Plato's works, show the large volume of activity in these areas in the sophistic period and the first half of the fourth century, even as they supersede all previous work.

The logical works of the so-called Aristotelian *Organon*, which give the "tools" for use in the exercise of a theoretical science, are practical in a different sense from ethics and politics: they are not properly philosophy at all in the Aristotelian scheme, but a tool for use in it. (The Stoics would later make logic one of the three parts of philosophy, alongside physics and ethics.) Thus the *Categories* and *On Interpretation* lay out the necessary foundations of language and the logic of statements or predi-cations. The *Prior Analytics* set forth the valid forms of syllogism or combination of propositions into a basic argument. The *Posterior Analytics* discuss the structure of a science, the identification of first principles through induction, and the practice of the science proper through deduction of further truths from these. The *Topics* and *Sophistical Refutations* examine the nature, devices, and fallacies of dialectic, the verbal strategies whereby one discovers the truths of science. These texts together constitute a field of logic, first articulated by Aristotle and used by Europeans from the middle ages to the early twentieth century, though it was superseded in antiquity by the further developments of the Stoics. They reflect disputes both within the Academy and against the Sophists, descended ultimately in a complex genealogy from the poem of Parmenides.

The theoretical fields, finally, include the scientific study of material and immaterial objects. The latter, which in Platonic fashion are the superior, include mathematics (which Aristotle largely leaves to the Academy) and the study of being or essence, which he demonstrates in the *Metaphysics*, offering a more sophisticated and, according to some scholars, tentative alternative to the Platonic theory of forms. In *Metaphysics* 1 Aristotle casts his project as a continuation of Pre-Socratic wisdom: previous philosophers have always tried to study the first principles but have failed on various counts. Although Aristotle is clearly forcing his predecessors into the straitjacket of his own views, and so probably distorting them, his histories of Pre-Socratic thought in *Metaphysics* book 1 and, similarly, *Physics* book 1 provide some of our oldest and best evidence for these thinkers. The scientific study of material objects, finally, is demonstrated in the works on *Physics, Generation and Corruption*, the *Heavens*, and the many aspects of the natural life sciences, which constitute the largest part of the Aristotelian corpus. Although many particular claims of Aristotelian natural science were being discarded already in the early modern period, his work remains valuable as examples of what we still recognize as a scientific method.

Aristotelian studies, the practical and productive as well as the theoretical, are characterized by an empirical approach to information, and some works, such as the *History of Animals* and the *Politics*, seem to be based on data collected and studied previously at a more basic level. The biological works use many examples gathered in the field by Aristotle or his friends during his travels to the Troad and Lesbos in the 340s; the *Politics* is possibly based on a research project in the Lyceum into 158 different Greek regimes, of which the surviving *Constitution of the Athenians* might be an example.

At the same time, Aristotle's science is shaped by a number of general theories that Aristotle, surely without intent, projects onto his data. One famous example is his model of the hylomorphic compound, central to his ontology, which analyzes all particular things as unities of a form, or immaterial object of thought or definition, with particular masses of matter. This hylomorphic model is, then, the basis for analyzing virtually everything, including the governance of a household, where the husband is like the form and the wife like the matter, or, similarly, procreation, in which the male seed or form is implanted into the female environment where it becomes instantiated in a particular bit of matter. By contrast with the empiricist Hippocratic doctors, who recognized a union of female seed with male, Aristotle appears to use an *a priori* model, as misleadingly "philosophical" as the cosmological speculations from which the Hippocratics tried to distance themselves. Many other Aristotelian concepts, such as the theory of four causes and the distinction between potential and actuality, pervade and shape his perceptions.

Both during Aristotle's lifetime and after his death in 322, other members of the Lyceum applied and extended his thought, largely without significant new direction. Aristotle's immediate successor Theophrastos worked and wrote in all areas that had interested Aristotle. Two lengthy botanical treatises survive, *Enquiry into Plants* in nine books and *Causes of Plants* in six books (a seventh may be lost and the extant *On Odors* may be the eighth), as well as a number of shorter treatises (including *Metaphysics, On Fire, On Stones*). More than a dozen further Peripatetics, active from the late fourth century to the mid-second, left enough fragments and titles to be edited in the edition of Wehrli (1944–59; republished [2]1967–78), which is gradually being replaced by new editions under the leadership of Fortenbaugh (2000–). From what we can tell, their work was largely oriented to the collection and analysis of information within the fields defined by Aristotle, though Straton, successor to Theophrastos as head of the school, stands out for his innovations in physics.

# 8 Greek Knowledge in 323

At the death of Alexander in 323, traditionally the end of the classical period, Greek knowledge lay mainly in the custody of the Academy and Lyceum, which had taken a range of stimuli from Sokrates, the Sophists, and their Pre-Socratic predecessors. The rhetorical school of Isokrates, which survived right through the period under the leadership of Isokrates himself until his death in 338 at age 98, educated myriads of statesmen and generals into the traditional conventions but did not change the contours of humanist knowledge from their sophistic shape. The schools of the Hellenistic period, yet to be founded in Athens by Epikuros of Samos in about 307/6 and Zenon of Kition in the same decade, would make the personal ethics of happiness more central to their philosophical systems: philosophical activity would be conducted for the sake of ethics, whereas for Plato and Aristotle happiness had been situated to a large extent in the very engagement in philosophical activity. Empirical research into the fields of medicine, astronomy, and literature would continue, with possible links to migrating Peripatetics, in the eventual new center of Greek knowledge, the library of Alexandria.

## Further reading

Several recent handbooks offer chapter-length overviews, with further bibliography, of topics handled here in very brief form:

Barnes, J. (ed.) (1995) *The Cambridge companion to Aristotle* (Cambridge: Cambridge University Press) (Cambridge Companions)

Brunschwig, J., & G. E. R. Lloyd (eds) (2000) *Greek thought: a guide to classical knowledge* (orig. *Le savoir grec: dictionnaire critique* Paris 1996) (Cambridge MA: Belknap Press of Harvard University Press) (Harvard University Press Reference Library)

Furley, D. (ed.) (1999) *From Aristotle to Augustine* (London: Routledge) (Routledge History of Philosophy 2)

Kraut, R. (ed.) (1992) *The Cambridge companion to Plato* (Cambridge: Cambridge University Press) (Cambridge Companions)

Long, A. A. (ed.) (1999) *The Cambridge companion to early Greek philosophy* (Cambridge: Cambridge University Press) (Cambridge Companions to Philosophy)

Lloyd, G. E. R. (ed.) (1978) *Hippocratic Writings* (Harmondsworth: Pelican Books)

Sedley, D. (ed.) (2003) *The Cambridge companion to Greek and Roman philosophy* (Cambridge: Cambridge University Press) (Cambridge Companions to Philosophy)

Shields, C. (ed.) (2003) *The Blackwell guide to ancient philosophy* (Oxford: Blackwell) (Blackwell Philosophy Guides)

Taylor, C. C. W. (ed.) (1997) *From the beginning to Plato* (London: Routledge) (Routledge History of Philosophy 1)

Primary texts can be found in the following editions and translations:

Barnes, J. (1984) *The complete works of Aristotle: the revised Oxford translation*, 2 vols (Princeton: Princeton University Press) (Bollingen Series 71, 2)

Cooper, J. M. (ed.) (1997) *Plato: complete works* (ed., with intro. and notes; associate ed. D. S. Hutchinson) (Indianapolis: Hackett)

Diels, H. (1951) *Die Fragmente der Vorsokratiker*, revised by W. Kranz, 3 vols (Berlin: Weidmann [6]1951–2 with numerous repr.)

Dillon, J., & T. Gergel (eds) (2003) *The Greek sophists* (Harmondsworth: Penguin)

Fortenbaugh, W. W., et al. (eds) (2000–) (Rutgers University Studies in Classical Humanities) – Fragments of the Peripatetics (New Brunswick NJ: Transaction Publishers)

Kirk, G. S., & J. E. Raven (1983) *The Presocratic philosophers: a critical history with a selection of texts* (Cambridge: Cambridge University Press [2]1983)

Wehrli, F. (1967–9) *Die Schule des Aristoteles: Texte und Kommentar*, 10 vols; 2 Suppl. vols (Basel: Schwabe [2]1967–78)

# Bibliography

Bett, R. (1989) "The sophists and relativism" in: *Phronesis* 34: 139–69

Classen, C. J. (1981) "Aristotle's picture of the sophists" in: Kerferd, G. B. (ed.) (1981) *The sophists and their legacy: proceedings of the 4. International Colloquium on Ancient Philosophy; held in cooperation with Projektgruppe Altertumswissenschaften der Thyssen-Stiftung at Bad Homburg, 29. Aug.–1. Sept. 1979* (Wiesbaden: Steiner) 7–24 (*Hermes* Einzelschriften 44)

Eucken, C. (1983) *Isokrates: Seine Positionen in der Auseinandersetzung mit den zeitgenössischen Philosophen* (Berlin: de Gruyter) (Untersuchungen zur antiken Literatur und Geschichte 19)

Farrar, C. (1988) *The origins of democratic thinking: the invention of politics in classical Athens* (Cambridge: Cambridge University Press)

Fowler, R. L. (1996) "Herodotos and his contemporaries" in: *JHS* 116: 62–87

Gill, M. L. & P. Pellegrin (eds) (2006) *A companion to ancient philosophy* (Oxford: Blackwell) (Blackwell Companions to Philosophy)

Guthrie, W. K. C. (1969) *A history of Greek philosophy*, vol. 3: *The fifth-century enlightenment* (Cambridge: Cambridge University Press)

Hadot, P. (1979) "Les divisions des parties de la philosophie dans l'antiquité" in: *Museum Helveticum* 36: 201–23

Hankinson, R. J. (2003) "Philosophy and science" in: Sedley 2003: 271–99

Kahn, C. H. (1996) *Plato and the Socratic dialogue: the philosophical use of a literary form* (Cambridge: Cambridge University Press)

Kerferd, G. B. (1981) *The sophistic movement* (Cambridge: Cambridge University Press)

Kerferd, G. B. (1997) "The sophists" in: Taylor, C. C. W. (ed.) (1997) *From the beginning to Plato* (London: Routledge) 244–70 (Routledge History of Philosophy 1)

Laks, A. (2005) "Remarks on the differentiation of early Greek philosophy" in: Sharples, R. W. (ed.) *Philosophy and the sciences in antiquity* (Aldershot: Ashgate) 8–22

Lloyd, G. E. R. (1966) *Polarity and analogy: two types of argumentation in early Greek thought* (Cambridge: Cambridge University Press; repr. Bristol: Bristol Classical Press 1987)

Lloyd, G. E. R. (1972) "The social background of early Greek science" in: Daiches, D., & A. Thorlby (eds) (1972) *Literature and western civilisation*, vol. 1: *The classical world* (London: Aldus) 381–95; repr. in: Lloyd, G. E. R. (1991) *Methods and problems in Greek science* (Cambridge: Cambridge University Press) 121–40

Lloyd, G. E. R. (1979) *Magic, reason and experience: studies in the origin and development of Greek science* (Cambridge: Cambridge University Press)

Lloyd, G. E. R. (1992) "Democracy, philosophy, and science in ancient Greece" in: Dunn, J. (ed.) (1992) *Democracy: the unfinished journey 500 BC to AD 1993* (Oxford: Oxford University Press) 41–56

Long, A. A. (1984) "Methods of argument in Gorgias' *Palamedes*" in: *He archaia sophistike: the sophistic movement: Praktika tou protou Diethnous Symposiou Philosophias gia ten Archaia Sophistike…ton Sept. tou 1982…Hellenike Philosophike Hetaireia* (Athens: Kardamitsas) 233–41 (Athenaike Philosophike Bibliotheke)

Long, A. A. (1988) "Socrates in Hellenistic philosophy" in: *CQ* 38: 150–11 (repr. in: Long, A. A. (1996) *Stoic studies* (Cambridge: Cambridge University Press) 1–34)

Longrigg, J. (1993) *Greek rational medicine: philosophy and medicine from Alcmaeon to the Alexandrians* (London: Routledge)

Nails, D. (2002) *The people of Plato: a prosopography of Plato and other Socratics* (Indianapolis: Hackett)

Raaflaub, K. A. (1989) "Die Anfänge des politischen Denkens bei den Griechen" in: *Historische Zeitschrift* 248: 1–32

Schiappa, E. (2003) *Protagoras and logos: a study in Greek philosophy and rhetoric* (Columbia SC: University of South Carolina Press [2]2003)

Schibli, H. S. (1990) *Pherekydes of Syros* (Oxford: Clarendon)

Sedley, D. (ed.) (2003) *The Cambridge companion to Greek and Roman philosophy* (Cambridge: Cambridge University Press) (Cambridge Companions to Philosophy)

Stokes, M. C. (1971) *One and many in Presocratic philosophy* (Cambridge MA: Harvard University Press) (Publications of the Center for Hellenic Studies)

Thomas, R. (2000) *Herodotus in context: ethnography, science, and the art of persuasion* (Cambridge: Cambridge University Press)

Vander Waerdt, P. A. (ed.) (1994) *The Socratic movement* (Ithaca NY: Cornell University Press)

Vlastos, G. (1991) *Socrates: ironist and moral philosopher* (Cambridge: Cambridge University Press)

Vlastos, G. (1994) *Socratic studies* (ed. M. Burnyeat) (Cambridge: Cambridge University Press)

CHAPTER TWENTY-TWO

# From Classical to Hellenistic Art

## Steven Lattimore

## 1 Art and Events

In 514, the young Athenian aristocrat Harmodios and his lover Aristogeiton assassinated Hipparchos, brother of the tyrant of Athens (Aristotle *Ath. Pol.* 18–19; Hdt. 6.109, 123; Pausanias 1.8.5; Thuc. 6.54–9). Their intention was to bring down the tyranny; ultimately they did so even though their motives had been personal rather than civic and they themselves were killed by the tyrant's followers. His brother's death caused the tyrant to become more repressive, which led to his expulsion in 510 and a sudden turn toward democracy. Proponents of this new government remembered the martyrs with such gratitude that they gave them the honor of a hero cult. Their shrine in the agora contained an unprecedented monument: statues of the tyrannicides by Antenor, one of very few Archaic artists whose name was remembered by posterity.

In 490, the memory of Harmodios and Aristogeiton inspired the Athenian general Kallimachos to give battle to the Persians at Marathon and die gloriously in a victory commemorated by numerous monuments. It is, however, uncertain whether Kallimachos had seen Antenor's statues, now often thought to have been set up after 490. In that case, they were only briefly on display before being carried away as booty by the Persian invaders of 481–479. When the Athenians reoccupied their ravaged city, replacement of the Tyrannicide Group was a top priority; new statues by Kritios and Nesiotes were installed in 477/6. These bronzes are lost, but their appearance is known from Roman versions; while the concept of intentionally exact Roman "copies" has become suspect, there are reasons to believe that the Tyrannicides were reproduced accurately (Figure 22.1). By the Hellenistic period, Antenor's statues had been returned from Persia for display beside their replacements. The pairs probably looked very much alike; Kritios and Nesiotes may have aimed at replication, possibly using Antenor's master molds. Accordingly, it has been suggested that we have Roman copies from both monuments.

**Figure 22.1** Harmodios and Aristogeiton (The Tyrannicides). Museo Archeologico Nazionale, Naples. © Scala/Art Resource, NY.

By convention, Classical art begins in 480, when the tide turned against the Persian invaders; the destruction debris of pre-Classical Athens helps to clarify the chronology of stylistic change; concomitantly, physical devastation and the elation of victory, accompanied by heightened Greek chauvinism, combined to give the Athenians a dynamic new outlook which at least some other Greeks shared (Pollitt 1972: 15–43). This understanding of the transition from Archaic to Classical art has been challenged by claims that there is more evidence for deep changes c. 500, and that such changes reflect momentum within art itself rather than the overall environment (Carpenter 1973; Hallett 1986). In the context of this debate, Kritios' and Nesiotes' Tyrannicides can be dated just after the Persian War – but are difficult to distinguish from pre-war (perhaps just barely) predecessors.

What did they look like? Facing slightly away from each other (probably), the heroes advanced toward their victim – whose part was played by the spectator. This attention to drama and psychology is Classical. The statues retain their air of menace; I doubt that any classicist can see a photo of the Tyrannicides without feeling a chill. The striding poses, taken from established heroic iconography, are contrasted for Early Classical characterization. Harmodios, winding up for a devastating over-arm blow, displays the impetuousness of youth. More cautiously, Aristogeiton prepares an underarm thrust and uses a cloak to shield himself or his beloved. He is bearded, his hair plain, his musculature less supple than that of beautiful curly-haired Harmodios, whose beard has not yet grown. Both figures, however, display the pronounced articulation of late Archaic art as well as faint Archaic smiles.

## 2   The End of Archaic

Two statues from the Athenian akropolis probably also made just after 479 are more Classical: the Kritios Boy (named for its resemblance to Harmodios), a quietly standing nude youth departing from the *kouros* format by shifting the preponderance of his weight to one leg; the Angelitos Athena, similarly innovative in stance and replacing the elaborately stylized linen *chiton* and mantle of the *kore* with the severe – and naturalistically rendered – woolen *peplos*. Both statues appear to have influenced later sculptors. Another akropolis statue, however, never again displayed after the sack, reminds us of how much was changing shortly before 480: the Euthydikos *kore*, whose dress is traditional but carved with inattentiveness that can only be willful; characterizing the sturdy figure underneath the patterned folds is what interested the artist, and the thrust of the girl's nipples embodies his impatience with Archaic style. The face even more clearly breaks with tradition; the fullness of eyelids and mouth are in reaction against the linearity of such details in earlier sculpture, but the artist cannot have been unaware of the resulting expression, which has given his *kore* the nickname "Pouting Girl." If tumultuous and exhilarating events caused artists to experiment and rebel, to prefer the newest techniques and trends, for Athenians the catalyst may have been not the pan-Hellenic campaign against Xerxes but Marathon or even the establishment of democracy.

Preliminary concentration on Athens seems inevitable. Historical circumstances make Athenian artifacts (including the Athenian Treasury at Delphi, now convincingly dated to the 480s – although its sculpture would seem earlier) invaluable in documenting what must ultimately be regarded as the full Classical revolution, c. 480. Additionally, Athens monopolized red figure vase painting, not the most prestigious medium but the most fully preserved, where unmistakable elements of post-Archaic style appear not only before 480 but before 500. In his Sack of Troy – another monument that may be either before or after 480 – the Kleophrades Painter has dramatized the catastrophe by using Archaic explicit action along with heightened suspense and pathos through Classical latent action and inaction. Kassandra, fully nude, clings for sanctuary to the Palladion; her body contrasts with the stiff, impenetrably draped statue (as though the sculptor of Euthydikos' *kore* had carved her naked and hung her old-fashioned garment next to her). The Ilioupersis in Archaic art had typically highlighted the brutality of the triumphant Greeks, but the Kleophrades Painter depicts the Trojans with new empathy and resourcefulness – derived, some scholars understandably believe, from awareness of the sack of his own city (or, if earlier than 480, that of Miletos, a famous Athenian sorrow?). Whether or not the painting is connected with any specific event, it marks the culmination of this community with the Other. During the fifth century, victory over Troy, Greek atrocities de-emphasized, became a stock analogue, especially in Athens, for triumph over Persia.

# 3   Beyond Athens

Classical Athens, however unique and sometimes hated, was also inclusive and representative of all Greece. In no other Greek city are we so aware of the presence and contributions of Greeks from elsewhere. Additionally, a number of important Athenians were, or at least were reputed to be, of partly non-Athenian (even non-Greek) origins; artists were no exception. By the late Archaic period, Greek sculptors like Antenor, learning from Egypt, began to master the techniques of large-scale bronze casting; the islanders of Aigina were particularly famous for their accomplishments. While Aigina and Athens were by now deadly enemies – indeed, at war in 481 – the signature of a contemporary Aiginetan sculptor was found on the Athenian akropolis; so was a bronze warrior's head assumed to be Aiginetan work of the 480s because of the similarity to marble heads decorating the Temple of Aphaia on Aigina. At this date, it was usually the long-established practice of stone carving that influenced the style of the younger medium. In a wealthier Greece after 480, however, bronze became more commonly used than marble for single statues, and its technical advantages led to more active and complex poses pioneered in metal, then used in stone.

The Aphaia temple may have been built as early as 500 or (as stratigraphy suggests) as late as the 470s. Pedimental decoration was under way when – undoubtedly on the east, probably on the west – the themes of the sculptural program were changed to Trojan wars: on the west the ten-year war, on the east the earlier expedition led by Herakles and the Aiginetan Telamon. The east pediment received its final decoration later than the west and shows a more advanced style, closer to Classical; instances of tired, mannered drapery tend to belong to the west, the more Classical-appearing heads and dynamic poses to the east. The expensive change to Trojan-War themes must have been strongly motivated, and commemoration of victory over Persia – at Salamis the Aiginetans played an even more glorious role than detested Athens – is the most plausible explanation. Many scholars date the replacements to the 480s, but if the east pediment at least is post-war, the anti-Persian theme is still a possibility, presumably adding to a sculptural program originating as anti-Athenian propaganda with aristocratic, anti-democratic emphasis.

The Tomb of the Diver at Poseidonia (Paestum) is another monument dated around 480 – probably slightly later, but here the connection with events is unimportant; while the Greeks of Sicily repelled a Carthaginian invasion around the time the mainland Greeks defeated Xerxes, the Greek cities of Italy were little affected by either barbarian threat. What is instead of interest is the adaptation of a non-Greek practice: the decoration of a tomb's interior with figural scenes of funerary significance. The walls depict an all-male symposium enlivened with musical and amorous rapture. On the underside of the lid, a nude youth dives from a massive masonry platform into a puddle of green water between two schematic trees. The obvious overall parallels are Etruscan tombs depicting banqueting and drinking. The Tomb of Hunting and Fishing at Tarquinia depicts a diver commonly cited as the prototype for the Poseidonia figure – but this is problematic; since some individual elements of the Etruscan painting have parallels in Greek vase painting, so might the diver. Whatever his origins, the Poseidonia diver – isolated, unlike the Etruscan youth – is the most meaningful motif on the Greek tomb and must be the soul plunging into the ocean of oblivion (although other interpretations have been suggested), perhaps from the Pillars of Herakles. The symposiasts have parallels in vase painting, but their figures are defined by areas of color rather than by interior detail, and their faces seem more individualized than those on Attic vases: a true Early Classical touch. Overall, in this single example of fifth-century Greek free (non-ceramic) painting yet discovered, Poseidonian artists display the charm and originality for which their Archaic temples – and those of the West Greeks generally – are admired.

The Temple of Athena built at Poseidonia around 500 is particularly attractive and striking for its integration of Ionic elements into the Doric order. This may further illustrate the open-mindedness exemplified by the Tomb of the Diver; conversely, it may reflect settlers' consciousness that all Greek styles were "theirs" rather than foreign. And the West Greeks came from all regions of the homeland. Most, whatever their origins, built Doric temples, but the large Ionic temples of the 470s at Lokroi and Metapontion have no mainland parallels from the entire Classical era. Even fiercely Dorian Syracuse had an Archaic Ionic temple.

Theron of Akragas, one of several Dorian tyrants in early fifth-century Sicily united by ties of blood or marriage, probably began the immense (over 100 m) Olympieion in the 480s, although some date the start of construction before 500, while others consider it a monument for the victory over the Carthaginians at Himera in 480. This decisive battle, in which Theron played a key role, occasioned other victory temples, and it has been speculated that some of the Olympieion's most unusual features were of Carthaginian origin, also that some workmen were Carthaginian prisoners; meaning and style could have evolved during the long period of intermittent construction. The order was Doric but included many Ionian elements, and the size may have been inspired by the comparably large Ionic temple at Ephesos and the Ionic temple-like Didyma sanctuary. At Akragas, however, there was no peristyle but an ashlar screen wall punctuated with half-columns, and this appears a West Greek idea. Statues, now variously called Giants, Atlantes, or Telamones, served as optical and perhaps physical supports (their exact location has been much debated), an innovative Doric version of Ionian caryatids and probably, like them, alluding to captives – specifically Carthaginians from Himera. The Olympieion was unfinished when Carthage obliterated Akragas, the second city of Sicily, in 406.

# 4   Architectural Developments

The most significant Athenian buildings of the Early Classical period were constructed in their agora, where the increasingly radical democracy decided policies that began to dominate Greek affairs. In purely architectural terms, however, the fifth-century Athenians built no political structure comparable to the enormous circular assembly hall already standing in the agora of West Greek Metapontion. Moreover, there is uncertainty about the nature and even identity of the agora in which the statues by Kritios and Nesiotes were set up; there is a growing consensus that the "Old Agora" of the Peisistratids was not that of Classical Athens, north of the Areopagos. The shift may have coincided with the establishment of the democracy in 508 – but there have also been suggestions that the new agora dates from immediately after Athenian reoccupation (once again: before or after 480?). It is uncertain, however, whether archaeological and stylistic evidence would permit the lower dating of the Royal Stoa, in any case the first Athenian stoa, whose Doric order was appropriated from religious architecture. More clearly of the new era, the *tholos* or roundhouse, where the *prytaneis* carried out their business and were fed at public expense, was constructed in the 460s; its circular plan apparently had a traditional connection with dining going back to Archaic temporary structures. Around the same time, the Athenians built a new stoa, the Stoa Poikile. The paintings that gave this popular building its name (not just "Painted" but "Fancy") have not survived, but an important and influential architectural innovation can be restored: exterior Doric colonnade, Ionic columns in the interior. The Athenian Stoa at Delphi – little more than a display-case for trophies – was long dated just after the Persian War but now appears to have been built around mid-century, for spoils from fellow-Greeks rather than Persians (Walsh 1986). The exterior (and sole) order is Ionic.

The earliest agora, wherever situated, was the original home of Athenian dramatic performances. In the 490s, tragic drama was moved to a new setting, the sanctuary of Dionysos on the south slope of the akropolis, where a theater of sorts was provided by shaping the earth so that large audiences could look down from rudimentary seating onto the actors and chorus in the orchestra. Specialists increasingly believe that this orchestra, and consequently the "auditorium," were rectangular or trapezoidal rather than circular; while this may be true of early theaters around Attika and elsewhere, the Theater of Dionysos probably had a circular orchestra, which would explain the rounded corners of rectilinear designs. Outside Attika, the earliest and most enthusiastic following for drama was among the West Greeks, and Syracuse had one of the first theaters.

It has been remarked that during the Classical period West Greek temples become more "conventional": more alike and more like those of the mainland; the closest match is certainly between the second Temple of Hera at Poseidonia and the contemporary Temple of Zeus at Olympia (470–456). It may well be that influence flowed from the west to the mainland, rather than vice versa. Libon of Elis, architect of the ambitiously large – and beautifully designed – Olympia temple, is otherwise unknown, from a state with no distinctive architectural tradition; he might have received training in the west, or from visiting West Greek architects (Klein 1998: 364–5). By now, lavishly funded West Greeks had replaced Peloponnesians as the dominant athletes at Olympia, and the western cultural presence was correspondingly impressive.

## 5   Sculpture and Painting

The pedimental sculpture from Libon's temple is the best preserved we have and on the east shares a theme with Aischylos' *Oresteia*, presented a year or so before the temple's completion: the line of Pelops. It depicts the suspenseful waiting just before a fatal chariot race (itself the subject of several tragedies). This choice of moment is entirely Early Classical, as are the differentiation and characterization of the figures; Pelops is youthful and confident, Oinomaos in the prime of life and masterful, the seer (perhaps Iamos) aged and worried – anticipating the horrible history of Pelops' descendants which Aischylos would dramatize. In the west pediment, there is explicit action in the Archaic manner, but the graphic details of the centaurs' onslaught against Lapith women are Early Classical. The workshop of the pediments has never been conclusively identified but on the west shows numerous links with Athens (Barron 1984). The same sculptors made the interior metopes, six over each porch depicting the Labors of Herakles with as much psychological subtlety as convincing action; the long-suffering hero ages before our eyes as he (like the Lapiths of the west pediment) battles for civilization. These reliefs did not follow the Canon of Twelve Labors; they established it.

The Labor of the Nemean Lion had been a favorite motif in Archaic art, showcasing virtuosity in depicting physical exertion and ferocity; at Olympia the lion has already succumbed and the hero, still adolescent at the beginning of his toils, stands pensively over it. Around this time, Herakles and the lion were similarly depicted by a vase painter of a school thought to be strongly influenced by free painting; several Olympia metopes have a pictorial look, and Oinomaos' bared teeth may be a borrowing from Polygnotos of Thasos, who introduced this motif to painting and flourished in the 460s. Pausanias describes in detail his ambitious tableaux in the Knidian *lesche* ("clubhouse") at Delphi, the Stoa Poikile, and several other Athenian buildings; he was said to be a sculptor also, but no details survive. Writers record Polygnotos' intimacy with Athens (he was given citizenship) and tell anecdotes, which mainly painters seemed to attract – perhaps because painting was the most prestigious of the arts, clearly ranking higher than architectural sculpture. Prestige makes the influence of painting on monuments such as the Olympia temple all the more plausible – but not inevitable. Vase painting, while not unappreciated, was not formally acknowledged as an art form (or even mentioned) in either Greek or Roman testimonia. Again, this does not mean that the vase painters would immediately have become tame imitators of ascendant free painting. Experiments in figure drawing by the red figure "Pioneers" c. 510 may correspond to the innovations Pliny the Elder (*Naturalis Historia* 35.56) attributes to the contemporary free painter Kimon of Kleonai. But the literary sources supply no free-painting counterpart to the black figure painters of the early fifth century, whose devices for indicating three-dimensional space anticipate Polygnotos by decades. Possibly Polygnotos was the last free painter who could learn from vase painting; clearly he revolutionized his medium. For his epic themes, he used huge casts of characters, deploying them on different levels to suggest space; when we find these features combined in vase paintings, the direct influence of Polygnotos is more than likely.

The Niobid Painter's name vase is the most fascinating such painting. The terrain suggested by multiple ground-lines is schematic but solid enough to support and sometimes partially conceal many figures in a variety of three-dimensional poses. On one side are Apollo and Artemis shooting down the children of Niobe. As with the Olympia pediments, an action scene is juxtaposed with a quieter yet more exciting pendant. Athena, Herakles, and nine armed men wait as though expecting momentous events (Figure 22.2). Anatomical details unique in the Niobid Painter's work

**Figure 22.2** Vase painting of Herakles and other heroes, by the Niobid Painter. Photo: Hervé Lewandowski. © Réunion des Musées Nationaux/Art Resource, NY. Louvre, Paris, France.

suggest that at least some figures were borrowed, and all have a power and presence usually beyond him – calling to mind the fame of Polygnotos for *ethos*, "character." There is no agreement on any identification, but possibly the Niobid Vase reproduces a Polygnotan painting of Theseus, recumbent in the lower center, about to be rescued from the Underworld by Herakles standing above him.

Several statues datable to Polygnotos' time perhaps give us a better idea of his *ethos* than do vase paintings. The bronze charioteer from Delphi survives from a monument commemorating the equestrian victories of a Sicilian tyrant in the 470s. The life-size statue rewards close inspection. The columnar aspect is complicated by torsion toward the right; the intricate variations of the linen tunic above the belt complement the turn and contrast with the heavy folds below. The face is not designed to project one specific emotion but to enable the onlooker to read its expression variably; it can appear triumphant, but also apprehensive.

The most spectacular marble statue of the 470s (as usually dated) also probably depicts a victorious charioteer (Bell 1995) and was discovered in the ruins of Motya, a Carthaginian city in Sicily the Greeks destroyed in 397. Certainly Greek work, the statue may have been recent plunder from Akragas; it has been identified as Theron or, more plausibly, his famed charioteer Nikomachos – but also as the Carthaginian general Hamilcar killed at Himera. The swaggering youth turns sharply left in a pose similar to Angelitos' Athena, and the clinging linen tunic emphasizes the motion while conspicuously modeling genitals and buttocks.

Debates over the Motya youth continue, with due attention to his insistent sexuality. Both statements apply to the bronze Warriors A and B found in the sea near Riace, in

Calabria, at the southern tip of Italy. Hardly an eminent fifth-century sculptor has not been proposed as the maker of one or both. The warriors are probably a pair rather than fragments of a larger group; eliminating some identifications, this would create another intriguing juxtaposition: confrontational Warrior A and Warrior B with milder countenance and more relaxed stance (a forerunner rather than derivation of Polykleitan poses?). Such suggestions as Agamemnon and Menelaos or Tydeus and Amphiaraos are speculative but appropriate. These awe-inspiring statues, combined with awareness of Polygnotan ensembles, suggest how immense is the loss (unless, improbably, the Riace bronzes are remnants) of Onatos' contemporary group; from a major thoroughfare, a visitor to Olympia saw on a semi-circular base the seven Achaian challengers of Hektor (as in Homer *Iliad* Book 7) and across the way Nestor faced them holding the lots. The way Early Classical statues "come to life" parallels the development of drama, specifically the multiplication of individual players to enact the narratives.

# 6   Imperial Athens in the Greek World

The Riace Warriors are sometimes assigned to a monument at Delphi commemorating Marathon: early work of Pheidias. Despite some intriguing evidence, this seems doubtful, and our surest approach to the great Athenian is through his creation of two enormous statues of which descriptions and replicas survive. Some stylistic and iconographic details of these, however, indicate some truth in the ancient tradition that gave Pheidias a major role in supervising the Periklean building program on the akropolis, at least in its initial phase. That began in 450/49, possibly because formal peace with Persia freed the Athenians from a vow not to rebuild desecrated shrines (the historicity of both peace and vow is disputed); peace might have made it easier – if provocative – to use both Athenian and allied funds for the embellishment of an increasingly imperial city.

The Athenian empire began as a voluntary alliance formed against Persia in 478; the allies were Ionians and held their meetings on Delos, their traditional religious center. Their annual contributions to allied defense were kept there under Apollo's protection until 454/3 (some scholars argue for the 460s), when the treasury was moved from the island to Athens, probably to the akropolis and presumably for security against foreign raids. Athens now completely controlled both the finances and other activities of the "League." This changed relationship is symbolized by the statue of Athena Parthenos, dedicated in 438, the centerpiece of the building program and the only component expressly attributed to Pheidias himself. Rather than a cult statue, it was the most costly of votives, fashioned of gold and ivory over a wooden core and standing 11.5 m tall. Small copies show the goddess wearing the aegis over a belted woolen tunic – a format started by the Angelitos Athena (possibly juvenile work of Pheidias) – and equipped, as often before, with a spear, shield, and helmet. Other aspects, however, point toward an additional antecedent. Apollo's cult statue on Delos stood c. 8.0 m, made in the mid-sixth century of wood overlaid with gold. Along with this overall similarity, the iconographic program of the Parthenos makes sufficient references to Apollo's decoration (e.g., Apollo held the three Graces in his right hand, Athena held Nike) to send (like Aischylos' *Eumenides?*) the emphatic message that the power has now passed to Athens (Fehr 1979).

A few years later Pheidias would design an equally immense gold-and-ivory statue of Zeus for the temple already waiting at Olympia; the building for Athena Parthenos, begun in 447, was even larger – hardly by chance. The Parthenon was a temple in name only, since there is no evidence for an altar or cult activity; this may have facilitated innovation. The main architect was Iktinos, of unknown, perhaps non-Athenian origins. His eight-column Doric façade was reminiscent of Archaic Ionic temples, but its broad, low proportions were an attractive novelty. The interior was equally original, showcasing the statue with a colonnade in back as well as along the sides and providing a separate rear chamber with four soaring Ionic columns, possibly topped by the first Corinthian capitals. Exceptionally, all metopes (an all-time high ninety-two) received carved pictorial decoration (the large number of columns reduced their size in relation to the pedimental sculpture, an aesthetic improvement). On the west they depicted an Amazonomachy (also on Athena Parthenos' shield); on the south, Lapiths battling centaurs; on the north, the sack of Troy; on the façade, the Olympians against the Giants. Cumulatively, the metopes celebrate victory over the enemies of civilization, and the dominance of Athena in both pediments above designates Athens as leader of the forces of order.

Still more pictorial decoration was furnished by a continuous frieze of Ionic antecedents uniquely positioned above the interior walls looking outward; again, the intention may have been to surpass spectacularly the Olympia temple with its Doric interior friezes. Viewed through the colonnade (bright paint, standard for Greek sculpture, would have enhanced visibility), it shows a procession almost certainly that of the Panathenaia, although discrepancies from the actual event have caused ceaseless controversy; the ceremony depicted was not so august as to preclude a few decorous flirtations (Younger 1997: 126–32). The assembly of gods on the façade must allude to all the cults of Athens; the juxtaposition of gods and worshippers makes the frieze an enormous votive relief (votive reliefs began their greatest era in the late fifth century, especially in Athens). It has been suggested that the frieze also commemorates Marathon, openly depicted in other sculpted and painted monuments of fifth-century Athens. A more controversial theory is that the frieze represents not the Panathenaic procession but an Athenian legend.

This vast sculptural program has enough stylistic unity to indicate a single supervising artist, of genius. He must be Pheidias, although much of the oversight and perhaps some actual carving would eventually have been left to pupils. The Parthenon figure style is marked by dignified but sensual faces with fleshy cheeks, full lips, and huge round eyes; male torsos with a power that seems to burst from within; robust female forms whose three-dimensionality is accentuated by clinging, spiraling drapery folds that work like chiaroscuro. Drapery also adds balance and variety to compositions already benefiting from smooth and convincing poses. In all these features and others, the sculptures depend on expert observation of reality but just as clearly declare the intention of going beyond nature to recreate it in idealized form.

There is more than a personal style involved; the Parthenon has made the transition (some metopes incompletely) from Early to High Classical, of which it may be called the first and greatest example. Again, there is no unanimity over the reasons for the changes (nor do all scholars acknowledge this transition). It is difficult to believe that the trend away from Early Classical naturalization and individualization toward a generalization and impassiveness that at times almost revive the Archaic spirit came about through some inevitable aesthetic impulse within the company of Greek sculptors or artists more generally. Conversely, there are difficulties in attributing the origins of the High Classical style too exclusively to the Pheidian school and whatever inspiration it derived from the achievements and ideology of Periklean Athens.

High Classical was not limited to Athens. While some forerunners among the Olympia sculptures could be due to the presence of Athenian sculptors, Polykleitos of Argos was a contemporary of Pheidias and a paradigmatically High Classical artist. Replicas of his Doryphoros (spear bearer) of the 440s combine with various testimonia to characterize him as a more formal artist than Pheidias, especially concerned with perfecting balanced poses and ideal proportions for the male body (the proportions of his Doryphoros are so convincingly athletic that the statue was recently used by athletic authorities to determine appropriate physical proportions for discouraging the use of steroids). Very influentially, the Doryphoros places a relaxed right arm over the supporting leg and a flexed left arm over the remarkably unburdened free leg; this chiastic ("X-shaped") rhythm is popular in contemporary Greek prose. This timeless, impassive statue has been seen as an updated *kouros*. Both the High Classical style and Polykleitos, however, are too complex to explain just in terms of reactionary tendencies. Polykleitos was an intellectual artist and emphasized numerical proportions and their relation to moral qualities in his lost treatise, *Kanon*. This suggests his work is analogous to music, an especially respected branch of Greek art; it is often thought that behind *Kanon* is the influence of the philosopher Pythagoras.

Pythagorean thought was extremely popular in the west and may have influenced the choice of male/female confrontations for the metopes of Temple E at Selinous in Sicily (Østby 1988). Their location over the inner porches may have preceded or followed this arrangement at Olympia; the West Greek transition to High Classical was halting and uneven, and these reliefs have consequently been dated as early as 470 and as late as 450. The best (Figure 22.3) probably depicts the Sacred Marriage between Zeus and Hera. The god, rising from his seat with an eager expression, is in an awkward, undignified position; the goddess on the viewer's left (the superior side) dominates him by both her standing pose and her majestic face. The arguably humorous effect may have been inspired by the seduction scene in *Iliad* Book 14. The god's head is commonly compared to the nobler Artemision Bronze, a roughly contemporary work probably representing Poseidon, not Zeus (there is also a possibility that the metope depicts Persephone and Hades).

High Classical style also appears in painting, most notably in the Achilles Painter, a contemporary of Pheidias whose early work includes a sharply individualized older man but whose idealized Achilles c. 440 evokes both Polykleitos and the Parthenon frieze. He also excelled in outline drawing on a white background, the preferred technique for funerary vases which may sometimes resemble free painting; toward 400, the Group R workshop depicted strikingly three-dimensional figures by skillful use of outline, a talent attributed to the free painter Parrhasios of Ephesos. These are (like the Niobid Painter's spatial experiments) ominous for the future of vase painting, whose full success required that naturalism be tempered with respect for the two-dimensional wall of the vessel.

Painting for theatrical performances was said to be an invention of Sophokles, and Aischylos' *Oresteia* required a structure eventually known as a *skene* which painted

**Figure 22.3** Metope from Selinous depicting Zeus and Hera (?). Museo Archeologico, Palermo. Scala/Art Resource, NY.

flats converted into different settings. Practically nothing is known of such painting (some conjectures have been based on vase paintings), which presumably attempted some sort of illusionism; Agatharchos of Samos practiced this art in fifth-century Athens (closer dating is difficult) and may have experimented with perspective.

The history of the Classical *skene* is notoriously obscure, but it is almost certain that throughout the fifth century the *skene*, however elaborate (probably incorporating a low stage), was temporary. The theory that Aischylos' *Persai* in 472 utilized the most fabulous example, Xerxes' abandoned tent, seems (sadly) untenable, but the tent remains in play, e.g., as the suggested model for the *tholos*. With the advent of the Periklean building program, the citation and appropriation of imperial Persian architecture and architectural decoration have been plausibly proposed for both the overall design of the akropolis and specific features, notably the Parthenon frieze. The Odeion of Perikles, built adjacent to the theater in 442, is not only the monument most directly associated with Perikles but the one for which antiquity expressly records a Persian model: Xerxes' tent. While this connection is uncertain, the pyramidal roof and interior forest of columns resulted in a Persian look. Around this time, probably under Persian influence, Athenian ceremonies became more elaborate and overtly imperial, and the Odeion, too large to be simply a concert hall, was built with these in mind.

The Propylaia gave the akropolis a suitably ceremonial entrance. Almost unthinkably large and complicated for a gateway, it was designed by Mnesikles, built with many modifications from 437 to 432, and left unfinished but capable of ushering in visitors magnificently and directing them toward the Parthenon by various visual correspondences. Like the Parthenon, the Propylaia presented a Doric façade; the interior was more emphatically Ionic, with soaring columns lining the main entranceway. As with stoas, a full, idiosyncratically Athenian Ionic order completed the sequence; the Temple of Athena Nike was built in the 420s, the Erechtheion was started then but constructed largely during the following two decades. The architect, especially for the former, is often identified as Kallikrates, to whom the Ionic elements of the Parthenon have also been attributed.

# 7  Wartime Art

Starts and stops in construction now reflect the heavy expenditures of the war that began in 431. A unique sculpture found on the akropolis has been variously associated with the outbreak of the Peloponnesian War, its later course, and Sophokles' lost *Tereus* – and plausibly attributed to Alkamenes (the dedicant) (Figure 22.4). Tereus' wife Prokne, daughter and sister of Athenian kings, is preparing to take revenge on her adulterous barbarian husband by murdering their young son Itys. The stiff columnar folds of her old-fashioned-looking drapery serve as a foil for the contorted figure of Itys, who senses danger and presses as close as possible against his mother; the danger is the knife in his mother's right hand, and the disturbance he creates among the regular folds reveals his hiding place like a searchlight. A small figure on the nearby Erechtheion frieze has a similar pose, and Prokne is often compared to the Erechtheion caryatids – possibly later work by the same Alkamenes.

Close in date to all these (c. 420) is a mighty statue of Nike at Olympia, which an inscription identifies as a commission by the Ionian Paionios for Athens' Messenian allies, commemorating their share in the startling victory over Sparta in 425. She was designed to be seen from below, as a flying figure about to alight on a tall pillar, and her impetus is conveyed both by the heavy drapery billowing behind and by the transparent, windblown garment with thin folds that model the body even more revealingly than where it is uncovered.

The Prokne and Nike are diverse developments of the sculpture of the Parthenon. Around the same time or even slightly earlier, the direction taken by Paionios was followed further by the sculptors who carved the parapet of the Athena Nike temple. The frieze consists mainly of Nikai leading bulls to sacrifice and depicts, unusually, the

**Figure 22.4**  Prokne with Itys, Athens Akropolis Museum. DAI, Athens. Neg. No. 1975/420.
Photographer: Hellner.

act of slaughter; the figures wear clinging drapery whose calligraphic folds, like chiaroscuro in painting, bring to three-dimensional life bodies that are not always anatomically credible. The overall effect is of unreal sensuous beauty at odds with the subject matter and the motive for the monument. This Rich Style, as it is often called, based on the combination of filmy drapery, modeling lines, and a variety of complex, active poses, originated in post-Periklean Athens – perhaps largely the creation of non-Athenian sculptors – and became predominant in Greek sculpture well into the fourth century. Its use outside Attika can often be connected with direct Athenian influence; conversely, local versions (Peloponnesian, West Greek, Ionian) developed. In free-standing sculpture, there is an increasing tendency to privilege a single viewing angle, a rhetorical approach. The Rich Style is used both for subject matter for which its prettiness might be thought unsuitable, such as battles, and for softer, emphatically feminized themes, especially Aphrodite and Maenads. The Meidias Painter, who flourished shortly before 400, specialized in the latter and his work is often cited as the painted equivalent of the Nike parapet. As for free painting, around this time Parrhasios of Ephesos portrayed Theseus (the greatest Athenian hero, robust and indestructible); it was said (by a later painter) that he appeared to have been fed on roses.

The Rich Style has analogies in late fifth-century architecture, especially the Athenian version of the Ionic order that culminated in the lacy Erechtheion. There is comparable mannered prettiness in contemporary literature, most notably the jingles and flourishes of Gorgianic rhetoric. Euripides, whose verses are occasionally precious, has a number of his characters express a fervent wish to escape – and the most plausible overall explanation for this emphasis on sheer beauty which variously thrills, seduces, and soothes is escapism, as several scholars have suggested (again, a transition is not universally acknowledged). The Rich Style appears at a time when, especially among the Athenians, there was good reason for escapism; there is good evidence as well. Interest in magic increased noticeably, and religion became more emotional and personal. Aphrodite and Dionysos were particular favorites, and the cult of the healer-savior hero-god Asklepios expanded rapidly and was memorably introduced to Athens in 420.

Escapism was clearly a factor but not the only one. Throughout the Peloponnesian War, the spirit of Aristophanes continues irrepressible, and the Athenians were capable of confidence, even euphoria, down to their final defeat by Lysander in 405 – another way of explaining the gorgeousness of the Nike parapet, with its characterization of Victory as a desirable woman, the more available for being pluralized. Thucydides recorded Athenian mood swings, also noting that the plague resulted in increased cynicism and selfishness (although Athenians continued capable of extraordinary self-sacrifice), caused conspicuous consumption, and created *nouveaux riches*. The emphasis on private rather than civic life, often called the hallmark of the fourth century, has begun, along with corresponding trends in material culture; Olynthos, expanded along a grid plan after 432 and destroyed by Philip of Macedon in 348, offers especially full evidence. Houses became larger toward 400, also more elegant, with peristyle courts, pebble floor mosaics, and wall painting (some foreshadowing the "First Pompeian Style"). Spending on family tombs, especially in Athens, reached obsessive levels.

Of several major Peloponnesian temples built in the late fifth century, only that of Apollo Epikourios at Bassai, because of its remote location high in the Arkadian mountains, is complete enough to have permitted extensive anastylosis (Figure 22.5). Construction was coeval with the Peloponnesian War, beginning in 429 and completed shortly before 400 – and sponsored by mercenary soldiers. Their architect was Iktinos, whose temple was remarkably different from the Parthenon and comparably original. The austere exterior, lacking most subtle refinements of mature Doric (even sculptural decoration!), served as a foil to the wild landscape – but more intentionally to the surprises of the interior. Unprecedentedly, the scale increases because of tall Ionic half-columns along each side; at the back, the last two flank a free-standing column surmounted by the first known Corinthian capital. Whether or not such capitals were used previously in the Parthenon, they derive from Athenian use of akanthos decoration, notably on the akropolis.

This colonnade supported an equally unusual continuous frieze; facing the interior, this was undoubtedly even harder to see clearly than the Parthenon frieze. Its battles with centaurs and Amazons are a familiar subject never depicted with such melodramatic violence. Some stylistic elements, especially male torsos, reflect the Parthenon, but the execution must be local (a number of Arkadian sculptors are known by name); although there are examples of skillful work (notably in foreshortening), many female figures are pudgy, many poses are exaggerated or rigid, and the clinging drapery is often inept.

Three statues found in Rome were once attributed to the Bassai pediments before it was determined that these held no sculpture; they certainly belong to a pedimental group depicting the slaughter of Niobe's children. The most surprising is a kneeling girl reaching for an arrow in her back and succeeding only in displacing so much of her garment that she becomes the first large-scale nude in Greek art (the Ludovisi

**Figure 22.5** Temple of Apollo Epikourios at Bassai. © Bettmann/CORBIS

Throne with its famous flute girl is not comparable and may ultimately be proved a fake). Her anatomy is not very feminine and there are other oddities of proportions; viewing from below might have ameliorated some of these problems.

Two monuments sum up the confusion in Greece following the end of the Peloponnesian War. Spartan arrogance soon led many Greeks to ally themselves with Athens – not for war against Persia, as in 478, but for war against Sparta with Persian assistance. The Spartan leader Lysander died in a defeat by former allies in 395, after commemorating his decisive victory of 405 with an enormous group of bronze statues at Delphi; this vanished monument appears to have been innovative and influential.

Dexileos was among the Athenian cavalrymen honored by burial in a public monument after the battle of Korinth in 394/3, where Sparta defeated Athens and former allies. His family also set up a cenotaph with a large *stele*, which survives complete and among Attic *stelai* is unique in recording his birth-date (in the archon-ship of Teisandros, 414/13: *IG2²* 6217; Dexileos was therefore too young to be tainted by the notorious support given the Thirty Tyrants by most Athenian caval-rymen); unusual in depicting a battle scene (Dexileos on a rearing horse about to spear a fallen enemy); and interesting for its stylistic links. The figures resemble and probably cite a now-fragmentary Athenian relief of the later fifth century, close to the Parthenon frieze, and the clinging drapery shares a number of features with the Bassai sculptures. Despite its very high relief, however, the treatment of space is much flatter than on those earlier bas-reliefs and the drapery folds are more mechanical. These peculiarities combine with emphatic diagonals to create a chilly dignity softened by the youthful face and not inappropriate to a hero's tomb. A corresponding sober version of the Rich Style to commemorate a woman is Hegeso's funerary stele dated 400, where transparent drapery reveals the body without denying the matron respectability.

# 8   The Fourth Century

Richness characterized many early fourth-century buildings in sanctuaries, such as the *tholos* at Delphi (probably c. 380, possibly earlier); its function, like that of most *tholoi* other than that of the Athenian agora, is much disputed. The Delphi example, Doric on the outside, combined an interior Corinthian colonnade (occasionally claimed as earlier than Bassai) with a profusion of decorative carvings and dark stone to offset white marble. The architect may have been Argive, as was more probably the designer of the larger *tholos* of the Asklepios sanctuary at Epidauros, similar but still more ornate. It was begun c. 370, around the time the deity's temple was completed, small but again featuring an elaborate interior with a gold and ivory cult statue. The sculpture of both pediments depicts Trojan War fighting and furnishes one of the last major examples of Rich Style clinging and billowing drapery; one mounted Amazon recalls Dexileos. Something new, however, is the raw pathos of several heads, notably that of Priam at the moment of his murder, and the emotional effect is heightened by the contorted spiral poses of several figures.

A reaction away from Rich Style sculpture is well represented by two obviously popular versions of the healing cult's chief divinities: the Asklepios Giustini (c. 380) and the Hope Hygieia (c. 360s). The dense drapery of the former, especially, has an architectural, almost abstract quality that has sometimes suggested fifth-century dating; Hygieia combines a like formality with greater naturalism. Both are commonly attributed to Peloponnesian artists – perhaps more resistant to the Rich Style than Athenians and Ionians – but occasionally to the Athenian Kephisodotos. To commemorate peace with Sparta, probably in 371 (slightly earlier and later dates are also argued), he was commissioned to make a bronze group for the Athenian agora: Eirene (Peace) holding the infant Ploutos (Wealth); the old motif of nurturer with child was given new allegorical meaning. The figures, known from copies, form an ensemble of great compositional subtlety, more three-dimensional than usually supposed. Eirene's drapery is a derivation from the style of Pheidias' successors simplified to complement a pose with increased complexity and tension, at the same time enlivened by small naturalistic folds suggesting the actual behavior of cloth.

Painting also seems to have turned away from the flamboyant and exquisite toward a quieter and more solid naturalism. The point of Euphranor's gibe about Parrhasios' Theseus was to contrast his own version of the hero as beef-fed. Probably Athenian and apparently active toward the middle of the fourth century, Euphranor was eminent as both sculptor and painter; his famous representation of the 362 battle of Mantineia conflated history by, impossibly, depicting Xenophon's cavalryman-son Gryllos killing Epameinondas. In vase painting, Athenian contemporaries of the Meidias painter perpetuated a more sober style that continued as the fourth-century mainstream; the red figure schools of south Italy, which began as a mid-fifth-century offshoot of Attic painting and never embraced the Rich Style, now produced some of the best work of the early fourth century.

The art of the period sometimes called Late Classical (c. 370–330) is particularly difficult to sum up. The instability of these years encouraged a search for order that resulted in more introspective and consciously intellectual art than the Rich Style. Artists sought to express reality through individualization, naturalism, and illusionism – approaches emphatically rejected by Plato, the greatest fourth-century seeker of order. There is, however, something Platonic in the proliferation of personifications in early fourth-century art, especially when they convey allegorical meaning. Personifications are prevalent on document reliefs, an institution that began in Periklean Athens (with Persian antecedents) and during the fourth century spread to other Greek states. Since these artifacts are dated and also do not pretend to great originality, they have been used for refining the chronology of major sculpture (e.g., Eirene with Ploutos), although with inconclusive results.

Ploutos reaches toward Eirene; she looks past him, her expression of gentle melancholy typically fourth-century. The overall effect, surely intentional, makes the allegory poignant; lasting peace was elusive at a time when Theban military successes were changing the face of the Peloponnese. The Arkadian federal capital Megalopolis, founded c. 370, soon lived up to its name with the construction of a theater accommodating about 20,000 spectators, very symmetrical and possibly the first with a round configuration. By the end of the century almost all Greek cities and major sanctuaries had permanent theaters – the most beautiful at Epidauros toward 300. Many had *skenai* with forward-projecting wings, probably influenced by the configuration of the Stoa of Zeus, built c. 430 in the Athenian agora. In the 330s, the Theater of Dionysos received the earliest stone auditorium. Megalopolis remained the largest theater yet was essentially an annex to the roofed council house called (after the man who funded it) the Thersileion, which featured concentric rectangles of interior supports arranged so as to offer the clearest possible view of the speakers' platform. Undoubtedly influenced by several Athenian meeting places, it surpassed them in size (length 66 m) and probably refinement; its destruction by King Kleomenes III of Sparta in 223 leaves most details uncertain.

# 9 Famous Artists and Patrons

The Greek world in the fourth century was more prosperous (with many exceptions), more commercial and urban than in the fifth (Hammond 1986: 521–32); it was also less purely Greek, more international. Maussollos, satrap of Karia, commenced the urbanization of his capital at Halikarnassos around the time Megalopolis was built but made his own future tomb the focal point; construction of the Maussolleion (as it was eventually called) probably began before his death in 353 and continued under his successors. The artists and architects employed were Greek, but the monument's main features recall non-Greek tombs from Asia Minor, especially Lykia: an Ionic colonnade stood on a high podium, both lavishly adorned with free-standing and relief sculpture, surmounted by a stepped pyramid (reflecting both local tradition and Egyptian influence?) with a chariot on top. It is commonly supposed that Maussollos was depicted in the chariot, and as commonly and reasonably agreed that this figure has not survived. The ruler, however, could have been portrayed more than once among the hundreds of statues and is the probable subject of a colossal (height 3 m) statue of an individualized mortal; he has an imposing countenance, set off by un-Hellenic facial hair and swept-back locks, and a burly body whose authoritative stance is made the more dramatic by dense, deeply carved drapery. "Maussollos" foreshadows mid-Hellenistic baroque and has occasionally been re-dated to that era. The free-standing sculpture shows a wide range of styles, as do the three pictorial friezes: a chariot race, an Amazonomachy, a centauromachy. The latter two are not likely to perpetuate triumph-over-barbarism symbolism (nor to have been chosen as conventional décor); rather, all three motifs had probably taken on funerary significance.

Whether or not the artists came to the Maussolleion already famous, their work there apparently advanced their careers. Pytheos, a sculptor-architect, went subsequently to his small native city of Priene and designed the Temple of Athena Polias, which has strong affinities with the Maussolleion in both architectural and sculptural details. Pytheos eschewed the previous expansiveness of Ionic buildings (including the Maussolleion) in favor of compactness, purity, and careful proportions; in all this, he was probably influenced by Doric practice – although he was known as a chauvinistic detractor of the Doric order. He was rewarded by posterity's recognition of Athena Polias as the canonical Ionic temple. Priene is notable for many well-preserved fourth-century and Hellenistic public buildings, also houses; their front porch-forecourt arrangement differs from the plan at Olynthos and elsewhere and appears to be a specialty of this part of Asia Minor extending back into the Archaic period and perhaps the Bronze Age.

Skopas of Paros, a more famous sculptor than Pytheos, worked with him on the Maussolleion; we know that on one later occasion he was a notable architect, since

Pausanias says that he designed the temple of Athena Alea at Tegea. Despite its size (only slightly smaller than the temple of Zeus at Olympia), this was the first Peloponnesian temple entirely of marble. The interior orders were purely decorative, engaged Corinthian half-columns supporting a second tier of small Ionic half-columns; this influential innovation, combined with rich moldings, gave the cella intricately articulated walls without encroaching on its spaciousness. The style of the pedimental sculptures was unusual, to judge from the heads; massive proportions, hard-breathing mouths, and large, upward-rolling eyes combine to produce an effect of powerful passion. Probably Skopas made the designs and assistants were responsible for the uneven execution. We can at least cite the Tegea heads as exemplars (along with descriptions of lost paintings) of passion in fourth-century art, forerunners of such Hellenistic works as the Altar of Pergamon.

The Athenian Praxiteles, younger kinsman (son?) of Kephisodotos, probably did not work on the Maussolleion (Vitruvius *De Architectura 7 praef.* 12–13 states this possibility), but his most remarkable statue was made for East Greek Knidos nearby – and can only be explained in terms of its location. Aphrodite came to the Greeks from the Near East, and Knidian proximity to cults emphasizing her fertility and sexuality resulted in the commission of Praxiteles' statue c. 340, the earliest fully nude female (except for the dying Niobid, an architectural figure) in large-scale Greek sculpture. Her Asian affinities explain not only her nudity but the motif: Aphrodite, preparing for her bath, holds her hand over her genitals, to draw attention to them while shielding the mortal onlooker from their full power. The statue's fame and popularity in copies and variants appear to date only from the late Hellenistic period (paradoxically, the lovely oval face was immediately influential), along with anachronistic bashful-bather interpretations. Praxiteles' Aphrodite was a great goddess, not a startled and embarrassed woman. Since she survives only in copies, ideas about Praxiteles' work have also been much influenced by a supposed original, the Hermes with infant Dionysos. But despite its similarity to the Eirene (see above), this superlative group displays too many stylistic and technical anomalies for a sure connection with Praxiteles, and attributions based on it have become suspect. It nevertheless appears, as before, that Praxiteles favored female and youthful male subjects and epitomized the quiet and intimate side of fourth-century art.

The Marsyas Painter's vase depicting Peleus' conquest of Thetis among the Nereids is contemporary with Praxitelean sculpture and often understandably cited as comparable. The mood recalls the Meidias Painter (see above), but the figures are larger and given more individual attention; both drapery and female nudity are attractive, naturalistic, and three-dimensional. It must nevertheless be admitted that such Athenian work is usually less lively than West Greek painting, which draws much inspiration from the theater (most explicitly in a crude but vigorous school of comic painting at Poseidonia). The Dareios Painter's name vase (330s) has a remarkable multi-figure scene inscribed "Persai"; it probably refers to a lost tragedy (contemporary or revived from the early fifth century?) in which the King receives news of Marathon.

The vase may also allude to the Asian exploits of Alexander, whose death in 323 conventionally begins the Hellenistic age in both art and history; since so many of his policies continued those of his father, one might also mark the transition by Philip's overwhelming victory at Chaironeia in 338. The crucial point is that any date for the beginning of Hellenistic art will be based – far more completely than in the case of the transition to Early Classical – on historical events. Rather than stylistic revolution, there is continuity of most trends beginning before 350; not a few sculptures have been dated to the fourth century but also the third and even second.

The artist epitomizing the long, gradual transition is Lysippos of Sikyon. He was evidently an established sculptor by the 360s; in maturity, he excelled at portraying Alexander as well as Alexander's ancestor and role model, Herakles; he outlived his royal patron to work for the Diadochoi close to 300; many eminent pupils (including three sons) further developed such Lysippan specialties as unprecedented naturalism and complex poses of both action and repose whose three-dimensionality demanded multiple viewing angles. Lysippos' famous Apoxyomenos (athlete cleaning himself with strigil), generally recognized in a plodding Roman copy, shows what he himself had achieved c. 320.

Alexander also extensively patronized Apelles of (probably) Kos, most admired of Greek painters, renowned on a par with Pheidias. Like Lysippos a skilled portraitist with allegorical interests, he added the sensuousness of Praxiteles, painting nude not only Aphrodite but Alexander's favorite (subsequently his own) mistress. Scholars' inevitable wishes to find pictorial traces of his work have occasionally linked Apelles with the Alexander Mosaic. This Pompeian pavement somehow captures in the intractable medium of tessellation the compositional subtlety and powerful atmosphere of a lost painting showcasing the opposing Macedonian and Persian kings. Philoxenos is more commonly and plausibly credited with the original, but this remains speculative, as does the usual identification as Issos; it may be that battle, freely varied (witness Euphranor's Mantineia! – see above), or it may be generic.

# 10   Macedon

Greek artists worked for Macedonian patrons as early as the end of the fifth century, when King Archelaos engaged Zeuxis, Parrhasios' great rival, to decorate his palace at Pella. As partial compensation for the loss of his paintings, adjacent villas preserve pebble mosaics made about a century later, including a stag hunt by the greatest ancient mosaicist, the first to sign his name: Gnosis. Hunting, a Macedonian and especially royal passion, is also the theme of a painting decorating the façade of the "Tomb of Philip II" at Vergina; similarities to the Alexander Mosaic (there are major differences also) have prompted some scholars to assign it to Philoxenos. Inside another Vergina tomb is depicted Hades abducting Persephone, a masterly painting sometimes attributed to Philoxenos' teacher Nikomachos.

Study of the rich material from Macedon shows how many specifics of the transition to Hellenistic art are uncertain. Most notably, many believe "Philip's" tomb misidentified, dating it about two decades after his death (even the identification of Vergina as ancient Aigai has been challenged) (Faklaris 1994). The barrel-vaulted construction may postdate Alexander's eastern conquests (it was almost certainly Macedonians who in the 320s built a stadium at Nemea with a barrel-vaulted entranceway), and some grave furnishings also seem closer to 300 than 336. The association with Philip still has defenders, some claiming that reconstruction of the male occupant's skull (drawing on forensic medical technology) shows a traumatic

**Figure 22.6** Grave stele found near Ilissos River, Athens. National Archaeological Museum, Athens. © Alinari/Art Resource, NY.

right-eye injury such as Philip received in 354. The right eyebrow of a miniature ivory head from the tomb bears a scar; the identification as Philip – and of several other heads as Alexander – is probable but not universally accepted.

Macedonians may have been not only patrons but makers of early Hellenistic art. This possibility is most readily conceded for metal work, such as the spectacular finds from the Derveni tombs in which Attic and Italiot as well as "northern" elements have been detected. As for painting, the decoration of tombs presumably had parallels above the ground, since some of its characteristics appear in later Italian wall painting; and we know that Macedonians employed famous Greek painters. The tomb painters, however, worked in close coordination with the architects, and of a distinctively Macedonian architecture there is little doubt.

The non-Hellenic practice of building tomb chambers with magnificent decoration and furnishings resulted in the preservation of notable Hellenic (or Macedonian) art. Ironically, around the same time (probably 317) a Macedonian-appointed ruler of Athens decisively legislated against elaborate funerary practices, including sculpted monuments. Demetrios of Phaleron's decree may have been immediately prompted by the erection of the Kallithea Monument just outside Athens; recently discovered and only preliminarily published, this huge structure combines statuary and architecture in the manner of the Maussolleion. So ended an interesting, often moving genre of Athenian art capable of producing an occasional masterpiece. The Ilissos Stele of the 330s (Figure 22.6), commemorating a youth mourned by an elderly man and a child, sensitively groups perfectly executed figures in illusionistic space; this is as beautiful and emotionally powerful as any Greek work that has come down to us.

# Further reading

Boedeker, D., & K. A. Raaflaub (eds) (1998) *Democracy, empire, and the arts in fifth-century Athens* (Cambridge MA: Harvard University Press) (Center for Hellenic Studies Colloquia 2)
Castriota, D. (1992) *Myth, ethos, and actuality: official art in fifth-century B.C. Athens* (Madison WI: University of Wisconsin Press) (Wisconsin Studies in Classics)
Cohen, B. (ed.) (2000) *Not the classical ideal: Athens and the construction of the other in Greek art* (Leiden: Brill)
Havelock, C. M. (1995) *The Aphrodite of Knidos and her successors: a historical review of the female nude in Greek art* (Ann Arbor: University of Michigan Press)
Hurwit, J. M. (1999) *The Athenian acropolis: history, mythology, and archaeology from the Neolithic era to the present* (Cambridge: Cambridge University Press)
Miller, M. C. (1997) *Athens and Persia in the fifth century BC: a study in cultural receptivity* (Cambridge: Cambridge University Press)
Pugliese Carratelli, G. (ed.) (1996) *The Greek world: art and civilization in Sicily and Magna Graecia* (trans. A. Ellis et al.) (New York: Rizzoli)
Ridgway, B. S. (1999) *Prayers in stone: Greek architectural sculpture ca. 600–100 B.C.E.* (Berkeley: University of California Press) (Sather Classical Lectures 63)
Robertson, M. (1975) *A history of Greek art*, 2 vols (London: Cambridge University Press)

# Bibliography

Barron, J. P. (1984) "Alkamenes at Olympia" in: *Bulletin of the Institute of Classical Studies of the University of London* 31: 199–211
Bell, M., III (1995) "The Motya charioteer and Pindar's *Isthmian* 2" in: *Memoirs of the American Academy in Rome* 40: 1–42
Carpenter, R. (1973) Review of Pollitt 1972 in: *American Journal of Archeology* 77: 349
Faklaris, P. B. (1994) "Aegae: determining the site of the first capital of the Macedonians" in: *American Journal of Archeology* 98: 609–16
Fehr, B. (1979) "Zur religionspolitischen Funktion der Athena Parthenos im Rahmen des delisch-attischen Seebundes, I" in: *Hephaistos* 1: 71–91

Fehr, B. (1980) "Zur religionspolitischen Funktion der Athena Parthenos im Rahmen des delisch-attischen Seebundes, II" in: *Hephaistos* 2: 113–25

Fehr, B. (1981) "Zur religionspolitischen Funktion der Athena Parthenos im Rahmen des delisch-attischen Seebundes, III" in: *Hephaistos* 3: 55–93

Hallett, C. H. (1986) "The origins of the classical style in sculpture" in: *JHS* 106: 71–84

Hammond, N. G. L. (1986) *A history of Greece to 322 B.C.* (Oxford: Clarendon [3]1986)

Klein, N. L. (1998) "Evidence for west Greek influence on mainland Greek roof construction and the creation of the truss in the archaic period" in: *Hesperia* 67: 335–74

Østby, E. (1988) "The sculptural program of temple E at Selinus" in: *Praktika tou XII Dienthnous Synedriou Klasikes Archaiologias, Athena, 4–10 Septemvriou 1983*, vol. 3 (Athens: Hypourgeion Politismou kai Epistemon 1988) 200–8

Papadopoulos, J. (1996) "The original kerameikos of Athens and the siting of the classical agora" in: *GRBS* 37: 107–28

Pollitt, J. J. (1972) *Art and experience in classical Greece* (Cambridge: Cambridge University Press)

Raubitschek, A. E. (1949) *Dedications from the Athenian Akropolis: a catalogue of the inscriptions of the sixth and fifth centuries B.C.* (with the collaboration of L. H. Jeffery) (Cambridge MA: Archaeological Institute of America)

Stewart, A. (1993) *Greek sculpture: exploration* (new ed.) (New Haven: Yale University Press)

Walsh, J. (1986) "The date of the Athenian stoa at Delphi" in: *American Journal of Archeology* 90: 319–36

Younger, J. G. (1997) "Gender and sexuality in the Parthenon frieze" in: Koloski-Ostrow, A. O., & C. L. Lyons (eds) (1997) *Naked truths: women, sexuality, and gender in classical art and archaeology* (London: Routledge) 120–53

# CHAPTER TWENTY-THREE

# Warfare in the Classical Age

## *John W. I. Lee*

## 1   Introduction

This chapter surveys warfare amongst the poleis (city-states) of mainland Greece from about 500 to 340. It begins on land, with examination of troop types and equipment, training and tactics, logistics and medical care, the role of slaves and non-combatants, and religion. There follow discussions of sieges and fortifications, as well as navies and sea power. Lastly, it outlines the transition from the Classical period to the Hellenistic, and suggests some profitable future paths for Greek warfare studies. Although it concentrates on the practical aspects of war-making, the survey also indicates the most significant connections between warfare and developments in other aspects of Greek civilization. Classical warfare was as much a political, social, and cultural phenomenon as a purely military one, and readers are encouraged to consult this chapter in conjunction with the relevant other chapters of this *Companion*. It also bears remembering that significant regional variations in military practices and ideology existed throughout the period, and while space constraints make it necessary here to emphasize features common to the polis world, it would be more accurate to speak of Greek "ways" rather than a "way" of war.

Armed conflict was an ever-present feature of ancient life, so it is no surprise that evidence for how the Greeks fought their wars appears throughout Classical literature. For descriptions of military organization and tactics, as well as for narratives of battles and campaigns, our major sources are the contemporary historians Herodotos, Thucydides, and Xenophon. Of these three, Xenophon (c. 427–355), a professional soldier with several decades of wide-ranging military experience, deserves particular attention not only for his historical writings, the *Hellenika* and *Anabasis*, but also for his technical treatises on horsemanship, cavalry, and hunting. The *Anabasis* is also noteworthy for the way in which it foregrounds the experiences of common soldiers, presaging the modern war memoir. A different approach appears in the fourth-century writer Aineias Taktikos, whose handbook on city defense and sieges comes in the form of a staccato series of general guidelines, backed up by historical examples. Other Classical authors, amongst them the comic playwright Aristophanes, provide passing references that help in recovering the details of equipment and logistics. Finally, inscriptions on stone and metal are important sources, especially for Athens, where a number of lengthy texts furnish valuable information on Athenian naval administration and on the commemoration of Athens' war dead. All this textual evidence demands careful analysis, for it sometimes tells us more about how the Greeks preferred to depict military matters than about how they actually were (van Wees 1995: 153–78).

Archaeological evidence is equally valuable in reconstructing Classical warfare, but here too there are challenges of interpretation. Depictions of warfare in sculpture and on painted pottery may seem straightforward enough at first glance, but as with literary authors, sculptors and potters were often more concerned with presenting an ideal vision of warfare than with historical accuracy. To give just one example, the many nude or nearly-nude warriors who appear on painted pottery reveal more about the Classical aesthetic of heroism and physical perfection than they do about how real soldiers dressed for combat. Excavated finds of armor and weapons, especially from graves and from the panhellenic sanctuary of Olympia, allow us to see how the Greeks girded themselves for battle, but there is precious little archaeological evidence for many of the more mundane aspects of military equipment, such as footwear and knapsacks. Some important items of Greek equipment, including wooden shields and leather corselets, are virtually absent from the archaeological record, and must be reconstructed using a combination of scattered literary references, surviving metal fittings, and practical calculations.

## 2  Hoplites and Phalanxes

Citizen armed forces were the hallmark of Classical warfare, and the pre-eminent foot soldier of the period was a heavily armed citizen militiaman, the *hoplites* or hoplite. The name derives from Greek *ta hopla*, tools or equipment – a hoplite was someone comprehensively geared up with the full tackle of war (Lazenby & Whitehead 1996: 27). Citizen hoplites furnished their own arms and armor. Because this equipment was expensive, and because the ideology of the Classical polis closely linked military service and political power, possession of hoplite gear also marked a man's political and economic status (Raaflaub 1999: 135–6).

For protection, Classical hoplites could choose amongst several styles of hammered bronze corselet or breastplate (*thorax*), and a variety of close-fitting bronze helmets that covered the head, neck, and face. Fabric or leather padding under both armor and helmet eased chafing and cushioned against enemy blows. Some men wore bronze greaves, akin to soccer or football shin guards. The standard hoplite shield (*hoplon* or *aspis*), a concave disk roughly a meter in diameter, built of thin bronze sheeting over a wooden core, offered durable but heavy (7–8 kg) protection. The hoplite shield boasted a double grip, consisting of an arm-band (*porpax*) and a hand-grip (*antilabe*). This grip helped distribute the weight of the shield across its bearer's left arm, but restricted his freedom of movement. Altogether, a full set of hoplite defensive equipment probably weighed in the order of 20 kg or more, a heavy burden considering that the average adult Greek male of the fifth century may have weighed only about 70 kg.

**Figure 23.1** Hoplite: a citizen hoplite taking leave of his family. He wears a bronze helmet and greaves, along with a leather or linen corselet. Note the arm-band (*porpax*) of his shield, and his sword slung on a baldric. Attic stamnos (wine jar), c. 450 BCE. © The Trustees of The British Museum, London.

**Figure 23.2** Phalanx: hoplites, probably Greek mercenaries, advancing in phalanx formation. Nereid monument, Lykia (Asia Minor), early fourth century BCE. © The Trustees of The British Museum, London.

There were ways to reduce this load. By 450, composite corselets of bronze and leather were appearing, and by the end of the fifth century, jerkins (*spolades*) of laminated linen or leather had become common. So too had the *pilos*, a lighter, open helmet, of bronze or even stiffened felt, that covered only the skull. Some hoplites were still sporting extensive metal armor in the mid-fourth century, but the overall trend of the Classical period was toward a progressive lightening of the panoply. This made hoplites more mobile, and thus better able to cope with the challenges of difficult terrain and enemy skirmishers. Lighter panoplies were also cheaper, meaning that more citizens could equip themselves as hoplites and enjoy the attendant political status.

For offense, the hoplite carried in his right hand a bronze- or iron-tipped thrusting spear (*dory*), some 2.0–2.5 m long and weighing about 1.5 kg. A sharp foursided end-spike (*sauroter*) allowed the spear to be jabbed upright into the ground for easy stowage in camp, and in combat enabled even broken spears to remain effective weapons. A hoplite whose spear broke could also draw his secondary weapon, a short iron sword (*xiphos*). Several types of cutting and thrusting sword, none more than 0.6 m long and weighing on average about 1 kg, saw widespread use during the Classical period. Perhaps the most distinctive was the *machaira* or *kopis*, a curved single-edged blade resembling a machete. As a last resort, a soldier might carry a dagger or concealable knife (*encheiridion*).

Classical hoplites fought in a densely packed infantry formation, the phalanx. Phalanx formations allowed each man in line about one meter of space, and were generally drawn up eight ranks deep (Pritchett 1971: 134–54). In such close order, the large hoplite shield could protect not just its bearer, but also the man to his left. Simultaneously, though, the need to preserve orderly files and ranks largely restricted phalanxes to open, level terrain. In an advance, phalanxes tended to drift to the right, as each man sought to edge behind the shield of the man to his right for greater protection.

Most hoplites were militia rather than professionals, and the majority of phalanx armies received minimal training and possessed little tactical organization. The Athenians, for example, divided their phalanx into ten tribal regiments (*taxeis*), each comprising an uncertain number of companies (*lochoi*), but with rare exceptions neither the *taxis* nor the *lochos* undertook independent movement on the battlefield. The strength of these units apparently varied depending on how many men were enrolled for a given campaign. When called up, men served alongside their neighbors and relatives, increasing unit cohesion. Metics, or resident aliens, also stood with Athenian citizens in the phalanx (Xenophon *Poroi* 2.2–4). Some basic drilling, including gymnastics and dance as well as rudimentary weapons practice, probably went on during the fifth century, but the Athenians did not enact a comprehensive program of military training, the *ephebeia*, until sometime in the mid-fourth century. Other Greeks, amongst them the Argives, Boiotians, Korinthians, and Megarians, also divided their hoplites into *lochoi* of several hundred men apiece. These units generally did not maneuver independently in battle, and there exists little evidence that they received systematic military preparation. A number of poleis, however, did form small units of picked troops (*epilektoi*), who were able to train constantly because they were subsidized at public expense. *Epilektoi* sometimes fought as the front rank of a hoplite line, while at other times they formed together as an assault group or reserve. The most famous of these elite units was the Theban Sacred Band (379–338), composed of pairs of lovers stationed side by side.

The Classical Spartan army was unique in possessing a developed tactical organization and a systematic military upbringing, the *agoge*. The *agoge* was designed to inculcate toughness, resourcefulness, austerity, and discipline. Beginning at age seven, Spartan male citizens, or Spartiates, were segregated by age classes, housed in barracks, and subjected to an incessant cycle of athletic and military exercises. Ritualized homosexual relationships between youths in the *agoge* and older men fostered group cohesion and helped socialize young males. At age twenty, a Spartiate joined a common mess (*syssition*), often being introduced by his older lover. For much of their lives, Spartiates lived and ate together with the members of their *syssition*.

These *syssitia* were not tactical units. Rather, several of them together made up the *enomotia* ("sworn band"), the basic unit of the Spartan tactical system. In the fifth century, according to Thucydides, four *enomotiai* of 32 men each formed a company (*pentekostys*) of 128 men, and four companies (*pentekostyes*) a regiment (*lochos*) of 512. There were apparently five *lochoi* of Spartiates in the late fifth century, with perioikoi (Spartan subject allies) organized in separate units (Singor 2002: 279–82). In contrast, Xenophon in the fourth century describes two (or possibly four) 40-man *enomotiai* making up a *pentekostys*, two *pentekostyes* a *lochos*, and two *lochoi* a brigade, or *mora* (Anderson 1970: 225–51; Lazenby 1985: 6–10). Six *morai* seem to have constituted the whole army, with Spartiates and perioikoi now serving together. Thucydides and Xenophon agree that each sub-unit had its own regular officers, and that sub-units could maneuver independently of the phalanx. Both also note the existence of the Skiritai, a unit of picked troops that guarded the flanks of the phalanx. Although scholars continue to debate the details, the essential point is that Sparta alone of the Classical poleis had a true tactical organization with a defined command hierarchy, enabling its phalanx to move flexibly on the battlefield.

Phalanx warfare between poleis was in the ideal a highly ritualized affair. Before joining battle, hoplite armies would draw up opposite each other on a suitable field. Cavalry and light troops, if present, were relegated to the flanks or rear. After speeches and sacrifices, the phalanxes, each singing its traditional war hymn (*paian*), lumbered forward to confront each other head-on. Exactly what happened then has been the subject of numerous reconstructions, none universally accepted (Krentz 1994: 45; Raaflaub 1999: 149 n. 12). Probably men began by thrusting with spears over the wall of their own shields, trying for the eyes and exposed limbs of their enemies. As spears shattered and ranks broke down, there would be cutting and stabbing with swords and broken spear-ends, followed possibly by a brutal shoving match (*othismos*), with hoplites in the rear ranks pressing their comrades forward into the foe. Eventually one phalanx would break, men casting aside shields and weapons in flight. Most casualties were inflicted at this stage, as the winning army cut down its panicked opponents. Yet the victors did not often engage in sustained pursuit, preferring rather to claim possession of the field and erect a trophy (from *tropaion*, the turning point of the struggle). The losers, in return, asked for the return of their dead under a truce. This act both signified the defeated side's acceptance of the results of the battle, and obliged the winners to perform a conciliatory religious act; indeed, not to return bodies when asked was deemed the foulest sacrilege.

This pattern of agonal (from *agon*, struggle) warfare, according to scholarly consensus since the mid-1980s, was created early in the Archaic period by the agrarian middling classes of the developing poleis. As poleis grew, they faced constant border disputes over scarce agricultural land. Farmers, being the majority of citizens, sought therefore to limit conflict and maximize farming time by giving primacy to the single-day decisive battle. The archetypal hoplite *agon* clearly defined winners and losers; with a trophy set up and bodies returned, everyone could get back to the real work of farming. The phalanx and its interlocking shields nicely encapsulated the communitarian ethos of the polis, while its exclusion of light troops and cavalry neatly reflected the farmers' desire to downplay the importance of both the landless poor and arrogant aristocrats. Such was the dominance of this agrarian world-view that "after the creation of the hoplite panoply, for nearly two and a half centuries (700–480) hoplite battle *was* Greek warfare" (Hanson 1999: 239).

Recent research, however, challenges this consensus. Re-examination of the Archaic evidence suggests that as late as 600, archers and other missile infantry were *not* excluded from the phalanx. Archers feature beside hoplites on painted vases until c. 480, and into the late sixth century hoplites themselves are shown carrying javelins. Archaic hoplite battle may have comprised a wide, fluid range of combats, including individual and small-group duels, rather than a single massed collision of phalanxes (van Wees 2000: 149–56). What is more, some of the so-called protocols of hoplite warfare, particularly the placement of battlefield trophies, appear on closer examination to be innovations of the Classical rather than the Archaic period (Krentz 2002: 32). The notion of phalanx battle as a limited, ritualized contest may have evolved fully only during the Classical period.

This new interpretation has much going for it. Warfare indeed became more prolonged and destructive during the fifth century, and it may well be that "a new, nostalgic ideology of war" developed in response (Krentz 2002: 25). The emphasis on close-quarter infantry battle rather than missile combat suited the increased opposition of "Greek" and "barbarian" that followed the Persian invasions of 490 and 480–479 (Hall 1997: 44; Tuplin 1999: 55–6). Persians were weak and effeminate; they fought from a distance, using bows or horses. Greeks were strong and manly, ready to fight man-to-man with shield and spear. Athenian victory at Marathon in 490, where a pure hoplite army routed a larger Persian force of archers and cavalry, represented the perfect symbol of this opposition. At least in the case of Athens, valorizing the agrarian hoplite phalanx also provided a potent ideological tool for internal political struggles. In the late fifth century, Athenian elites looked back to a fictitious "ancestral constitution" (*patrios politeia*) to critique the perceived failures of Athenian government (Roberts 1994: 65–70). So too Athenian farmer-hoplites, threatened by the military and political prominence of the Athenian navy during the mid-fifth century, appealed to an ancestral way of war and the legend of Marathon as proof that they, not the navy's landless rowers, represented the true spirit of Athens. The creation of a hoplite ideology may thus stand as the first important socio-military development of the Classical period.

The current model of hoplite warfare certainly places proper emphasis on the limited nature of early polis conflict. Archaic war was border war, simply because in mountainous Greece the seizure of fertile borderlands was by far the most attractive reason to seek battle. Most Archaic poleis, lacking navies, could not have transported their troops far afield even if they wanted to. War was seasonal because soldiers, whether hoplites or poorer light infantry, had to work for a living much of the year. Classical hoplites, in contrast, fought more often, further from home, and in a whole new range of environments. The largest poleis now had the populations and financial resources to deploy thousands of hoplites on distant campaigns, and to sustain them there for months at a time. Throughout the fifth century, hoplite marines perched precariously on the pitching decks of warships during naval battles all across the Aegean and splashed ashore in amphibious assaults on beaches hundreds of miles from home. Over the course of the Peloponnesian War and into the fourth century, hoplites fought in cities and in hill country, sometimes at night or in winter rain and snow; they built field fortifications, endured sieges and ambuscades, and plodded through forced marches.

The scale and tactical complexity of pitched battle also increased markedly during the fifth and fourth centuries, as states and alliances put larger forces into the field and commanders learned new tricks and tactics. The largest battles – amongst them Delion in 424, Mantineia in 418 and again in 362, and Koroneia in 394 – saw armies of up to ten thousand men apiece confront each other. Sometimes complex maneuvers carried the day, but tactical tricks could also be potential disasters. At Mantineia in 418, when the Spartan king Agis tried to extend his phalanx line by moving two companies to his left, he nearly threw his whole army into confusion (Thuc. 5.71–2). Often victory came down to a head-on shoving match. It was not uncommon for one portion of a phalanx to push back the enemy while another portion gave ground. This happened at Delion, where the Athenians won on their right and center, but lost on their left (Thuc. 4.96). At Koroneia the Thebans smashed the allied left flank of Agesilaos' Spartan army and pushed forward to take the Spartan camp; on the right, Agesilaos routed Thebes' Argive allies, then wheeled his phalanx completely around to confront and crush the Thebans (Xenophon *Hellenika* 4.3.16–19). The greatest tactical triumph of Classical hoplite battle came at Leuktra in 371. The Theban general Epameinondas took the unusual step of drawing up his left flank fifty deep rather than the customary eight, echeloning the center and right of his phalanx away from the opposing Spartan line, and screening his whole formation with cavalry. The Theban left, spearheaded by the Sacred Band, smashed into the Spartan right. The Spartans at first held their own, but soon gave way before Theban numbers. The Spartan king Kleombrotos and 400 Spartiates were killed, the first time in nearly two centuries that the Spartans had suffered a defeat in a hoplite battle (Xenophon *Hellenika* 6.4.8–15). Epameinondas used similar tactics at Mantineia in 362, this time combined with a preliminary attack by cavalry and light troops. The Thebans were victorious again, but Epameinondas died in the fighting.

## 3   Light Infantry: Peltasts, Archers, and Slingers

While hoplites remained the mainstay of Greek armies throughout the Classical period, from the Peloponnesian War onward new types of soldiers made their presence increasingly felt on the battlefield. Most prominent among these were the peltasts. Like hoplites, peltasts take their name from their equipment. The *pelte* was a crescent-shaped single-grip shield of Thracian origin, made of wicker or of animal hide stretched over a wooden frame. The term peltast (*peltastes*) at first specifically denoted a Thracian warrior armed primarily with javelins and carrying the *pelte*. During the Archaic period, Thracian peltasts served as mercenaries for a variety of Greek states (Best 1969: 3–9). During the Classical period, several different types of shield were lumped together as *peltai*, and "peltast" became a generic designation for

**Figure 23.3** Peltast: non-Greek warrior carrying a Thracian *pelte* and a javelin or spear. Interior of an Athenian red figure kylix, c. 470–460 BCE. Courtesy of the Arthur M. Sackler Museum, Harvard University Art Museums, Bequest of David M. Robinson. Photo: Photographic Services.

any javelin-armed, lightly protected infantry. Peltasts from Thrace remained in demand and could command high wages for their skills. Increasing numbers of Greek soldiers, however, were also equipped as peltasts.

Greek or non-Greek, a peltast needed training. Throwing the javelin (*akon*), for one thing, demanded constant practice. Javelins, their metal points smaller and better balanced than hoplite spearheads, varied in length from 1.25 to 2.25 m (Snodgrass 1964: 136–9). The maximum effective range for a running throw was probably no more than about 45 m, and many throws may have been at distances half that or less. For better range, a peltast could wrap one end of a leather thong (*ankyle*) around his javelin shaft, looping the other end around the first two fingers of his throwing hand. With the thong securely attached, a peltast would release his grip on the loop as his arm reached full extension, increasing the effective length of his arm and therefore the force of the throw (Harris 1963: 30).

Peltast units deployed in loose formations, harassing their opponents from afar while evading close combat. This style of fighting required extensive tactical training – learning to obey trumpet calls or other signals to advance and retreat, and perhaps practicing attack drills – as well as skill with the javelin. Peltast units could vary in size to suit tactical necessities. On level ground, groups as large as 600 men were stationed to protect the flanks of a phalanx. In difficult terrain, ad hoc companies of one or two hundred were more useful. Small peltast detachments also excelled as scouts and advance guards.

Peltasts were at their best facing unsupported hoplites in hilly or broken terrain. In summer 424, for instance, a mixed force of Athenian hoplites and light infantry, including several hundred peltasts, launched an amphibious assault on the rocky island of Sphakteria in the southwest Peloponnese. The 420 Spartan hoplites defending Sphakteria tried to brush aside the Athenian light troops and come to grips with their hoplite opposites. Instead, the Athenian hoplites hung back, while the peltasts and other skirmishers ran forward to launch a withering barrage of projectiles at the Spartan ranks. The Spartans in their heavy armor could not pursue the light troops across the rugged landscape of Sphakteria. Under constant attack, they fell back to one end of the island, where they were cornered and forced to surrender. Only 292 survived to be taken in chains to Athens (Thuc. 4.28–38).

Although unable to stand head-on against an unbroken phalanx, peltasts could fight effectively at close quarters against surprised or demoralized hoplites. At Amphipolis in 422, for example, the Spartan general Brasidas deployed a force including Myrkinian and Chalkidian peltasts to catch a larger Athenian hoplite army in the flank. The peltasts routed and pursued the hoplites, killing about six hundred Athenians along with their commander Kleon (Thuc. 5.7–11). On this occasion, peltasts functioned as a sort of medium infantry, nimble enough to escape attack if necessary, but also confident enough to enter melee combat under the right circumstances.

Properly trained peltasts, then, were mobile and versatile troops. So successful were they during the Peloponnesian War that by the early fourth century some terrified hoplites were refusing to fight peltast forces. Yet there were techniques to counter a peltast threat. Spartan phalanx commanders, for example, learned to dispatch their youngest, speediest hoplites to pursue and run down the attackers. The Spartan army had some success with this tactic during the Korinthian War, particularly in the fighting around Korinth in 390. Nonetheless, that same year the Athenian general Iphikrates, with a crack unit of peltasts, scored a resounding victory over a regiment of Spartan hoplites at Lechaion, just outside Korinth. The Spartans, some six hundred strong, were on their way home for a religious festival when Iphikrates and his men attacked using the characteristic combination of javelins and evasion. The Spartans repeatedly dispatched their fastest men in disorganized pursuit, but these soon fell back, unable to catch the peltasts. Under constant attack, and with Athenian hoplite reinforcements in sight, the Spartans broke and ran, some plunging into the sea to escape (Xenophon *Hellenika* 4.5.11–18). Of the 600 Spartans who set out that day, 250 perished. Ironically, had the Spartans not scored previous successes against peltasts, they might have better controlled their pursuit; as it was they were so overconfident that each man ran out at his own speed.

Other light troops, amongst them *akontistai* (javelineers) and *gymnetai* ("unarmored"), carried javelins but no shields. Later military manuals classified javelineers as true light troops (*psiloi*), in contrast to shield-carrying peltasts, who were considered intermediate between *psiloi* and hoplites (Onasandros *Strategikos* 17; Arrian *Tactica* 3.1–4). In practice, javelineers performed much the same functions as peltasts, using similar shoot-and-evade tactics, and Classical writers often used *psiloi* and *peltastai* interchangeably (Best 1969: 43–9). *Akontistai* were prominent in naval battles, especially in enclosed waters, where their missiles could inflict serious damage on enemy crews.

Less widely utilized than peltasts were archers, many from marginal regions like Crete, or from "barbarian" areas like Scythia. Classical archers employed both the simple one-piece bow and the composite bow, built up from layers of wood and horn. Greek bows were for the most part weak, as archers used a simple two-fingered pull and drew to the breast only. The Scythians, employed as policemen and auxiliaries at Athens, utilized a more complex grip and drew to the shoulder, but this technique was far more difficult to master (Snodgrass 1999: 83–4). The Cretans, too, developed better techniques, along with larger, stronger bows and long (up to 10 cm), tanged arrowheads (Snodgrass 1999: 40). The maximum effective range of ancient bows was probably around 150–200 m, though few men could manage more than five arrows a minute for any length of time (Gabriel & Metz 1991: 68). Weak bows also meant low penetrating power. Hoplite armor and shields were normally impervious to arrows except at very close range, so an archer's best chance was to hit unprotected flesh.

These technological limitations kept archery from becoming a major factor in Classical warfare. There were also cultural prejudices: after the Persian Wars, some rejected archery – a Persian specialty – as unmanly and unfair. As a Spartan captured at Sphakteria caustically remarked, an arrow "would be worth a great deal if it could pick out good and noble men from the rest" (Thuc. 4.40). Nonetheless, well-trained archers made excellent skirmishers and scouts, as even the Spartans understood: within a year of defeat at Sphakteria, Sparta had raised its first force of bowmen. Archery was also effective in sieges and urban fighting. During the final stages of the civil strife at Kerkyra in 425, for instance, the men of one faction climbed atop an enemy-occupied building, broke holes in the roof, and in a barrage of arrows shot down their opponents within (Thuc. 4.48). Navies too employed archers to great advantage. Athenian triremes regularly carried four apiece on deck; in battle these men targeted opposing officers, steersmen, and rowers. The importance of missile troops in naval warfare probably underlies the 1,600-strong corps of archers, not including Scythian policemen, which the Athenians had in service at the beginning of the Peloponnesian War. The Athenians also deployed several hundred mounted archers, probably to help protect the farmland of Attika from invading ravagers.

Slingers often fought alongside peltasts and archers on the Classical battlefield. The best slingers hailed from the fringes of the polis world, places like Akarnania, Malis, and Elis. Rhodians also gained fame for their slinging skills. The deceptively simple-looking sling was in the right hands deadlier than the bow. It consisted of no more than two lengths of twisted gut or sinew, even wool strips in a pinch, joined by a central pocket, with the end of one length secured around the slinger's wrist or middle finger. To throw, the slinger grasped both lengths firmly in one hand, placed a missile in the pocket, whirled the sling vertically or horizontally, and released his hand when it pointed at his target. This is far more difficult than it sounds, and slinging, even more than archery or javelin-throwing, demanded intensive training and practice. Expert slingers employed a variety of different casting techniques in addition to the stereotypical overhead whirl. At short range, they could operate even in confined spaces, using a single underhand whip of the wrist to fling heavy (30 g) projectiles with killing force (Lee 2001: 16).

Sling ammunition included round stones, clay pellets, and almond-shaped cast lead bullets. Bullets became increasingly common during the fifth and fourth centuries.

**Figure 23.4**   Lead sling bullet with a winged thunderbolt on one side, and on the other the inscription "Take that." Fourth century BCE, found in Athens. © The Trustees of The British Museum, London.

Some states produced them in bulk, although given a suitable mold slingers could quickly make new bullets from scrap lead even in field conditions (Xenophon *Anabasis* 3.4.17). Numerous excavated fourth-century examples from Olynthos in northern Greece show state manufacturers' inscriptions ("of the Olynthians"), as well as witty tag-lines like *aischron doron* – "an unpleasant gift." Lead bullets greatly enhanced effective range: Rhodian slingers using them were able to shoot perhaps 200 m, outdistancing even Persian archers (Xenophon *Anabasis* 3.3.17; 3.4.16). Slingers fought both on land and at sea. They were considered especially useful in siege operations, and slingers trained to use the underhanded whip throw could be extraordinarily effective in urban combat.

Peltasts, archers, slingers, and other light infantry represented powerful new forces in Classical warfare. Their equipment and formations enabled them to operate on ground wholly unsuited to the hoplite phalanx, while their ability to strike from a distance and rapidly withdraw confounded hoplites reliant on melee weapons. Sphakteria and Lechaion represented the salient examples of what light troops could do to unaccompanied hoplites, and similar scenes occurred with distressing results, for the hoplites at least, throughout the late fifth century. Nonetheless, missile-firers could never entirely displace hoplites from the battlefield. As Xenophon noted, "not even all the slingers in the world could stand at close quarters against a few men with hand-to-hand weapons" (Xenophon *Kyroupaideia* 7.4.15).

Hoplites could resort to short-range missile tactics themselves, notably at Solygeia in 424, where Korinthians rained down a hail of stones on an attacking Athenian phalanx (Thuc. 4.43). Yet the best solution to the threat of missile troops was to form integrated armies of hoplites, light infantry, and eventually, cavalry. The rudiments of such cooperation were in place as early as 458, when Athenian hoplites and *psiloi* massacred part of a retreating Korinthian army near Megara (Thuc. 1.106). The Peloponnesian War made it abundantly clear that unaccompanied hoplites ran great risks. Armies consequently fielded more light troops, and commanders learned to use them. By the early fourth century, the Spartan king Agesilaos was maneuvering his army as an articulated whole. In an attack, peltasts and other skirmishers could screen advancing hoplites, protecting them against missile fire until they were able to close in on an enemy force. Light troops could also cover changes in formation, flank marches, and withdrawals (Xenophon *Anabasis* 3.4.15). In urban fighting, like that between Athenian democrats and oligarchs during 404–403, slingers and archers could clear streets or pin down defenders, preparing the way for an assault with spears and swords (Xenophon *Hellenika* 2.4.12–19).

# 4  Cavalry

Although aristocrats kept horses throughout Greek history, most Classical poleis had little in the way of a cavalry tradition. Horses were expensive, and the mountains and ravines of southern Greece did not encourage mounted warfare. In hoplite circles during the early Classical period, disdain for Persian horsemen may have smeared cavalry with some of the "barbarian" mud thrown at archery. Horses, nonetheless, oozed glamor in a way that bows never could, and if some Athenians distrusted their wealthy aristocrats (*hippeis*) as undemocratic, the young horsy set throughout Greece still garnered enormous prestige from owning, displaying, and racing thoroughbreds (Spence 1993: 202–10).

The Athenians raised their first mounted corps early in the fifth century, and by the Peloponnesian War fielded a thousand horsemen, each of the ten Athenian tribes contributing a squadron. Athens also boasted a small unit of mounted archers from the 430s until the early fourth century. The Spartans did not organize their first cavalry force until 424, and Spartan armies often relied on allied or mercenary horsemen. The Spartan army did have an elite infantry unit of 300 *hippeis*; despite their name, these fought solely on foot. In central and northern Greece, open plains made for good horse country and much larger cavalries could appear. The Boiotians deployed about 1,000 cavalry in the fifth century; the cities of the Chalkidike peninsula together had at least as many, as did the kingdom of Macedon, while the Thessalians could assemble a force of thousands.

Classical cavalry were equipped to fight on horseback with both melee and missile weapons. Athenian troopers were typical in carrying a combination of javelins, thrusting spears, and short swords. Xenophon in the mid-fourth century recommended a slashing saber (*machaira*) and two javelins suitable for both throwing and thrusting (Xenophon *De Equitandi Ratione* 12.11–12), but probably every experienced rider had his own preferences. Defensive equipment also remained unstandardized. Some wealthy men splurged on customized bronze breastplates and helmets, along with thick, high leather boots. Others, out of preference or economy, traded metal protection for the comfort and flexibility of leather jerkins. Not much use was made of armor for horses.

**Figure 23.5** Cavalry: horseman carrying two javelins. Note the lack of stirrups. Hirmer Verlag, Munich.

Cavalry required both individual and unit training. Ancient riders did not enjoy the benefit of stirrups, and so needed greater skill to control their mounts. Nevertheless, well-trained men were perfectly capable of throwing javelins or handling sabers and spears from horseback. Along with individual drills, units maneuvered and practiced battle formations over a variety of terrain. The majority of our evidence on cavalry training concerns Athens, but similar measures were probably undertaken by other Greek states with large mounted contingents. Other poleis provided little or no formal training. The Spartans during the fourth century, for instance, seem to have largely neglected the matter. Wealthy men paid for the horses, but the riders were chosen at the last minute from amongst the least fit and aggressive Spartans (Xenophon *Hellenika* 6.4.10–11).

Scholars generally accept that cavalry became a decisive arm on the Greek battlefield only in the late fourth century, with the rise of the Macedonian lancers of Philip and Alexander. Yet cavalry performed significant military functions throughout the Classical period, and the fifth and fourth centuries witnessed some important innovations. Horsemen were far more mobile than hoplites or light infantry, and saw increasing use in raiding, scouting, and patrolling. In pitched battles, cavalry could screen hoplite advances, make flanking maneuvers, and pursue routed foes. Just as peltasts scored signal successes against unsupported hoplites, cavalry were particularly effective when an opposing phalanx was bereft of horsemen. After a seesaw hoplite struggle at Solygeia in 424, for instance, the Athenians finally won the day through the arrival of their cavalry. The same year at Delion, the Boiotians threw the Athenian phalanx into panic by sending two squadrons of cavalry on a threatening flanking movement. Ultimately, as combined arms tactics evolved during the late fifth and early fourth centuries, cavalry units became indispensable components of Greek armies. Several poleis even deployed *hamippoi*, specialized light infantry mixed into cavalry units for mutual support (Spence 1993: 57–60).

## 5    Mercenary Soldiers

Mercenaries had long been part of warfare in the eastern Mediterranean world. During the early Classical period several poleis recruited small numbers of specialist light infantry, amongst them Thracian peltasts, Cretan archers, and Rhodian slingers. A few states also sought out hoplite mercenaries, many from the mountainous uplands of Arkadia. Sparta enrolled modest contingents of professional hoplites on several occasions during the Peloponnesian War, usually for missions considered too dangerous or distant for Spartiate citizens. The Spartan general Brasidas, for instance, took with him a thousand Peloponnesian mercenaries on his campaign in northern Greece (424–422); Brasidas also had 700 helot hoplites, who gained freedom in return for their service.

   During the late fifth century, mercenary hoplites were much sought after by the Persian governors and local dynasts of western Asia Minor, to complement their light infantry and cavalry levies. A loyal hoplite bodyguard was also a fashionable status symbol. When the young Achaimenid prince Kyros was summoned to Babylon in 404, for instance, he took along the 300 hoplites of his personal guard and their Arkadian commanding officer. The Lykian dynast Arbinas, likewise, prominently depicted his hoplite guards in official art (Childs & Demargne 1989). The numbers of Greek mercenaries in Persian service increased substantially during the last quarter of the fifth century, primarily because of the political and economic disruptions of the Peloponnesian War. Persian gold beckoned invitingly to poverty-stricken or exiled Greeks, and by the end of the century, thousands of hoplite mercenaries served as city garrisons throughout Persian-controlled Ionia. In 401, some twelve thousand of these men joined the young prince Kyros in his failed attempt to seize the Persian throne from his elder brother Artaxerxes. The mercenaries, who became known as the "Cyreans," managed to stick together despite the death in battle of their employer, successfully reaching Byzantion in 399 after an epic trek out of the heart of the Persian empire.

   The Cyreans were the most visible sign of the increased presence of Greek mercenaries in the Aegean world, but they were not alone. The Persian demand for hired hoplites continued throughout the Classical period, but the fourth century for the first time witnessed widespread employment of Greek mercenaries by Greeks. Because of the new emphasis on combined arms, many of these were peltasts and other light troops. A significant proportion, however, were hoplites. Hardened professional soldiers of whatever sort were better trained and disciplined than citizen militia (Parke 1933: 77–9). In citizen eyes, mercenaries were also expendable, and therefore just the thing for carrying on a war while preserving citizen lives. Nonetheless, mercenaries never entirely displaced citizen hoplites. Even in the later fourth century, polis militias still mustered when danger threatened close to home, and citizen-soldiers still fought and died on Greek battlefields.

The expansion of mercenary service into mainland Greece carried in some cases significant political consequences. Hired soldiers could help protect a polis, but in the hands of an ambitious commander they could become agents of tyranny. The fourth century witnessed a new generation of mercenary-supported military autocrats, most notably Dionysios I of Syracuse (c. 430–367), who skillfully used hired soldiers to build and maintain his Sicilian empire. The Athenians, with their powerful democratic traditions, successfully kept their mercenary commanders from creating private armies. Many small poleis were not so lucky, judging from the amount of attention the fourth-century military handbook writer Aineias Taktikos devotes to forestalling coups and factional strife.

Classical attitudes toward mercenaries were mixed but overarchingly negative. In the fifth century, the euphemism *epikouros* ("helper") often designated the hired soldier, presumably to camouflage the embarrassing truth that he fought for pay. By the early fourth century, partly in reaction to the exploding number of mercenaries in mainland Greece, the derogatory *misthophoros* ("pay-taker") had entered common use (Parke 1933: 20–1). Orators like Isokrates and Demosthenes played on Greek prejudices against the working poor to portray mercenaries as immoral, wandering, plundering scoundrels, a threat to civic virtue and the integrity of the citizen soldier. Aristotle judged mercenaries lacking in the true courage characteristic of citizen-soldiers (Aristotle *Nicomachean Ethics* 3 1116b15). Aineias Taktikos (13.1–4) was more sanguine: mercenaries were a fact of life; they could be controlled, and they had their uses. For their part, mercenary units were sometimes more tolerant than the civilian Greeks who reviled them. The Cyreans, for instance, welcomed to their ranks both Greeks and non-Greeks, political exiles and renegades, gentlemen adventurers, ex-slaves, and at least one former professional boxer.

# 6   Logistics and Medical Care

Classical armies in general lacked developed supply and service apparatus. In citizen hoplite forces, soldiers usually provided and prepared their own food. At Athens, for instance, "Report with three days' rations" was a standard instruction (Aristophanes *Peace* 1183). The staple ration was bread or boiled porridge, supplemented by olives, cheese, onions, and wine. Given the difficulties of terrain, and the limited capacity of pack animals and wagons, armies sometimes attempted to synchronize their movements with harvest time, so that soldiers could forage on enemy territory. Alternatively, commanders could arrange with locals along a march route to furnish markets where soldiers could buy provisions. The best option, especially on longer expeditions, was seaborne supply in the form of cargo vessels carrying grain and other foodstuffs. These efforts were not always successful, and Greek armies were often hampered by their decentralized logistical systems. The Spartans were an exception. Their army possessed dedicated supply officers, and formalized common messes. On one occasion, the Spartans were even able to dispatch portable fire-pots to help revive a detachment isolated on a cold, rainy ridge (Xenophon *Hellenika* 4.5.4).

Medical services were of varying quality. In the fourth century, the Spartans had doctors (*iatroi*) accompanying their units. The Athenians may have had some doctors in public service, and mercenary forces sometimes included professional surgeons, but in other armies medics were selected ad hoc from amongst the ranks (Salazar 2000: 68–74). Generals and officers got the best care, while ordinary sick or wounded soldiers frequently had to rely on comrades or attendants to carry them from the field and take care of them. Military doctors could extract missiles and bind wounds, but were largely helpless against gangrene and infections.

## 7  Slaves, Servants, and Other Non-Combatants

Male slaves and servants often accompanied Classical armies, although they may have been less ubiquitous than has usually been supposed (van Wees 2001: 60). These attendants carried arms and armor, gathered firewood, cooked and cleaned, and evacuated and tended the wounded. Wealthier citizen hoplites at Athens possessed a single slave attendant, while each Spartan soldier could count on the services of one or more helot. Poorer mercenaries generally did not have attendants. In exceptional circumstances, slaves could be armed for pitched battle, while in urban fighting they might help defend their masters' homes. Some slaves also served as rowers in the Athenian and other navies. Helots too could be armed, and as the Classical period wore on, the Spartans increasingly used freed helot hoplites to supplement their dwindling citizen troops.

Non-Greek fighting women, the Amazons, constitute a prominent motif of Classical art, often as mythical stand-ins for the Persians. The participation of real Greek women in warfare, however, receives only rare mention in ancient sources. In Classical Greece, many of the military functions performed by female auxiliaries in other societies were the responsibility of slave or helot attendants. Still, women did on occasion accompany Classical armies. The Athenians besieging Samos in 440/39, for instance, allegedly brought courtesans (*hetairai*) along with them (Athenaios 572F), while Thucydides records that 110 women bakers served alongside the 480 defenders of Plataiai (Thuc. 2.78). In mercenary armies, women could become valued and vocal members of the soldiers' community, as Xenophon demonstrates in the *Anabasis*, his memoir of life with the Cyreans. Women also participated in urban combat, hurling tiles and stones from rooftops against invading troops.

## 8  Religion and Warfare

Rituals, vows, and sacrifices accompanied all stages of Classical warfare (Pritchett 1979). Upon leaving home, armies made preliminary offerings to seek divine favor and to delineate the transition from peace to war. On the march, there were rites for crossing borders and rivers. Commanders often relied on the services of professional diviners (*manteis*) to find the most auspicious moments for maneuvers or attacks. Before battle, there were animal sacrifices (*sphagia*) to furnish a symbolic beginning to the bloodletting, and soldiers marched into the fray singing the *paian*, a hymn to Apollo. This god was especially associated with mercenaries, and at the Temple of Apollo at Bassai in Arkadia, excavators have unearthed numerous miniature votives of arms and armor, striking evidence for the religious devotions of Arkadian professional soldiers on their way to and from war (Fields 1994: 104–8). On the battlefield, a victorious army set up a trophy (*tropaion*), an image of Zeus, lord of victory. Returning home, soldiers made individual votive offerings and sacrifices to fulfill vows made before setting out. There were drink offerings (*spondai*) to mark peace treaties, while the victors consecrated a tenth part (*dekaten*) of their spoils – often in the form of captured arms and armor – at local temples or at the great shrines of Delphi and Olympia (Burkert 1985: 267).

## 9  Fortifications and Siege Warfare

From the seventh century onward, poleis girded their citadels (*akropoleis*) with defensive walls, and by the Classical period virtually every polis, with the notable exceptions of Sparta and Elis, had a fortified akropolis. The akropolis walls protected temples and civic buildings, and in time of war served as a temporary refuge for citizens. Circuit walls covering the entire urban area of a polis were rare at first, but became increasingly common from the mid-fifth century onward. Most Greek walls were of quarried granite or limestone. Ashlar masonry, regular rectangular blocks in courses of equal height, eventually became one of the most common building methods. Walls frequently consisted of two ashlar facings enclosing a rubble core, sometimes with ashlar transverses for greater strength. Mud brick was occasionally employed when local stone was unavailable or of poor quality. The city walls of Athens, destroyed by the Persians in 480, were hurriedly rebuilt using recycled gravestones, bits of sculpture, and other rubble.

City walls were both a military advantage and a vivid symbol of polis sovereignty. They were also amongst the most expensive and labor-intensive projects a state could pursue. In 401, to cite an extreme example, Dionysios I of Syracuse conscripted 60,000 workers and 6,000 yoke of oxen to construct a 6 km wall with towers in two weeks. The total cost of this has been estimated at around 300 talents, the equivalent of almost two million daily wages for an average worker (Camp 2000: 46–7). At the other end of the scale, the akropolis walls of Halai in central Greece, with a circuit of roughly 0.5 km, went through many decades of patchwork building and modification. Once erected, walls required regular maintenance and sometimes, especially after earthquakes, extensive repairs.

Several poleis constructed Long Walls, paired extensions of a circuit wall running from an inland city to a port or beach. The best known of these, dating from the mid-fifth century, connected Athens with its port of Piraeus some seven kilometers to the southwest. Along with a third wall stretching south to the beach at Phaleron, the Athenian Long Walls enclosed several square kilometers of relatively open land, space for refugees from the Attic countryside during wartime. The countryside itself was dotted with numerous freestanding towers, which served as agricultural storehouses and slave quarters, lookout and signaling posts, and temporary refuges from raiders. Finally, elaborate border defense fortifications appeared in the fourth century. The Athenians, for instance, constructed a chain of forts, including Phyle, Oinoe, and Eleutherai, to cover the mountain passes leading into Attika from the north. There was also the so-called Dema Wall, perhaps built as early as the first quarter of the fourth century to cover the western approaches to Attika.

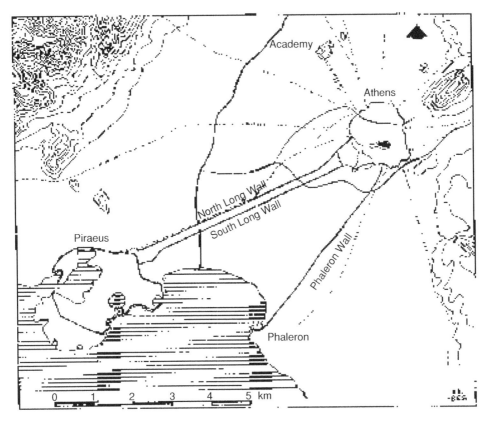

**Figure 23.6** The Long Walls connecting Athens and its port of Piraeus. In Piraeus were the dry docks, yards, and warehouses of the Athenian navy. John M. Camp, *The Archaeology of Athens* (New Haven and London: Yale University Press). Used with permission.

For much of the Classical period the Greeks lagged far behind in poliorcetic, or siege, technology, and defenders held the upper hand in siege warfare. The Athenians enjoyed a reputation as expert besiegers, but aside from being the first Greeks to deploy battering rams, at Samos in 440, they were not particularly successful. Indeed, their siege of Poteidaia (432–430) at the start of Peloponnesian War was typical: the Poteidaians surrendered only when food ran out. For their part, the Peloponnesians attacking Plataiai in summer 429 attempted a succession of different techniques (Thuc. 2.75–8). Blockading the town with a palisade of felled fruit trees, they began to heap up an earthen ramp to surmount the defensive walls. The Plataians countered by heightening their walls and undermining the ramp. When the Peloponnesians brought up battering rams, the defenders dropped heavy beams on chains to snap off some ram heads, and used lassoes to grab and disable others. Ultimately, although the Peloponnesians were able to collapse portions of the Plataian wall, they were unable to capture the city. They settled for a blockade, which took two years to starve the defenders into submission.

The Peloponnesian War saw further technological innovations. At Delion in 424, for example, the Boiotians devised a primitive flamethrower to drive Athenian defenders from a wooden fort (Thuc. 4.100); the Spartans used a similar device successfully on at least one other occasion (Thuc. 4.115). The greatest danger to fortifications, however, came from within. A gate left unguarded at night or opened by traitors within could provide attackers quick access to the city. Stealthy attackers could also scale unpatrolled walls at night or be smuggled into the city by a sympathetic faction. So serious were these threats that Aineias Taktikos devoted the majority of his handbook on siege warfare to discussing countermeasures against them. Getting past the walls, however, did not necessarily equal capturing the city, as the 300 Theban attackers of Plataiai discovered in 429. Let into the town by traitors, they made the mistake of grounding arms in the marketplace rather than immediately going house to house and arresting any who might oppose them. The Plataians soon recovered their courage and fought back, building street barricades and cutting holes through mud-brick house-walls to encircle the confused Thebans. Only a handful of attackers escaped, while 180 were captured and executed. The Macedonians let into Olynthos by traitors in 348 did not make the same mistake, but even so extensive urban fighting was required to subdue the city (Lee 2001).

The fourth century saw the advantage shift slowly to the offensive. The Carthaginians were the first to use mobile siege towers that overtopped defensive walls, at Selinous and Himera in 409. Dionysios I of Syracuse borrowed the idea to take Carthaginian-held Motya in 397. Dionysios also introduced the first bolt-shooting artillery. The earliest version, a sort of oversized crossbow called the *gastraphetes*, could reach perhaps 185–230 m. By around 375, this had grown into a mounted bolt-thrower (*oxybeles* or *katapaltes*) powered by winches and levers, able to propel a 1.25 m missile up to 275 m. The size and range of bolt-throwers continued to increase, and by the 350s some had been modified into stone-throwers (*lithoboloi*). These machines were effective against personnel, but not powerful enough to knock down walls or towers. Only during the 340s did torsion artillery, powered by twisted sinew or hair, come into use. Using bolts or heavy (15 kg) stones, torsion engines could shoot to ranges of 370 m or more (Marsden 1969: 12–17, 86–91). At closer ranges, with much heavier stones (up to 36 kg), they could breach most fortifications.

The development of siege artillery dramatically influenced military architecture. Tall artillery towers, designed to mount multiple defensive batteries with wide fields of fire, replaced or were retrofitted over earlier archery platforms and bastions. The number of towers in any given length of wall also increased significantly. Masonry was rusticated, left with an unfinished convex surface to deflect stone shot. Besiegers responded with larger mobile towers, more powerful artillery, and better engineering, inaugurating a race between attackers and defenders that would continue unabated into the Hellenistic period.

Given the advantages enjoyed by defenders in siege warfare throughout much of the period, why did Classical armies still sally forth to meet invaders in pitched battle? The obvious explanation is that citizen-soldiers sought to protect their fields and orchards from invading ravagers. Yet matters are not so simple. Agricultural devastation was time-consuming and often ineffective, and troops dispersed for ravaging were vulnerable to counterattack. Even the repeated Spartan invasions of Attika during the Peloponnesian War seem to have caused relatively little permanent damage (Hanson 1998: 174–84). The real damage, it has been argued, was to the pride and territoriality of citizen-farmers, who saw trespassers on *their* land, mucking about in their crops and defiling their ancestral shrines. Ravaging, in sum, was more symbolic than practical, intended to goad citizen-hoplites out of their walls and into pitched battle. This incitement usually worked. In fact the Athenians at the start of the Peloponnesian War were unusual precisely because they withdrew behind the Long Walls and did not sally forth to confront the Spartans. Perikles, indeed, experienced great difficulty convincing his fellow citizens to stick with this passive strategy (Thuc. 2.21).

Even if ravaging did not always cause irreparable long-term damage, the short-term damage could be significant. Successive repeated invasions coupled with semi-permanent occupation could do real harm, as the Athenians discovered later in the war when the Spartans established a fortress at Dekeleia in northeast Attika from which they could raid the countryside and offer sanctuary to escaping slaves. The Athenians at least had a naval lifeline which kept grain ships coming into the Piraeus until the last months of the war. Smaller poleis were not so fortunate. Even localized, temporary agricultural destruction could mean starvation for some, and so their citizens probably marched out to battle as much for practical economic reasons as for symbolic ones. If nothing else, they could delay the enemy long enough to evacuate the countryside. City walls were there to provide a fallback position if necessary, but the first thing to do was undertake an active defense against the invader.

# 10   Naval Warfare

Perhaps the single most important development of Classical warfare was the rise of strategic naval power. Beginning in the early fifth century, fleets of oared galleys presented a radical military challenge to the hoplite-dominated, limited war ethos of the polis. The development of naval warfare also had profound effects on the politics, society, and economy of its foremost practitioner, Athens.

Classical Greeks ascribed the building of the first navy to the legendary King Minos of Crete, said to have been the first ruler to aim at thalassocracy, imperial control of the seas. Polykrates, tyrant of Samos in the mid-sixth century, was the first historical figure to organize and deploy a significant fleet. Aigina and Korinth were other early naval powers. Even Sparta took to the sea in the sixth century, amongst other things sending a ship-borne army to overthrow the Athenian tyrant Hippias in 510.

At the beginning of the fifth century, the Athenians were not known for naval power. In fact, they had to borrow ships from Korinth to carry on a feud with Aigina in the early 490s. Nonetheless, one of the first major foreign policy decisions of the Athenian democracy was to dispatch, in 499, a force of twenty ships to aid the Ionian revolt against Persia. The real start of Athenian naval dominance came in 483/2 with the construction, at the urging of the politician Themistokles, of a fleet of more than one hundred large oared galleys. In 480, this formed the backbone of the combined Greek force that defeated a much larger Persian navy in the straits between Salamis and Attika, and subsequently enabled Athens to become dominant in the Delian League, an anti-Persian defensive alliance established in 479. As the Persian threat receded in the following three decades, the Athenians took advantage of their naval supremacy to reshape the Delian League into their own Aegean maritime empire.

Empire brought Athens unprecedented power and prosperity, but it also prompted the hegemonic rivalry with Sparta that culminated in the Peloponnesian War. During the war, naval power was Athens' lifeline, enabling the Athenians to shelter behind their Long Walls, import food, and conduct far-flung amphibious operations while refusing hoplite battle against the superior Spartan army. Overconfidence in the abilities of their fleet, however, led the Athenians to undertake the disastrous Sicilian expedition of 415–413. Even so, in the last decade of the war their reconstituted fleet continued to excel at sea. The Spartans responded by building, with Persian assistance, a navy of their own. Although repeatedly trounced by the Athenians, the Spartans scored a war-winning naval success in 404, surprising the Athenian fleet on the beach at Aigospotamoi in the Hellespont. Reduced to just twelve ships at the end of the Peloponnesian War, the Athenian fleet rebounded in the fourth century, and Athens played a leading, though no longer imperial, role in a second Aegean naval confederacy. Although never nearly as mighty as they had been in the fifth century, the Athenians remained a naval power to be reckoned with until the very end of the Classical period – their last sea battle, a defeat at Macedonian hands, came in 322 off Amorgos in the Cyclades.

The standard warship of all Classical Greek navies was an oared galley, the *trieres* or trireme. The vessel took its name from the arrangement of its 170 rowers into three levels, closely packed one above the other. Thirty-odd other crewmen, including the captain, a helmsman, sailors, hoplite marines, and archers, perched precariously on deck. Some 35 m long and less than 5 m at the beam, the trireme was optimized for speed and maneuverability. So light was its construction that the vessel had to be held together by tensioned ropes (*hypozomata*) fitted low down in the hull. Much valuable information on trireme performance comes from an experimental reconstruction, the

**Figure 23.7**    Reconstruction of Athenian trireme (1992) under oar at Poros. Photo: Alexander Guest. Courtesy: Trireme Trust.

*Olympias*, built by an international team in the 1980s (Morrison et al. 2000). Rowers on this vessel have achieved short-burst speeds of more than nine knots. Sea trials of *Olympias* have also highlighted the trireme's instability, as even a single person walking across the deck can cause significant pitching.

Although it used sails for long-distance travel, in battle a trireme was propelled by its rowers. The vessel attacked by smashing into enemy ships with its bow-mounted ram, a cast bronze prow flared at the end to prevent sticking in a holed opponent. Ancient sources mention two primary offensive tactics, the *diekplous* ("sailing through and out") and the *periplous* ("sailing around"). How these worked in practice remains uncertain. Some picture trireme combat as a series of individual dogfights, with swifter vessels turning tightly to hit the sterns of slower opponents (Whitehead 1987: 183–5). More likely, fleets maneuvered as units, either outflanking a shorter enemy line in the *periplous*, or, in the *diekplous*, sailing line-ahead to punch through an enemy formation. Either way, great skill on the part of helmsmen and rowers was required to time and execute attacks properly. Successful ram strikes could cause severe damage, shattering oars and pulverizing rowers at the point of impact, although the ships themselves were so buoyant that they tended to float even when disabled and could often be recovered after battle by the winning side.

Ramming tactics were particularly associated with the Athenian navy, which possessed light, fast ships, expert crews, and able commanders. These tactics had not developed overnight. At Salamis in 480, for instance, the inexperienced Greeks, fearing the skilled Phoenician rowers of the Persian fleet, lured their opponents into a narrow strait, where their hoplite marines could more easily grapple and board the Persian ships. As the Athenians became practiced in trireme warfare in the decades after Salamis, they embarked fewer marines, only ten per ship, against the forty carried by vessels of other states, and increasingly emphasized maneuver over boarding. There were other tactical viewpoints, though. During the Eurymedon campaign of the mid-460s, for example, the Athenian general Kimon modified his ships with broader decks and gangways to carry more hoplites. This may have been as much a political as a military decision, as Kimon sought to promote the glory of the hoplites at the expense of poor rowers (Strauss 2000: 321–3).

By the start of the Peloponnesian War, maneuver reigned supreme in Athenian naval circles, ramming and boarding being considered rather old-fashioned. The Athenians displayed their skills abundantly in the first years of the war, notably in the Gulf of Korinth, where a flotilla under Phormion repeatedly defeated larger Peloponnesian squadrons. In one battle Phormion's triremes literally sailed in circles around a frightened Peloponnesian convoy before closing in for the kill (Thuc. 2.83–4). So formidable were the Athenians that a 40-ship Peloponnesian fleet on the way to assist Mytilene in 427 fled rather than risk a fight after being sighted by a pair of Athenian triremes.

Athens' enemies, recognizing that maneuver required sea room and lighter, faster ships, found ways to fight back. The defenders of Syracuse, for example, won several naval battles by pinning the invading Athenian fleet in Syracuse's Great Harbor. In such confined waters, the Athenians found little space for their favored tactics. At close range, moreover, Syracusan archers, slingers, and javelin-throwers found easy targets on the Athenian triremes. The Syracusans unsuccessfully tried a fire ship on one occasion, and both sides employed artificial barriers, including sunken pilings and merchant ships, to protect their triremes. The Korinthians also discovered that Athenian ships, while optimized for high speed and quick turns, were vulnerable to frontal collisions. Exploiting this weakness by fitting their triremes with reinforced prows and training their crews to attack head-on, the Korinthians managed to fight the Athenians to a draw at Erineos in 413. The Syracusans quickly adopted the design and the tactic for their battles in the Great Harbor, with stunningly successful results (Thuc. 7.34–6).

There was more to naval power than sea battle. By controlling piracy, collecting tribute, and escorting merchant shipping, navies made maritime empire possible. Until the very end of the Peloponnesian War, the Athenian navy ensured Athens' survival by protecting the vital grain convoys that sustained the city even when the Spartans occupied the countryside. Through commerce raiding, the Athenians also caused some economic difficulty for their opponents, particularly the Korinthians. Furthermore, fleets enabled states to move ground forces quickly and easily over long distances, using specialized troop carriers as well as cavalry transports capable of carrying up to thirty horses (Morrison et al. 2000: 153–7). Seaborne troops could suppress revolts, launch lightning amphibious raids, establish outposts in enemy territory, or, as in the Sicilian expedition, conduct large-scale invasions. In the later stages of the Peloponnesian War, the Athenians even resorted to arming sailors as peltasts to mount improvised amphibious operations (Xenophon *Hellenika* 1.2.1).

There were several strategic limitations on naval power. Their light construction and cramped confines meant triremes were not sea-going vessels. Each day, crews had to find a port, or at least a shelving beach where they could draw up their ships and disembark to eat and sleep. This made blockades difficult to maintain. The Spartans trapped on Sphakteria in 425–424, for instance, received supplies via small boats despite a strong Athenian naval presence (Thuc. 4.26). More ominously, a fleet drawn up on shore was virtually helpless against surprise attack, particularly if rowers scattered in search of provisions. The Athenians at Aigospotamoi lost their fleet, and thus the Peloponnesian War, this way. Even if a safe anchorage was at hand, triremes could not remain on station indefinitely. Extended immersion caused hulls to become waterlogged, significantly reducing performance. Unless brought into dry-dock regularly for drying and cleaning, triremes were in serious trouble.

Triremes represented the acme of Classical technology, and they were expensive. A fleet required not only ships, but also spare parts, equipment, and supplies such as pitch and paint. Athens, with a navy averaging roughly 150–200 triremes over the course of the fifth and fourth centuries, had to maintain an extensive complex of ship sheds, building yards, and warehouses in its port of Piraeus. Paying for all this required the Athenians to draw on the resources of their wealthiest citizens (Gabrielsen 1994). In the fifth century, individual trierarchs were responsible for outfitting and maintaining a ship and its crew. Although not professionals, they were expected to accompany their vessels into battle. Such was the expense involved that by the end of the fifth century joint trierarchies, where two or more men combined to pay for a ship, became increasingly common. During the mid-fourth century a further series of reforms created twenty symmories of sixty men apiece, with each symmory financing an equal proportion of the fleet.

Without trained crews, triremes were little more than expensive firewood. Given that a fleet of 100 ships required 17,000 rowers, finding enough oarsmen was a constant concern. In the Athenian navy, a mix of poorer citizens and hired foreigners manned the oars. Some slaves also served as rowers, although the extent of their use remains disputed. Only the state triremes *Paralos* and *Salaminia* mustered all-citizen crews (Jordan 1975: 173–84). Rowers could receive up to a drachma a day in state pay, with additional bonuses often provided by trierarchs. To forestall desertion, men received only half their wages on enlistment, the rest being distributed upon return to Piraeus. Even so, in the last years of the Peloponnesian War, the Spartans, aided by Persian subsidies, managed to entice numbers of hired rowers away from the Athenian fleet with offers of higher pay.

For the thetes, poor Athenian citizen oarsmen, naval service carried powerful political implications. Just as some fifth-century hoplites appealed to the legend of Marathon to justify their claims to represent the true spirit of Athens, so too could thetes point to Salamis and to Athens' maritime empire as evidence of their importance to the polis. Rowing together in triremes provided thetes with a shared identity and experience, while the close association of trireme crews fostered political consciousness and discussion (Strauss 1996: 313). The rise of sea power went hand in hand with the development of radical democracy in fifth century Athens. Indeed, an elite writer ("The Old Oligarch") of the period reluctantly admitted that "the poor and ordinary people [of Athens] rightly have greater power than the well-born and the rich, because it's the ordinary people who row the ships and bring power to the city" (Pseudo-Xenophon *Ath. Pol.* 1.2). If no marble edifices glorified rowers and triremes, the thetes could point to still more impressive symbols of their glory: the arsenals and dockyards of Piraeus, and the prows of their triremes, carrying names such as *Eleutheria* ("Liberty") and *Parrhesia* ("Freedom of Speech").

## 11 Macedon and the End of Classical Warfare

The last decades of the Classical period saw the rise of a new military powerhouse, the kingdom of Macedon. Full treatment of Macedonian and Hellenistic warfare is beyond the scope of this survey, but it is important to point out how developments in the Classical period laid the foundations for Macedonian success. The integrated army of Philip II of Macedon, with pikemen, lancers, and light infantry working together, drew inspiration from the combined arms tactics that Greek commanders had been deploying since the late fifth century. Philip perfected combined arms tactics, forging his kingdom's excellent cavalry into an offensive hammer and equipping his infantry with a long (3.5–4.5 m) pike (*sarissa*) that far outreached the hoplite spear. The *sarissa* phalanx became an anvil upon which the Macedonian cavalry would smash its opponents. Philip also drew on Classical developments in siege engineering to create his own siege train, including powerful new torsion artillery. The true revolution in Macedonian warfare was logistical. Philip trained his men to march faster while carrying more, and backed them up with a supply system combining careful planning and advance requisitions. It was this logistical capability that made possible the lightning successes of his son Alexander the Great (Engels 1978).

# 12 Conclusions and Future Directions

The Classical period witnessed significant innovations in the Greek practice of warfare. These included the new prominence of light troops, resulting in the creation of combined arms tactics; greater "professionalization," epitomized by the widespread employment of mercenaries; a shift from defensive to offensive superiority in siege warfare, made possible by better engineering and torsion artillery; and the rise of strategic naval power, with its concomitant political and social effects at Athens. It is also possible that the ideology of hoplite battle, rather than being an Archaic invention, reached its fullest expression only in the Classical period.

Each of these topics invites further investigation. The origins and development of the hoplite phalanx, in particular, deserve restudy in light of the recent research noted above. So too does the relationship between hoplite ideology and the rise of the Athenian navy in the fifth century. In doing so, scholars must remain aware of the biased and prescriptive nature of the ancient textual and material evidence. More sophisticated archaeological work, as well as re-analysis of finds from earlier excavations, may help shed light on siege warfare and urban combat. In some cases, practical experimentation may help resolve long-standing questions, for instance the effective ranges of javelins, bows, and slings.

Since the mid-1990s, much attention has focused on pitched battle, especially amongst hoplites. While this work should continue, there exists also a pressing need for further research on the non-battle aspects of warfare, including logistics, social and community relationships within armies, and the roles of women and other non-combatants. More work is needed on the economic impact of agricultural devastation, and on the aftereffects of war, including post-combat trauma, military commemoration, and public memory. There should also be increased emphasis on the connections between military changes and developments in other aspects of Greek civilization. Too often the study of warfare is dismissed as mere "military history," technical research without wider significance for understanding the totality of Greek life. An integrated approach, explaining not just how the Greeks fought, but also how they wrote about war and depicted it in art, how they shaped armed force to fit their societies, and how war influenced their political and social organization, will go a long way toward removing this stigma.

## Further reading

Raaflaub (1999) is a good short introduction emphasizing the links between warfare and Greek society. For longer overviews consult Ducrey (1986a, 1986b) and Garlan (1975). For more advanced research, the five volumes of Pritchett's *Greek state at war* (Pritchett 1971–91) are an indispensable starting point. For ancient texts, see the excellent translations of Strassler (1996) (Thucydides), Dillery (2001) (Xenophon), and Whitehead (1990) (Aineias Taktikos). Sage (1996) provides a useful selection of translated primary sources, including inscriptions and other texts not otherwise readily available to students. Childs & Demargne (1989), along with Lissarague (1990), offer valuable studies of the representation of warriors in Greek art.

On the equipment, tactics, and ideology of hoplite warfare, start with Hanson (2000b), Mitchell (1996), and the essays collected in Hanson (1991) and van Wees (2000). Krentz (2002) and van Wees (2000) challenge the current view of hoplite warfare, as restated by Hanson (2000a). Anderson (1970) focuses on the fourth century, with treatment of logistics, generalship, training, and the interaction between hoplites and other arms. Ogden (1996) offers an excellent analysis of homosexual relations and combat cohesion in Greek armies. For the Spartan army in particular, Lazenby (1985) remains the best book-length study, although Singor (1999) and Singor (2002) are essential reading. Van Wees (2001) offers a provocative new interpretation of the connection between the rise of the hoplite phalanx and political change at Athens.

Snodgrass (1999) gives a good overview of Classical arms and armor. Jarva (1995) and Baitinger (2001) (in German) are more scholarly, but still accessible. On peltasts see Best (1969), and on slingers see Pritchett (1991); for cavalry, start with Spence (1993) and Gaebel (2002). Parke (1933) remains the best treatment of mercenary soldiers in classical Greece. For fortifications, see Lawrence (1979) and Adam (1981) (in French); on urban warfare see Lee (2001). On the development and construction of siege artillery see Marsden (1969); on agricultural devastation see Hanson (1998).

On trireme warfare and the reconstructed trireme *Olympias*, see Morrison et al. (2000). Recent research suggests that the *Olympias* reconstruction is inaccurate in several respects, and plans are afoot to build a second trireme; for details and updates see the web site of the Trireme Trust (http://www-atm.physics.ox.ac.uk/rowing/trireme/).

# Bibliography

Adam, J.-P. (1981) *L'architecture militaire grecque* (Paris: Picard) (Grandes manuels Picard)

Anderson, J. K. (1970) *Military theory and practice in the age of Xenophon* (Berkeley: University of California Press)

Aymard, A. (1967) "Mercenariat et histoire grecque" in: Aymard, A. (1967) *Études d'histoire ancienne* (Paris: Presses Universitaires de France) (Publications de la Faculté des Lettres et Sciences Humaines de Paris-Sorbonne: Série "Études et methods" 16) 487–98

Baitinger, H. (2001) *Die Angriffswaffen aus Olympia* (Berlin: de Gruyter) (Olympische Forschungen 29)

Berent, M. (2000) "Anthropology and the classics: war, violence, and the stateless *polis*" in: *CQ* 50: 257–89

Best, J. G. P. (1969) *Thracian peltasts and their influence on Greek warfare* (trans. I. Rike) (Groningen: Walters-Noordhoff) (Studies of the Dutch Archaeological and Historical Society 1)

Bugh, G. R. (1988) *The horsemen of Athens* (Princeton: Princeton University Press)

Burkert, W. (1985) *Greek religion: archaic and classical* (trans. J. Raffan) (Oxford: Blackwell)

Camp, J. McK. (2000) "Walls and the *polis*" in: Flensted-Jensen et al. 2000: 41–57

Childs, W. A. P., & P. Demargne (1989) *Fouilles de Xanthos*, vol. 8: *Le monument des Néréides: le décor sculpté* (Paris: Klincksieck)

Christ, M. R. (2001) "Conscription of hoplites in classical Athens" in: *CQ* 51: 398–422

Dillery, J. (2001) *Xenophon: Anabasis* (trans. C. L. Brownson; revised by J. Dillery) (Cambridge MA: Harvard University Press) (Loeb Classical Library)

Ducrey, P. (1986a) *Warfare in ancient Greece* (trans. J. Lloyd) (New York: Schocken)

Ducrey, P. (1986b) "Les fortifications grecques: rôle, fonction, efficacité" in: Leriche & Tréziny 1986: 133–42

Engels, D. (1978) *Alexander the Great and the logistics of the Macedonian army* (Berkeley: University of California Press)

Fields, N. (1994) "Apollo: god of war, protector of mercenaries" in: Sheedy, K. (ed.) (1994) *Archaeology in the Peloponnese: new excavations and research: meeting entitled "Archaeology in the Peloponnese: Research in the new decade": selected papers* (Oxford: Oxbow) 95–113

Flensted-Jensen, P., T. H. Nielsen, & L. Rubinstein (eds) (2000) *Polis and politics: studies in ancient Greek history presented to M. H. Hansen* (Copenhagen: Museum Tusculanum)

Gabriel, R., & K. Metz (1991) *From Sumer to Rome: the military capabilities of ancient armies* (New York: Greenwood)

Gabrielsen, V. (1994) *Financing the Athenian fleet: public taxation and social relations* (Baltimore: Johns Hopkins University Press)

Gaebel, R. (2002) *Cavalry operations in the ancient Greek world* (Norman: University of Oklahoma Press)

Garlan, Y. (1975) *War in the ancient world: a social history* (trans. J. Lloyd) (London: Chatto & Windus) (Ancient Culture and Society)

Hall, J. M. (1997) *Ethnic identity in Greek antiquity* (Cambridge: Cambridge University Press)

Hanson, V. D. (ed.) (1991) *Hoplites: the classical Greek battle experience* (London: Routledge)

Hanson, V. D. (1996) "Hoplites into democrats: the changing ideology of Athenian infantry" in: Ober, J., & C. W. Hedrick (eds) (1996) *Demokratia: a conversation on democracies, ancient and modern* (Princeton: Princeton University Press) 289–312

Hanson, V. D. (1998) *Warfare and agriculture in classical Greece* (Berkeley: University of California Press; revised ed., first published 1983 (Pisa: Giardini) (Biblioteca di Studi Antica 40))

Hanson, V. D. (1999) *The other Greeks: the family farm and the agrarian roots of western civilization* (Berkeley: University of California Press [2]1999)

Hanson, V. D. (2000a) "Hoplite battle as ancient Greek warfare" in: van Wees 2000: 201–32

Hanson, V. D. (2000b) *The western way of war: infantry battle in classical Greece* (with an intro. by J. Keegan) (Berkeley: University of California Press [2]2000)

Harris, H. A. (1963) "Greek javelin throwing" in: *G&R* 10: 26–36

Holladay, A. J. (1988) "Further thoughts on trireme tactics" in: *G&R* 35: 149–51

Hunt, P. (1998) *Slaves, warfare, and ideology in the Greek historians* (Cambridge: Cambridge University Press)

Jarva, E. (1995) *Archaiologia on archaic Greek body armour* (Rovaniemi: Pohjois-Suomen Historiallinen Yhdistys) (Studia Archaeologica Septentrionalia 3)

Jordan, B. (1975) *The Athenian navy in the classical period: a study of Athenian naval administration and military organization in the fifth and fourth centuries B.C.* (Berkeley: University of California Press) (University of California publications: Classical Studies 13)

Krentz, P. (1994) "Continuing the *othismos* on the *othismos*" in: *Ancient History Bulletin* 8: 45–9

Krentz, P. (1997) "The strategic culture of Periclean Athens" in: Hamilton, C. D., & P. Krentz (eds) (1997) *Polis and polemos: essays on politics, war, and history in ancient Greece in honor of Donald Kagan* (Claremont CA: Regina) 55–72

Krentz, P. (2002) "Fighting by the rules: the invention of the hoplite *agon*" in: *Hesperia* 71: 23–39

Lawrence, A. W. (1979) *Greek aims in fortification* (Oxford: Clarendon)

Lazenby, J. F. (1985) *The Spartan army* (Warminster: Aris & Phillips)

Lazenby, J. F. (1987) "The diekplous" in: *G&R* 34: 169–77

Lazenby, J. F., & D. Whitehead (1996) "The myth of the hoplite's *hoplon*" in: *CQ* 46: 27–33

Lee, J. (2001) "Urban combat at Olynthos, 348 BC" in: Freeman, P. W. M., & A. Pollard (eds) (2001) *Fields of conflict: progress and prospect in battlefield archaeology: proceedings of a conference held in the department of archaeology, University of Glasgow, April 2000* (Oxford: Archeopress): 11–22

Leriche, P., & H. Tréziny (eds) (1986) *La fortification dans l'histoire du monde grec: Actes du colloque international, La fortification et sa place dans l'histoire politique, culturelle et sociale du monde grec (Valbonne, décembre 1982)* (Paris: Éditions du CNRS) 305–13

Lissarague, F. (1990) *L'autre guerrier: archers, peltastes, cavaliers dans l'imagerie attique* (Paris: La Découverte) (Images à l'appui 3)

Marsden, E. W. (1969) *Greek and Roman artillery: historical development* (Oxford: Clarendon)

McNicoll, A. (1986) "Developments in techniques of siegecraft and fortification in the Greek world ca. 400–100 B.C." in: Leriche & Tréziny 1986: 305–13

Mitchell, S. (1996) "Hoplite warfare in ancient Greece" in: Lloyd, A. B. (ed.) (1996) *Battle in antiquity* (London: Duckworth & The Classical Press of Wales) 87–105

Morrison, J. S., J. F. Coates, & N. B. Rankov (2000) *The Athenian trireme: the history and reconstruction of an ancient Greek warship* (Cambridge: Cambridge University Press [2]2000)

Munn, M. H. (1993) *The defense of Attica: the Dema wall and the Boiotian war of 378–375 B.C.* (Berkeley: University of California Press)

Ober, J. (1985) *Fortress Attica: defense of the Athenian land frontier, 404–322 B.C.* (Leiden: Brill) (*Mnemosyne* Suppl. 84)

Ober, J. (1996) *The Athenian revolution: essays on ancient Greek democracy and political theory* (Princeton: Princeton University Press)

Ober, J., & C. W. Hedrick (eds) (1996) *Demokratia: a conversation on democracies, ancient and modern* (Princeton: Princeton University Press)

Ogden, D. (1996) "Homosexuality and warfare in classical Greece" in: Lloyd, A. B. (ed.) (1996) *Battle in antiquity* (London: Duckworth) 107–68

Parke, H. W. (1933) *Greek mercenary soldiers from the earliest times to the battle of Ipsus* (Oxford: Clarendon)

Pritchett, W. K. (1971–91) *The Greek state at war*, parts 1–5 (part 1 originally issued 1971 as *Ancient Greek military practices*, part 1, reissued 1974 as *The Greek state at war*, part 1) (Berkeley: University of California Press)

Raaflaub, K. A. (1996) "Equalities and inequalities in Athenian democracy" in: Ober & Hedrick 1996: 139–74

Raaflaub, K. A. (1997) "Soldiers, citizens and the evolution of the early Greek *polis*" in: Mitchell, L., & P. J. Rhodes (eds) (1997) *The development of the polis in archaic Greece* (London: Routledge) 49–59

Raaflaub, K. A. (1999) "Archaic and classical Greece" in Raaflaub, K. A., & N. Rosenstein (eds) (1999) *War and society in the ancient and medieval worlds: Asia, the Mediterranean, Europe, and Mesoamerica* (Cambridge MA: Harvard University Press) 129–61 (Center for Hellenic Studies Colloquia 3)

Ridley, R. T. (1979) "The hoplite as citizen: Athenian military institutions in their social context" in: *L'Antiquité Classique* 48: 508–48

Roberts, J. T. (1994) *Athens on trial: the antidemocratic tradition in western thought* (Princeton: Princeton University Press)

Rosivach, V. (2002) "*Zeugitai* and hoplites" in: *Ancient History Bulletin* 16: 33–43

Sage, M. M. (1996) *Warfare in ancient Greece: a sourcebook* (London: Routledge)

Salazar, C. F. (2000) *The treatment of war wounds in Graeco-Roman antiquity* (Leiden: Brill) (Studies in Ancient Medicine 21)

Singor, H. W. (1999) "Admission to the *syssitia* in fifth-century Sparta" in: Hodkinson, S., & A. Powell (eds) (1999) *Sparta: new perspectives* (London: Duckworth & The Classical Press of Wales) 67–89

Singor, H. W. (2002) "The Spartan army at Mantinea and its organisation in the fifth century BC" in: Jongman, W., & M. Kleijwegt (eds) (2002) *After the past: essays in ancient history in honour of H. W. Pleket* (Leiden: Brill) 235–84 (*Mnemosyne* Suppl. 233)

Smith, F. (1990) "The fighting unit: an essay in structural military history" in: *L'Antiquité Classique* 59: 149–65

Snodgrass, A. M. (1964) *Early Greek armour and weapons from the end of the bronze age to 600 B.C.* (Edinburgh: Edinburgh University Press)

Snodgrass, A. M. (1999) *Arms and armor of the Greeks* (Baltimore: Johns Hopkins University Press; originally published as *Arms and armour of the Greeks* (Ithaca NY: Cornell University Press 1967) (Aspects of Greek and Roman life))

Spence, I. G. (1993) *The cavalry of classical Greece: a social and military history with particular reference to Athens* (Oxford: Clarendon)

Strassler, R. (ed.) (1996) *The landmark Thucydides: a comprehensive guide to the Peloponnesian war: a newly revised edition of the Richard Crawley translation with maps, annotations, appendices, and encyclopedic index* (intro. V. D. Hanson) (New York: Free Press)

Strauss, B. (1986) *Athens after the Peloponnesian war: class, faction and policy, 403–386 BC* (Ithaca NY: Cornell University Press)

Strauss, B. (1996) "The Athenian trireme, school of democracy" in: Ober & Hedrick 1996: 313–25

Strauss, B. (2000) "Democracy, Kimon, and the evolution of Athenian naval tactics in the fifth century BC" in: Flensted-Jensen et al. 2000: 315–26

Tritle, L. A. (1989) " '*Epilektoi*' at Athens" in: *Ancient History Bulletin* 3: 54–9

Tritle, L. A. (2000) *From Melos to My Lai: war and survival* (London: Routledge)

Trundle, M. F. (1999) "Identity and community among Greek mercenaries in the classical world: 700–322" in: *Ancient History Bulletin* 13: 28–38

Tuplin, C. (1999) "Greek racism? Observations on the character and limits of Greek ethnic prejudice" in: Tsetskhladze, G. R. (ed.) (1999) *Ancient Greeks west and east* (Leiden: Brill) 47–75 (*Mnemosyne* Suppl. 196)

van Wees, H. (1995) "Politics and the battlefield" in: Powell, A. (ed.) (1995) *The Greek world* (London: Routledge) 153–78

van Wees, H. (2000) "The development of the hoplite phalanx: iconography and reality in the seventh century" in: van Wees, H. (ed.) (2000) *War and violence in ancient Greece* (London: Duckworth) 125–66

van Wees, H. (2001) "The myth of the middle-class army: military and social status in ancient Athens" in: Bekker-Nielsen, T., & L. Hannestad (eds) (2001) *War as a cultural and social force: essays on warfare in antiquity* (Copenhagen: Kongelige Danske Videnskabernes Selskab) 45–71 (Historisk-filosofiske Skrifter 22)

Whitehead, D. (1990) *Aineias the Tactician: how to survive under siege* (Oxford: Clarendon)

Whitehead, D. (1991) "Who equipped mercenary troops in classical Greece?" in: *Historia* 40: 105–13

Whitehead, I. (1987) "The periplous" in: *G&R* 34: 178–85

# CHAPTER TWENTY-FOUR

# The Greek World, 478–432

## *Thomas Harrison*

## 1   Introduction

If we are dependent on Thucydides to construct a historical narrative of the Peloponnesian War itself – Thucydides 'wrote the history of the Peloponnesian War'
(Thuc. 1.1, with Loraux 1986) – we are scarcely less so for the period immediately
preceding it: the roughly fifty years from the last major battles of the Persian wars,
Plataiai and Mykale (479), and the establishment of the Athenian naval alliance (478)
through to the beginning of conflict. Thucydides' account can sometimes, of course,
be supplemented, qualified or confirmed from other sources: Athenian decrees
(M&L; for translations, Fornara, Osborne 2000), the pamphlet known as the 'Old
Oligarch' ([Xenophon] *Ath. Pol.*), and later sources such as the *Parallel Lives* of
Plutarch (especially of Perikles, Kimon, Aristeides), the derivative 'universal history'
of Diodoros (largely based for this period on the fourth-century Ephoros of Kyme),
or (with caution) Athenian drama. We are reduced, however, almost exclusively to
fighting scholarly skirmishes on ground that the historian has chosen for us. We must
attempt, moreover, not only to test the details of his account in sequence in a kind of
commentary, but – as a prerequisite for writing any kind of narrative – to grasp
Thucydides' account as a whole.

Thucydides' account of the period in Book 1 of his *Histories* is no straightforward
sequential narrative. It is presented instead through a series of digressions, each taking
a further chronological step back, embedded within his more detailed account of the
immediate run-up to conflict. First, his account of the immediate professed causes for
the war (1.23), the flashpoints of Epidamnos and of Poteidaia (1.24–65), leads to a
first debate at Sparta and to the Spartan decision that Athens had broken the terms of
their treaty (1.66–88). This decision then leads to a more extended narrative of the
growth of Athenian power (the digression known as the 'pentakontaetia', or 'the fifty
years', 1.89–117) stepping further back in time to the end of the Persian wars,
bringing us back to the brink of war and to the conference of all Sparta's allies to

confirm the decision for war (1.118–25). A subsequent period of diplomatic posturing provides the narrative hook for a further step back, to accounts of the careers
and falls of Pausanias and Themistokles (1.126–38), pivotal figures not only in the
Persian wars but also in the shape of the following half-century; this concludes, as
does Book 1 of the *Histories*, with Perikles' recommendation to the Athenians to
reject the seemingly small demands made of them as the thin end of the wedge
(1.139–45).

Thucydides' approach might on first reading appear disjointed. The structure of
the book has indeed been seen as the result of the order of the work's composition
and of clumsy surgery on earlier drafts; his account of the pentakontaetia has been
criticized not only for its lack of chronological clarity (for which Thucydides blames
his predecessor Hellanikos, 1.97; all subsequent dates in this chapter should be
understood to be approximate at best: see, e.g., Lewis 1992b: 499–505, Rhodes
1992a: 44–5, Badian 1993b) but also for its omissions, most notoriously of the Peace
of Kallias that may or may not have been agreed between Athens and Persia (449; see
recently Badian 1993a). Such criticisms, however, fail to reflect the differences
between Thucydides' objectives and those of his modern critics. In particular, the
focus of the pentakontaetia is not to record all that his protagonists 'did or suffered'
in that period (cf. Aristotle *Poetics* 1451b), but specifically on the twin themes laid out
in an early programmatic statement (1.23; with Rood 1998; also Connor 1984):

> As to the reasons why they broke the truce, I propose first to give an account of the
> causes of complaint which they had against each other and of the specific instances where
> their interests clashed: this in order that there should be no doubt in anyone's mind
> about what led to this great war falling upon the Hellenes. But the real reason for the war
> is, in my opinion, most likely to be disguised by such an argument. What made war
> inevitable was the growth of Athenian power and the fear which this caused in Sparta.
> (trans. R. Warner)

This focus is sustained by a series of similar authorial statements throughout Book 1.
The first debate at Sparta concludes with a statement (which also effects a transition
into the pentakontaetia) that the Spartan decision for war was made less on the basis
of the speeches (the professed motives, in other words) than because they were 'afraid
of the further growth of Athenian power' (1.88). Similar ideas conclude the pentakontaetia: Athens' growth in power had reached a point where it was beginning to
encroach on Sparta's relationship with her allies (1.118). And the final chapter of
Book 1 recalls the distinction of 1.23, tacitly invoking again the distinction between
professed causes and the underlying reason for conflict: 'these, then, were the causes
of complaint and the differences which occurred between the two powers before the
outbreak of war . . . ' (1.146). This focus demands of the reader a detachment from
the cut-and-thrust of the diplomatic demands of the various protagonists. Rather
than seeking to indict one party or another for infringing the terms of their earlier
treaty, the Thirty Years' Peace (cf. de Ste. Croix 1972: e.g., 290 focusing esp. on
7.18), Thucydides' concern – like Herodotos' in the case of the Persian wars (Harrison 2002; cf. Sealey 1957) – is to give a 'thick description' of the movement to
war, and of the growing sense of the inevitability of conflict (e.g., 1.33, 44) – clearly a
self-fulfilling prophecy.

# 2   The Growth of Athens' Power

Thucydides' twin themes of 1.23 must, for convenience's sake, be sorted into two parallel plots: the growth of Athens' power, her *arche* or empire, on the one hand; Sparta's developing fear on the other.

Athens' empire grew out of the wartime alliance against the Persians (Brunt 1953–4). As Thucydides paraphrases baldly in the course of his '*Archaeology*', 'the Hellenes – both those who had fought in the war together and those who had revolted from the King of Persia – split into two divisions, one group following Athens and the other Sparta' (1.18). This split occurred through a change, apparently piecemeal, in the leadership of the naval campaign which sought to take the war into the King's own territory. The campaign in Cyprus and Byzantion was under the leadership of the Spartan Pausanias (1.94). His perceived arrogance, however, especially to those Ionians until recently under Persian rule, led to the Ionians' seeking Athenian protection. Complaints to Sparta, meanwhile, led to Pausanias' recall; by the time that a successor, the unfortunate Dorkis, was sent out to take over the command, the allies were no longer willing to accept Spartan command (1.95). The new dispensation was quickly sealed: with the establishment of a league treasury (at Delos) and treasurers (the hellenotamiai), and the fixing of the contributions to be made – which states should contribute ships and which money (1.96) – and, as we learn from the Aristotelian *Constitution of the Athenians*, by a solemn oath 'to have the same friends and enemies', sealed by the sinking of weights to the bottom of the sea ([Aristotle] *Ath. Pol.* 23).

The Spartans, crucially in Thucydides' account, were not unhappy with this outcome. As Thucydides' Athenian representatives at Sparta declare, '[this empire] came to us at a time when you were unwilling to fight on to the end against the Persians' (1.75); Thucydides ascribes to the Spartans, in his own words, the fear that their leaders would, like Pausanias, be corrupted by far-flung commands, the sense that the command was a burden, and the conviction that the Athenians were both capable and well-disposed to Spartan interests (1.95). (This complex picture of Spartan motivation should be read, however, alongside their secret sense of grievance over the Athenians' rebuilding of their walls, 1.92: see further below.) The Athenians' leadership is also, in Thucydides' account, initially with the consent of her allies: 'our allies came to us of their own accord and begged us to lead them' (as the Athenians at Sparta say again: 1.75). There is an almost immediate slippage, however. The allies were 'at first autonomous and deliberated in common councils', but implicitly this was short-lived (1.97). The report of the Athenians' crushing response to the attempted secession of Naxos – 'the first allied state to be enslaved contrary to what had been established' (1.98), the first of many – prompts a grim anatomy of the changing dynamics of the relationship between Athens and her allies in which allied laziness and Athenian harshness combine to entrench an inequality in strength (1.99):

> The chief reasons for these revolts were failures to produce the right amount of tribute or the right number of ships, and sometimes a refusal to produce any ships at all. For the Athenians insisted on obligations being exactly met, and made themselves unpopular by

bringing the severest pressure to bear on allies who were not used to making sacrifices and did not want to make them. In other ways, too, the Athenians as rulers were no longer popular as they used to be: they bore more than their fair share of the actual fighting, but this made it all the easier for them to force back into the alliance any state that wanted to leave it. For this position it was the allies themselves who were to blame. Because of this reluctance of theirs to face military service, most of them, to avoid serving abroad, had assessments made by which, instead of producing ships, they were to pay a corresponding sum of money. The result was that the Athenian navy grew strong at their expense, and when they revolted they always found themselves inadequately armed and inexperienced in war.

This pattern is further exemplified by Thucydides' sketch of subsequent relations between Athens and her allies: the revolt of Thasos, in part over a dispute over the control of the rich mines on the mainland of Thrace (1.100–1); the expansion (and subsequent contraction) of the alliance on the Greek mainland in the period of the so-called 'First Peloponnesian War' (461–446; see further below); or Athens' involvement in the war between two allies, Samos and Miletos, and her subsequent suppression of a Samian revolt (1.115–17), a conflict that, Thucydides comments, came close to depriving the Athenians of their control of the sea (8.76). The same development of alliance to empire is also, though, sketched in the overlapping accounts of the protagonists (all of which, we must remember, are put into their mouths by Thucydides himself: e.g., Stadter 1973, Rood 1998: 46–8, now Laird 1999: 143–52). For the Athenians, fear of Persia gives way to a sense of their own honour and to self-interest (1.75); others' hostility then prevents them from letting go of their empire. The Mytileneans, in the context of their revolt against Athens, justify their earlier failure to revolt (to the Spartans whose help they are soliciting) in terms again of a development of Athenian imperialism from innocent beginnings (3, 9–14). By the time that they realized the change they were powerless (3.10; cf. Hermokrates, Thuc. 6.76): 'when we saw that they were becoming less and less antagonistic to Persia and more and more interested in enslaving their own allies, then we became frightened.'

This developmental model is not beyond criticism (most radically: Robertson 1980). Other sources suggest, in particular, an earlier date for Athenian imperial intent. Herodotos is explicit that Pausanias' hybris was held up as a pretext (*prophasis*) for the Athenians to take the leadership (8.3). His account of the Persian wars, most probably written in its final form in the early years of the Peloponnesian War (Fornara 1971b, Hornblower 1991: 2–26), shows the Greek allies not only fighting against their Persian enemies but jostling amongst themselves for pole position come the peace. The Athenian general Miltiades, to take one example from many, in encouraging his fellow Athenian Kallimachos to cast his vote for battle against Persia, the battle of Marathon, makes the claim that Athens' survival would lead to her becoming the first of the cities of Greece (Hdt. 6.109; cf. 9.102). Athens' contribution to the Ionian Revolt is represented as motivated, at least in substantial part, by a desire for the wealth of Asia (5.97; cf. 5.49). And the Athenians' angry rejection of the suggestion that *their* colonists might be transplanted from Ionia to mainland Greece (the Ionians, with the Samians, Chians and Lesbians in the vanguard, are instead incorporated into the alliance against Persia; cf. [Aristotle] *Ath. Pol.* 24) already has a certain proprietorial air. (His account of Leotychidas and the Spartans' taking their leave from the war against Persia, while Xanthippos, the father of Perikles, and the

Athenians head for the Peloponnese, might, on the other hand, be taken to support Thucydides' portrait of Spartan acquiescence, to mark the crucial parting of the ways in the wartime alliance, 9.114.)

The presence of a pattern, if not of a critique, of incipient Athenian imperialism in Herodotos' *Histories* is now virtually an orthodoxy among Herodotean scholars (e.g., Fornara 1971b, Stadter 1992, Moles 1996, 2002; cf. Meiggs 1972: 5), but is yet to be established in historical narratives of the empire (cf. Fornara & Samons 1991: 76–113). That the Athenian empire or *arche* formed part of 'a larger sequence in which Athenian behaviour had already become pronouncedly aggressive' (Fornara & Samons 1991: 102) is also suggested by a number of what we might term 'proto-imperial' ventures in the sixth and early-fifth centuries: the Peisistratid tyrants' interest in Sigeion, for example, that of the Philaids in the Chersonese, or the curious and ultimately unsuccessful enterprises of Miltiades after Marathon (Hdt. 6.132; cf. 8.112.3; Hornblower 1984; Fornara & Samons, 1991: 76–113, Mills 1997: 69; cf. Calame 1996: 223–7); these ventures, undertaken by individuals, with varying degrees of polis sanction, to establish family fiefdoms, may precede the formal foundations of the fifth-century League but they are surely connected to it.

Further evidence of an early imperial intent can be gleaned from a dramatic source, Aischylos' *Persians* (a dramatization of the Persians' hearing of the news of their defeat at Salamis), first performed in 472, only a few years into the alliance's life (Gow 1928, Harrison 2000). A number of relevant themes emerge from the play: the idea that Athens' role is pivotal to the survival of Greece (lines 233–4), an idea which was unsurprisingly controversial (cf. Hdt 7.139) and which, as we know from Thucydides, served as a regular justification of Athenian rule over her allies (Thuc. 1.73–4, 5.89, 6.83; cf. Lysias 2.2); or the use of the ethnic term 'Ionians' to embrace both the Athenians and their allies (so, 'the Ionian people do not run away from battle', line 1025; cf. lines 178, 563, 950–1, 1011, Thuc. 1.94, Solon F 4a West), resonant of the Athenians' proprietorial embrace of the Ionians in Herodotos' account (9.105–6). Perhaps most significant, however, is the play's implicit analogy between Persian and Athenian empires, reflecting as it does the Athenians' consciousness of their status as an imperial power at this early date. In one scene of the play, the chorus of Persian elders heaps praise on their former King Dareios (in contrast to his son Xerxes) for his many conquests in the Greek world, listed with relish. At the end of the passage, however, we learn that Dareios' conquests are the Athenians' gains at the time of the play's production. 'Now there is no doubt', they conclude, 'that through wars we are enduring the gods' reversal of our fortunes' (lines 904–7). The dramatic motive of the list, it emerges then, has been to arouse the Athenian audience's pride in their own achievements: the Persians' losses are their gains, but the Athenians are protected from the fall that the Persians have suffered by their democracy and piety.

How can this picture be reconciled with that of Thucydides? Thucydides' portrayal of the origins of the empire is still notably cynical. The allied request for protection from the hybristic Pausanias was, he notes for example, welcome to the Athenians, 'who made up their minds to put a check on Pausanias and to arrange matters generally in a way that would best suit their own interests' (1.95; cf. Hdt. 8.3, Plutarch *Aristeides* 23). The alliance's initial purpose of ravaging the King's land was a pretext, or professed motive (*proschema*), disguising an Athenian desire either to subjugate the allies or to compete with Sparta (1.96). Thucydides' account of the early actions of the League under the leadership of Kimon (1.98) – the mopping up of a Persian position at Eion on the river Strymon, clearing the island of Skyros of Dolopian 'pirates' and replacing them with Athenian settlers, the defeat of Karystos on Euboia, and (climactically) the enslavement of Naxos – suggests only the briefest period of innocence. The Mytileneans' later claim that they were useful to Athens as an example of a willing ally shows also a distinctly critical approach to allied 'consent' (3.11). (The Mytileneans' characterization of the shift in the nature of the alliance is also of a *relative* change: the Athenians became *more* interested in enslaving their allies, 3.10.) Thucydides' conviction in his developmental model of imperialism, coupled with his start date (in part perhaps a homage to his predecessor, Herodotos; for the complexity of his attitude to Herodotos see Hornblower 1996: 19–38, 122–45), have possibly had the effect of downplaying the Athenians' original imperial intentions.

This is not, however, to deny any evolution in the relationship between Athens and her allies. The transfer of the league treasury from Delos to Athens (454), reflected in the beginning of records of the sixtieth share (or 'quota') dedicated to Athena (the so-called Tribute Lists), or the removal of the pretext of a war against Persia by the Peace of Kallias (or the de facto conclusion of hostilities with Persia) would surely have confirmed the suspicion of those who, like Thucydides' Mytileneans, perceived a shift towards Athens' enslaving of her own allies. Every successive revolt – especially the flurry in the period of the 'First Peloponnesian War' – would, in the light of its suppression, have ratcheted up both allied resentment and Athenian cynicism and attempts at self-vindication. A shift in the character of the empire has also traditionally been dated by the onset of a new harshness in the language of Athens' imperial decrees, a shift from speaking of Athenian allies to the 'cities which Athens rules' (Meiggs 1972: 152–74; cf. Finley 1978: 103). There may, however, have been a substantial time lag before the harsh realities of empire were reflected in harsh language; such language may to a large extent be dependent on context (see now Low 2005); and we anyway lack earlier inscriptions to serve as a control. (On the single-most hotly debated issue, the 'three bar-sigma', above, Chapter 3, Excursus.)

A further issue is the popularity of the empire among the allies. Thucydides gives us, at least in the period of the Peloponnesian War, an unreservedly negative picture: 'our empire is a tyranny', Perikles tells the assembled Athenians (2.63), a tyranny that it would be unsafe for the Athenians to give up even should they want to. This is an impression confirmed by the Old Oligarch ([Xenophon] *Ath. Pol.*) and reflected in Aristophanes (cf. Forrest 1975). The concern of much modern scholarship has been to break down the question of popularity into thematic parts: to weigh any advantages to the allies against disadvantages, to construct in the words of a famous essay by Moses Finley a 'balance sheet' of Athenian imperialism (Finley 1978).

On the negative side, then, we might list: the burden of tribute paying, and its association with political subjection (e.g., Hdt. 1.27 on Alyattes; R&O 22 for the Second Athenian Confederacy's eschewal of the term *phoros*, perhaps euphemistic but reflective also of a different balance of power); the presence of garrisons (Isokrates 7.65), or Athenian magistrates in allied cities (M&L 45 paragraph 4, [Aristotle] *Ath. Pol.* 24); the establishment of settlers or 'cleruchs' (literally, allotment-holders) on allied land (Brunt 1966), designed not only for security but also to 'make citizens without land into hoplites' (Antiphon F 61); the possible imposition of Athenian coinage on her allies (M&L 45; cf. Figueira 1998: esp. 319–423); or interference in the judicial independence of an allied city, the demand for example that cases for which the punishment was death should be heard in Athens (Antiphon 5.47, M&L 52; cf. M&L 31 for legal privileges granted to Phaselites, Thuc. 1.77 for an Athenian defence). The frequency of revolts from Athenian rule – which we may trace not only from Thucydides' narrative but also from tracking changes and omissions in a given city's record of tribute payment (Osborne 2000: 86–7) – might suggest that such burdens were felt keenly; the frequency of revolts cannot be taken, however, as a reliable measure of the level of discontent as revolt clearly depends on other factors, Athenian military reversals, or the presence of a Spartan army at the gates (so Brasidas in Thrace in 424: Thuc. 4–5.24).

On the positive side, we might include defence against the real and continuing threat of Persia or from pirates. The imposition of Athenian coinage on all allied cities might have had a positive aspect, a kind of 'common market' for goods and services across the Aegean world (see esp. [Xenophon] *Ath. Pol.* 2.8, Thuc. 2.38, Hermippos F 63 Kassel & Austin, though the cosmopolitan flavour of Athens in [Xenophon] is probably pejorative; cf. Hdt 1.135). It is crucial also to distinguish between different elements in allied poleis. Thucydides' and the Old Oligarch's impression of the empire as a tyranny was, in a now classic article of Geoffrey de Ste. Croix (de Ste. Croix 1954–5; cf. Bradeen 1960; Quinn 1964; Fornara 1977), argued to be the result of these authors' aristocratic leanings, and those of their contacts in the allied cities. This is a theory supported by a range of suggestive evidence. Allied revolts were often followed by the imposition of democratic regimes (e.g., Erythrai: M&L 40), just as Sparta saw to it that her allies were oligarchic in government (Thuc. 1.18, Aristotle *Politics* 1307b22; Isokrates later makes explicit that tribute was the price for the guarantee of democracy, 12.68). When the Athenians crushed the revolt of the Mytileneans, they chose (reversing their original decision, and overruling the advice of Kleon, Thuc. 3.39: 'Do not put the blame on the aristocracy and say that the people were innocent') to kill only the (anyway large number of) supposed ring-leaders of the revolt. A number of sources highlight the contacts maintained between aristocrats in the allied cities and in Athens (so, the Old Oligarch, in a confusing passage, [Xenophon] *Ath Pol.* 1.14–15), and between prominent pro-Athenians amongst the allies and leading Athenians: these connections are seen both as crucial for the maintenance of allied rule (Plato *Seventh Letter* 332B–C) and, by the Mytileneans, as a way of ensuring continued independence (Thuc. 3.12). (To be a leading pro-Athenian or *proxenos* was sometimes a vulnerable position: Thuc. 3.70, M&L 52, *IG*1³ 19, 27.)

Our balance sheet can also (more tendentiously perhaps) include less material advantages and disadvantages to the allies: on the negative side, evidence of opportunistic or selfish motives; on the positive side, evidence of benign intentions on the Athenians' part, or (from the allies' point of view) any sense of kinship or religious identity that might have mitigated political subjection.

Evidence for benign intentions – a civilizing mission even – might be detected in the oath sworn by the Athenian generals of 439 (in the wake of the destructive war against Samos) 'to do and advise and say only what is good for the people of Samos' (M&L 56.15–23). 'Did the men who swore that oath', one modern historian has asked (Forrest 1975; cf. Meiggs 1972: 193), 'have their tongues in their cheeks, all of them? Or did one or two of them have a tear in their eye?' Such idealism, first – even if we presume it to be in good faith – need not exclude opportunism (Harrison 2005; cf. Hornblower 1991: 144); the motives of an imperial power, as Thucydides appreciated in speaking of the pretext of revenge against Persia (1.96), are not black and white. Clearly also we should be wary of believing claims that are so clearly a part of an Athenian justification for empire (esp. Mills 1997: ch. 2; contrast de Ste. Croix 1972: 44 on Lysias 2.55–6). We should be similarly wary of the claims of protection from Persia or piracy, both probably contemporary Athenian claims (Thuc. 5.89; Lysias 2.56–8; Isokrates 12.69; Xenophon *Poroi* 5.5; Plutarch *Kimon* 8.3–7; Thuc. 1.4.2, though see Hornblower 1991: 21–2) and both often embedded unquestioned in modern narratives (Meiggs 1972: 69, Nixon & Price 1990: 138, Hornblower 2002: 17–18; cf. Hornblower 1991: 150; for piracy, see esp. M&L 30 (= Fornara 63) with de Souza 1999: 26–30). (By contrast, a reasonable modern rationalization of the clearing of 'pirates' from Skyros is that it had an economic motive, to safeguard the route to the Black Sea and thereby the grain supply from the Crimea: Davies 1993: 46, 77.)

A different problem arises when we turn to the allies' sense of belonging, our lack of evidence for allied opinions. There are ample suggestions that a sense of Ionian kinship between Athens and her allies formed a part of the city's official version: the initial location of the league treasury at Delos; the speech of Athena in Euripides' *Ion* 1569–94, prophesying the foundation of Athenian colonies and speaking of the glorious name of the Ionians – seemingly a kind of charter myth for the Delian League; Kimon's naming of one of his sons Oulios after an Ionian cult title of Apollo; or a number of passing references in Thucydides (the allies are said to have been conscious of their kinship when they asked Athens for help against Pausanias, 1.94; cf. 1.71; 1.124; 4.61). We can scarcely tell, however, whether – or how soon – such talk of kinship wore thin (cf. Davies 1993: 69). We are on slightly firmer ground when it comes to the religious obligations demanded by Athens of her allies: the cow and the panoply, for example, that the Athenians demanded to be brought to the Panathenaia. These gifts were, in time, demanded of all allies, and the demand reiterated with a little menace (M&L 40.2–8; 46.41–3; 49.11–13; 69.55–8). A later demand for the donation of first fruits for Eleusis suggests a lack of conviction that any but Athenian allies would want to contribute (M&L 73). For any such religious links to have been effective in binding together Athens and her allies depends on a pre-existing goodwill (which any compulsion would surely have eroded). It might be better then to see such religious tributes (from the Athenian's point of view) as the rewards of empire, as a request for fitting honour with scant concern for allied feelings (Parker 1996: 151).

This is perhaps a note that is too rarely sounded in accounts of Athenian imperialism, dominated, implicitly at least, by the question of the rights and wrongs of the empire (a concern that we have inherited from Thucydides, but which is in part informed by submerged analogy to modern empires: Harrison 2005). In Perikles' last speech (2.59–64) Thucydides shows us an Athens frozen in self-destructive introspection. Elsewhere, however, we can glimpse an almost limitless ambition and an unabashed pride (cf. Hölscher 1998 on artistic material). Athens' imperial drive leads her far further afield than the world of her Aegean allies: to respond to the request of the Libyan Inaros, for example, for help in his revolt against Persian rule in Egypt

(459–454), a venture that ends in the destruction of up to 250 ships together with their crews (Thuc. 1.104–10; cf. Thuc. 1.111 for a request from the Thessalian Orestes); to undertake a great naval show of strength through the Black Sea, 'bringing the whole sea under their own control' (Plutarch *Perikles* 20); to settle colonies at Amphipolis in Thrace, again initially with great losses (4.102; cf. 1.100) or, jointly, in Thourioi in southern Italy (Diodoros 11.90; 12.10–11); or to make speculative alliances as far abroad as Egesta in western Sicily (M&L 37), or with Leontinoi and Rhegion in the east of the island (M&L 63), alliances that foreshadow Thucydides' account of their over-reaching and disastrous expedition to Sicily (415–413; Thuc. Books 6–7; cf. 1.36). Athenian pride is perhaps no more clearly evidenced, however, than in the words placed in Perikles' mouth in the course of his funeral oration (2.41; cf. Andokides 3.37):

> Athens comes to her testing time in a greatness that surpasses what was imagined of her. In her case, and her case alone, no invading enemy is ashamed of being defeated, and no subject can complain of being governed by people unfit for their responsibilities. Mighty indeed are the marks and monuments of our empire that we have left. Future ages will wonder at us, as the present age wonders at us now. We do not need the praises of a Homer, or of anyone else whose words may delight us for the moment, but whose estimation of facts will fall short of what is really true. For our adventurous spirit has forced an entry into every sea and into every land; and everywhere we have left behind us everlasting memorials of good done to our friends or suffering inflicted on our enemies.

## 3   Sparta's Fear: The Causes of War

Thucydides' twin plots of the growth of Athenian power and of Spartan fear are intertwined. The founding act of Athenian imperialism, in Thucydides' account, is the rebuilding of the walls of Athens after their destruction (1.89–93; cf. 1.143; Andokides 3.37–8; [Xenophon] *Ath. Pol.* 2.14–16). Themistokles had argued that, if the Athenians became a seafaring people, they would have every advantage in adding to their power, and that they could go down to the Piraeus (the walls of which were completed) and take to their ships to defend themselves (1.93; cf. Spartan fears, 1.90). (Athenian leadership was later consolidated by the building of the Long Walls joining Athens and the Piraeus, beginning 1.106, seen as crucial by the Korinthians, 1.69.) The initial building of the city walls takes place, however, in the face of Sparta's (and Sparta's allies') opposition: the professed reason for their opposition was a concern for the defence of Greece in the event of another Persian invasion, so that the Persians would have no defensible base; their real reason (mirroring Themistokles' advice to the Athenians, 1.93) was fear of Athenian enterprise (1.90). The Spartans showed no open displeasure in the event, we are told; their request to the Athenians not to rebuild their walls had been 'friendly advice', no more; they were friendly to Athens because of her role in the Persian wars; and yet, 'the Spartans had not got their own way and secretly felt aggrieved because of it' (1.92). We might add that, the Athenians' hurried construction of the wall, Themistokles' filibustering in Sparta, or his instruction to keep the Spartan ambassadors in Athens (even, if necessary, by constraint) until the walls had reached a defensible height, all suggest at least a suspicion that Sparta might have sought to prevent the building of the walls. Themistokles' eventual revelation to the Spartans of the extent of the walls is accompanied by a rousing statement of Athenian independence, and (ironically in the light of the later Athenian empire) of how alliances must be on the 'basis of equal strength' (1.91).

This account of early tensions between Athens and Sparta can be supplemented a little from other sources. Competition between the two leading cities in Greece is a recurrent subplot throughout Herodotos' *Histories* (esp. Moles 1996, 2002), climaxing in their competition for Ionian defections at the battle of Mykale (9.102) or the testy debate on the future of the Ionians (9.105–6; see above). Diodoros records a debate in Sparta (early in the 470s) at which a member of the council of elders, the *gerousia*, narrowly persuaded his fellow Spartans not to go to war to fight for leadership of the naval alliance; 'it was not in Sparta's interests, he declared, to lay claim to the sea' (Diodoros 11.50; cf. [Aristotle] *Ath. Pol.* 23.2; for scepticism, see Lewis 1992a: 100). This tentative status quo whereby the Greek world was divided into two spheres of influence seems to have held, albeit tentatively, for much of the 470s and 460s, reinforced by the dominance of the pro-Spartan Kimon in Athens and a rash of conflict between Sparta and her Peloponnesian allies (see below). Tension erupts again, at least into our sources, at the time of the secession of Thasos from the Athenian alliance (464/3): the Spartans had promised the Thasians (secretly from the Athenians) that they would invade Attika, Thucydides tells us, and they would indeed have done so had it not been for the major earthquake and the subsequent revolt of the helots at Ithome (1.101). Even so Athens gave help to Sparta in the suppression of the helots, but their help was met with Spartan distrust (possibly because of the contemporary political changes at home, the reforms of Ephialtes: the relative chronology is uncertain): the Spartans grew afraid of the enterprise and unorthodoxy of the Athenians, thought that 'they might listen to the people in Ithome and become the sponsors of some revolutionary policy' (1.102), and so dismissed them from the Peloponnese – a snub that sealed the division, may well (depending on the chronology) have hastened democratic reforms in Athens, and led to Athens' forming an alternative alliance with Sparta's enemy, Argos (Thuc. 1.102).

There follows a complex phase of muted hostilities between Athens, on the one hand, and Sparta and her allies on the other, sometimes known (and referred to above) as the First Peloponnesian War. Though it may, in a number of the causes of conflict, foreshadow the later Peloponnesian War (itself arguably a more complex series of conflicts; Thucydides makes the case for seeing the whole period of 27 years as one war, 5.26), it is not comparable either in character or in intensity (Holladay 1977). It is a war mainly carried on between Athens and Sparta's Peloponnesian allies, the main focus being the expansion of Athens' sphere of influence on the Greek mainland (in particular, her 461 alliance with Megara, Thuc. 1.42), an apparent attempt to create a territorial block to the Korinthian Gulf in the west and preventing Spartan intervention north of the Peloponnese (Davies 1993: 82–3 on 1.107). Spartan intervention is selective. Their ostensible reason for sending fifteen hundred of their own hoplites in 458 was to support the Dorians against the Phokians. On their return, however, they hesitated in Boiotia, in part to coincide with an abortive oligarchic coup in Athens (1.107). The Athenians, conscious of the planned coup, marched out to fight at Tanagra; their defeat was not so conclusive as to give further momentum to any plotting; it also did not prevent the Athenians from marching out, only 62 days later, to subjugate Boiotia at the battle of Oinophyta. Further hostilities between Athenians and Spartans took place without any direct contact: in 448, in the so-called Sacred War, the Spartans gave Delphi back to the Delphians, and the Athenians promptly returned it to the Phokians (Thuc. 1.112). The Spartans' final intervention was more decisive: an invasion of Attika under the leadership of Pleistoanax. (The Spartans took their time, however: Thucydides tells us intriguingly of a Persian attempt to encourage an invasion of Attika through bribery: 1.109.) Unlike those of the first phase of the Peloponnesian War (the so-called Archidamian war), this invasion was effective in extracting a quick settlement, in large part due to the circumstances in which it was fought: in the light of the revolt from Athens of Boiotia, Euboia and Megara (1.114–15). The Thirty Years' Peace brought about the return of all the remaining 'places which they had seized from the Peloponnesians' (Nisaia, Pagai, Troizen, Achaia), in return for an implicit acceptance of the two parties' different spheres of influence (cf. Lewis 1992a: 137).

Tension scarcely abated in the aftermath of this settlement. The Peloponnesians seem to have come close to war with the Athenians at the time of Athens' intervention in Samos; Thucydides' Korinthians claim that they had openly opposed war, arguing that Athens should be left alone to discipline her allies (1.40). By the middle of the 430s we find ourselves embroiled in the 'causes of complaint' and 'specific instances where their interests clashed' of Thucydides 1.23: in particular, the disputes over Kerkyra and Poteidaia (1.24–65). What these disputes have in common is that both take place at points of overlap between the Peloponnesian and Athenian alliances, and that both involve Korinth: Kerkyra was a disenchanted colony of Korinth before Athens, mindful of her naval strength and of the inevitability of a war (cf. M&L 58, the Kallias decree, putting Athenian finances on a war footing from 434/3), formed a defensive alliance with her; Poteidaia was again a colony of Korinth and a member of the Athenian league. Thucydides' selection of these two episodes for detailed treatment fits with his foregrounding of Korinth throughout Book 1; it is Korinth's threat to find other allies that finally galvanizes Sparta into war (1.33, 42, 68–71; 118). Other cities' grievances are, conversely, downplayed: in particular, Aiginetan complaints that their promised independence was being infringed by the Athenians (Thucydides adds that the Aiginetans worked behind the scenes to foment war, 1.67, and the Athenians are later said to have blamed the Aiginetans for starting the war, Thuc. 2.27; cf. Andokides 3.6), and those of the Megarians, in particular (they are said to have listed 'a number of other grievances') at their exclusion from the harbours of Athens and her allies.

The precise meaning and significance of this exclusion, and of the 'Megarian Decrees' (most probably a trade ban) that Perikles insists adamantly that Athens should not repeal, has been the subject of heated debate (e.g., de Ste. Croix 1972: ch. vii). Other sources, mostly with a tendentious focus on the discreditable motives of Perikles, have been cited in support of the importance of Megara as a cause of war (Plutarch *Perikles* 29–31, Aristophanes *Acharnians* 524–39, *Peace* 606–9; Diodoros 12.39; Andokides 3.8). None of these, however, gives us reason to doubt Thucydides' conviction that the Megarian Decrees (though they may have been a significant *grievance*) were significant *as a cause of war* primarily as a diplomatic line in the sand.

# 4   Other Narratives

Finally, we can construct, albeit patchily, a variety of non-Thucydidean narratives of the period between the wars.

Our knowledge of internal Spartan affairs suggests a number of recurrent themes, but little evolution: problems with their helot population (even before Ithome, 1.128); a lack of any clear leadership, due to various difficulties in the two royal houses (the exile of Demaratos, the disgrace of Leotychidas and of the regent Pausanias, the minority of Pleistarchos and Archidamos); the beginnings of a decline in Spartan manpower (Cawkwell 1983, Hodkinson 1983); a renewed rash of conflict with her allies in the Peloponnese in the 470s and 460s. This last we learn of from a surprising source. Herodotos records an oracle given to the mantis Teisamenos of Elis, prophesying that he would win five important 'contests'; these were not, as he thought, athletic victories but military ones (9.33; 35): the battle of Plataiai, the battle against the Messenians at Ithome, Tanagra, and (between Plataiai and Ithome apparently) 'that at Tegea, against the Tegeans and the Argives ... that at Dipaia against all the Arkadians except the Mantineans'. These clashes may be linked to developing democratic movements in some of the cities of the Peloponnese as well as to the mischief-making of the Athenian Themistokles, now exiled in Argos but known to have visited other parts of the Peloponnese (Thuc. 1.135; Forrest 1960). Some insight into the nature of Sparta's leadership can be gained from Thucydides' account of the Spartan decision to go to war (1.79–87), setting the measured caution of Archidamos against the tub-thumping speech of the ephor Sthenelaïdas ('let no one try to tell us that when we are being attacked we should sit down and discuss matters', 1.86); the Spartans' vote was only narrowly in favour of war, but the impression given is that Sthenelaïdas' boorish voice was the dominant one. By contrast, the Athenians are apparently united behind the stance of (the unopposed) Perikles (1.140–4) – who already has the kind of grasp of his city's resources to which Archidamos aspires.

Of Athens' internal affairs much more can be said (esp. above, Chapter 17). On the basis of the Aristotelian *Athenaion Politeia* (supplemented, in particular, with details from Plutarch's *Lives* of prominent Athenians), we can construct a narrative both of a series of political leaderships (or of pairings of popular and conservative politicians, e.g., [Aristotle] *Ath. Pol.* 41) and of a series of democratic reforms – all again intertwined with Athens' relationships with Sparta and with her own allies. The dominance of Themistokles (a period associated with imperial expansion and an uncompromising approach to Sparta) gives way, especially in the light of Themistokles' ostracism in the late 470s, to the Kimonian era of further expansion but rapprochement with Sparta. Kimon's fall, probably in the light of his support of Sparta's suppression of the helots (see above), leads to a realignment of Athens vis-à-vis Sparta, in particular an alliance with her enemy Argos (reflected in the eternal friendship of Argos and Athens in Aischylos' *Suppliants*; cf. Thuc. 1.102), and may have given impetus to the democratic reforms of Ephialtes (462/1). The principles of Ephialtes' reforms, and an uncompromising attitude to Sparta, were then consolidated in the subsequent years of Perikles' dominance.

Such a demarcation of the period into distinct political phases and the classification of leading political figures into two opposed camps may, however, have been less clear in reality than on the pages of the *Athenaion Politeia*. Modern narratives of Athenian politics in the period are often based on a fragile tissue of hypothesis. So, for example, that Perikles as a young man was *choregos* for (i.e., the sponsor of) Aischylos' 472 play the *Persians* (seen by some as a play written in support of Themistokles) is taken as evidence that Perikles was, in some sense, his political successor (e.g., Podlecki 1999: ch. 2). It is by no means obvious, however, that sponsorship should be construed as implying political support (Wilson 2000), that political alignments were ever anything other than shifting and provisional (e.g., Connor 1971), or indeed that the *Persians* can be legitimately interpreted as a 'party political' play (Harrison 2000: chapters 2; 9). Later ancient sources often seem to embellish the contrasts between two leading figures: Plutarch's picture, for example, of the principled opposition of Thoukydides son of Melesias to the Periklean building programme ascribes anachronistic motives to his characters (Plutarch *Perikles* 11–14). Occasionally, moreover, we are reminded that our evidence is almost hopelessly fragmentary: the mention, for example, of the otherwise unknown Archestratos as a collaborator (with Perikles) of the democratic reformer Ephialtes should make us wary of supposing that Perikles was somehow the inevitable or natural successor of Ephialtes' position ([Aristotle] *Ath. Pol.* 35; cf. 25).

Even the nature of Ephialtes' democratic reforms is uncertain. It hinges on one short passage of the *Athenaion Politeia*:

> Ephialtes, son of Sophonides, became champion of the people, a man who appeared to be uncorrupt and upright in political matters. He attacked the Council of the Areopagos. First he eliminated many of its members, bringing them to trial for their conduct in office. Then in the archonship of Conon (462/1), he took away from the council all those powers which it had accrued which gave it guardianship of the constitution, giving some to the council of the 500, some to the people and some to the jury-courts. (trans. P. J. Rhodes)

The emphasis on Ephialtes' incorruptibility and the fact that his reforms were prefaced by attacks on the Areopagites' 'conduct in office' suggests that 'those powers which [the council of the Areopagos] had accrued' consisted (but perhaps not exclusively) in the right to conduct the processes of *dokimasia* and *euthynai*, the scrutiny of officials before and after their term of office (Sealey 1964, Wallace 1974, Cawkwell 1988, Rihll 1995). An underlying cause may have been a decline in the Areopagos' reputation following the introduction in 487 of election by lot to the archonship (the Areopagos was made up of former archons; cf. Badian 1971). Other, broader conclusions can also be reached. First, the framing of Ephialtes' reforms in terms of the removal of accretions is suggestive of a need to represent democratic reforms as conservative. Aischylos' *Eumenides* (458), similarly, represents in its conclusion the foundation of the Areopagos by Athena with precisely the limited role (judging homicide) ascribed to it after Ephialtes' reforms. Second, it should not be supposed that the issue of accountability was – as in contemporary democracies – one that failed to engage the broader public. Their importance is clear, not only from Ephialtes' subsequent assassination by an Aristodikos of Tanagra ([Aristotle] *Ath. Pol.* 25: cf. Stockton 1982), or from Thucydides' report of oligarchic plotting (1.107) – of a party in Athens 'who hoped to put an end to the democracy and the building of the Long Walls' – but also from dark references in the *Eumenides*: the chorus' prayer, for example, that 'the growling of factional strife, hungry for evil, never be heard in this city, and that the earth not drink citizens' black blood', or that the 'citizens might enjoy shared pleasures, a unanimity of thought in their loves and hatreds' (Aischylos *Eumenides* 976–88). If Aischylos' dream of unanimity also implied a recommendation to go no further (cf. Dover 1957; Dodds 1960; Macleod 1982), however, or in Athena's words to 'make no innovations in the laws' (681–710), it was not a warning that was heeded. The Ephialtic revolution initiated a wave of subsequent changes recorded by the author of the *Athenaion Politeia*: the opening of the archonship to the Zeugite class (the third of Solon's property classes), the introduction of jury pay to compensate the poorer Athenians for lost income, and finally the citizenship law of 451/0, intended to limit the bounty of empire to those born of two Athenian parents (cf. Patterson 1981).

Finally, this account so far might suggest a straightforwardly binary view of the fifth-century Greek world as dominated by two superpowers (and which envisages the fourth century as untidily fragmented in the aftermath of the Peloponnesian War). This is a view that is encouraged by our inevitable reliance on Thucydides (and our own desire for a controllable narrative), and one that was perhaps attractive in the era of the Cold War; it does not, however, adequately describe the *reality* of fifth-century history. The central events of Thucydides' narrative of the causes of war could be told from a Korinthian perspective. But from the account of Diodoros and from Pindar's homages to leading figures of the Greek world, we can see glimmers of yet other perspectives: the Syracusan Gelon's victory over the Carthaginians at Himera, represented by Pindar as equivalent to Salamis or Plataiai (*Pythian Odes* 1.72–80; cf. Diodoros 11.1.4, 20.1, 24.1–2) and the decline of the Syracusan dynasty from a position of dominance in Sicily at the time of Gelon's victory (Diodoros 11.25.5) to moral decrepitude only 14 years later (Diodoros 11.67–8; Asheri 1992); or the jostling for position of the different cities of Boiotia, climaxing in our period in the formation of a federal organization in Boiotia after the Athenians' expulsion (*Hellenika Oxyrhynchia* 16). In addition, however, to telling the narratives of other cities, we might also tell different types of narrative: of a new wave of federal organizations (*Hellenika Oxyrhynchia* 16; M&L 42; cf. Lewis 1992a: 120) foreshadowing those of the Hellenistic period and indicative of our areas of ignorance; of the appropriation of aristocratic ideals by the masses and the erosion of an archaic elite culture (Ober 1989); of the intellectual revolution of the Sophists and medical writers (e.g., de Romilly 1992, Lloyd 1979); of the formation of a Panhellenic cultural identity forged in the Persian wars (E. Hall 1989, J. Hall 2002); or of the sudden expansion in geographical knowledge, reflected in the writings of Hekataios, Herodotos and others (Davies 1992: 25–7). If the Peloponnesian War was, in Thucydides' words, 'the greatest movement (*kinesis*) yet known in history' for Greeks and Barbarians, that was in part because of these last two developments.

# Bibliography

Asheri, D. (1992) 'Sicily, 478–431 B.C.' in: *CAH*² 5 147–70

Badian, E. (1971) 'Archons and *strategoi*' in: *Antichthon* 5: 1–34

Badian, E. (1993a) 'The peace of Callias' in: Badian, E. (1993) *From Plataea to Potidaea: studies in the history and historiography of the pentecontaetia* (Baltimore: Johns Hopkins University Press) 1–72 (revised from Badian, E. (1987) in: *JHS* 107: 1–39)

Badian, E. (1993b) 'Toward a chronology of the pentecontaetia down to the renewal of the peace of Callias' in: Badian, E. (1993) *From Plataea to Potidaea: studies in the history and historiography of the pentecontaetia* (Baltimore: Johns Hopkins University Press) 83–107 (revised from Badian, E. (1988) in: *Classical Views/Etudes de monde classique* ns 7: 289–320)

Bakker, E. J., J. F. I. de Jong, H. van Wees (eds) (2002) *Brill's companion to Herodotus* (Leiden: Brill)

Bradeen, D. W. (1960) 'The popularity of the Athenian empire' in: *Historia* 9: 257–69

Brunt, P. A. (1953–4) 'The Hellenic league against Persia' in: *Historia* 2: 135–63

Brunt, P. A. (1966) 'Athenian settlements abroad in the fifth century B.C.' in: Badian, E. (ed.) (1966) *Ancient society and institutions: studies presented to Victor Ehrenberg on his 75th birthday* (Oxford: Blackwell) 71–92

Calame, C. (1996) *Thésée et l'imaginaire athénien: légende et culte en Grèce antique* (préf. P. Vidal-Naquet) (Lausanne: Payot ²1996)

Cawkwell, G. (1983) 'The decline of Sparta' in: *CQ* 33: 385–400

Cawkwell, G. L. (1988) '*Nomophylakia* and the Areopagus' in: *JHS* 108: 1–12

Connor, W. R. (1971) *The new politicians of fifth-century Athens* (Princeton: Princeton University Press)

Connor, W. R. (1984) *Thucydides* (Princeton: Princeton University Press)

Davies, J. K. (1992) 'Greece after the Persian wars' in: *CAH*² 5 15–33

Davies, J. K. (1993) *Democracy and classical Greece* (Cambridge MA: Harvard University Press ²1993)

De Romilly, J. (1992) *The great sophists in Periclean Athens* (trans. J. Lloyd) (Oxford: Clarendon)

De Ste. Croix, G. E. M. (1954–5) 'The character of the Athenian empire' in: *Historia* 3: 3–41

De Ste. Croix, G. E. M. (1972) *The origins of the Peloponnesian War* (London: Duckworth)

De Souza, P. (1999) *Piracy in the Graeco-Roman world* (Cambridge: Cambridge University Press)

Dodds, E. R. (1960) 'Morals and politics in the "Oresteia" ' in: *PCPhS* 186 (ns 6): 19–31 (repr. in: Dodds, E. R. (1973) *The ancient concept of progress, and other essays on Greek literature and belief* (Oxford: Clarendon) 45–63)

Dover, K. J. (1957) 'The political aspect of Aeschylus' *Eumenides*' in: *JHS* 77: 230–7 (repr. in: Dover, K. J. (1987) *Greek and the Greeks: collected papers*, vol. 1: *Language, poetry, drama* (Oxford: Blackwell) 161–75)

Figueira, T. J. (1998) *The power of money: coinage and politics in the Athenian empire* (Philadelphia: University of Pennsylvania Press)

Finley, M. I. (1978) 'The fifth-century Athenian empire: a balance-sheet' in: Garnsey, P. D. A., & C. R. Whittaker (eds) (1978) *Imperialism in the ancient world* (Cambridge: Cambridge University Press) 103–26

Fornara, C. W. (1971a) *Herodotus: an interpretative essay* (Oxford: Clarendon)

Fornara, C. W. (1971b) 'Evidence for the date of Herodotus' publication' in: *JHS* 91: 25–34

Fornara, C. W. (1977) 'IG I² 39.52–57 and the "popularity" of the Athenian empire' in: *CSCA* 10: 39–55

Fornara, C. W., & L. J. Samons (1991) *Athens from Cleisthenes to Pericles* (Berkeley: University of California Press)

Forrest, W. G. (1960) 'Themistocles and Argos' in: *CQ* 10: 221–41

Forrest, W. G. (1975) 'Aristophanes and the Athenian empire' in: Levick, B. (ed.) (1975) *The ancient historian and his materials: essays in honour of C. E. Stevens on his seventieth birthday* (Farnborough [Hamphire UK]: Gregg) 17–29

Gow, A. S. F. (1928) 'Notes on the *Persae* of Aeschylus' in: *JHS* 48: 132–58

Hall, E. (1989) *Inventing the barbarian: Greek self-definition through tragedy* (Oxford: Clarendon) (Oxford Classical Monographs)

Hall, J. (2002) *Hellenicity: between ethnicity and culture* (Chicago: University of Chicago Press)

Harrison, T. (2000) *The emptiness of Asia: Aeschylus' Persians and the history of the fifth century* (London: Duckworth)

Harrison, T. (2002) 'The Persian invasions' in: Bakker et al. 2002: 551–78

Harrison, T. (2005) 'Through British eyes: Athenian imperialism and modern historiography' in: Goff, B. E. (ed.) (2005) *Classics and colonialism* (London: Duckworth)

Hodkinson, S. (1983) 'Social order and the conflict of values in classical Sparta' in: *Chiron* 13: 239–81

Hodkinson, S. (2000) *Property and wealth in classical Sparta* (London: Duckworth & The Classical Press of Wales)

Holladay, A. J. (1977) 'Sparta's role in the first Peloponnesian war' in: *JHS* 97: 54–63

Hölscher, T. (1998) 'Images and political identity: the case of Athens' in: Boedeker, D., & K. A. Raaflaub (eds) (1998) *Democracy, empire, and the arts in fifth-century Athens* (Cambridge MA: Harvard University Press) 153–83 (Center for Hellenic Studies Colloquia 2)

Hornblower, S. (1984) 'Introduction: the archaic background to the fifth-century empire' in: Hornblower, S., & M. C. Greenstock (eds) (1984) *The Athenian empire* (Harrow: London Association of Classical Teachers) ii–v (Lactor 1)

Hornblower, S (1991) *A commentary on Thucydides*, vol. 1: *Books I–III* (Oxford: Clarendon)

Hornblower, S (1996) *A commentary on Thucydides*, vol. 2: *Books IV–V.24* (Oxford: Clarendon)

Hornblower, S. (2002) *The Greek world, 479–323 B.C.* (London: Routledge [3]2002) (Routledge History of the Ancient World)

Laird, A. (1999) *Powers of expression, expressions of power: speech presentation and Latin literature* (Oxford: Clarendon)

Lewis, D. M. (1992a) 'Causes of war' in: *CAH*[2] 5 370–80

Lewis, D. M. (1992b) 'Chronological notes' in: *CAH*[2] 5 499–505

Lloyd, G. E. R. (1979) *Magic, reason and experience: studies in the origin and development of Greek science* (Cambridge: Cambridge University Press)

Loraux, N. (1986) 'Thucydide a écrit la guerre du Péloponnèse' in: *Métis* 1: 139–61

Low, P. (2005) 'Looking for the language of Athenian imperialism' in: *JHS* 125: 92–111

Macleod, C. W. (1982) 'Politics and the *Oresteia*' in: *JHS* 102: 124–44 (repr. in: Macleod, C. W. (1983) *Collected essays* (Oxford: Clarendon) 20–43)

Meiggs, R. (1972) *The Athenian empire* (Oxford: Clarendon; repr. with corrections Oxford: Clarendon 1979)

Mills, S. (1997) *Theseus, tragedy, and the Athenian empire* (Oxford: Clarendon) (Oxford Classical Monographs)

Moles, J. (1996) 'Herodotus warns the Athenians' in: Cairns, F., & M. Heath (eds) (1996) *Papers of the Leeds International Latin Seminar 9: Roman poetry and prose, Greek poetry, etymology, historiography* (Leeds: Cairns) 259–84 (ARCA Classical and Medieval Texts, Papers and Monographs 34)

Moles, J. (2002) 'Herodotus and Athens' in: Bakker et al. 2002: 33–52

Nixon, L., & S. Price (1990) 'The size and resources of Greek cities' in: Murray, O., & S. Price (1990) *The Greek city: from Homer to Alexander* (Oxford: Clarendon) 137–70

Ober, J. (1989) *Mass and elite in democratic Athens* (Princeton: Princeton University Press)

Osborne, R. (2000) (ed.) *The Athenian empire* (trans. and ed. with notes by R. Osborne) (London: London Association of Classical Teachers [4]2000) (Lactor 1)

Parker, R. (1996) *Athenian religion: a history* (Oxford: Clarendon)

Patterson, C. B. (1981) *Pericles' citizenship law of 451–450 B.C.* (New York: Arno) (Monographs in Classical Studies)

Podlecki, A. J. (1999) *The political background of Aeschylean tragedy* (London: Bristol Classical Press [2]1999)

Quinn, T. J. (1964) 'Thucydides and the unpopularity of the Athenian empire' in: *Historia* 13: 257–66

Rhodes, P. J. (1992a) 'The Delian league to 449 B.C.' in: *CAH*[2] 5 34–61

Rhodes, P. J. (1992b) 'The Athenian revolution' in: *CAH*[2] 5 62–95

Rihll, T. E. (1995) 'Democracy denied: why Ephialtes attacked the Areiopagus' in: *JHS* 115: 87–98

Robertson, N. (1980) 'The true nature of the Delian league, 478–461 B.C.' in: *AJAH* 5: 64–96, 110–33

Rood, T. (1998) *Thucydides: narrative and explanation* (Oxford: Clarendon) (Oxford Classical Monographs)

Sealey, R. (1957) 'Thucydides, Herodotus and the causes of war' in: *CQ* 7: 1–12

Sealey, R. (1964) 'Ephialtes' in: *CPh* 59: 11–22 (repr. in: Sealey, R. (1967) *Essays in Greek politics* (New York: Manyland Books))

Stadter, P. A. (ed.) (1973) *The speeches in Thucydides: a collection of original studies with a bibliography [of scholarship on the speeches in Thucydides, 1873–1970, by W. C. West III]* (Papers presented at a colloquium sponsored by the Dept. of Classics of the University of North Carolina at Chapel Hill, March 26–27, 1972) (Chapel Hill: University of North Carolina Press)

Stadter, P. A. (1992) 'Herodotus and the Athenian *archē*' in: *Annali della Scuola Normale Superiore di Pisa, Classe di Lettere e Filosofia* 22: 781–809

Stockton, D. L. (1982) 'The death of Ephialtes' in: *CQ* 32: 227–8

Wallace, R. W. (1974) 'Ephialtes and the Areopagus' in: *GRBS* 15: 259–69

Wilson, P. (2000) *The Athenian institution of the khoregia: the chorus, the city, and the stage* (Cambridge: Cambridge University Press)

# CHAPTER TWENTY-FIVE

# The Peloponnesian War and its Aftermath

## Karl-Wilhelm Welwei

## 1  'The Greatest Upheaval for Greeks and Barbarians Alike' (Thucydides 1.1)

### The escalation of tensions

During late summer or early autumn of 432, about a year after the naval battle off the Sybota Islands near Kerkyra, Sparta reached a decision which would change the course of Greek history: the Spartan Assembly (*apella*) voted to support the motion of the ephor Sthenelaïdas declaring that Athens had broken the terms of the 'Thirty Years Peace' of 446 (Thuc. 1.87). The escalation of tensions only a year after Sybota illuminates the degree to which the political and economic spheres of interest of Athens and Sparta as the dominant powers in Greece were on a collision course. In 433/2 the treaties concluded by Athens with Leontinoi in Sicily and Rhegion in southern Italy were an indication of her growing interest in the Greek West (*IG*1³ 53, 54; Fornara 124, 125). From the Athenian perspective, however, the northern Aegean Sea was the most pressing problem, since Perdikkas II of Macedon sought to exploit the on-going conflict between Athens and Korinth for his own expansionist aims. He tacitly supported Poteidaia, the Chalkidians and Bottiaians in their desire to defect from the Delian League and he also sought by diplomatic means to explore the possibility of support from Sparta and Korinth (Thuc. 1.57). Athens feared the loss of access to the mineral resources and the timber for ship building from Thrace. She therefore demanded that the citizens of Poteidaia, a Korinthian colony but also a member of the Delian League, should dismantle their fortifications and expel the Korinthian appointed magistrates (*epidamiourgoi*).

After futile negotiations in Athens the Poteidaians secured a Spartan promise that Peloponnesian troops would invade Attika in case of an Athenian attack. Poteidaia rejected the Athenian ultimatum and allied herself with the Bottiaians and the Chalkidians, who had left their coastal cities and settled in Olynthos relying on the promise of Perdikkas II. Consequently the Athenians reinforced their contingent considerably, which was primarily sent out to counter the threat from Perdikkas II (Thuc. 1.56–65). Now they laid siege to Poteidaia. Tensions intensified when, on the motion of Perikles, the Athenian People's Assembly (*ekklesia*) passed the Megarian Decree (Thuc. 1.67.4; 1.139.1–2; Aristophanes *Acharnians* 515–55; *Peace* 605–9; Fornara 123). It excluded the Megarians from all markets and harbours of the Delian League as well as from the Athenian *agora* (Kagan 1969: 251–72). The decree effectively embargoed Megarian and Korinthian imports of Thracian timber and mineral resources.

The anticipation of a great war was an important factor in the political plans of Perikles (Thuc. 1.144.3; Plutarch *Perikles* 8.7). In Sparta meanwhile the ephor Sthenelaïdas and his political supporters, fearful of growing Athenian power, assessed the situation similarly. Thucydides (1.86.5) characterizes the situation as critical when he writes that in the debate Sthenelaïdas took a clear position from the outset by demanding that the Spartans declare war. The Megarian Decree represented a provocation of Sparta as the hegemon of the Peloponnesian League. This became plain in the complaints of the Korinthians, Megarians, and other Spartan allies before the Spartan assembly of 432 (Thuc. 1.68–71). King Archidamos, however, warned – persuasively, it appears (Thuc. 1.80–85) – against declaring war at this point, on the grounds that Sparta was inadequately prepared for war. In the end Sthenelaïdas proposed that the Assembly should merely 'state' its view that Athens had broken the terms of the Peace of 446. In an unusual move designed to emphasize the seriousness of his proposal concerning the alleged violation of the truce, he required the Spartiates to vote 'individually' by grouping themselves in the *apella* according to their vote instead of the customary vote by acclamation (Thuc. 1.87.1–3).

The Spartan leadership then convened a meeting of their allies. After further debate it was decided that war was the only option (Thuc. 1.125), but this was not as yet a declaration of war.

In the following winter Spartan negotiators in Athens demanded the expulsion of the 'Accursed', which refers to a curse incurred by the Alkmeonid Megakles (a distant ancestor of Perikles), who had ordered the execution of the followers of Kylon who sought asylum at a sanctuary on the akropolis after an unsuccessful coup d'état in the late seventh century (Hdt. 5.71; Thuc. 1.126). Perikles of course was an Alkmeonid and the Spartans attempted to undermine his political clout by this diplomatic manoeuvre, which naturally drew an Athenian rejection.

In further negotiations Sparta demanded that the Athenians lift the siege of Poteidaia, restore Aigina's autonomy (which had been subjugated in 458/7), repeal the Megarian Decree, and grant autonomy to all members of the Delian League. The Spartans ultimately signalled their willingness to enter into negotiations by reducing their criteria for peace to a repealing of the Megarian Decree (Thuc. 1.139). Perikles, who thought war was inevitable, persuaded the Athenian *ekklesia* to reject the Spartan demands (towards the end of the winter of 432/1: Thuc. 1.144–5).

It was, however, neither of the hegemonic leaders of their respective leagues who was the first to engage in military action: war erupted with the Thebans' (unsuccessful) attack on Plataiai, a long-time ally of Athens (Thuc. 2.2–5). Athens and Sparta now intensified their preparations for war, but some time passed before the first strike of a Peloponnesian army in Attika. Sparta evidently realized even before negotiations broke off that there was no hope for compromise on the part of Athens in the question of autonomy for her allies. This explains why Sparta ultimately only insisted on the repeal of the Megarian Decree: it was a matter of prestige and she could not abandon it without a loss of face. The many events leading up to the outbreak of war do not permit simple allocation of guilt (Meyer 1997: 23–54). Time and again actions and reactions from both hegemonic powers confronted their respective decision-making bodies with problems of great complexity. Even the leading players were unable to assess realistically the consequences of their decision.

## The Archidamian war

The strategies and aims of war were dictated by the opponents' assets: The sheer striking power of the Peloponnesian army stood against the naval strength of the Delian League. Sparta intended to invade Attika and devastate the Attic regions, whereas Athens sought to avoid an open battle with the superior Peloponnesian army of hoplites. On the one hand the Athenians planned to transfer the country residents out of the endangered regions into the triangular safety zone marked by the fortresses of Athens, Phaleron, and Piraeus; on the other hand they tried to remain in control of the sea and of their own allies and to raid the enemies' coastal lines in order to interrupt the lines of supply (Lewis 1992: 380–8).

By late May or early June the Peloponnesians under king Archidamos invaded Attika. The king once again offered peace talks, which were refused by Athens (Thuc. 2.12). Above all the invasion had a devastating psychological effect on the Athenian citizens who helplessly watched as the Peloponnesians pillaged and laid waste to their land (Thuc. 2.13–23). In order to secure Athenian trade Perikles ordered the seizure of the island of Aigina and the expulsion of its inhabitants. Naval operations were to secure the continuity of Athenian connections with Kerkyra and the Hellespont (Thuc. 2.25–7, 31–2). Despite an especially serious setback during the summer of 430 operations on the island of Zakynthos and in Akarnania continued in efforts to protect Athenian interests in the West.

During the second Peloponnesian invasion of Attika an epidemic reached Piraeus from the Near East and claimed numerous victims (Thuc. 2.48–54; Rubel 2000: 120–56). The *ekklesia* voted to sue for peace despite Perikles' objections, but the Spartans rejected it. The desperate and war-weary Athenians deposed Perikles as *strategos* and fined him for 'deceiving the people' (Thuc. 2.65.3). Although he was re-elected in the spring of 429, he died soon afterwards of the 'plague', without having influenced the on-going war again.

Ever since the ostracism of Thoukydides son of Melesias (not to be mistaken for the historian Thucydides son of Oloros) in 443, Perikles was the pre-eminent figure in Athenian politics because of his undisputed personal integrity and his authority as a statesman, which he maintained without undermining the strength of the Athenian democracy. He was single-mindedly focused on the advancement of the interests of his polis (Kagan 1991: 91–116). He proved incapable, however, of mastering the great crisis of 432/1 because he embraced vague political theories about the inevitability of wars between rival powers. His death paved the way for the rise of 'new politicians' (Connor 1971) like Kleon and Nikias, who were wealthy entrepreneurs, to play a prominent role in Athens. Kleon, owner of a large tannery, lacked Perikles' sophistication, but was accepted by many in the *ekklesia*, despite his rough manners. He had strongly criticized the strategies of Perikles and, like other Athenian politicians, was confronted with the problem of the stalemate in the war effort. Nikias, who held leases of silver mines and owned some 1,000 slaves, became one of the most important *strategoi* while at the same time avoiding military risks. He did not, however, succeed in influencing the *ekklesia* on a permanent basis. It was the trust of the *demos*, however, which remained the basis of a leading role in the polis. Every politician therefore had to reckon with the ever-present possibility of political defeat in the *ekklesia* despite previous successes in votes.

The fortunes of war kept changing over the course of the following years. In 429 a small Athenian squadron commanded by Phormion operated with great success in the Korinthian Gulf (Thuc. 80–92), and Poteidaia was forced to surrender during the winter of 430/29 (Thuc. 2.70). Chalkidike nonetheless remained a source of danger for Athens. Although in 429 Peloponnesian troops did not invade Attika, they laid siege to Plataiai for the long term. In 428 Mytilene and three other poleis on the island of Lesbos seceded (Thuc. 3.2–6), but the Athenians brutally crushed the revolt and took bloody revenge despite another Peloponnesian invasion of Attika. Kleon in particular whipped up the emotions of the *ekklesia*, which – one of the darkest moments of Athenian democracy – voted to execute all male citizens of Mytilene and to enslave the women and children. The next day the resolution was modified, but still about one thousand so-called ring-leaders were put to death (Thuc. 3.27–50). After the surrender of Plataiai in 427 the Spartans, urged on by their allies, displayed similar cruelty by ordering the execution of 285 surviving enemy combatants (Thuc. 3.52–68). In the summer of that year the ever increasing brutality reached its peak on the island of Kerkyra as certain subversive elements amongst its citizens caused civil war (Thuc. 3.69–81). They had bought their way out of Korinthian captivity on the promise of forcing an alliance between Kerkyra and Korinth. Thucydides analyses these events and lays bare both the destructive forces set loose during the war within many poleis and the abandoning of traditional values amongst their citizens (Thuc. 3.82–3).

In 427 the theatre of warfare expanded into the West. An Athenian squadron was dispatched in an unsuccessful effort to support Leontinoi against Syracuse (Thuc. 3.86) and had to retreat, after the Sicilian Greeks succeeded in settling their quarrels at the conference of Gela following a rousing speech made by Hermokrates of Syracuse (Thuc. 4.58–65).

The Athenian intervention, however, had far-reaching effects in respect to the strategic importance of Aitolia, Kerkyra, Kephallenia, Akarnania, and Zakynthos. By 426 these new plans came to life under the *strategos* Demosthenes, who sought to extend Athenian influence over Aitolia by a surprise attack designed to exert pressure on the Spartan allies in Boiotia (Roisman 1993: 23–32). In 425 Demosthenes, who accompanied the *strategoi* although he held no office, scored an unexpected success when the 40 triremes, which were to support the Athenian forces on Sicily, were delayed by inclement weather off the Peloponnesian coast near Pylos. Before their departure they set up a base at Koryphasion, the promontory of Pylos. Under the command of Demosthenes the garrison was manned with five trireme crews, who faced a siege when 420 Spartiates and *perioikoi* (non-citizen freemen in Lakonia) occupied the island of Sphakteria south of Koryphasion. In the end the

Lakedaimonians were surrounded by Athenian reinforcements and Sparta proposed peace negotiations, which, however, were rejected (Thuc. 4.2–23). The dominant speaker in the *ekklesia* was Kleon, who assumed the command of the Athenian forces in Pylos when the siege continued, but Demosthenes was the de facto commander of the operations which succeeded in overpowering the Lakedaimonians. The capture of 292 Lakedaimonian hoplites, including about 120 Spartiates, marked a turning point in the fortunes of war (Thuc. 4.26–41; Kagan 1974: 219–59). Victory now appeared within reach for the Athenians. In order to meet the expenses of the war they raised the *phoros*, the tribute of their allies, to c. 1,460–1,500 talents (M&L 69; *IG*1³ 71; Fornara 136) and planned major offensives against Megara and the Boiotians in 424. In the last analysis the failure of these expeditions was largely the result of inadequate means of communication (Roisman 1993: 42–51). Especially the Athenian defeat near Delion in Boiotia in 424 represented a serious set-back (Thuc. 4.90–9).

In the same year the conquest of the Spartan island of Kythera raised hopes in Athens, but the Spartan Brasidas was able to advance into Thrace with a small force of mercenaries and helots who, for the first time in Spartan history, served as hoplites. By capturing Amphipolis and some other poleis he scored a direct hit against Athenian naval supremacy (Thuc. 4.102–16). The Spartans made overtures to the Persian Court even before Brasidas' campaigns, but these proved fruitless (Thuc. 4.50). A willingness to come to an arrangement grew steadily in both poleis. In Athens the hope of victory diminished rapidly, and the Spartan leaders were eager to ransom the soldiers who had been captured on the island of Sphakteria. In the spring of 423 a one-year armistice agreement was concluded (*Staatsverträge* 183) which was favourable for Athens. It was not, however, renewed when it expired in 422 because Brasidas did not wish to put his successes in Thrace in jeopardy – in defiance of orders from the ephors. Kleon now assumed the Athenian command in Thrace but fell in the defeat at Amphipolis. Brasidas died of his wounds after the battle and received a hero's honours in Amphipolis (Thuc. 5.6–11). In sum Brasidas was a strict proponent of Spartan *Machtpolitik*. The slogans of freedom which gained him political success in some of the Thracian poleis were merely a means towards achieving his goals. Leading Spartans, however, considered his far-reaching strategic plans to be a danger to the political order of Sparta.

After the battle of Amphipolis politicians who recommended a peace arrangement forced the issue in both Athens and Sparta. In the spring of 421 they reached a settlement which was to establish a 50-years' peace. The Peace of Nikias, named after the most important Athenian negotiator, provided in essence that both poleis were to acknowledge the mutual spheres of interest of pre-war days and that any conflicts were to be settled by arbitration. The treaty also included concessions on the part of both sides (Thuc 5.18–19; *Staatsverträge* 188). The Athenians retained Nisaia, the harbour of Megara, while Thebes remained in possession of Plataiai. Athens was to leave Koryphasion, the promontory of Pylos, whereas Sparta was obliged to withdraw from Skione, a polis which was in revolt against Athens and which the Athenians had already decided to destroy.

This agreement was a clear indication that the Spartans had failed to make good on their professed goal of 'liberating the Hellenes' from Athenian hegemony, which they considered a tyranny. On the other hand Athens achieved less than had been predicted by Perikles. At the beginning of the war, in 431, the willingness of Perikles to incur a far greater risk than Athens was able to handle had had its motives in his overestimating Athenian military power. After his death, none of the politicians was able to deliver on his plans (Thuc. 2.65).

## The unstable peace and the Athenian expedition to Sicily

After the settlement of the Peace of Nikias the situation throughout Greece remained volatile. The Spartan commanding officer in Amphipolis refused to surrender the city and other poleis in Thrace to the wrath of Athens (Thuc. 5.21). The Boiotians did not give up the Attic frontier post of Panakton and the Korinthians did not succeed in linking their old colonies of Poteidaia and Kerkyra to the *metropolis*, the mother city (Korinth). Moreover it was uncertain whether the peace between Sparta and Argos, which reached its term in 421, could be renewed (Kagan 1974: 19–32; 1981). As her most important allies did not ratify the Peace of Nikias, Sparta changed her course and settled for a defensive alliance with Athens which was supposed to last 50 years (Thuc. 5.23; *Staatsverträge* 189). The reaction to this new development was an alliance between Mantineia, Argos, and Elis. Soon Korinth and the Chalkidians joined them (Thuc. 5.28–31; *Staatsverträge* 190). In the spring of 420 the Spartans formed an alliance with Boiotia because of growing discord with Athens (Thuc. 5.39.2–3).

Alkibiades exploited this new situation for his own daring coup: after his entering office as *strategos* in 420 he negotiated a 100-year alliance between Athens, Argos, Elis, and Mantineia (Thuc. 5.43–7; *Staatsverträge* 193; *IG*1³ 83). When the conflict between Argos and Sparta intensified, the Spartan leaders were determined to thwart further disintegration in the Peloponnesian League.

In the battle of Mantineia of 418 the Spartans under King Agis II succeeded in defeating the Argives and their allies – including an Athenian contingent – and in disrupting the new 'Quadruple Alliance' (Thuc. 5.64–74). They were unable, however, to impose a lasting pro-Spartan regime on Argos. In these years Sparta and Athens pursued their policy of strength with utmost brutality. In 417/16 the Spartans occupied the city of Hysiai near Argos and killed all captured citizens (Thuc. 5.83). The Athenians also showed their disregard for all rules of conduct. In the winter of 417/16 they executed all male citizens of the island of Melos and enslaved the women and children, because Melos was not willing to give up her neutrality. In his famous 'Melian Dialogue' Thucydides in masterly fashion transformed the negotiations of the summer of 416, when the Athenian envoys conveyed their demands, into a paradigm of an unscrupulous policy of terror (Thuc. 5.85–111).

Alkibiades probably did not participate in the action against Melos. In 416 he strengthened the position of the Athenian partisans in Argos once again. Furthermore he saw the chance of a large-scale Athenian intervention on Sicily, when in the winter of 416/15 the Elymian city of Segesta (or Egesta) in western Sicily sought support in Athens against the polis Selinous, which was allied with Syracuse (Thuc. 6.6). According to Alkibiades, who had been raised in the house of his uncle Perikles, a new struggle for power against Sparta was inevitable anyway. He pleaded for a preventive strike in order to thwart a coalition of Athens' enemies in Sicily and Greece proper (Thuc. 6.16–18). As to the 'Sicilian Expedition', he succeeded in carrying the day against the warnings of the more cautious Nikias. The *ekklesia* voted for the expedition with Alkibiades, Nikias, and Lamachos as *strategoi autokratores* (generals with plenipotentiary powers) and on equal terms, and it instructed them to protect Segesta and generally to deal with the Sicilian Greeks 'in a way that serves Athens best' (Thuc. 6.8.2). For Athens it was a daring undertaking (Kagan 1974: 191; 1981). It is true that up to that point Sparta had been unable to gain the upper hand in Greece, even with the support of new allies in the West. But even if the Athenians had been successful in incorporating the Sicilian Greeks into the Delian League, Athens' military and logistic potential would not have been sufficient to control the vast maritime space between the Carthaginian and Persian spheres of interest.

Shortly before the departure of the Athenian expeditionary force herms (stelai displaying an erect phallus and a bust of Hermes with a small altar for common people's offering) were mutilated one night (Thuc. 6.27–9) – an act allegedly planned by perhaps a dozen perpetrators: Athens was in turmoil (Rubel 2000: 178–232). Hermes was considered to be the patron god of travellers, and therefore none of the sailors in the Athenian fleet wanted to share the triremes with blasphemers. Moreover, in public opinion it was linked to an alleged conspiracy against democracy. Denunciations and incriminations created further confusion. Alkibiades, who was perceived as a typical champion of the Athenian *jeunesse dorée* ('gilded youth'), was accused of another sacrilegious act, the profanation of the Mysteries of Eleusis (Plutarch *Alkibiades* 19; Andokides 1.11–18). At first no action was brought against Alkibiades, but he was soon recalled. While returning to Athens he fled to Sparta. There he is said to have divulged some of Athens' far-reaching, but not in every respect believable plans of conquest and to have advised the Spartans permanently to occupy the Athenian fortress of Dekeleia (Thuc. 6.53; 6.88.9–93).

After some initial successes Nikias and Lamachos began to besiege Syracuse. In 414, however, Lamachos fell in battle at Epipolai, the plateau near Syracuse (Thuc. 6.101.6). When the surrender of Syracuse seemed to be imminent, the arrival of Gylippos, who had been sent by Sparta, turned the scales in favour of the besieged (Thuc. 7.1–7). He circumspectly organized the defence of the city, so that it was now the Athenians who found themselves under siege. After a belated and futile attempt by the fleet to break through the lines, and after a further delay due to a lunar eclipse, the Athenians had to retreat to the interior of Sicily and surrendered after a short while. Nikias and the renowned commander Demosthenes, who had been sent with reinforcements to Sicily, were executed. About 40,000 men – combatants and non-combatants – retreated in disarray (Thuc. 7.75.5). Several thousand managed to flee to Katana, but numerous men who had surrendered individually to the Syracusan soldiers were enslaved, against the customs of Greek warfare. About 7,000 men were captured as prisoners of war. For 70 days they were held in the notorious quarries of Syracuse in unspeakable conditions. Most of them died of hunger and exhaustion. Those prisoners who survived were also sold into slavery (Thuc. 7.87), with the exception of the Athenian citizens and their Greek allies from Sicily and southern Italy, who were left in the quarries and whose fate is unknown.

The largest Athenian operation of the Peloponnesian War failed (Kagan 1974: 353; 1981), but the war was yet not lost for Athens. One of the first reactions to the Sicilian disaster was the appointment of ten *probouloi* (preliminary advisors) who were to prevent precipitous resolutions by the *ekklesia*. But this must not be perceived as the victory of the oligarchic forces within Athenian society. Athens' main goal remained her hegemony over the Delian League. One of the important measures was the introduction of a 5 per cent import and export tariff replacing the *phoros* (tribute). Even after the 'Sicilian Expedition' Sparta did not consider herself as the master of the situation, although her designs of 432/1 seemed to be on the verge of succeeding.

## The fall of the Athenian thalassocracy

In the late summer or early autumn of 414, after Athenian raids on Peloponnesian coastal regions, Sparta declared that the Athenians had broken the Peace Treaty of 421. In 413 the Spartans occupied Dekeleia as a key position in Attika. Their main targets were agricultural production and the silver mines of Laureion.

Dekeleia became the headquarters for King Agis II. There, in the winter of 413/12, he met with envoys from Euboia and Lesbos who appealed for help in the matter of their intended secession from the Delian League. In Sparta a similar request was the subject of debates between the Spartans and envoys from Chios and Erythrai. The satrap Tissaphernes also explored whether he might find common ground with Sparta (Thuc. 8.5; Kagan 1987: 28). Making the most of the current pressure on Athens, he wanted to gain Spartan consent to the renewed claim of the Achaimenid king Dareios II to dominion over the Greek poleis in Asia Minor. In 412/11 the agreement was drafted in three treaties (Thuc. 8.18; 8.37; 8.58; *Staatsverträge* 200, 201, 202; Lewis 1977: 90–109). In return Sparta received Persian subsidies to build and sustain a fleet which could match that of Athens. In order to expand the war Sparta tried to support secession movements within the Delian League in 412. The Spartans were successful in Chios and Miletos (Thuc. 8.6–12; 8.14; 8.16–17), whereas the Athenians were able to crush the revolt of Samos and to regain control over Mytilene and Methymna on Lesbos (Thuc. 8.23). All things considered, the Athenians prevailed in Ionia, but they had to give up the blockade of Miletos and lost some of their influence over the coastal regions of Asia Minor. Yet once more they reclaimed the initiative: the Spartans began to distrust Alkibiades, who now fled to the Persian satrap Tissaphernes. In order to exploit the Persian interest in the Hellenic disputes for his own purposes, he attempted to persuade the satrap to adopt a policy of creating an appearance of being supportive of the causes of both Athens and Sparta. Alkibiades' next step was to suggest to the officers and to the rank and file of the Athenian fleet based on the island of Samos that he would be able to negotiate an alliance with Persia, including Persian subsidies if an oligarchic regime was established in Athens (Thuc. 8.45–54). His proposals were favourably received by a group of relatively wealthy Athenians who were not content with democracy. Not knowing that Alkibiades used them for his intrigues, they sent Peisandros, one of their leaders, to Athens with instructions to organize an oligarchic coup d'état. With the help of chosen *hetairoi* (members of socio-political groups of men) he intimidated the citizens, until he reached his aim in May of 411. A commission of thirty *syngrapheis* (authors) was formed, who were to draw up laws and proposals, allegedly in the best interest of the political order of the polis. According to Pseudo-Aristotle *Ath. Pol.* 29.2 twenty men were added to the ten *probouloi* of 413 of this committee (Fornara 148; Heftner 2001: 130–48). Arrangements were made for the establishment of a new Council of the Four Hundred, which was of course dominated by the most eager of the oligarchic conspirators. The Council of the Four Hundred never accomplished its ostensible task of bestowing full citizenship upon only a select five thousand men and subsequently showed its true colours as a regime of terror (Thuc. 8.63–71).

Meanwhile in Samos Thrasyboulos and Thrasyllos upheld Athenian democratic principles. They enabled Alkibiades to return to Samos, where he was appointed *strategos* by the crews of the fleet. In September successful Spartan naval operations off the east coast of Euboia led to the fall of the Four Hundred, who tried in vain to enter into negotiations with the Spartans (Thuc. 8.89–93). A new regime of the Five Thousand was proclaimed, but it never became reality (Andrewes 1992: 479–81). After the Athenians had lost Euboia, operations shifted to the Hellespont, regions important for the Athenian grain supply. In the spring of 410 the Athenian fleet under the command of Alkibiades scored a splendid victory off Kyzikos in the Propontis (Xenophon *Hellenika* 1.1.11–23; Diodoros 13.50–1; Kagan 1987: 238–46). Now the Spartans sued for peace, but their proposal on the basis of the *status quo*, which would obviously have required major Athenian concessions (Bleckmann 1998: 396–404), was rejected by the *ekklesia* (Diodoros 13.52.2–53.2; Philochoros *FGrHist* 328 F 139, F 140).

In late 408 or more probably early 407 Alkibiades returned to Athens in triumph (Fornara 159) and was appointed *strategos autokrator* (effectively commander-in-chief of the Athenian forces). He left the bulk of his fleet at Notion, the harbour of Kolophon, to join the Athenian forces at Phokaia with some troops and a few triremes in order to coordinate the operations against Phokaia and other poleis in northern Ionia. During his absence he appointed Antiochos, the *kybernetes* (helmsman) of his own ship, to be his lieutenant at Notion. Antiochos was defeated by the Spartan *nauarchos* (admiral) Lysander, who set up a trap for the Athenian triremes. Alkibiades lost his office or was not re-elected as one of the ten *strategoi* (Xenophon *Hellenika* 1.5.12–14; Diodoros 13.71.2–4; *Hellenika Oxyrhynchia* 4.1–4; Ellis 1989: 91–3). After his term of office ended, Lysander also had to hand over his command to Kallikratidas, who was defeated and fell in the battle off the Arginousai Islands, situated between Lesbos and the mainland (Xenophon *Hellenika* 1.6.24–38). This last Athenian victory was followed by the scandalous and tragic trial against the *strategoi*, who could not rescue numerous ship-wrecked sailors due to a rising windstorm in the course of battle (Xenophon *Hellenika* 1.7.1–35; Rubel 2000: 307–41). The victorious *strategoi* were tried before the highly emotional *ekklesia* and condemned to death.

In 405 Lysander, at that time *epistoleus* (lieutenant) of the newly appointed *nauarchos*, commanded the Spartan fleet. He had about 200 triremes at his disposal thanks to Persian subsidies, which he obtained primarily because of his good relations with the Achaimenid prince Kyros. At Aigospotamoi in the Hellespont Lysander struck hard and fast, outwitting the incompetent Athenian naval command nearly without a fight. Contrary to the customs of war the captured 3,000 Athenians were ordered to be executed (Xenophon *Hellenika* 2.1.15–32; Diodoros 13.105–6.7). Athens was no longer able to equip a new fleet. In the following weeks Lysander captured the last Athenian positions within the territories of the Delian League with the exception of Samos, which resisted a while longer. He ordered all Athenians to return to Athens, now under siege, in order to increase the famine there in the hope of accelerating the end of the war. In the spring of 404, after a prolonged siege, he forced the Athenians into submission. Athens had to tear down the 'Long Walls' to some extent and to dismantle the fortifications of Piraeus. Furthermore she had to hand over all triremes except twelve and to suffer the return of her exiles. The Delian League had ceased to exist. Athens had to comply with the Spartan command and to pay tribute, thereby acknowledging the Spartan hegemony. On her part Sparta rejected demands made by the Thebans and Korinthians to destroy the city of Athens, enslave the citizens and sell their slaves (Xenophon *Hellenika* 2.2.19–23). This request was presumably not only a result of the long-lasting hatred between Athens and her rivals, but also an indication of fear that Sparta could become too powerful by installing a regime closely attached to her (Lotze 1964: 45–6; Powell 2001: 198).

# 2  The Spartan Hegemony

## *The consequences of the Peloponnesian War*

The Athenian defeat had immeasurably affected the entire Greek world. The Athenians' fending off the invasion of Xerxes and the role of hegemon of the Delian League, which included the entire Aegean area, had already severely strained Athens, almost beyond its limits. Sparta could not fill the gap caused by the Athenian surrender and the collapse of the Delian League. The Spartans, to begin with, lacked the manpower required for their new role as the sole hegemonic power. They were not able to seize and to continue the ways and means which the Athenians had created in successive stages during the 'Pentekontaetia' in order to control immense spaces. But as the new hegemonic power in Hellas the Spartans could not retreat from the obligation to guarantee the autonomy of the Ionians against the Great King's claim to dominion. Therefore the dualism between Athens and Sparta in the time of the 'Pentekontaetia' led nearly inexorably to confrontation between Sparta and Persia after Sparta had supported the unsuccessful revolt of prince Kyros the Younger against his brother, King Artaxerxes II (Xenophon *Hellenika* 3.1.1; *Anabasis* 1.8.26–7; Diodoros 14.23.6–7; Deinon *FGrHist* 690 F 17). The Spartans above all did not possess a clear concept of how to meet the requirements of the new situation, although many Spartiates were able greatly to broaden their political horizon, as they had to evaluate the situation in the entire eastern Mediterranean as well as in the West.

In the Greek West Sparta could exert only a small measure of influence. Moreover the success of Syracuse in warding off the Athenian forces in 413 had failed also to stabilize the political situation in Sicily. The Segestans were once again threatened by Selinous and they appealed to Carthage for help in 410. In Syracuse the danger which arose from the on-going Carthaginian operations brought with it the rise of Dionysios I. After denunciation of the elected generals he was appointed *strategos autokrator* in 406 (Berger 1992: 41–3). By the following year he had his personal bodyguard and founded 'the most powerful and enduring of the tyrannies in Greek history' (Diodoros 13.96.4). He quickly built up Syracusan military power and went to war against Carthage in 398. By 392, when peace was established after several reversals, Dionysios had forced the Carthaginians out of the main regions of Sicily and confined them to the western part of the island (Diodoros 14.96.3; *Staatsverträge* 233). His last two wars against Carthage, however, were less successful (c. 384–374; 368–366). After his death in 367 his son and successor Dionysios II concluded the wars and established peace. Although Dionysios I did not remove the institutions of the assembly and the council, his gradually expanding rule certainly broke the constitutional framework of the polis (Lewis 1994: 136). There is an obvious contrast between the organization of his political power and the regional alliances or large-scale federations of small and medium-sized poleis in Greece proper and the border areas. Of course these so-called *koina* were organized along different lines. The founding of the Chalkidian League in particular, which was set in motion by Olynthos, and the Boiotian League, formed in 446 after the battle of Koroneia in 447, characterize the new political developments of the early fourth century. Rivalries amongst some of the poleis in the structural framework of the *koina*, however, as well as factional strife (*stasis*) within the citizen communities of a *koinon* could never be entirely overcome by 'federal' institutions. This may have been inevitable: despite the existence of central authorities and a common citizenship, poleis remained autonomous within the *koina*, and this meant that even with the proliferation of *koina*, the Greek world remained as unstable as ever (Beck 1997: 251–4). Partisan struggle within the *koina* and their poleis only encouraged outside intervention. These problems also complicated the Spartans' hegemony after the Peloponnesian War.

Sparta, the leading power of the Peloponnesian League, which was of course a hegemonic alliance (*symmachia*), cannot be regarded a stabilizing factor in the Aegean or mainland Greece. Necessary internal reforms in Sparta failed because of the Spartiates' commitment to the so-called 'Lykourgan Order (*kosmos*)'. From their point of view full citizenship combined with their system of land ownership (*klaros*) was the prerequisite to Spartan military supremacy, whereas the number of the full citizens, the equals (*homoioi*), decreased rapidly. Furthermore, shortly after the end of the Peloponnesian War, rivalries within Sparta already prevented the steering of a clear course in political dealings with Athens. A few weeks after the surrender, a commission of 30 Athenians (*hoi triakonta*, 'The Thirty') was appointed by Lysander, to draw up a new constitution and to rule the polis until this task was accomplished (Xenophon *Hellenika* 2.3.11). A regime of terror resulted instead, under the leadership of Kritias (Plato's uncle, as it happens). The Thirty bestowed full citizenship on only 3,000 Athenians. The opponents of the 'Thirty' were rallied in Boiotia by Thrasyboulos. After an unsuccessful attempt to overthrow the regime, a small contingent of exiles managed to break through to Piraeus. There Kritias fell in battle. Now a new regime, that of 'The Ten' replaced the 'Thirty'. After the intervention of the Spartan king Pausanias democracy was restored (Dössel 2003: 89–146), although oligarchic supporters of the toppled regime established a separate state in Eleusis. The renewal of the Athenian democracy took place according to the principles of decision making which were developed in the fifth century. After the fall of the 'Four Hundred' in 411 a general revision of the 'ancestral' laws had been initiated, and this was completed in 399. Closely connected with this revision is the introduction of new procedures for the introduction of new legislation. It was now to be entrusted to a body of *nomothetai* (law-givers). With regard to the jurors in the *dikasteria* (law-courts) the drawing of names by lot was newly regulated in the course of further innovations. Continuing tension within the polis community caused by the regime of the 'Thirty' and the resulting anti-oligarchic propaganda still had an effect on the trial of Sokrates in 399. The swift yet brutal reunification with Eleusis cleared the path for internal consolidation. The serious problems of Spartan foreign policy in 401/400 were the prerequisites which made possible the new beginning of Athenian democracy. The political situation in the Mediterranean and the Aegean Sea had now changed.

## Sparta's conflict with Persia and the Korinthian War

By the end of the Peloponnesian War Lysander had established dekarchies (*dekarchiai*) in the former Athenian sphere of interest (Xenophon *Hellenika* 3.5.13; 6.3.8; Plutarch *Lysander* 13). These were commissions consisting of ten men who ruled as oligarchic regimes. They were not accepted by the citizens of their poleis and had to be propped up either by Spartan garrisons under a *harmostes* (commander) or by the Achaimenid prince Kyros the Younger, before his revolt against his brother Artaxerxes II and death. In Lysander's mind these oligarchies were to serve Sparta's interests as instruments of her *Machtpolitik*. They were closely attached to his adherents, but he could not establish a rule of his own outside of Sparta (Bommelaer 1981: 209–11). Although Lysander was defeated in Sparta's internal controversies over the Athenian reorganization after the Peloponnesian War, he could eventually influence the Spartan process of decision making considerably, when, around 400, Agesilaos II ascended to the throne (Xenophon *Hellenika* 3.3.1–4; Plutarch *Agesilaos* 3; Cartledge 1987: 99–115).

In influential Spartan circles it was already recognized government by dekarchies was not suited to win the trust of the polis communities. The dekarchies in Asia Minor were abolished (Xenophon *Hellenika* 3.4.2), even if after 402 Spartan garrisons, consisting chiefly of mercenaries and *neodamodeis* (emancipated helots), continued at places of strategic importance. After the defeat of Kyros at Kounaxa in 401 the victorious Artaxerxes ordered the satrap Tissaphernes to collect tribute from the Ionian poleis that had supported Kyros. These cities turned to Sparta as the 'protector of all Hellenes' (Xenophon *Hellenika* 3.1.3). Sparta reacted swiftly but, owing to her limited resources, she could not send more than 1,000 *neodamodeis* and 4,000 allied combatants under the command of the Spartiate Thibron to Asia Minor (Xenophon *Hellenika* 3.1.4–8). In 399/8 Derkylidas operated successfully in the Ionian regions, but he settled for an armistice on account of the Persian predominance. Consequently Artaxerxes did not waive his claim to dominion over the Greek poleis of Asia Minor (Xenophon *Hellenika* 3.2.12–20; Diodoros 14.39.5–6). In 396 the Spartan king Agesilaos II took over command in view of the Persian naval threat. As for the conflict with Persia he spread the slogan of a Panhellenic War, but in 394, before the sea battle of Knidos, he had to return home with most of his soldiers (Hamilton 1991: 71–103). Near Knidos the Persian fleet under the command of the former Athenian *strategos* Konon won a decisive victory over the Spartans (Xenophon *Hellenika* 4.3.11–12; Diodoros 14.83.5–7).

In mainland Greece, the so-called Korinthian War broke out in 395. It arose from a boundary dispute between the Phokians and the Opuntian Lokrians to the east of them (or the Ozolian Lokrians situated west of them). The Phokians were supported by Sparta; the Lokrians won assistance from Thebes and its Boiotian League. The Spartans suffered a serious defeat near Haliartos in Boiotia, when Lysander began the battle before the arrival of the reinforcements under the command of King Pausanias and fell fighting (Xenophon *Hellenika* 3.15. 17–25; Plutarch *Lysander* 22). Not only did the Spartan attack on Boiotia fail: Athens and the Boiotian League, which had formed an alliance even before the Spartan assault (Harding 14; R&O 6), concluded a *symmachia* also with Argos and Korinth. The offer of Persian subsidies was the predominant prerequisite to this coalition, which was joined by further *symmachoi* (Diodoros 14.82). The coalition's main target was Sparta and it aimed at removing the Spartan hegemony at all costs. For the Athenians, however, new perspectives opened up to show them a way out of political isolation. The possibility of again becoming a major naval power was within reach (Badian 1995: 82–4). The pre-war events draw attention to the on-going internal conflicts in Greece. While Agesilaos successfully waged war against Persia, new constellations of power emerged which posed a serious threat to Spartan supremacy. Before the Korinthian War the conspiracy of Kinadon, a *hypomeion* (Spartan without civic rights), highlighted the internal problems of Sparta (Xenophon *Hellenika* 3.3.4–11). Again after Lysander's death, the Spartans were perturbed by rumours of his alleged revolutionary designs (Diodoros 14.13.2–3; Plutarch *Lysander* 24–6; *Agesilaos* 20). After the Persian victory of Knidos, when Sparta was threatened on several fronts, large Persian naval contingents appeared in Greek territorial waters for the first time since the invasion of Xerxes. The Spartan victories at the Nemea River near Korinth (Xenophon *Hellenika* 4.2.18–23) and a few weeks later at Koroneia in Boiotia (Xenophon *Hellenika* 4.3.15–20; Diodoros 14.84.1–2; Plutarch *Agesilaos* 18–19) did not compensate for the disaster of Knidos. Konon and the satrap Pharnabazos were clever enough to know how to exploit the Spartan difficulties by referring to the autonomy of the Greek cities in Ionia (Xenophon *Hellenika* 4.8.1). They forced most of the Spartan garrisons out of Asia Minor and the Aegean islands. In the end the Spartans were able to maintain their sphere of influence merely in the Hellespont.

Sparta was ready to acknowledge the Persian dominion over the Greeks of Asia Minor. She expected, however, that Persia would respect the autonomy of the poleis in the Aegean Sea and 'elsewhere', i.e., in mainland Greece (Xenophon *Hellenika* 4.8.14). A settlement with Persia would have prevented a further strengthening of Sparta's foes in Greece. During autumn and winter of 392/1 Sparta granted far-reaching concessions to Athens in order to break up the enemy coalition, but negotiations failed (Philochoros *FGrHist* 328 F 149; Urban 1991: 70–8). The situation in Korinth aggravated the Spartan problems: anti-Spartan groups strove for a union between Korinth and Argos. They reached their aim presumably only when a Spartan *mora* (battalion of hoplites) was annihilated by a troop of soldiers consisting primarily of peltasts (lightly armed mercenaries) under the command of the Athenian Iphikrates in 390 (Whitby 1984: 306–8). All over Greece the defeat of a Spartan *mora* in open battle was sensational news. As the theatre of war shifted to the eastern Aegean regions, however, the defining factor was that Athens had become Sparta's main enemy. The Spartan leadership realized that a war on several fronts would stretch their scarce resources. In the winter of 388/7 the *nauarchos* Antalkidas, who had already submitted proposals for peace to the Persian Court in 392, forced the issue in Sardis and Susa. The result of his efforts was the so-called Peace of

Antalkidas or King's Peace, which was confirmed by an oath taken by the Greeks in Sparta in 386 (Xenophon *Hellenika* 5.1.35–6; Diodoros 14.110.3; Plutarch *Agesilaos* 23; *Staatsverträge* 242): it was considered, however, a *prostagma* (diktat) of the Great King (Isokrates 4.175). All Greek poleis in Asia Minor as well as Klazomenai and Cyprus were to be 'owned' by the Great King. All other poleis were to be autonomous, with the exception of Lemnos, Imbros, and Skyros, which remained under Athenian control (Xenophon *Hellenika* 5.1.31). Moreover the Great King threatened to wage war against any Hellenes who were not willing to comply with these terms. In respect of mainland Greece Sparta was the true winner of the agreement, even if she was not acknowledged as the *prostates* (protector) of the peace by the Great King (Seager 1994: 118; Buckler 2003: 177). The Argives had to withdraw their troops from Korinth. The 'experiment' of the union between Argos and Korinth had failed. The Korinthians again became Spartan *symmachoi*. In Boiotia the supremacy of Thebes appeared to be broken as a result of the dissolution of the Boiotian League. By this time the Athenians owned a larger fleet and were able to set their sight beyond the limits set by Spartan hegemony. There was not a chance, however, of restoring their former empire.

Sparta on the other hand lost her strategic positions in Asia Minor and the Aegean regions. The Spartans faced the problem of defending their hegemony on the Greek mainland with severely limited resources. These strains intensified owing to political mistakes concerning the treatment of their allies. The Spartans were intent on making an example of those who had proved themselves to be unreliable allies during the Korinthian War. After the Spartans had forced the Mantineians to give up their city and to return to their old settlements in 385 (Xenophon *Hellenika* 5.2.1–7; 6.4.18; Diodoros 15.5; 15.12; Nielsen 2002: 390–1) they intervened in Olynthos in 382, which had gained power as the centre of a *koinon*. The course taken to eliminate the growing threat to her supremacy elucidates Sparta's military problems once again. Sparta left it to the discretion of her *symmachoi* either to provide soldiers or to make payments (Xenophon *Hellenika* 5.2.20–2). This was an important innovation within the Peloponnesian League, which was re-arranged to form ten districts. Even before war over Olynthos got under way, Spartan transgressions provoked general indignation. Marching to the Chalkidike, a force under the command of Phoibidas seized the Theban Kadmeia, aided by Theban traitors (Xenophon *Hellenika* 5.2.25–6; Diodoros 15.20.1–2; Plutarch *Pelopidas* 5; *Agesilaos* 23–4; Harding 32).

Olynthos surrendered in 379. The Spartans dissolved the Chalkidian League but in December of 379 they suffered a defeat which marked a turning-point. Theban exiles succeeded in overpowering their foes in Thebes and forced the Spartan garrison on the Kadmeia to withdraw (Xenophon *Hellenika* 5.4.1–12; Diodoros 15.25; Plutarch *Pelopidas* 6–13; Buck 1994: 72–8). Spartan countermeasures were confined to a small advance into Boiotia by King Kleombrotos in 378 and to the establishment of a garrison at Thespiai. From there the *harmostes* Sphodrias undertook an unsuccessful raid on Piraeus by his own decision and provoked further tensions (Xenophon *Hellenika* 5.4.20–3). The advances into Boiotia in the years 378 and 377, undertaken by King Agesilaos, failed as well. All things considered, the action of Sphodrias had succeeded in only one respect: the re-establishment of the Boiotian League.

It was during these years that Athens' determined policy of forming alliances wherever possible began paying dividends. After concluding several bilateral treaties the Athenians issued a general appeal to join the newly founded *symmachia*, the Second Athenian Naval League. They promised all members freedom to choose their constitutions at their own discretion and not to suffer the presence of Athenian garrisons and *archontes* (supervising magistrates). According to the terms of the King's Peace, the poleis situated in the Persian sphere of interest were excluded (Harding 34; R&O 22; Cargill 1981: 14–47). The purpose of the new *symmachia* was – last but not least – also to keep Spartan power at bay (Dreher 1995: 276).

In 376/5 the Athenians strengthened their position considerably on account of their victories over Spartan fleets off Naxos and Alyzeia (Xenophon *Hellenika* 5.4.60–1, 62–6). They nevertheless longed for peace as much as the Spartans because of the high financial burden imposed on them. At the conference in Sparta Athens obtained full recognition of the Second Athenian Naval League in 375 (Diodoros 15.38). The treaty was a *koine eirene* (common peace) (Jehne 1994: 57–64). Peace, however, did not last long: Sparta and Athens were drawn into *stasis* on Kerkyra. The conflict escalated because of the expansionist designs of the Boiotian League, which in turn provoked powerful Spartan intervention in Phokis (Xenophon *Hellenika* 6.1.1). In July 371 a conference in Sparta, which took place at the initiative of Athens, ended in failure. The Thebans, members of the Second Athenian Naval League, demanded recognition of their hegemonic position in Boiotia, but they found themselves excluded from the new Common Peace because of Agesilaos' opposition. A few weeks later the Spartan campaign, which was intended to force the Thebans to accept the terms of the Common Peace, ended in disaster. On the battle-field of Leuktra the right wing of the Spartan phalanx, about twelve men deep, was crushed by the Thebans' left wing, which had 50 rows of hoplites, a new and unexpected tactical move thought up by Epameinondas (Xenophon *Hellenika* 6.4.12–15; Diodoros 15.50–5; Plutarch *Pelopidas* 23). About 400 of the 700 Spartiates died, among them King Kleombrotos (Buckler 2003: 278–95). It was not only the superior tactics of Epameinondas, however, which proved fateful for Sparta. Ever since 404 the Spartans had overextended themselves. They had to assume the historical task of protecting the Greeks of Asia Minor, as well as the role of Greece's sole hegemonic power. These were challenges which could no longer be met by what had proved successful during the Peloponnesian War. Sparta moreover lacked sensitivity in dealing with her allies. Agesilaos' stubborn claim to hegemonic power provoked the final and fateful confrontation with Thebes. There were other options available, and even on the eve of the battle of Leuktra the Spartiate Prothoos advised avoiding the conflict with Thebes by respecting the principle of autonomy (Xenophon *Hellenika* 6.4.2–3). General outrage at Thebes, however, precluded a rational examination of his proposal. In the final analysis the Spartans paid the price for their almost hysterical reaction to the crisis by losing their hegemony. Agesilaos, who largely determined Spartan foreign policy, embodied the fatal continuity of Spartan *Machtpolitik* in the face of inadequate means. Even before the battle of Leuktra Sparta could not prevent the Boiotian League from gaining strength. Moreover they had to reckon with a new power in Thessaly. Iason (Jason) of Pherai, elected *tagos* (duke) by the Thessalians, pursued his own ambitious plans (Xenophon *Hellenika* 6.1.12; Tuplin 1993: 121). Considering the demographic development in Sparta, the policy of confrontation was totally irresponsible in 371. Ever since 480/79 the number of Spartiates had been on the decline, ultimately decreasing to about 10 per cent of the earlier numbers: after the battle of Leuktra only about 800 full citizens remained to perform civic duties and bear arms (Lévy 2003: 269).

   Leuktra proved one of the great turning-points in Greek history. Leading Athenians realized this at once and invited all parties to a peace conference in Athens in 371. The Thebans, however, declined to attend and Athens failed in preventing Thebes' and the Boiotian League's expansionist policies. The internecine conflicts amongst the Greeks continued until Macedonia rose to being the dominant power in Greece.

## Further reading

Extensive treatment of this period: *CAH*² 5 and *CAH*² 6. A recent general account of the Peloponnesian War: Kagan (2003) (rounding out his five-volume treatment, 1969–87). De Ste. Croix (1972) deals with pre-war events in a somewhat idiosyncratic way, blaming the Spartans for the outbreak of the war and ascribing little importance to the 'Megarian Decree'. Lazenby (2004) attributes the Spartans' victory to their capability of manning their fleet. Bleckmann (1998) discusses the final period of the war. On the political developments in Athens, Connor (1971) and Davies (1993) are still essential. A very useful study of the regime of the 'Thirty': Krentz (1982). On individual politicians, Will (2003) (Perikles) and Gribble (1999) (Alkibiades). A comparative study of Athens and Sparta: Schulz (2003); cf. also Dreher (2001) and Schubert (2003). Hodkinson (1993) deals in a concise study with the consequences of the Peloponnesian War on Sparta. Strauss (1987) discusses Athenian policy after 404. On small and medium-sized poleis, e.g., Tomlinson (1972), Legon (1981), Salmon (1984), and especially Gehrke (1986). Buckler (2003) examines for the first time the history of the Aegean region in the fourth century up to 336.

## Bibliography

Andrewes, A. (1992) 'The Spartan resurgence' in: *CAH*² 5 464–98

Badian, E. (1995) 'The ghost of empire: reflections on Athenian foreign policy in the fourth century BC' in: Eder, W. (ed.) *Die athenische Demokratie im 4. Jahrhundert v. Chr.: Vollendung oder Verfall einer Verfassungsform? Akten eines Symposiums, 3.–7. August 1992, Bellagio* (Stuttgart: Steiner 1995) 79–106

Beck, H. (1997) *Polis und Koinon: Untersuchungen zur Geschichte und Struktur der griechischen Bundesstaaten im 4. Jahrhundert v.Chr.* (Stuttgart: Steiner) (*Historia* Einzelschriften 114)

Berger, S. (1992) *Revolution and society in Greek Sicily and southern Italy* (Stuttgart: Steiner) (*Historia* Einzelschriften 71)

Bleckmann, B. (1998) *Athens Weg in die Niederlage: Die letzten Jahre des Peloponnesischen Kriegs* (Stuttgart: Teubner 1998) (Beiträge zur Altertumskunde 99)

Bommelaer, J.-F. (1981) *Lysandre de Sparte: histoire et traditions* (Paris: de Boccard) (Bibliothèque des Écoles françaises d'Athènes et de Rome 240)

Buck, R. J. (1994) *Boiotia and the Boiotian league, 423–371 B.C.* (Edmonton: University of Alberta Press)

Buckler, J. (2003) *Aegean Greece in the fourth century BC* (Leiden: Brill)

Cargill, J. (1981) *The second Athenian league: empire or free alliance?* (Berkeley: University of California Press)

Cartledge, P. (1987) *Agesilaos and the crisis of Sparta* (London: Duckworth)

Cartledge, P. (2002) *Sparta and Lakonia: a regional history 1300–362 B.C.* (London: Routledge ²2002)

Caven, B. (1990) *Dionysius I: war-lord of Sicily* (New Haven: Yale University Press)

Connor, W. R. (1971) *The new politicians of fifth-century Athens* (Princeton: Princeton University Press)

Davies, J. K. (1993) *Democracy and classical Greece* (London: Fontana ²1993) (Fontana History of the Ancient World)

De Ste. Croix, G. E. M. (1972) *The origins of the Peloponnesian War* (London: Duckworth)

Dössel, A. (2003) *Die Beilegung innerstaatlicher Konflikte in den griechischen Poleis vom 5.–3. Jahrhundert v. Chr.* (Frankfurt: Lang) (Europäische Hochschulschriften, Reihe 3, 954)

Dreher, M. (1995) *Hegemon und Symmachoi: Untersuchungen zum Zweiten Attischen Seebund* (Berlin: de Gruyter) (Untersuchungen zur antiken Literatur und Geschichte 46)

Dreher, M. (2001) *Athen und Sparta* (Munich: Beck) (C. H. Beck Studium)

Ellis, W. M. (1989) *Alcibiades* (London: Routledge) (Classical lives)

Gehrke, H.-J. (1986) *Jenseits von Athen und Sparta: Das Dritte Griechenland und seine Staatenwelt* (Munich Beck)

Gribble, D. W. (1999) *Alcibiades and Athens: a study in literary presentation* (Oxford: Clarendon) (Oxford Classical Monographs)

Hamilton, C. D. (1991) *Agesilaus and the failure of Spartan hegemony* (Ithaca NY: Cornell University Press)

Heftner, M. (2001) *Der oligarchische Umsturz des Jahres 411 v. Chr. und die Herrschaft der Vierhundert in Athen: Quellenkritische and historische Untersuchungen* (Frankfurt: Lang)

Hodkinson, S. (1993) 'Warfare, wealth, and the crisis of Spartiate society' in: Rich, J., & G. Shipley (eds) *War and society in the Greek world* (London: Routledge 1993) 146–76

Jehne, M. (1994) *Koine Eirene: Untersuchungen zu den Befriedungs-und Stabilisierungsbemühungen in der griechischen Poliswelt des 4. Jahrhunderts v. Chr.* (Stuttgart: Steiner) (*Hermes* Einzelschriften 63)

Kagan, D. (1969) *The outbreak of the Peloponnesian war* (Ithaca NY: Cornell University Press)

Kagan, D. (1974) *The Archidamian war* (Ithaca NY: Cornell University Press)

Kagan, D. (1981) *The peace of Nicias and the Sicilian expedition* (Ithaca NY: Cornell University Press)

Kagan, D. (1987) *The fall of the Athenian empire* (Ithaca NY: Cornell University Press)

Kagan, D. (1991) *Pericles of Athens and the birth of democracy* (New York: Free Press)

Kagan, D. (2003) *The Peloponnesian war: Athens and Sparta in savage conflict, 431–404 BC* (New York: Viking)

Krentz, P. M. (1982) *The thirty of Athens* (Ithaca NY: Cornell University Press)

Lazenby, J. F. (2004) *The Peloponnesian War: a military study* (London: Routledge) (Warfare and History)

Legon, R. P. (1981) *Megara: the political history of a Greek city-state to 336 B.C.* (Ithaca NY: Cornell University Press)

Lévy, E. (2003) *Sparte: histoire politique et sociale jusqu'à la conquête romaine* (Paris: Éditions du Seuil)

Lewis, D. M. (1977) *Sparta and Persia* (Leiden: Brill) (Cincinnati Classical Studies 2, 1)

Lewis, D. M. (1992) 'The Archidamian war' in: *CAH²* 5 370–432

Lewis, D. M. (1994) 'Sicily, 413–368 B.C.' in: *CAH²* 6 120–55

Lotze, D. (1964) *Lysander und der Peloponnesische Krieg* (Berlin: Akademie-Verlag) (Abhandlungen der Sächsischen Akademie der Wissenschaften zu Leipzig, Philologisch-historische Klasse 57, 1)

Meyer, E. A. (1997) 'The outbreak of the Peloponnesian War after twenty-five years' in: Hamilton, C. D., & P. M. Krentz (eds) *Polis and polemos: essays on politics, war, and history in Ancient Greece, in honor of Donald Kagan* (Claremont CA: Regina 1997) 23–54

Nielsen, T. H. (2002) *Arkadia and its poleis in the archaic and classical periods* (Göttingen: Vandenhoeck & Ruprecht) (Hypomnemata 140)

Powell, A. (2001) *Athens and Sparta: constructing Greek political and social history from 478 B.C.* (London: Routledge ²2001)

Roisman, J. (1993) *The general Demosthenes and his use of military surprise* (Stuttgart: Steiner) (*Historia* Einzelschriften 78)

Rubel, A. (2000) *Stadt in Angst: Religion und Politik in Athen während des Peloponnesischen Krieges* (Darmstadt: Wissenschaftliche Buchgesellschaft) (Edition Universität)

Salmon, J. B. (1984) *Wealthy Corinth: a history of the city to 338 BC* (Oxford: Clarendon)

Schubert, C. (2003) *Athen und Sparta in klassischer Zeit: Ein Studienbuch* (Stuttgart: Metzler)

Schulz, R. (2003) *Athen und Sparta* (Darmstadt: Wissenschaftliche Buchgesellschaft) (Geschichte kompakt, Antike)

Seager, R. (1994) 'The Corinthian war' in: *CAH²* 6 97–119

Strauss, B. S. (1987) *Athens after the Peloponnesian war: class, faction, and policy, 403–386* (London: Croom Helm)

Tomlinson, R. A. (1972) *Argos and the Argolid from the end of the Bronze Age to the Roman Occupation* (London: Routledge & Kegan Paul) (States and Cities of Ancient Greece)

Tuplin, C. (1993) *The failings of empire: a reading of Xenophon* Hellenica 2.3.11–7.5.27 (Stuttgart: Steiner) (*Historia* Einzelschriften 76)

Urban, R. (1991) *Der Königsfrieden von 387/86 v. Chr: Vorgeschichte, Zustandekommen, Ergebnis und politische Umsetzung* (Stuttgart: Steiner) (*Historia* Einzelschriften 68)

Whitby, M. (1984) 'The union of Corinth and Argos: a reconsideration' in: *Historia* 33: 295–308

Will, W. (2003) *Thukydides und Perikles: Der Historiker und sein Held* (Bonn: Habelt) (Antiquitas, Reihe 1, Abhandlungen zur alten Geschichte 51)

CHAPTER TWENTY-SIX

# The Greek World, 371–336

## *Bruce LaForse*

## 1   Introduction

The decisive Theban defeat of Sparta at Leuktra in 371 shocked the Greek world. It upset the balance of power, such as it was, and shook almost to the breaking point nearly every existing alliance. Sparta would never again regain her former prominence; Athens pulled back from Thebes and aligned with her old enemy Sparta; Thebes suddenly found herself on a seemingly unobstructed path to dominance not merely of Boiotia but of the Peloponnese and even northern Greece. Yet less than a decade later, after the battle of Mantineia in 362, in the words of the contemporary historian Xenophon, "there was even more confusion and disorder in Greece . . . than before" (*Hellenika* 7.5.27). Within three years the balance of power would shift north with the phenomenal rise of Macedonia under Philip II.

Beginning with the Peloponnesian War the Greek states embarked on a series of lengthy and debilitating internecine wars. These wars were often funded and eventually even refereed by the Persian Great King. The Athenian navy had effectively shut out Persia from Greek affairs since the mid fifth century. But after the Athenian disaster at Syracuse the Great King again began to play an increasingly important role in the Greek world. Persian coffers financed Lysander's victory over Athens in 404 and with the King's Peace of 387/6 the Great King became the official arbiter of Greek political affairs. Yet after wrecking Athens' imperial might the Spartans themselves were unable to wield power for much more than a generation, despite Persian backing, when they faced a resurgent Athens at the head of a new sea league and a new Theban-led democratic Boiotian Confederacy, the brainchild of the brilliant Epameinondas. Throughout the period the quest for hegemony caused alliances to shift with breath-taking rapidity; this year's friend frequently was next year's enemy.

Paradoxically, and perhaps understandably, this same period of Greek disunity saw a widespread popularity of panhellenic rhetoric; the theme permeates the works of contemporary writers such as Xenophon and Isokrates. Panhellenism urged Greeks to set aside their competition for hegemony and instead work together against Persia. This had deep emotional appeal for fourth-century Greeks on two levels. First, it drew directly on the Greek successes against Xerxes of the previous century, victories which ushered in the era of Greek self-rule and imperialism. This spoke to the humiliation many Greeks must have felt at the increasingly central role Persia played in Greek affairs. Second, and more importantly, it also addressed mounting Greek frustration at individual cities' inability to relinquish hegemonic dreams for the sake of greater Greek unity or even simply for peace. In fact no major Greek state ever voluntarily gave up its pursuit of hegemony, nor were there serious factions within individual cities which advocated a panhellenist foreign policy. Strong though its appeal may have been on an emotional level, panhellenism rarely had any lasting impact on a practical level. The speeches of Isokrates, for example, which call for a panhellenic expedition against Persia are for the most part thinly disguised propaganda for an alliance dominated by one state or another, usually his native Athens.

By the middle 350s, in the wake of the battle of Mantineia and the Social War, it seemed evident that no Greek state was powerful enough to win a military hegemony. Both Isokrates 8 (*On the Peace*) and Xenophon (*De Vectigalibus*) wrote treatises urging the Athenians to abandon their efforts to regain their former imperial greatness via military means. Instead both writers exhorted the Athenians to gain prestige by winning commercial prominence and by striving to defend the independence of all Greek cities. Athens, of course, continued to pursue an aggressive if not imperialist policy in the northern Aegean. This brought her into conflict with the rising power of Philip II of Macedon. The famous orator and statesman Demosthenes championed anti-Macedonian sentiment in Athens and urged the Athenians to act aggressively to protect their interests in the north, especially the vital grain route to the Black Sea. His rhetoric drew on panhellenic sentiment, but with Philip replacing the Great King as the barbarian threat to Greek freedom. Indeed, Demosthenes hoped Persia would play a key role in the struggle on the Greek side (Diodoros 9.71).

## 2 Thebes

The relatively small group of men who were responsible for the rise of Thebes, led by the anti-Spartan conspirators of 379, remained dominant after the battle of Leuktra (Buckler 1980: 34–45, 130–8). Of these men Pelopidas and Epameinondas were the most important. Both were of aristocratic families and superb soldiers; but where Pelopidas was wealthy, outgoing, and a family man, Epameinondas was poor, an austere student of Pythagoreanism, unmarried, and devoted to intellectual pursuit (Diodoros 15.39.2; 16.2.3). Both men were innovative military thinkers; Pelopidas was the first to deploy the elite Sacred Band as a tactical unit, instead of scattering its members in the regular hoplite ranks. Epameinondas made novel use of the already traditionally deeper than usual Theban line by placing the Thebans on the left at Leuktra to face the elite of the Spartan line. Perhaps more significantly he recognized that the key to destroying Sparta's power was not simply to defeat her army but to damage Sparta's infrastructure so badly that the system would collapse. This he achieved with his unprecedented invasions of Lakonia. These mark him as the true guiding hand of Theban preeminence.

Yet Epameinondas does not seem to have had the usual imperial ambitions for Thebes. While it was a top priority to secure Boiotia from foreign invasion, most notably Spartan, Epameinondas did not institute any of the practices typical of an imperial hegemon. There were no taxes or tribute collected, no oaths demanded, nor did he dictate an ally's form of government. Epameinondas refrained from executing Greek captives or selling them into slavery, an exceedingly rare example of practical policy motivated by panhellenic spirit (Diodoros 15.57.1; Xenophon *Hellenika* 7.1.42; Pausanias 9.15.3). His moderate political stance may have stemmed in part from his personal asceticism. A number of anecdotes survive illustrating his Pythagorean self-restraint. He shunned wealth so much that he supposedly owned only one cloak and had to stay inside, naked, when it was being cleaned; he ate frugally; he treated women as equals; he was incorruptible by money, power, or sex (Ailianos *Varia Historia* 5.5; Plutarch *Moralia* 192d–4c). In fact, unlike the case for most other great figures of ancient Greece, no parallel historical tradition survives that is hostile to Epameinondas. The worst unfriendly writers such as the Athenians Xenophon and Isokrates can do is simply omit most of Epameinondas' accomplishments from their works altogether (Diodoros 15.88; Buckler 1980: 263–77 on sources for Theban hegemony).

Not all Thebans shared Epameinondas' highly unusual benevolence toward fellow Greeks. While he was away with the short-lived Boiotian fleet in 364 the Thebans destroyed Orchomenos, their long-time nemesis in Boiotia (Diodoros 15.79.3–6). In establishing their control over the Boiotian Confederacy the Thebans had also dealt harshly with rivals such as Plataiai and Thespiai (Diodoros 15.46.6). Yet the Theban decision not to construct a political apparatus, like Sparta's Peloponnesian League or the Second Athenian Sea League, meant they lacked a crucial means for effective control of their allies. There was nothing like the Second Athenian League's *synhedrion* or council of allies, for example, through which Thebes' allies could voice their opinions or, more importantly, settle internal disputes. That the lack of such a mechanism was a serious drawback became increasingly apparent as various Peloponnesian cities, newly released from Spartan control, leapt to settle old scores or to expand at the expense of their neighbors. Elis and Arkadia, for example, quarreled over possession of Triphylia, a dispute that would eventually split Thebes' allies and lead to war (Buckler 2003: 299; 1980: 73–4, 220–7; Cartledge 1987: 310–11).

With the various Peloponnesian states suddenly enjoying much more control over their own destinies a more active and ambitious Theban presence might have maintained at least a semblance of the stability Sparta had imposed on the Peloponnese. But with the Thebans content to let the Peloponnesian cities to a large degree pursue their own courses there was more infighting and competition for prominence than ever. Some cities, such as Korinth, stayed loyal to Sparta. The Mantineians, whom Sparta had dispersed into villages in 385, refounded their city with stout walls and, along with the Tegeans, led a democratic movement to form an Arkadian League (Xenophon *Hellenika* 6.5.3–6). Sparta's traditional Peloponnesian foe Argos supported the Arkadians as did Elis, which hoped to get back territories the Spartans had seized from it about 30 years earlier, most notably the above-mentioned Triphylia (Xenophon *Hellenika* 6.5.23). When King Agesilaos of Sparta mobilized to invade Arkadia, the Arkadians asked Athens for help but the Athenians stayed neutral. The

Arkadians then turned to Thebes. Although it was late in the year (probably 370), the Thebans agreed to help. A promise of ten talents from Elis to help finance the expedition was an added inducement (Xenophon *Hellenika* 6.5.19–20).

Epameinondas set out with about 7,000 Boiotian hoplites and perhaps another 10,000 troops from Euboia, Phokis, Lokris, and Akarnania. The troops already in Arkadia probably numbered about 20,000, giving Epameinondas a total of about 40,000 hoplites, with perhaps another 30,000 light-armed and auxiliary forces (Xenophon *Hellenika* 6.5.23; Plutarch *Agesilaos* 31; Diodoros 15.62; Hanson 1999: 79–82). In the meantime, Agesilaos had already ravaged portions of Arkadia (the Arkadians stayed within their walls awaiting the arrival of the Thebans) and returned to Lakonia, thinking it too late in the year for further campaigning (Xenophon *Hellenika* 6.5.21).

Epameinondas split his huge force and approached Lakonia from four directions. As expected, large numbers of Lakonian helots and periokoi joined the invaders. For the first time in 600 years Lakonia felt the fire and sword of an invader. Famed for disdaining defensive walls, the Spartans spread their thin manpower to defend key positions in the city (Plutarch *Agesilaos* 31.1–3). The flooded Eurotas river also helped protect the city itself; the rest of Lakonia, however, was thoroughly ravaged and looted. The physical damage inflicted in Lakonia, though extensive, was not permanent, nor was it as serious as the lasting blow to Spartan prestige and pride (Xenophon *Hellenika* 6.5.27–32; Diodoros 15.65.5; Buckler 1980: 75–82).

Epameinondas' next step did cause lasting damage, however. Although much of his original force had probably been content to loot Lakonia and return home, Epameinondas led his Boiotians and remaining allies into Messenia and founded near Mt. Ithome a new capital city of Messene. He invited all former Messenians, their descendents, and anyone else interested to join the new community (Diodoros 15.66; Pausanias 4.22.3). He stayed for several months, long enough for walls to be built and the city to be secure from Spartan counter-attack, before leading his army back to Thebes (Plutarch *Agesilaos* 32.8, *Pelopidas* 24.1; Ailianos *Varia Historia* 13.42; Buckler 1980: 86–90).

The expedition had been enormously successful: an Arkadian League, democratic and friendly to Thebes, was securely in place as an obstacle to Sparta's north; the loss of Messenia, which had for centuries supported materially the Spartan ruling class, crippled Sparta while at the same time the new Messenian state served as a hostile barrier to the west. Yet when he got back to Thebes, Epameinondas found himself on trial, charged with retaining his command illegally after his term as boiotarch had expired while he was still in the field. He was also criticized for not burning the city of Sparta. He responded that he would gladly suffer execution so long as the Thebans would inscribe in public an epitaph which noted how he had forced the Thebans to defeat the Spartans at Leuktra, freeing both Thebes and much of Greece, and that he had refounded Messene as a check on Sparta. The charges were dropped without a vote being taken (Nepos *Epaminondas* 8.3–5).

Over the next few years Epameinondas led several subsequent invasions of the Peloponnese with much less dramatic results. Although the Arkadian League would split and the Thebans eventually found themselves fighting former allies, the overall effect of Epameinondas' policy of weakening Sparta was lasting. In 368 the Arkadians founded a new community based in the new walled city of Megalopolis to serve as the political headquarters of the League (Diodoros 15.72.4). The Thebans sent a force to protect the city as it was being built. Within a few years of Leuktra Sparta thus found herself surrounded by a ring of fortified cities: Messene, Megalopolis, and Mantineia. Though the Thebans did not seize direct political control of the Peloponnese, and despite the occasional unruliness of their allies there, Boiotia would never again be vulnerable to an invasion by Sparta.

# 3   Athens

The Theban victory at Leuktra shocked and greatly distressed the Athenians. The Thebans had played a prominent role in the early days of the Athenian Sea League but as their power increased the Athenians had grown chary of their one-time partner against Spartan oppression (Harding 33; Diodoros 15.28). Theban behavior in more recent years – such as the razing of Plataiai in 373 – had sharpened Athenian wariness though the two cities remained allies (Diodoros 15.46.4–6; Xenophon *Hellenika* 6.3.1; Isokrates 4). At a peace conference at Sparta immediately before Leuktra Epameinondas had provoked Spartan ire by refusing to sign the treaty on behalf merely of the Thebans instead of the Boiotians. The Athenians had no doubt looked forward to what they expected would be a thorough – and satisfying – thrashing of the Thebans by the Spartans at Leuktra. The Thebans, on the other hand, do not seem to have developed a reciprocal mistrust. They had contemplated sending their wives and children to Athens for safety at the start of the Leuktra campaign (Diodoros 15.52.1). Immediately after the battle they sent a garlanded herald to Athens with news of their victory and an invitation to join them in taking vengeance on the Spartans. The Athenians gave no answer to the herald and even refused to grant him the customary hospitality (Xenophon *Hellenika* 6.4.19–20).

Thebes, not Sparta, now became the Athenians' main worry. In the wake of Leuktra they convened a peace conference at Athens that reaffirmed once again the terms of the King's Peace. The Thebans were not included; indeed, the treaty added a provision that required all signatories to come to the defense of one another, an Athenian attempt to involve all states in the maintenance of the Peace against continued Theban expansion (Xenophon *Hellenika* 6.5.1–2). Nonetheless in 370 the Euboian cities and Akarnania left the League and joined the Theban side (Xenophon *Hellenika* 6.5.23). In 369, the year after Epameinondas had detached Messenia from Sparta and in the face of his second invasion of the Peloponnese, the Athenians allied themselves with Sparta (Xenophon *Hellenika* 6.5.33–49; 7.1–14).

Sparta had implemented her hegemony through the King's Peace (387/6) which granted her, as enforcer of the Peace, Persian political and financial backing. In return Sparta recognized Persian claims to the Greek cities of Asia Minor. Subsequently, Athens forced Sparta to share the enforcer's role by the success of her Second Sea League and by her smashing victory over the Spartan fleet in 375 at Naxos (Xenophon *Hellenika* 5.4.61; Diodoros 15.34.3). In 367, having hobbled Sparta and won over a number of Athenian allies, Thebes stood ready to make her own case to the Great King to be anointed protector (prostates) of his Peace. When it became known that Sparta had sent an embassy to the King at Susa seeking aid, the other Greek states followed suit. The Theban envoy, Pelopidas, enjoyed several advantages in the negotiations. Most obvious of these was that Thebes had convincingly demonstrated her military superiority. But alone among the ambassadors from leading Greek states Pelopidas could boast of Thebes' long history of friendship with Persia, dating back to the active assistance she had given Xerxes in 480/79. This is a striking and perhaps unique instance of a Greek publicly renouncing panhellenic ideals. Pelopidas persuaded the King to back Thebes as the enforcer of a new King's Peace that would recognize an independent Messenia and call for the Athenians to beach their fleet (Xenophon *Hellenika* 7.1.33–40; Diodoros 15.76.3). The Peace was not an immediate success among the Greeks – both Athens and Sparta rejected it – but winning the King's recognition was significant for Thebes (Diodoros 15.76.3; Buckler 2003: 327–32; Stylianou 1998: 485–9). Not long afterwards most of Sparta's remaining allies in the Peloponnese made peace with Thebes. In addition the Great King agreed to build a fleet for Thebes (Diodoros 15.79.1; 16.40.1; Buckler 1980: 169–75). The Theban ships would both counterbalance Athenian power and deter the King's often-restive satraps along the Aegean coast.

The focus of Athenian interest post-Leuktra was in the Aegean. A primary goal was to regain Amphipolis, which in 367 made an alliance with the Chalkidian League, a recent defection from the Athenian League (Cargill 1981: 168). Another goal was to prevent Theban expansion beyond Thessaly and Macedonia. While Sparta clearly was the Thebans' main concern they did not entirely ignore other areas in the mainland. They had been active in the north, chiefly under Pelopidas, though he was killed in battle in 364 (Diodoros 15.80.1–6). They had intervened in Thessalian affairs, eventually isolating Alexandros the tyrant of Pherai, and taken a hand in the dynastic struggle in Macedon, stymieing Athenian ambitions in the area (Diodoros 15.67.3–4; Plutarch *Pelopidas* 26). For their part, the Athenians backed contenders for the thrones of the Macedonian and assorted Thracian kingdoms, assisted satraps rebelling against the Persian King, and kept a fleet operating in the region to insure the safe passage of grain ships between the Black Sea and Athens. The results of this activity were generally favorable. Timotheos wrested Samos from Persian control in 365 (Diodoros 15.9; Isokrates 15.111). He also won over Pydna, Methone, Poteidaia, and Torone (Demosthenes 4.4; Isokrates 15.113; Diodoros 15.81.6). A grateful satrap ceded Sestos, a key city in the Chersonese, in return for Athenian assistance against the Persian King (Isokrates 15.112). But in 364 Athenian interests suffered a setback when Epameinondas launched the fleet Persia had built for Thebes. There was no battle, but the presence of a rival naval power dealt a blow to Athenian prestige and encouraged a series of defections from the Athenian League, including Byzantion, Chios, and Rhodes (the last two probably rejoined the League soon afterwards, however).

The Athenian about-face after Leuktra called into question the anti-Spartan purpose of their League. Modern opinion is divided as to how closely the Athenians adhered to the founding principles of the League. After 371 there were few, if any, new members added. Instead, the Athenians made bilateral treaties with new allies. They did establish garrisons and settle Athenian citizens in various allied towns and territories, for example, Samos and Sestos, though perhaps not in any League member (Cargill 1981: 146–60; Harding 69; R&O 52). They also collected funds from allies, calling the exactions (if so they were) "contributions" (*syntaxeis*) instead of "tribute" (*phoros*), the old fifth-century imperial term. Again, it is not clear if these were mandatory for League members. In any case, enforced exactions and settlements on bilateral allies probably did little to inspire the confidence of the League members in Athenian intentions overall.

In 357 the Athenian commander Chares intervened in a Thracian dynastic dispute and won over the Chersonese for the Athenians (Demosthenes 23.173; Harding 64; R&O 47). The Euboian cities also returned to the League (Diodoros 16.7.2; Harding 65, 66; R&O 48, 69). But in the same year Rhodes, Chios, and other League members joined Byzantion in an open revolt against the Athenians, initiating what modern historians call the Social War (from the Latin term for allies, *socii*). The satrap of Karia, Maussolos, supported them with a fleet and installed garrisons on Rhodes and Chios. The rebels plundered Imbros and Lemnos and besieged Samos. Chares sailed to Samos but was defeated by the rebels early in 356. A reinforced fleet again was defeated off Embata in the territory of Erythrai (Diodoros 16.7.3–4). Short of funds, Chares entered the service of the rebellious satrap Artabazos and inflicted a major defeat on forces loyal to Persia. In response the Persian King complained to the Athenians; there was a report as well that the King was readying a fleet of 300 ships to assist the enemies of Athens. As a result the Athenians made peace with their rebellious allies in 355 (Diodoros 16.22). The causes of the Social War are unclear. Demosthenes says that Maussolos was the prime mover (Demosthenes 15.3). It may not have been difficult for the ambitious satrap to exploit League members' discontent with the Athenians' aggressive actions in the Chersonese and on Samos. Athenian commanders such as Chares, whose efforts to raise money amounted to little more than outright plundering, also damaged Athens' reputation (Sealey 1993: 106–8; Cartledge 1987: 311; Cargill 1981: 161–88). Philip II would soon follow in Maussolos' footsteps. In the event it was a defeat for the Athenians; they had to recognize the independence of key cities such as Byzantion while at the same time deferring to Persia.

In the decade after Leuktra there were ongoing hostilities in the Peloponnese involving the Spartans, Arkadians, Eleians, and other cities in a constantly changing series of alliances. The Athenians for the most part were content to play a secondary role. They sent troops to harass the various Theban invasions and were active chiefly around Korinth and the Isthmus. In 366, angry that they had received no help when the Thebans had retained the long-disputed northeastern Attic border town of Oropos, the Athenians made a defensive alliance with the Arkadians, even though the Arkadians were at war with Athens' other key ally Sparta (Xenophon *Hellenika* 7.4.1–3; Diodoros 15.76.1). Also in 366, perhaps as a result of the King's Peace Pelopidas had negotiated the year before, Korinth and Phleious made peace with Thebes (Xenophon *Hellenika* 7.4.6–11). Nothing was left of Sparta's Peloponnesian League. A war between Elis and the Arkadian League led to fighting in the sanctuary at Olympia, the loss of much Eleian territory, and ultimately a split in the Arkadian League itself along democratic and oligarchic lines (Harding 56; R&O 41). The Thebans decided to invade Arkadia in 362 (Xenophon *Hellenika* 7.4.28.5–27). Her allies now included Tegea, Megalopolis, Messenia, Argos, and Sikyon. On the other side were Mantineia, Elis, Achaia, Sparta, and Athens. The two armies met near Mantineia and though the Thebans carried the day Epameinondas was killed. The battle of Mantineia marked the end of Theban predominance. While no longer the major player in Greek affairs, the Thebans had united Boiotia and dismantled Sparta's power.

# 4 Persia

During the fourth century the western region of the Persian Empire was divided into three, or at times four, major administrative districts or satrapies. In the northwest was Hellespontine Phrygia with a capital at Daskyleion; to the south was Lydia, which included Ionia and whose capital was Sardis; in the southwest was Karia with a traditional seat inland at Mylas, though later a new center was created at coastal Halikarnassos. Karia had been ruled since 390 by the indigenous Hekatomnid dynasty. There were other small dynasts who held their land, fief-like, at the pleasure of the King, such as Syennesis in Kilikia, and the descendants of prominent Greek exiles such as Demaratos and Themistokles in Mysia and the Troad. There were also regions that had resisted Persian rule, such as Pisidia and Lykia. For the most part an individual community operated with considerable freedom and could choose its own form of government and collect its own revenues. Democracies, oligarchies, and tyrannies existed side by side. Leagues of cities or small personal empires were tolerated. Individual satraps could be rivals for local control of territory. During the fourth century under the King there was probably greater opportunity for local and native peoples to attain high rank than there had been under fifth-century Athenian Empire. There were even women rulers in Karia and the Troad. The bottom line for the Persian King, it seems, was the regular payment of annual tribute and the willingness to provide military service when required (Hornblower 1994a: 45–96; Ruzicka 1997).

Artaxerxes II (404–359) was interested in the Greek world mainly as a source of mercenaries. While Sparta, Athens, and Thebes maneuvered for Hellenic preeminence, Artaxerxes II's chief concern was to bring Egypt, which had rebelled in 404, back under Persian rule. None of his attempts succeeded. He also faced a series of satrapal revolts in the west during the 360s. The satrap of Kappadokia, Datames, put in charge of an expedition to Egypt, retreated to his satrapy and prepared to revolt when he got wind of an intrigue against him at the royal court. Loyal satraps Autophradates of Lydia and Maussolos of Karia besieged Ariobarzanes, rebellious satrap (or perhaps regent for Pharnabazos' heir, Artabazos) of Hellespontine Phrygia. The Athenians briefly aided Ariobarzanes while the Spartan king Agesilaos served as mercenary commander in Egypt. It was in this climate that Artaxerxes financed the Theban fleet. By 362 all the western satraps were in revolt, as was Phoenicia and, of course, Egypt. The crisis with the satraps was settled swiftly, however, when the satraps chose Orontes as their leader and he promptly betrayed them to the King. By the time Artaxerxes II died all of the western Anatolian satraps were back in the fold. The focus on Egypt and the confusion caused by the satrapal revolts had allowed smaller dynasts, such as Hermeias of Atarneos, considerable scope to operate independently and to expand their rule (Hornblower 1994b: 209–33; Ruzicka 1997).

Artaxerxes III Ochos (359–338) is generally regarded as having been a much stronger and more competent ruler than his father. He ruthlessly eliminated potential rivals for the throne within his family. His word carried weight; when he ordered the western satraps to disband their mercenary armies they did so with alacrity. The one rebellious satrap, Artabazos of Hellespontine Phrygia, after some initial successes, eventually was forced to flee to Macedon. Similarly, Idrieus of Karia and the Athenians were quick to do as Artaxerxes III ordered. By 352 he was ready to tackle Egypt. His first attempt failed, as did a second, which fell short even of making inroads into the Levant. But in 345, with the King himself in command, Persia recaptured Sidon and as an example burnt it to the ground and executed its king. Once in Egypt Artaxerxes III's commanders Bagoas and the Rhodian Mentor scored an initial success in a relatively minor battle at the Pelusiac branch of the Nile in the eastern section of the delta; the Egyptian king Nektanebo II fled in panic to Memphis. By 343 Egypt was at last back under Persian domination. Artaxerxes III then dispatched Mentor to western Anatolia, where he restored order rapidly. Hermeias of Atarneos was defeated and captured and the other dynasts brought to heel. The growing power of Philip II of Macedon in Thrace and the Hellespont was Artaxerxes III's next concern. When Philip laid siege to Perinthos in 340 Artaxerxes III directed his satraps to assist the city, and Philip's effort eventually failed. Artaxerxes III died in 338, having lived long enough to hear of Philip's victory at Chaironeia but not of Philip's goal for his new League of Greek states based at Korinth: the freeing of the Greek cities of Anatolia from Persian rule.

# 5   Macedonia

Philip II of Macedonia is one of the most remarkable figures in European history. He came to power in one of his country's darkest hours, and though Macedonia had never previously played anything greater than a minor political, military, or economic role, he made it the preeminent power in the Aegean, poised to challenge the mighty Persian Empire. Yet his achievements have been overshadowed by those of his famous son Alexander the Great. Philip's reputation has also suffered because the sources for his reign are either fragmentary or vociferously hostile. The speeches of the Athenian orator and statesman Demosthenes, who bitterly opposed Philip, supplemented by those of Demosthenes' Athenian political rival Aischines, are the primary contemporary sources. These are not, of course, historical accounts, nor can the historian expect them to be at all times truthful and accurate. Demosthenes saw Philip as a dangerous barbarian invader who threatened Greek freedom in much the same way Xerxes and the Persians had in 480. He urged the Athenians to emulate their forebears' brilliant victories at Marathon and Salamis and to rally the other Greek states to defend Greece against the terrible foreign peril. Though Demosthenes' view has often colored subsequent assessments of Philip, recent interpretations have recognized a broader and perhaps more balanced opinion of Philip in antiquity. The freedom of the individual Greek cities that Demosthenes ostensibly championed had, for the past half century or so, produced a seemingly unending and fruitless state of war. There was no shortage of Greeks leery of Athenian imperial ambitions and willing to ally themselves with Philip; many of these were happy to accept him as a fellow Greek. Isokrates, for example, called on Philip to reconcile the warring Greek states so that they could once again take on the Persian Empire (see his two letters to Philip, Isokrates *Letters* 2 and 3). Demosthenes himself sought chiefly to rebuild Athenian imperial might; freedom for the Greeks to him meant freedom to contend for hegemony, to rule other Greeks. Whether one sees Philip as the destroyer of Greek freedom or the bringer of stability, the transformation he wrought in

Macedonia, which gave him the means to dominate Greece, was nothing short of remarkable.

Philip's formidable military and diplomatic skills and his affable personality were admirably suited to take advantage of the ongoing political disarray among the Greek states. He fully utilized Macedonia's resources, which he was quick to augment, so that unlike the Greek powers he had no need to seek the financial support of Persia. He was highly attuned to what motivated men and was able to instill confidence in his own troops in the uncertain early days of his reign or after a rare defeat. More than once he won a key ally by dangling precisely the right bait, such as Amphipolis to the Athenians or Poteidaia to Olynthos. Similarly he understood the importance of what the modern world calls propaganda or simply good public relations. For example, he adeptly exploited his victory in the Sacred War, as the avenger of Apollo's looted sanctuary, to enhance his standing among Greeks. He also recognized the power of panhellenic sentiment when arranging Greek affairs after his victory at Chaironeia: a panhellenic expedition against Persia ostensibly was one of the main goals of the League of Korinth. At the same time he adroitly exploited Greek rivalries and enmities. He used the Greek custom of guest-friendship extensively and had many friends who were prominent figures in Greek states. He also had ties with less socially exalted though no less influential and useful people such as actors. For Philip religious festivals, weddings, victory celebrations were not merely occasions for lavish entertainments but more importantly opportunities to expand his network of friends and allies. This network not only spread his influence and advanced his cause in other cities but was also an indispensable source of intelligence and information (McQueen 1995: 125–7, 173, 181). His numerous marriages, besides their obvious role in strengthening alliances, were also a means of extending this network. All of these skills enabled him to use his two greatest assets, his superb army and the unparalleled – at least by any Greek state – wealth of his kingdom, to dominate the Greek world and to bring to an end the decades of internecine warfare that had plagued Greece.

Ancient Macedonia occupied a key strategic position in the northwest Aegean. To its north and west were the non-Greek Illyrian and Paionian tribes; to the east were the Thracians and the Greek cities of the Chalkidian peninsula; to the southwest was Greek Thessaly. Western or Upper Macedonia, a series of rugged mountains and upland plains, was home to half a dozen or so tribes, each with its own chief or king. The Macedonian royal house of the Argeads directly controlled Eastern or Lower Macedonia, a large coastal plain running from Mount Olympos north along the Thermaic Gulf and then east to the modern city of Thessaloniki. Drained in modern times and highly fertile now, much of the plain was probably marsh in antiquity. Relations between Upper and Lower Macedonia varied according to the strength of the individual king. Macedonia was rich in natural resources, offering good farmland and pasturage, significant mineral resources, and most importantly one of the ancient Mediterranean's best sources of timber and pitch used to construct ships (Borza 1990: 23–57).

The ethnicity of the ancient Macedonians is the subject of much scholarly debate and complicated by the politics of the modern Balkans. Unfortunately, the evidence is scanty. The fifth-century historian Herodotos records a tradition that the royal house of the Argeads originated in Argos (8.137–8). There is no earlier evidence for this, moreover Alexander I (c. 498–452), quite likely Herodotos' source, had good political reasons for claiming a Greek descent. In any case, it is clear generally that in the fourth century neither the Greeks nor the Macedonians themselves regarded Macedonians as Greek.

The evidence for Macedonian political and social institutions before the reigns of Philip II and Alexander the Great is exiguous. It seems that, advised informally by his companions, the king ruled as he thought fit. There was no assembly or council. Under a strong king Macedon did well and vice versa. There was no primogeniture; any male belonging to the royal house could make a play for the throne and since most kings took more than one wife there were usually many contenders. A dynastic change, therefore, was typically accompanied by instability and often foreign invasion (Borza 1990: 231–52). Characteristically, then, the death of Philip's father, Amyntas III (reigned 393–370), led to ten years of dynastic contention. A brief summary of this period leading to Philip's accession to the throne will not only show the depths from which he brought Macedonia but also involves virtually all of the major political forces and issues with which Philip himself would later have to deal: internal rivals, relations with Thessaly, potential intervention by Thebes, the long-standing interest of Athens in the region including the status of Amphipolis, the growing power of Olynthos, and the Chalkidian League, along with the almost ever present threat of invasion by a variety of barbarian neighbors.

Upon taking the throne Amyntas' eldest son, Alexander II (370–368), bought off a threatened invasion by the Illyrians (Diodoros 15.60.3; Isokrates 6.46). He exiled as a potential rival Ptolemaios of Aloros, an Argead and his late father's advisor and, reputedly, his mother Eurydike's lover (Plutarch *Pelopidas* 26.5). Alexander's abbreviated attempt to exert Macedonian influence in Thessaly only brought Pelopidas and the Thebans decisively into the region and allowed his rival Ptolemaios to return to Macedon in his absence. Pelopidas arranged a settlement between the two that also provided for hostages to be sent to Thebes, including the youngest son of Amyntas III, the later Philip II (Plutarch *Pelopidas* 26.3–5). Alexander was assassinated in 368 and Ptolemaios took control of the throne as regent for Alexander's younger brother Perdikkas III (Diodoros 15.71.1).

When Perdikkas III came of age in 365 he assassinated Ptolemaios (Diodoros 15.77.5). He then entered a struggle between Athens and the Chalkidian League for control of Amphipolis, at first helping Athens. But when the Athenians were on the verge of taking the city, Amphipolis turned to Perdikkas, who sent a Macedonian force to garrison the city (Diodoros 16.3.3; Aischines 2.29). In retaliation the Athenians, under Timotheos, captured the Macedonian coastal towns of Pydna and Methone (Aischines 2.30; Demosthenes 4.4) as well as Torone and Poteidaia (Diodoros 15.81.6). They also developed ties with the Molossians, Greeks living to the west of Macedon, and with the Odrysian Thracians to the east (Cargill 1981: 92; Sealey 1993: 88–9). In the face of these challenges Perdikkas made improvements in the army and reportedly reorganized the kingdom's finances. But disaster struck in 360/59 when the Illyrians mounted a massive invasion. Perdikkas died on the field of battle, along with 4,000 Macedonians (Diodoros 16.2.4–5). The throne passed to the youngest of Amyntas III's sons, Philip.

Philip succeeded his brother in dire circumstances. The Illyrians were preparing to follow up their victory, and the Paionians, another neighboring barbarian tribe, were threatening to invade as well (Diodoros 16.2.6). To the east the Thracians were backing a competing claimant to the Macedonian throne while the Athenians backed yet another. Philip bought time in which to rebuild his army by removing the Macedonian garrison from Amphipolis and declaring to the Athenians that he had no interest in that city (Diodoros 16.3.3–4). The Athenians failed to move promptly to take Amphipolis but dropped their support of Philip's rival. Generous bribes persuaded the Thracians and Paionians to back off as well. In spring of 358 Philip and his new army inflicted a stunning defeat on the Illyrian king who had defeated and killed Perdikkas. The new army numbered 10,000 infantry and 600 cavalry, much larger numbers than earlier Macedonian armies; the Illyrians suffered some 7,000 killed. Philip continued to expand his army as his domains increased (Diodoros 16.4.3–7; Borza 1990: 198–202). By the end of his reign he could field an army of up to 30,000 infantry and 4,000 cavalry.

Besides building up the Macedonian army to an unprecedented size Philip also changed its tactics and equipment. He armed the infantry with the sarissa, a 6-meter pike. Its length was twice that of the Greek hoplite's spear and required two hands to wield, but the increased reach also obviated the need for heavy armor; this made the Macedonian phalanx more flexible and maneuverable than the Greek hoplite line. Philip was a pioneer in the use of cavalry as a striking force, deploying both light cavalry and the elite Companion Cavalry, a heavier armed unit made up of Macedonian nobles. Philip also broke new ground by developing a corps of engineers that specialized in siege warfare. It has become traditional to ascribe at least some of the inspiration for Philip's military reforms to the time he spent as a hostage in the Thebes of Pelopidas and Epameinondas (Plutarch *Pelopidas* 26.4–5). As Philip consolidated his hold on Macedonia and added new territories to his realm, he acquired the resources to pay his troops generously. He turned his army into a fulltime, highly trained professional force (Diodoros 16.3.2; Polybios 18.29–30; Borza 1990: 202–6; Pritchett 1971: 134–54).

Following his victory over the Illyrians Philip took control of the western Macedonian cantons of Orestis and Lynkos (Diodoros 16.8.1; Ellis 1994a: 733). He also married Olympias, the daughter of a Molossian leader and later the mother of Alexander the Great (Plutarch *Alexander* 2.1–6). By these two moves Philip secured the border and key passes to the west of his kingdom while adding more population and resources. In similar and soon to be typical fashion, Philip married Philinna of the Aleuadai family of Larisa in 358 to strengthen his ties within Thessaly (Plutarch *Alexander* 10.1; cf. Athenaios 557B–E)

In the east the Athenians had their hands full with the Social War and Philip took full advantage. In 357 he captured Amphipolis after a brief siege. He soon added Pydna (Demosthenes; 20.63), Poteidaia, and Methone (Demosthenes 5), as well as all the Thracian territory between the Strymon and Nestos rivers, including the city of Krenides (which he renamed Philippoi). The latter gave him access to the prolific gold and silver mines in the region around Mount Pangaion and dramatically improved the kingdom's financial footing (Diodoros 16.8.6–7). That same year (356) marked the birth of an heir, Alexander, and saw Philip's entry in the four-horse chariot race at Olympia victorious (Plutarch *Alexander* 3.8–9; Borza 1990: 210–16).

With his borders secured and the royal coffers well stocked Philip looked to expand his kingdom. He supported (his in-laws) the Aleuadai of Larisa in a war with their Thessalian neighbor Pherai and quickly became a dominating force in Thessaly

(Diodoros 16.14.2). The dominant aristocratic families of Thessaly recognized that Philip was uniquely capable of unifying the country. They granted him revenues from market dues and harbor fees to help administer a league of Thessalian cities, and allowed him to garrison some important towns with Macedonian troops (Demosthenes 1.22; 6.22; McQueen 1995: 108–9). Philip got the use of the superb Thessalian cavalry and control of the Thessalian votes on the Amphiktyonic Council, the body which administered the panhellenic sanctuary at Delphi and played a key role in Greek affairs. This activity in Thessaly soon drew Philip into the affairs of the central Greek states. In 356 the Amphiktyonic Council, under the influence of the Thebans, declared war on the Phokians (Diodoros 16.23.2–5; Buckler 2003: 397–406). Other Greek powers lined up to support one side or the other. The Phokians seized control of the sacred precinct at Delphi and over the course of the war melted down many of the numerous gold and silver offerings to the god in order to pay a mercenary army (Diodoros 16.24.3; 30.1). Their opponents thus could claim to be punishing temple robbers. The war reached Philip when the Phokians, who were allied to Philip's Thessalian enemy Pherai, moved the conflict to Thessaly. They inflicted a rare defeat on Philip in 353. A year later, however, with his soldiers wreathed with Apollo's laurel, Philip smashed the Phokian army at the battle of Crocus Field. He executed captured enemy soldiers as temple robbers – by drowning – and hanged their commander (Diodoros 16.35.2–6). The victory confirmed Philip's hold on Thessaly and established his reputation among the Greek states both as a defender of the gods and as a formidable military power.

In the early 350s Philip had combined with Olynthos to limit Athenian influence along the coast of Macedonia and the Chalkidian peninsulas (Diodoros 16.8.3; Harding 67; R&O 50). Near the end of that decade, however, the Olynthians grew alarmed at Philip's increasing power and made overtures to Athens (Harding 80). Philip invaded in 349, picking off Chalkidian cities one by one (Diodoros 16.52.9). Despite a series of brilliant speeches (the three *Olynthiacs*) by the Athenian orator Demosthenes, the Athenians failed to respond in time and in 348 Philip took Olynthos and razed it (Diodoros 16.53.1–3).

Philip had now transformed Macedon into the most powerful state in the Greek world. Although he still had several seasons of campaigning to do around his eastern and northern borders, it is at this time that he may well have begun to think about invading Asia. Mainland Greece had little in the way of wealth or resources, apart from soldiers, to offer him. The Persian-controlled cities of western Anatolia were wealthier and more accustomed to foreign domination; moreover, the western satraps had within recent memory shown how tenuous the Persian Great King's rule could be (Ellis 1994a: 751–2; Ellis 1976: 128–30; Buckler 2003: 516–20; cf. Isokrates *Letter 3* 13; Diodoros 16.52.2). For the time being, however, affairs in Greece, and Athens in particular, demanded his attention.

Much of Philip's new dominance had come at the expense of Athens. Though they still dreamed of getting their hands on Amphipolis and other former possessions in the northern Aegean the Athenians now held only the Chersonese. Fear of Philip's increasing sway might have offered some prospects for new allies, but the Athenians' failure to come to the assistance of the Olynthians doubtless encouraged many Greek states to consider carefully the benefits of friendship with Philip. Even within Athens itself there were those who advocated making some sort of accommodation with

Macedon. Demosthenes was not one of them. He argued, if not always in practical ways, for the continuation of an Athenian imperial presence in the north Aegean and he spearheaded the resistance to Philip (see his *Philippics*). There was a brief period as the Sacred War was dragging to its conclusion when Philip and Athens agreed to a treaty, the Peace of Philokrates, named after the chief Athenian negotiator (Sealey 1993: 143–57; Ellis 1994a: 751–9; Buckler 2003: 436–40, 458–61). But almost immediately after the agreement was signed Philip characteristically exploited a factional rift among the Phokians to get control of the pass at Thermopylai (Diodoros 16.59.3). With this key route into Greece in Philip's hands the Athenians panicked and took measures to protect Attika from imminent invasion (Aischines 3.80). Even when Philip did not invade, the Athenians regretted the Peace. They were uneasy about the treatment of the Phokians, their long-time ally in the Sacred War and who had surrendered when Athens had made peace with Philip. They also repented giving up any claim to Amphipolis as the agreement had demanded. Though the two sides refrained from active hostilities the Peace of Philokrates almost immediately became a dead letter. When Philip made alliances in the Peloponnese designed to keep Sparta weak – he displaced Thebes in this role – the Athenians began to try to stir up opposition to Philip in Greece (Aischines 2.79; Demosthenes 19.10–11, 303–6). Philip offered to make a Common Peace (*koine eirene*) open to all Greek states. The Athenians revived their demand for Amphipolis and renewed their military support of tribes hostile to Philip in the north Aegean. Campaigning in the Chersonese and Propontis in 340, Philip laid siege unsuccessfully to Perinthos and Byzantion, which were aided by Athens and Persia. He did, however, capture the Athenian grain fleet, and the Athenians formally renounced the Peace of Philokrates (Diodoros 16.75–7). A year later the Amphiktyonic Council, with the Athenians and Thebans abstaining, declared war on Amphissa, a town near Delphi (Demosthenes 143–53; Aischines 3.113–29). In anticipation of Philip's advance into central Greece Demosthenes engineered an alliance with Athens' neighbor and long-time enemy Thebes (Diodoros 16.85.1–2). After settling affairs in Amphissa Philip took his army to Boiotia, where he met and defeated a combined Athenian and Theban force at Chaironeia in 338 (Diodoros 16.85–6; Polyainos 2.7; Frontinus *Strategemata* 2.1.9). Philip treated the Athenians leniently, dissolving what was left of their Sea League but allowing them to keep their navy, perhaps expecting to put it to use in his upcoming invasion of Asia Minor (Diodoros 15.87.3; Borza 1990: 216–25; Ellis 1994b: 773–81; Sealey 1993: 194–8).

After Chaironeia Philip convened a meeting of Greek states at Korinth and proclaimed a Common Peace and military alliance that formed the basis for a new Hellenic League with himself as hegemon or leader (Diodoros 16.89; Harding 99; R&O 76; cf. Harding 138; Justin 9.5.1–2; Buckler 2003: 510–15). Only Sparta, isolated and harmless, refused to participate. It is not known when Philip decided to invade Asia Minor, or the extent of his ambitions once in Persian-held territory, but making such an expedition a central purpose of the League made good political sense in 337. The idea had been bandied about for decades, not least in the writings of Isokrates, and the more general concept of acting on behalf of the Greeks remained a potent rhetorical device. However tepidly and reluctantly the Greeks may have given their support to the project when it came time to contribute troops and money, nobody would be able, at least publicly, to find fault with the scheme, so powerful was its emotional appeal. But Philip would not live to lead the expedition. He was assassinated in 336 at an international gathering at Aigai (near the modern village of Vergina) to mark the marriage of his daughter Kleopatra to Alexandros of Molossos. The assassin was a member of Philip's bodyguard, angry that Philip had decided against him in a dispute with one of Philip's generals (Diodoros 16.91–5). As that general happened to be the father of Philip's latest wife, a recent marriage that had brought about the estrangement of Olympias, there has been speculation from antiquity to the present day, most likely unfounded, about a plot. One of the royal tombs discovered at Vergina in 1977 may well be that of Philip (Andronicos 1984; Borza 1990: 256–66).

Philip transformed Macedonia from a backwater into the most powerful state in the Aegean. With his deft handling of the situation facing him at his accession to the throne Philip demonstrated at the outset his almost uncanny political and diplomatic skills. Unifying Macedonia and effectively marshalling its rich resources gave Philip the means – primary among them a large, well-trained professional army – to put an end to the internecine strife that had long plagued the Greek world. Far from needing to court Persian financial assistance, Philip supplanted the Great King as the power broker among the Greek states. While the traditional Greek city-states such as Athens, Sparta, and Thebes had each failed to bring a lasting political stability to the Greek world, Philip, monarch of what had been a backward, semi-barbarous country almost on the periphery of Greek affairs, had succeeded. Although he has long been thought of as the conqueror of Greece, it seems likely that subduing and bringing stability to the warring Greek states was to Philip only a necessary preliminary step toward his ultimate goal of invading Persian-held Anatolia. The extent of his plans, and whether they were on the scale that his son eventually carried out, is matter for speculation.

# Further reading

*CAH*[2] 6 has comprehensive, up-to-date scholarly essays on all aspects of fourth-century history and includes a thorough bibliography. Tritle (1997) has much briefer though no less excellent essays on each of the period's major powers. Buckler (2003) provides an excellent narrative overview of the period from one scholarly viewpoint. This volume is also a useful counter-balance and supplement to the more narrowly focused and specialized studies of various states and eras, such as Cargill (1981) and Sealey (1993) on Athens, Cartledge (1987) and Hamilton (1991) on Sparta, as well as Ellis (1976) and Borza (1990) on Macedonia. Buckler (1980) remains the standard treatment of Thebes. Hanson (1999) offers a highly readable, meticulously researched, if somewhat romantic account of Epameinondas. Harding usefully collects a variety of ancient sources, including inscriptions, translated and with brief commentary. R&O provides up-to-date texts, translations, and full commentaries on important fourth-century inscriptions.

# Bibliography

Andronicos, M. (1984) *Vergina: the royal tombs and the ancient city* (trans. L. Turner) (Athens: Ekdotike Athenon; repr. 1987 etc.)

Borza, E. N. (1990) *In the shadow of Olympus: the emergence of Macedon* (Princeton: Princeton University Press)

Buckler, J. (1980) *The Theban hegemony 371–362 B.C.* (Cambridge MA: Harvard University Press) (Harvard Historical Studies 98)

Buckler, J. (2003) *Aegean Greece in the fourth century* BC (Leiden: Brill)

Cargill, J. (1981) *The second Athenian league: empire or free alliance?* (Berkeley: University of California Press)

Cartledge, P. (1987) *Agesilaos and the crisis of Sparta* (Baltimore: Johns Hopkins University Press)

Cook, J. M. (1983) *The Persian empire* (London: Schocken)

Ellis, J. R. (1976) *Philip II and Macedonian imperialism* (London: Thames & Hudson)

Ellis, J. R. (1994a) "Macedon and northwest Greece" in: *CAH²* 6 723–59

Ellis, J. R. (1994b) "Macedonian hegemony created" in: *CAH²* 6 760–90

Hamilton, C. D. (1991) *Agesilaus and the failure of Spartan hegemony* (Ithaca NY: Cornell University Press)

Hammond, N. G. L., & G. T. Griffith (1979) *A history of Macedonia*, vol. 2: *550–336 B.C.* (Oxford: Clarendon)

Hanson, V. D. (1999) *The soul of battle: from ancient times to the present day, how three great liberators vanquished tyranny* (New York: Free Press)

Heskel, J. (1997) "Macedonia and the north, 400–336" in: Tritle 1997: 167–88

Hornblower, S. (1994a) "Persia" in: *CAH²* 6 45–96

Hornblower, S. (1994b) "Asia Minor" in: *CAH²* 6 209–33

McQueen, E. I. (1995) *Diodorus Siculus, the reign of Philip II: the Greek and Macedonian narrative from book XVI: a companion; translation and commentary* (London: Bristol Classical Press) (Bristol Classical Press Classical Studies Series)

Pritchett, W. K. P. (1971) *Ancient Greek military practices* (Berkeley: University of California Press) (The Greek State at War 1)

Roy, J. (1994) "Thebes in the 360s BC" in: *CAH²* 6 187–208

Ruzicka, S. (1997) "The eastern Greek world" in: Tritle 1997: 107–36

Schwenk, C. (1997) "Athens" in: Tritle 1997: 8–40

Sealey, R. (1993) *Demosthenes and his time: a study in defeat* (Oxford: Oxford University Press)

Stylianou, P. J. (1998) *A historical commentary on Diodorus Siculus Book 15* (Oxford: Clarendon)

Tritle, L. A. (ed.) (1997) *The Greek world in the fourth century: from the fall of the Athenian Empire to the successors of Alexander* (London: Routledge)

Worthington, I. (ed.) (2000) *Demosthenes: statesman and orator* (London: Routledge)

Yardley, J. C., & R. Develin (1994) *Justin:* Epitome of the *Philippic History* of Pompeius Trogus (trans. J. C. Yardley; intro., explanatory notes R. Develin) (Atlanta GA: Scholars) (The American Philological Association Classical Resources Series 3)

CHAPTER TWENTY-SEVEN

# The Conquests of Alexander the Great

*Waldemar Heckel*

## 1 Introduction

On the seventh day of the Attic month Metageitnion (= 2 August) 338, Philip II, with his son Alexander commanding the cavalry on the left, defeated a coalition of Thebans and Athenians at Chaironeia, destroying the vaunted Theban Sacred Band and, as many writers of the nineteenth and twentieth centuries have commented, dealing the fatal blow to 'Greek liberty'. Today we may be more circumspect about the nature of Greek 'freedom', but the fact remains that Chaironeia was a turning-point in Greek history. Philip promptly consolidated his gains on the battlefield by forging the League of Korinth (R&O 76), which he was designated to lead as its *hegemon* in a crusade of vengeance against Persia. But dynastic politics, following on the heels of personal misjudgement, supervened, and in 336 the Macedonian king fell victim to an assassin's dagger before he could witness his statue carried into the theatre at Aigai (Vergina) along with those of the twelve Olympians (Willrich 1899; Badian 1963; Kraft 1971: 11–42; Bosworth 1971a; Fears 1975; Develin 1981). The ceremony was to have been a fitting tribute to a descendant of Herakles about to embark upon a Panhellenic war of conquest. The undertaking and the greatness that its fulfilment held in promise were to be Alexander's inheritance.

## 2 Prelude to Conquest

Straightaway, it was necessary for the new king to establish his authority. Rivals for the throne, and their supporters, were swiftly despatched: first of all, two sons of Lynkestian Aëropos, Arrhabaios and Heromenes, were publicly executed on charges of complicity in the assassination (Arrian [all references in this chapter are to *Anabasis* unless another work by Arrian is referred to] 1.25.1). The murderer himself, Pausanias of Orestis, had been killed in flight by the king's bodyguards. If there was any truth to the charge that the Lynkestians had conspired with him (Bosworth 1971a), they appear to have given little help (unless they supplied the horses that were meant to facilitate his escape), nor was it clear if they sought the throne for a member of their own family, or for Amyntas son of Perdikkas (Plutarch *Moralia* 327c). The vagueness in the reporting of their alleged crime is doubtless Alexander's doing; for it suited his purpose to eliminate all contenders, including the hapless Amyntas. Indeed, it is hard to credit the existence of such a conspiracy without dismissing its perpetrators as inept, if not downright stupid. The Lynkestians ought to have secured the support of Antipatros, the powerful father-in-law of their brother, Alexandros. But clearly they did not. Alexandros was reportedly the first to proclaim Alexander 'King', doubtless at the urging of Antipatros, who proved his own loyalty and bought the life of his daughter's husband by abandoning Arrhabaios and Heromenes. Even in later years, when distrust had tainted the relationship between king and viceroy, no charge of conspiring to kill Philip or prevent Alexander's accession was ever levelled against him. Amyntas son of Perdikkas, too, appears to have been eliminated swiftly – certainly he was dead by the spring of 335 (Arrian 1.5.4). A companion of his, Amyntas son of Antiochos, fled Macedonia and took service with the Persian king, but it is unlikely that this occurred *before* the death of Perdikkas' son. The latter was a nephew of Philip II and rightful heir to throne, whose claims the state, in need of strong leadership to combat external foes, had swept aside in the years that followed the death of Perdikkas III in 360/59 (Hammond & Griffith 1979: 208–9). Married to Philip's daughter by an Illyrian wife, the discarded heir had lived quietly, without incurring suspicion; in all likelihood, he became the victim of the aspirations of others and of his own bloodline (see, however, Ellis 1971, rejected by Prandi 1998; but: Worthington 2003a: 76–9).

Elsewhere, Attalos, guardian of Philip's last wife Kleopatra-Eurydike, may have been perceived as a threat. But, in this case as well, stories that Attalos was conniving with the Athenian Demosthenes and other Greeks (Diodoros 17.5.1), if they are true, point only to the desperation of his situation. So weak was his position that he could not even persuade his own father-in-law, Parmenion, to side with him, though together they commanded a substantial force in northwestern Asia Minor. Alexander's agent, Hekataios, secured Attalos' elimination, something that could not have been achieved without Parmenion's acquiescence. Some scholars have been misled into attributing too much power to Attalos; for his influence with Philip must be explained by the fact of his relationship to Kleopatra-Eurydike (Heckel 1986a: 297–8). His remark at the wedding feast in 337, that the marriage would produce 'legitimate heirs' to the throne, marked him for execution when Alexander became king. It was the tactless utterance of a drunken man, but fatal nonetheless. His relatives by blood and marriage, though hardly contemptible, could do little to save him and found it expedient not to try. Parmenion obtained a more suitable husband for his widowed daughter in the taxiarch, Koinos son of Polemokrates. The father-in-law and his sons received high offices in the expeditionary force (Heckel 1992: 13–33; 299–300).

Domestic problems were, moreover, balanced by defection in the south and challenges on the northern and western marches of the kingdom. In western Greece, Akarnania, Ambrakia and Aitolia openly declared themselves hostile to Philip's settlement (Roebuck 1948: 76–7); the Peloponnesians too evinced wide-spread disaffection. But Alexander made a rapid foray into Thessaly, effected by means of cutting steps into Mt Ossa ('Alexander's Ladder'), and induced the Thessalians to recognize him as Philip's heir as *archon* of their Thessalian League, thereby also gaining a voice in the Amphiktyonic Council. With the added moral authority, the new king granted independence to the Ambrakiots, and then moved south into Boiotia pre-empting military action there. The Athenians saw to their defences and sent an embassy to Alexander; Demosthenes was said to have abandoned the embassy at Kithairon, fearing the king's wrath (Diodoros 17.4.6–7; cf. Plutarch *Demosthenes* 23.3, in the context of Alexander's destruction of Thebes). Now, too, the League of Korinth declared Alexander its *hegemon*, but the sparks of disaffection were yet to ignite into full-scale rebellion.

In the north, Alexander turned against the so-called 'autonomous' Thracians and the Triballians, tribes dwelling near the Haimos range and beyond to the Danube. South of the Haimos, the Thracians sought to blockade Alexander's force by occupying the high ground and fortifying their position with wagons. Unable to resist the attacking Macedonians, even after pushing the empty wagons into the path of the on-coming enemy, they were dispersed with heavy casualties. The Triballians responded by transferring their women and children to the Danubian island of Peuke, which their king, Syrmos, defended with a small but adequate force. The remainder of the Triballians evaded the Macedonian army as it hastened north, and occupied a wooded area near the River Lyginos, less than a day's march from the Danube. But Alexander turned back and dealt with them, using his skirmishers to dislodge the Triballians from the forest before catching them between two detachments of cavalry and attacking their centre with the phalanx. Some three thousand were killed; the remainder escaped into the safety of the woods.

An attempt on Peuke failed: the ships which Alexander had brought up from the Black Sea were insufficient in numbers and the banks of the island too well defended. Instead the Macedonians launched an attack on the Getai who lived on the north bank of the river. After destroying their town and devastating their crops, they forced the Getai to come to terms. Syrmos too sent a delegation asking for terms; possibly, Alexander demanded that he contribute a contingent to serve in his expeditionary army, in which some 7,000 Illyrians, Odrysians and Triballians are found in 334.

To the west, the Illyrians, inveterate enemies of Macedon, threatened the kingdom's borders as Glaukias son of Bardylis allied himself with the Taulantian chief, Kleitos. At Pellion Alexander displayed what a superior army led by a brilliant tactician could do. The campaign was a textbook example of speed and manoeuvre: the discipline of Alexander's troops mesmerized the Illyrians, outwitting them with a display of drill that turned them into spectators when they ought to have been taking counter-measures (Fuller 1960: 225). But the preoccupation with northern affairs gave new impetus to the anti-Macedonian party in central Greece. The reckoning was long overdue, and the consequences for Thebes devastating.

Encouraged by rumours that Alexander had been killed in Illyria and by the false hope of Athenian aid, the Thebans besieged the Macedonian garrison established on the Kadmeia after Chaironeia (Wüst 1938: 169; Roebuck 1948: 77–80). The king's response was swift, far more so than they could have imagined; for Alexander bypassed Thermopylai and arrived before the gates of Thebes within two weeks. Negotiations amounted to little more than posturing by both sides and Thebes, abandoned by the very Athenians who had incited the rebellion, was quickly taken, though not without great bloodshed. The city was razed and the survivors enslaved, all as later – and doubtless contemporary – apologists claimed by the decision of a council of Alexander's allies. Many of these were Boiotians and Phokians with a long history of enmity towards the city, but it could also be argued that it was condign punishment for a century and a half of collaboration with Persians (*medismos* or 'Medism'). So it proved both a warning to other cities in Greece that Alexander would not tolerate rebellion and a symbolic beginning of the campaign against the true enemy of Greece and its supporters.

The Athenians, for their part, hastened to display contrition, foremost among them the very self-serving politicians who had fomented the uprising from the safety of the *bema*. Nevertheless, their prominence diverted the young king's wrath from the common citizens: instead he demanded the surrender of ten orators and generals. In the event, only the implacable Charidemos was punished with exile, although Ephialtes fled to Asia Minor in the company of Thrasyboulos; several of the others outlived Alexander to rally their citizens to another disastrous undertaking in 323/2. It is important to note, however, that whereas the destruction of Thebes could be justified with reference to the city's history of Medism, any hostile act against the Athenian state as a whole would have undermined Alexander's Panhellenic propaganda (Will 1983: 37–45; Habicht 1997: 13–15).

## 3 The Conquest of Asia Minor

The Asiatic campaign began in spring 334: in fact, it was a continuation of the initiative launched in spring 336 but postponed by Philip's murder and the unrest in Greece. The advance force under Parmenion, Attalos and Amyntas had faltered and was now clinging to its bases on the Asiatic side of the Hellespont. Attalos' execution had doubtless undermined the morale of the army, but the setback had as much to do with the vigorous resistance by the forces of Memnon the Rhodian (Judeich 1892: 302–6; Ruzicka 1985 and 1997: 124–5). Cities that had proclaimed their support of Philip – some with extravagant honours for the Macedonian king – reverted to a pro-Persian stance (R&O 83; 84; 85), and it was doubtless the lacklustre performance of the first Macedonian wave that persuaded Dareios III that a coalition of satraps from Asia Minor was sufficient to confront the invaders. For Dareios, in addition to securing his claim to the Persian throne, had been preoccupied with an uprising in Egypt (Anson 1989; Garvin 2003: 94–5; but Briant 2002: 1042 urges caution; on Khababash see Burstein 2000).

The army that crossed the Hellespont comprised 12,000 Macedonian heavy infantry, along with 7,000 allies and 5,000 mercenaries; the light infantry were supplied by Odrysians, Thracians and Illyrians, to the number of 7,000, as well as a thousand archers and the Agrianes, for a grand total of 32,000. To these were added 5,100 cavalry (thus Diodoros 17.17.3–4; but other estimates range from 34,000 to 48,000 in all). At the Graneikos River, to which the coalition of satraps had advanced after their council of war in Zeleia, the 'allied' forces confronted a Persian army that included a large contingent of Greek mercenaries. By choosing to stand with the Persian forces they had disregarded an order of the League and committed high treason, and Alexander was determined to make an example of them (Arrian 1.16.6). Distrusted by their employers, the mercenaries were not engaged until the battle was already lost (McCoy 1989). Nevertheless, they paid a heavy price in the butchery that followed, and those who surrendered were sent to hard labour camps in Macedonia, stigmatized as traitors to a noble cause and denied whatever rights might be granted prisoners-of-war. This stood in sharp contrast to Alexander's clemency on other occasions, and it would be almost three years before he relented and authorized their release. For their part, the Persian cavalry and light infantry fled as the victors turned to deal with the mercenaries. Arsites, in whose satrapy the disaster had taken place, escaped and thus bought enough time to die by his own hand. Panoplies from the battle were sent to Athens with the dedication, 'from Alexander son of Philip and all the Greeks, except the Lakedaimonians', maintaining the pretence of a common cause while directing criticism at the Spartans for their refusal to join the League.

Victory at the Graneikos cleared the path for the conquest of the Aegean littoral. Many states came over voluntarily, while others were prevented by the presence of Persian forces from declaring for the Macedonian conqueror. This should not be seen as enthusiasm for Macedonian 'liberation' but rather as an opportunity for the enemies of the existing regimes to overthrow their political masters. Far different was the case of Mithrenes, the *hyparchos* of Sardis, who surrendered the city despite its superb natural defences (Briant 1993: 14–17). The death of Spithridates at the Graneikos had left Lydia without a satrap (cf. Egypt after the death of Sauakes at Issos), and Mithrenes, making a realistic appraisal of the Persian military collapse in Asia Minor, was motivated by self-preservation and the hope of favourable treatment. Alexander received him honourably, although it would be late 331 before he reaped as his reward the unenviable task of ruling Armenia. To the Aeolic cities, not directly in the army's path, the king sent Alkimachos – a prominent Macedonian and, apparently, a brother of Lysimachos – to establish democracies. Alexander meanwhile turned his attention to Miletos and Halikarnassos, where resistance continued; for the Persian navy still dominated the eastern Aegean and Dareios' general Memnon had concentrated his forces in that area. Miletos was taken with relative ease, when the Macedonians controlled the access to the harbour before the Persian fleet could arrive. Nevertheless, Alexander decided at this point to disband his fleet – its strength, quality and loyalty were all suspect – and concentrate on engagements by land. The decision, though baffling to some at the time, would prove to be a wise strategic move and an economic blessing.

At Halikarnassos, Memnon and Orontopates directed a stubborn defence, inflicting casualties on the besiegers and setting fire to their siege-towers (Fuller 1960: 200–6; Romane 1994: 69–75). But the city was quickly cordoned off and eventually taken; for Alexander found a less costly, political means of gaining control of Karia. He had received envoys from neighbouring Alinda, where Ada, the ageing sister of Maussolos, and rightful queen of Halikarnassos, was residing. Some time after the death of her husband (also her brother), Idrieus, Ada had been deposed by yet another brother, Pixodaros (Hornblower 1982: 41–50; Briant 2002: 706–7; for Ada in particular Özet 1994). When Pixodaros died shortly before the Macedonian invasion, the administration of the satrapy was given to Orontopates, who appears to have married the younger Ada, a bride once offered to Alexander's half-witted sibling, Arrhidaios (Plutarch *Alexander* [all references in this chapter are to *Alexander* unless another work by Plutarch is referred to] 10.1–3; French & Dixon 1986). By restoring the former queen to her kingdom, and by accepting her as his adoptive mother, Alexander earned the goodwill of the Karians. Sufficient forces were left with Ada to compel the eventual surrender of Halikarnassos, thus freeing Alexander to proceed into Pamphylia. But the act of reinstating Ada, like the king's treatment of Mithrenes, was a departure from the official policy of hostility to the barbarian. Few in the conquering army will have cared about the Hekatomnid record of philhellenism.

Over the winter of 334/3, Alexander campaigned in Lykia and Pamphylia, rounding Mt Klimax where the sea receded, as if it were doing obeisance (*proskynesis*) to the future king of Asia (Kallisthenes *FGrHist* 124 F 31), just as the Euphrates had lowered its waters for the younger Kyros in 401 (Xenophon *Anabasis* 1.4.18). This apparent foreshadowing gained credence in spring 333 when Alexander slashed through the Gordian knot with his sword and claimed to have fulfilled the prophecy that foretold dominion over Asia for the man who could undo it. While prophecies could be carefully scripted by the spin-doctors, mastery over Asia would require military victory over Dareios III, who, by the time Alexander had entered Kilikia, had amassed an army on the plains of northern Mesopotamia at Sochoi. Alexander's own advance had been methodical, aiming clearly at the coastal regions that might give succour to the Persian fleet and the satrapal capitals with their administrative centres and treasure houses. Near Tarsos he fell ill, collapsing in the cold waters of the River Kydnos, perhaps stricken with malaria (Engels 1978b: 225–6). That Dareios interpreted the Macedonian's failure to emerge from Kilikia as cowardice (Curtius 3.8.10–11) may be attributable to the sources who wished to depict the Persian king as a vainglorious potentate whose actions in the field belied his boastful pronouncements. On the other hand, it is not unlikely that the Persians had a genuine expectation of victory – after all, a larger army under the younger Kyros had been crushed at Kounaxa in 401 despite the valour of the Ten Thousand (Xenophon *Anabasis* 1) – and underestimated both the Macedonian army and its youthful commander. Impatient and eager to force a decision upon an enemy he regarded as shirking battle, Dareios entered Kilikia via the so-called Amanic Gates and placed himself astride Alexander's lines of communication. By doing so, the Persian king had abandoned the more extensive plains which offered him the chance of deploying those mobile troops that could most harm the enemy and negated his numerical superiority by leading his forces into the narrow coastal plain between the Gulf of Issos and the mountains.

Alexander, who had advanced south of the Beilan Pass (Pillar of Jonah; for the topography see Hammond 1994) and approached what would in the Middle Ages be known as Alexandretta (Iskenderum), now turned about to confront the Persian army, marching first in column and then spreading out to occupy the plain south of the Pinaros River. Despite his initial error in allowing himself to be lured onto a battlefield more favourable to the smaller Macedonian army, Dareios made good use of the terrain, which he strengthened in one spot by means of a palisade. The Greek mercenaries gave a good account of themselves, as did the cavalry posted by the sea, but the battle was decided on the Persian left, where Alexander broke the Persian line and advanced directly upon Dareios. The Great King was soon turned in flight, a move that signalled defeat and *sauve qui peut*. The slaughter was great, but the enemy leader escaped, ultimately, to the centre of his empire to regroup and fight another day (Seibert 1987: 450–1 dismisses charges of 'cowardice').

# 4   Defeat of the Great King

The fortunes and paths of the two kings now moved in different directions. Dareios returned to Mesopotamia, intent upon saving the heart of the empire and rebuilding his army. For this purpose, he summoned levies from the upper satrapies, which had not been called up in 333, perhaps from overconfidence that the victory would be easily won without them. Alexander meanwhile stuck doggedly to his strategy of depriving the Persian fleet of its bases and gaining control of the lands that supplied ships and rowers. For it was clear that most served Persia under compulsion and would defect once their home governments had acknowledged the power of the conqueror. Tyre proved a stubborn exception – not out of loyalty to Persia, but rather in hope of gaining true independence as a neutral state. But Alexander could not afford to leave so prominent and powerful an island city unconquered. The siege and capture of Tyre were one of the king's greatest achievements and a monument to his determination and military brilliance. After seven months, the city succumbed to a combined attack of the infantry on the causeway, built with great effort and loss of life, and a seaborne assault on the weakest point of the walls. The king's naval strategy was already paying dividends; for the Cypriot rulers had by now defected and joined with the other Phoenicians to blockade the Tyrian ships in their harbour, while a second flotilla carrying soldiers and battering rams gained undisputed access to the walls. The defenders repelled an attack after the initial breach was achieved, but they were soon overwhelmed and the city paid a heavy price for its defiance of Alexander (Fuller 1960: 206–16; Romane 1987).

To the south, Gaza represented the final obstacle to the Macedonian strategy. It too was captured after a two-month siege. Its garrison commander, Batis, was allegedly dragged around the city by Alexander in imitation of Achilleus' punishment of Hektor. This has generally been dismissed as fiction, though perhaps unjustly. The form of punishment and Alexander's personal role may well be literary invention on the part of Kleitarchos, if not of Kallisthenes of Olynthos, but there is a strong suspicion that behind this story there lurks an element of truth: Batis was doubtless subjected to cruel punishment for his opposition to Alexander (and we might add that Alexander was twice wounded in the engagement), just as later Ariamazes was crucified for his defiance.

In Egypt, the Macedonian army faced no resistance, since Persian authority in the satrapy had collapsed (Briant 2002: 861). If the populace welcomed Alexander as liberator, they did so out of hatred for Persia, which had harshly re-integrated Egypt into the Persian empire after roughly sixty years of independence under the kings of the Twenty-Eighth to Thirtieth Dynasties, and because, like the native populations of other regions, they were helpless to do otherwise. Alexander himself was recognized as the legitimate pharaoh – whether or not an official crowning took place in Memphis (Burstein 1991) – and the earthly son of Amun, both in the Nile Delta and by the high priest of the god at Siwah in the Libyan Desert. Thus Egypt began a new era of foreign rule. The pharaonic titles were accepted by Alexander, just as they were conferred by his subjects, as recognition of the irresistible conqueror and his achievement. Neither side was truly deceived, but the process reaffirmed order and the continuation of the patterns of everyday life; for Alexander, like his Persian predecessors, would reside elsewhere and govern through satraps and nomarchs. The reality was clear to both Alexander and the Egyptians, but for the Macedonians Alexander's new role and the nature of his relationship with Amun were deeply disturbing.

The journey to the oracle of Amun at Siwah in the Libyan Desert represents a critical point not only in Alexander's personal development but also in the king's relationship with his men – common soldiers and officers alike. Although there is a tradition that Alexander was 'seized by an urge' (*pothos*) to visit the oracle and thus emulate his mythical ancestors, Perseus and Herakles, the journey cannot have been an impulsive act. Some have argued that the king sought divine approval for his new city on the Canopic mouth of the Nile. It is most likely that the journey was in some way connected with Alexander's role as pharaoh, and such an interpretation finds curious support in Herodotos' account of Kambyses. Certainly the story that the Persian king sent an army to destroy the shrine, and that this army was buried in the desert sands (Hdt. 3.26; Plutarch 26.12), is as apocryphal as the one about his killing of the Apis calf – a patent fabrication that still commands the belief of some Classical scholars. The kernel of truth is surely that Kambyses consulted the oracle once he became master of Egypt. Whatever the fate of his envoys, the Herodotean account defies credulity. But Alexander must have known that, as Pharaoh, he would be recognized as son of Amun. Whether the trip was made solely to consolidate his position in Egypt, or for a more ambitious purpose, cannot be determined. What is certain is that his men soon equated his acceptance of Amun as his divine father with a rejection of Philip (cf. Hamilton 1953). The first rumblings of discontent occurred before the army left Egypt; in the coming years, as the army made its weary progress eastwards, Alexander's apparent repudiation of his Macedonian origins was to become a recurring cause of complaint.

The conquest of the Levantine coast and Egypt had given Dareios time to regroup. In 331 he moved his army from Babylon, keeping the Tigris River on his right and then crossing it south of Arbela, where he deposited his baggage. From here he marched north, bridging the River Lykos, and then encamped by the Boumelos (Khazir) in the vicinity of Gaugamela. As the Persian king was choosing his battle-field, Mazaios, who had once been satrap of Abarnahara (the land beyond the river), approached the Euphrates near Thapsakos with some 6,000 men. This force was far too small to prevent Alexander's crossing and was probably intended to harass and observe the enemy, and Mazaios quickly withdrew in the direction of the Tigris. Alexander, for his part, had been informed by spies about Dareios' location and the size of his army; at any rate, he had banished any thought of proceeding directly to Babylon, a move which would have created supply problems and allowed Dareios to position himself astride his lines of communication for a second time. Furthermore, Alexander was eager for a decisive engagement.

In 331, Dareios was not Alexander's only worry. During his second visit to Tyre, on the return from Egypt, the king received word of unrest in Europe, where the Spartan king, Agis III, had organized a coalition and defeated Antipatros' *strategos* in the Peloponnese, Korrhagos (for the background to the war see McQueen 1978). Agis was besieging Megalopolis with an army of 22,000 just as Antipatros was attempting to suppress a rebellion by Memnon, *strategos* of Thrace. Despite the timing, there is no good reason for suspecting that the uprisings were coordinated, or that Memnon had been in communication with Agis (*pace* Badian 1967). In fact, Antipatros was able to come to terms with Memnon far too quickly for the Thracian rebellion to benefit Agis. Nor can the actions of the *strategos* have been regarded as treasonous; for the truce allowed him to retain his position, and Alexander appears to have taken no retaliatory action against him. Freed from distractions in the north, Antipatros led his forces to Megalopolis and re-established Macedonian authority with heavy bloodshed: 3,500 Macedonians lay dead, and 5,300 of the enemy, including Agis himself. But when Alexander confronted Dareios at Gaugamela the affairs of Europe were only beginning to unravel (Borza 1971; Wirth 1971; Lock 1972; Badian 1994).

In his address to the troops, Alexander told them that they would be facing the same men they had defeated twice before in battle, but in fact the composition of the Persian army at Gaugamela was radically different and included the skilled horsemen of the eastern satrapies. And, this time, the Persians would be fighting on terrain of their own choosing. With vastly superior numbers, Dareios expected to outflank and envelop the much smaller Macedonian army, which numbered only 47,000. Furthermore, the Macedonians were confronted by scythe-chariots and elephants. But the Macedonians advanced *en echelon*, with the cavalry on the far right wing deployed to prevent an outflanking manoeuvre there; behind the main battalions of the *pezhetairoi*, Alexander stationed troops to guard against envelopment. By thrusting with his Companions against the Persian left, Alexander disrupted the enemy formation as the heavy infantry surged ahead to strike at the centre. But in so doing, the infantry created a gap, which the Scythian and Indian horsemen were prompt to exploit. But the barbarians rode straight to the baggage of the field camp, eager for plunder and acting as if their victory was assured. Had they struck instead at the Macedonian left, where Mazaios was putting fearsome pressure on the Thessalian cavalry under Parmenion's command, they might have turned the tide of battle. Instead they were soon following their king in flight, struggling to escape the slaughter that emboldens the victor.

Defeat at Gaugamela left the heart of the empire and the Achaimenid capitals at the mercy of the invader. Mazaios, who had fled to Babylon, now surrendered the city and its treasures to Alexander, thus earning his own reward. The king retained him as satrap of Babylonia, though he took the precaution of installing Macedonian troops and overseers in the city. The administrative arrangements, like the ceremonial handing over of the city, were the same as those at Sardis, except that at that uncertain time Alexander was not yet ready to entrust the Iranian nobility with higher offices. In Susa, the king confirmed the Persian satrap Aboulites, who had made formal surrender after Gaugamela: but, again, native rule was fettered by military occupation as its Persian commandant, Mazaros, was replaced by the Macedonian Xenophilos (Heckel 2002).

In the closing months of 331, anxiety about Agis' war in the Peloponnese helped to buy the Persians time. The need to await news of events in the west kept Alexander in Babylonia and Elam longer than he had planned, a delay exploited by the Persian satrap, Ariobarzanes, who occupied the so-called Persian Gates (for location and topography, Speck 2002; also MacDermot & Shippmann 1999) with an army of perhaps 25,000 (40,000 infantry and 700 horse, according to Arrian 3.18.2). But his efforts, like those of the Ouxians shortly before, proved futile. Alexander circumvented the enemy's position and was soon reconstructing the bridge across the Araxes, which the Persians had destroyed in an effort to buy time. Perhaps the intention was to facilitate the removal or even the destruction of the city's treasure; for the best Ariobarzanes could do was delay Alexander's force while Parmenion took the heavier troops and the siege equipment along the more southerly wagon road to Persepolis. But no such measures were taken, and Tiridates surrendered the city and its wealth to the conqueror.

## 5   From Panhellenic Crusader to Great King: Propaganda and its Consequences

Vengeance had been the theme exploited, first by Philip and then by Alexander, and the war against Persia the justification for allied service under the Macedonian *hegemon*. The mandate of the League could be enforced before the troops even reached Asian soil. Thebes, which had a long history of Medism, was accused once again of collaboration with Persia, and indeed of advocating alliance with the Great King to overthrow the tyrant who was oppressing Greece, Alexander (Diodoros 17.9.5). The city's destruction was at once an act of terror and vengeance. On similar grounds, Parmenion had destroyed Gryneion in the Hellespontine region and enslaved its population (Diodoros 17.7.8; Bosworth 1988a: 250). And, not surprisingly, Alexander's propagandists depicted the crossing into Asia as the beginning of another chapter in the ongoing struggle between East and West. The king sacrificed to various gods and heroes associated with the Trojan War, including an *apotropaic* sacrifice to Protesilaos, the first of the Achaians to leap ashore and to meet his fate there. Thereafter he hurled his spear into Asian soil, and leaping onto the Asian shore, proclaimed it 'spear-won land' (Mehl 1980–1; Zahrnt 1996). The message was unmistakable: more than a mere punitive expedition, this was to be a war of conquest, and it was to be a Panhellenic effort (Seibert 1998; cf. Flower 2000). But Alexander had no sooner embarked on this fine-sounding mission than it became clear to him that propaganda and expediency were destined to clash. Slogans might prove useful for the enlistment of troops or creating ardour amongst the rank and file, but victory over the enemies' military forces did not guarantee the political acquiescence of the conquered peoples.

Hardly had he consigned Greeks who had served as mercenaries of the Great King to hard labour camps, for their collaboration with the enemy, before he accepted the surrender of Sardis by the Persian, Mithrenes, whom he treated with respect and kept in his entourage. It was a clear indication of what could be accomplished without recourse to battle, and the friendly treatment of the defector would induce others to follow his example. In the same campaigning season, Alexander dismissed the allied fleet. Militarily and economically, this was a good move, but the political implications were otherwise. The leader of the League of Korinth had rejected the participation of one of its most powerful members. Furthermore, he followed this gesture with an equally confounding one when he allowed Ada to return to Halikarnassos as its rightful queen and accepted her as his adoptive mother. From the very beginning, Alexander had recognized that he might conquer without reaching an accommodation with the barbarian, but he would do so more easily and rule the empire more securely if he did so. Hence, the orientalizing tendencies of the king, which were to cause so much anxiety in the years that followed Dareios' death, were already in evidence in 334/3. But Alexander was doing little more than applying the methods of Philip to the Asiatic sphere.

For the conservative Macedonians and Greeks, it was a disturbing trend, but Alexander's progressive moves reveal a political talent that rivalled his military genius. No opportunity was wasted. The decision to send the newly-weds back to Macedonia, where they could kindle the enthusiasm of their countrymen for the war and return with reinforcements, was a fine public-relations exercise, to say nothing of its impact on the Macedonian birth-rate. In spring 333, Alexander was quick to exploit the prophecy of the Gordian knot, even if his rashness forced him to find a desperate solution. After the king's death there were those who said that he had cheated by cutting the knot with his sword, but no one said so at the time. The respectful treatment of the Persian women captured at Issos showed that Alexander was the consummate master of propaganda, whether it was directed towards the Greeks, the Macedonians, or the barbarians. Not every victory would be gained on the battlefield. So much was clear to the young conqueror, although the soldiers and the majority of their commanders failed to appreciate their leader's approach. Whatever political advantages accompanied the king's recognition as 'Son of Amun', the troops saw only the rejection of Philip II and the inflated ego of a man to whom success came too soon and too easily.

It would indeed be easy to reduce the king's actions to those of a young man corrupted by fortune; for thus he is represented in some of the extant accounts. But this is to deny Alexander an awareness of the political reality. He more than anyone understood that the rhetoric which had fuelled the campaign in the first place must give way to a policy of *rapprochement* if the fruits of his military successes were not to be squandered. Nevertheless, he was prepared to employ different forms of propaganda in his dealings with two conflicting groups – the victors and the vanquished. But, when the fighting stopped, the consequences of this studied duplicity would confront him.

In truth, that confrontation occurred even before the war was officially ended. The flight of Dareios from Gaugamela and the surrender of Babylon and Susa made Alexander *de facto* ruler of the Persian Empire. Although one final attempt was made to impede the king's progress at the Persian Gates, the capture of Persepolis was more or less symbolic. Indeed, for the Greeks, the entry into the city was, like that of the armies of the First Crusade into Jerusalem in 1099, the culmination of the campaign and the fulfilment of the purpose for which they had crossed into Asia. But for Alexander it was a public-relations nightmare. As long as Dareios lived and continued to be recognized as Great King, the war remained unfinished and the eastern half of the empire unconquered. Greek allies, mindful of the League's propaganda, demanded the destruction of the city in the hope of sating their hunger for revenge and booty. Victorious and laden with spoils, they expected to be demobilized. To deny the soldiers of League, as well as his Macedonian veterans, the right to plunder would be a failure to acknowledge their sacrifices, but Parmenion rightly advised that Alexander should not destroy what was now his (Arrian 3.18.11). Hence the king compromised, allowing his troops to pillage while still reserving the greatest treasures for himself; for even in the suburbs there were enough spoils to go around. But, if the destruction of the palace was an act of policy, it was an unfortunate miscalculation. Alexander may have attempted to limit the physical destruction while satisfying the expectations of the Greeks back home; the symbolism of the act was, however, seared into the hearts of Iranians for centuries (Balcer 1978; Shabazi 2003: 19–20).

## 6    Guerrilla Warfare in Central Asia and the End of Persian Rule

In vain Dareios summoned reinforcements from the Upper Satrapies, despite the fact that Alexander was delayed at Persepolis awaiting news of the outcome of Agis' war and the clearing of the passes through the Zagros. When in May 330 Alexander finally crossed the Zagros into Media, Dareios had little choice but to retreat to solitudes of Central Asia, following the caravan route (later to be known as the 'Silk Road') that led from Rhagai through the Caspian Gates (the Sar-i-Darreh pass) between the Great Salt Desert and the Elburz mountains. But the cumbersome train of women and eunuchs, and the other *impedimenta* of royalty, made slow progress, while Alexander closed the distance between himself and his prey. Dareios thus felt compelled to decide the matter in battle, with an army that had dwindled to fewer than 40,000 barbarian troops and 4,000 Greeks. And these lacked the fighting spirit or the leadership to decide the matter on the battlefield: Bessos, satrap of Baktria and Sogdiana, and the chiliarch Nabarzanes were intent upon flight to Baktra (Balkh), where new forces could be enlisted for a guerrilla war against Alexander; Dareios had lost all authority. He was arrested and placed in chains, allegedly of gold, as if to mitigate the crime, and his remaining followers slipped away to make submission to the advancing conqueror. Finally, in a vain hope of buying time or winning Alexander's goodwill, the conspirators murdered their king and left him by the roadside. Arrian dates Dareios' death to the month Hekatombaion in the archonship of Aristophon, that is, July 330 (Arrian 3.22.2; Bosworth 1980a: 346 suggests a miscalculation and postpones the event to August). Not long after, Alexander reached Hekatompylos and dismissed the remainder of his allied troops. The pressure to declare an end to the Panhellenic war had been mounting since the fall of Persepolis, and some forces had been sent home from Ekbatana. Despite the loss of the allied contingents, there was still a ready supply of mercenary soldiers and regular reinforcements from Macedonia and Thrace. Furthermore, since the king was anxious to bring about an accommodation with the Persian aristocracy, and indeed to present himself as the legitimate successor of Dareios III, it was necessary to abandon the slogans of Panhellenism and vengeance.

Those who supported Bessos hastened in the direction of the Merv Oasis and the Upper Satrapies of Baktria and Sogdiana. Others, however, rejected Bessos and his clique. Bagisthanes, Antibelos (or, as Curtius 5.13.11 renders the name in Latin, Brochubelus) son of Mazaios, and Melon, the king's interpreter, had surrendered even before the conspirators seized Dareios. Now, upon Bessos' usurpation, the number and importance of these defectors increased: Phrataphernes, Autophradates, Artabazos and his sons, all found their way to Alexander's camp. The king did not

disappoint them, assigning to Phrataphernes the rule of the Parthians, and Autophradates the Tapourians. Artabazos and his sons remained with Alexander – he had
known them since they had taken refuge at Philip's court, and would reward them
later. Even the regicide Nabarzanes surrendered to Alexander and was pardoned
through the efforts of the younger Bagoas, an attractive eunuch who found favour
with Alexander (Badian 1958b). Perhaps he lived out his life in obscurity, although it
is possible that the 'Barzanes' who attempted to gain control of Parthia and Hyrkania,
and was subsequently arrested and executed, was in fact the former chiliarch (Heckel
1981: 66–7).

It soon became known that the regicide, Bessos, had assumed the upright tiara and
styled himself Artaxerxes V, and it is perhaps no mere coincidence that Alexander
adopted Persian dress at about the same time (Plutarch 45.1–3). At Sousia (Tus),
Alexander accepted the surrender of Satibarzanes, whom he confirmed him as satrap
of the Areians and sent back to his satrapy (in the vicinity of modern Herat)
accompanied by forty javelin-men under Anaxippos. These were soon butchered by
Satibarzanes' forces and Alexander, who had set out for Margiana, was forced to
divert his army to Artakoana. Caught off guard by the suddenness of his arrival, the
treacherous satrap fled to Baktria with 2,000 horsemen, but he soon returned to
challenge the Persian Arsakes, whom Alexander had installed in his place. Not much
later, Satibarzanes was killed in single combat with Erigyios.

Alexander himself followed the Helmand river valley eastward in the direction of
Arachosia. On the way, he encountered the Ariaspians, a people known also as the
'Benefactors' (*euergetai*) for the aid they gave Kyros the Great in the 530s; now they
provisioned another great conqueror over the winter of 330/29. In Arachosia, in the
vicinity of modern Kandahar (but cf. Vogelsang 1985: 60, for pre-Alexandrian
settlement), the king founded yet another Alexandreia in the satrapy abandoned by
the regicide Barsaentes, whom Sambos now sheltered. The Macedonians then
entered Baktria via the Khawak Pass, which led to Drapsaka (Qunduz). Their speed
and determination were beginning to take a toll on the barbarian leaders, who sought
reprieve by surrendering Bessos. The regicide was arrested, stripped naked and left in
chains to be taken (by Ptolemy) to Alexander, but the conspirators who betrayed him
were not yet ready to test the conqueror's mercy.

The punishment of Bessos – Alexander sent him back to Ekbatana to be mutilated
in Persian fashion (which involved the cutting off of the ears and nose) and then
executed – should have ended the affair. But the northeastern frontier was unstable,
and the semi-nomadic peoples there were inclined to trust the vastness of its open
spaces and its seemingly unassailable mountain fortresses. Furthermore, Alexander's
campaign to the Iaxartes, and the establishment of Alexandreia Eschate, to replace the
old outpost of Kyroupolis, threatened the old patterns of life and trade in Sogdiana
(Holt 1988: 54–9). Hence the local dynasts, Spitamenes, Sisimithres, Oxyartes,
Arimazes, took up the fight, and two years of guerrilla warfare followed before the
political marriage of Alexander and Oxyartes' daughter, Rhoxane, could bring stability to the region.

Alexander's treatment of Bessos had perhaps sent the wrong message: the rebels
should expect no clemency from the conqueror. Invited to a council at Baktra
(Zariaspa), the chieftains of Baktria and Sogdiana suspected treachery and renewed
their opposition. Spitamenes, perhaps an Achaimenid, emerged as the leader of the

resistance, striking at Marakanda while Alexander carried the war beyond the Iaxartes. Next he caught the force sent to relieve the town in an ambush at the Polytimetos, inflicting heavy casualties and inspiring the natives' hopes. But the following year, he was hemmed in by the contingents of Krateros and Koinos and eventually betrayed by his Scythian allies, who sent his head to the Macedonian camp while they themselves made good their escape into the desert.

In the late autumn of 328, large numbers of rebels and their families took refuge with Sisimithres on the so-called 'Rock of Chorienes', now known as Koh-i-nor (Chorienes was, in all likelihood, Sisimithres' official name; Heckel 1986b; but: Bosworth 1981; 1995: 124–39), frighteningly high and of even more imposing circumference and surrounded by a deep ravine. But Alexander induced his surrender through the agency of Oxyartes, who must have defected to the Macedonians in the hope of saving his family. By his voluntary submission Sisimithres averted a fate similar to that of Ariamazes, and he was allowed to retain his territory (probably the region of Gazaba), although his two sons were retained as hostages in Alexander's army. In early 327, Sisimithres was able to provision Alexander's army with supplies for two months, 'a large number of pack-animals, 2000 camels, and flocks of sheep and herds of cattle' (Curtius 8.4.19). Alexander repaid the favour by plundering the territory of the Sakai and offering Sisimithres a gift of 30,000 head of cattle. It was almost certainly at this point that the banquet at which Rhoxane was introduced to Alexander occurred, and the king took his first oriental bride.

Alexander had never entirely trusted mercenaries – perhaps he had bitter memories of their betrayal of Philip (Curtius 8.1.24) – and he found it convenient to settle not fewer than 10,000 of them in military outposts beyond the Oxos (Amu-darya). The king had, of course, founded numerous 'cities' throughout the east – several, though not all, named for himself – and would continue to do so in India: Plutarch (*Moralia* 328e: *De Fortuna Alexandri* 1.5) speaks of more than seventy, but many of these involved either the resettling of old cities (e.g., Alexandreia Troas, or Prophthasia at Phrada, modern Farah) or the establishment of military colonies (*katoikiai*), though some twelve to eighteen Alexandreias deserve serious attention (Stephanos Byzantios, entry 'Alexandreiai'; Fraser 1996; cf. Tarn 1997: 2 232–59). In Baktria and Sogdiana, the short-term prognosis for these settlements was not good: for the mercenaries felt abandoned in the solitudes of Central Asia and, prompted by the false news of Alexander's death in India, considered a bold escape to the west – thus imitating on a grander scale the achievement of the Ten Thousand – but the plan was suppressed in 326/5 and again, with great slaughter, in 323/2 (Holt 1988; cf. Tarn 1997). Paradoxically, Baktria and Sogdiana were destined to become an outpost of Hellenism between the Mauryan kingdom in the east and the Parthians in the west.

## 7 Conspiracy and Confrontation

The opposition to Alexander that manifested itself at the time of Philip's death had been silenced by swift and decisive measures, but the opponents remained. In the first year of the Asiatic campaign, the king found evidence of secret negotiations between Alexandros Lynkestes and representatives of the Great King. In winter 334/3, the Lynkestian was arrested on information divulged by a Persian agent named Sisenes

(Arrian 1.25). The theory that he had not been in treasonous contact with the chiliarch Nabarzanes and the exile Amyntas son of Antiochos, but was himself the victim of conspiracy devised by Alexander (thus Badian 2000), is unconvincing (see Heckel 2003a). At the time, however, Alexander's position was far from secure, and he was reluctant to test the loyalty of Antipatros by executing his son-in-law. The Lynkestian was nevertheless kept in chains for three years before being brought to trial.

Further dissatisfaction resulted from the king's acceptance of his 'divine birth' at Siwah. For the conquest and administration of the satrapy, Alexander's recognition by the priests of Amun was a political expedient. But the subtleties of politics were wasted on the conservative Macedonian aristocracy, which had grown to regard its king as first among equals. Like the king's later orientalisms, the decision to exploit native sentiment was regarded by the conquerors as a demotion of the victors and their practices. Hegelochos, perhaps a relative of Philip's last wife Kleopatra, appears to have plotted against the king in Egypt, but the plan came to naught and was disclosed only in 330, more than a year after the conspirator's death at Gaugamela. Philotas had also voiced his displeasure in Egypt, treasonous activity for a lesser man. His claim that Alexander's military success was due primarily to Parmenion's generalship did not sit well with the son of Philip of Macedon, perhaps because there was some truth in it. Before the final decision at Gaugamela, the remark was ignored but not forgotten. The echo of Philotas' boast would resound in Phrada in 330, when Parmenion had been left behind in Ekbatana.

In Alexander's camp there now occurred the first open signs of opposition to the king's authority and policies. The so-called 'conspiracy of Philotas' in the autumn of 330 was, if anything, an indication that many of the most prominent *hetairoi* had begun to question Alexander's leadership. At that time, a relatively unknown individual named Dimnos either instigated or was party to a conspiracy to murder the king. The details of this plot he revealed to his lover Nikomachos, and by him they were transmitted to Nikomachos' brother Kebalinos and ultimately to Alexander himself. Philotas' role is at best obscure: what we do know is that Kebalinos reported the plot to him and that he did not pass it on, later alleging that he did not take it seriously. He could perhaps point to the humiliation endured by his father, Parmenion, who falsely accused Philippos of Akarnania of planning to poison the king in Kilikia. But the fact remains that Philotas was already on record as having made boastful remarks which exaggerated his own achievements, and those of his father, and cast aspersions on Alexander's generalship (Arrian 3.26.1; Plutarch 48.1–49.2 provides the details). That this occurred in Egypt, after Alexander's acceptance of his role as 'Son of Amun', is significant; for it is a clear sign of how the orientalizing policies of the king were alienating the conservative commanders of the army. Hegelochos son of Hippostratos was also said to have harboured treasonous ambitions at this time (Curtius 6.11.22–9). Furthermore, in the deadly world of Macedonian politics, where assassination was a regular and effective tool, it was easily believed that anyone who knowingly suppressed knowledge of a conspiracy must in some way have approved of it. This, at least, was the substance of the charge against Philotas and, combined with his previous record of disloyalty, it was sufficient to bring about his condemnation and execution. Alexander nevertheless was careful to give the impression of legality to his actions, for he knew that the execution of the son would have to be followed by the father's murder. Charges were laid against Parmenion, and Polydamas the Thessalian was sent in disguise to Ekbatana, where the murder was carried out swiftly by men Alexander felt he could trust (see Badian 1960; Heckel 1977; Adams 2003).

The deaths of Philotas and his father gave Alexander the opportunity to eliminate Alexandros Lynkestes, who, if he was no longer a danger to the king, remained a political embarrassment. Antipatros appears not to have protested against the imprisonment of his son-in-law, and the king, who had now become truly the master of his growing domain, felt secure enough to execute the traitor. A lengthy incarceration will have given the Lynkestian time to rehearse a defence, but the hopelessness of his position rendered him confused and all but speechless.

The elimination of Philotas required a restructuring of the command of the Companion Cavalry. The king had learned that it was unwise to entrust so important an office to a single individual, and his solution was designed to limit the power of the hipparch while making conciliatory gestures to the old guard. Philotas' command was thus divided between Black Kleitos, who had saved the king's life at the Graneikos and whose sister had been Alexander's wet nurse, and the untried but unquestionably loyal Hephaistion. The latter appointment proved to be not merely a case of nepotism but an unsound military decision, and within two years the Companions were divided into at least five hipparchies, of which only one remained under Hephaistion's command.

The strain of combat and campaigning under the harshest conditions took its toll on soldiers and commanders alike. In summer 328, at a drinking party in Marakanda, the stress of combat mixed with personal resentment and political outlook into a deadly brew. The event that precipitated a quarrel between Alexander and Black Kleitos, the former commander of the 'Royal Squadron' (*ile basilike*) of the Companion Cavalry, was, on the face of it, innocent enough. A certain Pierion or Pranichos, who belonged to the king's entourage of artists, recited a poem that appears to have been a mock epic about one of their own – the harpist Aristonikos – who died in battle against Spitamenes (Holt 1988: 78–9 n. 118, plausibly). But the veteran warrior, Kleitos, took umbrage and faulted Alexander for allowing Greek non-military men to ridicule a Macedonian defeat at a function that included barbarians. And we must assume that there were greater issues at play: Kleitos had watched Alexander's transformation from a traditional Macedonian ruler to an orientalizing despot with disapproval, and the argument that ensued was as much a clash of generations and ideologies as the machismo of two battle-scarred veterans under the influence of alcohol.

The underlying tensions were not to subside. If anything, the marriage of Alexander to Rhoxane in winter 328/7, which had done so much to reconcile the barbarians with their conquerors, proved immensely unpopular with the army and its commanders – even more so, if there is any truth to claim that Alexander arranged for similar mixed marriages between his *hetairoi* and Baktrian women (*Metz Epitome* 31; Diodoros 17 index λ). Furthermore, the king's attempt to introduce the Persian practice of obeisance known as *proskynesis* at the court, for both barbarians and Macedonians, not only proved a dismal failure but increased the alienation of the Macedonian aristocracy.

Many scholars have seen Alexander's unsuccessful experiment with *proskynesis* as a thinly veiled demand for recognition of his divine status. This is, however, highly unlikely; for the Greeks themselves knew that the Great King was never regarded as divine and that *proskynesis* was merely part of the court protocol. That they considered it an inappropriate way of addressing a mortal ruler is another matter. If hostile sources chose to equate Alexander's adoption of the practice with a request for divine honours, that was a misinterpretation – either deliberate or unintentional – of the king's motives. (In view of his later demands, this is not entirely surprising.) Furthermore, the claim that *proskynesis* required the Macedonians to prostrate themselves before their king is equally nonsensical. Herodotos, in a famous passage concerning the practice (1.134.1), makes it clear that the extent of debasement was directly proportional to the status of the individual and was not restricted to the greeting of the Great King (cf. Xenophon *Anabasis* 1.6.10). If Macedonians like Leonnatos ridiculed the Persians for abasing themselves, it demonstrates merely that the conquered peoples approached their new sovereign as suppliants, thus humbling themselves before Alexander in a way that would not have been required of them at the court of Dareios, where the hierarchy was clearly established. The position of Persian nobles at the court of Alexander was yet to be determined and obsequious behaviour was a form of self-preservation. By contrast, Alexander would have required of his *hetairoi* little more than a kiss on the lips or the cheek, and it is perhaps a misunderstanding of this practice that led contemporary historians to claim that Alexander gave a kiss to his *hetairoi* only if they had previously performed *proskynesis*, when in fact the kiss and the *proskynesis* were synonymous. What is certain, however, is that the ceremony, which was intended to put the Persian and Macedonian on a roughly equal footing (Balsdon 1950: 382), and which suited Alexander's new role as Great King, was rejected by the Greeks and Macedonians, and that Kallisthenes of Olynthos was among the most vocal of those who voiced their objections. Nor is it difficult to understand that the nobles who had long regarded their ruler as *primus inter pares* would be reluctant to acknowledge that they, like the conquered enemy, were now 'slaves' (*douloi*) of the Great King.

The extent of the alienation can be seen in the so-called 'Conspiracy of the Pages'. The plot had its origins in a personal humiliation: Hermolaos son of Sopolis, while hunting with the king, had anticipated Alexander in striking a boar, an act of *lèse-majesté* (but: Roisman 2003: 315–16). For this he was flogged. But the view that he plotted to murder the king in order to avenge this outrage is simplistic, and it was recognized even at the time that there were larger issues at play. The Pages were the sons of prominent *hetairoi*, and their hostility towards Alexander was doubtless a reflection of the Macedonian aristocracy's reaction to his policies. The conspiracy itself came to naught: Eurylochos, a brother of one of the Pages, brought the news of the plot to the *somatophylakes*, Ptolemaios and Leonnatos, and the conspirators were arrested, tried and executed. But the episode revealed once again the extent of disaffection amongst the Macedonian aristocracy. The elimination of the conspirators also gave Alexander the opportunity of ridding himself of Kallisthenes (Aristotle's nephew), the official historian who, over the course of the campaign, had developed too sharp a tongue for the king's liking and had played no small part in sabotaging the introduction of *proskynesis*. As tutor of the Pages, he could be held responsible for their political attitudes, and, although there was no clear evidence to incriminate him, the suspicion of ill-will towards the king was sufficient to bring him down. If the king's friendship with Aristotle, perhaps already strained, mattered, he may indeed have intended to keep Kallisthenes in custody until his fate could be decided by a vote of the League of Korinth. The conflicting stories of the nature of his death reflect at least two layers of *apologia*. In the version given by Ptolemy, he was tortured and hanged, a punishment at once barbaric and appropriate to traitors (Arrian 4.14.3; cf. Bosworth 1995: 100); Chares of Mytilene says that he was incarcerated for seven months and died of obesity and a disease of lice (cf. Africa 1982: 4) before he could stand trial (Plutarch 55.9 = Chares *FGrHist* 125 F 15).

# 8   The Invasion of India

In spring 327, Alexander re-crossed the Hindu Kush and began his invasion of India, the easternmost limits of the Achaimenid Empire. The extent of Persian rule in Gandhara and the Punjab had doubtless declined since the age of Dareios I, but the response of the local dynasts to Alexander's demands for submission shows that they continued to recognize some form of Achaimenid overlordship (hence Arrian's use of the term *hyparchoi*), that is, that they regarded Alexander's authority as legitimate (cf. Bosworth 1995: 147–9). Not all came over willingly. In Bajaur, the Aspasians, who dwelt in the Kunar or Chitral valley, fled to the hills after abandoning and burning Arigaion (Nawagai); nevertheless the Macedonians captured 40,000 men and 230,000 oxen. More obstinate was the resistance of the Assakenoi, who fielded 2,000 cavalry, 30,000 infantry and 30 elephants. After the death of Assakenos, who may have been killed in the initial skirmish with Alexander, Massaga in the Katgala pass relied for its defence on Kleophis, the mother (or possibly widow) of Assakenos. Soon Kleophis sent a herald to Alexander to discuss terms of surrender, gaining as a result the reputation of 'harlot queen'; for she was said to have retained her kingdom through sexual favours (cf. Justin 12.7.9–11). The story that she later bore a son named Alexander is perhaps an invention of the late first century and an allusion to Kleopatra VII and Kaisarion (von Gutschmid 1882: 553–4; Seel 1971: 181–2). Ora (Udegram) and Beira or Bazeira (Bir-kot), other strongholds of the Assakenoi, fell in rapid succession. But a more strenuous effort was required to capture the rock of Aornos, which abutted on its eastern side the banks of the Indus River. Hence, it is probable that its identification with Pir-Sar by Sir Aurel Stein (Stein 1929; cf. Bosworth 1995: 178–80) is correct, though recently others have suggested Mt Ilam (Eggermont 1984: 191–200; Badian 1987: 117 n. 1).

In the meantime, the king had sent an advance force to bridge the Indus and secure Peukelaotis (modern Charsadda) with a Macedonian garrison. Ambhi (whom the Greeks called Omphis or Mophis), the ruler of Taxila – the region between the Indus and the Hydaspes – had already sent out diplomatic feelers to Alexander and he now welcomed the Macedonian army near his capital (in the vicinity of modern Islamabad); for he was prepared to exchange recognition of Alexander's overlordship for military help against his enemies, Abisares and Poros, who ruled the northern and western regions respectively. In return for Macedonian support, Philip son of Machatas was appointed as overseer of the region, with Ambhi (under the official name of 'Taxiles') as nominal head of the kingdom.

Abisares had known of Alexander's advance since, at least, winter 327/6, when he sent reinforcements to Ora. After the fall of Aornos in 326, natives from the region between Dyrta and the Indus fled to him, and he renewed his alliance with Poros. Though clearly the weaker partner in this relationship, Abisares could nevertheless muster an army of comparable size; hence Alexander planned to attack Poros before Abisares could join forces with him. In the event, Poros looked in vain for reinforcements, as Abisares made (token?) submission to Alexander and awaited the outcome of events. After the Macedonian victory at the Hydaspes, Abisares sent a second delegation, led by his own brother and bringing money and forty elephants as gifts. Despite his failure to present himself in person, as had been required of him, Abisares retained his kingdom, to which was added the hyparchy of Arsakes; he was, however, assessed for an annual tribute and closely watched by the satrap, Philip son of Machatas. Although Abisares is referred to as 'satrap' by Arrian, his son doubtless followed an independent course of action after Alexander's return to the west.

Poros meanwhile prepared to face the invader and his traditional enemy, Taxiles, at the Hydaspes (Jhelum), probably near modern Haranpur (Stein 1932; Wood 1997: 184–7; Fuller 1960: 180–4 for earlier theories). Here, Alexander positioned Krateros with a holding force directly opposite Poros and stationed a smaller contingent under Meleagros and Gorgias farther upstream; he himself conducted regular feints along the riverbank before marching, under the cover of night and a torrential downpour, to ford the river some 26 km north of the main crossing point, catching Poros' son, who had been posted upstream, off his guard. This was near modern Jalalpur and the wooded island of Admana. The main engagement was a particularly hard-fought and bloody one (Hamilton 1956; cf. Devine 1987), in which the Indian ruler distinguished himself by his bravery. The valiant enemy earned Alexander's respect, and was allowed to retain his kingdom. It had not always been so: Alexander had not always been so generous in his treatment of stubborn adversaries. The greater challenge lay, however, in the attempt to bring about lasting peace between the Indian rivals. Curtius claims that an alliance between Taxiles and Poros was sealed by marriage, the common currency in such transactions. But the arrangement was never entirely satisfactory. Though Taxiles was perhaps more to be trusted than Poros, Alexander needed a strong ruler in what would be the buffer zone at the eastern edge of his empire (cf. Breloer 1941).

Despite the popular view of Alexander as a man obsessed with conquest and intent upon reaching the eastern edge of the world – a view which will persist because the legend of Alexander has become so firmly rooted that it defies all rational attempts to change it – Alexander abandoned thoughts of acquiring new territory after his hard-fought victory over Poros. What he needed now was security, and he worked with his new ally himself to bring the neighbouring dynasts under Poros' authority. The Glausai were reduced by Alexander and their realm added to that of Poros, while Hephaistion annexed the kingdom of the so-called 'cowardly' Poros, between the Akesines (Chenab) and Hydraotes (Ravi) rivers. Garrisons were established in the region, but they comprised Indian troops and were responsible to Poros, not Alexander. Beyond the Ravi, the campaigns were either punitive or pre-emptive, depending on how Poros in his discussions with the king assessed their power or reported their activities. Sangala, indeed, was stubborn in its resistance, and the attackers paid a heavy price in casualties; but Sophytes (Saubhuti) made peace, perhaps relieved by the conqueror's suppression of the neighbouring Kshatriyas.

Nevertheless, the Hyphasis (Beas) marked the end of the eastward march – and Alexander knew it. He had, in truth, already determined to take the army elsewhere. After the victory at the Hydaspes, the king had established two cities, Boukephala and Nikaia, as outposts of his realm, and sent men into the hills to cut down trees for the construction of a fleet that would sail down the Hydaspes to the Indus delta, thus following a route known to the Greeks since the exploits of Skylax of Karyanda during the reign of Dareios I (Hdt. 5.44). His reasons for campaigning in the eastern Punjab were simple and practical enough. It was essential that Poros should control a strong vassal kingdom on the edge of Alexander's empire, and it was important to keep the men occupied and to place the burden of feeding his troops on the hostile tribes in that region rather than on his newly acquired friend Poros. Alexander's behaviour at the Hyphasis, when he withdrew into his tent and sulked because his troops would not follow him to the Ganges, was as much an act of dissembling as the larger-than-life structures that were erected at the river, designed to deceive posterity into thinking that the Macedonian invaders had been more than mere humans (Spann 1999; Heckel 2003b).

For Alexander the path to the Ocean was still open, but the need to secure the empire was not forgotten: the descent of the Indus waterway, conducted by land as well as on the river, shows that Alexander intended a systematic reduction of the area which would ensure Macedonian rule in the Punjab (Breloer 1941). The expedition was a show of force on the eastern side of the Indus to support Macedonian claims to rule the western lands adjacent to the river (Bosworth 1983). The Siboi, allegedly descendants of Herakles, were woven into the fabric of the Alexander legend more securely than into that of the empire. The Kshudrakas (Oxydrakai or Sudracae) and Malavas (Mallians) were deadly foes and long-time enemies of both Poros and Abisares. The sack of one of their towns – probably located at or near modern Multan (Wood 1997: 199–200) – nearly cost the king his life, and from this point, he was conveyed downstream by ship, displayed to the troops, in an attempt to stifle rumours that he had died and the 'truth' was being kept from them by the generals.

When the king recovered his strength, he turned his attention to Mousikanos, whose kingdom beyond the confluence of the Chenab is probably to be identified with ancient Alor. Mousikanos, surprised by the enemy's approach, surrendered and accepted a garrison. But Oxikanos (or Oxykanos), a nomarch of upper Sind (Eggermont 1975: 12 locates him at Azeika), resisted the invader and was eventually captured and, presumably, executed. Portikanos, ruler of Pardabathra, suffered a similar fate, but the arguments for identifying the two rulers as one and the same, as many scholars do (Smith 1914: 101 n. 3; Berve 1926: 2.293), are not compelling (Eggermont 1975: 9–10, 12). At Sindimana, the capital of the dynast Sambos, whom Alexander had appointed satrap of the hill-country west of the Indus, the inhabitants opened their gates to receive the Macedonians, but Sambos himself fled. Mousikanos, too, on the advice of the Brahmans, had rebelled soon after the king's departure, only to be hunted down by Peithon son of Agenor and brought to Alexander, who crucified Mousikanos and other leaders of the insurrection. What became of Sambos, we do not know, but Krateros' return to the west through the Bolan Pass may have been intended to root out the remaining insurgents; for it appears that Sambos controlled the profitable trade-route between Alor and Kandahar (cf. Eggermont 1975: 22).

# 9   Return to Babylonia

From Sind, Alexander explored the area of Patalene and the Indus Delta before sailing into the Indian Ocean, where he sacrificed to the same sea-deities whom he had propitiated at the Hellespont. But the road home, through the lands of the Oreitai and the Gedrosian Desert (for the route: Stein 1942; Strasburger 1952; Engels 1978a: 135–43; Seibert 1985: 171–8; cf. Hamilton 1972, for the Oreitai), would be a hard one, especially for the ill-provisioned camp-followers who had swollen the numbers of the Macedonian army. But the march was necessary if the king was to keep in contact with Nearchos' fleet, which had been instructed to sail from the delta to the straits of Hormuz (for early travel from the Persian Gulf to India, Casson 1974: 30–1, 45) and ultimately to the mouth of the Tigris; for at that time the river flowed directly into the sea, rather than joining the Euphrates, as it does today. The privations of the army were aggravated by the failure of certain satraps to provide the requisitioned supplies. The king's angry gesture of tossing Aboulites' coins at the feet of his horses (Plutarch 68.7) may suggest that the satrap had sent money instead of provisions. Nevertheless, Alexander reunited with Nearchos in Karmania and later again at the Tigris. The infamous Dionysiac procession, accepted or rejected by scholars (according to their personal views of Alexander) as evidence of his degeneration, may have been nothing more than well-deserved 'R & R' for the troops (Tarn 1997: 1 109, typically, 'a necessary holiday which legend perverted into a story of Alexander . . . reeling through Carmania at the head of a drunken rout').

Alexander's lengthy absence in Central Asia and the Indus valley had raised doubts about whether he would return, and in the heartland of the empire the administration of the lands and treasures was conducted with little regard for the king's pleasure or the empire's well-being. Among the worst offenders was Harpalos, the treasurer who had moved his headquarters from Ekbatana to Babylon, where he lavished gifts and titles upon first one Athenian courtesan, Pythionike, and after her death another, Glykera. Other charges against him involved sexual debauchery and illegal treatment of the native population. When he learned of Alexander's re-emergence from India, Harpalos fled westward, first to Kilikia and then on to Athens, taking with him Glykera and no small amount of the king's treasure. But Harpalos was only the most famous of the offenders and perhaps the most sensational in his offences. Others were quickly called to account, tried and in many cases deposed or executed. One scholar has labelled the actions a 'reign of terror' (Badian 1961) and the phrase is now employed by many scholars as a convenient shorthand for the events that followed the king's unexpected return from the East. Alexander's restoration of order is frequently interpreted as abuse of power, and criminals as 'scapegoats', and not all were executed or deposed from office. It is hardly surprising that the king, after a lengthy absence, should conduct an investigation into their affairs (a more balanced picture: Higgins 1980; cf. Müller 2003: 194–6; Worthington 2004: 172–3).

The house-cleaning was accompanied by further orientalizing policies: at Susa, mass-marriages of prominent *hetairoi* to the daughters of noble Persians were celebrated in conjunction with the legitimization of the thousands of informal unions of Macedonian soldiers with barbarian women. Not a 'policy of fusion', to be sure, or the creation of a 'mixed race', but rather a blueprint for political stability (Bosworth 1980b), if carried through by a capable leader committed to this vision of a new empire. This ceremony was soon followed by further integration of orientals into the military and the demobilization of some 10,000 Macedonian veterans. The process was regarded as an insult, even by those most eager to return home, and at Opis, for the first time, there was a genuine mutiny within the army. Once again Alexander showed himself a worthy son of Philip II, combining soothing words with largesse, while executing the ringleaders of the sedition. Notions of an appeal for universal brotherhood (Tarn 1933; 1997: 2 434–49) have, rightly, been debunked (Badian 1958a), but Alexander did not back away from his orientalizing policies; for he must now have given thought to establishing an administrative centre in Asia – possibly in Babylon (cf. Schachermeyr 1970) – and it appears that he elevated his best friend, Hephaistion, to the rank of chiliarch or 'Grand Vizier' (on the chiliarchy Collins 2001).

As it turned out, the *Alexanderreich*, buffeted by political storms and weighed down by the king's grandiose schemes, proved too flimsy a structure. Nor was the man himself emotionally prepared for what was to come. In the summer of 324, Nikanor of Stagira had proclaimed the Exiles' Decree at the Olympic festival (Diodoros 18.8.2–6; Zahrnt 2003), its demands far exceeding Alexander's prerogatives as *hegemon* of the League and their implications catastrophic for many states, Athens in particular. The danger of war with Macedon was heightened by the arrival of Harpalos and the lure of his money. But Alexander himself was soon plunged into personal tragedy, as Hephaistion died of fever and excessive drinking in Ekbatana (October 324). The king's grief knew no bounds and, although genuine, its Homeric displays were all too familiar. Anger was eventually directed against the Kossaian rebels, and mercy was in short supply. And in the months that followed, as he awaited the unfolding of events in Europe, including the possible confrontation between Antipatros and Krateros, who had been sent to replace him, Alexander turned his thoughts to funeral monuments, a hero-cult for Hephaistion, and a demand for his own divine recognition (Habicht 1970: 28–36). In June 323 he, too, died of illness in Babylon without designating an heir. It would not have mattered, for only three male relatives of the king remained, one of them as yet unborn, and the marshals of the empire had taken too equal a share in the burden of conquest to relinquish overall power to one of their own number. Even as he was destroying the empire's equilibrium, Alexander had been planning new expeditions to Carthage and Arabia (Diodoros 18.4.4; Högemann 1985). Thus his exit from life, and history, was at the same time an evasion of responsibility. Alexander (the Great) was as fortunate in death as he had been in life, as the burden of dealing with the consequences of his superhuman achievements fell on the shoulders of his all-too-human successors.

## Further reading

The number of works on Alexander in English alone is immense. The best modern treatments are Bosworth (1988a) and Bosworth in *CAH*[2] 6 791–875. Schachermeyr (1973) (in German) is unrivalled in any language; Wilcken (1967); Milns (1968) and Hamilton (1972) provide brief and reliable narratives; Cartledge (2004) takes a refreshing approach and is perhaps the best of the flood of Alexander volumes that appeared in that year; but cf. also Mossé (2004). The reader is also directed to the essays in Bosworth and Baynham (2000); Roisman (2003); Worthington (2003b); also the older collection of seminal works in Griffith (1966).

The major extant sources are available in English translation. See the Loeb translations of Arrian (Brunt 1976, 1983) and Diodoros, Book 17 (Welles 1963), the Penguin translations of Plutarch's *Life of Alexander* (Scott-Kilvert 1973), Q. Curtius Rufus (Yardley 1984), Arrian (de Sélincourt, rev. Hamilton 1971) and the Greek Alexander Romance (Stoneman 1991). For Justin's epitome of Pompeius Trogus, Yardley & Develin (1994). Commentaries on these authors can be found in Bosworth (1980a, 1995) (Arrian); Atkinson (1980, 1994) (Curtius), Hamilton (1969) (Plutarch); Yardley & Heckel (1997) (Justin). See also the specialized studies of Bosworth (1988b) and Baynham (1998). The important inscriptions of the age of Alexander: Harding; Schwenk (1985) (Athenian decrees: 338–322 BCE). See also Bellinger (1963) and Price (1991) for numismatic evidence. For a collection of readings in translation, arranged by theme, see Heckel & Yardley (2003).

Of equal importance are the fragments of the lost contemporary historians. These are collected in Jacoby, *FGrHist* 2B, and translated into English in Robinson (1953) (cf. Auberger 2001 for a Greek–French edition of the fragments). The lost historians are discussed in Pearson (1960). The relationships between lost and extant historians are treated (not in an entirely satisfactory way) by Hammond (1983, 1993).

The Macedonian background is discussed in Hammond & Griffith (1979); Errington (1990) and Borza (1990; cf. Borza 1999). For prosopographic details see Hoffmann (1906); Berve (1926) (both in German); Heckel (1992; forthcoming); Tataki (1998); cf. Müller (2003) for the power struggles at the Macedonian court. Military matters are discussed by Adcock (1957); Fuller (1960); Marsden (1964); Engels (1978a); Heckel (2003c) (general survey). Ashley (1998) is the work of an amateur historian, which contains much useful information but should be used with caution. Further information on Alexander in Central Asia and India can be found in Stein (1929); Eggermont (1975); Holt (1988). For women and dynastic marriage Macurdy (1932); Carney (2002); Ogden (1999).

# Bibliography

Adams, W. L. (2003) 'The episode of Philotas: an insight' in: Heckel & Tritle 2003: 113–16
Adcock, F. E. (1957) *The Greek and Macedonian art of war* (Berkeley: University of California Press) (Sather classical lectures 30)
Africa, T. (1982) 'Worms and the death of kings: a cautionary note on disease and history' in: *Classical Antiquity* 1: 1–17
Anson, E. M. (1989) 'The Persian fleet in 334' in: *CPh* 84: 44–9
Ashley, J. R. (1998) *The Macedonian empire: the era of warfare under Philip II and Alexander the Great, 359–323 B.C.* (Jefferson NC: McFarland)
Atkinson, J. E. (1980) *A commentary on Q. Curtius Rufus'* Historiae Alexandri Magni, *Books 3 and 4* (Amsterdam: Hakkert) (London studies in classical philology 4)
Atkinson, J. E. (1994) *A commentary on Q. Curtius Rufus'* Historiae Alexandri Magni, *Books 5 to 7.2* (Amsterdam: Hakkert) (*Acta Classica* Suppl. 1)
Auberger, J. (2001) *Historiens d'Alexandre* (textes traduits et annotés) (Paris: Belles Lettres)
Badian, E. (1958a) 'Alexander the Great and the unity of mankind' in: *Historia* 7: 425–44
Badian, E. (1958b) 'The eunuch Bagoas: a study in method' in: *CQ* 8: 144–57
Badian, E. (1960) 'The death of Parmenio' in: *TAPhA* 91: 324–38

Badian, E. (1961) 'Harpalus' in: *JHS* 81: 16–43

Badian, E. (1963) 'The death of Philip II' in: *Phoenix* 17: 244–50

Badian, E. (1967) 'Agis III' in: *Hermes* 95: 170–92

Badian, E (1987) 'Alexander at Peucelaotis' in: *CQ* 37: 117–28

Badian, E. (1994) 'Agis III: revisions and reflections' in: Worthington, I. (ed.) (1994) *Ventures into Greek history* (Second Australian Symposium on Ancient Macedonian Studies held at the University of Melbourne in July 1991, dedicated to Professor Nicholas Hammond) (Oxford: Clarendon) 258–93

Badian, E. (2000) 'Conspiracies' in: Bosworth & Baynham 2000: 50–95

Balcer, J. M. (1978) 'Alexander's burning of Persepolis' in: *Iranica Antiqua* 13: 119–33

Balsdon, J. P. V. D. (1950) 'The divinity of Alexander' in: *Historia* 1: 363–88

Baynham, E. J. (1998) *Alexander the Great: the unique History of Quintus Curtius* (Ann Arbor: University of Michigan Press)

Bellinger, A. R. (1963) *Essays on the coinage of Alexander the Great* (New York: American Numismatic Society) (Numismatic studies 11)

Berve, H. (1926) *Das Alexanderreich auf prosopographischer Grundlage*, 2 vols. (Munich: Beck)

Borza, E. N. (1971) 'The end of Agis' revolt' in: *CPh* 66: 230–5

Borza, E. N. (1990) *In the shadow of Olympus: the emergence of Macedon* (Princeton: Princeton University Press)

Borza, E. N. (1999) *Before Alexander: constructing early Macedonia* (Claremont CA: Regina) (Publications of the Association of Ancient Historians 6)

Bosworth, A. B. (1971a) 'Philip II and upper Macedonia' in: *CQ* 21: 93–105

Bosworth, A. B. (1971b) 'The death of Alexander the Great: rumour and propaganda' in: *CQ* 21: 112–36

Bosworth, A. B. (1980a) *A historical commentary on Arrian's* History of Alexander, vol. 1: *Commentary on Books I–III* (Oxford: Clarendon)

Bosworth, A. B. (1980b) 'Alexander and the Iranians' in: *JHS* 100: 1–21

Bosworth, A. B. (1981) 'A missing year in the history of Alexander' in: *JHS* 101: 17–39

Bosworth, A. B. (1983) 'The Indian satrapies under Alexander the Great' in: *Antichthon* 17: 37–46

Bosworth, A. B. (1988a) *Conquest and empire: the reign of Alexander the Great* (Cambridge: Cambridge University Press)

Bosworth, A. B. (1988b) *From Arrian to Alexander: studies in historical interpretation* (Oxford: Clarendon)

Bosworth, A. B. (1995) *A historical commentary on Arrian's* History of Alexander, vol. 2: *Commentary on books IV–V* (Oxford: Clarendon)

Bosworth, A. B. (1996) *Alexander and the east: the tragedy of triumph* (Oxford: Clarendon)

Bosworth, A. B. (2000) 'Ptolemy and Alexander's will' in: Bosworth & Baynham 2000: 207–41

Bosworth, A. B., & E. J. Baynham (eds) (2000) *Alexander the Great in fact and fiction* (Proceedings of a symposium held at the University of Newcastle (N.S.W., Australia) in July 1997) (Oxford: Oxford University Press)

Breloer, B. (1941) *Alexanders Bund mit Poros: Indien von Dareios zu Sandrokottos* (Leipzig: Harrassowitz) (Sammlung orientalischer Arbeiten 9)

Briant, P. (1993) 'Alexandre à Sardes' in: Carlsen, J., B. Due, O. Steen Due, B. Poulsen (eds) (1993) *Alexander the Great: Reality and Myth* (Final proceedings of the conference organized by the Accademia di Danimarca in Rome during the period 27–29 January 1992) (Rome: 'L'Erma' di Bretschneider) 13–27 (Analecta Romana Instituti Danici Suppl. 20)

Briant, P. (2002) *From Cyrus to Alexander: a history of the Persian Empire* (trans. P. T. Daniels) (Winona Lake IN: Eisenbrauns)

Burstein, S. M. (1991) 'Pharaoh Alexander: a scholarly myth' in: *Ancient Society* 22: 139–45

Burstein, S. M. (2000) 'Prelude to Alexander: the reign of Khababash' in: *Ancient History Bulletin* 14: 149–54

Carney, E. D. (2000) *Women and monarchy in Macedonia* (Norman OK: University of Oklahoma Press)

Cartledge, P. (2004) *Alexander the Great: the hunt for a new past* (London: Macmillan)

Casson, L. (1974) *Travel in the ancient world* (London: Allen & Unwin)

Collins, A. W. (2001) 'The office of chiliarch under Alexander and the successors' in: *Phoenix* 55: 259–83

Dani, A. H. (1994) 'Alexander and his successors in central Asia, part I: Alexander's campaign in central Asia' in: Harmatta, J., B. N. Puri, G. F. Etemadi (eds) (1994) *History of civilizations of Central Asia*, vol. 2: *The development of sedentary and nomadic civilizations, 700 B.C. to A.D. 250* (Paris: UNESCO) 167–88 (Multiple History Series)

Develin, R. (1981) 'The murder of Philip II' in: *Antichthon* 15: 86–99

Devine, A. M. (1987) 'The battle of the Hydaspes: a tactical and source-critical study' in: *The Ancient World* 16: 91–113

Eggermont, P. H. L. (1975) *Alexander's campaigns in Sind and Baluchistan and the siege of the Brahmin town of Harmatelia* (Leuven: Leuven University Press) (Orientalia Lovaniensia analecta 3)

Eggermont, P. H. L. (1984) 'Indien und die hellenistischen Königreiche: Zusammenschau einer westöstlichen Gesellschaft zwischen 550 und 150 v. Chr.' in: Ozols, J., & V. Thewalt (eds) (1984) *Aus dem Osten des Alexanderreiches: Völker und Kulturen zwischen Orient und Okzident: Iran, Afghanistan, Pakistan, Indien: Festschrift zum 65. Geburtstag von Klaus Fischer* (Cologne: DuMont): 74–83

Ellis, J. R. (1971) 'Amyntas Perdikka, Philip II, and Alexander the Great' in: *JHS* 91: 15–24

Engels, D. W. (1978a) *Alexander the Great and the logistics of the Macedonian army* (Berkeley: University of California Press)

Engels, D. W. (1978b) 'A note on Alexander's death' in: *CPh* 73: 224–8

Errington, R. M. (1990) *A history of Macedonia* (trans. C. Errington) (Berkeley: University of California Press)

Fears, J. R. (1975) 'Pausanias the assassin of Philip II' in: *Athenaeum* 53: 111–35

Flower, M. A. (2000) 'Alexander and Panhellenism' in: Bosworth & Baynham 2000: 96–135

Fraser, P. M. (1996) *The cities of Alexander the Great* (Oxford: Clarendon)

French, V., & P. Dixon (1986) 'The Pixodarus affair: another view: Appendix: The reliability of Plutarch' in: *The Ancient World* 13: 73–86

Fuller, J. F. C. (1960) *The generalship of Alexander the Great* (New Brunswick NJ: Rutgers University Press)

Garvin, E. E. (2003) 'Darius III and homeland defense' in: Heckel & Tritle 2003: 87–111

Griffith, G. T. (ed.) (1966) *Alexander the Great: the main problems* (Cambridge: Heffer) (Views and Controversies about Classical Antiquity)

Habicht, C. (1970) *Gottmenschentum und griechische Städte* (Munich: Beck ²1970) (Zetemata 14)

Habicht, C. (1997) *Athens from Alexander to Antony* (trans. by D. L. Schneider) (Cambridge MA: Harvard University Press)

Hamilton, J. R. (1953) 'Alexander and his so-called father' in: *CQ* 3: 151–7

Hamilton, J. R. (1956) 'The cavalry battle at the Hydaspes' in: *JHS* 76: 26–31

Hamilton, J. R. (1969) *Plutarch*, Alexander: *a commentary* (Oxford: Clarendon)

Hamilton, J. R. (1972) 'Alexander among the Oreitae' in: *Historia* 21: 603–8

Hamilton, J. R. (1973) *Alexander the Great* (London: Hutchinson)

Hammond, N. G. L. (1983) *Three historians of Alexander the Great: the so-called vulgate authors: Diodorus, Justin and Curtius* (Cambridge: Cambridge University Press)

Hammond, N. G. L. (1993) *Sources for Alexander the Great: an analysis of Plutarch's* Life *and* Arrian's Anabasis Alexandrou (Cambridge: Cambridge University Press) (Cambridge Classical Studies)

Hammond, N. G. L. (1994) 'One or two passes at the Cilicia–Syria border?' in: *The Ancient World* 25: 15–26

Hammond, N. G. L., & G. T. Griffith (1979) *History of Macedonia*, vol. 2: 550–336 B.C. (Oxford: Clarendon)

Heckel, W. (1977) 'The conspiracy *against* Philotas' in: *Phoenix* 31: 9–21

Heckel, W. (1981) 'Some speculations on the prosopography of the *Alexanderreich*' in: *LCM* 6: 63–70

Heckel, W. (1986a) 'Factions and Macedonian politics in the reign of Alexander the Great' in: *Anakoinoseis kata to 4. diethnes symposio Thessalonike, 21–25 septembriou 1983 = Papers read at the Fourth International Symposium held in Thessaloniki, September 21–25 1983* (Thessalonike: Hidryma Meleton Chersonesou tou Haimou) 293–305 (Institute for Balkan Studies 204)

Heckel, W. (1986b) 'Chorienes and Sisimithres' in: *Athenaeum* 64: 223–6

Heckel, W. (1988) *The last days and testament of Alexander the Great: a prosopographic study* (Stuttgart: Steiner) (*Historia* Einzelschriften 56)

Heckel, W. (1992) *The marshals of Alexander's empire* (London: Routledge)

Heckel, W. (2002) 'The case of the missing "phrourarch"' in: *Ancient History Bulletin* 16: 57–60

Heckel, W. (2003a) 'King and "companions": observations on the nature of power in the reign of Alexander the Great' in: Roisman 2003: 197–225

Heckel, W. (2003b) 'Alexander the Great and the "limits of the civilised world"' in: Heckel & Tritle 2003: 147–74

Heckel, W. (2003c) *The wars of Alexander the Great, 336–323 B.C.* (New York: Routledge, 2003) (Essential histories)

Heckel, W. (forthcoming) *Who's Who in the Age of Alexander the Great* (Oxford: Blackwell)

Heckel, W., & L. A. Tritle (eds) (2003) *Crossroads of history: the age of Alexander* (Claremont CA: Regina)

Heckel, W., & J. C. Yardley (eds) (2003) *Alexander the Great: historical sources in translation* (Oxford: Blackwell)

Higgins, W. E. (1980) 'Aspects of Alexander's imperial administration: some modern methods and views reviewed' in: *Athenaeum* 58: 129–52

Hoffmann, O. (1906) *Die Makedonen, ihre Sprache und ihr Volkstum* (Göttingen: Vandenhoeck & Ruprecht)

Högemann, P. (1985) *Alexander der Große und Arabien* (Munich: Beck) (Zetemata 82)

Holt, F. L. (1988) *Alexander the Great and Bactria: the formation of a Greek frontier in central Asia* (Leiden: Brill) (*Mnemosyne* Suppl. 104)

Hornblower, S. (1982) *Mausolus* (Oxford: Clarendon)

Judeich, W. (1892) *Kleinasiatische Studien: Untersuchungen zur griechisch-persischen Geschichte des 4. Jahrhunderts v. Chr.* (Marburg: Elwert; repr. Hildesheim: Olms 1987)

Kraft, K. (1971) *Der 'rationale' Alexander: bearbeitet und aus dem Nachlaß herausgegeben von H. Gesche* (Kallmünz: Lassleben) (Frankfurter althistorische Studien 5)

Lock, R. A. (1972) 'The date of Agis III's war in Greece' in: *Antichthon* 6: 10–27

MacDermot, B. C., & K. Shippmann (1999) 'Alexander's March from Susa to Persepolis' in: *Iranica Antiqua* 34: 283–308

Macurdy, G. H. (1932) *Hellenistic queens: a study of woman-power in Macedonia, Seleucid Syria, and Ptolemaic Egypt* (Baltimore: Johns Hopkins University Press)

Marsden, E. W. (1964) *The campaign of Gaugamela* (Liverpool: Liverpool University Press) (Liverpool Monographs in Archaeology and Oriental Studies 6)

McCoy, W. J. (1989) 'Memnon of Rhodes and the Granicus' in: *AJPh* 110: 413–33

McQueen, E. I. (1978) 'Some notes on the anti-Macedon movement in the Peloponnese' in: *Historia* 27: 40–64

Mehl, A. (1980–1) 'ΔΟΡΙΚΤΗΤΟΣ ΧΩΡΑ: Kritische Bemerkungen zum "Speererwerb" in Politik und Völkerrecht der hellenistischen Epoche' in: *Ancient Society* 11–12: 173–212

Milns, R. D. (1968) *Alexander the Great* (London: Hale)

Mossé, C. (2004) *Alexander: destiny and myth* (trans. J. Lloyd; with a foreword by P. Cartledge) (Baltimore: Johns Hopkins University Press)

Müller, S. (2003) *Massnahmen der Herrschaftssicherung gegenüber der makedonischen Opposition bei Alexander dem Grossen* (Frankfurt: Lang) (Europäische Hochschulschriften, Reihe 3, 974)

Ogden, D. (1999) *Polygamy, prostitutes and death: the Hellenistic dynasties* (London: Duckworth & The Classical Press of Wales)

Özet, M. (1994) 'The tomb of a noble woman from the Hekatomnid period' in: Isager, J. (ed.) (1994) *Hekatomnid Caria and the Ionian renaissance: acts of the International Symposium at the Department of Greek and Roman Studies, Odense University, 28–29 November, 1991* (Odense: Odense University Press) 88–96 (Halicarnassian Studies 1)

Pearson, L. (1960) *The lost histories of Alexander the Great* (New York: American Philological Association)

Prandi, L. (1998) 'A few remarks on the Amyntas "conspiracy" ' in: Will 1998: 91–101

Price, M. J. (1991) *The coinage in the name of Alexander the Great and Philip Arrhidaeus: a British Museum catalogue*, 2 vols (London: British Museum)

Robinson, C. A. (1953) *The history of Alexander the Great*, vol. 1, part 1: *An index to the extant historians*; part 2: *The fragments* (Providence RI: Brown University) (Brown University Studies 16)

Roebuck, C. (1948) 'The settlements of Philip II with the Greek states in 338 B.C.' in: *CPh* 43: 73–92

Roisman, J. (ed.) (2003) *Brill's Companion to Alexander the Great* (Leiden: Brill)

Romane, J. P. (1987) 'Alexander's siege of Tyre' in: *The Ancient World* 16: 79–90

Romane, J. P. (1988) 'Alexander's siege of Gaza' in: *The Ancient World* 18: 21–30

Romane, J. P. (1994) 'Alexander's sieges of Miletus and Halicarnassus' in: *The Ancient World* 25: 61–76

Ruzicka, S. (1985) 'A note on Philip's Persian war' in: *AJAH* 10: 84–95

Ruzicka, S. (1997) "The eastern Greek world" in: Tritle, L. A. (ed.) (1997) *The Greek world in the fourth century: from the fall of the Athenian Empire to the successors of Alexander* (London: Routledge) 107–36

Schachermeyr, F. (1970) *Alexander in Babylon und die Reichsordnung nach seinem Tode* (Vienna: Verlag der Österreichischen. Akademie der Wissenschaften) (Österreichische Akademie der Wissenschaften, Philosophisch-historische Klasse, Sitzungsberichte 268, 3)

Schachermeyr, F. (1973) *Alexander der Große: Das Problem seiner Persönlichkeit und seines Wirkens* (Vienna: Verlag der Österreichischen Akademie der Wissenschaften) (Österreichische Akademie der Wissenschaften, Philosophisch-historische Klasse, Sitzungsberichte 285)

Schwenk, C. J. (1985) *Athens in the Age of Alexander: the dated laws and decrees of 'the Lykourgan era', 338–322 B.C.* (Chicago: Ares)

Seel, O. (1971) *Eine römische Weltgeschichte: Studien zum Text der Epitome des Iustinus und zur Historik des Pompejus Trogus* (Nürnberg: Carl) (Erlanger Beiträge zur Sprach-und Kunstwissenschaft 39)

Seibert, J. (1985) *Die Eroberung des Perserreiches durch Alexander d. Gr. auf kartographischer Grundlage* (Wiesbaden: Reichert) (Beihefte zum Tübinger Atlas des Vorderen Orients, Reihe B, Geisteswissenschaften 68)

Seibert, J. (1987) 'Dareios III' in: Will, W. (ed.) (1987) *Zu Alexander dem Großen: Festschrift Gerhard Wirth zum 60. Geburtstag am 9.12.86*, vol. 1 (Amsterdam: Hakkert) 437–56

Seibert, J. (1998) '"Panhellenischer" Kreuzzug, Nationalkrieg, Rachefeldzug oder makedonischer Eroberungskrieg? – Überlegungen zu den Ursachen des Krieges gegen Persien' in: Will 1998: 5–58

Shabazi, A. S. (2003) 'Irano-Hellenic notes 3: Iranians and Alexander' in: *AJAH* ns 2: 5–38

Smith, V. A. (1914) *The early history of India from 600 B.C. to the Muhammadan conquest, including the invasion of Alexander the Great* (Oxford: Clarendon ³1914)

Spann, P. O. (1999) 'Alexander at the Beas: fox in a lion's skin' in: Titchener, F. B., & R. F. Moorton, Jr. (eds) (1999) *The eye expanded: life and the arts in Greco-Roman antiquity* (Berkeley: University of California Press) 62–74

Speck, H. (2002) 'Alexander at the Persian gates: a study in historiography and topography' in: *AJAH* ns 1: 1–238

Stein, M. A. (1929) *On Alexander's track to the Indus: personal narrative of explorations on the north-west frontier of India, etc.* (London: Macmillan)

Stein, M. A. (1932) 'The site of Alexander's passage of the Hydaspes and the battle with Poros' in: *Geographical Journal* 80: 31–46

Stein, M. A. (1942) 'Notes on Alexander's crossing of the Tigris and the battle of Arbela' in: *Geographical Journal* 100: 155–64

Strasburger, H. (1952) 'Alexanders Zug durch die gedrosische Wüste' in: *Hermes* 80: 456–93

Tarn, W. W. (1933) *Alexander the Great and the unity of mankind* (London: Milford) (The Raleigh Lecture on History, British Academy, 1933 = *Proceedings of the British Academy* 19: 123–66)

Tarn, W. W. (1997) *The Greeks in Bactria and India* (rev. ed. with new pref., bibl. by F. L. Holt [Chicago: Ares 1985], with additional bibl. by M. C. J. Miller [orig. publ. Cambridge: Cambridge University Press 1938]) (Chicago: Ares ³1997)

Tataki, A. B. (1998) *The Macedonians abroad: a contribution to the prosopography of ancient Macedonia* (Athens: Kentron Hellenikes kai Romaikes Archaiotetos, Ethnikon Hidryma Ereunon) (Kentron Hellenikes kai Romaikes Archaiotetos, Meletemata 26)

Vogelsang, W. (1985) 'Early historical Arachosia in south-east Afghanistan' in: *Iranica Antiqua* 20: 55–99

von Gutschmid, A. (1882) 'Trogus und Timagenes' in: *Rheinisches Museum für Philologie* 37: 548–55

Wilcken, U. (1967) *Alexander the Great* (trans G. C. Richards; pref., intro. to Alexander studies, notes, and bibliography by E. N. Borza) (New York: Norton)

Will, W. (1983) *Athen und Alexander: Untersuchungen zur Geschichte der Stadt von 338–322 v. Chr.* (Munich: Beck) (Münchener Beiträge zur Papyrusforschung und antiken Rechtsgeschichte 77)

Will, W. (ed.) (1998) *Alexander der Große: eine Welteroberung und ihr Hintergrund: Vorträge des Internationalen Bonner Alexanderkolloquiums, 19.–21.12.1996* (Bonn: Habelt) 91–101 (Antiquitas, Reihe 1, Abhandlungen zur alten Geschichte 46)

Willrich, H. (1899) 'Wer ließ König Philipp von Makedonien ermorden?' in: *Hermes* 34: 174–83

Wirth, G. (1971) 'Alexander zwischen Gaugamela und Persepolis' in: *Historia* 20: 617–32

Wood, M. (1997) *In the footsteps of Alexander the Great: a journey from Greece to Asia* (Berkeley University of California Press)

Worthington, I. (2003a) 'Alexander's destruction of Thebes' in: Heckel & Tritle 2003: 65–86

Worthington, I. (ed.) (2003b) *Alexander the Great: a reader* (London: Routledge)

Worthington, I. (2004) *Alexander the Great: man and god* (Harlow: Pearson Longman)

Wüst, F. R. (1938) *Philipp II. von Makedonien und Griechenland in den Jahren von 346 bis 338* (Munich: Beck) (Münchener historische Abhandlungen, Reihe 1, Allgemeine und politische Geschichte 14)

Yardley, J. C., & R. Develin (1994) *Justin:* Epitome of the *Philippic History* of Pompeius Trogus (trans. J. C. Yardley; intro., explanatory notes R. Develin) (Atlanta GA: Scholars) (The American Philological Association Classical Resources Series 3)

Yardley, J. C., & W. Heckel (1997) *Justin:* Epitome of the *Philippic History* of Pompeius Trogus, vol. 1: *books 11–12: Alexander the Great* (trans., appendices J. C. Yardley; comm. W. Heckel) (Oxford: Clarendon) (Clarendon Ancient History Series)

Zahrnt, M. (1996) 'Alexanders Übergang über den Hellespont' in: *Chiron* 26: 129–47

Zahrnt, M. (2003) 'Versöhnen oder Spalten? Überlegungen zu Alexanders Verbanntendekret' in: *Hermes* 131: 407–32

# Index

The asterisk before a name indicates that there is a separate entry for that name in this index. **Bold** indicates a table. *Italic* indicates a figure.

Made in the USA
Las Vegas, NV
22 April 2021